W9-BWZ-969

TOURO COLLEGE LIBRARY
Kings Hwy

WITHDRAWN

THE OXFORD HANDBOOK OF

PHILOSOPHY OF
LANGUAGE

THE OXFORD HANDBOOK OF

PHILOSOPHY OF LANGUAGE

Edited by

ERNEST LEPORE

and

BARRY C. SMITH

TOURO COLLEGE LIBRARY

Kings Hwy

CLARENDON PRESS · OXFORD

KH

OXFORD
UNIVERSITY PRESS

Great Clarendon Street, Oxford OX2 6DP

Oxford University Press is a department of the University of Oxford.
It furthers the University's objective of excellence in research, scholarship,
and education by publishing worldwide in

Oxford New York

Auckland Cape Town Dar es Salaam Hong Kong Karachi
Kuala Lumpur Madrid Melbourne Mexico City Nairobi
New Delhi Shanghai Taipei Toronto

With offices in

Argentina Austria Brazil Chile Czech Republic France Greece
Guatemala Hungary Italy Japan Poland Portugal Singapore
South Korea Switzerland Thailand Turkey Ukraine Vietnam

Oxford is a registered trade mark of Oxford University Press
in the UK and in certain other countries

Published in the United States
by Oxford University Press Inc., New York

© the several contributors 2006

The moral rights of the author have been asserted
Database right Oxford University Press (maker)

First published 2006

All rights reserved. No part of this publication may be reproduced,
stored in a retrieval system, or transmitted, in any form or by any means,
without the prior permission in writing of Oxford University Press,
or as expressly permitted by law, or under terms agreed with the appropriate
reprographics rights organization. Enquiries concerning reproduction
outside the scope of the above should be sent to the Rights Department,
Oxford University Press, at the address above

You must not circulate this book in any other binding or cover
and you must impose the same condition on any acquirer

British Library Cataloguing in Publication Data

Data available

Library of Congress Cataloging in Publication Data

The oxford handbook of philosophy of language / edited by Ernest Lepore and Barry C. Smith.
p. cm.
Includes index.
ISBN-13: 978–0–19–925941–0 (alk. paper)
ISBN-10: 0–19–925941–0 (alk. paper)
1. Language and languages—Philosophy. I. Lepore, Ernest, 1950- II. Smith, Barry C. P107.O98 2006
401—dc22 2006016274

Typeset by Laserwords Private Limited, Chennai, India
Printed in Great Britain
on acid-free paper by
Biddles Ltd., King's Lynn, Norfolk

ISBN 978-0-19-925941-0

3 5 7 9 10 8 6 4 2

7/29/08

This volume is dedicated to the memory of
Donald Davidson

PREFACE

Philosophy of language is usually presented as a deep-end subject. One is expected to jump in and eventually get the hang of it. And yet it can be a very technically demanding area of philosophy for the beginner. It is surely not special in this regard. However, it seems to us that it has lagged behind other sub-areas of philosophy in presenting its key concerns in accessible form, with the result that there is a considerable gap between the professional literature and understanding of the novice. Professional philosophers often advise students to read classic papers in the area such as 'On Sense and Reference', 'On Denoting', 'Meaning', 'Truth and Meaning', the second chapter of *Word and Object*, 'General Semantics', 'The Logic of Demonstratives', 'The Meaning of "Meaning" ', any chapter of *Naming and Necessity*. However, in each of these readings students will encounter aspects of the discussion that are opaque and that presuppose detailed knowledge of other parts of philosophy of language. This is by no means a criticism. These articles were not written for novices. But this is a problem if it deters the interested student from pursuing these topics further. It is all the more unfortunate for there is much about the philosophy of language that is deeply engaging and can be made accessible to every philosophy student. One gains the best understanding by first getting to grips with some of the fundamental debates in philosophy of language. By focusing on a particular debate and acquiring a thorough and detailed mastery of it one is able to extend that understanding to other areas, gradually working one's way into the field as a whole.

In our view, the right way to present these debates is not by trying to produce introductory material but rather by having philosophers involved in these debates set out the issues clearly, show what is at stake and argue for the position they take. In this way we hope the current volume will engage those working at a high level while also enabling others to appreciate what is going on in several areas of contemporary discussion. Here, in one volume, are the leading thinkers expressing their own views, and providing much of the material needed to understand both classic and contemporary debates.

We might begin with an awkward question: what is the philosophy of language? In asking this question we run the dangerous risk of looking for an *a priori* demarcation of a subject matter. Or, as our friend Jerry Fodor would put it, we should not be trying to bore the reader by trying to say who gets to call his or her research *real* philosophy of language. The good news is that we're doing neither. In assembling this volume we sought to discover what advances have been made in the philosophy of language both in terms of its history and in its most recent incarnations. But it's easy to see how we could have ended up addressing a less fruitful issue. Philosophy of language has been squeezed from at least two sides during the past twenty years or so. On one side, post-modernists are sometimes interpreted as saying there is nothing interesting to say in the philosophy of language. Richard Rorty in the third edition of his once influential *The Linguistic Turn* essentially apologizes for having led a genera-tion of philosophers into thinking about language—into thinking that language had something philosophically interesting to teach us. On the other side, linguists believe that substantial progress on language can only take place in *their* discipline. Barbara Partee recently told one of us that philosophers can no longer do interesting work in semantics since sophisticated knowledge of syntax is needed to achieve real results. So what is left for philosophy of language?

In its heyday, during the latter half of the twentieth century, philosophy of lan-guage was believed to occupy a central position in philosophy because it offered to deliver the ultimate route to metaphysical reality, or a refutation of skepticism, a challenge to Cartesianism, and a solution to the problem of other minds. Much was promised on behalf of philosophy of language but the accounts of language on offer were often shaped by the ambitions of philosophers pursuing one or more of these agendas. The skeptical outlook of post-modernism provided a useful correct-ive to some of the more fanciful claims made by epistemologists and metaphysicians on behalf of philosophers of language but shared with them—albeit in pessimistic vein—an unshakeable belief in the importance of language to reality. Meanwhile, on the other side, in logic, linguistics, psychology, and computer science, progress was being made on the nature of the natural language phenomena and the tools needed to investigate them. Another development of the late twentieth century was the rise of the philosophy of mind, which gradually displaced philosophy of language as the fastest growing part of the discipline. Many issues of meaning recurred there or were transformed by their new setting. But recently there has been a rapproche-ment between philosophy of mind and philosophy of language, with many of the interesting questions targeting the links between mind and language. And through its connections with other branches of philosophy and work in neighboring discip-lines, philosophy of language has enjoyed something of a resurgence recently, with a stronger sense of the issues worth pursuing, a sense that progress can be made, a keener focus on the topics of central concern to the study of language, and the need for such work to be informed by empirical results in linguistics and psychology.

Instead of serving other philosophical projects, the philosophy of language now focuses on its primary concern: the nature of natural language and the extraordinary capacity of human beings to use it to express and communicate their thoughts about the world and other subject-matters. The way language works, how specific linguistic devices function to achieve their effects, how we come to know these properties of expressions, and how we exploit them in our talk: all this is pursued by contempor-ary philosophers of language. And as well as pursuing detailed accounts of particular expression types, attention is also given to the nature of language and the nature of meaning. Rival accounts of the meaning and reference of certain expressions are now routinely tested against the rich descriptions of the phenomena linguistics provides, while the scope and limits of linguistic meaning are assessed against the background of work in psychology on the acquisition of language and its use in communication.

Philosophy of language continues to take seriously the special place language plays in our lives as an object and source of knowledge, as an interface between minds, and as an anchor between experience and reality. All of these topics were pursued by the late Donald Davidson. We are glad to be able to include an essay by him and would like to dedicate this volume to him. He would have expressed his disagreement with many of the views expressed here, but such disagreement is the stuff of philosophy. As Michael Dummett once put it, when philosophers have disciples it signals the end of doing philosophy.

In what follows we have organized the essays into sections. The volume starts with a historical section dealing with the impact of Frege and Wittgenstein on the subject. This continues with a discussion of Russell and other twentieth-century philosophers, and their legacy to philosophy of language. Having established the historical background we turn to a consideration of the nature of language as a social, psychological, or platonic object. Contrasting conceptions of language are discussed and this sets the stage for treatments of various linguistic phenomena in the subsequent essays.

The next section contains a collection of essays on the nature of meaning, covering normative and naturalistic accounts of the constitution of meaning, including discussions of rule-following, teleosemantics, conceptual-role semantics, truth-conditional and intention-based semantics. Special concerns are raised about the boundaries of linguistic meaning: indeterminacy and external dependence, holism, and the character of propositional content. The limits of semantics and the essential involvement of pragmatic considerations in the fixing of meaning are explored alongside a relevance-theoretic account of utterance meaning.

The following section moves to the nature of reference, with essays focusing on the semantic properties of proper names, natural kind terms, and predicates. Consideration is given to whether reference itself is a property of expressions or an act of intentional agents.

Next, there is an examination of the formal methods used in semantic theory to provide accounts of particular linguistic phenomena, and an investigation of a central concept employed by many semantic theories, namely truth.

Detailed treatments of the workings of language, including phenomena such as sentence structure, compositionality, opacity, tense, and plural constructions are addressed in the following section, along with an examination of the logical forms of language, natural language quantifiers and the interpretation of other logical constants.

Departures from the literal use of declarative sentences are considered in a section on the varieties of speech act. Here, non-declarative uses of language are explored along with metaphor and the performative aspects of language.

The final section tackles a number of topics in the epistemology and metaphysics of language, surrounding the relations between language, mind, and world. Topics include the nature and object of our knowledge of language, the basis of the human capacity for meaningful speech, the relation of language to reality, and the contents we share in virtue of being linguistic communicators. We end with a late essay by Donald Davidson that offers a culmination of his thinking on the practice of interpreting one another and the limits to any theory of language.

The essays assembled here represent work that has shaped and continues to shape current debates in philosophy of language. Further issues beyond those tackled here continue to emerge: issues concerning the semantics of taste predicates,[1] relativist semantics,[2] use theories of meaning,[3] the nature of testimony,[4] the relations between thought and language,[5] and more besides. This shows the healthy state of contemporary philosophy of language and strongly suggests that we won't run out of things to do. The Handbook presents those who wish to understand and those who wish to contribute to these debates with a firm grounding in the discussions that have taken place so far. And although we have still not said what philosophy of language is, in bringing together this collection of papers we hope to have shown it.[6]

Ernest Lepore
Barry C. Smith

---

[1] Peter Lasersohn, 'Context-dependence, Disagreement and Predicates of Personal Taste', *Linguistics and Philosophy* (2006).

[2] John McFarlane, 'Relativist Semantics?', *Proceedings of the Aristotelian Society* (2004), and Paul Boghossian, *Fear of Knowledge* (Oxford University Press, 2006).

[3] Paul Horwich, *Meaning* (Oxford University Press, 1999) and *Reflections on Meaning* (Oxford University Press, 2005).

[4] Elizabeth Fricker, 'Second-hand Knowledge', *Philosophy and Phenomenological Research* (2006).

[5] Jerry A. Fodor, 'Language, Thought and Compositionality', *Mind and Language* (2001), and Peter Carruthers, 'The Cognitive Function of Language', *Behavioral and Brain Sciences* (2002).

[6] Thanks for comments and advice to Jerry Fodor, Barbara Partee, and Ophelia Deroy.

Contents

PART IV   THE NATURE OF REFERENCE

PART V SEMANTIC THEORY

PART VI LINGUISTIC PHENOMENA

PART VII VARIETIES OF SPEECH ACT

PART VIII   THE EPISTEMOLOGY AND METAPHYSICS OF LANGUAGE

LIST OF CONTRIBUTORS

Kent Bach San Francisco State University

Thomas Baldwin University of York

Dorit Bar-On University of North Carolina, Chapel Hill

Michael Beaney University of York

Anne L. Bezuidenhout University of South Carolina

Daniel Boisvert California State University, Bakersfield

Emma Borg University of Reading

David Braun University of Rochester

Elisabeth Camp University of Pennsylvania

Herman Cappelen University of Oslo

Robyn Carston University College London

David J. Chalmers Australian National University

Donald Davidson formerly University of California, Berkeley

Josh Dever University of Texas, Austin

Dorothy Edgington University of Oxford

Katalin Farkas Central European University, Budapest

Michael Glanzberg University of California, Davis

Kathrin Glüer University of Stockholm

Mark Greenberg University of California, Los Angeles

Gilbert Harman Princeton University

Richard G. Heck Brown University

James Higginbotham University of Southern California

Jennifer Hornsby Birkbeck College, University of London

Jeffrey C. King University of Southern California

Ernest Lepore Rutgers University

Peter Ludlow University of Michigan

Kirk Ludwig University of Florida

Fraser MacBride Birkbeck College, University of London

Robert May University of California, Irvine

Alexander Miller University of Birmingham

Peter Pagin University of Stockholm

David Papineau King's College, University of London

Paul Pietroski University of Maryland

George Powell University College London

Marga Reimer University of Arizona

Mark Richard Tufts University

R. M. Sainsbury University of Texas, Austin, and King's College, University of London

Barry Schein University of Southern California

Stephen Schiffer New York University

Gabriel Segal King's College, University of London

Keith Simmons University of North Carolina, Chapel Hill

Barry C. Smith Birkbeck College, University of London

David Sosa University of Texas, Austin

Robert J. Stainton University of Western Ontario

Zoltán Gendler Szabó Cornell University

Charles Travis King's College, University of London

Alan Weir Queen's University, Belfast

George Wilson University of Southern California

PART I

THE HISTORICAL CONTEXT

CHAPTER 1

FREGE'S CONTRIBUTION TO PHILOSOPHY OF LANGUAGE

RICHARD G. HECK AND ROBERT MAY

1.1 WHENCE A PHILOSOPHY OF LANGUAGE?

GOTTLOB FREGE'S contributions to philosophy of language are so numerous and so fundamental that it is difficult to imagine the field without them. That this should be so was not, however, Frege's original intent. Frege was trained as a mathematician, and most of his non-foundational mathematical work lay at the intersection of geometry and complex analysis. That makes it at least somewhat surprising that he should have made any contribution to the study of language, let alone one so profound. But mathematics, in Frege's time, was itself in a state of upheaval, many of its most basic notions being subjected to a thorough re-examination. Among the central issues in Frege's intellectual environment was how we should understand the relation between geometry and arithmetic, the latter understood in a broad sense, as including the theory of all numbers, natural, real, and complex.[1] Though by no means universal, it was a common view that geometry was the more fundamental of the disciplines. In part, this view derived from Kant, who had famously argued that even

---

[1] Frege's relation to his mathematical environment has been the subject of much recent work. See (Wilson, 1995) and (Tappenden, 1995a, 1995b, 2000).

our knowledge of basic number theory is founded upon pure *a priori* intuition of roughly the same sort that he claimed underlay our knowledge of the axioms of Euclidean geometry. The view had other sources, too. For example, it was as common then as it is now to think of the complex numbers as points (or perhaps vectors) in the Euclidean plane. Such a treatment of the complex numbers would suggest, again, that geometrical knowledge is more basic than arithmetical knowledge.

Frege, like many mathematicians of his time, rejected this Kantian view. His strategy for refuting Kant was to demonstrate that "... arithmetic is a branch of logic and need not borrow any ground of proof whatever from either experience or intuition" (Frege, 1964, §0) by identifying a small set of recognizably logical principles, defining the basic logical notions using strictly logical vocabulary, and then proving axioms for arithmetic[2] using only recognizably logical means of inference. This view is what has come to be known as *logicism*.

Frege quickly realized that he could not carry out this program unless he had some way to keep track of precisely which assumptions were being made in a given proof, and which means of inference were being used.

To prevent anything intuitive from penetrating here unnoticed, I had to bend every effort to keep the chain of inference free of gaps. In attempting to comply with this requirement in the strictest possible way, I found the inadequacy of language to be an obstacle; no matter how unwieldy the expressions I was ready to accept, I was less and less able, as the relations became more and more complex, to attain the precision that my purpose required.   (Frege, 1967, pp. 5–6)

And so it was that Frege was led to invent his begriffsschrift,[3] his "conceptual notation". The invention consisted of two parts: a formal notation in which actual statements of mathematics could be written, and a detailed enumeration of a small number of modes of inference to be employed in formal arguments.[4] What made the system work was that the two parts were properly balanced: the formal notation was sufficiently articulated that it could be determined which modes of inference could be applied in a given case simply by examining the *forms* of the representations. That is, the logical relationships between propositions were sufficiently exhibited in the notation that one could check whether a proof was correct—and, in particular, whether all necessary assumptions had been made explicit—purely mechanically. Of the innovations that made this possible, perhaps most familiar today are Frege's dual notions of scope and binding and how they are used to represent generality.

---

[2] Frege never presents an explicit axiomatization of arithmetic, but there is a case to be made that he had one that was only slightly different from the now standard axiomatization due to Dedekind and Peano. See (Heck, 1995).

[3] We will use the lowercase 'begriffsschrift' to refer both to Frege's formal language and to the logical theory stated in that language. Context should disambiguate these uses. We will of course use upper case when referring to Frege's book.

[4] Arguably, Frege recognizes but one rule of inference, *modus ponens*, in *Begriffsschrift*. He does not clearly identify the other rules an adequate formalization would require—namely, universal generalization and substitution—and it is not clear that he regards them as rules of *inference*. See (Frege, 1979a, p. 39), where he refers to *modus ponens* as "[t]he rule of inference".

Indeed, one would be hard pressed to challenge the claim that it is Frege's conception of logical form that constitutes his most significant contribution to the study of language.

The reception of Frege's work among his colleagues was generally lukewarm.[5] This was especially so in the uncomprehending reaction by logicians of his day to *Begriffsschrift*, a volume we now rightly regard as firmly entrenched in the pantheon of thought about logic. Traditional logic—deriving from Aristotle but, just before Frege's time, thoroughly updated by George Boole and his followers (Boole, 1847, 1854)—had been quite incapable of articulating enough of the logical structure of actual mathematical statements to make their logical relations plain. Nowhere was this more evident than with generality. Nonetheless, neither Ernst Schröder (the leading German member of the Boolean school) nor John Venn (he of the Venn diagram) could see any real value in Frege's new notation.[6] Frege penned several pieces in the years immediately following the publication of *Begriffsschrift* comparing his new logic to that of the Booleans (Frege, 1972a, 1972c, 1972d, 1979a, 1979b); not surprisingly, in response Frege touts the importance of his treatment of generality. More generally, Frege emphasizes that the begriffsschrift, inclusive of the treatment of generality, provides us with something more than just an alternative (if albeit superior) notational device. As Russell would remark somewhat later in a famous appendix to *The Principles of Mathematics* that is devoted to Frege's thought:

Frege's work abounds in subtle distinctions, and avoids all the usual fallacies which beset writers on Logic. His symbolism, though unfortunately so cumbrous as to be very difficult to employ in practice, is based upon an analysis of logical notions much more profound than Peano's, and is philosophically very superior to its more convenient rival.   (Russell, 1903, p. 501)

From the early 1880s on, explicating this "symbolism" became a central focus of Frege's writings, and this required Frege to become more precise about the conceptual underpinnings of logic. Thus, while almost none of Frege's most well-known doctrines are fully present in *Begriffsschrift* (though their kernels often are), they have all emerged in full force a decade and half later at the time of *Grundgesetze*. These doctrines—most notably, the articulations of content embedded in the concept–object and sense–reference distinctions—emerge as Frege struggled to carry the logicist program forward. In large part, these developments spawned from Frege's understanding that, in order to derive the postulates of arithmetic from the laws of logic, he would have to operate in a setting in which proofs could be given rigorously and reliably. The logicist program simply could not be carried out otherwise. It was for this purpose that Frege had to clarify fundamental notions of logic and semantics: they were essential to articulating the relation between the language in which proofs are carried out, his begriffsschrift, and the mathematical

---

[5] Of course, Russell and Wittgenstein are well-known exceptions. Among purely mathematical colleagues, the only one who seems to have had much time at all for Frege's work was Peano, and his interest seems to have been short lived.

[6] Their reviews of *Begriffsschrift* are reprinted in (Frege, 1972b).

claims he intended to be proving. Insofar as we speak of Frege's philosophy of language, then, it can only be understood properly if we keep clearly in mind that it was, first and foremost, a philosophy of logic that was an integral part of a larger scientific project, the project of logicism.

The treatment of generality is to a large extent the catalyst for the emergence of Frege's characteristic philosophical doctrines. This is so because Frege regarded his treatment of generality as demonstrating why logic is so important to the study of mathematics in general and to logicism in particular. Frege recognized that logical rigor depends, first and foremost, upon our being able to articulate the structure of sentences, and what Frege understood profoundly was that how sentences containing words of generality *compose* is fundamentally different from how sentences containing no such words compose. This difference Frege saw as a structural difference in conceptual content, and we must come to terms with this point if we are to begin to understand what Frege means by "conceptual contents" or, to use his later terminology, "thoughts": we must grasp that thoughts are, *qua* contents, compositionally complex. Nonetheless, compositionality for Frege is neither a metaphysical principle nor a psychological one. Rather, it is a semantic principle, integral to our understanding of how thoughts can be expressed by language. As such, compositionality ranks as the distinctively *linguistic* contribution Frege's philosophy of logic makes to philosophy of language, not just as a guiding maxim but also in particular aspects of Frege's more detailed proposals.[7]

Our plan for the remainder of the paper is as follows. In section 1.2, we discuss Frege's apparently metaphysical doctrine that concepts are 'unsaturated'. We argue that it is primarily a semantic thesis, an essential ingredient of Frege's conception of compositionality. In section 1.3, we discuss Frege's conception of truth. We argue that his seemingly puzzling doctrine that sentences denote objects, namely, truth-values, emerges from considerations about the logic of sentential connectives and the semantics of predicates and embodies an understanding of why, as Frege sees it, logic is so intimately concerned with the notion of truth. In section 1.4, we turn to Frege's notion of a thought and, more generally, the distinction between sense and reference. Our first goal is to explain the philosophical pressures that lead Frege to draw this famous distinction. We then raise an interpretive question that has not previously been clearly recognized, namely: how does distinguishing the sense of 'the Morning Star' from that of 'the Evening Star' allow Frege to explain why sentences containing these two names express different thoughts? Answering this question will require us to clarify yet further Frege's conception of compositionality.

---

[7] There is much of interest in Frege's work that we shall not have space to discuss. We shall only touch very briefly upon Frege's treatment of intensional contexts (Frege, 1984f, opp. 36ff), barely mention his discussion of indexicality (Frege, 1984h, opp. 65ff), and, sadly, ignore his notion of a criterion of identity (Frege, 1980a, §§62ff) and his discussion of presupposition (Frege, 1984f, opp. 39ff). That is not, of course, because we think there is nothing of value in these discussions. There is. But we have tried here to focus upon Frege's most general doctrines, which in turn shape his particular analyses.

1.2 CONCEPTS

In the logic developed by Boole, sentences were constructed from predicates using a small number of operators corresponding to traditional forms of judgment, such as universal affirmative judgments, which are of the form 'All *F*s are *G*'. Proper names, such as 'Socrates', were regarded as predicates, that is, as being of the same logical type as expressions like 'is mortal'. Thus, the famous argument

> All humans are mortal.
> Socrates is a human.
> Therefore, Socrates is mortal.

might have been represented as:[8]

> All *H* are *M*.
> All *S* are *H*.
> All *S* are *M*.

The correctness of the argument then follows from the validity of the form of syllogism known as Barbara.

Frege's way of representing generality required him to reject this traditional identification of names and predicates. As Frege saw the matter in *Begriffsschrift*, a sentence may be regarded as constructed from an *argument* and a *function*. In the case of 'Socrates is mortal', for example, we may take the argument to be 'Socrates' and the function to be "the part that remains invariant in the expression" when we replace 'Socrates' by other names, such as 'Plato' or 'Thales' (Frege, 1967). Frege would then represent the sentence 'Socrates is mortal' in his logic, as: $M(s)$, and the generalization "Everything is mortal" as: $M(x)$, where the singular term 'Socrates' has been replaced by a variable. Note the absence of the quantifier: Frege's view, at this time, was that generality is indicated by "letters", that is, by variables (Frege, 1967, §1). The "concavity" in the more explicit representation

$$\underset{\mathfrak{a}}{\vphantom{|}}\!\!\!\!\cup\ M(\mathfrak{a})$$

serves, Frege says, only to "delimit[] the scope that the generality *indicated by the letter* covers" (Frege, 1967, §11, our emphasis).

Built into Frege's logical notation, then, is an asymmetry between expressions that occur as functions and those that occur as arguments. It is obvious that this early distinction, between function and argument, has much in common with Frege's later distinction between concept and object, but there are two important differences.

First, Frege speaks in *Begriffsschrift* as if functions and arguments are (parts of) *expressions*: when we replace 'Socrates' with other names in the expression 'Socrates is mortal', the function we discover is "the part that remains invariant in the

---

[8] The second premise could, of course, also be taken to be: Some *S* are *H*.

expression" (Frege, 1967, §9, our emphasis). It would be uncharitable, we think, to saddle Frege with the view that expressions are functions: more reasonable is the supposition that he was, at that time, no clearer about the distinction between use and mention than were any of his contemporaries. But we find Frege distinguishing use from mention more carefully just a couple years later. When Frege introduces the notion of a concept in "Boole's Logical Calculus and the Begriffsschrift", written about 1881, he speaks not of replacing the *expression* '2' by other *expressions* in the *sentence* '$2^4 = 16$' but rather of replacing the *object* 2 by other *objects* in the *content of possible judgement* $2^4 = 16$. The concept *fourth root of 16* is thus discovered in the *content* $2^4 = 16$: it is what remains invariant in the content when we vary imagine 2 replaced by other objects (Frege, 1979a, pp. 16–7). So already by 1881, Frege no longer regards concepts as parts of expressions that remain invariant when other parts are varied but rather as what such parts of expressions *denote*.[9]

Second, Frege insists in *Begriffsschrift* that the distinction between function and argument "has nothing to do with the conceptual content [of an expression]; it comes about only because we view the expression in a particular way" (Frege, 1967, §9). The distinction between function and argument is thus not absolute in the way Frege insists, in his later work, that the distinction between object and concept is: one may regard 'Socrates' as the argument and 'is mortal' as the function; but one may equally regard 'is mortal' as the argument and 'Socrates' as the function. Note that we have *not* said that one can regard 'ξ is mortal' as the argument and the second-level concept '$\Phi(Socrates)$' as the function, which is how Frege would have seen the matter in his later work: there is no notion of second-level concept to be found in *Begriffsschrift*.[10]

Frege's view had begun to change in this respect too already by 1881, largely in response to Boole's assimilation of names to predicates. Consider this passage:[11]

If ... you imagine the 2 in the content of possible judgement $2^4 = 16$ to be replaceable by something else, by -2 or by 3 say, which may be indicated by putting an x in place of the 2:

$$x^4 = 16,$$

the content of possible judgement is thus split into a constant and a variable part. The former, regarded in its own right but holding a place open for the latter, gives the concept '4th root of 16' ... And so instead of putting a judgement together out of an individual as subject and an already formed concept as predicate, we do the opposite and arrive at a concept by splitting up the content of possible judgement.   (Frege, 1979a, pp. 16–7)

---

[9] This change is noted explicitly by Philip Jourdain in his 1912 summary of Frege's doctrines (Jourdain, 1980, p. 204), on which Frege provided extensive commentary.

[10] And similarly, there is no distinction between first- and second-order quantification. There is but one axiom of universal instantiation, proposition 58, and it is used indiscriminately to justify both what we would regard as first-order inferences and what we would regard as second-order inferences.

[11] Frege speaks almost entirely of concepts in this paper, not of functions. But it is clear that this difference is only terminological: Boole speaks of concepts, and Frege is speaking as he does. Indeed, Frege's examples of functions in *Begriffsschrift* are generally examples of concepts (or predicates).

The view Frege is expressing here is very close to his mature view: the concept *fourth root of 16* is that part of the content $2^4 = 16$ that remains constant when one varies 2, "regarded in its own right but *holding a place open for*" a suitable argument (Frege, 1979a, p. 16, our emphasis). Concepts must therefore be fundamentally different from objects: "In the case of a concept it is always possible to ask whether something, and if so what, falls under it, questions which are senseless in the case of an individual" (Frege, 1979a, p. 18).

There is, however, an important difference between how Frege explains the 'unsaturatedness'[12] of concepts *circa* 1881 and how he explains it in his mature writings. As we have seen, Frege introduces the claim that concepts are unsaturated, in 1881, by asking us to imagine replacing the number 2 in the *content* $2^4 = 16$ with other objects. Frege also regards predicates—that is, expressions that designate concepts—as being unsaturated:

[I]n the begriffsschrift, [designations of properties] never occur on their own, but always in combinations which express contents of possible judgement. . . . A sign for a property never appears without a thing to which it might belong being at least indicated, a designation of a relation never without indication of the things which might stand in it.   (Frege, 1979a, p. 17)

But, in this paper, Frege seems to regard the unsaturatedness of predicates as a consequence of the unsaturatedness of what they designate. The roles are reversed in Frege's mature work. Once he has made the distinction between sense and reference, Frege can no longer speak of replacing the number 2 in the content of the sentence '$2^4 = 16$'—that is, in the thought it expresses—for he denies that objects occur in thoughts.[13] And so, when Frege is attempting to explain his doctrine that functions are unsaturated in "What is a Function?" he first explains his conception of a functional *expression* by asking us to consider sequences of expressions like 'sin 0', 'sin 1', 'sin 2' (Frege, 1984i, op. 665),[14] much as he did in *Begriffsschrift*. The difference, of course, is that Frege no longer regards functions as expressions but as what functional expressions denote.[15] That is to say: what Frege explains first is his view that functional *expressions* are unsaturated; he then explains the unsaturatedness of functions in terms of the unsaturatedness of predicates. Thus, Frege writes in "Comments on Sense and Meaning":[16]

[12] Frege does not use this terminology until 1882, in a letter to Anton Marty we quote below. The only earlier hint of that terminology—or, rather, of the alternative terminology of "incompleteness"—is in a footnote in "Boole's Logical Calculus", where Frege says that, in a concept, "one simply doesn't have anything complete" (Frege, 1979a, p. 17, fn).

[13] See the famous exchange about Mont Blanc and its snowfields in Frege's letter to Russell of 13 November 1904 (Frege, 1980b, p. 163) and Russell's reply of 12 December 1904 (Frege, 1980b, p. 169).

[14] We shall cite Frege's published papers, as reprinted in (Frege, 1984a), by the page number in the original publication.

[15] There is no general agreement about how Frege's technical term '*Bedeutung*' and its cognates should be translated. We shall here generally translate it as 'denotation' but sometimes as 'reference', and we shall use the latter exclusively when contrasting *Bedeutung* with sense.

[16] The translation has the last word of the first sentence being "them", as if it were anaphoric on 'empty places'. It is clear, however, that what Frege means is, as he puts it in *Function and Concept*, that "the argument does not belong with a function" (Frege, 1984c, op. 6).

[O]ne can always speak of the name of a function as having empty places, since what fills them does not, strictly speaking, belong to it. *Accordingly* I call the function itself unsaturated, or in need of supplementation, *because* its name has first to be completed with the sign of an argument if we are to obtain a meaning that is complete in itself.   (Frege, 1979c, p. 119, our emphasis)

One finds similar remarks in *Function and Concept* (Frege, 1984c, opp. 5ff), "On Concept and Object" (Frege, 1984e, opp. 194–5), and "What Is a Function? " (Frege, 1984i, opp. 665). So we take it that this aspect of Frege's view stabilized by 1891: the unsaturatedness of *predicates* is what is basic; the unsaturatedness of *functions and concepts* is to be explained in terms of the unsaturatedness of predicates.

Predicates are not unsaturated in the very same way that concepts are: Frege does not, in his mature work, regard predicates as themselves being functions from, say, names to sentences.[17] By insisting that predicates are unsaturated, Frege is expressing his deeper insistence on the fundamental syntactic distinction between names and predicates. It is clear enough that this claim has withstood the test of time, embedded as it is not only in contemporary logic but in syntactic theory, as well. The claim that the *denotations* of predicates are unsaturated, on the other hand, is often regarded as simply bizarre, and even Frege's most sympathetic interpreters rarely seem to know what to make of it. It can easily seem as if Frege is projecting—and that is the perjorative use—his syntax onto the world. But this impression is the result of our mistaking for a metaphysical doctrine what is, in Frege's hands, primarily a semantic one. If the fact that predicates are unsaturated is to have any consequence whatsoever for the nature of what they denote, then surely such consequences must issue from the nature of the *connection* between predicates and what they denote, that is, from something about the *semantics* of predicates.

What it means for predicates to be unsaturated is that they must always occur with an appropriate number of arguments: a sentence does not contain the one-place predicate 'is mortal' unless those words occur with an appropriate argument. If so, then the semantic clause for a predicate ought, one might well suppose, to reflect this fundamental syntactic fact about it. It is only a slight exaggeration to say that, on Frege's view, the question what 'is mortal' denotes need not be answered at all, since the predicate 'is mortal' can never occur on its own but only together with an appropriate argument. The semantic clause for 'is mortal' should therefore begin not:

'is mortal' denotes . . . ,

but rather:

⌜Δ is mortal⌝ denotes . . . ,

where 'Δ' is a syntactic variable ranging over expressions that might occur as arguments.[18] This suggestion accords with Frege's own practice: witness

---

[17] Of course, Frege did regard predicates as functions in *Begriffsschrift*, but that was for a different reason, namely, that he thought functions were expressions. As we shall see below, it is a delicate question to what the unsaturatedness of the *senses* of predicates amounts.

[18] More formally, 'Δ' ranges over what may be called 'auxiliary names': we suppose that the language can always be expanded by the addition of a new name, whose reference may then be any object one

his stipulations regarding the primitive expressions of the formal language of *Grundgesetze*.[19] A Frege-inspired clause for 'is mortal' would thus take the form:[20]

(1) $\ulcorner \Delta$ is mortal$\urcorner$ denotes the True iff, for some x, Δ denotes x and x is mortal.

But while clauses like (1) directly reflect the unsaturatedness of predicates, it is not clear what they imply about predicates' denotations, since they do not explicitly assign denotations to predicates at all. The most obvious way of doing so would be:

(2) The predicate 'is mortal' denotes the concept *mortality*.

But, of course, this will not do, for it leads directly to the infamous problem of the concept *horse*. Nevertheless, it is clear that Frege thought that a relation between a predicate and a concept was at least implied by a clause like (1). In section 5 of *Grundgesetze*, for example, Frege explains the meaning of the horizontal by the following postulate:

— Δ is the True if Δ is the True; on the other hand, it is the False if Δ is not the True,

and he takes this stipulation to be sufficient to assign a function as denotation of the horizontal. "Accordingly," Frege continues, " — ξ is a function whose value is always a truth-value . . .".

While Frege leaves matters at this pass, we can be more precise. Consider the relation that holds between a one-place predicate and its denotation. Since this is a relation of 'mixed level', taking as arguments an object—the predicate itself—and a concept, an expression denoting the relation between a predicate and its denotation must take as arguments a proper name denoting the predicate and a predicate denoting the concept.[21] This predicate, being unsaturated, must occur with an argument, which in this case will be a bound variable, there being nothing else for it to be. Thus, a 'denotation clause' for a predicate that is compatible with Frege's commitments would have to have the following form:[22]

(3) $denotes_x$('ξ is mortal', x is mortal)

---

wishes. Formally, a truth-definition using such a device requires us to quantify over languages that expand the original one. See (Heck, 1999) for discussion, and the appendix of that paper for a sketch of a formal of a theory of this kind.

Frege uses some such device, and we have borrowed this use of Greek capitals from him. It is not clear, however, how Frege regarded these expressions, whose use he never explains. Sometimes, they seem to act like meta-linguistic variables ranging over objects; but then they also occur in quotation-marks, as in the semantic clause for identity in §7 of *Grundgesetze*, which suggests that they are substitutional variables. Auxiliary names let us have the best of both worlds.

[19] We will quote one of these below, that for the horizontal. It is in no way exceptional. Regarding the other primitives, the clause for negation is in § 6; identity, § 7; the first-order universal quantifier, § 8; the smooth breathing, § 9; the definite article, § 11; the conditional, § 12; and the second-order universal quantifier, § 24.

[20] We will take up Frege's view that sentences denote truth-values below.

[21] The concept *horse* problem surely does make itself felt in these informal remarks. The point is that it need not make itself felt in the formal semantics.

[22] To be fully faithful to Frege's intentions, the clause would better be formulated so that it explicitly assigned a function to the predicate, but we'll glide past that complication.

Now, suppose we formulate our semantic theory using clauses of this form rather than clauses of form (1). To characterize the truth of atomic sentences, we will also need a principle governing the composition of simple sentences, say:[23]

(4) $\Phi(\Delta)$ denotes the True if, and only if, for some ϕ and for some x, denotes$_x$ $(\Phi(\xi), \phi x)$ and denotes (Δ, x) and ϕx.

We can now prove:[24]

(5) *denotes*$_x(\Phi(\xi), \phi x)$ iff, for every Δ, $\Phi(\Delta)$ denotes the True iff, for some x, *denotes*(Δ, x) and ϕx.

It follows that (1) is indeed sufficient to determine the denotation of 'is mortal', since (1) just is the right-hand side of the relevant instance of (5). It might therefore be thought that the question whether the semantics of predicates should be given by clauses like (1) or instead by clauses like (3) is of no real significance. We can take the latter as basic, in which case (3) and (4) obviously imply (1); or we can take (1) as basic, define denotation using (5), and then prove both (3) and (4). In that case, we would regard (1) as assigning a denotation to 'is mortal' as directly as it is possible to assign one, since, as already noted, (1) is the right-hand side of an instance of (5).

From Frege's perspective, however, the question whether (1) or (3) is more fundamental is critical. In a letter to Anton Marty, written in 1882, the language of unsaturatedness first appears explicitly, when Frege writes:[25]

A concept is unsaturated in that it requires something to fall under it; hence it cannot exist on its own. That an individual falls under it is a judgeable content, and here the concept appears as predicative and is always predicative. In this case, where the subject is an individual, the relation of subject to predicate is not a third thing added to the two, but it belongs to the content of the predicate, which is what makes the predicate unsatisfied. (Frege, 1980b, p. 101)

What should we make of this claim that concepts are essentially 'predicative'? that is, that predication itself somehow "belongs to the content of the predicate"? To understand what Frege is suggesting, we must understand what contrast he is trying to draw. What, then, is the other case, the case where the subject is *not* an individual? As Frege sees it, "the linguistic schema of subject and predicate . . . contains what are logically quite different relations" (Frege, 1980b, p. 101). One he calls "subordination": it is the relation between concepts expressed in such sentences as 'Humans

---

[23] Here '$\Phi(\xi)$' is a syntactic variable ranging over predicates, with ξ indicating the argument-place. It is here that it becomes important that Δ is an 'auxiliary name' and does not just range over such names as are available in the language itself. Note, however, that our being able to give this definition in no way depends upon our using the device of auxiliary names. The same trick could be pulled using satisfaction.

[24] For the proof, we also need a principle stating that every predicate denotes at most one concept: $denotes_x(\Phi\xi, \phi x) \wedge denotes_x(\Phi\xi, \psi x) \rightarrow \forall x(\phi x \equiv \psi x)$. But we need such a principle anyway, since we'd otherwise not be able to prove, say, that '0 = 1' is false: For that argument, we need to know that '=' denotes *only* the relation of identity. With this principle in place, we could then introduce an expression *true-of*(t,y), read 't is true of y', as equivalent to: $\exists F(denotes_x(t, Fx) \wedge Fy)$.

[25] Frege's use of the traditional terminology here is, presumably, in deference to Marty.

are mortal'. The other he calls "falling under": it is the relation between an object and a concept expressed in such sentences as 'Socrates is mortal'. The case where the subject is not an individual is thus the case traditional logic takes as fundamental. And in *that* case, Frege insists, the relation between subject and predicate *is* a "third thing added to the two", namely, the relation of "subordination", which we would symbolizes thus:

$$\forall a(\Psi a \rightarrow \Phi a)$$

By thus reducing subordination to the conditional, Frege is able to "reduce [Boole's] primary propositions to his secondary ones" (Frege, 1979a, p. 17).

Part of what Frege is claiming is thus that what we would call 'atomic' sentences are what are fundamental for logic. As he writes a decade or so later: "The fundamental logical relation is that of an object's falling under a concept: all relations between concepts can be reduced to this" (Frege, 1979c, p. 118). If atomic sentences are *truly* fundamental, however, then they cannot assert the existence of a *relation* between the subject and the predicate. The correct analysis of 'Socrates is mortal' is not: *falls-under* (M,s): that is, in effect, simply a version of the traditional view. The correct analysis is just: M(s). It is in that sense that concepts must contain the relation of predication within themselves. But a theory that takes the semantics of predicates to be given by clauses like (3) does *not* treat "the relation of subject to predicate" as something that "belongs to the content of the predicate"; on the contrary, it is a "third thing", recorded in (4), that must be "added to the two". Frege's doctrine that concepts are unsaturated is thus, as suggested above, primarily a semantic thesis, not a metaphysical one.

That the denotations of predicates—concepts—are unsaturated and so are fundamentally different from the denotations of proper names—objects—is Frege's central point in "On Concept and Object" (Frege, 1984e). We can now see both why Frege held it to be almost incoherent to hold otherwise and why expressions like 'the concept *horse*' should not seduce us into thinking that concepts are objects after all.

For Frege, effacing the concept–object distinction would beg the question of composition: if both predicates and proper names denoted objects, the question what bound them together and related them to truth would remain open. In striking contrast, taking the denotations of predicates to be functions from objects to truth-values provides a definite and precise answer to that question. Moreover, as Frege emphasizes, this answer can be generalized by extending the compositionality of concepts through a hierarchy of functions,[26] forming what we would characterize today as a type-hierarchy in which "[a]n object falls under a first-level concept [and] a [first-level] concept falls within a second-level concept" (Frege, 1984e, op. 201). It

---

[26] Concepts for Frege are those functions, at any level, that map their arguments to truth-values. Frege's hierarchy is defined, however, in terms of the arguments of functions, not their values, so there are functions at higher levels of the hierarchy that do not have truth-values as their values. Most notable is the second-level concept that is the denotation of the 'smooth-breathing' operator, which forms names of extensions of concepts (or, more generally, of value-ranges).

is thus Frege's reduction of compositionality to function-application that lies at the heart of his conception of logical form.

Both these aspects of Frege's view remain familiar to us today. The former corresponds to taking predicates to denote characteristic functions, while the latter corresponds to taking generality words like 'every' or 'some' to denote generalized quantifiers, functions from characteristic functions (or the sets they determine) to truth-values.[27] There are, of course, alternatives. If, in "On Concept and Object", Frege was responding to the mistake of taking predicates to denote objects, he did not envisage denying that predicates denote at all. Donald Davidson, for one, is well known for urging us not to take the step of assigning an entity to a predicate as its denotation (Davidson, 1984, p. 18). Opposition of this kind is sometimes motivated by ontological scruples—by a preference for desert landscapes, as Quine famously put it (Quine, 1953, p. 4)—but there is a more immediate concern, too, namely, whether the resulting treatment of predication is adequate to the empirical data. The issues between broadly Fregean and broadly non-Fregean accounts of predication are varied and subtle, and which we prefer will depend in part upon the context in which we are operating. In logic, the decision may well be a result of pragmatic choices in linguistic design. In linguistics, it will be rather empirical considerations about syntax, semantics, and their relation that are likely to come to the fore.[28] Adjudicating these matters goes far beyond what we can attempt here. But even if we abandon Frege's claim that predicates denote, what cannot be escaped is the demand that we "do justice at once to the distinction and to the similarity" between the modes of composition exhibited in 'Socrates is mortal' and in 'Everyone is mortal' (Frege, 1984e, p. 201). Frege's insight that such an account is semantically indispensable remains a watershed in the history of semantics.

1.3 TRUTH

For Frege, then, the concept denoted by the predicate 'is mortal' is a function. Its arguments are objects, such as Socrates. But what are its values? By the principle of compositionality, the denotation of 'Socrates is mortal' is the result of applying the function denoted by 'is mortal' to the object denoted by 'Socrates'. So the question what the values of concept-functions are is equivalent to the question what the denotations of sentences are. Frege's answer to that question, famously, is that sentences denote truth-values. But what kinds of things are truth-values? Since the distinction between concepts and objects is both absolute and exhaustive, there are but two possibilities, and famously he opts for the latter: sentences denote either the

---

[27] The most well-known characterization in terms of characteristic functions is found in (Montague, 1974). See also (Lewis, 1970). For discussion of generalized quantifiers, see (Higginbotham and May, 1981), (Barwise and Cooper, 1981), and (Keenan and Stavi, 1986), among a considerable literature.

[28] For some of the consequences of this choice for the semantics of natural language, see (Larson and Segal, 1995), (Chierchia and McConnell-Ginet, 1990), and (Heim and Kratzer, 1998).

True or the False, and it is these objects that are the values of concept-functions. These claims may seem bizarre, but they are central to Frege's understanding of the special role truth plays in logic, a topic to which he devoted several essays (Frege, 1979e, 1979f, 1984h). Truth-values are also central to Frege's philosophy of language, where their role in the emergence of the sense–reference distinction is critical.[29]

Frege's reasons for his view of truth commence with considerations concerning the particular role sentences play in his formal system. As Frege describes his system in *Grundgesetze*, the horizontal, negation, and the conditional are all explicitly presented as truth-functional operators, in a strong sense: each of them really does denote a *function* whose arguments and values are *truth-values*.[30] Negation, for example, is the function that maps the True to the False and the False to the True. It needs no emphasis how important and enduring Frege's conception of the sentential connectives has proven to be. But it was not the way he originally conceived of them. Although something very much like truth-tables appear in *Begriffsschrift*, the words 'true' and 'false' are not used in that connection. Frege speaks not of a content's being true or false but of its being "affirmed" or "denied", so that a conditional, for example, is said to "deny" the case in which the antecedent is "affirmed" and the consequent is "denied". Moreover, there is no indication in *Begriffsschrift* that Frege regarded the sentential operators as (being or denoting) functions.[31] So the expressions Frege would later regard as truth-functional connectives he regarded in *Begriffsschrift* neither as functional nor as specially concerned with truth-values.

Frege's discovery of the notion of a truth-function likely results, at least in part, from his reading Boole in the early 1880s. It was central to Boole's treatment of the sentential connectives that he regarded them as expressing functions, and one can well understand why that idea would have appealed to Frege. But if these operators are to be taken as expressing functions, the question arises[32] what the arguments and values of these functions are. Boole's answer, contrary to what seems to be a popular myth, was not "truth-values". In fact, the Booleans disagreed among themselves about what the correct answer was, and Boole's own view varies.[33] But, whatever the arguments and values were, they had to be classes of some sort: that much was

---

[29] There is a famous argument, the so-called "slingshot", that derives the claim that sentences denote their truth-values from compositionality and a handful of other claims. See (Neale, 2001) for extensive discussion. The argument has sometimes been ascribed to Frege, but we know of no evidence he ever formulated it and so will leave it out of account.

[30] Since, for Frege, the truth-values are objects, these functions are defined for non-truth-values as well. But because negation and the conditional embed horizontals, they may, in effect, be regarded as defined only on the truth-values.

[31] Øystein Linnebo argues that Frege relies upon a quite traditional form-content distinction in *Begriffsschrift*, and the logical machinery belongs to the 'form' of a proposition (Linnebo, 2003). If so, then the notion of a function clearly belongs to the content side and so wouldn't have been applied to such logical notions as the conditional.

[32] It will only arise for Frege once his views about what functions are have changed and he no longer regards them as expressions. As noted above, this change was well under way by 1881.

[33] Boole's view in *The Mathematical Analysis of Logic* (Boole, 1847) is that the possible values of sentential variables are something like sets of circumstances: these are basically possible worlds as understood in the model theory of propositional modal logic. This was an important idea, to be sure, and some of the earliest investigations of modal logic were undertaken by members of the Boolean school,

demanded by how Boole proposed to reduce the calculus of judgements (roughly, sentential logic) to the calculus of classes (roughly, monadic first-order logic). So while Frege may have borrowed the idea that the sentential connectives denote functions from Boole, the idea that they denote *truth*-functions is original to Frege. So far as we know, the first fully explicit appearance of the notion of a truth-function, as described above, is in Frege's 1891 lecture *Function and Concept* (Frege, 1984c, opp. 20–21, 22, 28), but we find Frege starting to use the terms 'true' and 'false' in connection with the arguments of the conditional as early as 1881 (Frege, 1979a, p. 11). Why does Frege so quickly settle upon this answer to the question what the arguments and values of his sentential connectives are?

Both in *Begriffsschrift* and in *Grundgesetze*, a form of Leibniz's Law applies to sentential variables: if the identity-statement connecting S and T is true, then S can be substituted for T. Under what circumstances, then, is an identity-statement connecting two sentences to be regarded as true? In *Begriffsschrift*, Frege's stated view was that '$p \equiv q$' is true only if p and q have the same conceptual content. If so, however, substitution will be possible only rarely. But, we believe, Frege came to realize that much more extensive substitution ought to be possible in his formal language: we ought to be able to substitute any true sentence for any other true sentence, *salva veritate*. Frege's reading of Boole probably played an important role here, too: Boole's logic is formulated as an algebraic system, and substitution of equals is one of its most basic principles. Such extensive substitution would be permitted if we regarded sentences as referring to their truth-values and re-interpreted the "sign for identity of content": then all true sentences name the same thing, '$p = q$' may be taken to be true so long as p and q have the same truth-value, and substitution may proceed apace; the material biconditional has thus been reduced to identity. But identity here is *objectual* identity, so sentences must denote objects, namely, the True or the False.

If the True and the False are objects, the question then arises which objects they are. Frege's answer is that they can be any objects at all, so long as all true thoughts refer to the same object, all false thoughts refer to the same object, and true thoughts refer to a different object than do false thoughts. In section 10 of *Grundgesetze*, Frege argues that if any pair of distinct value-ranges satisfies these conditions, then every pair of distinct value-ranges does so.[34] Although Frege's particular implementation is vitiated by its being embedded in an inconsistent system—the proof that the third clause is satisfied in any given case will depend on the identity-criteria for value-ranges, and these, unfortunately, are given by the Basic Law V—the underlying idea

---

such as Hugh MacColl, around the turn of the twentieth century. (Thanks to Stephen Read for this information.)

Boole's later view, in *Laws of Thought* (Boole, 1854), is the one Schröder elaborates in his review of *Begriffsschrift* (Schröder, 1972, p. 224): The semantic value of a sentence-letter is taken to be the set of times when it is true. Frege has a lot of fun with that suggestion, but it too has a contemporary echo, in tense logic.

[34] Value-ranges are the only option, since they are the only objects (other than truth-values, if truth-values are not value-ranges) in the domain of theory. See (Wehmeier and Schroeder-Heister, 2005) for a careful analysis of this argument, which turns out to contain a subtle flaw.

is nevertheless clear and widely employed: obviously, there is no significant difference between letting the truth-values be 0 and 1 and letting them be 27 and 34.

If, as we have seen, Frege argues for taking the truth-values to be objects by pointing to their role in logic, he is, of course, also aware that, in natural language, the word 'true' appears as an adjective: "Grammatically, the word 'true' looks like a word for a property" (Frege, 1984h, op. 59). Frege argues, *via* the so-called regress argument, that such a property must be indefinable:

> For in a definition certain characteristics would have to be specified. And in application to any particular case the question would always arise whether it were true that the characteristics were present. So we would be going round in a circle.   (Frege, 1984h, op. 60)

This circularity would be particularly endemic, Frege observes, to truth defined as correspondence:

> [W]hat ought we to do so as to decide whether something is true? We should have to inquire whether it is *true* that an idea and a reality, say, correspond . . . And then we should be confronted by a question of the same kind, and the game could begin again. So the attempted explanation of truth as correspondence breaks down.   (Frege, 1984h, op. 60)

The breakdown would be in evidence even if we delimited our definition, as we properly should according to Frege, to the truth of sentences or, better, of thoughts. Having said this, however, Frege is quick to note that it does not follow that truth is not a property of thoughts. "With every property of a thing," Frege says, "there is tied up a property of a thought, namely truth" (Frege, 1984h, op. 61). On the other hand, ascribing this property to a thought does not result in a different thought with new content but simply gives one the same thought back, or so Frege claims.[35] Perhaps, then, truth is "something which cannot be called a property in the ordinary sense at all" (Frege, 1984h, op. 61).

Some commentators have taken Frege to be arguing here that there is no property that all and only the true thoughts have.[36] But there is, we think, little evidence that he thought there can be no property that all and only the true thoughts have, and the regress argument simply does not establish this strong claim: if truth-values are the references of sentences, then "denotes the True" is a truth-predicate. Defenders of the interpretation just mentioned therefore take Frege to be arguing, more generally, that there can be no 'semantic meta-perspective' on logic: we cannot really speak of such a relation as that of denotation. This suggestion seems to us desperate: the suggestion that Frege abjures all properly semantic discourse is simply at odds with too much of what he has to say about logic and, in particular, with the plain sense of Part I of *Grundgesetze*.[37] But there is nonetheless a puzzle here. Doesn't the regress

---

[35] Even on Frege's own view, this is incorrect or, at least, inexact. As Dummett notes, the equivalence of A and "It is true that A" cannot be maintained if one allows sentences not to have truth-values, as Frege does (Dummett, 1978b, pp. 4–5).

[36] The view mentioned is particularly associated with Thomas Ricketts (Ricketts, 1986, 1996). See also (van Heijenoort, 1967), (Dreben and van Heijenoort, 1986), (Weiner, 1990), and (Goldfarb, 2001). See (Stanley, 1996) and (Tappenden, 1997) for criticism and development of contrary views.

[37] See (Heck, 2006) for development of this claim. Some reason for it will also emerge below in section 1.4.

argument apply *mutatis mutandis* to the suggestion that truth, regarded as a property of thoughts, can be defined in terms of "denotes the True"? If not—if truth, regarded as a property of thoughts, *is* in the end definable—then what is Frege trying to establish with the regress argument?

The earliest presentation of the regress argument is in a draft of a textbook on logic, written in 1897. At the opening of the paper, Frege emphasizes that logic, as he understands it, is concerned with truth in a way no other science is:

> Of course all the sciences have truth as their goal, but logic is concerned with 'true' in a quite special way, namely in a way analogous to that in which physics has to do with the predicates 'heavy' and 'warm' and chemistry with the predicates 'acid' and 'alkaline'... [L]ogic is the most general science of the laws of truth.   (Frege, 1979f, p. 128)

He then goes on to present the regress argument. What Frege is arguing, we suggest, is not that there is no property that all and only the true thoughts have but that logic's special concern with truth cannot properly be understood if truth is regarded as *fundamentally* a property of thoughts: there may be such a property, but it is not what specially concerns logic.

Logic, Frege insists, "is not concerned with how thoughts, regardless of truth-value, follow from thoughts..." (Frege, 1979c, p. 122). Rather, the premises and conclusion of an inference are always *judgements*, and judgement, as Frege understands it, is essentially directed at truth: to make a judgement is to acknowledge the truth of a thought (Frege, 1984h, op. 62).[38] Logic's special concern with truth is thus a consequence of its special concern with judgements and of judgement's intimate relation to truth. It is here that the regress argument becomes relevant: isn't *acknowledging* something itself simply making a judgement? If so, then to acknowledge the truth of the thought that $2 + 3 = 5$ is simply to judge that this thought is true. But then that judgement too must be regarded as the acknowledgement of the truth of the thought judged—that is, of the truth of the thought that it is true that $2 + 3 = 5$—but to acknowledge the truth of that thought is simply to judge that the thought that it is true that $2 + 3 = 5$ is true, and so on *ad infinitum*. What the regress argument is intended to establish is thus that the intimate relation between judgement and truth cannot be understood in terms of judgements' *predicating* truth of thoughts.[39]

---

[38] It is now widely agreed that this claim is what drives the regress. See (Ricketts, 1986) and (Kemp, 1995), for instance.

[39] There is, in fact, some evidence that Frege himself once so regarded judgement:

> We can imagine a language in which the proposition "Archimedes perished at the capture of Syracuse" would be expressed thus: "The violent death of Archimedes at the capture of Syracuse is a fact".... *Such a language would have only a single predicate for all judgements, namely, "is a fact".... Our ideography is a language of this sort, and in it the sign is the common predicate for all judgements.*   (Frege, 1967, §3)

The emphasis is Frege's.

Frege has another argument for this same claim. This argument—which we might call the argument from content-redundancy—purports to show that one can predicate truth of a thought without making a judgement:[40]

One can say . . . : 'The thought that 5 is a prime number is true'. But closer examination shows that nothing more has been said than in the simple sentence '5 is a prime number'. The truth claim arises in each case from the form of the assertoric sentence, and when the latter lacks its usual force, e.g. in the mouth of an actor upon the stage, even the sentence 'The thought that 5 is a prime number is true' contains only a thought, and indeed the same thought as the simple '5 is a prime number'. It follows that the relation of the thought to the True may not be compared with that of subject to predicate.   (Frege, 1984f, op. 34)

Frege makes a similar claim shortly after he presents the regress argument in "Thoughts" and then remarks that what "explains why . . . nothing seems to be added to a thought by attributing to it the property of truth" is the fact that we do not need to use the word 'true' to express a judgement (Frege, 1984h, op. 63). Rather, we may express our acknowledgement of the truth of a thought simply by asserting a sentence that expresses that thought (Frege, 1984h, op. 62).

What, then, is judgement? What, in particular, distinguishes one's *judging* that $2 + 3 = 5$ from one's merely *entertaining* the thought that $2 + 3 = 5$? Frege often notes that, if one is merely entertaining a thought, then it does not matter whether its parts refer to anything: it is only if we are concerned to evaluate the thought—to decide whether we should assert it or deny it—that the references of the parts matter (Frege, 1984f, opp. 32–3).[41] But, for Frege, reference is essentially compositional: if it matters whether the parts refer, and if so to what, then that must be because it matters whether the whole refers, and if so to what; "in every judgement, no matter how trivial, the step from the level of thoughts to the level of reference [is] taken" (Frege, 1984f, op. 34). We may thus distinguish judgements from mere entertainings of thoughts by insisting that judgements are "advances from a thought to a truth-value" (Frege, 1984f, op. 35): when one judges that $2 + 3 = 5$, one is not just entertaining the thought that $2 + 3 = 5$; one is attempting to *refer* to something, namely, the True. The relation between a thought and its truth-value, on Frege's view, is thus not that of an object to a property but "that of sense to reference" (Frege, 1984f, op. 34).

This view is immune to Frege's regress, even if we do take the next step and define 'It is true that p' as: the thought that p denotes the True. The regress, as noted above,

---

[40] We borrow the term 'content-redundancy' from Gary Kemp (Kemp, 1998). Kemp understands the argument differently from how we do, but we think he was right to highlight the connection between it and the regress argument.

See also the "Logic" of 1897, where Frege writes:

[I]t is really by using the form of an assertoric sentence that we assert truth, and to do this we do not need the word 'true'. Indeed we can say that even where we use the form of expression 'it is true that . . .' the essential thing is really the assertoric form of the sentence.   (Frege, 1979f, p. 129)

Frege might also have mentioned that 'it is true that p' can occur as antecedent of a conditional, in which case the thought that p need not be asserted.

[41] Frege makes similar remarks in his other discussions of the regress argument and the argument from content-redundancy (Frege, 1979f, p. 130; 1984h, op. 63).

is driven by a 'predicational' conception of judgement, according to which making a judgement is ascribing truth to a thought. The view just outlined rejects that conception of judgement. The view is *not* that judging that *p* is ascribing the property *denoting the True* to the thought that *p*: that would indeed re-instate the regress. Rather, the view is that judging that *p* is attempting to refer, by thinking that *p*, to the True.

It is, of course, obvious that this conception of judgement—that is, of belief and, correlatively, of assertion—could use further development. Unfortunately, Frege says little more about it. But that is, we suggest, because his main concern was not with judgement itself but with logic. The point that matters to Frege is that truth-values are properly understood as the references, or semantic values, of sentences: that claim, as we saw earlier, is central to his treatment of the sentential connectives; since the semantic values of sentences are the values of concept-functions, it is central also to his conception of concepts and so to his understanding of composition. Here again, Frege's basic point has survived. The role truth plays in logic is indeed more fundamental than is suggested by the familiar phrase 'the truth-predicate'. The truth-values do indeed enter logic, in the first instance, as the semantic values of sentences, because the most basic notion of logic, that of a valid inference, cannot be explicated except in terms of the notion of truth.

1.4 THOUGHTS

Truth-values, on Frege's view, are thus the references of sentences. But this doctrine gives rise to a problem, one that is most obvious if we translate Frege's term '*Bedeutung*' using its ordinary English equivalent, 'meaning'. The problem is this: "If . . . the truth-value of a sentence is its meaning, then on the one hand all true sentences have the same meaning and so, on the other hand, do all false sentences" (Frege, 1984f, op. 35). Frege's solution to this problem is, familiarly, to claim that the thought expressed by a sentence is distinct from its "meaning". But, as we shall see, Frege was not content simply to draw this distinction. His commitment to the principle of compositionality, and his subtle appreciation of the demands it imposes, led him to an account of what thoughts are and how they are expressed by sentences whose influence continues to be felt today.

The problem just mentioned is discussed in detail in *Function and Concept*:

What '$2^2 = 4$' means is the True just as, say, '2^2' means 4. And '$2^2 = 1$' means the False. Accordingly, '$2^2 = 4$', '$2 > 1$', and '$2^4 = 4^2$' all mean the same thing, viz. the True . . . The objection here suggests itself that '$2^2 = 4$' and '$2 > 1$' nevertheless tell us quite different things, express quite different thoughts.   (Frege, 1984c, op. 13)

Sentences cannot "mean" their truth-values, the claim is, because otherwise all true sentences would have to "tell us" the same thing. Frege's insight is that there is no incompatibility here at all. This objection poses no special problem for his view, he argues, because it stems from a much weaker assumption:

[L]ikewise '$2^4 = 4^2$' and '$4 \times 4 = 4^2$' express different thoughts; and yet we can replace '2^4' by '4×4', since both signs have the same meaning. Consequently, '$2^4 = 4^2$' and '$4 \times 4 = 4^2$' likewise have the same meaning. We see from this that from sameness of meaning there does not follow sameness of the thought expressed. If we say 'the Evening Star is a planet with a shorter period of revolution than the Earth', the thought we express is other than in the sentence 'the Morning Star is a planet with a shorter period of revolution than the Earth'; for somebody who does not know that the Morning Star is the Evening Star might regard the one as true and the other as false. And yet both sentences must have the same meaning; for it is just a matter of interchange of the words 'the Evening Star' and 'the Morning Star', which mean the same thing, i.e. are proper names of the same heavenly body.   (Frege, 1984c, opp. 13–14)

What Frege is arguing here is that the principle that the "meaning" of a complex expression is determined by the "meanings" of its parts—that is, the principle of compositionality—together with the principle that the "meaning" of a proper name is its bearer, already implies that the thought expressed by a sentence is not determined by its "meaning". If so, then it is no objection to his view that '$2^4 = 4^2$' and '$2 > 1$' have the same "meaning" that they express different thoughts.

There were a host of good reasons for Frege to endorse the premises behind this argument. (We revert now to speaking of denotation and reference rather than of "meaning".) The principle of compositionality falls out of his treatment of concepts as functions; the thesis that sentences denote their truth-values we have just discussed; and Frege had held that the "content" of a proper name was its bearer even early on in *Begriffsschrift*. There is, of course, one other assumption that is needed: that "...'$2^4 = 4^2$' and '$4 \times 4 = 4^2$' express different thoughts". This assumption has, of course, been much discussed in contemporary philosophy. At least until his correspondence with Russell, however, Frege does not seem even to have considered the possibility that it might be denied.[42]

If we accept that premise, as Frege did, then the argument we have been considering may not pose a problem for his view, but it does suggest a question, one Frege formulates in a letter to Peano as: "How can the substitution of one proper name for another designating the same object effect such changes? " (Frege, 1980b, p. 169). Frege's solution to this problem is, famously, to distinguish sense from reference. The distinction makes its first appearance in *Function and Concept*, immediately following the passage quoted above:

We must distinguish between sense and reference. '2^4' and '4×4' certainly have the same reference, i.e. are proper names of the same number; but they have not the same sense; consequently, '$2^4 = 4^2$' and '$4 \times 4 = 4^2$' refer to the same thing, but have not the same sense (i.e. in this case: they do not contain the same thought).   (Frege, 1984c, op. 14)

Although the formulation in terms of sense and reference does not crystallize in Frege's writings until the early 1890s,[43] it is clear that Frege is aware of the distinction

---

[42] See again the exchange about Mont Blanc and its snowfields, mentioned above in note 13.
[43] For some speculations on the dating, see (Sundholm, 2001).

as early as *Die Grundlagen*,[44] and, as we shall see below, some of the machinery he deploys is already present in *Begriffsschrift*.

Though its application to identity-statements is extremely significant, it's important to observe that the distinction between sense and reference does not emerge from any particular concern with identity-statements. At the time of *Begriffsschrift*, Frege treats mathematical equality as a notion distinct from 'identity of content', the latter being the notion governed by Leibniz's Law. But Frege must quickly have realized that this view is incompatible with a central tenet of logicism, namely, that there are no arithmetical notions with irreducibly mathematical content. When, in "Boole's Logical Calculus" (written, again, no more than two years later), Frege is demonstrating how actual mathematical arguments can be formalized in the begriffsschrift, he takes the logical principles that, in *Begriffsschrift*, had governed 'identity of content' now to govern arithmetical equality (Frege, 1979a, p. 29). In *Die Grundlagen*, Frege overtly takes the step of reducing arithmetical equality to the general notion of objectual identity governed by Leibniz's Law (Frege, 1980a, §65). Identity-statements then take pride of place within Frege's mathematical project, logicism: "... [I]dentities are, of all forms of proposition, the most typical of arithmetic" (Frege, 1980a), he tells us. But now there is a problem: Frege must explain why '$2 + 2 = 4$' expresses something more than a mere triviality; he must solve what has become popularly known as 'Frege's Puzzle'.[45] But there is also something else Frege must show, which he intimates in the passage from *Function and Concept* displayed above, namely, why '$2^4 = 4^2$' expresses a different true thought than does '$4 \times 4 = 4^2$'. The two puzzles are not the same, for in the latter case, unlike the former, substitution does not transform something of substance into a triviality: both '$2^4 = 4^2$' and '$4 \times 4 = 4^2$' have non-trivial thought contents.[46]

Although the sense–reference distinction is centrally implicated in accounting for both puzzles, a confluence that Frege thought highlighted its utility and importance, the reflections that led Frege to recognize the role this distinction played in resolving these two puzzles are quite different, as befits the difference between them. Whereas the puzzle about identity-statements arises for Frege from deep concern about a foundational mathematical issue—how equalities *qua* identities can express substantive mathematical content—the latter raises a more general semantic issue—how sentences express thoughts. For how are we to understand how the parts of a sentence contribute to determining the thought it expresses if sentences

---

[44] The notion that a single number may be given to us in different ways plays an important role in the central sections of *Die Grundlagen* (Frege, 1980a, §§62–67).

[45] Frege's awareness of this issue is no doubt due to his colleague Johannes Thomae, who argued in (Thomae, 1880) that equalities would express trivialities if they were regarded as identities. Thomae took it as a distinct advantage of his formalist approach, on which arithmetic propositions are regarded as rules for the manipulation of formal symbols, that this problem does not arise. See (May, 2001) for elaboration.

[46] This could be doubted, on the ground that '4^2' is *defined* as '4×4'. But there are obviously plenty of other examples.

expressing different thoughts can be composed in the same way from parts with the same references? The fact that Frege illustrates the problem with arithmetical examples shows that he views this matter as a semantic issue at the very foundations of logic: it is an issue about the meaningfulness of expressions of the begriffsschrift.[47] But Frege did not take the issue to be limited to logic; rather he took it to be endemic, to be found in any language whose sentences express thoughts, including natural languages.

The crucial insight, for Frege, is that the distinction between sense and reference is not a distinction between content and something else but a distinction *within* content. In his initial remarks about content in *Begriffsschrift*, Frege talks of sentences' having "possible contents of judgement" as their "conceptual content" (Frege, 1967, §8). But, in a famous passage from the preface to *Grundgesetze*, Frege emends this view, saying that he has "split" content into a complex of thought and truth-value (Frege, 1964, op. x).

A fair bit of effort has been expended trying to discover in what sense the earlier notion of conceptual content contained both the later notions within it. What difficulties have emerged may arise in large part from trying to see the break as structural, as if the notion of conceptual content were a kind of hybrid of the notions of thought and truth-value. But perhaps the break was functional: Frege had tried to use the one notion of conceptual content to do work for which he later decided two notions were needed. The rub came when conceptual content was asked to play a role more aptly enacted by truth-values. No doubt the peculiarities of taking conceptual contents as the denotations of sentences—so that negation and the conditional would be regarded as functions from conceptual contents to conceptual contents—would have been evident to Frege.[48] But the important point for present purposes is that there is no mystery about the way in which conceptual content was asked to play the role later played by thoughts: that is its most explicit theoretical purpose in *Begriffsschrift*, so much so that Frege would not, we think, have confused his readers had he simply continued using the term "conceptual content" instead of switching to the new term "thought". In any event, the notion of a thought that Frege deploys in his discussion in *Function and Concept* is not one for which he would have had to search very far: the distinction between the sense and reference of *sentences*—that is, the distinction between thought and truth-value—was ready to hand. The problem the puzzle about substitution posed for Frege was therefore not that he could not see

---

[47]   The issue is especially pressing for Frege since arithmetical equations, on his view, can be expressed by formulae of what we might call the 'pure' begriffsschrift. But it would arise even if that were not so.

[48]   It is not clear whether Frege ever regarded conceptual contents as the values of the functions with which he identified concepts. Frege does not express a view on this matter in the papers on Boole. It is striking, however, that, during this period, he regards concepts as *intensional*, in the sense that there may be two concepts both true only of Venus (Frege, 1979a, p. 18). It therefore seems that Frege was not by then taking truth-values to be the denotations of sentences. The matter is complicated, however, since Frege could have done so and still regarded concepts as intensional if he took functions generally to be intensional. Unfortunately, he does not express a view on that question in the papers on Boole.

how to allow that two sentences can have the same truth-value but express different thoughts.[49] Rather, the question the puzzle posed was *why* the two sentences express the different thoughts they do.

Frege took himself to have shown that the thought expressed by a sentence is not determined by the references of its parts. If not, it must presumably be determined by something else about the parts,[50] which we might as well agree to call their *senses*: "The names, whether simple or themselves composite, of which the name of a truth-value [that is, a sentence] consists, contribute to the expression of the thought, and this contribution of the individual [component] is its *sense*" (Frege, 1964, §32). So far, then, the notion of a name's sense is purely programmatic, but, as it happens, Frege also had the resources to make it somewhat less so ready to hand. In his discussion of identity-statements in *Begriffsschrift*, Frege remarks that:[51]

[T]he need for a sign for identity of content rests upon the following consideration: the same content can be completely determined in different ways; but that in a particular case *two ways of determining* it really yield the *same result* is the content of a *judgement*. Before this judgement can be made, two distinct names, corresponding to the two ways of determining the content, must be assigned to what these ways determine.   (Frege, 1967, §8, Frege's emphasis)

The idea that a proper name has both a "content", taken to be the object it denotes, and an associated mode of presentation (its *Bestimmungsweise*, in the terminology of *Begriffsschrift*) is thus present early on in Frege's thinking. The key insight, here again, was that this need not be regarded as a distinction between content and something else but can instead be regarded as a distinction within content itself.[52] From the perspective thus reached, Frege can therefore write in "On Sense and Reference":

It is natural . . . to think of there being connected with a sign . . . , besides that which the sign designates, which may be called the reference of the sign, also what I should like to call the *sense* of the sign, wherein the mode of presentation is contained.   (Frege, 1984f, op. 27)

This suggestion, that a name's sense "contains" a mode of presentation of the object it designates, gives the otherwise programmatic notion of sense at least some substantial content: the senses of the parts of a sentence determine the thought it expresses because senses present the objects the thought concerns, and such objects may be presented in different ways. Of course, how much illumination is thus provided depends upon how much we takes ourself to know about ways in which objects may be presented.

---

[49] In (Thau and Caplan, 2001), Michael Thau and Ben Caplan make this sort of suggestion. While we disagree, and disagree more generally with their reading of Frege on identity—see (May, 2001) and (Heck, 2003)—it should be clear that we do think they were right to emphasize how important Frege's view that truth-values are the referents of sentences is to the emergence of the distinction between sense and reference. The connection has been underappreciated.

[50] An assumption is being made here to which we shall call attention later, namely, the assumption that the *sentence* expresses a thought.

[51] Similarly, Frege writes in *Die Grundlagen*: "Why is it . . . that we are able to make use of identities with such significant results in such diverse fields? Surely it is . . . because we are able to recognize something as the same again although it is given in a different way" (Frege, 1980a, pp. 38–40).

[52] This was first observed by Ignazio Angelelli (Angelelli, 1967, p. 67).

Infamously, Frege never says very much more about what modes of presentation are, nor about what the sense of a name is, than he does in the passages we have cited. In much of the secondary literature, especially the older secondary literature, it is assumed that a mode of presentation is a condition an object must satisfy if it is to be the denotation of an expression. If so, then, in some sense,[53] every proper name will be equivalent to a definite description 'the ϕ', where ϕ abbreviates the mentioned condition. Part of what motivates this interpretation is the fact that the only examples Frege gives of modes of presentation are just such conditions.[54] But that does not show that modes of presentation *must* be descriptive conditions, only that they *may* be.

A deeper reason to endorse the descriptive interpretation of modes of presentation derives from Frege's insistence that sense determines reference.[55] There are stronger and weaker interpretations of this doctrine. On the weaker interpretation, Frege means only that reference supervenes on sense, that is, that any two expressions that have the same sense must also have the same reference. On the stronger interpretation, what Frege is claiming is that a name has the reference it does *because* it has the sense it does. One can see why the stronger interpretation might lead one to suppose that the sense of a name had to be something like a description: if a name's having the sense it does is to explain its having the reference it does, then the sense of the name must at least determine some condition that an object must satisfy if it is to be the name's reference. Moreover, the condition must be to some extent independent of the name's referring to the object it does: obviously, if the sense incorporated the reference somehow, the name's having that sense wouldn't explain its referring to the object it does.[56] But we know of no convincing evidence in favor of the stronger interpretation, and the weaker interpretation suggests no particular conception of what sense is.

The true reason the descriptive interpretation of the notion of sense was once so popular, however, is probably that it is simply not obvious what the alternatives are.

---

[53] In *Naming and Necessity* (Kripke, 1980), Saul Kripke famously insisted that, for both Frege and Russell, descriptions 'give the meaning' of names in some sense strong enough to license substitution everywhere, in particular, in modal contexts. We know of no evidence that Frege held any such view. Even if the descriptive interpretation were correct, then, Frege need not have been vulnerable to the arguments in Lecture I of *Naming and Necessity*.

[54] See, for example, (Frege, 1984f, op. 27, fn). There is one passage that may be an exception:

[I]f both Leo Peter and Rudolph Lingens understand by 'Dr Gustav Lauben' the doctor who is the only doctor living in a house known to both of them, then they understand the sentence 'Dr Gustav Lauben was wounded' in the same way; they associate the same thought with it.   (Frege, 1984h, op. 65)

It is not obvious that Frege is suggesting that Peter and Lingens both associate the description 'the only doctor living in such-and-such a house' with the name 'Dr Gustav Lauben'. He could be suggesting, instead, that their grasp of the sense of the name is to be found in their acquaintance with him—not in Russell's sense, of course, but in a sense close enough to Russell's that some, such as Gareth Evans (Evans, 1982), have thought it might do similar work.

[55] As expressed in such remarks as: "The regular connection between a sign, its sense, and its reference is of such a kind that to the sign there corresponds a definite sense and to that in turn a definite reference, while to a given reference (an object) there does not belong only a single sign" (Frege, 1984f, op. 27).

[56] It may be that some such line of thought is at the bottom of Dummett's conception of sense. See (Dummett, 1978a).

How else are we to characterize modes of presentation? Nonetheless, we agree with most scholars of Frege's work that the descriptive interpretation is a misinterpretation.[57] We suggest, moreover, that if one seeks illumination about the notion of sense, one should not look for a direct answer to the question "What is the sense of a name?" There is no such answer to be found in Frege. What is to be found is a theory of logic and language in which the notion of sense has an important role to play. And it, like many other theoretical notions, inherits its content from the broader theoretical framework in which it makes its home.[58]

Running through our discussion has been the claim, which Frege makes in numerous places, that the sense of a sentence is a thought. It is perhaps tempting to suppose that for Frege a thought just is the sense of a sentence, as if his remark in *Grundgesetze*, "The sense of a name of a truth-value I call a *thought*" (Frege, 1964, §2), were meant to be definitional. But it is not. For Frege, the notion of a thought is fundamentally a cognitive one. Like the earlier notion of conceptual content, it emerges from Frege's distinction between cognitive events, such as one's making a judgement or considering an hypothesis, and what it is that one judges or considers.[59] Frege insists, as against the 'psychologistic' logicians, that we must recognize in such episodes something objective that may be considered at one time and at another time judged, or affirmed by one person and denied by another. It is the objective element in such episodes that Frege calls a *thought*. Thoughts, that is, remain for Frege 'possible contents of judgement', to use the terminology of *Begriffsschrift*, or, to use more modern terminology, possible contents of propositional attitudes.

The distinction between thought and judgement is especially evident in natural languages, for these have speakers who have cognitive attitudes towards thoughts.[60] Speakers may judge thoughts, as well as know and believe them. Thus, in identifying thoughts as the senses of sentences, Frege is establishing a connection between language and cognition: he is claiming that with each sentence there is associated as its sense a possible content of a cognitive attitude. That naturally suggests that each sentence has a particular belief associated with it as the belief a literal utterance of that sentence would express. One might wonder, however, what justifies

---

[57] Dummett was perhaps the first explicitly to reject this interpretation (Dummett, 1981a, ch. 5, appendix). See also (McDowell, 1977) and (Evans, 1985).

[58] Space limits how much we can say about this broader framework here. See (Dummett, 1981a, chs. 5–6) for one classic discussion, as well as (Merrick, 2004), for a more recent one. Given Frege's ontology of concepts and objects, if asked what senses are, then they are clearly objects. But this can be construed as a theoretical claim, rather than a metaphysical one: senses are objects just because this is where they slot into the theory, not because there is an independent argument for their existence.

[59] Frege's most complete discussion of such issues is in (Frege, 1984h), but similar themes surface in many other places, for example, in his various efforts to write a piece on "logic" (Frege, 1979e, 1979f, 1979d) and in the introduction to *Grundgesetze* (Frege, 1964).

[60] It is less evident in logic, where the basic laws (axioms) are taken to be self-evident, and hence judged true universally. As Frege notes, however, the distinction is needed nonetheless, since thoughts can occur embedded within other thoughts, for example, as the antecedents of conditionals, where they need not be judged. (This is one reason to be unhappy with Frege's early use of the terms 'affirmed' and 'denied' rather than 'true' and 'false' in explaining the conditional.)

Frege's claim that thoughts are thus associated with the *sentences* of a language as opposed to the weaker claim that each speaker associates a thought with each sentence she understands, different speakers possibly associating different thoughts with the same sentence.[61] Only if the stronger claim can be defended, one might argue, can the notion of sense be regarded as a *linguistic* notion as opposed to a merely psychological one.

How Frege arrived at his point of view about this matter seems clear enough. It was important to Frege that thoughts should be objective. He insisted, as against those who would confuse thoughts with "ideas", that it must be possible for you to believe the very same thing I do, or again to believe its negation.[62] But it was equally important to Frege—in large part because he was so impressed by the use of language as a tool of communication, in particular, as a tool of joint scientific inquiry—that we *express* such agreement and disagreement in our use of language. If Smith says "Aristotle was Greek" and Jones says "Aristotle was not Greek", Jones appears to contradict Smith. But that would not be so if the thought Jones associated with the sentence he uttered was not the negation of the thought Smith associated with the sentence he uttered. Someone who knew that Smith and Jones associated different thoughts with the sentence "Aristotle was Greek" might rationally regard both of them as speaking truly. For example, if Jones took the sentence to express the thought that the teacher of Alexander the Great was Greek whereas Smith took it to express the thought that the greatest student of Plato was Greek, their apparent disagreement might be merely verbal in the sense that, if they were apprised of this fact, they would no longer regard themselves as disagreeing.

That said, however, Frege was aware that to require speakers always to assign the same senses to their words is to set a high standard, one that is not always met in everyday communication. We might take this to indicate that the notion of sense incorporates an idealization, so that the sense of a name is, say, what speakers would, perhaps after reflection and consultation with other speakers, acknowledge as a standard to which they were willing to subject their own usage of the name. Sense would be constant from speaker to speaker by convention.[63] Frege's view is different. His view is that we should simply recognize that, strictly speaking, those who associate different senses with a given proper name speak different languages and that communicability hews to weaker criteria than speaking the same language. Linguistic

---

[61] The issue we are raising here does not concern context-dependence. It arises as much for arithmetical statements as for empirical ones. But there are, of course, issues about context-dependence that do arise in this area, which Frege famously discusses in "Thoughts" (Frege, 1984h, opp. 64–6). See the next footnote for some references to the extensive secondary literature on that discussion.

[62] There is a long-standing dispute how extensive Frege's commitment to the shareability of thoughts is. The orthodox view, for a long time, was that it is exceptionless, so that the very idea of a thought only one person could entertain would be incoherent: see, for example, (Perry, 1993). That view was challenged, however, in the 1980s by Gareth Evans (Evans, 1985), and Evans's view has become the new orthodoxy. But the issue remains open. For some recent reflections, see (May, 2005a).

[63] This sort of view is most strongly associated with Dummett, who writes: "The notion of sense is ... of importance, not so much in giving an account of our linguistic practice, but as a means of systematizing it" (Dummett, 1981a, p. 105).

variation is a normal occurrence, and, as Frege himself notes, it is often unimportant that speakers should all associate the same sense with a given proper name. Whether an object falls under a given concept does not depend upon how the object is presented. It follows that communication can succeed between speakers who technically do not speak the same language so long as they can determine that they are speaking about the very same things: "So long as the reference remains the same," Frege writes, "variations of sense may be tolerated" (Frege, 1984f, op. 27, fn).[64]

But only to a point. It is not *always* unimportant whether the sense is the same for different speakers. The limits of tolerance are to be found where the thought itself matters. A contemporary philosopher might suspect that such cases are to be found most prominently where we attribute propositional attitudes. And, indeed, Frege famously regards sentences of the form 'N believes that S' as asserting a relation between N and the thought that S, which he takes to be the denotation of the phrase 'that S'.[65] Such cases are undoubtedly of interest, and they have of course been much discussed. But for Frege, the crucial case is always that of *logic*. And so it is no surprise that Frege follows his remark that "such variations of sense may be tolerated" with the warning that "they are to be avoided in the theoretical structure of a demonstrative science and ought not to occur in a perfect language" (Frege, 1984f, op. 27, fn).

Why not? The following passage contains a hint:

As if it were permissible to have different propositions with the same wording! This contradicts the rule of unambiguousness, the most important rule that logic must impose on written or spoken language. If propositions having the same wording differ, they can do so only in their thought-content. Just how could there be a single proof of different thoughts? (Frege, 1984g, op. 385 fn)

On Frege's view, logic is the enterprise of showing how true thoughts follow from other true thoughts. But showing this must meet the highest standards, those of proof. The criterion of sense-invariance is part of how we insure the reliability of proofs. If a given sentence, standing as the conclusion of a proof, could be associated with more than one thought, how could we be certain just which thought had been proven? That is why Frege is at pains to insist, in *Grundgesetze*, that his stipulations concerning the significance of his primitive expressions completely determine which thoughts are expressed by the sentences of his formal language. Referring to a much-discussed argument in the preceding sections, Frege writes in section 32:[66]

In this way it is shown that our eight primitive names have denotation, and thereby that the same holds good for all names correctly compounded out of them. However, not only a denotation, but also a sense, attaches to all names correctly formed from our signs.

---

[64] See also (Frege, 1984h), which contains a somewhat more extensive discussion of this issue.

[65] We are simplifying substantially. Frege's actual view is that, in certain contexts, expressions do not have their usual references but instead denote what are usually their senses, which Frege calls their "indirect" references (Frege, 1984f, opp. 47–8).

[66] The elided material concerns sentences containing free variables—what Frege calls "Roman marks"—and is orthogonal to our concerns.

Every such name of a truth-value [that is, every well-formed sentence] *expresses* a sense, a thought. Namely, by our stipulations it is determined under what conditions the name denotes the True. The sense of this name—the *thought*—is the thought that these conditions are fulfilled. Now a proposition of begriffsschrift consists of the judgement-stroke and of a name . . . of a truth-value. . . . It is now asserted by such a proposition that this name denotes the True. Since at the same time it expresses a thought, we have in every correctly-formed proposition of begriffsschrift a judgment that a thought is true; and here a thought certainly cannot be lacking.   (Frege, 1964, §32)

Frege is thus claiming that the theorems proven in *Grundgesetze* have been guaranteed to express completely determinate thoughts.[67]

To the extent that Frege was concerned with language as a tool of communication between inquiring minds, it was to codify those aspects of language that allow it to operate as such in a rigorous, reliable, and sound fashion. Frege's goal, more precisely, was to isolate those aspects of language that are required for *reasoning*. All communication involves the communication of thoughts, Frege would insist, but if we are to ascertain whether communication abides by the laws of thought—that is, the laws of logic—then it must be insisted that there be no variation of sense, so that we are dealing with just one language throughout. Otherwise the following sort of exchange might occur: Jones might prove a certain thought and then communicate it to Smith who, as it happens, actually associates a different thought with that same sentence; Smith then correctly derives some other thought from that one and then communicates it back to Jones, who in turn associates a different thought with *that* sentence, one that does not actually follow from the thought that he associated with the original sentence. Consequently, Frege insists, "we must really stipulate that for every proper name that there shall be just one associated manner of presentation of the object so designated" (Frege, 1984h, op. 65), although this condition may be relaxed (with the concomitant variation of language within a 'speech community') when not so much is on the line in our communicative interactions.[68]

That languages are defined by the relation between certain linguistic forms (namely, sentences) and the thoughts they express is a central Fregean doctrine. But for Frege, thoughts are complexes, made up of senses, and so it is the composition of those senses that will define the language. Thus, it is not just that speakers associate thoughts with sentences; languages, including the sense relevant to logic, are individuated in part by what senses their expressions have. For Frege, the principle of compositionality is thus a *linguistic* rather than a psychological principle; how thoughts compose to express truths plays out through an account of linguistic meaning. In this regard, that

---

[67] Frege also takes himself to have shown, earlier in *Grundgesetze*, that the axioms of his theory are true and that his rules of inference preserve truth. It follows that, if there is at least one false sentence, not every sentence is a theorem, whence the theory is consistent. Frege apparently understood that the argument he is summarizing had this consequence, for in his response to Russell's letter informing him of the contradiction he writes: "It seems accordingly . . . that my law V . . . is false, and that my explanations in sect. 31 do not suffice to secure a meaning for my combinations of signs in all cases" (Frege, 1980b, p. 132).

[68] For further elaboration, see (May, 2005b).

(M) The Morning Star is a planet

expresses a different thought than

(E) The Evening Star is a planet

does is a linguistic fact. And with this observation, we are close to an appreciation of Frege's solution to his famous puzzle. But we still lack one piece.

Grant that 'the Morning Star' and 'the Evening Star' are associated with different modes of presentation, so that they have different senses. How does that fact explain why (M) and (E) express different thoughts? That Frege intends such an explanation is clear from his language in *Function and Concept*:

'2^4' and '4×4' certainly have the same reference, i.e. are proper names of the same number; but they have not the same sense; *consequently*, '$2^4 = 4^2$' and '$4 \times 4 = 4^2$' refer to the same thing, but have not the same sense (i.e. in this case: they do not contain the same thought).   (Frege, 1984c, op. 14, our emphasis)

It is clear enough that Frege supposes that the sense of a sentence is determined by the senses of its parts. This assumption will deliver the conclusion that 'the Morning Star' and 'the Evening Star' have different senses. But it will not deliver the explanation Frege wants; it will not, that is to say, license his use of the term 'consequently'. If the sense of a sentence is determined by the senses of its parts, then the fact that (M) and (E) contain parts with different senses makes it *possible* that they should have different senses, but it in no way requires that they should. What Frege seems to be saying, however, is precisely that (M) and (E) express different thoughts *because* they contain parts with different senses.

What is at issue here is the difference between the claim that the sense of the sentence is *determined by* the senses of its parts and the much stronger claim that the sense of the sentence is *composed of* the senses of its parts. These claims differ because the former allows that the sense of the sentence might be something above and beyond the composed senses, so that in principle two different compositions of senses could converge on the same thought, just as two different compositions of references may converge on the same truth-value. On the latter conception, however, the composition of those senses into a whole determines a thought as the sense of the sentence by *being* that thought.

To make his argument concerning (M) and (E) stick, Frege must show that distinguishing the senses of names from their references is sufficient to account for such sentences' expressing different thoughts. Frege therefore must opt for the stronger interpretation of the principle of compositionality—the one that is arguably more deserving of the name—and regard thoughts as being composed of senses. Frege explicitly states this view in *Grundgesetze*: "If a name is part of the name of a truth-value, then the sense of the former name is part of the thought expressed by the latter name" (Frege, 1964, §32). But it is most vividly expressed in the opening remarks of Frege's last published essay:

It is astonishing what language can do. With a few syllables, it can express an incalculable number of thoughts, so that even if a thought has been grasped by an inhabitant of the

Earth for the very first time, a form of words can be found in which it will be understood by someone else to whom it is entirely new. This would not be possible if we could not distinguish parts in the thought corresponding to the parts of a sentence, so that the structure of the sentence can serve as a picture of the structure of the thought.   (Frege, 1984b, op. 36)

Unfortunately, it is not at all obvious how to apply mereological notions to thoughts: Frege himself, following up the remark just cited, warns that "...we really talk figuratively when we transfer the relation of whole and part to thoughts..." (Frege, 1984b, op. 36). The problem is no secret. It is all well and good to say that the sense of 'The Morning Star is a planet' contains the sense of 'the Morning Star' and the sense of 'is a planet' as parts (Frege, 1984f, op. 27, fn). But this is not enough without an answer to the question how the parts are bound together, that is, without an account of how senses cohere to form thoughts. The sense of 'John loves Mary' cannot be a mere agglomeration of the senses of the parts, lest 'Mary loves John' have the same sense—which, sadly, it does not.

Frege was well aware of this need, writing in "On Concept and Object":[69]

[N]ot all parts of a thought can be complete; at least one must be 'unsaturated' or predicative; otherwise, they would not hold together. For example, the sense of the phrase 'the number 2' does not hold together with that of the expression 'the concept *prime number*' without a link.   (Frege, 1984e, op. 205)

Frege insists that his terms 'complete' and 'unsaturated' are but "figures of speech", meant in the context of the essay "to give hints" to the reader (Frege, 1984e, op. 205). But one natural way to understand Frege's suggestion is to take the senses of predicates to be unsaturated in the very same way that their references are: the sense of a predicate is a function from the senses of names to thoughts. Thus, not only does 'is a planet' *refer* to a function, it also *expresses* one, namely, the one that maps the sense of 'Venus' to the thought that Venus is a planet; the sense of 'Sirius' to the thought that Sirius is a planet; and so forth. Compositionality for senses would then reduce to function-application, again in tandem with references. But this will not do. For one thing, it is not clear that it is coherent to regard senses *qua* functions as parts of a thought, however far we stretch that notion. Certainly to do so would break down the parallelism with reference, for we do not take concepts to be parts of truth-values.[70] But even if this leaves us unfazed, it still remains that, if the senses of predicates are functions, then the senses of the parts merely *determine* the sense of the whole. Without additional extrinsic stipulation, a 'sense-function' could map distinct arguments onto the same thought, and then there is no explanation of why (M) and (E) express distinct thoughts.[71]

---

[69] Similar remarks can be found in the late essay "Negation" (Frege, 1984d). It is worth noting that, in remarks following the passage we quote, Frege effectively rejects the suggestion that thoughts are structured *if* the structure is conceived as some kind of framework into which senses slot, since we would then have to explain in what respect the structure itself is 'unsaturated', and no progress has been made.

[70] In "On Sense and Reference", Frege suggests that the references of the parts are parts of the reference of the whole (Frege, 1984f, opp. 35–6), but he later takes the suggestion back (Frege, 1979g, p. 255).

[71] For further discussion of the functional interpretation of the senses of predicates, see (Dummett, 1981b, ch. 13) and (Dummett, 1991a, ch. 6). The first point we made is to be found in Dummett, but the

There is, however, a more promising way of understanding Frege's intentions. What we are going to suggest is that the unsaturatedness of the senses of predicates is parasitic on the unsaturatedness of their references. More precisely, our suggestion will be that what binds the sense of a predicate and the sense of a name together into a thought is the interaction of two more fundamental forces: the determination of sense by reference and the composition of references.[72]

Let us think first about straightforwardly functional expressions, say '$\xi^2 - 1$' and '$(\xi + 1)(\xi - 1)$'. These have the same reference, for they have the same value for every argument. They have different senses, however, because the value the function has for a given argument is determined in different ways: in the one case, we multiply the argument by itself and then subtract one; in the other, we multiply the result of increasing the argument by one by the result of decreasing it by one. These two ways of describing a single mapping from arguments to values correspond to the senses of the two expressions: the sense of a functional expression is a particular way in which values may be associated with arguments. It is thus tempting to think of the senses of these expressions as what are sometimes called 'functions-in-intension', that is, as arithmetic functions individuated intensionally rather than (as is nowadays common) extensionally. We are not suggesting that we should succumb to this temptation. But there is an idea here that is worth preserving, namely, that, since the sense of a functional expression is *a way in which a function may be given to us*, any such sense will inherit the 'unsaturatedness' of its referent. We can use this fact to explain how senses compose.

If the sense of a functional expression is 'unsaturated', then it must, in some sense, 'need completion' by something else. We suggest that what 'completes' the sense of a functional expression is simply an *object*. It might seem as if that's impossible, since we would then be unable to distinguish the sense of, say, '4^2' from that of '$(2 \times 2)^2$'. And if the sense of 'ξ^2' were a function from objects to thoughts, then of course the objection would be conclusive, but we are *not* saying that the sense of 'ξ^2' is such a function or, for that matter, that it is any kind of function at all. It certainly does not follow from the fact that the senses of predicates are unsaturated that they are functions: predicates are unsaturated, too (Frege, 1984i, opp. 663–4), but they are certainly not functions. What we *are* suggesting is that the sense of 'ξ^2' needs to be completed by an object *because* 'ξ^2' *denotes a function*, and that function needs to be completed by an object. But when an object is provided as argument, it must be given to us in some particular way. What distinguishes the sense of '4^2' from that of '$(2 \times 2)^2$' is how that object is given to us. Let's suppose that the sense of '4' presents 4 as the successor of 3. Then the sense expressed by '4^2' may be characterized as follows: to one who understands it, the expression '4^2' presents an object as the number that

---

latter is not. Still, Dummett's positive conception of what thoughts are for Frege is very close to ours, and that conception plays an important role in Dummett's discussion.

[72] If so, then the composition of senses is mediated by their relation to their references, and it becomes extremely natural to regard sentences containing parts without reference as exhibiting a grave semantic defect. Compare (Evans, 1985).

results if the successor of 3 is multiplied by itself. The expression '$(2 \times 2)^2$' presents that same object in a different way.

It now becomes extremely tempting to say that the sense of a functional expression is completed by the sense of a name. Such an interpretation, the Siren notes, can be defended using the same move we just made: deny that the senses of functional expressions are functions that take senses as arguments. The difficulty, however, is that it would then be impossible to explain how the sense of 'ξ^2' is completed in a sentence like: $\forall x\ (x^2 > x)$, the problem being that variables do not have senses. On our reconstruction—it is hard to call it an 'interpretation'—there is no such problem: the sense of the expression will be completed in virtue of its *reference*'s being completed through the semantic analogue of variable binding.[73] Nonetheless, there is something right about the proposal, for there is a clear sense in which, on our view, the sense of a functional expression is *indirectly* completed by the sense of a name. What completes the sense of a functional expression is, most fundamentally, an object. But when we think of an object as the value of ξ^2 for some particular argument, we must think of the argument in some way. We will then be thinking of an object as the result of applying a function that is given to us in a certain way to an object that is given to us in a certain other way.

It should now be clear enough what we want to say about the senses of predicates and how they are bound together with the senses of names to form thoughts. Consider our sentence (M), 'The Morning Star is a planet'. The sense of the predicate 'is a planet' we identify with a way of presenting a function from objects to truth-values.[74] It needs to be completed by an object because the function it denotes needs to be completed by an object. The sense of the name 'the Morning Star' determines an object, and so the sense indirectly completes both the sense and the referent of the predicate. The references of the expressions can then compose, via function-application, to determine a truth-value for the whole sentence (the True, in this case). To entertain the thought expressed by (M) is thus to think of an object given in a certain way as being mapped to the True by a function given in a certain way. The thought expressed by (M) is thus, to a first approximation, that the last celestial body visible in the morning is mapped to the True by the function that maps all and only planets to the True. Or, much more precisely, albeit much less informatively: that the Morning Star is a planet. To entertain the thought expressed by (E), on the other hand, is to think of an object given as the first celestial body visible in the evening as being mapped to the True by the function that maps all and only planets to the True. The thought expressed is thus: that the Evening Star is a planet. The sentences

---

[73] A similar answer is available to the functional interpretation: since the sense of 'ξ^2' is, on that view, a function, its argument-place can be bound by a higher operator.

[74] Of course, a finer analysis would distinguish parts within the predicate, too, recognizing at least the tense as another component. So something like a mode of presentation of the present would also enter. How such context-dependence is to be handled in a broadly Fregean framework is a much discussed and very difficult question: for discussion, see (Perry, 1993), (McDowell, 1977), (Burge, 1979), (Evans, 1985), (Heck, 2002), and (May, 2005a).

(M) and (E) therefore express different thoughts and do so for just the reason that Frege cites: they are made up of parts with different senses.

In the end, then, no 'sense-glue' is needed to bind the parts of a thought together. The sense of a name is bound to the sense of a predicate because the sense of the name determines an object and the sense of the predicate determines a function which, being unsaturated, may be completed by that object. It follows that, absent reference-failure, a thought will have one of the two truth-values, and the senses of the parts will, through how they determine the references of the parts, determine under what condition that value will be the True. That is to say, the familiar Fregean doctrines that thoughts are truth-evaluable and that they determine truth-conditions emerge, on our account, as consequences of deep features of Frege's conception of how senses combine to form thoughts. The same cannot be said for the alternative interpretation that takes the senses of predicates to be functions. There is, of course, nothing in that view that *precludes* thoughts from being truth-evaluable or from determining a truth-condition. But since thoughts are values of the functions with which the senses of predicates are identified, it will be impossible to characterize those functions absent an antecedent conception of what thoughts are (Dummett, 1981b, ch. 13). One will then have no alternative but to take it as axiomatic that thoughts are truth-evaluable and that they determine truth-conditions, and so will be unable to explain these facts.

In section 1.2, we were at pains to emphasize that Frege's doctrine that concepts are unsaturated is primarily, and perhaps even entirely, semantic rather than meta-physical. What it is for an object to fall under a concept will be, for Frege, illumin-ated by an account of linguistic meaning. Something similar can now be said about Frege's conception of thoughts. We emphasized earlier that, for Frege, the notion of a thought is fundamentally a cognitive one. That is *not* to say that it is fundament-ally a *psychological* one, and Frege would vehemently have denied that it was. It is, indeed, as much a manifestation of Frege's genius as anything we know how carefully he separates these two claims. Both the danger, and Frege's strategy for avoiding it, are visible in his account of how thoughts cohere. The danger is that we will reach for the easy solution that appeals to some psychological analogue of predication—some notion of 'applying a concept to an object'—seems to offer. The strategy for avoiding this danger is to occupy and steadfastly refuse to abandon the semantic perspective that pervades Frege's mature writings. Such a psychological notion may be needed to explain how or why we are able to *entertain* the thoughts we do, but it is not, Frege insists, needed to explain how the parts of a thought cohere. That, too, is to be illuminated by an account of linguistic meaning.

1.5 Closing Remarks

From Frege, what endures? If we were to distill his contribution to the study of language down to its essence, it would be his recognition of the necessity of compositionality to an account of truth and meaning. Although Frege never elaborated a formal theory of truth for begriffsschrift, as Tarski did for the calculus of classes, he did develop an informal theory that is no less mathematical for being informal[75] and which remains the first demonstration of how a compositional theory of truth for a language of reasonable expressive power can be given. The central aspects of Frege's semantic theory remain with us, if not always in their particulars, then at least in their guiding ideas. Thus, underlying Frege's conception of concepts as unsaturated is his insistence that the semantics of predicates must reveal the role they play in determining truth-values; underlying his conception of thoughts is his insistence that the semantics of sentences must reveal the role their constituent parts play in composing entities that have truth-values.

As uncontentious as these doctrines may seem to us today, Frege's notion of sense still raises the hackles of many. But the underlying idea has persisted here as well: in a slogan, "No reference without information". Thus, though the terminology differs, it is quite commonly held that, to use a proper name to speak of an object, a speaker must be in possession of conceptual information about the name's reference: the speaker must have a way of thinking of it, a dossier of information about it, a body of knowledge concerning it, a guise through which she thinks of it, or—suggestive of the Fregean heritage—a mode of presentation of it.[76] How close a given view is to Frege's is largely a function of how much information about the reference a speaker is required to have. But, whatever the other differences between them, these contemporary views all deny that the information the speaker associates with the name determines its reference.[77] It is here that the fundamental difference between 'new' theories of reference and Frege's is to be found.

Frege himself no doubt would have viewed these newer accounts of sense, with their appeal to inherent subjectivity and speaker to speaker variability, as heralding a new psychologism no less pernicious than the old.[78] Contemporary writers are liable to dismiss this concern, and their tendency to do so is, we believe, indicative of a more fundamental change from Frege's views, one concerning how language itself is conceived. For Frege, languages are inherently interpreted systems, characterized by the association between senses and symbols. Today, on the other hand, we are used to thinking of languages without this tight bond between syntax and semantics. The

---

[75] For a defense of this way of reading Part I of *Grundgesetze*, see (Heck, 2006). This kind of reading originates, of course, with Dummett (Dummett, 1981a). In application to the full begriffsschrift, Frege's theory of truth is inevitably flawed, since there is no consistent (classical) theory of truth for that language. Indeed, the part of the theory concerned with the smooth breathing, from which names of value-ranges are formed, is exceedingly peculiar. The remainder of the theory, however, is clean and familiar, differences from Tarski being due to Frege's different treatment of quantification.

[76] There are more versions of this view than we can reasonably cite here. For a few different versions, see (Grice, 1969), (Schiffer, 1978), (Evans, 1982), (Salmon, 1986), (Castañeda, 1989), and (Forbes, 1990). Some, notably Michael Devitt (Devitt, 1996) and Saul Kripke (Kripke, 1980) have proposed that a mere causal link to the object is sufficient, even in the absence of information about the bearer. That view represents a complete break with Frege, but it remains a minority position.

[77] The *locus classicus* of such arguments against Frege is of course the second lecture of *Naming and Necessity* (Kripke, 1980).

[78] And Frege's premier modern exponent, Michael Dummett, would agree with him (Dummett, 1991b).

resulting perspective has proved extraordinarily fruitful. Meta-logic, as we know it, would not be possible without the idea that a fixed language can have various interpretations,[79] and the question how syntax and semantics are related is among the most difficult and, therefore, most fruitful posed by contemporary linguistic theory. This change in how language is conceived places the notion of sense itself in a very different perspective: if languages are conceived as Frege conceived them, then sense is semantic by definition; for languages conceived as they are today, sense not only need not be semantic, it need not even be linguistic.

In this regard, the contemporary debate about reference seems to us to be one piece of a more general discussion that continues to animate the philosophy of language: how we are to fit into a very different conception of language the very real semantical insights that Frege bequeathed to us.[80]

References

Angelelli, I. (1967). *Studies on Gottlob Frege and Traditional Philosophy*. Reidel, Dordrecht.

Antonelli, A. and May, R. (2000). Frege's New Science. *Notre Dame Journal of Formal Logic*, 41: 242–70.

Barwise, J. and Cooper, R. (1981). Generalized Quantifiers and Natural Language. *Linguistics and Philosophy*, 4: 159–219.

Boole, G. (1847). *The Mathematical Analysis of Logic*. Macmillan, Barclay, and Macmillan, Cambridge.

—— (1854). *The Laws of Thought*. Dover Publications, New York.

Burge, T. (1979). Sinning against Frege. *Philosophical Review*, 88: 398–432.

Castañeda, H.-N. (1989). *Thinking, Language, and Experience*. University of Minnesota Press, Minneapolis.

Chierchia, G. and McConnell-Ginet, S. (1990). *Meaning and Grammar: An Introduction to Semantics*. MIT Press, Cambridge MA.

Davidson, D. (1984). Truth and Meaning. In *Inquiries Into Truth and Interpretation*, pages 17–36. Clarendon Press, Oxford.

Demopoulos, W., editor (1995). *Frege's Philosophy of Mathematics*. Harvard University Press, Cambridge MA.

Devitt, M. (1996). *Coming To Our Senses*. Cambridge University Press, Cambridge.

Dreben, B. and van Heijenoort, J. (1986). Introductory Note to 1929, 1930, and 1930a. In Feferman, S., Dawson, J., and Kleene, S., editors, *Collected Works*, volume 1, pages 44–59. Oxford University Press, Oxford, 3rd edition.

Dummett, M. (1978a). Frege's Distinction between Sense and Reference. In (Dummett, 1978c), pages 116–44.

—— (1978b). Truth. In (Dummett, 1978c), pages 1–24.

—— (1978c). *Truth and Other Enigmas*. Duckworth, London.

—— (1981a). *Frege: Philosophy of Language*. Harvard University Press, Cambridge MA, 2nd edition.

---

[79] Frege's famous dispute with Hilbert was, most fundamentally, over how languages are to be characterized (Antonelli and May, 2000).

[80] Thanks to Bill Demopoulos, Michael Glanzberg, Øystein Linnebo, and Kai Wehmeier for helpful comments on drafts of this material.

_____ (1981b). *The Interpretation of Frege's Philosophy*. Harvard University Press, Cambridge MA.

_____ (1991a). *The Logical Basis of Metaphysics*. Harvard University Press, Cambridge MA.

_____ (1991b). The Relative Priority of Thought and Language. In *Frege and Other Philosophers*, pages 315–24. Clarendon Press, Oxford.

Evans, G. (1982). *The Varieties of Reference*. Clarendon Press, Oxford.

_____ (1985). Understanding Demonstratives. In *Collected Papers*, pages 291–321. Clarendon Press, Oxford.

Forbes, G. (1990). The Indispensability of *Sinn*. *Philosophical Review*, 99: 535–63.

Frege, G. (1964). *The Basic Laws of Arithmetic: Exposition of the System*. University of California Press, Berkeley CA. Ed. and tr. by M. Furth.

_____ (1967). Begriffsschrift: A Formula Language Modeled upon that of Arithmetic, For Pure Thought. In van Heijenoort, J., editor, *From Frege to Godel: A Sourcebook in Mathematical Logic*, pages 5–82. Harvard University Press, Cambridge MA. Tr. by J. van Heijenoort.

_____ (1972a). Applications of the Conceptual Notation. In (Frege, 1972b), pages 204–8. Tr. by T. W. Bynum.

_____ (1972b). *Conceptual Notation and Related Articles*. Oxford University Press, New York.

_____ (1972c). On the Aim of the Conceptual Notation. In (Frege, 1972b), pages 90–100. Tr. by T. W. Bynum.

_____ (1972d). On the Scientific Justification of a Conceptual Notation. In (Frege, 1972b), pages 83–9. Tr. by T. W. Bynum.

_____ (1979a). Boole's Logical Calculus and the Concept-Script. In (Frege, 1979h), pages 9–52. Tr. by P. Long and R. White.

_____ (1979b). Boole's Logical Formula-Language and my Concept-Script. In (Frege, 1979h), pages 47–52. Tr. by P. Long and R. White.

_____ (1979c). Comments on Sense and Meaning. In (Frege, 1979h), pages 118–25. Tr. by P. Long and R. White.

_____ (1979d). Introduction to Logic. In (Frege, 1979h), pages 185–96. Tr. by P. Long and R. White.

_____ (1979e). Logic (1879–1891). In (Frege, 1979h), pages 1–8. Tr. by P. Long and R. White.

_____ (1979f). Logic (1897). In (Frege, 1979h), pages 126–51. Tr. by P. Long and R. White.

_____ (1979g). Notes for Ludwig Darmstaedter. In (Frege, 1979h), pages 253–7. Tr. by P. Long and R. White.

_____ (1979h). *Posthumous Writings*. University of Chicago Press, Chicago. Trans. by P. Long and R. White.

_____ (1980a). *The Foundations of Arithmetic*. Northwestern University Press, Evanston IL, 2nd revised edition. Tr. by J. L. Austin.

_____ (1980b). *Philosophical and Mathematical Correspondence*. University of Chicago Press, Chicago. Ed. by G. Gabriel, *et al*. Tr. by H. Kaal.

_____ (1984a). *Collected Papers on Mathematics, Logic, and Philosophy*. Basil Blackwell, Oxford. Ed. by B. McGuinness.

_____ (1984b). Compound Thoughts. In (Frege, 1984a), pages 390–406. Tr. by P. Geach and R. H. Stoothoff.

_____ (1984c). Function and Concept. In (Frege, 1984a), pages 137–56. Tr. by P. Geach.

_____ (1984d). Negation. In (Frege, 1984a), pages 373–89. Tr. by P. Geach and R. H. Stoothoff.

_____ (1984e). On Concept and Object. In (Frege, 1984a), pages 182–94. Tr. by P. Geach.

_____ (1984f). On Sense and Meaning. In (Frege, 1984a), pages 157–77. Tr. by M. Black.

_____ (1984g). On the Foundations of Geometry: Second Series. In (Frege, 1984a), pages 293–340. Tr. by E. H. W. Kluge.

_____ (1984h). Thoughts. In (Frege, 1984a), pages 351–72. Tr. by P. Geach and R. H. Stoothoff.

_____ (1984i). What is a Function? In (Frege, 1984a), pages 285–92. Tr. by P. Geach.

Goldfarb, W. (2001). Frege's Conception of Logic. In Floyd, J. and Shieh, S., editors, *Future Pasts: The Analytic Tradition in Twentieth-Century Philosophy*, pages 25–41. Oxford University Press, New York.

Grice, H. (1969). Vacuous Names. In Davidson, D. and Hintikka, J., editors, *Words and Objections: Essays on the Philosophy of W. V. Quine*, pages 118–45. Reidel, Dordrecht.

Heck, R. (1995). Definition by Induction in Frege's *Grundgesetze der Arithmetik*. In (Demopoulos, 1995), pages 295–333.

_____ (1999). *Grundgesetze der Arithmetik* I §10. *Philosophia Mathematica*, 7: 258–92.

_____ (2002). Do Demonstratives have Senses? *Philosophers' Imprint*, 2. http://www.philosophersimprint.org/002002/.

_____ (2003). Frege on Identity and Identity-Statements: A Reply to Thau and Caplan. *Canadian Journal of Philosophy*, 33: 83–102.

_____ (2006). Frege and Semantics. In Ricketts, T., editor, *The Cambridge Companion to Frege*. Cambridge University Press, Cambridge.

Heim, I. and Kratzer, A. (1998). *Semantics in Generative Grammar*. Blackwell, Malden MA.

Higginbotham, J. and May, R. (1981). Questions, Quantifiers, and Crossing. *The Linguistic Review*, 1: 41–79.

Jourdain, P. E. B. (1980). Gottlob Frege. In (Frege, 1980b), pages 179–206. Ed. by G. Gabriel, *et al.* Tr. by H. Kaal.

Keenan, E. and Stavi, J. (1986). A Semantic Characterization of Natural Language Determiners. *Linguistics and Philosophy*, 9: 253–326.

Kemp, G. (1995). Truth in Frege's 'Law of Truth'. *Synthese*, 105: 31–51.

_____ (1998). Meaning and Truth-Conditions. *Philosophical Quarterly*, 48: 483–93.

Kripke, S. (1980). *Naming and Necessity*. Harvard University Press, Cambridge MA.

Larson, R. and Segal, G. (1995). *Knowledge of Meaning*. MIT Press, Cambridge MA.

Lewis, D. (1970). General Semantics. *Synthese*, 22: 18–67.

Linnebo, Ø. (2003). Frege's Conception of Logic: From Kant to *Grundgesetze*. *Manuscrito*, 16: 235–52.

May, R. (2001). Frege on Identity Statements. In C. Cecchetto, e., editor, *Semantic Interfaces: Reference, Anaphora, and Aspect*. CSLI Publications, Stanford.

_____ (2005a). Frege on Indexicals, forthcoming in *Philosophical Review*.

_____ (2005b). The Invariance of Sense, forthcoming in *The Journal of Philosophy*.

McDowell, J. (1977). On the Sense and Reference of a Proper Name. *Mind*, 86: 159–85.

Merrick, T. (2004). *Frege's Concept–Object Distinction: Much Ado About Nothing or a Significant Neo-Kantian Principle?* PhD thesis, University of California, Irvine.

Montague, R. (1974). *Formal Philosophy: Selected Papers of Richard Montague*. Yale University Press, New Haven.

Neale, S. (2001). *Facing Facts*. Oxford University Press, Oxford.

Perry, J. (1993). Frege on Demonstratives. In *The Problem of the Essential Indexical, and Other Essays*, pages 3–32. Oxford University Press, New York.

Quine, W. V. O. (1953). On What There is. In *From a Logical Point of View*, pages 1–18. Harvard University Press, Cambridge MA.

Ricketts, T. (1986). Objectivity and Objecthood: Frege's Metaphysics of Judgement. In L. Haaparanta and J. Hintikka, editors, *Frege Synthesized*, pages 65–95. Reidel, Dordrecht.

_____ (1996). Logic and Truth in Frege. *Proceedings of the Aristotelian Society, sup. vol.*, 70: 121–40.

Russell, B. (1903). *The Principles of Mathematics*. Cambridge University Press, Cambridge.

Salmon, N. (1986). *Frege's Puzzle*. MIT Press, Cambridge MA.

Schiffer, S. (1978). The Basis of Reference. *Erkenntnis*, 13: 171–206.

Schröder, E. (1972). Review of Frege's *Conceptual Notation*. In (Frege, 1972b), pages 218–32.

Stanley, J. (1996). Truth and Metatheory in Frege. *Pacific Philosophical Quarterly*, 77: 45–70.

Sundholm, G. (2001). Frege, August Bebel, and the Return of Alsace-Lorraine: The Dating of the Distinction between *Sinn* and *Bedeutung*. *History and Philosophy of Logic*, 22: 57–73.

Tappenden, J. (1995*a*). Extending Knowledge and Fruitful Concepts: Fregean Themes in the Foundations of Mathematics. *Noûs*, 29: 427–67.

_____ (1995b). Geometry and Generality in Frege. *Synthese*, 102: 319–61.

_____ (1997). Metatheory and Mathematical Practice in Frege. *Philosophical Topics*, 25: 213–64.

_____ (2000). Frege on Axioms, Indirect Proof, and Independence Arguments in Geometry: Did Frege Reject Independence Arguments? *Notre Dame Journal of Formal Logic*, 41: 271–315.

Thau, M. and Caplan, B. (2001). What's Puzzling Gottlob Frege? *Canadian Journal of Philosophy*, 31: 159–200.

Thomae, J. (1880). *Elementare Theorie der analytischen Functionen einer complexen Veränderlichen*. L. Nebert, Halle.

van Heijenoort, J. (1967). Logic as Calculus and Logic as Language. *Synthese*, 17: 324–30.

Wehmeier, K. and Schroeder-Heister, P. (2005). Frege's Permutation Argument Revisited. *Synthese*, 147: 43–61.

Weiner, J. (1990). *Frege in Perspective*. Cornell University Press, Ithaca NY.

Wilson, M. (1995). Frege: The Royal Road from Geometry. In (Demopoulos, 1995), pages 108–59.

CHAPTER 2

WITTGENSTEIN ON LANGUAGE: FROM SIMPLES TO SAMPLES

MICHAEL BEANEY

THE so-called 'linguistic turn' that took place in philosophy in the first half of the twentieth century is most strongly associated with the work of Ludwig Wittgenstein (1889–1951). If there is a single text that might be identified as the source of the linguistic turn, then it is Wittgenstein's first book, the *Tractatus Logico-Philosophicus*, published in German in 1921 and in an English translation in 1922. Wittgenstein proclaimed there that "All philosophy is 'critique of language'" (*TLP*, 4.0031),[1] and this remained his view throughout his subsequent work. Although he came to reject many of the doctrines of the *Tractatus* in his later writings, most notably, in his main book, the *Philosophical Investigations*, which was published posthumously in 1953, he continued to believe that an understanding of language held the key to the solution—or better, dissolution—of philosophical problems. Philosophy, he famously remarked, "is a battle against the bewitchment of our intelligence by means of language" (*PI*, §109).

---

[1] In the citations from the *Tractatus* that follow, I have used the translation by Pears and McGuinness. But occasionally, as here, I have made slight modifications to that translation.

On his early view, the meaningfulness of language is ultimately grounded in the necessary existence of what Wittgenstein called 'simple objects'. At the most basic level, these simple objects ensure that names have meaning. Wittgenstein gave no examples of simple objects, but he regarded their existence as a precondition for propositions to have sense. It was this idea, in particular, that he came to reject in his later work. Instead, he argued, the meaning of terms is given by their *use*, the use of language being something that is open to view. Particular uses of language might indeed presuppose the existence of certain kinds of things, which he called 'samples', such as the standard metre, but these were to be understood as *means* of representation rather than as *what* is represented (cf. *PI*, §50). Throughout his work, in other words, Wittgenstein was concerned with the foundations of language; the crucial shift lay from the appeal to simples to the appeal to samples, and a corresponding shift from assumptions about what lies hidden to appreciation of what is visible to all in our linguistic practices. In what follows, I will first outline the main elements of Wittgenstein's early conception of language, before considering his critique of that conception and his later views.

2.1 WITTGENSTEIN'S CONCEPTION OF LANGUAGE IN THE *Tractatus*

In his preface to the *Tractatus*, Wittgenstein singles out just two philosophers as having influenced his work: Gottlob Frege (1848–1925) and Bertrand Russell (1872–1970). From Frege Wittgenstein inherited the assumptions that logic was essentially Fregean logic and that function-argument analysis held the key to the analysis of propositions (cf. *TLP*, 3.318, 5.47). From Russell Wittgenstein drew inspiration from the theory of descriptions, which he endorsed, and the theory of types, which he rejected. The theory of descriptions motivated his logical atomism, and his critique of the theory of types was articulated through his distinction between saying and showing.

The most significant difference between Wittgenstein, on the one hand, and Frege and Russell, on the other hand, lay in their view of the relationship between logic and language. According to Frege and Russell, ordinary language was logically deficient in various ways, and at least for scientific purposes, needed to be replaced by a logical language. In his introduction to the *Tractatus*, Russell suggested that Wittgenstein shared this view: "Mr Wittgenstein is concerned with the conditions for a logically perfect language—not that any language is logically perfect, or that we believe ourselves capable, here and now, of constructing a logically perfect language, but that the whole function of language is to have meaning, and it only fulfils this function in proportion as it approaches to the ideal language which we postulate" (*TLP*, x). But this misrepresents Wittgenstein's position. According to Wittgenstein, "all the pro-positions of our everyday language, just as they stand, are in perfect logical order" (*TLP*, 5.5563). He was indeed concerned with the conditions for a logically perfect language, but these were at the same time the conditions for our ordinary language to express the senses it does.

It is true that Wittgenstein also said that all philosophy is 'critique of language' (as noted above). But there is no inconsistency here. What Wittgenstein objected to was the fact that the same word can signify in different ways, and so belong to different 'symbols', as he put it (*TLP*, 3.323). It is this that he held responsible for many of the confusions in philosophy (*TLP*, 3.324). To avoid such errors, he wrote, "we must make use of a sign-language that excludes them by not using the same sign for differ-ent symbols and by not using in a superficially similar way signs that have different modes of signification: that is to say, a sign-language that is governed by *logical* gram-mar—by logical syntax" (*TLP*, 3.325). What Wittgenstein was advocating, then, was not an ideal language but an ideal *notation*—a notation that made clear the logical form of every proposition.

This indicates why Wittgenstein was so impressed by Russell's theory of descrip-tions. After remarking that all philosophy is 'critique of language', Wittgenstein goes on: "It was Russell who performed the service of showing that the apparent logical form of a proposition need not be its real one" (*TLP*, 4.0031). What is inadequate about ordinary language is its surface grammatical form, not its underlying logical form; and it was the task of philosophy to reveal the logical form of propositions. What Wittgenstein clearly had in mind in commending Russell was his theory of descriptions, according to which propositions of the grammatical form of (1) are seen as having the more complex logical form of (2), which can be formalized in modern Fregean (i.e. quantificational) logic as (3):

(1) The *F* is *G*.
(2) There is one and only one *F*, and whatever is *F* is *G*.
(3) $\exists x(Fx \,\&\, \forall x(Fy \rightarrow y = x) \,\&\, Gx)$.

As far as Russell was concerned, the significance of this analysis lay in showing how propositions containing definite descriptions, i.e. denoting phrases of the form 'the *F*', could have meaning and a truth-value even if the denoting phrase itself failed to denote anything. As Russell himself put it, "The central point of the theory of descriptions was that a phrase may contribute to the meaning of a sentence without having any meaning at all in isolation" (1959, 64). According to Russell, 'the *F*' has meaning if and only if it denotes something, but sentences containing the phrase can still have a meaning even if the phrase itself lacks meaning as long as the sentence can be rephrased to show its 'real' meaningful constituents.[2] The problems that arise in the case of phrases that fail to denote anything are solved by 'analysing away' the relevant phrase.

---

[2] I gloss over here the differences between Russell's use of 'sentence' and Wittgenstein's use of 'proposition' ('Satz'). For Wittgenstein, "a proposition is a propositional sign in its projective relation to the world" (*TLP*, 3.12). So it may be most accurate to say that what Russell means by 'sentence' is what Wittgenstein means by 'propositional sign'. But I shall not pursue this further here.

This opens up the possibility of a whole programme of analysis, recasting the propositions of a given domain into their correct logical form. Frege had first suggested such a programme in offering his logicist analysis of number statements, as part of his general project of demonstrating how arithmetic can be 'reduced' to logic; and Russell showed how logical analysis might be extended in developing his theory of descriptions. But it was Wittgenstein who radically generalized the idea to encompass the whole of language. Any proposition, if it has sense, according to Wittgenstein, must be analysable—at least in principle—to reveal its underlying logical form. Ordinary language is indeed misleading, since the underlying logical form of a given proposition cannot simply be read off from its surface grammatical form. Even a proposition as apparently simple as a proposition of the form 'The F is G' has a hidden complexity. In fact, on the Russellian analysis, it is a conjunction of three simpler propositions, of the form 'There is at least one F', 'There is at most one F' and 'Whatever is F is G'. This suggested to Wittgenstein that any complex proposition could be uniquely analysed into simpler propositions, the most basic of which he called 'elementary propositions'.

How do we know when we have reached the elementary propositions and uncovered the logical form of a proposition? Wittgenstein gave no examples of a completely analysed proposition. But he did think that he could specify the essential characteristics of logical analysis and elementary propositions and draw conclusions about what the world must be like for these characteristics to obtain. As mentioned above, Wittgenstein saw all propositions as analysable in function–argument terms. "Like Frege and Russell I construe a proposition as a function of the expressions contained in it" (*TLP*, 3.318).[3] He regarded complex propositions as functions (more specifically, truth-functions) of elementary propositions, and elementary propositions as functions of names. These elementary propositions, he argued, must be logically independent of one another, since if they were not, and one proposition, say, could be deduced from another, then the latter would possess an internal complexity requiring further analysis (cf. *TLP*, 4.211, 5.13, 5.134). Wittgenstein also drew metaphysical conclusions from his views on logical analysis. One of the most striking of these was his doctrine that there must be simple objects. Take any elementary proposition, regarded as a function of a certain set of names. If any of these names fails to denote, then according to Russell's theory of descriptions, they must be treated as definite descriptions and 'analysed away'. But this would mean that the proposition is not, after all, elementary. So in any elementary proposition, all names must denote and the objects they denote must necessarily exist.

What we have been considering so far is Wittgenstein's logical atomism, motivated by generalizing the programme of logical analysis instigated by Frege and Russell. The main theses of his logical atomism can be summarized as follows:

(A) Every genuine proposition is uniquely and completely analysable into, i.e. is a truth-function of, elementary propositions. (Cf. *TLP*, 3.25, 4.221, 5, 5.3.)

---

[3] This is more true of Frege than it is of Russell, who construed analysis primarily in mereological, i.e. whole-part, terms. Cf. Beaney, 2003, §6; Levine, 2002.

(B) Each elementary proposition is a function of names. (Cf. *TLP*, 4.22, 4.221, 4.24.)

(C) Each simple name denotes a simple object, which is its meaning (*Bedeutung*). (Cf. *TLP*, 3.203, 3.22.)

These three theses, however, were only part of the conception of language that Wittgenstein articulated in the *Tractatus*. The other part is what Wittgenstein called in his *Notebooks* his 'theory of logical portrayal' (cf. *NB*, 15). Taken together these constitute what is generally referred to as his picture theory of language.[4] Central to this theory is the idea that (genuine) propositions are pictures (*Bilder*) which depict a possible state of affairs (cf. *TLP*, 4.01), the state of affairs depicted being the sense of a proposition. The inspiration for the picture theory apparently came from a model that was used in a Paris law-court to represent a motor car accident, although Wittgenstein was also influenced by Hertz's conception of *Bilder* in science.[5]

Wittgenstein explains what he sees as the essential properties of pictures from 2.1 to 2.225 of the *Tractatus*, and elaborates on the idea of propositions being pictures from 4.01 to 4.125. The key theses of his theory of logical portrayal can be stated as follows:

(D) A picture presents a possible state of affairs, which is its sense (*Sinn*). (Cf. *TLP*, 2.11, 2.201, 2.202, 2.221, 4.021, 4.022, 4.031, 4.1.)

(E) A picture is composite, and its elements are correlated with the objects of reality that they represent. (Cf. *TLP*, 2.13, 2.131, 2.1514, 4.032, 4.04.)

(F) A picture is a fact. It is the fact that the elements of a picture are related in a determinate way that represents how things in the world are related. (Cf. *TLP*, 2.141, 2.15, 4.0311.)

(G) A picture has both form and structure, its structure being the connection of its elements, and its form being the possibility of this structure. (Cf. *TLP*, 2.15, 2.033.) What it has in common with the reality it represents is 'pictorial form' (*TLP*, 2.151, 2.17) or 'logical form' (*TLP*, 2.18), which is what allows it to depict the world. (Cf. *TLP*, 2.16, 2.161, 2.17, 2.18, 4.12.)

(H) A picture is true if it agrees with reality, false if it does not. (Cf. *TLP*, 2.21, 2.222, 4.06.)

(I) What a picture represents it does so independently of its truth or falsity. (*TLP*, 2.22; cf. 4.061.)

(J) In order to tell whether a picture is true or false we must compare it with reality. (*TLP*, 2.223; cf. 4.05.)

(K) No picture is true *a priori*. (Cf. *TLP*, 2.224, 2.225, 3.04, 3.05, 4.463, 4.464, 6.113.)

(L) There is an internal relation between a picture and the possible state of affairs that it represents. (Cf. *TLP*, 4.014, 4.023.)

---

[4] Some commentators, e.g. Kenny (1973, ch.4) have seen the picture theory as comprising *only* the theory of logical portrayal. But the theses of logical atomism are essential to the overall conception, so it seems right to include these as well. Cf. Hacker, 1981, §§3–4.

[5] The *Notebooks* record the moment when the seed of the picture theory was sown; *NB*, 7. On Hertz's influence on Wittgenstein, see e.g. Janik, 1994.

(M) The logical form that a picture and what it represents have in common, and the
internal relation that holds between them, can only be shown. (Cf. *TLP*, 4.12,
4.121, 4.122, 4.124, 4.125.)

Many of the numbered remarks in the *Tractatus* that set out Wittgenstein's picture
theory may need detailed clarification, but the vision of language that emerges from
them is clear enough in outline. According to Wittgenstein, language is the totality of
propositions (cf. *TLP*, 4.001), and every proposition can be shown, through analysis,
to be a function of elementary propositions, each of which pictures a possible state
of affairs, which constitutes its sense, and makes contact with reality at the level of its
constituent names, whose meanings are the simple objects they denote. This vision
was subjected to devastating critique in the *Philosophical Investigations*. But there are
several core features of his account that we can regard as transformed in his later
work rather than repudiated outright. The two most significant of these, reflected in
theses (L) and (M) above, were Wittgenstein's conception of internal relations and
his distinction between saying and showing.

A property is internal, Wittgenstein writes, "if it is unthinkable that its object
should not possess it" (*TLP*, 4.123). By extension, a relation is internal if it is unthinkable that the objects between which the relation holds should not be so related. Wittgenstein gives the example of two shades of colour: "This shade of blue and that one
stand, eo ipso, in the internal relation of lighter to darker. It is unthinkable that *these*
two objects should not stand in this relation." (*Ibid.*) An internal relation is thus a
constitutive, i.e. necessary or essential, relation. Something that stands in an internal
relation to something else would not be what it is without that relation obtaining.

Consider, then, the case of pictures—or genuine propositions (i.e. propositions
that have sense), which Wittgenstein conceives as logical pictures (cf. the main
remarks numbered 3 and 4 of the *Tractatus*). For anything to be a picture of
something else, it must have something in common with what it depicts: this is
what Wittgenstein calls its 'pictorial' or (with propositions in mind) its 'logical' form.
The relation that a picture has to what it depicts, in virtue of this shared form, is an
internal relation. Without such a relation, a picture could not be the picture it is.

According to Wittgenstein, however, *that* a picture stands in an internal relation
to what it depicts cannot be said but only shown. Consider the following attempt to
state that an internal relation obtains:

(4) Proposition P pictures a possible state of affairs S.

If we understand 'P' at all, then we will know what state of affairs it pictures, so
(4) does not tell us anything. (4) does not itself present a (merely) possible state of
affairs: if P does indeed picture S, then it could not be otherwise. According to Wittgenstein, therefore, (4) lacks sense. But it is not gibberish. It does seem to express the
internal relation that obtains between P and S. What Wittgenstein suggests, then, is
that propositions such as (4) represent an illegitimate attempt to say what can only,
in fact, be *shown*.

The distinction between saying and showing is one of the most important ideas
in the *Tractatus*, and its motivation and the various uses to which it is put require

clarification of the whole range of issues with which Wittgenstein was concerned. A full account would have to explain its connection, for example, with Wittgenstein's critique of Russell's theory of types, which he also regarded as an illegitimate attempt to say what could only be shown (through an appropriate notation). But the essential point is this. For a picture to depict, or a proposition to say something, various conditions must be met. According to Wittgenstein, however, these conditions cannot themselves be represented, but can only be shown.

Notoriously, in the final two remarks of the *Tractatus*, Wittgenstein writes:

My propositions serve as elucidations in the following way: anyone who understands me eventually recognizes them as nonsensical, when he has used them—as steps—to climb up beyond them. (He must, so to speak, throw away the ladder after he has climbed up it.)

He must transcend these propositions, and then he will see the world aright.   (6.54)
What we cannot speak about we must pass over in silence.   (7)

These remarks have generated a great deal of controversy. On the traditional view, although the propositions of the *Tractatus* are indeed nonsense, strictly speaking (i.e. on the *Tractatus* conception of sense), they can still be regarded as 'illuminating' nonsense, to use a term of Hacker's.[6] There are ineffable necessary truths about the nature of the world and the conditions that obtain for our ordinary (genuine) propositions to have the sense they do, and the propositions of the *Tractatus* are an attempt to express these truths. They may be metaphysically loaded and philosophically problematic, but they are nevertheless taken by Wittgenstein to be *truths*.

In recent years, however, a school of interpretation has developed that challenges this traditional view.[7] On this new 'therapeutic' reading,[8] the so-called 'framing' remarks of the *Tractatus* (the ones at the end just quoted and a similar remark made in the preface) are treated very seriously. The appeal to the idea of 'illuminating' nonsense is criticized as 'chickening out' or as being insufficiently 'resolute'.[9] Instead, it is argued, Wittgenstein's propositions must be regarded, quite literally and without qualification, as nonsense, the point of the *Tractatus* being to get us to recognize the illusory nature of the metaphysical pronouncements that we might be tempted to make. The saying/showing distinction is played down in favour of the sense/nonsense distinction: nonsense is nonsense, and however sophisticated, no amount of showing can turn it into sense.

As I see it, however, this new reading is flawed at its core. There is much to be gained by probing at Wittgenstein's distinctions between sense and nonsense, and saying and showing, and the associated methodological notion of elucidation, in particular. But there is little evidence that Wittgenstein regarded what he was

---

[6] Hacker, 1986, 18.

[7] See e.g. Diamond, 1991a, 1991b; Ricketts, 1996; Goldfarb, 1997; Conant, 2002.

[8] I adopt here the term used by McGinn (1999, 492), who distinguishes the new 'therapeutic' reading from the traditional 'metaphysical' reading, and develops her own 'elucidatory' reading as an intermediate position.

[9] Diamond (1991a, 181) uses the phrase 'chickening out'; Goldfarb (1997, 64) prefers to talk of 'resolute' rather than 'irresolute' interpretations.

trying to show in the *Tractatus* as entirely illusory as opposed to merely ineffable. In the preface alone, Wittgenstein writes that "the *truth* of the thoughts that are here communicated seems to me unassailable and definitive" (*TLP*, p. 4). On the new reading, the distinction between sense and nonsense is emphasized, but the proposition that there *is* such a distinction does not itself have sense, according to the picture theory. So even on the new reading, there is at least one thing that can only be shown, and hence at least one ineffable truth. Of course, Wittgenstein later rejects his earlier views, and in particular, his *Tractatus* conception of sense, as a consequence of which the distinction between saying and showing is no longer required to do the work it did. He is also critical of his earlier metaphysical pronouncements. But he does not reject them as complete nonsense. Rather he sees them as misguided attempts to express grammatical rules. So something of his earlier conception of showing might still be regarded as remaining. Metaphysical propositions are indeed an attempt to express something. It is just that they do so in a very misleading way, and the task of philosophy is to clarify what is actually going on.

In my view, then, the conception of showing is more robust than the *Tractatus* conception of sense, and in privileging the latter, the new reading distorts Wittgenstein's thought and makes a virtue out of his central vice.[10] The metaphysical remarks in the *Tractatus* are only characterized as nonsense because of the restricted conception of sense imposed by the picture theory. Once this theory is rejected, then the way is open to offer a different account of what these remarks are trying to do. This was the task that Wittgenstein undertook in his later work. By repudiating the picture theory of language and broadening his conception of logic, he was able to recognize and emphasize that there are many different kinds of propositions, doing different work in different contexts. The task of clarification is not something that can be done once and for all.

2.2 WITTGENSTEIN'S CRITIQUE OF HIS EARLIER CONCEPTION OF LANGUAGE

The first flaw that Wittgenstein detected himself in his *Tractatus* conception of language concerned his doctrine of the logical independence of elementary propositions. A proposition as apparently simple as 'A is red', ascribing the colour red to an object A, might seem to be a good example of an elementary proposition. But 'A is red' excludes 'A is green', 'A is yellow', and so on, and so is not logically independent. At the time of the *Tractatus*, Wittgenstein had merely assumed that such propositions remained to be analysed (cf. *TLP*, 6.3751; *NB*, 81, 91); but this did raise the question as to what their underlying logical form might be.

---

[10] For more detailed criticisms of the new reading, see Hacker, 2000, 2003. An account of the debate is provided in Nordmann, 2005, 77–91.

In his 1929 paper, 'Some Remarks on Logical Form', Wittgenstein attempted to find an analysis, but came to the conclusion that propositions such as 'A is red' should be seen, after all, as elementary, but with numbers somehow entering into their logical forms to reflect the degrees of quality involved (such as position along a spectrum). However, since the logical relations between such propositions could not be represented within the truth-functional logic he had taken for granted in the *Tractatus*, he felt forced to conclude, too, that the necessary rules "cannot be laid down until we have actually reached the ultimate analysis of the phenomena in question" (*RLF*, 37). This contradicted one of the most basic assumptions of the *Tractatus*—the view, as he put it, that "logic must take care of itself" (*TLP*, 5.473; *NB*, 2; cf. *TLP*, 5.551), and this was not a view that he wished to give up. Indeed, it was to prove equally fundamental to his later thought. Wittgenstein disowned his 1929 paper before the time even arrived to present it at the meeting for which it had been commissioned,[11] and he saw no alternative but to abandon the requirement, at least in its general form, that elementary propositions be logically independent. Instead, he came to believe, elementary propositions should be seen as divided into *Satzsysteme*—systems of propositions, only one member of a system being applicable on a given occasion. Propositions from different systems will be logically independent, but propositions within a particular system will contradict one another (cf. *WVC*, 63–4; *PR*, 110–13, 317).

Wittgenstein's recognition of the problem of colour exclusion brought with it the realization, then, that there were logical inferences that could not be handled within the *Tractatus* theory of truth-functions (cf. *WVC*, 64), inferences such as the following:

(5) A is red; therefore A is not green.

(6) B is 2 m tall; therefore B is under 3 m.

The rules for the logical connectives were thus only part of a far more complex system of syntactical rules than he had earlier thought (cf. *WVC*, 74, 76; *PR*, 109, 111); and the new project that this then suggests—providing an account of the logic of the various *Satzsysteme*—was to develop into the elucidation of language-games that became such a central feature of his later work (cf. *PG*, 211–12).

In a conversation recorded by Waismann in 1929, Wittgenstein remarked that he had earlier had two conceptions of an elementary proposition, one of which was "completely wrong", the one concerning logical independence, and the other of which still seemed correct—that "in analysing propositions we must eventually reach propositions that are immediate connections of objects without any help from logical constants" (*WVC*, 73–4). By the time of the *Philosophical Investigations*, this conception, too, had been rejected—or more accurately, perhaps, had been transformed as Wittgenstein thought through the implications of his recognition of *Satzsysteme* or language-games. He retained his concern with the foundations of language, but the appeal to necessarily existent *simples* underpinning the whole

---

[11] This paper was to have been read at the Joint Session, but when the time came, Wittgenstein talked about infinity instead (cf. Anscombe's note to *RLF*, 31).

of language was replaced by the appeal to varying sets of *samples* for each of the language-games that actually make up our language. In my view, this is the key development in Wittgenstein's thought, exhibiting both the underlying continuity and the crucial discontinuity between his early and later philosophy.

The transformation can be illustrated by returning to the case of colour. In a conversation also recorded by Waismann in 1929, Wittgenstein remarks that statements about colour can be represented in geometrical terms—assigning them a position along certain colour axes (precisely the possibility that underlies the conception of a *Satzsysteme*). Two diagrams are given, one a two-dimensional figure with a red–blue x-axis and a black–white y-axis (see Diagram 1), and the other a three-dimensional double cone, with a main black–white z-axis and the four pure colours at the points of its central xy-plane (see Diagram 2; which I have filled in by making use of similar diagrams elsewhere; *PR*, 278; *WLL*, 8).

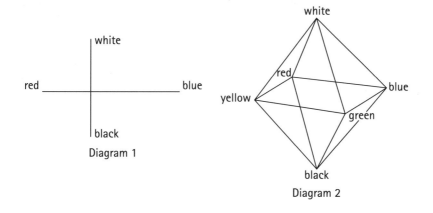

Diagram 1

Diagram 2

"Every statement about colours", Wittgenstein remarks, "can be represented by means of such symbols. If we say that four elementary colours would suffice, I call such symbols of equal status *elements of representation*. These elements of representation are the 'objects'" (*WVC*, 43). We can define 'orange', for example, as what lies between red and yellow. To say that something is orange, then, is to say that it has a colour between red and yellow, where red and yellow are treated as two of the elementary colours that fix the logical space of colour representation. Within a year Wittgenstein is talking of these 'elements of representation' as samples, and the shift is complete. He writes: "What I once called 'objects', simples, were simply what I could refer to without running the risk of their possible non-existence; i.e. that for which there is neither existence nor non-existence, and that means: what we can speak about *no matter what may be the case*" (*PR*, 72). He now recognizes that "what we can speak about *no matter what may be the case*" are the elements of representation, which belong to the symbolism itself. He goes on: "If I want to tell someone what colour some material is to be, I send him a sample, and obviously this sample belongs to language" (*PR*, 73). A particular set of objects may indeed be presupposed by a given language-game, then, but these objects are not the simples of the *Tractatus* but the samples that function as the elements of representation.

In the key work of his later period, the *Philosophical Investigations*, Wittgenstein's main discussion of simples and samples occurs in §§39–64. He starts by mentioning his *Tractatus* conception that "a name ought really to signify a simple", and taking 'Excalibur' as his example, presents an argument for simples that is essentially the same as that sketched above (see p. 43). However, in response, he now argues that this is to confuse the *meaning* of a word with its *bearer* (§40), and suggests instead that the meaning of a word is its *use* (§43). In §46 he quotes the passage from Plato's *Theaetetus* (201e1–202b5) in which Socrates presents the conception of 'primary elements', which Wittgenstein remarks is similar to his own earlier notion of simple objects. The crucial idea here is that primary elements can only be named and not described, descriptive language being seen as the compounding together of names. In his critique of this, he first explains that what counts as 'simple' or 'complex' depends on the context (§§47–8), and then makes a similar point about the idea of a 'name' itself: that whether a word counts as a name or not depends on what is done with it. "For naming and describing do not stand on the same level: naming is a preparation for description. . . . We may say: *nothing* has so far been done, when a thing has been named. It has not even *got* a name except in the language-game" (§49). In §50 we then arrive at what is undoubtedly the clearest expression of the transition from simples to samples, and the underlying continuity:

What does it mean to say that we can attribute neither being nor non-being to elements?—One might say: if everything that we call "being" and "non-being" consists in the existence and non-existence of connexions between elements, it makes no sense to speak of an element's being (non-being); just as when everything that we call "destruction" lies in the separation of elements, it makes no sense to speak of the destruction of an element.

One would, however, like to say: existence cannot be attributed to an element, for if it did not *exist*, one could not even name it and so one could say nothing at all of it.—But let us consider an analogous case. There is *one* thing of which one can say neither that it is one metre long, nor that it is not one metre long, and that is the standard metre in Paris.—But this is, of course, not to ascribe any extraordinary property to it, but only to mark its peculiar role in the language-game of measuring with a metre-rule.—Let us imagine samples of colour being preserved in Paris like the standard metre. We define: "sepia" means the colour of the standard sepia which is there kept hermetically sealed. Then it will make no sense to say of this sample either that it is of this colour or that it is not.

We can put it like this: this sample is an instrument of the language used in ascriptions of colour. In this language-game it is not something that is represented, but is a means of representation. . . . And to say "If it did not *exist*, it could have no name" is to say as much and as little as: if this thing did not exist, we could not use it in our language-game.—What looks as if it *had* to exist, is part of the language. It is a paradigm in our language-game; something with which comparison is made. And this may be an important observation; but it is none the less an observation concerning our language-game—our method of representation.   (*PI*, §50.)

Now it might seem implausible to deny that it makes sense to say that the standard metre is a metre long, for surely the standard metre *is* a metre long? Let us assume, however, that the only way we have of determining whether something is a metre long or not is by measuring it against the standard metre. To say that something is a metre long, then, is to say that when laid against the standard metre, it can be seen to be the same length. But since this operation cannot be carried out with respect to the standard metre itself, it cannot make sense to say that the standard metre is a metre long. Just as it is illegitimate to attribute either being or non-being to any simple (on a certain conception of being), so too it is illegitimate to say of any sample that it either possesses or lacks that property of which it is a sample.

But surely, it might be objected, if we can speak of something being the same length as the standard metre, then it must make sense to talk about the standard metre being a certain length. Have I not just talked of a sample being a sample *of* a property, implying that it possesses that property itself? In reply, let us consider the following pattern of inference:

(7) (a) Y is the same length as X.
   (b) The length of X is one metre.

   (c) The length of Y is one metre.

Assuming that (a), (b) and (c) have sense, the inference is clearly valid. But what if 'X' is replaced by 'the standard metre'? According to Wittgenstein, (b) now lacks sense, so what happens to the inference? Does a *gap* not open up? If so, and such inferences underlie the use of samples, then how can we judge anything by means of them? However, in this case, (b) simply drops out altogether, being no longer required for the validity of the inference: (c) can be directly inferred from (a). If Y is the same length as the standard metre, then it is one metre long. On Wittgenstein's account, (b) is now the expression of a *rule*, licensing the passage from (a) to (c), rather than a premise in itself.

Compare the following analogous case:

(8) (a) P
   (b) P → Q

   (c) Q

Within propositional logic, this, too, is a valid form of inference. But now consider replacing 'Q' by 'P ∨ Q'. We can now infer (c) directly from (a): (b) is no longer a required premise, but is simply an expression of the *rule* licensing the inference (i.e. "From 'P' infer 'P ∨ Q' ").[12] The essential idea here is the insight that lay at the heart of Wittgenstein's account of logic in the *Tractatus* (and which underlies natural deduction systems of logic). As he articulated it then, logical propositions such

---

[12] If the rule has to be formulated as a premise, then we generate the so-called 'paradox of inference', first formulated (though not under that name) by Lewis Carroll (1895).

as 'P → P ∨ Q' are tautologies which do indeed reflect rules licensing inferences, without themselves possessing sense or being required as premises (cf. *TLP*, 6.1, 6.1201, 6.1221). They simply *show* that a certain inference is valid (cf. *TLP*, 6.1264). Although he came to reject not only the conception of sense in contrast to which logical propositions were seen as senseless (and its supposed metaphysical underpinnings), but also the idea that all logical propositions are truth-functional tautologies, he continued to believe that logical propositions—understood as expressions of rules licensing inferences—lacked sense. Although there may be many different ways in which ordinary propositions have sense, according to Wittgenstein, to attribute sense to expressions of rules as well is to obscure their essential role.

This fundamental point has not always been appreciated. Kripke, for example, has argued that Wittgenstein is just wrong in denying that it makes sense to say that the standard metre is a metre long.[13] According to Kripke, 'The standard metre is a metre long' is a paradigm example of a contingent *a priori* truth. It is contingent because it is possible for the particular object that plays the role of the standard metre *not* to be one metre long (e.g. if it is heated slightly), and it is *a priori* because knowing that this is a definition, it can be judged to be true "without further investigation" (1980, 56). But Kripke simply confuses two different uses of a proposition of the form 'X is a metre long'. It is true that if 'the standard metre' just serves to denote a particular lump of matter, then it is only a contingent truth that it has the particular length it does at a given time. And we might also accept, on some conception of the *a priori*, that if the proposition functions as a definition or rule of inference, then we can know *a priori* that it is true. But Wittgenstein's point is that such propositions cannot perform both of these functions at the same time, and his concern in §50 is with the second. When samples—qua samples—serve as elements of representation, it makes no sense to say that they have the property of which they are the sample.

Of course, we might still be reluctant to say that 'The standard metre is a metre long' (when talking about its role as a sample) is *senseless*. For the proposition is not nonsense, and if we have liberated ourselves from the restricted conception of sense of the *Tractatus*, then why can we not admit that it has sense, even if in a different way? To answer this, we need to recognize just how deep Wittgenstein's insight about samples goes. Judgements of 'sense', too, can only be made in implicit comparison to samples of propositions that are used with sense. Even if there are lots of different ways in which we can say things about the world, communicate our views, and so on, it remains the case that propositions that reflect rules of grammar—just like the logical propositions of the *Tractatus*—do not do any of these things. These rules are what are involved *in* doing them. So in comparison even with the wide range of propositions that do have sense when used in these ways, 'grammatical propositions' are different. It is this difference that Wittgenstein wants to express in

---

[13] Kripke, 1980, 54–7.

characterizing them as lacking sense. And this brings out, I think, a deep continuity with the *Tractatus*. His conception of logic may have broadened to include what he alternatively now also calls 'grammar', and as we have seen, there is a crucial shift from simples to samples, but his basic conception of the distinction between 'ordinary' and 'logical' propositions remained constant.

2.3 Wittgenstein's Later Conception of Language

From the publication of the *Philosophical Investigations* in 1953 until the early 1970s Wittgenstein's private language argument (as articulated, in particular, in *PI*, §§243–315) was widely seen as the most important argument of his later philosophy. Certainly, it provoked the most debate, although topics such as his conception of a language-game were also discussed.[14] In the late 1970s and 1980s, partly influenced by lectures given by Saul Kripke, which were published as a book in 1982, Wittgenstein's discussion of rule-following, which in the *Investigations* immediately preceded the private language argument (*PI*, §§185–242), took centre-stage.[15] In my view, the private language argument is indeed rooted in the earlier rule-following considerations. But both discussions must themselves be seen in the light of Wittgenstein's critique of his *Tractatus* conception of language, and in particular, of the shift from simples to samples.

To appreciate this, let us return to Wittgenstein's example of the colour sepia, and imagine being introduced to this colour by being presented with a sample of it—for example, by being given a piece of card painted the right shade of reddish brown. It might be tempting to suppose, on something like Wittgenstein's conception of simple objects in the *Tractatus*, that as long as the relevant object is somehow before us (even if our apprehension is assumed to occur at some deep unconscious level), we will know exactly what it is and be able to recognize it in the future. As he put it in the *Tractatus*, "If I know an object I also know all its possible occurrences in states of affairs" (*TLP*, 2.0123). Knowledge of the simple objects, according to Wittgenstein, was what enables me to understand propositions whose senses just are the possible states of affairs that are pictured.

But this conception, Wittgenstein came to realize, is deeply misguided. For no definition of a term by mere presentation of some object can guarantee that I understand the meaning of that term. If I am simply given the sample and told "This is sepia", with no further words of explanation, then how am I to know what to do

---

[14] For a good indication of the range of topics discussed during this period, see the collections edited by Pitcher (1966) and Klemke (1971).

[15] Kripke, 1982. The shift in emphasis was marked, in particular, by the collection edited by Holtzman and Leich (1981), and the second volume of Baker and Hacker's commentary on the *Investigations* (1985).

with it? How will I realize that it is a sample of *colour*? The opening pages of the *Investigations* contain a sustained attack on the idea that ostensive teaching alone can initiate someone into the use of language. Ostensive definitions are not illegitimate, but the understanding of them presupposes certain background knowledge. As Wittgenstein's example of 'tove' at the beginning of *The Blue Book* shows, until we appreciate the context, there is no way of knowing what an ostensive definition is defining. If we hold up a pencil and say "This is tove", do we mean 'pencil', 'round', 'wood', 'one', 'hard' or what? (cf. *BB*, p. 2). "So one might say: the ostensive definition explains the use—the meaning—of the word when the overall role of the word in language is clear. Thus if I know that someone means to explain a colour-word to me the ostensive definition "That is called 'sepia'" will help me to understand the word" (*PI*, §30).

But even if I know that I am being introduced to a particular colour, how do I know how similar something must be to the sample I am given for it to count as 'sepia'? However many further samples I am given, making clearer not only what is meant by 'sepia' but also what is not meant by 'sepia', is there not always the possibility of coming across a new shade which I will describe 'wrongly'? This is essentially the problem with which Wittgenstein deals in his discussion of rule-following in the *Investigations*. The main example he takes here, introduced in §185, concerns getting someone to continue a series of numbers by adding 2 each time. Here too we can imagine having taught them by presenting them with a range of samples of such additions, and as Wittgenstein suggests, tested them up to 1000. But they might still, when they come to 1000, continue the series with 1004, 1008, 1012, and so on. Since it is always a possibility that there will come a point at which they will diverge from how we would have continued the series, how can we ever be sure that we mean the same by our words, or indeed, how can I know myself what I mean, for who knows how I might go on in the future?

The key point here is that there will always be some 'interpretation' of the rule or order that will reconcile its initial or sample applications with its later divergent application. Perhaps 'sepia' was all along taken to mean 'reddish brown or ochre', or the instruction 'Add 2' was understood to involve, as *we* would put it, adding 2 up to 1000, 4 up to 2000, 6 up to 3000, and so on (cf. *PI*, §185). So how can any expression of a rule tell us how to correctly apply it in all cases, since different interpretations can always be offered? Wittgenstein characterizes the sceptical paradox in §201: "no course of action [can] be determined by a rule, because every course of action can be made out to accord with the rule". However, what this shows, he goes on to argue, is that "there is a way of grasping a rule which is *not* an *interpretation*, but which is exhibited in what we call "obeying the rule" and "going against it" in actual cases" (*Ibid.*). He admits that there is an inclination to say that any action that exhibits grasp of a rule is itself an 'interpretation'. But, he suggests, "we ought to restrict the term "interpretation" to the substitution of one expression of the rule for another" (*Ibid.*).

What is being rejected here, then, is the idea that an 'interpretation' is required to connect an apprehension of some rule-formulation with the supposedly appropriate action. 'Interpretations' do not mediate between grasping a rule and acting in accord with it, just as 'meanings' do not mediate between our understanding of words and our using them: their meaning *is* their use, and our use of them exhibits our understanding of them. Wittgenstein's doctrine that meaning is use and his conception of rule-following as a practice are inextricably linked. It is in this context that his controversial next section becomes clear:

And hence also 'obeying a rule' is a practice. And to *think* one is obeying a rule is not to obey a rule. Hence it is not possible to obey a rule 'privately': otherwise thinking one was obeying a rule would be the same thing as obeying it.   (*PI*, §202.)

These remarks have been frequently misinterpreted. By 'practice' Wittgenstein means 'practice as a fundamental human activity' rather than 'practice of a community' (though community practices may well constitute the vast majority of such activities); and by 'privately' he does not mean 'in isolation from other people' but something more like 'by reference to one's own interpretation'. Wittgenstein is not alluding to what might be termed 'contingent privacy', but to a kind of 'necessary privacy'.[16] What he is criticizing is the idea that obeying a rule involves some essential process of 'interpreting' the rule—in the sense of generating or consulting some 'mental representation' of the rule. What counts as following a certain rule is governed by what we do, not by what we think.

The essential message here is also the message of the private language argument, which can be seen as developing the rule-following considerations by focusing on the possibility that our knowledge of the meaning of a term is constituted by our possession of some private mental object. But we are no better off appealing to a private mental sample, as it might be put, than a public one (such as a sample of colour). According to Wittgenstein, it is not just that, since no one else has access to any of my 'private' mental objects, there would be no way for them to verify that I have it or to understand what I mean when I refer to it. I cannot even know myself what I mean. For how do I know that the object is not always changing? To judge whether it has changed or not, I must have some means of identifying it. But if the criteria for this are 'public', then the supposed object is not, after all, inaccessible to others. And if the criteria can only be given 'privately', using terms which themselves refer to private mental entities, then we are no further forward. Once again, according to Wittgenstein, what I mean by a given term, even a sensation term, is determined by my *use* of the term, and not by any private act of ostensive definition.

That Wittgenstein's private language argument is also rooted in his concern with the role of samples is clear from his earlier discussion in the *Investigations* of the supposed indestructibility of whatever it is—whether simples or samples—that guarantees that our basic terms have meaning. He writes, for example:

---

[16] These misconstruals are characteristic of the so-called 'community interpretation' of Wittgenstein's remarks on rule-following, as propounded by Kripke (1982), in particular. For a detailed critique, see Baker and Hacker, 1984. That Wittgenstein's target is 'necessary' rather than 'contingent' privacy applies equally to his private language argument, as *PI*, §243 makes clear.

But what if no such sample is part of the language, and we *bear in mind* the colour (for instance) that a word stands for?—"And if we bear it in mind then it comes before our mind's eye when we utter the word. So, if it is always supposed to be possible for us to remember it, it must be in itself indestructible."—But what do we regard as the criterion for remembering it right?—When we work with a sample instead of our memory there are circumstances in which we say that the sample has changed colour and we judge of this by memory. But can we not sometimes speak of a darkening (for example) of our memory-image? Aren't we as much at the mercy of memory as of a sample? (For someone might feel like saying: "If we had no memory we should be at the mercy of a sample".) Or perhaps of some chemical reaction. Imagine that you were supposed to paint a particular colour "C", which was the colour that appeared when the chemical substances X and Y combined.—Suppose that the colour struck you as brighter on one day than on another; would you not sometimes say: "I must be wrong, the colour is certainly the same as yesterday"? This shews that we do not always resort to what memory tells us as the verdict of the highest court of appeal.   (*PI*, §56)

On Wittgenstein's view, we can indeed use our memory to judge what colour something is on a given occasion. But if *all* we had to rely on was our memory, without any actual samples of red to appeal to in explaining what we meant by 'red', then the language-game of using 'red' would soon break down. "For suppose you cannot remember the colour any more?—When we forget which colour this is the name of, it loses its meaning for us; that is, we are no longer able to play a particular language-game with it. And the situation then is comparable with that in which we have lost a paradigm which was an instrument of our language" (*PI*, §57).

On Wittgenstein's later conception of language, then, it is samples rather than simples that secure the meaningfulness of our linguistic practices, where these samples are seen as instruments of the language, constituting the means of representation. To say that these samples are 'indestructible' (as Wittgenstein did of simples in the *Tractatus*) is just a misleading way of saying that without these samples, the relevant language-game could not be played. Samples are essential in teaching someone the language-game, and in elucidating what we mean. Our own understanding of the language-game is manifested in what we do—in our use of the relevant terms, and in our appeal to samples, ostensive definitions and rule-formulations in explaining what we mean. To utilize Wittgenstein's earlier distinction, this understanding is thus *shown* in our practice. We might indeed attempt to *say* what it is we know when we understand a particular term, by appealing to a sample, giving an ostensive definition or formulating a rule, but this is only one expression of that understanding, and does not in itself constitute that understanding. Although Wittgenstein does not himself make use of the distinction between saying and showing in his later work, associated as it no doubt was in his mind with his earlier metaphysics, the underlying idea remained. Our understanding of the meaning of terms—our mastery of a given language-game—is *shown* in our linguistic behaviour.

2.4 CONCLUSION

In the *Tractatus*, Wittgenstein assumed that there was a single underlying logic to our thought and language—essentially that articulated by Frege. Influenced by Russell's theory of descriptions, he was led to the conclusion that there were simple objects that necessarily existed as the condition for language to have meaning. But in his later work he came to see that Fregean logic did not provide the logic of our language, and that there were, in fact, an indefinite number of different (but often overlapping) 'language-games', each with its own set of rules or 'logic'. His conception of logic was broadened to cover what he termed the 'grammar' of language-games. These language-games were dependent not on simples but on samples, whose existence was necessary to the language-game in which they played a role but which did not exist 'necessarily' in any absolute sense. If the samples of a given language-game were ever destroyed or ceased to be, then the relevant language-game would simply break down.

Throughout his life, however, he insisted on a sharp distinction between propositions with 'sense' and 'logical' propositions. The latter do not 'picture' possible states of affairs, as he put it in the *Tractatus*, or in more general terms, tell us anything about the world or impart genuine information, but simply express the rules of grammar that govern our use of language. A sentence such as 'This is sepia', for example, can thus be used in two basic ways. It can be used to describe something as sepia, or to explain what 'sepia' means by identifying a sample of the colour. To describe something as 'sepia' is to assert that it is similar in colour to a sample of sepia. To use Wittgenstein's earlier language, it is to assert an internal relation. For something to be sepia is for it to stand in the relevant relation of similarity to samples of sepia. It would not be the colour it is without that relation obtaining. As in the case of the distinction between saying and showing, Wittgenstein may have been reluctant to use the term 'internal relation' in his later work, but the essential idea remained.[17] To describe something as sepia presupposes that 'sepia' has meaning, a meaning that can be explained by giving an appropriate ostensive definition, identifying a sample of sepia. To say 'This is sepia' in giving an ostensive definition, however, is to do something quite different from using the sentence in describing something as sepia. In this case what is expressed is a rule of grammar, a rule that licenses us to describe something as sepia in virtue of being internally related to a sample of sepia. This fundamental distinction between ordinary contingent propositions and 'logical' or 'grammatical' propositions lay at the heart of his conception of language in both his early and later work.

---

[17] Two passages where he does use the term 'internal relation' occur in *PI*, ɪɪ, p. 212, and in *RFM*, pp. 363–4.

In discussing the nature of philosophy, Wittgenstein spoke of the need to find 'the liberating word' [*das erlösende Wort*], which gives expression to what has been lurking unarticulated in our consciousness (*BT*, 302). In my view, 'from simples to samples' is the phrase that encapsulates most neatly the development in Wittgenstein's thought. The development was significant, with major ramifications, but that the transition can be represented by a mere vowel change shows, I hope, that underlying this development was a fundamental continuity.

REFERENCES

Baker, G. P. and Hacker, P. M. S. (1984). *Scepticism, Rules and Language*, Oxford: Blackwell.

_____ (1985). *Wittgenstein: Rules, Grammar and Necessity*, Oxford: Blackwell.

_____ (2005). *Wittgenstein: Understanding and Meaning*, 2nd edn., rev. by P. M. S. Hacker, 2 vols., Part I: Essays, Part II: Exegesis §§1–184, Oxford: Blackwell; 1st edn. published as one vol. 1980, and as two vols. in paperback 1983.

Beaney, Michael (2003). 'Russell and Frege', in N. Griffin, ed., *The Cambridge Companion to Russell*, Cambridge: Cambridge University Press, 2003, 128–70.

Beaney, Michael and Reck, Erich H. (2005). eds., *Gottlob Frege: Critical Assessments*, 4 vols., London: Routledge.

Block, Irving (1981). ed., *Perspectives on the Philosophy of Wittgenstein*, Oxford: Blackwell.

Carroll, Lewis (C. L. Dodgson) (1895). 'What the Tortoise Said to Achilles', *Mind* 4, 278–80; repr. in *Mind* 104 (1995), 691–3.

Conant, James (2002). 'The Method of the *Tractatus*', in Reck, 2002, 374–462.

Copi, Irving M. and Beard, Robert W. (1966). eds., *Essays on Wittgenstein's Tractatus*, London: Routledge.

Crary, Alice and Read, Rupert (2000). eds., *The New Wittgenstein*, London: Routledge.

Diamond, Cora (1991). *The Realistic Spirit*, Cambridge, Mass.: MIT Press.

_____ (1991a). 'Throwing Away the Ladder: How to Read the *Tractatus*', in Diamond, 1991, 179–204.

_____ (1991b). 'Ethics, Imagination and the Method of Wittgenstein's *Tractatus*', in R. Heinrich and H. Vetter, eds., *Bilder der Philosophie*, Vienna: Oldenbourg, 1991, 55–90; repr. in Crary and Read, 2000, 149–73.

Goldfarb, Warren (1997). 'Metaphysics and Nonsense: on Cora Diamond's *The Realistic Spirit*', *Journal of Philosophical Research* 22, 57–73.

Hacker, P. M. S. (1981). 'The Rise and Fall of the Picture Theory', in Block, 1981, 85–109.

_____ (1986). *Insight and Illusion*, rev. edn., Oxford: Oxford University Press.

_____ (2000). 'Was he Trying to Whistle it?', in Crary and Read 2000, 353–88.

_____ (2003). 'Wittgenstein, Carnap and the New American Wittgensteinians', *Philosophical Quarterly* 53, 1–23.

Holtzman, S. H., and Leich, C. M. (1981). eds., *Wittgenstein: To Follow a Rule*, London: Routledge.

Janik, Allan (1994). 'How did Hertz influence Wittgenstein's Philosophical Development?', *Grazer Philosophische Studien* 49 (1994/5), 19–47.

Kenny, Anthony (1973). *Wittgenstein*, London: Penguin.

Klemke, E. D. (1971). ed., *Essays on Wittgenstein*, Urbana: University of Illinois Press.

Kripke, Saul A. (1980). *Naming and Necessity*, Oxford: Blackwell.

_____ (1982). *Wittgenstein on Rules and Private Language*, Oxford: Blackwell; earlier version in Block, 1981, 238–312.

Levine, James (2002). 'Analysis and Decomposition in Frege and Russell', *Philosophical Quarterly* 52, 195–216; repr. in Beaney and Reck, 2005, vol. IV, 392–413.

McGinn, Marie (1999). 'Between Metaphysics and Nonsense: The Role of Elucidation in Wittgenstein's *Tractatus*', *Philosophical Quarterly* 49, 491–513.

Nordmann, Alfred (2005). *Wittgenstein's Tractatus: An Introduction*, Cambridge: Cambridge University Press.

Pitcher, George (1966). ed., *Wittgenstein: The Philosophical Investigations*, London: Macmillan.

Reck, Erich H. (2002). ed., *From Frege to Wittgenstein*, New York: Oxford University Press.

Ricketts, Thomas (1996). 'Pictures, Logic, and the Limits of Sense in Wittgenstein's *Tractatus*', in Sluga and Stern, 1996, 59–99.

Russell, Bertrand (1959). *My Philosophical Development*, London: George Allen and Unwin; publ. Unwin Paperbacks, 1985.

Sluga, Hans and Stern, David (1996). eds., *The Cambridge Companion to Wittgenstein*, Cambridge: Cambridge University Press.

Wittgenstein, Ludwig (1979). *NB, Notebooks 1914–1916*, 2nd edn., ed. G. H. von Wright and G. E. M. Anscombe, tr. G. E. M. Anscombe, Oxford: Blackwell; 1st edn. 1961.

––––– , *TLP, Tractatus Logico-Philosophicus* (1961, 1974). tr. D. F. Pears and B. McGuinness, London: Routledge; orig. tr. C. K. Ogden, London: Routledge, 1922.

––––– , *RLF* (1929), 'Some Remarks on Logical Form', in Copi and Beard, (1966), 31–7; orig. in *Proc. Aris. Soc. Supp.* (1929), 162–71.

––––– , *WVC, Ludwig Wittgenstein and the Vienna Circle* (1979). conversations recorded by Friedrich Waismann, ed. B. McGuinness, tr. J. Schulte and B. McGuinness, Oxford: Blackwell.

––––– , *PR, Philosophical Remarks* (1975). ed. R. Rhees, tr. R. Hargreaves and R. White, Oxford: Blackwell.

––––– , *PG, Philosophical Grammar* (1974). ed. R. Rhees, tr. A. Kenny, Oxford: Blackwell.

––––– , *WLL, Wittgenstein's Lectures, Cambridge 1930–1932* (1980). ed. Desmond Lee, Oxford: Blackwell.

––––– , *BB, The Blue and Brown Books* (1958). 2nd edn., Oxford: Blackwell, 1974.

––––– , *RFM, Remarks on the Foundations of Mathematics* (1956). 3rd edn., ed. G. H. von Wright, R. Rhees and G. E. M. Anscombe, tr. G. E. M. Anscombe, Oxford: Blackwell, 1978.

––––– , *BT, The Big Typescript: TS 213* (2005) ed. and tr. C. G. Luckhardt and M. A. E. Aue, Oxford: Blackwell.

––––– , *PI, Philosophical Investigations* (1956). 3rd edn., tr. G. E. M. Anscombe, Oxford: Blackwell, 1978.

CHAPTER 3

....

PHILOSOPHY OF LANGUAGE IN THE TWENTIETH CENTURY

....

THOMAS BALDWIN

DURING the first half of the twentieth century philosophy took a 'linguistic turn' (the phrase, which comes from Gustav Bergmann,[1] was made famous by Richard Rorty as the title of an anthology of papers in which this development is set out and assessed).[2] The first clear signal of this development was Ludwig Wittgenstein's remark in his *Tractatus Logico-Philosophicus* (1921) that 'All philosophy is "Critique of Language"' (4.0031), and this work by Wittgenstein (which I discuss in Section 3.2) remains a classic presentation of the thesis that philosophy can only be undertaken through the critical study of language. Thus during the twentieth century philosophical approaches to language, the kinds of theorizing now known as 'philosophy of language', have been developed in a context in which language has been taken to be a primary resource for philosophy, and as a result there has been a two-way relationship in which conceptions of language and of philosophy have been developed together. But one theme has been central: that language is not just the contingent expression of some wholly independent reality; instead there is an internal relation between the two. What remains controversial is the nature of this internal relation and thus of the role of language in our conception of reality. One

[1] G. Bergmann, *Logic and Reality*, University of Wisconsin Press, Madison, 1964, p. 177.
[2] R. Rorty, *The Linguistic Turn*, University of Chicago Press, Chicago, 1967.

common position, especially associated with logical empiricists of the 1930s, was that the traditional conception of *a priori* truth should be reinterpreted as analytic truth, understood as the truth of a statement merely in virtue of the meaning of the words employed in it. Where this position is taken and analytic truth inherits the traditional role of the *a priori* in providing the categorial structure of our knowledge of the world, a linguistic version of transcendental idealism is implied. Critical discussion of this implication has been one of the central themes of late twentieth-century philosophy of language.

In this case the debate concerns the role of language in the context of metaphysical debates about idealism and realism. But philosophy of language has also transformed debates in other areas of philosophy, most notably epistemology and philosophy of mind. Questions about empirical evidence have been formulated as questions about the role of 'observation-sentences' and as to whether sense-experience has a content which transcends language; and these questions intersect with others as to how far language is the accomplishment of thought and feeling, rather than the expression of mental states whose content is independent of language. I shall characterize some of these debates below, but first I turn to discuss Frege's philosophy of language.

3.1 FREGE

In his book *Frege: Philosophy of Language* Michael Dummett claimed that at the end of the nineteenth century Frege initiated a 'revolution' in philosophy by making the philosophy of language the foundation of philosophy in place of epistemology, which had occupied this place since the time of Descartes.[3] Although Dummett did not initiate the phrase 'philosophy of language',—see, for example, William Alston's 1964 book of this title[4]—there is no doubt that by this claim he helped to raise consciousness of the philosophy of language and its importance. In thinking about it, one question is clearly whether philosophy needs a 'foundation' at all, and this question will recur in several contexts in this essay. But for the moment it is Dummett's claim about Frege's achievement which requires attention. For when one turns to Frege himself one finds nothing like Dummett's claim that philosophy of language is to be the foundation of philosophy; instead Frege's frequent claim is that by his work in logic he aims 'to free thinking from the fetters of language by pointing up the logical imperfections of language'[5].

In fact this point is no great objection to Dummett, since his claim is one about Frege's achievement and not one about his intentions, and a way to see what Dummett had in mind is to consider the slightly paradoxical claim with which Frege introduces his first great work, his *Begriffsschrift* (1879), in which he broke with tradition

---

[3] M. Dummett, *Frege: Philosophy of Language*, Duckworth, London, 1973, p. 665
[4] W. Alston, *The Philosophy of Language*, Prentice-Hall, Englewood Cliffs NJ, 1964.
[5] From Frege's unpublished 'Logic' essay, probably written in 1897; p. 149 in his *Posthumous Writings*, ed. H. Hermes, F. Kambartel, and F. Kaulbach, trans. P. Long and R. White, Blackwell, Oxford, 1979.

by starting from a truth-functional sentential logic and then went on to introduce first-order predicate logic with quantifiers. Frege writes here:

If it is one of the tasks of philosophy to break the domination of the word over the human spirit by laying bare the misconceptions that through the use of language often unavoidably arise concerning the relations between concepts and by freeing thought from that with which only the means of expression of ordinary language, constituted as they are, saddle it, then my ideography, further developed for these purposes, can become a useful tool for the philosopher.[6]

Frege characteristically talks here of freeing thought from language; but in fact his method of doing so is precisely to propose his new 'ideography', his new concept-notation (*Begriffsschrift*), which is first-order predicate logic set out in an idiosyncratic way. So the contrast between language and pure thought turns out to be a contrast between ordinary language with all its misleading superficial similarities and the logician's analytic reformulation of the language in such a way as to make the underlying logical inferences transparent. It is this latter contrast, between ordinary language and a logically reconstructed language, which is going to be fundamental to twentieth-century philosophy of language; for the core of Frege's position is that logic, by breaking the domination of ordinary language over the human spirit, can liberate philosophy to explore the world unfettered by misconception.

This gets us some way towards Dummett's thesis. But Dummett had a broader claim in mind. He regularly writes of philosophy of language as 'theory of meaning' and his claim is that Frege had a theory of meaning which, whether or not Frege appreciated it, provided a new foundation for philosophy. What Dummett has in mind here is not Frege's logical theory but his theory of 'sense' (*sinn*) and 'reference' (*bedeutung*). The starting point for this theory is Frege's insight that the fundamental phenomenon of meaning is the expression of a thought by a complete sentence, and not the way in which words such as names and predicates refer to objects and properties. Frege singles out as one of his fundamental principles the principle that one should 'never ask for the meaning of a word in isolation, but only in the context of a sentence';[7] so the meanings of words, including names, are to be thought of in terms of their potential contribution to the meaning of sentences in which they occur. At this point Frege introduces his next fundamental point, that the concept of truth is fundamental to an account of the meaning of a sentence; so the meanings of words comprise their contribution to the conditions under which sentences in which they occur are true. It is in developing this insight that Frege introduces his distinction between sense and reference. The reference of a sentence, he says, is that aspect of the sentence which is fixed by the objects and properties referred to in the sentence, and this, he says, is its truth-value,—its truth, if it is true, or its falsehood if it is false. But it is clear that this is not a complete account of the meaning of a sentence,

---

[6] From the preface to G. Frege, *Begriffsschrift*, Halle, 1879, p. 7 in the English translation edited and translated by J. van Heijenoort, *Frege and Godel*, Harvard University Press, Cambridge MA, 1970.

[7] G. Frege, *Foundations of Arithmetic*, trans. J. Austin, Blackwell, Oxford, 1950, p. x of Frege's 'Introduction'.

since it is obviously not the case that all true sentences have the same meaning; so the conception of the sense of a sentence is employed to capture a further way of discriminating among sentences which differ in meaning despite having the same truth-value. For Frege, the way to make this further discrimination is to characterize the different conditions under which sentences are true, i.e. their truth-conditions. For, intuitively, although the sentences 'snow is white' and 'grass is green' have the same truth-value because they are both true, the conditions under which they are true differ: in one case, the condition is that snow is white, in the other case, it is that grass is green. So, it seems, as far as sentences are concerned, the sense/reference distinction is a distinction between the truth-conditions and the truth-value of a sentence.

But this notion of truth-conditions, which is central to twentieth-century philosophy of language, is tricky; for there is a sense in which all sentences with the same truth-value have the same truth-condition. Because snow is in fact white and grass is in fact green, it follows that 'snow is white' is true if and only if grass is green and 'grass is green' is true if and only if snow is white. This external, 'extensional', way of identifying truth-conditions is, however, clearly not what Frege has in mind. Instead he takes it that the sense of a sentence is given just by that account of the conditions under which it is true which is implied by the meaning of the words which occur within it.[8] So the conception of a sentence's truth-conditions which captures its sense is a conception of these conditions whose specification is internal to the language and does not depend on extraneous non-linguistic facts such as that snow is white and grass is green. This point implies that for Frege there is a crucial interdependence between sentence-meaning and word-meaning. On the one hand, sentence-meaning is conceptually fundamental: the meaning of a word just comprises its contribution to the meaning, that is, the truth-conditions, of sentences in which it occurs. But, on the other hand, for any given sentence, the account of its meaning is dependent on that of the meanings of the words which occur within it. Furthermore word-meaning again requires the distinction between sense and reference. For while the truth or falsehood of a sentence, and thus its reference, depends only on the relationships among the objects and properties referred to by the words which occur within the sentence, the sense of the sentence depends also on the way in which these objects and properties are described in the sentence, and thus, as Frege puts it, on the sense as well as the reference of these descriptions. Frege illustrates his point with a famous example: even though the Morning Star is the Evening Star, the sense of the sentence 'The Morning Star is the Evening Star' differs from that of 'The Morning Star is the Morning Star' since the former, unlike the latter, expresses a remarkable astronomical discovery; so in respect of phrases such as 'The Morning Star' and 'The Evening Star' we also need to distinguish sense from reference.

As we will see below, this final point has been a focus for debate throughout the twentieth century. But that debate should not overshadow the other two basic claims which Frege introduced into the philosophy of language: the fundamental status

---

[8] G. Frege, *The Basic Laws of Arithmetic*, trans. M. Furth, University of California Press, Berkeley CA, 1967, §32 (p. 90).

of sentence-meaning vis-à-vis word-meaning and the central role of the concept of truth in the elucidation of sentence-meaning. Both of these have been disputed and in recent years the second in particular has come under pressure (see Sections 3.8 and 3.9). Frege himself recognized that there was more to the meaning of a sentence than its truth-conditions, but he argued that distinctions of meaning which do not affect questions of truth, such as that between 'and' and 'but', should be set to one side, as questions of 'tone' or 'force'.[9] Whether this is appropriate is a matter to which I shall return towards the end of this essay; for most of the twentieth century, most philosophers have accepted Frege's position on this matter. But I want to return to Dummett's claim, that this 'theory of meaning', or rather the very idea of providing a theory of this kind, provides a new foundation for philosophy. What Dummett has in mind here is that a systematic account of the meaning of language of the kind that Frege offers provides the basis also for an account of the content of thoughts: in a later work he takes it that this claim is the distinctive mark of 'analytical philosophy': 'what distinguishes analytical philosophy, in its diverse manifestations, from other schools is the belief, first, that a philosophical account of thought can be attained through a philosophical account of language, and, secondly, that a comprehensive account can only be so attained'.[10] In fact this claim is not exclusive to 'analytical philosophers': it is characteristic of Heidegger's later philosophy and equally of the writings of Merleau-Ponty and Derrida, though I shall not pursue their approaches to it here. Nonetheless the suggestion that language is the fundamental form of intentionality, and thus that an account of the meaning of language is central to an account of the content of thought, has been central to much twentieth-century philosophy. Indeed one might well say that it is only through the recent development of alternative theories of 'mental representation' (functionalist, teleological etc.) that the domination of philosophy by the philosophy of language has been finally broken.

As I have indicated, Dummett acknowledges that his account of Frege's achievements is not one of Frege's express intentions, though he points to the fact that when, in the *Foundations of Arithmetic*, Frege turns to present his own account of what numbers are, he does so precisely by defining the sense of sentences, especially identity statements, in which number words occur.[11] But it is in fact questionable whether even Dummett's imputation to Frege of a 'theory of meaning' is appropriate, since Frege's distinction between sense and reference is presented by him, not as a systematic theory comparable to his theory of number, but only as an elucidation (*erläuterung*) of the basic concepts that occur in this theory.[12] Furthermore there is one qualification to the account of Frege given so far which does need to be introduced. I have described Frege's conception of the sense of a sentence as a conception of its truth-conditions. This is, however, a simplification of his position,

---

[9] G. Frege, 'Thoughts', trans. P. Geach and R. Stoothof, in his *Collected Papers*, ed. B. McGuiness, Blackwell, Oxford, 1984, p. 357.

[10] M. Dummett, *Origins of Analytical Philosophy*, Duckworth, London, 1993, p. 4.

[11] G. Frege, *Foundations of Arithmetic*, note 7, p. 73.

[12] This point has been especially urged by Joan Weiner; see *Frege in Perspective*, Cornell University Press, Ithaca NY, 1990.

for it omits his 'Platonism' according to which the sense of a sentence is an abstract object. The background to this is his use of a mathematical model for the semantic structure of a sentence which leads him to think of sentences as functional expressions. For this leads him to treat sentences as names whose reference and sense must both be objects of some kind. There is no problem here about the reference; for the reference of a sentence, as we have seen, is its truth-value, and this can be readily conceived as an abstract object. But what of its sense? How can its truth-conditions be an object? Frege argues that the sense of a sentence cannot be a physical object, nor, equally a psychological state; hence, he infers, it too is an abstract object, a 'thought'.[13] But since this is to be a mode of presentation of the reference of the sentence, its truth-value, it turns out that this object is just an abstract specification of the conditions under which a sentence which expresses the thought is true. So in the end the conception of the sense of a sentence as a Platonic thought is not in conflict with the truth-conditional account of it; but, equally, it looks to be an undesirable addition to it.

3.2 Wittgenstein's Tractatus Logico-Philosophicus

I started this chapter with a reference to the conception of philosophy as 'critique of language' presented by Wittgenstein in his *Tractatus Logico-Philosophicus*; and, following on from the previous section, one might well say that the position which Dummett attributes to Frege is really that of the young Wittgenstein. It is not surprising that there is this profound similarity, for Wittgenstein arrived at his position in his *Tractatus* precisely by simplifying and radicalizing the views advanced by Frege, whose work he praises in his preface. While retaining the fundamental 'context' principle that gives primacy to sentence-meaning over word-meaning (3.3), and the emphasis on truth in an account of meaning (4.024: 'To understand a statement means to know what is the case if it is true'), Wittgenstein denies that sentences are names. Thus he rejects Frege's Platonist conception of the thoughts expressed by sentences as abstract objects and instead reconceptualizes thoughts in a functional way as anything which provides a 'logical picture' of a fact (3). This then enables him to deepen the link between thought and language by maintaining that it is precisely language, with its meaningful sentences, which performs this function of representing facts (4). For sentences represents facts by specifying the states of affairs whose existence constitutes a fact, and since a specification of these states of affairs just is an account of the conditions under which the sentence is true, an account of the truth-conditions of a sentence, as determined by its constituent expressions, will reveal its semantic function, the fact which it purports to represent. So the truth-conditional

---

[13] Frege develops this conception of thoughts most fully in his paper 'Thoughts' (note 9).

conception of meaning fits neatly with the functional conception of the thoughts expressed in language.

Wittgenstein's conception of the sense/reference distinction is also a radical simplification of Frege's position. Where Frege assigns both sense and reference systematically to sentences and to their semantic constituents, such as names and predicates, because Wittgenstein denies that sentences are names, he denies that they have any reference at all. Nonetheless he holds that they do have a sense, though this is not an object of any kind but comprises instead their truth-conditions which identify the fact they purport to represent. By contrast, the semantic constituents of a sentence, which are primarily names, have a reference, the object they name, but no sense at all. Since the objects thus referred to by the names which occur in a sentence are the objects which combine in the states of affairs whose existence the sentence represents, it turns out that collectively they constitute the conditions for the truth of the sentence, and thus its sense. So for Wittgenstein sense and reference are mutually interdependent even though they are exclusive, in that no expressions have both sense and reference. Although this simplified account of meaning has obvious attractions, it does need to deal with the point raised by Frege in connection with our understanding of the expressions 'the Morning Star' and 'the Evening Star' which led him to maintain that names have sense as well as reference (see Section 3.1). Insofar as Wittgenstein addresses this point, he suggests that one cannot understand two names which are names of the same object without knowing that they are names of the same object (4.243); by itself this is unconvincing, but his references to Russell suggest that he takes it that Russell's theory of descriptions (see Section 3.3) provides a way of saving the appearances which suffices to provide an alternative solution to Frege's problem.

This is only a brief sketch of Wittgenstein's austere account of language. His conception of logic must now be introduced. For Wittgenstein logic is not just a way of systematizing valid formal inference; it is also integral to the representation of truths since true thoughts are logical pictures of facts. The association here is familiar from the case which Wittgenstein takes to be paradigmatic, namely sentential logic, where the theorems are tautologies and vice-versa. Wittgenstein generalizes this case to language in general, to affirm that semantic structure is just logical structure. Wittgenstein then adds to this two further claims: first, that the only kind of possibility is logical possibility, and thus that the only kind of necessity is logical necessity (6.375). So the traditional philosophical task of exhibiting and defending necessary connections, essential truths and so on devolves upon logic. But, and this is the second claim, because there are no logical objects (4.0312—Wittgenstein remarks that this is his 'fundamental thought'), this task does not lead to the identification of fundamental logical truths; on the contrary, because there are no logical objects, there are no logical truths. Hence there can be no 'philosophical propositions' (4.112) to express the logical connections that might be thought to capture the point of traditional philosophical claims about necessity and essence. Instead the only way in which logical points can be exhibited is by undertaking a logical analysis of the language involved which clarifies the concepts involved in such a way that supposed necessary connections either 'show' themselves, or are undermined, without the need for explicit statement of a logical truth. Thus philosophy is to be thought of as a therapeutic activity which employs a logical analysis of language to effect a critique, not so much of language as such, as of the typical misunderstandings of ordinary language which give rise to traditional philosophical puzzles. When language is understood properly it will be seen that the only substantive unanswered questions which can be formulated are 'scientific' questions: 'beyond' science there are no further undiscovered metaphysical truths even though there remains the perennial task of understanding why the illusory appearance of such truths arises and thereby dispelling it.

It is easy to see why this conception of philosophy as, in effect, a logical philosophy of language was both captivating and challenging. In the present context there are a few further aspects of it to pursue briefly. The first concerns the structure of beliefs, desires, and similar psychological states. Wittgenstein faces an apparent problem here: for on the one hand he takes it that the only structure available is that expressible in a truth-functional logic (5); but, on the other hand, it is obvious that sentences of the form 'a believes that p' are not truth-functional. Wittgenstein's remedy for this is the thesis that the form of 'a believes that p' is '"p" says p' (5.542). This is enigmatic, but I take it that Wittgenstein's proposal is that belief has the form 'a's belief says p', i.e. that the appearance of non-truth-functionality is to be removed by treating beliefs as having a structure comparable to that of sentences so that they can be correlated with the possible states of affairs they represent in much the way that sentences are correlated with facts through a correlation of words and objects. This is not quite the view that beliefs just are sentences, but it implies that insofar as the mind involves propositional contents (believing that so-and-so and the like), it is at least language-like. Hence it implies that the philosophy of mind is to be based upon the philosophy of language. The second issue concerns the relation between epistemology and the philosophy of language. Wittgenstein says that theory of knowledge is just the philosophy of psychology (4.1121), and thus just concerns the question about the logical form of belief and knowledge which I have been discussing. This dismissive remark, however, does not capture an important implication of his approach, which is that evidential relations can only be logical. So his position implies that epistemology is just an application of his logical philosophy of language: it combines an account of the logical form of the sentences in which we ascribe belief and knowledge with an account of the logical relationships between the sentence-like beliefs thus ascribed.

These points show how Wittgenstein's early conception of philosophy is critical of traditional conceptions of the mind and of the structure of knowledge. And yet he also represents himself as an upholder of ordinary language which is, he says, logically well-ordered just as it is (5.5563). Wittgenstein's resolution of this tension is that, despite being well-ordered, ordinary language often disguises logical form because its superficial structure has evolved for reasons which have nothing to do with logic (4.002). Hence the task of philosophy is non-trivial: logical analysis is not straightforward, as indeed Wittgenstein's treatment of belief exemplifies; nonetheless it is supposed, in the end, to display the inferences which our understanding of our own ordinary language leads us to endorse. This resolution rests on the assumption that truth-functional logic captures not just one way in which the representation of facts can be accomplished, that which is appropriate for natural science, but the only way in which this can be accomplished. One of the main developments in his thought is his subsequent recognition that this belief is mistaken, and thus that ordinary language, so far from being answerable to the demands of this logic, shows us its limitations. (see Section 3.7).

3.3 RUSSELL

Apart from Frege, the other philosopher whose influence Wittgenstein acknowledged in the preface to the *Tractatus* was 'my friend Bertrand Russell'. By this time Russell had already acknowledged the impact of the ideas of 'my friend Ludwig Wittgenstein' in the preface to his 1914 Harvard lectures published as *Our Knowledge of the External World*.[14] Indeed it is striking to compare the traditional approach to philosophy Russell followed in his classic introductory book *The Problems of Philosophy*[15] which was written in 1911, just before he met Wittgenstein, with the 'logical-analytic method' recommended in these 1914 lectures. In the earlier book Russell begins by discussing 'appearance and reality' and ends with a sympathetic discussion of the possibility of speculative metaphysics; whereas he starts his lectures with the bold claim that 'every philosophical problem . . . . is found either to be not really philosophical at all, or else to be . . . logical'.[16]

Most of Russell's previous work had been directed to the development of a logical theory which could vindicate the logicist thesis that mathematics is logic. As Frege's work shows, logic is inseparable from an analysis of language, so one would expect Russell's development of his logic to bring with it a philosophy of language. In practice, as we shall see, this is true; but it took some time for Russell himself to recognize this point because he initially regarded logic as a theory about inferences between propositions which he conceived as non-linguistic structures composed of the entities meant by words—'a proposition, unless it happens to be linguistic, does not itself contain words: it contains the entities indicated by words. Thus meaning, in the sense which words have meaning, is irrelevant to logic'.[17] Propositions, so conceived, are fact-like; indeed for Russell facts just are true propositions. Contemporary philosophers sometimes write of 'Russellian propositions', and it is this early conception of Russell's that they have in mind, whereby propositions include objects and properties rather than descriptions, psychological representations or abstract modes of presentation of them.

[14] B. Russell, *Our Knowledge of the External World*, Open Court, London, 1914.
[15] B. Russell, *The Problems of Philosophy*, Williams and Norgate, London, 1912.
[16] *Ibid.*, note 14 p. 33
[17] B. Russell, *The Principles of Mathematics*, George Allen and Unwin, London, 1903, p. 47.

Although it was only under Wittgenstein's influence that Russell explicitly adopted a conception of propositions as representations, linguistic or mental, this change was anticipated by earlier developments in his position whereby his officially non-linguistic logic became irretrievably enmeshed with questions of language, especially in the context of questions about the logic of propositions which include 'denoting concepts' such as 'a man', as it occurs in the proposition that *I met a man*. When first discussing this case in 1903 Russell says that the proposition is not 'about' the concept 'a man' which, he says, occurs in it; instead it is about a man denoted by this concept—'an actual man with a tailor and a bank-account or a public-house and a drunken wife'.[18] This insistence on what the proposition is 'about' is, I take it, a way of saying that the proposition's truth does not consist in a fact about the concept 'a man' but, instead, consists in a fact about an actual man, even though this man does not occur in the proposition itself. In his attempt to capture this point systematically Russell says that the concept 'a man' denotes the disjunction of all men—Tom or Dick or Harry etc.....; but he does not have a satisfactory account of the way to get from this disjunctive 'object', as he calls it,[19] to facts involving particular disjuncts in which the truth of the proposition consists. Not surprisingly, therefore, Russell swept this theory away in his famous 1905 paper 'On Denoting'[20] in which he returns to the issue he had previously grappled with. And significantly he now starts the paper by explaining that he wants to discuss what he calls 'denoting phrases' such as 'a man', and not 'denoting concepts' as before, so that throughout the paper linguistic concerns are prominent even though he still employs his non-linguistic conception of the proposition expressed by a sentence as the basic bearer of truth.

Russell begins with a brisk account of the truth of propositions expressed by sentences such as 'I met a man' in which, without argument, he introduces quantifiers and gives a substitutional account of the truth of the propositions thereby expressed.[21] According to Russell this involves a 'reduction' of propositions whose expression involves the denoting phrase 'a man' to propositions whose expression does not involve this phrase, a procedure which, he says, 'leaves "a man", by itself, wholly destitute of meaning, but gives meaning to every proposition in whose verbal expression "a man" occurs'.[22] Russell's main concern in the paper is then to extend this approach to the propositions expressed by sentences which include denoting phrases of the form 'the so-and-so' by reducing these propositions to the propositions expressed by sentences which start by asserting that some property is uniquely instantiated, so that the proposition expressed by 'The F is G' is understood as that expressed by 'There is just one F and it is G', where the truth of this latter proposition is handled in accordance with his substitutional account of quantifiers.

[18]   *The Principles of Mathematics*, note 17, p. 53.

[19]   *Ibid.*, note 17, p. 53.

[20]   B. Russell, 'On Denoting', *Mind*, ns. 14 (1905) 479–93; reprinted in *The Collected Papers of Bertrand Russell*, Vol. 4, Routledge, London, 1994, pp. 415–27.

[21]   Russell does not explain whether he took the idea of a quantifier from Frege, or from the Boolean tradition in which it was also employed, or thought it up for himself.

[22]   'On Denoting', note 20, p. 416.

Having presented this hypothesis Russell attempts to argue for it against alternatives which he ascribes to Meinong and to Frege. His argument is notoriously difficult to understand;[23] but the details do not matter here, nor indeed does it matter whether Russell's position is to be preferred to that of Frege.[24] What does matter is the way in which Russell's theory of descriptions, as it has come to be known, contributed to the development of the philosophy of language.

The key to this is the thesis that, like the phrase 'a man', the phrase 'the man' is what Russell comes to call an 'incomplete symbol' because it is a phrase which 'has no meaning in isolation' in the sense that it fails to name an object which occurs directly as a constituent of the Russellian proposition expressed by a sentence in which it occurs. Instead the phrase indicates that the proposition expressed by a sentence such as 'The butcher is drunk' is one whose truth depends on the truth of a proposition obtained by making the substitutions specified by the quantifiers in a complex propositional function which is identified by the logical analysis of the original proposition. It is the negative claim here which is important, for phrases of the form 'the so-and-so', as in 'The butcher is drunk', certainly appear to be ways of referring to an object, a butcher, about which something further is then affirmed; hence Russell's theory legitimated the thought that the logical analysis of language can show that appearances such as this are deceptive, that surface grammar is not a sure guide to logical form and thus to the structure of the facts in which the truth of propositions consists. In part this is just an extension of the liberation from surface grammar accomplished by Frege in his *Begriffsschrift*; but because Russell's theory concerns putative referring expressions, its implications are more striking. It is surely this aspect of Russell's work that Wittgenstein had in mind in the *Tractatus* when, in order to substantiate his claim that 'All philosophy is "Critique of Language"', he adds 'Russell's merit is to have shown that the apparent logical form of a statement need not be its real form' (4.0031).

Russell uses this new theory in several related ways. In 'On Denoting' he uses it to suggest that we can have 'knowledge by description' about things with which we are not acquainted. This suggestion is made in the context of a traditional foundationalist epistemology which holds that knowledge has to be grounded in the immediate and infallible presence to consciousness of some self-identifying items with which we are thereby acquainted, such as sense-data. Because we are plainly not acquainted in this way with physical objects, this epistemology seems irredeemably sceptical. But Russell proposes that when we interpret sentences which appear to involve reference to physical objects in accordance with his theory, it does not matter that we are not acquainted with them; as long as we can have knowledge that there are physical

[23]   See P. Hylton, *Russell, Idealism, and the Emergence of Analytic Philosophy*, Clarendon Press, Oxford, 1990, ch. 6.

[24]   In connection with Frege there are two issues to be distinguished: (i) Frege's treatment of definite descriptions as complex names; (ii) Frege's way of attributing sense as well as reference to names, including complex names. For a recent comparison of the positions of Frege and Russell, see T. J. Smiley, 'The Theory of Descriptions' in *Studies in the Philosophy of Logic and Knowledge*, eds. T. Baldwin and T. Smiley, Oxford University Press, Oxford, 2004.

objects related somehow to the sense-data with which we are acquainted, we can have 'knowledge by description' of the physical world. In developing this point, he suggests that this kind of use of a definite description involves a 'logical fiction', the fiction that the description is a way of referring to a suitable object; for once a sentence using the description is interpreted in accordance with his theory the putative reference to a physical object is eliminated and it will become clear that the proposition expressed just concerns the instantiation of some properties. This fictionalist application of a philosophy of language, which looks back to Hume, has become increasingly important during the twentieth century. But in Russell's case the situation is complicated by the fact that the properties involved in his descriptive analysis are typically properties whose instantiation requires the existence of objects just like the one putatively referred to. So although his theory of descriptions removes the appearance of reference to an object it does not remove the commitment to the existence of objects of that kind. But Russell takes a further step when he adds his theory of classes to his theory of descriptions: for according to his theory of classes sentences which include expressions which seem to refer to classes should be treated as abbreviations of sentences which just concern propositional functions, which he informally identifies with properties and with which he takes us to be readily acquainted. So in this case there is a reduction of classes to properties, and as Russell gets more confident about this logico-linguistic technique he develops the idea of a 'logical construction' which rests on the hypothesis that by introducing a language which replaces our ordinary talk of physical objects with apparent reference to classes of sense-data and their properties, and then applying his logical theories to this latter language, he can show that there is no need to suppose that knowledge of the physical world requires a problematic inference from appearances to some real but unperceived cause of these appearances. Instead such inferences are just to be thought of as inferences from actual sense-data to further similar potential sense-data. Thus by following his maxim that 'wherever possible logical constructions are to be substituted for inferred entities', [25] he uses his philosophy of language to move the goalposts for his epistemology.

This conception of a logical construction and of the reform of language will be important later. For the moment I just want to use it to elucidate an important disagreement between Russell and Wittgenstein. In the *Tractatus*, as I have mentioned, Wittgenstein cites Russell in support of his claim that the surface grammar of ordinary language can be misleading as to its logical form while also affirming that nonetheless in practice ordinary language is well-ordered as it is. In his 1922 introduction to the *Tractatus*, however, Russell attributed to Wittgenstein a concern, not with the logical analysis of ordinary language, but with the construction of a 'logically perfect language' whose structure would be completely transparent with respect to logical form and its relationship with the world. Wittgenstein protested to Russell that this had not been his aim; but one might at first wonder whether there is a

---

[25] 'The Relation of Sense-Data to Physics' (1914), reprinted in *The Collected Papers of Bertrand Russell*, Vol. 8, Allen and Unwin, London, 1986, p. 11.

substantive issue here, since Russell's logically perfect language might be taken to be just the result of a Wittgensteinian logical analysis of ordinary language. The grounds for Wittgenstein's complaint become clear, however, once one considers what motivates Russell's conception of a logically perfect language. For this is motivated not just by logic, but also by epistemology: Russell's aim is to characterize a language which has the means to express our knowledge of the physical world while satisfying his fundamental principle that every proposition we can understand must be composed wholly of constituents with which we are acquainted.[26] According to Russell, an ideal language which employs the method of logical construction enables one to satisfy these requirements. But Wittgenstein did not accept any such motivation: as we have seen, his attitude to epistemology was generally dismissive. Hence he was deeply dismayed to find Russell attributing to him a position which implies that language should be adapted to accord with what he regarded as an extraneous and improper external requirement; for him, the critique of language is essentially an internal critique only.

After 1919 Russell radically modified his philosophy. He rejected the conception of acquaintance that had been fundamental to his epistemology and philosophy of language and he sought to develop in its place a functionalist theory of language that relies mainly on causation to fix meaning. He attempted, as we might say now, to 'naturalize' his philosophy of language (and mind) believing that 'we shall be wise to build our philosophy upon science'.[27] Because psychological theory then was somewhat rudimentary, he did not have the resources to develop the position in a persuasive way and, I think, only Frank Ramsey really appreciated at the time what he was attempting to do. There is no space here for a detailed account of these later, neglected, writings by Russell, but once one does investigate them one readily finds anticipations of later 'externalist' conceptions of mind and language.[28]

3.4 LOGICAL EMPIRICISM

It is an important, and striking, fact that the group of thinkers who next took up and developed the positions advanced by Wittgenstein and Russell were scientists, the group of philosophically engaged scientists who gathered under the leadership of Moritz Schlick in Vienna and published their manifesto *The Scientific World-Conception*[29] in 1929. In this work they called for a programme of radical intellectual

---

[26] 'Knowledge by Acquaintance and Knowledge by Description' (1911), reprinted in *The Collected Papers of Bertrand Russell*, Vol. 6, Routledge, London, 1992, p. 154.

[27] B. Russell, 'The Philosophy of Logical Atomism' (1924), reprinted in *Logic and Knowledge* ed. R. C. Marsh, George, Allen and Unwin, London, 1956, p. 339.

[28] The key text is *The Analysis of Mind* (George, Allen and Unwin, London, 1921). For discussion of this work, see my introduction to the 1995 edition of the book.

[29] O. Neurath, R. Carnap, and H. Hahn, *Wissenschafliche Weltasffassung. Der Wiener Kreis*, Wolf, Vienna, 1929.

and social reform in order to implement a properly scientific understanding of the world. Although their programme had several sources, such as the ideas of Ernst Mach, they were clearly inspired by statements in Wittgenstein's *Tractatus* such as that 'the totality of true statements is the totality of natural science' (4.11); and since Wittgenstein was at this time living in Austria some of them met with him for philosophical discussion. As well as the emphasis on natural science, they liked his account of logic and mathematics as 'tautologies' with no substantive truth of their own and, most of all, they liked his account of philosophy as just logical analysis of language. For right from the start they were emphatic in repudiating old-style metaphysics, with its pretension to provide knowledge of higher, non-scientific, truths. Nonetheless they also differed with Wittgenstein on two significant points. While Wittgenstein had held that fundamental points about logical form could only be 'shown' through analysis of the use of language and not 'said', that is, stated as philosophical propositions, the logical empiricists, while accepting that the illusions of metaphysics often arose from the attempt to express these points as if they were claims about the world, argued that they could be sensibly expressed as statements about language itself, as an account of what Carnap called 'the logical syntax of language'. This move greatly enhanced the emphasis on language which one finds in the writings of the logical empiricists. The second difference arose from their primary concern with science, especially natural science. For despite Wittgenstein's claim quoted above about natural science, he was, as we have seen in Section 3.2, dismissive of epistemology and thus provided no account of the role of observation in vindicating scientific claims. The logical empiricists, by contrast, sought to bring their empiricist emphasis on the role of observation in science right into their account of language. The way in which they sought to do this was to maintain that there is an internal link between meaning and empirical verification: the Fregean thesis of the *Tractatus* that 'to understand a statement means to know what is the case if it is true' (4.024) becomes the verificationist thesis that 'understanding a statement and knowing the way of its verification is one and the same thing'.[30]

These two points bring the position of the logical empiricists close to that of Russell, albeit with verification substituted for acquaintance. One indication of this is that, like Russell, the logical empiricists were not much interested in ordinary language; instead they wanted to construct, or characterize, a language which would be ideal for science. Such a language would gain its meaning through the empirical criteria by which simple statements are verified and falsified, and also through the rules governing the use of logical and mathematical terminology whose role is to facilitate reasoning and calculation, not to capture a special type of non-empirical truth. The task of philosophy is then conceived to be the detailed characterization of such a language: the enlightened philosopher will practise 'a strict scientific discipline, namely that of the logic of science as the syntax of the language of science'.[31] But one qualification should be introduced at once. Once embarked on this project, it became

---

[30] M. Schlick, 'Meaning and Verification' in *Essential Readings in Logical Positivism*, ed. O. Hanfling, Blackwell, Oxford, p. 40.

[31] R. Carnap, *The Logical Syntax of Language*, Routledge and Kegan Paul, London, 1937, p. 332.

clear that there are many different ways of characterizing an ideal language, and this plurality of candidates gave rise to the question as to whether one should be seeking just one ideal language. In response to this there developed an interesting compromise: on the one hand, it was acknowledged that there can be a variety of languages with different logical systems which are to be assessed in a given context on pragmatic criteria, since, as Carnap put it, 'in logic there are no morals';[32] but, on the other hand, as far as empirical concepts go, it was argued that primacy attaches to the 'physical language', the language which describes physical phenomena, as opposed to a 'phenomenalist language' which describes the contents of experience. We shall see below why the logical empiricists gave a special status to physical language; equally we shall see that the distinction here, between logical and empirical concepts, is one that comes to be called into question.

Several issues which are central to subsequent philosophy of language arise within the context of logical empiricism. One concerns the nature of non-scientific language. It was all very well to dismiss metaphysics as nothing but meaningless pseudo-science, but moral language cannot be similarly dismissed. The response of Ayer and others was to propose that this language is misunderstood if it is regarded as used to make claims, true or false, about reality. Instead this language needs to be recognized as a way of expressing feelings such as disgust or enthusiasm and of encouraging or prescribing others to act in certain ways.[33] This position gave rise to the 'emotivist' theory of ethics[34] which exemplified clearly one way in which the philosophy of language then dominated philosophy: the philosophical study of morality was the study of the language of morals. To some extent, indeed, this approach persists within ethics, or rather 'metaethics' as it is often now called. But contemporary discussions as to how far moral language is descriptive or expressive are now rooted not in empiricist presumptions but in debates about the role of moral judgements as reasons for action: those who hold that there is only an external connection between moral judgement and motivation treat moral language as descriptive of moral truth whereas internalists who hold that this connection is internal tend to construe moral language as fundamentally expressive of feelings and desires.[35]

A different group of questions, rather closer to the core of logical empiricism, concerns the nature and limits of empirical verification. The question of limits arose from the critical rhetoric of the logical empiricists, that because the putative statements of theology and speculative metaphysics are unverifiable they are meaningless pseudo-statements which are at best expressive of certain feelings. For this clearly required a test of verifiability. Ironically it turned out that no sensible test could be devised and thus that by its own standards the question of verifiability

---

[32] R. Carnap, *The Logical Syntax of Language*, note 31, p. 52.

[33] A. J. Ayer, *Language, Truth and Logic*, Gollancz, London, 1936, ch. 6.

[34] This is slightly inaccurate; at the start of the twentieth century the emotivist position was worked out by the Uppsala School of philosophers, most notably Axel Hagerstrom and in the 1920s the position was also sympathetically discussed in Cambridge, most notably by Duncan-Jones. But the position had little general support until it was taken up by the logical empiricists.

[35] For a good survey of the recent debate, see M. Smith, *The Moral Problem*, Blackwell, Oxford, 1994.

was meaningless; and with this the suggestion that meaningfulness is a matter of verifiability was quietly dropped.[36] A much more productive debate focused on nature of empirical verification, the 'protocol-sentence' debate, so-called because the logical empiricists called records of observations 'protocols'. On one side of this debate was Schlick, who held that since observation is fundamentally a matter of individual subjective experience these protocol-sentences should aim to capture, in so far as this is possible, experiences of this kind. On the other side of the argument was Oscar Neurath who observed that Schlick's position implies that the meaning of a person's protocol-sentences is private to that person since this meaning is dependent upon experiences which cannot be shared. Neurath then argued that this conclusion is untenable, partly because it would undermine the possibility of providing an objective basis for scientific knowledge, but more radically because the very idea of such a private language is incoherent since language requires classifications and distinctions which necessarily transcend any individual speaker's application of them.[37] Neurath's discussion of this point is very brief, but prescient; I return to this issue of a 'private language' below in connection with Wittgenstein's later philosophy of language (see Section 3.7). Neurath's own conclusion was that protocol-sentences, the records of observation, must therefore be expressed in an intersubjective 'physical' language; and that empirical inquiry is largely a matter of preserving the coherence of the protocol-sentences which stimulation of our sense-organs causes us to affirm with the non protocol-sentences which express the explanatory theories we accept.

Neurath was generally thought to have won this debate—Carnap, for example, changed sides in the course of it on the issue of the protocol language—but whether Neurath's coherentist account of scientific knowledge was satisfactory remained disputed. Carnap discussed this issue in *The Logical Syntax of Language* (1934), and this discussion is especially important because of his account here of the role of the analytic/synthetic distinction in empirical inquiries. Carnap begins by accepting that there can be no question of simply inducing explanatory theories and laws from observations because 'the system of hypotheses is never univocally determined by empirical material, however rich it is'.[38] Hence, he argues, scientific inquiry involves 'conventions', the postulation of general rules which enable scientists to make predictions of protocol-sentences from hypotheses and thereby assess these hypotheses in the light of the protocol-sentences they actually affirm. Because of the complexity of scientific theories, however, this assessment is always provisional: there will always be ways of modifying a theory to save a given hypothesis even when predicted protocol-sentences are not confirmed: hence 'there is in the strict sense no refutation (falsification) of an hypothesis' (Carnap alludes here to Duhem's famous discussion

---

[36] The classic discussion of this point is C. G. Hempel, 'Problems and Changes in the Empiricist Criterion of Meaning', reprinted in *Aspects of Scientific Explanation and Other Essays*, Free Press, New York, 1965.

[37] O. Neurath, 'Protocol Sentences', reprinted in *Essential Readings in Logical Positivism*, ed. O. Hanfling, Blackwell, Oxford, pp. 160–8.

[38] *The Logical Syntax of Language*, note 31, p. 320.

of this point).[39] How, then, should the scientist proceed? Carnap here introduces the analytic/synthetic distinction: the analytic 'L-rules' are the rules of logic and mathematics which are essential for the derivation of predicted protocol-sentences from scientific hypotheses and these are not normally called into question in the course of scientific inquiry even though their adoption is fundamentally a matter of convention. By contrast the synthetic 'P-rules', the hypotheses of the scientific theory at issue, are to be considered revisable in the light of observation, although, because of the underdetermination of theory by observation, no unique revision is usually implied and pragmatic considerations of 'simplicity, expedience and fruitfulness' will guide the development of scientific research.[40] Thus the analytic/synthetic distinction separates the scientific hypotheses that are up for assessment from the rules for inference and calculation which provide the background connections. Despite this role for the distinction between the analytic and synthetic, however, Carnap maintains that the distinction is fundamentally only practical: 'in this respect, there are only differences of degree; certain rules are more difficult to renounce than others';[41] and he goes on to add, concerning an analytic sentence S that 'it may come about that, under the inducement of new protocol-sentences, we alter the language to such an extent that S is no longer analytic'.[42]

Carnap's position on this matter fits with his tolerant attitude to alternative logics, since that attitude implies a willingness to revise one's logic. But it is one thing to revise one's logic in the light of progress in logical theory, such as Frege's insights into the need for quantifiers, and quite another to allow that such revisions can be justified by empirical discoveries (by 'the inducement of new protocol-sentences'). For, as Carnap here acknowledges, this implies that there is no deep difference in kind between the analytic truths of logic and mathematics and the synthetic truths of natural science. But without a difference in kind here, the presumption that the philosophy of language provides a warrant for treating certain truths as distinctively non-empirical and necessary because they are analytic 'tautologies' whose truth arises merely from the meaning of the logical words which occur within them is undermined. Once the meaning of our logical vocabulary is regarded as answerable to empirical investigations, a logic-based philosophy of language offers no basis for *a priori* necessity and, more generally, no longer provides a foundation for scientific inquiry.

3.5 QUINE

The philosopher who grasped the significance of this aspect of Carnap's position was his American disciple, Willard van Quine, who had worked with Carnap on the English translation of *The Logical Syntax of Language*. In his famous paper 'Two Dogmas of Empiricism' in which he attacks the 'dogma' that there is a difference of

---

[39] *The Logical Syntax of Language*, note 31, p. 320.   [40] *Ibid.*   [41] *Ibid.*   [42] *Ibid.*

kind between analytic and synthetic truths Quine presented his position as if for this reason alone it involved a radical critique of logical empiricism.[43] As Quine knew perfectly well, however, this dogma had not been Carnap's position in *The Logical Syntax of Language*. Nonetheless there was a genuine disagreement between them, arising from Quine's willingness to think through the implications of this new thoroughgoing empiricism. An important instance of this concerned the role of linguistic convention. Carnap, like other logical empiricists, held that the adoption of a system of logic is fundamentally a matter of linguistic convention, so that logical truth is 'truth by convention', even if these conventions are revisable in the light of empirical investigations. Quine observed, however, that the logical implications of a logical truth cannot themselves be a matter of linguistic convention, on pain of requiring an infinite number of such conventions, and thus that the role of convention in logic can amount at most to the adoption of certain fundamental principles.[44] And he further argued that once these conventions are acknowledged to be vulnerable to empirical investigations, it is a mistake to think of logical truth as 'truth by convention' at all; instead we should recognize that 'conventionality is a passing trait, significant at the moving front of science but useless in classifying sentences behind the lines. It is a trait of events and not of sentences.'[45]

Despite this disengagement from the voluntarist aspect of logical empiricism, however, Quine's empiricism is very much in accord with its linguistic aspect. Thus his account of the evidence for science is couched in terms of the role of 'observation sentences', which are the old 'protocol-sentences' under a new name. Furthermore, despite the fact he holds that logic is revisable in the light of empirical inquiries, Quine (who was a distinguished logician) still assigns logic a central place in his philosophy of language. For example, he holds that questions of ontology are dependent on questions of logic since 'to be is to be the value of a variable'[46]—that is, the ontological commitments of a theory are dependent on its logical structure since they concern the kinds of thing whose existence is logically required for the truth of the theory. This position requires a way of making logical structure explicit, and for Quine this end is achieved by 'regimenting' the theory in a 'canonical notation' (a version of the logical empiricists' ideal language) which does justice to all the scientific implications of the theory. Quite what these implications are may well be disputed, but it is an important implication of Quine's rejection of the analytic/synthetic distinction that scientific disputes cannot be divorced from disputes about the appropriateness or not of a notation or language. A case in point concerns psychology and the attribution of propositional attitudes such as belief. Because Quine holds that from a scientific standpoint there is no substance to

[43] W. V. Quine, 'Two Dogmas of Empiricism' in *From a Logical Point of View*, Harper Row, New York, 1953.

[44] W. V. Quine, 'Truth by Convention' (1936), reprinted in *The Ways of Paradox*, Random House, New York, 1966, esp. pp. 96–8.

[45] W. V. Quine, 'Carnap and Logical Truth' (1954), reprinted in *The Ways of Paradox*, Random House, New York, 1966, p. 112.

[46] W. V. Quine, 'On What There Is' in *From a Logical Point of View*, Harper Row, New York, 1953, p. 15.

talk of beliefs, he denies that a canonical notation for psychology needs to include existentially quantified variables whose values are beliefs or their contents. Many will disagree with Quine on this issue, but whichever side one takes on this debate, however, the point to grasp here is that for Quine, the choice of theory is inseparable from the choice of language, as Quine indicates clearly: 'If we are limning the true and ultimate structure of reality, the canonical scheme for us is the austere scheme that knows no quotation but direct quotation and no propositional attitudes but only the physical constitution and behaviour of organisms. ... If we are venturing to formulate the fundamental laws of a branch of science, however tentatively, this austere idiom is again likely to be the one that suits.'[47]

Yet Quine is also responsible for a sceptical argument which calls into question the significance of questions about language. This is his argument for the essential 'indeterminacy of translation', whose conclusion is that in disputes about translation or meaning, there is no 'objective matter to be right or wrong about'.[48] The starting point for this sceptical conclusion is the application of his all-embracing empiricism to questions about meaning. Quine holds that these questions are best conceived as questions about the way in which translation from a foreign language into one's own language is to be achieved; but he argues that the empirical evidence available to us when we seek to do this is so inadequate that it radically underdetermines the choice between competing ways of translating the foreign language. The evidence will comprise observations of the behaviour of native speakers, consisting primarily but not exclusively of observations of their linguistic behaviour, and also observations of their environment and interactions with it and each other. But, Quine argues, if we make different assumptions about what native speakers perceive, believe, want and are trying to do, we can match this evidence to quite different translations of individual statements by making compensating adjustments throughout schemes of translation. In effect, Quine is here applying to linguistic theory Duhem's general point about the underdetermination of theory by empirical evidence (see §5) except that Quine extends Duhem's thesis by arguing that it applies however much evidence is adduced. Quine then infers from this that questions about the meaning of individual utterances are radically indeterminate. Although their meaning is determinate relative to a scheme of translation which makes good sense overall of a speaker's behaviour, because there is an ineliminable plurality of workable but incompatible schemes, when considered by themselves utterances have no determinate meaning. Hence, he concludes, the question of what a speaker means on some occasion lacks objective truth. So when seeking scientific explanations of behaviour it is a mistake to employ a psychology which attributes meanings to the utterances of speakers. Further, since the attribution of beliefs and other propositional attitudes to agents is dependent upon the attribution of meaning to their utterances, these also lack objective truth. So it is equally a mistake to invoke these attitudes in a

[47] W. V. Quine, *Word and Object*, MIT Press, Cambridge MA, 1960, p. 221.
[48] *Ibid.*, note 47, p. 73.

scientific psychology—which explains Quine's position on this matter, encountered just above.

Not surprisingly, this argument has attracted a good deal of criticism. Some critics reject the underdetermination thesis, arguing that once the presumptions inherent in the enterprise of understanding others and the implications of syntax are taken into account a pragmatic choice between competing schemes of translation can usually be made on empirical criteria in much the way that a choice between competing physical theories can be made. In both cases, where the evidence is insufficient, the choice of scheme or theory is indeed underdetermined; but this should be regarded as a challenge which demands further empirical investigation and not as a proof, in the case of linguistic theory, that questions about meaning and translation are inherently non-empirical. Other critics reject Quine's move from the underdetermination thesis, which is essentially epistemological, to the metaphysical thesis that meaning itself is radically indeterminate, which is a form of sceptical antirealism about meaning and content. These critics note that in physics Quine does not endorse a similar conclusion; instead he holds that because physical theory gives an ineliminable explanatory role to unobserved entities a lack of decisive evidence here for choosing one theory rather than another does not warrant an antirealist attitude to the postulation of such entities. Thus one issue within psychology and linguistics is whether there are grounds within these sciences for assigning an explanatory role to contents and meanings; if there are such grounds, then, contrary to the way in which Quine presents the matter, a realist attitude to meaning and content remains consistent with his sceptical epistemological considerations. So at this point the issue becomes one as to whether there are good independent reasons for preferring Quine's austere behaviourist psychology to psychological theories which draw on contents and meanings to account for behaviour, including speech. Current cognitive science and our ordinary ways of understanding each other strongly suggest that content and meaning do have explanatory roles. But one question here is whether these explanatory roles can be incorporated into the framework of natural science which includes physics and its laws of nature, or whether they belong within a different 'hermeneutic' mode of inquiry in which we make sense of each other as rational agents rather than as physical organisms. For if there is a genuine opposition here, one might acknowledge that Quine was right to hold that meanings and propositional attitudes do not belong within the realist ontology of natural science while still defending the objectivity of meaning in the light of the possibility of hermeneutic inquiries which provide empirically determinate conclusions about meaning.

3.6 DAVIDSON (AND DUMMETT)

This last suggestion, which harks back to nineteenth century German debates about the status of the *Geisteswissenschaften*, was especially championed by Quine's pupil, Donald Davidson, who argued that the demands of rationality and intelligibility imply that mind and language are 'anomalous', in the sense that these indefinitely pervasive aspects of thought and language cannot be accommodated within the strict laws of natural science.[49] But far from abjuring the approach to the philosophy of language which I have so far been discussing, which might well be thought to bring with it the presumption that the study of language belongs with natural science, Davidson developed his alternative position which rejects this presumption in the context of a philosophy of language which deliberately brings together elements from this approach, starting with the Fregean thesis that 'meaning is truth-conditions'.

Since this thesis has to be combined with the familiar point that the meaning of a sentence is determined by the meaning of the words which occur within it it is natural to suppose there needs to be a fundamental theory of word meaning, a theory of reference, which generates specifications of the truth-conditions of sentences in terms of the objects and properties referred to by the words which occur within them. Indeed as we saw in Section 3.1 some such presumption seems essential if one is to be able to identify that account of the truth-conditions of a sentence which gives its meaning, since truth-conditions by themselves are much too coarse-grained to constitute meanings. Davidson's insight, however, was to see that this presumption is not in fact necessary, in that the work done by the theory of reference could actually be subsumed within the construction of a theory about truth-conditions. The person whose work he appropriated to this end was Alfred Tarski, a Polish logician whose work was closely associated with the logical empiricist programme. Tarski developed a way of 'defining' truth for a language by providing a recursive specification of truth-conditions for each sentence of the language. For Tarski this was a way of defining truth in terms of meaning, since he took it that these metalinguistic specifications of the truth-conditions of sentences of an object-language had to satisfy the requirement that the sentence in the metalanguage was a translation of the sentence in the object-language. Davidson, however, proposed that the direction of explanation here be reversed: that truth be taken as fundamental, and that the meaning of a sentence be defined as that account of its truth-conditions which is generated by an adequate theory of truth, where adequacy is assessed without invoking presumptions about the meaning of sentences or the reference of terms within them.[50]

How, then, is adequacy to be defined? Here Davidson took over from Quine the idea of coming to understand, or interpret, as he calls it, a previously unknown language by observing the speakers of the language. Davidson's proposal was that we can model the strategy of a linguist in this situation by thinking of her as attempting to construct a systematic account of the truth-conditions of the sentences of the language, a 'theory of truth', which takes account of the structure of these sentences. Although the linguist has to start with guesswork—tentatively, assigning meanings (referents) to words and phrases in the light of her observations of the contexts in

---

[49] See Davidson's 1970 paper 'Mental Events', reprinted in his *Essays on Actions and Events*, Clarendon Press, Oxford, 1980.

[50] Davidson first presented this position in his 1967 paper 'Truth and Meaning', reprinted in his *Inquiries into Truth and Interpretation*, Clarendon Press, Oxford, 1984. His best statement of it is his 1973 paper 'Radical Interpretation', also reprinted in *Inquiries into Truth and Interpretation*.

which native speakers use simple sentences in which these words occur—Davidson argues that she has two unavoidable but legitimate presumptions to guide the development of her theory of truth: 'charity'—the presumption that, by and large, native utterances are true, insofar as they include some truth claim, as most utterances do; and 'humanity'—the presumption that the natives are generally rational, and thus that the interpretation of their utterances should lead to the imputation of perceptions, beliefs and desires which take account of the observable environment and show how their behaviour is motivated action. Davidson then claims that the combination of these two presumptions with the holistic requirement that the linguist's theory should yield plausible truth-conditions for all the sentences of the language suffices for the adequacy of the resulting theory. These conditions capture all the evidential resources that are available to us as we come to understand each other and, Davidson argues, there is no reason to think that there is any inescapable indeterminacy in the application of this procedure even though of course in some cases our actual evidence may be insufficient.[51] For this reason, even though we do not construct a theory of this kind as we interpret others, a theory of truth which satisfies these requirements provides a model which makes explicit the considerations on which we depend. Because such a theory would be adequate for the purpose of interpreting others it is sufficient to yield an account of the meaning of the language they use.

This position was famously criticized by Michael Dummett,[52] who argued that it was too 'modest' in that it failed to provide a satisfactory account of a speaker's understanding of their own language. Dummett's point can be expressed in terms of Frege's distinction between sense and reference (see Section 3.1): according to Dummett, Davidson's account of meaning is only an account of reference and omits the element of sense which is essential if one is to capture the way in which the speaker understands the language. Dummett then goes on to argue, in a way which departs from Frege (as he acknowledges), that an account of sense requires one to include within one's theory of meaning for a language sufficient detail to generate a specification of the kinds of evidence whose recognition speakers treat as warranting the assertion of appropriate sentences of the language. For Dummett, therefore, the primary goal of a theory of meaning should be an account of the 'assertibility-conditions' of the sentences of the language, although by adding what it is that these conditions are evidence of it should also be possible to arrive at an account of the truth-conditions of the sentences and thereby provide a specification of their meaning.

This position resembles the verificationist account of meaning advanced by the logical empiricists, and it is therefore vulnerable to some of the criticisms which

---

[51] In his 1997 paper 'Indeterminism and Antirealism', reprinted in *Subjective, Intersubjective, Objective*, Clarendon Press, Oxford, 2001, Davidson explains why he takes it that, nonetheless, an element of Quine's indeterminacy thesis is correct (pp. 75 ff.), namely that which concerns the essential 'inscrutability' of reference. I am not persuaded by Davidson on this point but I shall not pursue it here.

[52] Dummett first articulated this criticism in his papers 'What is a Theory of Meaning? (i)' (1975) and 'What is a Theory of Meaning? (ii)' (1976), both of which are reprinted in *The Seas of Language*, Clarendon Press, Oxford, 1993. For a later statement of the criticism, see *The Logical Basis of Metaphysics*, Duckworth, London, 1991, esp. ch. 5.

arise from discussions of that position, in particular the objection that because the evidence for or against a statement is indefinitely complex and depends on a range of intersecting beliefs and hypotheses, the position leads back to Quine's sceptical conclusion that sentences have no definite meaning by themselves. Dummett responds to this criticism by drawing a distinction between the 'canonical evidence' ('criterion') for the application of a concept, knowledge of which he takes to be a prerequisite for understanding, and evidence which is only indirectly relevant in the light of other assumptions. Hence, he maintains, it is possible to provide determinate assertibility-conditions for individual sentences, based on the canonical evidence which defines the concepts employed there. But Dummett's critics argue that this response fails to acknowledge the inescapable pragmatism inherent in the relationship between evidence, assumptions and hypotheses identified by Duhem, Carnap and Quine; and once one looks at the ways in which scientific concepts alter in the face of new kinds of evidence it is hard to retain confidence in the conception of some distinctively canonical evidence which defines these concepts. Adapting Quine's remark about conventionality, quoted earlier, the truth is that 'canonical status is a passing trait, significant at the moving front of science but useless in classifying evidence behind the lines. It is a trait of events and not of evidence.'

However even if Dummett's own proposal for a theory of meaning is for this reason problematic, the question as to whether he succeeded in identifying a serious weakness in Davidson's philosophy of language remains to be addressed. As Dummett has acknowledged, the way in which Davidson defines the adequacy of a theory of truth in terms of the procedure of radical interpretation shows that the notion of evidence does in fact play an important role in Davidson's position. Although this role does not imply that an adequate theory of truth is based on a theory of canonical evidence, Davidson argues that it does imply that such a theory of truth can play the role of a theory of sense. For it implies that it is only that systematic account of the truth-conditions of the sentences of the language (and thus also of the reference of the words of the language) which meets the combined requirements of charity and humanity which provides a specification of their meaning. So, contrary to Dummett's charge, for Davidson, meaning is not just a matter of reference and truth-conditions if this is understood to imply that any specification of the truth-conditions of a sentence, or of the reference of a term, provides an account of its meaning. Instead, Davidson's method of radical interpretation yields privileged specifications of truth-conditions which show the sense of the terms in question. Hence Davidson's position does, after all, accommodate both sense and reference.

Davidson's position became the established philosophy of language for the last quarter of the twentieth century. Many of those who accepted it, however, did not accept all the ways in which he proceeded to develop it, and it is worth looking briefly at some of these points since they illustrate one way in which the philosophy of language has remained central to philosophical debate. A good case to start with is Davidson's account of first person authority, the epistemic authority we accord to a thinker concerning what it is that he thinks or feels. In Russell's work at the start of the twentieth century this authority was thought of as deriving from the immediate acquaintance we each have with our own thoughts and feelings, a kind of acquaintance which we do not have with the thoughts and feelings of others. This conception of acquaintance was effectively criticized by later philosophers such as Neurath on the grounds that it treats the conceptualization and recognition of thoughts and feelings as if it were just a matter of having them; as a result many philosophers came to doubt the very idea of first person authority or to argue that it should be re-interpreted as a mistaken interpretation of the distinctive role of a subject who makes it true that he has a thought by avowing it, for example, by saying 'I intend to go to New York tomorrow.'[53] For Davidson, however, the way to approach the issue is to go back to the situation of the linguist who seeks to understand someone ('the native') whose language she does not understand. For in this situation, Davidson argues, the linguist has no choice but to start from the presumption that the native's utterances express thoughts which the native knows that he has. For the linguist can only interpret the native insofar as she starts from the presumption that the native's utterances are intelligible in the light of the native's own understanding of them, for example that the native knows what he is doing when he says 'I intend to go to New York tomorrow.' So the hypothesis that the native does not generally know what he is thinking when he speaks will undermine the possibility of interpretation by implying that the native's behaviour is largely unintelligible.[54]

Davidson's discussion of this point connects with the claim that thought and language are intimately related, so much so that one cannot have thoughts without a language which others can interpret. This is probably the most controversial aspect of his philosophy since it implies that the ascription of thoughts (such as beliefs and desires) to brute animals is a mistake. Davidson bases his position on the claim that thoughts belong within networks linked by inferential connections and that one cannot make the relevant inferences without the capacity to recognize that one has the thoughts in question. For example, he suggests, in being surprised by what one sees, one is recognizing that what one sees conflicts with what one has believed. He further argues that this capacity to recognize one's own thoughts depends on the ability to distinguish between how things are and how one thinks that they are, and that this ability requires the capacity to communicate with others who show one the need to make this distinction for oneself in just the way that one makes it with respect to them. The first part of this argument, which ties the capacity for thought to the capacity for self-conscious rational inference can be questioned; critics argue that simple thoughts, and even capacities such as that for surprise, can be linked by causal dispositions which do not require the higher-order thoughts Davidson demands.

[53] This position was famously advanced by Gilbert Ryle in *The Concept of Mind*, Penguin, Harmondsworth, 1963, p. 175.

[54] See D. Davidson 'First Person Authority' (1984), reprinted in *Subjective, Intersubjective, Objective*, Clarendon Press, Oxford, 2001.

If the critics are right (as I think they are), then thought and language need not be as interdependent as Davidson maintains. But this point can be detached from the second part of Davidson's argument, according to which the capacity for self-consciously objective thought depends on language. This is a thesis which Davidson came to call his 'triangulation' thesis: thinkers get their conception of an objective world, a world distinct from anyone's subjective conception of it, including their own, by recognizing through the ways in which they understand what others are saying about them that because those others apply to them the distinction which they themselves draw with respect to others between their thoughts and the world, there is a general distinction between the world and anyone's thoughts about it. So objective thought depends upon the intersubjectivity of language. The opposite also holds: intersubjective communication depends on the possibility of interpreters making sense of each other within a world which they take to be independent of the perspectives of each speaker, that is, within a world which they take to be objective. Thus the triangle 'Self/Other/World' is fundamental to the possibility both of intersubjective communication and objective thought, and it is language which forms the base of this triangle, the connection between oneself and others.[55]

Davidson's work shows clearly how philosophy of language remains central to philosophical debate at the end of the twentieth century, though it does not have quite the foundational role within philosophy that Dummett had in mind when praising Frege's revolutionary insights at the start of the century. Before moving on, however, there is one final twist in the tale to add, namely Davidson's sceptical thesis that 'there is no such thing as a language, not if a language is anything like what many philosophers and linguists have supposed'.[56] This thesis, which is distinctive of Davidson's late writings, seems paradoxical from someone whose philosophy depends on his philosophy of 'language' in the ways I have intimated. But the qualification in the passage cited is crucial: Davidson is just rejecting the conception of language that was characteristic of the logical empiricists and their successors, the conception of language as a network of conventional rules which speakers tacitly invoke as they seek to communicate their thoughts to their audience.[57] A classic formulation of this position had been presented in 1969 by David Lewis.[58] Lewis had started by developing an insight of Hume's, that conventions of any kind can emerge where there are regularities in behaviour which are recognized as providing solutions to problems of social coordination. For these regularities acquire the status of conventions once they give rise to mutual expectations about the intentions with which this

---

[55] See D. Davidson, 'Rational Animals' (1982), reprinted in *Subjective, Intersubjective, Objective*, Clarendon Press, Oxford, 2001, p. 105.

[56] D. Davidson, 'A Nice Derangement of Epitaphs' (1986), reprinted in *Truth, Language and History*, Clarendon Press, Oxford, 2005, p. 107.

[57] Davidson emphasizes that his scepticism is primarily directed at philosophical, and not ordinary, conceptions of language in 'The Social Aspect of Language' (1994), reprinted in *Truth, Language and History*, Clarendon Press, Oxford, 2005.

[58] D. Lewis, *Convention*, Harvard University Press, Cambridge MA, 1969.

behaviour is initiated. Lewis then argued that since linguistic behaviour provides a solution to the problem of coordinating the beliefs and actions of different people by providing a way of communicating to each other their beliefs, commands, wishes and so on, language is a network of communicative conventions of this kind. Although this proposal provides a prima facie plausible general account of the evolution of linguistic behaviour,[59] Davidson argues it leads one to expect much greater uniformity of linguistic practice than one actually finds: he argues that we all have our own personal idiolects and when we speak with others we constantly adjust our vocabulary and syntax in order to facilitate communication without much attention to conventional rules. A compromise suggestion might be that in learning a language one is initiated into a network of default conventions from which one can later detach oneself for the purposes of humour or local circumstances; but Davidson rejects this too. According to Davidson, therefore, communication and understanding are essentially practical skills whose exercise varies from context to context; they do not draw on any familiarity with a shared set of general conventions whose function would be to act as 'a portable interpreting machine set to grind out the meaning of an arbitrary utterance'.[60]

I return below to the issue of context-specific considerations which Davidson emphasizes here. But one might well ask here whether this new emphasis on the piecemeal interpretation of personal idiolects is consistent with his earlier account of radical interpretation with its emphasis on the construction of a systematic theory of truth for a language. In part Davidson's response to this will be to observe that he had always maintained that his account of radical interpretation was always conceived to be just a theoretical model to illustrate the considerations which have a role in a theory of meaning; it was never his view that speakers actually proceed as radical interpreters of this kind. Yet this does not explain why radical interpretation is a good model of linguistic communication if this is as context specific and unsystematic as he maintains in his later work; and I think that, as he himself intimates, his views did change on this matter over the course of his career. Whether this was a change for the better remains a matter of dispute, but one aspect of this final position is worth further notice: Davidson came to think that nothing in the linguistic practices of speakers and their audience must be shared—'meaning something requires that by and large one follows a practice of one's own, a practice that can be understood by others. But there is no fundamental reason why practices must be shared.'[61] This thesis certainly puts him at odds with most philosophers of language of the twentieth century; as Davidson himself notes, it is a significant disagreement with Wittgenstein's later philosophy of language, to which I now turn.

---

[59] This approach is developed in detail by Jonathan Bennett in *Linguistic Behaviour*, Cambridge University Press, Cambridge, 1976, esp. ch. 7.

[60] 'A Nice Derangement of Epitaphs', note 53, p. 107.

[61] D. Davidson, 'The Social Aspect of Language' (1994), reprinted in *Truth, Language and History*, Clarendon Press, Oxford, 2005, p. 125.

3.7 WITTGENSTEIN'S PHILOSOPHICAL INVESTIGATIONS

At the time of the publication in 1921 of his *Tractatus Logico-Philosophicus* Wittgenstein believed that it provided final solutions to the problems of philosophy. By 1930 he had revised this judgement, and during the following decade he worked on a new series of philosophical 'investigations' which, by 1945, he had distilled into a manuscript which we know as part I of his *Philosophical Investigations*. This was published posthumously in 1953, along with some later reflections that he was not able to integrate into the earlier manuscript as he had intended and which now appear as Part II of the book.

I have chosen to discuss this later work of Wittgenstein's out of historical sequence mainly because doing otherwise would have interrupted the narrative I have hitherto constructed; but there is also a sense in which it is particularly towards the end of the twentieth century that the issues he discusses here concerning the way in which our ordinary everyday language should be understood have come to be salient within the philosophy of language. Nonetheless, as he himself suggests, the best way to approach this book is by comparing it with his earlier one, the *Tractatus*. As before, philosophy is conceived as a critique of language, or rather, as he now puts it: 'Philosophy is a battle against the bewitchment of our intelligence by means of language' (I: ¶109). So philosophy is essentially an activity which aims, as before, at clarity, the kind of clarity which brings 'peace' because 'philosophical problems *completely* disappear' (I: ¶133), a result to be attained by an investigation which transforms disguised nonsense into patent nonsense (I: ¶464). This kind of philosophical investigation is therefore 'grammatical' (I: ¶90); and since its primary aim is to clear away misunderstandings it is an essentially descriptive inquiry which does not seek to advance any positive theses; instead 'it leaves everything as it is' (I: ¶124).

So far the only apparent contrast with the *Tractatus* is the substitution of a concern with grammar for his earlier emphasis on logic. This might seem to be just a difference of idiom, but it signals the fact that Wittgenstein has come to reject the conception of representation invoked in the *Tractatus* according to which the possibility of meaningful language was supposed to depend at a fundamental level upon the use of basic, logically independent, sentences involving simple names of things. Wittgenstein now takes that belief to rest on a misguided presumption that there is a single essence for language which is most clearly manifested by the use of language in the exact sciences where one might indeed hope to find some such sentences dealing with basic physical parameters. Hence he begins his *Philosophical Investigations* with an invitation to his readers to stand back and consider the huge variety of ways in which language is in fact used (I: ¶23), most of which tolerate vagueness and a lack of precision. So the kind of clarity he now seeks in order to bring an end to philosophical dispute is not that which arises from a logical analysis of ordinary language undertaken in order to identify basic sentences and simple names on which language is thought to depend. Instead the kind of 'perspicuous representation' he now seeks

(I: ¶122) involves careful descriptions of the 'grammar' of ordinary language whose aim is to exhibit both the implications inherent in our actual use of language and the external conditions under which these uses of language make sense, including points which we normally take for granted because they are too familiar for us to think them worthy of notice. Since philosophical problems arise from misunderstandings of our ordinary everyday language, it is that language which needs to be understood properly as it is, and not by reference to a misguided conception of how it has to be:

When I talk about language (words, sentences, etc.) I must speak the language of every day. Is this language somehow too coarse and material for what we want to say? *Then how is another one to be constructed?*   (I: ¶120)

This turn to ordinary language for its own sake was not entirely new: G. E. Moore's late writings about knowledge and certainty, for example, had already pointed in the same direction.[62] Wittgenstein's emphatic affirmation of the value of the ordinary nonetheless marks a striking change of direction when considered in the light of the tradition I have so far been discussing. As I have indicated, one aspect of this change is a turn from the implicit monism of that tradition which treats the language of the exact natural sciences as the fundamental model of meaning to an open-ended pluralism which recognizes a variety of different 'language-games', as Wittgenstein calls our meaningful practices in which language and conduct are interwoven (one can also think of this is as a radicalization of Carnap's tolerant attitude to variety among logical systems—see Section 3.4). Wittgenstein holds that different language-games have their own distinctive grammars, and we do not need to suppose that these differences are in principle to be regulated by some master language-game; instead coherence is to be achieved by piecemeal inquiries, by understanding and noting differences, so that once we have characterized a particular language-game there will come a point where our investigations can cease and we can say *'this language-game is played'* (I: ¶654). In this later period, therefore, Wittgenstein was particularly hostile to the presumption that all language-games are answerable to the natural sciences, and in the very last section of Part II of the *Philosophical Investigations* he inveighs against the *'conceptual confusion'* which afflicts psychology as a result of this presumption (II: §xiv).

Despite this emphasis on the irreducible variety of language-games, Wittgenstein does make one general point about language-games, namely that they all involve the following of 'rules', though since he argues that there is no single essence of 'game' (I: ¶67), it would be a mistake to think of 'rule-following' as some single fundamental structure. Nonetheless since he says that rules determine what is, or is not, to count as the same (I: ¶225), the implication is that all language-games involve judgements of some kind about what is the same or different and that their rules provide the concepts which are employed in these judgements. Wittgenstein then makes two key points. First, if one is engaged in a game of any kind, including a language-game, it

[62] See, for example, Moore's paper, 'Four Forms of Scepticism', which dates from the 1940s and is reprinted in his *Philosophical Papers*, George Allen and Unwin, London, 1959.

must be possible to mistake the application of a rule. This point is clear in the case of classification: it only makes sense to suppose that someone is classifying objects in some way if the person involved can make a mistake in doing so. Secondly, he observes that any statement of a rule can be interpreted in such a way that what looks like a mistake when the rule is applied to a new case is actually in accordance with the rule. If we are doing arithmetic and the rule is simply 'add 2', someone who has been trained successfully in the application of the rule to numbers less than 1000 but then gives the answer '1004' when told to 'add 2' to 1000 can provide a deviant interpretation of the operation of addition which justifies their answer (I: ¶185). Hence, Wittgenstein suggests, there is a 'paradox' here: 'no course of action could be determined by a rule, because every course of action can be made out to accord with the rule' (I: ¶201). (See George Wilson, 'Rule Following, Meaning, and Normativity,' Ch. 7. this volume.)

Wittgenstein infers from this that following a rule is not just a matter of acting in accordance with an explicit instruction, or indeed a rule-book, since their interpretation is inescapably indeterminate. Instead, he suggests, the way to understand the situation is to start from our natural capacity to note similarities and draw distinctions; what then needs explanation is the way in which the exercise of this capacity counts as following a rule by allowing for the possibility of our making a mistake, the possibility, that is, that our actual judgement differs from that which is appropriate to the circumstances in the light of the rules, the concepts, employed in the judgement. As we have seen, it is no good looking to instructions or precedents by themselves to identify the rule; and Wittgenstein is equally insistent that it is no good imagining that an agent's subjective impressions, such as visual imagery, can identify a rule where these external facts fail. Instead his proposal is that we have to put all these materials in the context of the games which are regulated by the rules in question, and let the rules be identified through the common practices of those who participate, which will of course include reference to rule-books and precedents (I: ¶199). So where language is involved, the rules which characterize the concepts expressed are those manifested by the practices of the speakers engaged in the language-game in question, which will include the cases which are picked out as paradigms, the types of evidence taken to be relevant, the authority of different speakers, the general point of the language-game and the implications, both theoretical and practical, taken to follow from some judgement.

Just exactly what this involves, and whether it is correct, remain matters of much dispute.[63] A key question is how it is that these practices can define a rule when examples, rule-books etc, are by themselves inadequate. Wittgenstein gives his answer to this question through his descriptions of a great variety of language-games in the first hundred sections of the *Philosophical Investigations*—the answer summed up in the slogan 'the meaning of a word is its use in the language' (I: ¶43); I shall not

---

[63] Saul Kripke's discussion of this aspect of Wittgenstein's work has been especially influential and controversial: see S. A. Kripke, *Wittgenstein on Rules and Private Language*, Harvard University Press, Cambridge MA, 1982.

pursue the matter here. But an important implication of Wittgenstein's position is expressed by his remark that we have rules only where there is agreement (I: ¶224); for this implies that language must be shared, a point which, as we have seen (§7), is denied by Davidson. Nonetheless Wittgenstein denies that truth itself is ever just a matter of agreement among speakers (I: ¶241). So Wittgenstein, like Quine (see §6), rejects the idea of 'truth by convention', even concerning what one might suppose to be '*a priori*' principles of a language-game. As he explains in his notes *On Certainty*[64] even where a presumption, such as that the earth has existed for very many years, has a special status in our ways of gathering and assessing evidence so that it functions like a river-bed along which the stream of ordinary thought can flow, we still allow that it can itself be called into question—'the river-bed of my thoughts may shift' (*On Certainty* ¶97). But one point which Wittgenstein does take from his discussion of rule-following is that because this is essentially a practice, there cannot be 'private' rules (I: ¶202). What this means becomes clear when Wittgenstein invites his readers to consider the hypothesis that someone might employ a 'private language' to classify his own 'immediate private sensations' in such a way that others cannot understand the language (I: ¶243). This would be a language employed by someone who classifies his sensations purely on the basis of his subjective experiences, of how he feels at the time, without relying on their physical causes or his subsequent behaviour, since facts of these two kinds would in principle permit others to understand his classifications. Wittgenstein does not explain the significance of this hypothesis, but the implication is that there is an important philosophical tradition which conceives of subjective experience, and consciousness in general, on the assumption that a private language of this kind is possible; and we have only to think of the works of Descartes to recognize this assumption in practice.

Wittgenstein argues that this hypothesis is empty, for the reason that the speaker's use of his 'language' does not constitute a rule-governed practice within which it makes sense to suppose that the speaker can make a mistake. For the basis of the speaker's classification of his sensations is to be just his subjective experiences, but, like all examples, taken individually these experiences do not by themselves determine what is to count as having the same type of sensation on some other occasion. Hence it follows that although, when he has a sensation, the speaker no doubt thinks of himself as classifying it in accordance with a rule he initiated on some earlier occasion, the only content for his current judgement that this is the same sensation as that which he had before is one fixed by his own current assessment of the subjective similarity between his present and his past experience; but since this assessment also constitutes his current judgement, the judgement is infallible. Yet that implies that the situation here is such that he cannot make a mistake, and thus that no judgement is actually being made; as Wittgenstein puts it, 'whatever is going to seem right to me is right. And that only means that here we can't talk about "right" ' (I: ¶258).

As with his rule-following argument, it remains a matter of dispute just what this argument implies, especially concerning 'Robinson Crusoe'-type situations in which

---

[64] *On Certainty*, Blackwell, Oxford, 1969.

individual thinkers are *de facto* isolated, but I shall not pursue the matter here.[65] Instead I want to briefly indicate the way in which he uses his new philosophy of language (if one can so speak) to offer a new way of thinking about psychological concepts. As we have seen, Wittgenstein holds that our conception of psychological states has to include reference to the situations which prompt them and to the behaviour to which they give rise; but he is no physicalist or behaviourist, although he is often misrepresented as such. For these positions do not provide for the special role of first-person judgements which he takes to be distinctive of psychological concepts.[66] This may appear a surprising point for him to insist upon, since it might be thought to lead back to the position of the Cartesian philosophers whom he has criticized because of their assumption about the essential privacy of consciousness. But his claim is not that there is no phenomenon of first-person authority with respect to the mind; only that it has been radically misunderstood by those who think of sensations and other mental states as inner states with essential features which are privately presented to the subject. And the deep mistake here, he suggests, is a failure on all sides to appreciate properly the distinctively non-descriptive grammar of the language-games in which we employ psychological concepts (I: ¶304). The Cartesian recognizes the phenomenon of first-person authority, but because he construes the language-game as essentially descriptive he misconstrues the phenomenon in terms of epistemological privacy; the behaviourist and physicalist rightly reject privacy, but because they too assume that psychological concepts are just used to describe states and processes, they fail to acknowledge first-person authority at all. Wittgenstein's claim, then, is that we need a new approach, one which involves 'a radical break with the idea that language always functions in one way, always serves the same purpose: to convey thoughts—which may be about houses, pains, good and evil, or anything else you please' (I: ¶304).

Wittgenstein goes on to offer several suggestions of this kind, embodying different accounts of the role of different first-person judgements. In the case of expressions of intention, decision and the like, he suggests, the special position of the speaker simply reflects the fact that expressing our own intentions and decisions is a way of making up our mind what to do in the first place or of reaffirming our plans.[67] So our authority here is in the first instance practical, a matter of our own responsibility for ourselves, and only derivatively epistemological. In the case of sensations such as pain Wittgenstein's suggestion is that what is distinctive about a speaker's first-person judgements ('It hurts', 'I am in pain') is that they are expressions of pain; so instead of thinking of their authority as dependent upon the speaker's unique ability to recognize his own sensations, they should be seen as a conceptualization of the

---

[65] Wittgenstein discussed Robinson Crusoe-type situations in lectures given in 1934–5, and his lecture notes are included in the collection *Philosophical Occasions* (eds. J. Klagge and A. Nordmann, Hackett, Indianapolis, 1993); see esp. p. 237. For a good general discussion of the 'private language argument' see M. Budd, *Wittgenstein's Philosophy of Psychology*, Routledge, London, 1989.

[66] Wittgenstein's clearest statement of this point is in his *Remarks on the Philosophy of Psychology*, Vol. II (Blackwell, Oxford, 1980), ¶63. But it is implicit in the latter part of his *Philosophical Investigations*.

[67] *Remarks on the Philosophy of Psychology*, Vol. II ¶275–6.

involuntary expressions of pain ('Ow!') which provide us with our basic evidence for the ascription of pain. Indeed the speaker's grasp of the concept of pain, as expressed in his first-person judgements about himself, is dependent upon an ability to make judgements about himself and others that are appropriate to these other kinds of evidence and to their implications (I: ¶310). Finally, Wittgenstein draws on an observation made by Moore concerning the special status of first-person expressions of belief, namely that it is nonsensical for me to say 'I believe that it is raining, though it is not raining' even though others can sensibly point out that I am mistaken. Again, the special status of these first-person expressions of belief is not a matter of epistemological privilege; instead, Wittgenstein suggests, they reflect the fact that it is a mark of the language-game of belief that I express my beliefs by saying 'I believe that it is raining' just as much as by saying 'It is raining' (II: §x).

These cases show Wittgenstein's new pluralist approach to the 'grammar' of ordinary language at work. Whether or not one accepts all the details of his account,—and it is interesting to compare his approach and conclusions with of Davidson which I described above (Section 3.6),—I think it is indisputable that Wittgenstein's investigations of psychological concepts exemplify a new and fruitful way in which the philosophy of language has contributed to the philosophy of mind.

3.8 Ordinary Language Philosophy

Wittgenstein's emphasis in these later writings on the grammar of our ordinary language-games was part of a broader turn to 'ordinary language', which reached its zenith in the work of the three major Oxford philosophers of the early post-1945 period, Gilbert Ryle, John Austin and Peter Strawson. In different ways, they all took it that there are implications in our ordinary uses of language which are of central importance for an understanding of the concepts we employ but which have often been neglected in philosophical discussion of these concepts.

Ryle was the oldest of this trio and, having been on friendly terms with Wittgenstein during the 1930s, was familiar with his new approach to philosophy.[68] In presenting this approach, however, Ryle retained the word 'logic' to describe the implications inherent in the ordinary use of language while insisting that this logic of ordinary language is essentially informal: 'the logic of everyday statements . . . cannot in principle be adequately represented by the formulae of formal logic'.[69] But it is a fair criticism of Ryle that his account of this 'logic' is altogether too unstructured to be persuasive. A characteristic case is provided by his discussion of the freedom

---

[68] See R. Monk, *Ludwig Wittgenstein: the Duty of Genius*, Jonathan Cape, London, 1990, p. 275. Monk tells the story how, when asked how many people understood his philosophy, Wittgenstein replied 'Two—and one of them is Gilbert Ryle', p. 436.

[69] 'Ordinary Language' (1953), reprinted in his *Collected Papers* II, Hutchinson, London, 1971, p. 316.

of the will in *The Concept of Mind*.[70] Ryle starts by maintaining that 'In their most ordinary employment "voluntary" and "involuntary" are used, with a few minor elasticities, as adjectives applying to actions which ought not to be done' (p. 67). So 'In this ordinary use, then, it is absurd to discuss whether satisfactory, correct or admirable performances are voluntary or involuntary' (p. 68). But philosophers have not heeded this constraint, with the result that 'The tangle of largely spurious problems, known as the Freedom of the Will, partly derives from this unconsciously stretched use of "voluntary"' (p. 69). Ryle here moves too quickly from the linguistic phenomena he adduces uncritically to his conclusion. To say this is not to say that we require a formal logic to identify the implications inherent in ordinary language; but what is needed is a critical discussion, if not a theory, which enables one to distinguish different kinds of implication and to assess what significance they have, if any.

Austin's work can be seen as providing part of this critical discussion. His paper 'A Plea for Excuses' covers some of the same ground as Ryle's brisk discussion of the voluntary, but now with an unsurpassed ear for the implications inherent in the different idioms employed in discussions of responsibility.[71] Yet Austin qualifies the significance of appeals to ordinary language: it is not, he says, the 'Last Word', since the distinctions it employs may incorporate old errors or fail to take account of new discoveries which rely on 'the resources of the microscope and its successors'.[72] Nonetheless, because it is the 'first word' its implications should help us to call into question the ways in which philosophical issues have been approached—Austin remarks that his interest in excuses was prompted by dissatisfaction with traditional discussions of free will.[73] But Austin's contribution went well beyond this kind of critical scrutiny of Ryle's appeal to the logic of ordinary language. For starting from his account of utterances such as 'I promise' as 'performative utterances' through which we make promises rather than simply describe them, Austin was led to develop a theory of speech acts, of the things which we do by our utterances.[74] I shall not try to describe this theory, but there are two aspects of it that merit brief notice. First, Austin's emphasis on the variety of things which we do with language and his attempt to characterize this variety in some detail can be seen as a way of developing Wittgenstein's emphasis on the variety of our language-games. They share the view that one of the characteristic mistakes of philosophy has been to think that language is fundamentally descriptive; and they also agree that one of the best ways to identify this mistake is to attend to verbs whose first-person present tense use is in some respects different from that of other uses of the verb, though Austin shows that this is by no means a distinctive characteristic of psychological verbs. Second, Austin discusses at

---

[70] *The Concept of Mind*, Hutchinson, London, 1949; page references are to the 1963 edition published by Penguin, Harmondsworth.

[71] 'A Plea for Excuses' (1956), reprinted in his *Philosophical Papers*, Clarendon Press, Oxford, 2nd edn, 1970.

[72] *Ibid.*, note 71, p. 185.

[73] *Ibid.*, note 71, p. 180.

[74] Austin set out his position in his 1955 William James lectures which were published posthumously as *How to Do Things with Words*, ed. J. Urmson, Clarendon Press, Oxford, 1962.

length the different ways in which a speaker's putative performance of a speech act is 'to some extent a failure', or, as he says, 'infelicitous'.[75] Since the successful perform-ance of a speech-act will be one which avoids these infelicities, it follows that Austin's account of this matter is an important contribution to disentangling Ryle's undiffer-entiated conception of the implications inherent in the use of ordinary language.

A different contribution to this task had been made a few years earlier by Strawson. Strawson began his career by taking the case for ordinary language right into the enemy camp, the study of formal logic. In his 1952 *Introduction to Logical Theory* he affirmed that alongside the study of formal logic there is 'the study of the logical features of ordinary speech' which is much more complex than formal logic, for it involves logical relations beyond those of entailment and contradiction, but, he con-cludes, 'It is none the less true that the logic of ordinary speech provides a field of intellectual study unsurpassed in richness, complexity, and the power to absorb.'[76] Strawson had begun his argument for this conclusion two years earlier when he pub-lished 'On Referring',[77] his famous critical study of Russell's theory of descriptions (see Section 3.2). The core of Strawson's critique of Russell was that Russell's the-ory fails to do justice to the way in which we use definite descriptions to refer to things. Strawson argues that reference is a fundamental linguistic act, one whereby we identify, or single out, some one thing which we can then go on to describe, and he emphasizes the role of the context of utterance in enabling the speaker to identify the thing he is talking about. This point is central to his criticism of Russell. For, Strawson argued, because he failed to appreciate the role of context, Russell took it that reference could be achieved only by names which were guaranteed to single out one and the same object in any context, which Russell called 'logically proper names'. Since definite descriptions fail this requirement, it was inevitable that Russell should construe them as merely descriptive; but, Strawson argued, this was a mistake. Rus-sell's conception of a logically proper name is illusory and once the contribution of context to determining reference is correctly understood, Strawson argued, there is no reason to deny that in utterances of a sentence such as 'The table is covered with books' the phrase 'the table' is being used by the speaker to refer to some one table which he believes to be identifiable in the context, so that the statement made by this utterance is true if that table is covered with books and false if it is not. Strawson further claimed that where there is in fact no table which can be identified from the context of utterance, the question of the truth and falsity of the speaker's statement does not arise since the speaker's use of the sentence to make a statement is 'spuri-ous'; no statement is in fact made. So that there is such a table is something which is 'implied' by the speaker's success in making a statement at all, true or false. It is this type of implication that Strawson had in mind when he wrote in the *Introduction to Logical Theory* of logical relations beyond entailment, and he here calls it 'presupposi-tion', which is how it is now commonly described.[78]

---

[75] *How to Do Things with Words*, note 74, p. 14.
[76] *Introduction to Logical Theory*, Methuen, London, 1952, pp. 231–2.
[77] 'On Referring' (1950), reprinted in his *Logico-Linguistic Papers*, Methuen, London, 1971.
[78] *Introduction to Logical Theory*, note 76, p. 175.

Subsequent discussion has refined many of the points at issue between Strawson and Russell. On one side, Kripke's distinction between rigid and non-rigid designators supports a general distinction between names and definite descriptions which counts in favour of Russell's approach;[79] on the other side, the role of context in determining the reference of phrases with demonstratives is now well understood and readily incorporates descriptions conceived in the way that Strawson proposed.[80] At the same time however other ways of thinking about the issue have been developed with the result that the debate now has many more than two sides and I shall not pursue it further here.[81] Instead I want to turn back to the very idea of ordinary language philosophy and discuss some of the issues it raised for the philosophy of language, in particular the question as to whether an account of meaning should take a concern with the conditions under which what is said is true as fundamental. The tradition I described in the first parts of this chapter, running from Frege to Davidson (Section 3.1–3.6), did take this view—hence the attention throughout to truth-conditions; but this presumption is called into question by the philosophers of ordinary language. For it is central to their approach that meaning encompasses a great variety of implications which extend well beyond those which are grounded in questions of truth and falsity. One response to this challenge would be to say that it was never part of the truth-conditional tradition to hold that the emphasis on truth was exhaustive of meaning: Frege's conception of the 'tone' of an expression such as 'but', for example, was precisely intended to capture implications arising from its use which are not inherent in the truth-conditions of sentences in which it occurs. But this does not meet the point; for the ordinary language philosophers deny that in the characterization of meaning priority is to be given to those aspects of meaning which give rise to questions of truth and falsity. To accept this priority is to assume that language is basically descriptive—the assumption which Wittgenstein and Austin reject.

At this point (*c.* 1960) in the development of the philosophy of language, therefore, there was an opportunity for a sustained debate about the role of truth in the determination of meaning. The issue was raised in 1957 by Stanley Cavell, who had studied with Austin and been deeply influenced by his own study of Wittgenstein, in a famous paper 'Must We Mean What We Say?';[82] and Strawson later devoted his 1969 inaugural lecture 'Meaning and Truth' to this question, describing it as a 'Homeric struggle' between the protagonists of a truth-conditional approach and the ordinary language philosophers who emphasized instead the primacy of speech and communication, amongst whom he not surprisingly included himself.[83] Yet the debate did not really take off. Why not? Partly because Davidson's conception of radical interpretation (§7) provided a way of approaching the issue that combined an emphasis

---

[79] See S. Kripke, *Naming and Necessity*, Harvard University Press, Cambridge MA, 1972.

[80] See R. Stalnaker, 'Pragmatic Presuppositions' (1974), reprinted in *Context and Content*, Oxford University Press, New York NY, 1999.

[81] See the special centenary issue of *Mind* 114 (October 2005).

[82] The original version of Cavell's paper was published in *Inquiry* 1 (1958). He later published a revised version in his collection *Must We Mean What We Say*, Charles Scribner's Sons, New York NY, 1969.

[83] P. Strawson, 'Meaning and Truth' (1969), reprinted in his *Logico-Linguistic Papers*, Methuen, London, 1971; for the 'Homeric struggle' see p. 172.

on truth-conditions with sensitivity to the intentions and beliefs of speakers, and therefore seemed to provide a way of combining the approaches which Strawson sought to oppose. But the main reason the debate stalled derived from the work of a philosopher who belonged to the ordinary language tradition and yet propounded a subtle compromise which, at least for a time, defused the radical challenge posed by that tradition—Paul Grice.

Grice began his career in Oxford at a time when ordinary language philosophy was dominant and was being used to criticize traditional philosophical debates. Some of these uses were sophisticated, some less so; and Grice wanted to find a way of drawing distinctions between them. The position he first discussed was one to the effect that when someone says 'The book looks red' the speaker implies either that he doubts that the book in question is red or that he thinks that it is not red; otherwise he would have said 'The book is red' instead. Hence, on this view, where these implications are not satisfied, the speaker's utterance says nothing true or false at all.[84] Clearly, if this is right, then traditional philosophical debates about appearance and reality are misconceived, since they assume that it makes sense to suppose that, for example, things that are red normally look red, and thus that one can describe how things appear to one without any implication of doubt or denial concerning the way they really are. Grice felt that these debates were indeed being cut off too quickly, and, he argued, the critic here mistakes something which might well be implied in the course of a conversation for an implication which is either presupposed in Strawson's sense, as a condition of truth or falsity, or strictly implied by what is said. Implications of the first kind Grice called 'conversational implicature', and one mark of them, as opposed to the others, is that a speaker can explicitly cancel them without any incoherence, e.g. in the case envisaged by saying 'The book looks red, and I have no doubt that it is red'.

Having introduced this distinction, Grice went on to develop a sophisticated account of conversational implicature whose basic principle is that speakers normally seek to cooperate with their audience by saying things which are relevant to the context in which their conversation is taking place, and thus that there are many things which are in this way conversationally implicated by utterances without being part of what is strictly said. For example, if a colleague asks me how a student whom I am teaching is progressing and I just reply 'His handwriting is very clear', I thereby 'implicate' by my remark that the intellectual quality of his work is not good; but the implicature is just conversational, for I can obviously go on to cancel it without incoherence by adding 'and what he writes is very interesting'.[85] Through the plausibility of this account Grice succeeded in creating a broad consensus in favour of

---

[84] H. P. Grice, 'The Causal Theory of Perception' (1961), reprinted in part in his *Studies in the Way of Words*, Harvard University Press, Cambridge MA, 1989; see esp. pp. 227–8. The view being criticized had been advanced by A. Quinton in 'The Problem of Perception', *Mind*, 64 (1955), 28–51. Grice's argument does not apply to the very different way in which Austin criticized traditional discussions of appearance and reality in *Sense and Sensibilia* (Clarendon Press, Oxford, 1962), esp. lectures VII, VIII.

[85] See 'Logic and Conversation' (1967), reprinted in a revised version in *Studies in the Way of Words*, note 84.

the thesis that there is a clear distinction between conversational implicature, on the one hand, which is inherently dependent upon the speaker's wish to take advantage of the audience's ability to grasp what the speaker is trying to communicate by saying what he does in the light of the context of the conversation, and 'what is said', on the other hand, by the use of a sentence on some occasion, which Grice takes to be determined by general conventions governing the use of language, and which is therefore not dependent upon the conversational context in which the sentence occurs.

Grice went on to offer an account of meaning of this latter kind, what is said or 'literal meaning' as it is often called, in terms of a speaker's intention to induce within her audience a belief whose content identifies what is said through her intention that the audience should recognize from her utterance that she has the intention to induce the belief in question;[86] and David Lewis then showed that this account is precisely that which his own account of the conventional status of language would lead one to expect (see Section 3.6).[87] As we have seen, there are those, such as Davidson, who deny that language is in this way conventional; but this disagreement is not crucial here, for Davidson still subscribes to Grice's distinction between conversational implicature and literal meaning.[88] And as long as that distinction is retained, it is easy to argue that a concern with truth-conditions must retain a central place in the philosophy of language as a way of capturing what is said by the utterance of a sentence on some occasion. Thus precisely by his sensitivity to ordinary conversational uses of language Grice appeared to have defused the threat which ordinary language philosophy posed to traditional truth-oriented philosophy of language.[89]

3.9 THINGS FALL APART

In recent years, however, the debate has been revived. Doubts about the Gricean compromise come from many directions. I will just indicate a few and will not attempt to resolve the issues thereby raised.

First, Strawson's doubts about the way in which standard systems of formal logic represent the logic of ordinary speech have become increasingly difficult to dismiss. A key focus of debate has been the understanding of conditionals, sentences of the form 'if p, then q'. As well as criticizing Russell's theory of descriptions in his *Introduction to Logical Theory* Strawson had also here criticized the standard truth-conditional treatment of the logic of conditionals on the grounds that focusing on

---

[86] See 'Meaning' (1957), reprinted in *Studies in the Way of Words*, note 84.
[87] See *Convention*, note 58, pp. 155–6.
[88] See 'A Nice Derangement of Epitaphs' (1986), reprinted in *Truth, Language and History*, Clarendon, Oxford, 2005, p. 91.
[89] Of course not everyone was persuaded. A notable dissenter is Charles Travis; see *Unshadowed Thought*, Harvard University Press, Cambridge MA, 2001.

the truth or falsity of conditional sentences misrepresents their role in inference.[90] Grice responded to Strawson, arguing that once normal conversational implicature is brought into the discussion, the objections to the standard account can be set aside.[91] But Grice's response did not end the debate, and an important new approach to conditionals was initiated by Ernest Adams, who argued that the best way to think about conditionals is to concentrate on the conditions under which their assertion is warranted, which Adams identified as situations in which there is a high probability of the truth of the consequent given the truth of the antecedent.[92] This intuitively plausible claim then suggests that conditionals be thought of as propositions whose probability matches the conditional probability identified by Adams. But David Lewis proved that this cannot be: there can be no conditional proposition whose probability matches the conditional probability of the consequent given the antecedent.[93] This result suggests to some (though not to Lewis himself) that, for conditionals at any rate, truth-conditions are not the fundamental requirement for an account of meaning as the standard tradition supposes.[94] It is then a matter for further debate whether accepting this conclusion would be a serious challenge to the standard tradition; but it is certainly unnerving to find the truth-conditional approach to meaning strongly challenged on its home ground of logic.

A second area of unhappiness has developed around the significance of identity statements. Frege's famous discussion of the need to capture the cognitive value of the discovery expressed as 'The Morning Star is the Evening Star' and his suggestion that this is best accommodated by recognizing that names have sense as well as reference (see Section 3.1) have been the topic for sustained debate. Many philosophers, most notably Saul Kripke, have argued that it is a mistake to assign sense as well as reference to proper names; and thus that there needs to be a different strategy for handling the cognitive value of identity-statements which capture important discoveries.[95] But, it is also acknowledged, Grice's notion of conversational implicature is too weak for this task, since it is cancellable. Hence some further dimension of meaning seems required, one which captures the informational content conveyed by the utterance of a sentence in context but is less closely tied to truth-conditions than Frege's conception of sense. This issue has been sharpened by some further cases advanced by Jennifer Saul in which she tests our judgements concerning cases in which a person has two names which are associated with different roles which are supposed to be kept separate from each other: she focuses on our judgements about

---

[90] *Introduction to Logical Theory*, note 76, pp. 85 ff. Many other philosophers had expressed dissatisfaction about this matter, notably G. E. Moore and C. I. Lewis.

[91] See 'Indicative Conditionals', in his *Studies in the Way of Words*, note 84.

[92] E. Adams, *The Logic of Conditionals*, Dordrecht, 1975.

[93] D. Lewis, 'Probabilities of Conditionals and Conditional Probabilities' (1976), reprinted in his *Philosophical Papers*, Vol. ii, Oxford University Press, New York, 1986.

[94] See D. Edgington, 'Do Conditionals have Truth-Conditions?' (1986), reprinted in *Conditionals*, ed. F. Jackson, Oxford University Press, Oxford, 1991.

[95] See *Naming and Necessity*, note 79. For a good discussion of the issue here, see N. Salmon, *Frege's Puzzle*, MIT Press, Cambridge MA, 1986.

Clark Kent/Superman. Even when we are familiar with this identity, she observes, we hesitate to accept inferences such as:

> Superman leaps more tall buildings than Clark Kent
>
> So: Superman leaps more tall buildings than Superman

> Clark Kent went into a phone booth, and Superman came out
>
> So: Clark Kent went into a phone booth, and Clark Kent came out

A Fregean strategy for vindicating our hesitation by interpreting the use of names here as expressive of a role, as 'Superman *qua* Superman' or 'Clark Kent *qua* Clark Kent', is counterintuitive when we think of our normal use of names. It certainly produces the wrong results if we think of a speaker who is uninformed about the identity. Equally, however, it is not clear how to handle our hesitations as just a matter of conversational implicature alone. Instead, as before, there seems to be some informational content which is conveyed by the use of the different names but which is neither a matter of 'what is said' nor of what is just conversationally implicated.[96]

The concept that is often used to describe these contextual implications is 'pragmatics', so that the debate here is conceived as one about the respective merits of truth-conditional semantics versus informational pragmatics. In thinking about this debate it is important to acknowledge from the start that some of the ways in which context contributes to meaning are readily accommodated within a broad truth-conditional semantics; this applies particularly to the ways in which context of utterance fixes the reference of indexical and demonstrative expressions.[97] The issue, however, is how far this can be extended to apply to cases in which the contribution of context is of a rather different kind: rather than contributing suitable objects to what is said, the context enables communication to be successfully achieved despite the fact that speakers say things which are literally false. Thus, to take an example from a recent paper by Dan Sperber and Deirdre Wilson,[98] suppose you offer me supper and I accept, saying 'Thanks, I haven't eaten.' On the face of it, what I say is false; but in the context what I communicate is that I have not yet eaten this evening. This phenomenon of 'loose talk' is ubiquitous in ordinary conversation, and we use our common sense all the time to understand each other without any need to correct or qualify our statements.[99] A first thought about it may be that one can construct conceptions of what is said such that the appearance of literal falsehood is dispelled by adding extra parameters and qualifications. In my judgement, however, the phenomena are too varied for this strategy to be persuasive.[100] An alternative line of thought is that what we have here are just Gricean conversational implicatures, and thus a

---

[96] Jennifer Saul, 'Substitution and Simple Sentences', *Analysis* (57), 1997.

[97] David Kaplan's work has shown how this is to be done; see his essay 'Demonstratives' in *Themes from Kaplan*, eds. J. Almog, H. Wettstein and J. Perry, Oxford University Press, New York, 1989.

[98] Dan Sperber and Deirdre Wilson, 'Truthfulness and Relevance', *Mind*, 111 (2002), pp. 583–632.

[99] The hero of Mark Haddon's novel *The Curious Incident of the Dog in the Night-Time*, Christopher Boone, has Asperger's syndrome and cannot stand loose talk. As Mark Haddon shows, this makes conversations with him very unnatural and tedious.

[100] See Francois Recanati, *Literal Meaning*, Cambridge University Press, Cambridge, 2004.

phenomenon which is not a threat to truth-conditional semantics, but a complement to it. In fact, the phenomena here cannot all be captured by Grice's theory (e.g. the conversational implication that I haven't yet eaten this evening cannot be sensibly cancelled in the simple conversation above); but it is plausible to hold that an extended Gricean theory will do so.[101] Once such a theory is seen to be effective, however, it poses a challenge of a different kind: namely that if what we want is an account of the basis of our understanding of each other, then truth-conditional semantics is not what is wanted. Instead we need an account of the way in which pragmatic skills are employed in conversational contexts to work out what is relevant for the purpose of communication with others. Sperber and Wilson put the point as follows:

Of course hearers expect to be informed and not misled by what is communicated; but what is communicated is not the same as what is said. Whatever genuine facts such a convention or maxim <sc. of truthfulness> was supposed to explain are better explained by assuming that communication is governed by a principle of relevance.[102]

Sperber and Wilson suggest, then, that a pragmatic theory of communication can supplant, and not merely complement, truth-conditional semantics as the proper basis for a philosophy of language for the twenty-first century. And what then would be the proper place for semantics? I leave the last word on this with the greatest linguistic theorist of the twentieth century, Noam Chomsky: 'It is possible that natural language has only syntax and pragmatics.'[103]

---

[101] Cf. Sperber and Wilson 'Truthfulness and Relevance', note 98.

[102] *Ibid.*, note 98, p. 583.

[103] N. Chomsky, 'Language as a Natural Object' in *New Horizons in the Study of Language and Mind*, Cambridge University Press, Cambridge, 2000, p. 132.

TOURO COLLEGE LIBRARY

PART II

THE NATURE OF LANGUAGE

CHAPTER 4

PSYCHOLOGISM

CHARLES TRAVIS

'PSYCHOLOGISM' is a term of abuse. It has been used recently of several different flaws. The main ones run in roughly opposite directions. One flaw does away with a phenomenon absolutely central to thought. The other inflates the demands of that phenomenon, thus deciding too much in advance as to what thought must be. I will call the phenomenon *answerability*. I begin with a simple, intuitive, idea of it. Elaboration will be needed. But in due time.

Thinking something so is a special sort of stance, or attitude, towards things being as they are. Where one thinks something so, there is, first, that which one thinks so. Whether what one thus thinks so *is* so—whether things are as one thus thinks them—can be determined only by things being as they are; what one's stance is towards. A stance of this sort is eligible for a particular kind of correctness. In terms of it, there are, for any such stance, two ways for things to be in being as they are. If things are the one way, then in taking that stance one thinks correctly in this sense. If they are the other, one thus thinks incorrectly. Where the world works this way, a stance it makes correct on any taking of it, it makes correct on all. *Perhaps* one who finds chocolate banal is no more correct or incorrect than one wholly in thrall to it. That would thus be a stance without the features just mentioned. So it would not be the special sort of stance that thinking something so is.

Thus is such correctness decided (if at all) solely by how things are. Factors peculiar to a taking of the stance can play no role. Properly spelled out, the correctness involved here is truth. The sort of eligibility for truth I have just described is what I mean by answerability—being answerable to things being as they are.

Now for two opposing thoughts, each of which has driven a very great deal of philosophy, each of which is difficult to give up. Again these are intuitive ideas. Again elaboration will come. The first begins with the idea that we—let that be we

* I am grateful to Barry Smith for a pleasant and fruitful editorial process, from which I and the reader have both benefited greatly.

humans—are thinkers of a special, *parochial*, sort. Not all thinkers need think as we do. It continues: the parochial sort of thinker one is shapes how it is open to one to be answerable to the way things are. In particular, it helps to determine what it is in things being as they are to which one *can* be answerable; the sorts of aspects of things being as they are with which it is possible for one to have that sort of rapport. So if, so to speak, a Martian is as different from us as any thinker could be, then there will be things we can think so that the Martian cannot, and, perhaps, vice-versa. There will be cases where the Martian cannot see what it is we are answerable to; and vice-versa. For all of which, the thought goes, we are, in those cases, thinking things *so*; being answerable.

Where the parochial is assigned the wrong work in making us answerable to what we are, it instead abolishes the answerability it was meant to make for. For it will then intrude on, or compromise, what was to be the sole province of things being as they are. The resulting stances (if any) will not fit the required notion of correctness. The world will lose the *sole* authority such correctness calls for. Making the parochial thus intrude is one thing that has been called psychologism.

The second thought is that there can be no answerable stances except those available, in principle, to any thinker. So (minimally) we cannot think it *so* that P if a Martian could not grasp when things would be as we thus thought. That is why these are opposing thoughts. A *very* great deal of philosophy has been a working-out of this second thought. As we shall see, this second thought places heavy demands on answerability. The stronger the demands, the more the range of (genuinely) answerable stances shrinks. If, developing this second thought, some supposed area of answerability seems to disappear—we are apparently left, say, without stances that it is *so* that such-and-such caused such-and-such—there are two possible reactions. One is to accept the loss. The other is to save that region of presumed answerability by enlarging the powers and workings of *The Mind*, that is, the common property of all who qualify as thinkers—so that the Martian turns out after all to be able to take those stances that seemed, for a moment, lost.

If there are risks in seeing the parochial as working to make aspects of the way things are available for us to be answerable to, there are risks in the enlargement of The Mind as well. Enlargement may become inflation. It may banish some of the plasticity our thought requires. Building too much into The Mind narrows the ambit of empirical psychology. That sin in the opposite direction might also be called psychologism. Such psychologism would be specialized scientism—a mistaken insistence as to how empirical investigation *must* turn out.

Just how might the parochial threaten answerability? What constraints on answerability might it violate? I will pursue that question by developing Frege's conception of answerability, and his correlative views on psychologism of the first sort. Compared to prior philosophers, such as British empiricists, Frege is a minimalist in the demands he sets on answerability. If he is ever less than minimalist, that is something that flows out of his particular conception of logic. I will then turn to Wittgenstein's (last) conception of answerability, by which Frege is not quite minimalist enough. That will allow us to see how the pursuit of answerability might lead to psychologism of the second kind.

4.1 GRUNDLAGEN

For Frege, psychologism is confusing the psychological with the logical. That would be psychologism of our first form: involving (our) psychology in (presumed) standards of correctness in a way such as to frustrate any suitable form of answerability to *how things are*. Frege's first attempt at spelling out the transgression that yields such loss was in *Grundlagen der Arithmetik*.[1] There the crucial transgression is a form of privacy: making the way in which a (supposed) judgment is answerable graspable, in principle, by no more than *one* thinker. The idea of this particular transgression continued to play a role in Frege's thought; for it matters to his conception of what logic is, in a way soon to be spelled out. As an account of psychologism, though, this idea lacks the right generality. It leaves many untouched who Frege meant to target. Moreover, it flows less obviously, or directly, from the idea of answerability itself than later Fregean elaborations. By the time of *Grundgesetze der Arithmetik*,[2] Frege's attention was thus focused elsewhere. Nonetheless, this first idea merits some expansion.

Frege introduces the idea in the preface to *Grundlagen*, where he vows

always to separate sharply the psychological from the logical, the subjective from the objective;

never to ask for the meaning of a word in isolation, but only in the context of a proposition.

and comments:

In compliance with the first principle, I have used the word 'idea' always in the psychological sense, and have distinguished ideas from concepts and from objects. If the second principle is not observed, one is almost forced to take as the meanings of words mental pictures or acts of the individual mind, and so to offend against the first principle as well.[3]

The cogency or import of the context principle is not the issue here. What matters is the sin into which one might be tempted: taking the meanings of words to be 'ideas', by which he means "contents of an inner world", such as sense impressions, creations of imagination, experiences, feelings, moods, inclinations, and wishes.[4] Here is the crucial feature of ideas which makes the sin here a sin:

The sense impression of green which I have exists only through me; I am its bearer. It strikes us as nonsense that a pain, a mood, a wish should occur on their own, without a bearer. An experience is not possible without an experiencer. . . .

Thus

Ideas must have a bearer.

Every idea has only one bearer; no two people have the same idea.

---

[1] In English, *The Foundations of Arithmetic*, J. L. Austin, trans., Oxford: Basil Blackwell, 1950.

[2] In English, *The Basic Laws of Arithmetic*, M. Furth, trans., Berkeley and Los Angeles: University of California Press, 1967.

[3] *Ibid.*, p. x.

[4] "Der Gedanke", *Logische Untersuchungen*, Göttingen: Vandenhoeck und Ruprecht, 1966. The quotes which follow are an extract of pp. 40–3 of that edition. My translation.

So if meanings were ideas, then no two people could take words to have the same meaning; no two people could attach the same understanding to given words.

What happens if meanings are ideas? The simplest thought would be that then all we ever talk about are ideas (our own, if we can grasp what we say). There is a second, more encompassing, idea. Meaning (as Frege sees things) fixes when words would say what is so—just how they are answerable, how the way things are matters to them. Where meanings are ideas, it takes ideas to identify the conditions on such correctness. So for any given words, if they *are* answerable, then at most one person, in principle, can grasp how. At most one person can mean words to answer in that way. So at most one can *think* what is so answerable. Two people can thus neither contradict nor endorse each other's views. Wherever meaning works like that, Frege tells us, there can be neither genuine disputes nor genuine shared knowledge:

There could be no science which was in common to many ... but I would have perhaps my science, namely the totality of thoughts whose bearer I am, another would have his science. Each of us would concern himself with the contents of his own consciousness. A contradiction between both sciences is then impossible; and it is really idle to dispute over truth, almost as ridiculous as if two people disputed whether a hundred mark note was real, when each meant the one in his pocket, and each understood the word 'real' in a different sense.[5]

One thing this stresses is that if there were answerability under these conditions, each thinker would be answerable to what was, essentially, his own private tract of reality—some expanse of the way things are that was in principle inaccessible to anyone else. So for no thinker would there be another whose views (or information) as to what was right could matter to whether this first thinker was.

That is a terrible situation. If we were all in it, would that abolish answerability, so logic, *tout court*? If someone were in it, would it abolish answerability for him? Might there be private answerability? Or is that very idea incompatible with what logic must be? Frege certainly thought this last thing. To see why, we need to spell out how the mere supposition of private conditions of correctness is destructive of answerability itself.

Frege remarks that if everything were an idea (so if meanings were) then "psychology would also rule logic and mathematics".[6] That, he takes it, would make logic at most a collection of psychological truths. But, he remarks, "neither logic nor mathematics has the task of investigating ... contents of consciousness belonging to individuals."[7] So it is an error to see logic as psychology. That might be called psychologism. Just where does this error lie? Genuine psychology is answerable. That is not the trouble. But, for Frege, logic has a special content. Its task is to set out precisely what truth, so what answerability, as such is. To do that it must say what it would be for a *thought* to be true. It will not do merely to say what it would be

---

[5] "Der Gedanke", *Logische Untersuchungen*, Göttingen: Vandenhoeck und Ruprecht, 1966. The quotes which follow are an extract of p. 43. of that edition. My translation.

[6] *Ibid.*, p. 50.   [7] *Ibid.*

for such-and-such thoughts to be true (or, more properly, to be in some particular condition). Nor can it be that whether thoughts in general, or some given thinker's thoughts, do answer (are true), given the world's being as it is—or whether they are in that condition of which logic speaks—depends on some thinkers' psychologies. That would be precisely not to have the matter decided solely by the world; so it would not be answerability at all. So logic would not have explicated the notion that is its proper subject. And, Frege tells us, things do thus go wrong when meanings are ideas. He expresses the key idea as follows:

The words 'true' and 'false', as I understand them, would apply only in the area of my consciousness . . . Then truth would be limited to the content of my consciousness, and it would be doubtful whether anything at all similar occurred in the consciousness of others.[8]

If 'true' and 'false' have a sense in which I might take my private stances to be true or false, then that is not a sense in which any other stances might be true. So there can be no saying what it is for a *thought* to be true. So there can be no proper logic. At most a logic might try to say what it is for, say, *my* thoughts to be what *I* understand by true. But *a* logic—one among others—would not unfold the laws of truth (the task Frege assigns logic). For *they* apply, intrinsically, to *any* thought. They say precisely what answerability as such demands. To be a thought just *is* to be answerable. What *a* logic explicated could not be answerability as such, so nor truth. That is a sketch of a story of how loss of publicity loses answerability, and of how, conversely, if there could be genuinely answerable private stances, then that would abolish logic. It remains to spell out details.

For Frege, laws of logic are *the* most general truths; arrived at by abstraction from less general ones. They mention *nothing*, insofar as it is possible to abstract away from such mention; to generalize instead. Such truths have nothing but their structure to make them true. So they can speak to thought, or thoughts, only in this way: their structure reflects (is an image of) the structure of a system to which both they, and the thoughts to which they speak, belong; a system structured by inferential relations, and by commonalities in ways of representing (or in what would thus be represented). This idea yields an alternate route to the above point.

So conceiving logic, let us try to suppose answerability a private matter. So the thoughts each thinker thinks are available only to him. One thinker's thoughts, if they were that, might form a system. By abstraction, one could reach most general thoughts within it. But these thoughts would be most general only relative to it. For each thinker, there would be a different such system. So to be most general within some one such system would not yet be to be most general *tout court*. Further, no one such system contains a negation, or any other logical compound, of anything in any other. This is to say that there are no inferential relations between the elements of one such system and those of another. Thus no principles of logic span two such systems. Rather, the most general truths of one system reflect nothing of the structure of another; nor of its inferential properties. Nor are there any truths save

[8] *Ibid.*, p. 43.

those belonging to one such system or another. So no truth speaks, in the way a most general truth would speak, to *all* thought. (There *is* no maximal generality *tout court*.) But a law of logic was to be a partial characterization of what *truth* is; that is, of what it is for a *thought* (full stop) to be true. If answerability is a private matter, no thought does that. So no thought says what a law of logic would. There *is* no logic. The idea now runs: thoughts not subject to logic are subject to *no* genuine standard for having answered. No matter how things are, one might just as well say that they did answer as that they did not—or, once logic is abandoned, say both. Such 'thoughts' would not be answerable, so not thoughts at all. That is a *reductio* on the idea that answerability is a private matter.[9]

There is a more minimalist case against private answerability. In explaining what answerability is we needed, crucially, the idea that what is answerable is a *stance there is to take*, where what the stance is is identifiable independent of any particular taking of it; identifiable by that to which the stance is answerable. Where a stance must be identified in terms of ideas, it is, essentially, a stance only one person could take. That erodes distance between the *stance* and a particular thinker's taking it, and, again, a particular taking of it. That, one might argue, deprives us altogether here of the idea of a stance there is to take. Which would make it impossible to say what, in this case, answerability comes to. There are thus several different cases that might be developed—but still need to be.

4.2 GRUNDGESETZE

The idea was: things are *judged* to be some way only where whether things are that way depends exclusively on how things are. This dependence on the way things are, most straightforwardly elaborated, would mean: if things were otherwise, they might not be as judged. That idea, though, does not quite serve Frege's purpose. Instead, we might try to identify answerability in terms of what must *not* share the role to be played by the way things are. That is Frege's strategy in *Grundgesetze*. The rough idea is: thinking cannot make it so. An answerable stance is answerable to something in particular: to whether things are thus and so. Such a connection between stance and world is answerability only where whether things are in fact that way could not be changed by different reactions towards, or senses for, their being so. Historically, most worries about psychologism have been about transgressing that requirement.

Frege expresses this particular condition as follows:

There is no contradiction in something's being true which everybody takes to be false. . . . If it is true that I am writing this in my chamber on the 13th of July, 1893, while the wind howls outside, then it remains true even if all men should subsequently take it to be false. If

---

[9] The argument goes through on the weaker assumption that answerability *may* be a private matter. Thoughts for which it is cannot form a system with thoughts available to other thinkers. So, again, nothing can say what a law of logic was meant to.

being true is thus independent of being acknowledged by somebody or other, then the laws of truth are not psychological laws.[10]

In a later unpublished fragment,[11] he elaborates this theme:

If anyone tried to contradict the statement that what is true is true independently of our recognizing it as such, he would by his very assertion contradict what he had asserted. . . .

To elaborate: if something were true only for him who held it to be true, there would be no contradiction between the opinions of different people. So to be consistent, any person holding this view would have no right whatever to contradict the opposite view: he would have to espouse the principle *non disputandum est*. He would not be able to assert anything at all in the normal sense, and even if his utterances had the form of assertions, they would only have the status of interjections—of expressions of mental states or processes, between which, and such mental states or processes in another person there could be no contradiction. And in that case his assertion that something was true only for us and through being recognized by us would have that status too. If this view were true . . . there would be no science, no error, and no correction of error; properly speaking there would be nothing true in the normal sense of the word. For this is so closely bound up with that independence of being recognized as true . . . that it cannot be separated from it.[12]

Transgressing *Grundlagen*'s demands on answerability would eliminate the science that we know. Does it leave room for private science—for each person, his own physics? If *Grundlagen's* demands are genuine demands on answerability, then no. What is at stake in *Grundgesetze* is very clearly answerability as such. What would be lost with it can be no less than science full stop. What Frege demands is, as he sees it, essential for anything's being either true or false. So it is a minimal condition for logic. In fact, he suggests, logic is no more than an elaboration of what comes into play when the demand is met.

For something to be true is one thing; for everyone to think so is another. So, perhaps *ceteris paribus*, either thing might occur without the other. More generally, where a stance undertakes to answer to things being thus and so, its truth should be compatible with any views or perceptions by anyone as to whether things *are* that way. This idea comes into play only after it has been fixed to what the stance in question *is* answerable. What different views of things would not change is whether things, as they are, are *that* way. The views that cannot change things are, crucially, views as to how things are. They might also be views about how to think about how things are. Or they might simply consist in a particular (non-obligatory) way of thinking of how things are; a way of viewing things. What such views cannot change is whether that which is so according to any answerable stance is so.

Frege's example, that the wind howled on a certain day, is particularly compelling in part because of its subject matter. Suppose the judgment were that everyone now thinks the wind howled. That would be answerable to what all present earthlings

[10] *Grundgesetze*, p. 13.
[11] "Logic" (1897), *Posthumous Writings*, H. Hermes, F. Kambartel and F. Kaulbach, eds., Oxford: Basil Blackwell, 1979.
[12] *Ibid.*, pp. 132–3.

think (as to the wind's howling). That actual thinkers in fact have certain attitudes is as much part of how things are as anything, so part of what there is to be answerable to. Trivially, where a stance is answerable to *such* a feature of reality, whether it in fact *answers* to how things are depends in some way on the attitudes certain thinkers in fact take. If it is correct, then, had those thinkers not had those attitudes, it would have been incorrect. That is what it is like for such a stance to depend on how things are. What answerability demands here, the idea is, is that whether such a stance is correct cannot depend on how, or what, or whether, *one* thinks about the way things in fact are—one's views, or preferences, in taking, or evaluating, these stances towards so-and-so's attitudes; as if thinkers with different ways of viewing things might equally correctly take either the stance in question, or the opposing one. What must not be is that one may correctly take the stance if one thinks in one way, but also correctly reject it if one thinks in another.

Suppose Sid takes *andouilletes* to be disgusting. Is that an answerable stance? That may well depend on its ambitions. The stance may undertake no more than disgust at *andouilletes*. In that case, not. For otherwise either all those disgusted by them, or all those not, would be getting something wrong as to how things are. But in matters of taste for *andouilletes*, if anywhere, *non disputandem est*. Suppose, though, that Sid's attitude is part and parcel of a view that denies what I just said—a view on which there *is* something observer-independent to get right as to what is disgusting and what is not. So it is part of his stance that *amateurs* of *andouilletes* are getting something wrong. Then his stance may be both answerable and false. *Andouilletes* are not disgusting in the way he means. A stance may *undertake* to be answerable: to take it is to take oneself to be answerable, and in a certain way—to mean to bind oneself to how things are. Whether a stance *is* answerable is sometimes decided by whether it undertakes to be. How could a stance which undertakes to be answerable, for all that, fail to be? By failing some requirement on answerability, of course. Section 4.4 will present an idea by which such failure is none too easily suffered.

One can see both the core idea of *Grundlagen* and that of *Grundgesetze* as different attempts to work out the intuition that answerability requires a distinction between—in fact, logical independence of—thinking something so, and thereby being right. That distinction goes missing, the *Grundlagen* idea is, when what being right would be is something private. In *Grundgesetze* it shows up in the stability of what is thought so under certain variations in attitudes towards that being so: an answerable stance-to-be-taken, correct on any taking of it, is, *ipso facto*, correct on all. That is the mark of the answerable. *Grundgesetze*'s demand on answerability more directly, and fully, touches the target of concern to Frege. His concern was that there should be something for logic to be about—genuine *thoughts* that such-and-such is so; and, most particularly, that logic itself should be answerable, but not to any fact about (particular) psychologies. Logic presents a special case of answerability. Here are some preliminary remarks on how.

For Frege, a law of logic is, to begin with, true. So it is answerable: for each such law, to a specifiable aspect of how things are. Second, Frege insists that there is no *explaining* why a law of logic is true (except in terms of other laws of logic). He tells us,

The question why and with what right we acknowledge a law of logic to be true, logic can answer only by reducing it to another law of logic. Where that is not possible, logic can give no answer. If we step away from logic, we may say: we are compelled to make judgments by our own nature and by external circumstances: and if we do so we cannot reject this law . . . I shall neither dispute nor support this view; I shall merely remark that what we have here is not a logical consequence. What is given is not a reason for something's being true, but for our taking it to be true.[13]

A law of logic depends on, is hostage to, *nothing*. It does not hold by virtue of things being one way rather than another. That is how there is no explaining it. It is only a very special case of that to say that it in no way depends on facts of human psychology. It equally cannot depend on facts about meteorology. But in any event it will be a form of psychologism (the second sort just mentioned) to make a logical truth depend for its truth on anyone's attitudes. These two points mean that answerability does not always mean a liability to vary in correctness according to how things are. Thus the *via negativa* of *Grundgesetze*: identifying it in terms of what must *not* matter.

For a law of logic (or anything) to be hostage to nothing is for there to be no such thing as things being other than it has them. If there is no such thing as, say, being F without being G—for example, being a conjunction but not subject to conjunction elimination—that means that being G is just part of what being F is (what it is to be F). A model might be: there is no such thing as a married bachelor; being unmarried is part of what it is to be a bachelor. Or: there is no such thing as a conjunction that might be true without both its conjuncts so being: nothing would so count; that is part of what it is for something to be a conjunction. (This supposes these claims true.)

So the truth of laws of logic is part of what it is to be something or other. What? A superficial answer would be: logical laws involve certain logical constants—conjunction, disjunction and so on; their truth is part of what it is for something to be what those constants form—a conjunction, for example. There are problems with that view. What makes something a logical constant, to begin with? If disjunction *is* one, how can we be so sure that there is really no such thing as *disjunction* behaving differently than it would if the laws Frege takes for laws of logic are true? It is, in any case, not Frege's view.

Frege tells us,

The meaning of the word 'true' is unfolded in the laws of being true.[14]

Logical laws (the laws of truth) are thus part of what it is for something to be true; that is, part of what it is to be answerable. It is clear how this is meant to work in the case of propositional logic. Where there is answerability, a certain notion of correctness applies; one on which (on Frege's view) what is answerable has, outright,

[13] G. Frege, *Grundgesetze*, p. 15.   [14] "Der Gedanke", p. 31.

precisely one of two values: correct, incorrect. One can define the usual trivial functions of these values (the usual truth functions). One can then define compound thoughts (compound answerable stances), and the connectives that form them, in terms of these functions. If we regard the laws of (propositional) logic as holding of (so, for Frege, as being) such compounds, then that they hold is a trivial consequence of the nature of that particular sort of correctness such that to be answerable is to admit of it.

This view of the matter sets up some small distance between laws of logic and the thoughts they concern. There is a natural truth-functional correspondent of conjunction. That the laws of logic hold of conjunction *defined as that truth-functional connective* is, perhaps, just part of what answerability is. So, perhaps, there is no such thing as things being otherwise in *that* respect. But *is* conjunction nothing other than what is so defined? Must anything that would ever count as conjunction be that? One *might* think: we have an intuitive idea of conjunction which *may* be adequately captured in that way, at least for some purposes, but then again, *could* turn out (sometimes) not to be. Such might depend on what the world is like. Perhaps, at least, it is not quite right that there is simply no such thing as *conjunction* behaving other than in this truth-functional way—nothing that would *ever* so count. If not, and if, for logic, conjunction is truth-functional by *fiat*, then logic treats conjunction at one remove. *Its* conjunction is at best a proxy for *conjunction*. Our conjunctive thoughts are subject to the relevant laws only where, and insofar as, they are correctly viewed as so definable. Plausibly, Frege failed to note the distance here because it seemed inevitable to him that conjunction was so definable. The point, though, begins to suggest a view of logic very different from Frege's. We will return to that in the last section.

There is one more strand in Frege's view. For Frege, logical laws are the most general truths. If they are *most* general, then they make no mention of such things as functions, or connectives, or thoughts, or anything else. So there is nothing but their structure to make them true. If the law is no more than an unfolding of what being true is, thus of answerability, then the relevant unfolding is in that structure. To be *that* law is to be so structured; to be so structured is to be true just where that law is, which is to be true *simpliciter*. That what is *so* structured is true *where* it is, so true full stop, is simply part of what being answerable, or being true, is. Where truth depends on structure in the way the truth of a law of logic does, there is thus no such thing as things being otherwise with respect to it.

If, by virtue of their generality, logical laws do not mention anything, how can they be *about* thoughts, or thought? How can there be, in fact, anything to which they answer? Here is one response. Logical laws are true in virtue of their structure. But a thought *has* a structure only insofar as it belongs to a system of thoughts. The elements of which it is structured are nothing but reflections of particular samenesses in ranges of thoughts—what is in common, for example, to the thoughts Fa, Fb, Fc, ... A thought's structure is thus a reflection of the structure of the system to which it belongs. And so it is for a law of logic. Its structure reflects the most general structure of *the* system to which it belongs; the most general, so the hardest, most non-negotiable, network of truth-preserving paths within and through that structure. By its structure it identifies those paths. It is thus answerable to the structure of that system. (If there is the distance between logical laws and actual thoughts that we began to notice above, Frege is not entitled to this view. But that is an issue for later.)

To what system does a law of logic belong? A thought belongs to the same system as a given thought if it is logically related to it—if there might be an argument leading from the one to the other, or involving both, or a thought compounded of both. For Frege, a law of logic is (must be) related to *every* thought: it bears on each thought in unfolding in part what it is for that thought to be answerable. What it did not relate to logically simply would not be a thought. So every thought belongs to the system it does. So there is but one system to which all thoughts belong.

4.3 THE MARTIAN PRINCIPLE

How can demands on answerability limit the role of special design in shaping it? Here is one line of thought. Suppose that a special design—ours, say—is essential for being able to detect a certain thing to which to be answerable—things being, or not being, F, say. So without that design, no such thing to answer to could come in view. Without it we would have detected nothing to be answerable to at that place where we in fact do. The Martian can, in principle, see no *such* thing to which thought might answer. There are, then, two sorts of special design (ours and the Martian's). With the one, one would detect a certain way things might or might not be—or so it would seem to one so designed. With the other, one would detect no such thing. Is there, then, in fact such a thing to which to be answerable? Each design offers a standard by which that question might be answered. By that standard, there are just those ways for things to be which one so designed might recognize. By the standard of the first design, there is such a thing to which to answer. By that of the second, there is not. By that standard, those of the first design are condemned to suffer an illusion. They suppose themselves to be taking answerable stances which, in fact, are answerable to nothing.

Which design, if either, yields the right answer to the question? Is there really, in the way things are, something to be answerable to, which the first design then allows one to detect? Or is there not? We will get nowhere on this question (the idea is) while relying on the one, or on the other, design. It is already clear what answer such reliance would yield. Each design gives us only a thoroughly parochial view of the matter. So if the question has an answer, it will have to be what is the right answer by the standards of some third design. That will have to be a third *special* design. For if the question were settled merely by the answerability conferred by *The* Mind—what any thinker must be like—then it would be settled already by what we and the Martian share in common, as it is not. But a third special design, if it yields a result at all, only makes our problem arise anew. It gets us no farther. *It* cannot supply an answer to our question when we did not have one already. So there is no answer to that question. Put otherwise, there is no answerable stance that could be such an answer.

For nothing could make that stance correct outright, aside from some parochial way of thinking of things. So it is not a fact that those with the first design are thereby enabled to be answerable to something; that their apparent answerable stances are in fact that.

This line of thought suggests what I will call the Martian Principle: No thinker, or stance, could be answerable to anything to which any other thinker in principle could not be. For any answerable stance, any thinker whatever could, in principle, grasp what it was to be answerable to what that stance is, and could thus take a stance answerable to that.[15] How might one transgress this principle?

Consider, for example, Noam Chomsky's relation to the principle. Chomsky, he tells us, deals in the empirical. Empirical psychology or linguistics is, by definition, concerned with the parochial. As Frege reminds us, experiment is otiose if the question is what any thinker (or language user) *must* be. But psychology's involvement with the parochial may seem non-threatening to one persuaded of the Martian principle. For it aims for *explicit* accounts of parochial capacities and sensibilities. And one might think an explicit account would make the parochial eliminable: in its explicitness, it would not require a parochial sensibility for grasping it; its issue would be just those perceptions, or intuitions, which it originally took the relevant parochial sense to see (or feel). The *eliminably* parochial—what one could, in principle, do without—is no threat to the Principle.

Chomsky certainly aims for explicitness. But is it an explicitness that makes the parochial eliminable? His interest is in a specifically human (thus parochial) language faculty. But there are various ways to be interested in it. Chomsky's interest is, for one thing, in explicit grammars of specific languages (and in constraints on the form of any such). Such a grammar would eliminate reliance on one sort of intuition, peculiar to speakers of its language: intuitions about the syntactic shapes occurring in that language. It would do so in this way: by a finite set of principles (graspable not just by those speakers) it would generate individuating descriptions of each such shape. Those descriptions would be available to one not sharing the native speaker's intuitions *as to how his sentences are shaped*. The speaker has a feel for when well-formed strings are syntactically different. Given an ability to match such surface strings to the structures the grammar provides for them, one could rely on the grammar for identifying, by those structures, just where there are such differences, and how each such difference relates systematically to others. One need no longer consult the native speaker's feelings. For argument's sake, suppose the Martian, too, is thus served. Chomsky is also (perhaps more) concerned with universal grammar: an account of the general form of the syntactic shapes of *any* human language. We can think of a universal grammar as a schema which became the grammar of a particular human language when values were assigned parameters in it. Let us suppose the Martian equally well served by that theory.

---

[15] Bernard Williams endorses this idea in *Descartes: The Project of Pure Enquiry*, Harmondsworth: Penguin Books, 1978, see especially chapter 2. The idea is elaborated by Adrian Moore in *Points of View*, Oxford: Oxford University Press, 1997.

The Martian might be *that* much better off. There remain at least two problems. First, individuating descriptions of syntactic structures need not enlighten us as to the representational roles of those structures, insofar as they are dedicated to specific ones. So the Martian may well remain unenlightened on that score, thus unable to speak or understand a human language. One might wonder whether a theory of those roles which met the psychologist's normal standards of explicitness, thus relieving human beings (in principle) from reliance on a feel for what happens when a given such role is played, would, necessarily, also enlighten the Martian.

The second problem is one on which Chomsky has been explicit. It is that of making out which shapes occur in some language one encounters—what it is that given humans are up to syntactically. To eliminate the parochial in this domain, one would need (at the least) a discovery procedure for grammars—some set of principles which, for given non-syntactic (in fact, non-linguistic) facts about what the speakers were up to, would predict the syntactic shapes of the sentences they produce. What a universal grammar would say about such procedures is just this: 'Assign values to *these* parameters as, here, a normal human would.' To which a Martian could only reply, 'Thanks, pal.'

On this problem there is one point of agreement between Chomsky and Quine. It is highly unlikely, at best, that any Martianly accessible discovery procedure would predict the presence, in any language, of syntactic shapes of the complexity and subtlety which, Chomsky has argued, humans are prepared to *recognize* in the grammars of human languages. The moral Quine draws is that there are no such shapes in human languages. Or, more cautiously, that there can be no fact of the matter as to whether any given such shape is *the* shape of some sentence or not. That reflects Quine's adherence to the Principle. The moral Chomsky draws is that there are (most likely) no discovery procedures for human grammars. That is to say, in this special case, our ways of telling what our fellows are up to do not reduce to Martianly accessible principles. They rely ineliminably on the parochial. It was in arguing precisely this that Chomsky effected his initial radical re-orientation of focus in linguistics. That aligns Chomsky with such philosophers as John McDowell, and against such others as Quine, Michael Dummett and Bernard Williams. It manifests his firm rejection (and resolute transgression) of the Martian Principle.

Where some area of purported answerability is unquestionably the real thing, adherence to the Principle might lead one to the conclusion that The Mind—the common possession of all thinkers—is a richer and more elaborate affair than one would have thought. Where the purported area can be made to seem open to doubt, the Principle might be used to show that there is no genuine answerability there at all. There might be less of that than one would have thought.

Empiricists, such as Hume, or Quine, are notorious for theses of the second sort. Hume, for example, entertains such a thought about our stances as to one thing's having caused another. He does aim to describe that parochial endowment which yields our *perceptions* as to what causes what. But he makes it difficult to think of this endowment as a *capacity* to *detect* things in the world to which to answer. Quine takes such a view of stances as to what words mean. In each case the conclusion might flow directly from the Principle. In fact, though, typically for an empiricist, Hume and Quine each appeal to two different ideas. The first is that all answerability must ultimately be answerability to the observable; the second is that the argument from illusion is a tool for identifying what really is observable. By that argument, it is not observable that P if anything that might count as such an observation admits of ringers: a situation which, if one were in it, would be not detectably different from that of the supposed observation, but in which not P. For if there are ringers, then the situation putatively of observation might be one in which not P—which could not be so where one had *observed* that P. The upshot in the causal case is that no more than events and their concatenations are observable. In Quine's case, it is that no more is (relevantly) observable than behaviour in a highly attenuated sense: bodily move-ments and emissions (notably of noises). Neither causation nor meaning is plausibly constructible from such materials.

The Principle so applied thus means that neither our attitudes towards causes, nor those towards what words mean, have anything suitable to which they could be answerable; so are not answerable. If there were causes, or things words mean, that is what these stances would answer to. Since they answer to nothing, there are neither causes, nor things words mean.

These specifically empiricist ideas may be an unnecessary detour. Adopting a suggestion by Bernard Williams, perhaps they both just follow from the Martian Principle.[16] Here is a sketch of the idea for the argument from illusion. That argument would be blocked just where, though there is a ringer for the observing situation with respect to P—say, with respect to observing a pig standing before one—there is no doubt that one's situation is *not* a ringer; nothing one need establish to establish that it is not. That is needed since if one did need to establish something, that would be in order to *conclude* that P (that there is, in fact, a pig before one), which is precisely what one does not need to do where this is something one can just observe. But, plausibly, facts of the required form—that such-and-such does, or does not need establishing—if there are such facts, would be visible only to a thinker of a certain special design (ours, say). We (humans, readers of this essay, or whatever) have, perhaps, our shared sense of what ought to be doubted. We cannot expect a Martian to share this. So, by the Martian Principle, there are no such facts. So the argument from illusion is valid.

The Martian Principle is thus perhaps prior to, and more general than, traditional empiricism. Empiricism, though, does highlight one feature of it. The empiricist idea is that where a stance purports to be answerable to the world in some particular way, we can step back from the stance and turn our gaze to the world to see whether there is, in it, anything to which to be answerable in that way. Our investigation will be philosophic, not scientific. Our tools are the argument from illusion, not physical measuring devices. Crucially, though, we can examine the world while the scrutinized stance itself remains *sub judice*, thus without deploying it. We look to the world as it is anyway, independent of how it would be if such stances, or their

---

[16] See Bernard Williams, especially pp. 66–7.

negations, really answered to it. The world, so viewed, must turn up something to which the stance might be answerable. Or, the idea is, there is no such thing. That, we may now note, is also the *modus operandi* of the line of thought that led us to the Martian Principle. On that line of thought, there is a special design which, if taken as conferring a cognitive *capacity*, permits detection of some features of the world to which one might be answerable. But, the idea is, there is a question as to whether the design can be taken in that way: as conferring a capacity rather than a mere illusion of one. That question, the line goes, must be settled by what there really is to answer to, as visible without aid (or interference) of that special design. Unsurprisingly, that idea, whether in its special empiricist form, or more generally, tends either to reduce the scope of our answerability, or to inflate the powers of The Mind (or both).

The Martian Principle lies on one side of two opposing intuitions. One is that, for any *answerable* stance, that to which it is answerable would be just the way it is no matter how anyone was designed to think about such things. No thinker's design could change which stances answered and which did not, among the answerable stances there are to take. (Everything would have been coloured just the way it is no matter how we were designed to think.) The other intuition is: where we are answerable, that to which we are answerable must be identified by what we are prepared, or equipped, to recognize. The phenomenon we thereby think about cannot be other than what we are equipped to acknowledge it to be. (Roughly, being coloured green cannot *diverge* from what we would understand by, or recognize as, being coloured green.) Correct intuitions cannot conflict. The next section explores how these two may be reconciled.

4.4 INVESTIGATIONS

There is an idea with which one might oppose the Martian Principle. Wittgenstein expresses it in *Investigations* §136:

What a proposition is is in one sense determined by the rules of sentence formation (of the German language, for example), and in another sense by the use of the sign in the language game. And the use of the words 'true' and 'false' may be among the constituent parts of this game; and if so it *belongs* to our concept 'proposition' but does not 'fit' it. As we might also say, check *belongs* to our concept of the king in chess (as so to speak a constituent part of it). To say that check did not *fit* our concept of the pawns, would mean that a game in which pawns were checked, in which, say, the players who lost their pawns lost, would be uninteresting or stupid or too complicated or something of the kind.[17]

Truth may *belong* to a stance: it may be part of the stance, not just that things are thus and so, but that *it* is answerable (to whether they are). Truth and falsity may, in that way, belong to its ambitions. Suppose that, taking these ambitions

---

[17] Ludwig Wittgenstein, *Philosophical Investigations*, Oxford: Basil Blackwell, 1953.

to be achieved—holding the words, or stances, answerable as they would thus be understood to be—yields sufficiently orderly results: the stance belongs to a range of stances such that if one supposes them to be answerable to something, it is then not too stupid or complicated to sort out those which then would be correct from those which would then not be. As it may be, the stance is that the lake is blue; there is another that it is not blue; if precisely one of these *must* be the correct one, it is not too stupid to suppose that, with information enough, one could say which. And so, more or less in general, through some impressive enough range of related stances. If this condition is met, the idea is, the stance *is* answerable; there is no further way for it to fail to be, so no further requirement to be met. In particular, satisfying the Martian Principle is no such requirement..

The core of the idea is that the only intelligible questions there are as to answerability are resolvable by what is visible to those taking, or able to take, the relevant stances. Answerability, or lack of it, does not turn on what would be visible of the world, or of the stance's relation to it, only, or *even*, to a thinker differently designed, or from some viewpoint independent of what enables the taking of that stance itself. *Grundgesetze* proposed necessary conditions on answerability; ones whose satisfaction it takes no such foreign form of thought to see. The present idea is, roughly, that such conditions are also sufficient, all that answerability demands. (This is not to say that answerability, or its absence, is always settled by what takers of the stance in fact do say as to what is too stupid, what not. One can be wrong as to just how stupid a given way of treating stances really is.) To put things imagistically, a special design may, in a special way, articulate the way things are into particular ways things are; different special designs might do that differently; the articulations in things that one special design makes visible need not be visible to a thinker embodying another.

Despite this reference to *different* special designs, the main use for this idea is in resisting challenges to our answerability posed by philosophers of our own design, such as Hume and Quine. If the idea is right, then it is an adequate response to such challenges to point to the manifest discipline and coherence of the stances within the challenged area: its being not too stupid, or complicated to treat them as what they represent themselves as being—answerable stances; its being clear enough just how they would thus be treated. If causal stances are answerable, for example, it is clear enough when to say the man on the next stool spilled Sid's beer, when to say it was rather Sid himself, and that where the barmaid pushed the man who bumped the beer, there are two things to say as to who it is who spilled the beer. The idea just is that no more than that is needed to show that Hume was wrong. Similarly, if, by our ordinary standards in such matters, 'livid' means pale, and not purple, with rage, then there is no way for Quine to be right about meaning. Martians, of course, have a right to this idea as well. That matters to us precisely so far as we can see enough about their taking stances to raise specific questions as to whether such-and-such among these are answerable. That need not be very far.

This idea is not answerability by fiat. A stance can take itself to be answerable but fail to be. The world may be not what it was supposed. We assign weight to cheeses, taking ourselves to be dealing in a stable feature of them. If measurements of their weights turn out to vary wildly and unpredictably, it will perhaps turn out that there is no stable feature of a cheese that its weight might be (given what weight was supposed to be); so nothing to which these particular stances might be answerable, so no facts as to what cheeses weigh. That would be, conspicuously, a *mundane* discovery; something the world might teach us in teaching us how it was—a physical, and not a philosophical, discovery.

The idea does, though, exclude the Martian Principle. It allows special design to make thinkers so designed *aware* of something there is in fact to which to be answerable—simply by making us so designed as to satisfy the above requirements in some particular way. By design, we take, or may take, stances which hold themselves answerable in some sufficiently determinate way; it is not too stupid, or etc., to regard them as doing what they thus purport to. Within these bounds, special design may operate *ad lib*. Nothing invisible to us, nor anything on the order of the Martian Principle, would show that expressions of such stances 'really' fall short of saying how things are.

Since Wittgenstein that idea has been most prominent in the work of John McDowell. He insists, for example, that special design may locate for us a phenomenon of memory which may yield non-inferential knowledge of the past, a phenomenon of kindness, facts about which are intrinsically motivating (in a certain way), or a phenomenon of knowledge, including, sometimes, ways of standing towards, say, the pig's being in the sty, which are proof against the argument from illusion. That memory sometimes yields non-inferential knowledge of the past is part of the concept—not in the strong sense that the concept as such somehow makes that *true*, but simply in that, as things stand, it is part of what memory is to be presumed to be. We take stances aimed at answerability to what fits that conception. Is it too stupid to take those stances to be answerable in the way they aim to be—too disorderly to suppose there to be such a phenomenon for them to be about? Patently not. So those stances are answerable to what they purport to be: there is, in fact, *that* phenomenon of memory.

Where special design shapes answerability, *what* those so designed are answerable to is fixed by what they are thus equipped to recognize as to how the relevant form of answerability would work. That captures the second of our pair of opposing intuitions; and thus may seem to threaten the first—that where a stance is answerable, what it answers to if correct is what would be so no matter how, or what, or whether, anyone thought. But the threat is only apparent. For insofar as the second idea captures what answerability is, it is part of the way a stance undertakes to work in undertaking to be answerable. So if the stance does work as it aims to, then any role for what we are prepared to recognize, for our responses, for agreement among us, or for any other feature of our (perhaps special) design, is confined to fixing *what it is* to which we are thus answerable, and not, of any such thing, whether that is so. And now the Wittgensteinian idea applies. Is it too stupid to regard these stances as achieving that aim? Is their behaviour too disorderly for that? If not, then they do achieve it.

An issue, so far suppressed, must now surface. Frege's idea about howling wind was: for each answerable stance, there is the way things are according to it; whether things are *that* way cannot depend on what, or how, one thinks as to their being so. But there are several notions of a way things are. Sid said that the wind is howling. To say that *is* to say what way he said things were: such that the wind was howling. It is that, that is, on one understanding of *the way spoken of*. Now, *is* the wind howling? When would it be? When, for example, howling, and not merely whistling? The answer might be: it depends on what you understand (mean) by howling wind. There is (suppose) a way of thinking of wind howling on which the wind Sid spoke of qualifies as doing that; but also another way of thinking on which it does not. Whether that is right depends on that wind. But suppose it is. Then a further question arises. Should Sid be taken to have spoken of howling wind on the first understanding? On the second? Perhaps on neither in particular? More generally, should the way *that* wind was be counted as the way Sid said it was in saying it to be howling? Or should it not?

If special design makes wind howling something we can think about, then it *cannot* ever work to determine whether wind is howling. That would undermine answerability in just the way Frege suggests. But, without doing that, it can work to point us to answers to the above questions. By its lights, for example, taking Sid to have spoken on the first understanding may be the only reasonable thing to do. It is free to shape our answerability so long as all that it shapes is what we are committed to in thinking, say, that wind is howling—how, for purposes of that commitment, wind howling must be thought of. When, one might ask, should it count as shaping answerability rather than that to which some stance stands in a mere pretence of answerability? Wittgenstein's answer is: it shapes *answerability* (and nothing less) for what represents, or takes, itself as answerable, provided it is not too unreasonable, or foolish, to hold otherwise. That is, *count* it as working towards answerability when it is not too stupid to.

For all *that* latitude, Wittgenstein's idea still collides with the Martian Principle. It was meant to. It is opposed accordingly by Michael Dummett.[18] Dummett's opposition helps exhibit what is at stake. It shows up in his insistence on the possibility of what he calls a 'theory of meaning'. Such a theory, for a given language, targets this phenomenon: fluent speakers of the language can recognize, of indefinitely many novel cases, when it has been used correctly; notably, when given words would have described correctly what they were used of. He insists on two conditions of success for such a theory. First, it must consist of a set of stated principles which generate, from specified inputs, everything competence would allow one to recognize of novel cases—all there is to be recognized, given the language as it is. (The theory must specify what inputs it requires; these will presumably consist in facts about the novel cases, other than facts about what words of the language mean.) Second, the principles must be adequate to serve, in principle, as a cognitive prosthetic for the

---

[18]   See his "What is a Theory of Meaning?" (I and II), in *The Seas of Language*, Oxford: Oxford University Press, 1993.

Martian: perhaps the Martian cannot, unaided, get the hang of what we are on to in recognizing what we do as to what is describable as what; but (considerations of time, attention, and so on, aside) he could operate the principles so as to derive all that we can see intuitively.

Accepting Wittgenstein's idea, one would want to ask why we should think that our sense for what is describable as what can be captured in such a theory. The phenomenon is that there is a range of facts we are prepared to recognize. With Wittgenstein's idea in place, it is not required, for there to be such facts, that they follow from any such set of principles—that there be, even in principle, a prosthetic for the Martian. To insist on that would be to demand more for answerability than answerability itself demands. So to a philosopher like McDowell, Dummett's insistence will look like no more than armchair psychology; thus psychologism of our second sort. Dummett in fact supports his view with a very sweeping claim: any ability to recognize some range of facts is representable as theoretical knowledge, that is, captured by some set of principles. He does not appeal to any special facts about our *linguistic* competence. That heightens the impression of psychologism of this second sort.

Things look otherwise with the Martian Principle in place. Then, where a (supposed) capacity to *recognize* failed Dummett's demands there would be no such capacity at all. In the case of meaning, we were meant to be able to recognize a certain range of *facts*—such-and-such was correctly described as mauve, say. But if a Martian cannot grasp what it would be for such a fact to obtain, or when it would, then there *are* no such facts. Our stances were meant to be *answerable*; but, failing what Dummett insists on, there would be nothing for them to answer to. The fact was meant to be that you *cannot* call that mauve; that it is not true to say so. But, by the Principle, without a cognitive prosthetic for the Martian, there *are* no facts as to what is, and is not, correctly called mauve. If the principle moves Dummett, he understandably insists on what he does.

Is Dummett guilty of psychologism (not Frege's target, but that other form)? That depends on whether the Martian Principle is correct. We have seen one intuitive case for it. How might a case be built against? The general form of a case would look like this: the Principle's rationale rests on envisioning a certain alleged way of failing of answerability; but when we try to do the indicated envisioning, we find that there is really nothing there to be envisioned. Conversely, whatever we *can* envision we can accommodate without being pushed towards the Principle. What the Principle tries to envision is some state of affairs—some way things 'really are'—visible only from (what turns out to be) an imaginary vantage point, one outside of, and neutral between, all special designs. But there is no such vantage point; *a fortiori*, nothing visible from it. What we *can* envision are mundane ways of being under an illusion of answerability—of failing at what we in fact aim at in aiming at that. The Principle rests on the idea of an ultramundane way of suffering illusion; a way that would not frustrate anything we can recognize to be our aims or interests. But, the idea is, there is no such way.

We sometimes, for one purpose or another, classify some things as mauve, others as taupe, others as heliotrope, and so on. We take ourselves thus to be saying how some things *are*. The Principle tries to raise a certain spectre of illusion: in a certain special way we may not be doing what we suppose ourselves to be doing in so classifying things. Our stances here rest on certain expectations of the world; but some of these may, in fact, be disappointed. We may be let down in unnoticed ways; moreover, in ways in principle beyond our ken. We certainly *can* be let down by the world. There *is* such a thing as having one's expectations dashed. But, the thought is, to be let down as to what *we* expect of the world is to be let down in a way representable by *us* as obtaining, from the parochial perspectives available to us in the positions we, in fact, occupy. Perhaps if we looked harder at the things we are classifying, we would notice that what looked mauve one moment looked taupe the next, change being so disorderly here that there is really no point in insisting, in the way we had, that the things in question really *are* mauve, taupe, or etc.

Such intelligible, here discoverable, disappointment does nothing to move us towards the Martian Principle. There is no need yet for the source of our disappointment to be visible to a Martian. Such disappointments happen. But it is enough for disappointment that *we* are capable of grasping them. The disappointment that yields the principle need be no disappointment to us at all. It *would* be nothing we could recognize as such. It is meant to be what *ought* to disappoint us if we could but see the world from some unattainable vantage point—if we could but be the purely neutral observer. But why call that disappointment? Just *what* expectations of ours are dashed here? Precisely what did we suppose ourselves to be doing, in taking the supposedly answerable stances we do, that we in fact are not doing? Just *what* are the relevant stances meant to be, which they are not? Plausibly, nothing they undertook in undertaking to be answerable. If that is so, then there is no reason to accept the Martian Principle.

This, though, must be read as a scheme for a case, and not the case itself. Such a case would need to be detailed beyond our present limits. What matters here most is how the Martian Principle matters to issues of psychologism, and just what makes it seductive.

4.5 NOUVEAUX ESSAIS

The Martian Principle seems, all too often, to present us with a choice: either we are much less answerable than we supposed; or we share much more in common with the Martian than one would have thought. To put this second option in other terms: there is much more to what any thinker would have to be (to be a thinker at all) than seemed at first; much more structure to The Mind, as opposed to merely minds of particular designs. Our current sense of philosophy's task makes us rightly chary of the first option. So the principle militates towards more detailed and elaborate specifications of what any thinker must be. (The problem is not just about moral facts, or facts about so-called 'secondary qualities'. As McDowell has noted, it extends to the correct expansion of such-and-such arithmetical series—a purely arithmetical problem when, but only when, it has been fixed which series is in question. In fact, it arises for any descriptions of sublunary affairs.)

Dummett, moved by the Martian Principle, is led to *a priori* conclusions about how empirical psychology must turn out. If one shares Wittgenstein's more relaxed view of answerability, one will, with McDowell, find this a particular kind of psychologism—not Frege's target, but what we can now see as lying at an opposing pole: *a priorism*, or scientism. One lands at that pole when, to avoid being Frege's target, one ascribes more to The Mind than it rightfully possesses. From a Wittgensteinian perspective, one cannot insist *a priori* that, say, our appreciation of when something is properly called a chair—a specifically human sensibility—must be reducible to principles which say when something *is* to be called a chair, and which could be applied to decide this without reliance on those very human sensibilities. Dummett insists otherwise; a second form of psychologism just in case the Martian Principle itself is.[19]

On Frege's view, logic concerns what any thinker must be. There are two elements in that idea. First, there is the idea that the laws of logic apply to any thought whatever—whether Martian, or ours. Second, there is the idea that the laws of logic capture something one must be prepared to recognize in order to be a thinker at all. Each of these ideas bears various understandings. Might the second form of psychologism lie hidden in either?

The first idea may be innocuous. It can be a valuable insight that the sort of thing a statement of a law of logic undertakes to say is different in kind from, say, the sort of thing a definition in physics undertakes. The latter aims to say what something—perhaps a certain physical quantity—*is to be supposed to be* (in given circumstances, for given purposes). It is consistent with its ambitions that subsequent events should show that, while those suppositions are not right of anything, the quantity it aimed to define is definable in some other way. Definitions in physics represent themselves as such as to be replaceable by others, should the facts so dictate. That feature identifies, in part, what it is they do say. (The point is Hilary Putnam's.) By contrast, a statement of a law of logic aims to say—represents itself as saying—what is hostage to nothing; so what is never to be retracted, what nothing would ever count as making, or showing, false. Such a statement *may* succeed in what it aims at. If so, it is correctly treatable as answerable as it purports to be. So to treat it is to treat *what* it states as what depends on nothing. That treatment is correct *if* the statement can be taken at face value. For it thus to be correct is just what it is for a way things are to depend on nothing. What *can* be so treated need not be a world-independent matter.

---

[19] McDowell portrays Dummett, in such matters, as positing 'hidden mechanisms'—sets of principles which somehow *guide* our intuition. It bears emphasis that hidden mechanisms are the target of *Grundlagen* only if they function to form hidden standards of *correctness*, not if their role is mere psychological explanation. Insisting on such explanation may be scientism. But that is not Frege's target.

As with definitions in physics, this feature of the ambitions of a statement of logic helps fix just what its content is. To state what is hostage to nothing, it must state, so undertake to state, nothing that could be falsified by any way patterns of entailment in the world turn out to be. A logical law must thus not be about conjunction, for example, insofar as conjunction is something open to *proving* to be truth-functional or not. So if the fact to which a statement of logic answers is that conjunction elim- ination holds, that fact may come to little more than what it is for that rule to hold within a given calculus. In the one case, it simply is not that calculus without that rule. As for logic itself, it is simply not the conjunction *logic* is concerned with unless that rule applies to it (for all of which, some, or all, conjunctive thoughts we think might not involve *that* conjunction). Such restriction of the import of the law may prove the price that must be paid for depending on nothing.

It can also be part of the content of a law that it is, whatever else it may be, some- thing universally valid (something holding, say, of *all* thought). That is a demand that *might* be satisfied vacuously. Suppose the law is, or means, that a disjunction follows from either of its disjuncts. Then it might be true of any thought, whether Martian or human, that wherever a disjunction occurs in such thought, it is so related to other thoughts, which are its disjuncts. That is compatible with no disjunct ever occur- ring in Martian thought at all. Perhaps disjunction is not a form in which Martian thought can be answerable. The idea here is not that Martians might think disjunctive thoughts, but not ones for which the law holds. Precisely not: that *would* conflict with the universal scope of the law. Rather: the law holds universally by virtue of this: what it would not hold for cannot count as instancing what it applies to.

This, though, is not how Frege sees things. For him, logic limns features that any thought whatever must have; features that follow from the mere idea of answerabil- ity. So whatever a principle about disjunction tells us, Martian thought encompasses disjunction. That might consist in an insistence that Martian thought, whatever it is, and whether Martians think disjunctive thoughts or not, can be formed into dis- junctions: one can take any two Martian thoughts and disjoin them, the result being something thinkable. (But by whom?) The principle then applies. This commits Frege to a view of what disjunction really is. What for him follows from the mere idea of answerability is that the calculus of truth functions applies to anything that could possibly count as thought. The extra premise is that disjunction could not but be a certain truth-functional connective.

There is now the second idea: one could not be a thinker at all without grasping the laws of logic, that is, without being prepared to recognize that to which a statement of them answers. So here are particular cases of answerability which must not be beyond the grasp of the Martian, even if the Martian Principle is not true in general. What the Martian must be prepared to recognize in the case of propositional logic would be that any thought (available to him) can be put in truth-functional combination with any other, and that the results are *thoughts* with the indicated truth-values. Notably, he can recognize, of any thought he can think, that such-and-such is a negation of it. For Frege (by the move discussed) this just amounts to recognizing conjunctions, disjunctions, etc., and recognizing them as truth-evaluable in the way they in fact are.

There will be parallel things to recognize in the case of predicate logic, though it is more difficult to say just how they follow from the idea of answerability. All of this would be just part of recognizing a thought as a *thought*—that is, as answerable.

Frege tells us that one cannot recognize anything to be any way without thereby, or therein, finding a certain thought true.[20] So one cannot judge at all without judging as to truth, thus without grasping what truth is. He also tells us that truth, though indefinable, is unfolded in the laws of logic (that is, of truth). So one must grasp them to know what truth is, so to judge, or think things, at all. We have just had an idea of what such grasp would come to. It would align Frege with Leibniz, who, in the *Nouveaux Essais*, argues, contra Locke, that knowledge of logical laws cannot be acquired, since one cannot begin on the project of learning anything—one cannot so much as think—unless one already recognizes certain basic laws.[21] Leibniz thought that we can do that because we have certain innate ideas, which, he insists, is equivalent to innate knowledge of certain principles. (This is a particular notion of *part of the concept*, shared by Kant and Frege.) Leibniz thus ascribes to us a specific logical competence—part of our human design, without which we would not be thinkers at all.

The ideas are thus, first, that certain forms of thought must be available to any thinker. (Whatever thoughts he thinks, these are combinable truth-functionally into *thoughts*.) And, second, any thinker must be able to recognize the truth-functional structure of the range of thoughts he can think, and the truth-values and truth-functional dependencies that this imposes on certain elements in that range. (There will be a parallel point for predicate logic.) Is there in this, perhaps, a subtle form of the psychologism of which Dummett's ideas about meaning stand accused?

I close with a speculation. In taking an answerable stance, one employs a conception of just *how* it is answerable. The stance is, in part, that it is answerable in a certain way. Part of any such particular conception is a conception of what answerability itself would be. Again, such a conception must be at work whenever we consider whether a stance has, or should count as having, answered. Frege spells out considerable specifics of what the operative notion must involve. Logic—the laws of truth—*is*, for him, that spelling out. We do recognize our notions of being true and being false in Frege's unfolding of them—though one might haggle over where, on our conception, those laws apply. (One might well resist, for example, the idea that any answerable stance *must* be either true or false, and any reading of the laws that forces that idea on us.)

But is there, in these respects, only *one* way of conceiving answerability? Is it really so that nothing could *ever* count as answerability, but in a different form—that there is flatly no such thing as that? Since Frege, we have come not to expect our concepts to work like that. Even in the case of vixens, it is not quite right to say that there is simply no such thing as something counting as a vixen but not a female fox. (Perhaps

---

[20] "Der Gedanke", p. 34.

[21] G. W. Leibniz, *New Essays on Human Understanding*, Paris: Garnier-Flammarion, 1966. This argument is one main point of book I. See also "On Locke's Essay on Human Understanding" (1696), collected in *New Essays on Human Understanding*, A. G. Langley, trans., La Salle, Illinois: Open Court, 1949. There is a suggestion that Frege thought this in *Der Gedanke*, pp. 61–2.

'female' turns out to be not quite *le mot juste* for that one side of a familiar recognizable distinction.) Answerability is, perhaps, the most central concept in our thinking,
and thus an exception to the rule that concepts alone do not make things true. (For
there to be such a thing as being F, and for such-and-such propositions to be true
is, except in particular circumstances, not just two sides of a single coin.) One need
not doubt answerability's centrality. One might doubt that the normal plasticity of
thought ossifies in the face of that centrality when it comes to thinking about answerability. To the extent that it does not, Frege's picture of logic is a very subtle form of
psychologism.

References

Dummett, M. A. E. (1993). "What is a Theory of Meaning?" (I and II), *The Seas of Language*,
    Oxford: Oxford University Press.
Frege, Gottlob. (1950). *The Foundations of Arithmetic* (1884) J. L. Austin, trans., Oxford: Basil
    Blackwell.
_____ (1967). *The Basic Laws of Arithmetic*, v.1 (1893) M. Furth, trans., Berkeley and Los
    Angeles: The University of California Press.
_____ (1918–19). "Der Gedanke", *Beiträge zur Philosophie des deutschen Idealismus* v. 2,
    pp. 58–77.
_____ (1979). "Logic" (1897), *Posthumous Writings*, H. Hermes, F. Kambartel, F. Kaulban,
    eds., Oxford: Basil Blackwell.
Leibniz, G. W. (1966). *New Essays On Human Understanding* (1751), Paris: Garnier-
    Flammarion.
_____ (1949). "On Locke's Essay on Human Understanding" (1696), in *New Essays On
    Human Understanding*, A. G. Langley, trans., La Salle: Open Court.
McDowell, J. (1998). "Might There Be External Reasons?", *World, Mind and Ethics*,
    J. E. J. Altham and Ross Harrison, eds., Cambridge: Cambridge University Press, 1995,
    pp. 387–95 (reprinted in McDowell, *Mind, Value and Reality*, Cambridge, MA: Harvard
    University Press).
_____ (1996). "Two Sorts of Naturalism, *Virtue and Reasons*, R. Hirsthouse, G. Lawrence,
    W. Quinn, eds., Oxford: Oxford University Press, pp. 149–79 (reprinted in *Mind, Value
    and Reality*).
_____ (1998). "Antirealism and the Epistemology of Understanding", *Meaning and
    Understanding*, H. Parret and J. Bouveresse, eds., Berlin: de Gruyter, 1981, pp. 225–48
    (reprinted in McDowell, *Meaning, Knowledge and Reality*, Cambridge, MA: Harvard
    University Press).
Moore, A. (1997). *Points of View*, Oxford: Oxford University Press.
Williams, B. A. O. (1978). *Descartes, The Project of Pure Enquiry*, Harmondsworth: Penguin.
Wittgenstein, L. (1952). *Philosophical Investigations*, Oxford: Blackwell.

CHAPTER 5

LANGUAGE AS INTERNAL

ANNE L. BEZUIDENHOUT

ACCORDING to internalist conceptions of language, languages are properties of the
mind/brains of individuals and supervene entirely on the internal states of these
mind/brains. Hence, languages are primarily to be studied by the mind and/or
brain sciences—psychology, neuroscience, and the cognitive sciences more generally
(including linguistics and philosophy). This is not to deny that other sciences may
contribute to our understanding too (e.g. evolutionary biology). The internalist
conception of language is most associated with Chomsky, who has argued for it in
many of his writings. See Chomsky (1986, 1990a,b, 1993, 1995, 2000). Chomsky
calls this conception 'I-language' (where 'I' stands for 'internal' and 'individual')
and he contrasts it with a conception that he labels 'E-language' (where 'E' stands
for 'external'). Chomsky thinks that only I-languages are proper objects for scientific
study. (For more on what Chomsky takes to be the prospects for and the requirements on a science of language, see entry by Stainton on 'Meaning and Reference:
Some Chomskian Themes'.)

Chomsky argues that one part of the human brain is specialized for language.
This language system has an innate specification. All normal humans, in virtue of
their membership in the species *Homo sapiens*, are born with their language systems configured in the same way. Call the initial state of the language system S_0.
A universal grammar (UG) is a theory of S_0. Language acquisition on this view is
the development and maturation of the language system in the brain. A language is

Thanks to Robert M. Harnish for reading two earlier drafts of this entry and offering excellent advice
for improving the presentation of my arguments. There are undoubtedly still places where he would
see room for improvement, but this is a much better piece for having had his critical eye pass over it.
Thanks also to Rob Stainton and Ernie Lepore for their suggestions. They too are not to be blamed for
any remaining infelicities.

simply the mature state of an individual's language system. Call this mature state S_m. Of course, language development requires exposure to linguistic input. A child growing up in an English-language environment will end up speaking English, a child in a Japanese-language environment will end up speaking Japanese, and so on. (Talk of English-language speakers is simply a shorthand way of talking of a group of speakers whose language systems are very similar. Languages are more properly thought of as *idiolects*. A language is a "way to speak and understand" (Chomsky, 1993: 49)). What is theorized about in a grammar for one's language is what one knows when one knows a language—i.e. one's linguistic competence. (For more on this, see Smith's entry, 'What I know when I know a Language'). That is, a grammar for one's language is a theory of S_m, the mature state of one's language system.

Connectionists, such as Elman (1999); Seidenberg (1997); Seidenberg, MacDonald, and Saffran (2002), have been critical of various aspects of Chomsky's views. They are not persuaded by Chomsky's "poverty of the stimulus" argument for the innateness of what is described by UG. Thus, they think that far more of language has to be learned and far less is pre-programmed than Chomsky assumes. They also think that Chomsky's focus on linguistic competence is misplaced. They think that language acquisition must be studied in the context of linguistic performance (i.e. of language production and comprehension). This is because factors that influence performance are also important in acquisition. For example, sensitivity to the functional or pragmatic roles of expressions is important in acquisition. Moreover, the statistical properties of words that have been shown to affect performance, such as frequencies of use, also play a role in acquisition (see Saffran *et al.*, 1996).

However, it is important to note that these critics of Chomsky are as committed to an internalist conception of language as is Chomsky. Languages are still properties of the mind/brains of individuals according to this connectionist view. It is just that the mature state of a competent speaker of a language is achieved via a route different from the one envisaged by Chomsky. Multiple constraints are at work, and some of the mechanisms involved in language learning (e.g. those involved in learning to segment a stream of speech into words, or the ones involved in perceiving phonemic contrasts) are the same mechanisms that are at work in learning and performing other *non*-linguistic perceptual tasks. Nevertheless, these connectionists would not deny that the changes being wrought are changes to an individual brain, and that the end result of this process will be a competent adult speaker of a language in the internalist sense.

Connectionists think that Chomsky's emphasis on competence, as opposed to performance, is misplaced. However, their conception of performance is as internalist as Chomsky's conception of competence. Linguistic performance involves the interaction of multiple cognitive "systems"—perceptual systems, general learning systems, motor systems, memory systems, etc. But all of these are internally individuated. Also, although these connectionists emphasize the role of experience in language acquisition, this does not make them externalists. Chomsky too sees a role for experience. All parties to this debate agree that users of a language are embedded in a wider world, and that this wider world impinges on language users in some way.

Internalists agree that had one's experience been different one would have ended up with a different language—with a different S_m. But two people have similar languages if they share something internal, not if they have similar experiential histories. Perhaps it is possible in some cases for different histories to lead to the same internal state S_m. Then these people would share a language, despite having different histories.

5.1 INTERNALISM VS. EXTERNALISM

There are various views about the nature of language and meaning that can be labeled 'externalist', and Chomsky has been critical of them all. It is useful to see Chomsky's anti-externalism as directed towards two distinct targets, which can be called *language externalism* and *semantic externalism* respectively. Language externalists deny that languages are objects whose properties supervene on the internal states of an individual's mind/brain. E-languages are not psychological objects, but exist independently of language users. Semantic externalists on the other hand deny that the referential or intensional properties of the expressions in a language can be fixed independently of the physical and/or social environments of the speakers of that language.

It is possible to be a language externalist but a semantic internalist. For instance, one might hold that languages are abstract objects, and so not psychological in nature, but also hold that linguistic expressions have their reference-fixing properties independently of the physical and/or social contexts of language users. On this view, a single expression-type would have the same reference-fixing powers across different physical/social contexts. It is also possible to accept at least a modified form of language internalism and yet to be a semantic externalist. On this view, which is arguably the view held by Fodor (1987, 1990), languages are systems of mental representations in the mind/brains of individuals. However, while the computational and conceptual role properties of these representations supervene on the internal states of individuals, the referential or intensional properties of these mental representations depend on the wider physical context of language users.

5.1.1 Chomsky's Critique of Language Externalism

Language externalists deny that languages are systems of internal mental representations. (The way in which 'representation' is here understood is broad enough to cover both the traditional symbol system view according to which the things with representational properties are mental *symbols* and the connectionist view according to which objects and properties are represented in a distributed way by *networks of interconnected nodes*. Thus both Chomsky's view and the connectionist view count as internalist conceptions of language.) According to one version of language externalism, languages are systems of abstract rules, where the rules for a language generate all the (possibly infinite) grammatical strings for that language. This is a view of language defended by Katz (1981). Katz argues that such abstract objects can be studied independently of any psychological investigations of language users. Of course, language users must be able to represent one (or more) of these abstract languages in their mind/brains. However, the question as to which of these E-languages a speaker has actually mastered is a completely separate question from the question as to the properties of these abstract objects.

This abstractionist conception of language treats natural languages as akin to the artificial, constructed languages of formal logic. One internalist response will be that constructed languages bear very little resemblance to natural languages. Logical notation strives to eliminate ambiguity, vagueness and other such properties that are characteristic of natural languages. Formal languages are designed for special purposes and need not be constrained by the conditions imposed on human languages by the architecture of the mind/brain. So, using formal logic as a model for natural language is not helpful, as it gives us no purchase on questions about how language is acquired, how it is represented in the brain, or on how our knowledge of language plays a role in language production and comprehension. See Chomsky (2000: 12). The abstractionist might reply that the abstract rules that he posits will reflect the way knowledge is represented and organized in the brain. Language in this sense is an abstract structure that is an image of the causal structures in the mind/brain. However, such an approach concedes the conceptual primacy of I-languages. As Chomsky (2000: 73) says: "Since the language in this sense is completely determined by the I-language, though abstracted from it, it is not entirely clear that this further step [of abstraction] is motivated."

Croft (2000: 2) raises a second problem. If languages are abstract systems of rules then languages are *abstract particulars*. But then languages can't be objects of scientific theorizing, since science is concerned with types, or at any rate with particulars only as instances of types. The abstractionist is likely to respond that it is possible to make generalizations about languages on the basis of a study of abstract particulars. The study of language is like the study of geometry or any other formal, mathematical science and has its own laws or rules. However, such laws would not be empirical laws or generalizations and hence the study of natural languages would not be a part of natural science. On the face of it this is problematic, since human languages share some of the characteristics of other animal communication systems, and to take the study of human languages out of the arena of natural science is to forgo the opportunity to see human languages as evolutionarily continuous with other animal communication systems. Of course, formal sciences can be applied to the natural world, and so a formal science of language could be applied to human and animal communication. But the critic of abstractionism is likely to feel that this reverses the order of investigation. Human languages should in the first instance be thought of as psychological constructs that can be studied by naturalistic means. Insights from other parts of natural science (e.g. ethology, evolutionary biology) might then prove relevant to the study of human languages. When we start with logic and mathematics as the model for human languages we are pointed in the wrong direction.

Another conception of language that denies its psychological nature is the conception that identifies languages with the *products* of linguistic acts, namely with sets of written or spoken or signed expressions (words, phrases, and sentences). Structuralists, hermeneuticists, deconstructionists and others who think that texts are the primary objects of study presumably would advocate such a conception of language. Note that what is produced by a linguistic act is an expression-*token* rather than an expression-*type*. As Smith (1999: 37–8) notes, if languages are identified with sets of *actual* expression-tokens, then languages will not be coherent objects of scientific study, because such sets will consist of both grammatical and ungrammatical strings. One might try to avoid this problem by identifying languages with those possible expression-tokens that conform to certain rules of correct usage. The trouble with this is that if these rules are thought of as abstract, then this view collapses into the abstractionist view discussed in the previous paragraph. On the other hand, if these rules are thought of as mentally represented, then this view is not after all a competitor to internalism.

One might suggest that languages be identified with the linguistic acts themselves, rather than the products of these acts. On this conception, languages would be sets of *utterances*. This view faces problems similar to those just mentioned. Actual utterances are dated particulars (events) and include both correct and incorrect uses of language. If one tries to exclude utterances that involve incorrect uses by appeal to rules for correct usage, then once again the view collapses into either abstractionism or internalism, depending on the nature of the rules that are invoked. Besides, utterances, in virtue of being intentional actions of speakers, are internally related to the mental states that produced these actions, and thus this view treats languages as psychological objects that depend on language users.

Yet another externalist conception of language that is the target of Chomsky's attacks is the "commonsense" view of language advocated by Dummett (1986, 1989). According to this view, languages are social practices that are governed by social conventions. Dummett writes: "The natural choice for the fundamental notion of a language, from the viewpoint that sees language as a practice, is a language in the ordinary sense in which English is a language, or, perhaps, a dialect of such a language" (1986: 473). Dummett is concerned to argue against Davidson (1986), whom he takes to be denying that there are languages in the ordinary sense. Davidson instead takes idiolects as primary (as does Chomsky, although their reasons for making this choice are very different). Dummett protests by saying: "Oppressive governments, such as those of Franco and Mussolini, attempt to suppress minority languages; under such regimes teachers punish children for speaking those languages in the playground . . . Bretons, Catalans, Basques, and Kurds each declare that their language is the soul of their culture. The option does not seem to be open to us to declare that such governments and such peoples are under the illusion that there is anything they are suppressing or cherishing"(1986: 465). Dummett also argues that languages in this sense are independent of any particular speakers of the language (1986: 473), and that such a conception is needed to make sense of Putnam's principle of the division of linguistic labor (462), and more generally of the idea that we can be mistaken about the meanings of the words in our language. Only if languages are independent of individuals does it make sense to say that we have a partial, and partially erroneous, grasp of our own language (468–9).

Chomsky does not deny that there is this commonsense conception of language, or that it is invoked in various sorts of social contexts. However, he is skeptical that this commonsense conception can play a role in the language sciences. He writes: "The concept of language that Dummett takes to be essential involves complex and obscure sociopolitical, historical, cultural, and normative-teleological elements. Such elements may be of some interest for the sociology of identification within various social and political communities and the study of authority structure, but they plainly lie far beyond any useful inquiry into the nature of language or the psychology of users of language" (2000: 49). Chomsky thinks that this social conception of language will be unable to explain certain facts about the structures of languages. For example, consider the ways in which we interpret the pronouns 'herself' and 'her' in the following sentences:

(a) Mary$_i$ expects e_i to pay for herself$_i$.
(b) I wonder who$_i$ Mary$_{*i/j}$ expects e_i to pay for herself$_i$.
(c) Mary$_i$ expects e_i to pay for her$_{*i/j}$.
(d) I wonder who$_i$ Mary$_j$ expects e_i to pay for her$_{j/k}$.

In (a), 'herself' must be coreferential with 'Mary', whereas in (b) it cannot refer to Mary but must refer to someone else. On the other hand, if we replace the reflexive pronoun by 'her', we get a different pattern of co-reference. In (c), 'her' would have to refer to someone other than Mary, whereas in (d), 'her' can refer to either Mary or some other contextually salient female. These facts about the binding properties of pronouns do not seem to be explicable by appeal to any social norm, custom, or practice. Chomsky's answer as to what explains these facts is that certain principles (the principles described in Binding Theory) are built into the initial state of our language systems, and "when certain options left undetermined in the initial state are fixed by elementary experience" (2000: 50), then we have no choice but to interpret examples (a)–(d) in the way we do.

Of course, linguists who hold a social conception of language could graft Chomsky's account of such patterns of co-reference onto their social accounts of other aspects of language (e.g. onto accounts of the ways in which power relations determine linguistic choices). So, in this sense Chomsky's account is not incompatible with social accounts. But the point is that there does not seem to be a purely social explanation for linguistic patterns such as those illustrated in (a)–(d). Following such patterns in one's use of language is not like following the rules of the road or other such social conventions. Learning a language is not like learning the rules of the road, and we couldn't decide to change the way we speak in the same way that we could decide to start driving on the opposite side of the road (as the Swedes did starting on early Sunday morning on September 3, 1967) or decide to start using a metric system of weights and measures (as they did in South Africa starting on September 15, 1967).

Chomsky also thinks that the study of language in Dummett's social sense would come dangerously close to the "study of everything", and so language in this sense "is not a useful topic of inquiry" (2000: 50). Furthermore, there are certain facts about language acquisition that Dummett cannot explain. We say that a child of five is on its way to acquiring a language, say English. But if all adult speakers were to die, and all the five-year-old children were somehow to survive, then whatever these children are speaking would be a human language. Chomsky writes: "Ordinary usage provides no useful way to describe any of this, since it involves too many disparate and obscure concerns and interests, which is one reason why the concept that Dummett adopts is useless for actual inquiry" (2000: 49). (For more on Chomsky's critique of the commonsense conception of language, see the entry by Stainton on 'Meaning and Reference: Some Chomskian Themes'.)

Finally, Chomsky thinks that Dummett's conception of language as a social practice leads to the idea that learning a language is learning how to engage in such a practice, and thus that knowledge of language is a learned ability to engage in such practices. Chomsky attributes a similar idea to Kenny (1984: 138), who argues that to know a language is to have the ability to speak, read, talk to oneself, etc. Dummett and Kenny appear to think that knowing a language is just like knowing how to ride a bike. Linguistic knowledge for these philosophers is knowledge-how rather than propositional knowledge-that. Chomsky (2000: 50–2; 1990: 586–8) thinks this is an absurd view. For one thing, he thinks that it is possible to lose the ability to speak English (e.g. because one is a sufferer of Parkinson's disease) and then to recover that ability (e.g. because one is given a drug that enhances the levels of the chemical L-Dopa in one's brain). He thinks that if Dummett and Kenny maintain that the Parkinson's patient's ability to speak English was there all along (because the patient's knowledge of English was there all along), they will simply have invented a special meaning for the word 'ability' different from the commonsense one. Call ability in this special sense 'K-ability'. Chomsky thinks that K-abilities are introduced merely to avoid the problem that one can lose and regain the ability (in the commonsense sense) to speak a language. Besides, even if knowledge of language involves know-how, know-how cannot be completely analyzed in terms of abilities or dispositions. All know-how involves an irreducible cognitive element (2000: 52). Chomsky writes: 'knowing-how involves a crucial cognitive element, some internal representation of a system of knowledge' (Chomsky, 1990: 565). (For more on Chomsky's notion of knowledge of language, see Smith's entry, 'What I know when I know a Language).

5.1.2 Chomsky's Critique of Semantic Externalism

As noted above, semantic externalists deny that the referential or intentional properties of the expressions in a language can be fixed independently of the physical and/or social environments of the speakers of that language. Chomsky opposes both physical and social versions of semantic externalism. The former version of semantic externalism is associated with work in psychosemantics by Dretske (1981, 1988) and

Fodor (1987, 1990), but also with arguments offered by Putnam (1975). According to this view, to determine the semantic properties of words, we have to take account of the external, causal relations that hold between words and the world. Putnam's Twin-Earth thought experiments are meant to dramatize this point.

Suppose that Fred and Twin-Fred are two individuals who are molecule for molecule duplicates of each other. Fred lives on Earth, where the substance that fills the lakes and seas and falls as precipitation has the chemical structure H_2O. Twin-Fred lives on Twin-Earth, where the substance that fills the lakes and seas and falls as precipitation has the chemical structure XYZ. Also, suppose that Fred and Twin-Fred are ignorant about the chemical composition of the stuffs they call 'water' (either because they live in a time prior to the discovery of the chemical composition of these substances, or because they are exceptionally naive and uneducated people). Since Fred and his twin are molecule-for-molecule duplicates, their language systems are identical from the internal perspective. However, Putnam argues, in Fred's mouth 'water' refers to the substance on Earth whose chemical composition is H_2O, whereas in his twin's mouth the word refers to the substance on Twin-Earth whose chemical composition is XYZ. So, it seems, the referential properties of our terms depend on our relations to external objects, and do not supervene on our internal psychological states. The exact nature of this external, causal relation is a matter of some dispute, and Dretske, Fodor and others have given different answers to this question.

Chomsky (2000: 148–55, 189–94) argues that we should not put too much weight on these Twin-Earth cases. For one thing, such thought experiments appeal to our intuitions, but we can have no intuitions about such cases, because they are framed using technical terms, such as 'extension' or 'reference'. These terms mean exactly what their inventors tell us they mean (2000: 148–9). Moreover, our intuitions here are malleable. If Fred and Twin-Fred were to switch places, unbeknown to themselves and to the others with whom they interact, nothing about the behavior of either would change, and others would treat them as before, as though no switch had taken place. This suggests that 'water' in their mouths means the *same* thing, something that can be characterized from the internal perspective—perhaps something like *the stuff that fills the lakes and seas and falls as precipitation*. (Externalists would dispute Chomsky's internalist characterization of such switching cases. They are happy to assert that after such a switch Twin-Fred's uses of 'water' would refer to H_2O and Fred's to XYZ. Externalists disagree amongst themselves as to whether at least some post-switch uses of such natural kind terms would retain their old, pre-switch meanings. This would depend on such factors as the length of time the person has spent in the new environment, as well as on the context in which the term is being used—e.g. whether it is being used to describe something perceptually present or to reminisce about something from pre-switch days. See Ludlow (1995) and Gibbons (1996) for differing views on this matter.)

If what is at issue is whether or not attributions of meaning to linguistic symbols sometimes appeal to factors beyond the internal resources of the users of those symbols, then Chomsky concedes that sometimes they do. Sometimes we make meaning attributions in a way that overrides the speaker's own internal perspective. Moreover, we don't need exotic examples to show that this is so. Suppose someone is talking to you in 2006 about the battle for Baghdad and the war against Saddam but as the conversation evolves you begin to suspect that your interlocutor is a seriously disturbed ex-soldier who believes the previous Gulf War is still raging. Does one take an external perspective and regard the person as making false claims about the war in Iraq in 2006, or does one adopt the speaker's own perspective and regard him as making true claims about a war that ended more than ten years ago? In different circumstances one might make different decisions about this. Chomsky thinks that the way in which meaning attributions vary with circumstances "is a legitimate topic of linguistic semantics and ethnoscience", but a scientific psychology of language "will proceed along its separate course" (2000: 154).

Chomsky is generally critical of the enterprise of philosophical semantics. He suggests that there is no semantics in the philosopher's sense. Language has only a syntax and a pragmatics. The only notion of semantics that makes sense is *lexical* semantics, and that is a thoroughly internalist enterprise. It does not purport to be characterizing word–world relations, but at most word–word relations. See Chomsky (1995: 26–7). Furthermore, an internalist might argue that it is incoherent to try to theorize about word–world relations. To ask about how words refer to items in the world, we would need some way of characterizing objects in the world that is independent of our linguistic means of referring to them. But such an independent characterization is impossible. Thus this word–world relation cannot be scientifically studied. Only internal aspects of language are scientifically tractable. (For more on Chomsky's critique of the idea that semantics studies word–world relations, see the entry by Stainton on 'Meaning and Reference: Some Chomskian Themes'.)

Chomsky is also critical of the social form of semantic externalism associated with the work of Putnam (1975) and Burge (1979, 1989b). According to this view, the semantic properties of the words of language depend on features of the social environment of the speaker. So, for example, when someone with a pain in his thigh complains to his doctor that he has arthritis, because he does not realize that arthritis is a disease of the joints, his doctor will take him to have expressed a false belief about arthritis, not a true belief about a disease that afflicts joints and other bones equally. Thus it seems as though the semantic properties of an individual's words depend on facts about the linguistic community to which he belongs. As Putnam (1975: 227) says: " 'meanings' just ain't in the *head*!"

Related to this idea of the externalist individuation of meanings is Putnam's thesis of "the division of linguistic labor". This thesis is that we do not always know (or fully know) the meanings of our own words, and in these cases we defer to experts. Thus 'elm' and 'beech' mean two different things in my idiolect, even though the entries in my mental lexicon for these two words contain the same information—something like *deciduous tree*. These words have different meanings because I live in a linguistic community in which there are experts whose knowledge of elms and beeches is sufficiently rich that they are able to tell elms and beeches apart, and to whom I am disposed to defer, when the need arises to be more precise than my own internal resources allow. (For more on semantic externalism see the entry by farkas on 'Semantic Internalism and Externalism').

Burge (1989b), in arguing that there is a social aspect to language, makes a similar point. He distinguishes between concepts and conceptions. Concepts are individuated widely, although conceptions are internalist. My concepts *elm* and *beech* are distinct, even if the conceptions associated with my words 'elm' and beech' are identical. The references of my words 'elm' and beech' are different and hence they must express different concepts. But nothing in my head fixes reference or individuates concepts. Others are often in a better position to determine empirical features of the referents of my terms, and their activity thus plays a role in determining the reference of my words and hence in individuating my concepts.

Chomsky is skeptical about the scientific worth of the social semantic externalist's idea that there is a division of linguistic labor, and the claim that there are experts to whom we defer to determine the referents of our terms. He also denies that the meanings of an individual's words are determined in any interesting sense by community norms. Chomsky identifies three senses in which we can speak of a misuse of language. He calls these the 'individual', the 'community', and the 'expert' senses of misuse of language (2000: 70–3, 143). The first sort of misuse is a case in which a speaker uses a word not in accordance with his own I-language. For example, due to a slip of the tongue one might say 'odd hack' instead of '*ad hoc*'. Such a notion of misuse can be explained from the internal perspective. In the example given, the vowel sounds in the two words are interchanged during the process of articulation.

A second sort of misuse is when speakers use words in ways that violate some sort of community standard. For example, many people say things like 'Me and him are going to the movies', but language purists like William Safire object to these uses on the grounds that these are not correct uses of English. Chomsky thinks that such misuses and their corrections "may be of interest for the study of the sociology of group identification, authority structure, and the like, but they have little bearing on the study of language . . . to say that one variety of English is "right" and another "wrong" makes as much sense as saying that Spanish is right and English is wrong" (2000: 71).

Finally, Chomsky agrees that one's lexical entries for 'elm' and 'beech' may be indistinguishable, and this may lead to misuses, in the sense that one applies these terms in ways that do not accord with the uses of the experts to whom one is disposed to defer. However, Chomsky denies that this establishes that meanings are individuated widely, by reference to one's linguistic community. For one thing, the expert to whom one defers about elms and beeches may be an Italian gardener who corrects one's usage through reference to technical Latin names that one shares. In other words, the network of 'experts' that one relies upon might not line up in any straightforward way with any linguistic community to which one can plausibly be said to belong. So, the fact that one has a disposition to be guided by expert knowledge does not support the social theory of reference.

Burge (1989a) claims that an examination of work in cognitive psychology shows that even practicing scientists assume that concepts/meanings are individuated widely. Patterson (1991) takes issue with this. She discusses the models that are used by developmental psychologists working on children's acquisition of semantic knowledge. She shows that these scientists are not committed to describing the concepts a child attaches to words in terms of the concepts normally attached to those words in the child's linguistic community. The semantic content of the child's representational states is thus not individuated with reference to linguistic environment in the way Burge claims it is. Patterson's arguments support Chomsky's claim that scientific work in linguistics and cognitive science more generally is conducted from an internalist perspective, as there is "no realistic alternative" (2000: 156; see also 158–63).

5.2 THE CONNECTION BETWEEN INTERNALISM AND INDIVIDUALISM

We have seen that internalism about language is the view according to which language supervenes on the internal psychological and/or neurological states of an individual. Such a view is in opposition to externalist conceptions of various sorts, such as abstractionist, product-oriented and commonsense conceptions of language. Chomsky's internalism is connected to his acceptance of individualism. According to individualism, the individual and his idiolect are the primary objects of scientific study. We can of course make generalizations across language users, provided that the individual users live in a homogeneous environment. But the order of explanation is from the individual level to the social level, rather than vice-versa. Thus social generalizations are explained by appeal to facts about individuals.

For example, the pronunciation of English vowel sounds has changed a great deal since the time of Chaucer. In particular there were dramatic shifts in pronunciation that occurred some time during the fifteenth century. This is traditionally known as the Great Vowel Shift. Linguists explain this shift by appeal to facts about how vowel sounds are articulated in the mouth. The long vowels became articulated with the tongue higher up in the mouth. So what may look to be a sociological fact (namely how words are pronounced in some linguistic community) is explained by appeal to a physiological fact about individuals (namely how sounds are articulated in the mouth and the fact that changes in the place of articulation of one sound will force a compensatory change in the place of articulation of other sounds).

One could argue that there are certain social generalizations that cannot be accounted for in individualist terms. For example, speakers choose to use polite forms of address when talking to those in authority. Here it seems we cannot explain the speaker's linguistic choices without appeal to social factors, such as power relations, and the social institutions that realize and sustain these power relations. An individualist would respond that the real explanation lies at the level of the individual and his mental states, for the speaker would not behave in the way he does unless he wanted to. The anti-individualist might reply that the individual's wants are them-selves socially constructed. The individualist in turn is likely to respond that the social forces at work here have nothing to do with language or linguistic choices in particular. They are equally at work (if at all) in explaining people's choices of dress, foods to eat, places to dine, movies to watch, and so on. Thus any such social explanations are orthogonal to the concerns of linguists. This is not to say that these social explanations are uninteresting or misguided. It is simply to say that they are not aimed at a level of explanation that would account for linguistic choices in a way that they wouldn't equally account for non-linguistic choices.

Chomsky does not deny that individuals live in social environments and that these social environments can have an impact on language. For example, Chomsky does not deny that the way in which one speaks can be socially stigmatized, because one's language differs from the language of those in power. Chomsky is sometimes taken to be claiming that the social factors influencing language that are studied by socio-linguists are uninteresting or unimportant. But Chomsky strenuously denies that this is his view (2000: 156). On the contrary, he thinks that these topics may be among the most important that face humanity. However, he also thinks that these topics are unlikely to yield to scientific study, and that insights here are more likely to come from the study of literature or from branches of learning other than natural science. Chomsky argues that the forces that drive social life are too diverse and obscure, and even if we could identify them, they are likely to prove irrelevant to the ques-tions of concern to the language sciences (namely to questions about how language is acquired, how it is represented in the brain, and how it is used in production and comprehension). Chomsky also thinks that inasmuch as we do make scientific pro-gress in this field (e.g. in theories of discourse processing) it will be because we've adopted an internalist perspective.

Chomsky's own writings on all the topics discussed above are very clear and access-ible. The essays collected in Chomsky (2000) are especially recommended for further study. The commentaries on Chomsky's ideas by Smith (1999) and by Stone and Davies (2002) are also excellent sources for further information on these topics. The former contains useful characterizations of empirical findings (e.g. about language impairment) that support Chomsky's position. The latter contains a challenge to Chomsky's naturalism and to his privileging of the methods of science in the study of natural language.

REFERENCES

Burge, T. (1979). 'Individualism and the Mental', *Midwest Studies in Philosophy* 4: 73–121.
_____ (1989a). 'Individuation and Causation in Psychology', *Pacific Philosophical Quarterly* 70: 303–22.
_____ (1989b). 'Wherein is Language Social?' in A. George (ed.) *Reflections on Chomsky* (Oxford: Blackwell), 175–91.
Chomsky, N. (1986). *Knowledge of Language: Its Nature, Origin and Use* (New York: Praeger).

_____ (1990a). 'Language and Mind', in D. H. Mellor (ed.), *Ways of Communicating* (Cambridge: Cambridge University Press), 56–80.

_____ (1990b). 'Language and Problems of Knowledge', in A. Martinich (ed.) *The Philosophy of Language*, 2nd edition (Oxford: Oxford University Press), 581–99.

_____ (1993). *Language and Thought* (Wakefield, RI: Moyer Bell).

_____ (1995). 'Language and Nature', *Mind* 104: 1–61.

_____ (2000). *New Horizons in the Study of Language and Mind* (Cambridge: Cambridge University Press).

Croft, W. (2000). *Explaining Language Change: An Evolutionary Approach* (Harlow: Longman Linguistics Library).

Davidson, D. (1986). 'A Nice Derangement of Epitaphs', in E. Lepore (ed.), *Truth and Interpretation: Perspectives on the Philosophy of Donald Davidson* (Oxford: Blackwell), 433–446.

Dretske, F. (1981). *Knowledge and the Flow of Information* (Cambridge, MA: MIT Press).

_____ (1988). *Explaining Behavior: Reasons in a World of Causes.* (Cambridge, MA: MIT Press).

Dummett, M. (1986). 'A Nice Derangement of Epitaphs: Some Comments on Davidson and Hacking', in E. Lepore (ed.) *Truth and Interpretation: Perspectives on the Philosophy of Donald Davidson* (Oxford: Blackwell), 459–76.

_____ (1989). 'Language and Communication', in A. George (ed.) *Reflections on Chomsky* (Oxford: Blackwell), 192–212.

Elman, J. (1999). 'Origins of Language: A Conspiracy Theory', in B. MacWhinney (ed.) *The Emergence of Language* (Hillsdale, NJ: Lawrence Erlbaum Associates), 1–27.

_____ (1987). *Psychosemantics: The Problem of Meaning in the Philosophy of Mind.* (Cambridge, MA: MIT Press).

_____ (1990). *A Theory of Content and Other Essays* (Cambridge, MA: MIT Press).

Gibbons, J. (1996). 'Externalism and Knowledge of Content', *Philosophical Review* 105: 287–310.

Katz, J. (1981). *Language and Other Abstract Objects* (Totowa, NJ: Rowman and Littlefield).

Kenny, A. (1984). *The Legacy of Wittgenstein* (Oxford: Blackwell).

Ludlow, P. (1995). 'Social Externalism, Self-Knowledge and Memory', *Analysis* 55: 45–9.

Patterson, S. (1991). 'Individualism and Semantic Development', *Philosophy of Science* 57: 15–35.

Putnam, H. (1975). 'The Meaning of "Meaning" ', *Mind, Language and Reality: Philosophical Papers* vol. 2 (Cambridge, Cambridge University Press), 215–71.

Saffran, J., Aslin, R. and Newport, E. (1996). 'Statistical Learning by 8-Month-Old Infants', *Science* 274: 1926–8.

Seidenberg, M. (1997). 'Language Acquisition and Use: Learning and Applying Probabilistic Constraints', *Science* 275: 1599–603.

_____ , MacDonald, M. and Saffran, J. (2002). 'Does Grammar Start where Statistics Stop?' *Science* 298: 553–4.

Smith, N. (1999). *Chomsky: Ideas and Ideals* (Cambridge: Cambridge University Press).

Stone, T. and Davies, M. (2002). 'Chomsky among the Philosophers', *Mind and Language* 17: 276–89.

CHAPTER 6

LANGUAGES AND IDIOLECTS: THEIR LANGUAGE AND OURS

JAMES HIGGINBOTHAM

WHEN my eldest son, some years ago, volunteered about some escapade or another, "It was so fun," I was astonished. I knew that people said, "It was a fun thing to do," as though *fun* could be a nominal modifier. But "It was so fun?" Sounds like, "It was so water." Ridiculous. However, as I was to learn, the word *fun* has in my lifetime adopted adjectival behavior (not yet recorded by Cambridge, or Merriam-Webster). The younger generation, therefore, did not learn their grammar lesson properly. They got it wrong. But is it wrong? After all, that generation merely extended the word *fun* from its use as an abstract mass noun, like *information*, to an adjective, presumably taking their cue from already prevalent nominal compounds such as *fun thing*, or *fun fur*. Anyway, who says *fun* is only a Noun?

We are all used to novel words. But my son and his peers had not just extended the vocabularies they were taught; rather, they had created something that, to my ears, perceptibly conflicted with what had been established. Unlike simple extensions of vocabulary, then, theirs was a *deviant* addition. Other examples abound, such as *paranoid* as a transitive adjective meaning *greatly afraid of* ("I'm paranoid of snakes"). The reader's experience will surely provide still more. Besides additions, historical studies especially reveal many examples of deviant *subtractions*, linguistic departures that actually shrink linguistic resources, such as the loss of infinitives in Greek. Or consider the obligatoriness in contemporary English of subject-raising with *become*, replacing the expletive subject *it* with the subject of the non-finite complement clause. The alternation with *seem*, as in (1) and (2), used to be permitted with *become*, as in (3) and (4); but (4) is ungrammatical in contemporary English:

(1) It sometimes seems that the accounts are illegible.
(2) The accounts sometimes seem to be illegible.
(3) The accounts sometimes become illegible.
(4) It sometimes becomes that the accounts are illegible.

To complete the circle of possibilities, there are examples of what may be called deviant *replacements*, where one form or construction alters its significance, to be replaced by another that acquires the significance that it used to have. The history of the tense systems of the Romance languages is a well-known example. In all of these cases of historical change (or, in the case of adjectival *fun*, of historical change in the making) learners project something other than the grammars to which they were exposed. My examples have involved semantics and syntax; but of course they are rife in phonology as well.

Historical phenomena apart, an elementary survey of the stratification of language by social class, geographical region, and other variables rapidly reveals cases where *x*'s speech is, from *y*'s point of view, deviant in one or another respect; that is, neither merely extending or contracting *y*'s resources, but perceptibly at odds with *y*'s grammar. My son's "It was so fun," or the common use of *livid* to mean *flushed* rather than *pale*, are cases in point; likewise the vulgar use of *fish* to include lobsters. In all of these cases the same question arises: are the deviant mistaken, or are they merely different? The question is often symmetrical, as deviation can be, but need not be, a two-way street: if I don't use *fun* as an adjective I am merely conservative; but if I use *livid* to mean exclusively *pale*, I may deviate from my neighbor, as she, who uses it only to mean *flushed*, deviates from me.

Thus far I have spoken of developed languages. But languages are learned, and learned over substantial time. Hence the question arises how to think of what we apprehend in learners as merely partial grasp or understanding. Even mature speakers lack a comprehensive understanding of many terms that they themselves may use, and hear used: in my case of terms such as *carburetor, tort, enzyme*, and on and on. From this point of view, grammatical construction, meaning, and pronunciation confront both the individual speaker and her potential critics as objective matters, which they may or may not get right.

At the same time, criticism of the vulgar use of *livid, fun*, or *fish* seems out of place in a description of what goes on in the user of language; that is, the nature of her internalized grammar. The deviant speaker's meaning can be as definite as anyone else's; and where it is indefinite (as in, say, my hazy use of *tort*) I should be as resentful of being upbraided by the legally knowledgeable as they would be for my know-it-all correction of their philosophical sloppinesses.

We have, then, a genuine dialectic. Language, on the one hand, is a social phenomenon, showing changes over time and space, and reflecting the interlocking social concerns and expertise of a variety of human endeavors, a "division of linguistic labor," in Hilary Putnam's memorable phrase. On the other hand, there is the grammar of the individual speaker at a particular time, and in a particular setting, through which are expressed such thoughts as we may possess and apprehend. How should one think of these factors in an account of language and thought? This article is devoted to an investigation of that foundational issue. The issue is foundational along at least three dimensions: (i) as it concerns the factual or evidential background that goes into the explanation of linguistic phenomena; (ii) as it bears upon some normative aspects of language, including deviant speech in the sense illustrated above; and (iii) as it influences our view of the relations between the thought a person expresses and the linguistic forms she uses.

Let us say that a conception of language, as bearing on the questions just mentioned, is *idiolectal* to the extent that social phenomena—deviant speech, partial understanding, historical change, and the like—are to be viewed as deriving from the interactions of the several grammars of individuals, without any essentially social residue, and say that it is *social* to the extent that it relies upon social variables. Even with these rough and ready labels we may clarify some issues.

First of all, a social conception of language does not deny the existence of idiolects; rather, idiolects would be construed as idiolects *of* a common language, and would for example take this article as written in an idiolect of English, reflecting its author's particular style and background. Diversity in speech, as in much else, has its place within community. When my English friends say that something costs "fifty quid," I understand them to mean it costs fifty pounds. *I* wouldn't say "fifty quid," and I wouldn't expect them to refer to an American ten dollar bill as a "sawbuck." But we are, in our different ways, speaking English.

Second, there are many aspects of social life for which a social conception of language is essential. If we think of "languages" in the sense of languages recognized at the United Nations, or languages in which it is possible to give expert testimony in court, take a written driving test in the state of California, or publish a daily newspaper, then broad sociopolitical divisions among languages come to the fore. These, however, are not of any obvious interest in the scientific project of describing the organization of human speech along the familiar dimensions of semantics (and pragmatics), syntax (including morphology), and phonology (including at least parts of phonetics). Moreover, and crucially for our dialectic, they come on the social scene only *after* the fundamentals of human first languages, the ordinary medium of communication, are in place. Thus, if we take native linguistic competence in Noam Chomsky's sense as the target of linguistic explanation, then the sociopolitical dimension of language appears to drop out of the picture.

Third, it is commonplace to say that languages are *conventional*; that is, that a language belongs to a population because of the intertwining, and mutually agreeing and reinforcing, mental states and dispositions of its members.[1] Conventions are essentially among several individuals; hence the social conception may inherit

---

[1] Lewis (1975) is an important exposition of this view.

plausibility from the assumption of conventionality. Certainly, some relatively sophisticated aspects of language, many of them pragmatic, are conventional, as conventional as the use of "Please" and "Thank you." In further support of the conventionalist view, we may observe that, just as the exchange of commodities for money requires agreement on value given and value received, so the successful exchange of thoughts in communication requires intent to line up with interpretation. The hearer must interpret the speaker as the speaker intends to be interpreted, and the speaker must intend something that the interpreter is able to grasp as intended. From these points alone, however, it does not yet follow that language is conventional in a strong sense; that is, that more than on-the-spot agreement is at stake in communication.[2] And anyway, as I will suggest below, there is a distinct possibility that communicative success of the ordinary sort is brought about by other means.

Social dimensions of language, then, are not to be dismissed just because there is individual variation; but neither are they to be swallowed whole just because of the advanced human social organization that gives a point of sorts to the political demarcation of languages, or because of appeals to convention.

I have opposed the social conception of language to the idiolectal, one whose units, at a natural extreme, are the dialects of individuals at times, and perhaps relative to style of speech, and social occasion. Units intermediate between the individual-at-a-time and the wider society are possible as well, and find their place in Linguistics in the study of such phenomena as "code-switching," or the intermingling of diverse forms, for instance from English and Spanish in casual speech in some urban settings in America. My exposition, however, will chiefly concern the extreme idiolectal view. That view, as well as the intermediate cases just envisaged, often draws force from examples such as those I have given, of *livid, fish*, and the like. It pronounces, with justification in many cases: nobody is "right," and nobody is "wrong." They have their language and we have ours; and that's all.

However, a point to be noted at the very beginning is that an idiolectal conception of language does not at all imply the absence of external, including social, features in the individuation of the forms and meanings attaching to a particular person's idiolect. So much, even if in the end it is but an empty reminder, is a matter of logic. It is granted that where a social conception sees idiolects as variations within a larger scheme, an idiolectal conception takes the scheme itself to be built up through such regularities as present themselves in common background and interaction among individual speakers. But the individual is not therefore to be considered as if in isolation. People can depend upon one another for their words and their grammars. To take a simple analogy: the properties of a pine forest, whether it grows or contracts, flourishes or withers, its density and fecundity, arise from the properties of its individual trees and saplings; it by no means follows that what goes on with an individual tree is independent of its neighbors.

---

[2] I take this point from (my understanding of) Davidson (1986).

A further disclaimer: to say that a conception of language is idiolectal is to say that generalizations over "the language" are summary accounts that are made true or false through the states and transitions between states of individuals. But that is not to say that the summary accounts are in any sense reducible to statements about individuals, in practice or in principle. Reducibility in practice of, say, the advent of obligatory pronominal subjects in French is out of the question, and would be so even if we possessed an exhaustive list of utterances in French from Roman times to the present. But reducibility in principle is also questionable, as learners and those from whom they learn are tied by relations of authority and love (among others) that are essentially social, and whose influence is substantial.

An idiolectal conception of language is compatible with a substantive role for external things—objects, including other people—in the characterization of idiolects. Illustrations of this role are not hard to come by. The point of looking outward from the individual is pretty evident for the case of reference to perceptually encountered objects: had the world been significantly different, a person with the same molecular history would have acquired, and called by the same familiar names, different physical and other concepts (see Burge (1986) for careful elaborations). An idiolectal conception of language is by no means committed, and has some reason to be opposed, to internalism, and to *individualism* in Burge's sense; that is, to the view that the organization of the body, abstracting from external things, is constitutive of any linguistically significant aspect of language (for discussion of various senses of internalism, see Bezuidenhout, this volume; and see both Bezuidenhout and Farkas, this volume, for exposition and analysis of individualism and anti-individualism in the sense of Burge). It remains to examine several areas where, as I shall argue, internalism fails.

First of all, consider my son's extension of *fun* to an adjective, presumably by some internalized formula, or lexical entry, such as (5):

(5) *fun*: adj., true of an activity x iff for a person to engage in x is fun for that person.

I may have any number of reasons for "correcting" my son: perhaps he'll miss a question on an English achievement test. But these reasons for my action have no tendency to show that he was somehow linguistically wrong in extending *fun* as in (5), or that I am right in not doing so. Similar remarks go for the person whose *livid* means *flushed*, and those who call lobsters fish.

On the other hand, there are active linguistic mistakes that are not so readily dismissed. Thus, to deploy an example due to Burge (1982), many people believe, falsely, that two parties have made a contract only if their agreement is supported in written form. In learning otherwise, they stand, and conceive themselves to stand, corrected. The critical point is that they change their views for *cognitive* reasons; that is, because, in point of fact, contractual obligation is created by open mutual understanding, to which written documents bear only an evidentiary relation. Their semantic divergence, then, is not a mere difference between them and others, but a real error, properly classified as such by those who are corrected.

All of us have been, and presumably still are, in the following linguistic bind. We have assigned a meaning to some word or expression that gets it wrong, in major or minor ways. But we *intend* the meaning of those around us, from whom we derived the expression in the first place. We are therefore incoherent, as there is no single meaning we intend. Consider the plight of Adam, who is ready to say (2):

(2) Smith and Jones have an open oral agreement, but no contract.

If we evaluate Adam's *contract* according to his internal lexical entry, he speaks truly, or so we may suppose. But if we evaluate that word according to the public meaning, *which Adam also intends*, he contradicts himself. How then do we evaluate Adam's statement?

One answer would be: go for the personal lexical entry. But that answer overlooks the point that Adam doesn't intend to deploy just his own personal understanding of the expression 'contract'; and of course it omits that Adam, once appraised by the lawyers, takes himself to have been corrected, and changes his views for good reason. Just as lopsided would be: go for the public word. For that would omit that Adam in saying (2) gave voice to a definite belief of his, namely that Smith and Jones's agreement had not been written down. It is not that there is just one thing that Adam said and intended to say in saying (2), and we have a dilemma about which it is. Adam is just in a bind.

If the above is correct, then besides the cases where linguistic differences are merely differences, one side or another of which may be "correct" for one or another extraneous purpose, there are cases where one's internalized assignment of meaning goes astray; and in those cases the speaker's intentions actually conflict with their internal assignments of meaning. The difference between the cases, it is to be stressed, is itself owing to differences in the thoughts of individual speakers. If I don't care how icthyologists use the word *fish*, I shall not change my ways just because of some pedant's alleged correction, and if I don't mind being etymologically challenged I shall not refrain from saying that someone red with anger was "livid with rage." But for those cases that I care about for good reason, my intentions in speaking, and the form of my lexical entries, will reflect my position as one user among many of an expression we have in common. I am not bowing to authority, but recognizing, in language as elsewhere, substantial differences in knowledge.

In support of internalism, it is sometimes presupposed that the individual speaker is an infallible authority on what her words mean. Of course, individual speakers *are* in an important sense authorities on the meanings of their words. So the presupposition to be questioned is not that people, or those of appropriate maturity anyway, have first-person authority over their meanings, as they do over their beliefs, desires, and intentions, but rather that, if language is idiolectally based, then a speaker's words must mean *whatever* she thinks they mean; that is, that it is her conception of what they mean that endows them with such meaning as they have. On a non-internalist view, however, the speaker's contribution is only part of the story. In language as elsewhere, one's conception of things may deviate from a norm to which one is already committed (for further discussion of the normativity of meaning, see Wilson, this volume).

In illustrating the non-internalist view I have been speaking of an extreme case, namely of an actual mistake in the interpretation of an expression. More common is the case of merely partial understanding. Suppose the car won't go properly. I take it to the mechanic, and am told there is "a leak in the gasket." I can convey this information to others even though *I* don't know what a gasket is. In so doing, I am no mere parrot, as I would be if in Iceland I should repeat to an Icelander something said to me in Icelandic, without the least comprehension of what it was. Rather, so the example suggests, I am using, and intending to use, a word *with its meaning*, even if I myself have only a slender understanding of what that meaning is. And so it would be for me, and no doubt the reader, with many other words. No amount of internal investigation of us will determine what we meant.

I have remarked that, as a matter of logic, internalism is not implied by an idiolectal conception of language, and have subsequently argued by example that it fails in general anyway, on account of a variety of cases of errors and incomplete understanding on the part of the mature speaker. These phenomena apart, there are serious questions about the acquisition of a first language, whose answers, insofar as they can be discerned, are critical for understanding the role of social phenomena in the speech of individuals. I shall put some of these questions very abstractly, illustrating below with reference to a particular representative example.

Linguistic theory, as I am considering it here, aims to describe and to explain the genesis under normal conditions of the internalized grammars of human beings, their linguistic competence in Chomsky's sense. The objects of explanation are widely various, and all but a few of them arise in the context of ongoing theory. We would view aspects of linguistic competence as social, in one good sense, to the degree that the notion of *success*, together with motivational factors, *intending to speak as others do*, for instance, come into the picture; indeed, we have appealed to these notions in advancing a non-internalist idiolectal conception of language, supported by examples such as those given. However, it cannot be decided a prior what role, if any, these notions play in the growth of language in normal human children, or in the basic structures and interpretations of expressions that come in the fullness of time. For it is perfectly conceivable that assignments of structure and meaning, even as made in rational response to external speech and perceptual situations, proceed *blindly*; that is, without motivation, or any recognizable striving for success. Success indeed is achieved (emphatically not "success in communication," as communication may succeed or fail for adventitious reasons, but rather success in grasping the levels of linguistic structure and their interactions, which are revealed only through a theoretical construction on the basis of the perceptual and linguistic evidence), but it would be the kind of "success" associated with, say, the maturation of small motor control, rather than self-conscious learning. In much of the contemporary literature, the picture of language is not that of the learner's passing through stages of partial learning, or of learning only part of the language to be acquired, but rather as passing through a triggered sequence of individual competences, tending toward a steady state, thereafter elaborated only little. To this extent an internalist idiolectal view of acquisition and competence would be strengthened.[3]

To choose one case for the purposes of illustration, consider the English *resultative* construction, illustrated by (6) and (7):

(6) John wiped the table clean.

(7) Mary called the waiter over.

It's evident that if (6) is true then the table comes to be clean as a result of John's wiping it; likewise that (7) means that the waiter comes to be "over (to her)" as a result of Mary's calling him; hence the name of the construction. Two notable points: (i) the resultative construction is very common in some languages (English, Chinese, Dutch), absent or very nearly absent in others (Italian, Japanese); (ii) it is *lexically particular*, in the sense that not every construction that fits the kind of meaning attaching to (6) and (7) is acceptable. For point (i), we need to explain how the speaker of English comes to know about the construction and its meaning, and why speakers of Italian, say, don't have it, or bother to make it up. For (ii), as noted in various work, including especially Bowerman (1982), we need to explain the unacceptability of (8) and (9) (the latter actually volunteered by a child speaking English):

(8) John wiped the table dirty.

(9) I pulled [the papers] unstapled.

Obviously, a table can become dirty as a result of wiping it; and papers can come unstapled as a result of pulling on them. But (8) and (9) are odd, to put it mildly.

The resultative construction is not universally attested, and therefore must be acquired. The child learning English, or Chinese, hears *instances* of it, and must somehow recognize them as such. The instances must be generalized, through some procedure. Once these matters are in place, this particular aspect of ordinary competence is set. The intellectual process, guided by some prior conception of the nature of human language, may or may not, for all that has been said, be guided also by social factors. But even if it is not so guided; that is, even if it represents only the flowering of a native capacity under appropriate conditions, it will support communication: for, all that is required is that the learner wind up in the right place; that is, the same place more or less as everyone else. No appeal to convention in any serious sense is wanted, or so it would appear.

Further questions, if anything more difficult than those just considered, arise in connection with linguistic differences, and the child's volunteering e.g. of the unacceptable (9). From the fact that the child learning Italian hears only sparse instances of the resultative, it by no means follows that the construction is generally excluded; but such is the case. Likewise, the child learning English has to tailor the generalization of the resultative, so as to exclude (8) and (9) among others. But how is this feat accomplished? In the Italian case, the system that would generate the

---

[3] For a recent survey, see Guasti (2004).

resultative construction has to be put out of commission. In the English case, it's a matter of tailoring usage. Whether social features play a role in either remains open.

In this article I have reviewed several prominent considerations in favor of an idiolectal, but non-internalist, conception of language, insofar as linguistic investigation is concerned with the nature and genesis of the grammars of speakers, acquired under normal conditions, and the relations between the thoughts they express and the meanings they conceive expressions to have. That is not to deny that essentially social conceptions are wanted for other purposes. However, if I am right, appeals to language as convention, or to success in communication, do not of themselves carry much force against the idiolectal conception. Conversely, that conception does not support internalism as much as may at first appear. The complexity of the relations between language and thought, exemplified by the phenomena of linguistic error and partial understanding, makes work for the theory of meaning and the acquisition of meaning, in the individual and in interpersonal communication.

REFERENCES

Bowerman, M. (1982). "Starting to Talk Worse: Clues to Language Acquisition From Children's Late Errors." In Strauss, S. (ed.), *U-Shaped Behavioral Growth*. New York: Academic Press.

Burge, T. (1979). "Individualism and the Mental," in French, P. *et al.* (eds.), *Midwest Studies in Philosophy, vol. 4: Studies in Metaphysics*. Minneapolis: University of Minnesota Press.

_____ (1989). "Wherein is Language Social?" George, A. (ed.), *Reflections on Chomsky*. Oxford: Basil Blackwell. pp. 175–91.

Chomsky, N. (1986). *Knowledge of Language: Its Nature, Origins, and Use*. New York: Praeger.

Davidson, Donald (1986). "A Nice Derangement of Epitaphs." In LePore, E. (ed.), *Truth and Interpretation: Perspectives on the Philosophy of Donald Davidson*. Oxford: Basil Blackwell. pp. 433–46.

Guasti, M.-T. (2004). *Language Acquisition: The Growth of Grammar*. Cambridge, MA: The MIT Press.

Higginbotham, J. (1991). "Remarks on the Metaphysics of Linguistics." *Linguistics and Philosophy* 14, 4. pp. 555–6.

_____ (1988). "Knowledge of Reference." In George, A. (ed.), *Reflections on Chomsky*. Oxford: Basil Blackwell. pp. 153–74.

Lewis, D. (1975). "Languages and Language." Gunderson, K. (ed.), *Minnesota Studies in the Philosophy of Science, vol. 7*. Minneapolis: University of Minnesota Press. Reprinted in Lewis, *Philosophical Papers*, vol. I. Oxford: Oxford University Press pp. 163–88.

PART III

THE NATURE OF MEANING

CHAPTER 7

RULE-FOLLOWING, MEANING, AND NORMATIVITY[1]

GEORGE WILSON

AT §138 of the *Philosophical Investigations*, Wittgenstein raises an objection to the view that the meaning of a word is determined by its use—a view which, with qualifications, he has seemed in earlier remarks to endorse. He says, "But we *understand* the meaning of a word when we hear or say it; we grasp it in a flash, and what we grasp in this way is surely something different from the 'use' which is extended in time!" Moreover, as he indicates in §139, what we grasp in understanding seems to determine how the word, so understood, is to be applied. In raising this concern, Wittgenstein seems to be thinking of Frege's views on sense and his own views at the time of the *Tractatus*. These considerations lead him to investigate what it is that might come before our mind when we mean or understand a word. He notes that, when I understand the word "cube," what comes before my mind may be, for instance, a mental picture of a cube. However, he argues that a picture or something like a picture can not determine how the associated word is meant to be applied. Even if the picture has been evoked with the intention that it serve as a sample of a cube, in the absence of a method or procedure for matching shaped objects to the sample, the picture tells one nothing about how the word "cube" is correctly ascribed to potential instances.

[1] Thanks to Brian Bowman, Michael Glanzberg, Barry C. Smith, Karen Wilson, and Mark Wilson for helpful advice and to Brooke Roberts for help with the Suggested Further Readings.

Wittgenstein does allow that a *method* or *procedure* or a *rule* for applying a word (or for continuing a series) can also, in a certain sense, come before a person's mind at a given moment, but this prompts him to explore what that certain sense might amount to. In his subsequent remarks (§141–§187), Wittgenstein discusses various aspects of what it is to grasp a general rule, to be guided by a rule, and to follow it successfully. However, the major recurring theme in these and subsequent remarks (§188–§242) is the difficulty of seeing how a rule for applying a word in an unbounded range of cases can be (i) something that is somehow present to a speaker's mind and (ii) something that determines in advance how the word in question ought to be applied.

At the beginning of §201, these difficulties culminate in a notorious philosophical impasse. Wittgenstein says, "This was our paradox: no course of action could be determined by a rule, because every course of action can be made out to accord with the rule. The answer was: if everything can be made out to accord with the rule, then it can also be made out to conflict with it. And so there would be neither accord nor conflict here." In this remark, the word "rule" refers to the expression of a rule—a form of words that is supposed to be governed by a substantive rule for applying it correctly. The paradox says that, since any action can be interpreted as being either in accord or in conflict with the rule, it makes no sense to suppose of any action that it is in accord or conflict with the rule, i.e. either the expression of the rule or the substantive rule that is meant to determine the instances of accord and conflict.

In the very next sentence of §201, Wittgenstein says that the paradox is "based on a misunderstanding," and he hints at a way in which the paradox is to be avoided. Thus, in understanding 'the rule following considerations,' one wants an account of at least the following three matters. What exactly is the apparent paradox about rule following that Wittgenstein mentions in §201? How, according to Wittgenstein, is the paradox to be resolved or otherwise defused? And finally, what is the bearing of the paradox and its proper resolution on questions of what it is to mean something by a word? These questions and Wittgenstein's discussion of them have intrigued many important philosophers of language since *Philosophical Investigations* and *Remarks on the Foundations of Mathematics* were published. Saul Kripke, Crispin Wright, and John McDowell, to name only a few, have written extensively and influentially on the topic. Unfortunately, the secondary literary is vast, complex, and often confusing. Any brief strategy of summary and explication is bound to be inadequate, ignoring a host of valuable exegetical and philosophical contributions that the literature on the subject contains.

Nevertheless, here is the strategy that I will follow in this entry. Kripke's reading of Wittgenstein in his book, *Wittgenstein: On Rules and Private Language* (WRPL) is probably the best known commentary on the rule following considerations, and it has influenced a wide range of other commentators on Wittgenstein. In fact, many of these authors partially define their own positions in reaction to disagreements they have with basic aspects of Kripke's exposition. The situation is further complicated by the fact that there are deep divisions about how Kripke's book itself is to be understood. I will start out by delineating an interpretation of Kripke on Wittgenstein, an interpretation that seems to me to stand the best chance of fitting at least the basic concerns and insights expressed in the *Investigations*. In doing so, I will sketch a conception of meaning and truth conditions against which Wittgenstein's remarks are plausibly directed, and I will explain how Kripke's reconstruction of Wittgenstein can be read as incorporating a broad attack on that conception. It is well known that Kripke's account involves the staging of a Skeptical Argument for a Skeptical Conclusion about meaning, and this is an argument that Kripke says Wittgenstein accepts. The interpretation with which I will open offers what I will call "the (merely) dramatic reading of the Skeptical Argument." The reader should be warned from the outset, however, that this explication of Kripke is controversial, and later in the entry I will sketch a common alternative approach to understanding Kripke's Wittgensteinian argument. The Skeptical Conclusion, on this second exegetical approach, is decidedly more radical, and I will dub it "the melodramatic reading of the Skeptical Argument."

7.1 The Dramatic Reading of the Skeptical Argument

So, we begin with the conception of meaning whose credentials are to be investigated. At least for those *basic* general terms that speakers have learned either by ostension or by direct inductive training, the following conception is intuitively quite natural. (I) If a speaker means something by a general term 'Φ', then the speaker has adopted a rule that specifies the standards of correctness for 'Φ' as she proposes to use it. The rule, we may suppose, has for her the form: 'Φ' (as I shall use it) is to be ascribed to an object o just in case o satisfies *those conditions*, where the conditions are given by some property or properties that the speaker has suitably in mind. These conditions are comprised of properties that exist independently of language and are exemplified (when they are), independently of our ability to ratify the relevant facts. (II) It is also natural to suppose that speakers come to adopt such 'semantic' rules *privately* or *individualistically*. That is, the 'defining' conditions for 'Φ' must be given by properties that are epistemically available to the speaker, properties that are somehow represented within her experience or as a part of her wider mental life. It is only on the basis of being able to grasp or pick out the conditions in such a privileged way that the speaker is able to form the particular intention mentioned above. Of course, an individual speaker is likely to expect that other speakers will have adopted the very same semantic rule for their uses of 'Φ', and it may be the speaker's further intention, in using 'Φ', that she is to be using it with the same set of standards of correctness that other speakers also employ. However, for any one speaker, the standards for her use of 'Φ' will have been set in place by her private adoption of the semantic rule in question. (III) The speaker is guided in her application of 'Φ' by her internal intuitive apprehension of the standards of correctness that have been settled for the term by her acceptance of the intended rule. She judges in a particular instance that the pertinent test item has features in virtue of which it realizes the conditions that she has in mind for 'Φ', and her grasp of those conditions form a part of the *reasons* for which she judges as she does. This is the core of the conception under scrutiny, and (I) through (III) describe an individualistic version of what Kripke calls 'classical realism,' classical realism about *truth (or satisfaction) conditions* in this case.

Extending the core conception somewhat, two further theses should be added. (IV) As the speaker employs the term in question, she will intend, in ascribing 'Φ' to an object *o*, to express the proposition that *o* satisfies the 'defining' conditions C. (V) Moreover, it is also natural to suppose that 'Φ', as the speaker uses it, has the meaning that it does *in virtue of* the fact that she has adopted the semantic rule and the fact that her ensuing application of 'Φ' is governed by her sustained commitment to that rule. That is, the speaker's commitment to the rule determines what has to be the case in order for 'Φ', as the speaker uses it, to apply correctly to an arbitrary item *o*, and it is *because* the speaker has this continuing commitment to the rule that 'Φ', as she uses it, means what it does. With an eye to returning to §201, we may say that the speaker's adoption of a particular semantic rule for 'Φ' assigns a truth-conditional *interpretation* to the speaker's use of 'Φ'. It assigns conditions C as the interpretation of 'Φ' within her idiolect. Theses (I) through (V) give us an individualistic version of classical realism about *meaning*. (V), in particular, expresses a truth conditional theory of meaning conceived in individualistic terms.

Classical realism about meaning is closely akin to an unmodified form of 'the contractual model of meaning' that Crispin Wright, in his early writings on rule following, took as the principal foil of Wittgenstein's critical remarks on meaning and understanding. This is the view, in Wright's words, that "...grasping the meaning of an expression [is] grasping a general pattern of use, conformity to which requires certain determinate uses in so far unconsidered cases. The pattern is thus thought of as extending *of itself* to cases which we have yet to confront" (Wright 1981, p. 34). Presumably the 'general pattern of use' mentioned in this passage reflects the truth or satisfaction conditions for the expression, as these are construed by the classical realist. Wright agrees, as do many other expositors of Wittgenstein, that the rule following considerations represent some sort of fundamental criticism of or challenge to this conception of meaning as individualistic semantic rule following. Commentators differ about which aspects of the conception (I through V) are under attack, and they differ about the nature of the criticisms that Wittgenstein mounts against it. Some commentators believe that the target of the attack includes significantly more than the individualistic version of classical realism, but they generally agree at least that this view is rejected—whether it is rejected as false or as philosophically defective in some other crucial way.

At the heart of Kripke's discussion in *WRPL* is a characteristic structure of argument directed at classical realism about truth conditions and meaning. The strategy is embodied in the so-called "Skeptical Argument," and it can be understood to proceed in the following manner. Consider any speaker S who is supposed to have done something that constituted her having adopted a semantic rule for a term 'Φ'. Kripke constructs an argument, based on considerations derived from Wittgenstein, which is meant to show that there is not and could not be any fact of the matter about what semantic rule, if any, S has thereby adopted. That is, let us begin by supposing that S has adopted a specific semantic rule, a rule that purports to establish conditions C as the standards of correctness for her use of 'Φ'. So, C purports to give the satisfaction conditions for S's use of 'Φ', and they are established as such by S's acceptance of her rule. However, Kripke's Wittgenstein argues that it is possible to construct an unlimited range of related but non-equivalent semantic rules, incorporating the potential truth conditions $C_1, C_2, \ldots Cn \ldots$ respectively, such that there are simply no facts at all about S and her use of 'Φ' that determines which, if any, of these possible rules the speaker has actually adopted. In other words, there is no fact of the matter about whether the (classical realist) truth conditions that S has putatively established for her use of 'Φ' are C or C_1 or C_2, and so on. If the speaker's word is "blue," for example, then the admissible alternatives, depending upon the course of the speaker's earlier applications, might include 'blue', 'navy blue', 'blue or green', or 'blue and three-dimensional', Goodman's 'bleen',[2] etc. There will be nothing in the speaker's history—either in her external behavior or in her overall psychological state—that makes it the case that for her 'Φ' is governed by C and not by one or another of the idiosyncratic alternatives. More specifically, the unbounded set of alternative satisfaction conditions can be constructed in such a way, that for any new candidate o for 'Φ' ascription, o will satisfy some of the conditions in the constructed set, and it will fail to satisfy some others. Therefore, since, according to the Skeptical Argument, it is factually indeterminate as to which, if any, of these conditions govern S's use of 'Φ', it will correspondingly be indeterminate, in any new case, whether or not 'Φ', as S uses it, is true or false of an arbitrary item o.

Kripke's skeptic does not doubt that the speaker takes herself to have a definite semantic intention that 'Φ' is to be ascribed to something just in case it satisfies the conditions that she has in mind. But, which are the conditions that she, in so intending, 'has in mind?' What are the facts about S that determine that her semantic intention is directed at conditions C (as we are supposing) instead of C_1 or C_2, etc? Or, perhaps her intention is directed at no determinate conditions at all. In the Skeptical Argument, Kripke's Wittgenstein maintains that there simply is no defensible answer to this meta-semantic question. The various types of fact about S that might seem to establish which properties she has in mind and at which her semantic intention for 'Φ' is directed do not succeed in accomplishing that task. Some initially promising answers turn out to yield intuitively wrong results. They pick out a set of conditions which plainly are not the intuitive satisfaction conditions of 'Φ'. Other proposals fail to discriminate between the 'right' satisfaction conditions and a number of surprising alternative conditions that intuitively are 'wrong'. And other proposals fail in other crucial ways. If all of the *prima facie* viable proposals have been

---

[2] A term introduced by Nelson Goodman in "The New Riddle of Induction", reprinted in *Fact, Fiction, and Forecast*, 4th edition (Cambridge: Harvard University Press, 2005), p. 79 "bleen" applies to emeralds examined before time t just in case they are blue and to other emeralds just in case they are green.

investigated and rejected, then the global skeptical conclusion has been sustained: for any speaker S and general term 'Φ', there are no facts that determine which semantic rule, if any, governs S's use of 'Φ'. This is the (merely) dramatic version of the Skeptical Argument.

Kripke works through this argument using an example in which a speaker is supposed to have meant addition by the term "+". We begin by making the assumption that the speaker has learned to perform addition in some notation, e.g. has mastered a computational procedure for adding any pair of numbers in Arabic notation. The speaker, taking herself to have learned the relevant procedure, intends to fix the satisfaction conditions for statements of the form 'l + m = n' in terms of the procedure in question. It is her intention that a particular instance of this statement form is true just in case the application of this procedure to 'l' and 'm' yields 'n' as its result. But, what are the facts about the speaker in virtue of which it is a computational procedure for *addition* that she has mastered and in terms of which she means to establish the satisfaction conditions for her use of "+"? What are the facts about her that rule out the apparent possibility that she has mastered some oddball algorithm that agrees with the results of an algorithm for addition throughout a certain initial range of cases but diverges beyond that range and that *this* is the algorithm upon which her semantic rule for "+" is based.

The first proposal that Kripke considers is the idea that the speaker mentally accepts some sentence or some other symbolic representation that formulates the algorithm she purportedly has learned. There is surely a difference between mastering an algorithm (a computational procedure) and knowing how to provide a statement of it. On the present proposal, the speaker frames for herself a set of 'instructions' that specify the computational procedure that she is supposed to carry out from case to case. However, such a proposal only sets in motion the regress of interpretations emphasized repeatedly by Wittgenstein. The relevant instructions will themselves imbed certain crucial general terms whose standards of correctness in S's idiolect have to have been settled in order for those instructions to describe a determinate algorithm. So, now let 'Φ*' be such a term imbedded in the instructions that S has offered to herself. We can ask again, "What are the facts about S and her use of 'Φ*' that establish satisfaction conditions for this term?" After all, the original question was meant to be a general question about any term whatsoever, and this proposal has merely shifted the focus from one targeted term 'Φ' to a related term 'Φ*' contained in the would-be explication. Surely, it can't be that the answer for 'Φ*' is itself to be given in terms of still another set of instructions that the speaker gives for its employment. Otherwise, the obvious endless regress will ensue.

In an especially influential part of his discussion, Kripke goes on to examine the idea that it is facts about the way in which S is *disposed* to calculate when confronted with a problem of the form 'l + m = what?' that determines the arithmetic procedure upon which the intended satisfaction conditions for "+" are based. In its crudest form, the dispositionalist account proposes that the procedure in question can simply be 'read off' from the series of calculations that S would actually produce if she were posed, *per impossible*, an exhaustive series of basic 'addition' problems.

But, the crude account fails immediately for at least two different reasons. First, the speaker's computational dispositions are themselves finite. For certain enormously long 'addition' problems, the speaker may have no dispositions to execute the needed calculations whatever. She might fall into paralyzing confusion, quit, or die before she had proceeded very far at all. So in these cases there simply are no values that the speaker is disposed to produce in the course of her computational activity. Second, the speaker may, in fact, be disposed to make recurrent errors. Intuitively, the procedure she has actually mastered dictates for any given problem how the required calculation would be carried out correctly. The procedure or the rules that are embodied in that procedure are 'normative' in this sense. But the speaker may well be disposed to execute some of these calculations incorrectly. If we were to read off the procedure she intended to be following directly from her flawed attempts to carry it out, then the speaker could never make a computational mistake. Anything she was disposed to do would, by definition, constitute an instance of the procedure she was trying to execute. The procedure she was performing would turn out to be, not a procedure for adding, but a procedure that corresponded to whatever aberrant arithmetic mapping tracked her actual calculations—the correct calculations and the incorrect ones alike.

Kripke spends a fair amount of space examining refined versions of the dispositionalist account, versions in which the intended calculation procedure is to be read off some idealization of the speaker's actual computational dispositions. His conclusion is that these refinements will either fail for reasons similar to the problems that defeat the original crude version or the idealized specifications of the speaker's disposition will become circular by stipulating, in effect, that the computational dispositions are to be the ones that the speaker *would* have if the algorithm she intended to be following, in using "+", were an algorithm for *addition* (and not some other arithmetic operation).

A third proposal that Kripke scrutinizes holds that the content of the speaker's semantic intention is fixed by the qualitative character of some experience the speaker undergoes in association with having the relevant intention. But, this proposal is defeated by the same considerations that are exemplified in Wittgenstein's example of a speaker who entertains a picture of a cube when the meaning of the word "cube" has come before his mind. At best, the putative experiences could provide samples or illustrations of how a computation for "+" should go, and, in the absence of a general specification of how the samples and illustrations are themselves to be interpreted and deployed, they do nothing on their own to determine for S how "+" is to be applied from instance to instance. This is still another case in which Wittgenstein's regress of interpretations objection comes into play.

In a similar vein, Kripke discusses other possible responses to the skeptic and develops considerations, suggested by themes in Wittgenstein, that are meant to show that none of these proposals can succeed either. Thus, the pattern of case-by-case argument is the one that was sketched out earlier. If all of the possible answers have been considered and defeated, then there is no fact of the matter as to whether it is S's mastery of addition or her mastery of some related but non-standard arithmetic operation that fixes for her the satisfaction conditions of her use of "+". As Kripke himself emphasizes, the overall argument he presents is an indeterminacy argument. There are no facts about the speaker S that determine what the satisfaction conditions for her use of 'Φ' might be. If the conclusion of the argument is right, then, within the framework of classical realism about meaning, it follows from (III) that there will be no factually determinate content to the rule or general semantic intention that is supposed to be providing psychological 'guidance' to S in her various ascriptions of 'Φ'. By (IV), there will also be no fact of the matter about whether the speaker's ascriptions of 'Φ' to an arbitrary item *o* are true or not. Finally, by (V), there will be no fact of the matter about what S means by 'Φ'. It will be utterly indeterminate what meaning 'Φ' expresses within S's idiolect. Several related skeptical conclusions will have been established, and the individualist version of classical realism about meaning—meaning as private rule following—will be in shambles.

This framework yields a Kripkean reading of the paradox that Wittgenstein mentions in §201. It is clear in context that Wittgenstein's initial use of "rule" in §201 refers to the expression of a rule, e.g. to the verbal order, "Add 2." Then, because it has come to seem as though there is no fact of the matter about which possible semantic rule—which truth conditions—assigns a determinate 'interpretation' to the expression, there can be no fact of the matter about which items are in accord or conflict with the predicate, 'the result of adding 2 to x yields y.'

Wittgenstein goes on to say,

It can be seen that there is a misunderstanding here from the mere fact that in the course of our argument we give one interpretation after another; as if each one contented us at least for a moment, until we thought of yet another standing behind it. What this shews is that there is a way of grasping a rule which is *not* an *interpretation*, but which is exhibited in what we call 'obeying the rule' and 'going against it' in actual cases.   [*PI* §201]

As noted before, the dramatic reading suggests that an 'interpretation' here can be construed as a classical realist semantic rule which is intended to govern the form of words in question. We can think of one possible alternative interpretation after another, any one of which might 'content us for a moment,' but it is utterly indeterminate as to which of these various incompatible interpretations actually serves to define accord and conflict for the pertinent expression. This should show us that meaning something by an expression is not, in general, a matter of privately assigning it a semantic rule, and understanding the meaning of the expression, as used by another, is not, in general, a matter of knowing which semantic rule the other speaker has adopted for it. At least in a range of basic cases, meaning or understanding the expression of a rule must be something that is *exhibited* in the behavior that we count as obeying or going against that 'rule.' Naturally, this elucidation of what Wittgenstein means here by "interpreting an (expression of) a rule" is contentious, but it yields an apparently coherent account of what he says in §201.

The argument just outlined, being directed at an individualistic version of classical realism about meaning, seems to me to correspond rather well with the philosophical themes and commentary that Wittgenstein elaborates in the setting of the rule following remarks. Moreover, according to Kripke, a version of the Private Language

Argument will fall out as a more or less direct consequence of this Skeptical Conclusion. A private language is a language that contains terms that apply to objects which only the given individual can experience and whose truth conditions and meaning only that individual can establish, presumably by private ostensive definition. But, this means that the truth conditions and the meaning of such a term, as used by the speaker, is established by the speaker's individualistic adoption of a semantic rule directed at the properties of the objects that are accessible to him alone. However, the possibility of the successful adoption of such a rule has already been foreclosed by the prior argument to show that individualistic versions of classical realist truth conditions and meaning are incoherent. If sensations are private objects and the basic terms that are ascribed to them have their meaning fixed by private ostensive definition, then terms for sensations in an idiolect acquire their meaning in accordance with classical realism individualistically construed. But, if individualistic classical realism has already been refuted, then the idea of a private language is an illusion. Or, in any case, this is Kripke's intriguing suggestion.

As noted above, Crispin Wright agrees that Wittgenstein's remarks are directed at an individualistic version of classical realism, but the argument that Wright derives from Wittgenstein is apparently quite different. Bob Hale has provided a succinct re-formulation of Wright's argument:

> The difficulty here is to see how it can be justified to describe the situation [of the speaker S] in terms of *recognizing* what her supposed pattern [standard of correctness] requires her to say, in any particular case, as opposed to her merely being *disposed* to apply 'Φ' (or not, as may be). The former description is justified only if there is a distinction to be drawn between S's going on as the pattern demands on the one hand, and on the other her merely *seeming* to do so. But S cannot make this distinction for herself, since it is bound to seem to her that her sincere and considered application of 'Φ' conforms to the requirements of the pattern: and by hypothesis, the distinction is not to be made out on the basis of others' assessment of her performance.   (Hale 1997, p. 382)

However, the extent of the difference between this argument and the one that Kripke develops depends partly upon how a certain ambiguity in such a formulation is resolved. When it is claimed that 'S cannot make this distinction for herself,' this could mean either that S herself cannot epistemically discriminate between, on the one hand, the cases in which she is actually using 'Φ', as she intends, in accordance with her previously adopted standard of correctness and, on the other, the cases in which it merely seems to her that her present use is being governed by those standards. On this interpretation of Wright's argument, there *is* a genuine distinction of fact as to whether or not, in a given use of 'Φ', the speaker is following her pre-established standard of correctness. The difficulty is supposed to be that the speaker is utterly unable to *know*, from instance to instance, which of the two possibilities has been realized. It is therefore impossible that she is genuinely *guided* by any determinate standard of correctness at all. Her grasp of the standards cannot be among the reasons for her judgments involving 'Φ'. On an alternative reading, it is the very idea that there is a genuine distinction here that is taken to be mistaken. There is no fact of the matter as to whether any of the speaker's particular applications of 'Φ' are governed by one possible semantic rule rather than another out of an indefinitely large range of incompatible but admissible alternatives. In other words, there is no fact of the matter as to which standard of correctness S has pre-established for her subsequent employment of the term. If Wright has the second interpretation in mind, then his original argument may need to be supplemented with some of the considerations that are brought forward in the course of Kripke's Skeptical Argument. From this perspective, Wright's Wittgenstein and Kripke's hold substantially similar positions both about the critical target of the rule following considerations and about the basic argumentative line of attack that Wittgenstein develops.

It is true that Wright tends to frame his conception of the issue as an epistemological one: how does S *know* what the rule requires of her in any particular case? And, he opposes this epistemological question to the more purely constitutive question that he takes Kripke to be posing on Wittgenstein's behalf. However, Wright supposes that Kripke is putting forward what I call below 'a melodramatic version' of the Skeptical Argument and not the merely dramatic version before us. What is more he agrees that Wittgenstein rejects the idea that the epistemological question is to be answered along the following lines. At each stage of possible application, there is an 'autonomous requirement' that the rule supplies for the case in question, and S has the capacity to muster an intuitive grasp of what that specific autonomous requirement amounts to. Certainly, this line of thought has important affinities to the rejection of classical realism about truth and meaning that Kripke discerns in Wittgenstein.

However, the discussion so far has focused only on *individualistic* versions of classical realism, and, in the contemporary philosophical setting, it is natural to wonder whether *social* or *community-based* versions of classical realism might be invulnerable to the skeptic's arguments. If it is only the individualism that is the source of the skeptical problems, then the interest of Kripke's Wittgensteinian argument will be substantially mitigated. That is, the following conjunction of views may well seem to be potentially viable. First, consider a term 'Φ', as it is used in the linguistic practices of an interacting community of speakers. Isn't there a determinate fact about the satisfaction conditions and the meaning of 'Φ', when it figures as an element in the community's shared language? Wasn't it precisely the individualism that is presupposed in the original skeptical argument that created the basis for the skeptical challenge just outlined? Won't we find that there *are* facts about the community and its co-operative practices that establish what 'Φ' means in the shared language—what classical realist satisfaction conditions it has? Let us suppose, for a moment, that this is so. Then, second, we might propose that 'Φ', as used by an individual member of the community, means what the community means by 'Φ' if the linguistic behavior of that individual and his dispositions to relevant linguistic behavior stand in the right kind of alignment with the meaning-constituting practices of the community as a whole. In other words, 'Φ', as the competent individual speaker uses it, inherits its satisfaction conditions from the satisfaction conditions that have been established by communal practice.

However, Kripke indicates that he believes that Wittgenstein rejects such a social version of classical realism as well. In particular, he states that it is likely that objections can be developed to the first strand of the social version that will be analogues to several of the objections to the individualistic version of classical realism about truth conditions (see *WRPL* p. 111). More specifically, Kripke seems to think that the truth condition determining facts will have to arise from facts about the community's collective dispositions in using 'Φ', and he holds that such appeals to the collective dispositions of the community will face analogues of the problems that defeated similar appeals to the dispositions of the individual. Of course, Kripke allows that Wittgenstein's account of meaning does insist on recognizing the social dimension of linguistic use, but the social aspect so recognized will not provide for classical realist satisfaction conditions for terms in the community's language. Hence, the meanings of terms *in a given language* will not derive from classical realist truth or satisfaction conditions either. Whether Kripke is right about Wittgenstein's outlook on this point or not, his discussion does not explore the exegetical or substantive issues that are raised by the topic at any length. This is an area in which further clarification and elaboration are needed. Nevertheless, it is plain that the Skeptical Conclusion in *WRPL* embraces skepticism about any version of classical realism, individualistic or social.

Here again Crispin Wright is in agreement with Kripke. His version of Wittgenstein also rejects community based versions of classical realism, although his arguments are different from Kripke's and are elaborated in much greater detail. Throughout the various versions he has set out (1980, 1981), he attempts to extend and modify his original argument against individualistic classical realism. These arguments against the social version turn on the idea that there is for the linguistic community as a whole no genuine distinction to be drawn, on the one hand, between overall agreement in ascribing a term which arises out of a genuine conformity to community standards of correctness and, on the other, a mere *de facto* consensus which only seems to so arise, an agreement based on nothing more than a fortunate similarity in linguistic dispositions.

7.2 THE SKEPTICAL SOLUTION

Of course, if someone accepted the Skeptical Argument just outlined *and* also accepted the classical realist truth conditional theory of meaning, then it would follow that there is no fact of the matter about what *meaning* a term expresses, either for the individual speaker or in the language of a particular speech community. Now, in fact, some of Kripke's formulations of the Skeptical Conclusion seem to affirm some such non-factualist thesis about meaning. For example, Kripke characteristically states that the Skeptical Argument establishes that there is no fact about the speaker that *constitutes* his meaning *such and such* by 'Φ'. For instance, he says, ". . . I choose to be so bold as to say: Wittgenstein holds, with the skeptic, that there is no fact as to whether [by "+"] I mean plus or [some related arithmetic operation]"(*WRPL*, pp. 70–1). But, the dramatic reading of the Skeptical Argument purports to show, in the first instance, only that there can be no fact as to what classical realist satisfaction conditions a given term might have. Even if this notable result is right, non-factualism about meaning will not follow unless the classical realist truth conditional theory of meaning is presupposed. That is, one might maintain that the meanings of terms in a speaker's idiolect or a community's language simply are *not* based upon classical realist satisfaction conditions at all, and that classical realism about meaning ought to be rejected and replaced with some alternative account. And yet, this *is* also an idea that Kripke thinks that Wittgenstein favors: Kripke's exposition of Wittgenstein's response to the Skeptical Conclusion proceeds by this very strategy. The Skeptical Conclusion is said to be embraced by Wittgenstein, but a Skeptical Solution is offered to contain its destructive impact on the concept of 'meaning'. A critical part of the 'solution' is to adumbrate a quite different notion of what it is for a term (or sentence) to have meaning within a linguistic community. Kripke explains the matter in this way:

> Nevertheless as Dummett says, "the *Investigations* contains implicitly a rejection of the classical (realist) Frege-*Tractatus* view that the general form of explanation of meaning is a statement of the truth conditions." In the place of this view, Wittgenstein proposes an alternative rough general picture . . . Wittgenstein replaces the question, "What must be the case for the sentence to be true?" by two others: first, "Under what conditions may this form of words be appropriately asserted (or denied)?"; second, given an answer to the first question, "What is the role, and the utility, in our lives of our practice of asserting (or denying) the form of words under these conditions".   (*WRPL*, p. 73)

So the idea that meaning is based on classical realist truth or satisfaction conditions *is* repudiated and replaced. Indeed, it is the errors of classical realism that embody for Kripke's Wittgenstein the 'misunderstanding' that is supposed to resolve the paradox referred to at the outset of §201. But, to repeat, it is hard to see how a Skeptical Conclusion about the factual indeterminacy of meaning (non-factualism about meaning) can be thought to follow from the Skeptical Argument and how it can be a conclusion that Kripke supposes that Wittgenstein accepts. Within Kripke's reconstruction, it is important to distinguish the Skeptical Conclusion, which is endorsed by Wittgenstein, from something he calls "the skeptical paradox," which is not. The skeptical paradox is the 'insane and intolerable' conclusion which the Skeptical Solution is meant to block. According to the dramatic reading at least, the paradox states that there is no fact at all about what anyone means by any term, and the Skeptical Conclusion says only that there is no fact about the speaker or about the linguistic community which establishes one potential satisfaction condition for 'Φ' rather than another as (the basis of) its meaning. But, Kripke's varying formulations do not always make it easy to keep the content of these distinct theses straight. This reading of the Skeptical Conclusion does not entail the skeptical paradox, and hence, it doesn't entail non-factualism about meaning. Whether such a Skeptical Conclusion deserves to be regarded as a kind of skepticism at all is, naturally, a further question.

The Skeptical Solution offers an account of what it is for terms to have meaning in a language which does not explain their meaningfulness in terms of truth or satisfaction conditions at all. Rather, a term means what it does in virtue of its language-games uses in the speech community. This is essentially the view that engendered the rule following worries in the first place. According to Kripke's skeptical solution, the view that 'meaning is use' claims that a term 'Φ' has the meaning that it does in language L in virtue of the assertability and deniability conditions for 'Φ' ascriptions that systematically prevail among the competent 'Φ' users in L. Or rather, the meaningfulness of 'Φ' depends jointly upon the practices of justified 'Φ' assertion in L and the larger language-game role that 'Φ' assertions, so regulated, have for members of the speech community in question. In this way, the Skeptical Solution makes no explanatory appeal to truth conditions in its account of meaning. Let us say that a theory of meaning that rejects classical realist accounts of truth conditions and explains the meaningfulness of an expression in terms of assertability conditions is 'antirealist.' So, the Skeptical Solution is paradigmatically antirealist in this specific sense. Still, antirealist accounts do not deny that 'Φ' ascriptions 'have truth or satisfaction conditions,' at least in some deflationary sense of the phrase. If 'Φ' is meaningful in L, then a sentence in L that says that

'Φ' is true of *o* in L if and only if *o* is Φ

expresses a truth, and it will be accepted as a commitment concerning 'Φ' ascriptions by masters of 'Φ' within the speech community for L. Such a sentence can be said to give the 'satisfaction conditions' for 'Φ' in L, but the conditions in question are minimalist in nature, and they inherit whatever normative consequences they have from the prior imperatives of the assertability and deniability conditions that govern 'Φ' within the community. In other words, satisfaction conditions of this ilk are explained in terms of a more fundamental concept of meaningfulness (in use) and not, as in classical realism about meaning, the other way around.

However, these considerations only underscore the dilemma about how the Skeptical Conclusion ought to be construed. Again, the consensus view is that it is a thesis embracing the non-factualist status of meaning, and Kripke's text repeatedly, but not consistently can seem to support such an interpretation. Nevertheless, if the skeptical paradox is blocked by the Skeptical Solution, as described above, then it is puzzling how meaning ascriptions could fail to state or report facts in some sense. Indeed, it would seem that correct meaning ascriptions about individual speakers should describe facts about their apparent mastery of the community's assertability conditions for the term and their linguistic responsiveness to its role and utility in the relevant language games. Of course, it is not to be expected that necessary and sufficient conditions for meaning ascriptions concerning 'Φ' are to be given in terms of the assertability conditions and linguistic role of 'Φ', but, if the Skeptical Solution makes sense at all, then these features of the term's use should surely figure as the subject matter of correct meaning ascriptions. And, given that they have such a subject matter, these ascriptions should surely enjoy some sort of factual standing. Thus, although Kripke's Wittgenstein is widely reputed to be some kind of nonfactualist about meaning, this is not an obvious upshot of the version of the dramatic reading of the Skeptical Argument. How this discrepancy in the text of *WRPL* is to be explained remains an open question.

7.3 THE MELODRAMATIC READING
OF THE SKEPTICAL ARGUMENT

Since most commentators on Kripke have taken the Skeptical Argument to aim directly at a non-factualist Skeptical Conclusion, they have naturally supposed that the argument proceeds according to a significantly different strategy from the one heretofore portrayed. This is the interpretation of Kripke's reconstruction of Wittgenstein that I propose to call "the melodramatic reading." The content of the Skeptical Conclusion on this reading (non-factualism about meaning) is the same as the skeptical paradox in the dramatic reading. Here, for example, is Crispin Wright's summary characterization of his version of Kripke's Skeptical Argument:

Roughly, the conclusion that there are no facts of a disputed species [i.e. about meaning] is to follow from an argument to the effect that, even if we imagine our abilities idealized to the point where, if there were any such facts to be known, we would certainly be in possession of them, we *still* would not be in a position to justify any particular claim about their character. So we first, as it were plot the area in which the facts in question would have to be found if they existed and then imagine a suitable idealization, with respect to that area, of our knowledge acquiring powers; if it then transpires that any particular claim about those facts [about meaning] still proves resistant to all justification, there is no alternative to concluding that the 'facts' never existed in the first place.   (Wright 2001, pp. 94–95)

There are two key components to this approach. First, there is a delineation of a totality of genuine facts in terms of which the factual status of correct meaning ascriptions is potentially to be justified. Second, there is an account of how such 'justifications' may be legitimately carried out. Naturally, there are a number of possible views about how the totality of basic genuine facts might be characterized, but several authors believe that this totality consists of all facts that are describable in non-semantic and non-intentional terms. These philosophers argue, as we will see below, that both semantic and intentional 'facts' cannot, for present purposes at least, be treated as primitive and, hence, that their factual status requires a suitable justification. Given a delineation of the factual base, correct ascriptions of meaning, e.g. 'Φ, as S uses it, means *so and so*' can be understood to describe or express facts only if it is possible to demonstrate that the facts that they purportedly describe are reducible to or supervene upon suitable segments of the naturalistic base. Thus, when the skeptic challenges us to 'justify' the factual status of meaning ascriptions, we are being challenged to demonstrate how the facts that true meaning ascriptions purportedly describe are reducible to or supervene upon a suitable selection from the admissible range of basic facts. The main line of the non-factualist Skeptical Argument then proceeds by surveying the potentially relevant factual domains within the base and arguing, for each case, that the purported facts of meaning cannot plausibly be shown to reduce to or supervene upon facts drawn from that domain. This version of the Skeptical Argument is, as before, a case-by-case argument, and the types of fact that are considered under the individual cases are roughly the ones that I outlined in presenting the dramatic version. And also as before, the range of cases considered is supposed to exhaust the plausible justifying possibilities.

The central line of reasoning in this version of the Skeptical Argument cannot get started if meaning facts are deemed to be primitive, that is, genuinely factual but not determined by any more basic level of fact. However, this alternative is rejected by Kripke as 'desperate' and 'completely mysterious' (*WRPL* p. 51). What he means by this reaction is that, if meaning facts are, in this sense, primitive—if we respond to the skeptic in this way—then we have explicitly precluded ourselves from being able to give any sort of philosophical explanation of some of meaning's crucial features, for example, that speakers normally know directly and with a high degree of certainty what they mean by the terms in their language, and that the meaning of a term carries with it an unbounded range of normative consequences for the speaker's prospective linguistic behavior. If we say that meaning facts are simply primitive and *sui generis*, then we return to the problem that motivated the rule following considerations in the first place. We apparently have no way of explaining how facts about what a speaker means by a term can be grasped by the speaker immediately and in a moment and how they determine how the term is to be applied over an indefinite range of possible candidates. So meaning facts, if they exist, should be shown to have some type of naturalistic grounding, a grounding that might make it possible to explain their principal epistemological and normative properties. On the other hand, as the argument moves from one case to another, it is argued that meaning facts cannot be derived from the basis delineated for that case. Wright (1984), McDowell (1984, 1992), and Soames (1998b), among many others, take this or a variant of it to be the underlying strategy of the Kripke's Skeptical Argument.[3]

Warren Goldfarb (1989), who accepts this as the proper reading of Kripke's Skeptical Argument, argues forcefully that it is implausible that Wittgenstein in his later writings accepted any such tendentious conception of 'the totality of genuine facts.' That conception derives from a contemporary form of naturalism with which Wittgenstein would have been unlikely to have had much sympathy. Correlatively, Goldfarb finds it implausible that Wittgenstein had the project of certifying the factuality of meaning by the 'justifying' tactics here envisaged. However, the issues are delicate and complicated. Paul Boghossian (1989) and Scott Soames (1998a, 1998b) think that the scope of this version of the skeptical challenge is considerably broader than a question about the factual status of linguistic meaning. Focusing for the moment on sentences in an idiolect or a communal language, the skeptic does want to know, in the first instance, what are the facts that constitute its being the case that a given sentence P expresses one proposition rather than another from an open range of admissible alternatives. But, in the same way and on the same grounds, the skeptic can and does ask, concerning a given state of believing, desiring, intending, and so on, "What are the facts in virtue of which it is true of a specific concrete psychological

---

[3] Soames (1998a) suggests that Kripke's presentation contains important strands of both the dramatic and melodramatic versions of the argument and that there may not be a consistent overall reading of *WRPL*. The proposal strikes me as plausible.

state that it expresses one certain propositional content rather than any one of a range of counterintuitive alternatives?" For Boghossian, Soames, and others, this skeptical challenge is a natural and unavoidable generalization of the more limited challenge that is directed at linguistic meaning. If this generalized form of the challenge is granted to be plausible, then it is plausible as well that any suitably general answer to the challenge will have to be restricted to justifications of factuality that appeal only to facts that can be described in purely non-intentional terms.

In pursuing the issues raised by this proposal, it is important to keep different questions in focus. On the one hand, one can wonder whether the more encompassing challenge, taken on its own terms, is intelligible and legitimate. Much contemporary philosophy of mind will allow that it is, as the proliferation of theories of mental content amply attests. The case-by-case considerations that figure in the non-factualist version of the Skeptical Argument, where they are sound, raise legitimate problems for various theories of linguistic and mental content. On the other hand, since exegesis of Wittgenstein is in play, one can also wonder whether this is a challenge that Wittgenstein himself would have countenanced, and that idea is extremely dubious. The proposed generalization of the challenge rests on the idea that, for example, a person believes that P at t just in case there is an inner state s of the person, realized at t, that is an instance of believing (rather than wanting or intending) and which has the proposition that P as its content. The skeptical challenge is extended to s and its putative content 'that P.' This is an idea that seems deeply at odds with much of what the later Wittgenstein says and suggests about the propositional attitudes, and it seems an improbable foundation for his explicitly expressed concerns about meaning and following a rule. Finally, one can ask whether Kripke believes that Wittgenstein adopted such a perspective. The textual evidence in WRPL for a positive answer to this question is equivocal at best.

Given the conclusion of the non-factualist reading of the Skeptical Argument (even on its narrower reading), there are no facts that true meaning ascriptions can describe. But, Kripke's Wittgenstein does not hold that meaning ascriptions are themselves meaningless, and he grants, in addition, that there must be some substance to the practice of treating many of them as 'correct'. In particular, he certainly doesn't endorse the utterly self-defeating Skeptical Paradox thesis that no one ever means anything by an expression. The chief role of the Skeptical Solution is now to explain, in the face of non-factualism, how these theses can be maintained. The proponent of the non-factualist version of the Solution denies that meaning ascriptions even *purport* to describe facts and claims instead that they have some other type of standard linguistic function. It is highlighted in the Skeptical Solution that there are a range of circumstances in which members of the community will be taken to be justified in asserting and denying meaning ascriptions, despite the non-descriptive function they are supposed to serve. Thus, meaning ascriptions, like other expressions in the language, will have characteristic assertability conditions, and they will have a characteristic role or utility in the relevant language games of linguistic instruction, encouragement, and correction. So, in the terms of the Skeptical Solution, ascriptions of meaning will have a distinctive kind of meaning, and it is allowed that there is a distinction between those that are defeasibly warranted in the speech community and those that are not.

Nevertheless, many writers have charged that non-factualism about meaning is incoherent or otherwise self-defeating. For example, since the truth-value of an arbitrary sentence is jointly determined by the facts about what it means and the facts about its subject, Crispin Wright points out that non-factualism about meaning threatens to give rise to a global non-factualism about the truth or falsity of any statement whatsoever. We will not pursue that question here. However, Scott Soames (1998a) has raised a different objection to the basic strategy of the non-factualist version of the Skeptical Argument. Suppose that we grant the success of each part of the case-by-case argument. That is, we grant that it is impossible to *demonstrate* the truth of intuitively correct meaning ascriptions from the totality of basic non-intentional facts considered for that case. In other words, we cannot *derive* the relevant statements about meaning from the designated configuration of non-intentional facts even working within the background of a set of true *a priori* principles concerning mind and language. Should such a conclusion convince us that facts about meaning do not supervene upon the non-semantic, non-intentional base? After all, we presumably start out with the strong conviction that (a) meaning ascriptions *are* somehow factual, and we may very well believe that (b) every domain of genuine fact must supervene upon a naturalistic base.

At the same time, we are likely to be much less confident that, in any given case, we can identify a minimal but adequate naturalistic base with significant accuracy, and, even more importantly, we may be deeply unsure that we are in a position to construct a derivation that *demonstrates* that the wanted supervenience obtains. It is an open possibility that the semantic does supervene upon the non-intentional even though we are in no position to demonstrate, from one case to another, how this might be so. Therefore, our inability to answer the skeptic in his own terms may quite reasonably fail to trump our intuitive conviction in (a) and (b) above. In the same way, we might conclude that we are unable to demonstrate from facts about our immediate sensory impressions that there is a mind-independent world to which we have perceptual access and about which most of our ordinary sensory impressions are veridical. The philosophical failure to construct the desired derivation is hardly likely to shake our conviction in an external world about which our senses provide us with generally reliable information. Hence, even on the most favorable scenario, the skeptical challenge about facts of meaning may fail to convince in a manner that is characteristic of similar projects of overly ambitious philosophical skepticism.

7.4 THE OBJECTIVITY OF JUDGMENT AND THE NORMATIVITY OF MEANING

John McDowell (1984, 1992) has given special emphasis to an issue that has remained implicit in the discussion so far. Any account of meaning, mental content, truth conditions, and the explanatory connection between them must be adequate to validate our intuitive conception of the objectivity of judgment. In a famous passage, he explains that notion in the following way:

The idea at risk is the idea of things being thus and such anyway, whether or not we choose to investigate the matter in question, and whatever the outcome of any such investigation. That idea requires the conception of how things could correctly be said to be anyway—whatever, if anything, we could in fact go on to say about the matter; and this notion of correctness can only be the notion of how a pattern of application that we grasp, when we come to understand the concept in question, extends, independently of the actual outcome of any investigation, to the relevant case.   (McDowell, 1984, p. 46)

So, this is a constraint on the 'objectivity of judgment' that any satisfactory theory must satisfy. However, he argues, all of the approaches presented so far fail to fulfill this objectivity constraint in a plausible manner. Take, for example, classical realism about truth and satisfaction conditions. This is a prime instance of one sort of approach (McDowell dubs it "Scylla") that McDowell unequivocally repudiates. Classical realism is designed to ensure that the constraint on the objectivity of judgment is satisfied, but it does so by grounding objectivity on an inflated and ultimately incoherent explanatory basis In its individualistic version, the user of a term 'Φ' is supposed to pick out a pertinent property about which the speaker forms a suitable semantic intention. How does this epistemic operation proceed? For a certain type of Platonist, the speaker has immediate intuitive access to the world of properties (*qua* universals) and has the capacity to focus directly on and to form an intention about one property to the exclusion of the others. Having supposedly formed the requisite intention, the speaker is thereafter guided, again in a direct and immediate way, by the particular consequences that it engenders. McDowell regards this approach as hopelessly mythological. For him, it is simply a version of the theoretical picture of rule following that Wittgenstein ridicules as "the operation of a super-rigid yet ethereal machine." (See the remarks on machines at *PI* §193–4).

The alternative here is to allow that our grasp of properties is mediated by our experiences and by the operation of appropriate mental activities. The often postulated activity of abstracting a specific property out of some range of perceptual experiences is a familiar, albeit schematic, instance of a mediated approach. However, the activity of abstraction (or whatever psychological process is proposed to do its work) can deliver a mediating mental product which represents one property rather than another only if the activity and its product have been subjected by the speaker to a specific and fitting interpretation. And now, if we ask what is it that determines which, if any, interpretation of the abstraction process the speaker has had in mind, then we are launched on the familiar infinite regress of interpretations that Wittgenstein regularly invokes. So, McDowell agrees with Kripke and Wright that classical realism, at least in its individualistic version, can't get off the ground. Moreover, although McDowell goes on to stress the crucial contribution of social practice to meaning, it is plain that he does not intend to be defending a social or community wide version of classical realism about meaning or truth conditions.

At this stage of his argument, McDowell may be in greater agreement with Kripke than he supposes. McDowell believes that *WRPL* is to be read as representing the melodramatic reading of the Skeptical Argument and so has Wittgenstein embracing a radical non-factualism about meaning ascriptions. But, of course, if Kripke had in mind only the merely dramatic reading of the Skeptical Argument, then Kripke and McDowell both read Wittgenstein as opposing classical realism about meaning and truth conditions. That is, both philosophers have the ambition of repudiating classical realism without collapsing into a paradoxical non-factualism. Thus, McDowell states,

When we say "'Diamonds are hard' is true if and only if diamonds are hard", we are just as much involved on the right hand side as the reflections on rule-following tell us we are. There is a standing temptation to miss this obvious truth, and to suppose that the right-hand side somehow presents us with *a possible fact* [my italics], pictured as an unconceptualized configuration of things in themselves. But we can find the connection between meaning and truth illuminating without succumbing to this temptation.   (McDowell, p. 74)

The temptation here is to imagine that the constraints imposed by our concepts have the sort of 'Platonistic autonomy' that classical realism about truth and meaning characteristically affirms.

Of course, Kripke maintains that the rejection of classical realism requires the reconstructive surgery of a Skeptical Solution, while McDowell thinks that no such philosophical reconstruction is called for here at all. McDowell criticizes Kripke for failing to grasp the crucial role in Wittgenstein's dialectic of his rejection of what McDowell calls 'the master thesis'—the thesis that meaning and understanding is always a matter of 'interpretation.' And yet, as the earlier presentation of the merely dramatic version of the Skeptical Argument indicates, Kripke's Wittgenstein can be read as rejecting a 'master thesis' that is expressible in those very words, and the rejection of that thesis is crucial to the resolution of the central paradox in #201. Nevertheless, it is unlikely that Kripke and McDowell will understand such a 'master thesis' in the same way. For Kripke, the master thesis, in the setting of his account of Wittgenstein, will simply constitute a succinct expression of classical realism. For McDowell, it is the wider thesis that words and sentences have the meanings that they do only because an individual speaker or the linguistic community as a whole has somehow *assigned* their content to them. On his view, when the underlying basis of Wittgenstein's rejection of such a master thesis has been fully grasped and assimilated, then we can see how it is intelligible to deny classical realism without reneging on our intuitive commitment to the objectivity of judgment and without elaborating some positive theory of truth and meaning. Naturally, an amplified conception of McDowell's master this and of the considerations that, in his opinion, motivate rejecting it are crucial to his distinctive approach to these issues. Some critics, e.g., Gary Ebbs in *Rule-Following and Realism*, have argued that, under critical pressure, McDowell's position either veers back toward the metaphysics and epistemology of a social version of classical realism or winds up itself committed to at least a modest form of anti-realism. I don't have the space to explore these delicate questions here.

If classical realism is a chief example of the Scylla that McDowell thinks that one has to avoid, then antirealist accounts of meaning, such as Kripke's Skeptical Solution, represent the equally threatening Charybdis. McDowell insists that antirealist accounts simply fail to satisfy his objectivity constraint. (On his reading of the later writings, McDowell thinks that Wittgenstein has achieved the 'perfectly satisfying' intermediate account that avoids the overinflated semantic realism of Scylla and the failure to ensure the objectivity of judgment characteristic of Charybdis.) According to the Skeptical Solution, ascriptions of meaning to a term are warranted by the bare facts about the actual ongoing linguistic practices of the speech community. These will include facts about the circumstances under which members of the community endorse or reject the ascription of a term to its candidate instances; facts about the way in which a term is taught, including the character of expressions of criticism and agreement in teaching; and facts about the procedures that are in actual practice employed to ascertain the warrant of particular ascriptions. Finally, the Skeptical Solution also posits that it is relevant to what a term means for the community that the acceptance and rejection of various such ascriptions have characteristic consequences within the relevant language-games and, therefore, have a certain role or utility within these settings. Out of materials of these sorts, McDowell urges, it is impossible to construct a positive account of meaning that has any hope of satisfying his objectivity constraint. He maintains that there is simply no way in which we can explain, in the framework of antirealism, how it is that a speaker can be committed to a determinate normative pattern of application that covers an unbounded range of actual and possible ascriptions of the term, settling their correctness conditions across the range. This is the heart of McDowell's challenge to antirealist accounts of meaning. The challenge seems especially formidable if one agrees with McDowell that a fully adequate antirealist account should have application to linguistic meanings *and* to the contents of propositional attitudes. He concludes from this adequacy condition that the Skeptical Solution must accept that facts about linguistic usage, taken at 'the basic level,' are purely non-intentional. However, even if the requirement that the 'basic level' facts must be non-intentional is relaxed, it still can seem that the difficulty for the antirealist of satisfying the objectivity constraint is daunting. In my opinion McDowell has raised an important challenge for antirealist accounts to answer, but he gives the further impression that it is pretty obvious that the challenge can't be met.

I don't believe that this is so obvious. The issue can be illustrated in the following way. In the passage quoted above, McDowell gives the impression that an antirealist account of meaning that partially but centrally explains meaning in terms of assertability conditions is unable to introduce and sustain "a notion of correctness" for 'Φ' ascriptions such that the correctness, in this sense, of a particular 'Φ' ascription is independent of any actual investigation of the question. But, on first impression at least, this claim is too strong. For example, let P be a proposition that says that an object o is Φ at t. We stipulate that P is 'counterfactually warranted at t' if a competent investigator of 'Φ' ascriptions *would* be warranted in asserting P if he *were* to apply to o at t a standardly accepted test procedure for 'Φ' ascriptions. As far as I can see, there is no reason why the Skeptical Solution cannot allow that there will be a fact of the matter as to whether P has counterfactual warrant at t even though no one has actually investigated the relevant case at all. Having counterfactual warrant at a time is a property that marks its instances as being, in a certain sense, 'correct,' albeit in a restricted and conditional way. Admittedly, the property of having counterfactual warrant falls far short of serving as a surrogate for an intuitive conception of 'objective truth.' For one thing, warranted assertability is a defeasible notion and so is the concept of 'being counterfactually warranted.' That is, a proposition can be counterfactually warranted at a time although the warrant that it has counterfactually might turn out to be defeated by additional and more far reaching considerations concerning either o or the epistemic standing of the test procedure itself. Nevertheless, the fact remains that it constitutes a simple notion of 'correctness' for propositions that seems to be independent of all actual investigations of the matter.

Now, it is likely that McDowell intends to be appealing to a significantly stronger conception of investigation independence. If so, it becomes important to have the envisaged strengthening spelled out. Having counterfactual warrant might fail to be investigation independent in the hypothetical stronger sense, but the antirealist framework of the Skeptical Solution also has richer resources. It leaves conceptual space for concepts of propositional 'correctness' that are richer and more robust than the concept of 'having counterfactual warrant.' After all, in the Skeptical Solution, the meaning of a term is not grounded merely upon its *de facto* assertability conditions but also on its role or utility in the language games in which it figures. What is more, even simple language games will include community practices of counting, measuring, matching to a sample, etc. It certainly seems possible that these materials will yield various more robust concepts of 'propositional correctness'. Let 'R-correctness' stand in for an arbitrary one of these more robust notions. It is an open question whether the pattern described in the previous paragraph won't repeat. That is, it will generally be an open question whether the fact that propositions—say 'Φ' ascriptions—that are R-correct are investigation independent in the strengthened sense as well. The point here is not to make a prediction about how these questions might play out. The point is that such a debate will not be settled by anything less than an extended, detailed investigation of the pertinent concepts of 'correctness' and 'investigation independence' and how they turn out to be related. Hence, it is not obvious, as McDowell suggests, that an antirealist account of meaning must clash with the intuitive investigation independence of certain antirealist notions of 'propositional correctness'.[4]

However, McDowell may mean to be arguing a somewhat different point. His view may be that an antirealist account of meaning must conflict with at least some of

---

[4] These and related questions are explored at great length in Crispin Wright's *Truth and Objectivity*.

our fundamental intuitions concerning objective truth. Thus, the reference to invest-igation independence may be intended to highlight just this one significant facet of the richer and more fundamental concept of 'truth.' This claim does seem likely to be true. It might even be, for instance, that our intuitive concept of 'objective truth' incorporates a classical realist view of truth or satisfaction conditions. Still, what are we to conclude if this or something similar turns out to be right? Surely, the antire-alist believes that some basic strands in the intuitive concept of 'objective truth' are defective. This is almost certainly the perspective of any serious antirealism about meaning and truth. So, once again, the prospects that McDowell's discussion can settle the case against antirealism are not very promising. The disagreements between McDowell and the antirealist at this juncture seem to be roughly equivalent to the most fundamental divisions in philosophical opinion about the nature of truth.

Kripke introduces the idea that meaning is normative in the following well-known passage:

> What is the relation of this supposition [the supposition that I mean addition by "+"] to the question how I will respond to the problem '68 + 57'? The dispositionalist gives a *descriptive* account of this relation: if '+' meant addition, then I will answer '125'. But this is not the proper account of the relation, which is *normative*, not descriptive. The point is *not* that, if I meant addition by '+', I will answer '125', but if I intend to accord with my past meaning of "+", I *should* answer '125'.   (*WRPL*, p. 37)

A lot has been written about what this normativity of meaning could amount to, but, in its broadest features, the notion is clear enough. If a person or linguistic com-munity means something by a term, then they are thereby committed to standards of correctness that govern their prospective application of the term. If some item *o* is a candidate for possible 'Φ' ascription, then depending upon the facts about what the relevant standards are and the relevant facts about *o*, a speaker who is com-mitted to the standards *should* (or *should not*, as the case may be) ascribe 'Φ' to *o*. Having said this much about the general concept of 'the normativity of meaning,' almost everything else is potentially in dispute. What kind of thing is a standard of correctness? Indeed, what sort of correctness is supposed to be in question here? And, in what sense are speakers committed to the standards in question? Are these commitments that individual speakers adopt, by forming and acting upon certain semantic intentions? Or, are these commitments imposed upon the speaker because of his participation in certain social institutions of the community? Or, is it some combination of the two? Giving a positive theory of the normativity of meaning that answers these questions has proved to be very difficult, and it is unlikely that there can be a positive theory that is neutral between the different approaches to meaning, truth conditions, and rule following that have been the subject of this entry.

References

An excellent anthology is *Rule-Following and Meaning*, edited by Alexander Miller and Crispin Wright, Chesham, England: Acumen Press, 2002. When papers included in this anthology are cited in the entry, page references are to the reprinted versions in the anthology.

Baker, Gordon and Hacker, P. M. S. *Scepticism, Rules, and Language* (Oxford: Blackwell, 1984).

——— *Wittgenstein: Understanding and Meaning* (Oxford: Blackwell, 1980).

Blackburn, Simon. "The Individual Strikes Back." *Synthese* 58 (1984), pp. 281–301. Kluwer Academic Publishers. Reprinted in *Rule-Following and Meaning*.

——— "Wittgenstein's Irrealism." In J. Brandl and R. Haller (eds.) *Wittgenstein: Eine Neubewehrung* (Vienna: Holder-Pichler-Temsky, 1990).

Boghossian, Paul A. "The Rule-Following Considerations." *Mind* 98 (1989), pp. 507–49. Reprinted in *Rule-Following and Meaning*.

Brandom, Robert. *Making it Explicit* (Cambridge, MA: Harvard University Press, 1994).

Byrne, Alexander. "On Misinterpreting Kripke's Wittgenstein." *Philosophy and Phenomenological Research* 56 (1996).

Davies, David. "How skeptical is Kripke's 'Sceptical Solution'." *Philosophia* 26 (1998).

Diamond, Cora. *The Realistic Spirit: Wittgenstein, Philosophy, and the Mind.* (Cambridge, MA: MIT Press, 1991), Chapter 7.

Dummett, Michael. *Frege: Philosophy of Language* (Cambridge, MA: Harvard University Press, 1993).

——— *Truth and Other Enigmas* (Cambridge, MA: Harvard University Press, 1981).

Ebbs, Gary. *Rule-Following and Realism* (Cambridge, MA: Harvard University Press, 1997), Chapter 5.

Fitch, G. W. *Saul Kripke* (Chesham, England: Acumen Press, 2004), Chapter 7.

Forbes, Graeme. "Scepticism and Semantic Knowledge." *Proceedings of the Aristotelian Society*, 1983–4, pp. 223–37. Blackwell Publishers. Reprinted in *Rule-Following and Meaning*.

Gibbard, Allan. "Meaning and Normativity." In E. Villanueva (ed.) *Philosophical Issues* 5 (Atascadero, CA: Ridgeview Publishing Co., 1994), pp. 95–115.

Ginet, Carl. "The Dispositionalist Solution to Wittgenstein's Problem about Understanding a Rule: Answering Kripke's Objections." In P. A. French, T. E. Uehling, and H. K. Wettstein (eds.) *Midwest Studies in Philosophy, Volume XII: The Wittgenstein Legacy* (Notre Dame: University of Notre Dame Press, 1992).

Goldfarb, Warren. "Kripke on Wittgenstein on Rules." *Journal of Philosophy* (1985), pp. 471–488. Reprinted in *Rule-Following and Meaning*.

——— "Wittgenstein on Understanding." In P. A. French, T. E. Uehling, and H. K. Wettstein (eds.) *Midwest Studies in Philosophy, Volume XII: The Wittgenstein Legacy* (Notre Dame: University of Notre Dame Press, 1992).

Hacker, P. M. S. *Wittgenstein: Meaning and Mind* (Oxford: Blackwell, 1989).

Hale, Bob. "Rule-Following, Objectivity, and Meaning." In B. Hale, and C. Wright (eds.) *A Companion to the Philosophy of Language* (Oxford: Blackwell, 1997).

Heal, Jane. *Fact and Meaning* (Oxford: Blackwell, 1990).

Hoffman, Paul. "Kripke on Private Language." *Philosophical Studies* 47 (1985).

Horwich, Paul. "Meaning, Use and Truth." *Mind* 104 (1995), pp. 355–68. Oxford University Press. Reprinted in *Rule-Following and Meaning*.

——— "Critical Notice of Kripke's *Wittgenstein on Rules and Private Language*." *Philosophy of Science* 51 (1984).

——— "Wittgenstein and Kripke on the Nature of Meaning." *Mind and Language* 5 (1990).

——— *Meaning* (Oxford: Oxford University Press, 1998).

Johnston, Mark. "Objectivity Disfigured." (Appendix 3), In J. Haldane and C. Wright (eds.) *Reality, Representation, and Projection* (Oxford: Oxford University Press, 1993).

Koethe, John. *The Continuity of Wittgenstein's Thought* (Ithaca, NY: Cornell University Press, 1996)

Kremer, Michael. "Wilson on Kripke's Wittgenstein." *Philosophy and Phenomenological Research* 60 (2000).

Kripke, Saul. *Wittgenstein on Rules and Private Language* (Boston: Harvard University Press, 1984).

Malcolm, Norman. "Wittgenstein on Language and Rules." *Philosophy* 64 (1989).

McDowell, John. "Meaning and Intention in Wittgenstein's Later Philosophy." In P. A. French, T. E. Uehling, Jr., and H. K. Wettstein (eds.), *Midwest Studies in Philosophy, Volume XII: The Wittgensteinian Legacy* (Notre Dame: University of Notre Dame Press, 1992).

——— "Non-Cognitivism and Rule-Following." In S. Holtzmann and C. Leich (eds.) *Wittgenstein: To Follow a Rule* (London: Routledge and Kegan Paul, 1981).

——— "One Strand in the Private Language Argument." *Grazer Philosphiche Studien* 33/4 (1989).

——— "Reply to Wright." In C. McDonald, B. Smith, and C. Wright (eds.) *On Knowing One's Own Mind* (Oxford: Oxford University Press, 1998).

McDowell, John. "Wittgenstein on Following a Rule." *Synthese* 58 (1984), pp. 325–63. Kluwer Academic Publishers. Reprinted in *Rule-Following and Meaning*.

McGinn, Colin. "Wittgenstein, Kripke, and Non-Reductionism about Meaning." In McGinn's *Wittgenstein on Meaning* (Oxford: Blackwell, 1984), pp. 150–64. Reprinted in *Rule-Following and Meaning*.

McGinn, Marie. "Kripke on Wittgenstein's Sceptical Problem." *Ratio* (1984).

_____ *Wittgenstein and the Philosophical Investigations* (London: Routledge Press, 1997), Chapter 3.

Miller, Alexander. "Horwich, Meaning, and Kripke's Wittgenstein." *Philosophical Quarterly* 50 (2000).

_____ "Rule-Following, Response-Dependence and McDowell's Debate With AntiRealism." *European Review of Philosophy* 3 (1998).

Millikan, Ruth Garrett. "Truth Rules, Hoverflies, and the Kripke-Wittgenstein Paradox." *The Philosophical Review* 99, no. 3 (1990), pp. 323–53. Reprinted in *Rule-Following and Meaning*.

Peacocke, Christopher. "Rule-Following: The Nature of Wittgenstein's Arguments." In S. Holtzmann and C. Leich (eds.) *Wittgenstein: To Follow a Rule* (London: Routledge and Kegan Paul, 1981).

Pears, David. *The False Prison* volume 2 (Oxford: Oxford University Press, 1988).

Pettit, Philip. "The Reality of Rule-Following." *Mind* 99 (1990), pp. 1–21. Oxford University Press. Reprinted in *Rule-Following and Meaning*.

Soames, Scott. "Facts, Truth-Conditions, and the Skeptical Solution to the Rule-Following Paradox." In J. Tomberlin (ed.) *Philosophical Perspectives* 12: *Language, Mind, and Ontology* (1998a).

_____ "Part One: Ludwig Wittgenstein's *Philosophical Investigations*." In *Philosophical Analysis in the Twentieth Century: Vol. 2, The Age of Meaning*, (Princeton: Princeton University Press, 2003), pp. 1–63.

_____ "Skepticism About Meaning: Indeterminacy, Normativity, and the Rule-Following Paradox." *Canadian Journal of Philosophy*, supp. Vol. 23 (1998b).

Thornton, Tim. "Intention, Rule-Following, and the Strategic Role of Wright's Order-of-Determination Test." *Philosophical Investigations* 20 (1997).

Wilson, George M. "Kripke on Wittgenstein on Normativity." *Midwest Studies in Philosophy* 19 (1994), pp. 366–90. Reprinted in *Rule-Following and Meaning*.

_____ "Semantic Realism and Kripke's Wittgenstein." *Philosophy and Phenomenological Research* 83 (1998).

Wilson, Mark. "Predicate Meets Property," *The Philosophical Review* 91 (1982).

Wittgenstein, Ludwig. *Philosophical Investigations* (Oxford: Blackwell Publishing, 1958).

_____ *Remarks on the Foundations of Mathematics*. Ed. R. Rhees, trans. G. E. M. Anscombe (Boston: The MIT Press, 1983).

Wright, Crispin. "Critical Notice of Colin McGinn's *Wittgenstein on Meaning*." *Mind* 98 (1989), pp. 289–305. Oxford University Press. Reprinted in *Rule-Following and Meaning*.

_____ "Does PI §§258–60 Suggest A Cogent Argument Against Private Language?." In J. McDowell and P. Petit (eds.) *Subject, Thought and Context* (Oxford: Oxford University Press, 1986).

_____ "Kripke's Account of the Argument Against Private Language." *Journal of Philosophy* 81 (1984).

_____ "Meaning and Intention as Judgment Dependent." In Wright's "Wittgenstein's Rule-Following Considerations and the Central Project of Theoretical Linguistics", in A. George (ed.), *Reflections on Chomsky* (Oxford: Blackwell, 1989), pp. 246–54. Reprinted in *Rule-Following and Meaning*.

_____ *Rails to Infinity* (Cambridge, MA: Harvard University Press, 2001).

_____ "Realism, Antirealism, Irrealism, Quasi-Realism." *Midwest Studies in Philosophy* 12 (1998).

_____ "Rule-Following, Meaning, and Constructivism." In C. Travis (ed.) *Meaning and Interpretation* (Oxford: Blackwell, 1986).

_____ "Self-Knowledge: The Wittgensteinian Legacy." In C. McDonald, B. Smith, and C. Wright (eds.) *On Knowing One's Own Mind* (Oxford: Oxford University Press, 1998).

_____ *Truth and Objectivity* (Cambridge, MA: Harvard University Press, 1992).

_____ *Wittgenstein on the Foundations of Mathematics* (London: Duckworth, 1980), Chapters 2 and 12.

_____ "Wittgenstein's Later Philosophy of Mind: Sensation, Privacy, and Intention." In K. Puhl (ed.) *Meaning-Scepticism* (Berlin: De Gruyter, 1991).

Zalabardo, José L. "Kripke's Normativity Argument." *Canadian Journal of Philosophy* 27, no. 4 (1997), pp. 467–88. University of Calgary Press. Reprinted in *Rule-Following and Meaning*.

C H A P T E R 8

....

NATURALIST
THEORIES OF
MEANING

....

DAVID PAPINEAU

NATURALIST theories of meaning aim to account for representation within a naturalist framework. This programme involves two ideas: representation and naturalism. Both of these call for some initial comment.

To begin with the former, representation is as familiar as it is puzzling. The English sentence 'Santiago is east of Sacramento' represents the world as being a certain way. So does my belief that Santiago is east of Sacramento. In these examples, one item—a sentence or a belief—lays claim to something else, a state of affairs, which may be far removed in space and time. This is the phenomenon that naturalist theories of meaning aim to explain. How is it possible for one thing to stand for something else in this way?

Sentences can represent, and so can mental states. By and large, naturalist theories of meaning take mental representation to be basic, and linguistic representation to be derivative. Most such theories aim first to account for the representational powers of mental states—paradigmatically beliefs—and then to account for the representational powers of sentences in public languages by viewing the latter as in some sense 'expressing' mental states.[1]

Most naturalist theories of meaning also subscribe to some version of the 'language of thought' hypothesis. That is, they assume that the vehicles of mental

---

[1] The view that mental representation is more basic than public language allows that creatures without any public language might nevertheless have mental representations. But at the same time it leaves open the possibility that many human mental representations may be developmentally or even constitutively dependent on surrounding linguistic practices.

representation are inner items with sentence-like structure, at least to the extent that they are constructed from recombinable word-like components ('concepts') which carry their representational content from use to use.

It is not clear how far these commitments—to the primacy of mental representation over public linguistic representation, and to an inner language of thought—are essential to naturalist theories of meaning. One can imagine versions of the theories to be discussed below that relax either or both of these assumptions. Still, most existing naturalist theories do work within this framework, and it will be convenient to take it as given in what follows.

What about the requirements of 'naturalism'? At its most general, naturalism says that the methods and ontology of the natural sciences are sufficient for understanding reality. A naturalist theory of meaning would thus aim to bring the phenomenon of representation within the scope of the natural sciences. However, naturalism in this general sense is a very open-ended doctrine. There are many different branches of natural science—from physics and paleontology to meteorology and zoology—each with its own methods and ontologies. Without some further specification of what counts as a 'natural science', it is unclear that 'naturalism' imposes any genuine requirements at all. In particular, it is unclear why our everyday pre-theoretical understanding of representation should not already qualify as naturalistic, without the help of any further theoretical analysis.

Contemporary naturalism normally also endorses some version of physicalism. But it is not clear that even this further commitment imposes any substantial methodological constraints on theories of representation. Contemporary physicalism only requires that non-physical properties must 'supervene' on physical properties (in the sense that any non-physical differences between things must derive from physical differences) not that they be type-identical with physical properties (Fodor, 1974). Again, this leaves it unclear why our everyday pre-theoretical understanding of representation should be in need of help from further 'naturalistic' theorizing. After all, our everyday pre-theoretical understanding of representation already seems in perfectly good accord with the requirement that representational facts should supervene on physical ones.

Still, even if 'naturalism' as such does not impose any strong reductive demands, it is not difficult to motivate theories which aim to account for representation in terms of such basic scientific categories as causation, spatio-temporal correlation, functional isomorphism, or biological function. Representational facts appear radically unlike facts found in other branches of science. A pattern of marks on paper, or a state in some psychological system, somehow reaches out and lays claim to some possibly distant state of affairs. How is the trick done? And how do these representational relations interact with other features of the natural world? If some theory can answer these questions by reducing representational relations to other familiar categories, then that would clearly constitute an achievement, whether or not such a theory is mandated by the methodological requirements of 'naturalism'.

From this perspective, the proof of the naturalistic approach to meaning will be in the eating. Naturalists will seek some *a posteriori* reduction of representation to other scientifically familiar categories, and aim thereby to show how representational relations play a role in the scientifically described world. If this project succeeds, then that will be its own vindication. Of course, it remains open that no such reduction is possible. In that event, thinkers of strongly naturalist inclinations may wish to argue that representational relations should be eliminated from our world view, on the grounds that nothing in reality answers to our everyday conception of representation.[2] Others, however, will maintain that our everyday conception of representation is acceptable in its own right, even if no reduction to other scientific categories is possible. Fortunately, we can leave this issue open here. Our main business is with the prior question of whether any of the naturalistic theories so far proposed does constitute a plausible scientific reduction of representation.

8.1 INFERENTIAL ROLE SEMANTICS

One family of naturalist theories of meaning take the representational content of mental states to be constituted by their *inferential role*. (Harman, 1982, 1987; Block, 1986. See also Cummins, 1991; Peacocke, 1992, for related approaches see also Conceptual Role Semantics.)

Take the concept *dog*. This bears inferential relations to various other concepts, including *animal, mammal,* and *pet*. Inferential role semantics takes the total set of such inferential relations to fix the content of *dog*. This can be seen as involving two elements: first, the cognitive role (the connotation, the sense) of *dog* is identified with this set of inferential relations; given this, the referential value (the extension, the denotation) of *dog* is equated with that entity, if any, whose real-world relations to the referents of *animal, pet* and so on are isomorphic to the inferential relations *dog* bears to these other concepts.

An initial problem for any theory of this kind is to avoid conceptual holism and consequent problems for the public communicability of concepts (Fodor and Lepore, 1992). Different subjects are unlikely ever to embed a concept in exactly the same set of inferential relations—given my particular views about dogs, I will no doubt infer some different things from applications of the concept *dog* than you will. If the cognitive identity of any concept depends on the totality of inferential relations it enters into, then it would seem to follow that different individuals will rarely share the same concept. But this seems inconsistent with the existence of public languages, and in particular with the fact that a *word* like 'dog' expresses the same concept in the mouths of different individuals.

The obvious response to this problem is to say that not all inferential liaisons contribute to the cognitive identity of concepts. This would then allow different

---

[2] This eliminativist position is defended in Churchland, 1989. An alternative to outright eliminativism about representation is offered by 'minimalist' or 'disquotationalist' views which hold that the truth predicate does not refer to any substantial property, but is rather a device for endorsing claims without asserting them (cf. Horwich, 1990).

individuals to display idiosyncratic inferential dispositions without this automatically rendering their concepts incommensurable. The trouble with this suggestion, however, is that there seems no principled way of distinguishing those 'analytic' inferential liaisons that contribute to the identity of concepts from the 'synthetic' ones that do not (Quine, 1951). Moreover, even if there were some way of making this distinction, the original problem is likely to remain, for there is no obvious reason why individuals should coincide even in those analytic inferential liaisons that do fix the cognitive identity of concepts.

Another major problem facing inferential role theories is the apparent circularity of the way they explain reference. The idea is that the referent of *dog* is that entity which is appropriately related to the referents of *animal, pet* and so on. But what determines the referents of the latter concepts? If their referents are explained in the same way, as depending on the inferential relations that these concepts bear to yet other concepts, then there would seem nothing to tie down the overall structure of inferentially related concepts to the real world. At best that structure could be seen as representing *any* set of entities that bear relations that are isomorphic to the inferential relations between the concepts. But then it seems that *dog, animal, pet* and so on will come out as representing many different things—structures of atoms, stars, or whatever—as well as the kinds they actually represent. For surely there are many structures of atoms, stars, and other things that are related in ways that are isomorphic to the inferential relations between *dog, animal, pet* and so on.[3]

In the face of this problem, the natural move is to allow that some concepts have their reference fixed by something other than their inferential role. But this move will then require some explanation of representation that goes beyond purely inferential role semantics. It remains possible that inferential role semantics alone can explain the content of *some* concepts, once the contents of others have been explained in some different way. However, I shall not pursue this possibility here, since it leaves inferential role semantics with only a derivative part in explaining reference, and moreover still facing the problem of conceptual holism.

8.2 CAUSAL THEORIES

Another family of naturalist theories of meaning aims to explain the representational content of mental states in terms of the conditions that *cause* those states, and which those states therefore indicate (Stampe, 1977; Dretske, 1981, 1988; Fodor 1990). At its simplest, such a theory might start by equating the content of any belief-like mental state B with that condition C which is causally responsible for all tokens of B.

This simple theory is clearly too crude, however, since it lacks the resources to explain *misrepresentation*. Misrepresentation by a belief-like state occurs when the

---

[3] Cummins (1992) is prepared to embrace such a referentially promiscuous notion of representation, at least for the purposes of cognitive science.

state is tokened, but its truth condition does not obtain. However, if the state's truth condition is simply the range of circumstances that cause the state to be tokened, then it is unclear how the state *can* be tokened and yet its truth condition not obtain.

To make the problem clear, take a state that intuitively represents the presence of a snake. Such a state will often be caused, not by real snakes, but also by glimpses of slithery animals, toy snakes, and so on. The problem for the simple causal theory is that it has no obvious way of excluding these misleading extra causes from this state's truth condition. So the causal theory seems to end up implying, absurdly, that all tokenings of this belief-like state are true.

Fred Dretske (1981) develops a version of indicator semantics that is designed to account for misrepresentation. He argues that the truth condition of a belief-like state B should be identified specifically with the causes of tokens of B that occur during 'the learning period', that is, during the period when the disposition to produce tokens of B is reinforced by experience. This then leaves room for tokens of B produced outside the learning period to misrepresent, since they might or might not be due to the same causes that operated during the learning period.

While Dretske's theory does leave room for misrepresentation, it faces other difficulties. For one thing, it presupposes a sharp distinction between the learning period (when misrepresentation is impossible) and subsequent tokenings of B (which can misrepresent), even though there seems no principled basis in psychological learning theory for such a demarcation. Another problem is that there seems no good reason why the causes that do operate during the learning period should automatically be included in B's truth condition: for example, a child might learn to represent snakes by observing toy snakes or pictures of snakes, yet toy snakes and pictures of snakes are not part of the truth condition of *snake*.[4]

Jerry Fodor (1990) defends a different version of indicator semantics. His basic idea is to discriminate fundamental from derivative causes of B, and to equate truth conditions with the fundamental causes. By way of example, note that the belief *there's a cow* can be caused by cows, but also by horses at some distance. However, the relationship between horses and this belief is only derivative, argues Fodor, in that horses wouldn't cause this belief if cows didn't, whereas cows would still cause this belief even if horses didn't. According to Fodor's *asymmetric dependence theory*, B represents C just in case (i) C causes Bs and (ii) for any other D that causes Bs, D wouldn't cause Bs if C didn't cause Bs, while C would still cause B even if D didn't. On this account, then, the belief that *there's a cow* represents cows but not horses, because of the asymmetric way this beliefs depends on the cows and horses respectively.

The basic worry about this theory is that it seems in danger of implicitly supposing what it is supposed to explain. Who says that cows would still cause the mental state that actually has the content *there's a cow*, even if horses didn't? After all, it is pretty inevitable that people are always going to mistake a few horses for cows. So if

---

[4] Dretske (1988) adds a teleological component to his causal theory of representation, but difficulties relating to the learning period remain.

some state were never caused by horses, then surely it would follow that it couldn't mean *there's a cow*. However, if this is right, then Fodor's counterfactuals will fail to discriminate cows from horses as the referent of *there's a cow*, since neither horses nor cows would cause this state if the other didn't. In the light of this objection, it looks as if Fodor must implicitly be holding fixed the actual content of the mental state when he insists that cows would still cause this state, even if horses didn't. But this would be illegitimate, in a context where the counterfactuals are supposed to provide a metaphysical reduction of representational content.

8.3 SUCCESS SEMANTICS

All causal indicator theories share one important feature. They focus on the conditions that *give rise* to belief-like representations, aiming to equate truth-conditional content with some distinguished subset of these 'input' conditions. A different family of theories does things the other way around. Instead of starting with the conditions that give rise to representations, they focus on the *consequences* of representations. Such 'output-orientated' theories include success semantics and teleosemantics. I shall discuss success semantics in this section and teleosemantics in the following sections.

According to success-semantics, the truth condition of any belief is that circumstance which will ensure the satisfaction of whichever desire combines with the belief to prompt action. (Ramsey, 1927; Appiah, 1986; Whyte, 1990; Dokic and Engel, 2002.)

More intuitively, what makes it the case that you believe p is that you behave in a way that will satisfy your desires *if* p. For example, you believe that there is beer in the fridge if you go to the fridge when you want a beer.

Success semantics has no difficulty accommodating misrepresentation. Because it analyses truth conditions in terms of results, rather than causes, it carries no implication that beliefs will generally tend to be true. The content of a belief is fixed by the behaviour it generates, not by the causes that give rise to it. As long as it makes me go to the fridge, my state will have the content that there is beer there, even if this state is characteristically caused when there is no beer in the fridge. Success semantics thus creates ample room for beliefs to be false, even typically false.

One obvious problem facing success semantics is that many beliefs will only combine with desires to generate behaviour if they are conjoined with yet further beliefs. (Consider, for example, the belief that the sun has nine planets.) To deal with this, success semantics needs a more complicated formulation: the truth condition of any belief is that circumstance which will ensure the satisfaction of whichever desire it combines with to prompt action, *on the assumption that any other beliefs involved in generating that action are true*.

However, as it stands this is obviously inadequate as a reductive account of truth-conditional content, since the last clause assumes the notion of truth. The most promising way for success semantics to overcome this difficulty is to regard the connection between truth conditions and desire satisfaction as being imposed simultaneously on all the beliefs in a thinker's repertoire. We get the truth condition for all these beliefs by solving a set of simultaneous equations, so to speak. The 'equations' are the assumptions that the truth condition of each belief guarantees desire satisfaction, if all other relevant beliefs are true. The 'solution' is then a collective assignment of truth conditions that satisfies all those equations.

There is another obvious objection to success semantics. In explaining truth conditions, it assumes the notion of desire satisfaction. But desire satisfaction is itself a representational notion, and so cannot be taken for granted by a reductive theory of representation.

The natural response to this difficulty is to find some independent account of desire satisfaction (Whyte, 1991.) One possibility is to equate satisfaction conditions for desires with those circumstances that typically *extinguish* the desire—my desire is a desire for beer because it is beer that makes that desire go away. An alternative is to equate satisfaction conditions with those results that are *reinforcing*—that is, which make it more likely that the behaviour prompted by the desire will be repeated next time the desire is activated.

However, it is not clear that either of these suggestions is fully satisfactory. The equation of satisfaction conditions with extinguishing circumstances has difficulties with desires that are fuelled by their own satisfaction (salted peanuts) or quenched by their non-satisfaction (sour grapes). Again, the explanation of satisfaction in terms of reinforcement seems to rule out the possibility of desire content where there is no reinforcement learning, even though this would seem a real possibility, both for primitive creatures with limited behavioural flexibility and for humans in respect of their more abstract desires.

8.4 TELEOSEMANTICS[5]

One way of understanding teleosemantics is as a combination of success semantics with a teleological account of desire satisfaction. (Cf. Papineau, 1993, ch. 3.) So conceived, teleosemantics embraces the connection between truth conditions and desire satisfaction articulated by success semantics, and then deals with the problem of explaining desire satisfaction by equating satisfaction conditions with the *biological functions* of desires. (The notion of biological 'function' invoked here is in turn explained in aetiological-selectional terms: the biological functions of desires are those results in virtue of which the desires have been favoured by past processes of natural selection.)

This approach to teleosemantics is 'top-down', in that it takes a realistic attitude to human belief-desire psychology, and then seeks a naturalistic account of representation for the human beliefs and desires it is thus committed to. Ruth Millikan has developed a more generalized 'bottom-up' version of teleosemantics, aimed in the

---

[5] I would like to thank Graham MacDonald for helping to develop these comments on teleosemantics.

first instance at representation in organisms far simpler than human beings (1984, 1993). Millikan starts by distinguishing mechanisms that *produce* mental representations from those that *consume* them. The producing mechanisms are paradigmatically the sensory processes that give rise to cognitive representations. The consumer mechanisms are those that use these representations to direct behaviour in pursuit of some biological end. Millikan then considers the biological functions of mental representations. Biological functions are in the first instance always a matter of effects. So the function of a mental representation must lie in the way it contributes to the biological end of the mechanism that consumes it. More specifically, its function will be to enable the consumer mechanism to achieve its end by gearing behaviour to circumstances. Given this, argues Millikan, we can think of the representation's truth condition as the circumstance that enables it to fulfil this function—that is, as the circumstance in which the behaviour it prompts is designed to produce the consumer mechanism's end.

Millikan's version of teleosemantics coincides with the version that builds on success semantics if we equate the consumer mechanism for a *belief* with the decision-making process that uses that belief to select behaviour that will satisfy currently active *desires*. Given this, the association of a success condition with a belief can be viewed as one example of the way Millikan's analysis fixes the content of any belief-like representation. At the same time, Millikan's version of teleosemantics is far more general than the success-semantics alternative, in that it can also deal with representation in creatures who lack the cognitive complexity of full belief-desire psychology.

Millikan's bottom-up strategy has the obvious advantage of more general applicability, and moreover avoids the danger that everyday belief-psychology may offer a misleading picture of actual human cognitive structure. On the other hand, a full account of mental representation will need to cover human cognition too, and the top-down approach via success semantics offers one possible account of this. In the end, perhaps the two approaches are best thought of as complementary rather than competing.

In what follows I shall ignore the differences between these versions of teleosemantics and concentrate on issues that arise for both. The next subsection will focus on the output-orientation of teleosemantics, while the final subsection will be concerned with teleosemantics' commitment to selectional functions.

8.4.1 Teleosemantics and Outputs

One strength of teleosemantics is that it inherits the ability of success semantics to deal with misrepresentation. Since teleosemantics is also output-based, it coincides with success semantics in imposing no requirements on how representations are caused, nor on the reliability of the mechanisms which produce them. A representation can have the content that p, in the sense that resulting behaviour will be successful if p, even if its producing mechanisms are highly prone to give rise to the representation when not-p.

Moreover, now that we are thinking of representation from a specifically biological perspective, this divergence between truth-conditional content and typical causes is no longer merely an abstract possibility. Consider a small mammal which can form a representation which will lead it to behave in a way appropriate to an eagle being overhead. According to teleosemantics, this representation will have the content 'eagle overhead', since its purpose is to prompt behaviour which will be advantageous specifically in that circumstance. However, given the relative biological costs of false positives and negatives in this context, we can expect that the mechanisms which produce this representation will err generously on the side of caution, and frequently trigger the representation in circumstances where no eagle is in fact overhead.

Not everybody regards this input-independence as an obvious virtue in teleosemantics. If the small mammal's representation is triggered by any moving shadow, say, would it not be better to interpret its content as 'moving shadow' rather than 'eagle overhead'?

This reaction is bolstered by the following well-known thought-experiment due to Paul Pietroski (1992). The kimu are simple creatures, with very limited sensory abilities, whose only enemies are the snorf, who hunt them every day at dawn. A mutation endows one of the kimu with a disposition to sense and approach red things. This disposition is a biological advantage to its possessors, since it leads them to climb a nearby hill every dawn, the better to observe the red sunrise, and means that they thereby avoid the marauding snorf, who do not climb hills. As a result, the disposition spreads through the kimu population.

Now, consider the state a kimu gets into when it is stimulated by something red. It seems natural to credit this state with the content *red*. But an output-based teleosemantics argues differently. Nothing good happens to the kimu just because they approach something red. Most of their red-approaching behaviour is just a waste of time. It is only when this behaviour takes them away from the dangerous snorf that it yields any biological advantage. So an output-based teleosemantics will deem the state in question to represent *snorf-free*, or *predator-free*, or some such. This strikes many as strongly counter-intuitive. After all, by hypothesis the kimu's senses are tracking the presence or absence or redness, not the presence or absence of snorfs.

Still, advocates of teleosemantics can respond that these intuitions depend on reading more into Pietroski's scenario than is justified by his description. Pietroski says that the kimu evolve some state that is triggered by redness and which has the advantage of keeping them away from the snorf. Given this specification, it is natural to think of the kimu as having some general-purpose visual *system* which gathers items of visual information which informs an open-ended range of behavioural projects directed at different possible ends (such as avoiding blood, or finding post-boxes, or indeed wanting to see red things). However, this extra structure in fact takes us significantly beyond what Pietroski's description actually requires, and it is open to teleosemanticists to argue that their theory is quite able to explain why an organism with all this extra structure would be representing redness rather than snorf-freeness: if the organism's visual states inform a *range* of different behaviours directed at different ends, then the content of any such state needs to be fixed as some condition that assists in the achievement of *all* those ends, and this may well come out as redness. On the other hand, if we do stick to a minimal understanding of the snorf, as having only a special-purpose visual sensitivity that brings no advantage except snorf-avoidance, then it's not so clear that there is anything wrong with the output-based reading of their states as representing *snorf-freeness*: after all, if these states never do anything except trigger simple avoidance behaviour, it seems natural enough to read them as representing the danger they are designed to avoid.

It might seem unclear why teleosemantics is forced to focus exclusively on output conditions and ignore input conditions in explaining content. What would be wrong with a hybrid input–output theory which starts with the relationship between input conditions (red surfaces) and representations (the kimu state), and then says that such a correlation constitutes representation if it has the function of guiding behaviour in pursuit of biological ends? Something like this approach has been explored by a number of writers (Neander, 1995; Dretske, 1988; Millikan, 2004). However, it is not clear that this leads to a substantial alternative to a purely output-based teleosemantics. Remember that many different input circumstances will be correlated to a greater or lesser degree with any given representation-type—including all those causes that systematically give rise to misrepresentations. So, even if we start with input conditions, we still face the task of explaining what picks out the representation's genuine content from all the other potentially informational input-representation correlations. And then we will be back where we started, if the only answer is that content corresponds to that correlation which is a matter of biological design. For the biological function of representation is to guide behaviour in pursuit of biological ends, and so an appeal to biological design can do no other than pick out as content that circumstance required for the organism's behaviour to yield biological success (which for the kimu will once more be *snorf-freeness* rather than *redness*).[6]

8.4.2 Teleosemantics and Selection

According to teleosemantics, representational content depends on biological design, and biological design requires a history of natural selection. This prompts an obvious query. What about creatures who have no such history? Will they not be able to represent?

This worry is normally pressed with the help of the 'swampman' thought experiment (Davidson, 1987). Suppose that lighting strikes a steamy marsh deep in the tropical jungle, and that by miraculous coincidence a perfect molecule-for-molecule

---

[6] Teleosemantics is often charged with an inability to ascribe determinate contents to cognitive states using only considerations of biological design (cf. Fodor, 1990). An initial response to this charge is that only those input-representation correlations that are *used* in pursuit of biological *ends* qualify as representational. The adequacy of this response depends in large part on how far the relevant notion of biological end can be rendered unequivocal. (Neander, 1995; Papineau, 1988, 2003.)

replica of a human being assembles itself out of the organic materials available in the swamp. By hypothesis, this 'swampman' will lack any history of natural selection, and so, according to teleosemantics, will not be possessed of any representational powers. Yet intuitively it seems that swampman will be perfectly capable of at least some forms of mental representation. After all, it will be physically just like a normal human, so will be equally capable of visually registering its surroundings and making appropriate behavioural responses. So it looks as if teleosemantics has gone wrong somewhere, if it denies that swampman has any representational capacities.

The standard teleosemantic response to this difficulty is to bite the bullet and maintain that swampmen will indeed be incapable of representation. Maybe everyday intuition says that swampmen can represent. But a good theoretical account should be allowed to overturn a few everyday intuitions. Just as our modern concept of fish excludes whales, despite any naive intuitions to the contrary, so should a developed concept of representation be allowed to exclude swampmen. According to this line of thought, then, we should replace our naive concept of representation by the theoretically more powerful selection-based notion, even at the cost of overturning intuitions about swampmen. (Cf. Millikan, 1996; Neander, 1996; Papineau, 1996.)

However, there is room for an alternative and more irenic defence of teleosemantics against swampman worries. The alternative strategy is to leave the concept of representation as it is, and focus instead on the status of teleosemantics as an *a posteriori* reduction of representational facts—that is, as a scientific theory that reveals the selectional nature of representation, just as chemistry reveals the nature of water to be H_2O. From this perspective, it is no argument against teleosemantics that representationally competent swampmen are consistent with our everyday concept of representation; you may as well oppose modern chemistry on the grounds that XYZ-composed water is consistent with our everyday concept of water. The fact that swampmen with representations can be *imagined* does nothing to undermine the central teleosemantic claim that in the *actual* world representational facts consist of selectional facts. Of course, if there were plenty of actual swampmen, then things would be different, for they would then provide concrete evidence that teleosemantics is false. But as long as swampmen remain merely imaginary, they are no more relevant to teleosemantics than imaginary molecular make-ups are relevant to chemistry (Papineau, 2001).

Let me conclude this discussion of teleosemantics by addressing one further worry about the appeal to selection. Teleosemantics takes all representation to depend on histories of natural selection. The most familiar kind of such natural selection is the intergenerational selection of genes. However, it is surely unlikely that all representation can be explained in terms of such *genetic* selection. After all, most human beliefs and desires are products of ontogeny rather than phylogeny. No genes have been selected specifically to foster those specific beliefs or desires.

Fortunately for the teleosemantic project, the ascription of a selectional function to some trait does not always require that specific genes have been selected because they give rise to those traits. There are ways in which biological items can have aetiological-selectional functions even though they have no specific genetic basis. In particular, there are two theoretical possibilities that often go unnoticed in this context. The first, emphasized by Millikan, appeals to a many-layered account of functions. The second appeals to non-genetic selection. Together these greatly expand the range of items that possess aetiological-selectional functions.

Multi-layered functions first. Millikan notes that one kind of function is a *relational* function, which is a function to do something only when bearing a certain relation to something else. The chameleon's skin-colour mechanism has the relational function of making the chameleon's skin-colour match that of its environment, whatever that colour may be. Given a specific colour to adapt to, this mechanism then generates traits with *derived* functions. When the chameleon is sitting on a brown plant, its skin colour has the derived function of matching it to the brown environment. Note that this brown skin may have never been produced before, but even so will have a derived function, in virtue of the fact that the skin-colour mechanism has been selected to produce whatever colour will match the background.

This analysis in terms of multi-layered functions can be applied to novel representations within a compositional syntactical system. Consider the famous dance of the bees, which acts as a signal to other bees, 'telling' them where to go to find nectar. A particular dance will be adapted to the current location of the nectar, and so will have a derived function. Again, the dance that indicates this specific direction may never have occurred before. Rather, it owes its functionality to the function of a *system* that has yielded a reproductive advantage in the past. Analogously, we can expect that many features of human cognition can be viewed as having biological functions, not because they themselves have been selected for, but because they are products of a system that has been so selected.

The other possibility to which teleosemanticists can appeal is non-genetic selection. There are two possibilities worth mentioning in this context. One is *selection-based learning*. This doesn't involve the differential reproduction of organisms over generations, but the differential reproduction of cognitive or behavioural items themselves during the development of a given individual. Such ontogenetic selection takes place, for example, when behaviour is moulded by experience during learning. In such cases we can think of the items selected as having the function of producing those effects in virtue of which they were favoured by the learning mechanism.

A second kind of non-genetic selection is *non-genetic intergenerational selection*. Many traits are passed from parents to children by channels other than the sexual transmission of genetic material: these traits will include the possession of parasites, the products of imprinting mechanisms, and the many cognitive and behavioural traits acquired from parents via social learning. A number of biological theorists are currently interested in the way in which such non-genetically inherited traits can be naturally selected through the normal Darwinian process of differential reproduction of organisms (Jablonka and Lamb, 1999; Mameli, 2004). Non-genetically inherited traits that become prevalent in this way will have functions, namely, the effects which favoured their possessors. It seems highly possible, though this is an area that has yet to be properly explored, that functions of this kind could do much to explain the contents of sophisticated mental representations. After all, it seems a natural enough thought that certain non-genetically inherited ways of thinking are an advantage to their possessors because they make them sensitive to certain features of the environment. On the other hand, it remains an open question how many features of human thought are in fact due to differential reproduction of offspring resulting from such advantages.

It should be said that there is as yet little detailed work showing how teleosemantics might analyse sophisticated human modes of cognition by appealing to functions other than those deriving directly from the selection of genes. True, Millikan (1984) has indicated how her notion of an adapted proper function can be used to account for the representational contents of elements in complex representational systems. And Dretske (1988) has focused on selection in learning as one means by which to explain how cognitive states can be teleosemantically targeted on specific contents. Still, much remains to be done in applying teleosemantics to specifically human modes of cognition.

Perhaps this is inevitable. Detailed analyses of representational powers in terms of aetiological functions must rest on an adequate empirical knowledge of the cognitive mechanisms involved. There is no question of identifying the functions of cognitive items if we don't know what kinds of mechanisms process these items and how those mechanisms develop in individuals. From this perspective, the teleosemantic project is not so much a theory of content for sophisticated human representation, but a methodology which promises to explain content piecemeal, in the wake of empirical discoveries about human cognitive architecture.

References

Block, N. (1986). 'Advertisement for a semantics for psychology.' *Midwest Studies in Philosophy* 10.

Cummins, R. (1991). *Meaning and Mental Representation*. Cambridge, Mass: MIT Press.

Churchland, P. (1989). *A Neurocomputational Perspective: The Nature of Mind and the Structure of Science*. Cambridge, Mass: MIT Press.

Davidson, D. (1987). 'Knowing One's Own Mind.' *Proceedings and Addresses of the American Philosophical Association* 60.

Dokic, J. and Engel, P. (2002). *Frank Ramsey: Truth and Success*. London: Routledge.

Dretske, F. (1981). *Knowledge and the Flow of Information*. Cambridge, Mass: MIT Press.

——— (1988). *Explaining Behaviour*. Cambridge, Mass: MIT Press.

Fodor, J. (1974). 'Special Sciences: Or, The Disunity of Science as a Working Hypothesis.' *Synthese* 28.

——— (1990). *A Theory of Content and Other Essays*. Cambridge, Mass: MIT Press.

——— and Lepore, E. (1992). *Holism: A Shoppers' Guide*. Oxford: Blackwell.

Harman, G. (1982). 'Conceptual Role Semantics.' *Notre Dame Journal of Formal Logic* 23.

——— (1987). '(Nonsolipsistic) Conceptual Role Semantics' in LePore, E. (ed.) *Semantics of Natural Language*. New York: Academic Press.

Horwich, P. (1990). *Truth*. Oxford, Blackwell.

Jablonka, E. and Lamb, M. (1999). *Epigenetic Inheritance and Evolution*. Oxford: Oxford University Press.

Mameli, M. (2004), 'Nongenetic Selection and Nongenetic Inheritance?', *British Journal for the Philosophy of Science* 55.

Millikan, R. (1984). *Language Thought and Other Biological Categories*. Cambridge, Mass: MIT Press.

____ (1993). *White Queen Psychology and Other Essays for Alice*. Cambridge, Mass: MIT Press.

____ (1996). 'On Swampkinds.' *Mind and Language* 11.

____ (2004). *Varieties of Meaning*. Cambridge, Mass: MIT Press.

Neander, K. (1995). 'Malfunctioning and Misrepresenting.' *Philosophical Studies* 79.

____ (1996). 'Swampman Meets Swampcow.' *Mind and Language* 11.

Papineau, D. (1993). *Philosophical Naturalism*. Oxford, Blackwell.

____ (1996). 'Doubtful Intuitions.' *Mind and Language* 11.

____ (1998). 'Teleosemantics and Indeterminacy.' *Australasian Journal of Philosophy* 76.

____ (2001). 'The Status of Teleosemantics, or How to Stop Worrying about Swampman.' *Australasian Journal of Philosophy* 79.

____ (2003). 'Is Representation Rife?' *Ratio* 16.

Peacocke, C. (1992). *A Study of Concepts*. Cambridge, Mass: MIT Press.

Pietrowski, P. (1992). 'Intentional and Teleological Error.' *Pacific Philosophical Quarterly* 73.

Ramsey, F. (1927). 'Facts and Propositions'. *Aristotelian Society Supplementary Volume* 7.

Stampe, D. (1977). 'Toward a Causal Theory of Linguistic Representation' in P. A. French, T. E. Uehling, Jr., and H. K. Wettstein (eds.) *Midwest Studies in Philosophy: Studies in the Philosophy of Language* 2. Minneapolis: University of Minnesota Press.

Quine, W. (1951). 'Two Dogmas of Empiricism.' *Philosophical Review* 60.

Whyte, J. (1990). 'Success Semantics.' *Analysis* 50.

____ (1991). 'The Normal Rewards of Success.' *Analysis* 50.

CHAPTER 9

....

TRUTH AND MEANING

....

GABRIEL SEGAL

THIS chapter is not the first work to go by the name "Truth and Meaning". It is preceded by a homonymously titled paper published by Donald Davidson in 1967, a seminal paper on the topic of truth-theoretic semantics for natural languages. It seems appropriate that "Truth and Meaning" (Davidson, 1967) should loom large in this article. I will say something about previous work in the area, go on to discuss Davidson (1967) and related papers of his and then discuss some issues arising. I begin with the work of Gottlob Frege.

9.1 SEMANTICS 1879–1965

....

9.1.1 Gottlob Frege

Truth has nearly always been seen as the core notion in the study of meaning and representation. Gottlob Frege produced the most influential work in the area (Frege, 1987).[1,2] Frege's chief interest was in the construction of the Begriffsschrift, an

---

[1] Bibliographic dates in the text are those of English translations. See bibliography for original publication dates.

[2] The first semantic theorist appears to have been the Czech priest, Bernard Bolzano (1781–1848) who anticipated many ideas of both Frege and Tarski. Like Frege, he was keen to distinguish 'subjective' (i.e. mental) representations from 'objective' representations (Fregean senses) and both of those from objects represented (Fregean referents) (Bolzano, 1972). And, like Tarski, he does semantics by providing truth conditions: "[a proposition in itself is true] when every object that falls under the subject concept

artificial formal language for use in mathematics and science.[3] The key feature of the Begriffsschrift was its logical perfection. Entailment relations among sentences of the Begriffsschrift had to be capable of being made completely explicit. It was a language in which one could construct logical proofs. And logic is all about truth, as Frege himself made clear: "The word 'true' indicates the aim of logic as does 'beautiful' that of aesthetics or 'good' that of ethics" (Frege, 1956, p. 289).

Fregean semantics is based upon the specification of relations between expressions and entities. At the level of extension, singular terms refer to objects; predicates, connectives and quantifiers refer to functions of various types; and sentences refer to truth-values. Frege insists that in the Begriffsschrift every significant expression must have a referent. Expressions that do not, as it were, really have a referent, such as "the greatest prime number", had to be assigned a referent arbitrarily.[4] And Frege thought of senses as entities as well: for an expression to be meaningful was for it to relate to a special kind of meaning-entity, a sense.

It is not entirely clear what Frege thought about the prospects of providing formal semantics for natural languages. He certainly thought that natural languages were imperfect representational systems, considered from a logical point of view. Natural languages have expressions with no real referent. And natural languages have further problems not shared by the Begriffsschrift. It was important for Frege that logically well-behaved predicates be completely defined: each one must be either true or false of each object. Predicates of natural languages often fail to meet this requirement. Vague predicates, like "is bald" are neither true nor false of borderline instances.[5] And Frege thought that some predicates are "incompletely defined" in the sense they only apply to objects of certain categories; so, for example, the number three is neither in nor out of the extension of "woman".[6]

However, Frege certainly presents the appearance of someone who thinks that natural languages do have some kind of formal semantics, particularly in his later work. In Frege (1952) and (1956) he sketches semantic accounts of various natural-language constructions, including different types of opaque contexts, subordinate clauses, counterfactuals and indexicals. A somewhat neglected but fascinating paper (Frege, 1977) is revealing both in respect of his motivation for thinking of natural languages as subject to formal treatment and in respect of his ideas about the methodology for carrying it out. The article merits some detailed discussion. It begins thus (p. 56):

---

of the proposition has a property that falls under its predicate concept" (Bolzano, 1935) See Coffa (1991, ch. 2) for discussion. For discussion of differences between Bolzano and the other two, see Textor (1997). (Thanks to Peter Simons for most of this footnote.)

   [3] By a "formal language", I mean, roughly speaking, a language with a computable syntax and one in which "the sense of every expression is unambiguously determined by its form" (Tarski, 1956, p. 166). I do not mean an uninterpreted one.

   [4] There are good reasons to think that this aspect of Frege's views is deeply problematic. See Segal (2005) for discussion.

   [5] Or so it seems to many of us. For an alternative view, see Williamson (1994).

   [6] Letter to Paeno 29.9.1896. in Frege (1980).

It is astonishing what language can do. With a few syllables it can express an incalculable number of thoughts, so that even a thought grasped by a terrestrial being for the very first time can be put into a form of words which will be understood by someone to whom the thought is entirely new. This would be impossible, were we not able to distinguish parts in the thought corresponding to the parts of a sentence, so that the structure of the sentence serves as an image of the structure of the thought.... If, then, we look upon thoughts as composed of simple parts, and take these in turn, to correspond to the simple parts of sentences, we can understand how a few parts of sentences can go to make up a great multitude of sentences, to which, in turn, there correspond a great multitude of thoughts.[7]

He then goes on to discuss the nature of specific compound thoughts, introducing and talking about various truth-functional compounds. He also devotes some time to the issue of how these compound thoughts are expressed in language, and many of his examples are drawn from natural language. Among the compound thoughts he discusses are "hypothetical compounds". A hypothetical compound is true if and only if either the antecedent is false or the consequent is true. A hypothetical compound thought is thus a material implication, which we now sometimes write "$\rightarrow$". Frege says that a hypothetical compound can be expressed by sentences of the form "If B, then A". He immediately anticipates the objection that "this does not square with linguistic usage" and goes on to offer a complex response, which develops in a fascinating manner (p. 69):

It must once again be emphasised that science has to be allowed its own terminology, that it cannot always bow to ordinary language. Just here I see the greatest difficulty for philosophy: the instrument it finds available for its work, namely ordinary language, is little suited to the purpose, for its formation was governed by requirements wholly different from those of philosophy. So also logic is first of all obliged to fashion a usable instrument from those already to hand. And for this purpose it initially finds but little in the way of usable instruments available.

The instrument we need for philosophy is a logically perfect language. This language would contain suitable means for expressing complex thoughts, including, for example, hypothetical compounds. Logic looks to ordinary language for its instruments and initially finds but little of use. Notice that he says "initially". He does not say that "after a thorough search" of ordinary language, we find but little of use. He then immediately proceeds with the search via a defence of his interpretation of "If B, then A". He discusses the example "If I own a cock which has laid eggs today, then Cologne Cathedral will collapse tomorrow morning" (p. 70), which he says is true (presumably because the antecedent is false). He anticipates the objection that it is not true, because there is no connection between antecedent and consequent. He says his account is not designed to "square with ordinary linguistic usage, which is generally too vague and ambiguous for the purposes of logic" and immediately goes on:

---

[7] In the same passage he says that talk of thoughts having parts is "figurative". I do not think this significantly affects the point, which could be put in terms of a thought's semantic properties rather than its parts.

Questions of all kinds arise at this point, e.g. the relation of cause and effect, the intention of a speaker who utters a sentence of the form "If B, then A", the grounds on which he holds its content to be true. The speaker may perhaps give hints in regard to such questions arising among his hearers. These hints are amongst the adjuncts which often surround the thought in ordinary language. My task here is to remove the adjuncts and thereby to pick out, as the logical kernel, a compound of two thoughts which I have called a hypothetical compound thought.

Here is how I understand that. If someone utters "If B, then A", then, when we consider what is going on with respect to ordinary usage, we have to take into account various things. For example we need to consider what thoughts the speaker wants to get across to his audience. Does he, for instance, mean to convey that there is a relation of cause and effect between A and B? The speaker might give hints in respect of these issues. Frege might have in mind such things as that the speaker may take advantage of the conversational context in order to convey the desired message. So the context might, for example, make it clear that the speaker does think that there is causal relation between A and B and wants his audience to know that he thinks this. But that thought, the one about a causal connection, is an adjunct to 'the' thought. I take 'the' thought to be the thought literally expressed by the words uttered.[8] That thought is the logical kernel of what is conveyed in the use of ordinary language. The logical kernel of the ordinary language use of "If B, then A" is thus the hypothetical compound.

So the view is something like the following. Ordinary language is unsuitable for logic because its formation suited it for other things. For example, it is a flexible and efficient instrument for conveying thoughts in conversational contexts. It can rely on such contexts in a way that logic cannot. So initially when we look to ordinary language, we don't find instruments useful for logic. But, when we look harder, we do find them. We notice, first, that natural language is productive: that we can use old words in new combinations to convey thoughts, even previously unexpressed or unthought thoughts. We infer that natural language must have a compositional semantics, that the meaning of complex expressions must be determined by the meanings of the component expressions and the way they are put together. So we must look for the compositional structure of language, which is not obvious at casual inspection. The way to find it is to strip away the adjuncts accompanying linguistic usage and reveal how combinations of words strictly and literally express thoughts. For example, sentences of the form "If B, then A" appear not to allow for compositional semantics, since they seem not to be truth-functional: the semantic value of a sentence of the form "If B, then A" appears not to depend on the semantic values of its component parts and their mode of combination. But after careful investigation, we find that actually it is truth-functional after all.[9]

---

[8] One criterion he uses for distinguishing adjunct thoughts from sense is that the former can vary from context to context while the latter cannot.

[9] Just this view was given a detailed defence in H. P. Grice's seminal "Logic and Conversation" (Grice, 1975). The similarity with Frege's "Compound Thoughts" is striking. The latter was first published in translation in 1963, in *Mind*. Grice's collected papers (Grice, 1989) contains not one mention of Frege.

It seems then, that Frege thought that natural languages, logically imperfect as they are, are formal at least in parts—and presumably very significant parts, since it is the formal parts of language that allow us to express an incalculable number of thoughts.

Much work in the twentieth century developed Frege's ideas. A great deal of that work continued with the assumption that semantics is fundamentally concerned with the assignments of entities (objects, sets, functions and truth-values) to expressions. So, for example, those who tried to develop a formal account of sense did so by treating senses as functions of various kinds; the sense of a predicate, for example, was often seen as a function from possible worlds to extensions (e.g. Carnap, 1947).

9.1.2 Alfred Tarski

A notable exception was Alfred Tarski, who described himself as "being a mathematician (as well as a logician, and perhaps a philosopher of a sort)" (Tarski, 1944, p. 369). Tarski's semantics came in the form of truth definitions (or "T-theories"). A truth definition for a particular language, L, is the definition of a predicate, say "is T", that is true of all and only the true sentences of L.[10] Tarski was concerned to develop truth definitions that are "materially adequate" and "formally correct". The former requirement means that "is T" must apply to all and only the true sentences of the language, the latter means that the definition must be consistent. Tarski's famous "Convention T" is a sufficient condition for material adequacy (Tarski, 1956 p. 188). To a reasonable approximation, Convention T says that a truth definition will be materially adequate if it entails all instances of the famous (T) schema:

(T) "s" is true iff p

where "s" would be replaced by an object-language sentence and "p" by a translation of that sentence in the meta-language.

As Davidson observes (1984, p. xiv), Tarski deploys the notion of meaning, in the guise of translation, in his analysis of truth. The requirement that p translates s is part of what ensures the material adequacy of the truth definition. The way it works is as follows. Suppose that s is true. Since p is a translation of s, it must have the same truth-value as s, and so it must be true too. (Assume that there are no indexicals in s.) Since (T) is true, ["s" is T] and p must have the same truth-value. So ["s" is T] is also true. So T applies to s. Conversely, if s is false, then p is false. If p is false ["s" is T] is false and so T does not apply to s. So T applies to all and only the true sentences of L.

Tarski provided a materially adequate and formally correct truth definition for a specific artificially constructed, formal language, which he called the "the language of the calculus of classes" and I will call "LC" for short. LC is a language for expressing the Boolean algebra of classes, consisting in some elements of first-order logic, variables ranging over classes and an expression for class inclusion. In providing this

---

[10] Contemporary theorists are used to using "is T" to instantiate the predicate and I will continue the tradition, though Tarski used either "is true" or "is a member of the class Tr".

truth definition, Tarski produced the first proper formal semantic theory for a whole language.

Tarski defined truth in terms of satisfaction. Satisfaction is a relation that holds between expressions and objects or sequences of objects. Roughly speaking, it is the converse of the relation of being true of. For example, an object satisfies the predicate "is white" iff the predicate "is white" is true of the object.[11] Tarskian semantics provides an alternative to the Fregean model whereby every expression has to relate to some entity. Instead of saying that "is white" extends over the set of white things, or that it refers to a function that maps all and only white objects onto The True or whatever, we say (Tarski, 1956, p. 190):

(W) For every a, we have a satisfies the sentential function "x is white" if and only if a is white

Compare Davidson's discussion of the expression "the father of" (1984, p. 18). Davidson considers the proposal that the expression refers to a function that maps people onto their fathers. He points out that the postulated object of reference is not doing any explanatory work. What we need to know is how the expression "the father of" contributes to the semantics of complex expressions in which it features.[12] This can be stated as follows: a complex term consisting of "the father of" prefixed to a term, t, refers to the father of the person to whom t refers. "It is obvious," Davidson remarks "that no entity corresponding to 'the father of' is, or needs to be, mentioned in stating this theory."[13]

To give the flavour of a T-theory, I provide a small, semi-formalized sample theory, T*, for a baby language fragment, L* below.[14]

L* Syntax
Singular terms
a
b

Predicates
G
H

Functor
F

Connective
&

Using "f", "t", "p", "s", and "c" (with subscripts where necessary) as typed variables ranging over object-language expressions of the categories functor, singular term,

---

[11] See Quine (1970a) for a clear and simple introduction to Tarskian semantics.
[12] Quine makes much the same point in Quine (1960, p. 239).
[13] Note that saying that "the father of" refers to a function from people to their fathers wouldn't suffice as an explanation of the semantics of the expression either. For we would need also to say how the referent of "the father of" interacts with the referent of t to determine a referent for "the father of" $^\wedge$t.
[14] T* is a bit anachronistic in that it is more post-Davidsonian in style than purely Tarskian.

predicate, sentence and connective, respectively, and "$^\wedge$" for concatenation, we can express rules for forming complex expressions as follows:

$(f)(t)(f^\wedge t$ is a singular term$)$
$(p)(t)(p^\wedge t$ is a sentence$)$
$(c)(s_1)(s_2)(s_1^\wedge c^\wedge s_2$ is a sentence$)$

T*
(A1) $(x)(x$ satisfies "a" iff $x =$ Donald Davidson$)$
(A2) $(x)(x$ satisfies "b" iff $x =$ Alfred Tarski$)$
(A3) $(x)(x$ satisfies "G" iff x is a mathematician$)$
(A4) $(x)(x$ satisfies "H" iff x is a philosopher$)$

   Composition axioms

(A5) $(t_1)(t_2)(f)(x)($if $t_1 = f^\wedge t_2$ then $(x$ satisfies t_1 iff $(\exists y)(y$ satisfies t_2 and x is the father of $y)))$
(A6) $(s)(p)(t)($if $s = p^\wedge t$ then $(s$ is true iff $(\exists x)(x$ satisfies t and x satisfies $p)))$
(A7) $(s_1)(s_2)(s_3)($if $s_1 = s_2^\wedge c^\wedge s_3$, then $(s_1$ is true iff s_2 is true and s_3 is true$))$

Notice that the L has infinitely many sentences, since the syntactic rules for complex singular terms and sentences are recursive. So we can have "fa", "ffa", "Ha&Gb", "Ha&Gb&Ha" and so on. This infinite collection of sentences may be very boring. But for all that, T* interprets them all. Here is an edited down derivation of a T-theorem, for "HFa".

 (i) "Hfa" is true iff $(\exists x)(x$ satisfies "fa" and x satisfies "H"$)$ (A6)
(ii) "Hfa" is true iff $(\exists x)(x$ satisfies "fa" and x is a philosopher$)$ (A4)
(iii) "Hfa" is true iff $(\exists x)(\exists y)(y$ satisfies "a" and x is the father of y and x is a philosopher$)$ (A5)
(iv) "Hfa" is true iff $(\exists x)(\exists y)(y =$ Donald Davidson and x is the father of y and x is a philosopher$)$ (A1)
 (v) "Hfa" is true iff the father of Donald Davidson is a philosopher (iv)

There is one important matter in respect of which T* might be held to go against Tarski's grain. For it may be that the truth definition Tarski provides for LC should be considered as model-theoretic, in which case it would differ significantly from T*. The question warrants a digression.

   Model theory is a branch of logic that defines notions of validity, consistency etc., in terms of interpretations relative to models. A sentence has a model if there is a possible assignment of objects, relations etc. to its non-logical vocabulary under which it comes out true. With this notion one can define, for example, logical consequence: "A sentence X follows logically from the sentences of the class K if and only if every model of the class K is also a model of the sentence X" (Tarski, 1956, p. 417). Tarski argued that model theory provides the best formal account of the intuitive notion of logical consequence. He was also the first theorist to give a rigorous formal treatment of a model theory and explore its general properties.

Now Tarski's definition of truth for LC is completed on p. 195 of Tarski (1956) and neither it nor any of the preceding discussion makes any mention of truth or interpretation relative to a model. Rather, with the exception of variables, every expression of the language has a fixed interpretation and every sentence is true or false, period, not true or false relative to model. However Tarski quickly goes on to introduce the notion of truth relative to a model ("domain"): "In the investigations ... in the methodology of the deductive sciences ... another concept of relative character plays a much greater part than the absolute concept of truth and includes it as a special case. This is the concept of *correct or true sentence in an individual domain a*" (Tarski's emphasis). He then goes on explicitly to develop a model theory for LC in which both truth and satisfaction are relativized to models.

According to one interpretation, Tarski would have regarded the preceding definition of absolute truth as really elliptical for a definition of model-relative truth. For, in LC the only non-logical terms are class-theoretic. Evidently, models in which these terms don't have their normal interpretations are of no interest. Therefore a definition of absolute truth and a definition of truth relative to a canonical set of models in which the terms have their normal interpretations, come to the same thing. So there would have been no need for Tarski to make explicit the extra parameter in his descriptions of satisfaction and truth.

I tend to the view, however, that that interpretation gets Tarski backwards. For Tarski, a model was a set of real objects, and absolute truth was the limiting case where a sentence is true relative to the set of all objects.[15] Tarski's primary notion of truth was that of absolute truth. That is why he added this footnote to the initial discussion of relative truth (Tarski, 1956, p. 199):

The discussion of these relativised notions is not essential for the understanding of the main theme of this work and may be omitted by those readers who are not interested in special studies in the domain of the methodology of the deductive sciences.

Moreover, in his one philosophical paper on truth, Tarski (1944), he discussed his conception of truth at length without saying anything to the effect that really he thinks of it as a relation between sentences and models, with the real world, the world where snow is white, being just one model among others. In fact, he mentions models just once, towards the end of the paper, in saying that his semantic methods are useful in the construction of the important meta-mathematical notion of a model. So it appears that he regarded the business of providing a definition of absolute truth for a language as distinct from the business of giving an account of the logic of that language. Only the second enterprise requires the notion of truth in a model.[16]

Tarski provided examples for natural language, like (W) above and his famous (S), below, merely as an informal aid to understanding the formal semantics.

(S) "Snow is white" is true iff snow is white.

---

[15] Thanks to Peter Simons for pointing this out to me.
[16] For discussion of the distinction between absolute and model-theoretic semantics see Davidson (1973); Lepore (1983); and Higginbotham (1988).

He had grave doubts that materially adequate, formally correct truth definitions could be given for natural languages. For one thing, he did not think that natural languages have determinate, precise syntactic properties (Tarski, 1944, p. 349). For another, liar sentences appear to pose a huge threat to the formal correctness of any truth definition of a natural language, since they will drive the definition to inconsistency. Thus if (L) is the sentence:

(L)   (L) is not a true sentence

We can prove (L')

(L')   (L) is a true sentence is true if and only if (L) is not a true sentence.[17]

9.1.3 Segue

Prior to the late 1960s, many theorists shared Tarski's scepticism about the prospects of fruitfully applying the apparatus of formal semantics to natural languages.[18] This is not surprising since natural languages—paradoxes or no—look distinctly casual. Typically, a formal semantic theory specifies semantic properties of atomic expressions of a language, and it contains the means to show how the semantic properties of complex expressions derive from those of their component parts and syntactic structure. Formal semantic theories only apply to languages that have the right kind of syntactic structure: it is best if each complex expression has a unique logical form of a type that allows the theory to get a grip, permitting it to compute the semantic properties of the complex from those of the components and that logical form. The phonological and orthographic perceptible forms of natural language are not logical forms and do not correspond to them one-one. The orthographic form (0) provides a familiar illustration:

(0) Everyone loves someone

The visible form of (0) can associate with either of two logical forms, one for each of the two possible interpretations. Further, (0) doesn't appear to have the right kind of structure for semantics: semantics likes constituent structure, and we can't see whether e.g. "Everyone loves" is a constituent of (0). And further still, semantics typically needs expressions to be categorized, as they are in L*, and the components of (0) don't wear their categories on their sleeves.

9.1.4 W. V. Quine

Davidson's tutor, W. V. Quine was famously sceptical about the prospects of any kind of serious semantics for natural languages. His thesis of the 'indeterminacy

---

[17] Tarski (1956, p. 158).

[18] At a casual glance Bertrand Russell appears to be doing semantics for natural languages in Russell (1905) when he offers his theory of descriptions. But a close look at his formulations supports the view that he is only talking about the content of the proposition that we affirm when we assert a sentence of the form "The F is G". He does not explain how it is that semantic properties of the words in the sentence interact with the sentence's syntactic structure so that it expresses that proposition. Russell himself later claimed (Russell, 1959), that he had had no interest in natural language in 1905.

of translation' was that there is no fact of the matter about when two expressions have the same meaning (e.g. Quine, 1960, 1970b).[19] One of the conclusions he drew from this was that there are no such things as meanings, or Fregean senses. Many of his arguments for the indeterminacy of translation involve reflections on the radical interpreter, this being an imaginary field linguist confronted with a previously unknown language, 'Jungle', who takes on the task of translating it into his own, using only evidence from Jungle speakers' behaviour. According to Quine, semantic facts about Jungle are exhausted by facts that would be available to the radical interpreter.

A facet of Quine's methodology that I expect was important for Davidson was the shift of focus of the theory of sense away from the endeavour to say what kinds of things senses are and towards the idea of trying to interpret an object-language sentence by looking for a synonymous sentence of the home language. Applying the methodology led Quine to the conclusion that there are no such things as senses anyway, so any endeavour to say what kind of objects they are would obviously be doomed to failure. Since there are no synonymous sentences, the endeavour to do semantics by finding synonyms also cannot succeed as stated. But what remains a possibility is that one might find a range of candidate translations that are as good as each other, better than any other candidates, and good enough for their purpose, the purpose of getting along with native speakers. Quine saw such an enterprise as a practical one. For him, since there are no facts of the matter about what a sentence means, there are no facts for a semantic theory to describe and semantic theory cannot be science. Davidson accepted the premise that there would be no unique best translation, but rather a range of equally good ones. And he accepted that there would be no hidden facts of the matter in virtue of which one of a range of equally acceptable translations would be right and the others wrong. But he drew no further sceptical conclusions. Rather his view was: let a thousand flowers bloom. All of the best translations would be right.

Although many theorists of the early and middle years of the twentieth century were sceptical about the prospects of formal semantics for natural languages, there were a few exceptions. Davidson (1984, p. 29) cites Yehoshua Bar-Hillel and Evert Beth, both in Schilpp (1963), as examples. I should add that Carnap himself, in his reply to Bar-Hillel (*ibid.*, p. 941), expresses sympathy with Bar-Hillel's appeal for the use of formal methods in the study of natural language. He says that it would be a good idea to use a formal meta-language for the study of natural language and he offers and briefly develops the analogy of studying clouds by comparing them to precise geometrical shapes (*ibid.*, p. 942). I am not sure how to interpret him, exactly, but as far as I can see he does not think of natural languages as approximations

---

[19] See Weir (this volume) for a discussion of Quine's arguments for indeterminacy of translation. For further exegesis and critique see Segal (2000).

to formal languages, nor would he agree with the 'logical kernel' view that Frege expressed in "Compound Thoughts" (see also Carnap's replies to Beth and Strawson in that volume).[20]

In another landmark development in the 1950s and 1960s, Noam Chomsky developed arguments that natural languages had at least formal syntax, that sentences have imperceptible tree-like constituent structures determining their grammatical properties (Chomsky, 1957, 1964), and thereby founded scientific linguistics.

In the mid to late 1960s and early 1970s, a small number of philosophers took the view that, in spite of appearances, natural languages really are formal and that they are proper subjects of formal semantic theories.[21] Worthy of particular note for their influence in this regard are Richard Montague and Donald Davidson (papers collected in Davidson (1984) and Thomason ed. (1974)).[22] Both Montague and Davidson offered concrete proposals about the nature of natural language semantics, drawing on earlier work in the formal tradition. Montague developed his formal programme in some depth and detail, developing a model-theoretic semantics whereby expressions are related to entities relative to models. But he said very little about how to explain the gap between the casual, sometimes sloppy appearance of natural language and its underlying formality. In other words, he did not say in virtue of what a particular formal description was true of a piece of language, nor how one could tell whether it was. Davidson, by contrast, offered lengthy systematic answers to both of those questions.

9.2 DONALD DAVIDSON

9.2.1 How can a Natural Language be a Formal Language?

If natural languages are really formal, then we need to find their logical forms. Davidson's account of logical form goes something like this. We rework Quine's tale of the radical interpreter as follows. The radical interpreter's job is to construct a theory of meaning for an object language, L. The interpreter's job is done if he comes up with a theory that systematically yields correct interpretations of what an L-speaker says. An interpretation is correct if it would fit in with a correct overall interpretation of the L-speaker's speech and other behaviour. An overall

---

[20] Katz and Fodor (1963) and Katz and Postal (1964) also took a formal approach to semantics, constructing formal representations of expressions of natural languages. They did not, however, adopt a truth-theoretic perspective.

[21] Chomsky has never shown much enthusiasm for the latter idea, and certainly doesn't think that the typical apparatus of the Fregean tradition provides the means for a correct account of linguistic meaning. See, e.g. Chomsky (1995).

[22] David Lewis was of similar mind, see in particular Lewis (1970).

interpretation is correct if and only if it obeys the principle of charity: it maximizes the speaker's rationality by making as much as possible of what he says come out reasonable and true. There will be no unique best theory, by these lights, but a number of equally good ones. But that is not a problem, since we should regard all of them as true, saying the same thing in different ways. Davidson offers the ('rough') analogy of Fahrenheit and Centigrade: the actual assignments of numbers to temperatures by the two scales are different, but the pattern of assignments is the same (Davidson, 1984, p. 225). Similarly, theories of meaning capture "the semantic location" of each sentence in "the pattern of sentences that comprise the language" (1984, p. 225). By "the semantic location" of a sentence in the pattern of sentences, Davidson means its logical location: the entailment relations it bears to the other sentences (Davidson, p.c.).

So, for Davidson, the logical forms of a natural language, L, are an abstraction from L speakers' behaviours. A sentence's logical form is a form that would allow a theory of meaning to apply to it. This means that a theory of logical form has two constraints to meet. One is that it must assign forms that allow the theory of meaning to provide an interpretation of each L sentence. And the second is that it must assign forms that account for logical relations among L sentences. Davidson also thought, at least at certain times, that logical forms would be Chomskyan deep structures (Davidson, 1984, p. xv). Under that assumption, there would be a third source of constraint on the theory of form: it would need to account for expressions' grammatical properties as well.[23]

9.2.2 Truth Theories and the Philosophical Program

What sort of theory would serve the interpreter's purpose? Davidson defines a theory of meaning for L as a theory which, if it were explicitly known, would allow the knower, in principle, to interpret all the sentences of L. Davidson saw that a T-theory has some of the properties that a theory of meaning ought to have. A T-theory is a finite formal theory with axioms specifying semantic properties of atomic expressions from which follow theorems specifying semantic properties of complex expressions. Moreover, T-theorems pair object-language sentences with meta-language sentences that could be used to specify their meanings.

However, T-theories appear to lack one crucial property that a theory of meaning ought to have. They do not actually say what any object-language expression means. To make the point vivid consider (1) (a) and (b):

(1)   a. "Les elephants ont des oreilles" is true iff elephants have ears
       b. "Les elephants ont des oreilles" is true iff pigs have curly tails

---

[23] Notice that it is *a priori* entirely possible that the three enterprises could come apart. A theory of interpretation might assign one set of forms, while a theory of logic assigned a second one and a theory of syntax a third. For discussion see Larson and Segal (1995), pp. 67–76, and Neale (1994). Davidson and Segal discuss the issue of whether a theory of meaning should account for logical relations in Fara (1997).

Let us call a theory that provides a correct characterization of "true" a "truth theory" and one that also meets Tarski's translation constraint, a "T-theory". We can suppose that (1) (a) and (b) are theorems of different truth theories, the first of which, is interpretive, hence T-theoretic, and the second of which is not. We can suppose further that both theories are true and provide correct characterizations of "true". If the only information about the object-language to which you had access was the information in the truth theories, then you would not be able to tell that (1a) is interpretive and (1b) is not. Thus even if a T-theory has the property of interpretivity it does not itself say that it has that property.

A T-theory is not a theory of meaning. Moreover the information provided by a T-theory falls far short of what the interpreter requires. For what he would need to know to distinguish the interpretive from uninterpretive truth theories are such things as that: "Les elephants ont des oreilles" means that elephants have ears. But that is just the sort of information that a theory of meaning is supposed to provide. Let us call this "the information problem".

In spite of the information problem, Davidson claimed, a T-theory can in some interesting sense 'do duty for' a theory of meaning. His idea was to redescribe what it takes for a truth theory to be interpretive in a way that doesn't implicate linguistic semantic notions. In this way, he could get a philosophical account of meaning, something that might very roughly be expressed along the lines of: s means that p iff a truth theory with property X entails that s is true iff p.

The X that Davidson settled on in the mid seventies, had, I believe two conditions. The truth theory had to be lawlike and maximally simple. The lawlikeness requirement was intended to rule out cases like (1b). It is a little difficult to see what kind of law Davidson has in mind. But it does seem right that (1a) is less accidentally true than (1b). For example, (1a) supports counterfactuals and (1b) does not: "les elephants ont des oreilles" would be true even if pigs lacked curly tails, but would be false if elephants lacked ears.

The simplicity requirement was meant to rule out cases like (2):

(2) "La neige est blanche" is true iff snow is white and [either snow is black or snow is not black]

So Davidson's claim might be informally expressed as (D):

(D) A sentence s of a language L means that p iff a theorem of a maximally simple, lawlike truth theory for L says that s is true iff p.

So what the interpreter would need to know is that his truth theory is lawlike and maximally simple.[24]

---

[24] In fact, it is not obvious that knowing a truth theory and knowing that it meets the two constraints would provide enough information for the interpreter, even if D is true. He would also have to know that (D) is true. However, (D) itself is the important claim. The view I am outlining here is the one Davidson appeared to hold in papers collected in Davidson (1984). Davidson explicitly mentions lawlikeness in (1984), pp. xiv, 26, and174. He does not, as far as I know, explicitly mention simplicity in Davidson (1984), but I think he had it in mind as part of the empirical nature of the theory. He does acknowledge the simplicity constraint in his "Reply to Segal" in Zeglen (1999) where he also explains how his views

It seems to me that the simplicity requirement is in fact redundant for reasons to do with the notion of the interpretivity of a truth theory. Let me explain. A proper exposition of a T-theory involves a specification of a logic, or a set of 'production rules' (Larson and Segal, 1995, p. 35) with which to conduct the derivations. Now, if the theory comes with a standard logic, such as first-order predicate calculus with identity, then it will be overproductive. That is, it will be able to prove lots of uninterpretive T-theorems such as (2). So we must either construct T-theories that do not yield uninterpretive theorems or find some means of picking out only the interpretive theorems.

Taking the former approach, one might develop a theory that uses only very limited logical apparatus. It is possible in that manner to rule out the derivation of many uninterpretive theorems. But it is very difficult or impossible to rule them all out by this means because, typically, one has to prove uninterpretive theorems on the way to proving interpretive ones: observe the first three lines of the little partial derivation above. Taking the latter approach involves specifying specific procedures for the derivation of theorems, often called "canonical derivations", which are guaranteed to produce only interpretive theorems. A mixed approach is also possible, whereby one would specify a limited logical apparatus—just enough to prove the desired theorems and no more—and specify a canonical proof procedure as well.[25]

Which approach one prefers will depend on one's conception of the aims of semantic theory. For example, if you think the theory ought to account for logical relations among L sentences, then you will need more than the few rules that are required to prove T-theorems. If you don't, but think rather that the main aim of the theory is to get the right theorems, then you might prefer to stick to the limited logic. (For discussion see Larson and Segal (1995), pp. 34–7 and Fara (1997).)

In any event, the point here is that the locus of a T-theory's interpretivity is only the canonically derived T-theorems. And those will not include examples like (2), the proof of which uses procedures that are not required for proving the desired sort of theorems and therefore would not be used in a canonical proof.

So, where Davidson might have claimed (D), I would propose that he might equally have claimed (D'):

(D') A sentence s of a language L means that p iff a canonical theorem of a lawlike truth theory for L says that s is true iff p.

have shifted in respect of the question of how a truth theory can do duty as a theory of meaning. At that point, he claimed that the interpreter would not have to know either a T-theory nor that a known theory was T-theoretic.

[25] Both the pure canonical derivation and the mixed approach work for T-theories of fragments of natural language that have so far been developed. But large portions of natural language remain as yet beyond the scope of T-theory and I am not aware of any proof that those methods would work if T-theories of the relevant constructions are developed. I think it is likely that they would, since there is no special reason to suppose that the new theories will differ significantly in their logical character from those already at large. But you never know with this sort of thing.

9.3 COGNITIVISM VERSUS
INSTRUMENTALISM

Davidson adopts an instrumentalist stance towards reference and other semantic notions. Reference and satisfaction are the interpreter's tools and nothing more. And the interpreter's job is to discover charitable interpretations and nothing more. Here is a characteristic quote: "The crucial point on which I am with Quine might be put: all the evidence for or against a theory of truth (interpretation, translation) comes in the form of facts about what events or situations in the world cause or would cause speakers to assent to or dissent from each sentence in the speakers repertoire" (Davidson, 1984, 230). Later, in Fara (1997) Davidson clarified the stricture on evidence. He said that he allowed that other sorts of evidence might be helpful in the discovery of semantic facts. But other kinds of evidence could never be used to adjudicate between truth theories that are equally good at providing charitable interpretations. He said that evidence in the form of facts about what events or situations in the world cause or would cause speakers to assent to or dissent from sentences in the speaker's repertoire is sufficient for deciding the correctness of a theory of meaning. Language, he said, is a social phenomenon and evidence about what someone's words mean must be socially available. The alternative is that each would just be speaking their own language and there would be no assurance that anyone else could understand it. He said that, on his view, what people mean is determined by the public circumstances in which they speak.[26]

To me, it seems wrong to claim that evidence of a certain, circumscribed sort is always sufficient to adjudicate between rival theories of a given range of phenomena. Such claims would be out of place if we were considering theories of planetary motion or optics or any other natural phenomenon. Semantic phenomena are perfectly real natural phenomena as well. Given this, we cannot know what kinds of evidence will help us discover them by telling us which of two or more rival theories is right. As Chomsky has pointed out (in various places, including Chomsky, 2000), making a priori stipulations about the range of evidence available to theories of language amounts to an unmotivated methodological dualism. The study of language and mind generally should meet the same standards as scientific study of other phenomena.[27]

Psycholinguistics, the branch of cognitive psychology founded by Chomsky, is consistent with a different and, in my view, more attractive picture than Davidson's. In this picture, what I mean by an expression is determined by certain cognitive states of mine that are associated with it. These states are not determined by my speech dispositions. Rather they are part of the mechanism that explains these dispositions.

---

[26] The line of thought Davidson voices here also derives from Quine.

[27] For discussion, see Segal (1999) and Davidson's reply in the same volume.

I will sketch out this alternative and then argue that it does not suffer from any problems about how one person can know what another means.[28]

In the Chomskyan picture, language is not really a social phenomenon. The rules of language are in people's heads, or, more precisely, represented in the minds of individual speakers. We may not be conscious of these representations. But they are there anyway. The representations enter into the explanation of various syntactic, semantic and phonological data all of which concern human cognition and action: how speech sounds are perceived and produced, judgements people make about what sentences do and don't mean, whether certain strings of words seem deviant and so on.

For example, consider (3):

(3)   a. The tourists wanted to lick them
      b. The zookeeper asked the tour leader which lion the tourists wanted to lick them

In (3a) "them" cannot refer back to the tourists, but must have its interpretation fixed by something else in the context. The same string of words as (3a) occurs in (3b). But in that case "them" can be interpreted as referring back to tourists (although it doesn't have to be). A possible explanation for this goes roughly as follows (from Chomsky, 1986, pp. 164–84). Suppose that the logical forms of the sentences are as partially depicted in (4):

(4)   a. [The tourists]$_j$ wanted to lick them$_k$
      b. The zookeeper asked the tour leader which lion [the tourists]$_k$ wanted PRO to lick them$_k$

PRO is a hidden element, present in the logical form but not pronounced or written, that works rather like a pronoun meaning *one*. The subscripts are also hidden but real elements of the logical form and they determine the relations of co-reference: co-indexed terms must co-refer. There are rules that govern the possibilities of co-indexing and these do not allow the co-indexing of expressions that have too little linguistic material of a specifiable sort between them. In (a) there is too little between "the tourists" and "them" for co-indexing to be permitted. But in (b), the presence of PRO permits the possibility of co-indexing and hence co-reference.[29]

Suppose, for the sake of argument, that that explanation is along the right lines. If we did not know the relevant rules, then we would have no reason not to interpret "them" in (a) as referring back to the tourists. If we want to explain our judgements in terms of linguistic rules, then we have to suppose that the rules are guiding those judgements. And the easiest way to make sense of that is to suppose that we know them, if not consciously, then unconsciously, or that they are represented in what Chomsky calls our "language faculty", that is, the cognitive systems that underlie our linguistic capacity.

---

[28] The exposition below is partly drawn from unpublished joint work with Richard Larson.

[29] Note that "co-reference" means *co-reference as determined by the syntax*. Suppose I mistake a shopkeeper for a customer and say "the shopkeeper ought to help him". Then "him" can refer to the shopkeeper. But the reference is determined by contextual factors, not co-indexing.

With that picture in place, we can offer a different account of semantic theory from Davidson's. Logical forms are not abstracted from speech behaviour but rather are the structures that our language faculties represent complex expressions as possessing. Semantic rules are a subset of the rules represented by our language faculties. And if we suppose that the rules we represent constitute a compositional semantic theory, then we can explain our remarkable capacity to understand new sentences. We can explain how "with a few syllables" [we] "can express an incalculable number of thoughts, so that even a thought grasped by a terrestrial being for the very first time can be put into a form of words which will be understood by someone to whom the thought is entirely new" (compare the first quote from Frege, 1923, above).

With the development of Chomskyan linguistics and the rise of cognitivism in the latter part of the twentieth century, a number of theorists adopted Davidson's insight that a T-theory (or some elaboration of one) was the right sort of theory for semantics, but deployed the insight within a more cognitivist perspective.[30] The next section sketches the specific approach adopted by Larson and Segal (1995).

9.3.1 Semantics from a Cognitivist Perspective

If we want to explain semantic competence in terms of knowledge of a T-theory, the information problem resurfaces. Since a T-theory does not say what any expression means, knowing a mere T-theory would not appear to suffice for semantic competence.

From the cognitivist perspective, the information problem can be solved by exploiting Chomsky's distinction between competence and performance, the distinction between having a body of knowledge (competence) and having the means to deploy the knowledge in relation to specific tasks (performance).

To illustrate the distinction between competence and performance, Chomsky (Chomsky, 1986) invited us consider a case of temporary aphasia. In such cases, a subject temporarily loses some or all of their capacity to speak and understand. The capacities then return. Since the subject does not have to relearn the language, it is very natural to suppose that they retained their linguistic knowledge, but merely could not access it. If we suppose that during the aphasic period they lacked the knowledge, it would be very difficult to explain how they suddenly regained it.

As a second illustration, please consider (5) and (6):

(5) The philosopher the linguist the psychologist agreed with argued with abstained.
(6) The cat hunted in the attic sneezed.

When initially confronted with such examples, most speakers judge them to be garbled or meaningless. However, they are perfectly grammatical and meaningful.

---

[30] The idea that semantic competence might be explained in terms of unconscious knowledge of a T-theory occurs in Harman (1972) and Harman (1974). The proposal has been pursued in detail by James Higginbotham in a number of articles, e.g. Higginbotham (1985), (1986), (1989). The most detailed treatment is Larson and Segal (1995).

To understand (5), note that the philosopher abstained—it was the philosopher with whom the linguist argued—and that the psychologist agreed with the linguist. (6) is easy to understand in the right sort of context, such as: "One cat was hunted in the cellar, the other was hunted in the attic. The cat hunted in the attic sneezed." The idea is that normal English speakers unconsciously know syntactic and semantic rules that generate legitimate structures and meanings for (5) and (6), but are unable to apply this knowledge to these particular cases.[31]

What bridge the gap between competence and performance are performance systems: cognitive systems that have access to the internally represented syntactic and semantic theories and apply the information to particular linguistic tasks such as speech and understanding. These systems get tangled up when confronted with examples like (5) and (6). And it is these systems that are impaired in temporary aphasias.

Not a great deal is known about performance systems. It is fairly clear that they must include at least a parser—something that accesses the axioms of the syntactic and semantic theories and applies them to build up representations of the structure and meaning of complex expressions.

There are presumably other performance systems too. For example, there may be one that identifies the referents of indexicals, and combines such information with information about the semantics of sentence types to derive the truth conditions of utterances of context-sensitive sentences. There may also be one or more performance systems concerned with pragmatics, involved in inferring speaker meaning from literal meaning and context.

Larson and Segal (1995, pp. 37–42) apply the distinction to the information problem roughly as follows. They suggest that performance systems have access to an internally represented T-theory and use this theory to produce representations of meanings of words and sentences. They do this because they use the T-theory precisely on the assumption that it is interpretive. To put it crudely, they use the p on the right-hand side of a T-theorem to interpret the s on the left.

The proposal might appear to be some sort of confidence trick. After all, there is a considerable difference between the information provided by a T-theory and the information that a given T-theory is interpretive. By what right do these performance systems merely get to assume that their local T-theory is interpretive, given that establishing the interpretivity of a candidate T-theory is such a big task?

But the question is: interpretive of which language? The contents of a subject's internalized T-theory simply determine how they will understand language. For example, when they encounter a linguistic sign, a written or spoken sentence, for instance, then the performance systems will automatically provide an interpretation for it, based on the contents of their T-theory. If a canonical theorem of the T-theory has it that "les elephants ont des oreilles" is true iff elephants have ears, then the subject will automatically take "les elephants ont des oreilles" to mean that elephants have ears.

---

[31] For defence of this claim see Segal (1994).

One speaker will understand another, then (*ceteris paribus*), if the contents of their internalized theories are the same in respect of the words and sentences that they use in their communications. That we often can understand one another is not a mystery. Rather, it is to be expected, given the overall design of human linguistic systems. If adult semantic competence consists in knowledge of a T-theory, then acquiring semantic competence is acquiring a good T-theory, one that will allow you to understand others in your environment. Hence it is the business of language-acquisition mechanisms to ensure that what gets encoded in the language faculty is a T-theory that is interpretive for ambient bits of language. So, for example, when a French child learns "rouge", she learns that "rouge" applies to any object x iff x is red. She doesn't learn that "rouge" applies to x iff x is the colour of raspberries, nor that "rouge" applies to x iff [x is red & [either snow is black or snow is not black]].

So that is how a mere T-theory can do duty for a theory of meaning: the T-theory is unconsciously known by a speaker, linguistic performance systems within the speaker have access to the theory and use it to interpret linguistic forms.

On Larson and Segal's account, we get (M1) and (M2) in place of Davidson's (D):

(M1) A sentence S means that p for individual I iff it is a canonical theorem of I's internalized T-theory that S is true iff p.

(M2) What an expression E means for I is given by the canonical clause for E in I's internalized T-theory.[32]

In this picture, the fundamental notion of meaning is idiolectic and in no metaphysically essential way social or publicly accessible. Davidson (and others whom I have encountered) worry that this makes communication a mystery. Davidson's own view, as explained above, is that what a person means by their words must in principle be determined by publicly observable facts. The worry is that if it were not, then other speakers could never really know what she meant.

But the worry is misplaced. Consider first the actual epistemic situation of real speakers. If someone utters something in a language you understand, then you will automatically hear it as having a certain meaning. The same applies to written words. Try not to understand "all philosophers are idiots" as saying that all philosophers are idiots.[33] You understand the sentence as you do because performance systems that have access to your internalized semantic theory automatically provide you with interpretations of linguistic signs that you encounter. Whether the interpretation they provide is correct depends on whether the speaker's idiolect coincides with the hearer's (or reader's). In normal cases, the hearer will have no reason for doubts and will accept the automatically-provided interpretation of the words. In special cases she may not: she may have reason to believe that the speaker is speaking a different language and that the similarity of signs is merely coincidental.

Now let us suppose that there is an element of doubt: the speaker appears to have said, for example, that all philosophers are idiots. But maybe he is speaking a

---

[32] (M1) and (M2) are meant to be empirical rather than *a priori* claims.

[33] I am not suggesting the quoted sentence is true. My tactic works better if the sentence that you are trying not to understand is startling.

different language from the hearer's. That is a genuine epistemic issue. But it makes no interesting difference to the epistemological situation of whether meanings are constituted by publicly observable facts about behaviour or by internal representations of rules. Note first that the typical hearer has not in fact observed the relevant observable facts—the linguistic behavioural history of the speaker—any more than they have observed the hearer's internal representations. So in either case the speaker must, if they want to find out what the speaker meant, do some research.

In Davidson's picture, they would need to explore behavioural dispositions. One might expect that the hearer could do this reasonably successfully and, up to reasonable inductive confidence, come to know the relevant dispositional facts. So for example, he might check that the speaker applies "philosopher" to certain specific philosophers, assents to "these days philosophers often work at universities" and so on. But the hearer could never get 100 per cent conclusive evidence about the relevant dispositions, because the disposition has infinitely logically possible manifestations which might in principle undermine the hypothesis that best fits the finite data. Gruelike examples come to mind.

In Larson and Segal's picture the research project would be to find out the content of the relevant internalized rules. The ordinary hearer presumably would not endeavour to discover the rules represented in the speaker's language faculty. However they might reasonably be expected to do something similar: to investigate whether the idea that the speaker associates with "philosopher" is the idea of a philosopher, where an idea is taken to be part of what causes behaviour. If it is, and if the speaker has the relevant further beliefs, then he will be disposed to apply "philosopher" to certain specific philosophers, to assent to "these days philosophers often work at universities" and so on. In this case, the process is one of confirming a theory about unobservables using observable evidence. And the hearer could come to know that the hypothesis was correct. Of course that sort of knowledge falls short of absolute certainty. But that is the same in the Davidsonian scenario.

The same applies if the hearer becomes a cognitive semantic theorist and endeavours to test the hypothesis that the speaker has a representation in his language faculty which states that (x) (satisfies "philosopher" iff x is a philosopher). If that is the case, then the speaker will be disposed, if his performance mechanisms are functioning properly and if he has the relevant further beliefs, to apply "philosopher" to certain specific philosophers, to assent to "these days philosophers often work at universities" and so on. This is again a process of theory confirmation of a sort that can yield knowledge, in the ordinary, undemanding sense of "knowledge".

9.4 CONTEXT AND THE LIMITS OF FORMALITY

Before concluding, I want briefly to consider one objection to formal truth-theoretic approaches to natural language semantics. According to Tarski, recall, a language is formal if the sense of every expression is unambiguously determined by its form. I noted that one reason that natural languages don't appear to be formal is due to ambiguity. The standard move for a formal semanticist is to deal with structural ambiguity, such as that exhibited by (0) above, by claiming that (0) is just the surface form of two different sentences with two different logical forms. Analogously what appear to be ambiguous words like "book" are held to be surface forms of distinct words: "book$_1$", a verb meaning to make a reservation; "book$_2$", a noun referring to a form of written work.

But for a wide range of cases, such moves do not appear particularly plausible. Here is a nice example, borrowed from Charles Travis (p.c.). A watermelon is green on the outside and red on the inside. Now consider two utterances of (7) in two different contexts:

(7) That is a red one

In both contexts, the same melon, m, is being picked out by the demonstrative. In the first context, a greengrocer is helping a customer find one of those melons that is red inside. The utterance is true. In the second context, an artist is looking for a melon with a green outside and his colour-blind and ignorant friend, mistaken about m's exterior colouring, utters (7). In that case, the utterance is false. The utterances have different truth conditions even though they are utterances of what appears to be a single expression. Moreover the whole notion of satisfaction now becomes problematic. Does m satisfy "red" or not?

One could try to deploy the normal methods. As just mentioned, one ploy would be to claim that "red" is ambiguous, in one sense meaning *red on the outside* and in another, *red on the inside*. But few would believe that. And the problem generalizes beyond that solution. Blue ink in a bottle can look black. One can imagine contexts in which "black" is truly applied to the ink and others in which it is not. It's not just a matter of insides and outsides.

Another standard ploy that one might try in this case would be to appeal to the distinction between semantics and pragmatics, as Frege did in his defence of the truth-functional account of "If B, then A". One could claim that, strictly and literally speaking, (7) is true even as uttered in the artist's studio. What (7) means is something like: *That one is red in some way or other*. And that is true, since m is red on the inside. When the artist's friend utters (7), however, he conveys an adjunct thought to the effect that m is red in a contextually relevant way, which would be: red on the outside. We think the utterance is false because we focus on the adjunct thought, rather than the thought strictly and literally expressed.

This proposal leads to some counterintuitive consequences, since it makes it very easy for something to be red. Suppose, for example, that there is a species of brown mushroom with two similar-looking subspecies. One subspecies has characteristic tiny red dots on the underside of its cap and the other has corresponding yellow ones. As a result, people classify them as "red" and "yellow". Suppose that the artist is assembling a scene for a still life that he wants to paint. I offer to go home and fetch a mushroom that I think will fit in nicely. It is one of the brown ones with tiny red dots.

The artist asks me what colour it is and I say "It is red." On the suggested account, my utterance is strictly and literally true. But that does not really seem right. When I bring the mushroom, the artist might well exclaim: "It is brown, not red." Suppose I then show him the red dots and say "Look, it is red." The pragmatic proposal would predict that the artist might well respond with something like: "Oh, I see. It is red, strictly speaking. It is just not red in the way you had led me to expect." But that is not the sort of response one would anticipate.

Maybe, in spite of such consequences, the pragmatic proposal could be defended. But I am tentatively inclined to doubt that and to accept Travis's account of the examples. In that case, we must recognize that our language faculties allow us to be the final arbiters of how linguistic expressions ought to apply to the world. Whether a mushroom or a watermelon is properly called "red" does not depend only on the meaning of the term "red" and the colour of the object. It is up to the participants in the conversation (just the speaker, in my view) to determine what manner of being red is to decide the matter.

None of that precludes expressions from making stable semantic contributions across different contexts. Obviously "red" means *red* both in the greengrocer's shop and in the artist's studio. Semantic theory, therefore, has to be modified to take account of the interaction of context and context-independent semantic properties of words in determining conditions of satisfaction and truth.[34] I don't think, however, that this requires any major departure from standard truth-theoretic methods. It just means predicates work rather like indexicals, with extensions varying across contexts.[35,36]

REFERENCES

Bolzano, B., (1972). *Theory of Science*, ed. and trans. R. George, University of California Press: Berkeley and L.A. Originally published 1837.
____ (1935). *Der Briefwechsel B. Bolzano's mit F.Exner*, ed. E. Winter. Prague: Royal Bohemian Society of Sciences. Letter dated 18.12.1834.
Chomsky, N., (1957). *Syntactic Structures*, Mouton and Co, The Hague.
____ (1986). *Knowledge of Language: Its Nature, Origin and Use*, Praeger: New York.
____ (1995). "Language and Nature", *Mind* 104: 1–61.
____ (2000). *New Horizons in the Study of Language and Mind*, Cambridge University Press: Cambridge.
Carnap, R., (1947). *Meaning and Necessity: A Study in Semantics and Modal Logic*, Chicago.
Coffa, J. A., (1991). *The Semantic Tradition from Kant to Carnap*, Cambridge University Press: Cambridge.
Davidson, D., (1965). "Theories of Meaning and Learnable Languages", reprinted in Davidson 1984.

[34] For similar thoughts, see Pietroski (2003).
[35] For one implementation of this idea, see Szabo (2001). See also Travis (1997) for discussion.
[36] Many thanks for very helpful discussion to Emma Borg, Donald Davidson, Alexander George, Richard Heck, Keith Hossack, Shalom Lappin, Ernie Lepore, Guy Longworth, Mark Sainsbury, Peter Simons, Jason Stanley, Mark Textor and Charles Travis. Donald Davidson died while I was writing this article. He was an inspiration and a friend and I will miss him.

—— (1967). "Truth and Meaning", reprinted in Davidson 1984.

—— (1973). "In Defence of Convention T", reprinted in Davidson 1984.

—— (1984). *Inquiries into Truth and Interpretation*, Clarendon Press: Oxford.

Frege, G., (1879). *Begriffsschrift* Halle. Translated as *Conceptual Notation and Related Articles* (trans. T.W. Bynum) Oxford.

—— (1952). "On Sense and Meaning" (trans. M. Black) in *Translations from the Philosophical Writings of Gottlob Frege*, eds. Geach, P., and M. Black, Rowman and Littlefield: New Jersey. Originally published 1879.

—— (1956). "The Thought: A Logical Enquiry", *Mind* 65: 289–311. Originally published 1918.

—— (1977). "Compound Thoughts", in Frege, G., *Logical Investigations*, trans. P. Geach and R. H. Stoohoff, Blackwell. Originally published 1923.

—— (1980). "Philosophical and Mathematical Correspondence", ed. Gabriel, G., *et al.*, abridged for the English version by McGuinness (trans. Kaal, H.), Blackwell: Oxford.

Fara, R., (1997). "The Segal Discussion", a video interview with Donald Davidson, Philosophy International Publications.

Grice, H. P., (1975). "Logic and Conversation", in Cole, P. and Morgan J. (eds.) *Syntax and Semantics*, Academic Press: New York, 41–58.

—— (1989). *Studies in the Ways of Words*, Harvard University Press: Cambridge MA.

Harman, G., (1972). "Logical Form", *Foundations of Language*, 9: 38–65.

—— (1974). "Meaning and Semantics", in M. Munitz and P. Unger eds., *Semantics and Philosophy*, New York University Press: New York, 1–16.

Higginbotham, J., (1985). "On Semantics", *Linguistic Inquiry*, 16: 547–93.

—— (1986). "Linguistic Theory and Davidson's Program in Semantics", in E. LePore, ed. *Truth and Interpretation: Perspectives on the Philosophy of Donald Davidson*, Blackwell: Oxford, 29–48.

—— (1988). "Contexts, Models and Meanings: A Note on the Data of Semantics", in R. Kempson, ed. *Mental Representations: The Interface between Language and Reality*, Cambridge University Press: Cambridge 29–48.

—— (1989). "Knowledge of Reference", in A. George ed., *Reflections on Chomsky*, Basil Blackwell: Oxford, 153–174.

Katz, J. and Fodor, J., (1963). "The Structure of a Semantic Theory", *Language* 39: 170:210.

Katz, J. and Postal, P., (1964). *An integrated theory of linguistic descriptions*, Cambridge: MIT Press.

Larson, R. and Segal, G., (1995). *Knowledge of Meaning: An Introduction to Semantic Theory*, MIT Press: Cambridge MA.

Lepore, E., (1983). "What Model-Theoretic Semantics Cannot Do" *Synthese* 54: 167–187.

Lewis, D., (1970). "General Semantics", *Synthese* 22: 18–67.

Neale, S., (1994). "Logical Form and LF", in Otero, C. (ed.), *Noam Chomsky: Critical Assessments*, (London: Routledge), 788–838.

Pietroski, P., "The Character of Natural Language Semantics", in Barber A., ed., *The Epistemology of Language*, (Oxford University Press: Oxford) (2003) 217–256.

Quine, W. V., (1960). *Word and Object*, MIT Press: Cambridge, MA.

Quine, W. V., (1970a). *Philosophy of Logic*, Prentice-Hall: Englewood.

Quine, W. V., (1970b). "On the Reasons for the Indeterminacy of Translation", *Journal of Philosophy* 67: 178–83.

Schilpp, P., (1963). *The Philosophy of Rudolph Carnap*, Open Court, La Salle: Illinois.

Segal, G., (1994). "Priorities in the Philosophy of Thought", *Proceedings of the Aristotelian Society*, supp. vol. 48: 107–30.

Segal, G., (1999). "How a Truth Theory can do Duty as a Theory of Meaning", in Zeglen, ed. 1999.

_____ (2000). "Four Arguments for the Indeterminacy of Translation", *Knowledge, Language and Logic: Questions for Quine*, eds. A. Orenstein and P. Kotatko, Kluwer Academic Publications, 131–41.

_____ "Intentionality", in *The Oxford Handbook of Contemporary Analytic Philosophy*, edited by Frank Jackson and Michael Smith (Oxford: Oxford University Press 2005) 283–309.

Szabo, Z., (2001). "Adjectives in Context." In I. Kenesei and R. M. Harnish eds., *Perspectives on Semantics, Pragmatics, and Discourse*. Amsterdam: John Benjamins, pp. 119–46.

Tarski, A., (1931). "The Concept of Truth in Formalized Languages", reprinted in Tarski, 1956.

_____ (1956). *Logic, Semantics, Mathematics*, translated by J. H. Woodger, Oxford University Press: London.

_____ (1944). "The Semantic Conception of Truth", *Philosophy and Phenomenological Research* 4: 341–75.

Textor, M., (1997). "Bolzano's Sententialism", in *Grazer Philosophische Studien*, 53 181–202 (Special Volume: *Bolzano and Analytic Philosophy*).

Thomason, R., (ed) (1974). *Formal Philosophy: Collected Papers of Richard Montague*, Yale University Press: New Haven.

Travis, C., (1997). "Pragmatics" in Hale, B. and C. Wright eds., *A Companion to the Philosophy of Language*, Blackwell: Oxford and New York.

Russell, B., (1905). "On Denoting", *Mind*, 14: 479–93.

_____ (1959). *My Philosophical Development*, George Allen and Unwin: London.

Weir, A., this volume "Quine on Indeterminacy".

Williamson, T., (1994). *Vagueness*. Routledge: London and New York.

Zeglen, U., ed. (1999). *Donald Davidson: Truth, Meaning and Knowledge*, Routledge: London and New York.

CHAPTER 10

....

MEANING HOLISM

....

PETER PAGIN

10.1 BACKGROUND

....

THE term 'meaning holism' (together with variants like 'semantic holism' and 'linguistic holism') has been used for a number of more or less closely interrelated ideas. According to one common view, meaning holism (MH) is the thesis that what a linguistic expression means depends on its relations to many or all other expressions within the same totality. Sometimes these relations are called 'conceptual' or 'inferential'. A related idea is that what an expression means depends, mutually, on the meaning of the other expressions in the totality, or alternatively on some semantic property of this totality itself. The totality in question may be the language to which the expressions belong, or a theory formulation in that language. In this sense MH is contrasted for example with so-called atomistic theories, according to which each simple expression can have a meaning independently of all other expressions, or molecular theories according to which there are meaning dependencies but restricted to smaller parts and often unidirectional.

Meaning holistic ideas were introduced into analytic philosophy in the early 1950s, in works by Carl Gustav Hempel (1950) and Willard Van Quine (1951), both concerned with the meaning of theoretical sentences in the formulation of a scientific theory. Hempel articulated an idea of interdependence among expressions:

In order to understand "the meaning" of a hypothesis within an empiricist language, we have to know not merely what observation sentences it entails alone or in conjunction with subsidiary hypotheses, but also what other, non-observational, empirical sentences are entailed by it, and for what other hypotheses the given one would be confirmatory or disconfirmatory. In other words, the cognitive meaning of a statement in an empirical language is reflected in the totality of its logical relationships to all other statements in that language, and not to the observation sentences alone.   (Hempel, 1950: 181)

Hempel's idea was a way of accounting for the fact that in general, a theoretical sentence does not alone, but only together with other theoretical sentences, imply observation sentences. This, sometimes called *confirmation holism*, or *epistemological holism*, was even more emphasized by Quine. In setting out his views on sentence meaning, he employed the more austere notion of *empirical content*. Roughly, the empirical content of a sentence is the set of possible experiences that confirm it. Quine then characterized 'total science' metaphorically as a field of force with observation sentences at the periphery, confronting experience, and theoretical sentences in the interior:

> If this view is right, it is misleading to speak of the empirical content of an individual statement—especially if it is a statement at all remote from the experiential periphery of the field.   (Quine, 1951: 43)

> The unit of empirical significance is the whole of science.   (Quine, 1951: 42)

This has often been taken as implying that it is the whole theory formulation that has meaning in the first place, and that theoretical sentences and sub-sentential expressions, have meaning (but not empirical content) in a derivative way. So understood, it is one example of the idea that the meaning of individual expressions depends on the totality to which they belong.

Hempel's view, though clearly anticipating later holistic ideas, did not have a great influence, but Quine's did. In particular, it has been correctly pointed out that if you combine confirmation holism with a form of *verificationism*, or some similar epistemic conception of sentence meaning, then a form of meaning holism results, provided the meaning of a sentence is understood as something like its *total contribution* to the empirical content of the theory. Because of confirmation holism, the contribution of a theoretical sentence depends on the contributions of other sentences, and therefore the meaning of the sentence depends on the meaning of other sentences. This source of meaning holism has received much attention.

Other important meaning holistic ideas were proposed in Wilfrid Sellars's work on language games (1963). On Sellars's view, the meaning of an expression is determined by the set of rules governing the kinds of 'moves' that can be made with it in the game. There are three kinds of move: *language entry moves*, which lead from observation to the acceptance of a sentence, *intra-language moves*, which are inferential transitions from sentences to a sentence, and *language exit moves*, which lead from accepted sentences to action. Since, on Sellars's view, sameness of meaning consists in sameness of role in a language game, an intuitively holistic conception results.

Sellars's work inspired what has come to be called *conceptual role* or *inferential role semantics*, suggested for instance in works by Harman (1974), Field (1977), Block (1986) and Brandom (1994). In a narrower sense, *inferential* role semantics is concerned with the meaning of sentences only, and identifies it with its role in a set of correct or accepted inferences or inference patterns, whereas *conceptual* role semantics is concerned also with sub-sentential expressions, and with the roles not only in inferences proper, but also roles in relation to perception and action. In Harman and Block the theories are concerned with *mental* language, that is, a system of mental representations having its own syntax-like structure. Again, the holistic element consists in the idea that the *conceptual role* of a mental representation relates it directly or indirectly to all or at least many other mental representations in the same system, and since meaning is or is determined by conceptual role, representations are mutually dependent for meaning.

Yet other holistic ideas were suggested in Donald Davidson's theory of *radical interpretation* (1967, 1973). According to Davidson, a correct semantic theory for the language of a particular speaker is a theory that results from methodologically correct *interpretation* of the utterances of that speaker. Such interpretation is holistic in the sense that only *whole* theories can be tested by the interpretation method. Although the semantic theory will ascribe meaning to individual sentences of the language, the possible empirical evidence for any particular ascription is too weak to fully support it. The accumulated evidence can justify the whole theory, but parts of the evidence cannot fully justify parts of the theory. This connects with the idea of interdependence when the structure of the language and the theory is taken into account (see Section 10.2) given that, as on Davidson's view, meaning is *determined* by methodologically correct interpretation. Related ideas were formulated by Dennett (1971) and Lewis (1974).

Holism of this kind is sometimes connected with a kind of *belief holism*, according to which a subject cannot have a particular belief without having many related beliefs. For instance, Davidson puts it like this:

There are good reasons for not insisting on any particular list of beliefs that are needed if a creature is to wonder whether a gun is loaded. Nevertheless, it is necessary that there be endless interlocked beliefs. The system of such beliefs identifies a thought by locating it in a logical and epistemic space.   (Davidson, 1975: 157)

Belief holism has seemed plausible (see Section 10.4), but the role of meaning or content has not always been clear (see next section).

MH has also had its critics. Davidson's holism in particular was criticized by Michael Dummett (1976, 1991), who concentrated on the issue of language learning. Other attacks on holism include Fodor, 1987 and above all Fodor and Lepore, 1992, who stressed questions of communication and psychological generalizations. Fodor and Lepore's attack on holism gave rise to an intense discussion of the topic during the 1990s. Unfortunately, the definitions of MH in these discussions have varied quite a bit, and to some extent the discussions have suffered from it. Before looking at the arguments, the question of definition therefore needs some attention.

10.2 Defining Meaning Holism

10.2.1 Indirect Definitions

In the case of belief holism, the stress is on the conditions for a person to have a belief with such and such a content. This is clearly a different question from that concerning how belief states depend on each other for having their content fixed. If there is a dependence, so that one belief state cannot have a particular content unless it is somehow connected to other belief states with appropriately related contents, then belief holistic claims follow. But the converse doesn't hold. There can be other reasons for belief holism than MH. For instance, it is reasonable to claim that to have a belief that a gun is loaded the believer must minimally be able to distinguish guns from other things. This may then be combined with two further claims: first, that the only way of having that ability is having a grasp of functional features of guns (as distinct from perceptual features), and second, that grasp of functional features requires further beliefs. The need for having further beliefs is then *epistemic* rather than *semantic*: other beliefs are needed for some particular cognitive capacity. If the dependence of some beliefs on others isn't semantic in nature, we don't have an example of MH.

An analogous point can be made regarding the ascriptions of beliefs to speakers or of meaning to their words. It is reasonable to hold, with Davidson, that interpretation of a speaker is a holistic enterprise, precisely because the evidence at each point by itself is so weak. But unless it is also held that an expression has some particular meaning just *because* this is what it can correctly be interpreted as meaning, MH doesn't follow. You might hold that it is merely a matter of empirical fact that a certain method of interpretation is reliable for finding out what human speakers mean by their words. That these words have those meanings may however depend on quite different factors, and there need be no holism involved. You will then affirm interpretation holism for epistemological reasons and reject MH itself.

Similarly, Dummett's definition of meaning holism suffers from a failure of distinguishing purely semantic issues. According to Dummett, meaning holism is the view that you have to know an entire language in order to know the meaning of any single expression in that language (1991:221). (A similar formulation can be found in Wittgenstein's *Philosophical Investigations*, #199, but the exegetical issues are too difficult to be discussed here). Exactly what knowing an entire language amounts to in this context is not so clear (e.g. knowing the meanings of all the simple parts and all syntactic operations), but either way there can be several reasons why knowledge of an entire language is necessary for knowing the meaning of any single expression. It can be because of semantic dependencies between expressions, but it can also be because of cognitive peculiarities of the human mind, having to do with its capacity of grasping concepts (cf. Tennant, 1987), and in that case the view does not have much to do with MH.

In general, if a definition of MH is given, not in terms of what meaning expressions have or how their meaning is determined, but *indirectly*, in terms of conditions on having meaning at all, or on being related in a certain way to things having meaning, then there is a possibility that those conditions are met for *non*-semantic reasons.

In fact, this holds of the official definition of meaning holism given in Fodor and Lepore (FL) 1992. According to FL (1992: 1–2), a property is *atomic* just if it is possible for exactly one thing to have it. A property is *anatomic* just if it is necessary that if one thing has it, then at least two things have it. A property is *holistic* in the sense of FL just if it is necessary that if one thing has it, then *lots* of things have it. In this

terminology, meaning holism is the view that the generic property of having meaning, or intentional content, is holistic. Let's call this *FL-holism*. FL-holism is indeed
a consequence of other definitions in terms of meaning determination, but in itself
does not distinguish between semantic and non-semantic reasons why lots of things
must be implicated. As FL seem to have acknowledged (Fodor and Lepore, 1993:
318), it may be that for any system to be *mental*, that system must have a lot of *states*
that can be characterized as mental. Then add the views that mental states are individuated by their intentional content, and that nothing can have meaning or content
unless there is a system with mental states. FL-holism results, because of metaphysical
or nomological facts about the mental, not for semantic reasons.

10.2.2 Definitions in Terms of Inferential Role

Although it is common to characterize holism as the view that the meaning of an
expression is its role *in the language*, this is not in itself a holistic view in any interesting sense. The *role* of 'and' in English may be said to be exactly that of expressing the
truth function of conjunction, which is not holistically characterized at all. Similarly,
the role of the name 'Ernest Hemingway' may be to contribute to truth conditions of
sentences exactly by referring to Ernest Hemingway. In general, describing the meaning of an expression in terms of its semantic contributions to more complex expressions is often part of holistic views, but as long as the role in question can be specified
without reference to the meaning of any other expression, it is not itself holistic.

Another issue is whether MH shall be characterized in terms that are independent
of any particular meaning theory, or whether some particular theory or kind of theory may be presupposed. For instance, according to the definition given by Louise
Antony (1993: 140), meaning holism is the view that 'conceptual connections constitute content'. This definition apparently presupposes some form of conceptual role
semantics, since the general idea of semantic interdependence between expressions
does *not* imply that if two expressions are interdependent for meaning, there is also
a conceptual connection (in any ordinary sense of this phrase) between them. Given
Antony's definition, MH is false if conceptual role semantics is false.

This situation is even clearer in Michael Devitt's definition. Devitt (1996: 10)
assumes a conceptual/inferential role semantics for sentences, and defines meaning
holism as the view that *all* the inferential relations a sentence participates in together
constitute its meaning. Devitt himself is opposed to holism in this sense, and prefers
'localism', the view that only a distinguished subset of this total inferential set constitute the meaning of the sentence. Devitt openly assumes an inferential role semantics
for both definitions. But even with this assumption in place, it is worth while to consider the relation between Devitt's definition and the idea of interdependence, not
least since holism in this sense plays a central role in the arguments of Fodor and
Lepore and in subsequent discussion.

Assume the view that there is an interdependence for meaning between *any* two
expressions in a language. That is, for any two expressions, whatever meaning is given

to the one constrains what meaning can be given to the other. Call this *total pair holism*. Assume further, that if two sentences stand in a relevant inferential relation, they are interdependent for meaning in this sense, and also that interdependence is a transitive relation (if s and s' are interdependent, and also s' and s'', then so are s and s''). Now it is clear that total pair holism does not imply Devitt holism, for it may well be enough that for each sentence only a small subset of its total inferential set is relevant for meaning interdependence, and that yet because of the transitivity of interdependence, total pair holism results. In fact, it is enough that each sentence is relevantly related to just two other sentences (number the sentences consecutively, and let each odd-numbered sentence s_n be relevantly inferable from exactly s_{n-1} and s_{n+1}; then because of the transitivity, all sentences are semantically interdependent).

Neither does Devitt holism imply total pair holism, for it is in principle possible that the language is partitioned into isolated 'inferential' sets of sentences, such that no two sentences of different inferential sets are inferentially related. Then total pair holism is false, even though Devitt holism may be true.

Thus, Devitt holism and total pair holism are logically independent. It is plausible that as a matter of general tendency (assuming inferential role semantics), the more other sentences a particular sentence is relevantly inferentially related to, the closer the language will be to instantiate total pair holism. Moreover, if the language in question contains logical vocabulary, it is not partitioned into isolated inferential sets, for any two sentences will be inferentially related to, among other things, their conjunction. Still, these two ideas of holism are clearly different.

10.2.3 Holism as a Principle of Meaning Determination

Even when we turn to the idea of interdependence itself, there are a number of issues to be clarified. First, some formulations of holism, like Antony's, suggest that what gets determined, or constituted, are the meanings or contents themselves. But it is unclear whether anyone really thinks so, and it is an implausible view anyway. Meanings, if they are entities at all, are abstract, and it is not plausible that whenever some abstract entities are essentially related to each other, they are also 'constituted' by that relation. For instance, it does not make much sense to say that the number 5, or the concept of that number, is constituted by the fact $5 + 27 = 32$, or that the proposition that p is constituted by the fact that it is equivalent with the proposition that $(p\&q)\vee p$, even though these relations may well be called 'conceptual'. That which is constituting must in some way or other be prior to that which it constitutes, and when it comes to abstract objects, the only ideas of priority that seem plausibly applicable are those of part–whole relations or inductive definitions. For instance, we might say that the number 5 is constituted by being the successor of the number 4, or that the proposition that $p\&q$ is constituted by being the conjunction of p and q. But such constitution is obviously not holistic.

What can plausibly be said to be determined or constituted according to MH is rather the expression–meaning *relation*. That is, *what* meaning an expression has may be determined or constituted in a holistic way. But it is then highly misleading, or outright false, to say that what meaning a sentence has is determined by its inferential relations to other sentences. Only a sentence that *has* a meaning can be at all inferentially related to other sentences. It simply cannot be (even though suggested by many formulations in the literature) that inferential relations between sentences precede the meaningfulness of their relata.

Rather, the proper basis for presenting MH along the idea of interdependence, is to say that expressions in a language (public or mental) have certain *non*-semantic properties and stand in certain *non*-semantic relations to each other, such that the semantic properties of the sentences depend on, get determined or constituted by, or supervene on, these non-semantic properties and relations. Call this *the determination base*. In Davidson's case the determination base consists of sentences being *held true* by the speaker (or in later works, preferred true), or in general *held true under certain circumstances*, together with the syntactic relations of constituent structure. In the case of Brian Loar (1981) it is a matter of causal relations between physical (neural) states.

Properly stated, inferential role semantics is a theory of how the meanings of sentences get determined by what inferences the speaker, or thinker, *accepts*. The relation that holds between two sentences just in case a particular speaker accepts the inference from the truth of the first to the truth of the second, is itself *non*-semantic. It is a fact about speaker psychology, not about inferential properties of the sentences. Given such non-semantic facts, it is up to the theory to say how the inferential properties themselves, and further semantic properties, get determined. One such principle of determination is precisely that if an inference is accepted as valid, then it is to *be* valid. That is, the sentences involved must be assigned meaning to the effect that the accepted inferences come out as valid. Call this the *Validating Principle*. This principle seems often tacitly taken for granted in the literature in cases where the difference between being valid and being accepted as valid isn't noted. It *is* noted, and emphasized—for example in Boghossian 1993, 1994.

In Davidson's framework the principle is in a sense approximated. The method of interpretation is summed up under the title 'the principle of charity'. In its simplest version this is the principle of *maximizing* truth among the sentences held true by the speaker. That is, assign meaning so that as much as possible of what the speaker says comes out as true. This is a *best approximation* principle. Since all speakers in fact have a number of false beliefs, it is not in general possible (given that interpretation is constrained by the need of respecting the constituent structure of sentences) to find an interpretation that makes true all the sentences held true. According to the principle of charity, an interpretation that gives the best approximation is correct.

The Validating Principle induces a kind of generalized implicit definition. Normally, in an implicit definition you have a number of sentences containing mostly words that are already interpreted, but also one or more that are not. By stipulating that the sentences shall be true, the previously uninterpreted words must get some meaning (if there is one) such that the sentences in fact come out true. This was the case with Hilbert's implicit definition of the terms 'point', 'line' and 'plane' by means of his axioms of geometry (Hilbert, 1899). This is also the best way of understanding Hempel's suggestion. Theoretical sentences of a scientific theory contain previously understood expressions, and also theoretical terms specific to the theory itself. These terms, such as 'quark' and 'boson' in particle physics, can be seen as implicitly defined by means of the theory formulation. Some of its sentences are to be true, and some are held to follow from others. This totality of accepted truths and inferences together implicitly define the terms specific to the theory. Since the terms are connected, both by co-occurring in the same sentences and by occurring in inferentially related sentences, the meaning assigned to one term must match the meanings assigned to others, so that the desired truths and validities result. That is, we have interdependence.

Usually, meaning determination principles are thought of synchronically: for instance, the meaning of a speaker's sentences at a time t is taken to depend on his attitudes at time t, not on his *revisions* of those attitudes at later times. However, *dispositions* to make revisions can be taken into account. For instance, the *strength* with which a speaker holds a particular sentence true (his unwillingness to give it up), may be relevant to meaning determination.

This applies to the connection between MH and Quine's claim in Two Dogmas of *unrestricted revisability*, i.e. that any statement held true can be given up in the face of recalcitrant experience (Quine 1951:43). The connection is not simple, but it is important to note that MH, as a meaning determination principle, can accommodate both restricted and unrestricted revisability. On a restricted revisability alternative, a particular proposition p cannot be assigned to any sentence s as held true by speaker S, if S is disposed to give up his attitude to s under particular circumstances. Typically, you would prefer this alternative if you believe in an unrevisability version of the analytic/synthetic distinction and think that some propositions, for example the proposition *that bachelors are unmarried*, can only be expressed by an analytic sentence.

10.2.4   The Primacy of the Whole

The semantic idea, exemplifying more general holistic ideas, that there is some whole with semantic significance that has priority of the semantics of parts—individual linguistic expressions—is not always easy to make sense of. There does not, for instance, seem to be any relevant semantic property of a *language* by which a language can be the 'whole' in question.

The idea, often attributed to Quine (cf. Okasha, 2000), that the meaning of theoretical sentences consist in their contribution to the empirical content of the theory does, on closer inspection, reduce to a kind of inferential role semantics: some sentences are taken as together entailing certain observation conditionals (that is, conditionals with observation sentences as antecedent and consequent) or observation categoricals (universalized observation conditionals), whereas the various observation sentences are just accepted or rejected. Therefore, this idea does not really give rise to a different kind of meaning holism. The primacy of the whole boils down to the primacy and relative independence of observation sentences (cf. Quine, 1986b).

An alternative is the *nihilist* view, which does seem to have been Quine's (Quine, 1986a), that sentences without empirical content, including many theoretical sentences, don't have any meaning at all. On this alternative, too, meaning is assigned to individual observation sentences, not just to the totality.

10.2.5 The Network Metaphor

As in the Davidson quotation above, and for example also in Block 1998, MH is sometimes characterized by saying that the meaning of a sentence, or a belief state, is given by its place in a 'network', 'web', 'pattern', 'space', or 'system' of sentences or beliefs. The network metaphor is not cashed in, however, but only used as an illustration. The illustration is somewhat misleading, since it suggests that—like the nodes in a network are pairwise connected with lines—the relevant interconnections between expressions consist in a large number of *binary* relations, and also that a metric of *distance* between the nodes can be defined on that basis, so that we have a well-defined notion of a *location* in the network (directly connected expressions are supposed to be 'closer' than indirectly connected ones). By contrast, the relations actually considered in theories of meaning determination are more complex.

10.2.6 The Combinatorics of Interdependence

The general idea of interdependence of meaning determination is only that the assignment of meaning to one or more expressions constrains the assignment of meaning to others. This again means that some combinations of expression-meaning pairs are ruled out. For example, with respect to a miniature language of three singular terms and three one-place predicates, for which there are three possible objects of reference to the terms and three possible concepts expressible by the predicates, the set M of possible combinations of meaning assignments has exactly $3^6 = 729$ members, since each of the six expressions of the language has three possible meanings. If we say that expression t_1 cannot have meaning m_3 while expression F_2 has meaning m_6, then this excludes all meaning distributions that include pair, of assignments, which is exactly $3^4 = 81$ distributions (three possible meanings to each of the remaining four expressions). All proper subsets of M define restrictions that rule certain combinations out. For instance, the restriction that all expressions must have *different* meanings leaves only $(3!)^2 = 36$ admissible distributions (combining $3 \cdot 2 \cdot 1$ possible distributions over the terms freely with as many possible distributions over the predicates).

By means of such combinatorial ideas we can give a *measure* of interdependence. Let's say that a *total distribution* gives a meaning to each of the expressions of the language (for sake of simplicity, ignore lexical ambiguity). For an expression e the assignment number $N(e)$ is the total number of meanings given to e by the different admissible total distributions. For instance, in the example $N(e) = 3$ for all simple e if all possible total distributions are admissible, but also after imposing the *different meanings* restriction: in either case there are three possible meanings a particular simple expression can have. Let $N(L)$ be the number of admissible total distributions to the language L, and $N(E)$ the number of admissible distributions to syntactically *simple* expressions. If we simplify matters by assuming that the language has a compositional semantics, and fix the semantic significance of syntactic operations, then the meanings of complex expressions will be uniquely determined by the meanings given to simple expressions and their mode of composition. Then $N(L) = N(E)$, for if there are, say, 36 admissible distributions over simple expressions, there cannot be 37 admissible total distributions. For if so, there are two distributions giving the same meanings to simple expressions but differing over the meaning of some complex expression, thus violating the assumption of compositionality (given that the significance of syntax is fixed).

Now we want to give a measure of interdependence by computing the degree to which possible distributions are excluded. Since it cannot be assumed that $N(e)$ is the same for all expressions e, we shall have to give an interdependence measure for each e, and then define the total measure as an average. First, then, we specify the maximum number of admissible total distributions. We get the maximum number if meaning assignments to individual expressions can be freely combined. Where k is the number of simple expressions of L we have

$$Max(L) = N(e_1) \cdot N(e_2) \cdot \ldots \cdot N(e_k)$$

which in the example is 3^6. Then we define $DI\,(L, e)$, the degree of interdependence of L with respect to e, as follows:

$$DI(L, e) = \frac{Max(L) - N(L)}{Max(L) - N(e)}$$

When meaning assignments can be combined freely we have no interdependence at all, which amounts to setting $N(L) = Max(L)$. In this case $DI(L, e) = 0$ for any expression e. When interdependence is maximal, any assignment of meaning to one expression uniquely determines the assignment of meaning to any other expression. Then $N(L) = N(e)$, for any simple expression e: there cannot be two total distributions d_1 and d_2 that assign the same meaning m to some expression e, for then there is at least one expression e' that gets different meanings by d_1 and d_2. In that case, assigning m to e does not uniquely determine the meaning of e', contrary to assumption. In case of maximal interdependence, when $N(L) = N(e)$, we have $DI(L, e) = 1$ (note that $DI(L, e)$ is undefined in case $N(e') = 1$ for all $e' \neq e$, since then $Max(L) - N(e) = 0$; this is intuitively right, since if there isn't more than one possible meaning for any single expression, there is no measurable degree of interdependence either). Values between 0 and 1 correspond to intermediate degrees of interdependence, the higher the more interdependent. In the example, with the *different meanings* restriction in force, giving 36 admissible total assignments, we have

$$DI(L, e) = \frac{729 - 36}{729 - 3} \approx 0{,}995$$

for each e.

Finally, we define $DI(L)$, the degree of interdependence of L, as the *average* of the expression-relative values:

$$DI(L) = \overline{DI(L, e_i)}, 1 \leq i \leq k$$

(where the bar denotes average value). We have the highest degree of interdependence for L, $DI(L) = 1$, in case $DI(L, e) = 1$ for all e. Again, values between 0 and 1 correspond to intermediate degrees of interdependence, the higher the more holistic. Total pair holism is not of highest degree, since it only says that the assignment of meaning to an expression *constrains* the assignment to any other. This is best understood as a *lowering* of N-values, as follows: let $N(e'|e)$ be a conditional value, the (highest) number of admissible assignments to e' given an admissible assignment to e. We can now interpret total pair holism as the view that for all e, e' in L, if $N(e') > 1$, then $N(e'|e) < N(e')$.

We can now define MH in terms of degree of interdependence. Following some suggestions in the literature, we should define MH as the view that $DI(L) = 1$ (for any L). However, it might be more reasonable to require only a value close to 1. One can also go for a definition in terms of conditional assignment numbers. Finally, one can disregard numbers altogether and focus on the mechanisms that bring interdependence about.

10.2.7 Meanings and the Mechanisms of Determination

The main idea in the literature of a determination mechanism has the following form: first, assign a basic property to some sentences, like being accepted as true (or accepted as true under certain circumstances), or to some inferences, like accepted as valid (or as valid under certain circumstances). Second, require a certain semantic dependence of complex expressions on their proper parts, like that the semantics be compositional. Third, assume some syntactic analysis of the sentences. Optionally, one can also fix the semantic significance of syntactic operations, or just let that be determined together with the meanings of the expressions.

The meaning determining factors are then a combination of non-semantic facts and structural constraints. Now assume that available semantic values are ordinary objects as values for singular terms, ordinary familiar concepts as values for predicates, familiar concepts of concepts as values for quantifiers, and so on. That is, assume *standard meanings*.

Assume further that the general determination principle is the *Validating Principle*. (That is, we assume that the Validating Principle is a *true* principle of meaning determination, not that it is accepted by the speaker.) Because of the Validating Principle, the meanings assigned to constituents of a sentence that is held true must fit together so that—given the way the world is—the sentence comes out true. Because of this, the constituent parts cannot be assigned meaning independently of each other. And this is repeated for sentence after sentence, inference after inference, that is to come out true or valid. (This is like solving a system of mathematical equations, where numerical values are to be assigned to free variables so that the equations come out true.) Then the following might happen:

(a) We have underdetermination: more than one total meaning assignment fulfils the requirements.
(b) We have unsatisfiable overdetermination: no total meaning assignment fulfils the requirement.

There are now basically two options available. The first option is to keep standard meanings and adjust the evidence. For instance, with respect to underdetermination we can require *more* non-semantic facts, sharpen the structural constraints, or simply accept the underdetermination. With respect to unsatisfiable overdetermination we can take Davidson's option and *discount* some sentences or inferences accepted by the person as mere mistakes. The hope is that such a process eventually yields a unique total meaning assignment, which is the *best approximation*. Clearly, with finding a best approximation for assigning familiar meanings there will be several sets of non-semantic facts that determine the *same* total meaning assignment as outcome. That is, we have a *many–one correlation* between determination bases and total meaning assignments.

The second option is to take the non-semantic facts to determine a unique meaning assignment *anyway*. That will then have the consequence that the meanings assigned to expressions are *other* than the familiar ones. That is, we reject standard meanings in favour of some *non-standard* semantics with differently individuated, perhaps more *fine-grained* meanings. (In terms of the system of equations analogy, this corresponds to the need of introducing numbers of a new kind, like complex numbers in relation to the reals, in order that the equations come out true.) What meanings will this give us? That is unclear. Perhaps meanings defined in terms of *sense data*, or perhaps meanings defined in terms of neural network activation patterns, as in Paul Churchland's (1991, 1993, 1998) *state space semantics*. According to Ned Block (1986, 1993, 1995), inferential role semantics is a semantics for *narrow mental content*. Narrow content is a *non-representational* kind of content, determined completely by *speaker–internal* factors, the main purpose of which is to serve for psychological explanations. However, if the relevant kind of meaning is non-representational, then the concepts of truth and falsity don't apply, and then something else than the Validating Principle is needed to effect the determination.

If we abstract from the Validating Principle and simply consider a total meaning assignment as a (non-constant) function of a base of accepted sentences or inferences, then it is clear that a subject cannot change his mind arbitrarily much without inducing meaning changes. The total meaning assignment cannot stay fixed through *all* changes in acceptance attitudes. But beyond this consequence, not much follows concerning the relation between meaning and acceptance (meaning and belief). For instance, it does *not* follow from the general idea that if some particular expression e is to have some particular meaning m, then some particular inference i must be accepted, so that acceptance of i is *constitutive* of e meaning m. The function from bases to meaning assignments might simply be more complicated.

Further, it is often assumed in the literature that if you have a holistic inferential role semantics for mental content (i.e. Devitt holism), then *any* change of belief (any change of acceptance of sentences or inferences) will change the contents of *all* the beliefs of the subject. This is the *Instability* or *Total Change Thesis*. The Total Change Thesis is extremely strong. It is stronger than the assumption of a *one–one correlation* between determination bases and total assignments, for the obtaining of a one–one correlation allows different total assignments to overlap. The Total Change Thesis does imply a maximal degree of semantic interdependence. For if assigning a meaning to one expression e does not determine the meaning of another expression e', but allows e' to be assigned both m_1 and m_2, then e can retain its meaning while e' changes from m_1 to m_2, and precisely this was ruled out.

It is unclear what determination mechanism would make the Total Change Thesis true. Probably it is assumed that a change of meaning of one word somehow infects its environment by inducing a change of meaning in all words co-occurring with it in sentences in the determination base. As the infected words spread the change via contact in other sentences, total change eventually results. But the mechanism of this induction is unspecified. It is indeed true that the Validating Principle *can* effect total semantic change in exceptional cases, but the Total Change Thesis requires this to happen every time.

One can try simply to identify the determination base with *Fregean sense*, since the determination base does something that Fregean sense does too, viz. determine reference. One can characterize the *determination base role* of an expression by constructing it from the expression's occurrences in accepted inferences, so that any change somewhere in the determination base does induce changes in the roles of other expressions in accordance with the infection scenario (for suggestions, see Berg, 1993 and Pagin, 1997). Then a high degree of *sense*-interdependence between different expressions automatically results, because of the identity. However, selecting an expression's role in the determination base as its meaning is a rather extreme form of non-standard semantics. It is not a *content* or *meaning* in any intuitive sense of those terms. The truth of MH or the Total Change Thesis cannot simply be stipulated by decreeing that one or other holistic property be called 'meaning' or 'sense'.

Accepting the identity gives one a reason for the claim that because of holism, the meaning of an expression cannot be *specified* except by specifying the meaning of every expression in the language (see e.g. Davidson, 1967: 22). This claim does not follow from the premise that meaning determination is holistic in any of the senses given here. It must be distinguished from the claim that the conditions for a particular expression to *have* a particular meaning cannot be specified without specifying the corresponding meaning conditions for other (possibly all other) expressions. This claim, by contrast, does follow.

It seems that belief in the Total Change Thesis tacitly relies on the assumptions that (a) there is a one–one correlation between determination bases and total meaning assignments, and (b) meanings are so finely *individuated* that maximum interdependence can be upheld. But neither (a) nor (b) is true in all versions of MH.

10.3 ARGUMENTS AGAINST MEANING HOLISM

Two main arguments have been levelled against MH, Dummett's language learning argument, and Fodor and Lepore's instability or total change arguments. In addition, Fodor and Lepore have a related argument that MH is incompatible with semantic compositionality.

10.3.1 The Language Learning Argument

Dummett (1976: 42–45, 1991: 221) has argued that if meaning holism is true, then a language cannot be learnt incrementally, that is, by learning small parts of the language at a time. This is so, according to Dummett, since one cannot know the meaning of any expression without knowing the entire language. But, the argument concludes, if we cannot learn it incrementally, it is a mystery how we can learn it at all.

The thesis that we cannot learn a language incrementally does follow from Dummett's definition of holism (see Section 10.2), but not, or at least not straightforwardly, from more standard definitions. The difference between them may be used for countering the argument. Although Dummett's learnability thesis is correct with respect to some definitions of holism and some definitions of knowledge, it is incorrect with respect to others.

With respect to a version of MH that supports the Total Change Thesis, it is correct that one must know the entire language for understanding any expression in it, at least if learning a new expression automatically changes the determination base. With respect to a definition of knowledge by which you cannot know what an expression means unless you know all the facts that determine its meaning and how that is done, Dummett's thesis is again correct even for weaker versions of MH.

But if a *reliabilist* conception of knowledge may be employed, and weaker versions of MH are acceptable, then Dummett's claim is incorrect. If associating the right meaning with an expression as the result of a reliable learning process is enough for knowledge, then it is possible for speakers to know what an individual expression means even from knowledge of a small fragment of the language containing it. This holds provided that, first, we have a version of MH that allows standard meanings, and second, we have a meaning determination principle that is normally *conservative*, that is, by which the meaning assigned to an expression usually remains the same as the language is extended with new expressions (cf. Pagin, 1997). This indeed does hold for Davidson's principle of charity, since speakers do not normally perform large scale beliefs revisions as part of learning new words.

A different response to Dummett is proposed in Bilgrami, 1986 and in Dresner, 2002 but prefigured already in Davidson, 1965. All hold that learning can be gradual in the sense that a subject can have *partial knowledge* of the meaning of an expression and gradually increase it. Dresner suggests an algebraic framework for representing partial knowledge of meaning, and a way of making the notion of partial knowledge precise, and also refers to empirical studies. The general idea is that a speaker can know some but not all of the restrictions on admissible interpretations of lexical items.

A variant of the language learning argument concerns the possibility of communication (Dummett, 1973: 599). The assumptions are that communication succeeds only if the hearer knows what the speaker says, and that in order to know this the hearer must know the speaker's language. On these assumptions we have the same difficulties, and the same possible countersuggestions, with communication as we have with original language learning. Cf. Tennant, 1987, Shieh, 1997.

10.3.2 The Total Change Arguments

In Fodor, 1987: 55–60 and in Fodor and Lepore, 1992: 11–22 (see also Putnam, 1986) three arguments against MH are extracted from the Total Change Thesis. First, two persons cannot disagree on anything, and they cannot agree on anything unless they agree on everything. This makes communication impossible except between persons that agree on every belief anyway, and therefore don't need it. Second, one person cannot change his mind about anything, for changing one's mind also changes the content of the belief. Third, because of these facts, we cannot make true intentional generalizations, and hence no good intentional explanations.

It is widely agreed both that these consequences do follow from the Total Change Thesis (given that the determination base consists of accepted sentences and inferences), and that they are unacceptable. However, several authors, including McLaughlin (1993), Pagin (1997), and Jackman (1999), have pointed out that the Total Change Thesis does not follow from MH (even though true of some versions). In particular there may be a many–one correlation between determination bases and total meaning assignments, allowing for the desired meaning stability across determination base variations.

Another point discussed, especially between FL (1992, 1999) and Churchland (1993, 1998), is whether it can be enough, for example for successful communication, that the meanings assigned to an expression by speaker and hearer are *similar*, even if not identical. If it is enough, we could live with the truth of the Total Change Thesis. However, the discussion has been somewhat distorted by the conflation of two different issues. On the one hand we have the question whether communicative success is compatible with meaning difference, in some respect and to some extent, between speaker and hearer. On the other hand we have the question whether intersubjective identity *or* similarity is definable in the first place, given that the determinants of meaning are (like neural activation patterns) *wholly internal* to the speakers. The first question is the point of departure, but the discussion has come to concern the second. Several commentators, like Tiffany (1999), have regarded FL as victorious on the second point, but the original question remains.

10.3.3 The Compositionality Argument

In FL, 1991: 332–7, Fodor and Lepore argue that an inferential role theory must be combined with acceptance of the analytic/synthetic distinction, and since this distinction cannot be upheld (in a principled way), inferential role semantics should be given up. The justification for the combination claim involves the principle of compositionality.

On FL's understanding, if the inference from 'x is a brown cow' to 'x is danger-ous' is part of the meaning of 'x is a brown cow', and meaning is compositional, then it must follow from the meanings of the components of 'x is a brown cow' and the mode of composition, that the inference to 'x is dangerous' is part of its mean-ing. But intuitively it doesn't, since acceptance of the inference depends only on the speaker's beliefs, not the meanings of the components. In order to avoid this conclu-sion, FL argue, inferential role semantics must be restricted to identifying meaning with role in *analytic* inferences, like from 'x is a brown cow' to 'x is an animal'. Hence acceptance of the analytic/synthetic distinction.

There are two reasons why this might seem unpersuasive. The first concerns the relevance of the analytic/synthetic distinction. Assume that what FL mean, by say-ing that meaning *is* inferential role, at bottom is that the Validating Principle applies to accepted inferences. Any inference accepted as valid must come out as valid after meaning assignment. But here, coming out as valid does not mean coming out as logically valid, or as conceptually valid. The Validating Principle requires only that accepted inferences lead from true premises to true conclusions, *given* the facts of the world, not that they come out true or valid *independently* of facts. Hence it is not required that accepted, meaning constitutive inferences are analytically valid. That the inference is only contingently correct is not a problem.

The second reason concerns contingent validity. The real problem with FL's 'brown cow' example is rather that the inference isn't even contingently valid. Given the Validating Principle, this would force an assignment of non-standard meaning to 'brown cow', and, given compositionality, also to 'brown' and 'cow'. They could not mean *brown* and *cow*, respectively, for a speaker accepting the inference. This problem with the Validating Principle was noted above, and it can be circumvented by replacing it with some weaker principle that can accommodate mistaken beliefs, in particular a principle that allows a many–one relation between determination bases and total meaning assignments.

10.4 ARGUMENTS FOR MEANING HOLISM

There have not been many arguments for MH, and those presented have usually relied on controversial assumptions. One kind consist of arguments for the truth of certain meaning theories, which are then assumed to be holistic. For instance, in Bilgrami 1998 it is argued that we need appeal to inferential role for solving Fregean co-reference problems, and since inferential role semantics is holistic, MH is true.

Another kind consists of arguments that need to be combined with a meaning theory of a certain kind to yield MH. For instance, it is common to regard the combination of Quine's confirmation holism with *verificationism* as an argument for MH. However, this argument is not endorsed by Quine himself (cf. Quine, 1986a). Moreover, few post-positivist philosophers have been verificationists, and those that have been, like Dummett, Prawitz and Cozzo, have tended to be anti-holists, favouring the view that only what counts as a *direct* or *canonical* verification is meaning determining, not every possible verification. MH will follow only if everything accepted as a verification takes part in meaning determination.

A similar situation holds as regards appeal to belief holism. There is a strong intuitive support for belief holism, as has been brought out by Stephen Stich:

Shortly before her death, Mrs. T had lost all memory about what assassination is. She had even forgotten what death itself is. She could, however, regularly respond to the question, "What happened to McKinley?" by saying, "McKinley was assassinated." Did she, at that time, believe that McKinley was assassinated? For just about everyone to whom I have posed this question, the overwhelmingly clear intuitive answer is no. One simply cannot believe that McKinley was assassinated if one has no idea what an assassination is, nor any grasp of the difference between life and death.   (Stich, 1983: 56)

Although these intuitions are widely shared, we get an argument for MH only if there is further support for the view that belief holism results for reasons of semantic interdependence between belief states, rather than for epistemological or other reasons.

A related appeal to change over time is made in Block (1995), building on Putnam 1983. Block argues to the effect that changes in belief induce changes in narrow mental content. This is advertised as an argument for holism, even though the argument only considers the change of content of one particular term ('grug'). The underlying idea seems to be that since *small* changes of belief suffice for changes in narrow content, changes in belief will induce *many* changes in narrow content. A very similar argument, concerning cognitive content, is given in Segal, 2003.

Two related arguments have been presented, but not endorsed, by Fodor and Lepore. The first (FL, 1991: 340) is an argument for the conclusion that inferential role semantics is holistic, and the second (1992: 23–4) for belief holism, or FL-holism with respect to belief. The 1991 version runs as follows.

(1) The meaning of an expression is at least partially constituted by the expression's inferential relations.
(2) There is no principled distinction between those of its inferential relations that constitute the meaning of an expression and those that don't.
(3) Hence, the meaning of an expression is constituted by *all* of its inferential relations, hence by all of its role in a language.

This argument and its later variant have received much attention, and a large part of the discussion has been concerned with the second premise. FL think of the second premise as expressing a claim about the analytic/synthetic distinction, and the 1992 version has the rejection of a principled analytic/synthetic distinction explicitly as its second premise. Several authors (e.g. Boghossian, 1993; Rey, 1993) have tried to defend the analytic/synthetic or constitutive/non-constitutive distinctions. FL themselves accept the second premise and have consequently argued against the first.

Three problems with this argument deserve mention. First, as several commentators have pointed out (concerning this or the later version; see especially Perry, 1994), the structure of the argument is unclear. Some kind of slippery slope or sorites argument is suggested, but exactly how it is to come out as valid remains unspecified (this connects with the third problem). Second, the conclusion is what is here called Devitt holism, and there is a big step from there to interdependence versions of MH, and especially to the Total Change Thesis that FL employ for their *reductio* of MH. Third, it is not clear whether anyone endorses the argument (hence unclear whether anyone is committed to clarifying the structure). In addition, as was pointed out above, the analytic/synthetic distinction is irrelevant if meaning is assigned in accordance with the Validating Principle.

Finally, an argument due to Glüer (2001) trades on the difficulties with the Validating Principle. As mentioned above, it has the consequence that, *if* speakers make mistakes, strange non-standard meanings result. In Fodor's own information–theoretic setting this is known as the *disjunction problem*: occasionally mistaking a cow for a horse results in 'horse' meaning *horse or cow* (Fodor, 1992, chapters 3 and 4), and in a normative setting it is an aspect of the *rule-following* problem. In order to avoid non-standard meanings the Validating Principle must be replaced by some principle that filters out mistakes.

In both the normative and the information–theoretic settings, it has proved difficult to find principles that work. Glüer's argument for holism then has the following form: there is a filtering principle that works in a holistic context, viz. the *best approximation* principle, and since no working non-holistic filtering principle exists, MH is true. Basically, therefore, the argument is that MH provides the only way of securing standard meanings.

References

Antony, L., (1993). 'Conceptual Connection and the Observation/Theory Distinction', in J. Fodor and E. Lepore (eds.), *Holism: A Consumer Update, Grazer Philosophische Studien* 46.

Berg, J., (1993). 'Inferential Role, Quine and Mad Holism', in J. Fodor and E. Lepore (eds.), *Holism: A Consumer Update, Grazer Philosophische Studien*, 46.

Bilgrami, A., (1986). 'Meaning, Holism and Use', in LePore (ed.), *Truth and Interpretation. Perspectives on the Philosophy of Donald Davidson*, Blackwell, Oxford.

_____ (1998). 'Why Holism is Harmless and Necessary', *Philosophical Perspectives*, 12, *Mind, Language and Ontology*: 105–26.

Block, N., (1986). 'Advertisement for a Semantics for Psychology', *Midwest Studies in Philosophy*: 615–78.

_____ (1993). 'Holism, Hyper-Analyticity and Hyper-Compositionality', *Mind and Language*, 8: 1–26.

_____ (1995). 'An Argument for Holism', *Proceedings of the Aristotelian Society*, 95: 151–69.

_____ (1998). 'Holism, Mental and Semantic', *Routledge Encyclopedia of Philosophy*.

Boghossian, P., (1993). 'Does Inferential Role Semantics Rest upon a Mistake', *Mind and Language*, 8: 27–48.

—— (1994). 'Inferential Role Semantics and the Analytic/Synthetic Distinction', *Philosophical Studies*, 73: 109–22.

Brandom, R., (1994). *Making it Explicit*, Harvard University Press, Cambridge, MA.

Churchland, P. M., (1991). *A Neurocomputational Perspective*, MIT Press, Cambridge, MA.

—— (1993). 'State Space Semantics and Meaning Holism', in *Philosophy and Phenomenological Research*, 3: 667–72.

—— (1998). 'Conceptual Similarity across Sensory and Neural Diversity: The Fodor/Lepore Challenge Answered', *Journal of Philosophy*, 95: 5–32.

Cozzo, C., (1994). *Meaning and Argument. A Theory of Meaning Centred on Immediate Argumental Role*, Almqvist and Wiksell International, Stockholm.

Davidson, D., (1965). 'Theories of Meaning and Learnable Languages', in Davidson, *Inquiries into Truth and Interpretation*, Clarendon Press, Oxford, 1984.

—— (1967). 'Truth and Meaning', *Synthèse* 17: 304–23. Reprinted in Davidson, *Inquiries into Truth and Interpretation*, Clarendon Press, Oxford, 1984.

—— (1973). 'Radical Interpretation', *Dialectica* 27: 313–28. Reprinted in Davidson, *Inquiries into Truth and Interpretation*, Clarendon Press, Oxford 1984.

—— (1975). 'Thought and Talk', in S. Guttenplan (ed.), *Mind and Language*, Oxford University Press. Reprinted in Davidson, *Inquiries into Truth and Interpretation*, Clarendon Press, Oxford, 1984. Page reference to the reprint.

Dennett, D., (1971). 'Intentional Systems', *Journal of Philosophy*, 68: 87–106.

Devitt, M., (1996). *Coming to Our Senses. A Naturalistic Program for Semantic Localism*, Cambridge University Press, Cambridge.

Dresner, E., (2002). 'Holism, Language Acquisition, and Algebraic Logic', *Linguistics and Philosophy*, 25: 419–52.

Dummett, M., (1976). 'What is a Theory of Meaning? (II)', in Evans and McDowell (eds.), *Truth and Meaning*, Oxford University Press. Reprinted in Dummett, *The Seas of Language*, Clarendon Press, Oxford 1993. Page references to the reprint.

—— (1981). *Frege. Philosophy of Language*, second edition, Harvard University Press, Cambridge, MA.

—— (1991). *The Logical Basis of Metaphysics*, Duckworth, London.

Field, H., (1977). 'Logic, Meaning and Conceptual Role', *Journal of Philosophy*, 74: 379–409.

Fodor, J., (1987). *Psychosemantics. The Problem of Meaning in the Philosophy of Mind*, MIT Press, Cambridge, MA.

Fodor J. and Lepore E., (1991). 'Why Meaning (Probably) isn't Conceptual Role', *Mind and Language*, 6: 328–43.

—— (1992). *Holism. A Shopper's Guide*, Basil Blackwell, Oxford.

—— (1993). 'Replies', in J. Fodor and E. Lepore (eds.), *Holism: A Consumer Update*, Grazer Philosophische Studien, 46.

—— (1999). 'All at Sea in Semantic Space: Churchland on Meaning Similarity', *Journal of Philosophy*, 96: 381–403.

Glüer, K., (2001). 'Alter Hut kleidet gut. Zur Verteidigung des semantischen Holismus', in M. Seel, J. Liptow, G. Bertram (eds.), *Holismus in der Philosophie*, Velbrück Wissenschaft Verlag, Weilerswist.

Harman, G., (1974). *Thought*, Princeton University Press, Princeton, NJ.

—— (1982). 'Conceptual Role Semantics', *Notre Dame Journal of Formal Logic*, 23: 242–56.

Hempel, C. G., (1950). 'Problems and Changes in the Empiricist Criterion of Meaning', *Revue internationale de Philosophie*, 11. Reprinted in L. Linsky (ed.), *Semantics and the Philosophy of Language*, University of Illinois Press, Urbana, IL, 1970. Page references to the reprint.

Hilbert, D., (1899). *Die Grundlagen der Geometrie*, Leipzig.

Jackman, H., (1999). 'Moderate Holism and the Instability Thesis'. *American Philosophical Quarterly*, 36: 361–69.

Lewis, D., (1974). 'Radical Interpretation', *Synthèse*, 23: 331–44.

Loar, B., (1981). *Mind and Meaning*, Cambridge University Press, Cambridge.

McLaughlin, B., (1993). 'On Punctate Content and Conceptual Role', *Philosophy and Phenomenological Research* 53.

Okasha, S., (2000). 'Holism about Meaning and About Evidence: In Defence of W.V. Quine', *Erkenntnis*, 52: 39–61.

Pagin, P., (1997). 'Is Compositionality Compatible with Holism?', *Mind and Language*, 12: 11–33.

Perry, J., (1994). 'Fodor and Lepore on Holism', *Philosophical Studies*, 73: 123–38.

Prawitz, D., (1995). 'Quine and Verificationism', *Inquiry*, 37: 487–94.

Putnam, H., (1983). 'Computational Psychology and Interpretation Theory', in Putnam, *Philosophical Papers III: Representation and Reality*, 405–26, Cambridge University Press, Cambridge.

_____ (1986). 'Meaning Holism', in L. E. Hahn and P. A. Schilpp (eds.), *The philosophy of W. V. Quine*, expanded edition: 427–31, Open Court, Chicago, IL.

Quine, W. V., (1951). 'Two Dogmas of Empiricism', *Philosophical Review*, 60: 20–43. Reprinted in Quine, *From a Logical Point of View*, second edn, Harvard University Press, Cambridge, MA, 1980, Page references to the reprint.

_____ (1986a). 'Reply to Roger F. Gibson, Jr', in L. E. Hahn and P. A. Schilpp (eds.), *The Philosophy of W. V. Quine*, expanded edition, Open Court, Chicago, IL.

_____ (1986b). 'Reply to Hilary Putnam', in L. E. Hahn and P. A. Schilpp (eds.), *The Philosophy of W. V. Quine*, expanded edition, Open Court, Chicago, IL.

Rey, G., (1993). 'The Unavailability of What we Mean: A Reply to Quine, Fodor and Lepore', in J. Fodor and E. Lepore (eds.), *Holism: A Consumer Update, Grazer Philosophische Studien*, 46.

Segal, G., (2003). 'Ignorance of Meaning', in A. Barber (ed.), *Epistemology of Language*, Oxford University Press, Oxford.

Sellars, W., (1963). 'Some Reflections on Language Games', in Sellars, *Science, Perception and Reality*, Routledge and Kegan Paul, London.

Shieh, S., (1997). 'Some Senses of Holism: An Anti-Realist Guide to Quine', in R. Heck (ed.), *Language, Thought and Logic*, Oxford University Press, Oxford.

Stich, S., (1983). *From Folk Psychology to Cognitive Science*, MIT Press, Cambridge, MA.

Tennant, N., (1987). 'Holism, Molecularity and Truth', in B. Taylor (ed.), *Michael Dummett. Contributions to Philosophy*, Martinus Nijhoff, Dordrecht.

Tiffany, E., (1999). 'Semantics San Diege style', *Journal of Philosophy* 96: 416–29.

Wittgenstein, L., (1953). *Philosophical Investigations*, Blackwell, Oxford.

CHAPTER 11

....

INDETERMINACY
OF TRANSLATION

....

ALAN WEIR

W.V. QUINE'S thesis of the indeterminacy of translation is the theory which launched a thousand doctorates. During the 1970s it sometimes seemed to be as firmly entrenched a dogma among North American philosophers as the existence of God was among medieval theologians. Although now subject to much more by way of critical appraisal, Quine's work is still, rightly, at the forefront of contemporary philosophy of language. Moreover though propounded and defended by the doyen of analytical philosophy, as hard-nosed a logician as one can find, Quine's questioning of the determinacy of meaning is of interest to a much wider audience than logicians. Indeed the idea of indeterminacy of meaning has more than a whiff of smoke-filled cafés on the banks of the Seine about it, though Quine's arguments for indeterminacy belong firmly to the tradition of logical empiricism.

Doubts such as Quine's about the scientific credentials of the concept of meaning,[1] were common among the logical empiricists (or positivists) of the Vienna Circle, including Quine's mentor Rudolf Carnap. But after Carnap had absorbed Tarski's work on truth, he moved into a resolutely semantic phase. The classic positivist position—logic and mathematics admit of no empirical confirmation but are nonetheless respectable ('non-metaphysical') because true by virtue of *meaning*—could then be held in good faith, now that meaning had been passed as scientifically respectable. Moreover philosophy as conceptual analysis, as the tracing of the meaning connections among expressions and thereby among the concepts they express, only makes sense if there are fairly determinate and fine-grained relations of

---

[1] Or, if expressing things this way veers too close to self-refutation, of the scientific credentials of expressions such as 'synonymy' and 'meaning' as we usually use them.

sameness and difference of meaning, at least if one thinks that concepts are essentially linguistic. Hence Quine's claim that meaning is radically indeterminate threatens to deconstruct logical empiricism and to demolish analytical philosophy, construed as a philosophy of conceptual analysis, from within.

So what is the indeterminacy thesis? It is very tempting, of course, to apply a little reflexivity and deny that there is any determinate thesis of indeterminacy of translation; to charge Quine with championing a doctrine which has no clear meaning, or which is hopelessly ambiguous. Such a charge is, I will argue in Section 11.1, false. His meaning is fairly clear and there is widespread agreement on what the thesis amounts to. In the second section I will look at Quine's 'argument from below' for indeterminacy, in Section 11.3 at the 'argument from above', with concluding remarks in Section 11.4.

11.1

The *locus classicus* for the exposition of Quine's thesis of indeterminacy of translation is chapter 2 of *Word and Object* (Quine, 1960). Quine starts with an 'uncritical' presentation of the doctrine:

two men could be just alike in all their dispositions to verbal behaviour under all possible sensory stimulations, and yet the meanings or ideas expressed in their identically triggered and identically sounded utterances could diverge radically, for the two men, in a wide range of cases.   (Quine, 1960, p. 26)

(Women were language-less, in the early 1960s.) However he rejects this version as meaningless:

a distinction of meaning unreflected in the totality of dispositions to verbal behaviour is a distinction without a difference.   (*Ibid.*)

This makes it look as if some form of behaviourism is a background presupposition of Quine's argument and he does say:

We are concerned here with language as the complex of present dispositions to verbal behaviour.   (1960, p. 27; see also 1987, p. 5)

Quine certainly eschews 'mentalism', if we define this as a rejection of the supervenience of semantics on behaviour. For 'no distinction of meaning without a difference in behaviour', just is, in slogan format, the supervenience of semantics on behaviour. One motive here is a publicity requirement on language use. Language is a social art, Quine emphasizes. We acquire it by observing through ordinary sensory means the verbal behaviour of our peers as they attempt to communicate with us and each other. Quine moves, therefore, to a less mentalistic formulation of the indeterminacy thesis:

the infinite totality of sentences of any given speaker's language can be so permuted, or mapped onto itself, that (*a*) the totality of the speaker's dispositions to verbal behavior remains invariant, and yet (*b*) the mapping is no mere correlation of sentences with *equivalent* sentences, in any plausible sense of equivalence however loose.   (*Ibid.*)

What could the plausible sense of equivalence be? A third formulation is introduced to help clarify:

The same point can be put less abstractly and more realistically by switching to translation. . . . [M]anuals for translating one language into another can be set up in divergent ways, all compatible with the totality of dispositions, yet incompatible with one another.   (*Ibid.*)

The discussion then focuses on the thought experiment of radical *translation*, of the predicament of a linguist faced with a community speaking a language which has no discernible affinities with any known to linguists (a bit like Aberdonians, but even more so). Quine introduces his famous example of 'Gavagai':

A rabbit scurries by, the native says 'Gavagai', and the linguist notes down the sentence 'Rabbit' . . . as tentative translation   (1960, p. 29)

This might make it look as if the indeterminacy thesis is concerned solely with *translation* between languages, perhaps only with translation of alien, putatively incommensurable, cultures; or that it is an epistemological thesis, expressing sceptical doubts as to whether we can ever know what others mean, at least if they speak a radically different language.

   This would be a grave mistake. Quine's second formulation, in terms of permutations of one's own language, is the most fundamental one. His thesis is not an epistemological one but a metaphysical one and it concerns an indeterminacy in the meaning of the expressions of one's own language—

On deeper reflection, radical translation begins at home.   (Quine 1969a, p. 46; see also 1960, p. 78)

Indeterminacy of translation is merely a corollary of the main thesis, albeit one which is pedagogically useful. The radical translation thought experiment helps one to bracket mentalistic assumptions and focus on the purely behavioural data which are available to linguist and language learner alike.

   In what sense, then, do the permutations map sentences to non-equivalent sentences while leaving behavioural dispositions untouched? If Quine is indeed assuming some form of behaviourism, this is puzzling. Say that two sentences of a speaker's language are *behaviourally equivalent* iff the totality of the speaker's verbal dispositions towards the one is the same as that towards the other (spelling this out in detail has complications which we will pass over). Then Quine in the above quotation seems to be saying that there are behaviourally equivalent sentences which are nonetheless non-equivalent in some plausible sense. What sense can this be?

   Could it be that they differ objectively in meaning, though they are behaviourally equivalent? As we have seen, a mentalist could say this, could take the thesis to be a rejection of the supervenience of meaning on verbal behaviour. But Quine cannot say this since for him any distinction in meaning must be reflected in a distinction in dispositions to verbal behaviour. On the other hand, to say only that they are syntactically distinct sentences is merely to affirm the existence of synonyms which Quine, by the time of *Word and Object* (Quine, 1960) sees is fairly platitudinous.[2] Similarly dismissed by Quine as platitudinous are the theses that translation is often rough, there being no precise synonym, and that many sentences are vague (see again 1960, pp. 41, 73–4).

Quine's indeterminacy thesis is far more radical than this. One more radical claim which might be taken to interpret the thesis is the assertion that two behaviourally equivalent sentences can be non-equivalent in the sense of *intuitively non-synonymous*. That is, they can be objectively alike in meaning yet we think they differ; our beliefs about synonymy are fallible (1960, pp. 36, 63). This seems plausible for a behaviourist, though it goes against what one might call an extreme Cartesian view of the mind. On the latter view, the mind, including the meanings our mind gives to words, is transparent to us so that we have infallible, privileged access to all our mental states and can thus tell whether two words express, on our lips, the same idea or not.[3]

However the more of our intuitions Quine holds to be erroneous, the more radical (and less plausible) his position becomes. In fact the following version of indeterminacy:

countless native sentences admitting no independent check . . . may be expected to receive radically unlike and incompatible renderings under the two systems.   (1960, p. 72)

illustrates just how radical Quine's doctrine is. It embodies the thesis Quine most often has in mind when arguing for indeterminacy of meaning: —two sentences can be behaviourally equivalent yet distinct in truth-value—the one is true if and only if the other is false. A variant of this thesis applied to names and predicates is the thesis of *ontological relativity* or *inscrutability of reference*:[4] two names can be behaviourally equivalent and yet stand for different objects, two predicates can be behaviourally equivalent yet true of different things.

But how can this possibly be? If sentence *p* is behaviourally equivalent to sentence *q* then surely, for Quine, *p* means the same as *q*. Yet if they are incompatible in the above sense, we have P iff not Q, where P and Q are the sentences named by *p* and *q* respectively. But the following rule *R* is surely constitutive[5] of the notions of meaning and truth:

$$\frac{p \text{ means the same as } q}{p \text{ is true iff } q \text{ is true.}}$$

[2] In 'Two Dogmas of Empiricism' (Quine, 1951) Quine notoriously expressed a strong scepticism about the notion of synonymy. But in *Word and Object* he introduces a notion of 'stimulus synonymy' which, he says, is quite close to our intuitive notion of synonymy in the case of highly observational sentences. Two syntactically distinct sentences can, for Quine, be stimulus synonymous for a given individual (and for a linguistic community, if thus synonymous for each speaker in the community).
[3] Plausible though the anti-Cartesian view is, it is rejected by Wittgenstein (1922, 4.243) and, following Frege, Dummett (1981, p. 95).
[4] For Quine, these two terms are pretty much synonymous, at least for him in 1992 (1992, pp. 51–2).
[5] Or if not constitutive, at least one we would be most loath to give up.

From the premise that two sentences mean the same we can conclude that the one is true iff the other is (relative to a background context which removes any ambiguity and fixes reference for any context-relative terms). Quine agrees with Tarski that 'p is true iff P' and 'q is true iff Q' are constitutive of the concept of truth. Putting all these things together (using the symmetry of 'iff') we derive, from the premises that p means the same as q and that P iff not Q:

$$Q \text{ iff } q \text{ is true [Tarski]; iff } p \text{ is true } (R); \text{ iff P [Tarski]; iff not Q}$$

And the transitivity of 'iff' (A iff B and B iff C entails A iff C) gives us Q iff not Q which leads, in standard logic, straight to contradiction. More directly, from rule R we conclude that the one sentence is true iff the other is whereas Quine maintains that the one is true iff the other is false; and these two claims are surely contradictory.

Similarly 'the referent of $\langle t \rangle = t$' is another disquotational Tarskian truth about reference—here substitutions for parameter "$\langle t \rangle$" canonically name substitutions for parameter "t". The analogue R' of R (if two names mean the same, their referents are identical) plus the assumption that t means the same as u yields (with 'Ref($\langle t \rangle$)' standing for 'the referent of $\langle t \rangle$'):

$$t = \text{Ref}(\langle t \rangle)\,[\text{Tarski}]; = \text{Ref}(\langle u \rangle)\,[R']; = u\,[\text{Tarski}]$$

so that $t = u$ even though, according to Quine we can have $t \neq u$. For example, if 'Poppy' names your pet rabbit then Quine holds, as we shall see, that the singular term 'Poppy's left ear' is identical, in point of objective meaning, with 'Poppy' hence, by the above argument, Poppy = Poppy's left ear, even though we know they are distinct, one being a proper part of the other. A similar argument can be given for the indeterminacy of the extension of predicates: 'gavagai' can be interpreted as true of all and only rabbits or as true of all and only the undetached observable parts of rabbits, and so on.

Is Quine's position simply contradictory then? There is an explicit answer for reference, in the doctrine of ontological relativity, though one he seems to shy away from in the case of truth. For reference, Quine takes the above argument to be a *reductio ad absurdum* of some of the underlying assumptions, in particular, of the assumption that meaning and reference are absolute. Rather, insofar as sentences without empirical content can be said to have meaning at all, it is only relative to some one among many possible interpretations of the language into some background language (the *meta-language* in which we talk of the *object language* in question; it may be a completely different one or an extension of the object language):

unless pretty firmly conditioned to sensory stimulation, a sentence S is meaningless except relative to its own theory; meaningless inter-theoretically.   (1960, p. 24)

reference *is* nonsense, except relative to a coordinate system. . . . What makes sense is to say not what the objects of theories are, absolutely speaking, but how one theory of objects is interpretable or reinterpretable in another.   (1969a, pp. 48, 50)

What Quine's view seems to comes down to, then, is this. If p and q have no empirical content, they do not have meanings but have one or other interpretation imposed or projected onto them, although the two sentences never get the same interpretation in one in the same projection, if the equivalence P iff not Q holds. Similarly a term such as 'Gavagai' may have a determinate layer of meaning, to do with rabbit features being present—'It's rabbitish', as it were—but it does not segment occasions into rabbits, rather than undetached rabbit parts, and so forth. Such a segmentation is *our* projection onto a world which, in itself, does not come packaged into separate objects.

Relativity alone, however, will not save Quine from contradiction. The argument above will go through with the various notions relativized to an interpretation I: 'means$_I$ the same as', 'is true$_I$' and so on. The Tarskian schema then becomes $\ulcorner p$ is true$_I$ iff P*$\urcorner$, where P* is any sentence such that p means$_I$ the same as p^*.[6] Further, rule R then becomes R^*:

$$\frac{p \text{ means}_I \text{ the same as } q}{p \text{ is true}_I \text{ iff } q \text{ is true}_I.}$$

In order to block the inference to:

Q iff p is true$_I$ [Tarski]; iff q is true$_I$ (R^*); iff P [Tarski]; iff not Q

(granted that p and q are alike in all objective aspects of meaning) we need, as in the previous paragraph, to deny that if sentences have the same meaning then there is some interpretation I in which they mean$_I$ the same.

The claim that p means the same as q, then, Quine has to read as something like:

There is a sentence r such that there is an interpretation I in which p is interpreted by r and also an interpretation I^* such that q is interpreted by r in I^*; but it need not be the case that $I = I^*$.

If, therefore, we step back from our object language at time t and talk about it at $t + 1$ in what is in effect a metalanguage, we can say that there is an interpretation I of 'rabbit' and 'undetached rabbit part' (as used at t) in which the former is true of all and only the rabbits, the latter of all and only the undetached rabbit parts. But since 'rabbit' and 'undetached rabbit part' mean the same, there is another interpretation I^* in which 'rabbit' is given the interpretation 'undetached rabbit part' has in I so that 'rabbit' is true of all and only undetached parts of rabbits (and we can let 'undetached rabbit part' have the set of rabbits as its extension in I*). There is, though, no interpretation I^{**} in which 'rabbit' is true of all and only the rabbits *and* all and only the undetached proper parts of rabbits, that is indeed absurd.

The upshot of Quine's indeterminacy thesis is the relativity of reference and, if he is consistent, of truth. Hence Quine must be placed firmly in the camp of the anti-realists. True, Quine is prepared to assent to current scientific theory and hence to affirm its truth, since he accepts $\ulcorner p$ is true iff P$\urcorner$; he has a deflationary, disquotational

---

[6] The trivial homophonic interpretation H in which each sentence translates itself will always be admissible hence so too will the disquotational schema $\ulcorner p$ is true$_H$ iff P$\urcorner$; in this transparent case, we can drop the subscript on 'true'.

view of truth (Quine, 1960, pp. 24–5). But he is wrong in thinking this makes him a realist, in anything like the traditional sense. An instrumentalist who accepts current scientific theory (as instrumentalists generally did) and is prepared to accept the legitimacy of at least a disquotational conception of truth (as most were, post Tarski) would not disagree in the least with Quine on truth. The realist, however, believes that our theoretical conjectures are determinately and absolutely true or determinately and absolutely false, whether or not we have any means of finding out which. But for Quine, once we reach the theoretical realms where meaning, he claims, is indeterminate, truth and reference are relative, not absolute.

Just as a diagram can be read as a gavagai looked at one way, a duck another, though the objective figure is the same, so a theory can be true interpreted one way, false interpreted another though the objective facts (that is, for an empiricist such as Quine, the *empirical* facts) and the meaning of the theory remain the same. Hence there is no sense to the claim that it is one or the other independently of us: as regards the theoretical component of a theory whose empirical consequences are true, it is *we*, by our way of reading that theoretical component, who make it true$_I$ or false$_{I*}$.

The objective world is, for Quine, an ensemble of occasions possessing, as wholes, objective, observable features and some sort of structured articulation of a general, highly abstract, nature. But the segmentation of such occasions into distinct objects so as to instantiate in a particular way the abstract structure, objects which we suppose possess non-observable, underlying microscopic natures—all this is a human construction answering to no corresponding objective reality; it is a colourization of an intrinsically monochrome scene, as it were, and one which could equally well be effected in a number of different ways (though perhaps not by us). Such a view embodies a relativistic antirealism (one might even read Kantian overtones into it) which Quine himself shrinks from, at least as regards the notion of truth. (Quine, 1960, pp. 24–5; 1975, pp. 327–8.)

11.2

Indeterminacy, then, is a bold thesis with far-reaching metaphysical consequences. Does Quine give us good reason for thinking it true? He has two main arguments for indeterminacy of meaning, which he terms the argument from below and the argument from above, respectively (1970, p. 183). Both hinge on the assumption that the only meaning a sentence can have, on its own, is empirical meaning which he characterizes in terms of his concept of *stimulus meaning*. A sentence's stimulus meaning is a pair consisting of the affirmative stimulus meaning together with the negative stimulus meaning. The former is the set of stimulations which would prompt assent to the sentence on being queried on it, the latter the set of stimulations which would prompt dissent. In *Word and Object*, Quine treated stimulations as physical events or 'patterns' just outside the sensory organs (1960, p. 31). Translation then should match sentences with approximately identical stimulus meanings: the natives would assent to 'Gavagai' on being prompted with pretty much the same stimulations as we would assent to 'Rabbit', likewise for dissent.

Quine's empirical meanings, then, are not distal objects:

It is important to think of what prompts the native's assent to "Gavagai?" as stimulations and not rabbits. Stimulation can remain the same though the rabbit be supplanted by a counterfeit.   (1960, p. 31)

and similarly a rabbit may fail to stimulate assent because of poor lighting etc. Later on, he despairs of intersubjective stimulations; placing them just outside the sensory organs will not work because of differences in orientation and anatomy among different subjects (Quine, 1974, pp. 23–4). He therefore re-defines stimulations as patterns of firings of sensory receptors (1992, pp. 2, 40) and accepts, because of the lack of homology of sensory nerve networks (Quine, 1974, p. 24, fn. 2), that there can be no intersubjective stimulations. This is a major change in his position: translation of observation sentences is no longer based on objective sameness and difference of stimulus meanings but has become a much more hermeneutic business, a matter of empathetic placing of oneself in the subject's shoes and figuring out what translation makes best sense from that perspective (Quine, 1992, p. 42).

Could Quine not have held firm to a naturalistic account of observational meaning? He acknowledges, in response to Davidson's suggestion of a more distal meaning in external physical objects:

I could place the stimulus out where Davidson does without finessing any reification on the subject's part. But I am put off by the vagueness of shared situations.   (1992, p. 42)

However all the basic terms of Quine's semantic theory, for example terms such as 'assent', are vague and vagueness on its own is no bar to externalizing Quine's stimulus meanings while still avoiding reification on the subject's part. I will try to externalize Quine's notion of stimulus meaning using the concept of the *co-presence* of two objects. Firstly, consider any region of the universe which is exactly congruent to me, now, in some posture or other I could adopt (whether I am actually filling that region or not). An actual occasion (for me) can be defined as the mereological complement of such a region, that is, every bit of the universe which is not part of the region congruent with me—the region's 'cosmic complement' (Quine, 1995, p. 71). Occasions for human speakers, then, actual or possible,[7] are cosmic doughnuts with humanoid holes at their core.

Suppose my current overall neural state, minus its receptor cell fringes, grounds a determinate disposition to respond to sentence S with assent (dissent) given the pattern of receptor firing which would be induced by my insertion, as it were, into

---

[7]   Quine, of course, debars possibilia, such as possible events, from his ontology. 'Certainly it is hopeless nonsense to talk thus of unrealized particulars and try to assemble them into classes. Unrealized entities have to be construed as universals' (1960, p. 34). Unfortunately Quine also refuses to admit universals or attributes into his ontology. Here we have a straight inconsistency in his position.

a particular occasion O. For Quine this means the *receptor cell pattern*[8] which would result from such an insertion belongs to the affirmative (negative) stimulus meaning of S. But by the same token my total neural state will likewise ground the disposition to assent (dissent) if I am inserted in *occasion O*. We can take the meanings, then, to be composed of the external occasions, not the internal neural firings.[9] These 'occasion meanings' take account of orientation and are just about as idiosyncratic as Quinean stimulus meanings. No occasion in the occasion meaning of any of my sentences can belong to the meaning of any of yours, unless you have the misfortune to be shaped, down to the last wrinkle, like me. Moreover there is still no reification, no segmentation of the occasions into component objects.

We can, however, make sense, with some charitable reading, of the idea of a proper part *p* of an occasion O being observable. Imagine *p* excised from O and replaced with something else without altering the rest of O, thereby yielding a variant occasion O*. (Here again there is vagueness: we need to discount sufficiently insignificant changes in [O minus *p*] as not really involving a change in the rest of O and perhaps look only to fairly natural ways of replacing one part with another.) If there is a sentence S such that my response to S is different for O compared to that for O* then *p* is observable.

We can extend observationality to a notion of weak observationality, relative to an occasion O. Where the occasions are mine, consider occasions O* in which we punch out (conceptually) a me-shaped hole in reality not too far from the me-shaped hole which defines O. If *p* is observable at O* then it is weakly observable at O (so observationality is a special case of weak observationality). Thus if I am standing in front of my house, the front is observable to me, but there is a position round the back, no further (or not much further) from the centre of mass of the house than my current position is and from which the back is observable. Hence the back is weakly observable.[10] But no houses a few streets away, obscured by intervening houses, are even weakly observable. Clearly the notion is vague, dependent on the vague notion of the viewer standpoint for weak observationality being 'not too far away' from that for the occasion.

Occasions are time slices of the entire physical universe, minus their (potential) observer core. Ordinary 'external' physical bodies overlap some series of occasions (again we can leave the length of occasions, the 'specious present', vague). A necessary condition for two bodies being '*co-present*' as I will call it, is that they overlap the same occasions. Thus most, if not all, ordinary everyday 'external' bodies

---

[8] But what can such a 'pattern' be other than an attribute of the nervous system, despite Quine's rejection of such entities? Similar problems of consistency arise when trying to make sense of 'dispositions' while remaining faithful to Quine's official nominalistic rejection of properties.

[9] There will be a difference for those Quinean observation sentences which are keyed to internal states (such as pain states) but for which I have no determinate disposition keying them to external states. These will no longer count as observational; but that is as it should be.

[10] 'Weak observationality' is a fairly basic approximation to more sophisticated notions which utilize concepts such as expectation in conditionals such as the one in: [I perceive the whole house, on looking at the front, only if, were I to go round the back and discover the front was a mere façade, as in a movie set, I would be greatly surprised].

here on earth are not co-present with, for example, the chair I am sitting on—their beginnings or endings do not coincide with its creation or destruction. But some non-salient stretches of spacetime are; perhaps some on far-off planets would be relatively salient to us if we were aware of them. However we can rule them out by requiring, in addition, that stages of α and of β must also be weakly observable in exactly the same occasions, if α and β are to be co-present. If we have two bodies which either do not overlap the same occasions or are such that there is an occasion O on which the stage of α (say) which is part of O is weakly observable at O but the corresponding stage of β is not then they are not co-present; let us say in such cases that they are 'stimulus-distinct'.

I return then, to the argument from below, the argument for relativity of reference and ontology. Define an admissible permutation of an interpretation I to be a permutation of the domain of individuals of I which maps individuals to co-present individuals. For example, a permutation p might be the identity mapping except that it swaps over Poppy the rabbit with Poppy's left ear. From any such interpretation I we can create a new permuted interpretation I_p. If α is the referent of singular term t in I then $p(\alpha)$ is its referent in I_p, if $\{x : \varphi x\}$ is the extension of predicate F in I then $\{x : \exists y \varphi y \ \& \ x = p(y)\}$ is its extension in I_p.[11] It is easy to show that I and I_p are materially equivalent, that is, S is true in I iff true in I_p, for all sentences S.[12] Material equivalence is clearly (but see footnote 13) a necessary condition on any two interpretations of a language being equally good. A second constraint one could add, I will call it 'stimulus equivalence', is that no singular term is assigned stimulus-distinct individuals on the two interpretations and no predicate has stimulus-distinct extensions in the sense that there is a member of one extension which has no stimulus equivalent correlate in the other.

Quine, in Word and Object (1960, §12) argues that there is a multiplicity of equally good interpretations of the singular terms and predicates of our language, no pair of which can be combined into a single coherent interpretation. There is nothing in our verbal behaviour which could differentiate between an interpretation of 'gavagai' as segmenting occasions into [rabbits, against a background], on the one hand, versus [a grouping of undetached rabbit parts, against a background] on the other. But what does Quine mean by equally good interpretations? I read his original argument, the one developed in Word and Object §12, as invoking something along the lines of stimulus-equivalence, as developed in my 'externalized' reconstruction above. But in his later writings there is a tendency for him to follow Davidson (1979, p. 229)

---

[11] It is routine to extend this to relational terms, to second-order languages and to intensional languages.
[12] Note that this will be true even if the variant interpretation does not change the interpretation of what Quine calls the 'apparatus of individuation', terms for identity, definite and indefinite articles, numerals and attributions of number—the number of Fs is n—and so on. Some of Quine's earlier arguments appealed to compensating re-interpretations of such terms, see 1960, p. 53, 1969a, pp. 32–3. See 1964, p. 215 for 'reduction' construed as material equivalence given by an effective mapping.

and Putnam (1981, pp. 32–5, 217–18) and drop anything like stimulus equivalence, retaining only material equivalence as generated by arbitrary permutations.[13]

If material equivalence is the only constraint on rating interpretations as equally good then indeed reference is wholly indeterminate, since any old permutation will produce a materially equivalent one and so 'Hilary Putnam' is as correctly interpreted as referring to the Andromeda Galaxy as to Hilary Putnam. That this conclusion has been accepted is testament to the engaging tendency of philosophers in the grip of theories to transform a reductio ad absurdum of a cherished assumption into a proof of that very absurdity. For the assumption that material equivalence is the sole criterion for equivalence of interpretations is vastly less plausible than the thesis that the Andromeda Galaxy is nothing like as good a candidate for the referent of 'Hilary Putnam' as Hilary Putnam himself. More generally, how can two stimulus-distinct objects α and β be equally good candidates for referent of a term t given that there is at least one sentence S (which we can assume contains t) with occasion O in its occasion meaning and in which parts of α (say), are observable parts of O (and so α contributes to our assent to—or dissent from—S) whereas no part of β is an observable part of O and hence makes no contribution? The reason Poppy the rabbit is a better candidate for membership of the extension of 'rabbit' than Lucy the cat is that there are occasions when I say 'the rabbit is going to chew that wire', occasions on which Poppy is present otherwise I would not say that, yet (fortunately for the rabbit) occasions on which the cat is not.

It will not do to respond that the terms featuring in any additional constraints could themselves be re-interpreted in different ways: 'stimulus-equivalence' could be re-interpreted so that the Andromeda Galaxy and Hilary Putnam are stimulus-equivalent.[14] Certainly if one assumes from the outset that no term has determinate reference one will be hard put to show that many terms have determinate reference. But we are engaged here in a sub-species of naturalized epistemology in which we are trying to explain a special type of knowledge: of meaning. Our task is to assume determinate reference and extension relations, e.g. between 'Hilary Putnam' and Hilary Putnam (and nothing else), 'stimulation' and stimulations and so forth and then go on to show how speakers could grasp a language with such reference relations. This is not, prima facie, an impossible feat so long as one does not deny the theorist the right to assume determinate reference relations at the outset. But it is certainly no trivial feat as Quine's original arguments, for a more moderate form of indeterminacy of reference, show.

Gareth Evans (Evans, 1975) mounted an interesting counter-argument against Quine. Evans notes that Quine tends to consider only the simplest one-word contexts

[13] See for example, Quine, 1995, pp. 71–3; Quine, 2000, pp. 419, 420. General permutations—'proxy functions'—emerged in Quine, 1964. As we shall see Quine goes even further, in his 'argument from above', and effectively abandons material equivalence itself, but only for theoretical terms.

[14] Davidson (1979, p. 237) and Putnam (1978, p. 126 and 1981, p. 36) respond along those lines against which see Kirk (1986, pp. 118–27).

in which names and general terms might occur. In more complex contexts such as 'brown gavagai', we might have hard behavioural evidence that 'gavagai' segments occasions up in one particular fashion (assuming that the native's 'brown' is stimulus synonymous with our 'brown'). For instance, if natives dissent from 'brown gavagai' in the presence of a largely white rabbit with a brown ear but assent in the presence of a mostly brown rabbit, we can conclude 'gavagai' is not true of any and every undetached rabbit part.

Evans seems to me to be onto a genuinely explanatory account of the nature of at least some forms of predication. Nonetheless any admissible permutation function p which maps objects only onto co-present objects will get round Evans' point. For the extension of 'gavagai' in an interpretation H_p which is a variant of the homophonic interpretation H[15] will be the set of all p-images of rabbits, so including perhaps some rabbit ears; the extension of 'brown' will be all p-images of brown things. Suppose p, for example, is the permutation above which permutes our mostly white rabbit Poppy with its brown left ear, swapping the two round leaving all else untouched. So Poppy's ear satisfies 'gavagai' according to H_p but not 'brown' hence H_p is entirely consonant with the speakers dissent from 'brown gavagai' in the presence of that rabbit. True the extension of 'brown' under H_p is more heterogeneous, by our lights, than under the homophonic H, consisting of all but one of the brown things plus a white thing with a brown part and this is counter-intuitive; but nothing like as counter-intuitive as under the Putnam/Davidson reading of indeterminacy, in which 'brown' could be true of black holes.

Quine's arguments for indeterminacy from below, then, particularly in their earlier form, suggest strongly that one is forced to give up either the supervenience of semantics on the behavioural, perhaps indeed on the physical, or else give up determinacy of reference. Quine chooses the latter course.

11.3

Quine's argument from above is an argument for the indeterminacy of meaning of theoretical sentences, an argument which he often based on the *underdetermination of theory by evidence* (see, in particular, Quine, 1970 and 1975). This occurs when we have two theories T and T* which are empirically equivalent—that is if T entails an empirical sentence E so does T* and vice-versa—yet incompatible (so that there is a theoretical, non-empirical sentence A such that T entails A but T* entails $\sim$A).[16]

Trivial examples of underdetermination arise when we take a given theory and swap round two theoretical terms—e.g. swap 'electron' with 'molecule' in the axioms of

---

[15] i.e. H('W.V. Quine') = W.V. Quine, H('tree') = the set of all trees, and so on.

[16] More complexly one might add the requirement that T is empirically equivalent to T* only if, for all observation sentences E, the probability (or degree of confirmation or some such) of T given E equals that of T* given E; but I will stick with the simpler, purely deductive, definition which is to be found in Quine, 1970, p. 179 (expressed, equivalently, in terms of compatibility rather than entailment).

the theory so we now end up saying that molecules are smaller than electrons, have negative charge etc. Quine focuses on more complex examples in which we know of no simple permutation of predicates which would turn T into a 'merely terminologically' different T*. Suggested examples of such theories include two versions of Newton's gravitational theory, one interpreting gravitation in terms of fields of force which exist at every point in space, the other in terms of action at a distance. These are clearly incompatible, yet observationally there would be no difference between the two. Another example is a theory T which says time is linear but cyclical with infinitely many exact repetitions of each epoch, while T* says there is only one epoch but the topology of time is circular (see Newton-Smith, 1978, pp. 78–9; see also pp. 84–5). Or T posits a 'multiverse' comprising a vast plurality of mini-universes each expanding from a Big Bang but according to different parameters, only one set of which determines the mini-universe we are in and can observe. And so on.[17]

How does underdetermination lead to indeterminacy? Quine's argument is that since T and T* have the same empirical content, in addition to the trivial identity mapping translating P by itself for all members of T and T*, there will also be translations of T into T* and T* into T which preserve empirical content (do not map a sentence into one with distinct empirical content) and so are equally good, yet map sentences (such as the conjunction of the axioms of T) onto incompatible sentences (such as the conjunction of the axioms of T*).

Some objected to Quine that there was no more here than the usual scientific uncertainty:—in linguistics as in physics the theory outruns the evidence. Quine replied (e.g. at 1970, p. 180; 1987, pp. 9–10) that the thesis is a stronger metaphysical one. Fix all the physical facts—choose either T or T* as the correct theory; there is still no unique correct interpretation and hence no determinate fact of the matter. A counter-reply to this is that perhaps the physical facts are not all the facts or, if this is so by definition of 'physics', perhaps future physics will differ from current physics in such a way as to render indeterminacy implausible. Quine would accept this possibility, seeing his philosophical views as part of science, not prior to and more fundamental than it, and so fallible like the rest of science.

There is a puzzle about Quine arguing to indeterminacy from underdetermination, however, since underdetermination is surely a highly realist thesis:—it says there can be two theories which are empirically indistinguishable. But if they can also be equally explanatory, how could we ever know which, if any, is correct? From the sceptical standpoint of the realist (of a certain type), the answer is we cannot know; but from an empiricist viewpoint, surely such theories would be

---

[17] In the last two cases, although *we* cannot make any crucial experiments distinguishing the two hypothesis, it may be that different sets of observations sentences, construed as abstract objects which need be grasped by no observer, are true in each case. This problem can be avoided if we image a multiverse in which all mini-universes bar our own last only a few nano-seconds or have tiny spatial dimensions. There might be theoretical reasons for positing such a multiverse, for example resolving the 'fine-tuning' problem of why the 'brute' parameters of the universe seem so exactly fitted for the development of stable complex molecules and so life. Here the empirical equivalence of the two theories is less clear on the more nuanced notions of equivalence which appeal to confirmation or the like.

indistinguishable and hence not two theories but one. Quine's later work reveals an increasing acceptance of this argument and the related idea that there is no significant underdetermination of theory by evidence. He sways between *ecumenical* views on truth—any two empirically equivalent theories can be rendered compatible by terminological readjustments and incorporated into a wider whole—and a *sectarian* view according to which we should plump for one such and reject the other as meaningless.[18] The latter seems his more favoured view but, reflecting on the situation, he acknowledges we can flip from sectarian adherence to one theory to similarly ardent adherence to the other (1992, pp. 99–100; real sectarians do not behave like this!); so his reflective position seems hard to distinguish from the ecumenical one.[19]

If realism is wrong and there is no genuine underdetermination, what of the argument from above? It still goes through because the background assumptions used to derive indeterminacy from underdetermination—*holism* and *verificationism*—are sufficient to yield indeterminacy on their own.[20] Verificationism is the empiricist view that the only literal meaning is empirical meaning, empirical content. Holism, for the purposes of this argument, is the view that no theoretical sentence has empirical meaning or, more moderately, that most theoretical sentences do not, though some (the conjunction of the axioms and boundary conditions of an empirical theory, for instance) do. This more moderate holism is Quine's later view and is extremely plausible. Together they yield the characteristic Quinean views that synonymy is an empty relation amongst most theoretical sentences, since they have no meanings of their own to relate, and that there are permutations of the theoretical language which send some sentences to empirically equivalent but incompatible, intuitively non-synonymous, ones.

For example, let N be the conjunction of Newton's three laws of motion plus his inverse square gravity law. N has no empirical content, it entails no empirical hypotheses independently of further auxiliary hypotheses and boundary conditions. Neither does its negation $\sim N$: without further hypotheses we have no predictions as to which objects are violating the laws. So both have the same (null) meaning according to Quine! We did not need to appeal to underdetermination here.

Indeterminacy from above, and the resultant rejection of realism, follow from the highly plausible holist thesis, if verificationism is true. But verificationism is obviously incompatible with realism and fairly easily dismissed by the realist. Empirical content is not all there is to meaning even on fairly behaviouristic premises. Where O is an observational sentence then (O & O) and (O ∨ O) are both logically equivalent

---

[18] See Quine, 1992, §42. One reason against accepting a combined theory in which one renders the two formally incompatible but empirically equivalent theories consistent by terminological readjustment is that the resultant theory will be 'bloated'. Quine favours theories which are more elegant and have less 'fat'—this is what rules out adding 'The Absolute is Lazy' to an empirically acceptable theory—so long as they entail the right observational consequences in a simple, acceptable fashion.

[19] A very useful charting of Quine's oscillations on this matter is to be found in Gibson, 1988, ch. 5.

[20] See Quine, 1969b, pp. 80–1, though the argument is already pre-figured in Section V of 'Two Dogmas', Quine 1951. The point is made by Føllesdal (1973), pp. 290–1 and endorsed, as I read him, by Quine, 1986a pp. 155–6, though for a different reading and more on holism, see Peter Pagin, 'Meaning Holism', this volume.

hence identical in empirical content. But they have different syntactic structures, one being constructed using &, the other ∨ (inclusive disjunction). Moreover Quine himself, in his verdict matrix theory of the connectives, provides a behaviouristic account of how such connectives have meaning and how they differ in meaning (1960, §13). If, then, we require for the synonymy of two sentences not only sameness of empirical content but also that operators with the same meaning occur at the same nodes in the structure of the sentences then we can fairly easily show how empirically equivalent sentences have different meanings. Quine's argument from above, then, is not incontrovertible, though it is much more difficult to show how empirically equivalent sentences could differ in truth-conditions (as (O & O) and (O ∨ O) do not) as well as in meaning.[21]

11.4

Quine's moderate holism explains his tolerant attitude, despite his behaviouristic outlook, to the failure of behaviourist reductions of key notions such as assent, dissent and, in his philosophy of perception, perceptual similarity. As in any other science, theoretical concepts cannot be defined in more empirical (for instance, behavioural) terms—such as moderate holism. Nor can we always expect illuminating definitions in terms of other theoretical notions.

But if that is so, why not accept the notions of analyticity or synonymy, even though they are not non-trivially definable nor fully behaviourally reducible, and with them a whole host of other notions, such as concept, proposition, belief, all individuated in a fine-grained way? Quine might appeal to the supervenience of the psychological on the physical and claim to have shown that supervenience fails for all these notions; for example, synonymy relations are not fixed even when all physical facts are fixed. But he showed this only granted the very identification of meaning with empirical content which is being challenged as resting on reductionist premises. Quine's ultimate answer here seems to be that he can see no point to the introduction of these notions (see Quine, 1986, p. 207).

Certainly, those traditional notions of analyticity and synonymy can play no role in the establishing of Quine's highly empiricist, antirealist metaphysics, since they can be used to undermine it. This means that his radical empiricism, which he thinks of as breaking free from older metaphysics by being continuous with modern science and making no prior philosophical presuppositions, in fact itself presupposes, rather than establishes, the correctness of the old empiricist, verificationist metaphysics. Nonetheless both the argument from above and from below yield important illumination even for those who do not accept that meaning is indeterminate. For they show

---

[21] The idea here is close to Carnap's notion of 'intentional isomorphism'. Quine, 1960, §42, criticizes the use of such an idea, see especially the paragraph pp. 205–6, but the criticism is arguably question-begging in that it assumes that the indeterminacy thesis is true.

that if synonymy is as fine-grained as we are pre-theoretically inclined to think it is, we must modify or abandon some central tenets of a naturalistic empiricism which many find highly attractive.

REFERENCES

Works by Quine cited

Quine, W. V. (1951). 'Two Dogmas of Empiricism', in *From a Logical Point of View* (Cambridge: Harvard University Press), 2nd revised edition (1961), pp. 20–46.

____ (1960). *Word and Object* (Cambridge Mass.: MIT Press).

____ (1964). 'Ontological Reduction and the World of Numbers', in W. V. Quine, *The Ways of Paradox and Other Essays* (2nd edition), (Cambridge, Mass.: Harvard University Press, 1976).

____ (1969). *Ontological Relativity and Other Essays* (New York: Columbia University Press).

____ (1969a). 'Ontological Relativity', in W. V. Quine, 1969, pp. 26–68.

____ (1969b). 'Epistemology Naturalized', in W. V. Quine, 1969, pp. 69–90.

____ (1970). 'On the Reasons for Indeterminacy of Translation', *The Journal of Philosophy*, 67, pp. 178–83.

____ (1974). *The Roots of Reference* (La Salle, Illinois: Open Court).

____ (1975). 'On Empirically Equivalent Systems of the World', *Erkenntnis*, 9, pp. 313–28.

____ (1986a). 'Reply to Gibson', in L. E. Hahn and P. A. Schilpp (eds.) *The Philosophy of W.V. Quine* (La Salle, Illinois: Open Court), pp. 155–7.

____ (1986b). 'Reply to Hellman', in L. E. Hahn and P. A. Schilpp, pp. 206–8.

____ (1987). 'Indeterminacy of Translation Again', *The Journal of Philosophy*, 84, pp. 5–10.

____ (1992). *Pursuit of Truth* (Cambridge, Mass.: Harvard University Press).

____ (1995). *From Stimulus to Science* (Cambridge, Mass.: Harvard University Press).

____ (2000). 'Responses', in P. Kotatko and A. Orenstein (eds.), *Knowledge, Language and Logic: Questions for Quine* (Dordrecht: Kluwer).

Useful monographs on Quine

Gibson, Roger, (1988). *Enlightened Empiricism* (Tampa: University of South Florida Press).

Hookway, Christopher, (1988). *Quine* (Cambridge: Polity Press).

Kirk, Robert, (1986). *Translation Determined* (Oxford: Clarendon Press).

Orenstein, Alex, (2002). *W.V. Quine* (Princeton: Princeton University Press).

See also

Miller, Alexander, (1998). *Philosophy of Language* (London: UCL Press), ch. 4.

Other works cited

Davidson, Donald, (1979). 'Inscrutability of Reference', in Donald Davidson, *Inquiries into Truth and Interpretation* (Oxford: Clarendon Press, 1984, pp. 227–41).

Dummett, Michael, (1981). *Frege: Philosophy of Language* (Second Edition), (London: Duckworth).

Evans, Gareth, (1975). 'Identity and Predication', *The Journal of Philosophy*, 72, pp. 343–63.

Føllesdal, Dagfinn, (1973). 'Indeterminacy of Translation and UnderDetermination of the Theory of Nature', *Dialectica*, 27, pp. 289–301.

Newton-Smith, W. H. (1978). 'The Underdetermination of Theory by Data', *Proceedings of the Aristotelian Society*, supplementary volume, 52 pp. 71–91.

Pagin, Peter, (2006). 'Meaning Holism', this volume.

Putnam, Hilary, (1978). *Meaning and the Moral Sciences* (London: Routledge, Kegan and Paul).

_____ (1981). *Reason, Truth and History* (Cambridge: Cambridge University Press).

Wittgenstein, Ludwig, (1922). *Tractatus Logico-Philosophicus* (London: Routledge and Kegan Paul).

CHAPTER 12

INTENTION-BASED SEMANTICS

EMMA BORG

THERE is a sense in which it is trivial to say that one accepts intention-(or convention-) based semantics.[1] For if what is meant by this claim is simply that there is an important respect in which words and sentences have meaning (either at all or the particular meanings that they have in any given natural language) due to the fact that they are used, in the way they are, by intentional agents (i.e. speakers), then it seems no one should disagree. For imagine a possible world where there are physical things which share the shape and form of words of English or Japanese, or the acoustic properties of sentences of Finnish or Arapaho, yet where there are no intentional agents (or where any remaining intentional agents don't use language). In such a world, it seems clear that these physical objects, which are only superficially language-like, will lack all meaning. Furthermore, it seems that questions of particular meaning are also settled by the conventions of intentional language users: it's nothing more than convention which makes the concatenation of letters 'a'^'p'^'p'^'l'^'e' mean *apple*, rather than *banana*, in English.[2] So, understood as the minimal claim that intentional agents, with a practice of using certain physical objects (written words, sounds, hand gestures, etc.) to communicate certain thoughts, are a *prerequisite* for linguistic meaning, the idea that semantics is based on both intention and convention seems indisputable. I will label a theory which

---

[1] Intention-based semantics (IBS), as practised by, say, Grice, is a different project from convention-based semantics as practised by, say, Lewis. However, the two projects are often thought to be intimately connected, with convention providing a key component in IBS accounts of sentence, as opposed to speaker, meaning (see Schiffer, 1972, and next section).

[2] This platitudinous sense of a dependence on convention is stressed at the outset by Lewis, 1969: 1–2.

recognizes this preconditional role for speaker intentions an A-style intention-based semantics and we will explore one such account in Section 12.1.[3]

This relatively trivial form of appeal to speaker intentions in determining semantic content can, however, be distinguished from a more pervasive form of appeal. On this picture, intentional agents are not only a prerequisite for linguistic meaning, they also play a fundamental role in determining the semantic content of an expression in a current communicative exchange. In this way, the route to grasp of meaning must go via a consideration of a current speaker's state of mind. I will label any theory which assigns this more substantive role to speaker intentions a B-style intention-based semantics and we will look at one form such a theory might take in Section 12.2. Then, in Section 12.3, I want to highlight three points of difference between A-style and B-style theories and suggest, in Section 12.4, that it is the characteristics of A-style intention-based semantics which appear better suited to providing a semantic theory for natural language.

12.1 A-Style Intention-Based Semantics (A-Style IBS)

The intention-based semantics (IBS) story really starts with the work of Paul Grice. In a number of seminal papers, Grice put forward an account which aimed to show that all semantic notions attaching to a public language could be reduced to psychological notions.[4] Grice's idea was to show how claims about sentence meaning could be explicated in terms of speaker-meaning, and then show how speaker-meaning could be understood purely in terms of (non-semantic) speaker intentions. These moves, if successful, would reveal linguistic meaning as posing no further problems than the more fundamental notion of mental content.[5] Furthermore, if the reductive IBS programme were twined with a reductive, naturalistic account of intentionality, then we would have an account which successfully showed us how to find a place for linguistic meaning in the ordinary, physical, scheme of things. It would show us how the meanings of our words and phrases can be explained, ultimately, by appeal to physical facts alone.

A key notion in Grice's account is, then, that of utterer's meaning—the idea that *by uttering some linguistic item x, a speaker, U, meant that p*. This notion of utterer's

---

[3] I introduce the labels 'A-style' and 'B-style' in order to abstract from exegetical questions concerning which theorists hold which position. Such exegetical issues will be touched on, but certainly not settled, below.

[4] Grice, 1989: Essay 5, 91. This claim that the Gricean project is reductive in nature has been questioned by some, cf. Avramides, 1989: ch.1.

[5] We might note that Fodor, 1989: 423 also endorses IBS: "[W]e don't know how IBS *could* be true. But IBS is the metaphysics we require to explain how there could be intentional laws; and it's the metaphysics that the computational theory of the mind presupposes. So we know IBS *must* be true. So we know that IBS *is* true."

meaning is explained via the speaker's intentions: an agent means something by a given act only if she intends that act to produce some effect in an audience, at least partly by means of the audience's recognition of that intention. It is for this reason that we might think of the intentions in question as reflexive or self-referential: they are intentions which are satisfied when they themselves are recognized.[6] This gives us the form of analysis for utterer's, or speaker's, meaning, which forms the heart of Gricean IBS:

   (UM) U utterer-means that p by x iff for some audience A, U intends that:

   (i)   by uttering x, U induce the belief that (U believes that) p in A
   (ii) A should recognize (i)
   (iii) A's recognition of (i) should be the reason for A's forming the belief that (U believes that) p.[7]

One point we should clarify with respect to the Gricean programme is the status of at least some of these deliveries of utterer's meaning as genuinely *semantic,* for one of the primary distinctions contemporary philosophy of language has borrowed from Grice is the distinction between sentence meaning and utterer's meaning, and the view that while the former is the proper subject of semantics, the latter is the proper subject of pragmatics. So we could be misled into thinking that UM only offers an analysis of pragmatic, not semantic, content.

   Grice himself did not use the terminology 'semantics' and 'pragmatics', preferring instead to distinguish between 'what is said' and 'what is implicated'.[8] 'What is said', in Grice's favoured sense, is intended to pick out the 'central meaning' of a sentence, s, something which we might think qualifies as the semantic content of that sentence.[9] Implicatures, on the other hand, are pragmatically conveyed propositions which may diverge from the literal meaning of the sentence uttered in significant ways. Grice distinguishes between conventional and non-conventional implicatures, but the general notion is easiest to see with reference to a specific kind of non-conventional implicature, namely conversational implicatures.

---

   [6] See Bach, 1987. One issue here concerns the existence of apparently successful speakers who are unable to entertain the kind of higher-order intentions UM requires, e.g. autistic speakers who seem capable of producing meaningful linguistic utterances despite apparent theory of mind deficits, see Laurence, 1996; Glüer and Pagin, 2003. Although I can't explore this point here, it seems that whether or not autistic speakers do constitute genuine counterexamples to the Gricean project will depend on the precise role played by speaker intentions. If we treat Grice's account as an A-style theory then it might be that such speakers could exploit a pre-existing system of conventional meaning, even while being unable to form the intentions required by UM.

   [7] UM receives a range of subtly different formulations, both within Grice's work and across other IBS accounts; for instance, the addition of the parenthetical 'U believes that' in clauses (i) and (iii) occurs in Grice's 1989: Essay 6, 123, version of the definition. However, for our purposes, I think these subtle variations can be ignored.

   [8] Grice, 1989: Essay 6, 118.

   [9] Grice, 1989: Essay 5, 87–8 suggests that his privileged notion of 'what is said' is tied to the syntactic constituents of a sentence. Thus we should not conflate the Gricean notion with a perhaps more intuitive notion of 'what a speaker says by uttering a sentence' (which connects to judgements of indirect speech reports); see Saul, 2002.

Conversational implicatures occur when a speaker wilfully flouts what Grice takes to be a quite general principle of good communication: "make your conversational contribution such as is required, at the stage at which it occurs, by the accepted purpose or direction of the talk exchange in which you are engaged".[10] For Grice, this general principle subsumes such maxims as 'be as informative as required', 'don't utter what you believe to be false' and 'be relevant'. So if an otherwise competent speaker utters a sentence, the conventional meaning of which flouts one of these maxims in the current context of utterance, her audience will be licensed in inferring that the speaker does not mean to convey what the sentence itself says. Instead she should be taken as conveying some alternative, implicated proposition. For instance, imagine that I am looking at a list of marks for essays by students from Year 1, a year which contains the notoriously lax Smith. Seeing no mark next to Smith's name, I might utter "Well, someone didn't hand in an essay again." Now, the quite general literal proposition my sentence expresses seems, in this context, to flout Grice's maxim of quantity, which states roughly that a speaker should aim to convey as much relevant information as possible.[11] For there is a much more informative proposition I could have produced in this context, namely that *Smith didn't hand in an essay again*. Yet so long as my audience are aware of this fact they will be able to infer that, although I literally express only a quite general proposition, I actually intend to conversationally implicate the more informative proposition directly concerning Smith.

There is obviously much to be said about implicatures, but the important point to notice from our current perspective is simply that the existence of implicatures entails that there will be a notion of utterer's-meaning which will not be relevant to the core IBS project. This will be the case whenever a speaker intends to convey an implicature, for here, though the speaker intends to produce a belief in her audience via some utterance, the belief she intends to produce diverges from the conventional content of the sentence uttered.[12] However, the claim of Gricean IBS is that we can also isolate a notion of UM which *does* deal with genuinely semantic content, namely those instances of the schema which deal with what is said by a sentence, or its 'time-less meaning'.[13] It is at this point in the Gricean system, then, that many proponents of IBS make the connection to some notion of *convention*.[14] UM will deliver what we might think of as the genuinely semantic content of a sentence where there is a convention among a community of speakers to use an expression of type x in the way specified by the given instance of UM. Conventional speaker intentions are con-stitutive of meaning: what matters for an expression coming to have a given meaning in a given community is that the expression be used by one speaker to convey a cer-tain meaning and that this use be picked up by the community, so that there comes to be a convention of using this word in this way. Notice, however, that this is an answer to a constitutive question concerning the kind of thing linguistic meaning

---

[10] Grice, 1989: Essay 2, 26.   [11] *Ibid.*, 28–33.   [12] *Ibid.*: Essay 14, 221.
[13] *Ibid.*: Essay 6, 121.   [14] E.g. see Schiffer, 1972: chs 5 and 6.

is. It does not as yet entail anything about the route current interlocutors need take to recover the semantic content of any expression. Specifically, it seems that there is no requirement that hearers have access to, or reason about, the mental states of a *current* speaker.[15]

If this is correct, then the role accorded to speaker intentions in the Gricean project is a preconditional one. It is an A-style IBS and thus allows that an audience may grasp the semantic content of a sentence even if they know nothing of the current speaker's aims or intentions.[16] However, it seems that we could also envisage an alternative kind of intention-based account—one which accords a much more thorough-going role to speaker intentions. To see this let us turn now to a different kind of approach, drawn from Sperber and Wilson's relevance theory.[17]

12.2 B-STYLE INTENTION-BASED SEMANTICS (B-STYLE IBS)

According to relevance theory, there is an integral role for current speaker intentions to play in determining the truth-conditional content of an utterance.[18] For both Grice and Sperber and Wilson (henceforth 'S&W') a linguistic production is simply a (good) piece of evidence about what the speaker means and to grasp this meaning the addressee must engage in some inferential reasoning. However, for S&W, what the addressee reasons about is not (directly) the intentions of the speaker but rather the machinations of relevance, which in turn serve to make speaker intentions evident:

[E]very act of ostension communicates a presumption of its own optimal relevance—Ostensive behaviour provides evidence of one's thoughts. It succeeds in doing so because it implies a guarantee of relevance. It implies such a guarantee because humans automatically

---

[15] I'm grateful to Kent Bach and Jim Higginbotham for stressing this point.

[16] That this is the Gricean view is suggested by Neale, 1992: 500–2, who writes: "[One might think] that Grice's project gets something 'backwards': surely any attempt to model how we work out what someone means on a given occasion will progress from word meaning plus syntax to sentence meaning, and from sentence meaning plus context to what is said, and from what is said plus context to what is meant. And doesn't this clash with Grice's view that sentence meaning is analysable in terms of utterer's meaning? I do not think this can be correct . . . It is no part of Grice's theory that in general a hearer must work out what U meant by uttering a sentence X in order to work out the meaning of X. Such a view is so clearly false that it is difficult to see how anyone might be induced to subscribe to it or attribute it to another philosopher . . . Grice himself is explicit on this point: 'Of course, I would not want to deny that when the vehicle of meaning is a sentence (or the utterance of a sentence), the speaker's intentions are to be recognized, in the normal case, by virtue of a knowledge of the conventional use of the sentence (indeed, my account of nonconventional implicature depends on this idea' (*SITWW*, pp. 100–1). Importantly, an *analysis* of sentence meaning does not conflict with this idea."

[17] As we will see in the next section, it unlikely that such an intention-based semantics would in fact be endorsed by Sperber and Wilson, thus a straightforward ascription of the position to them would be misplaced.

[18] See S&W, 1986; Carston, 2002.

turn their attention to what seems most relevant to them. [Our] main thesis ... is that an act of ostension carries a guarantee of relevance, and that this ... *principle of relevance* makes manifest the intention behind the ostension.[19]

Relevance here is a technical term (though clearly related to the natural language homonym), whereby an interpretation is relevant just in case the cognitive cost of processing the event which demands the attention of the agent is outweighed by the cognitive benefits of that processing (where benefits include deriving or strengthening new assumptions, and confirming or rejecting previous assumptions).[20] 'Optimal relevance' states that the first interpretation which crosses the relevance threshold is the right one; that is, that the first relevant interpretation the addressee arrives at is the one the speaker intended to communicate.

So, the key to assessments of meaning seems to be the actions of an inferential mechanism aimed at articulating speaker intentions connected to a particular communicative act.[21] However, despite the apparently central role for speaker intentions on this kind of picture, there are questions to be raised about classifying this account as a form of IBS. For a start, one might wonder exactly how integral the appeal to speaker intentions really is within relevance theory. For S&W emphasize the role of the relevance mechanisms in a processing account, i.e. they couch the theory in terms of the (potentially sub-personal) cognitive mechanisms underlying linguistic comprehension. Yet if the assumption is that as a brute psychological fact both addressee and hearer have the same, relevance directed, psychological mechanisms, it's not clear that the addressee ever need move to the more reflective step of judging the relevant interpretation as revelatory of the speaker's intentions (the thought is roughly that, on this account, recognition of intention becomes something of an epiphenomenon in the process of utterance interpretation).[22] If this construal were correct then, despite its Gricean heritage, relevance theory would end up more removed from IBS than it initially appeared. However, we should be clear that S&W also stress the importance of the mutual manifestness of intentions in making an act a genuinely communicative act: it is this factor which distinguishes genuine communication from all other forms of sub-personal co-ordination (like, say, the automatic accommodation agents make to avoid bumping into each other on the street). So, despite the autonomy of the psychological, relevance-directed mechanisms from speaker intentions, it still seems to be the case that recognition of speaker intentions is necessary for an act to count as genuinely communicative for S&W.

However, a more fundamental reason for resisting the classification of relevance theory as a form of IBS is that S&W explicitly state that semantics for them deals with

---

[19] S&W, 1986: 50.   [20] *Ibid.*: 47–50.   [21] S&W, 1986: 23.
[22] Kempson, 1986: 90 notes the potential irrelevancy of grasp of speaker intentions on a relevance theoretic account. This point is, I think, related to, though distinct from, the worry voiced by Bach, 1987 and 1999: 79, where he objects to accounts like S&W's on the grounds that they neglect the self-referential or reflexive nature of Gricean communicative intentions.

non-propositional/non-truth-evaluable items which are arrived at *without* appeal to speaker intentions. They write:

What are the meanings of sentences? Sentence meanings are sets of semantic representations, as many semantic representations as there are ways in which the sentence is ambiguous. Semantic representations are incomplete logical forms, i.e. at best fragmentary representations of thoughts ... One entertains thoughts; one does not entertain semantic representations of sentences. Semantic representations of sentences are mental objects that never surface to consciousness. If they did, they would be entirely uninteresting (except, of course, to semanticists). Semantic representations become mentally represented as a result of an automatic and unconscious process of linguistic decoding. They can be used as assumption schemas to identify first the propositional form and then the explicatures of an utterance. It is these explicatures alone that have contextual effects, and are therefore worthy of conscious attention.[23]

The picture of linguistic comprehension which emerges in S&W's project is then as follows. Imagine that A and B are discussing the problems in retaining valuable colleagues, A points at C and says "She's leaving". To understand this communicative exchange an addressee needs to engage in three stages of processing:

Semantic decoding $\Rightarrow$ incomplete logical form

Pragmatic inference (1) $\Rightarrow$ proposition expressed/explicature (e.g. *C is leaving the university*)

Pragmatic inference (2) $\Rightarrow$ implicature (e.g. *A isn't happy about this*)

Semantic decoding yields something incomplete here because we need to look to the context of utterance to discover *what* C is leaving. Only once we've found this out do we get a truth-condition for the sentence A produced. Clearly, then, by their own lights, relevance theory is *not* a form of IBS, since semantics for S&W deals with propositional schemas, or incomplete logical forms, which are arrived at simply through decoding and not through any sensitivity to speaker intentions. However, on a perhaps more standard reading of 'semantics', where it deals with complete propositions, or truth-conditions, it looks as if relevance theory *is* a form of IBS, since complete propositions are (in general) arrived at only after some pragmatic inference, aimed at articulating speaker intentions, has taken place (i.e. they emerge only at the level of pragmatic inference (1), which delivers the explicature of the utterance).[24]

So, if we take 'semantics' (as is common in philosophy, especially among formal semanticists) to concern complete propositions or truth-conditional content, it does seem plausible to label *both* Grice's programme and the relevance-based account

---

[23] S&W, 1986: 193. 'Explicature' is S&W's technical term for the literal meaning of an utterance, a level of complete (propositional or truth-conditional) content recovered via certain contextual enrichments of the incomplete logical form of the sentence uttered.

[24] Kempson, 1986: 102 writes: "The semantic component of a grammar neither completely specifies the propositions to be paired with any given sentence, nor is restricted to specifying such propositions. The semantic component of a grammar indeed does not provide a semantic theory for a language at all in the philosophical sense."

sketched in this section as forms of IBS, for on both accounts semantic content depends on the intentional states of speakers. However, according to the (A-style) position of §1, the crucial intentions concern conventional use and are thus independent of the intentional states of a current speaker. While, according to the (B-style) position of this section, the crucial intentions include those belonging to the current speaker. So, now we can ask which kind of account is better equipped to provide a semantic theory for a language—that is to say, what is the role of speaker intentions in an appealing intention-based semantics?

12.3 THREE POINTS OF DIFFERENCE

We have two different kinds of approach, both of which accord a central role to speaker intentions. According to the reading of Grice offered in Section 12.1, speaker intentions play a preconditional role in determining linguistic meaning, though this does not necessarily entail anything about the route by which a current interlocutor recovers literal meaning. According to the relevance-based account outlined in Section 12.2, on the other hand, it is access to current speaker intentions which provides the route to grasp of semantic (i.e. truth-evaluable) content in any current linguistic exchange. To help us decide which version of IBS is more feasible, I want now to highlight three points of difference between the two accounts. Then, in the next section, I'll argue that it is the characteristics of A-style IBS which prove more attractive.

(i) *Are sentences or utterances the primary bearers of semantic content?*

As we have already seen, our two opposing accounts take different stances in respect of this question. For Grice, although the notion of speaker meaning is crucial, semantic content attaches not at the level of utterances but at the level of sentences, for it is only at this more abstract level that the idea of conventional speaker meanings can emerge. If we concentrate just on a single utterance, though we might be able to specify utterer's meaning we cannot establish sentence-meaning. For S&W, however, it is usually the utterance which forms the first point at which truth-conditional (semantic) content can be recovered. It is speech acts, or ostensive acts in general, which connect most directly with intentional states, and which thus provide the point at which something truth-evaluable may be recovered. So our two accounts focus on different items as the primary locus of literal linguistic meaning: for A-style accounts it is some fairly abstract notion of a sentence-type, while for B-style theories it is the much more concrete and context-bound notion of an utterance which is paramount.

(ii) *What kind of cognitive processes are involved in recovering semantic content?*

Again, it seems that our two varieties of IBS will differ in the answers they give to this question. According to an A-style account, it seems possible that the processes by which meaning is recovered may run along exhaustively (or at least predominantly) mechanistic or syntactic trails. An interlocutor can grasp the semantic content of a sentence via a grasp of its syntactic parts and knowledge of the conventional use of those parts. This sort of procedure looks like it might be given a fairly mechanistic explanation, akin to simple decoding. Whereas, given the more pervasive appeal to speaker intentions in a B-style approach, no such mechanistic route to meaning will be available. For the B-style theory, grasping semantic content will be an essentially *reason-based* or *inferential* activity.[25] Coming to grasp propositional or truth-evaluable content will be a process of reasoning about the state of an interlocutor's mind, based on past and present evidence of their nature and interests, together with other (mutually known) background beliefs.

This yields another, related, difference: the kinds of inferential processes licensed by B-theories on route to semantic content will not be simple, deductive inferences, but rather all-things-considered, abductive inferential moves.[26] What the addressee has to reason her way to is the most fitting or relevant interpretation of some utterance given features of the context of utterance, background beliefs about conventional behaviour and social mores, and about the specific aims and objectives of the speaker and of this conversational exchange. Thus the reasoning will be a form of inference to the best explanation, an 'all-things-considered process' which could, in principle appeal to any aspect of the agent's knowledge. Clearly, though, one crucial aspect of the inferential procedure will be the addressee's ability to ascertain the intentional states of the communicative agent. Thus, to use currently popular terminology, to grasp the semantic content of a sentence like 'The apple is red', the B-style IBS theorist suggests one needs more than simple decoding processes, one also needs an ability to *mind-read*. For instance, in this case, one needs to appeal to current speaker intentions to determine in which respect the apple is claimed to be red (e.g. its skin or its flesh).

This seems very different to the approach of the A-theorist, who (at least prima facie) claims that assessments of literal meaning need invoke no capacity for mind-reading. For the A-theorist, to grasp the meaning of a sentence what matters is that the agent undertake the correct computation or translation procedure, and this will be a predominantly mechanistic procedure—something which can be undertaken *without* appeal to rich features of the context of utterance (such as speaker intentions) and without appeal to non-deductive inference procedures (i.e. abductive or all-things-considered reasoning).[27]

---

[25] Certain distinctions are suppressed here for reasons of space. For instance, Recanati, 2002 has argued that, while it is right to think of linguistic comprehension as inferential in a broad sense (i.e. as involving reason-based manipulations of conceptual representations, but manipulations which occur potentially subpersonally and with a high degree of automaticity), it is a mistake to see it as inferential in a narrow sense, as he suggests S&W do (i.e. as a consciously inferential process).

[26] See Josephson and Josephson, 1994 for a detailed discussion of abductive reasoning.

[27] There is an important question to be addressed here concerning the recovery of truth-evaluable content for context-dependent expressions, such as demonstratives and indexicals. Determining semantic content for such expressions appears to require relativization to a context and, it may be argued, the

Of course, things are complex here, for it is not simply the case that the B-style IBS theorist must claim *all* aspects of understanding of meaning are inferential, while the A-style IBS theorist must claim *all* aspects of linguistic understanding are mechanistic. Instead the truth lies somewhere in between: the B-theorist may claim that some (initial) aspect of linguistic comprehension is simply decoding. Thus, as we've seen, she may claim that phonetic or orthographic or syntactic processing, up to the point of logical form representation, is a simple act of decoding—mapping input received via the senses to internal representations purely on the basis of the form of this input. However, what the B-theorist will then claim is that the result of this decoding process radically underdetermines analyses of propositional content and that to arrive at this richer level of interpretation there must be an ineliminable appeal to current speaker intentions (thus it is only by working out that the speaker of 'the apple is red' intends to convey, say, that the apple is red *on its skin* that one grasps the semantic content in play). A-theorists, on the other hand, come at things from the other direction: though there may be an element of rich, inferential processing required prior to grasp of what *a speaker says by a given utterance*, this inferential processing occurs post-semantically and is not relevant for judgements of literal linguistic meaning. For them it is the brute, mechanistic process that reveals literal linguistic meaning, with rich inferential processing appealing to speaker intentions occurring only as a possible adjunct to a more fundamental process of linguistic interpretation. So, though both accounts allow a role for both decoding and inference, the difference in emphasis is clear.

(iii) *Is linguistic meaning a species of general ostensive behaviour?*

This difference between decoding and inference surfaces again in the kind of phenomenon each approach takes understanding of language to be. B-style IBS accounts see linguistic meaning as in important respects non-unique; linguistic acts form a subset of a much wider ranging phenomenon, namely ostensive behaviour per se. Thus there will be no difference *in kind* between pointing at a cake while licking one's lips and asking the baker for a slice.[28] Both actions require the addressee to employ her theory of mind to attribute those intentional states to the agent which best explain the action. Though the types of intentions recognized in, or the amount of evidence supplied by, each case may be slightly different (perhaps being more specialized in the case of utterance interpretation) linguistic communication is not a radically different kind of ostensive act.[29]

For A-style IBS accounts this assimilation of language to communicative behaviour in general is, if not mistaken, then at least misleading. Though words and

features of the context which are relevant (e.g. the referential intentions of the speaker) require mind-reading to recover. However, for reasons of space, I will leave the discussion of what I would term 'overt context-sensitivity' to one side for now; see Borg, 2004a; 2004b, ch.3.

[28] Grice, 1989: Essay, 14; Schiffer, 1972: 7–13.

[29] As Carston, 1999: 104 notes: "[T]he use of a linguistic system, or some other code, for ostensive purposes provides the relevance-constrained inferential mechanisms with information of a much more fine-grained and determinate sort than is available otherwise."

mimes may both serve to get one's message across (and thus at one, very broad, level of brushstroke may be classified together), to treat the former as a mere subset of the latter runs the risk of underestimating the considerable differences between the two forms of communication. With the emphasis they place on the exhaustive nature of mechanistic processes, the formal theorist claims that linguistic meaning is fundamentally special. No matter how easy it is to interpret the dog whining by the door as 'saying' it wants to go out, or the pre-linguistic child pointing to the ice-cream as communicating that she wants to eat it, neither of these communicative actions belongs to the same kind as uttering 'I want to go outside' or saying 'I would like that ice-cream.' Though utterances and actions may equally serve to get one's message across, according to the formal theorist, they are exploiting very different processes of comprehension when they do so.[30]

There are, then, substantial differences between our two varieties of IBS. B-style IBS accounts take the intentional states of a current speaker to be crucial in establishing semantic content, thus they take utterances to be the primary bearers of semantic content, with sentence-level meaning (should it be required) abstracted from here. Grasp of semantic content will be a richly inferential, all-things-considered process, and they treat linguistic acts as not essentially different in kind to other types of communicative act, like mimes or gestures. On each of these points A-style IBS accounts can diverge.

12.4 A-STYLE VS. B-STYLE INTENTION-BASED SEMANTICS

It seems to me that, though intention-based approaches may ultimately have a crucial role to play in studies of language use, the mistake made by B-style accounts is to think that a theory of literal truth-conditional or propositional content can or should be simply subsumed within a theory of communication. To see this, I want to explore (in reverse order) what I think is wrong with the three characteristics of B-style IBS accounts enumerated in the last section, and, conversely, what might be right about A-style accounts.

(i) *Is linguistic meaning a species of general ostensive behaviour?*
It's all very well to claim that linguistic acts belong to a much wider group of communicative acts in general (acts which include gestures, mimes, picture drawing, facial expressions, etc.) for at some degree of generalization all such acts clearly do share a common profile. However, we must ask whether grouping these acts together, simply on the basis of similarity at a very general level of description, really results in the most perspicuous categorization. One reason for thinking that this is not the case

---

[30] This point is also made by Laurence, 1996: 298–9.

is that such a categorization serves to disguise what seem to be some fundamental differences between communicative acts in general and linguistic acts in particular. Linguistic acts, uniquely in this area, have a crystallized component to their meaning, an element which they carry with them across all contexts and which may be accessed by a competent language user even if she has no access at all to the speaker's original intentions. Thus, if I come across the sentence 'Snow is white' it seems I can recover the proposition this sentence expresses (or consider the conditions under which an utterance of this sentence would be true) even if all I know about the sentence's producer is that they spoke English (and thus I have no access to the beliefs and desires which prompted production of the sentence). Yet these genuinely code-like qualities seem very different to the properties of other communicative acts, which depend on context in a far more constitutive way. A raise of the eyebrows may indicate surprise or consternation or nothing, and which it is, and what the agent is surprised or upset about, are factors which can *only* be settled by finding something out about the context of production. The meaning of a non-linguistic ostensive act seems ineliminably tied to its context in a way that the meaning of a linguistic act is not. Furthermore, it seems that the kinds of processes involved in the comprehension of the two cases are radically different, which brings us to the next point.

(ii) *What kind of cognitive processes are involved in recovering semantic content?*

B-style IBS accounts claim that semantic content is arrived at via inferential processes generating hypotheses about speaker intentions. However, while this may seem a reasonable claim concerning what a speaker succeeds in communicating via her linguistic production, it seems to ignore the degree of autonomy which literal meaning possesses. What is literally meant seems to be independent of what the speaker intends her utterance to mean. Furthermore, it seems that the rich, inferential route to semantic content predicted by the B-style theory is at odds with an independently plausible picture of the kind of cognitive architecture which underlies linguistic comprehension. Specifically, it seems that an A-style account can allow, while a B-style theory cannot allow, that our semantic abilities are underpinned by a specific module for language.[31]

At its broadest, modularity of mind claims simply that the mind is composed of a number of discrete or encapsulated modules, each dedicated to some aspect of human intelligence, and each operating with its own deductive rules and representations. In Fodor's original account of modularity there were thought to be six primary modules (with each potentially containing yet smaller sub-modules), namely the 'input systems', consisting of the five senses plus language. Modules subserve a non-modular 'central processing unit', or general intelligence, which engages in the kind of open-ended, abductive processing (utilizing the outputs of the mechanistic, computational modules) which is paradigmatically human. Fodorian modules are characterized by a number of properties, including being domain

---

[31] See Fodor, 1983; Borg 2004b, ch.2.

specific (each is dedicated to its own, specialized task), informationally encapsulated (modules are 'opaque', they don't have access to information not contained within that module), they are fast and their processing is mandatory. Finally, they are associated with hardwired neural systems and exhibit specific patterns of acquisition and loss.

Now there is, it seems, some evidence that grasp of literal, semantic content for sentences is the kind of ability which deserves a modular explanation; that is to say, literal linguistic comprehension displays the characteristics of a module. For instance, linguistic comprehension is 'switched on' only by a very specialized kind of input, grasp of meaning is incredibly fast and it does indeed seem to be mandatory.[32] Furthermore, semantic understanding does seem to be associated with specific patterns of acquisition and loss. For instance, certain cognitive pathologies seem to show that an agent may retain semantic abilities even though they have lost a wide range of other cognitive skills (apparently including those associated with mind-reading). Thus certain patients with schizophrenia lose the ability to pick up on commonly conveyed meanings, instead displaying what we might class as a kind of 'over-literalism';[33] similarly, patients with Asperger's syndrome apparently show normal abilities in understanding literal sentence meaning but often fail to grasp the richer propositions speakers intend to communicate by their utterances (Asperger himself described his patients as 'talking like little professors'). Although I cannot properly rehearse all the empirical evidence here, such cases may lend support to the idea that linguistic comprehension in general, and semantic comprehension in particular, can be lost or preserved in isolation from other cognitive abilities, specifically including the ability to assess the mental states of others.

Yet claims of modularity for semantic comprehension seem to be in tension with the kind of picture given to us by B-style IBS. For advocates of such approaches, if they accept modularity at all, are required to see any module for linguistic understanding as a dedicated sub-module within a wider 'theory of mind module', responsible for intentional interpretation in general (since semantic interpretation is just a type of intentional interpretation).[34] Yet it seems that nothing like this could be a Fodorian module, since, as noted above, the kinds of cognitive processes involved in such intentional interpretation simply do not fit with the limited,

[32] As Fodor, 1983: 55.

[33] See Langdon, R, Davies, M, and Coltheart, M. 2002. 'Understanding minds and communicated meanings in schizophrenics', *Mind and Language*, 17: 68–104. As they write: "[I]t has been known for many years that patients with frontal lesions exhibit pervasive pragmatics deficits including (a) difficulty with formulating hints . . . (b) impaired ability to provide adequate information (e.g. when explaining a board game to a novice . . .) (c) failure to take account of a listener's interest when conversing . . . and (d) literal misinterpretations of sarcastic utterances . . . More recently it has been found that patients with frontal lesions also demonstrate general mind-reading deficits on story and cartoon versions of traditional theory-of-mind tasks and on a less traditional perspective-taking test of general mind-reading ability. Finally there is evidence from within the psychiatric literature that individuals who become poor pragmatic communicators later in life due to some form of late on-set neuropathology also turn out to be poor mind-readers. The primary example here . . . is schizophrenia" (76). However, it seems that none of these forms of cognitive impairment adversely affect sufferers handling of literal sentence meaning.

[34] See Sperber and Wilson, 2002.

computational processes of Fodor's modules. Indeed, the 'theory of mind module' shares several characteristics with the kind of thing Fodor has in mind for the (global) general intelligence: both will work on abductive, inference-to-the-best-explanation principles and both will require access to an indefinite range of information, including past and present perceptual information, knowledge of social behaviour and conventions, and assessments of intentional states. Finally, any account which places linguistic comprehension within a wider module dealing with communicative acts in general may face problems in explaining those cases where semantic abilities appear to remain in tact while other communicative abilities are lost. We can't hope to fully explore the modularity approach to the mind here, but we do reach at least a conditional claim: *if* we think that the hallmarks of modules include non-abductive processing and informational encapsulation, and we think that linguistic comprehension, up to and including semantic understanding, should be susceptible to a modular explanation, *then* we must reject B-style IBS accounts.[35]

(iii) *Are sentences or utterances the primary bearers of semantic content?*
It is certainly true that what interlocutors are concerned with, in the most part, are utterances. When we are interested in what we are being told, or how a linguistic act impinges on our cognitive life, what we want to deal with are utterances. However, the A-style theorist can cede all of this to her opponent while claiming that sentence meaning (as opposed to speaker meaning) remains a separate level of content (which perhaps is not even calculated in every communicative exchange, but which *could* be calculated in any case). This sentence level content will then have a distinct role to play, for instance it will give us a level of content which is not cancellable, that is, from which a speaker can rescind only at the cost of contradiction. This is in stark contrast to any pragmatically enriched or altered interpretation of an uttered sentence, which can be denied by a speaker without literal contradiction (though a charge of obfuscation may well be made). Furthermore, the sentence level content will be important for other purposes, like grasping the meaning of a written sentence abstracted from its context, or providing an analysis which reveals which arguments are formally valid and which go through only on the strength of background assumptions. So, we seem to have reasons to resist the B-theorists claim that utterances, not sentences, are the primary bearers of semantic content.

12.5 CONCLUSION

I have argued that, with respect to the three points of difference sketched in §3, it is the characteristics of the A-style approach which seem better suited to semantic

---

[35] The recognition of a tension between B-style IBS and Fodorian modularity does not necessarily conflict with our earlier recognition (n.5) that Fodor himself endorses IBS, for he ultimately holds that semantic content properly attaches only at the level of thought, rejecting the idea of a semantics for natural languages. See Fodor, 1989: 418–19; Fodor, 1998, ch. 6.

theorizing. If this is correct, then, if we want to develop an intention-based semantics for natural language, it seems that we should follow the weaker, A-style approach (here attributed to Grice) rather than assign any more substantive role to speaker intentions. Yet, if this is the case, a question might now emerge concerning the relation of IBS to other varieties of semantic theory; specifically, it is no longer clear to what degree IBS constitutes a genuine alternative to what we might think of as formal semantics (e.g. a truth-conditional approach, such as that instigated by Davidson). According to formal semantic theories the route to semantic content runs exclusively along syntactic trails. That is to say, all propositional or truth-conditional semantic content can be traced back to the syntactic level and it is delivered by formal operations over the syntactic representations of sentences.[36] Just as with an A-style IBS approach, the formal theorist will maintain that (formally described) sentences, rather than utterances, are the primary bearers of semantic content. She will also hold that the route to meaning runs (either exclusively or at least predominantly) via formal decoding processes and maintain that grasp of semantic content is a computational process (possibly underpinned by a discrete language faculty), rather than a richly inferential, abductive process. Following on from this, the formal theorist will maintain that linguistic meaning is a very different creature to ostensive or gestural meaning. So, with respect to characteristics like (i–iii) above, both A-style IBS and traditional formal approaches are entirely in agreement. Furthermore, it seems that a formal theorist could easily incorporate the kind of preconditional role for speaker intentions recognized by A-style IBS accounts. On a formal approach, just as on an A-style IBS account, it may be allowed that what makes a given physical item meaningful, and indeed what determines the precise meaning that it has, is its connection to the conventional, intentional practices of a community of speakers. One question we might need to go on to address, then, is: exactly what is the relationship between A-style IBS and formal semantic theories?

Finally, we might ask where this leaves B-style theories? If it is right to think that B-style IBS accounts are not plausible, does this mean that there is no role to be played by current speaker intentions in settling questions of meaning? The answer to this question, however, is clearly 'no'. For though I have argued for the retention of a level of propositional content divorced from current speaker intentions, and claimed this literal, sentence-level meaning is the proper subject of semantics, I certainly have not shown that appeals to current speaker intentions are unnecessary in an analysis of linguistic communicative acts. Indeed, far from it, hypothesizing about speaker intentions seems to be crucial to understanding our rich, informative, communicative behaviour. If this is right, it seems that though we might reject B-style intention-based *semantics* in favour of either an A-style or a formal approach, we may nevertheless recognize that B-style intention-based theories of *communication* may prove essential to a proper understanding of our

---

[36] For instance, the kinds of processes involved may be canonical derivations of truth conditions, see Larson and Segal, 1995.

linguistic behaviour as a whole: mind-reading may be the key to communication, even if it is not the key to linguistic meaning.[37]

REFERENCES

Avramides, A. (1997). Intention and Convention. In B. Hale and C. Wright (eds.) *Companion to the Philosophy of Language*. Oxford: Blackwell. 60–86.

_____ (1989). *Meaning and Mind: An Examination of a Gricean Account of Meaning*. Cambridge, MA: MIT Press.

Bach, K. (1987). On Communicative Intentions. *Mind and Language*, 2: 141–54.

_____ (1999). The Semantics–Pragmatics Distinction: What it is and Why it Matters. In K. Turner (ed.) *The Semantics/Pragmatics Interface from Different Points of View*. Elsevier Science. 65–83.

Borg, E. (2004a). Formal Semantics and Intentional States. *Analysis*, 64: 215–23.

_____ (2004b). *Minimal Semantics*. Oxford: Oxford University Press.

Carston, R. (1999). The Semantics/Pragmatics Distinction: A View from Relevance Theory. In K. Turner (ed.) *The Semantics/Pragmatics Interface from Different Points of View*. Elsevier Science: 85–125.

_____ (2002). *Thoughts and Utterances*. Oxford: Blackwell.

Fodor, J. (1983). *Modularity of Mind*. Cambridge, MA: MIT Press.

_____ (1989). Review of "Remnants of Meaning" by Stephen Schiffer. *Philosophy and Phenomenological Research*, 50: 409–23.

_____ (1998). *In Critical Condition*. Cambridge, MA: MIT Press.

Glüer, K. and P. Pagin. (2003). Meaning Theory and Autistic Speakers. *Mind and Language*, 18: 23–51.

Grice, P. (1989). *Studies in the Way of Words*. Cambridge, MA: Harvard University Press.

Kempson, R. (1986). Ambiguity and the Semantics–Pragmatics Distinction. In C. Travis (ed.) *Meaning and Interpretation*. Oxford: Blackwell. 77–104.

Larson, R. and G. Segal. (1995). *Knowledge of Meaning: An Introduction to Semantic Theory*. Cambridge, MA: MIT Press.

Laurence, S. (1996). A Chomskian Alternative to Convention-Based Semantics. *Mind*, 105: 269–301.

_____ (1998). Convention-Based Semantics and the Development of Language. In P. Carruthers and J. Boucher (eds.) *Language and Thought. Interdisciplinary Themes*. Cambridge: Cambridge University Press. 201–17.

Lewis, D. (1969). *Convention: A Philosophical Study*. Cambridge, MA: MIT Press.

[37] Thus S&W, 1986: 21 write: "[The Gricean definition of utterer's meaning] can be developed in two ways. Grice himself used it as the point of departure for a theory of 'meaning', trying to go from the analysis of 'speaker's meaning' towards such traditional semantic concerns as the analysis of 'sentence meaning' and 'word meaning' . . . [W]e doubt that very much can be achieved in this direction. However, Grice's analysis can also be used as a point of departure for an inferential model of communication, and this is how we propose to take it." Certainly, this quote undermines any categorization of relevance theory as a form of intention-based *semantics* as opposed to an intention-based theory of communication. However, we should also note that, despite their avowed interest in communication rather than semantics, relevance theorists do tend to draw some quite radical conclusions about philosophical semantics, claiming that the project of determining truth-conditional content on the basis of formal features of sentences alone is doomed to failure. Yet clearly *this* is a claim about sentence-meaning (the traditional subject of semantics) and not merely about communicated or speaker meaning.

Recanati, F. (2002). Does Linguistic Communication Rest on Inference? *Mind and Language*, 17: 105–126.

Saul, J. (2002). What is Said and Psychological Reality: Grice's Project and Relevance Theorists' Criticisms. *Linguistics and Philosophy*, 25: 347–372.

Schiffer, S. (1972). *Meaning*. Oxford: Oxford University Press.

Sperber, D. and D. Wilson. (1986). *Relevance: Communication and Cognition*. Oxford: Blackwell.

———— (2002). Pragmatics, Modularity and Mind-Reading. *Mind and Language*, 17: 3–23.

CHAPTER 13

....

PROPOSITIONAL CONTENT

....

STEPHEN SCHIFFER

To a first approximation, *propositional content* is whatever *that-clauses* contribute to what is ascribed in utterances of sentences such as

> Ralph believes *that Tony Curtis is alive.*
> Ralph said *that Tony Curtis is alive.*
> Ralph hopes *that Tony Curtis is alive.*
> Ralph desires *that Tony Curtis is alive.*
> 'Tony Curtis is alive' means *that Tony Curtis is alive.*

An account of propositional content is of foundational importance in the theory of linguistic and mental representation, but, as we are about to see, there are widely divergent opinions about what that account should be.

13.1 THE FACE-VALUE THEORY OF BELIEF REPORTS

....

It is not possible to theorize in any significant way about what that-clauses contribute to sentences such as those displayed independently of a consideration of the truth conditions of those sentences and of the contributions their other constituent expressions make to the determination of those truth conditions. For this reason, I shall begin by considering a theory of belief reports which I shall call the *face-value theory*. I call it that because it is a theory which appears well motivated when belief reports are taken at face value, and because the intuitive considerations which *prima facie* support the theory arguably give it the default status of a theory that must be defeated if it is not to be accepted, as is evidenced by the fact that those who have proposed alternative theories have motivated those alternatives by appeal to what they perceived to be problems with the face-value theory. Also, as we are about to appreciate, the face-value theory affords the primary way of motivating what may well be the currently dominant view—namely, that propositional contents are entities of a kind philosophers call *propositions*.

The face-value theory is about belief reports of the form

(1)   *A* believes that *S*,

and it makes two claims: first, that reports of this form are true just in case the referent of the '*A*' term stands in the belief relation to the thing to which the 'that *S*' term—the that-clause—refers, and second, that these that-clauses refer to propositions.

The first claim, which implies that (1) consists of a two-place transitive verb flanked by slots for two argument singular terms, is made plausible by its being the most straightforward way of accounting for the apparent validity of inferences like these:[1]

> Harold believes that there is life on Venus, and so does Fiona.
> So, there is something that they both believe—to wit, that there is life on Venus.
>
> Harold believes everything that Fiona says.
> Fiona says that there is life on Venus.
> So, Harold believes that there is life on Venus.
>
> Harold believes that there is life on Venus.
> That there is life on Venus is Fiona's theory.
> So, Harold believes Fiona's theory.
>
> Harold believes that there is life on Venus.
> That there is life on Venus is implausible.
> So, Harold believes something implausible—to wit, that there is life on Venus.

These inferences appear to be formally valid, and the most straightforward way of accounting for that formal validity is to represent them, respectively, as having the following logical forms:[2]

Fab & *Fcb*
$\therefore \exists x(Fax \ \& \ Fcx)$

$\forall x(Fax \rightarrow Gbx)$
Fab
$\therefore Gbc$

Fab

---

[1]   Here and elsewhere in this article I borrow wholesale from Schiffer (2003).

[2]   In what follows I represent 'Fiona's theory' as a logical singular term, rather than as a Russellian definite description; but nothing turns on this. The validity of the arguments would also be captured if that-clauses were represented as Russellian definite descriptions whose denotations were propositions.

$b = d$

$\therefore$ *Fad*

Fab

Gb

$\therefore$ $\exists x(Gx \,\&\, Fax)$

These are the forms the inferences enjoy if, but only if, (1) is composed of a two-place transitive verb flanked by slots for two singular argument terms.

The face-value theory's second claim, that that-clauses refer to propositions, gets its *prima facie* support in the following way. Consider

(2) Ramona believes that eating carrots improves eyesight.

If, as the face-value theory has it, the displayed occurrence of 'that eating carrots improves eyesight' is a singular term, then, obviously, its referent is *that eating carrots improves eyesight*, and, it would seem, we can straightway say the following things about this thing, *that eating carrots improves eyesight*, which is the referent of the that-clause singular term:

- *That eating carrots improves eyesight* is *abstract*: it has no spatial location, nor anything else that can make it a physical object.
- It is *mind- and language-independent* in two senses. First, its existence is independent of the existence of thinkers or speakers. *That eating carrots improves eyesight* was not brought into existence by anything anyone said or thought. Second, *that eating carrots improves eyesight* can be expressed by a sentence of just about any natural language but itself belongs to no language.
- It has a *truth condition*: *that eating carrots improves eyesight* is true iff eating carrots improves eyesight.
- It has its truth condition *essentially*: it is a *necessary truth* that *that eating carrots improves eyesight* is true iff eating carrots improves eyesight. The contrast here is with sentences. The *sentence* 'Eating carrots improves eyesight' is also true iff eating carrots improves eyesight, but that is a *contingent* truth that would have been otherwise had English speakers used 'carrots' the way they now use 'bicycles'.
- It has its truth condition *absolutely*, i. e., without relativization to anything. The contrast is again with sentences. The sentence 'Eating carrots improves eyesight' has its truth condition only *in English* or *among us*. There might be another language or population of speakers in which it means that camels snore; but *that eating carrots improves eyesight* has its truth condition everywhere and everywhen.

From all this we may conclude, by an obvious generalization, that things believed are what philosophers nowadays call *propositions*: abstract, mind- and language-independent entities that have truth conditions, and have their truth conditions both essentially and absolutely.

Such is the *prima facie* motivation for the face-value theory. We cannot properly assess it before we are told what account of propositions is to complement it, and on this there are competing views. We also cannot properly assess the face-value theory until we have taken account of the objections to it, and then taken account of the alternative theories that have been proposed in the light of those objections. But first we should look at the various ways in which the face-value theory might be completed.

13.2 PROPOSITIONS AND THE FACE-VALUE THEORY

Two philosophers may accept the face-value theory and therefore agree that the things we believe are propositions—abstract, mind- and language-independent entities that have truth conditions, and have their truth conditions both essentially and absolutely—but disagree about the further nature of those propositions. Here is a brief critical survey of some of the options.

13.2.1 Russellian Propositions and the Face-Value Theory

This conjunction—call it the *Russellian face-value theory*—is the theory that the face-value theory of belief reports is true and that the propositions to which that-clauses in belief reports refer are so-called *Russellian propositions*. The theory is suggested by J. S. Mill's theory of proper names;[3] it was explicitly held by Bertrand Russell around the time his landmark article "On Denoting" was published in 1905 (which is why the propositions in question are called Russellian); and it, or something close to it, was evidently also held by Gottlob Frege when he published his *Begriffsschrift* in 1879. Russellian propositions are structured entities whose basic components are the objects, properties, and relations our beliefs and assertions might be about. The simplest Russellian propositions are "singular propositions" like the proposition that Tony Curtis is alive, and it is common to represent such propositions as ordered pairs of the form $\langle x, \Phi \rangle$, where such a proposition is true iff x has the property Φ, false otherwise.[4] Thus, the Russellian proposition that Tony Curtis is alive may be represented by the ordered pair $\langle TC,$ the property of being alive$\rangle$, which, necessarily, is true iff Tony Curtis has the property of being alive, where Tony Curtis has the property of being alive iff Tony Curtis is alive. When the face-value theory is supplemented with the claim that the things we believe are Russellian propositions, then the resulting theory represents the logical form of

---

[3] Mill (1843).

[4] See Schiffer (2003: 18–19) for a technical discussion of the general form of Russellian propositions. Note that I said that for the Russellian the proposition that Tony Curtis is alive may be *represented* by the ordered pair $\langle TC,$ the property of being alive$\rangle$, not that the proposition *was* that ordered pair. It is merely a matter of arbitrary convention whether the Russellian represents the proposition that Tony Curtis is alive as $\langle TC,$ the property of being alive$\rangle$ rather than $\langle$the property of being alive, TC$\rangle$, so if it were claimed that the proposition was identical to an ordered pair, then the Russellian would have to say that it was indeterminate to which of two ordered pairs the proposition was identical. The most sympathetic statement of the Russellian position is that Russellian propositions are *sui generis* abstract objects that may be *represented* by ordered pairs of a certain kind.

(3) Ralph believes that Tony Curtis is alive

as

(4) B^2(Ralph, ⟨TC, the property of being alive⟩),

which is just a convenient way of revealing that 'believes' in (3) expresses the two-place belief relation, 'Ralph' refers to Ralph, 'that Tony Curtis is alive' refers to ⟨TC, the property of being alive⟩, and that, therefore, (3) is true just in case Ralph bears that belief relation to ⟨TC, the property of being alive⟩.

There are problems with the Russellian face-value theory of belief reports. These problems were first clearly stated in Frege's "On Sense and Reference," published in 1892, where he renounced the Russellian face-value theory he formerly held and supplanted it with a theory we will get to presently. Frege positions us to raise two objections to the Russellian face-value theorist's claim that (4) reveals (3)'s logical form.

(i) Suppose it transpires, for whatever reason, that the intended referent of 'Tony Curtis' never existed; there was no one actor who bore that name in any two films (the actor with that name in "Some Like It Hot" was a different actor who very closely resembled, in looks and Bronx accent, the actor of that name who starred in "The Boston Strangler," and so on). We would not thereby hold that (3) cannot possibly be true; we would think that even if Tony Curtis never existed, Ralph might nevertheless believe that Tony Curtis was alive. We might say

(5) Ralph believes that Tony Curtis is alive, but in fact there never was such an actor—the corrupt studio that produced the films that were supposed to star an actor named 'Tony Curtis' had a pool of look-alike actors whom they used interchangeably.

But apparently this is not something the Russellian face-value theorist can allow. According to her theory—at least as I have represented (4) as its account of (3)'s logical form[5]—if the proper name 'Tony Curtis' in (3) and (5) did not refer to a bearer of that name, then the occurrence of the that-clause in both (3) and (5) would fail to refer, and utterances like (3) and (5) could no more be true than could your utterance of 'Tony Curtis is alive' if the occurrence of 'Tony Curtis' in that sentence failed to refer to anyone. Call this *the problem of empty names*.[6]

(ii) Suppose that Ralph uses the name 'Tony Curtis' to refer to the film actor, that he uses the name 'Bernie Schwartz' to refer to a person he knew as a child in the Bronx but with whom he lost touch in adolescence, and that, entirely unbeknown to Ralph, one and the same person is the referent of both names in. Now, should Ralph insist

(6) I believe that Tony Curtis is alive, but I don't believe that Bernie Schwarz is alive [that little nogoodnik, Ralph thinks to himself, probably died of a drug overdose],

---

[5] The reason for the qualification my use of 'apparently' hints at is revealed just below, when I explain Russell's own reaction to the two Fregean objections in question.

[6] The problem can also arise for non-referring occurrences in that-clauses of other kinds of singular terms, but to keep things as simple as possible I shall present the Russellian's problem of empty singular terms only with respect to proper names.

we would without hesitation believe what he said—viz., that he believes that Tony Curtis is alive but does not believe that Bernie Schwartz is alive; we certainly would not regard him as making a contradictory statement. But, apparently, none of this can be true if the Russellian face-value theory is true. If, as I suggested, the theory implies that (4) gives the logical form of (3), then it cannot be true that Ralph does not realize that Bernie Schwartz is Tony Curtis, since he does realize that Tony Curtis is Tony Curtis, and the proposition that Bernie Schwartz is Tony Curtis is the very same proposition as the proposition that Tony Curtis is Tony Curtis. And, in the same way, the theory would apparently have it, Ralph's utterance of (6) cannot be true, since the statement he made in uttering it is the very same statement he would have made had he uttered the explicit contradiction

(7) I believe that Tony Curtis is alive, but I don't believe that Tony Curtis is alive.

There are three ways a Russellian face-value theorist might respond to the Fregean counterexamples without giving up her view that that-clauses refer to Russellian propositions, although, as we shall see, one of those ways does give up the face-value theory.

Bertrand Russell accepted the Fregean examples as counter-examples to the Russellian face-value theory *as presented above*, but he made a move that allowed him to continue to accept the Russellian face-value theory (i.e. the face-value theory together with the claim that that-clauses in belief reports refer to Russellian propositions). In my initial presentation of the Russellian face-value theory, I assumed that proper names like 'Tony Curtis' were genuine referring expressions, or *singular terms*, and I implicitly built that assumption into my initial characterization of the theory. If that-clauses refer to Russellian propositions and names are genuine singular terms, then names contribute nothing but their referents to the propositions referred to by the that-clauses in which those names occur and it follows, given the identity of Tony Curtis and Bernie Schwartz, that the proposition that Tony Curtis is alive = the proposition that Bernie Schwartz is alive. This makes clear that the truth of Ralph's utterance

(6) I believe that Tony Curtis is alive, but I don't believe that Bernie Schwarz is alive

is not inconsistent with the Russellian face-value theory *per se*, but only with that theory plus the claim that names are singular terms. Russell's strategy for dealing with the Fregean examples was to give up the claim that ordinary proper names were singular terms. In his groundbreaking paper "On Denoting," Russell had already argued that definite descriptions—expressions of the form 'the *F*'—are not singular terms but function so as to make sentences of the form 'The *F* is *G*' express general propositions of the form *there is something that is uniquely F and also G*. Russell now avoided the Fregean counter-examples by claiming that ordinary proper names functioned as disguised definite descriptions.

So suppose that in the ongoing examples we take 'Tony Curtis' and 'Bernie Schwartz' to mean the same, respectively, as 'the famous actor named "Tony Curtis"' and 'the kid I knew years ago in the Bronx named "Bernie Schwartz"'. Then Russell could respond to the two Fregean objections as follows. He could respond to the first objection by saying that

(3) Ralph believes that Tony Curtis is alive

means the same as

(8) Ralph believes that the famous actor named 'Tony Curtis' is alive,

and that it is no objection to the Russellian face-value theory that (8) may be true even if there was no famous actor named 'Tony Curtis'. And he could respond to the second objection by saying that (6) means the same as

(9) I believe that the famous actor named 'Tony Curtis' is alive, but I don't believe that the kid I knew years ago in the Bronx named 'Bernie Schwartz' is alive

and that it is no objection to the Russellian face-value theory that (9) may be true.[7]

Most philosophers believe that Saul Kripke demolished Russell's description theory of names in his enormously influential book *Naming and Necessity*. Kripke raised three objections.

(a) A consequence of Russell's theory is that the reference of a name n as used by a speaker S is always determined by some definite description S associates with n. Kripke offered the following counterexample to this consequence. The name 'Kurt Gödel' may be a name of Kurt Gödel in Ralph's idiolect even though the only definite description Ralph associates with the name is 'the person who proved the incompleteness of arithmetic'. Now suppose that it transpires that the man who was Albert Einstein's friend and whom everyone called 'Kurt Gödel' had stolen the proof from a certain Schmidt and published it under his own name. Then the just-mentioned consequence of Russell's theory implies that the referent of 'Kurt Gödel', as Ralph uses that name, must be Schmidt, the person who in fact proved the incompleteness of arithmetic. Yet, Kripke claims, we have a clear intuition that the name 'Kurt Gödel' in Ralph's idiolect would still refer to Kurt Gödel, even though Kurt Gödel does not satisfy the only description Ralph associates with the name.

(b) A second consequence of Russell's description theory of names is that n cannot be a name of anything for a speaker S if S does not associate any definite description with n that is supposed by S to apply to the bearer of n. Kripke offered counter-examples to that consequence, too. He pointed out, for example, that a person might use the name 'Richard Feynman' as a name of the famous physicist Richard Feynman even though all she knows about Feynman is that he was a famous theoretical physicist who taught at Cal Tech, and thus associates no definite description at all with the name that is capable of fixing the name's reference.

(c) A third consequence of Russell's theory (or at least a consequence of it given Russell's own view of the truth conditions of sentences of the form 'The F is G') is that if n means the same as 'the F' for S, then the proposition expressed by 'n is

---

[7] Russell also claimed—as he had to in order to avoid the Fregean objections—that typical uses of pronouns and demonstratives also functioned as disguised definite descriptions. See e.g. Russell (1910a).

G' will be true in an arbitrary possible world w just in case in w something is both uniquely F and also G, regardless of whether the F in w is the thing n names in the actual world. For example, suppose that for Jones 'Kurt Gödel' means the same as 'the person who proved the incompleteness of arithmetic', then the proposition that Kurt Gödel died in Princeton would be true in a possible world in which Gödel died somewhere other than Princeton but in which Britney Spears was the person who proved the incompleteness of arithmetic and she died in Princeton. Kripke argued persuasively—some would say he *proved*—that this gets the truth conditions of the propositions expressed by sentences containing names wrong: the proposition that Kurt Gödel died in Princeton is true in any possible world w only if the person who is actually Kurt Gödel died in Princeton in w, regardless of whether or not he proved the incompleteness of arithmetic in w. According to Kripke, proper names are what he called *rigid designators*: they designate the thing they actually designate in every possible world in which they designate anything. What this means is that if a name n refers to x in the actual world, then for any possible world w, the proposition expressed by a sentence S containing n, $S(n)$, is true iff in w x satisfies the condition expressed by $S()$. For example, since 'Kurt Gödel' rigidly designates a certain man, the proposition expressed by 'Kurt Gödel was a hockey player' is true in an arbitrary world just in case in that world the man whose name in the actual world was 'Kurt Gödel' is a hockey player in that world, no matter whether in that world some other person proved the incompleteness of arithmetic. But if Russell's description theory of names were correct, names would not be rigid designators, since Russell's account has the referent of a name in a possible world w be whatever satisfies the definite description that actually fixes the name's reference, and in the typical case that description can be satisfied by different things in different possible worlds. For example, as already noted, if the proposition expressed by 'Kurt Gödel died in Princeton' were the proposition that the person who proved the incompleteness of arithmetic died in Princeton, then in a possible world in which Britney Spears was the person who proved the incompleteness of arithmetic, 'Kurt Gödel', as we use it in the actual world, would refer in that world to Britney Spears, and the proposition expressed by 'Kurt Gödel died in Princeton' would be true in that world only if in that world Britney Spears died in Princeton.

None of these objections is conclusive as stated. The first two counterexamples ignore the role that might be played by meta-linguistic descriptions like 'The person called "Kurt Gödel" by those from whom I acquired that name', and there are versions of the description theory of names according to which names are rigid designators. I do not, however, believe that any of these responses to Kripke can in the end make any sort of description theory of names plausible. In any case, it is not possible to discuss these responses in this article.[8]

The second way of responding to the Fregean examples without giving up the Russellian face-value theory is a response advanced by such contemporary

---

[8] See e.g. Loar (1976) and Stanley (1997).

theorists as David Kaplan, Nathan Salmon, Scott Soames, and David Braun.[9] These theorists offer a two-pronged argument to show that the Fregean examples are not counterexamples. The first prong argues that the case for the Russellian face-value theory is made compelling by Saul Kripke's work on proper names and natural kind terms, Hilary Putnam's work on natural kind terms, and David Kaplan's work on demonstratives.[10] The second prong argues that the force of the Fregean examples can be explained away. Both prongs have problems. The first prong relies mostly on two claims that are taken to be established: that the description theory of names is false and that names typically function as rigid designators.[11] These two claims do indeed seem to be true, but they fall very short of establishing the Russellian face-value theory; they are easily accommodated by any of the other theories we are about to consider. The second prong is equally problematic. The theorists in question disagree among themselves as to how best to explain away our Fregean intuitions, and there is I believe a systematic objection to all their attempts based on a difficulty they encounter in attempting to explain how one can rationally believe and disbelieve one and the same proposition. According to the Russellian face-value theorist who recognizes that proper names are singular terms, it is true (pretending the Superman story to be fact) that Lois Lane rationally believes both that Superman flies and that Superman does not fly. This is so because she rationally believes both that Superman flies and that Clark Kent does not fly, and, since Clark Kent = Superman, it follows for this theorist that the proposition that Superman flies = the proposition that Clark Kent flies. The theorist explains Lois's rationality in believing and disbelieving that Superman flies by appeal, in effect, to the Fregean notion of modes of presentation: Lois believes Superman to fly when she thinks of him under a mode of presentation which identifies him as a superhero who goes about in a caped spandex outfit and she believes Superman not to fly when she thinks of him under a mode of presentation which identifies him as a nerdy bespectacled newspaper reporter, and this is possible because she does not realize that the two modes of presentation are modes of presentation of the same person.

The problem is that this explanation does not generalize to cover the theory's commitment to its being the case that *you*, who are in the know about Superman/Clark Kent, rationally believe both that Lois realizes that Superman is Superman and that Lois does not realize that Superman is Superman. You rationally believe this because you rationally believe both that Lois realizes that Superman is Superman and that Lois does not realize that Clark Kent is Superman, and, for the theorist in question, the proposition that Superman is Superman = the proposition that Clark Kent is Superman. But we cannot explain your rationally believing and disbelieving the same proposition by appeal to the fact that you have two modes of presentation of Superman/Clark Kent which you fail to realize are modes of

---

[9] Kaplan (1978, 1989); Salmon (1986, 1989, 1995, forthcoming); Soames (2002); and Braun (1998).

[10] Kripke (1980); Putnam (1975a); and Kaplan (1978, 1989).

[11] These theorists would make the same claim, *mutatis mutandis*, about other ostensible singular terms such as pronouns and (at least) single-word demonstratives ('this', 'that', etc.), but to keep things simple, I am restricting attention to proper names.

presentation of the same person. You, being completely in the know, do not have two such modes of presentation. Anyway, this is what I take to be the core of one compelling objection to the Russellian face-value theory on the assumption that names are singular terms.[12]

The third way a Russellian face-value theorist might respond to the Fregean counterexamples without giving up her view that that-clauses refer to Russellian propositions entails accepting that the counterexamples are counterexamples and giving up the face-value theory. I allude to what I have elsewhere called the *hidden-indexical theory of belief reports*.[13] This is probably the only sane option for a theorist who wants an account of the semantics of

(1) *A* believes that *S*

according to which substitution instances of 'that *S*' refer to Russellian propositions and Fregean intuitions about the truth-values of belief reports are respected, so that, for example, nothing prevents

(6) I believe that Tony Curtis is alive, but I don't believe that Bernie Schwarz is alive

from being true, notwithstanding that the proposition that Tony Curtis is alive = the proposition that Bernie Schwarz is alive. The hidden-indexical theory holds, first, that that-clauses in sentences of form (1) refer to Russellian propositions, and, second, that a literal utterance of (1) states that

(10) For some mode of presentation *m* of the proposition that *S*, *A* believes that *S* under *m* and *m* is of type Ψ^*

where Ψ^* is some contextually determined type of mode of presentation to which implicit reference is made in the utterance of (1). For example, in uttering 'Lois believes that Superman flies', one might mean that Lois believes ⟨Superman, the property of being a thing that flies⟩ under a mode of presentation which identifies Superman as a superhero. I call this theory the *hidden*-indexical theory because the reference to the contextually determined type of mode of presentation is not carried by any expression in (1), and I call it the hidden-*indexical* theory because the implicit reference to a type of mode of presentation is context dependent, potentially varying from one context of utterance to another.

While the hidden-indexical theory may be the best way for the proponent of Russellian propositions to go, it has problems. Here are four of them.

First, the theory has the same problem of empty names that confronts the Russellian face-value theory. Intuitively,

(5) Ralph believes that Tony Curtis is alive, but in fact there never was such an actor—the corrupt studio that produced the films that were supposed to star

---

[12] See Schiffer (forthcoming) and the replies of Braun (forthcoming) and Salmon (forthcoming).

[13] I first proposed a version of this theory in Schiffer (1977). A slightly different version was independently presented in Crimmins and Perry (1989) and more fully elaborated in Crimmins (1992). I am critical of the theory in Schiffer (1992) and, most recently and most completely, in Schiffer (2003: 39–42). My present presentation of the theory is an abbreviated version of what I say in Schiffer (2003).

an actor named 'Tony Curtis' had a pool of look-alike actors whom they used interchangeably

may be true, but it cannot be true if the hidden-indexical theory is correct, since (given that names are referring expressions) if Tony Curtis did not exist, then the that-clause in (5) would fail to refer to any proposition, and thus (5) would express no complete proposition.

Second, the theory is committed to an implausible error theory: it must hold that ordinary speakers are in error about what they are stating when they make belief reports. The sentence 'It's raining' does have a hidden-indexical semantics, and, as one would expect, a speaker uttering 'It's raining' knows that she is stating that it is raining at such-and-such place, where the place is determined by her referential intentions. No one who utters 'It's raining' would suppose that he simply means that it is raining. Yet one uttering, say, 'I believe that $1^2 + 1^2 = 4$' is in no way aware of stating *that for some m, he believes that $1^2 + 1^2 = 4$ under m and m is of type Ψ^**. Yet that is what the speaker would mean if the hidden-indexical theory were correct. One would think that if in uttering a sentence a speaker were implicitly referring to a thing and saying something about it, she would be aware of that.

Third, the theory makes it difficult to account for the validity of inferences such as

> Harold believes everything that Fiona says.
> Fiona says that there is life on Venus.
> So, Harold believes that there is life on Venus.

Should we read the first premise as saying (11) or (12)?

(11) For any p and any m, if Fiona says p under m, then Harold believes p under m.
(12) For any p, if Fiona says p under some m, then Harold believes p under some m'.

I shall leave it to the reader to see that either reading makes for big problems in accounting for the validity of the displayed inference.[14]

Finally, the theory has a problem in accounting for the logical form of sentences of form

(1) *A believes that S.*

Should the hidden-indexical theory agree with the face-value theory that 'believes' in (1) expresses a *two*-place relation that holds between a believer and a proposition, or should it disagree with the face-value theory and maintain that 'believes' in (1) expresses a *three*-place relation that holds among a believer, a proposition, and a mode of presentation under which the believer believes the proposition? Either way there is a problem. If it is claimed that 'believes' expresses the three-place relation, then 'μ', construed as a name of a mode of presentation in

(13) Ralph believes that Fido is a dog under μ,

---

[14] See Schiffer (2003: 41–2) and Salmon (1995).

would occur as an argument of the three-place belief relation. But it does not; it occurs as part of the adverbial phrase 'under μ', and thereby behaves semantically exactly like 'under the mistletoe' in

(14) Carmelina kissed Ralph under the mistletoe,

and no one supposes that kissing is a three-place relation holding among kissers, kissees, and things under which kissers kiss kissees.[15] If, on the other hand, the hidden-indexical theory claims that 'believes' is, as it appears to be, a genuinely two-place relational predicate, and that therefore 'μ' merely occurs as part of the adverbial phrase 'under μ', then it becomes very difficult to explain why a literal utterance of

(15) Ralph believes that Fido is a dog

must mean that

(16) For some m, Ralph believes $\langle$Fido, doghood$\rangle$ under m and m is of type Ψ^*

where Ψ^* is some contextually determined type of mode of presentation. If 'believes' in (15) merely expresses the two-place belief relation, then the compositional determination of (15)'s meaning should allow one simply to state, without further adverbial embellishment about modes of presentation, that Ralph believes the proposition that Fido is a dog.

13.2.2 Fregean Propositions and the Face-Value Theory

Frege's response to the objections he produced to the Russellian face-value theory led him to the view that the propositions we believe and assert are structured propositions whose basic components are not the objects and properties our beliefs and assertions may be about but are rather what he called *modes of presentation* of those objects and properties. For Frege, the proposition that Tony Curtis is an actor may be represented as the order pair $\langle m_{tc}, m_A \rangle$, where m_{tc} is a mode of presentation of Tony Curtis and m_A is a mode of presentation of the property of being an actor, and where $\langle m_{tc}, m_A \rangle$ is true in an arbitrary possible world w just in case in w there is a thing x and property Φ such that m_{tc} is a mode of presentation of x, m_A is a mode of presentation of Φ, and x instantiates Φ.[16] This allows Frege to say that the name

---

[15] See the test for whether a phrase is adverbial in Schiffer (1992: 518–19). What if the hidden-indexical theorist concedes the adverbial status of 'under μ' in (13) but claims that 'believes' in 'A believes that S' expresses a three-place relation $B^3(x, p, m)$ which is instantiated just in case x believes p under m? (Eliza Block raised this response in conversation.) Then the hidden-indexical theorist could claim that the proposition expressed in uttering (15) (see below in the text) is not (16), but is rather the conceptually equivalent proposition *that $\exists m[B^*(Ralph, \langle Fido, doghood \rangle, m)$ & m is of type $\Psi^*]$.* The problem with this response is that it is hard to see how it avoids inconsistency. If 'believes' in 'A believes p' is a three-place relational predicate, then so must it also be in 'A believes p under m'. But the mooted response is motivated by the concession that 'believes' in the latter sentence form is a two-place relational predicate. It would seem, then, that the 'believes' in 'A believes p' is three-place only if it is also three-place in 'A believes p under m', and that returns us to the objection in the text.

[16] More exactly, for any possible world w, a Fregean proposition $\langle m, m' \rangle$ is

'Bernie Schwartz' is associated with a different mode of presentation m_{bc} of Tony Curtis, so that the proposition that Bernie Schwartz is an actor may be represented as the distinct proposition $\langle m_{bc}, m_A \rangle$. In this way—and this was for Frege the main *raison d'être* of Fregean propositions—nothing prevents

(6) I believe that Tony Curtis is alive, but I don't believe that Bernie Schwarz is alive

from being true. So that is how Frege avoids the problem that reports like (6) raise for the Russellian face-value theorist. And he can avoid the problem of empty names presented by the fact that a belief report may be true even though its that-clause contains a name which has no bearer by claiming that the mode of presentation to which the occurrence of the name refers need not be a mode of presentation of anything, that is, that there need not be anything of which that mode of presentation is a mode of presentation.

There are problems with the Fregean face-value theory—the theory which claims both that the face-value theory is correct and that the propositions we believe are Fregean propositions. One problem is that the Fregean theory is incomplete absent an account of what modes of presentation are supposed to be.[17] Although Frege was appealing to our pre-theoretic notion of a thing's appearing to us, or of our thinking of a thing, in a certain way, that pre-theoretic notion is not able to do all that Frege needs it to do. Frege needs modes of presentation for every kind of thing we might think about—numbers, properties, abstract entities like nations and languages, etc.—and he needs things that can account for how a person may believe that Tony Curtis is an actor while disbelieving that Bernie Schwartz is an actor, notwithstanding that Tony Curtis is Bernie Schwartz; he needs things that can be available as referents of singular terms in that-clauses even when they present nothing (as they must if Fregeans are to avoid a problem of empty names); and he needs things that will not preclude names from being rigid designators of their bearers. There is disagreement among Fregeans about what modes of presentation are, and there is not to date an unproblematic account of what exactly Fregean propositions are supposed to be.

A second problem is that the Fregean face-value theory is very implausible, even if Fregean propositions are the objects of belief. For consider this belief report:

(17) Most British citizens believe that Osama Bin Laden is alive and hiding in the mountains of Afghanistan.

---

true in *w* iff in *w*: there is a thing *x* and property Φ such that *m* is a mop of *x* & *m'* is a mop of Φ & *x* instantiates Φ;

false in *w* iff in *w*: there is a thing *x* and property Φ such that *m* is a mop of *x* & *m'* is a mop of Φ & *x* does not instantiate Φ; and

neither true nor false in *w* iff in *w*: it is not the case that there is a thing *x* and property Φ such that *m* is a mop of *x* & *m'* is a mop of Φ.

On this account, an utterance of a name will "rigidly designate" its referent just in case the mode of presentation expressed by the utterance of the name is a mode of presentation of the same thing in every possible world in which it is a mode of presentation of anything.

[17] The same is of course true of attempts, such as those considered above, to incorporate "modes of presentation" into Russellian theories.

We have no trouble understanding (17), and we have no trouble in supposing it might be true; but it is very unlikely that it is true if the that-clause in (17) refers to a Fregean proposition, for whatever modes of presentation are taken to be, it is extremely unlikely that there are modes of presentation of Bin Laden, Afghanistan, the hiding relation, being alive, etc. such that most British citizens think of those things under precisely those modes of presentation. Yet if the Fregean face-value theory were true, then there would have to be such modes of presentation in order for (17) to be true. In fact, it should be obvious on reflection that, contrary to what the Fregean face-value theory entails, we can understand true belief reports without having to know exactly how the believer thinks of the objects and properties her belief is about.

The foregoing objection to the Fregean face-value theory is evidently decisive, but a proponent of Fregean propositions might hang onto them by rejecting that part of the face-value theory which claims that that-clauses in belief reports always refer to that-clauses. The idea would be that the meaning of a belief report permits but does not require that-clauses to refer to Fregean propositions. In uttering

(18) Ralph believes that Fido is a dog

it *may* be that there are modes of presentation m_F and m_D of Fido and doghood, respectively, such that the speaker is referring to the Fregean proposition $\langle m_F, m_D \rangle$ by her utterance of 'that Fido is a dog', but, the idea continues, it is more likely that what would be asserted in an utterance of (18) would either be that

(19) There are modes of presentation m and m' such that m is a mode of present-ation of Fido, m' is a mode of presentation of doghood, and Ralph believes $\langle m, m' \rangle$,

or, more plausibly, that

(20) There are modes of presentation m and m' such that m is a mode of presenta-tion of type Ψ of Fido, m' is a mode of presentation of type Ψ' of doghood, and Ralph believes $\langle m, m' \rangle$,

where Ψ and Ψ' are contextually determined types of modes of presentation.[18]

The attempt to hang onto Fregean propositions by revising the face-value theory is unpromising. Among its problems are these two. First, none of the inferences used to motivate the face-value theory p. 268 above) is valid when, as in (19) and (20), the that-clauses are quantified into and thus not occurring as singular terms (I leave the demonstration of this to the reader). Second, if the Fregean proposal at issue were correct, it should apply to

(21) Ralph said that Fido is a dog,

as well as to

---

[18] (20) is more promising for the Fregean than (19), because if what is asserted by an utterance of (1) is a proposition in the style of (19), then the Fregean cannot account for the truth of, say, 'Lois believes that Superman flies but does not believe that Clark Kent flies'. See Forbes (1990).

(18) Ralph believes that Fido is a dog;

but it is very implausible that what is asserted in an utterance of (21) can be that

(22) There are modes of presentation *m* and *m'* such that *m* is a mode of presentation of Fido, *m'* is a mode of presentation of doghood, and Ralph said ⟨*m*, *m'*⟩.

This is implausible because it is extremely unlikely that Ralph, in his utterance of 'Fido is a dog', will have said any such Fregean proposition. If he did mean some such proposition, then there would be a specification of what he said that is other than 'that Fido is a dog' and that refers to a Fregean proposition. But it is clear that there need be no such alternative specification of what he said.[19]

13.2.3 Propositions as Sets of Possible Worlds and the Face-Value Theory

Russellian and Fregean propositions are *structured* entities whose basic components are not themselves propositions, Russellians and Fregeans differing on what they take those basic components to be. There are also conceptions of propositions according to which the propositions we believe are unstructured. According to one such view, whose chief proponent is Robert Stalnaker,[20] propositions are sets of possible worlds. For example, on this view the proposition that snow is white is the set of possible words in which snow is white. The view allows for subtleties about how contextual factors may operate in communication to delimit the possible worlds to be considered in individuating a particular proposition. But the view has problems, the main one being that it is forced to say that there is just one necessarily true proposition, since any necessarily true proposition, being true in every possible world, must be identified with the set of all possible worlds. This is a problem because a person may believe the necessarily true proposition that dogs are dogs without also believing the necessarily true proposition that any planar map can be colored using at most four colors in such a way that no two adjacent areas are of the same color. Stalnaker has been resourceful in his efforts to ameliorate this highly counter-intuitive result,[21] but one may question whether he has been resourceful enough.

13.2.4 Pleonastic Propositions and the Face-Value Theory

This is the theory I advance in *The Things We Mean*, so I shall be very brief. *Pleonastic entities* are entities whose existence is entailed by what I call *something-from-nothing transformations*. These are conceptually valid inferences that take one from a statement in which no reference is made to a thing of a certain kind to a statement in

---

[19] This objection and its wording are borrowed from Schiffer (1992: 506, fn. 10).
[20] Stalnaker (1984).   [21] Stalnaker (1987).

which there is a reference to a thing of that kind. The property of being a dog, for example, is a pleonastic entity. From the statement

Lassie is a dog,

whose only singular term is 'Lassie', we can validly infer its pleonastic equivalent

Lassie has the property of being a dog,

which contains the new singular term 'the property of being a dog', whose referent is the property of being a dog. I call the entities these transformations introduce *pleonastic* entities because something-from-nothing transformations often take one from a statement to a pleonastic equivalent of it. Propositions, the things to which that-clauses refer, are also pleonastic entities. They have their something-from-nothing transformations, such as the one that takes us from

Lassie is a dog,

whose only singular term continues to be Lassie, to another of its pleonastic equivalents,

That Lassie is a dog is true

(more colloquially, 'It is true that Lassie is a dog'), which contains the singular term 'that Lassie is a dog', whose referent is the proposition that Lassie is a dog. Owing to the pleonastic nature of the propositions we believe and assert, the relation between a that-clause in a propositional-attitude report and the pleonastic proposition to which it refers is importantly different from the usual relation between singular terms and their referents: the contextual factors which determine the reference of a that-clause also individuate it in a way that allows the pleonastic proposition to which the that-clause refers to be both fine-grained and unstructured. Pleonastic propositions are individuated in part by what it takes to believe them, so that, say, the that-clauses in utterances of 'Ralph believes that Tony Curtis is alive' and 'Ralph does not believe that Bernie Schwartz is alive' may refer to propositions with the same possible-worlds conditions (both propositions will be true in an arbitrary possible world just in case Tony Curtis, i.e. Bernie Schwartz, is alive in that world) but differ because, e.g., in order to believe the proposition to which the utterance of 'that Tony Curtis is alive' refers, one must think of Tony Curtis as a movie actor. It is not for me to assess whether the face-value theory of belief reports is viable when combined with the further claim that the referents of that-clauses are pleonastic propositions.

13.3 OBJECTIONS TO THE FACE-VALUE THEORY

While several alternatives to the face-value theory have been proposed (see Section 13.4), there are surprisingly few published objections to it *per se* (although there are plenty of objections to packages of the face-value theory and this, that, or the other conception of propositions). At any rate, I am aware of only two objections to the theory that do not presuppose its being conjoined with some particular conception of propositions.

Any objection to either the existence of propositions or to their deployment in the theory of linguistic and mental representation is *eo ipso* an objection to the face-value theory, at least on the assumption that there are true reports.[22] Donald Davidson objected to the deployment:

Paradoxically, the one thing meanings [= abstract entities such as propositions] do not seem to do is oil the wheels of a theory of meaning—at least as long as we require of such a theory that it non-trivially give the meaning of every sentence in the language. My objection to meanings is not that they are abstract or that their identity conditions are obscure, but that they have no demonstrated use.[23]

But Davidson was assuming that there could be no compositional theory of propositions, and it has become well known since Davidson's article was originally published in 1967 that there are various ways of getting such propositions. Whether or not a proposition-deploying theory of meaning needs compositionally constructed propositions is, however, another question.[24]

Other prominent philosophers object to the existence of propositions. Some of these philosophers—such as Nelson Goodman, Paul Benacerraf, and Hartry Field[25]—object to all abstract objects, but they have no quarrel with propositions other than that they are abstract objects. Goodman seems simply to find abstract objects too mysterious to play any serious explanatory role, and, like many others, he can see no reason to believe in anything that cannot play an explanatory role. Benacerraf and Field worry about the possibility of knowledge and reliable beliefs about abstract objects, which ought to be possible if abstract objects exist. Willard Quine has no problem with abstract objects *per se*, provided they enjoy reasonably clear criteria of individuation—that is, criteria for determining when abstract objects x and y are the same or different.[26] So Quine tolerates sets, since set x = set y iff x and y have the same members. But propositions, he argues, have no clear criteria of individuation, and this because in order to have a criterion for saying whether two

---

[22] A theorist might allow that the face-value theory gives the correct semantics of belief reports while denying that there are any propositions for that-clauses to refer to. This theorist will therefore deny that there are any true that-clause-containing propositional-attitude reports, but she might try to sugar-coat this highly counter-intuitive consequence with a so-called fictionalist account of propositional-attitude reports, according to which a belief report may be true in the "belief story" even though no such report is literally true. See e.g. Crimmins (1998). These efforts are inspired by Hartry Field's ((1980) and (1989)) fictionalist account of numbers, according to which numerical sentences like '1 + 1 = 2' cannot be true, because numerals purport to be names of numbers and numbers do not exist, yet such sentences may be "true in the fiction of arithmetic." It will be a working hypothesis of this paper that there are at least some true propositional-attitude reports. After all, what is the point of trying to advance a fictionalist account of propositional-attitude reports if it is impossible for one to state anything?

[23] Davidson (1984a: 20–1).   [24] See Schiffer (2003: chs. 3 and 4).
[25] Goodman (1978); Benacerraf (1973); Field (1989).   [26] See e.g. Quine (1970).

sentences express the same or different propositions there would have to be a viable analytic/synthetic distinction, and, Quine argues, there can be no such distinction.

None of these objections to propositions is compelling. Goodman's "objection" is really just an expression of a distaste for abstract entities, and offers no *reason* for disbelieving in propositions or any other abstract entities. Benacerraf's objection presupposes an untenable causal theory of knowledge,[27] and Field's claim that there can be no accounting for reliable beliefs about abstract entities fails to take into account the best ways of accounting for such reliability.[28] Quine's argument from criteria of individuation is problematic in a few ways, but the principal way is its assumption that *F*s exist only if there are criteria for individuating *F*s, i.e. criteria that enable us to know whether *F*s *x* and *y* are the same or different. If this really were a requirement on the existence of *F*s, we should have to conclude that there are no restaurants: Le Poisson Rance, owned by Jean-Paul Gras, is located at 33 Waverly Place. Gras closes that restaurant, opens a restaurant with the same chef and menu at 14 Bleecker Street, and calls it Chez Gras. Is Chez Gras the same restaurant as Le Poisson Rance? We lack criteria of individuation for restaurants that enable us to give a determinate answer.[29] Propositions are merely in the same boat as restaurants.

There is an interesting objection to the face-value theory that has nothing to do with any problems about the existence of propositions.[30] According to the face-value theory, the that-clause in

(23) Jane believes that Slovenia will win the World Cup

refers to the proposition that Slovenia will win the World Cup, and this consequence seems confirmed by the fact that

(24) Jane believes the proposition that Slovenia will win the World Cup

is pleonastically equivalent to (23). After all, if the face-value theory is correct, then instances of 'that *S*' and 'the proposition that *S*' refer to the same proposition, so, it would seem, they ought to be intersubstitutable *salva veritate*. Now, if the face-value theory of belief reports is correct, then we should expect no less of the face-value theory of other propositional-attitude reports, such as, say, those of the form

(25) *A* hopes that *S*.

And if the face-value theory of (25) is true, then, reflecting back on (23) and (24), it would seem that we should expect (25) to be pleonastically equivalent to

(26) *A* hopes the proposition that *S*.

The trouble is, they clearly are not equivalent. Not only is

(27) Jane hopes that Slovenia will win the World Cup

---

[27] See Field (1989).

[28] See e.g. Hale and Wright (1992), and Schiffer (2003: ch. 2).

[29] I believe I got the restaurant example from Richard Grandy.

[30] So far as I am aware, the problem was first raised in Prior (1971: ch. 2). See also Bach (1997), Schiffer (2003: 92–5), and King (2002).

not equivalent to

(28) Jane hopes the proposition that Slovenia will win the World Cup;

(28) is not even grammatical![31] In short, if the face-value theory of (27) is correct, then its that-clause refers to the proposition that Slovenia will win the World Cup. But if it does, then should we not be able to replace *salva veritate* its that-clause with the co-referential singular term 'the proposition that Slovenian will win the World Cup'? Yet that, as the ungrammatical (28) reveals, is precisely what we cannot do.

It is not an option to maintain the face-value theory of belief reports while denying the face-value theory of hope reports. One reason (there are others) is that it is difficult to see how we can explain why a necessary condition for one's hoping that S is that one not believe that S if that-clauses in belief reports, but not in hope reports, referred to propositions. It would seem that if one is to hold the face-value theory of belief reports, then one will have to hold the face-value theory of hope reports and therefore maintain that the that-clauses in hope reports refer to propositions, even though 'the proposition that S' cannot be substituted for them. But can it plausibly be maintained that that-clauses in hope reports refer to propositions despite this failure of substitutivity? A definite answer may not now be possible, but at least three things should incline us to answer yes.[32] First, we cannot conclude that because the only semantic role of a singular term t in an utterance is to refer to x, that we can replace t *salva veritate* with any other singular term that also refers to x. As Paul Horwich pointed out to me (in conversation), instances of apposition provide clear examples where such substitutivity fails. For example, even if Pavarotti is the greatest tenor, we still cannot substitute 'the greatest tenor' *salva veritate* for Pavarotti in

(29) The Italian singer Pavarotti never sings Wagner

since

(30) The Italian singer the greatest tenor never sings Wagner

is not well formed. Second, if the substitutitivity facts in play showed that that-clauses in hope reports do not refer to propositions, then they also show that they do not refer to anything. For example,

(31) Jane hopes the sentence that Slovenian will win the World Cup

is as ungrammatical as (28). But it is unclear how one can account for the logical form of hope reports if their that-clauses cannot function as singular terms. Third, the case for taking that-clauses in belief reports to be singular terms is pretty compelling, as is the claim that whatever is going on with that-clauses in belief reports must also be going on with them in other propositional-attitude reports.

---

[31] 'Predicts', 'guesses', and other propositional-attitude verbs also produce ungrammaticality in the same way. In some cases—e.g. 'Jane fears/expects that Slovenia will win the World Cup'—grammaticality is preserved, but the meaning is drastically changed.
[32] Further considerations are offered in Schiffer (2003: 95).

Still, one cannot be confident that any face-value theory is correct absent a plausible account of why substitutivity fails when it does. If the that-clause in (27) refers to the proposition that Slovenian will win the World Cup, then why does not 'the proposition that Slovenian will win the World Cup' in (28) also refer to that proposition? We cannot be confident of what is going on with that-clauses until we can account for the asymmetry between belief and hope reports, and I am not aware of any plausible account of it.

13.4 NON-PROPOSITIONALIST ALTERNATIVES TO THE FACE-VALUE THEORY

In Section 13.1, we saw how proponents of Russellian and Fregean propositions might be motivated to seek alternatives to the face-value theory of belief reports. In this section I consider proposed alternatives that do not entail that believing is a relation to propositions or involve any other commitment to propositions. These alternatives fall into two classes: those which entail that believing is not a relation to things of any kind, and thus that that-clauses never function as singular terms (*non-relational accounts of believing*), and those which entail that believing is a relation to things other than propositions and that that-clauses may, and typically do, occur as referring to things of that kind (*non-propositional relational accounts of believing*).

13.4.1 Non-Relational Accounts of Believing

One already-noticed reason for supposing that 'believes' in belief reports expresses a relation between believers and the things they believe is the validity of inferences like

> Harold believes that there is life on Venus, and so does Fiona.
> So, there is something that they both believe—to wit, that there is life on Venus.

For how are we to read the quantification in the conclusion other than as saying that there *is* some *thing* that Harold and Fiona both believe? Well, it might be replied, in the same way we are to read the quantification in 'There are many things that don't exist—the Loch Ness Monster, God, Sherlock Holmes.'[33] The question is whether the quantification in the conclusion of the displayed inference ('there is something that they both believe') is, to use some jargon, *objectual* or *non-objectual*. A quantification of the form 'There is something that is *F*' is objectual if it entails that there *exists* some thing that is *F*, non-objectual if it does not have that entailment. One form of non-objectual quantification is so-called *substitutional quantification* wherein, for example, 'John is something' is true just in case some substitution instance of 'John

---

[33] Lycan (1979).

is X'—such as 'John is smart'—is true. But non-objectual quantification need not be substitutional; like objectual quantification, it might be a primitive form of quantification. Those who deny that believing is a relation will hold that that-clauses are not referring expressions and that quantifications like 'Ralph believes something' are non-objectual.

A compositional truth theory for a language L is a finitely statable theory of L which ascribes semantic properties to the finitely many words and expression-forming operations of L in such a way as to determine, for each of the infinitely many sentences of L that can be used to say something true or false, the condition, or conditions, under which an utterance of that sentence would be true. For many theorists, one big selling point for the relational account of believing, wherein the quantifications in question are objectual, is that it makes it easy to see how to accommodate belief reports in a compositional truth theory—that is to say, makes it easy to see how the truth-value of a belief report is determined by the semantic values the words composing the report have in that report. But what are we to make of the complex predicate 'believes that Slovenia will win the World Cup' in

(23) Jane believes that Slovenia will win the World Cup

if 'believes' is not occurring in that report as a relational predicate? No one should object to taking the predicate's extension to be the set of things that believe that Slovenia will win the World Cup, which allows us to say that (23) is true just in case the extension of 'Jane'—viz. Jane—belongs to the extension of 'believes that Slovenia will win the World Cup', which in turn entails that (23) is true iff Jane believes that Slovenia will win the World Cup. The problem is to see how the extension of that complex predicate is determined by the extensions of its component words if 'believes' does not occur in it as a transitive verb, and there must be such a determination if the language to which the report belongs enjoys a correct compositional truth theory.

There are two ways to respond to this "problem." One is to deny that belief reports can be accommodated in a compositional truth theory and to argue that natural languages neither have nor need compositional truth theories. This is the approach I took in *Remnants of Meaning*.[34] The other response, proposed most notably by Arthur Prior and Jaakko Hintikka, is to treat 'believes that' as a certain sort of operator. Neither response is promising.

Some will think that the approach which denies compositional semantics is problematic precisely because it denies compositional semantics, but there is another problem even if the denial of compositional semantics is unproblematic.[35] This problem is that no determinate sense can be made of the non-compositionalist's claim that that-clauses do not refer to propositions once this theorist has said all that she needs to say. The theorist in question does not deny that many belief reports are true, she does not deny that inferences like the one most recently displayed are valid, and she does not deny that any of the following may be true:

---

[34] See also Hofweber (2000).   [35] See Schiffer (2003: ch. 4).

That there is life on Venus is Harold's theory.

That there is life on Venus is true iff there is life on Venus.

That there is life on Venus has its truth condition both essentially and absolutely.

That there is life on Venus is implausible.

That there is life on Venus is one of many things that are implausible.

That there is life on Venus is abstract—i.e. has no physical attributes—and mind- and language-independent.

What then is the cash-value of the debate between this theorist and one who maintains that that-clauses refer to propositions? Well, it may be said that the first denies, while the second affirms, that propositions exist. But what can the cash-value of *that* debate come to, given all that the two theorists hold in common? What would count as a determinate resolution of this debate? The only concept of existence on which I feel I have any grip makes it difficult to deny that propositions exist, given the truth of all the that-clause-containing utterances the non-compositionalist is willing to acknowledge. But if it is acknowledged that propositions exist, then the view that that-clauses do not refer to them is not well motivated.

The operator account of 'believes that' promises to be a non-relationist account of believing which comports with compositional semantics. Trivially, 'believes that' is syntactically an "operator" in that it takes a sentence and makes a sentence. What those who propose an operator account of 'believes that' have in mind, however, is a way of giving a semantic rule governing the expression 'believes that' which yields a truth condition for every belief report. What rules of this sort are on offer? While Arthur Prior clearly advocated an operator account of 'believes that'—in part for the problems raised by examples like hope reports—he never actually proposed a semantics for the operator. Hintikka does provide an operator account that is modeled on the operator account of 'necessarily' in modal logic, but it is merely a notational variant of the view, discussed above, that believing is a relation to propositions construed as sets of possible worlds.

At this point in the development of our subject, there seems not to be any plausible non-relational account of believing.

13.4.2 Non-Propositional Relational Accounts of Believing

Most philosophers who deny that believing is a relation to propositions hold that it is a relation to things other than propositions. Since the things we believe have truth-values and other semantic properties, these alternative objects of belief must be linguistic, or quasi-linguistic, entities of some kind—sentences, utterances, mental representations, or whatever.

If believing is a relation to linguistic entities of some stripe or other, what stripe exactly is it? They cannot be public language sentence *types*, since too many sentence types (e.g. 'She isn't there yet') cannot have truth-values, while the things we believe must have, or at least be capable of having, truth-values. For this reason, Donald Davidson proposed his famous paratactic theory of propositional-attitude reports, which entails that believing is a relation to utterance tokens.[36] Davidson's idea runs as follows. Although Pierre is a monolingual speaker of French, I may speak truly in saying

(32) Pierre believes that snow is white.

According to Davidson, my utterance (32) really consists of two distinct utterances linked by parataxis, to be represented as

(33) Pierre believes that. Snow is white.

The claim is that my utterance of 'that' in (32) occurs as a demonstrative which refers to my utterance of 'snow is white' which immediately follows it. When I utter 'snow is white' in uttering (32), I am not asserting that snow is white. Rather, I utter it to produce an utterance with a certain content for the sole purpose of ascribing to Pierre a belief with the same content: my utterance of (32) is true, according to Davidson's paratactic theory, just in case Pierre has a belief with the same content as that of my utterance of 'snow is white' to which my utterance of the demonstrative 'that' refers.

The implausibility of Davidson's theory may be greater than its considerable ingenuity. There are several problems.

a. From a typical utterance of (32) we should expect to be able to infer

(34) There is something such that Pierre believes that it is white,

but

(35) There is something such that Pierre believes that. It is white.

is meaningless.

b. None of the inferences used to motivate the face-value theory are valid if Davidson's paratactic theory is correct.[37] I shall leave the demonstration of this to the reader.

c. The paratactic theory owes an account of utterance content which does not appeal to propositions. Davidson thought he had such a theory. He thought that a compositional truth theory for a language in the style of Tarski could serve as a meaning theory for the language, where a theory of meaning for a language L is, for Davidson, a finitely axiomatized theory knowledge of which would enable one to understand utterances in L.[38] But Davidson's proposal that a truth theory can serve as a meaning theory is highly problematic,[39] and any theory that presupposes it inherits its problems.

d. Even if Davidson's meaning theory were correct, it is not clear how it would help to explain the idea of a belief state's having the same content as an utterance token, since, on the face of it, Davidson's truth-theoretic account of meaning has no application to belief states. So even if Davidson has given a correct account of

---

[36] Davidson (1984a) and (1984b).   [37] See Burge (1986).
[38] Tarski (1956); Davidson (1984c).
[39] See Schiffer (1987: ch. 5) and Schiffer (2003: §8.2).

natural language meaning, he still owes an account of belief content which enables us to understand talk of a belief state's having the "same content" as an utterance token.

e. If Davidson's theory of (32) were correct, one would expect it also to be true of (32)'s French translation,

(36) Pierre croit que la neige est blanche.

But 'que' has no use in French as a demonstrative. Are we to suppose that while a paratactic treatment of (32) is correct, a paratactic treatment of (36) is not correct?[40]

f. An apparently pretty big problem with the claim that believing is a relation to utterance tokens is that there are more beliefs than there are utterance tokens. A person might have a belief which neither she nor anyone else has ever expressed, and which no one has ever attributed to anyone. Here it will be true that the person believes something, yet there is evidently no utterance token available to be what she believes.

g. One cannot know the *assertion made*, the truth stated, by (32) without knowing *what* Pierre believes, the *content* of his belief, where this includes, for example, knowing that he has a belief that is true if, and only if, snow is white. Davidson's account is in conflict with this datum. On his account, one can know the assertion made in the utterance of (32) without knowing the first thing about what Pierre believes, the content of his belief. According to Davidson, the only assertion made in (32) is made by the utterance of 'Pierre believes that', where 'that' occurs as a demonstrative which refers to a distinct utterance of 'snow is white'. The assertion made in the utterance of (32) is merely one that is true iff Pierre is in a belief state which has the same content as the referred to utterance of 'snow is white'. But that is something that could be known by a monolingual speaker of Pashto: she could know that Pierre was in a belief state whose content matched that of my utterance of 'snow is white' even though she had no idea of the content of that utterance. It should be clear that a version of this problem will infect any account which holds that a belief report is true just in case its subject is in a belief state with the same content as a certain expression or utterance to which reference is made in the report.

So much, then, for linguistic accounts of belief reports. A quasi-linguistic account has, however, been proposed which may seem to avoid the foregoing problems. Like Davidson's account, it crucially relies for its motivation on Davidson's idea that a truth theory can serve as a meaning theory. The theory is the same as the face-value theory of

(1) *A believes that S*

except that according to it that-clauses refer not to propositions but to what proponents of the theory call *interpreted logical forms* (ILFs).[41] Here a logical form, or

---

[40] It would seem that Davidson later abandoned his paratactic account of belief reports. In (2001a: 57–8) he wrote: "There is ... no plausible alternative to taking [the that-clause in a belief report] as a singular term which, by referring to an appropriate entity, specifies the relevant belief."

[41] Larson and Ludlow (1993) and Larson and Segal (1995). A similar proposal is made in Richard (1990).

LF, is a technical notion used in Chomskian linguistics to describe that level of the syntactic analysis of a sentence which is the proper object of semantic interpretation. An *interpreted* LF is a representation of the LF in which semantic values are paired with expressions in the LF, where those semantic values are of the kind that would enter into an extensional Tarskian truth theory for the language of the kind Davidson advocates. Simplifying, we might represent the ILF to which the that-clause in 'Ralph believes that Fido is a dog' refers as the set-theoretic entity

(37) $<<$'Fido', Fido$>$, $<$'is a dog', the set of dogs$>>$,

this ILF being true iff Fido belongs to the set of dogs, which is to say, iff Fido is a dog. Even this simplified toy model of an ILF must be considerably complicated just to get a simplified toy model for sentences with quantifiers, where those quantifiers may be treated syncategorematically, and thus not assigned semantic values,[42] or with pronouns and demonstratives, for which only tokens of those expressions may have semantic values. But (37) already gives us enough to object to the theory.

For one thing, ILF theory can be no more promising than its presupposition that a truth theory can serve as a meaning theory, and, as noted, it is arguable that that presupposition is problematic. A more immediate problem is close to the epistemological problem, (g), encountered by Davidson's paratactic theory. Suppose that the set of dogs = the set of things most loved by fleas. Then the ILF (37) = the ILF

(38) $<<$'Fido', Fido$>$, $<$'is a dog', the set of things most loved by fleas$>>$,

and it is clear that someone—say, a monolingual speaker of Japanese—could know that Ralph stands to (38) in the relation the ILF theorist takes to be the semantic value of 'believes' and not know that Ralph believes that Fido is a dog. It might seem that the ILF theorist can avoid this problem by taking properties, rather than sets, to be the appropriate semantic values of predicates, so that the ILF to which 'that Fido is a dog' refers is not

(37) but rather
(38) $<<$'Fido', Fido$>$, $<$'is a dog', doghood$>>$.

The trouble now is that this theory would be for all intents and purposes a propositionalist proposal whereby the propositions to which that-clauses refer are truth-conditionally equivalent to the Russellian propositions they determine—as (38) determines the Russellian proposition ⟨Fido, doghood⟩—and the linguistic components of ILFs play the role of Fregean modes of presentation.

---

[42] An expression is syncategorematic in the context of ILF theory if the truth theory for the language assigns it no semantic value but rather interprets it by a clause in the truth theory, in the way that, say, quantifiers and connectives are interpreted in standard truth definitions in predicate logic.

13.5 SUMMARY AND CONCLUSION

The topic of this paper is propositional content, the kind of content our thoughts and speech acts possess, which I provisionally identified as whatever that-clauses ascribe in propositional-attitude and speech-act reports. *Propositions*, of some stripe or other, are propositional contents, if the relevant generalization of the face-value theory of belief reports is correct, and that theory has a defeasible default status: it is the theory that must be defeated if it is not to be accepted, the only theory of the semantics of belief reports that enjoys direct intuitive support (alternatives to the face-value theory are motivated by perceived problems with the face-value theory).

One problem with the face-value theory is that it awaits a complementary account of propositions, and there are problems with the best known contenders. Problems some of these contenders confront when slotted into the face-value theory invite revisions of the face-value theory, such as the hidden-indexical theory of belief reports or the version of Fregeanism whereby that-clauses, in the typical case, partially characterize but do not refer to Fregean propositions. Yet these revisions were found to suffer from problems of their own. Another problem we saw the face-value theory encounter was the inability to preface the that clause in 'A hopes that S' with 'the proposition' and achieve thereby a sentence with the same truth-value ('A hopes the proposition that S' is not even grammatical), which is puzzling if 'that S' refers to the proposition that S. Well-known vagaries concerning substitutivity *salva veritate* prevent this from being on its own a decisive objection to the face-value theory, but in the absence of an account of why the substitutions fail in hope (and certain other) reports, one cannot be confident that the inability to substitute 'the proposition that S' for 'that S' does not cover a decisive objection, and such an account is not yet known. If the substitutivity problem does cover a decisive objection, the objection would be decisive to any referential account of that-clauses: 'A hopes the sentence/utterance/mental representation that S' is no more meaningful than 'A hopes the proposition that S'.

The substitutivity problem might suggest, as it suggested to Arthur Prior,[43] that believing is not a relation, and that, therefore, quantifications like 'Ralph believes something' are not *objectual* quantifications. But both versions of this tack proved problematic.

The most popular alternative to the theory that identifies propositional contents with propositions, and thus takes propositional attitudes to be relations to propositions, is the view that propositional attitudes are relations to linguistic, or quasi-linguistic, entities of some kind or other. Yet these accounts seem even more problematic than the propositionalist views they hope to supplant.

---

[43] Prior (1981).

On balance, my unprejudiced bet is on the theory I advanced in *The Things We Mean*, which holds that propositional contents are what I called pleonastic propositions. I suspect, however, that others might have a different opinion. I know that we have not reached the end of discussion on the problem of propositional content.

REFERENCES

Almog, J., Perry, J., and Wettstein, H. (eds.) (1989). *Themes from Kaplan* (Oxford University Press).

Bach, K. (1997). "Do Belief Reports Report Beliefs?" *Pacific Philosophical Quarterly* 78: 215–41.

Benacerraf, P. (1973). "Mathematical Truth," *Journal of Philosophy*, 70: 661–79.

Braun, D. (1998). "Understanding Belief Reports," *The Philosophical Review*, 107: 555–95.

Burge, T. (1986). "On Davidson's "Saying That" ", in E. LePore (1986).

—— (forthcoming). "Illogical, but Rational," *Noûs*.

Cole, P. (ed.) (1978). *Syntax and Pragmatics, ix: Pragmatics* (Academic Press).

Crimmins, M. (1998). "Hesperus and Phosphorus: Sense, Pretense, and Reference," *Philosophical Review*, 107: 1–47.

Davidson, D. (1984a). "Truth and Meaning," in Davidson (1984d): 20–36.

—— (1984b). "Moods and Performances," in Davidson (1984d): 109–21.

—— (1984c). "Truth and Meaning," in Davidson (1984d): 17–36.

—— (1984d). *Inquiries into Truth and Interpretation* (Oxford University Press).

—— (2001). "What is Present to the Mind?" in *Subjective, Intersubjective, Objective* (2001).

Everett, A. and Hofweber, T. (2000). *Empty Names, Fiction and the Puzzles of Non-Existence* (CSLI Publications).

Field, H. (1980). *Science without Numbers* (Princeton University Press).

—— (1989). *Realism, Mathematics, and Modality* (Blackwell).

Forbes, G. (1990). "The Indispensability of *Sinn*," *The Philosophical Review*, 99: 535–63.

Frege, G. (1879). *Begriffsschrift, eine der arithmetischen nachgebildete Formelsprache des reinen Denkens* (Halle).

—— (1892). "On Sense and Reference," *Zeitschrift für Philosophie und philosophische Kritik*, 100: 25–50.

Hale, B. and Wright, C. (1992). "Nominalism and the Contingency of Abstract Objects," *Journal of Philosophy*, 89: 111–35.

—— (eds.). (1997). *A Companion to the Philosophy of Language* (Blackwell).

Hofweber, T. (2000). "Quantification and Non-Existent Objects," in Everett and Hofweber (2000).

Kaplan, D. (1978). "Dthat," in Cole (1978).

—— (1989). "Demonstratives: An Essay on the Semantics, Logic, Metaphysics, and Epistemology of Demonstratives and Other Indexicals," in Almog *et al.* (1989).

King, J. (2002). "Designating Propositions," *Philosophical Review*, 111: 341–71.

Kripke, S. (1980). *Naming and Necessity* (Harvard University Press).

Larson, R. and Ludlow, P. (1993). "Interpreted Logical Forms," *Synthese*, 95: 305–55.

Larson, R. and Segal, G. (1995). *Knowledge of Meaning: An Introduction to Semantic Theory* (MIT Press).

Lepore, E. (ed.). (1986). (ed.) *Truth and Interpretation: Perspectives on the Philosophy of Donald Davidson* (Blackwell).

Loar, B. (1976). "The Semantics of Singular Terms," *Philosophical Studies*, 30: 353–77.

Loux, M. (ed). (1979). *The Possible and the Actual* (Cornell University Press).

Lycan, W. (1979). "The Trouble with Possible Worlds," in Loux (1979).

Mill, J. (1843, 1973). *System of Logic*, Book I (University of Toronto Press).

Prior, A. (1971). *Objects of Thought* (Oxford University Press).

Putnam, H. (1975a). "The Meaning of 'Meaning'," in Putnam (1975b).

——— (1975b). *Mind, Language, and Reality: Philosophical Papers*, vol. ii (Cambridge University Press).

Quine, W. (1970). *Philosophy of Logic* (Prentice-Hall).

Richard, M. (1990). *Propositional Attitudes: An Essay on Thoughts and How We Ascribe Them* (Cambridge University Press).

Russell, B. (1905). "On Denoting," *Mind* 14: 479–93.

——— (1910a). "Knowledge by Acquaintance and Knowledge by Description" in Russell (1910b).

——— (1910b). *Mysticism and Logic* (Unwin Books).

Salmon, N. (1986). *Frege's Puzzle* (MIT Press).

——— (1989). "Illogical Belief," *Philosophical Perspectives*, 3: 243–85.

——— (1995). "Being of Two Minds: Belief and Doubt," *Noûs*, 29: 1–20.

——— (forthcoming). "The Resilience of Illogical Belief," *Noûs*.

Schiffer, S. (1992). "Belief Ascription," *The Journal of Philosophy*, 89: 499–521.

——— (2003). *The Things We Mean* (Oxford University Press).

Soames, S. (2002). *Beyond Rigidity: The Unfinished Semantic Agenda of Naming and Necessity* (Oxford University Press).

Stalnaker, R. (1984). *Inquiry* (MIT Press).

——— (1987). "Semantics for Belief," *Philosophical Topics*, 15 (1987): 177–90.

Stanley, J. (1997). "Names and Rigid Designation," in Hale and Wright (1997).

Tarski, A. (1956). "The Concept of Truth in Formalized Languages," in *Logic, Semantics, Metamathematics* (Oxford University Press).

CHAPTER 14

CONCEPTUAL ROLE SEMANTICS

MARK GREENBERG AND GILBERT HARMAN

14.1 MEANINGS DETERMINED BY USE

CONCEPTUAL role semantics (CRS) is the view that the meanings of expressions of a language (or other symbol system) or the contents of mental states are determined or explained by the role of the expressions or mental states in thinking. The theory can be taken to be applicable to language in the ordinary sense, to mental represent-ations, conceived of either as symbols in a "language of thought" or as mental states such as beliefs, or to certain other sorts of symbol systems. CRS rejects the compet-ing idea that thoughts have intrinsic content that is prior to the use of concepts in thought. According to CRS, meaning and content derive from use, not the other way round.

CRS is thus an attempt to answer the question of what determines or makes it the case that representations have particular meanings or contents. The significance of this question can be seen by considering, for example, theories of mind that postulate a language of thought. Such theories presuppose an account of what makes it the case that a symbol in the language of thought has a particular meaning. Some conceptual role theorists have not clearly distinguished this kind of question from questions about the nature of the meanings or contents of various kinds of representations. CRS, as we understand it, is consistent with many different kinds of positions on the

We are indebted to Ram Neta and James Pryor for useful comments on a prior draft.

latter question. For example, as we discuss below, CRS has no commitment to the view that the meaning of a symbol should be *identified* with its conceptual role.

Some discussions of CRS (e.g. Sellars, 1963; Harman, 1974, 1975, 1987) suppose that CRS must limit the relevant uses to those involved in inference, in reacting to perception, and in decisions leading to action. (In Section 14.5 below, we discuss versions that take an even more limited view of relevant factors.) But it is best to begin discussion by interpreting "conceptual role" in the widest possible way, considering a great variety of uses of symbols in thought, in order to be able to ask which uses if any might be relevant to meaning or content and how they might be relevant (see Section 14.3).

We propose to use the phrase *conceptual role semantics* or *CRS* in a very broad sense, according to which CRS includes any theory that holds that the content of mental states or symbols is determined by any part of their role or use in thought. There is a common use of the term that is more limited. In this use, in order to count as a version of CRS, a theory must hold that the determinants of content include the role of the mental states or symbols *in inference* or in other purely internal mental processes. This restriction excludes information-based or indication theories of content (see Section 14.5 below). By contrast, on our broader use of the term CRS, information-based or indication theories count as special versions of CRS.

In what follows, we will sometimes use the abbreviation "CCRS" (core CRS) for the sort of CRS that takes the recognition of internal inferential and implicational relations to be crucial to the meaning or content of some expressions or syntactic constructions. CCRS allows for the relevance to content of other aspects of use, such as relations of symbols to perceptual input and to actions.[1] So, we will use the expression *CCRS* in the way that some theorists use the phrase *conceptual role semantics*.

Just how inclusive our broad understanding of CRS is depends on how broadly conceptual role or use is understood. For example, *teleological* theories of content give an important role to the evolutionarily determined "function" of symbols or symbol structures, where some such theories understand the notion of the function of a symbol or structure in a way that goes beyond the symbol's use or role as ordinarily understood (e.g. Dretske, 1988, 2000; Millikan, 1984, 1993; Neander, 1995; Papineau, 1987). We do not count such theories as versions of CRS. (We discuss these theories in Section 14.6.3 below.)

One other point is that we understand conceptual role in such a way that it might be externally or non-individualistically individuated. Thus, if we consider myself and my twin on Twin Earth (Putnam, 1975), it is arguable that my symbol for water and his symbol for twater have different conceptual roles. For example, they have different relations to properties in the world, as I have often applied my symbol to

---

[1] *Solipsistic* theories, according to which the *only* relevant conceptual role is inference (or other purely internal relations), are also special versions of CRS. We believe, however, that the only plausible versions of CRS do not restrict the relevant conceptual role to wholly external or wholly internal aspects of conceptual role.

H_2O, and he has often applied his to XYZ. If our uses are individuated externally, our uses are different since my uses are water-applications and my twin's are twater-applications.

When CRS is understood in our ecumenical way, much of the currently active debate concerning the determination of meaning and content is a debate between competing versions of CRS, such as between CCRS and information-based theories, rather than between CRS and other positions.

There are theorists, however, who reject CRS on even the most inclusive understanding of it. According to some such theorists (Searle, 1980; Bonjour, 1998), the content of mental states is intrinsic to them, not explained by their use or the use of any sort of mental symbols, and the content or meaning of words and other symbols derives from the content of mental states. Such theorists reject CRS on any understanding of it.

It is important to emphasize something from the start. CRS supposes that meaning or content is determined by (and so *supervenes* on) conceptual role, but that does not imply that meaning and conceptual role are the same thing. Nor does it imply that any difference in conceptual role entails a difference in meaning. For example, to the extent that "giving the meaning" of an expression is providing a paraphrase or translation of the expression, CRS implies that the adequacy of such a translation or paraphrase is determined by the way expressions in the relevant languages are used in thought. CRS does not imply that any difference in relevant usage automatically calls for a difference in translation. (We return to this point in Section 14.5.2 below.)

There are at least three broadly different ways in which symbols can be used—in communication, in speech acts like promising that go beyond mere communication, and in thinking. CRS takes the last of these uses, the use of symbols in thought, to be the most basic and important use for determining the content of symbols, where that use includes (at least) perceptual representation, recognition of implications, modeling, inference, labeling, categorization, theorizing, planning, and control of action.

In one view (e.g. Katz, 1966), linguistic expressions are used mainly for purposes of communication and do not have a significant use in thought. In this view, the content of linguistic expressions derives from the content of the non-linguistic thoughts they express and CRS is relevant to language only to the extent that it provides the correct story about the contents of non-linguistic thoughts. In a contrasting view (e.g. Sellars, 1969), ordinary linguistic communication involves "thinking out loud," people sometimes think in language (but not only in language), and the use of language in thought determines meaning. In the latter view, CRS applies directly to expressions in natural language as well as to other symbols used in thinking.

CRS need not claim that the content of all expressions is determined by their use. (Indeed, CRS does not claim that all expressions of a language have functions or uses. Such a claim would be very implausible for very long expressions that never occur.) Many conceptual role or use theorists (e.g. Ryle, 1961; Peacocke, 1992) claim that the contents of simple expressions, such as words, are determined by their conceptual roles, and that the contents of complex expressions, such as sentences, are determined by the contents of their components and the way in which they are combined (see Section 14.2.4).

More precisely, then, CRS holds that meaning and content (including the meanings of words and other symbols and the contents of mental representations) arise from and are explained by the role words, symbols, and other features of representation play in thinking of various sorts. CRS seeks to describe the relevant sorts of conceptual role and to explain how conceptual roles determine meaning and content.

In the next three sections, we examine CRS's treatment of a few fundamental issues (Section 14.2), consider diverse examples of ways in which representations are used in thought, (Section 14.3), and discuss how to investigate the relevance of conceptual role to content (Section 14.4). Next, in Section 14.5, we turn to information-based versions of CRS and the challenge that they pose to versions that recognize other aspects of conceptual role. Finally, we consider in Section 14.6 a number of important objections to CRS.

14.2 Understanding Meaning

14.2.1 Understanding Oneself

According to one plausible version of CRS, the basic understanding one has of the meaning of one's own words and expressions consists in one's being at home with one's use of those words and expressions. It is a kind of know-how: one knows how to proceed. One can have that basic kind of knowledge of meaning without having any sort of theoretical understanding of meaning and without being able to say what is meant in any interesting way.

We believe that a correct account of this sort of knowledge must reject the popular but obscure metaphor in which basic understanding of meaning involves "grasping" something, as if such understanding consisted in getting one's mental hands around something (Frege, 1982; Dummett, 1991; Peacocke, 1999; Fodor, 2004). According to our understanding of CRS, although one's meaning is determined by and explained by the way one uses words and other basic symbols, one's understanding of one's own meaning need not consist in having an understanding of the way one uses these items. (Nor need it consist in having an understanding of truth conditions or anything else.) It might consist simply in having symbols with the relevant conceptual roles.

14.2.2 Understanding Someone Else

Some CRS theorists (Sellars, 1962; Quine, 1953, 1960; Davidson, 1973; Field, 2001) suggest that to understand the meaning of an expression built from resources that one does not use oneself, one seeks to find a paraphrase or translation into an expression built from resources one does use.[2]

This might suggest treating " 'Nichts' means *nothing*" to a first approximation as a variant of " 'Nichts' is best translated into my system as 'nothing'." Let us call proposals that try to explain meaning statements (of the form '*e* means *m*') in terms of translation *translational accounts of meaning statements*. Various worries might be raised about such accounts. It might be objected that the suggested treatment can be shown to fail by comparing the translations into French of " 'Nichts' means *nothing*" and " 'Nichts' is best translated into my system as 'nothing' ". Sellars (1962) responds by rephrasing the proposal using "dot-quotation," where "·nothing·" is used to specify a type of expression that can appear in any language, categorized by its use in its language. Field (2001) notes that ordinary quotation often functions like Sellars' dot quotation (see also Recanati, 2001, p. 641). We will not here try to decide whether translational accounts might provide an adequate treatment of meaning statements. CRS is compatible with such proposals even if not committed to them.

14.2.3 Meaningfulness

Barry Stroud has observed (personal communication) that there is an ambiguity in the remark " 'Nichts' means *nothing*" between the claim that 'Nichts' has no meaning and the claim that 'Nichts' has a meaning and its meaning is *nothing*. In philosophical writing it is customary to use an italic font for the second interpretation, according to which the word is used to mention its meaning rather than to express that meaning, and a regular font for the first, as we have done above. In this chapter, we sometimes use italics in this way, to mention a meaning or content, and sometimes use it to mention an expression. Context will make it clear which role the italic font is playing.

We noted above that translation can be used to give an account of meaning statements. It also provides a sufficient condition for meaningfulness. If an expression *e* has an adequate translation into something meaningful in one's own system, *e* is a meaningful expression. Davidson (1974) appears to argue for the converse claim that an expression in another language is meaningful *only if* it has such a translation into one's own system. But even if the notion of translation provides the best account of meaning *statements* (of the form "*e* means *m*"), it does not follow that we must identify an expression's *being meaningful* with its having such a translation, and we should not do so, according to CRS. It is consistent with a translational account of meaning statements to hold that an expression in another

---

[2] Some versions of CRS give a prominent place to the notion of translation (e.g. Quine, 1953; Harman, 1990). There are at least two distinct ways in which translation can figure in such theories. First, the notion of translation can be used to address questions about meaning statements (see the text below) or about the nature of symbols' meanings or contents. Second, as we discuss in Section 14.4.2, considering translation can be a way of investigating the way in which conceptual role maps onto, or determines, content.

system is meaningful in virtue of its conceptual role in that system even if nothing has a corresponding role in one's own system.

14.2.4 Compositionality

It is widely assumed that meaning is compositional in the sense that the meaning of a compound expression is determined by the meanings of its parts and the way they are put together. Fodor and Lepore (2002) argue that CRS cannot accept such compositionality, because the use of a complex expression is not determined by the uses of its parts and the way they are put together. (This is obvious, if Ryle is right in arguing that only simple expressions have uses.) As we have emphasized, however, CRS need not identify meaning with conceptual role, nor need it hold that the contents of complex expressions are determined by their uses.

Once this point is recognized, compositionality presents no obstacle. For example, CRS can certainly allow that the *translation* of a compound expression is determined by the translation of its parts. Versions of CRS that accept a translational theory of meaning statements can therefore allow a form of compositionality of meaning. So can any other version of CRS that supposes that meanings of simple expressions are determined by, but not identical to, conceptual role. On such a view, the meanings of complex expressions are neither determined by nor identical to their uses, but are derived from the meanings of the simple expressions of which they are composed.

14.3 EXAMPLES OF USES OF SYMBOLS

We now describe some non-communicative uses of representations in maps, gauges, models and diagrams, mathematical calculations and other sorts of problem solving, lists, labels and naming, categorization of various sorts, inference, and planning. We also consider what features of these uses might be especially relevant to meaning or content, an issue we take up further in the following section.

14.3.1 Maps

Maps are used to communicate information about geographical areas but also perhaps more importantly in thinking about the geography of an area. A person might use a map in planning what route to take in order to get somewhere, perhaps drawing a line to sketch a possible route, maybe erasing it and trying another, in this way thinking by marking up the map. People use a map in order to get clear about relative locations or to estimate distances. Some people construct their own rough maps in order to get clearer about where things are, as a way of putting together various things they know. In this way people use printed maps on paper, maps on computer screens, and also internal "mental maps." Dropping breadcrumbs in order to indicate the way home is another way of using symbols to represent geographical features.

CRS might speculate that the representational content of maps is partly a function of ways in which maps are constructed on the basis of features of areas mapped and partly a function of the ways in which maps are used in planning routes and the like.

14.3.2 Gauges

A driver uses a fuel gauge in order to make sure there is enough gas in the gas tank. The driver uses a speedometer to tell how fast the car is going, perhaps to avoid a speeding ticket. People check thermometers in order to tell how hot an oven is or what it's like outside.

People also have internal gauges that indicate via hunger and thirst when they need food or drink. Sensations of pain function to indicate that parts of their bodies are suffering harm.

CRS might suggest here that what is indicated by the value of a certain feature of a gauge depends both on what the values of the feature normally depend on and how one reacts to various values of that feature. So, for example, hunger and thirst differ in content in that hunger normally arises from lack of food and normally produces the goal of eating, whereas thirst normally arises from dehydration and normally produces the goal of drinking.

14.3.3 Models and Diagrams

People use models and diagrams to help in planning marching band formations, football plays, battles, and seating arrangements. These are sometimes three-dimensional wooden constructions, sometimes sketches in pencil on paper, and sometimes internal "mental models." The spatial relations of marks can serve to represent other, non-spatial relations in a way that greatly aids thinking about those relations. Flow charts, pie charts, graphs, and Venn diagrams are examples.

CRS might suggest that the content of such models and diagrams derives in part from the role they play in planning. What makes a certain figure the representation of a band member, for example, might in part derive from the way the model in which it is a part is used to plan a marching band formation. What makes a certain rectangular piece of cardboard represent a desk might in part derive from its use in planning where a desk should go.

14.3.4 Mathematical Reasoning

People use representations of numbers to count and measure, calculate costs, balance checkbooks, and solve other problems. They do mathematics on paper and in their heads.

What makes certain symbols stand for amounts of money in a bank account might depend partly on how the symbols relate to various transactions involving that account. What makes certain mathematical symbols stand for mathematical addition or exponentiation or integration might be in part what are taken to be good calculations involving those symbols. Learning the meanings of such symbols might in part depend on learning how to use them in mathematical reasoning. (Of course, representations of numbers can also be used in a wide variety of other ways, for example as memory aids and passwords.)

14.3.5 Lists

People make shopping lists and other "to do" lists. They keep diaries and schedules of appointments. They make lists of whom to invite to parties. Their lists can be on paper and in the mind.

People solve problems or crimes by listing initial possibilities and ruling as many out as they can. Some puzzles can be solved in their heads, others require writing things down on paper. In trying to decide what to do, people make lists of considerations, trying to correlate those supporting one decision with others supporting another decision, so that the considerations can be crossed off, leaving easier problems.

CRS might suggest that what makes these things lists is at least in part that they are used in such ways. In support of this, notice that it is not the case that every sequence of representations is a list. For example, a sentence or a mathematical proof is not a list.

14.3.6 Envisioning Possibilities

In planning and related thinking people form representations of various possible scenarios, anticipating in their imagination or in some more external way what can happen and how others may react. It is possible that the conceptual role of certain terms includes the use of such terms in processes that model various possibilities and reasoning with these models. Relevant terms might include logical constants, modals (alethic, normative, and epistemic) like *may, might, can, must,* and *ought,* etc.

CRS might suggest that what makes representations representations of possibilities rather than representations of how one takes the world to be (beliefs) is the distinctive way in which the representations are formed and how they function in further thinking.

14.3.7 Reasoning and Implication

Reasoning often includes recognition of implications. How these deductive relations affect inference is not straightforward (Harman, 1995).

CRS might suggest that the meanings of certain terms is due in part to the role these terms play in recognizing implications. So, for example, CRS might suppose that a construction $C(\cdot, \cdot)$ functions as logical conjunction (*and*) for a person if and only if the person recognizes that $C(P, Q)$ immediately implies both P and Q and is immediately implied by them taken together. Similarly, CRS might suppose that the meanings of certain terms is connected to the recognition of certain immediate inconsistencies, so that one thing that makes a construction $N(\cdot)$ represent negation (*not*) is that P is treated as immediately inconsistent with $N(P)$. (Harman, 1986, appeals to notions of psychologically "immediate" implication and inconsistency. Peacocke, 1992, appeals to "primitively compelling transitions.")

14.3.8 Mental Models

People use representations to think about implications. Given some information, they draw physical or mental pictures from which they read off further information. In determining what follows from assumptions people form mental models of possibilities, using the assumptions to eliminate possibilities and conclude that what is implied is what is true in the remaining possibilities (Johnson-Laird and Byrne, 1991).

People have mental models of how things work. Their models of how thermostats in refrigerators work influence what they do in order to adjust their temperatures (Kempton, 1987; Norman, 1988).

People reason to causes and other explanations by envisioning possible causes, perhaps using complex mental models of possible causes. People reason by analogy, using a model of one area, such as the flow of water through pipes, to form a model in another area, such as the "flow" of electricity "through" wires (Holyoak and Thagard, 1994; Lakoff and Johnson, 1980). Such uses of symbols in figuring out how systems work or what the cause of an event is may in part determine what the symbols represent.

14.3.9 Labels

People put marks or labels on things in order to recognize them later. At the gym, one puts a colorful label on a lock in order to distinguish it from the other locks in the locker room. Walking in the woods, one puts a mark on a tree to recognize it as the tree at which one turned left. Labeling an object allows a way to refer to it later: it's the one with the label. One might even use an actual feature of an object as a label: it's the tree with the distinctively broken branch; its broken branch functions for one as a label. Numerals provide a common way of labeling many kinds of things: houses, contestants in sports events, automobiles, guns, complaints. Once items have been labeled, the labels can be used to manipulate objects for a variety of purposes. The letters and numerals on keyboards, telephones, and combination locks, and the icons on computer screens are some examples.

This sort of label—an identifying label—is used to mark a particular individual item. Proper names like *Peter, Chicago*, and *The Spirit of St. Louis* are also used as labels of that sort. Strawson (1974) discusses the functions such proper names or labels can have.

People also use labels to classify or categorize items. A bottle might be given a label with a skull and cross-bones on it to indicate that it contains a poison. Otherwise identical looking shakers might be labeled to indicate whether they contain salt, pepper, or sugar. Color-coding is a common way of labeling objects, such as files, in order to be able to classify them quickly. Items of clothing, such as uniforms, badges, priests' collars, or blind persons' canes, can function as labels to classify people. And the shape and color of road signs can serve as symbols to indicate the types of signs. Common nouns are sometimes used as labels of this second type. (We say more about classifying uses of labels in the next section.)

Although a label or name might be used to label several different items, identifying labels and proper names are not so used to classify the items as similar in some interesting way. There is no implication that the various people named *Peter* are similar except in having that name. The other sort of labels and common names are used to classify things as similar in certain respects. In this respect a proper name like *Sam* that is used as a name of several different people is multiply ambiguous in a way that a common name like *person*, which applies to any person, is not.

CRS might suggest that the two sorts of labels and names are semantically distinguished in part by these ways in which one uses them, how they are assigned and how we use them in negotiating the environment.

14.3.10 Categorization

As we remarked in the previous section, common names and labels can be used to categorize things in various ways. Labels can be used as warnings: "poison", "flammable", "soft-shoulder". Or to indicate an "exit". Traffic signs indicate directions and distances to desired goals, gas stations, rest areas, diners. The content of such signs and labels is indexical, indicating that this is poison or flammable, that this road has a soft-shoulder, that this points the way to the exit, etc.

CRS might suppose that what gives content to a categorization of something as poisonous is in part that assigning this category to something enables one to treat it in an appropriate and safe way, and similarly for other danger categories. CRS might also suggest that what gives content to the categorization of something as an exit is in part the use of such a categorization to enable a driver to use the exit as an exit by leaving the highway and similarly for other traffic signs.

People categorize certain geographical features of their environments as hills, mountains, rivers, lakes, fields, forests, plains, and so forth. CRS might suppose that these categorizations function in planning and practical reasoning in part by helping one get around in the world.

Symbols for categories of individual items have roles that are different in certain respects from symbols for categories of materials, substances, and stuff, as is indicated by different ways we use count nouns like *cat* and *mountain* and mass terms like *water* and *dirt* (Quine, 1960).

People also categorize living things in various ways, as one or another type of plant or animal. CRS might suggest that this sort of categorization plays a role within a proto-biology of the natural world, according to which cats are animals that are similar in their internal make-up, with similar organs arranged similarly, this proto-biology helping to guide behavior in interactions with cats and other living things.

Sometimes people categorize things in terms of function, artifacts like knives, watches, and pencils, for example. Parts of artifacts are also often categorized functionally, for example, the steering wheel and brakes of a car. CRS might suppose that the content of such categorizations depends in part on the way they facilitate the appropriate use of such artifacts.

Parts of living things are often categorized functionally, for example, eyes, hearts, and lungs. People are classified functionally as having certain occupations, as doctors, farmers, soldiers, teachers, and burglars. Such functional categorizations facilitate understanding of what things do and how they work.

Functional categorizations connect with evaluation and CRS might treat such connections as important to the meanings of the functional categories and the evaluational concepts. A good X is an X that functions well. Good eyes are good for seeing. A good knife cuts well. A car's brakes are good if they enable the car to stop quickly. A good safe-cracker is quick and quiet at getting a safe open. There is something wrong with an X that does not function well. An X ought to function in a certain way. There is something wrong with a teacher whose students do not learn. A bad farmer does not do well at farming. These same "conceptual connections" apply also to evaluations of people as people: a coward is not a full or good person, for example. Of course, it is less clear in the moral case how to treat being a person as a functional role. (We note some complications about functional classifications in the next section, below.)

14.4 Investigating Conceptual Role

We have now described some of the ways we use representations to think with. (We will mention others as we go along.) CRS is concerned with the various roles that aspects of our representations play in such thinking, and maintains that the content of those representations is determined by these roles.

14.4.1 Possibility Test

One way to investigate the contribution of use to meaning is to consider how a thinker describes certain imaginary possibilities. For example, one aspect of Mabel's use of concepts is her firm belief that all cats are animals. Other aspects include her firm beliefs that there are cats now, there have been cats in the past, and there will be cats in the future. Another aspect is the way she applies the concept *cat* to particular things. In order to assess the relative importance of these aspects of Mabel's use of *cat* we might ask her how she would describe the imaginary discovery that all the things that people like Mabel have ever called *cats* are really radio-controlled robots from Mars (Putnam, 1962; Unger, 1984). Her saying, "That would be to discover that cats are not really animals," would be evidence that her firm belief that cats are animals may not be as important to the content of her concept of a cat as other aspects of her use. In this kind of example, the way that the thinker describes certain imaginary possibilities is itself an aspect of the thinker's use of the concept. Rather than putting the point in terms of evidence, we could say that the way in which Mabel describes certain imagined cases plausibly makes a certain contribution to the content of her concept. We do not consider here the different question of the possible relevance to content of what Mabel would do if the imagined cases became actual.

A similar issue arises about Mabel's concept of a witch. Mabel applies this concept to various people and also accepts some general views about witchcraft, including the view that witches have magical powers of certain specified sorts. We can ask Mabel how she would describe the possible discovery that no one has the relevant magical powers. Would she describe this as showing that there are no witches or as showing that witches do not after all have magical powers? If Mabel says that this sort of discovery would show that there are no witches, that is some evidence that her acceptance of the general views is more important to the content of her concept of a witch than her judgments that various people are witches.

In sum, her characterization of such imagined cases might show that Mabel's acceptance of certain theoretical assumptions is more central to the content of her concept of a witch than it is to the content of her concept of a cat.

14.4.2 Translation Test

To know the meaning of someone else's words often includes knowing how to translate them into your language, and to understand what an experience is like for another person or what it is like to be that person often includes knowing how to translate that person's outlook into yours. So, another way in which CRS might study how conceptual role determines meaning is to see how it might determine good translation. This too is a useful heuristic.

14.4.2.1 *Color Concepts*

If Mabel applies certain words to objects on the basis of perception in ways that match your applications of your color terminology, that may be a reason to translate Mabel's words into your corresponding color words. If a bear's color perception works similarly to that of humans, allowing bears to make discriminations of color of the sort that humans make, that may be a reason to "translate" their color experience into ours—that is, to understand them as seeing colors much as we do. To the extent that a rabbit's color perception works in some other way, perhaps enabling the creature to make different sorts of discriminations between objects from the ones we make, it may be hard to translate rabbits' experience into ours and hard to gain understanding of how things look to them. Since there are such differences even among people, who may have one or another form of color blindness, or may be totally blind, a similar point holds there also. A congenitally blind person may have at best a very impoverished understanding of what perception of color is like for someone with normal human color perception.

What about the color words used by a congenitally blind person who relies on others for information about color? One kind of CRS might interpret the blind person's use of 'red' as meaning something like *having the perceptual feature that sighted members of my community call 'red'*. But CRS need not take this position. A different version of CRS might hold that the blind person's conceptual role for 'red', though different from a sighted person's, nevertheless manages (through reliance on sighted members of the community) to determine the same content had by sighted persons' 'red'.

What about someone who has normal color perception and terminology at one time but then loses color vision? CRS may be able to allow that the person still remembers how red looks. Perhaps CRS would understand this as a case in which the conceptual roles are still there but are blocked, as in a sighted person wearing a blindfold.

Some versions of CRS assume that there is a non-conceptual content of mental states that is not determined by considerations of conceptual (or functional role) (Block, 1998; Peacocke, 1983). Other versions of CRS claim to apply to all aspects of the phenomenal content of mental states. Consider a possible interpretation of Mabel's visual experience that attributes an inverted spectrum to her. This interprets the experience Mabel has looking at something red as like the experience you have when you are looking at something green, and similarly for other colors. Without special reasons for such an interpretation, a CRS that aims to explain phenomenal content would speak against it, holding that, if color concepts and words are functioning in the same way for both Mabel and you with respect to the external colors of objects, that contributes to making it the case that the non-inverted interpretation is the correct one.

There might be a consideration on the other side if Mabel's internal mechanisms were somehow inverted, so that what happens internally when Mabel sees red is like what happens internally when you see green, where the differences in internal mechanisms constitute differences in the internal use of symbols. Or this might not be relevant. If you accept this sort of CRS, you might approach this issue by trying to determine what would make for the best translation between Mabel's mental life and your own.

14.4.2.2 *Moral Concepts*

Consider a different sort of case, the interpretation of moral thinking and terminology of people in a different culture, call them *the Amarras*. Imagine (Dreier, 1990) that the Amarras make two contrasts, using the words *ret* and *wreng* for one contrast and *rit* and *wrig* for the other. The things the Amarras take to be *ret* are of the sort that you and other people in your society tend to consider morally right and the things the Amarras take to be *wreng* are of the sort you and yours tend to consider morally wrong. However, the Amarras do not take themselves to have reasons to be motivated toward what they take to be *ret* and do not take themselves to have reasons to be motivated to avoid what they take to be *wreng*. On the other hand, the Amarras do take themselves to have reasons to be motivated toward what they call *rit* and to avoid what they call *wrig*, although what they consider *rit* and *wrig* are quite different from what you and yours consider right and wrong, respectively.

How should you interpret their words *ret, wreng, rit*, and *wrig*? Which best correspond to your 'right' and 'wrong'? Should you translate them as agreeing with you about what is right and wrong while lacking your interest in doing what is right? Or should you translate them as thinking that different things are right or wrong from you? Suppose the latter option is better, so that *rit* and *wrig* are better translated as *right* and *wrong* than are *ret* and *wreng*. CRS can use that as an indication that the connection with motivational reasons is an important aspect of the meaning of moral terms like *right* and *wrong*.

Would this conclusion imply that people cannot believe certain things are right and wrong without being motivated to do what is right? What about someone who uses moral concepts and terminology in your way for years but eventually decides that morality is bunk and loses the motivations? And what about psychopaths who lack the sort of human sympathy that seems important for moral motivation (Blair, 1995)?

For CRS, such issues are similar to those that arise about the color concepts of non-normal perceivers and similar methods might deal with them. For example, Hare (1952) suggests that a moral sceptic's use of moral terminology might be such that the sceptic's 'good' is best interpreted as *the sort of thing you call 'good'*. On the other hand, a normative conceptual role theory (Greenberg, 2005) could hold that the fact that a sceptic *ought* to have the relevant motivations makes it the case that the sceptic's 'good' has the same content as others' 'good'.

14.4.2.3 *More or Less Functional Concepts*

Suppose you are trying to determine the meaning of a symbol T in Zeke's thought. Zeke tends not to apply T to something unless it has the function of collecting dust, crumbs, or other relatively small particles or objects from floors or other surfaces. This observation may suggest the hypothesis that T should be translated as 'broom'. However, Zeke uses T for anything that has that function, regardless of its construction or composition. For example, Zeke uses T for vacuum cleaners and sticky sheets of paper that are used to pick up dust. If you are inclined to conclude that *T* does not mean *broom*, that would indicate that your concept of a broom is not a purely functional concept.

By contrast, suppose Zeke tends not to apply *U* to an object unless the object has the function of slowing or stopping the system of which it is a part. This observation raises the hypothesis that *U* means *brake*. Also, Zeke uses *U* for anything that has that function regardless of its construction or composition. For example, Zeke uses *U* for tennis shoes when they are given the function of slowing bicycles and for electromagnetic fields when they are given the function of slowing space ships. If you are inclined to think that this aspect of *U*'s conceptual role does not undermine the hypothesis that U means *brake*, that would suggest that your concept of a brake is more of a functional concept than your concept of a broom.

There seems to be a spectrum of artifact concepts from predominantly functional ones, of which *brake* or *clock* may be examples, to concepts that are not only functional but have additional aspects. Although something must have a certain purpose in order to count as a typewriter, a drill, or a stapler, not just anything with that purpose is a typewriter, a drill, or a stapler. For some concepts, composition or construction seems to matter. For others, history is important. For example, arguably a musical instrument that is very like an oboe doesn't count as an oboe if it was independently developed by Australian aborigines. It is not part of the historical family of oboes. Thus, if Oscar uses a term for all oboe-like musical instruments, that term does not mean *oboe*.

In this section, we have illustrated how one can investigate conceptual role by considering imaginary possibilities and by asking how to translate expressions. A remaining question for CRS is whether it is possible (and if so, how) to give a systematic account of what determines which aspects of conceptual role are relevant to content and what their precise relevance is.

14.5 LIMITED VERSIONS OF CRS: INDICATION

In Section 14.3, above, we discussed a variety of ways in which symbols are used. We have mentioned relevant factors as perceptual input, inner mental processes, and output in the form of action. The first and third of these are concerned with relations between symbols and the world, the middle is concerned with relations of symbols to each other.

In this section, we turn to special versions of CRS that restrict the relevant conceptual role to the first of the three factors, namely perceptual input. Verification theories of meaning (e.g. Ayer, 1936; Quine, 1960) are an historical example of such a restricted CRS. We will be concerned with the more recent information-based or indication theories (Dretske, 1986, 2000; Fodor, 1987, 1990; Stampe, 1977). There is an active debate between such theories and CCRS (the kind of CRS that holds that inner uses are essential to determining content). We will suggest that information-based theories encounter a range of difficulties that push them to include inferential relations and actions in the relevant conceptual role.

14.5.1 Information-Based Theories

Information-based theories hold that the content of a symbol depends only on the information about the environment carried by an internal tokening of the symbol. So, an internal occurrence of a token of 'red' indicates or carries the information that there is something red in the environment, where such indication might be analyzed as a kind of counterfactual, causal, or nomic dependence.

One problem for such views is that it is difficult for them to do without intentional notions such as the *application* of a symbol to an object, i.e. using a symbol with the intention to characterize an object as falling under it, as in "That's Bill" or "That's a cow" (see Greenberg, 2001). The straightforward way to give an information-based account is to say, roughly speaking, that a symbol has content as it is the property whose instantiations normally or optimally covary with the symbol's *application* (e.g. Boghossian, 1989). Many things other than water—deserts, *thoughts of deserts*—may covary with the *occurrence* of my mental symbol for water. But, leaving aside mistakes, only water covaries with the *application* of the relevant mental symbol.[3] The problem is that the notion of an application of a symbol is plainly an intentional notion that, at least on the face of it, needs to be explained in terms of internal aspects of the use of symbols such as the intentions or other mental states that cause the occurrence of the symbol.

A different problem for standard informational theories is that they have fewer resources than other versions of CRS for dealing with such problems as necessarily co-referring expressions and necessarily co-instantiated properties. For example, an informational theory cannot appeal to inferential or implicational considerations to distinguish the concept of a unicorn from the concept of a gremlin (assuming unicornhood and gremlinhood are both necessarily empty). And, similarly, an informational theory cannot appeal to a concept's role in reasoning to solve the problem (Quine, 1960) of whether the concept refers to rabbits, undetached rabbit parts, or temporal stages of rabbits.

It is also natural to appeal to internal aspects of conceptual role to address the problem that not everything that carries information has meaning or content. For example, for a creature to have a concept of, say, red, it is not enough that there be some state or condition of the creature whose instances or tokens carry the information that there is something red in the environment. The relevant tokens

---

[3] We here ignore the different problem for information-based theories of what makes it the case that a symbol means *water* rather than, for example, certain patterns of nerve cell stimulations, or some other more proximal or distal correlate of the symbol's occurrence.

must figure appropriately in the creature's psychology. In response to this kind of problem, some theorists move away from pure information-based accounts by taking into account how the internal tokening of a symbol relates to other internal states in a way that might affect how the creature acts to satisfy its needs (Stalnaker, 1984, pp. 18–19; Dretske, 1986, 2000; Fodor, 1990, p. 130).

There are other issues on which even the purest information-based theories tend to appeal to internal aspects of conceptual role. For example, Fodor (1998, p. 35, 163–5; Fodor and Lepore, 2002, pp. 18–22) holds that what makes it the case that a complex symbol—one that is composed of other symbols arranged in a certain way—expresses a particular concept is the symbol's relations to the simple symbols of which it is composed. Another example is that it is difficult to see how to give an account of the content of logical constants without appeal to internal relations (Fodor, 1990, pp. 110–11).

Fodor's (1990) asymmetric-dependence theory, perhaps the best-known informational theory, attempts to deal with some of the problems discussed in this section,[4] but it has generated a battery of objections (Loewer and Rey, 1991) and few if any adherents, and we think it is fatally flawed (Greenberg, 2001).

Fodor and Lepore have argued that CRS must give up the extra resources available to versions of CRS that are not purely informational; we criticize this argument in the next section. (A terminological caution: Fodor and Lepore use the term "conceptual role semantics" or "inferential role semantics" for (roughly) the views that we are calling "CCRS"; thus, in their terminology, information-based theories of contents are rivals to conceptual role theories, rather than as in our terminology special versions of them.)

14.5.2 Fodor and Lepore's Dilemma

We have so far argued that it is not easy to see how meaning or content could be explained entirely in terms of information or indication without appeal to internal uses of terms. In other words, it is hard to see how CRS can avoid being CCRS.

We now consider an argument by Fodor and Lepore that is supposed to provide a threshold objection to any form of CCRS (Fodor, 2000; Fodor, 1998, ch. 4, 1990, pp. ix–xi; Fodor and Lepore, 1992). (See also the discussion of this argument in Sections 10.3–10.4 of the Meaning Holism chapter in this volume.) Fodor and Lepore begin by assuming plausibly that no two people accept exactly the same inferences and implications. Given that assumption, they argue that CCRS faces the following dilemma. Either

(a) every such internal aspect of the way one uses one's terms is relevant to the terms' content, or

---

[4] Fodor's asymmetric dependence theory is designed to do without the notion of an application of a concept (see Fodor, 1990, pp. 89–131). For Fodor on co-extensive and co-instantiated symbols, see his 1994, pp. 39–79; also his 1990, pp. 100–1; 1998, pp. 163–5.

(b) only some such internal aspects are relevant.

If (a), according to Fodor and Lepore it follows that no two people ever mean the same thing by any of their terms (or ever have thoughts with the same contents). This conclusion, they maintain, has the following implications, which they take to be absurd:

(c1) that no two people can ever agree or disagree with each other about anything

(c2) that intentional explanation collapses since no two people ever fall under the same intentional laws.

If (b), according to Fodor and Lepore it follows that CRS is committed to the analytic-synthetic distinction, a distinction that (according to them) has been decisively undermined by Quine.

However, Fodor and Lepore's presentation of their alleged dilemma is flawed. Consider their argument if horn (a) of the dilemma is chosen. That argument rests on, among other things, the following assumption:

(aa) that, if all aspects of internal use are relevant to meaning and the aspects of one person's internal use are not exactly the same as those of another person's, then the two people do not mean the same thing by their terms.

Assumption (aa) is indefensible because, as we emphasized at the beginning of this chapter, even if all aspects of internal use are relevant to meaning, there can be differences in such use without a corresponding difference in meaning. To say that a given aspect of internal use is relevant to meaning is to say that there is a possible case in which a difference in that aspect makes for a difference in meaning, not to say that a difference in that aspect always makes for a difference in meaning. (Similarly, whether the number of students in a class is odd or even depends on the number of students in the class, but that does not imply that two classes with different numbers of students cannot both have an even number of students.)

In response, Fodor and Lepore might try to argue that no plausible version of CCRS has the consequence that differences in the determinants of content do not imply differences in content. But such a response would require consideration of the merits of different possible versions of CCRS; the point we have made here is that Fodor and Lepore have failed in their attempt to offer an in-principle threshold objection to all versions of CCRS.

It is also worth noting that two people who mean different things by their terms can still use those terms to agree or disagree with each other. Mary can disagree with John by saying something that they both know is true only if what John said is false. Mary can agree with John by saying something that they both know is true only if what John said is true. To take a very simple example, suppose that Mary and John do not mean exactly the same thing by their color terms in that the boundaries between what counts for them as *red* and *orange* are slightly different and the boundaries between what counts for them as *green* and *blue* are slightly different. Still, they disagree about a color when John calls it *red* and Mary calls it *green*.

The claim that intentional explanation collapses if no two people have the same contents can also be disputed. It may be that intentional explanation requires only a notion of similarity of content (Harman, 1973, 1993; Block, 1986). Fodor (1998, pp. 30–4) has objected that, according to CRS, to have *similar* content is to be related to at least many of the *same* contents, which presupposes sameness of content. But CRS is not in fact committed to any such account of similarity of content.

Thus, horn (a) of the alleged dilemma for CCRS is harmless.

According to horn (b) of the alleged dilemma, the claim that only some aspects of internal conceptual role are relevant to meaning commits the CCRS theorist to an analytic-synthetic distinction of a sort that Quine is supposed to have shown to be untenable.

We have three things to say about this horn. First, there are coherent versions of CCRS that do not accept an analytic-synthetic distinction yet take some but not all aspects of internal conceptual role to be relevant to meaning. As we have observed in discussing (aa), from the claim that a given aspect of conceptual role, a certain belief for example, is part of what determines that a symbol has a given meaning, it does not follow that someone without the belief cannot have a symbol with the same meaning. Thus, the belief's relevance to the meaning of the symbol does not imply that the belief is analytic. (See also Section 10.4 of the Meaning Holism chapter.)

Second, various distinctions may qualify as some kind of analytic–synthetic distinction. Whether Quine's (or others') arguments undermine the particular distinction to which a given CCRS is committed depends on the details of each case. (See Rey, 1993, 1995 for discussion.) For example, Peacocke (2002) has made out a strong case that Quine's arguments do not apply to the particular kind of analytic-synthetic distinction to which Peacocke's (1992) version of CCRS is committed. Similarly, Fodor's own informational theory of content is committed to conceptual truth, though arguably not to an objectionable version of the analytic–synthetic distinction (e.g. Fodor, 1998, p. 14 and fn. 8).

Third, Quine's attack is aimed at a traditional notion of analyticity according to which analytic truths are *a priori*. But CCRS need not accept that knowledge of conceptual role is *a priori*. As we noted above (Section 14.2.1), a thinker can have a symbol with a certain conceptual role without having a theoretical understanding of how she uses the symbol.

We conclude that Fodor and Lepore have not yet refuted CCRS.

14.6 FURTHER OBJECTIONS TO CRS

According to CRS, conceptual role determines and explains content. Searle (1980, 1992) vigorously argues for the opposite view. Searle argues that mental states have intrinsic content that explains and is not explained by the conceptual roles such states have in thinking. Other symbols have derivative content by virtue of having some relation to the intrinsically contentful mental states. Linguistic representations are used to express people's thoughts. States of a computer program have derived content through people interpreting them as having content. A translation of a term into another language is good to the extent that the translation expresses an idea with the same intrinsic content as the idea expressed by the term being translated. Although we can appeal to linguistic use in assessing translations, that is not because use determines content but because content determines use, in Searle's view.

CRS denies that an explanation of conceptual role by appeal to intrinsic content has any force unless it reduces to some version of CRS. Perhaps explanations of particular occasions of the use of a mental symbol E will invoke m, the content of the symbol. But what explains E's having content m? In order to explain why E has the role it has, Searle would have to explain why it has content m, but his appeal to intrinsic intentionality has no resources to do so (though he thinks that biology may ultimately be able to explain intrinsic intentionality). In particular, what is wanted is an explanation of why something has a particular content that also accounts for why something with that content has a given role. CRS has an explanation of E's having content m that satisifies this condition (though, as we discuss in Section 14.6.3, there are difficult issues about, for example, whether and how actual use can explain a term's having a certain normative role). We now consider some worries about this explanation.

14.6.1 Circularity Objection

One worry about the explanation provided by CRS is that it might be circular. Consider the suggestion that the meaning of logical conjunction (*and*) is determined in part by the fact that one immediately recognizes that a conjunction implies its conjuncts. Fodor (2004) objects that any such account is circular because to recognize an implication presupposes thinking of the items in the implication relation as having content.

A defender of the suggestion might respond that the relevant recognition of implications does not involve such thoughts about symbols. It is enough that one is at home in using the symbols in the relevant way. One simply and directly treats a conjunction as implying its conjuncts. (See also the discussion in Section 10.2 of the Meaning Holism chapter.)

But in order to make such a response work it is necessary to show that the relevant conceptual roles can be specified without reference to the content of the symbols.

Peacocke (2002) offers a version of CRS that is explicitly circular in explaining aspects of conceptual role in terms of what a person is "entitled" to accept, where entitlement is a normative epistemological notion that is itself to be explained in terms of intentional content. More precisely, according to Peacocke, "there is a large circle of interrelated notions, including entitlement, knowledge, and even intentional content itself, each of whose elucidations ultimately involves the others."

A related objection is that conceptual roles are interrelated and cannot be specified in isolation from one another. A structuralist like Saussure (1916) says that one's concept of red is partly defined in terms of colors like green that are in a certain respect excluded by something's being red. Sellars (1956, section 19) writes that "one can have the concept of green only by having a whole battery of concepts of which it is one element." Similarly, Wittgenstein (1969) says, "When we first begin to *believe* anything, what we believe is not a single proposition but a whole system of propositions. (Light dawns gradually over the whole.)" How can the conceptual roles of concepts be specified if they are interdependent in this way?

One response to this problem (e.g. Peacocke, 1992, pp. 9–12) is to suppose that, where there is such interdependence, there is a system of connected conceptual roles. (Of course, in the case of color concepts, there are connections through perception to items in the environment in addition to the interconnections among those concepts.) Two people can be said to have the same color concepts to the extent that they both have systems of concepts that satisfy certain conditions. (Compare our discussion above about when people might count as having the same color concepts.)

This idea fits with Ramsey's (1931) suggestion that references to theoretical states and processes be replaced with existentially quantified variables in an overall theory. It also fits with the idea that conceptual roles are analogous to roles played by symbols in the running of computer programs.[5]

Such analogies open CRS up to objections on various fronts. One is that, if conceptual roles can be specified in the manner suggested, then it should actually be possible to build a robot directed by a computer program in which symbols have the relevant conceptual roles and therefore have the appropriate contents. While some defenders of CRS welcome that conclusion, Searle argues that it reduces CRS to absurdity.

14.6.2 Chinese Room Objection

Searle (1992) summarizes his basic argument against any computationally friendly version of CRS in the slogan that syntax is not enough for semantics. However, that slogan is misleading as an objection to CRS. The idea that syntax is not enough for semantics is obviously correct if what is meant is simply that expressions with different meanings might have exactly the same syntactic form. The sentences "Jack loves Mary" and "Sue hates Allen" mean different things but have exactly the same syntactic form, say, "(N (V N))". However, that obvious point by itself is no objection to computationally friendly CRS. CRS does not make the false claim that syntax in the ordinary sense is sufficient for semantics.

Searle takes conceptual role to be a purely syntactical matter in the following sense: conceptual role is to be defined entirely in terms of operations on certain symbols without any appeal to meaning or content. Of course, as emphasized above, conceptual role can also involve using symbols in relation to non-linguistic things in the world, as in perceptual responses or in practical reasoning leading to action. So Searle must understand "purely syntactic operation" to include these cases also.

Searle's famous "Chinese Room" argument tries to show that syntax in this second sense is not sufficient for understanding. The argument has a number of different

---

[5] It should be noted, however, that, as Peacocke (1992) recognizes, his account makes use of contentful notions in a way that cannot be eliminated through Ramsey's suggestion.

targets. For our purposes, we can treat the argument as seeking to show by example that a person can know how to use symbols and be at ease with their use without having any understanding of what they mean.

The argument begins by supposing, for the sake of *reductio*, that a given person who speaks and understands only a dialect of Chinese thinks using a system whose elements have specifiable conceptual roles. According to CRS, this speaker's understanding of Chinese consists in his or her being disposed to use and using the symbols in the right way. So, CRS is committed to thinking that any other person would have the same understanding of Chinese if the other person used those elements in the same way.

The argument continues as follows. We are assuming that the relevant conceptual roles are specifiable, so consider a specification of those roles. Given that specification, it would be possible in theory to construct a robot that would have a central processor running a program that would allow the robot to follow those rules. And, if that is possible, it is in theory possible to replace the central processor in the robot with a room containing a person knowing only English and so not knowing any Chinese, who nevertheless could blindly follow the rules. Although the person doing the processing might use the symbols in accordance with the rules, he or she would not understand the symbols. So, it seems that, contrary to CRS, the use of symbols in the relevant way is not sufficient for understanding the meaning of those symbols.

Searle's Chinese Room Argument has generated an enormous response (beginning with the responses to Searle, 1980, in the same issue of the journal). We will not try to summarize this response.

Instead we mention only the following possible response. It might be suggested on behalf of CRS that the role of symbols being used to simulate a person who has certain concepts (the Chinese speaker in the example) is not the same as the role of the symbols in the Chinese speaker that express the relevant concepts. The original Chinese speaker is using the symbols to think with. The person processing a simulation—*the simulator*, for short—is using the symbols to simulate someone who uses the symbols to think with. One sign of this is that the Chinese speaker does not normally think about the symbols whereas the simulator must think about them.

But can this response be developed without circularity? As formulated, the response is circular because it explains conceptual role in part by mentioning what the subject is thinking about, which is to explain conceptual role in terms of intentional content, whereas CRS seeks to do things the other way round, explaining intentional content in terms of conceptual role.

We think that the response to Searle is not circular: it is not the case that the differences in conceptual role between the Chinese speaker and the simulator show up only at the level of contentful descriptions (though that level offers an easy way of describing the differences). The problem is that Searle has given us a strong reason for thinking that the simulator's symbols, either on paper or in his mind/brain (if we assume that he fully internalizes the process) do not have the same conceptual roles as the symbols of the Chinese speaker. In particular, he tells us that the simulator has not been taught to speak and understand Chinese but has been taught to follow rules that capture the conceptual role of the Chinese speaker's symbols. The result is that the simulator's symbols should not have the same conceptual role of those of the Chinese speaker, but those of someone who is simulating the speaking of Chinese. The point is most obvious if we take the original case where the simulator is in a room and the input and output are slips of paper with marks on them. The symbols in the actual Chinese speaker's mind/brain are connected to certain perceptual states and actions. The candidate symbols in the simulator are connected to very different perceptual states and actions (perceptions of certain slips of paper with certain figures on them coming into the room and actions of making certain marks and passing slips of paper back out).

Even if we suppose that the simulator internalizes the whole process, including the room, and simply responds to utterances in Chinese with utterances apparently in Chinese, the problem remains.[6] Whether the simulator has the same conceptual role as the Chinese speaker depends on how the connections are organized, not just on whether the inputs and outputs are the same. So Searle faces a dilemma. If, on the one hand, he stipulates that the overall conceptual role of the simulator's symbols, including their internal organization, is now identical to that of the Chinese speaker, then he no longer will be able to rely on the strong intuition that the simulator does not understand Chinese. CRS theorists can plausibly maintain that a "simulator" who can interact with Chinese speakers and the world in just the way that Chinese speakers do—and whose internal symbolic organization is the same as that of Chinese speakers—understands Chinese.[7] (Theorists who believe that conceptual role cannot explain understanding may not be convinced, but the present point is only that the Chinese Room does not provide such theorists with a refutation of CRS.)

If, on the other hand, Searle stipulates that the Chinese thinker continues to manipulate symbols according to the now-internalized rules for simulating the conceptual role of the Chinese speaker, we lack good reason to think that the overall conceptual role of the simulator's symbols is the same as the overall conceptual role of the Chinese speaker's symbols. To put it in the intuitive way again, the relations of some of the simulator's symbols (the ones that are supposed to correspond to those of the Chinese speaker) will be controlled by other symbols (the ones that specify the rules for manipulating the former symbols). We have not been given reason to think that that is precisely how the Chinese speaker's symbols are organized. (And, once again, if it is stipulated that the simulator's internal states are organized in the same way as those of the Chinese speaker, it is plausible to claim that the simulator is no longer simulating, but speaking and understanding, Chinese.)

---

[6] The following response applies, *mutatis mutandis*, if we suppose instead that the Chinese speaker is in the room manipulating slips of paper.

[7] As noted above, same conceptual role is not necessary for same content, but it is sufficient. Searle's argument depends on claiming that the simulator has the same conceptual roles as the Chinese speaker (and therefore that CRS entails that he has the same contents as the Chinese speaker).

In sum, a set of instructions for taking symbols and manipulating them in a way that gives the simulator's symbols the same conceptual role as a Chinese speaker's mental symbols may be self-defeating. For part of the conceptual role of a Chinese speaker's mental symbols may be that they are not manipulated in accordance with that set of instructions.

14.6.3 Objections that Conceptual Role is Non-Factual

A related issue about CRS is whether it is a purely factual matter what the conceptual roles of a given person's symbols are. Some symbols, for example those in a computer program that is running on a particular computer, may have their conceptual roles in virtue of facts about design. Assume that it can be a completely factual matter whether someone has designed a system so as to instantiate a particular computer program.[8] In that case, to the extent that a symbol's conceptual role is determined by design facts, its conceptual role can be a purely factual matter. But CRS is supposed to apply to the content of concepts of someone who has not been designed or programmed by anyone.[9] Can it be in the same way a matter of fact whether such a person's concepts have the relevant conceptual roles?

Suppose CRS says that a person's concepts have the relevant conceptual roles as long as the system *can be interpreted* as instantiating the relevant conceptual roles. Kalke (1969) and Searle (1992) object that there will always be a way to interpret *anything* as running any given computer program. If they are right *even taking into account relevant external relations*, this version of CRS is in trouble. But once external relations are taken into account, it is far from obvious that they are right.

Apart from that worry, an actual system may break down or wear out or not have enough capacity to carry out certain tasks it is programmed to do. What distinguishes those aspects of the system that are defects or limitations from those that are part of the program, as it were? CRS needs to distinguish those aspects of a system that reflect conceptual roles of components and those aspects that reflect processing limitations, noise, damage, and mistakes. But how does such a distinction reflect facts about the system itself (Wittgenstein, 1953; Kripke, 1982)? Such issues have spawned a large literature (e.g. Boghossian, 1989; Horwich, 1990, 1998; Lewis, 1983; Millikan, 1990; Pettit, 1990; Pietroski and Rey, 1995; Soames, 1998).[10]

A different but related issue is whether actual dispositions to use symbols in thought are the right sort of thing to determine content. Some theorists have thought that conceptual role must have a normative element (Kripke, 1982). For example,

---

[8] This is to assume that it can be a factual matter what the content of a designer's intentions are.

[9] We have noted above that some theorists (e.g. Dennett, 1995; Millikan, 1984, 1993; Neander, 1995) appeal to evolution as a source of something that takes the place of design. A certain sort of learning might function similarly (Dretske, 1986, 1988). The worries in the following paragraphs may still apply.

[10] Greenberg (2001) shows that the so-called "disjunction problem" familiar from information-based theories of content (e.g. Fodor, 1990) is another way of presenting the same group of issues.

we mentioned above that Peacocke's (2002) version of CRS explains some aspects of conceptual role partly in terms of conditions that "entitle" someone to accept something, where entitlement is a normative notion. Apart from the circularity worry already discussed, one might also worry whether it could be a purely factual matter whether a certain normative condition obtains. Greenberg (2001, 2005) discusses a view that can be understood as a normative version of CRS—the view that a thought's having a certain content is in part explained not by the thinker's being disposed to use symbols in certain ways but by the thinker's being subject to standards requiring her to do so.

We will not try to answer the questions raised in this section, although we do not think they pose insuperable difficulties for CRS.

14.7 Summary

CRS says that the meanings of expressions of a language or other symbol system or the contents of mental states are determined and explained by the way symbols are used in thinking. According to CRS one's understanding of aspects of one's own concepts consists in knowing how to use one's symbols and being at ease with that use. Understanding expressions in other systems may involve interpreting or translating those expressions into corresponding symbols of one's own system.

Many different aspects of the way symbols are used are relevant to their meaning or content. There seem to be three main categories of uses, having to do with perceptual input, internal thinking, and output in action. Information-based or indication theories that attempt to rely only on perceptual input face difficulties that put pressure on them to rely on other aspects of conceptual role. Worries about CRS include possible circularity, how to respond to Searle's Chinese Room Argument, and whether there are facts about conceptual role. Whether these worries can be satisfactorily addressed is a matter of current debate.

REFERENCES

Ayer, A. J. (1936). *Language, Truth and Logic*. London: Gollancz.

Blair, R. J. R. (1995). "A Cognitive Developmental Approach to Morality: Investigating the Psychopath." *Cognition*, 57: 1–29.

Block, N. (1986). "Advertisement for a Semantics for Psychology," in *Midwest Studies in Philosophy* 10: 615–78. Minneapolis, MN: University of Minnesota Press.

—— (1998). "Is Experiencing just Representing?" *Philosophy and Phenomenological Research*, 58.

Boghossian, P. (1989). "The Rule-Following Considerations," *Mind*, 98: 507–49.

Bonjour, L. (1998). *In Defense of Pure Reason*. London: Cambridge University Press.

Davidson, D. (1973). "Radical Interpretation," *Dialectica*, 27: 313–28.

Davidson, D. (1974). "On the very Idea of a Conceptual Scheme," *Proceedings and Addresses of the American Philosophical Association*, 47: 5–20.

Dennett, D. (1995). *Darwin's Dangerous Idea*. New York: Simon and Schuster.

Dilthey, W. (1883). *Einleitung in die Geisteswissenschaften*. English translation by R. A. Makkreel and F. Rodi, *Introduction to the Human Sciences*. Princeton, NJ: Princeton University Press, 1989.

Dreier, J. (1990). "Internalism and Speaker Relativism," *Ethics*, 101: 6–26.

Dretske, F. (1986). "Misrepresentation," in Bogdan, R., editor, *Belief*. Oxford: Oxford University Press.

_____ (1988). *Explaining Behavior*, Cambridge, Mass: MIT Press.

_____ (2000). *Perception, Knowledge, and Belief: Selected Essays*. Cambridge: Cambridge University Press.

Dummett, M. (1991). *The Logical Basis of Metaphysics*. London: Duckworth.

Field, H. (2001). "Attributions of meaning and content," in H. Field, *Truth and the Absence of Fact*. Oxford: Clarendon Press, pp. 157–74.

Fodor, J. (1987). *Psychosemantics*. Cambridge, MA: MIT Press.

_____ (1990). *A Theory of Content and Other Essays*. Cambridge, MA: MIT Press.

_____ (1994). *The Elm and the Expert: Mentalese and its Semantics*. Cambridge, MA: MIT Press.

_____ (1998). *Concepts: Where Cognitive Science Went Wrong*. Oxford: Oxford University Press.

_____ (2000). *The Mind Doesn't Work That Way: The Scope and Limits of Computational Psychology*. Cambridge, MA: MIT Press.

_____ (2004). "Having Concepts: A Brief Refutation of the 20th Century," *Mind and Language*, 19: 29–47.

Fodor, J. and Lepore, E. (2002). *The Compositionality Papers*. Oxford: Clarendon Press.

Frege, G. (1982). "Über Sinn und Bedeutung," in Zeitschrift für Philosophie und philosophische Kritik.

Greenberg, M. (2001). *Thoughts Without Masters: Incomplete Understanding and the Content of Mind* (University of Oxford, D.Phil. Dissertation).

_____ (2005). "A New Map of Theories of Mental Content: Constitutive Accounts and Normative Theories," in E. Sosa and E. Villanueva (eds.), *Philosophical Issues*, 15.

Hare, R. M. (1952). *The Language of Morals*. Oxford: Oxford University Press.

Harman, G. (1973). *Thought*. Princeton, NJ: Princeton University Press.

_____ (1974). "Meaning and Semantics," in M. K. Munitz and P. K. Unger (eds.), *Semantics and Philosophy*. New York: NYU Press, pp. 1–16.

_____ (1975). "Language, Thought, and Communication," in K. Gunderson (ed.), *Language, Mind, and Knowledge: Minnesota Studies in the Philosophy of Science* VII. Minneapolis, Minn.: University of Minnesota Press, pp. 279–98.

_____ (1986). *Change in View*. Cambridge, MA: MIT Press.

_____ (1987). "(Nonsolipsistic) Conceptual Role Semantics," in E. Lepore (ed.), *New Directions in Semantics*. London: Academic Press, pp. 55–81.

_____ (1990). "Immanent and Transcendent Approaches to the Theory of Meaning," in R. Gibson and R. B. Barrett, eds., *Perspectives on Quine*. Oxford: Blackwell.

_____ (1995). "Rationality," in E. E. Smith and D. N. Osherson, eds., *Thinking: Invitation to Cognitive Science, Volume 3*. Cambridge, MA: MIT Press, pp. 175–211.

Holyoak, K. J. and Thagard, P. R. (1994). *Mental Leaps: Analogy in Creative Thought*. Cambridge, MA: MIT Press.

Horwich, P. (1990). "Wittgenstein and Kripke on the Nature of Meaning," *Mind and Language*, 5: 105–21.

_____ (1998). *Meaning*. Oxford: Oxford University Press.

Johnson-Laird, P. N. and Byrne, R. M. J. (1991). *Deduction*. Hillsdale, NJ: Erlbaum.

Kalke, W. (1969). "What's Wrong with Fodor and Putnam's Functionalism," *Nous*, 3: 83–93.

Katz, J. A. (1966). *The Philosophy of Language*. New York: Harper and Row.

Kempton, W. (1987). "Two Theories of Home Heat Control," in N. Quinn and D. Holland, eds. *Cultural Models in Language and Thought*. New York: Cambridge University Press.

Kripke, S. A. (1982). *Wittgenstein on Rules and Private Language : An Elementary Exposition*. Cambridge, MA: Harvard University Press.

Lakoff, G. and Johnson, M. (1980). *Metaphors We Live By*. Chicago: University of Chicago Press.

Lewis, D. (1983). "New Work for a Theory of Universals," *Australasian Journal of Philosophy*, 61: 343–77. Reprinted in *Papers in Metaphysics and Epistemology* (1999). Cambridge, UK: Cambridge University Press, pp. 8–55.

Loewer, B. and Rey, G., eds. (1991). *Meaning in Mind: Fodor and His Critics*. Cambridge, MA: Blackwell.

Millikan, R. G. (1984). *Language, Thought, and Other Biological Categories: New Foundations for Realism*. Cambridge, MA/London: Bradford Books, MIT Press.

_____ (1990). "Truth Rules, Hoverflies, and the Kripke-Wittgenstein Paradox," *Philosophical Review* 99: 323–53. Reprinted in her 1993, pp. 211–39.

_____ (1993). *White Queen Psychology and Other Essays for Alice*. Cambridge, MA: MIT Press.

Nagel, T. (1974). "What is it Like to be a Bat?" *Philosophical Review*, 83: 435–50.

Neander, K. (1995). Misrepresenting and Malfunctioning," *Philosophical Studies*, 79: 109–41.

Norman, D. (1988). *The Psychology of Everyday Things*. New York: Basic Books. Reprinted as (1998). *The Design of Everyday Things*. London: MIT Press.

Papineau, D. (1987). *Reality and Representation*. Oxford: Blackwell.

Peacocke, C. (1983). *Sense and Content*. Oxford: Oxford University Press.

_____ (1992). *A Study of Concepts*. Cambridge, MA: MIT Press.

_____ (1999). *Being Known*. Oxford. Clarendon Press.

_____ (2002). "Three Principles of Rationalism," *European Journal of Philosophy*, 10: 375–97.

Pettit, P. (1990). "The Reality of Rule-Following," *Mind*, 99: 1–22. Reprinted in (2002). *Rules, Reasons, and Norms*. Oxford: Oxford University Press.

Pietroski, P. and Rey, G. (1995). "When Other Things Aren't Equal: *Saving Ceteris Paribus Laws from Vacuity*," *British Journal for the Philosophy of Science*, 46: 81–110.

Putnam, H. (1962). "It ain't Necessarily So," *Journal of Philosophy*, 59: 658–71.

_____ (1975). "The Meaning of 'Meaning,'" in Putnam, H., *Mind, Language, and Reality* (Philosophical Papers, vol. II). Cambridge, UK: Cambridge University Press).

Quine, W. V. (1953). "The Problem of Meaning in Linguistics," in W. V. Quine, *From a Logical Point of View*. New York: Harper and Row, pp. 47–64.

_____ (1960). *Word and Object*. Cambridge, MA: MIT Press.

Ramsey, F. P. (1931). *The Foundations of Mathematics*. London: Kegan Paul, Trench, Trubner.

Recanati, F. (2001). "Open Quotation," *Mind*, 110: 637–87.

Rey, Georges (1993). The Unavailability of What We Mean," *Grazer Philosophische Studien*, 46: 61–101.

_____ (1995). "Keeping Meaning More in Mind", *Intellectica* 21: 65–80.

Ryle, G. (1961). "Use, Usage, and Meaning," *Proceedings of the Aristotelian Supplementary Volume*, 35: 223–30.

de Saussure, F. (1916). *Cours de linguistique générale*. Paris: Payot.

Searle, J. (1980). "Minds, Brains, and Programs," *Behavioral and Brain Sciences*, 3.

_____ (1992). *The Rediscovery of the Mind*. Cambridge, MA: MIT Press.

Sellars, W. (1956). "Empiricism and the Philosophy of Mind", in *Minnesota Studies in The Philosophy of Science, Vol. I: The Foundations of Science and the Concepts of Psychology and Psychoanalysis*, edited by Herbert Feigl and Michael Scriven (Minneapolis: University of Minnesota Press: 253–329).

_____ (1962). "Truth and Correspondence," *Journal of Philosophy*, 59: 29–56.

_____ (1963). "Some Reflections on Language Games," in his *Science, Perception, and Reality*. London: Routledge and Kegan Paul.

_____ (1969). "Language as Thought and as Communication," *Philosophy and Phenomenological Research*, 29: 506–27.

Soames, S. (1998). "Skepticism about Meaning: Indeterminacy, Normativity, and the Rule-Following Paradox," *The Canadian Journal of Philosophy*, Supplementary Volume 23, *Meaning and Reference*, Kazmi, A. A., ed., pp. 1–39.

Stalnaker, R. (1984). *Inquiry*. Cambridge, MA: Bradford Books, MIT Press.

Stampe, D. (1977). "Towards a Causal Theory of Linguistic Representation," in P. French, T. Uehling, and H. Wettstein (eds.), *Midwest Studies in Philosophy*, 2. University of Minnesota Press, Minneapolis, MN, pp. 42–63.

Strawson, P. F. (1974). *Subject and Predicate in Logic and Grammar*. London: Methuen.

Wittgenstein, L. (1953). *Philosophical Investigations*. Oxford: Blackwell.

_____ (1969). *On Certainty*. G. E. M. Anscombe and G. H. von Wright (eds.). D. Paul and G. E. M. Anscombe (trans.). Oxford: Blackwell.

CHAPTER 15

SEMANTIC INTERNALISM AND EXTERNALISM

KATALIN FARKAS

15.1 THREE CLAIMS ABOUT MEANING

IN a sense, the meaning of our words obviously depends on circumstances outside us. 'Elm' in English is used to talk about elms, and though I could decide—perhaps as a kind of code—to use the word 'elm' to talk about beeches, my decision would hardly change what other people mean by the word. The meaning of 'elm' depends on the practices or conventions of the language-speaking community, and these are certainly beyond my control. In this sense, it certainly looks as though meaning is determined by factors outside the individual. At the same time, it seems that it is up to me what *I mean* by my words; and in fact, the meaning of a word in the language is simply a result of what most of us mean by it. Another way of putting this point is that even if the meaning of an expression is determined by social agreement, grasping the meaning of the word is an individual psychological act. I may grasp the

I am grateful to Tim Crane and Zoltán Gendler Szabó for discussions and comments on earlier versions, and to Barry Smith for detailed and very helpful comments on the penultimate draft. I would also like to thank the support of the Hungarian OTKA (grant no. т046757) and the Philosophy of Language Research Group of the Hungarian Academy of Sciences.

usual public meaning correctly, or I may—willingly or accidentally—mean something different by the word, but it looks as though meaning in this sense depends entirely on me.

It is also plausible to assume that in some sense, our physical environment contributes to what our words mean. If I am right in assuming that before Europeans arrived at Australia, English had no word which meant the same as the word 'kangaroo' does nowadays, this is easily explained by the fact that people at that time hadn't encountered kangaroos. However, a further question is whether it would have been *possible* to have a word with the same meaning, if kangaroos had never existed, or no one had ever met them. And it seems the answer is yes. You can learn what 'kangaroo' means without ever having seen a kangaroo, say from descriptions or drawings; and descriptions and drawings can be made about non-existent creatures. If this were not so, we couldn't have words like 'yeti' or 'unicorn'. Thus the existence of kangaroos, though it in actual fact did play a role in a word acquiring its meaning, is not necessary for having a word with this meaning. This brings us to our first claim: meaning is independent from—social and physical—factors outside us.

The function of certain expressions in the language is to refer to things, and expressions refer to things in virtue of their meaning. This is so obvious that it almost defies explanation or supporting argument. If we use the word 'Morning Star' to talk about the Morning Star, what could possibly determine the fact that the expression refers to the Morning Star—rather than say, to Mont Blanc—, if not its meaning? What we learn when we learn the meaning of the expression is precisely that it is used to talk about a certain thing. And if two expressions like the 'Morning Star' and the 'Mont Blanc' refer to different things, this must be in virtue of the difference in their meanings.[1] Of course, there are names like 'Pegasus' which do not refer to anything, but this is also a consequence of their meaning; compare 'Pegasus' and 'Bucephalus'.

Here the claim that meaning determines reference is understood simply as the claim that sameness of meaning implies sameness of reference. A limiting case of this may be those theories which regard a name's reference as its only semantic feature—then the sameness of the only relevant semantic feature of a name automatically results in the sameness of reference. So our second claim about meaning is: meaning determines reference.

The truth-value of a sentence is determined by what the words in the sentence mean and how things are in the world. As Quine says in "The two dogmas of empiricism", the sentence 'Brutus killed Caesar' is true, but it would be false if either 'killed' meant the same as now 'begat' means, or if the world had been different in certain ways. It would also be false, we may add, if for example the name 'Caesar' referred to Octavius, instead of Caesar. We can see how the meaning of the words—by determining their references, by expressing certain relations or activities—collaborate to determine the conditions under which the sentence is true; and if those conditions

---

[1] McCulloch, 1995: 66 and McDowell, 1992: 309 give similar expressions to the obviousness of the idea that meaning determines reference.

obtain in a world, the sentence is true. We shall call the aspect of the meaning of a declarative sentence which is responsible for its truth-conditions its 'content', and our third important claim about meaning—which parallels the second—is that the content of a sentence determines its truth-conditions.[2]

15.2 THE TWIN EARTH ARGUMENTS

We have introduced three plausible claims: that what a speaker means by a word does not depend on social and physical factors outside her; that meaning determines reference; that the content of a sentence determines its truth-conditions. However, in an influential paper published in 1975, Hilary Putnam argued that the first statement is incompatible with the second two.

Putnam's particular case is very well known by now, but let us state it for the record. We are asked to imagine a planet we may call 'Twin Earth', which is just like Earth in most respects, with one difference. The transparent, colourless, odourless liquid which flows in the rivers of Twin Earth, and which people on Twin Earth who speak a language which sounds just like English call 'water', is not H_2O, but has a different complex chemical composition, which we shall abbreviate as XYZ. H_2O and XYZ are distinguishable only by using sophisticated chemical analysis, but in normal circumstances they look, smell and taste the same. Putnam's first contention is that XYZ is not water. If a spaceship travelled from Earth to Twin Earth, travellers from Earth may think first that Twin Earth has water; later, when chemical analysis is done, they would find that they had been wrong. Since XYZ is not water, our word 'water' does not refer to XYZ, and parallel considerations would show that the Twin Earth word 'water' does not refer to H_2O.[3]

Next we are asked to go back in time to say 1750, when the chemical composition of water was not known. Putnam maintains that the word 'water' had the same reference back then as it has now; the subsequent discovery that water is H_2O hasn't changed the meaning and hence the reference of 'water', but simply taught us something about the stuff we have been calling 'water' all along. If this is right, then already back in 1750 the word 'water' as used on Earth referred only to H_2O, and not to XYZ. And similar considerations about Twin Earth would show that their word 'water' referred only to XYZ, and not to H_2O.

[2] This formulation allows for the identification of the meaning of a declarative sentence with its content, and that, in turn, with its truth-conditions. In this case, the determination is trivial. However, it also allows the meaning to be richer or more fine grained than truth-conditions or whatever determines truth-conditions; and it also allows regarding truth-conditions as states of affairs, and distinguishes them from features of abstract entities or mental states.

[3] A scenario similar to Twin Earth is invoked by Strawson (in Strawson, 1959: 20): another sector of the universe reproduces this one. Strawson's point is that since these sectors agree descriptively, mere description is not sufficient to secure particular reference. Evans, 1982: 45 ff includes further discussion of this idea.

Now enter Oscar, an inhabitant of Earth who lived in 1750, and suppose that by some cosmic coincidence, there lived someone on Twin Earth, call him 'Twin-Oscar' (known to his friends simply as 'Oscar'), who was an exact, atom-by-atom replica of Oscar, and shared the same history throughout his lifetime. Oscar and Twin Oscar are internally the same. Two remarks should be made here. First, we set up the Twin Earth scenario in the usual way, assuming that Oscar and Twin Oscar are internal physical duplicates. Internal *physical* sameness entails internal sameness only if Oscar and Twin Oscar are entirely physical entities, an assumption many philosophers are happy to accept. However, if someone thinks that Oscar and Twin Oscar have also non-physical properties, the thought-experiment has to be modified by offering a different notion of internal sameness. Another problem is that Oscar's body contains a significant amount of H_2O, and if there is no H_2O on Twin Earth, Twin Oscar cannot be a physical duplicate of Oscar. The usual answer to this is that we could easily choose another substance which is not to be found in the human body.[4]

Oscar refers exclusively to H_2O by 'water', and Twin Oscar refers exclusively to XYZ by 'water'. If we retain the assumption that meaning determines reference—that is, sameness of meaning implies sameness of reference, and consequently difference in reference implies difference in meaning—, then the meaning of 'water' is different for Oscar and Twin Oscar. This means, however, that internal sameness does not imply sameness of meaning; meaning depends on factors outside the individuals.[5] Hence Putnam's famous slogan: 'Meanings ain't in the head.'

Let us run a slightly different version of the argument. Oscar and Twin Oscar are internally the same. When Oscar says 'Water quenches thirst', his sentence is true if and only if H_2O quenches thirst. The same sentence uttered by Twin Oscar is true iff XYZ quenches thirst. Thus the truth-conditions of their sentences are different. If we retain the assumption that content determines truth-conditions—that is, sameness of content implies sameness of truth-conditions, and consequently, difference in truth-conditions implies difference in content—, then the content of the sentence 'Water quenches thirst' is different for Oscar and Twin Oscar. This means, however, that internal sameness does not imply sameness of content: the content of (some of)

---

[4] Burge, 1979 stipulates sameness of non-intentional mental phenomena in addition to physical sameness for the subjects of his thought-experiment. A suggestion for a notion of internal sameness which is applicable to non-physicalist theories, and at the same time deals with the problem of the human body's containing H_2O, is found in Farkas, 2003. The idea is, briefly, that we could have a perfectly good Twin Earth argument for example about a disease, which is found only in the brain. Therefore the boundary between the internal and the external should not be drawn around the brain, or the body, or the skin, but should be formulated in terms of the subject's perspective. This has further consequences to the issue of self-knowledge.

[5] It may be objected that difference in meaning for internally qualitatively identical subjects does not entail that the difference is due to some *outside* factor: it could be due to the mere fact that we have two different individuals; for example, suppose that 'I' means something different for everyone simply because we are different individuals. (There could be an analogous view about intrinsic properties: 'being identical to Oscar' and 'being identical to Twin Oscar' could be regarded as an intrinsic property, which internal duplicates do not share.) For a defense of the view, see Searle, 1983 ch. 8; for discussion and criticism, Newman, *forthcoming*.

our sentences depends on factors outside the individual. And this is the view known as semantic externalism.

In the version of the Twin Earth argument just presented, we saw that—contrary to our initially appealing statement about meanings—features of our physical environment may play a constitutive role in determining the meaning of our words. Recall our earlier example about kangaroos; the Twin Earth argument suggests that if animals superficially similar to our kangaroos but with a different internal constitution lived on Twin Earth, they would not be *kangaroos*, and hence our word 'kangaroo' would not refer to them. If this is right, then—contrary to what seemed plausible to accept earlier—it wouldn't be possible to mean what we do by 'kangaroo' if kangaroos hadn't existed and had some sort of causal connection to us.

Putnam offers another argument to show that the other external feature we discarded originally, the social community, can have a similar role. To use Putnam's example: suppose that Oscar knows that elms and beeches are some sort of deciduous trees, but he has no further knowledge of the subject. Some people in Oscar's linguistic community—the 'experts'—know what the difference between an elm and a beech tree is, but Oscar is not one of them; he simply uses these words with the assumption that *someone* must know what the difference is. This phenomenon is called 'the division of linguistic labour'. It is still plausible, however, that the word 'elm' in Oscar's idiolect refers to elms only, and not to beeches; if he said 'there is an elm tree in my back garden', he would speak truly if and only if there was an elm tree in his back garden. Now imagine that Twin Oscar's linguistic community has the word 'elm' and 'beech' too, but as it happens, they are swapped: on Twin Earth, 'beech' refers to elms, and 'elm' refers to beeches. Thus we find Oscar and Twin Oscar in the familiar situation: despite their internal sameness, their words 'elm' refer to different things; the truth-conditions of their sentences 'there is an elm tree in my back garden' are different.[6]

Twin Earth arguments proceed by first pointing out that references are different for internally identical subjects, and then arguing further that difference in reference implies a difference in meaning. That *reference* is externally individuated or 'outside the head' is hardly a surprising claim; the view we are considering is interesting because it states the externality of *meanings* or *contents*. And this implication holds only if there is a determinate reference belonging to a meaning. So the assumption that meaning determines reference (or the parallel assumption that content determines truth-conditions) is crucial to these type of arguments for externalism.

We may wonder where this leaves direct reference theories, which hold—at least on one understanding—that nothing mediates between a name and its reference. [7]

---

[6] For similar arguments about belief contents, see Tyler Burge's classic paper, Burge, 1979. Although many defenders of externalism see the argument from natural kind terms and from the division of linguistic labour as making similar points, the two arguments are independent. For a view which favours the first, but not the second argument, see McCulloch, 1995, esp. pp. 175–81.

[7] See the entry on NAMES AND NATURAL KIND TERMS. On various interpretations of the direct reference claim, see Marti, 1995.

Externalists and internalists[8] could all agree that reference is externally individuated. If, as direct reference theories maintain, the name's *only* semantic feature is its reference, then there doesn't seem to be *another* semantic feature which can be claimed external, and hence direct reference theorists would apparently be prevented from being externalists in an interesting sense. However, there is more to this. Direct reference theorists may hold that various functions which have been traditionally assigned to the *meanings* of words—say accounting for the significance of the word, accounting for the primary function of the word to refer, contribution to the meaning or truth-conditions of sentences, etc.—are played by reference. And the thesis that whatever plays these functions does not supervene on the internal states of a speaker is externalist in a non-trivial sense.

Although Putnam's original argument was about meanings, a further important step in the history of the debate was when the externalist thesis was applied to mental contents.[9] Mental states like beliefs are similar to declarative sentences in that they also have semantic features: they can be true or false, and thus have truth-conditions, and can be about certain things in the world. The characteristic of a belief which is responsible for its semantic features is called its content, and just like in the case of sentences, content determines truth-conditions. Some have extended the externalist argument to mental content by assuming a close correspondence between belief content and what is expressed or asserted by uttering a sentence. With this assumption in place, we can reason as follows. Since Oscar's belief which he expresses by saying 'Water quenches thirst' is true iff H_2O quenches thirst, and Twin Oscar's belief which he expresses by using the same words is true iff XYZ quenches thirst, the truth-conditions, and hence the content of their respective beliefs, and hence the beliefs themselves, are different.

As the simple application of the same argument for an externalist conclusion about meanings and mental contents shows, the issues raised by these two varieties of content externalism are largely the same. Externalism is principally a view about the conditions for truth and reference, and invokes the same considerations whether it is the condition for the truth of a sentence, or for the truth of a belief is in question.[10] Notice also that our initial formulation of the problem about meaning has already involved a reference to mental states: Putnam characterized the internalist position as the claim that grasping the meaning of a word is an individual psychological act.[11] However, in what follows, we will keep language in focus, and merely indicate connections with questions about the mind.

---

[8] I call the opponents of externalists 'internalists'. They are also known as 'individualists'; this latter terminology is used in the entry LANGUAGE AS INTERNAL.

[9] The first occurrence of the extension I know of is in McGinn, 1977. See also e.g. McGinn, 1982, Burge, 1982. On various options of how the argument may be extended, see McDowell, 1992.

[10] Though externalism about other aspects of mental states—for example, externalism about attitudes, as it is developed in Williamson, 2000—has no parallel in the linguistic case.

[11] As Putnam points out, Frege for example holds that meanings are abstract, and not mental entities, and hence meanings would be 'outside' the head. What nonetheless makes Frege an internalist on Putnam's view, is the conviction that " 'grasping' these abstract entities was still an individual psychological act." (Putnam, 1975, 218).

15.3 Reference — Same or Different?

The argument presented so far has centred upon the following claims:

- Oscar and Twin Oscar refer to different things by the term 'water'; the truth-conditions for their sentences 'Water quenches thirst' are different.
- Meaning determines reference, content determines truth-conditions.

Let us now consider these steps and possible objections in more detail.

The first statement, even if it is not immediately intuitively obvious, is supported by the theory of natural kind terms advocated by Kripke and Putnam.[12] This theory can, of course, be criticized and ultimately rejected, and it can be claimed that 'water' has the same reference on Earth and Twin Earth.[13] But this in itself can be regarded as a conclusive refutation of externalism only if there aren't any *other* types of expressions which exhibit similar phenomena. In fact, there are such expressions. Suppose that long before Twin Oscar's time, there lived a philosopher on Twin Earth, called 'Aristotle', whose life and influence exactly paralleled those of our Aristotle. When Oscar and Twin Oscar use the name 'Aristotle', they clearly refer to different individuals; to say that both of them refer to both philosophers — and to any other philosopher on other planets whose life was similar — is very implausible. (If we accept Kripke's theory of proper names, we have a neat explanation of all this: Oscar refers to Aristotle, because there is a causal chain leading from some original baptism of Aristotle to his use of the name; whereas Twin Oscar refers to Twin Aristotle, since the causal chain leading to *his* use is leading from some original baptism of *Twin Aristotle*. See also the entry on NAMES AND NATURAL KIND TERMS.) But whether someone accepts Kripke's theory of names or not, the important thing to remember is that as long as we find words whose reference is different when used by internally identical Oscar and Twin Oscar, the starting point of the externalist argument is secured.

Searching for more cases of this sort we may consider so-called indexical expressions like 'you' or 'she'. Suppose that Oscar has a friend called Lucinda, and Twin Oscar has a friend who is an exact replica of Lucinda. When Oscar and Twin Oscar simultaneously use the sentence 'You are beautiful' speaking to their respective friends, Oscar refers to Lucinda, and Twin Oscar refers to Twin Lucinda. That the references are different is as obvious in this case as in the case of proper names. So can we run a Twin Earth argument with 'you'? As we have seen, after establishing the difference of reference for our internally identical subjects, the next step in a Twin Earth argument is to use the connection between meaning and reference to draw a conclusion about meaning. However, we encounter a problem here, since for example Putnam claims that in the case of indexicals, meaning does not determine reference.

Here are some reasons for this view. Ambiguity is the phenomenon when the same word has different meanings in a language; 'ball' could mean a festive event, or the

---

[12] Putnam, 1970 and 1975, and Kripke, 1972. For more details, see the entry on NAMES AND NATURAL KIND TERMS.

[13] For a criticism of externalism along these lines, see Mellor, 1977. See also the contributions on natural kinds in Pessin and Goldberg, 1996.

round object used in a football game. This is a clear sense in which a word has different meanings on different occasions. However, when we use the word 'you' in different contexts to refer to different people, it is not ambiguous in this way. On the contrary, the natural assumption is that the meaning of 'you' is the same in all its uses, and presumably this is what we learn when we learn the meaning of the word. In the discussion above, we assumed that the claim that meaning determines reference amounts to claiming that there is a determinate reference belonging to every meaning, and consequently, difference of reference implies difference in meaning. In the case of 'you', this does not seem to hold: 'you' could refer to different individuals on different occasions and yet, we just saw a good reason to believe that it has a constant linguistic meaning.[14]

So far we have seen that the externalist argument has contradicted one of our initial assumptions about meaning: that what we mean by our words does not constitutively depend on physical and social factors outside us. Now another initial thesis, that meaning determines reference, seems in danger too—or could we perhaps reconcile the present finding with our reasons for holding this thesis? Let us consider a case when someone uses the words 'I' and 'you' *in the same context*: for example Oscar saying to Lucinda 'I stand by you'. 'I' in this case refers to Oscar, 'you' refers to Lucinda, and this difference is due their different meanings. Thus we could preserve the force of the original argument if we said that the meaning of an indexical determines its reference *within a context*, or with respect to a certain context. Next we should see what consequences this has for the externalist argument.

15.4 SENSE DETERMINES REFERENCE

One of the first expressions of the idea that meaning should determine reference is found in Frege's famous paper, "On Sense and Reference": "to the sign there corresponds a definite sense and to that in turn a definite reference" (Frege, 1892: 25). Frege extended the sense/reference distinction to sentences; the sense of a sentence is a *thought*, and the reference of a sentence is its *truth-value*. The determination between sense and reference is upheld in the case of sentences: it is not only that thoughts *are* true or false, but also every thought has a fixed truth-value.

The central cases Frege usually has in mind are from mathematics and logic, and here the idea that each thought has a determinate truth-value is plausible indeed. Given that the Pythagorean theorem is true, no false sentence could express the same thought as the Pythagorean theorem does. If Frege had these kinds of examples in mind in the first place, it is easy to understand why he adopted the doctrine.

It is interesting though that Frege took the doctrine so seriously that he applied it also *outside* the realm of mathematics or logic. This is illustrated by the way he deals

---

[14] This is only one option; others do uphold the thesis that meaning determines reference for indexicals, and deny that indexicals have constant meaning. Yet another position distinguishes different semantic features of indexicals. For details, see the entry on INDEXICALS and some of the discussion below.

with an apparent counterexample in a later paper, "The Thought". He notes that the sentence "This tree is covered with green leaves" may be true now, but false in six months' time. But instead of concluding from this that thoughts do not have fixed truth-values after all, he chooses to hold that the sentence expresses two different thoughts on the two occasions.

The words "this tree is covered with green leaves" are not sufficient by themselves for the utterance, the time of utterance is involved as well. Without the time-indication this gives we have no complete thought, i.e. no thought at all. But this thought, if it is true, is true not only today or tomorrow but timelessly.   (Frege 1918: 103)

Some properties of thoughts may change—for example the property of being grasped by me or by someone else—, but the truth-value of a thought cannot. This suggests that according to Frege, *a thought has its truth-value essentially*. If two sentences differ in truth-value, they cannot express the same thought. The claim that thoughts determine their truth-value is an instance of the doctrine that sense determines reference. This, we can see now, is quite literally true: sense *alone* determines reference.

As we said, this has some plausibility for mathematics and logic. Consider, however, a sentence like

(1)   The inventor of bifocals was a man.

As it happens, the description picks out Benjamin Franklin, who was indeed a man. So the sentence is true. Since this statement is contingent, then there is another world where, say, Deborah Franklin invents bifocals, and where the sentence is false. Here we have a phenomenon which, at first sight, is similar to the one we encountered above about the tree and green leaves: the same sentence can be true in some circumstances (in our world) and false in others (in another possible worlds), so there is no determinate truth-value belonging to this sentence; an apparent counterexample to the claim that sense determines reference.

As a response, we could follow the Fregean recipe to the letter, and insist on the determination between sense and reference. This would mean that sentence (1) *expresses different thoughts in different worlds*. In other words, if we accept without qualification that thoughts have their truth-values essentially, then given that (1) is true, it is impossible to express the same thought by a false sentence. Hence in a world where Mrs Franklin and not Mr Franklin invented bifocals, the sentence could not express the same thought.

But contrary to this, it is standard to assume that in a world where (1) is false, its meaning or its sense or its content would nonetheless be the same. If this is right, then we cannot in general say that sense (or content) *alone* determines a truth-value; we also need the state of the world; that is, in this case, the fact that the inventor bifocals was a man. (An analogous reasoning holds for the description 'the inventor of bifocals': its sense *alone* is not sufficient to determine its denotation. We also need the world to make its contribution.)[15] When we say that sense determines reference, we understand it in this case as relative to some state of the world.

---

[15]   Here I am assuming the admittedly controversial thesis—in this case in agreement with Frege—that the semantic value of 'the inventor of bifocals' is the inventor of bifocals.

Now recall Frege's reasoning about the tree and the green leaves. The only thing established in this case was that the *truth-values* (references) of the sentences are different on the two occasions. From this, Frege concludes that the *thoughts* (senses) are different. If Frege—inspired originally by examples in mathematics and logic—assumes that sense *alone* determines reference, then his reasoning is valid, but it rests on a premise which is highly implausible outside mathematics and logic.

If, on the other hand, we reject this implausible application of the premise, and hold that sense alone need not determine reference outside mathematics and logic, then the reasoning is not valid. If [sense plus X] determine reference, then a difference in reference implies a difference *either* in sense *or* in X. But a difference in reference does not, in itself, entail a difference in sense.

Similar considerations apply to subsentential expressions. What is established in the Twin Earth case, at most, is that the extension—or, if you think the reference of 'water' is a property, then the property—is different on Earth and Twin Earth. Can we claim that sense always alone determines reference (or extension)? No. To be on the safe side, we must claim that [sense plus X] determines reference. Then if water has different references on Earth and Twin Earth, then, until further notice, this means that either sense or X is different.

In the case of the inventor of bifocals, we said that sense determines reference not on its own, but relative to (or together with) a state of the world. There is no immediate objection to extending the same strategy to indexicals: the suggestion would be that in the case of indexicals, meaning determines reference not only relative to the state of the world, but also relative to a context. In the case of contingent (non-indexical) sentences, difference in truth-value *within a world* implies difference of content; in the case of indexical sentences, difference in truth-value *within a context* implies difference in content. Frege held that thoughts have their *truth-value* essentially; but today, we say that contents (which inherit the role of Fregean thoughts) have their *truth-conditions* essentially. This move is motivated precisely by considerations about sentences like 'The inventor of bifocals': for we can say that the truth-value of the sentence may vary from world to world, but the truth-conditions, and hence the content, remain the same. There is nothing inherent in the notion of truth-conditions which would forbid to say that analogously, though the truth-value of an indexical sentence may vary from context to context, its truth-conditions remain the same. Truth-conditions do not have trivial individuation in the way truth-values do. After all, we could have said that the truth-conditions of 'The inventor of bifocals was a man' are different in this world and in the other one: its truth depends on Benjamin Franklin's gender in this world, and on Deborah Franklin's gender in the other. Nonetheless, we decided to regard this difference as not affecting truth-conditions.[16] Why not make similar decisions in other cases?

---

[16] Compare here the fact that the premise used in the externalist argument is often formulated by claiming that meaning determines *extension*, and that difference in extension implies difference in meaning. This is clearly not right: even if the extension of 'philosopher' were different, this would be no reason to think that it had a different meaning. The most we would say is that meaning determines extension-*conditions* (analogously to truth-conditions). If 'reference' is the extension of a denoting

The consequence of this is that the standard Twin Earth argument for externalism is inconclusive. Everyone should agree that at least in some cases, meaning determines reference only together with some factors which are not themselves constitutive of meaning. It requires a separate argument to show that the context in which a sentence is used is not among these further factors. In the absence of such argument, it is possible to hold *both* that the meaning of an indexical determines its reference (relative to some further factors), and that it is the same for internally identical subjects.

Concluding his discussion of natural kind terms, Putnam says that "Our theory can be summarized as saying that words like 'water' have an unnoticed indexical component" (Putnam, 1975: 234). Now even if Putnam's theory of natural kind terms is generally on the right lines, these terms do not function entirely analogously to indexicals. The reference of an indexical depends on the context of its *use*: if I travel from Budapest to London, the reference of 'here' shifts from Budapest to London. But if Oscar traveled to Twin Earth, the reference of his term 'water' would not—or at least not immediately—shift to XYZ[17] (and similarly, the reference of his term 'Aristotle' would not shift either). In the case of natural kind terms, what seems to matter is not the context of *use*, but the context of *acquisition*. Still, keeping in mind these differences, we could extend the previous treatment of indexicals to natural kind terms and names. We could for instance say that the meaning of 'water' is the same for Oscar and Twin Oscar, and that this meaning—together with some further factors, like features of the environment where they acquire the word, or causal chains between initial baptisms and use of terms—determines reference. Thus contrary to the conclusion of the classic Twin Earth argument, the two assumptions that meaning determines reference, and that meaning is internal, are not incompatible.[18]

15.5 EXTERNAL AND INTERNAL SEMANTIC FEATURES

Everyone agrees that at least in some cases, meaning determines reference only together with some further factors. Thus the idea that meaning determines reference, plus a mere difference in reference are not sufficient for the conclusion that meanings are different—the difference could be due to a difference in the further factors. There are, however, independent considerations which may show that in some cases where

expression, then meaning determines reference-conditions, and not reference. And the individuation of reference-conditions is also far from trivial.

[17] Though it may shift after a certain time. This is the phenomenon called 'slow-switching", see Burge, 1988.

[18] It should be noted that the question of what contribution the context makes to an utterance is a subject of intense debates. See the entries on THE DISTINCTION BETWEEN SEMANTICS AND PRAGMATICS and RELEVANCE THEORY: NEW DIRECTIONS AND DEVELOPMENTS.

the reference is different, so are the contents of sentences. Suppose that you and I run a race; we hit the finish pretty much at the same time, and we both exclaim: 'You lost'.[19] We disagree; and this disagreement is naturally understood as stating different things or having different beliefs. A further plausible explanation of this is that the content of our statements and those of our beliefs are different. Suppose Oscar travels to Twin Earth, and pointing to a glass of water, says 'That's water'. If Twin Oscar says the same, and we acknowledge that their terms refer to different things, then again, it seems they disagree, and the disagreement is straightforwardly explained as having different beliefs, and that, in turn, that their beliefs have different contents. If someone wants to hold that the contents of these beliefs are nonetheless the same, something more complex has to be said about the semantics of belief attribution.

In the first kind of situation, it is natural to say that in some sense, you and I say the same, and in some sense, we say something different. The sentence 'I thought I won; and she believed the same' is ambiguous: it allows us to assume that she thought that she won, or that she thought that I won. Two dimensional semantic treatments of indexicals try to capture this phenomenon by attributing two semantic features to indexical expressions: the first is constant throughout different uses, and hence makes the same contribution to the meaning of indexical sentences in every context. As we saw, this feature can be naturally regarded as the linguistic meaning of the indexical. The second feature may vary from context to context, depending on the actual reference of the indexical, making different contributions to the content of an indexical sentence. A further plausible thought concerns the relation between the two features: it is that the function of the constant meaning is to assign different contents to indexical sentences in different contexts.[20]

The relevance of this to the debate about externalism is that while the utterances of indexical sentences by internally identical subjects share the first feature, they may differ in the second feature. There are many details of this debate which are discussed elsewhere in this book,[21] we shall mention only a couple of points. First, can the two-dimensional treatment be extended to natural kind terms and names? While in the case of indexicals, it seemed plausible that uses of 'You lost' in different contexts are in some way similar, and some way different, and that *both* of these features are semantically important, the same is less obvious for names and natural kind terms. Suppose that someone holds the direct reference theory for names. Oscar and Twin Oscar have the same internal *physical* states; the symbols used by them may have the same *syntactic* features; but there is no *semantic* 'common factor' that their use of the name 'Aristotle' share. The only semantic feature of the name, its reference, is different. Of course, one can reject the direct reference theory for both names and natural kind terms, but the question remains: is there anything shared by say, Oscar's

[19] I owe this example to Zoltán Gendler Szabó.
[20] A classic treatment is Kaplan, 1977: he calls the first feature 'character', the second 'content'. Though the details vary a lot, an important, and to some extent similar reaction to externalism about mental content was to distinguish 'narrow' and 'broad' (or 'wide') mental contents. McGinn, 1982 and Fodor, 1987 are classic versions.
[21] See the entry on TWO DIMENSIONAL SEMANTICS.

and Twin Oscar's use of 'water' beyond physical or syntactic features—something that has to do with *meanings*?[22]

15.6 THE TRANSPARENCY OF MEANING

One reason why some philosophers have thought that there *is* an internal component to meaning is that certain features, which have been traditionally assigned to meanings, are apparently played by internally, and not by externally individuated aspects. One such feature is that meanings are known in a special way.[23] Michael Dummett writes

It is an undeniable feature of the notion of meaning—obscure as that notion is—that meaning is *transparent* in the sense that, if someone attaches a meaning to each of two words, he must know whether these meanings are the same.[24]

Knowing which of my words have the same or different meanings teaches me that I can express my desire for sparkling water by using the words 'sparkling water' or 'fizzy water', but not with 'still water'. Of course such endeavours may fail if I grasp some meanings incompletely or incorrectly—that is, if I mean something else by a word than everyone else does. But it is a common assumption in the externalist arguments that when meaning is externally individuated, this is not simply the widely agreed phenomenon, discussed in the first paragraph of this paper, of incomplete or mistaken understanding. If Oscar doesn't mean *elm* by 'elm', and *beech* by 'beech', but instead he means some idiosyncratic concept *elch,* which has both elms and beaches in its extension, no externalist conclusion follows.[25]

Let us consider indexicals first—it was agreed that they have both an internally and an externally individuated semantic feature. I can tell whether two indexicals have the same linguistic meaning or not, and this will guide me in my use of 'you' instead of 'I', or of 'now' instead of 'tomorrow', as the situation requires. In contrast, the content—the externally individuated feature—of an indexical sentence depends on the context of use, and if two contexts are indistinguishable, I may not be able to tell whether the content is the same or not. 'You are one minute older than your

---

[22] Stalnaker, 1995 argues (as a response to Loar, 1988) that there is no procedure which will result in a determinate, internally individuated content. A similar argument is in Section 10 of Block and Stalnaker, 1999. An argument against the view that mental content has an internal (as well as an external) component is in McDowell, 1986.

[23] The questions raised by knowledge of mental contents and knowledge of meanings are largely the same; and the issue of externalism and the knowledge of mental contents has inspired a very complex discussion, which I cannot hope to reproduce here. Some classic pieces are reprinted in Ludlow and Martin, 1998. Wright, Smith and MacDonald, 1998 includes further developments. A recent collection with contributions from many influential participants of the debate is Nuccetelli, 2003.

[24] Dummett, 1975: 131. Quoted in Boghossian, 1995: 33. As Boghossian notes, the surrounding discussion makes it clear that knowing whether meanings are the same or not should be non-empirical.

[25] For an argument of how the externalist argument can be refuted if we allow such cases to count as simply misunderstanding or incomplete understanding, see Crane, 1991.

twin' expresses different contents when addressed to Castor or to Pollux, but I may not be able to tell the difference; 'turning left here leads out of the labyrinth' expresses different contents when uttered at two different locations, but if the locations are indiscriminable, again I may be unable to tell the difference. Internally individuated features are transparent, while externally individuated features are not.

The phenomenon under discussion is the ability to tell whether two meanings are the same or not. This is stronger than the requirement of being able to tell, in some sense, what the meaning of a word is. Externalist theories of mental content were criticized on the ground that they cannot account for direct and non-empirical knowledge of our own thoughts. One standard response is the following. Beliefs about the content of our thoughts (e.g. the thought 'water is wet') arise from form-ing second-order thoughts ('now I am thinking that water is wet'). Since the content of the second-order thought inherits the content of the first-order thought, there is no possibility of mismatch between the content of these two thoughts. Oscar and Twin Oscar start out with different contents for their first-order thoughts, and the difference is inherited to their second-order thoughts, so they both will be right. The contextually self-verifying character of these second-order thoughts is sufficient to explain the direct and non-empirical character of self-knowledge. As Burge says: "We 'individuate' our thoughts, or discriminate them from others, by thinking those, and not the others, self-ascriptively. . . . Our epistemic right rests on this immediacy . . ."[26]

Burge points out, correctly, that in order to know the content of our thoughts, we do not need to know every empirical fact which makes it possible to have these thoughts. But even if we agree with this, it still may be objected that this theory provides a rather etiolated conception of self-knowledge, as an analogy will help to illustrate. I am always right in believing that *I am here*; a token of 'I am here' is contextually self-verifying in a similar way as second-order thoughts are. But even though I know I am here, I still may have no idea where I am. (This is of course not about the content of the thought 'I am here'; the point is an *analogy*, between knowing our location and knowing our thoughts.) It would not be particularly con-vincing to say that we individuate our locations, or discriminate them from others, by simply being at those locations, and not at others. This suggests that the impossib-ility of error because of the contextually self-verifying character of a judgment may not be sufficient to exclude ignorance. One way to spell out the idea that knowledge of my whereabouts is more than knowing that I am here, is to point out that what I lack in the case of not knowing my whereabouts, is an ability to discriminate between my present location and other locations. Analogously, a more robust knowledge of

---

[26] Burge, 1988: 656. See also Burge, 1996. Applied to meanings, the theory could be something like this: both Oscar and Twin Oscar are right when they say "I mean *water* by 'water'". It is of course required that the sentences expressing knowledge of meanings or contents should be understood; I do not express knowledge by saying that ' "Cantankerous" means cantankerous' if I don't understand what cantankerous means. One way to put the issue between externalists and internalists is to ask whether there is a danger that on the theory just presented, knowledge of meanings reduces to people's 'mouthpiecing' such statements without really understanding them.

meanings and contents would require an ability to discriminate among them, and this is what Dummett's transparency thesis requires. This kind of knowledge is called 'discriminatory' or 'comparative' knowledge of content.

On some externalist theories, there can be cases when we are unable to tell that two meanings are the *same*: on direct reference theories, for example, 'Hesperus' and 'Phosphorus' have the same meaning, but a perfectly competent user of the names may have no idea about this.[27] Are there cases where we cannot tell that the meanings of two words are *different*? Oscar and Twin Oscar's case poses no such problem: here the externally individuated meanings are possessed by two different language users. What we need is a single subject who can or cannot discriminate among different meanings. There are two ways to turn the Twin Earth scenario into such a situation. First, instead of imagining Earth and Twin Earth as two planets in the actual universe, we could conceive Twin Earth as a counterfactual scenario about Earth, and Twin Oscar as a counterfactual counterpart of Oscar. In the counterfactual situation, Oscar's word 'water' would have a different meaning. In the case of indexicals, we said that the same indexical sentence may express different contents in different contexts, but if the situations are indistinguishable, the subject may not be able to tell the difference. This applies to the counterfactual scenario we are considering: if Oscar had grown up on Twin Earth instead of Earth, his situation would be indistinguishable, and hence by the same reasoning it seems that he would not be able to tell the difference in his concepts.[28]

Alternatively, we could try to furnish an actual language user with both concepts. Suppose that Earth and Twin Earth are part of the actual universe, and Oscar is transported to Twin Earth, unaware, overnight. When he wakes up, nothing seems different, and he goes on with his life. The general view is that after a certain time, the meaning of his word 'water', as describing his ongoing experiences, switches to twater. But there is no reason to assume that the concept that figures in his memories of Earthly water experiences switches too: when he recalls swimming in the Pacific back on Earth, and says that 'The water was salty', his word refers to H_2O. Similar phenomenon arises about his word 'Aristotle': when he remembers having read Aristotle's *Categories* ten years before, he refers to Earthly Aristotle; when he discusses his recent encounter with Aristotle's *Metaphysics*, he refers to Twin Aristotle. If externalist theories are right, the meaning of 'Aristotle' is different on the two occasions; yet Oscar is in no position to find this out merely by introspection (and similar remarks apply to 'water').

Inability to tell that two meanings are the *same* need not be a consequence of all externalist theories; a view which combines externalism with Fregean senses[29] could

---

[27] A similar case is Kripke's famous Pierre, see Kripke, 1979.

[28] Burge uses counterfactual situations to set up his Twin type thought experiments for example in Burge, 1979. In Burge, 1988, he agrees that a person could not tell the difference between the actual and the counterfactual situation, but since he thinks that we could have knowledge of our thoughts even without being able to discriminate them from possible thoughts we might be thinking instead of them, he does not regard this as a problem.

[29] See Evans, 1982; McDowell, 1984.

hold that 'Hesperus' and 'Phosphorus' have indeed two different, object-dependent senses, and competent users of the name will be able to establish this merely by introspection. But the inability of telling that two meanings are *different* in certain situations—as illustrated by the slow-switching cases—is a consequence of all externalist theories. To see this, you merely have to assume that a single subject can be exposed to two different environments, and interactions with these environments result in acquiring different meanings. The differences in the environment, and the resulting difference in meanings cannot be traced to internal differences—otherwise we would not have a case of externalism. Hence the subject will not be able to tell merely by reflection the difference between these concepts. In contrast, an internalist will allow a difference in meanings only as long as it is traceable to internal differences.

It seems that internalism can provide a more robust account of knowledge of meaning than externalism can. But is there any reason to prefer the more robust account? Consider again the case where Oscar has been transported to Twin Earth, and his reports about his past experiences refer to Aristotle and water, the ones about his recent experiences to Twin Aristotle and twater. Oscar cannot discriminate between the two meanings of his word 'water', but he can discriminate the meaning of 'water' from the meaning of 'blood' or 'brandy'. The externalist then could say that this is sufficient to award Oscar a knowledge of meanings. However, the internalist will have an objection. Suppose that Oscar argues in the following way:

(1) 'Aristotle doesn't refer to the notions of form and matter in his definition of substance in the *Categories*.'
(2) 'Aristotle's discussion of substance relies on the notions of form and matter in the *Metaphysics*.'
(3) 'Therefore Aristotle has changed his views about substance between writing the *Categories* and the *Metaphysics*.'

This argument is mistaken; the question is, what sort of mistake is being made here. The internalist could say that it is a *factual* mistake: Oscar is wrong about the fact that the two books he read were written by the same person. But on the externalist view, though Oscar may make a factual mistake, he also makes a different kind of mistake: he equivocates on the word 'Aristotle'; in the first and the second premise, the word has different meanings. Of course we do make similar mistakes in arguments for example when a subject matter is complicated, when we don't quite understand the concepts, when we are in a hurry, when our judgment is discoloured by emotions, and so on. But even though Oscar is completely dispassionate on this topic, he is a perfectly competent user of all these words, the whole issue is quite simple, he has all the time in the world—he still won't be able find out this mistake simply by reflecting on the premises of his argument. [30]

Faced with this situation, we could simply draw the consequence that the kind of mistakes we are prone to in our empirical or perceptual judgments may affect also

---

[30] For other cases of mistakes, entailed by an externalist conception of mental content, see Boghossian, 1994.

our judgments about meanings or mental contents. My rationality is not threatened if I cannot tell Castor and Pollux apart just by looking; and similarly, this argument continues, it's entirely understandable if I cannot discriminate some of my meanings introspectively.[31] However, one might want to distinguish between factual mistakes and mistakes of reasoning of this kind.[32] And if someone thinks that therefore the consequences of the externalist view pose a serious threat to our rationality, she should object to the view which entailed it.

REFERENCES

Block, Ned and Robert Stalnaker (1999). "Conceptual Analysis, Dualism, and the Explanatory Gap." *Philosophical Review*, 108: 1–46.

Boghossian, Paul A. (1994). "The Transparency of Mental Content." *Philosophical Perspectives*, 8: 33–50.

Burge, Tyler (1979). "Individualism and the Mental." Reprinted in David M. Rosenthal (ed.), *The Nature of Mind*, Oxford University Press, 1991: 536–67 and in Ludlow and Martin, 1998: 21–82. Some sections are reprinted in Pessin and Goldberg, 1996: 125–41.

—— (1982). "Other Bodies," in Andrew Woodfield (ed.), *Thought and Object*. Oxford: Clarendon Press. Reprinted in Pessin and Goldberg, 1996: 142–60.

—— (1988). "Individualism and Self-Knowledge." *Journal of Philosophy*, 85: 649–63. Reprinted in Pessin and Goldberg, 1996: 342–54, and in Ludlow and Martin, 1998: 111–28.

—— (1996). "Our Entitlement to Self-Knowledge." *Proceedings of the Aristotelian Society*, 96: 91–116. Reprinted in Ludlow and Martin, 1998: 239–64.

Crane, Tim (1991). "All the Difference in the World." *Philosophical Quarterly*, 41: 1–25. Reprinted in Pessin and Goldberg, 1995, 284–304.

Dummett, Michael (1975). "Frege's Distinction between Sense and Reference," in *Truth and Other Enigmas*. London: Duckworth, 1978: 116–44.

Evans, Gareth (1982). *The Varieties of Reference*. Oxford: Clarendon Press.

Farkas, Katalin (2003). "What is Externalism?" *Philosophical Studies*, 112/13: 187–208.

Fodor, Jerry A. (1987). *Psychosemantics*. Cambridge, Mass.: MIT Press.

Frege, Gottlob (1892). "On Sense and Reference." Reprinted in A. W. Moore (ed.), *Meaning and Reference*. Oxford University Press, 1993: 23–42.

—— (1918). "The Thought." Reprinted in Simon Blackburn, and Keith Simmons, (eds.), *Truth*. Oxford University Press, 1999: 85–105.

Kaplan, David (1977). "Demonstratives," in Almog, J., Perry, J., and Wettstein, H. (eds.), *Themes from Kaplan*. Oxford University Press, 1989: 481–563.

Kripke, Saul A. (1972). "Naming and Necessity." Reprinted in book form by Blackwell, Oxford 1980.

—— (1979). "A Puzzle About Belief." Reprinted in Salmon, Nathan, and Soames, Scott (eds.), *Propositions and Attitudes*, 1988. Oxford University Press: 102–48.

Loar, Brian (1988). "Social Content and Psychological Content." Reprinted in Pessin and Goldberg, 1996: 180–92.

---

[31] See Owens, 1989. For further discussion of how such equivocations may be innocent, see Sorensen 1998.

[32] I have in mind the kind of distinction drawn in McDowell, 1995 (see esp. fn 5); mistakes which are, or not, results of 'misconducting oneself in the space of reasons'. Of course, McDowell would not subscribe to this point being used in an argument against externalism.

Ludlow, Peter and Norah Martin (eds.), (1998). *Externalism and Self-Knowledge*. Stanford: CSLI.

Marti, Genoveva (1995). "The Essence of Genuine Reference." *Journal of Philosophical Logic*, 24: 275–89.

McDowell, John (1984). "*De Re* Senses." *Philosophical Quarterly*, 34: 283–94.

_____ (1986). "Singular Thought and the Extent of Inner Space," in Pettit, Philip and John McDowell (eds.), *Subject, Thought and Context*. Oxford: Clarendon Press: 136–168.

_____ (1992). "Putnam on Mind and Meaning." *Philosophical Topics*, 20(1): 35–48. Reprinted in Pessin and Goldberg, 1996: 305–17.

_____ (1995). "Knowledge and the Internal." *Philosophy and Phenomenological Research*, 55: 877–93.

McGinn, Colin, (1977). "Charity, Interpretation and Belief." *Journal of Philosophy*, 74: 521–35.

_____ (1982). "The Structure of Content," in Andrew Woodfield (ed.), *Thought and Object*. Oxford: Clarendon Press: 207–58.

Mellor, D. H. (1977). "Natural Kinds." *British Journal for the Philosophy of Science*, 28: 299–312. Reprinted in Pessin and Goldberg, 1996: 69–80.

Newman, Anthony, (2005): "Two Grades of Internalism (Pass and Fail)." *Philosophical Studies*, 122: 153–69.

Nucetelli, Susana ed., (2003). *New Essays on Semantic Externalism and Self-Knowledge*. Cambridge, Mass.: MIT Press. Bradford Books.

Owens, Joseph (1989). "Contradictory Belief and Cognitive Access." *Midwest Studies in Philosophy*, 14, University of Minnesota Press: 289–316.

Pessin, Andrew and Sanford Goldberg (eds.), (1996). *The Twin Earth Chronicles*. Armonk, NY and London: M. E. Sharpe.

Putnam, Hilary, (1970). "Is Semantics Possible?" Reprinted in *Mind, Language and Reality*. Cambridge University Press, 1975: 139–52.

_____ (1975). "The Meaning of 'Meaning,'" in *Mind, Language and Reality*. Cambridge University Press. Reprinted in Pessin and Goldberg, 1996: 3–52.

Searle, John R. (1983). *Intentionality*. Cambridge University Press.

Sorensen, Roy (1998), "Logical Luck." *Philosophical Quarterly*, 48: 319–34.

Stalnaker, Robert (1995). "Narrow Content." Reprinted in *Context and Content*. Oxford: Clarendon Press, 1999 p. 195–210.

Strawson, Peter F. (1959). *Individuals*. Reprinted in 1993, London and New York: Routledge.

Williamson, Timothy (2000). *Knowledge and its Limits*. Oxford University Press.

Wright, Crispin, Barry C. Smith, and Cynthia Macdonald (eds.), (1998). *Knowing Our Own Minds*. Oxford: Clarendon Press.

CHAPTER 16

....

RELEVANCE THEORY NEW DIRECTIONS AND DEVELOPMENTS

....

ROBYN CARSTON

AND GEORGE POWELL

16.1 INTRODUCTION—AN OUTLINE OF RELEVANCE THEORY

....

As a post-Gricean pragmatic theory, Relevance Theory (RT) takes as its starting point the question of how hearers bridge the gap between sentence meaning and speaker meaning. That there is such a gap has been a given of linguistic philosophy since Grice's (1967) *Logic and Conversation*. But the account that relevance theory offers of how this gap is bridged, although originating as a development of Grice's co-operative principle and conversational maxims, differs from other broadly Gricean accounts in certain fundamental respects, and leads to a stance on the nature of language, meaning and communication which is at odds, not only with the view of Grice himself, but also with the view common to most post-Fregean philosophy of language.

We are grateful to Berry C. Smith for his patience and encouragements during our writing of this chapter, and for very helpful comments on our earlier version.

Relevance theory grounds its account of utterance interpretation within a general claim about cognitive design, the claim that human cognition is geared towards the maximization of *relevance*. For Sperber and Wilson (1986/95a), relevance is a potential property of inputs to cognitive processes. Any input may deliver a variety of different types of cognitive effect; it may, for instance, combine inferentially with existing assumptions to yield new conclusions (known as *contextual implications*), or it may provide evidence that strengthens existing beliefs, or it may contradict and eliminate already held information. At the same time, getting at the effects of a particular input demands processing effort. For Sperber and Wilson, relevance is, roughly speaking, a trade-off between cognitive effects and processing effort: the greater the ratio of effects to effort the greater the relevance of an input.[1] Given this notion of relevance, to claim that humans are geared towards maximizing relevance is to claim that we are designed to look for as many cognitive effects as possible for as little processing effort as possible. The idea is that, as a result of constant selection pressure towards increasing cognitive efficiency, we have evolved procedures to pick out potentially relevant inputs and to process them in the most cost-effective way (Sperber and Wilson, 1995b).

All communication, and linguistic communication in particular, makes use of this cognitive drive for relevance. Taking the case of linguistic communication, Sperber and Wilson's claim is that an utterance raises quite specific expectations of relevance in its addressee, that is expectations about the effects it will yield and the mental effort it will cost. Quite generally, an utterance comes with a presumption of its own optimal relevance; that is, there is an implicit guarantee that the utterance is the most relevant one the speaker could have produced, given her abilities and her preferences, and that it is at least relevant enough to be worth processing. That utterances carry this presumption motivates a particular comprehension procedure, which, in successful communication, reduces the number of possible interpretations to one: in essence, it licenses a hearer to consider possible interpretations in order of their accessibility (that is, to follow a path of least effort) and to stop as soon as he reaches one that satisfies his expectation of relevance.

Sperber and Wilson thus posit a powerful cognitively grounded machinery for the interpretation of utterances. Recent research within the relevance-theoretic framework suggests that the implications of such a machinery are far-reaching. As we discuss in Section 16.2, this approach to utterance interpretation supports a view of language and meaning which differs fundamentally from that common in the contemporary philosophy of language. Furthermore, it raises important questions about the relationship between communication and mental architecture, which we outline in Section 16.3.

Much work in relevance theory relies on the kinds of method and data familiar to linguistic philosophers: essentially introspection and native speaker intuitions on

---

[1] Sperber and Wilson distinguish between those effects which are beneficial to a cognitive agent (*positive cognitive effects*) and those which are not. Talking a little less loosely, therefore, relevance is a trade off between positive cognitive effects and processing effort. See Sperber and Wilson (1995b) and Wilson and Sperber (2004).

properties such as truth conditions, truth values, what is said, etc. Recently, however, relevance theorists have been at the forefront of a newly-emerging research field, experimental pragmatics, which aims to apply the empirical techniques of psycholinguistics to questions about utterance interpretation. Over the last few years, this new research methodology has thrown up interesting and sometimes surprising insights into the psychological processes underlying human communication and comprehension, some of which we discuss in Section 16.4.

16.2 Relevance Theory and the Semantics–Pragmatics Distinction

Where should the line be drawn between semantics and pragmatics? On one familiar view, endorsed both by Grice and by most contemporary philosophers of language, the outline answer is clear: semantics is concerned with what is variously called *the proposition (semantically/literally) expressed, what is said* or simply *the truth-conditional content* of an utterance, whereas pragmatics is concerned with the implicatures of an utterance. There are, however, respects in which, for all but the most hard-line truth-conditionalist, context contributes to propositional content. Grice, for instance, accepted that what is said by an utterance is determined, not only by the 'conventional meaning' of the sentence uttered, but also by disambiguation and assignment of values to indexical expressions (Grice, 1989: 25).

However, there has been much recent work within the relevance-theoretic framework arguing for the view that pragmatic contributions to propositional content go a great deal further than disambiguation and reference assignment. There are two key strands to this work: on the one hand, there has been research into lexical pragmatics which broadly defends the position that, not only those lexical items traditionally taken to be indexical, but more or less all lexical meaning is context-sensitive; on the other hand, there has been research into proposition-level context-sensitivity which supports the view that some pragmatic aspects of propositional content may not correspond to items present at any level of syntactic representation. This leads to a reassessment of the appropriate way to draw the distinction between semantics and pragmatics.

16.2.1 Relevance Theory and Lexical Pragmatics

While indexicals, such as 'she', 'those', 'here', clearly require the pragmatic supplying of a contextual value, it might seem that what are often known as *content words,*— nouns, verbs, adjectives, etc.—come with a fully specified, context-invariant, conceptual content as a matter of their lexically encoded meaning. However, according to the relevance-theoretic view, such words, although linguistically unambiguous, may communicate a range of distinct (though related) meanings in different contexts. Consider the following examples (adapted from Searle, 1983: 145):

(1) a. Pat *opened* the curtains.
   b. Bill *opened* his mouth.
   c. Sally *opened* her book to page 56.
   d. The child *opened* the package.
   e. The carpenter *opened* the wall.
   f. The surgeon *opened* the wound.

Although the lexically encoded meaning of the word 'open' is the same in these examples, it is understood differently in each case. As Searle points out, the contribution it makes to the truth conditions of quite literal utterances varies with the sentential context it occurs in. What constitutes opening a book is very different from what constitutes opening one's mouth, which is quite different again from what constitutes opening a package, etc. Given that the concept expressed by the use of a word may also vary with extralinguistic context (for instance, in a scenario in which a person's broken jaw has been wired together the process of opening the mouth is rather different from the usual one), a virtually indefinite range of different concepts can be communicated by uses of the verb 'open'. The upshot of the pragmatic process at work here is a *narrowing* of the linguistically encoded meaning to a more specific concept.

The opposite result occurs too, that is, the concept communicated by the use of a word in context may be broader than the linguistically given concept. Consider the different interpretations of the adjective 'flat' in the following examples (adapted from Wilson, 2004: 345):

(2) a. This ironing board is *flat*.
   b. My back garden is *flat*.
   c. He had a *flat* face and sad eyes.
   d. Holland is *flat*.
   e. The sea was *flat*.

As with narrowing, different degrees and types of *broadening* (or *loosening*) are appropriate in different circumstances, so that, for instance, the departure from true flatness is greater in the case of a whole country than in the case of one's back garden, and the flatness of a landscape is different in kind from the flatness of a face. Another variety of broadening involves what is often called 'category extension' and is typified by the use of salient brand names or person names (e.g. 'Hoover', 'Kleenex', 'Hitler', 'Chomsky') to denote a broader category (vacuum cleaners in general, the class of megalomaniac leaders with inhuman policies, etc.). In some cases, the communicated meaning may involve both an element of narrowing and an element of broadening; for instance, consider a depressed woman who says of her irresponsible husband 'Ken's a bachelor'. The concept she communicates is both narrower than the encoded meaning of the word 'bachelor' since it is confined to the stereotype of an easy-going, promiscuous kind of bachelor, but it is clearly also broader since it includes in its denotation certain married men whose behaviour is like that of the stereotypic bachelor (Carston 2002: section 5.2).

Two important and distinctive characteristics of the RT approach to these phenomena are: (a) the claim that the pragmatic process involved is not a matter of implicature derivation but rather of conceptual adjustment which contributes to the proposition explicitly communicated (the truth-conditional content of the utterance), and (b) while most other pragmatic approaches assume that narrowing and broadening are to be treated as distinct processes, the RT view is that they are simply different possible outcomes of a single pragmatic process which fine-tunes the interpretation of virtually every word. The model of lexical semantics that we assume essentially follows Fodor (1998): lexical forms map to mentally-represented concepts, that is, elements of a conceptual representation system or 'language of thought' (leaving aside indexicals to which this does not obviously apply). These concepts constitute the meanings of words as expression-types in a linguistic system, so that words can be thought of as inheriting the denotational semantics of the Mentalese concept that they encode. When the outcome of the lexical pragmatic process of meaning adjustment is a narrowing, the denotation of the concept communicated by the use of a word is a proper subpart of the denotation of the lexically encoded concept, and when the outcome is a broadening, the opposite relation between the denotations of encoded concept and communicated concept holds. When the adjustment involves both outcomes, the relation between the denotations of encoded concept and communicated concept is one of mere overlap.

How does this single unified account work? Recall the relevance-based comprehension procedure mentioned in the introduction, according to which an addressee follows a track of least effort in trying out interpretations, stopping once he has one that meets his expectation of relevance (that is, of sufficient effects for no gratuitous processing effort). This procedure is automatically applied to the on-line processing of attended verbal utterances: taking the schematic decoded linguistic meaning as input, processes of pragmatic enrichment at the explicit level occur in parallel with the derivation of the implications of the utterance. Central to the working of the procedure is a subprocess of 'mutual adjustment' of explicit content, contextual assumptions and contextual implications, a process guided and constrained by expectations of relevance. Here is a brief example involving the adjustment of explicit content in response to expected implications and where the outcome is a narrowing of a lexically encoded meaning:

(3) A (to B): Be careful. The path is *uneven.*

Given that the first part of A's utterance warns B to take care, B is very likely to expect the second part of the utterance to achieve relevance by explaining or elaborating on why, or in what way, he should take care. Now, virtually every path is, strictly speaking, uneven to some degree or other (i.e. not perfectly plane), but given that B is looking for a particular kind of implication, he will enrich the very general encoded concept UNEVEN so that the proposition explicitly communicated provides appropriate inferential warrant for such implications of the utterance as: B might trip over, B should take small steps, B should keep his eye on the path, etc. The result is a concept, which we can label UNEVEN*, whose denotation is a proper subset of the denotation of the lexical concept UNEVEN. (For much more detailed exemplification of the RT-based account of lexical adjustment, resulting in concept broadening, or narrowing, or a combination of the two, see Wilson and Sperber (2002).)

Finally, a distinctive RT claim in this context is that metaphorical and hyperbolic uses of words involve a kind of concept broadening (or loose use), so fall within this single process of lexical meaning adjustment. For instance, an utterance of the sentence in (4) could be taken as an ordinary broadening (if, say, it's known that a particular run, referred to by 'it', was a little less than 26 miles) or as hyperbolic (if it was considerably less than the length of a marathon) or as metaphorical for a long, arduous, exhausting experience, whether physical or mental.

(4) It was a *marathon*.

The idea is that there is no hard and fast distinction between these different degrees of loosening of the lexical concept MARATHON; rather, there is a continuum of cases from ordinary approximations through to the more radical broadening involved in comprehending metaphors. (See Wilson, 2004; Carston and Wilson, forthcoming.)

16.2.2 Relevance Theory and Reference

The primary domain of lexical pragmatics within RT has been the interpretation of predicate expressions. However, over recent years there has also been a certain amount of research from an RT perspective into the semantics and pragmatics of singular expressions (proper names, indexicals and demonstratives, both simple and complex) as well as definite descriptions.

While there is something very close to consensus among linguistic philosophers on the context-sensitivity of indexical and demonstrative expressions, there is much less agreement on how best to treat definite descriptions and proper names. As is well-known, the key question on definite descriptions over the last forty years has been how to analyse what Donnellan (1966) calls the referential–attributive distinction, i.e. how best to accommodate the apparent datum that a definite description 'the F' may be used either to talk about a particular antecedently identified individual or to talk about *whatever* happens to be uniquely F. As regards proper names, there are broadly three positions: those who consider names to be the natural language equivalent of logical individual constants, those who take them to be descriptive, i.e. to contribute properties to truth conditions, and those who see them as closely related to indexicals.

Donnellan's referential–attributive distinction has proved notoriously divisive within the philosophy of language. On the one hand, there seem to be good reasons to suppose that the distinction corresponds to a truth-conditional difference: the truth conditions of an utterance of a definite description sentence appear to alter according to whether the description is used referentially or attributively. On the other hand, there also seem to be good reasons to believe that definite descriptions are not ambiguous: although 'the man drinking a martini' may be used either referentially or attributively, it does not seem to be ambiguous in the way that, say, 'bank' or 'coach' is. But, of course, these two observations are hard to reconcile on standard philosophical assumptions: if (leaving aside indexical expressions) you identify the meaning of an expression with the contribution that expression makes to truth conditions, then it follows directly that an expression which is capable of making two different kinds of contribution to truth conditions has two different meanings, that is, is ambiguous.

However, as a number of researchers working within the relevance-theoretic framework have pointed out (e.g. Rouchota, 1992; Bezuidenhout, 1997; Powell, 2001), RT offers a natural way to reconcile these data. As discussed in the previous section, there is a key distinction drawn in Relevance Theory between, on the one hand, the linguistically encoded meaning of a particular expression and, on the other hand, the contribution that expression makes to truth-conditional content on an occasion of use. Given this distinction, the fact that a particular expression may make two distinct types of contribution to truth-conditional content is no evidence for its ambiguity at the level of linguistically encoded meaning. While differing in detail, all the above-mentioned RT accounts take the following position: that definite descriptions are linguistically univocal but truth-conditionally ambiguous. The gap between the encoded meaning of a definite description and what that description contributes to propositional content in a particular context is bridged by relevance-guided pragmatic inference.

Just as with definite descriptions, proper names have thrown up some notoriously thorny philosophical questions, of which the most attention has probably gone to Frege's puzzle on the informativeness of identity statements (for instance, 'Marilyn Monroe is Norma Jean Baker', 'Evan Hunter was Ed McBain'). There has been less work from a relevance-theoretic perspective on proper names than on definite descriptions, but Powell (1998, 2003) has addressed questions about proper names as part of a general RT-flavoured analysis of the semantics and pragmatics of singular expressions. On this analysis, all such expressions are profoundly context-sensitive: whether they make referential or descriptive contributions to truth conditions is not a matter of the encoded meanings of these expressions, but is rather a matter of broad context and pragmatic principles. Powell (2003) analyses the encoded meanings of singular expressions (including here definite descriptions) not in terms of their contribution to truth conditions, but rather in terms of their contribution to a hearer's mental representations. All these expressions, on this view, are marked as *individual concept communicators* by virtue of their linguistically encoded meaning. That is to say, they are marked as contributing to a hearer's mental representation a concept which, roughly speaking, is taken to be satisfied by a unique individual. Beyond that, the encoded meaning of these expressions is silent as to whether this concept should be *de re* (i.e. referential) or descriptive. Which constraints a particular singular expression lays on the concepts which may serve as its interpretation will vary according to the type of singular expression. In the case of a proper name 'N', the constraint on interpretation is simply that the individual concept should be of a bearer of 'N'. Which concept that is on a particular occasion will be determined by context and pragmatic inference. A definite description 'the F', on the other hand, encodes a rather more complex condition: it constrains interpretation to an individual concept of a unique F in a salient context. Again, which is the salient context and which the intended individual concept (and whether it is referential or descriptive) on any given occasion is determined pragmatically.

On this analysis, traditional philosophical puzzles with proper names, such as the informativeness of identity statements, disappear. Consider an utterance of:

(5) Evan Hunter was Ed McBain

The familiar problem is how such statements, which seem merely to predicate the identity of an individual with itself, can nevertheless be informative. On Powell's analysis, a hearer faced with the task of interpreting an utterance of (5) will access two individual concepts, one associated with the name 'Evan Hunter' and the other with the name 'Ed McBain'. So long as these two concepts are appropriately referentially anchored, they will be anchored to the same individual, since the names 'Evan Hunter' and 'Ed McBain' share a bearer. This does not, however, imply that the concepts share informational content. A person's 'Evan Hunter' concept might contain information such as *x is the author of 'The Blackboard Jungle'* while her 'Ed McBain' concept might contain information such as *x wrote the 87th Precinct novels*. Since these two concepts are associated with different information, when this person comprehends (5) she thereby gains access to new information, for instance, the information that the author of 'The Blackboard Jungle' also wrote the 87th Precinct novels. On this analysis, therefore, it is predicted that identity statements involving co-referring names are capable of being informative.[2]

16.2.3 Relevance Theory and Unarticulated Constituents

As discussed in the last two sections, recent research within relevance theory has supported the view that linguistic expressions of all sorts display profound context-sensitivity. But might context-sensitivity go even beyond this? Much attention has recently been paid to what Perry (1986) dubbed *unarticulated constituents*. The idea behind Perry's notion is that the proposition expressed by an utterance may contain constituents which do not correspond to anything in the syntax of the sentence uttered. Consider, for instance, the much-discussed sentence in (6):

(6) It's raining

It seems that if I utter (6) in London then I have said that it is raining in London, whereas if I utter (6) in Paris I have said that it is raining in Paris; it seems, in other words, as if any utterance of (6) will be true iff it is raining *at a particular location*

---

[2] The informativeness puzzle is not limited to uses of different co-referring names; it can also arise for identity statements involving different uses of the same name, as demonstrated by Kripke's Paderewski example (Kripke, 1979). It is interesting to note, however, that such cases only give rise to the puzzle in those instances where the one name is associated with two distinct individual concepts.

(and, in fact, the particular location is not always the place of utterance). Yet there is no constituent, at least in the overt syntax of (6), which corresponds to this location parameter.

How should one best account for this sort of datum? There are, broadly speaking, three types of response currently on the market. At one end of the spectrum are those who argue that features such as this location parameter form no part of the truth-conditional content of utterances. Cappelen and Lepore (2005), for instance, claim that the belief that such elements contribute to literal propositional content results from a confusion on the distinction between the proposition semantically expressed by an utterance and the speech acts the utterance is used to perform. On the middle path are those who accept that features such as the location parameter in (6) do indeed contribute to literal propositional content, but who argue that they must, therefore, be represented covertly in the syntax (e.g. Stanley, 2000). Recent research within the relevance-theoretic framework, however, has defended a third position, that at least some of these features do contribute to truth-conditional content, while at the same time being genuinely unarticulated, i.e. unrepresented in the syntax at any level of representation. Carston (2004a) defends a position on which the retrieval of such constituents is a purely pragmatic process, the result of relevance-guided inference.

The argument is essentially two-fold. First, any theory of content which aims to play a serious role in a wider theory of interpretation and communication, i.e. which lays claim to any degree of psychological plausibility, must be answerable to native speaker intuitions on such matters as truth conditions, truth values and what is said. This is taken to exclude positions such as that adopted by Cappelen and Lepore, on which the kind of minimalist propositions (indexical values being the only contextually provided elements) which are taken to constitute truth-conditional content will be generally inaccessible to intuition. Once one takes intuition seriously, there seems little way of avoiding the conclusion that the sorts of constituent under discussion do genuinely contribute to truth-conditional content. Second, according to relevance theorists, any attempt to tread the middle path leads to very problematic results.

Stanley (2000) finds support for his middle position from evidence that the postulated covert indexical elements, such as a location parameter in (6), can, like overt pronouns, enter into binding relations. Carston's (2004a) rejoinder starts from an argument first presented by Wilson and Sperber (2002), in which they pointed out that there is no principled limit to the number of covert elements that such a theory would have to posit. An utterance of (7), for instance, might express a proposition with a range of constituents corresponding to what is eaten, the time, place, manner of eating, and so on.

(7) I've eaten

On Stanley's analysis, each of these would have to correspond to a variable or indexical at LF (linguistic logical form), a theoretical prediction which Wilson and Sperber take to be a *reductio* of Stanley's position. Carston develops this one step further by showing that, although all of these hidden indexical elements would have to be present at LF, there would be many instances on which some of these elements would receive no value. Consider an utterance of (7) in response to the question 'Would you like some dinner?' While what was eaten and the time of eating might well be relevant (that the speaker has eaten a full meal and the eating took place in the recent past), the place and manner of eating would surely not be. It nevertheless seems that such an utterance would express a determinate proposition. This is not the sort of thing we expect of indexicals. Consider a standard use of an overt pronoun in an utterance of (8):

(8) She put the book on the table.

If 'she' does not receive a value in context, then clearly (8) does not express a complete proposition. So Stanley's hidden indexicals are, at the least, a very different kind of thing from the sort of indexicals we are used to.[3]

If relevance theorists are right, and (some of) these constituents do contribute to truth-conditional content while being genuinely unarticulated, this is another serious blow for hopes of building a truth-conditional theory of linguistic meaning, since it yet further breaks the link between sentence meaning and truth-conditional content. Rather, it fits with a view of the relation between encoded meaning and propositional content on which sentences encode not propositions but something more like propositional schemas or templates. These, then, must be pragmatically fleshed out in a context in order for the explicit content of the utterance to be recovered or, in many cases, in order that anything even minimally truth evaluable can be retrieved.

16.2.4 Conclusion

Where does the research discussed above leave us on the semantics-pragmatics distinction? There are two key elements to the relevance-theoretic view. First, relevance theorists take a view on pragmatic contributions to truth-conditional content which is fundamentally at odds with traditional views of the semantics–pragmatics distinction. On the RT view, there is, in principle, no limit to the effects of contextual information on propositional content: not only are all expressions context-sensitive, but context may also add constituents to propositional content which are entirely unrepresented in the syntax. Second, on the RT view, the processes which bridge the gap between linguistically encoded meaning and explicitly communicated meaning and those that bridge the gap between explicitly and implicitly communicated meaning (in Gricean terms, between what is said and what is implicated) are aspects of a single inferential process (seeking the optimally relevant interpretation); they occur in parallel and are subject to a mechanism of mutual adjustment as discussed in Section 16.2.1. This distinguishes relevance theorists from others who, while broadly sympathetic to the strong contextualist stance of RT, take some version

---

[3] For further arguments against the hidden indexical view, see Carston (2004b) and, from a different (non-RT) contextualist perspective, Recanati (2002a). Stanley's account has also come under some sustained fire from the opposite end of the spectrum, most recently from Cappelen and Lepore (2005).

of a multi-phase view of pragmatics on which the processes that mediate linguistic meaning and explicit content may be different in kind from those responsible for implicatures (see, for instance, Asher, 1999; Levinson, 2000; Recanati, 2002b, 2004).

Finally, given that the proposition explicitly expressed by an utterance is replete with pragmatically supplied content, only some of which is linguistically mandated, the rest being entirely pragmatically motivated, it is clearly not possible to draw a semantics–pragmatics distinction that coincides with the distinction between explicit utterance content and implicatures. According to the RT approach, the distinction has to be drawn between context-free linguistic expression-type meaning and what is communicated. That this is the only coherent way in which to draw the distinction is argued in more detail in Carston (forthcoming) (but see THE DISTINCTION BETWEEN SEMANTICS AND PRAGMATICS in this volume for a different view). It follows from this position that the long-standing Principles of Semantic Compositionality and Semantic Innocence hold, not at the level of the truth-conditional content of an utterance, but at the more schematic (often nonpropositional) level of linguistic expression-type meaning (see Powell, 2002).

16.3 Relevance Theory and Mental Architecture

While inferential pragmatics has its origins in the philosophy of language, the relevance-theoretic approach, on which it is construed as a mental processing system responsible for interpreting a kind of human behaviour (verbal and other ostensive communicative acts), sets it squarely within cognitive science. The result is an account which, while still very much concerned with the issue of the right distribution of labour between semantics and pragmatics in accounting for speaker meaning, is embedded in wider issues about human cognition. One of these is the question of cognitive architecture and the location of pragmatics within it: what sort of a system is responsible for pragmatic processing? is it task-dedicated or a more general problem-solving system? what other cognitive systems does it interact with? The account is receptive to considerations from evolutionary psychology concerning the kinds of cognitive systems that have been naturally selected to solve particular adaptive problems (is pragmatics one of these?). And it must answer to experimental findings about the nature and time-course of utterance comprehension; for example, results concerning which elements of conceptual information are activated at which points in the processing of ambiguous words, or metaphorical uses, or cases of implicature. Some of the ways in which relevance theory and such empirical work have begun to mutually inform each other are considered in the next section.

Probably the single most influential position on human cognitive architecture is that of Jerry Fodor (1983, 2000). On his view, the mind has a hybrid architecture: perceptual input systems, including language perception, and motor output systems are autonomous mental modules, while the central systems responsible for forming beliefs and making decisions are nonmodular. The processes of pragmatic inference are clearly a function of central systems: their goal is the fixing of a belief about a speaker's meaning (the content of her communicative intention) and they are highly context-sensitive. So the conclusion has to be that, while the phase of linguistically decoding an utterance may be carried out by a fast, automatic, informationally encapsulated system (a module), the inferential phase which bridges the gap between linguistic meaning and speaker meaning is nonmodular.

However, in recent years, there has been a shift towards a more modular (indeed a massively modular) view of the mind, albeit with a degree of relaxation of Fodor's criteria for what constitutes a modular system. This is largely a result of bringing evolutionary considerations to bear on hypotheses about the nature of mental architecture (see, for instance, Barkow, Cosmides and Tooby, 1995; Sperber, 1994b; Carruthers and Chamberlain, 2000). Natural selection favours specific solutions for specific problems. A cognitive procedure dedicated to dealing with a particular recurrent environmental problem is very likely to outperform a more general process applied to the same problem because the computations of the more general process must effect a compromise in order to deal with several distinct types of problem. Thus an evolutionary perspective suggests the increasing and refining of mental modularity rather than any kind of merging into more general systems and the crucial property of a modular system on this view is that it is a special-purpose mechanism attuned to regularities within a particular problem domain.

If the Fodorian central interpretive systems are to be reconstrued as consisting of such modular mechanisms the issue becomes whether or not pragmatic processes are executed by such a system. Currently there are two main positions on this question. One is that attributing a meaning (a special kind of intention) to a speaker falls within our broader capacity to attribute intentions, beliefs and other mental states to each other on the basis of any kind of purposive behaviour, whether communicative or non-communicative (variously known as a mind-reading ability or 'theory of mind') (see, for example, Bloom, 2002). The current relevance-theoretic view, however, is that pragmatic processes are carried out by a dedicated, domain-specific comprehension module with its own special principles and procedures. In support of this position, Sperber and Wilson (2002) point out some telling differences between general mind-reading and utterance interpretation.

First, while both of these kinds of mental state attribution clearly involve a metarepresentational capacity (the capacity to represent the mental representations of others), there is an important difference in the complexity of its application in the two cases. Ostensive communication involves an informative intention embedded in a communicative intention, so that a hearer has to recognize that the speaker *intends* him to *believe* that she *intends* him to *believe* a certain set of propositions (Sperber, 1994a, 2000), that is, four levels of metarepresentation, while in understanding ordinary actions a single level of intention attribution is usually sufficient. Furthermore, there is an interesting disparity here in the abilities of three-year-old children, many of whom are quite competent linguistic communicators while nevertheless failing standard *false belief tasks* that require them to attribute only a single-level epistemic state to an agent (see, for instance, Baron-Cohen, 1995; Scholl and Leslie, 1999). This dissociation of capacities is difficult to explain if the attribution of a meaning to a speaker is simply a function of a general capacity to attribute intentional states.

Second, while the range of intentions that can be reasonably attributed to an agent on the basis of some noncommunicative behaviour in a particular situation (e.g. extending an arm into a cupboard, walking up a flight of stairs) is generally quite limited, the physical setting of an utterance places few restrictions on its content and, given the gap between linguistic meaning and speaker meaning, there is a vast range of possible meanings that a speaker could be communicating. The standard procedure for recognizing and attributing an intention to someone on the basis of purposive behaviour (e.g. an intention to retrieve a bowl from the cupboard, an intention to reach the philosophy department on the third floor) involves observing the various effects of the behaviour, or consulting one's memory about the usual results of such a behaviour, and taking it that the desirable and predictable effects are the intended ones. This strategy would very seldom come up with the right result if applied to communicative behaviour because the desired effect just is the recognition of the communicator's intention: 'hearers cannot *first* identify a desirable effect of the utterance and *then* infer that the speaker's intention was precisely to achieve this effect' (Wilson, 2003: 116). The claim, then, is that the strategy pursued in figuring out what a speaker means by her communicative behaviour is the one given in the introduction: the comprehension process follows a path of least effort in accessing interpretations (at both the explicit and implicit levels) and it stops when the specific expectations of relevance raised by the particular utterance are satisfied. What underpins this strategy is the presumption of optimal relevance that accompanies all acts of ostensive communication and which is absent from other kinds of intentional behaviour. Thus distinct procedures are followed in the two kinds of intention-attribution.[4] In fact, the RT view is that pragmatics is one of a cluster of modules that make up what could be broadly thought of as our social cognitive capacity.

Finally, suppose that it is true that pragmatics is a fast, automatic system with its own idiosyncratic relevance-based procedure for solving its own specific problem, the next question is what is the domain of this module? Given what has been said so far, one might think it is acts of linguistic communication (verbal utterances). However, the RT view is that the domain of pragmatics is quite a lot wider than this—it is *ostensive stimuli* and these comprise any and all human actions which come with a particular complex kind of intention, an informative intention embedded in a communicative intention, including, for instance, acts of miming and other bodily gestures whose primary purpose is communicative. At this stage, it might seem that the domain of the module corresponds closely with what Grice (1957) called cases of

---

[4] This aspect of the RT view stands in clear contrast with the position taken by Donald Davidson, according to which the interpretation of any rational intentional action, whether communicative or non-communicative, is a thoroughly non-modular, holistic matter of attributing to the agent those beliefs and desires that make best sense of his overall life and conduct (Davidson, 1973, 1986).

non-natural meaning (as opposed to natural meaning), but again RT departs some-what from Grice. Wharton (2003) has pointed out that instances of natural human behaviours, such as spontaneous expressions of emotion - facial expressions, affective tone of voice—can be used by communicators as (or as components of) ostensive stimuli. For instance, a communicator conveying some positive news may openly let her audience see her spontaneous smile, or, in a different situation, may use a particular tone of voice which will calibrate the degree of anger her audience takes her to be conveying (both of these to be distinguished from the faking of a natural beha-viour as a means of communication). As Wharton says, an ostensive stimulus is often a composite of verbal behaviour (non-natural) and natural behaviour, both of which provide rich clues to the addressee in recovering the speaker's meaning.

16.4 RELEVANCE THEORY AND EXPERIMENTAL PRAGMATICS

So far we've been looking at the content of current theoretical research within the RT framework. In this section we turn to recent developments in research method-ologies. The methods used by RT-oriented researchers have standardly been those employed by most philosophers of language: introspection, intuition, analysis and argument. Recently, however, a growing number of researchers have been approach-ing questions on the nature of pragmatic processing via experimental techniques familiar to psycholinguists, but less familiar to theoretical pragmatists.

Within the RT framework, these techniques are being applied to questions surrounding so-called *scalar implicatures* (*scalar implications, scalar inferences* or sometimes just *scalars*). Very roughly, a scalar implicature arises when a speaker, by expressing a less informative proposition is taken to communicate the negation of a more informative proposition. Consider, for example, the following dialogue:

(9) PETER: Do you like Woody Allen's films?
     JANE: I like some of them.

It would seem that Jane's utterance communicates the proposition in (10):

(10) Jane does not like all of Woody Allen's films.

Yet this proposition does not appear to be part of the meaning of the sentence she has uttered. After all, there is no incompatibility between the proposition explicitly expressed by Jane in (9) and the proposition in (11):

(11) Jane likes all of Woody Allen's films.

Experimental methods have been applied to a number of distinct questions about scalar inferences such as (10): whether they are genuinely pragmatic or are auto-matically triggered by elements in the grammar; whether they should be treated as implicatures or rather as elements of explicitly communicated content; at what stage in development children begin to draw scalar inferences; and, cross-cutting these, whether the set of phenomena which have traditionally been treated as scalars form a coherent class, or whether different scalars should receive different types of analysis. Here we will focus on the first of these questions, since it has received particular attention in the recent literature.

Broadly speaking, there are two distinct approaches to the analysis of scalars currently on the market.[5] On the one hand, there are those who take scalar inferences to be triggered by elements in the grammar. Chierchia (2004), for instance, claims that the grammar delivers two distinct entries for each scalar term, with the logically weaker being filtered out according to linguistic context. Along similar lines, Levinson (2000) takes scalar implicatures to be default inferences, hence generated whenever a scalar term is used (with possible subsequent cancellation due to contextual incompatibility). On the other hand, there are those who think that scalar implicatures are purely pragmatic, that is, that they are generated on a case-by-case basis according to context and pragmatic principles. This latter view, advocated by, for instance, Carston (1998) and Sperber and Wilson (1995b), has become the dominant relevance-theoretic position on scalars.

A number of researchers have turned to experimental testing in an attempt to adjudicate between these two positions. Noveck and colleagues (e.g. Noveck and Posada (2003); Bott and Noveck (2004)) have used both psycholinguistic and neuropsychological methods to explore hearers' reactions to underinformative statements such as those in (12) and (13):

(12) Some cows are mammals
(13) Some books have pages

Subjects were asked to judge these sentences as true or false while both their response time and neural activity were measured. The key results come from subjects who judged the sentences to be false, since this judgment depends on retrieving a scalar interpretation. That is to say, in order to judge (12) false you have to take it as conveying the proposition in (14):

(14) Some but not all cows are mammals

Noveck and colleagues found evidence that those who gave such judgments took longer to reach an interpretation than those who did not. This is taken to favour the relevance-theoretic account of scalars, on which the retrieval of scalar interpretations is an effortful case-by-case matter, over default accounts, on which scalar interpretations are automatically triggered by the grammar. The relevance-theoretic view on scalars is also supported by a series of experiments conducted by Breheny and colleagues (Breheny, Katsos, and Williams (in press), Katsos, Breheny, and Williams (2005)), using a range of sophisticated techniques to investigate the role of context in scalar inference.

---

[5] We do not mean to suggest that adherents of each position would necessarily see themselves as fighting the same corner, merely that there are important similarities for our purposes.

In Section 16.2.1 above, we discussed ways in which a concept lexically encoded by a particular content word may be adjusted during interpretation. There has recently been interesting work conducted within the RT framework aimed at examining these processes from an experimental perspective and, in particular, at adjudicating between RT accounts and others currently available. Rubio (2005) uses on-line word-recognition tasks to show patterns of conceptual priming across time. Her results give preliminary support to the analyses of concept narrowing and concept loosening developed by Carston (2002). Beyond this, Rubio examines the time-course of activation and deactivation of a range of conceptual associates, that is, concepts related to the concept lexically encoded by the test word. Her results point to the interesting conclusion that some conceptual correlates are so closely associated to a particular content word that they will remain active during interpretation regardless of their contextual irrelevance. For instance, in the case of understanding a metaphorical use of 'John is a cactus', she found that the concept PLANT, a superordinate of CACTUS, remains active even after the metaphorical interpretation (for which it is irrelevant) has been recovered. This sort of finding has to be accommodated by RT and any other pragmatic theory which aims to capture the actual on-line processes of comprehension.

16.5 Future Directions for Relevance Theory

As discussed in the previous section, a growing number of researchers are committed to spelling out the empirical predictions of relevance theory and subjecting them to experimental testing. These include predictions that follow from the fundamental Cognitive Principle (human cognition tends to be geared to the maximization of relevance) and others flowing from the Communicative Principle (ostensive stimuli can be presumed to be optimally relevant) (see Van der Henst and Sperber, 2004). More generally, the emerging field of *psychopragmatics* is being energetically developed by pragmatists working in several frameworks, with RT being strongly represented among them (see Noveck and Sperber, 2004).

There are two other strands of empirical work in which ideas from RT are playing an increasing role. One is research into the development of communicative competence in children and its relation to their linguistic maturation, on the one hand, and to their developing mind-reading capacity, on the other. As touched on in Section 16.3, ostensive communication emerges earlier (from two years old) than the less metarepresentationally complex ability to attribute false beliefs to others (maturing at around four years old). Happé and Loth (2002) take this as evidence in favour of Sperber and Wilson's view of pragmatics as a modular mental system distinct from general theory of mind. However, one question that arises here is whether the child is manipulating the kind of complex layered intentions generally assumed to characterize ostensive stimuli, or whether some other earlier emerging aspect of mind-reading such as *joint attention* (arising around twelve months) is sufficient to explain early communication and comprehension (see Tomasello and Rakoczy, 2003; Breheny, 2006). Another interesting line of thought here concerns the degree of metarepresentational complexity of different kinds of *expectations of relevance* (crucial to the functioning of the RT comprehension procedure) that children and adults may have at different stages of development. It has been suggested that a young child may assume that any utterance directed at her just is optimally relevant to her, whereas more sophisticated expectations might make allowance for a speaker's fallibilities and/or ulterior motives (see Sperber, 1994a; Wilson, 2000). Clearly, the naive expectation requires no consideration of the speaker's beliefs or desires whereas the more sophisticated ones do. There is potentially fruitful work to be done in deriving explicit predictions from these ideas and testing them on communicators at different stages of development.

The other area of empirical investigation concerns people with atypical or impaired communicative capacities. These are usually looked at alongside, or as an aspect of, atypical or impaired mind-reading capacities, autism being a much-studied case in point. Autistic people are widely seen as lacking certain mind-reading abilities (in particular, but not only, the capacity to attribute epistemic mental states (Leslie, 1991; Baron-Cohen, 1995)) and many also have difficulty understanding non-verbal communication, non-literal verbal communication and the various facial and prosodic expressions of affect that often accompany verbal acts. In an early test of the RT prediction that irony is more metarepresentationally complex than metaphor, Happé (1993) showed that a group of autistic people who could understand similes had problems with both metaphor and irony, while another group who were able to handle metaphor could not grasp irony. She correlated this with the different levels of general mind-reading (in)capacities of the two groups as measured by performance on false belief tasks. More recently, Langdon *et al.* (2002) report similar results from studies of metaphor and irony understanding by people with right-hemisphere brain damage. However, on the basis of extensive testing of a group of schizophrenic people, their conclusion about the schizophrenic difficulty with metaphor is that it cannot be accounted for in terms of a theory of mind deficit. Their tentative suggestion here, based on the RT account briefly mentioned in Section 16.2.1, is that the problem lies with disorganization or degradation of the schizophrenic person's conceptual networks, which interferes with the kind of adjustment to the literal encoded concept that is necessary for metaphor understanding (Langdon *et al.*, 2002: 98). People with Williams Syndrome are generally thought to have good mind-reading capacities but, while they are often volubly communicative, recent work indicates atypical lexical processing and difficulty with certain kinds of metaphor understanding (Thomas *et al.*, unpublished data). This looks like another test-bed for RT ideas about lexical adjustment, including cases of metaphor.

On the one hand, RT has a wealth of ideas to offer to these various areas of empirical investigation; on the other, the theory itself has much to gain from the pressure for explicitness required in forming testable hypotheses and, of course, from the resulting evidence that may confirm or disconfirm its predictions. New directions for research within the relevance-theoretic framework will surely arise from this cross-fertilization between the theoretical and the empirical.

REFERENCES

Asher, N. (1999). Discourse Structure and the Logic of Conversation. In Turner, K. (ed.) *The Semantics/Pragmatics Interface from Different Points of View*. Oxford: Elsevier Science. 19–48.

Barkow, J., Cosmides, L., and Tooby, J. (1995). *The Adapted Mind: Evolutionary Psychology and the Generation of Culture*. Oxford: Oxford University Press.

Baron-Cohen, S. (1995). *Mindblindness: An Essay on Autism and Theory of Mind*. Cambridge, Mass.: MIT Press.

Bezuidenhout, A. (1997). Pragmatics, Semantic Underdetermination and the Referential/Attributive Distinction. *Mind* 106: 375–409.

Bloom, P. (2002). Mindreading, Communication and the Learning of Names for Things. *Mind and Language* 17: 37–54.

Bott, L. and Noveck, I. (2004). Some Utterances are Underinformative: The Onset and Time Course of Scalar Inferences. *Journal of Memory and Language* 51: 437–57.

Breheny, R. (2006). Communication and Folk Psychology. *Mind and Language* 21: 74–107.

Breheny, R., Katsos, N. and Williams, J. in press. Are Scalar Implicatures Generated by Default? An On-line Investigation into the Role of Context in Generating Pragmatic Inferences. *Cognition*.

Cappelen, H. and E. Lepore. (2005). *Insensitive Semantics*. Oxford: Blackwell.

Carruthers, P. and Chamberlain, A. (eds.) (2000). *Evolution and the Human Mind: Modularity, Language and Meta-Cognition*. Cambridge: Cambridge University Press.

Carston, R. (1998). Informativeness, Relevance and Scalar Implicature. In Carston, R. and Uchida, S. (eds.) *Relevance Theory: Applications and Implications*. Amsterdam: John Benjamins. 179–236.

_____ (2002). *Thoughts and Utterances: The Pragmatics of Explicit Communication*. Oxford: Blackwell.

_____ (2004a). Explicature and Semantics. In Davis, S. and Gillon, B. (eds.) *Semantics: A Reader*. Oxford: Oxford University Press. 817–845.

_____ (2004b). Truth-Conditional Content and Conversational Implicature. In Bianchi, C. (ed.) *The Semantics/Pragmatics Distinction*. CSLI. Stanford University. 65–100.

_____ forthcoming. Pragmatics, Semantics and Semantics/Pragmatics Distinctions. *Synthèse*.

Carston, R. and Wilson, D. forthcoming. Lexical Pragmatics and Relevance Theory. In Burton-Roberts, N. (ed.) *Advances in Pragmatics*. Palgrave.

Chierchia, G. (2004). Scalar Implicatures, Polarity Phenomena and the Syntax/Pragmatic Interface. In Belletti, A. (ed.) *Structures and Beyond*. Oxford: Oxford University Press.

Davidson, D. (1973). Radical Interpretation. *Dialectica* 27, 313–28. Reprinted in Davidson, D. (1984) *Inquiries into Truth and Interpretation*. Oxford: Clarendon Press. 125–39.

_____ (1986). A Nice Derangement of Epitaphs. In Lepore, E. (ed.) *Truth and Interpretation: Perspectives on the Philosophy of Donald Davidson*. Oxford: Blackwell. 433–446.

Donnellan, K. (1966). Reference and Definite Descriptions. *Philosophical Review* 75: 281–304.

Fodor, J. (1983). *Modularity of Mind*. Cambridge Mass.: MIT Press.

_____ (1998). *Concepts: Where Cognitive Science Went Wrong*. Oxford: Clarendon Press.

_____ (2000). *The Mind Doesn't Work That Way*. Cambridge, Mass.: MIT Press.

Grice, H. P. (1957). Meaning. *The Philosophical Review* 66: 377–88. Reprinted in H.P. Grice 1989: 213–23.

_____ (1967). Logic and Conversation. William James Lectures. Reprinted in H. P. Grice (1989): 1–143.

_____ (1989). *Studies in the Way of Words*. Cambridge: Harvard University Press.

Happé, F. (1993). Communicative Competence and Theory of Mind in Autism: A Test of Relevance Theory. *Cognition* 48, 101–19.

Happé, F. and Loth, E. (2002). 'Theory of Mind' and Tracking Speakers' Intentions. *Mind and Language* 17: 24–36.

Katsos, N., Breheny, R. and Williams, J. (2005). Interaction of Structural and Contextual Constraints during the On-line Generation of Scalar Inferences. Proceedings of the 27th Annual Meeting of the Cognitive Science Society, Stresa, Italy.

Kripke, S. (1979). A Puzzle about Belief. In Margalit, A. (ed.) *Meaning and Use*. Dordrecht: Reidel. 239–83.

Langdon, R., Davies, M. and Coltheart, M. (2002). Understanding Minds and Understanding Communicated Meanings in Schizophrenia. *Mind and Language* 17: 68–104.

Leslie, A. (1991). The Theory of Mind Impairment in Autism: Evidence for a Modular Mechanism of Development? In Whiten, A. (ed.) *Natural Theories of Mind: Evolution, Development and Simulation of Everyday Mindreading*. Oxford: Blackwell.

Levinson, S. (2000). *Presumptive Meanings*. Cambridge, Mass.: MIT Press.

Noveck, I. and Posada, A. (2003). Characterising the Time Course of an Implicature: An Evoked Potentials Study. *Brain and Language* 85: 203–10.

Noveck, I. and Sperber, D. (eds.) (2004). *Experimental Pragmatics*. Basingstoke: Palgrave.

Perry, J. (1986). Thought Without Representation. *The Aristotelian Society Supplementary Volume* 60: 137–51.

Powell, G. (1998). The Deferred Interpretation of Indexicals and Proper Names. *UCL Working Papers in Linguistics* 10: 143–72.

_____ (2001). The Referential–Attributive distinction—A Cognitive Account. *Pragmatics and Cognition* 9 (1): 69–98.

_____ (2002). Underdetermination and the Principles of Semantic Theory. *Proceedings of the Aristotelian Society* 102(3): 271–8.

_____ (2003). *Language, Thought and Reference*. University of London PhD thesis.

Recanati, F. (2002a). Unarticulated Constituents. *Linguistics and Philosophy* 25: 299–345.

_____ (2002b). Does Linguistic Communication Rest on Inference? *Mind and Language* 17: 105–26.

_____ (2004). *Literal Meaning*. Cambridge: Cambridge University Press.

Rouchota, V. (1992). On the Referential/Attributive Distinction. *Lingua* 87: 137–67.

Rubio, P. (2005). *Pragmatic Processes and Cognitive Mechanisms in Lexical Interpretation*. University of Cambridge PhD thesis.

Scholl, B. and Leslie, A. (1999). Modularity, Development and 'Theory of Mind'. *Mind and Language* 14: 131–53.

Searle, J. (1983). *Intentionality*. Cambridge: Cambridge University Press.

Sperber, D. (1994a). Understanding Verbal Understanding. In Khalfa, J. (ed.) *What is Intelligence?* Cambridge: Cambridge University Press. 179–98.

_____ (1994b). The Modularity of Thought and the Epidemiology of Representations. In Hirschfeld, L. and Gelman, S. (eds.) *Mapping the Mind: Domain Specificity in Cognition and Culture*. Cambridge: Cambridge University Press. 39–67.

_____ (2000). Metarepresentations in an Evolutionary Perspective. In Sperber, D. (ed.) *Metarepresentations: A Multidisciplinary Perspective*. Oxford University Press. 117–37.

Sperber, D. and Wilson, D. (1986/95a). *Relevance: Communication and Cognition*. Oxford: Blackwell. Second edition 1995.

——— (1995b). Postface. In Sperber, D. and Wilson D. 1995a: 255–279.

——— (2002). Pragmatics, Modularity and Mind-Reading. *Mind and Language* 17: 3–23.

Stanley, J. (2000). Context and Logical Form. *Linguistics and Philosophy* 25: 391–434.

Thomas, M. S. C., Van Duuren, M., Ansari, D., Parmigiani, C., and Karmiloff-Smith, A., unpublished data. The Development of Semantic Categories and Metaphor Comprehension in Williams Syndrome.

Tomasello, M. and Rakoczy, H. (2003). What Makes Human Cognition Unique? *Mind and Language* 18: 121–47.

Van der Henst, J-B. and Sperber, D. (2004). Testing the Cognitive and Communicative Principles of Relevance. In Noveck, I. and Sperber, D. (eds.) 2004: 141–71.

Wharton, T. (2003). Natural Pragmatics and Natural Codes. *Mind and Language* 18: 447–77.

Wilson, D. (2000). Metarepresentation in Linguistic Communication. In Sperber, D. (ed.) *Metarepresentations: A Multidisciplinary Perspective*. Oxford University Press. 411–48.

——— (2003). New Directions for Research on Pragmatics and Modularity. *UCL Working Papers in Linguistics* 15: 105–27.

——— (2004). Relevance and Lexical Pragmatics. *UCL Working Papers in Linguistics* 16: 343–60.

Wilson, D. and Sperber, D. (2002). Truthfulness and Relevance. *Mind* 111: 583–632.

——— (2004). Relevance Theory. In Horn, L. and Ward, G. (eds.) *Handbook of Pragmatics*. Oxford: Blackwell. 607–32.

CHAPTER 17

THE DISTINCTION BETWEEN SEMANTICS AND PRAGMATICS

ZOLTÁN GENDLER SZABÓ

WHEN we disagree, we want our disagreements to be substantive. Substantive disagreements require agreement about what the disagreement is about, which in turn requires mutual understanding. Lack of mutual understanding comes from two kinds of defects: hidden differences in how the parties understand some expression, or hidden differences in what they take to be the context in which their views are presented. The former defects are eliminable in principle and manageable in practice; the latter are something between troublesome and hopeless. So it is important to see how to tell them apart. One thing seems clear—these defects fall on opposite sides of the divide between semantics and pragmatics. This is one reason that the divide matters.

Let me elaborate. Suppose you say that the Evening Star is a star and I say it is not. Ideally, we know well enough what the world would have to be like for our respective views to be correct: if the shiniest celestial object visible in the sky just after sunset (discounting the Moon) is a sphere of hot gases radiating energy derived from thermonuclear reactions you are right; otherwise I am. If we agree about this much, our debate is certainly substantive. But things could be less than ideal and still good

I thank Kent Bach, Kati Farkas, Tamar Szabó Gendler, Ernie Lepore, Allyson Mount, and Barry C. Smith for their comments and objections.

enough for mutual understanding. Perhaps we don't both know which one of the shiny objects in the sky is the Evening Star, or what exactly makes one of those objects a star. Nonetheless, there is a clear sense in which we know what the world would have to be like for our views to be correct: if the Evening Star is a star you are right, if it isn't I am. Putting it this way is somewhat perplexing, for the statement does not move beyond the words you or I would use to present our respective views. But there is nothing wrong with that—mutual understanding does not require agreement about paraphrase.

But do we *really* agree that if the Evening Star is a star you are right and if it isn't I am? Suppose you take it that the English word 'star' applies to any celestial object visible at night from Earth by the naked eye (excepting the Moon and the occasional comets) and I take it that it applies to just those things that fit the astronomical definition, and suppose that we are unaware of this difference. Then we may be prepared to *say* that we agree that your view would be correct if the Evening Star is a star, mine if it isn't. Still, once we realize what is going on, we would stop putting things this way. We would still agree that you assent to 'The Evening Star is a star' and I do not, but given the fact that we attach different meanings to this sentence we would no longer use it without quotation in contrasting our views. We would conclude that we have a *verbal* disagreement about what the Evening Star is, which prevents us from seeing whether we also have a substantive disagreement about this matter. To achieve mutual understanding, we need to make sure that we interpret the linguistic expressions involved in stating our views in the same way.

Despite their bad reputation, verbal disagreements needn't be frivolous or trivial—it is just that they are usually unwanted. For example, I think that if you attach to the English word 'star' a meaning that allows you to say truly that the Evening Star is a star, you are mistaken about what this word means. (The mistake is common and a number of dictionaries are willing to comply.) But if we are concerned about what sort of thing the Evening Star might be we need not settle *this* disagreement, we can simply bypass it. To ensure mutual understanding, we may agree to distinguish between your word and mine by an index: we agree that for the purposes of our discussion we will mean by 'star$_1$' what you mean by 'star' and we will mean by 'star$_2$' what I do. Once we did that, we can see whether you are willing to assent to 'The Evening Star is a star$_2$' and whether I am willing to assent to 'The Evening Star is a star$_1$'. If either of these is the case, we might have a substantive disagreement; if neither is we have none.

This is a general method for filtering out verbal disagreements: locate the contentious linguistic expression (it needn't be a lexical item—we could disagree about the meanings of morphemes or phrases as well), clarify the different meanings the parties attach to it, introduce new expressions with the clarified meanings, and finally restate the disagreement using the new expressions. The process is arduous and often impractical. Still, when applied with care and caution it eliminates verbal disagreements. If all non-substantive disagreements were verbal, we would be in good shape: not only would we know what mutual understanding is (agreement about the meanings of linguistic expressions employed in stating our views), we would also have a sense of how to bring it about (eliminate verbal disagreements by replacing contentious expressions with new ones introduced by more or less explicit stipulation).

Unfortunately, things are not this tidy: there are disagreements that are neither substantive nor verbal. If I say 'The table looks good here' and you say 'The table looks terrible here' I may refer to a place next to the window and you to a place in the opposite corner from it, I may talk about the coffee table and you about the dining table, I may invoke low standards for looks and you high, I may attribute good looks to the table from my own perspective and you terrible looks from yours, I may speak in jest and you in all sincerity, and so on. In these cases, if we take ourselves to disagree our disagreement lacks substance, even if we are in full agreement about what these sentences mean. These misunderstandings are neither factual nor linguistic; to have a label, we might call them *contextual*.

There is no general recipe for bypassing contextual disagreements. Some of them are tied to specific linguistic expressions, such as the indexical 'here' in the above example. These may be replaced by appropriate descriptions: instead of saying 'The table looks good here' I may agree to present my view as 'The table looks good next to the window.' But then again, I may not. I might be reluctant to state my view in this way because I fear that it would then be misunderstood as suggesting that the table looks good *because* of its proximity to the window. Even if we make it clear that such a causal–explanatory link is not intended, I might remain reluctant. After all, the two claims are not necessarily equivalent and even if I believe both, I may want to be careful about which of my modal commitments I want to make explicit. But suppose I accept this new claim as an adequate way to state my view. It still looks like all I did was to replace one context-sensitive expression ('here') with another ('next to'). It is by no means clear whether there is a sentence containing no context-sensitive expressions I could use to state my view. And even if we carefully eliminate all context-sensitive expressions, we are still stuck with the possibility of contextual disagreements that are not tied to particular linguistic expressions. As any good censor knows, paraphrase cannot eliminate irony. Of course, we may agree, for the sake of our discussion, to cut out all forms of non-literal speech—assuming we have the same understanding of exactly what constitutes such speech. But we have no reason to assume that by adhering to this maxim, we maintain the ability to express ourselves fully. In sum: we don't know, even *in principle*, how we could bypass our contextual disagreements because we have no inventory of all the different ways in which context might influence interpretation.

Semantics is the study of linguistic meaning, or more precisely, the study of the relation between linguistic expressions and their meanings. Whenever we have a verbal disagreement, we disagree about the semantics of some expression we employed in stating our views. Pragmatics is the study of contexts of utterance, or more precisely, a study of the way context can influence our understanding of linguistic utterances. Whenever we have a contextual disagreement, we take ourselves to be in different contexts and the difference effects what we take ourselves to have done through our respective acts of stating our views. Settling on a shared meaning for the expressions we used may be hard, but settling on a shared take on the context is often harder.

Philosophy is full of recalcitrant debates where the impression that the parties are somehow speaking past each other is strong. Those of us who want to maintain that the debates (about skepticism, about ontology, about free will, and so on) are substantive must show not only that they involve no equivocation, but also that they are free of contextual confusion. This will be hard, unless we have some way to show that—at least in the relevant cases—the role of context is tightly constrained. The question about how to draw the distinction between semantics and pragmatics is philosophically important because to a large extent it determines how hard it will be to defend the legitimacy of philosophical debates.

The distinction between semantics and pragmatics I gave is nothing but a sketch; it is the intent of the rest of this paper to make it more precise. I will start in Section 17.1 by considering three alternative characterizations and explain what I find problematic about each of them. This leads to the discussion of utterance interpretation in Section 17.2, which will situate semantics and pragmatics, as I see them, in a larger enterprise. But the characterization of their contrast remains sketchy until the final section, where I discuss how truth-conditions and the notion of *what is said* fit into the picture.

17.1 HOW NOT TO DRAW THE LINE: SOME EXAMPLES FROM THE LITERATURE

The sketch of a characterization of the semantic/pragmatics distinction I gave (semantics is the study of linguistic meaning; pragmatics of the context of utterance) seems fairly innocent. Still, it differs significantly from a number of standard conceptions.[1] In this section, I will survey three alternatives—occasionally pausing to set the historical record straight. I will also point out features of these alternatives that make them, in my view, less desirable than the view I advocate.

17.1.1 The Semiotic Conception

The now-familiar distinction between syntax, semantics, and pragmatics can be traced to Charles Morris's short but influential 1938 book, in which he outlines the conceptual foundations for a general study of signs. Morris's starting point is the process in which something functions as a sign, a process he calls *semiosis*:[2]

---

[1] My characterization of pragmatics is identical to that of Stalnaker (1970): "Pragmatics is the study of linguistics acts and the contexts in which they are performed." (30) However, as I will elaborate in Section 17.3, I do not agree with Stalnaker's claim that semantics is primarily concerned with what is said by declarative sentences, that it is "the study of propositions" (32). Still, the way I suggest the semantics/pragmatics distinction should be drawn is probably closest to Stalnaker's view.

[2] Morris (1938): 3–4.

A dog responds by the type of behavior (*I*) involved in the hunting of chipmunks (*D*) to a certain sound (*S*); a traveler prepares himself to deal appropriately (*I*) with the geographical region (*D*) in virtue of the letter (*S*) received from a friend. In such cases *S* is the sign vehicle (and a sign in virtue of its functioning), *D* the designatum, and *I* the interpretant of the interpreter. The most effective characterization of a sign is the following: *S* is a sign of *D* for *I* to the degree that *I* takes account of *D* in virtue of the presence of *S*. Thus in semiosis something takes account of something else mediately, i.e. by means of a third something.

Semiosis is accordingly a mediated-taking-account-of. The mediators are *sign vehicles*; the takings-account-of are *interpretants*; the agents of the process are *interpreters*; what is taken account of are *designata*.

The term 'semiosis,' along with the idea that the process in which something is used as a sign is a process involving mediation, goes back to Charles Pierce. Pierce had the curious idea that this mediation (or 'thirdness') automatically guarantees that semiosis is not a physical or even psychological process:[3]

All dynamical action, or action of brute force, physical or psychical, either takes place between two subjects... or at any rate is a resultant of such actions between pairs. But by 'semiosis' I mean, on the contrary, an action, or influence, which is, or involves a cooperation of *three* subjects, such as a sign, its object, and its interpretant, this tri-relative influence not being in any way resolvable into actions between pairs...

Morris's attitude towards Pierce's irreducibility claim is complex. On the one hand, he often emphasizes the importance of mediation in semiosis—he even concedes the triadic nature of this relation defeats simple-minded attempts to reduce it into dyadic stimulus–response relations.[4] On the other, he also says that "of the triadic relation of semiosis, a number of other dyadic relations may be abstracted for further study,"[5] that these relations fall into three categories, which he calls the three "dimensions of semiosis," and that such a three-dimensional analysis is complete.[6] Corresponding to the three dimensions of semiosis, Morris distinguishes three branches of the general study of signs: *syntactics* (the study of relations between signs and signs), *semantics* (the study of relations between signs and their designata), and *pragmatics* (the study of relations between signs and their interpreters). He says that an axiomatic development may leave the triadic relation of 'mediately-taking-account-of' as primitive, but he also leaves no doubt that he thinks behavioristic reduction—presumably, through the reduction of the binary syntactic, semantic, and pragmatic relations—is possible.[7]

---

[3] Pierce (1931): Vol. 5, § 484.

[4] Morris (1946): 288. Behaviorism is supposed to be saved by pointing out that the link between stimulus and response is mediated by a reinforcing state.

[5] Morris (1938): 6–7.

[6] "...an individual sign is completely characterized by giving its relation to other signs, objects, and its users." Morris (1938): 11.

[7] Morris says that "from the point of view of behavioristics, to take account of *D* by the presence of *S* involves responding to *D* in virtue of a response to *S*." Morris (1938): 6. This, of course, is far from an acceptable behavioristic analysis: what it is to respond to something (especially, to something not present in one's immediate environment) needs further elaboration. It is this further analysis that is supposed to involve syntactic, semantic, and pragmatic relations.

Morris's definitions of semantics and pragmatics are subject to misunderstanding. Although semantics studies the relations between signs and the objects to which the signs are applicable, it surely does not study *all* these relations. The fact that the English word 'dog' applies to dogs is a semantic fact; the fact that most dogs would bark if one yelled 'dog' into their ears is not. Semantics is concerned only with those relations between 'dog' and dogs *in virtue of which* 'dog' is a sign that applies to dogs. This is why Morris emphasizes that we arrive at the relations semantics is concerned with by abstracting away from interpreters in considering the triadic relation underlying semiosis. Properly stated, Morris's view is that semantics is the study of the relations between one thing and another in virtue of which the former is a sign applicable to the latter, whereas pragmatics is the study of the relations one thing bears to another in virtue of which the former is interpreted as a sign by the latter.

Morris assigns a rather narrow scope to semantics. If semantics is the study of the sign-designatum relation, it must remain silent about the linguistic meanings of those expressions whose function is not to stand for something. According to Morris, these include prepositions, affixes, quantifiers, and logical connectives, all of which indicate (but not designate) syntactic relations to other signs in the language, as well as adverbs, such as 'fortunately' or 'certainly', which indicate (but again, do not designate) pragmatic relations involving the users of the sign.[8] It is not altogether clear whether Morris thinks that such expressions are meaningless—although they doubtless have a determinate function in language—or whether their meanings must be discussed by syntactics and pragmatics, respectively. Given his hostility towards the very notion of meaning—he thinks it can be dispensed with altogether and has no place in the language of semiotics—we should probably not expect much guidance from him on this matter.

Indexical expressions also fall outside the domain of semantics, as Morris understands the term, although his exact views on indexicals are a bit hard to pin down. At one point he claims that within the sentence 'That white horse runs slowly,' spoken in an actual situation with indexical gestures "'that' in combination with the indexical gesture serves as an indexical sign."[9] This seems to suggest that the demonstrative pronoun by itself (without the accompanying gesture) is not a sign at all. In a later work, however, he is willing to say that "terms such as 'it', 'this', 'I', 'now' are [...] singular signs like "proper names" but differing from proper names in that what they denote varies with the circumstances of production of the individual sign-vehicles of the sign-families to which they belong."[10] Here indexical expressions themselves have denotata, and the role of possible indexical gestures is simply to help to identify them. Either way, indexicals fall outside the purview of semantics: to spell out what a particular indexical sign stands for, we must bring in facts about the circumstances under which it is used, and this is a task for pragmatics.

Complementing his narrow conception of semantics, Morris's picture of pragmatics is broad and amorphous. Pragmatics, he writes, concerns itself with "the biotic aspects of semiosis, that is, with all the psychological, biological, and sociological

---

[8] Morris (1938): 27–8.   [9] *Ibid.* 19.   [10] Morris (1946): 77.

phenomena which occur in the functioning of signs."[11] Given how much in our lives is bound up with the use of signs, this is tantamount to a comprehensive theory of human interactions. Morris suggests that the concept of sign may prove as fundamental for the biological sciences as the concept of atom is for the physical ones.[12] The problem with this is not so much that it is false; it is rather that it comes at the wrong level of generality. Genes may well be the atoms of life and it may well be a good idea to think of them primarily as information carriers, or signs. But given how few useful generalizations apply equally well to genes, traffic signs and words, it is good news that the biological sciences are *not* in the business of looking for them.

There is another problem with Morris's way of drawing the distinction between semantics and pragmatics. His idea is that just as semantics abstracts away from the relation signs bear to their interpreters, pragmatics is supposed to neglect the relation signs bear to their designata. It is more or less clear what the former amounts to: we can say, for example, that the English noun 'dog' refers to dogs and in saying this we do not commit ourselves to anything specific about how particular speakers of English will on particular occasions interpret particular occurrences of this word. It is doubtless true that if 'dog' refers to dogs, then many speakers of English will on many occasions refer to dogs by 'dog,' and it is also clear that if all of them on all occasions used the word 'dog' to refer to cats, then it couldn't be the case that 'dog' refers to dogs. Still, there is no need to burden semantics with such facts: it is one thing to say what a word refers to and another to say *why* it refers to what it does. By contrast, it is not altogether clear how we can abstract away from designation in discussing the relation between signs and their interpreters. The fact that particular speakers of English use 'dog' on many particular occasions to refer to dogs is clearly an important fact about their relation to this word; without being able to state this fact much else will have to remain unexplained about this relation. There seems to be a fundamental *asymmetry* between semantics and pragmatics, in the sense that the former can operate in relative ignorance of the latter, but not the other way around.[13] This asymmetry is not captured by the semiotic conception, which is the main reason I believe we should not follow Morris in drawing the line between semantics and pragmatics.

17.1.2 The Indexical Conception

Perhaps the most influential conception of the relationship between semantics and pragmatics is presented in two papers by Richard Montague.[14] Montague does not regard his conception as new:[15]

---

[11] Morris (1938): 30.   [12] *Ibid.* 42.
[13] There is a similar asymmetry between syntax and semantics, which comes to the fore when we consider complex expressions. The semantics of a complex expression depends on its syntactic structure, but not the other way around.
[14] Montague (1968) and Montague (1970a).   [15] Montague (1968): 95.

The study of language (or *semiosis* or *semiotic*) was partitioned in Morris (1938) into three branches—syntax, semantics, and pragmatics—that may be characterized roughly as follows. Syntax is concerned solely with relations between linguistic expressions; semantics with relations between expressions and the objects to which they refer; and pragmatics with relations among expressions, the objects to which they refer, and the users or contexts of use of the expressions.

Despite the credit, this characterization is quite different from Morris's. First of all, it is drawn not within the general theory of signs but rather within the study of language, a much narrower domain. But within this narrower domain, pragmatics is supposed to deal with the entirety of the relation underlying semiosis.[16] In Montague's characterization, pragmatics does not abstract away from designata, and so it becomes an extension of semantics, not a distinct field. Here is how he puts it:

> Though Bar-Hillel (1954) suggested that pragmatics concern itself with indexical expressions, he was not wholly explicit as to the form this concern should take. It seemed to me desirable that pragmatics should at least initially follow the lead of semantics—or its modern version, model theory—which is primarily concerned with the notions of truth and satisfaction (in a model, or under an interpretation). Pragmatics, then, should employ similar notions, though we should speak about truth and satisfaction with respect not only to an interpretation but also to a context of use.

Bar-Hillel indeed said that the investigation of indexical languages belongs to pragmatics, but he never said that this is all there is to pragmatics.[17] By contrast, for Montague—at least "initially" (whatever that qualification may amount to)—pragmatics is nothing more or less than the systematic assignment of reference to expressions of an indexical language and the ensuing definition of truth relative to an interpretation and also to a context of use.[18]

This way of distinguishing semantics and pragmatics has its advantages. We know how to do semantics, at least for simple formal languages, and if pragmatics is just the extension of these techniques to slightly more complicated languages, we know how to do that too. By making pragmatics deal with generalizations of the semantic notions of truth and reference, Montague's distinction also captures the asymmetry in the relation between semantics and pragmatics, which escaped Morris. And, although by swallowing up semantics Montagovean pragmatics acquires considerable dimensions, its scope certainly does not include all the "biotic aspects of semiosis." All these are good things.

---

[16]   There are smaller differences as well. 'Semiosis' is a term Morris uses for the process when something functions as a sign, not as a synonym for 'semiotics'. Morris does not use the term 'reference'; he speaks of 'designation' instead. (This matters: empty names lack reference, but for Morris it is analytic that every sign has a designatum. He used 'denotatum' in roughly the way a Fregean might use 'reference'.)

[17]   Bar-Hillel (1954): 369.

[18]   The Montagovean view of the relation between semantics and pragmatics is echoed in Donald Kalish (1967). He writes: "Pragmatics, so conceived, is simply the extension of the semantical truth-definition to formal languages containing indexical terms." (p. 356) The misrepresentations of Morris's view and the claim that Bar-Hillel "identified" pragmatics with the study of indexical languages can also be found here.

Despite the advantages, there is a sense in which the indexical conception of the distinction between semantics and pragmatics is simply incomplete. Morris's definition tells us that semantics and pragmatics are parts of the general theory of signs and specifies their subject-matters: semantics is about relations between one thing and another in virtue of which the former is a sign *of* the latter, pragmatics about relations between one thing and another in virtue of which the former is a sign *for* the latter. By contrast, the indexical conception leaves the subject-matter of semantics entirely open and defines pragmatics in relation to it. Semantics studies something about non-indexical languages and pragmatics studies the same thing about indexical ones.

Montague, of course, did have quite a specific view about what semantics is, so perhaps the charitable thing to do is to interpret his distinction together with those additional views. Suppose we go along with Montague and assume that the task of semantics is to systematically assign what Carnap called extensions to all expressions of a non-indexical language relative to a model—then the task of pragmatics is to do the same for an indexical language. Now we have a substantive conception of the difference between semantics and pragmatics, but there is a new concern: once we consider natural languages (as opposed to tiny fragments of them Montague discussed), the idea that we could simply view pragmatics as an extension of ordinary semantics becomes illusory. Let me explain.

The theory of indexicals is typically pursued within the scope of what has come to be called *index-theory*. Indices are supposed to be abstract representations—usually *n*-tuples—of those features of the context of utterance that are relevant for the assignment of extensions to the expressions of the indexical language under consideration. If the language contains the pronouns 'I' and 'you', the indices will contain the speaker and the addressee of the utterance; if the language contains temporal indexicals, such as 'now' or 'next Thursday', the indices will contain the time of utterance, if the language contains spatial indexicals, such as 'here' or 'five miles to the North', the indices will contain the place of utterance, and so on. In order to apply Montague's techniques to natural languages, we would need to specify *all* these features of contexts of utterance that play a role in determining extensions. At one point, David Lewis used as indices 8-tuples of (i) a possible world, (ii) a moment of time, (iii) a place, (iv) a person (speaker), (v) a set of persons (speaker), (vi) a set of objects (available for demonstration), (vii) a segment of discourse, and (viii) an assignment function (a function assigning appropriate values to all variables used in the Tarskian semantics for quantification).[19] But he was well aware that even this was inadequate: our language may contain expressions whose interpretation apparently depends on orientation ('to the left'), or standards of precision ('hexagonal'), or salient relations ('Bill's book'), or salient domains ('every bottle'), or epistemic alternatives ('knows'), and so on. In each of these cases, we will need additional coordinates in our indices. The chances of listing all the features of the context

---

[19] Lewis (1970): 195.

upon which extensions in natural languages depend seem bleak.[20] Because of these difficulties, Lewis and many others gave up on the idea of representing contexts by indices.

Could Montague's view that pragmatics is an extension of semantics survive the abandonment of index-theory? Lewis proposed that we could represent contexts simply as triplets of a world, a time and a speaker (or, if our metaphysics allows it, as a world-bound time-slice of a possible speaker) and leave the other coordinates implicit.[21] Those who follow him no longer have a theory that looks anything like ordinary model-theoretic semantics. Instead of clauses such as (1), they have clauses like (2):

(1) The extension of 'here' in a model M relative to the index $\langle s, t, w, p \rangle$ is p.
(2) The extension of 'here' in a model M relative to the index $\langle s, t, w \rangle$ is the place where s is at t in w.

At first sight, the difference between (1) and (2) may appear inconsequential, especially if we add the informal gloss that the fourth coordinate of the index in (1) is supposed to be the place where s is at t in w. But it does matter. A model-theoretic semantics is supposed to define a function that assigns extensions to all expressions in the language under consideration from some formal structure. Given (1) alone, it is guaranteed that 'here' has a unique extension relative to an arbitrary index $\langle s, t, w, p \rangle$. Given (2) alone, we do not have a guarantee that 'here' has an extension relative to an arbitrary index $\langle s, t, w \rangle$ —if there is some speaker, time and world such that the speaker is at no place or at more than one place at that time in that world, (2) fails to determine the extension of 'here' relative to an arbitrary index. Leaving contextual coordinates implicit compromises the formal adequacy of the assignment of extensions.[22]

So pragmatics, as Montague conceives of it, may not be a completely straightforward extension of model-theoretic semantics. But this is not the real problem with the indexical conception. The main reason for its unpopularity is that it leaves out too much from the domain of pragmatics. Take for example the case where a waiter uses the sentence 'The ham sandwich is getting restless' to inform the cook that the person who ordered a ham sandwich ten minutes ago is eagerly awaiting his lunch. How is this fact to be accounted for on a Montagovean picture? Perhaps we can say that 'the ham sandwich' relative to the context of the utterance is interpreted

---

[20] Unless the intuition that the extensions of most of these expressions depend on context is mistaken; for an argument to this effect see Cappelen and Lepore (2005).

[21] Cf. Lewis (1981) and Lewis (1983).

[22] One way to react to this difficulty is to give up entirely the project of assigning extensions to indexical expressions relative to context. Instead, one might replace each and every clause of a semantic theory with a conditionalized schema whose antecedent specifies an arbitrary assignment to all the indexicals in the lexicon. Instead of the usual T-sentence for 'She is lazy', Higginbotham (1988) recommends that we include in our semantics the clause 'If x is referred to by "she" in the course of an utterance of "She is lazy" and x is female, then that utterance is true iff x is lazy.' In this way, he hopes to stay clear of the "morass of communicative context." (Higginbotham (1988): 40.)

as denoting a person, and thereby treat the phenomenon as a new sort of indexical-ity. But this is a dangerous strategy: after all, almost any definite description could be used in a similarly off way in some context, and if we allow that all of them are index-icals, we risk losing our intuitive grip on the very notion of indexicality. Or consider the sentence 'I will not forget this', which could be uttered as a simple prediction, as a threat, as a promise, and in many other ways. Identifying which of these is the case is part of interpreting the sentence in the context of utterance. If this is to be treated as a kind of indexicality, we need to represent the illocutionary force of the sentence in our model, which seems to be a bad idea. (Models are supposed to rep-resent what linguistic expressions are about, not how they are employed to various conversational effects.)

The examples could be multiplied. Many phenomena discussed in pragmatics text-books—presupposition, conversational implicature, rhetorical tropes, etc.—simply do not yield easily to indexical treatment. The problem is not primarily technical—it is not just that we would end up with a lot of odd indices to which to relativize inter-pretation. It is rather that, intuitively, many of the traditional problems of pragmatics are problems of utterance interpretation, not problems of the interpretation of lin-guistic expressions in context. The case of irony illustrates the point nicely. Suppose I utter the sentence 'He is a fine friend' contemptuously. The interpretation of my utterance must be sensitive to this fact, otherwise the addressee will misunderstand me in the worst possible way. But intuitively, the sentence itself means what it does quite independently of my manifest contempt. Utterance interpretation often goes beyond literal meaning, even literal meaning relativized to context. This is not cap-tured by the indexical conception—which is, I think, the main reason why we should not adopt it.

17.1.3 The Cognitivist Conception

It is a fairly natural idea to try to distinguish semantics and pragmatics on psy-chological grounds: perhaps different kinds of psychological mechanisms underlie different parts of the interpretation process, and these are subject to different kinds of inquiry. In their influential 1986 book *Relevance*, Dan Sperber and Deirdre Wilson proposed just such a distinction. On their view, semantics studies coding mech-anisms whereby linguistic expressions are paired with their meanings;[23] pragmatics concerns itself with inferential mechanisms whereby one can integrate this meaning with other information available from the context to arrive at the interpretation of an utterance. These mechanisms are fundamentally different:[24]

An *inferential process* starts from a set of premises and results in a set of conclusions which follow logically from, or are at least warranted by, the premises. A *decoding process* starts

---

[23] For Sperber and Wilson, the study of all the psychological mechanisms whereby certain acoustic signals are connected with meanings is grammar. Semantics is a part of grammar.
[24] Sperber and Wilson (1988): 12–13.

from a signal and results in the recovery of a message which is associated to the signal by an underlying code. In general, conclusions are not associated to their premises by a code, and signals do not warrant the messages they convey.

Unfortunately, the distinction is not as clear as it first seems. Since natural languages contain infinitely many expressions, pairing them with their meanings must proceed via a recursive function. Assuming that speakers do in fact compute the values of such a function when they determine the meaning of a particular expression, the cognitive mechanism they employ is, in a perfectly natural sense of the word, inferential. If inferential mechanisms employed in interpretation belong to pragmatics, all that remains within the scope of semantics is the study of lexical meaning.

This is clearly not Sperber and Wilson's intent. Although they don't dispute simple and empirically well-founded generalizations, like that one must know what 'snow' and 'white' mean (as well as how predication works) in order to know the meaning of 'Snow is white', they believe the process involved in moving from understanding words to understanding sentences those words compose differs fundamentally from ordinary inferential processes:[25]

A variety of species, from bees to humans, have codes which are to a greater or lesser extent genetically determined. These differ from inferential systems in two main respects: first, the representations they relate need not be conceptual, and second, the rules relating these representations need not be inferential. Human natural languages are case in point. If we are right, then linguistic knowledge does not contribute to the comprehension process in the way described above: by providing premises for inference.

Is it legitimate to seek to distinguish semantics and pragmatics on psychological grounds? A familiar objection to this very idea starts with Montague's contention that "there is no important theoretical difference between natural languages and the artificial languages of logicians."[26] Despite occasional overstatements to the contrary, this does not quite mean that linguistics is a branch of mathematics: what linguists are really interested in is which of the possible abstract formal structures are English, Swahili, or Bulgarian—and these are surely empirical questions.[27] Still, these are not questions of psychology; which populations speak which mathematically characterized language is a question about conventions, and as such, is a concern for sociology. There clearly are problems about what it is for an individual to have the capacity to speak and comprehend a language, and anti-psychologists about linguistics usually do not deny this. What they maintain instead is that the main business of linguistics—formally characterizing a range of possible languages and empirically determining which of these is used by which groups of people—can

---

[25] Sperber and Wilson (1988): 27. I take it that one aspect of the difference alluded to here has something to do with doubts whether our understanding of complex expressions can legitimately be called a kind of knowledge. The doubts are linked to the observation that our beliefs about what linguistic expressions mean do not appear to have justification—at least if we assume that justification requires reasons we could articulate.

[26] Montague (1970b): 222.

[27] For one of the clearest ways of outlining this conception of the subject-matter of linguistics, see Lewis (1968).

proceed independently of the psychological details. Indeed, if linguistics is concerned with languages as we ordinarily think of them—as essentially social phenomena—it is hard to see why the psychological details would matter. Presumably we all agree that Martians could learn English, even if they employed completely different psychological mechanisms to produce and interpret English utterances. In fact, later on, all the people could die out and the Martians could keep using English in their conversations. So, we could have English without any of the current psychological mechanisms connected with its use.

Cognitivists, like Sperber and Wilson, will not dispute the cogency of this argument but instead of concluding that psychology is irrelevant to linguistics, they conclude that linguistics is not primarily about public language.[28] For certain purposes the idiolects spoken by Martians would count as sufficiently similar to be called idiolects of the same language, and for other purposes they may not be, just as for certain purposes we would say that Chaucer and Poe spoke the same language and for others that they did not. And although the idiolect of a person does typically manifest itself in linguistic behavior—*performance*, as Chomsky calls it—the full range of such behavior provides us with a confusing set of data, which in its entirety does not yield to systematic theorizing. Nonetheless, underlying the cacophony, we have good reason to postulate a uniform, largely genetically encoded linguistic capacity of individual human beings—their *competence*—which is for linguistics to reveal. Perhaps semantics deals with certain aspects of utterance interpretation that are manifestations of linguistic competence (decoding process), while pragmatics is part of the study of certain aspects of performance (inferential process).[29] The human language faculty, the psychological system underlying linguistic competence, is a paradigm example of a *module*: it works fast, its principles are domain-specific, and it works in a way that remains largely inaccessible to consciousness and to other modules. The gist of Sperber and Wilson's view is that semantics and pragmatics study different processes involved in utterance interpretation, and that the subject matter of the former but not the latter are the workings of the linguistic module.[30]

Many cognitivists—famously including Chomsky himself—are reluctant to say that linguistic competence includes semantic competence. The reluctance is entirely natural: it is hard to see how the study of the relation between language and

---

[28] Chomsky (1986) introduced the distinction between *I-language* and *E-language*. The former is a natural object internal to the brain of an individual whose working is representable as a function-in-intension generating structural descriptions of (as opposed to mere strings of) expressions. The latter is something external to individuals, either a social object constituted by norms and conventions, or some abstract object, say, a set of sentences. According to Chomsky, the former is the proper object of the study of language, the latter is not.

[29] "Pragmatic theories [...] explicate the reasoning of speakers and addressees in working out the correlation in a context of a sentence token with a proposition. In this respect, a pragmatic theory is part of performance." Katz (1977): 19.

[30] Initially Sperber and Wilson defended the idea that pragmatic processes do not belong to any module. See Wilson and Sperber (1986). Lately their views have changed; cf. Sperber and Wilson (2002). What is crucial to our discussion here is that they do not belong to the *linguistic* module.

world could be part of individual psychology. The world, after all, could be quite different from the way it is—for example, it could be that rivers and lakes contain a curious substance XYZ superficially indistinguishable from our H_2O—without any relevant change in what is in our head. If semantics is really concerned with the question of what the English word 'water' represents, it must be sensitive to the difference between XYZ and H_2O, and hence, it must be outside the scope of cognitive linguistics. Here is a familiar argument to this effect. Suppose our semantics of Oscar's idiolect contains (3):

(3) 'Water' refers to water

Assuming—as it seems plausible—that not being H_2O, XYZ is not a kind of water, (3) is false on Twin-Earth (a planet just like ours, except that the substance in rivers and lakes is XYZ), and consequently cannot be part of an adequate semantics of the idiolect of Twin-Oscar. Oscar's and Twin-Oscar's idiolects have different semantics, even though (given that they are molecule-by-molecule duplicates) their individual psychology must be the same. So, semantics is not part of cognitive linguistics.[31]

There are ways to resist this conclusion but each carries considerable difficulties.[32] The particular path Sperber and Wilson chose involves rejecting the idea that semantics should tell us about how language is related to the world: the job of a semantic theory of (idiolects of) English is merely to assign mental representations to linguistic expressions. Those representations, of course, must stand in an appropriate relation to the world, and we may theorize about that relation as well. That theory, however, has nothing to do with language or communication—in particular, it is not a theory that articulates something that is supposed to be already tacitly known. Using capital letters to talk about the relevant mental representations, (4) is a common clause of the semantics of (idiolects of) English and Twin-English; (5) tells us what a particular mental representation refers to on Earth and (6) tells us what it refers to on Twin-Earth. Neither (5) nor (6) is part of semantics of idiolects on either planet.

(4) 'Water' expresses WATER
(5) 'WATER' refers to H_2O
(6) 'WATER' refers to XYZ

---

[31] Chomsky thinks the reference of 'water' is interest-relative. He points out that if we fill a glass from the tap and then dip a tea bag into it, we would be reluctant to call the content 'water'. By contrast, if we fill another glass from another tap that is connected to a reservoir into which tea has been dumped, we would probably not hesitate to call the content of this glass 'water'. Chomsky thinks this remains the case even if it turns out that the contents of the two cups are indistinguishable even for a chemist (Chomsky (1995): 22. I disagree: I think many of us would be reluctant to stand by both judgments upon learning the chemist's verdict; we might not know which one to give up, but that does not mean that they must have the same standing.

[32] The main options are: (i) argue that despite majority intuition XYZ *is* a kind of water, (ii) argue that false clauses can underlie semantic competence, (iii) say that 'water' contains a hidden indexical, (iv) say that semantics proper does not include lexical semantics, or (v) accept internalism about semantics, as Sperber and Wilson do.

Philosophers often doubt whether a theory that assigns one representation to another deserves the name 'semantics.' The idea bothers me too, but not as much as the suggestion that a theory that does establish links between representations and the world does *not* deserve that name.[33] But perhaps the complaint is merely verbal. Sperber and Wilson may fundamentally agree with Chomsky that there is one important line to be drawn: between speakers' linguistic competence and whatever else is involved in utterance interpretation. Sperber and Wilson think semantic processes belong to the former and Chomsky does not—but this is only because Chomsky understands 'semantics' as 'referential semantics' and Sperber and Wilson understand it as 'translational semantics.' They agree that translational semantics is part of linguistic competence and referential semantics isn't.[34]

This maneuver has a price. Cognitivists may have successfully drawn distinctions between translational semantics and pragmatics and between referential and translational semantics. Still, in order for these to make up a successful semantics/pragmatics distinction, they need to convince us that referential semantics and pragmatics do not overlap. That is, *none* of the pragmatic processes involved in utterance interpretation requires at any point information about what a certain word refers to or what the truth-conditions of a sentence might be. This is a strong claim, one that I am not much inclined to believe. But even if my inclination is wrong, it seems unwise to burden a simple distinction with such a theoretical baggage. I think the basic idea of the Sperber and Wilson distinction can be preserved without assuming the truth of cognitivism from the outset.

17.2 INTERPRETING UTTERANCES

I said that semantics is the study of linguistic meaning and pragmatics the study of context of utterance. This makes it seem as if they are about entirely different things. In a way, this is so: *primarily* expression types have linguistic meaning and expression tokens occur in contexts. Courtesies are extended in both directions, but tokens can only be said to have a certain linguistic meaning by extension, in virtue of being tokens of a type with that meaning, and types can only be said to occur in a context by extension, in virtue of being types to which a token that occurs in that context belongs.

Despite their differences there is a way to pull meaning and context together: they are the two sources of information used in *interpreting utterances*. An utterance is an action involving the articulation of a linguistic expression by an intentional agent, the *speaker*, directed at an intentional agent, the *addressee*. The interpretation of the utterance is a cognitive process whereby the addressee ascertains what the

---

[33] Fodor, a major proponent of the view that instead of (3), we need (4) and (5), takes his view to mean that while English has no semantics, Mentalese, of course, does. Cf. Fodor (1998): 9.

[34] This is the sort of view taken in the Introduction of Carston (2002).

speaker meant in making the utterance.[35] In paradigm cases, interpretation begins with the recognition of a certain acoustic event[36] and ends with knowledge about what the speaker meant in bringing that event about. In between the beginning and the end, the addressee relies on her ability to understand linguistic expressions (her knowledge of their linguistic meanings) and on her ability to track what is manifest in the situation (her knowledge of the context of utterance). When she does the former, she is engaged in semantic interpretation; when she does the latter, she is engaged in pragmatic interpretation.

What is speaker meaning, knowledge of which by the addressee is the postulated end point of interpretation? According to Grice's famous analysis, it is a certain effect the speaker intends to bring about in the addressee by means of the recognition of that intention.[37] That meaning something involves intentions to bring about recognition of intentions is an important insight that has been preserved in much of our current thinking. Nonetheless, we know that Grice's analysis is not exactly correct. The speaker may utter something; have the first-order intention to bring about a certain effect in the addressee, and the second-order intention that this response come about by means of the recognition of the first-order intention—still, he may also have a third-order intention that his second-order intention should remain unrecognized.[38] Fixing up Grice's characterization so that it can deal with such cases is hard and I will not attempt it here. All that is needed for our purposes is the acknowledgment that it requires the speaker having a certain intention to bring about a certain effect, and that beyond that it requires nothing but presence of some further intentions and perhaps the absence of others.[39]

If meaning something by an utterance primarily requires having an intention to bring about some effect in the addressee, it seems natural to say that *what* is meant by an utterance is just that effect. This is indeed Grice's view:

... to ask for a specification of what A meant [by making an utterance] is to ask for a specification of the intended effect (though, of course, it may not always be possible to get a straight answer involving a "that" clause, for example, "a belief that...").[40]

This is a bit surprising, for ordinary specifications of the intended effects of our utterances do not seem to be like that at all:

---

[35] I follow Levinson (1983): 72 in distinguishing between *addressee* (someone at whom an utterance is directed) and *hearer* (someone who heard the utterance, perhaps accidentally). The way I understand utterance interpretation, it is always a cognitive process of someone at whom the utterance is directed.

[36] I focus here on spoken language because the interpretation of written texts poses extra difficulties. Written language involves a code whereby certain marks are associated with linguistic expressions—a code that is unknown to illiterate but otherwise linguistically-competent people. More importantly, this code enables us to make "canned" utterances that can be directed at an indeterminate number of addressees, rendering the process of identifying the context against which the interpretation must take place particularly difficult.

[37] Grice (1957): 220.   [38] Examples of this sort were first raised in Strawson (1964).

[39] For discussion of how Grice's analysis might be improved, see Searle (1965); Grice (1967); Schiffer (1972); Bach and Harnish (1979); and Sperber and Wilson (1986).

[40] Grice (1957): 220.

(7) a. By uttering 'Watch out!' I meant to bring you to a halt.
   b. By uttering 'Well done.' I meant to make you proud.
   c. By uttering 'Who was that?' I meant to get you to tell me who you were talking to.
   d. By uttering 'Your wallet!' I meant to obtain your wallet.
   e. By uttering 'It is on the left' I meant to persuade you to turn left.

By contrast, if we focus not on what effects the speaker intends to accomplish *by* making the utterance, but rather on what the speaker intends to do *in* making it, we can easily get the impression that a straight answer must indeed involve a clause—not necessarily one headed by the complementizer 'that', but a clause nonetheless:

(8) a. In uttering 'Watch out!' I meant to warn you that the train is coming.
   b. In uttering 'Well done.' I meant to praise you for having succeeded.
   c. In uttering 'Who was that?' I meant to ask you who you were talking to.
   d. In uttering 'Your wallet!' I meant to command you to hand me your wallet.
   e. In uttering 'It is on the left.' I meant to inform you that the exit is on your left.

It is hard to resist the idea that Grice did not pay sufficient attention to Austin's distinction between *illocutionary* and *perlocutionary* acts.[41] There are two sorts of speaker meaning. Someone who understands my utterances *will* typically know the things stated under (7), but all he *must* know are the things stated under (8). I suggest that we should modify Grice's view and take the latter, rather than the former, to be the endpoint of utterance interpretation.[42]

I am not sure whether all specifications of what the speaker meant in uttering certain words can be brought into canonical form, like the ones under (8), but I am fairly confident that most can. If so, speaker meaning typically has two components: one is given by the main verb within the infinitival clause in the complement of 'mean' and the other by the clause in the complement of that verb. I call the first component the *illocutionary act* meant by the utterance, the second the *content* of that act.

So, a general theory of utterance interpretation is the study of how we normally get from our perceptions of certain sounds to our knowledge what the person making those sounds meant in making them. It is important that this theory studies *normal* processes—it does not investigate, for example, the arduous path followed by Champollion in deciphering the Rosetta stone. That process relies

---

[41] Austin (1962), esp. Lecture VII. The third of the tripartite distinction, the *locutionary act* is the mere utterance of a linguistic expression "with a certain sense and reference" (93). Grice's lapse has been stressed by Strawson (1964); Searle (1969); and Bach and Harnish (1979).

[42] Note that this does not call into question Grice's claim that one can only mean something if one has an intention to bring about a certain effect in the addressee. But the relevant effects are the illocutionary effects (the effect that the addressee understands the utterance), not the perlocutionary ones (further effects that are usually the point of the speaker's utterance). As Searle (1969): 46 notes, Grice's claim that speaker meanings are intended perlocutionary effects is problematic anyway: when I greet someone I undoubtedly mean something even though my utterance is typically without intended perlocutionary effects.

on information beyond meaning and context.[43] Although it is not as complex as hermeneutics, the theory of utterance interpretation is still an ambitious enterprise, one we have no clear idea how to pursue (hence philosophers' persisting interest in it). Conventional wisdom locates semantics in the middle of this picture: its inputs are linguistic expressions (something which must somehow be identified through parsing the noises that are the input of utterance interpretation) and its outputs are linguistic meanings (something which must somehow yield through further processing knowledge of what was meant in making the noises by the one who was making them). Since semantic knowledge is something speakers have independently of the particular situations in which they interpret utterances, this pairing is strictly context-independent. Context enters utterance interpretation *before* semantics does (in helping disambiguation, filling in elliptical expressions, etc.) or *after* semantics does (in helping to derive conversational implicatures, to determine the force of indirect speech acts, etc.).

The temporal language must be taken with a grain of salt here. There is no reason to assume that in interpreting a certain utterance we first determine (without any recourse to semantic knowledge) which linguistic expression was used, then determine (without any recourse to pragmatic knowledge) what that expression means, and then determine (again, without recourse to semantic knowledge) what the speaker meant in making the utterance. It is psychologically much more plausible to think the employment of our semantic and pragmatic knowledge is intertwined, e.g. that in order to disambiguate a sound we need to consider the meanings of the alternative expressions it may encode, or even what sort of implicatures the utterance of the alternative expressions may carry. But this does not alter the conceptual point that we can assign a linguistic meaning to an expression only after we know what the expression is, or the conceptual point that if the assignment of linguistic meaning to the expression occurs at all, it must occur before the entire process of utterance interpretation reaches its goal.

Does interpretation always have to involve a semantic component? Do we have to know what words, phrases, and clauses were uttered and what they meant if we are to ascertain what the speaker meant in uttering them? The answer is no—otherwise people with patchy knowledge of a language wouldn't be able to get along so well. It is an everyday experience of people interacting in a foreign-language environment that they may be perfectly clear about what an utterance meant despite hearty ignorance concerning the expressions that compose it. Indeed, it is a common experience to learn all but the first few hundred words of a new language *in situ* by understanding utterances in which they occur and then reasoning back to what their linguistic meaning must be. Although in practice these tend to be cases where we know the

---

[43] We should certainly avoid the temptation to say that context includes absolutely everything an addressee might employ to ascertain what a speaker meant. If context is understood so widely, then it is trivial that interpretation requires nothing beyond knowledge of context, and so, knowledge of linguistic meaning is deemed not to be an independent source of information for interpreting utterances. I return to this issue at the end of Section 17.3.

meaning of some of the words employed, it seems clear that, in a rich enough context, we could *in principle* bypass all semantics.[44]

What about interpretation without a pragmatic component? Can there be a situation where an addressee can interpret an utterance completely independently of context, exclusively on the basis of his linguistic knowledge? I think this is doubtful. Take a case of a math teacher announcing at the end of a calculation: "Four thousand eight hundred fifty three plus six hundred ninety four is five thousand five hundred forty seven." Clearly, the students know that the teacher meant to inform them that $4853 + 694 = 5547$. But the fact that she meant just that (and not something more, or something different) is something they know because they know that they are listening to their teacher in a class and not, for example, to an enraged costumer in a restaurant (who is complaining about the faulty addition on his bill) or an actor on stage (who plays an insane serial killer making plans). Perhaps there is such a thing as zero context, but the addressee still must know that he is in such a context, and *that* knowledge is not linguistic.

Let me summarize the picture advocated here. I suggest that we understand semantics and pragmatics as subfields within the general study of utterance interpretation, the process whereby the addressee determines what the speaker meant in uttering a linguistic expression. Typically but not always, such a process will include a component when the speaker associates linguistic expressions with their meanings: this is the subject-matter of semantics. This association is independent of the context in which the utterance takes place; the study of the various ways in which context influences utterance interpretation is the business of pragmatics.

Like the cognitivist conception, this picture avoids the problems that render the semiotic and the indexical conceptions implausible: unlike Morris's definitions, it accounts for the fact that semantics can be pursued in relative ignorance of pragmatics, but not the other way around, and unlike Montague's definitions, it does not neglect the fact that pragmatics is concerned with the interpretation of utterances, not merely the interpretation of linguistic expressions in context. It departs from the cognitivist conception in being neutral on the questions of whether semantic and pragmatic processes are fundamentally different and whether either is fully describable at the level of individual psychology.

---

[44] This is Grice's view as well. Searle criticized Grice's definition of speaker meaning on the grounds that it allows for this possibility. The intuition Searle relies on is exemplified in the following case. An American soldier in the Second World War wishes to convince the Italians who have captured him that he is a German officer by uttering the only German sentence he knows: 'Kennst du das Land wo die Zitronen blühen?' Intuitively, in making this utterance he does not mean to tell them that he is a German soldier. The conclusion Searle draws is that in order for a speaker to mean something, he must intend that his primary intention to convey something be recognized *in virtue of the addressee's semantic knowledge*; cf. Searle (1965): 49–50. Although I accept this intuition, I think the suggested revision of Grice's definition is much too radical. As Grice (1967): 101–2 points out, Searle's definition is much too restrictive. If a Port Said merchant standing in the doorway of his shop sees a British visitor and in a sweet tone with an alluring smile utters the Arabic translation of 'You pig of an Englishman', he does mean to suggest that the visitor should come into his store, and the visitor may well correctly interpret his utterance this way.

17.3 TRUTH-CONDITIONS AND WHAT IS SAID

Saying that semantics is concerned with linguistic meaning may simultaneously bore and annoy philosophers. It's a bit like "You should buy low and sell high"—true but unhelpful. Semanticists tend to talk more about truth-conditions than about meaning. I need to stick out my neck and say something about how truth-conditions fit into the picture I outlined; otherwise the main frontlines in the semantics/pragmatics wars remain hidden.

It is sometimes said that the linguistic meaning of an expression simply *is* what it contributes to the truth-conditions of declarative sentence where it occurs (in an extensional context). As it stands, this isn't quite right: there are meaningful subsentential expressions which contribute nothing to truth-conditions (such as 'by the way'[45]) and differences in linguistic meaning (say, between 'a(n)' and 'at least one'[46]) which do not affect truth-conditions. Semanticists who conduct their business in terms of truth-conditions are well aware of this, but they are sufficiently well-occupied by their central task not to worry much about peripheral cases. Still, if one wants to speak accurately, one has to be a bit more careful. We can say at most that the linguistic meaning of an expression simply *determines* what (if anything) it contributes to the truth-conditions of declarative sentence where it occurs (in an extensional context). Here is how David Lewis puts such a proposal:[47]

A meaning for a sentence determines the conditions under which the sentence is true or false. It determines the truth-value of the sentence in various possible states of affairs, at various times, at various places, for various speakers, and so on. [. . .] Similarly, a meaning for a name is something that determines what thing, if any, the name names in various possible states of affairs, at various times, and so on. [. . .] Similarly, a meaning for a common noun is something that determines which (actual or possible) things, if any, that common noun applies to in various possible states of affairs, at various times, and so on. We call the truth-value of a sentence the *extension* of that sentence; we call the thing named by a name the *extension* of that name; we call the set of things to which a common noun applies the *extension* of that common noun. The extension of something in one of these three categories depends on its meaning and, in general, on other things as well: on facts about the world, on the time of utterance, on the place of the utterance, on the speaker, on the surrounding discourse, etc. It is the meaning that which determines how the extension depends on the combination of other relevant factors.

---

[45] 'By the way' is hardly exceptional: Bach (1999) lists over a hundred such examples.

[46] That these expressions don't mean the same is plausible because unlike 'a(n)', 'at least one' cannot occur as the subject of a generic sentence ('At least one elephant never forgets' vs. 'An elephant never forgets') and can be part of a complex quantifier ('at least one but no more than five' vs. *'an but no more than five'). It is hard to believe that these syntactic contrasts have nothing to do with meaning.

[47] Lewis (1970): 193.

It is important that Lewis uses the term 'truth-condition' in a slightly non-standard way. He takes truth-conditions to be *all* the conditions other than linguistic meaning upon which the truth-value of a (declarative)[48] sentence depends. Call these *absolute truth-conditions*. Lewis would represent the absolute truth-conditions of 'I am now hungry' by a function that maps possible worlds, times, and individuals onto the truth just in case the individual is the speaker at that time in that world and (s)he is hungry. Truth-conditions are typically construed more restrictively: they specify the conditions involving the *subject-matter* of the sentence upon which its truth-value depends. Call these *relative truth-conditions*. The relative truth-conditions of 'I am now hungry' vary according to speaker and time of utterance: if the speaker is Socrates and the time of utterance is 5pm GMT January 6, 2006, they could be representable by the function that maps possible worlds onto the truth just in case Socrates is hungry at 5pm GMT January 6, 2006 in that world; if the speaker is Cromwell and the time of utterance is 1pm GMT March 11, 1256, they could be representable by the function that maps possible worlds onto the truth just in case Cromwell is hungry at 1pm GMT March 11, 1256 in that world, and so on for any possible individual and any possible time.[49] Lewis claims that linguistic meaning determines absolute truth-conditions, and consequently, that linguistic meaning *together with the context* determines relative truth-conditions. Since relative truth-conditions are typically called 'truth-conditions' or 'truth-conditional content', the view can be rephrased as follows: linguistic meaning plus context determine truth-conditional content. Call this the *standard view*.[50]

The standard view—at least in the version I find plausible—is not committed to the claim that semantic theory *aims* at the assignment of truth-conditional content relative to context. Semantics is supposed to tell us what linguistic expressions mean and truth-conditional content relative to context is *not* meaning. (As I mentioned above, the two obviously come apart in cases of meaningful expressions contributing nothing to truth-conditional content, such as 'by the way'. I suspect the divergence is much more widespread.)[51] Nonetheless, in many cases the best we can do in characterizing linguistic meaning is to show how it determines, together with context, the

---

[48] Lewis (1970): 220–6 sketches some proposals about how to extend this story to non-declaratives.

[49] Those who abhor non-actual possibilia can represent absolute truth-conditions by a relativized T-sentence and relative truth-conditions by unrelativized ones. For current purposes, nothing hangs on this.

[50] Some philosophers prefer to conduct the business of semantics in terms of propositions rather than truth-conditions. They don't deny that one can assign truth-conditions to declarative sentences, but they prefer to break this assignment into two parts: the assignment of propositions to sentences, and the assignment of truth-conditions to propositions. The first part (e.g. that 'Snow is white' expresses in English the proposition that snow is white) is an empirical matter which belongs to semantics; the second part (e.g. that the proposition that snow is white is true just in case snow is white) is a conceptual truth. Whether these philosophers are right is orthogonal to the issue whether the standard view is correct: linguistic meaning plus context may well determine truth-conditional content even if such a determination is not a purely semantic matter.

[51] I have argued in Szabó (2000) that the indefinite and definite articles have the same truth-conditional content, namely, that of the determiner 'some'. I did not say that the articles are synonymous—they most certainly are not.

truth-conditional content of an expression. Semantic interest in context and truth-conditions is merely instrumental.

The standard view has fallen into disrepute in many circles lately. The reason is that there are a host of putative counterexamples to it. These are all simple, meaningful, well-formed declarative sentences, each of which seems to lack truth-conditional content, even within a context of utterance. Here are some examples:

(9) a. Igor is tall. (compared to what?)
   b. Louise is taller. (than whom?)
   c. Kati is ready. (for what?)
   d. Hendryk arrived. (where?)

Intuitively, the parenthetical questions must be answered before we can assign truth-conditional content to these sentences and, it is claimed, the answers are usually not provided by the context in which they are uttered. From this, it is concluded that to these sentences (and many others) semantic theory must assign something *less* than truth-conditional content.[52,53]

One can object to these putative counterexamples in at least three ways. The first is to deny that these sentences are context-dependent. This might be the most plausible in the case of (9a): perhaps 'Igor is tall' is true in *any* context just in case Igor is tall. If so, 'Igor is tall' does not follow from 'Igor is tall for a soccer player', no matter what the context might be. People may, of course, convey the thought that Igor is tall for a soccer player by sincerely uttering 'Igor is tall' in the right context, but this has nothing to do with the truth-conditional content of the sentence. Defenders of this line will be forced to acknowledge that tallness is somewhat hard to detect: we may know that Igor is tall for an accountant, not tall for a basketball player—we may even be told that he is exactly 6'1". *In principle* one could know all these facts and still be ignorant whether Igor is tall. This is not particularly intuitive but it is not a fatal objection against those who deny the context-dependence of (9a). After all, verificationism is dead: semantics is one thing, epistemology another.[54]

The second option is to claim that the declarative sentence is elliptical: context must provide a linguistic expression of some sort to fill in a lacuna. This strategy

---

[52] Sperber and Wilson (1986): 188 suggest that we assign to such sentences subpropositional logical forms; Bach (1994): 269 says that they express propositional radicals.

[53] In addition to these sorts of cases many theorists (among them Sperber and Wilson, and Bach as well) claim that semantics underdetermines scope assignment. More generally, Levinson (2000) argues that all indexing at the level of logical form is underdetermined by semantics. These views require not merely the revision of our standard picture of the role of semantics in utterance interpretation, but also that of syntax. (Chapter 4 of Levinson (2000) is an attempt to replace Binding Theory by generalized conversational implicatures.) I set this issue aside, for even if it were true (contrary to the majority view among linguists) a defender of the standard view could simply retreat and claim that semantics assigns a *finite set* of (relative) truth-conditions to declarative sentences. This would be a concession, but not a fundamental one. (Note, for example, that one of the standard approaches that aims to capture the truth-conditional effects of focus already requires that we assign *two* semantic values to declarative sentences; cf. Rooth (1992).)

[54] For this sort of line see Cappelen and Lepore (2003) and (2005). They also provide detailed arguments against the positive case made in Searle (1978); Travis (1985), and others that the sort of underdetermination they see in (9a) is present in virtually every declarative sentence.

is most plausible in the case of (9b): the sentence when it occurs in the context of an utterance must be something like 'Louise is taller *than Rita*' or 'Louise is taller *than her*'—it's just that the words in italics remain unpronounced. Why think this? One might point at the fact that, just as paradigm cases of ellipsis, (9b) supports a strict/sloppy ambiguity:

(10) Vera visited her mother. Louise did too.
(11) Vera is shorter than her mother. Louise is taller.

(10) can mean either that Louise also visited Vera's mother, or that she also visited her own mother, and (11) either that she is taller than Vera's mother, or that she is taller than her own mother. If the right account of this involves the postulation of ellipsis in (10), the situation is likely to be the same in (11).

A third option is to postulate a hidden variable in logical form. A reasonable case can be made for this regarding (9c): perhaps at the level of logical form 'ready' is really 'ready for x' and in (9c) it is context that must provide an appropriate value for the variable. One reason to think so could be the observation that this variable is apparently available for binding from outside the clause; the most natural reading of (12) appears to be (13):

(12) Whatever comes her way, Kati is ready.
(13) For every x, if x comes her way, Kati is ready for x.

If we believe, as many syntacticians do, that binding phenomena must be captured at the level of logical form, it seems natural to demand the presence of an appropriate variable in (9c). Once we come this far, it is hard to resist the hidden variable proposal.[55]

Needless to say, these defenses of the standard view are controversial. And there are other examples for which they would be even more controversial, (9d) being one of them. Still, I don't think any of the standard examples from the literature provide robust enough evidence that the standard view is false. In fact, it seems that there is an *argument* that there won't be counterexamples to the standard view. It goes as follows. Everyone agrees that semantic theory should tell us what declarative sentences mean. Everyone agrees that declarative sentences are the sort of linguistic expressions for which the question of truth or falsity arises, that it *makes sense* to ask whether they would be true if uttered in a certain situation. Now, it might be (for all I know) that although the question makes sense, it cannot be answered because there is simply no fact of the matter about what the correct answer is. If there are such cases, let's set them aside: the challenge the sentences under (9) pose to the orthodox view is not *indeterminacy* but *underdetermination*.[56] But if there is a fact of the matter whether a declarative sentence is true or false, its truth-value depends on its meaning,

---

[55] For a similar argument for postulating domain variables in the logical form of nouns to capture domain restriction phenomena, see Stanley and Szabó (2000). For a detailed defense of the binding argument, see Stanley (2000).

[56] This point is very clearly made in Carston (2002): 20–1.

the context, and the facts it is about—nothing else. By telling what a declarative sentence means we specify something that determines relative to context what the facts would have to be for the sentence to be true.

As far as I can tell, there is only one way to resist this argument: by claiming that it presupposes an unreasonably broad conception of context. This is the charge formulated by Kent Bach in many places, among them in the following passage:[57]

Now if context were defined so broadly as to include anything other than linguistic meaning that is relevant to determining what a speaker means, then of course the speaker's intention would be part of the context. However, if the context is to play the explanatory role claimed for it, it must be something that is the same for the speaker as it is for his audience, and obviously the role of the speaker's intention in not the same for both.

It is certainly true that we should not construe context as including absolutely everything other than linguistic meaning that might play a role in determining what the speaker meant in making an utterance. In particular, we should not say that *what the speaker meant* is itself part of the context—doing so would rob context of its explanatory role. (Interpretation would be portrayed as a process whereby the addressee figures out what the speaker meant on the basis of information that includes, among other things, what the speaker meant.) But this restriction does not entail that context shouldn't include *any* information about the speaker's intentions.[58] It is, I think, perfectly legitimate to include in the context what the speaker meant *in uttering certain words that occur in the sentence he uttered*. So, for example, while it is illegitimate to assume that when the speaker utters the sentence 'She is hungry', it is part of the context of utterance that in uttering 'She is hungry' he meant to inform the addressee that Adele is hungry, it is *not* illegitimate to assume that in uttering 'she' he meant to refer to Adele. (Interpretation then is portrayed as a process whereby the addressee figures out what the speaker meant in making an utterance of a sentence on the basis of information that may include, among other things, what the speaker meant in uttering some of the constituents of that sentence.) The charge that such information has a different role for the speaker and the addressee seems beside the point: as long as the speaker made his intention to mean this or that in uttering a word manifest, it can be accessible to the addressee, and that is all that is required.[59]

---

[57] Bach (2001a): 30.

[58] I note here that Gauker (1998) explicitly argues for a conception of context that is thoroughly unintentional. Nonetheless, Gauker is no champion of underdetermination—although he advocates a rather stringent conception of context, but he also thinks meaning and context are sufficient for determining truth-conditional content.

[59] To capture the plausible idea that context is shared by the speaker and the addressee, we can identify it with some part of common ground. Following Stalnaker (2002), we can say that p is part of the common ground in a conversation iff the speaker and the addressee accept p, they both believe that they accept p, they both believe that they both believe that they accept p, . . . and so on. Unlike Stalnaker, I think context should not be thought of as *all* of the common ground, since the context would include propositions about linguistic meanings as well. Those who resist identifying context with part of the common ground sometimes object that the reference of indexicals is determined independently of everything the speaker

This leads the debate back to the question of whether the sort of incompleteness many claim to detect in, say, (9c) can be tied to a hidden variable associated with one of the constituents. If so, my response can stand: context may include the speaker's intention to mean 'ready for a fight' in uttering 'ready' within 'Kati is ready'. But those who view (9c) as a counterexample to the project of truth-conditional semantics will insist that 'ready' (and all other constituents of the sentence) are used *literally* to mean nothing more or less than what they always mean in every context.[60] If they are right then the relevant information needed in order to assign truth-conditions to (9c) will be nothing less than what the speaker meant in uttering the entire sentence, and this—I already conceded—cannot be part of the context of utterance.

Resolving this debate is not something I will attempt here. What is relevant for our purposes is something that both sides should readily concede: that the fate of the underdetermination challenge against truth-conditional semantics depends on subtle empirical questions, and neither the piling of putative counterexamples, nor some abstract argument, is likely to lead to a quick resolution. What I can offer here are a few remarks which may put this debate in clearer focus by distancing it from another equally taxing but quite independent disagreement concerning the notion of *what is said*.

The distinction between what someone said and meant in making a certain utterance is one of the cornerstones of our ordinary thinking about communication. The simplest cases when these come apart are mistakes: the speaker picks the wrong word (because her understanding of it is defective or because she is speaking carelessly), and she ends up saying something she does not mean. More complex but equally uncontroversial are cases discussed by Grice, where someone says something and thereby implicates something else, which she also means. And there are probably other sorts of cases as well.[61]

Somehow or other the standard view about semantics came to acquire the additional commitment that the truth-conditional content of a declarative sentence in a context (what semantic theory must specify) is identical to, or at least determined by, what a speaker in that context would say in uttering that sentence. If so, the debates over whether sentences such as (9a-d) have truth-conditional content are properly conducted by eliciting intuitions about what someone uttering these would say under various circumstances. This is, in fact, how most of the debate has been

---

and addressee may believe. Now, it is certainly true that the referent of 'I' is *not* Napoleon in an utterance of 'I order you to withdraw the troops' uttered in a psychiatric hospital by one patient to another, even if it is common ground between the speaker and the addressee that the utterer *is* Napoleon. But I take it that this phenomenon can be taken care of if we assume that among all the propositions in the common ground the one that actually fixes the reference of 'I' in the context of an utterance *u* is one that would have been expressed by the speaker's utterance of 'I am the speaker of this' (where the reference of the demonstrative is *u*).

[60] See Bach (2001b).

[61] Bach (2001b), for example, claims that there are cases when one says one thing and means something else instead (e.g. when one speaks metaphorically) and cases when one says something but means nothing at all (e.g. when one rehearses the words of others). Describing metaphor and rehearsal in these terms is more controversial than the examples in the main text.

conducted, which is unfortunate, since both the pedigree and the standing of the additional commitment are dubious.

Grice, who was the first to offer a systematic contrast between what is said and what is meant, offered little by way of written illumination concerning his views about the former notion. It is often assumed that he held what is said to be a proposition or truth-conditional content, but I cannot find solid evidence for this in Grice's writings. What Grice claims is that his intended notion of what is said by the speaker is "closely related to the conventional meaning of the words (the sentence) he has uttered" and it corresponds to "the elements of [the sentence], their order, and their syntactical character."[62] In addition, he also insists that what we say is always part of what we mean.[63] (According to Grice, in uttering the words 'He is a nice friend' ironically one does not say that he is a nice friend, one "makes as if to say" that he is.)[64] Whether he thought that the proper subject of semantics is what is said is rather hard to tell, especially because he does not use the term 'semantics' at all. In any case, the purported Gricean pedigree of the thesis that truth-conditional content is determined by what is said is questionable at best.

And things are little better in the case of Kaplan, who played a central role in popularizing the term 'what is said.' Kaplan was certainly committed to the view that 'what is said' designates a proposition semantic theory and is supposed to assign to declarative sentences relative to contexts. But his is not the ordinary notion of what is said *by a speaker*—it is rather the semi-technical notion of what is said *by a sentence*. Soames, who follows Kaplan in this regard makes this fully explicit when he writes "the fundamental task of a semantic theory is to tell us what sentences say in various contexts of utterance."[65] The terminology certainly suggests that what a sentence says in a context bears some intimate relation to what a speaker would say in that context in uttering the sentence, but the claim that this relation is always or even usually *identity* is not part of this conception.[66]

Whether or not it is traceable to a misattribution of lineage, the claim that what a speaker says in uttering a declarative sentence determines the truth-conditional content of the sentence in the context of utterance is assumed tacitly all the time in semantic theorizing. Is this assumption true? Following Austin, we should distinguish between a *locutionary* act of uttering a declarative sentence with a certain meaning and the *illocutionary* act of performing a speech act (typically an assertion) in uttering that sentence. Both of these can be described as saying something but they are certainly distinct acts; let us call them saying$_{loc}$ and saying$_{illoc}$.

What a speaker says$_{loc}$ in uttering a declarative sentence in a context is obviously what the semantic theory should assign to that sentence in the context—whether it is truth-conditional is not immediately clear. If you think 'Hendryk arrived' is

---

[62] Grice (1967): 25 and 87.   [63] *Ibid.*: 88 and 120.

[64] *Ibid.*: 34 and 53. Neale (1992) has argued, quite persuasively, that the reason why Grice insisted on this has to do with his large program of reducing linguistic meaning to speaker meaning.

[65] Soames (1989): 394.

[66] Nonetheless, it is true that this is often presupposed without argument in semantic theorizing. Soames (2002): 57 makes it explicit, but Soames (2005) goes on rejecting this picture.

semantically incomplete, you should say that what someone uttering this sentence said$_{loc}$ is *not* truth-conditional.[67] What a speaker says$_{illoc}$ in uttering a declarative sentence in a context is obviously truth-conditional—whether it is the content of the sentence uttered in the context is controversial. If you think 'Hendryk arrived' is semantically incomplete, you should say that what someone uttering this sentence said$_{illoc}$ is a proposition determined by pragmatic means.[68]

Given the inherent ambiguity of the notion of what is said by a speaker and the proximity of these to the semi-technical notion of what is said by a sentence, intuitions about what is said are of dubious value.[69] I think it is better to avoid such a slippery term when we debate whether declarative sentences have truth-conditional content in context. It would perhaps be better to settle whether truth-conditional semantics can be defended against the underdetermination examples before we sort out how the various notions of what is said relate to utterance interpretation.

17.4 CONCLUSION

The distinction between semantics and pragmatics, I argued, is the distinction between the study of linguistic meaning and the study of context of utterance. These are components of a general theory about how addressees normally determine what speakers mean in uttering linguistic expressions. Semantic knowledge is context-independent, but semantics does meddle with context to the extent that part of its task is to settle what the truth-conditional content of various expressions is relative to context. Context does not include absolutely everything other than linguistic meaning that might be relevant to the interpretation of an utterance, but it does include at least some information about speaker intentions.

REFERENCES

Austin, J. L. (1962). *How to Do Things with Words.* Cambridge, MA: Harvard University Press.

Bach, Kent (1994). 'Conversational Impliciture.' *Mind and Language,* 9: 124–62.

—— (1999). 'The Myth of Conventional Implicature.' *Linguistics and Philosophy,* 22: 327–66.

—— (2001a). 'You don't say.' *Synthese,* 128: 15–44.

—— (2001b). 'Speaking Loosely: Sentence Nonliterality.' In Peter French and Howard Wettstein eds., *Midwest Studies in Philosophy,* vol. 25: *Figurative Language.* Oxford: Blackwell, pp. 249–63.

[67] This is what Bach (2001) claims along with the claim that what is said must be what is said$_{loc}$.

[68] This is what Recanati (2001) claims along with the claim that what is said must be what is said$_{illoc}$.

[69] Our ordinary practice of indirect quotation certainly does not require that in reporting someone's utterance we use a clause that has the same truth-conditional content; see Capellen and Lepore (1997) for detailed arguments.

Bach, Kent and Robert Harnish (1979). *Linguistic Communication and Speech Acts.* Cambridge: Cambridge University Press.

Bar-Hillel, Yehoshua (1954). 'Indexical Expressions.' *Mind*, 63: 359–79.

Cappelen, Herman and Ernie Lepore (1997). 'On an Alleged Connection between Indirect Quotation and Semantic Theory.' *Mind and Language*, 12: 278–96.

____ (2003). 'Context-Shifting Arguments.' *Philosophical Perspectives: Language and Philosophical Linguistics*, 17.

____ (2005). *Insensitive Semantics: A Defense of Semantic Minimalism and Speech-Act Pluralism*, Oxford: Blackwell.

Carston, Robyn (2002). *Thoughts and Utterances.* Oxford: Blackwell.

Chomsky, Noam (1986). *Knowledge of Language: Its Nature Origin, and Use.* New York: Praeger.

____ (1995). 'Language and Nature.' *Mind*, 104: 1–61.

Fodor, Jerry (1998). *Concepts: Where Cognitive Science Went Wrong.* Oxford: Clarendon Press.

Gauker, Christopher (1998). "What is a Context of Utterance?' *Philosophical Studies*, 91: 149–72.

Grice, Paul (1957). 'Meaning.' In P. Grice *Studies in the Way of Words.* Cambridge, MA: Harvard University Press, 1989, pp. 213–23.

____ (1967). 'Utterer's Meaning and Intentions.' In P. Grice, *Studies in the Way of Words.* Cambridge, MA: Harvard University Press, 1989, pp. 86–116.

Higginbotham, James (1988). 'Contexts, Models and Meanings: A Note on the Data of Semantics.' In R. Kempson ed., *Mental Representations: The Interface between Language and Reality.* Cambridge: Cambridge University Press, pp. 29–48.

Kalish, Donald (1967). 'Semantics.' In P. Edwards ed., *Encyclopedia of Philosophy*, Vol. 7. New York: Collier-MacMillan, pp. 348–58.

Kaplan, David (1977). *Demonstratives: An Essay on the Semantics, Logic, Metaphysics, and Epistemology of Demonstratives and Other Indexicals.* In J. Almog, J. Perry, and H. Wettstein eds., *Themes from Kaplan.* Oxford: Oxford University Press, 1989, pp. 481–563.

Katz, Jerrold (1977). *Propositional Structure and Illocutionary Force.* New York: Crowell.

Larson, Richard and Gabriel Segal (1995). *Knowledge of Meaning: An Introduction to Semantic Theory.* Cambridge, MA: MIT Press.

Levinson, Stephen (1983). *Pragmatics.* Cambridge: Cambridge University Press.

____ (2000). *Presumptive Meanings.* Cambridge, MA: MIT Press.

Lewis, David (1968). 'Languages and Language.' In *Philosophical Papers*, Vol. 1. Oxford: Oxford University Press, 1983, pp. 163–88.

____ (1970). 'General Semantics.' In *Philosophical Papers*, Vol. 1. Oxford: Oxford University Press, 1983, pp. 189–229.

____ (1981). 'Index, Context, and Content.' In *Papers in Philosophical Logic*, Cambridge: Cambridge University Press, 1998, pp. 21–44.

____ (1983). 'Postscript to "General Semantics."' In *Philosophical Papers*, Vol. 1. Oxford: Oxford University Press, 1983, pp. 230–2.

Montague, Richard (1968). 'Pragmatics.' In R. H. Thomason ed., *Formal Philosophy*, New Haven: Yale University Press, 1974, pp. 95–118.

____ (1970a). 'Pragmatics and intensional logic.' In R. H. Thomason ed., *Formal Philosophy*, New Haven: Yale University Press, 1974, 119–47.

____ (1970b). 'Universal grammar.' In R. H. Thomason ed., *Formal Philosophy*, New Haven: Yale University Press, 1974, 222–46.

Morris, Charles (1938). Foundations of the Theory of Signs. In O. Neurath, R. Carnap and C. Morris eds., *International Encyclopedia of Unified Science*, Vol. 1–2. Chicago: University of Chicago Press.

—— (1946). *Signs, Language, and Behavior.* New York: Prentice Hall.

Neale, Stephen (1992). 'Paul Grice and the Philosophy of Language.' *Linguistics and Philosophy*, 15: 509–59.

Nunberg, Geoffrey (1993). 'Indexicality and Deixis.' *Linguistics and Philosophy*, 16: 1–43.

Pierce, Charles Sanders (1931). *Collected Papers*, Vol. 5. Cambridge, MA.

Recanati, Francois (2001). 'What is Said.' *Synthese*, 128: 75–91.

—— (forthcoming). 'Deixis and Anaphora.' In Z. G. Szabó ed., *Semantics vs. Pragmatics.* Oxford: Oxford University Press.

Rooth, Mats (1992). 'A Theory of Focus Interpretation.' *Natural Language Semantics*, 1: 75–116.

Schiffer, Stephen (1972). *Meaning.* Oxford: Clarendon Press.

Searle, John R. (1965). 'What is a Speech Act?' In S. Davis ed., *Pragmatics.* Oxford: Oxford University Press, 1991, pp. 254–64.

—— (1969). *Speech Acts.* Cambridge: Cambridge University Press.

—— (1978). 'Literal Meaning.' *Erkenntnis*, 13: 207–24.

Soames, Scott (1989). 'Direct Reference and Propositional Attitudes.' In J. Almog, J. Perry, and H. Wettstein eds., *Themes from Kaplan.* Oxford: Oxford University Press, 1989, pp. 383–419.

—— (2002). *Beyond Rigidity.* Oxford: Oxford University Press.

—— (2005). 'Naming and Asserting.' In Z. G. Szabó ed., *Semantics vs. Pragmatics.* Oxford: Oxford University Press.

Sperber, Dan and Deindre Wilson (1986). *Relevance: Communication and Cognition.* Cambridge, MA: Harvard University Press.

—— (2002). 'Pragmatics, Modularity, and Mindreading.' *Mind and Language* 17: 3–23.

Stalnaker, Robert (1970). 'Pragmatics.' *Synthese*, 22. Reprinted in *Context and Content: Essays on Intentionality in Speech and Thought.* Oxford: Oxford University Press, 1999.

—— (2002). 'Common Ground.' *Linguistics and Philosophy*, 25: 701–21.

Stanley, Jason (2000). 'Context and Logical Form.' *Linguistics and Philosophy*, 23: 391–34.

Stanley, Jason and Zoltán Gendler Szabó (2000). 'On Quantifier Domain Restriction.' *Mind and Language*, 15: 219–61.

Strawson, Peter F. (1974). 'Intention and Convention in Speech Acts.' In S. Davis ed., *Pragmatics.* Oxford: Oxford University Press, 1991, pp. 290–301.

Szabó, Zoltán Gendler (2000). 'Descriptions and Uniqueness.' *Philosophical Studies*, 101: 29–57.

Travis, Charles (1985). 'On What is Strictly Speaking True.' *Canadian Journal of Philosophy*, 15: 187–229.

Wilson, Deirdre and Dan Sperber (1986). 'Pragmatics and Modularity.' In S. Davis ed., *Pragmatics.* Oxford: Oxford University Press, 1991, pp. 583–95.

PART IV

....

THE NATURE OF REFERENCE

....

CHAPTER 18

THE ESSENCE OF REFERENCE

R. M. SAINSBURY

PEOPLE use words and concepts to refer to things. There are agents who refer, there are acts of referring, and there are tools to refer with: words and concepts. Reference is a relation between people and things, and also between words or concepts and things, and perhaps it involves all three things at once (I refer to Aristotle using the word "Aristotle"). It is not just any relation between an action or word and a thing; the list of things which can refer, people, words and concepts, is probably not complete (scenes in more recent movies can refer to scenes in less recent movies); and a complete account would need to speak of cases in which the reference relation seems to involve three terms in a different way from the one already mentioned (for such uses, I refer *you* to *the OED*). In the philosophy of language, it has been customary to think of reference as a two-place relation, with some object as the second term and a word or phrase as the first. Even if one believes that any such relation comes into existence thanks to the referential activities of speakers, one can hardly deny that it obtains. This relation is the topic of this chapter.

What is the essence of reference? Perhaps there is no essence.[1] Perhaps our notion of reference, even as used in philosophical theorizing, is too vague to have an essence, or else it bundles together a number of similar but distinct relations. If this were so, the concept of a *referring expression* would have no place in the best semantic description of a language: such a concept would be too vague, or would wrongly assimilate expressions with a number of distinct semantic functions. I reject such views, because

---

[1] In coming to prefer "The Varieties of Reference", rather than "The Essence of Reference" as his title for an intended lecture course, it may be that Evans was preferring a title which gave the best emphasis, rather than rejecting a title with a presupposition he had come to believe was defective (Evans, 1982: vi–vii).

I think that there is an essence: it is (I shall argue) constitutive of being a referring expression that how things are with its actual referent, if any, is what matters to the truth or falsehood, with respect to any world, of a range of sentences or utterances in which it occurs. The remainder of this chapter leads up to this conclusion.

In the previous paragraph, there was a natural transition from a question about the essence of reference to a question about what makes something a referring expression. An answer to the second question, suitably given in terms of how such an expression must function semantically, will provide an answer to the first: a referring expression is, necessarily, one whose function is to refer, so a suitable characterization of what it is to be such an expression is thereby a characterization of what it is to have that function, and so of what that function is. This should settle the question of whether it is the same function or a different one from that which relates other expressions (predicates, logical constants) to the world.

Here are a number of candidates for specifying part or the whole of what it is to be a referring expression. Most of them can be traced back to Russell's conception of a logically proper name, a name "in the proper strict logical sense of the word" (Russell, 1918: 201).

(1) A referring expression must be semantically simple.
(2) A referring expression must have just one referent.
(3) Understanding a referring expression is a matter of knowing who or what its referent is.
(4) Referring expressions are scopeless.
(5) Definite descriptions are not referring expressions.
(6) Referring expressions are "rigid designators".

I will describe the motivation for these various claims and will discuss their correctness. I conclude that only the last can be endorsed without qualification, and that even it does not constitute, but merely manifests, the essence of reference.[2]

18.1 SIMPLICITY

Concern with word–world relations goes back to some of the earliest moments in philosophy (certainly as far back as Aristotle and no doubt further). Where should one look for a notion of reference which sets it aside from other word–world relations? I do not know enough history to venture a confident pronouncement about where we first find such a distinction, but we do find it, in different ways, in both Frege and Russell.[3]

---

[2] A full understanding of reference requires appreciating its basis in pre-linguistic activity, and in particular its link with perceptual attention and tracking (see Campbell, 2002). These aspects cannot be addressed in the present chapter.

[3] Mill (1843) distinguished denotation from connotation, but his denotation would appear to be an undifferentiated word–world relation (adjectives and verbs unproblematically denote), and not a first intimation of the modern notion of reference. Thanks to Dean Buckner for alerting me to the difficulties of identifying the first appearance of the modern notion.

Frege's central distinction between concept and object leads to a distinction among expressions. We could think of a referring expression in Fregean terms as what he calls a proper name (Eigenname): an expression whose Sinn (sense) is supposed to determine an object as opposed to a concept as its Bedeutung (referent). In Frege's writing, the extension of "Eigenname" is wider than that of "referring expression" in present day usage, since for Frege whole sentences count as Eigennamen, having the special objects called truth-values as their referents (all being well). If, as I think best, we represent this divergence as a difference of doctrine rather than as a difference of subject matter, Frege must be taken to deny that a referring expression must be simple. He is fully explicit. Having said that a proper name is a designation having as its referent (Bedeutung) a definite object, he continues

The designation of a single object can also consist of several words or other signs.   (Frege, 1892: 158)

Russell, by contrast, held that reference requires simplicity:

The only kind of word that is theoretically capable of standing for a particular is a *proper name*.   (Russell, 1918: 200)

A name is a simple symbol (i.e. a symbol which does not have any parts that are symbols)...   (Russell, 1918: 244)

Since particulars are certainly among the things to which we can refer, these two Russellian claims entail that any word theoretically capable of standing for a particular is semantically simple. Even on the reasonable assumption that "standing for" and "referring to" are words for the same relation, this does not quite amount to thesis (1), for two reasons. First, there are expressions which are not "words" (but instead phrases made up of more than one word). We do no injustice to Russell's thought to replace "kind of word" by "kind of expression" in the first quotation. Secondly, the context makes plain that Russell had in mind only singular reference. It may be that we should understand his claim as that any expression which stands for just one particular must be semantically simple. This interprets the passage as neutral about whether expressions like "Russell and Whitehead" are referring expressions: they are clearly not simple, but if they refer at all, then, on the face of it, they refer to more than one object. On the proposed interpretation of Russell, they are therefore not precluded from counting as referring expressions.

These complex plural names (or expressions which appear to deserve this classification) strongly suggest that one should not accept (1) as it stands. The only alternatives to rejecting (1) are either to claim that the plural expressions are not semantic units at all, for they will "disappear" under "analysis", or else to regard them as Russellian definite descriptions, and so not referring expressions: definite descriptions along the lines "the set/sum/aggregate whose members/parts are Russell and Whitehead". While both options have been considered in the literature, both have difficulties which I regard as insurmountable (cf. Hossack, 2000; McKay, 2003).

If this is right, the only plausible thesis restricts simplicity to singular referring expressions. It is certainly true that many paradigms of singular referring expressions are semantically simple, proper names like "London" and demonstratives like "this". But complexity lurks close to the simple paradigms. There are apparently complex singular proper names, ones which contain proper names as parts. Most Westerners have names made up of other names: "Tony Blair" seems to be made up of the names "Tony" and "Blair". Some names of cities (like "Aix-en-Provence") display a seemingly similar feature. We are generally not fussy about the distinction between the name of a book or movie and its title, and titles are certainly often complex. Demonstrative phrases (like "That book", or "That book beneath this one") may contain all sorts of material (including possibly further demonstratives or other referring expressions).[4] Even our paradigms do not provide much basis for the thesis that all singular referring expressions are simple.

An argument for the simplicity of singular referring expressions could be constructed using Russell's theory of descriptions as a premise. The theory can be partially characterized as the claim that definite descriptions are not referring expressions. A definite description may have a denotation, and does so just if the predicate in the description is uniquely satisfied in the relevant domain, but for Russell a denotation is not a referent: unlike a referent, Russell believes, a denotation is not required for intelligibility. A complex expression owes its intelligibility to the intelligibility of its parts and their mode of combination. Hence even if a complex expression has a denotation, it cannot have a referent. The argument could be set out as follows:

(7) A referring expression owes its intelligibility to having a referent.

(8) A complex expression owes its intelligibility entirely to the meanings of its parts and how they are put together.

(9) Hence a complex expression does not owe its intelligibility to having a referent.

(10) So no complex expression is a referring expression.

Although I am not aware of encountering an explicit version of this argument, its availability may well explain the tendency for belief in the simplicity of referring expressions to be linked to the belief that such expressions require a referent.

The conclusion confronts, as possible counterexamples, complex demonstrative expressions, like "That man who broke the bank at Monte Carlo" (cf. Peacocke, 1975). Although such cases may be addressed in other ways (see note 4 above), they raise an issue of principle which should make one wary of (8) above. Although semantic complexity by definition requires that the meaning of the complex depend in some way upon the meaning of the parts, entire dependence is another matter. There might be additional dependence upon context, as the example of complex demonstratives suggests. The principle of compositionality which was appealed to may be correct for the "character" of an expression in Kaplan's sense (1977): that aspect of its meaning which is independent of context, and which serves

---

[4] There are views according to which all demonstrative expressions are as such simple, and the predicative material either does not introduce genuine content, or does not really belong with the demonstrative pronoun (for a view of the latter kind, see Lepore and Ludwig (2000)). This involves some departure from natural first thoughts, and it is with these that I am currently concerned.

to determine, in conjunction with the context which prevails on a particular occasion of use, the truth conditions of what is thereby said on that occasion. In this perspective, a complex expression of sound character, determined in the proper way by compositional features, may be used on a given occasion in such a way as to determine no truth conditional content, thanks to recalcitrance of context. Once context enters the picture, and "intelligibility" is understood in a way which factors in the contribution of context to what is said by the use of an expression, (8) becomes wholly implausible, and this argument for the simplicity of singular expressions collapses. The possibility remains open that though the character of a complex expression is a function of the character of its parts, the content is not, since it depends upon context.

18.2 UNIQUENESS

Uniqueness demands that, necessarily, a singular referring expression have at most and at least one referent. The "at most" condition has generally been taken for granted, though on the face of it nothing could be more counterintuitive. Many people and places have the same name. Every example of a name which I can think of has more than one bearer. There is Aristotle the philosopher, and Aristotle the tycoon, Paris, France and Paris, Texas; and so on. In this thought, names are individuated in a natural, more or less syntactic, way.[5] We could alternatively individuate names more semantically, in terms of the practices in which they are used, or in terms of their referents. One could be party to one use of a (syntactic) name without being party to some other use of the same name; yet one might rightly be said fully to understand the name, in the use to which one is party. The situation is similar in the case of demonstratives. Clearly the word "that" has been used of countless different things. This should neither disqualify it as a referring expression, nor defeat a suitable at-most thesis: in each use, "that" has at most one referent.

The idea that a singular referring expression has at most one referent invokes a more semantic individuation, which makes the claim close to trivial. In normal cases, ones in which there is no confusion or other kind of mistake, the discovery that a singular referring expression is used of more than one thing is simply the discovery that the same (syntactic) expression features in distinct practices. When we speak semantically of a referring expression, we thereby implicitly speak of a practice in which it is used; the relevant notion of a practice requires further clarification (see Section 18.3 below).

In the singular case, the at-most condition can be expressed:

if (in a given practice) a singular referring expression refers to x and to y, then $x = y$.

---

[5] Only more or less syntactic, because perhaps the natural criterion counts, for example, "London" and "Londres" as (regional variations on) the same name. Cf. Kripke (1972: 8, n. 9).

This tells us how we can properly express the condition for plural referring expressions, which in a sense refer to more than one thing. We can use plural variables, that is, variables which may properly be replaced by plural referring expressions, to write the condition much as before:

if (in a given practice) a plural referring expression refers to X and to Y, then X are Y.

If "the Apostles" refers to Matthew, Mark, Luke, . . . and John and also to the twelve Apostles, then Matthew, Mark, Luke, . . . and John are the twelve Apostles. If we use variables and an identity sign neutral between singular and plural, a single condition can do duty for both singular and plural referring expressions.

The "at-least" condition has been much more contentious. Frege was explicit that, for proper names (Eigennamen), in his broad use of this expression to include definite descriptions and whole sentences, there could be Sinn without Bedeutung:

It may perhaps be granted that every grammatically well-formed expression figuring as a proper name always has a sense. But this is not to say that to the sense there also corresponds a thing meant [Bedeutung]. . . . The expression "the least rapidly convergent series" has a sense, but demonstrably there is nothing that it means [i.e. it demonstrably has no Bedeutung].   (Frege, 1892: 159)

Almost everyone agrees that intelligible definite descriptions may lack a referent; this has historically been a reason for not counting them among referring expressions. It is much more controversial whether intelligible semantically simple proper names may lack a referent. On the face of it, Frege's claim of the possibility of Sinn without Bedeutung is not restricted to the semantically complex. This leaves open whether or not he was committed to such a restriction at a deeper level.

Frege is explicit that "Odysseus" has sense but no referent. According to Evans, Frege's

apparent willingness to ascribe sense to certain empty singular terms was equivocal, hedged around with qualifications, and dubiously consistent with the fundamentals of his philosophy of language.   (Evans, 1982: 38)

For Evans, Frege's fundamental idea was that the Sinn of a semantically simple expression is the mode of presentation of an object, and so not something available in the absence of an object. Frege's examples of simple expressions possessing Sinn but lacking Bedeutung belong to fiction, and Evans suggests that this shows that Frege is attempting to retain his fundamental idea: in fiction, we pretend that a name is associated with a mode of presentation of an object. According to Evans, this should have led Frege to say that we merely pretend that the name has Sinn (and so pretend that it has Bedeutung); he should not have said that it really has Sinn and really lacks Bedeutung.[6]

Whatever Frege's view may have been, there are plenty of philosophers, including Evans himself, who hold that, for most names and demonstratives, no intelligible use could lack a referent. The classic source is Russell:

---

[6] For disagreement with Evans's interpretation of Frege see Sainsbury, 2002: 9–13.

a name has got to name something or it is not a name.   (Russell, 1918: 243)

For many (though not for Evans himself), this amounts to the thesis that no intelligible referring expression lacks a referent, for referring expressions are often confined to the two categories just mentioned (names and demonstratives). [7] Let us for the moment confine ourselves to proper names. If it could be shown that these must always have referents, perhaps the considerations would extend to referring expressions more generally.

One argument for the view that proper names must have referents involves a picture of proper names as like tags, or labels. A vivid version is mentioned by Mill (1843: 29): a proper name functions in some respects like the chalk mark the robber placed on the doors of those houses which were to be burgled. Just as there can be no chalk mark on a door without a door, so there cannot be a name without a bearer. Such views need to address the apparent fact that there are familiar names without bearers (like "Santa Claus" and "Vulcan"). Mill in effect denied the phenomenon: "All names are names of something, real or imaginary" (Mill 1843: 32). Those who do not believe that there (really) are any merely imaginary things, like Vulcan or Santa Claus, cannot accept this position, literally understood.[8] The chalk-mark model is far from realistic, for whereas the chalk-mark cannot become detached from its door, names are often used and introduced in the absence of the bearer. This detachment makes it possible for an expression to present itself as if it were a name with a bearer when it is not, and for a speaker or hearer to have no good basis for telling that it has no bearer. This possibility, which is accepted both by those who hold that names, or referring expressions in general, must have bearers, and by those who deny this, is not mirrored in the chalk-mark view, which, accordingly, cannot be taken as a guide.

A common source of the view that proper names must have referents is that they are not descriptive. Kripke (1972) has persuaded many theorists that, contrary to a view commonly attributed to Frege, and, for "ordinary" proper names, to Russell, the meaning of a proper name is not given by a definite description, nor is a definite description essentially involved in fixing its referent. Taking for granted that definite descriptions can fail to refer to anything, this closes off one way in which a proper name could be intelligible yet have no referent, namely, by functioning like a definite description. The argument then requires the further claim that there is no other way in which a name could be intelligible while failing to have a referent, a claim for which I am not aware of an argument. On the face of it, a proper name could be intelligible thanks to being used in some systematic and coherent way, without being equivalent to a description yet also without having a referent. The slide from rejecting

---

[7] "The only words one does use as names in the logical sense are words like 'this' and 'that'" (Russell, 1918: 201).

[8] Mill was probably not paying much attention to the distinction between a name of an imaginary object and an expression which, we imagine, names an object. No theorist should have any problem accepting that there are expressions meeting the second condition (though there may be a terminological issue about whether they should count as names). Not every case of a name without a bearer does meet the second condition: Leverrier did not merely imagine that "Vulcan" named an object.

descriptive views to insisting that a name must have a referent emerges clearly in work by John McDowell.

McDowell (1977) argued, I think entirely persuasively, that the Fregean distinction between sense and reference does not entail that proper names are descriptive, or indeed that their sense is in any way analysable.[9] He says that we can distinguish between the claim that "Hesperus" stands for Hesperus and the claim that it stands for Phosphorus, even though Hesperus is Phosphorus, on the grounds that it is the former claim that will lead us to correct interpretations of the use of "Hesperus" in actual language. Although "Hesperus" does stand for Phosphorus, using this in interpreting speech may lead to misinterpretation. It would lead one to misrepresent one who assertively says "Hesperus is visible but Phosphorus is not visible" as making the absurd claim that Phosphorus is visible but Phosphorus is not visible. McDowell's point seems valuable, both as a defence of a non-descriptive Fregeanism, and for the more general feature that we cannot typically expect, within a single language, to be able to state the meaning of an expression in other terms. To think that we normally could do so would be to think that language has an enormous amount of built-in redundancy in its means of expression. Even if many languages display quite a measure of redundancy, it is certainly not enough to enable the meaning of every expression to be stated in other terms, and there can be no *a priori* argument against the possibility of a language entirely lacking such redundancy.

In the course of making these valuable points, McDowell introduces a pattern to be used to specify a name's role in language in the austere way he recommends: we quote the name, append "stands for", and then append a use of the name without quotation. If we follow this pattern, then on all reasonable views, we commit ourselves to the name having a referent. In defending a non-descriptive account of names, McDowell has defended a position on which every name must have a referent.

McDowell himself should have no grounds for preferring one rather than another of these equally austere ways of representing the crucial fact about the functioning of a name like "Hesperus":

(11) "Hesperus" stands for Hesperus

(12) For all x ("Hesperus" stands for x iff x = Hesperus).

The two sentences are equivalent in the classical logic which McDowell implicitly accepts; and (12) is as good as (11) from the point of view of providing correct accounts of the speech of users of a language containing "Hesperus". McDowell himself should therefore have no quarrel with a presentation of his view through a sentence like (12) rather than (11).

From other points of view, however, (12) is to be preferred to (11), for it can be true even when the target expression is a name with no bearer. On all reasonable views, " 'Vulcan' stands for Vulcan" is not true. It entails the falsehood that something is Vulcan. By contrast, within so-called negative free logic (NFL), "For all x

[9] This accords well with Frege's own observation: "In order to speak of the sense of an expression 'A' one may simply use the phrase 'the sense of the expression 'A' '' " (1892: 159). This suggests that Frege is disinclined to suppose that, in general, the sense of an expression can be specified in other terms.

('Vulcan' stands for x iff $x =$ Vulcan)" is true: "$x =$ Vulcan" is false of each thing, since any subject-predicate sentence with an empty referring expression is false, and so is "'Vulcan' stands for x". Within negative free logic, existential quantifier introduction is restricted, so that there is no inference from the truth of the quantified sentence (12) to the falsehood that Vulcan exists.[10]

If we reconstrue McDowell's article as an argument for the impossibility of names without bearers, it would need as a premise that classical logic, and in particular the notion of an individual constant which it incorporates, permits a correct expression of the function of proper names regarded as primitive terms (rather than as disguised definite descriptions). With this premise, nothing else is needed to arrive at the conclusion that every name must have a bearer, as is shown by the classical theoremhood of every sentence of the form "$\exists x\, x = a$". This hardly advances the issue, for, in the context, the only contested feature of classical logic is whether it is correct to model natural language proper names as expressions which, on every interpretation, are assigned a bearer. McDowell did not, I believe, intend his article as an argument for the conclusion that there cannot be empty names. Rather, this thesis struck him as a "complication" (McDowell, 1977: 172); we can properly see it as an artefact of the classical logical framework which he takes for granted.

Notions of pretence can be used to help render more plausible the view that every proper name must have a bearer. For example, in fiction, in pretending that certain events occurred, involving certain individuals, we pretend that certain expressions are proper names, that is, are expressions with referents (cf. Evans, 1982: ch. 10). A defence of this kind is required only if one is independently persuaded that every name must have a bearer. The reasons for this opinion considered so far have not been persuasive; a further possible reason, which I claim is also unpersuasive, will be considered in Section 18.3.

The more general thesis that any referring expression must have a referent might be reached by reflection on the role of reference in truth conditions. One line of thought involves the following steps:

(13) Reference is a relation which is characterized by its role in truth conditions.

(14) For properly constructed simple sentences in which a referring expression t is coupled with a predicate, F, the truth conditions are:
    "t is F" is true iff "t" has just one referent and it satisfies "F" and is false iff "t" has just one referent and it does not satisfy "F".

(15) If a properly constructed sentence is neither true nor false, it has a part which is not intelligible.

(16) The only way for a properly constructed simple sentence "t is F" to be neither true nor false is for "t" to fail to have a unique referent.[11]

---

[10] The application of negative free logic to semantics dates back to Burge (1974). See also Sainsbury (2002: XII). For an overview of free logics see Morscher and Simons (2001). By negative free logic I mean their NFL with a partial interpretation function and a total valuation function (see their p. 11).

[11] If "F" is not intelligible, nothing will satisfy it, so the intelligibility of "F" is not required in the argument. This rather artificial feature could be dispensed with.

(17) Hence an expression which plays such a role in the construction of simple sentences but which lacks a referent is not intelligible.

(18) Referring expressions can play such a role in the construction of simple sentences.

(19) So all intelligible referring expressions have a unique referent.

The truth conditions envisaged at (14), which may be called Strawsonian, have an obvious alternative: keep to the necessary and sufficient condition for truth, but regard falsehood as failure of truth. Such an account, which may be called Ockhamist, prevents the argument from going through: a simple sentence whose referring expression has no referent will be false.[12] So the argument needs to be supplemented with a case for Strawsonian truth conditions.

Strawson himself (1950) attacks something like this argument, which he ascribes to Russell. He insists, rightly in my view, on the importance of the distinction between a sentence and any statement which a sentence may be used to make on some specific occasion of its use. Being meaningful or intelligible is a property of sentences and other expressions and is common to various distinct uses to which they may be put. Something of this kind is required to do justice to indexicality. The same sentence (for example, "I am happy") can be used to make different statements, according to who uses the sentence and when. In this framework, (15) above will be rejected as some kind of category mistake. There is no inference from the fact that, in a specific use, no statement is made by a sentence, to the conclusion that the sentence or any part of it is meaningless. As Strawson says, the meaningfulness of the sentence "The present King of France is bald" is manifest by the fact that in the eighteenth century it could have been used to make a statement, even though it cannot now be used with this upshot.

Strawson's early work gave a new direction to the study of reference by stressing that it is a social phenomenon, essentially dependent upon speakers' intentions, which themselves implicitly presuppose "identifying knowledge" of particulars on the part of fellow members of the linguistic community. Following this line of thought, he summarized the "function" of proper names and various other singular terms, at least in their "primary" use: they are to introduce particular objects into discourse, enabling us to judge propositions concerning these objects (Strawson, 1974). Many theorists would accept this characterization. On one common use of the notion of a function, something can possess a function which it does not, or even cannot, perform. The function of a malformed heart is to pump blood, even if such a heart cannot in fact pump blood. So there could be names, or in general referring expressions, having as their function to enable us to introduce particular objects into discourse, yet incapable of fulfilling this function. The analogy suggests that they may still be classified as referring expressions. But talk of function leaves us in the dark about whether we should say that a non-referring referring expression can be understood, or whether it can be used in the expression of a proposition. Strawson said that

---

[12] Cf. Strawson, 1974: 58; 1961: 401; Ockham (Freddoso, 1998: 86).

although such expressions can be understood, they cannot be used in the expression of a proposition: "there is no true or false proposition asserted" (1974: 58). An argument for this position requires more than the premise that referring expressions have as their function to refer.

I have identified the following arguments for the view that names must have a referent:

(20) McDowell's argument from the correct austere semantic description of names.
(21) The argument from Strawsonian truth conditions.
(22) The argument from the function of names.

(20) rests on an unargued assumption of the adequacy of classical logical semantic categories for the description of natural language (an assumption which delivers the conclusion without need for the appeal to austerity). (21) rests on the assumption that these truth conditions are correct, as opposed to Ockhamist ones. (22) delivers the conclusion only on the assumption that everything which has a certain function fulfils it. The needed further assumptions are either false (as for (22)) or else controversial.[13]

Without the premise that names must have a referent, one could not hope to generalize to all referring expressions. But one might look elsewhere for arguments, in particular one might look to the notion of understanding. Here one must take proper note of the epistemic and social notions which, as Strawson suggested, are critical to name-using practices.

18.3 IDENTIFYING KNOWLEDGE, UNDERSTANDING, AND TRANSMISSION

The thesis that every referring expression has a unique referent is associated with the thesis that understanding a referring expression involves knowing to whom or what it refers. Proper names are, as usual, the paradigms. In a theory like Strawson's, which involves more than one semantic layer, *meaning* (a property of sentences) and *statement* (what emerges from the interaction of meaning with contextual features prevailing on a particular occasion on which the sentence is put to use), there is a prospect of extending the claim beyond the semantically simple. Understanding a *sentence* containing the expression "the present King of France" does not involve knowing who the King is; intuitively, there is no such fact. By contrast, it is not implausible to hold that understanding a *statement* made using a sentence which contains that expression does involve knowing who the King is. In a circumstance in which there is no knowing who, no statement is made by the use of that sentence. One such circumstance is there being no King.

---

[13] "Any existence claim that is felt to inhere in the meaning of singular terms is well eliminated." (Quine, 1960: 182) My thesis is that there is in any case no such existence claim, so nothing needing elimination.

Strawson claimed that linguistic reference is typically possible only in a social context in which it is mutually known that the members of one's speech community have or can immediately acquire independent knowledge of the particulars to which one wishes to refer. The use of a definite referring expression, or definite singular term,

> achieves its identificatory purpose by drawing upon what in the widest sense might be called the conditions of its utterance, *including* what the hearer is presumed to know or to presume already or to be in a position there and then to perceive for himself. . . . The possibility of identification in the relevant sense exists only for an audience antecedently equipped with knowledge or presumptions, or placed in a position of possible perception, which can be drawn on in this way.   (Strawson 1961: 399)

In using a sentence containing a demonstrative in an ordinary perceptual situation, for example using "That bull is about to charge" in the conspicuous presence of a large bovine, the speaker assumes that the hearer either had already seen the animal or could now come to see it. Unless the speaker presumes upon the hearer's access to this perceptual mode of identification, the utterance would not be a normal and appropriate use of the sentence.

Although Strawson's considerations are sometimes used to justify the view that understanding a referring expression involves identifying its referent, the ones just quoted do not involve so strong a claim. The uncontroversial claim, and the only one to which Strawson is committed in the passage quoted, is that (in normal circumstances) one who uses a referring expression must *presume* that her hearer knows or presumes this or that, or can identify an object as the intended referent. If these speaker-presumptions are presumptions only, and not knowledge, they may be false, and one way for them to be false is for the referring expression to lack a referent. Completing the argument requires two additions: that an understander should know the things the speaker presumes he knows; and that this requirement on understanding should reflect a feature of meaning: if understanding is impossible (for example because there is no "identifying fact" to be known), there is no meaning.

The link between meaning and understanding comes to the fore in the work of Gareth Evans (1982), who, developing some of Strawson's ideas, provides an account of the varieties of reference in terms of varieties of conditions required for understanding. Evans suggests that understanding is a form of knowledge. To understand a saying (an utterance with declarative force) is to know what the utterer has thereby said. On the assumption that the meaning of a sentence is derived from the meanings of its component words and their mode of combination, it is natural to think that the relevant knowledge of what has been said by an utterance is derived from knowledge relating to the meanings of the parts. In the case of proper names, simple referring expressions, a Strawsonian thought is that the relevant knowledge is "identifying knowledge", registering which object the expression refers to. The relevant knowledge might be identified in various, non-exclusive, ways. (a) It might be that one who understands a name, N, is able knowledgeably to answer the question "To whom or what does 'N' refer?". (b) It might be that an understander must be capable of answering this question without making use of the name in question (a non-linguistic answer, for example a pointing gesture, might be a limiting case). (c) It might be that the relevant knowledge can be expressed only in a de re way: concerning the object which is the referent of "N", the understander knows that it is the referent of "N".

On Strawson's own view, it would seem that knowledge of all the kinds (a)–(c) must obtain. If the understander brings to bear independent identificatory knowledge, then an answer to the question "To whom or what does 'N' refer" could be expressed independently of using the name. (One would not expect there to be a piece of identificatory knowledge available to every understander: the requirement is only that every understander possess some identificatory knowledge, and this may differ from understander to understander and occasion to occasion.) There would seem no barrier to expressing the knowledge thus made manifest in the de re style envisaged in (c).

These are plausible views, but they must be distinguished from closely similar weaker ones. As they stand, the views imply the impossibility of a referring expression which lacks a bearer. There is no knowing to whom or what a name refers unless it has a referent. Compare this claim: An understander must be able to give a knowledgeable answer to the question "To whom or what does 'N' purport to refer?" without using "N". This stays clear of de re attribution, but captures something very close to the Strawsonian answer. There is a requirement of independent knowledge of an independent fact of purported identification. "Santa Claus" purports to refer to Santa Claus. One who understands the name knows this, and also knows that, for example, "Santa Claus" purports to refer to a jolly bearded Lapp who brings children presents at Christmas. This seems to do justice to many of the things that struck Strawson about our use of referring expressions. What motivation is there for moving to stronger versions of the claim, versions which make it impossible for empty referring expressions to be understood? Answers independent of how we account for understanding have been considered and not found compelling. The same should be said for accounts which draw upon the nature of understanding.[14]

In considering what items of knowledge could be involved in, or identified with, understanding, we need to re-work a theme of the previous section, the one involved in the discussion of McDowell. In the truth theoretic tradition initiated by Davidson, a semantic account of a language would involve truth theoretic axioms which would deliver T-sentences, theorems of the form "s is true iff p", in which "p" states something which could properly be used to report what was said in a normal statement-making use of s. By delivering such T-sentences, the axioms are to meet the condition that if they were known, they would provide enough information to make understanding possible. In McDowell's framework considered in Section 18.2 above, it looked as if suitable truth theoretic axioms for names would follow the lines of "'Hesperus' stands for Hesperus", and so knowledge of them would be possible only for non-empty names. However, we saw that a theorist who believes that empty names deserve a non-descriptive semantic account can take over the non-descriptive

[14] A more detailed discussion of Evans's view is provided by Sainsbury, 2002: IX.

approach while denying the need for a referent. If understanding is to be identified with an actual or possible item of propositional knowledge, then, in a negative free logical framework, one can include such knowledge for empty names: for all x, "Vulcan" refers to x iff x is Vulcan. This contributes to meeting, even for empty names, a condition which Evans thought important: "there is some true proposition such that knowledge of its truth constitutes understanding the utterance" (Evans, 1982: 330). Admittedly, the condition is met in a rather abstract way: we get little philosophical enlightenment about what the relevant understanding consists in. For this we must look to another idea which Evans stressed: that of a name-using practice. This idea can also help address another issue: the relevant knowledge is not the timeless thing philosophers sometimes pretend. We need a context if a T-sentence is to have any determinate content, for example, one which will distinguish the practice of using "Vulcan" in the way we have presupposed, involving an astronomical context, and the practice of using it in the context of the ancient pantheon. We perhaps suppose that thinking requires no context, that somehow the relevant distinctions can be made in thought by willing them so; this is probably an illusion (cf. Burge, 1983: 83). Distinct name-using practices may be practices of using the same name (syntactically considered); in the example, one practice is supposed to relate to Vulcan, the lame god who worked in bronze, and another to Vulcan, the planet Leverrier claimed to have discovered.

If the notion of a name-using practice must be made secure in any adequate theoretical reflection on names, describing name-understanding in terms of propositional knowledge may not be maximally illuminating. Understanding certainly issues in propositional knowledge, knowledge of what speakers have said, but this does not guarantee either that understanders in fact derive it from propositional knowledge, or that talk of propositional knowledge throws the greatest light on understanding. An alternative view is that to understand a certain use of a name is simply to be party to the practice to which that use belongs. While this participation might involve propositional knowledge, there seems in general no reason to suppose that this is necessary. We can be party to the practice of bowing our heads on being introduced to someone for the first time, without so much as knowing that we behave in this way, let alone there being a proposition we know which summarizes the fact of our participation.

Kripke (1972) takes a stand on what determines the referent of a name which mirrors this approach to understanding. In Kripke's picture, a practice propagates outward from an initial baptism of an object. This causal propagation fixes the referent of the use of a name as the recipient of the baptism from which the use derives. On this picture of name-using practices, it may seem that the referent is again essential, and that no progress has been made towards recognizing the intelligibility of names without bearers.

Kripke's picture, however, has an apparently unmotivated feature. A baptism which, perhaps through some radical mistake, is the baptism of nothing, is as good a propagator of a new use as a baptism of an object. The baptism masks off the object's causal role. No doubt if a baptism succeeds in giving a name to an object, that object will be causally involved in the baptism. It does not follow that the object plays any significant role in determining the subsequent causal chain. Subsequent uses will be those which trace back in the right way to the baptism. If they do this, then they trace back to the baptised object; but that extra fact does not make a contribution to the unification of the practice. Hence there is no reason to think that a referent will play some specially significant part in the individuation of name-using practices: all the work can be done by baptisms, even in the absence of an object.[15]

Once we have to hand a notion of name-using practice individuated independently of the name's referent, we can use it to explain understanding a name in terms of immersion in that practice. This idea helps explain why we are, in ordinary life, so liberal in allowing new members into the practice. If someone who has not heard a certain name before is exposed to a few minutes of conversation in which the name is used, we normally do not balk at saying that the newcomer has come to understand the name. As with many other linguistic practices, our use of proper names, like other expressions, is marked by the slogan "newcomers welcome!"

Often, immersion in a practice will result in various kinds of knowledge, which may manifest that immersion. For example, we will normally learn something about the name's bearer. Such manifestations cannot be guaranteed: information may be scrambled, or indeed the name might be empty. Resistance to the view that understanding might be simply constituted by immersion, and might leave no trace in introspectible propositional knowledge, may stem from a general predilection for theories of the mind according to which one's mental life is in principle open to one's mental gaze. By contrast, if one is immersed in a practice, one individuated in terms of its baptism, aspects of the immersion may not be open to such gaze. In the present anti-Cartesian climate, the natural choice in such a conflict is simply to accept that immersion is not an introspectible property. It may also suggest counterexamples to KK. Understanding is knowledge, yet we may reasonably have knowledge-defeating doubts about whether we understand even though we in fact do.[16]

18.4 SCOPE

An alleged mark of a genuinely referential expression is that it is scopeless:

(23) if sentences which agree in everything, except the relative scope of two expressions, differ in meaning or truth conditions, neither expression is a referring expression.[17]

---

[15] See Sainsbury, 2002: XII. Evans (1982: 381) also holds that practices are not to be individuated by their referents.

[16] This is relevant to "Paderewski" cases: see Kripke, 1979.

[17] See Geach, 1972: 144. Geach explicitly considers only temporal and modal scopelessness. According to the present paper, referring expressions are temporally and modally rigid. This is consistent with their having significant scope interactions with, for example, negation. Kripke (1972) contrasts names and definite descriptions in relation to scope distinctions in modal contexts. In later work (Kripke, 1977: n.7), he is careful to avoid commitment to a general thesis of scopelessness.

I will suggest that although referring expressions manifest no significant scope distinctions with respect to temporal or modal operators, they at least could manifest such distinctions with respect to other operators, in particular negation. Although this is possible, I also think that the English "not" hardly ever exploits this possibility.[18]

A classic application of scope considerations to conclusions about reference derives from Russell's first presentation of his theory of descriptions (Russell, 1905). One could distil the argument as follows:

(24) Definite descriptions show significant scope variation with respect to negation.

(25) No referring expressions show significant scope variation.

(26) So definite descriptions are not referring expressions.

Russell's famous example was

(27) The King of France is not bald,

which he said was ambiguous between a reading on which the negation has wide scope relative to the definite description, so that the whole sentence is true, and a reading on which it has narrow scope, so that the whole sentence is false. One might contrast (27) with

(28) Aristotle is not bald,

which shows no such ambiguity.

There is no doubt that the two standard formalizations of (27) are scope variants (that is, they differ only in that one or more pairs of expressions differ in relative scope). It is a more controversial claim that the sentence is ambiguous in English. It seems to me that if we firmly discard our Russellian ear trumpets, we cannot hear (27) as false in normal contexts. There is no need to become embroiled in a dispute about intuitions of this kind; instead we can go directly to the theoretical issue, which can be expressed as follows. On a Russellian view, a description sentence, "The F is G", is true iff "the F" has a denotation (that is, a unique satisfier of "F") which satisfies "G" and is otherwise false. Falsity can arise in two ways: through "the F" failing to have a denotation, or through it having a denotation which fails to satisfy "G". It is irrelevant whether these distinct possibilities can or cannot be expressed, ambiguously or unambiguously, by English signs for negation.

By contrast, on a Strawsonian view, a sentence in which a name, "a", takes the place of the description is true iff "a" has a referent which satisfies "G" and is false iff "a" has a referent which does not satisfy "G". These conditions do not speak to the case in which "a" has no referent. There is nothing to correspond to the two ways in which, on the Russellian view, a sentence can be false. The generalization is this: referring expressions induce truth conditions for simple sentences following the Strawsonian pattern; impostors, expressions which may seem like referring expressions but which

---

[18] Ockham seems to have thought that uses of the Latin "non" exploit the possibility: "ista est neganda: 'Chimaera est non-homo', quia habet unum exponentem falsam, scilicet istam: 'Chimaera est aliquid'" (quoted by Henry, 1984: 102). Klima (2001: 201) claims that this distinction is common in medieval philosophy.

are really nothing of the sort, induce truth conditions for simple sentences following the Russellian pattern. What was initially presented as an issue about the scope of negation is really best seen as one concerning the pattern of truth conditions.

There is a simple prima facie reason to prefer applying the Russellian pattern to the case of sentences containing names. The Russellian pattern produces Ockhamist truth conditions: "*a* is *F*" is true iff "*a*" has a referent which satisfies "*F*" and is false otherwise. There are negative existential truths expressed using names, like "Vulcan does not exist". Applying the Ockhamist pattern, "Vulcan exists" is false, since "*a*" has no referent and the condition for truth fails; since negation turns a falsehood into a truth, "Vulcan does not exist" is true. The Strawsonian pattern would ensure that "Vulcan exists" has no truth condition. Special devices and theses may be applied to deal with this problem, but the Ockhamist perspective renders redundant such *ad hoc* moves.

Names contribute to the truth conditions of simple sentences rather as definite descriptions do: no referent, no truth. Assuming names count as referring expressions, this shows that present considerations do not establish that referring expressions and definite descriptions belong to exclusive categories. Those who believe that the semantics of proper names are given by definite descriptions believed this already. However, a similar argument can be run even for demonstratives, and so should persuade everyone who believes that there are *any* referring expressions. "This does not exist" is false, but it might have been true (assuming "this" to refer to a contingent being), that is, there is a world with respect to which it is true, that is, a world with respect to which "This exists" is false. World-relativized Ockhamist or free logical truth conditions deal with this in a smooth and obvious way, treating "This exists" as false with respect to such a world through lack of a referent; alternatives are complex and involve a loss of uniformity.

The Ockhamist approach can be applied to natural language negation by considering an apparent difficulty: why cannot we use

(29) Pegasus doesn't fly

to disabuse someone who has been deceived by the myth? Being parallel to "Vulcan does not exist", this ought to be true. Given the nature of the truth conditions, a free logician could say that natural language negation generates scope ambiguities, so that there is a false reading of (29). This would be to move from the possibility of scope distinctions with respect to negation, which I accept, to the further claim that these distinctions are needed in order to describe the behaviour of "not" in English. Though there are special cases in which we do need to recognize ambiguity, (29) is not one of them. The norm is that negation takes wide scope,[19] and (29) is indeed true. Were ambiguity universal, there would be a false reading of "Vulcan does not exist", which there does not appear to be. We can explain the phenomena better by appealing to two connected features. First, it is possible to overlook the distinction

---

[19] It is hard to hear "George Bush didn't meet with the King of France" as false, though the Russellian must claim that there is a false reading.

between truth and falsehood on the one hand and, on the other, fidelity or lack of fidelity to a myth or fiction. (29) is true, but is not faithful to the myth. Second, we need to bear in mind the defeasible presumption that referring expressions refer. One deceived by the myth would take it that "Pegasus" in (29) refers, and is believed by the speaker to refer, so an appropriate response would be: "What are the wings for? Just ornament?". A powerful move is needed to cancel the presumption, for example saying "Pegasus does not exist". The presumption can hold fictionally as well as genuinely. If we are both engaged in the myth, we are concerned with fidelity and not truth: we hold the presumption in the fictional or mythical way, and it is still right for you to dispute (29): you dispute its fidelity, not its truth. We cannot use (29) to disabuse, for either it will be taken as merely fictional, and so to be evaluated for fidelity rather than truth, or else, taken factually, it will not by itself be enough to cancel the presumption that referring expressions have referents.

A similar argument to the one about the scope of negation could be advanced using the possibility operator rather than negation, and the following contrasting pair:

(30) The teacher of Alexander might not have taught Alexander.
(31) Aristotle might not have taught Alexander.

It has been claimed that (30), unlike (31), is scope ambiguous. In the presence of the lemma about the scopelessness of referring expressions, this excludes definite descriptions from the category of referring expressions, while leaving open the possibility that proper names belong to it.

I claim that (30) is unambiguously true, and that the same goes for attempts to give the possibility operator wide scope in English, for example:

(32) It might have been that the teacher of Alexander did not teach Alexander.

On the other hand, there are examples which point in a different direction:

(33) George Bush might not have been the President of the USA

has only a true reading in normal use: it cannot say that he might not have been himself. This combination of views requires a pluralistic treatment of definite descriptions: in some uses, as in (32), they are rigid, in others, as in (33), they are not. The thesis that referring expressions are scopeless, when scope with respect to modal operators is the only issue, coincides with the thesis that referring expressions are rigid. I accept this thesis, and amplify it and argue for it in §6 below.

18.5 DEFINITE DESCRIPTIONS

Even if there is no general argument for the semantic simplicity of all referring expressions, it does not follow that every complex expression which is naturally regarded as a referring expression really is one. The most heavily debated category is that of definite descriptions, singular or plural expressions of the form "the so-and-so". Going back to Russell, there have been many specific arguments for the view that these are quantifier phrases rather than referring expressions (for the most thorough and detailed versions of these Russellian arguments, see Neale, 1990). At the same time, there has been plenty of rather unselfconscious talk of the reference of definite descriptions. For example Quine, who officially subscribes to Russell's theory of descriptions, says "In 'I saw the lion' the singular term is presumed to refer to some one lion" (Quine, 1960: 112), and that "in ordinary discourse the idiom of singular description" is used to "single out" an object (1960: 183). Strawson (1950) explicitly argues for treating definite descriptions as referring expressions. Kripke is officially a defender of Russell's theory of descriptions (Kripke, 1977), yet he is happy to talk of the referent of a definite description (Kripke, 1972: 24) and to treat names and descriptions as variants within the common semantic category of "designators".

There is little pre-theoretical pressure to make much of the distinction between proper names and definite descriptions; we owe to Russell the motivation for splitting up this apparently unified category. From his point of view, definite descriptions could not be referring expressions, that is, could not function in the way that logically proper names function. His many reasons include these:

(34) some definite descriptions have no referent, and these cannot be regarded as referring expressions; by "parity of form", the same holds for all.

(35) some can be used in negative existential truths, and these cannot be regarded as referring expressions; by "parity of form", the same holds for all.

(36) some can be used in informative (non-"tautologous") identity sentences, and these cannot be regarded as referring expressions; by "parity of form", the same holds for all.

Dualistic accounts of definite descriptions, typically expressed in terms of a distinction between "referential" and "attributive", suggest that all the "by parity of form" arguments are suspect. Turning to more specific issues, few would accept the validity of the last two reasons. Anyone who thinks that one can refer to contingent things, for example by some expression e, will believe that such a thing might not exist (or might not have existed). The most natural way to think about the semantics requires there to be a world with respect to which the sentence "e does not exist" is true. This is hard to square with (35). Frege took the fact that, to all appearances, there are informative identity sentences involving referring expressions as a datum in constructing the distinction between sense and reference; common sense is on his side. One would accordingly need theoretical justification for (36).

Though many would accept the validity of (34), it is not justified within a free logical perspective: a referring expression may lack a referent.[20] Russell also gave a significant reason for not regarding all definite descriptions as referring expressions: many are used quite correctly and normally, yet without a hint of a referential intention. Slightly elaborating an example used by Russell (1912: ch. 5), imagine someone

[20] "Nowhere has free logic had greater impact than in the logical theory of definite descriptions" (Lambert, 2001: 37).

drawing up the rules of a club, and writing: "The secretary shall be elected by simple majority vote of the members". There is no person-related "identifying information" that the utterer is bringing to bear or trying to invoke; nor is she intending her hearer to bring to bear some identifying information or other.[21] Another example of the absence of such intentions is a supposed proof by reductio ad absurdum that there is no greatest prime. A mathematician who starts the proof with "The greatest prime is odd or even" clearly has no referential intentions. The conclusion is that the only serious way to do justice to the supposedly referential nature of some descriptions is pluralistic: there are at least two kinds or uses of definite descriptions, and one is referential.

Such a pluralistic scheme naturally starts with a dualism of speakers intentions. Donnellan marks it thus:

A speaker who uses a definite description attributively in an assertion states something about whoever or whatever is the so-and-so. A speaker who uses a definite description referentially in an assertion, on the other hand, uses the description to enable his audience to pick out whom or what he is talking about and states something about that person or thing.   (Donnellan 1966: 285)

Donnellan provides both attributive and referential uses with positive characterizations. I will focus on the referential use, and speak of other uses simply as non-referential.

There are at least two kinds of referential intentions. One kind is object-involving, meeting a condition of the following form: there is an object, x such that the speaker intends that...x.... The other kind is not object-involving, meeting a condition of the following weaker form: the speaker intends that there be an object x such that...x....[22] It will be controversial to say what should fill the blanks. I think that the speaker should intend the truth or otherwise of what he says to turn on how things are with x. When the intentions are object-involving, the quantifier which governs this occurrence of "x" can be placed with widest scope, lying outside the content of the intention; in the non-object-involving case, the quantifier must be placed within the content of the intention. If there are empty referring expressions, we cannot require that the proper use of every referring expression should be animated by object-involving referential intentions. The relevant question is therefore whether it is plausible to think that normal uses of definite descriptions need to be animated by non-object-involving referential intentions. These do not preclude object-involving referential intentions; indeed, object-involving referential intentions normally guarantee the existence of non-object-involving ones, so if examples of these can be found, they will serve the purpose.

---

[21] It may be that these office-related descriptions form a separate category: they are referential, but refer to an office rather than to an office holder. This may be involved in the best way of handling the ambiguity of sentences like "The mayor comes up for election every year".

[22] Those who hear this as an intention to bring something into existence, and thus as inappropriate, may prefer to regard it as an abbreviation for: the speaker believes that there is an object x such that... and intends that...x....

A large range of expressions can be used with referential intentions, including quantifier phrases (as in "*Someone* has once again failed to close the door properly") and indefinite noun phrases. To count an expression as a referring expression, the practice of using the expression must contain a significant and typical period in which normal use of the expression requires having referential intentions and the expression is a perfectly adapted semantic tool for realizing them, with no irony or archness.

Some uses of definite descriptions fit this bill. Here is an example in which the referential intention is non-object-involving. You have a tennis court and you invite me over to play. We walk to the court together and I see that there is no centre net. I ask "Where's the net?" I have non-object-involving referential intentions: I intend that there be an object, namely the net, concerning which you realize that I am asking where it is. For my plan to work, you have to draw upon object-related knowledge: the net needs to be something of which you are aware. (I am hoping that you know, concerning the net, where it is; that is, that you know where the net is.) This is knowledge I must presume you to have in order for my question to be appropriate. By normal standards, I do not have object-involving intentions: I have never played on your court before, and have never had any causal contact, direct or indirect, with the net in question: it is not something I have seen or touched, or seen photographs of, and nor have I been party to any discussion in which it was referred to. It is consistent with my having the described intentions that there is no net and never has been one (the construction company went bankrupt before completing the job).

Cases in which there are non-object-involving referential intentions can be distinguished from cases in which there are no referential intentions at all. These are cases in which the speaker has no object-related knowledge, and does not count on the hearer having any. A clear example has already been given: the mathematician who non-assertively utters "The greatest prime is odd or even" in the course of his reductio. Other cases are descriptions used predicatively, for example "De Gaulle is the President of the Republic" (cf. Linsky, 1963: 80): a use of the definite description in such a sentence may not be animated by referential intentions. Other commonly cited examples are less clear. For example, Strawson quite reasonably suggests that uses of "the whale" are importantly different in "The whale is a mammal" and "The whale struck the ship". Normally, no one using the first would intend to refer to a particular whale; users would have neither object-involving nor non-object-involving whale-related referential intentions. In the case of the second, however, a normal context would contain a whale which was the object of the speaker's referential intentions. This does not settle whether or not the first sentence, as most naturally used, contains a referring expression. Perhaps "the whale" can also refer to a species, and perhaps a normal use of the first sentence involves referential intentions directed at that species.[23]

---

[23] Matters are more complicated than one might expect from the philosophical literature. For example, nouns apparently referring to species cannot always be happily prefixed by "the", as in: "Some Americans came to Africa to hunt lion", "Neanderthal man was probably exterminated by *homo sapiens*". See also Graff (2001).

Donnellan's own initial (and best-known) example of a non-referential use is introduced as follows:

Suppose . . . we come upon poor Smith foully murdered. From the brutal manner of the killing and the fact that Smith was the most gentle person in the world, we might exclaim, "Smith's murderer is insane".   (Donnellan, 1966: 285)

We are to assume that "Smith's murderer" abbreviates the definite description "the murderer of Smith".[24] Donnellan envisages that the evidence for the assertion is purely general (anyone who committed such a murder is insane). It may follow that the utterance in question was not driven by object-involving referential intentions. It does not follow that it was not driven by the weaker kind of referential intentions. That depends upon whether the speaker intended that, for some object x the truth of the remark should turn on how things are with x. Presumably that would be the normal intention, which is a (non-object-involving) referential intention in my scheme. This suggests that fidelity to Donnellan requires "referential" descriptions to be confined to those used with object-involving referential intentions. Further evidence is provided by his characterization of attributive uses, already cited:

A speaker who uses a definite description attributively in an assertion states something about whoever or whatever is the so-and-so.

This is certainly consistent with, and even suggestive of, the use of a definite description with a non-object-involving referential intention. I have suggested that we cut semantic reality more closely to its joints if we take non-object-involving referential intentions as the principal guide, on the side of use, to what expressions are to be counted as referring expressions.

The distinction between object-involving and non-object-involving referential intentions is "external" to the speaker: duplicates may differ in just this respect, one being in the presence of an object fit to be the target of object-involving intentions, the other not (perhaps thanks to Cartesian interference). In contrast, we would typically wish a constraint of the envisaged kind, one which determines what interpretive response is required by the hearer, to be within the control of the speaker. The speaker can control whether he intends the hearer's interpretation to be object-involving, and he can possess this intention even if he is animated merely by non-object-involving referential intentions. The speaker cannot control whether he succeeds in getting the hearer to attain an object-involving interpretation: that is a function of what is in their environment. This suggests that the significant break is between uses animated by referential intentions of either kind, and uses not so animated.

---

[24] It is unclear that genitives can properly be treated in this way; not, at least, if uniqueness is required. "John is Sally's child" can be true even if Sally has other children (cf. Graff, 2001). The same effect can obtain even when the definite description is in subject as opposed to predicate position: "John's leg was broken in his fall" can be true even if John has two legs.

Donnellan (1966) argued that we could recognize a referential use of a definite description "the F" by the fact that the speaker could thereby refer to something which is not F. If one takes this line, one will be tempted to count an utterance of "The man drinking martini is drunk" as true if Jones is drunk and is the object of the speaker's referential intentions, even if Jones has nothing but water in his martini glass. This ruling is not compulsory. In such a case, assuming the circumstances to be of the most ordinary kind, the speaker intended to refer to a martini-drinker but failed. We are not compelled to say that this failure really amounts to success in referring to a non-martini-drinker.

Many theorists (e.g. Kripke, 1977; Neale, 1990) have attempted to show that the direction Donnellan himself took at this point is misguided. Suppose (as before) that Jones is the object of the speaker's intentions and that there is also a unique martini drinker, Smith. One could not fault a hearer who took the utterance to be true just if Smith is drunk. If this is a faultless interpretation, it must have correctly identified what the speaker said. A hearer is not obliged, in order to reach a proper understanding, to chase through the various possible errors of which a speaker might be guilty. If this is accepted, Donnellan should not have allowed (and arguably did not allow) that the utterance would be true if Jones was drunk. Such criticisms should not, however, be regarded as counting against dualism (or pluralism) about definite descriptions, since dualism does not require the particular development which Donnellan envisaged.

Few doubt that there are referential uses of definite descriptions. The controversy is the impact of this fact on semantics. I believe that referential intentions show that referential semantics are appropriate: these will involve a reference condition of a familiar form, in the setting of a theory which will ensure that referring expressions are rigid (see Section 18.6 below).[25] The most straightforward way in which this effect can be achieved is by regarding "the" as ambiguous, and reserving a special axiom for the kind of "the" which enters into a phrase used with referential intentions. An alternative is to regard "the" as itself semantically underdetermined, while holding that contextual enrichment may lead either to referential truth conditions or some other. On this view we could think of "the" as having a constant meaning in rather the way a demonstrative pronoun like "that" or "I" does, and part of this constant meaning is a switch which says "If you detect referential intentions (or other relevant contextual material), interpret me as a referential definite description; if not, interpret me as a non-referential definite description".[26] In this chapter, I take no stand on which alternative is to be preferred.

[25] If the metalanguage has referring definite descriptions, the pattern will be: for all x, "the F" refers to x iff $x =$ the F; if not, the pattern could be Russellian: for all x, "the F" refers to x iff x is uniquely F. Even the Russellian condition may assign a referent rigidly, if other parts of the theory treat reference as a rigid relation.

[26] Evans (1982: 321–2) assumes that any account of definite descriptions which is dualist at the level of truth conditions will treat "the" as ambiguous. For underspecification approaches (which do not treat "the" as ambiguous) developed with greater finesse than the version given here, see Bezuidenhout (1997) and Recanati (1993).

18.6 RIGIDITY

In a Kripkean perspective, rigidity is understood in such a way that an expression may have as referent at a world an object which does not exist at that world.[27] This is made explicit in these words:

a rigid designator [has] the same reference in all possible worlds. I ... don't mean to imply that the thing designated exists in all possible worlds, just that the name refers rigidly to that thing.   (Kripke, 1972/80: 77–8)

To express the contingency of Kripke's existence, we need "Kripke does not exist" to be true with respect to some world. On his view, a world w in which Kripke does not exist is still one at which "Kripke" designates Kripke. Since Kripke is not among the things which exist in w, the sentence "Kripke does not exist" is true with respect to w. It follows classically that "Something does not exist" is true with respect to w, which will be distasteful to some kinds of non-Meinongians. On the assumption that something exists only if there is something that it is, we also get the truth with respect to w of "$\neg\exists x \, x = $ Kripke", and so, by classical reasoning, of "$\exists y \neg \exists x \, x = y$" (see Wiggins 1995). Most people would think that this last is something that ought to be true with respect to no world: how could there be something which is not identical to anything? No problem of this kind arises within NFL, if only because it does not accept classical existential generalization. The natural explanation of why "Aristotle exists" is false with respect to a world in which Aristotle does not exist is the same as the explanation of why "Vulcan exists" is actually false: the referring expression fails to refer. The upshot is that "Hesperus is Phosphorus" is contingent, though it may well often be intended as a shortened form of the necessary "if Hesperus exists, then Hesperus is Phosphorus".[28]

The intuitive idea behind rigidity is that actual referent (if any) projects onto all possibilities. We can make this precise without defining rigidity as sameness of referent at every world, and so without encountering the problems of the previous paragraph. A rigid expression with an actual referent refers to that object at each world at which the object exists, but refers to nothing at other worlds; a rigid expression with no actual referent has no referent at any world. One formulation of the general idea counts an expression e as rigid iff it meets the following condition:

(37) for all worlds w, all objects y, (e actually designates y and y exists in w) iff e designates y with respect to w.[29]

---

[27] Kripke's original words are: "Let's call something a *rigid designator* if in every possible world it designates the same object" (Kripke, 1972/1980: 48). Kaplan (1989: 569–7, n.8) chronicles some of Kripke's responses to accusations that he changed his view.

[28] Kripke's view also requires the necessity to be conditional, for even if "Hesperus" refers to Hesperus at a world in which Hesperus does not exist, Hesperus will not belong to any ordered pair in the identity relation at that world.

[29] Referring expressions are also temporally rigid. This needs to be defined along Kripkean lines, rather than following the structure of (37), since the referent of an expression at a time might be something which does not exist at that time.

Any reasonable approach to rigidity, and certainly (37), allows that empty expressions can be rigid. NFL should take advantage of this, classifying empty referring expressions as rigid, along with non-empty ones. A consequence is that it is strictly false that Vulcan might have existed. Since "Vulcan" has no referent with respect to the actual world, if it is rigid it has no referent with respect to any world, so there is no world with respect to which "Vulcan exists" is true.[30] Those who think this is the wrong result confuse genuinely possible worlds with epistemic duplicates. Kripke has given us the resources to handle this issue: there is a possible world which Leverrier (before he learned the bad news) could not distinguish from the actual world and in which there is a planet which, had he known about it, he would have counted as verifying his "Vulcan" hypotheses. This does not amount to a world at which Vulcan exists.[31]

The essence of reference is closely connected with, and ultimately explains, the rigidity of referring expressions. We find it in Evans's principle (P):

If S is an atomic sentence in which the n-place concept-expression R is combined with singular terms $t_1 \ldots t_n$, then S is true iff $\langle$ the referent of $t_1 \ldots$ the referent of $t_n \rangle$ satisfies R. (Evans 1982: 49)

The restriction to atomic sentences looks forward to a point Evans makes later in the book, namely that definite descriptions are not singular terms (singular referring expressions). The principle ought to be neutral on whether there are any semantically complex "singular terms". If there are, a sentence constructed out of these in the way Evans envisaged will not be atomic in the classical sense; we can just drop the restriction "atomic" from (P). The expression "singular term" is also less than ideal, for any plausibility the principle has extends also to plural referring expressions: no doubt "Russell and Whitehead wrote *Principia*" is true iff $\langle$the referent of "Russell and Whitehead", the referent of "*Principia*"$\rangle$ satisfies "wrote". We can simply replace "singular term" by "referring expression".

Are the definite descriptions lying between "$<$" and "$>$" themselves referring expressions, or are they to be understood in Russell's way?[32] This is connected with how we should understand the possible worlds truth conditions supplied by (P). Evaluating a sentence to which (P) applies at some non-actual world, w, should we count the referent with respect to w of some referring expression, t, as the referent of t with respect to w or the referent of t with respect to the actual world? If the definite

---

[30] One could accept that there might have been such a planet as Vulcan, if "such as" means one like Vulcan was supposed to be.

[31] McDowell argues for de re senses, characterizing these in terms which seem to amount to rigidity: they are senses for which it is not the case that they are indifferent to whether they have a referent or not (cf. McDowell, 1984: 283). On the view proposed here, referring expressions which refer have their referent essentially, and for those which do not refer, their failure to refer is essential. Yet McDowell supposes that the de re character of a sense, that is, its rigidity, will ensure that it has a referent.

[32] In a related discussion, Evans speaks of using "a metalinguistic definite description ('the referent of "the author of *Waverley*"') as a referring expression" (Evans, 1982: 53). However, compare "all uses of definite descriptions in this book, both formal and informal, are intended to be understood according to the [Russellian quantificationalist] proposal I have tentatively put forward" (Evans, 1982: 60).

descriptions are referring expressions in the metalanguage, and referring expressions are rigid, the same object is involved however we answer, and this is intuitively the right result. If the definite descriptions are treated in a Russellian way, it would be clarifying to insert "actual" at some point. The Russellian version of (P), making also the small adjustments recommended in the previous paragraph, would read:

If S is a sentence in which the n-place concept-expression R is combined with referring expressions $t_1 \ldots t_n$, then S is true iff for some x_1, t_1 refers to x_1 with respect to the actual world, ... and for some x_n, t_n refers to x_n with respect to the actual world and $\langle x_1, \ldots x_n \rangle$ satisfies R.

These metalanguage Russellized definite descriptions are in effect rigidified.

If the thesis that all referring expressions are rigid is correct, and if suitable metalanguage definite descriptions are used as referring expressions, we can leave Evans's formulation of (P) almost unchanged: the relevant reference is the referent of t with respect to the actual world, which will be the very same object as its referent with respect to w. I will adopt the convention that an underlined definite description is to be treated as a referring expression, in which case (P) has its neatest formulation thus:

(38) If S is a sentence in which the n-place concept-expression R is combined with referring expressions $t_1 \ldots t_n$, then S is true iff $\langle$ the referent of t_1 ... the referent of $t_n \rangle$ satisfies R.[33]

The concluding thesis of this paper is that an expression is a referring expression if and only if it satisfies principle (P), optimally formulated as (38). Satisfaction of the principle ensures that any referring expression is modally rigid, and explains the source of the rigidity. It remains to ask why this thesis should be accepted.

There are *ad hoc* reasons relating to examples, like those offered by Kripke for proper names. These have generally been found convincing, so I will be brief. Kripke says that when we come to consider whether under certain circumstances it would have been true that Aristotle did not teach Alexander, we need to consider circumstances containing Aristotle, that is, containing the very man Aristotle who is in fact the referent of "Aristotle" (Kripke, 1972/80: 62). This seems indubitable, and if it holds in general, as indeed it seems to do, suggests that "Aristotle" is rigid: when we use the name to speak of Aristotle, we intend to say something whose truth or falsehood, actual or counterfactual, depends on how things are with him. Since there was nothing special about this name it points to the general conclusion that all names are rigid.

It was important to Kripke to contrast the rigidity of names with the non-rigidity of many or most definite descriptions. The clearest examples of non-rigid definite descriptions are in predicative uses. One of Kripke's own examples (close to (33) above) is:

---

[33] Plurals are incorporated by taking the variables to be neutral in number and replacing "referent" by "referent or referents". A sequent satisfies a predicate by its members doing so, taken in their sequence-order.

(39) Someone other than the US President in 1970 might have been the US President in 1970. (Kripke 1972/80: 48)

For this claim to be plausible, we need to understand the structure thus:

(40) The x which was US President in 1970 is such that possibly $\exists y \ y \neq x$ such that y was the US President in 1970.

The natural truth conditions require the first occurrence of the definite description to be rigid. Normally, a definite description used with referential intentions is rigid. An utterance of "The teacher of Alexander did not teach Alexander" is obviously actually false. But how should we evaluate it with respect to other worlds? The answer which does justice to the referential intention is that it is true at just the worlds at which Aristotle did not teach Alexander: what matters is who was taught by the person who is in fact the referent of "the teacher of Alexander". The explanation is that this person is the target of the referential intentions, which are intentions to say something which would be true if and only if this person did not teach Alexander.

The explanation of the fact that definite descriptions in predicate position are typically not rigid is that they are not used with referential intentions. They serve to characterize how things are with something presumed already available. The fact that definite descriptions in subject position are often rigid is explicable in similar terms. As Strawson said, the role of a referring expression is typically to help a speaker introduce an object for the rest of the sentence to say something about. When there is such an object, the speaker intends how things are with it to be what matters to truth, actual and counterfactual (and with respect to other times). This is what is reflected by Evans's principle (P), and this is why referring expressions are modally rigid.[34]

REFERENCES

Bezuidenhout, Anne (1997). "Pragmatics, Semantic Underdetermination and the Referential/Attributive Distinction." *Mind*, 106: 1–34.

Burge, Tyler (1974). "Truth and Singular Terms." *Noûs*, 8: 309–25.

—— (1983). "Russell's Problem and Intentional Identity." *Agent, Language and the Structure of the World: Essays Presented to Hector-Neri Casteñeda, with His Replies*. J. E. Tomberlin (ed.) Indianapolis, Hackett: 79–110.

Campbell, John (2002). *Reference and Consciousness*. Oxford, Clarendon Press.

Donnellan, Keith (1966). "Reference and Definite Descriptions." *Philosophical Review*, 77: 203–15.

Evans, Gareth (1982). *The Varieties of Reference*. Oxford, Clarendon Press.

Frege, Gottlob (1892). "On Sense and Meaning." *Gottlob Frege: Collected Papers on Mathematics, Logic and Philosophy*. Brian McGuiness *et al.* (eds. and trans.) Oxford, Basil Blackwell (1984): 157–77.

Geach, P. (1972). *Logic Matters*, Oxford, Basil Blackwell.

Graff, Delia (2001). "Descriptions as Predicates." *Philosophical Studies*, 102: 1–42.

---

[34] My thanks to Ernie Lepore for helpful comments and editorial guidance on an early draft.

Henry, D. P. (1984). *That Most Subtle Question.* Manchester, Manchester University Press.

Hossack, K. (2000). "Plurals and Complexes." *British Journal for Philosophy of Science*, 51: 411–43.

Kaplan, David (1977). "Demonstratives." *Themes from Kaplan.* J. Almog, J. Perry and H. Wettstein (eds.). Oxford, Oxford University Press (1989): 481–563.

_____ (1989). "Afterthoughts." *Themes from Kaplan.* J. Almog, J. Perry and H. Wettstein (eds.).Oxford, Oxford University Press: 565–614.

Klima, G. (2001). "Existence and Reference in Medieval Logic." *New Essays in Free Logic. In Honour of Karel Lambert.* E. Morscher and A. Hieke (eds.). Dordrecht, Kluwer: 197–226.

Kripke, Saul (1972/1980). *Naming and Necessity.* Oxford, Basil Blackwell.

_____ (1977). "Speaker's Reference and Semantic Reference." *Midwest Studies in Philosophy, Volume II: Studies in the Philosophy of Language. Revised edition (1979): Contemporary Perspectives in Philosophy of Language.* P. A. French, T. E. Uehling, and H. K. Wettstein (eds.). Minneapolis, University of Minnesota Press.

Lambert, K. (2001). "Free Logic and Definite Descriptions." *New Essays in Free Logic. In Honour of Karel Lambert.* E. Morscher and A. Hieke (eds.). Dordrecht, Kluwer: 37–47.

Lepore, Ernest and Ludwig, Kirk (2000). "The Semantics and Pragmatics of Complex Demonstratives." *Mind*, 109: 199–240.

Linsky, L. (1963). "Reference and Referents". In C. E. Caton (ed.). *Philosophy and Ordinary Language* Urbana, University of Illinois Press, 74–89.

McDowell, John (1977). "On the Sense and Reference of a Proper Name." *Mind*, 86: 159–85.

_____ (1984). "De re senses." *Philosophical Quarterly*, 34: 283–94.

McKay, T. (2003). *Plurals and Non-Distributive Predication.* Draft version available on McKay's page at http://philosophy.syr.edu/.

Mill, John Stuart (1843). *System of Logic.* London, Parker.

Neale, Stephen (1990). *Descriptions.* Cambridge, Mass., London, MIT Press.

Morscher, E. and P. Simons (2001). "Free Logic: A Fifty Year Past and an Open Future." *New Essays in Free Logic. In Honour of Karel Lambert.* E. Morscher and A. Hieke (eds.). Dordrecht, Kluwer: 1–34.

Ockham, W. (Freddoso, ed. 1998). *Summae Logica II: Ockham's Theory of Propositions.* South Bend, Indiana, St Augustine's Press.

Peacocke, Christopher (1975). "Proper Names, Reference and Rigid Designation." *Meaning, Reference and Necessity.* S. Blackburn (ed.). Cambridge, Cambridge University Press: 109–32.

Quine, Willard V. O. (1960). *Word and Object.* New York, Technology Press of MIT and John Wiley and Sons Inc.

Recanati, François (1993). *Direct Reference.* Oxford, Blackwell Publishers.

Russell, Bertrand (1905). "On Denoting". *Mind*, 14: 479–93. Reprinted in *Logic and Knowledge*, R. C. Marsh (ed.). London, George Allen and Unwin (1956).

_____ (1912). *Problems of Philosophy.* Oxford, Oxford University Press (1959).

_____ (1918–19). "Lectures on the Philosophy of Logical Atomism." *Monist*, 28, 29. Reprinted in *Logic and Knowledge*, R. C. Marsh (ed.). London, George Allen and Unwin (1956): 177–281.

Sainsbury, R. Mark (2002). *Departing From Frege: Essays in the Philosophy of Language.* London, Routledge.

Strawson, Peter F. (1950). "On Referring." *Mind*, 59: 269–86.

—— (1961). "Singular Terms and Predication." *The Journal of Philosophy*, 58: 393–412.

—— (1974). *Subject and Predicate in Logic and Grammar*. London, Methuen.

Wiggins, David (1995). "The Kant–Frege–Russell View of Existence: Toward the Rehabilitation of the Second-Level View." *Modality, Morality and Belief. Essays in Honor of Ruth Barcan Marcus*. W. Sinnott-Armstrong, D. Raffman, and N. Asher (eds.). Cambridge, Cambridge University Press.

CHAPTER 19

PREDICATE REFERENCE

FRASER MACBRIDE

A *verb* . . . is a sign of something said of something else

(Aristotle)

Can we put the problem of philosophy thus? Let us write out all we think; then part of this will contain meaningless terms only there to connect (unify) the rest. I.e., some is there on its own account, the rest for the sake of the first. Which is that first, and how far does it extend?

(Ramsey)

The tendency to construe predication as a kind of, or analogous to, reference is one of the most persistent mistakes in the history of western philosophy

(Searle)

ARE predicates referring expressions? If only a convincing answer to this question could be found and put in place, so many other pieces of the philosophical puzzle might fit together: the objectivity of judgement, the unity of the sentence, the status of higher-order logic, the problem of universals. But what is the question asking? That all depends on what we mean by "predicate", and what we mean by "referring expression".

Thanks to audiences at the Universities of Leeds and York. For further discussion I am grateful to Kit Fine, Jane Heal, Jennifer Hornsby, Keith Hossack, April Jones, Mark Kalderon, Guy Longworth, Mike Martin, Joseph Melia, Alex Oliver, Gabriel Segal, Mark Sainsbury, Peter Simons, Mark Textor, and especially Barry C. Smith. I am also grateful to the Arts and Humanities Research Council who funded the period of leave during which this chapter was written.

It is in the fundamental union of predication that names and predicates find their contrasting but correlative roles. In the simplest form of sentence a name serves to pick out an object while the predicate supplies what the sentence says about the object so named. More generally, where a sentence consists of two or more names the predicate supplies what the sentence says about the objects thereby picked out (if they are different). Conceived in this way, predication may be represented by the neutral logical forms "*Fa*", "*Fab*" and "*Fabc*" (etc.); forms that depict predicate expressions with an upper case letter "*F*", and names with lower case "*a*", "*b*", "*c*". Our question then becomes whether the expressions that the "*F*" represents in "*Fa*" or "*Fab*" or "*Fabc*" refer.

This picture of predication operates at a high level of abstraction. Predicates are conceived as what the rest of sentence says about the object or objects named. But the rest of a sentence (in natural languages at least) may exhibit considerable complexity that a mere "*F*" is beggared to represent. It is true that some sentences contain only a name and an intransitive verb in finite form ("Socrates walks"), but these are far from being the rule. There are others that conjoin a name with an adjective or a substantive prefaced by the copula "is" or "is a" ("Socrates is wise", "Socrates is a man"). Then there are sentences that conjoin a name with another via a transitive verb ("Socrates loves Plato"). And there are sentences in which an adjective or a substantive is framed by the copula and a preposition or conjunction to relate one name to another ("Socrates is wiser than Plato", "Socrates is a teacher of Plato"). There are also more complex constructions in which (e.g.) an adjective is placed in attributive position to a substantive ("Socrates is a wise man") or an adverb is joined to a verb ("Socrates walks slowly").

In abstracting away from these and other contrasting differences between verbs, adjectives and substantives—in depicting the different predicative constructions to which they contribute as mere grammatical variations on what is logically represented by "*Fa*" or "*Fab*" or "*Fabc*"—the practice of picturing a predicate with a simple "*F*" risks neglecting semantically significant structure. Quine has sought to justify the practice of operating at this high level of abstraction, declaring these grammatical contrasts to have "little bearing on questions of reference" (see his 1960: 96). But Quine offers no argument for this claim, and it is difficult to avoid the suspicion that operating at such a high level of abstraction seems acceptable to Quine only because the formal languages that logicians have found fruitful to study lack the grammatical paraphernalia of verb, adjective and substantive. It may be that it is only by attending to differences among the more complex constructions of natural language—differences concealed beneath the coat tails of an "*F*"—that it is possible to settle (at least) some questions of reference. Simplicity and generality in a theory are nevertheless to be prized and what is often difficult to make out at ground level may be seen clearly in outline from a loftier perspective. Let us therefore begin our investigations by entertaining the hypothesis that predication is adequately represented by the neutral forms "*Fa*", "*Fab*", "*Fabc*" while remaining ready to test out and if necessary discard it.

Whether a predicate is a referential expression depends upon what reference is conceived to be. Even if it is granted that reference is a relation between words and worldly items, the referents of expressions being the items to which they are so related, this still leaves considerable scope for disagreement about whether predicates refer. One of Frege's great contributions to the philosophy of language was to introduce an especially liberal conception of reference relative to which it is unproblematic to suppose that predicates are referring expressions. According to this liberal conception, each significant expression in a language has its own distinctive semantic role or power, a power to effect the truth-value of the sentences in which it occurs. Frege took the semantic power of an expression to be determined by the presence of an extra-linguistic correlate or *semantic value*, a value to which the expression refers. So conceived, each significant expression in a language—whether a name, a predicate, a sentence or an expression of some other category—is a device for referring to its semantic value. Frege introduced this conception of reference because the systematic assignment of semantic values to expressions in a language provides the basis for a recursive determination of the truth-values of sentences in the language. In doing so, Frege anticipated the modern logician's notion of an *interpretation*, an assignment of entities to expressions that enables the logician to track and code the truth-sensitive features of a language, features vital to an appreciation of logical consequence and validity.

However, Frege also employed a far more demanding conception of reference— inchoate but still exerting of a powerful theoretical attraction of its own—that renders it far more problematic to suppose that predicates are referring expressions.[1] There are prototypical cases of referring expressions: "that mountain", "this river", "Alexander". What makes such expressions prototypical is the fact that—from an intuitive point of view—they are evidently used to identify the things about which we think and talk; they isolate and focus our attention upon features of the world drawn forth from the environmental backdrop. The prototypical cases, demonstratives, and names, thus provide a (provisional) model for conceiving of reference, reference being initially (at least) explained as the relation that obtains between a prototypical expression and the thing in the world it picks outs.[2] Since predicates do not belong to the class of prototypical cases it needs to be argued, rather than assumed, that the conception of reference that arises from considering the prototypical cases should be extended to cover predicates. Whether predicates belong to a more general category of referring expressions therefore depends upon the extent to which predicates are to be compared rather than contrasted with the prototypes, akin or analogous in their functioning to demonstratives or names where

---

[1] This interpretation of Frege—that identifies two distinct ingredients in his notion of reference—is owed to Dummett (1973, 1981).

[2] Of course we should also be prepared to countenance the possibility that, upon reflection, the notion of reference may become detached from the class of prototypical expressions relative to which it is often introduced. See Sainsbury "The Essence of Reference" (this volume) for a sustained discussion of reference *per se*.

these are conceived as referring devices. Are predicates referring expressions in this more demanding sense?

A Road Map

At first blush it may appear that a relational construal of predication—that likens predicates to names—is scarcely credible. For, from an intuitive point of view, it appears that a speaker of English can perfectly well understand "x is wise" or "y runs" without there being something that these predicates refer to. To understand "x is wise" and "y runs" the speaker need merely know when these predicates may be truly applied. He or she need merely know that "x is wise" applies to wise individuals, "y runs" to running things. This suggests that the semantic role of predicates consists in simply being true (or false) of objects picked out by names—predicates perform no additional role that demands them to have referents of their own. This conception of predication is introduced and developed in Section 19.1. Whether predication can be satisfactorily understood in such terms ultimately depends upon whether there are features of the use of predicates that are adequately explained if predicates are conceived as merely true (or false) of objects. Succeeding sections therefore explore whether there are such features of use. Section 19.2 considers whether the interaction between predicates and quantifiers forces the construal of predicates as referring expressions picking out elements of a domain over which quantifiers of the relevant form range. Section 19.3 discusses whether there are analogues of the notions of identity and identification familiarly associated with names that apply to predicates and supply analogous reasons for construing predicates as referring expressions. Finally, Section 19.4 investigates whether the prevalence of nominalizations in natural language, expressions like "wisdom" and "courage", provide evidence that the predicates from which these expressions are derived are referring. It is illuminating to begin our exploration of these issues from a consideration of the historical point of entry for analytic philosophy into the debate about predication.

19.1 OBJECTIVITY WITHOUT OBJECTS

It is now routine to separate the question whether a given stretch of discourse is objective—whether the statements of the discourse express truths that are independent of cognition in some fitting sense—from the question whether the discourse in question describes a domain of objects.[3] This separation of questions relies upon the

---

[3] This separation of issues gives rise to the dictum with which Kreisel is credited: "the problem in the philosophy of mathematics is the objectivity of mathematical statements, not the existence of mathematical objects".

veracity of the insight that objectivity does not require to be anchored in the existence of objects. But if this is an insight, it is hard won; for without the benefit of some of the most spectacular advances of analytic philosophy it might never have been achieved. And had these advances never been made, the question whether predicates are referring expressions might never have been a subject of controversy for us.

How can it be possible to make a statement about an objective reality true or false depending upon the character of that reality? One plausible answer is that it is possible because the different words that make up such a statement stand for different elements of reality, the whole true or false depending upon whether the elements of reality are arranged as stated. By so affirming the possibility of statements about a mind-independent reality the founders of analytic philosophy—Frege, Moore and Russell—sought to undermine the different forms of idealism that prevailed among their contemporaries. The doctrine that predicates are referring expressions (alongside others) thus became key to their revolt against idealism.

The significance of subsequent developments is thrown into relief against the backdrop of Russell evolving views upon reference.[4] In his *Principles of Mathematics* Russell had staunchly advocated a realist theory of meaning: "*Words* all have meaning, in the simple sense that they are symbols which stand for something other than themselves" (see his 1903: §51). This led Russell to admit a profligate ontology—that included "Numbers, the Homeric gods, relations, chimeras, and four-dimensional spaces"—to correspond to the many different words of our language. By holding to the being, if not the existence, of these different objects Russell was able to maintain the objectivity of statements about them; for "whatever can be thought of has being, and its being is a precondition, not a result, of its being thought of" (1903: §427).

Russell was to become sceptical of this ultra-realist theory because of the ontological excesses to which it gave rise. But he could not act upon such scruples to deny that many words have reference until some other means had been found of ensuring the objectivity of the statements to which these words contributed. Famously, the decisive breakthrough came when Russell discovered his theory of descriptions. Surface appearances suggest that phrases of the form "the ϕ" are referring expressions; the theory of descriptions shows that such appearances deceive us. This is because, according to the theory, contexts in which definite descriptions occur admit of eliminative paraphrase: "F(the ϕ)" is equivalent to "Exactly one thing is ϕ and whatever is ϕ is also F", a context in which "the ϕ" does not occur, referring or otherwise. In an echo of Russell's discovery, the early Wittgenstein was later to argue that the logical constants ("$\rightarrow$", "$\sim$" etc.) do not refer either, their role taken up and discharged by a truth-table notation from which the logical constants are absent (see Wittgenstein, 1922: 4.0312, 4.4414).

Despite these advances Russell continued to maintain that predicates are referring expressions. His reasons become evident in *The Problems of Philosophy*. There discussion is focused upon whether the preposition "in" is a referring expression:

---

[4] See also Frege, 1892: 61–2, 1906: 193 and Moore, 1898.

Suppose, for instance, that I am in my room. I exist, and my room exists; but does 'in' exist? Yet obviously the word 'in' has a meaning; it denotes a relation which holds between me and my room.   (Russell 1912: 50)

Why is it obvious that the word "in" refers to a relation? Russell invites us to entertain an alternative account of "in", an account whereby the preposition reflects the synthesizing activity of the mind:

Many philosophers, following Kant, have maintained that relations are the work of the mind, that things in themselves have no relations, but that the mind brings them together in one act of thought and thus produces the relations which it judges them to have. (1912: 51)

But to suppose that the use of the word "in" reflects the activity of the mind would be—absurdly—to undermine the objectivity of what Russell uses the sentence "I am in my room" to express:

It seems plain that it is not thought which produces the truth of the proposition 'I am in my room'. It may be true that an earwig is in my room, even if neither I nor the earwig nor any one else is aware of this truth; for this truth concerns only the earwig and the room, and does not depend upon anything else.   (1912: 51)

Russell so arrives at the conclusion that "relations ... must be placed in a world which is neither mental nor physical", elements of platonic realm that prepositions and transitive verbs pick out.

Russell's argument thus proceeds by elimination: either predicates are referring expressions or they reflect the activity of the mind; if predicates reflect the activity of the mind then the objectivity of statements about a mind independent reality is undermined; therefore predicates must be referring expressions. This argument fails if there is some alternative account of how predicates function that Russell has neglected to eliminate. But Russell saw no such alternative. He saw none because the dominant model of how expressions might function other than by referring was provided by the method of eliminative paraphrase embodied in the theory of descriptions. This method cannot be applied to eliminate predicates. For what are the equivalent contexts " . . . a" in favour of which predications of the form "Fa" are to be eliminated? There are no such contexts; predication is so fundamental a combination that no language that names or quantifies over objects could fail to incorporate a predicative device in order to say something about them.

19.1.1 A Disquotational Theory of Predication

But is there a third way that Russell neglected to consider? Is there a way of construing predicates that does not attribute a referential function to them but still respects the fact that predicates make an essential contribution to the statements they are used to make without undermining the objectivity of these statements? Quine saw it, or at least thought he did.

Like Russell, Quine was impressed by the theory of descriptions. However for Quine the theory revealed not only how expressions of a particular form ("the ϕ") contribute to the contexts in which they occur but without referring. For Quine the theory of descriptions also revealed that there is a great gulf between meaning and reference in general. But if an expression's being meaningful and an expression's bearing a referential function are different things then this opens up the possibility that a predicate may function "merely as a contextually meaningful word... a syncategorematic expression which *names* nothing, abstract or concrete" (Quine, 1939: 704).

However, in order for Quine to generalize legitimately in this way from the theory of descriptions it was also necessary for Quine to see the theory of descriptions as a limiting case. This is because the theory of descriptions shows how a certain form of expression makes a contextually significant contribution by *eliminating* them from the contexts in which they occur; consequently the significance of the contribution made by these expressions may be articulated without using them. But, as we have seen, predicates cannot be eliminated in this way. In order then to generalize from the example that the theory of descriptions provides it was therefore necessary for Quine to allow for the possibility that an expression may be contextually meaningful even if it cannot be eliminated from the contexts in which it occurs; in other words, an expression may be meaningful and make an objective contribution to the sentential contexts in which it occurs even if the only way to specify its contribution is by *using* the expression in question to say what it means.

This insight, if it is one, emerges in the course of a famous, or infamous, passage in which Quine dismisses the view of an imaginary realist (McX) who maintains that the adjective "red" picks out a universal held in common by different red things:

One may admit that there are red houses, roses and sunsets, but deny, except as a popular and misleading manner of speaking that they have anything in common... the word 'red' or 'red object' is true of each of sundry individual entities which are red house, red roses, red sunsets... That the houses and roses and sunsets are all of them red may be taken as ultimate and irreducible, and it may be held that McX is no better off, in point of real explanatory power, for all the occult entities which he posits under such names as 'redness'. (Quine 1948: 10)

In order to appreciate the significance of what Quine says here, two related confusions must be cleared away. First, even if, as Quine maintains, McX is wrong to think that there are universals ("occult entities") which appear under the *name* "redness" it does not follow that the *adjective* "red" is not a referring expression. After all, grammatically at least, adjectives are not names. Second, Quine characterizes himself as having argued "that we can use general terms, for example, predicates without conceding them to be names of abstract entities" (1948:12). But even if McX is mistaken in thinking that predicates are a special kind of *name*—names of abstract entities—this still leaves open the possibility that *predicates* are referring expressions which are not names.

Once these confusions are set aside, Quine's account comes (at a first approximation) to this. The contribution that "(is) red" makes to the contexts in which it occurs is fully captured by the use of the expression (outside quotation marks) to say what function "red" performs; there is no more to be said about "red" than that it is true of red things. The attempt to say any more about the contribution made by this adjective—that, for example, it refers to a universal—is to add nothing but metaphysical excess and mystery to what has already been said. More generally, there is no more to the contribution of predicates than is captured by the instances of the following 'disquotational' schema.[5]

(P) "F" is true of x iff x is (an) F

The disquotational theory of predication that Quine so presents appears to reduce the phenomenon of predication to a collection of trivialities.[6] For no one—not even the opponents of Quine who hold there is something more to be said about predication than the instances of (P) assemble—will wish to deny that the instances of (P) are true. Nevertheless the disquotational theory appears to offer something nontrivial, a third way of thinking about predication that allows predicates to make an objective contribution to the contexts in which they occur but without bestowing a referential function upon them.

Predicates are used to frame apt descriptions of how things are. "Red" is used to describe things that are red rather than some other colour, "square" is used to describe things that are square rather than some other shape, and so on. Predicates are used in this way to map the objective contours of reality. What is it that enables predicates to do so? The answer provided by the disquotational theory could not be more straightforward: "red" is true of every red thing and nothing else, "square" is true of every square thing and nothing else, and so on. But doesn't this just mean the adjectives "red" and "square" are used to apply to whatever things we may happen to call "red" or "square" rather than map objective contours? Doesn't this just undermine whatever confidence we may have had in the objectivity of the statements that "red" or "square" are used to make?

Not on the face of it. Each instance of the disquotational schema (P) mentions a predicate "F" and employing a bi-conditional specifies necessary and sufficient conditions for "F" to apply to an object x. A predicate "F" that appears on the left-hand side of an instance of (P) is thus paired with a description on the right-hand side of the circumstances in which it may truly be applied. Whether a predicate mentioned on the left-hand side of an instance of (P) makes an objective contribution to the contexts in which it occurs will therefore depend upon whether the circumstances described on the corresponding right-hand side are themselves objective. Now note that the right-hand side of instances of (P) describe circumstances that appear perfectly objective, an object's being red, an object's being square; there is no mention

---

[5] As it stands (P) applies only to adjectives and nouns. For present purposes I leave aside complications that arise from adapting (P) to cover the case of transitive and intransitive verbs and other predicative expressions.

[6] This theory is analogous to—but also to be distinguished from—Tarski's theory of truth that relies in similar fashion upon the schema (T) "p" is true iff p. Quine remarks on the parallel in his 1953c: 136–8.

on the right-hand side of the subjective interventions of speakers who call this or that "red" or "square". If appearances do not deceive us it follows that the objective contribution of the predicate mentioned on the corresponding left-hand side is thereby secured.

Of course, it is true that the disquotational theory uses the predicate that is mentioned on the left-hand side of an instance of (P) to specify on the right-hand side the circumstances in which the predicate applies. But it does not follow that the circumstances described on the right-hand side fail to be objective. Moreover, the practice of using a predicate that is also mentioned to describe the circumstances in which it applies appears to be all but inevitable. This is because, for at least the primitive predicates of our language, there may be no other way of describing what these circumstances are. Our capacity to provide a discursive description of the application of predicates must come to an end somewhere; we cannot always be expected to describe F-things without using the predicate "F". So in the end it may simply be "ultimate and irreducible" that some things are F and hence that "F" is true of them.

In response it may be suggested that so far from being inevitable the circularity the instances of (P) exhibit is avoided by a realist account of predication that construes predicates as referring devices. In place of (P) such an account will appeal to the instances of the following rule for predication.

(P^*) "F" is true of x iff x instantiates the referent of "F".

This rule appears to avoid the circularity inherent in (P) because its instances do not involve the use of a predicate to explain its own application conditions; the predicates whose application conditions are to be explained appear inside quotation marks on both right- and left-hand sides of (P^*)'s instances. But this is only possible because the instances of (P^*) incorporate auxiliary predicative machinery of their own—'instantiates the referent of "F"'—predicative machinery that *is* used to say how an object must stand to the referent of a predicate "F" in order for "F" to be true of it. In order to provide a fully general account of predicative expressions it follows that the realist must also provide an account of the conditions under which this auxiliary machinery is to be applied. But this brings the realist face to face with an uncomfortable dilemma. Either the application conditions of this auxiliary machinery will be accounted for by the instances of (P^*) or they will not. If the former is the case then there is a subset of (P^*)'s instances that exhibit the special form:

$(P^*\text{-})$ 'instantiates the referent of "F"' is true of x iff x instantiates the referent of 'instantiates the referent of "F"'.

If so, then the same predicative machinery that is mentioned on the left-hand side of some instances of (P^*)—i.e. those that exhibit the form $(P^*\text{-})$—is used to describe its own application conditions on the right. But then at least some instances of (P^*) exhibit the same kind of circularity that is inherent to instances of (P). Alternatively, the application conditions of this predicative machinery is to be explained by appealing to an additional principle of the following kind:

(P^{**}) 'instantiates the referent of "F"' is true of x iff x instantiates* the referent of 'instantiates the referent of "F"'.

Like instances of (P^*), instances of (P^{**}) make use of their own distinctive auxiliary predicative machinery ("instantiates* the referent of"). But then the realist is set upon the course of infinite regress. In order to achieve generality the realist must provide an account of the application conditions of this novel machinery. But to avoid circularity the realist must introduce further auxiliary machinery to do so ("instantiates** the referent of") and so on.

The difficulties the realist confronts here are a symptom of a point already noted: predication is a fundamental linguistic combination that cannot be eliminated; there is no getting away from the use of predicates. It is important not to overreact to this situation. From the fact that the realist cannot provide a reductive account of predication that treats predicates as referring devices it does not follow that predicative expressions do not refer. It only follows that the realist cannot fault (P) on grounds of circularity and that consequently the realist must provide some other grounds for preferring a referential account.

However even if (P) is not to be faulted for circularity there is a related charge of question begging that is worth considering. Quine denies that predicates are referring expressions and endeavours to account for their application conditions by using them. This provokes the suspicion that the issue of whether predicates refer is somehow being ignored. Here is one way of articulating the suspicion. It can be agreed upon all hands that the instances of (P) are true; no one will wish to deny that a predicate "F" is aptly used to describe F-things (if there are any). The instances of (P) may thus be taken to record a semantic achievement—that of being in a position to use predicates to aptly describe worldly things. But how is this achievement to be secured? The realist offers, in outline at least, a discursive account of how this can be done: a predicate "F" refers to a universal Φ, and so applies to the particulars that instantiate Φ (application is secured as the composition of reference and instantiation). By contrast, Quine offers no account of how we can succeed in co-ordinating predicates with the contours of an extra-linguistic reality. Instead Quine just affirms (P)'s instances. It consequently appears that Quine takes for granted what he seeks to establish—that predicates can be used without discharging a referential function.[7] For in the absence of such an account a mere appeal to instances of (P) can hardly be claimed to obviate the necessity to conceive predicates as referring expressions; we are simply left in the dark concerning whether the necessity for so-conceiving predicates indeed arises in the course of securing the semantic achievement recorded by (P)'s instances, or not.

It is critical to a proper appreciation of the disquotational theory Quine advocates that it be recognized not to beg the question in quite *this* way. For it is not so much the affirmation of (P)'s instances that provides the substance of this theory as the denial that there is anything else significant or general to be said about predication.

[7] See Armstrong, 1978: 16–7 and Hochberg, 1978: 139–40 for different versions of this complaint. See also the exchange between Devitt (1980) and Armstrong (1980).

According to Quine, there is no theoretical necessity to say anything other than (P); rather than being left in the dark by the disquotational theory we are led into darkness if we succumb to the temptation to say anymore. Whether the disquotational theory merits our acceptance turns upon whether this is truly so.

19.1.2 The Limits of Disquotationalism

Is there really nothing to be said but (P)? That depends (in part) upon what kinds of concern an account of predication is obliged to address. If our concern is that of the early analytic philosophers—that of securing the objectivity of scientific discourse—then it appears (P) cannot say enough. If there is a worry about whether a predicate "F" makes an objective contribution to the statements in which it occurs then there will likewise be a worry about the objectivity of what "F" is used to say; one cannot impugn a vehicle of expression without thereby impugning the content that the vehicle expresses. So if there is a concern about the objectivity of "F" as it appears on the left-hand side of a relevant instance of (P)—i.e. where "F" is mentioned—there will be no less of a concern about the objectivity of the circumstances of its own application that "F" is used to describe on the corresponding right-hand side. It appears therefore that (P) cannot say enough to assure us of the objective contribution of "F".

This concern about objectivity is related to another. Before stating the objection it is necessary—in order to avoid a distracting detail—to introduce a qualification to what has already been said. Reflect that the same string of sounds or letters in one language could mean something different in another language. It follows that merely disquoting a string and using it in one language may fail to describe its application conditions in another. Quine draws the conclusion that a string is never simply true of an object, but true in a language L, for appropriate L, of an object (see his 1953c: 134–5). He therefore recommends that (P) appear in the relative form:

(P_L) "F" is-true-in-L of a iff Fa

But this does not mean that what a predicate (relative to a given language) is used to state fails in some sense to be objective; it just means that the same string may mean different things in different languages. So even a realist account must recognize this form of benign linguistic relativity and allow what, from their point of view, constitutes the same predicate having different meanings in different languages, viz. the same predicative string referring to different universals in different languages. To accommodate this fact, reference must—like *being true of*—be framed relative to a language.[8] So , more fully, a realist account of this kind must state:

---

[8] This is not the only way to accommodate the relativity in question. For rather than qualifying the relations of reference and *being true of*, making them hold only relative to a language, predicative strings may be individuated more finely and indexed to a language. Then (P) may be written: "F_L" is true of a iff F_La. And (R) becomes: "F_L" is true of a iff a falls under the referent of "F_L".

(R) For any predicate "*F*" and language *L*, "*F*" is true-in-*L* of an object *a* iff *a* falls under the referent-in-*L* of "*F*".

We are now in a position to state the aforementioned objection. (P_L) is distinctively beset by difficulties familiar from discussion of Tarski's theory of truth.[9] This is because (P_L) is a schema, shorthand for a list of its instances. Because (P_L) merely provides an enumeration of its instances it fails to state what is common—by way of purpose or function—to its different instances. It no more states what predicates have in common than merely providing a list of friends states what friends have in common. Moreover because (P_L) does not state what its instances have in common, (P_L) provides no idea of how to apply the concept *predicate* to novel strings that are added to a language, or how to apply the concept to a new language. (P_L) provides no more guidance upon this matter than a mere list of existing friends guides one in applying the concept *friend* to someone new. It is therefore difficult to avoid the suspicion that the disquotational theory fails to provide the kind of insight that one might otherwise have expected of an account of predicates and predication.

By contrast, a referential account of predicates underpinned by (R) appears to avoid these difficulties. The instances of (P_L) collectively state what it takes for any given predicate to be true (in any given language in which it occurs) of an object: what it takes for "green" to be true-in-English of an object is that it be green, what it takes for "round" to be true-in-English of an object is that it be round, and so on. But the instances of (P_L) fail to state what it takes for predicates in general to be true of objects. This is why (P_L) fails to capture what is common among its different instances. A referential account of predicates appears to steal a march here upon its rival because it is able to attain a far higher level of generality. It is able to do so because it assigns a univocal purpose to predicates—to refer to universals. It is important to note how (R) achieves this higher-level of generality. Each instance of (P_L) both mentions *and* uses a predicate to specify its application conditions. Consequently, (P_L) is obliged to remain schematic rather than axiomatic; we cannot intelligibly replace a predicate both when it is mentioned and when it is used with the same bound variable. By contrast, (R) only mentions predicates. This is because it seeks to account for the application conditions of predicates not by using them but in a different way to (P_L)—by appealing to the referents of (mentioned) predicates and the capacity of objects to fall under these referents. Because predicates are only mentioned it follows that they may be uniformly replaced with a bound variable and (R) is correspondingly more general than (P_L).

Does (R) thereby steal a march upon its rival? Well for one thing it is questionable whether (R) achieves so much. We have already reflected that the application conditions of some predicates ("instantiates", "falls under") cannot—on pain of infinite regress—be specified without using the predicates in question. So it appears that (R) cannot succeed in full generality. For another thing, while generality is a theoretical virtue to be prized in the abstract it is unclear whether such generality as (R)

[9] See the criticisms of Tarski's theory of truth in (e.g.) Field, 1972 and Dummett, 1978: xx–xxi.

achieves is especially to be desired in the case at hand. For while (R) states what is uniform to a range of different predicates it says nothing about the application of a single one. We will not be able fill this gap—to specify the application conditions of a given predicate—until an account is forthcoming of how individual predicates pick out their referents. And, so far, the realist has supplied no more than a promissory note that a satisfactory account of this kind will be forthcoming. By contrast, (P_L) avoids the need to tackle such vexed issues: instead it supplies directly the application conditions for each given predicate of a given language. And while (P_L) offers no uniform account of predication, (P_L) provides a template for supplying application conditions for predicates, a template that—when impressed upon a particular language—is grasped as clearly by us as the expressions of the language to which it is applied.

Evidently the arguments that we have so far considered fail to be entirely satisfactory. Is the realist simply pursuing a craven desire for generality, seeking a form of objectivity so naive that only a primitive would otherwise be drawn to it? Or is the nominalist (Quine) failing to supply an explanation where reason demands one, making illicit appeal to the very phenomenon (our use of predicates) that vexes our understanding, trapping us off from reality by encircling us with our own words? That depends upon what is required of an account of how language is responsive and responsible to the world and its states. Since there is no such agreed account to fall back upon there appears little prospect—so far—of relief from the interminable dialectic of charge and counter-charge that prevails between realist and nominalist.

19.1.3 A Challenge for Disquotationalism

There is, however, an objection that arises concerning the use of (P_L), an objection that does not rely upon disputed background assumptions. The nominalist assumes that names are referring expressions. (P_L) is then used to show that there is no need to construe predicates as likewise referring; predicates need only be construed as strings that are true or false of the objects names pick out. If this method of argument is a good one then it appears that the same method may be deployed to show that there is no need to construe names as referring expressions. The nominalist must therefore either (i) abandon the use of (P_L) to show that predicates do not refer, or else (ii) demonstrate that there is a relevant difference between the different ways in which the method is deployed.

This case against the nominalist may be developed in the following stages. Let us begin by focusing our attention upon the collection of name-predicate sentences in English that exhibit the monadic form "Fa". Take "Socrates swims" as our target sentence. By nominalist lights, whether this sentence is true (or false) depends on whether "swims" is true (or false) of Socrates. In other words,

(1) "swims" is true of Socrates iff Socrates swims

If this construal of "Socrates swims" is accepted then "Socrates" occurs as a referring expression while it is merely the string "swims"—its referent being nowhere in sight—that is true (or false) of Socrates. But what stands in the way of turning this analysis on its head and offering the alternative construal?

(2) "Socrates" is true of swimming iff Socrates swims

If (2) is accepted then it is "swims" that occurs as a referring expression while "Socrates" is consigned to the role of a string true (or false) of swimming. Unless the nominalist supplies a principled reason for preferring (1) to (2), (1) can hardly be used to show that "swims" is not a referring expression.[10]

There are a number of responses available to the nominalist worth disentangling. The nominalist may begin by countering that (1) is to be preferred to (2) because we are *already* committed to names having reference. But if ordinary practice does already enjoin such a commitment then it should be possible to explain to us wherein this commitment consists—what it is about our use of names that constrains them to be counted referring expressions. The nominalist now encounters a dilemma. If it is not possible to give such an explanation then it remains an open possibility that it is not principle but prejudice that speaks in favour of (1). But if such an explanation can be given then we should be able to inspect directly whether the use of predicates is similarly, or at least analogously, constrained to names and decide upon that basis whether predicates are referring expressions. Either way analyses like (1) become redundant, unable to establish unaided that predicates are not referring expressions.

A second nominalist response seeks to bypass this concern by arguing that analyses like (2) founder when the realist applies them to more complex constructions. Take "Socrates is older than Plato" as our target. Because "is older than" is asymmetric this sentence says something different from, and incompatible with, "Plato is older than Socrates". When the disquotational strategy is applied to this sentence the analysis results

(3) "Socrates" and "Plato" are true of *being older than* iff Socrates is older than Plato

Obviously (3) is inadequate. It simply says that "Socrates" and "Plato" are true of *being older than* but provides no inkling of whether or how "Socrates" and "Plato" are true of this relation in such a way as to guarantee that it is Socrates that is older than Plato rather than the reverse. Hence (3) leaves us without the means for distinguishing between what is said by "Socrates is older than Plato" and "Plato is older than Socrates."

This objection is not insuperable. The realist can augment (3) with additional resources to get around this problem. He may add primitive operators ("in that order") to his *ideology* and use the order in which "Socrates" and "Plato" are written down to show the way in which they are true of *being older than*:

---

[10] Quine, who first raised an objection of this form, suggested a somewhat different *reductio*: "On what grounds, indeed, can we take issue with someone who even outdoes the nominalist and repudiates *everything*, the concrete as well as the abstract, by construing all words indiscriminately as syncategorematic expressions designating nothing?" (1939: 704; see also 1980: 165). Quine answers by arguing that expressions that occur in positions that are open to quantification cannot be construed as syncategorematic. Whether reference, or lack of it, can be linked in this way to the accessibility, or inaccessibility, of a position to quantification will be discussed in the next section.

(5) "Socrates" and "Plato" are true of *being older than* (in that order) iff Socrates is older than Plato

Of course appeal to additional ideological (primitive operators) or ontological resources (for example, ordered pairs) would do little to aid the realist if the nominalist had no corresponding need of these additions. But the nominalist does need them, and implicitly presupposes them. Applying the disquotational strategy of (1) to "Socrates is older than Plato" yields

(6) "is older than" is true of Socrates and Plato iff Socrates is older than Plato.

But this analysis provides no basis either for distinguishing between the case in which "is older than" is true of Socrates and Plato in such a way that Socrates is older than Plato, and the case in which it is true of them in such a way that Plato is older than Socrates. If we do not immediately notice this fact it is simply because we are habituated in English to using the order in which "Socrates" and "Plato" are written down to mark this difference (you may have relied upon this convention when scanning the left-hand side of (6)). But even if we are habituated in English to doing so this does not excuse the nominalist from recognizing that he or she already relies upon additional ideological resources—in this case relying upon an implicit convention about the use of word order in English—to make sense of relational constructions.[11]

The nominalist may make a far more basic objection: that (2) is grammatically precarious in a way that (1) is not; that ' "Socrates" is true of swimming' just isn't tolerable English. But whether one feels inclined to report a sense of queasiness (or not) can hardly be taken to settle this or any other philosophical issue; one needs a stronger stomach for doing philosophy. It remains an open possibility that our sense of grammatical unease arises from what is accidental—laid down by the contingencies of biological and historical development—rather than essential about the forms we speak. So once again the nominalist must provide an argument to show that (1) is to be preferred to (2).

This third response faces a further difficulty, a case of the pot calling the kettle black. Insofar as (2) is grammatically precarious, (1) appears no less questionable. Whoever says: ' "swims" is true of Socrates'? Nobody, I conjecture, outside a philosophy or a linguistics department. Following Strawson, one may endeavour to find a paraphrase of this latter construction that is more tolerable in ordinary language.[12] The availability of such a paraphrase is suggested by the familiar equivalence of the *oratio recta* construction ' "Socrates swims" is true' with the *oratio obliqua* 'It is true that Socrates swims'. This suggests that the *oratio recta* ' "swims" is true of Socrates' is equivalent to the *oratio obliqua* form,

---

[11] Davidson recognizes this requirement in his description of predicate satisfaction: "Thus 'Dolores loves Dagmar' would be satisfied by Dolores and Dagmar (in that order) provided Dolores loves Dagmar" (Davidson, 1969: 48). The problems faced by the nominalist and realist who employ the 'is true of' idiom do not end with the recognition of order. They must also introduce some device (ontological or ideological) to distinguish a collective from a distributive reading of "is true of".

[12] See Strawson, 1974: 9–11.

(7) It is true of Socrates that he swims.

But once this paraphrase is allowed there seems no reason to disallow the corresponding *oratio obliqua* form,

(8) It is true of swimming that Socrates does it

and so the intelligibility of the *oratio recta* construction ' "Socrates" is true of swimming'. Strawson concludes, "No distinction between subject and predicate is therefore marked by the availability of paraphrase in the 'true of' construction."

Nevertheless these paraphrases do highlight the fact that there is a grammatical asymmetry between (*a*) (1) and (7) and (*b*) (2) and (8). Whereas (1) and (7) employ the same expression ("swims") in the same grammatical category as it appeared in the original target sentence ("Socrates swims"), (2) and (8) convert the predicative "swims" into the noun phrase "swimming". The realist who employs (2) and (8) is obliged to do so because the relational expressions "x is true of y" and "it is true of x that" only accept names or noun phrases in their open positions. The nominalist who uses (1) and (7) does not demand that "swims" undergo this kind of transformation because he makes no attempt to place an expression picking out the referent of "swims" in the open positions of these relational predicates. By contrast, the realist cannot avoid doing so.[13]

This asymmetry suggests that the appearance is no more than superficial that (2) and its ilk—constructions in which it is predicates that pick out elements of reality—may be used to obviate the necessity of assigning reference to names. This is because the meta-language (the extended fragment of English) in which (2) is framed uses a name ("swimming") rather than a predicate to assign a referent to the predicate "swims". It follows that the realist cannot avoid assigning *some* names reference—names in the meta-language for the referents of object language predicates. But once it is allowed that some names have reference it is difficult to see what principled motive there can be for preferring (2) as an analysis to (1), that is, for denying outright that names in the object language ("Socrates") are referring expressions. The nominalist's use of (1) avoids this kind of awkwardness; (1) does not use predicates in the meta-language to assign referents to object-language names.

It is far from evident that this objection to (2) is critical. The objection plays upon what appears to be a meta-linguistic prejudice in favour of the nominal. However this appearance itself appears superficial, nothing more than the consequence of a grammatical fact already noted, that "is true of" requires names to be completed into a whole sentence; a fact that makes it grammatically inevitable that the referents of predicates—of which object-language names are true—are picked out by names in the meta-language. Of course if we grammatically blinker ourselves in this way then we won't be able to see logically right or left. But why would we want to blinker

---

[13] We catch our first glimpse here of the so-called paradox of the concept *horse*, a conundrum that arises from the fact that grammar often obliges us to use a name ("swimming") to talk about the referent of a predicate ("swims"), thereby (apparently) belying the predicative nature of what the predicate picks out. See Section 19.4.1 below.

ourselves in the first place? Why should we accept in advance that the use of the "is true of" idiom provides the touchstone for determining whether a word, of whatever kind, is a referring expression? Do we not thereby beg the question in favour of the view that it is only names that are referring expressions?

No doubt the nominalist will reply: there is no need to accept this in advance; whether the 'is true of' idiom turns out to perform the touchstone role will depend upon whether by its employment we succeed in saying everything that needs to be said about the relationship between predicative expressions and the world.[14] Does the nominalist thereby succeed in saying everything that needs to be said about this relationship? That depends upon whether there are features of the use of predicates that cannot be captured or understood if predicates are conceived as mere strings true (or false) of objects. Are there such features of use?

19.2 QUANTIFICATION AND REFERENCE

Names are paradigmatic devices of reference. By looking to see what features of use compel us to construe names as referring devices, we may hope to establish whether the same or analogous features compel us to construe predicates likewise. What makes names appear paradigmatic devices of reference?

In part it is the stereotypical interaction of names with the universal and existential quantifiers "every object is such that" and "some object is such that", what Quine has dubbed the "unequivocally referential idioms of ordinary language" (1960: 242). Why does Quine say so? Why are quantification and reference to be linked in this way? Because these quantifier phrases may be used to make explicit statements about what objects exists. It is because of the interaction between (*i*) singular sentences that involve only names and (*i*) quantified statements that may be parlayed as explicit statements about the existence of objects that (*iii*) there is reason to think that names pick out objects—the objects that are said to exist by quantified statements (1960: 240; 1969*b*: 94).

Focus upon the role of the existential quantifier. It is the operation of existential generalization that controls the interaction between singular statements in which names occur and general statements that feature the existential quantifier. When applied to "Socrates is wise" this operation licenses us to infer "someone is wise", or more formally, "$(\exists x)(x \text{ is wise})$". The name "Socrates" is thus extracted from the position in the original sentence in which it occurred and a quantifier phrase

---

[14] This is, effectively, the strategy Davidson employs when he argues that there is no need to assign predicates reference in order to generate an adequate truth theory for a first-order language; for this purpose, it is merely required that objects, or sequences of objects, satisfy ('satisfies' being the converse of 'is true of') predicates. He writes, "Here, the call for entities to correspond to predicates disappears when the theory is made to produce T-sentences without excess semantic baggage" (Davidson, 1977: 210). Davidson assumes here that predicates in natural language occur in positions that are not open to quantification. This assumption will be placed under scrutiny in the next section.

or bound variable inserted into the position left vacant by the name. The result-ing sentence is equivalent to the existence claim "There is an object which is wise." This transition makes sense if "Socrates" is a referring device that picks out a thing of the kind (a wise thing) that is then said to exist. In applying the operation of existential generalization to "Socrates is wise" we thereby *quantify over* what the name picks out; the object to which "Socrates" refers is assigned as a value to the variables of quantification. It follows—insofar as the validity of this operation is accepted—that there is no escaping the obligation to construe names as referring devices. So if a corresponding rule can be found, or indeed licensed, that applies to predicates—an operation that leads us to quantify over what these expressions stand for—then there can be no less of an obligation to construe predicates as referring devices.

Are there corresponding predicative operations of an appropriate form? Let us begin by considering where there is an operation that enables us to infer "$(\exists X)$(Socrates X)" from "Socrates is wise" by extracting " . . . is wise" from the latter sentence and inserting a bound variable "X" into the predicate position left vacant to yield the former quantified locution. Sometimes it has been claimed to be built into the very distinction between names and predicates that the former but not the latter are susceptible to quantification: "When we schematize a sentence in the predicative way "Fa", or "a is an F", our recognition of an "a" part and an "F" part turn strictly on our use of variables of quantification; the "a" represents a part of the sentence that stands where a quantifiable variable could stand, and the "F" represents the rest" (Quine, 1969b: 95). It follows that the very idea of quantification into predicate position is a contradiction in terms—predicates, by definition, are inaccessible to quantification. Quine has even gone so far as to claim that in a finite universe, where existential and universal quantification are eliminable in favour of finite disjunctions and conjunctions of atomic sentences, "the very distinction between names and other signs lapses in turn, since the mark of a name is its admissibility in positions of variables" (see his 1969a: 62).

These claims rest upon the questionable assumption that names and predicates cannot be distinguished by other means. In fact, if we simply rely upon the famil-iar formal and informal clues that we use to distinguish names from other sentence parts—to distinguish names from verbs, adjectives and other particles—it appears that English actually permits quantification into a variety of non-name positions. Suppose that whereas Socrates and Plato are both men, Socrates is also wise. It fol-lows that while there is something that Socrates and Plato both are (men) there is also something that Socrates is but Plato isn't (i.e. wise). Suppose too that Plato does whatever Socrates does. It follows that if Socrates scowls then Plato scowls too. In the former case we have an inference that depends upon quantification into both noun and adjective positions. In the latter case we have an inference that depends upon quantification into verb position. Since English permits inferences of this form it is difficult to see how their intelligibility can be denied.[15]

---

[15] See Geach, 1951: 132; Strawson, 1961: 80, 1974b: 64–5 and Dummett, 1973: 214–16.

But is quantification into noun or adjective position genuine predicate quantification? If a predicate is simply the rest of a sentence that remains once the name (or names) has been subtracted, then the predicate of "Socrates is wise" is not merely the adjective "wise" but the concatenation of the copula plus "wise". Predicate quantification proper must therefore involve the replacement of not just an adjective or noun but the entire predicate—copula included—with a bound variable or quantifier phrase. But quantification of this form does not appear to be allowable in English.[16] The position occupied by a predicate grammatically requires to be replaced by a predicate, otherwise the sentence in which it occurs is reduced to a list. So the bound variables or quantifier phrases that replace predicates must (if there are any) have the grammatical character of predicates too. But English contains no expressions of this form; it contains only pronouns and quantifier phrases that are noun-like. When these expressions are used to replace the predicate in "Socrates is wise" a sensible sentence is reduced to a nonsense list ("Socrates it", "Socrates something").

It is unclear what weight to place upon these considerations. On the one hand, noting the mere *absence* of a form of expression in English hardly establishes that such expressions—if they were to be introduced—would be unintelligible. On the other hand, a philosopher cannot simply stipulate that expressions—even if artificially introduced—bear the significance with which he or she would wish them to be invested; a philosopher may well be the victim of their own wishful thinking. However, there is evidence of a limited form of predicate quantification in English, namely in cases where the predicate is a verb that can be replaced with a quantificational pro-verb "do" or "does" (recall "Plato does whatever Socrates does"). What stands in the way of generalizing from such cases, treating pro-verbs as a species of a more generic form of variable and introducing pro-predicates as a further instance capable of standing in the place of predicates that are not verbs? It may only be the neglect—rather than the wisdom—of our ancestors that has prevented us from so doing until now.

There is another possibility. Rather than being neglectful perhaps the constructions our forebears envisaged already obviate the need to introduce a category of pro-predicates. It is the copula that supposedly separates an adjective or a noun from a predicate proper. Following Frege, however, the copula is often conceived as merely an auxiliary device without content of its own, a device for converting an adjective or noun into a verb phrase where grammar demands one (Dummett, 1973: 214). Alternatively, the copula may be conceived as the limiting and trivial case—akin to multiplying by 1 or adding 0—of a class of adjective and noun operators that include "—*was* . . . ", "—*looks* . . . " and "—*became* . . . " (Geach, 1980: 182). But if the copula is empty, or redundant, then there is nothing of substance to separate quantification proper from quantification into noun or adjective position. It is unclear what purpose the former might achieve that the latter does not already accomplish. More generally, it is unclear just what significance the distinction between predicates

---

[16] See Dudman, 1976: 80; Sen, 1982: 100; and Wiggins, 1984: 132.

and other predicative particles should bear. As Ramsey once remarked and Strawson has repeatedly emphasized, it is important to bear in mind when considering such matters "that the task on which we are engaged is not merely one of English grammar; we are not school children analysing sentences into subject, extension of the subject, complement and so on" (1925: 13).

Is the copula a mere grammatical device empty of content? Even though Frege suggested the idea, it is often thought that Frege himself supplied the deep reasons to the contrary (Dudman 1974: 80–1; Wright 1998: 81). Frege was concerned to mark the difference between a sentence and a mere list; the fact that the former but not the latter may be used to convey a judgeable content. He did so by reflecting that whereas a name is a complete expression, a predicate is essentially incomplete, an expression with a gap (or gaps) that results from the extraction of a name (or names) from an entire sentence. It is because a predicate is incomplete in this way that the insertion of a name (or names) into this gap (or gaps) yields a sentence that is capable of expressing a thought. Since it is a predicate with a copula (or a verb) that results from the extraction of a name (or names) from a sentence, rather than an adjective or noun (without a copula), it follows that Frege cannot elide the difference between a predicate and a noun or an adjective without undermining his own account of what distinguishes a sentence from a mere list.

Dudman and Wright's criticism rests upon a failure to appreciate what distinguishes—by Frege's lights—an incomplete from a complete expression. It is the fact that the former (predicates) but not the latter (names) have *argument positions*, positions that are shown to us by their successive occupation by *different* names—an appreciation of the incompleteness of the predicate "ξ scowls" thus arises from recognizing what is common to "Socrates scowls" and "Plato scowls", an appreciation of the incompleteness of "ξ admires ζ" arises from recognizing what is common to "Plato admires Socrates" and "Aristotle admires Plato", and so on. It is in this sense that Frege likened predicates to arithmetical functors, expressions of an incomplete kind that are recognized as the patterns common to (e.g.) "$2.0^3 + 0$", "$2.1^3 + 1$", and "$2.3^3 + 3$" (Frege 1891: 133). Because the notion of an expression with an argument position does not essentially rely upon the presence of the copula, Frege is correspondingly free to maintain the incompleteness of predicates while dismissing the semantic relevance of the copula. Even from the perspective of natural language this should have been apparent all along. For many sentences lack the "is" of copulation, featuring occurrences of intransitive and transitive verbs instead.

We have been discussing whether quantification into the position of adjective or noun is to be assimilated to or distinguished from predicate quantification. But, according to Quine's influential views, the *only* intelligible quantification is quantification into name position. So for many this is likely to appear an idle boundary dispute: if it is permissible in English to quantify into what appears to be adjective, noun or verb positions then appearances must deceive us; they must deceive us no less than if English permitted what appears to be quantification into predicate position. So if what appears to be an adjective or noun yields to a quantifier phrase—for example, in the operation that takes us from "Socrates is wise" to "Socrates is something"—this can only be because the adjective or noun is really a name and the copula a two place predicate that relates a name of one kind ("Socrates") to another ("wise") (1970: 67). If Quine is right about this then there is no possibility of quantifying into predicate position and consequently the possibility of so quantifying provides no basis for supposing that predicates refer.

19.2.1 Quine's Animadversions on Predicate Quantification

Is Quine right to insist that only quantification into name position is intelligible? He offers a battery of related reasons for doing so.[17] For present purposes it is important to bring into focus one key argument that Quine employs. It appeals to a link between quantification and naming:

Consider first some ordinary quantifications: '$(\exists x)(x$ walks)', '$(x)(x$ walks)', '$(\exists x)(x$ is a prime number)'. The open sentence after the quantifier shows 'x' in a position where a name could stand; a name of a walker, for instance, or of a prime number. The quantifications do not mean that names walk or are prime; what are said to walk or be prime are things that could be named *by* names in those positions. To put the predicate letter 'F' in a quantifier, then, is to treat predicate positions suddenly as name positions, and hence to treat predicates as names of entities of some sort.   (Quine, 1970: 66–7)

Predicates have attributes as their 'intensions' or meanings (or would if there were attributes), and they have sets as their extensions; but they are names of neither. Variables eligible for quantification therefore do not belong in predicate position. They belong in name positions.   (1970: 67)

The argument of these passages may be schematized in the form,

(A) Variables eligible for quantification occur only in name position.
(B) Predicates are neither names of their intensions (meanings) nor their extensions (sets).
(C) Variables eligible for quantification do not belong in predicate position.

This argument evidently begs the question. Take premise (B). Even if predicates are neither names of their intensions nor their extensions it does not follow that predicates cannot stand in a semantically significant relation—call it reference if you like—to other items. It remains open that (e.g.) predicates pick out—without being names—referents that are neither intensions nor extensions, worldly items that are available to fall within the range of a corresponding quantifier. Quine simply fails to engage with the Fregean thought that the referents of predicates are neither senses nor objects but concepts.[18]

---

[17] See Quine, 1947, 1953b and 1970: 66–8. Boolos, 1975 and Shapiro, 1991 develop the countervailing case for second-order logic. See MacBride, 2003: 135–42 for an overview and assessment of this debate.

[18] Frege's thinking about predicate reference will be explored in Section 19.4. See Heck and May "Frege and Semantics" (this volume) for further discussion of Frege's views.

Switch to (A). Since predicates occupy different positions in sentences to names this premise presupposes what the argument is intended to show. Quine supports this premise by asking us to consider "some ordinary quantifications: '$(\exists x)(x \text{ walks})$', '$(x)(x \text{ walks})$', '$(\exists x)(x \text{ is prime})$'" where the bound variable "x" figures in name position. He then generalizes from these examples: "The quantifications do not mean that names walk or are prime; what are said to walk or to be prime are things that could be named *by* names in those positions. To put the predicate letter "F" in a quantifier, then, is to treat predicates as names of entities of some sort." But this argument does not appear convincing either. Just because *some* quantifications—the "ordinary" ones in which the bound variable figures in name position—quantify over items that could be named by names in those positions it does not follow that *all* quantification quantify over items in just this way. Consequently it does not follow either that quantifying into predicate position is tantamount to treating predicates as names. Quine's argument against predicate quantification consequently fails.

If there is any substance to what Quine says, there must be another argument operating in the background of his thought that forges a more intimate connection between naming and quantification than a brute induction from ordinary cases provides. The following remark from "Reference and Modality" is suggestive of what this connection might be:

The connection between naming and quantification is implicit in the operation, whereby, from 'Socrates is mortal', we infer '$(\exists x)(x \text{ is mortal})$', that is, 'Something is mortal' .... The idea behind such inference is that whatever is true of the object named by a given singular term is true of something; and clearly the inference loses its justification when the singular term in question does not happen to name.   (Quine, 1953d: 145; see also 1939: 705–6)

The important phrase here is "whatever is true of the object named by a given singular term is true of something". How do we advance from the idea of a predicate being true of an object named to the idea of a predicate being true of something—an object for which we may lack a name altogether? Consider the sentence "Socrates is mortal." The role of the name "Socrates" is to pick out an object o. Once o is picked out the name "Socrates" drops away, its task completed ("the singular term is used purely to specify its object, for the rest of the sentence to say something about" (Quine, 1960: 142–3, 177)). The role of the predicate "is mortal" is then to be true (or false) of o regardless of how it is named—regardless of whatever else Socrates may be called. Because the predicate assumes a role that is independent of the accompanying name we are thus able to form the conception of a predicate true (or false) of an arbitrary object. It is then a short step to an appreciation of quantification itself, as what results from applying the predicate to each object in the domain.

But so far from sub-serving Quine's rejection of predication question, this account of how naming and quantification are connected leaves open the possibility that predicate positions are accessible to quantifiers. This is because nothing has been done to rule out the possibility that there are predicates and quantifiers similarly related. To make out this possibility, it need merely be established that (*i*) there is a basic class of predicates that refer to worldly items of which (*ii*) a further class of predicates are true (or false) independently of how these items are picked out. Once again, it is a short step from the idea of a predicate that is true (or false) of an arbitrary item of this kind to the idea of a quantifier that includes these items in its range.

It is important to appreciate what is unquestionably right about this line of thought: (*i*) *if* there is reason to conceive of predicates as referring expressions *then* there is a corresponding motivation to conceive of quantifier expressions that stand in predicate position as ranging over the items that predicates pick out. But it does not follow (*ii*) that if quantifiers are eligible to be placed in predicate position then predicates are referring expressions.[19]

Why? Because the idea that quantifiers of a given kind range over an associated domain of entities was arrived at *via* the assumption that expressions of the kind whose positions they occupy are independently conceived to be referential expressions, expressions that drop away once an object is picked out. So one may grant the connection between naming and quantification that Quine points to while doubting that quantification into the position of predicates involves quantification *over* items that predicates pick out, or, for that matter, anything else. The doubt can intelligibly be raised so long as it remains questionable whether predicates are referring expressions. *Contra* Quine, it appears that the accessibility of a position X to quantification cannot be used as a *test* for whether constant expressions that occupy X are referential.

19.2.2 Prior on Quantification

This criticism of Quine takes advantage of a gap in his argument—the gap that opens up because his conception of quantification runs the risk of being parochial, arising from reflection upon what may turn out to be the limited and special case of names. But one may also arrive at the same objection from a more principled standpoint. The most forceful and influential articulation of such a standpoint is owed to Prior (1971: 33–47). I distinguish two components of the view that I will call (*a*) *neutralism* and (*b*) *anti-formalism*.

According to neutralism, the mere use of a quantifier phrase does not of itself oblige us to construe the sentence in which the phrase occurs as making a statement about a domain of entities over which the quantifier ranges. Whether the quantifier is so committing will depend upon whether the constant expressions—names or predicates—that occupy the position bound by the quantifier are *already* committing. Neutralism thus rejects Quine's claim that a quantified statement is *eo ipso* a statement of existence. A quantified statement need only be construed as a statement of existence if the singular forms that gave rise to the quantified statement were

---

[19] Strangely Dummett recognizes (*i*) when he remarks "To construe the reference of predicates after the model of the name-bearer relation *entails* admitting second-level quantification as legitimate" (1973: 227) but evidently fails to appreciate (*ii*) when he later adds "there can be no reservation whatever about the existence of concepts, relations and functions provided that we are prepared to admit second-level quantification (1973: 245).

(implicitly) existence affirming in the first place. Prior goes far as to say: "I doubt whether any dogma, even of empiricism, has ever been quite so muddling as the dogma that to be is to be the value of a variable" (1963: 118).

Prior provides support for neutralism by appealing to examples from natural language. He asks us to consider, for example, the sentence "I hurt him by treading on his toe" and its existential generalization "I hurt him somehow." Since there is no need to construe the adverbial phrase "by treading on his toe" as a referring expression, there is no need to construe the quantifier phrase "somehow" that replaces it as ontologically committing either. The adverbial quantifier "somehow" simply does generally what the adverbial phrase "by treading on his toes" does singularly: "no grammarian would count 'somehow' as anything but an adverb, functioning in 'I hurt him somehow' exactly as the adverbial phrase 'by treading on his toe' does in 'I hurt him by treading on his toe'" (Prior, 1971: 37). Appeal is thus made to the idea that the role of a quantifier that binds a position X is to generalize upon the semantic function of the category of constant expressions that occupy X; *how* a quantifier generalizes depends upon *what* semantic function the corresponding category of constant expressions perform.

This conception is neutral because it does not presuppose that quantifiers generalize in a uniform way upon the categories of expressions whose positions they bind. This opens up the possibility that different categories of constant expressions perform different semantic functions and hence that different styles of quantifier generalize in different *sui generis* ways. Whether this possibility is realized will depend upon whether the similarities and differences that obtain among the different categories of constant expressions signal underlying differences of semantic function. So it cannot be assumed—by Quine or anyone else—that just because name quantifiers range over a domain of entities to which names refer, predicate quantifiers must range likewise over a domain. Whether predicate quantifiers carry with them an associated ontology, as name quantifiers do, will depend upon whether names and predicates function in relevantly similar ways, picking out elements of a domain.

The neutral component of Prior's view is open to a substitutional development.[20] Developed in such a way, a variable that occurs in a position X in a given sentence is thought of as a place marker for constant expressions of the grammatical class Ξ that are eligible to be inserted into X. The sentence that results from binding this

---

[20] Witness Marcus and Sellars' treatment of quantifiers and ontological commitment. Like Prior, Marcus advocates a neutral conception: "where we are *already* ontologically committed in some sense, then, all right: to be is to be the value of a variable" (see her 1971: 78). Marcus later adds the clarification: "There are even in ordinary use, quantifier phrases that seem to be ontologically more neutral, as in 'It is sometimes the case that species and kinds are, in the course of evolution, extinguished.' It does not seem to me that the presence there of a quantifier *forces* an ontology of kinds or species. If the case is to be made for reference of kind terms, it would have to be made, as for proper names, independently" (Marcus, 1978: 121–2). Sellars comes close to entertaining the same view when he remarks, "there is no general correspondence between *existentially quantified formulae* and *existence statements*. Only in those cases where the variable which is quantified is a variable of which the values are singular terms will a quantified formula be the counterpart of an existence statement" (Sellars, 1960: 255). Unlike Prior, Sellars and Marcus develop the neutral insight in a substitutional way.

variable with a universal quantifier is true if and only if every sentence that results from inserting a Ξ constant into X is true. The sentence that results from binding the variable with an existential quantifier is true if and only if at least one sentence that results from inserting a Ξ constant into X is true. This account of the quantifiers is neutral in the following sense. Whether a quantifier is ontologically committing will depend upon whether the class of constants that provide substitution instances for the variables it binds are referential expressions.

There is, however, no obligation to develop the neutral conception in this way, and Prior resists it. The substitutional treatment of quantifiers encounters a familiar difficulty. The sentence "I hurt him somehow" may be true even though there is no adverb in our language that specifies how it was done—how it was done may be literally unspeakable. So this sentence may be true even though there fails to be at least one sentence that results from inserting a constant into the position occupied by "somehow"; it is not a necessary condition of "I hurt him somehow" being true that such a sentence exists.

To avoid this difficulty Prior appeals to the anti-formalist component of his view. His view is anti-formalist in the sense that "I do not think that any formal definition of 'something' is either necessary or possible, but certain observations can usefully be made about the truth-conditions of statements of this sort" (1971: 35). Prior observes that it is a sufficient condition of "something is red-haired" being true that there is a true sentence in which "something" is replaced by a specific name. But it cannot be a necessary condition because "its truth may be due to the red-hairedness of some object for which our language has no name". The only way to supply a necessary condition is to *use* the quantifier "something" to rehearse the truth-conditions of the very contexts in which it occurs:

If we want to bring an 'only if' into it the best we can do, ultimately, is to say that 'For some x, x is red-haired' is true if and only if there is some red-haired object or person, but this is only to say that it is true if and only if, for some x, x is red-haired.   (1971: 36)

The same point is then carried over to apply *mutatis mutandis* to quantifiers that bind variables of other categories. "I hurt him somehow" is true if there is a true sentence in which "somehow" is replaced with a specific adverb. But it is true if *and only if* I hurt him somehow—a necessary condition is expressed by using the adverbial quantifier itself. There is no avoiding the use of even the name quantifiers to explicate the truth-conditions of the sentences in which they occur—there is no prospect of intelligibly *reducing* generality to something else. So there can be no objection to the use of predicative quantifiers to explicate the truth-conditions of the sentences in which they occur. And because there is no avoiding their use there is no necessity to explicate their truth-conditions by assigning a domain of entities for them to range over or, alternatively, a class of constants to provide substitution instances. By deploying this insight Prior endeavours to develop the neutral component of his view so as to avoid the pitfalls of a substitutional approach to the predicative quantifiers, but without thereby being obliged to treat predicative quantifiers as ranging over the elements of a domain.

Has Prior given a convincing account of the quantifiers? Prior provides precious little argument for his view. At one point he attempts to show that there is an absurdity in the opposing view he attributes to Quine, that quantified forms commit us to the existence of kinds of entities to which we are not committed by the singular forms that entail them: "The alleged emergence of these new ontological commitments has an almost magical air about it" (1971: 43). But this argument cannot be made to carry much weight. For Quine has no need to deny that singular forms are ontologically committing. Rather quantified forms are conceived by Quine as "explicitly presupposing entities of one or another given kind" that are "not explicitly presupposed" by their corresponding singular forms. This does not mean Quine must deny that these singular forms *implicitly* presuppose such entities or that he must be convicted of incoherence when he refuses to quantify over predicative expressions because—by his lights—they are not ontologically committing (*cf.* Quine, 1939: 706–7, 1953b: 102, 113). At other points Prior seems to write as if Quine were espousing a form of reductionism about generality to which Prior's own anti-formalism is an anti-reductionist antidote. But it hardly follows from the fact that, by Quine's lights, values must be assigned to variables in a semantic treatment of object language quantifiers that Quine is committed to the absurd view that devices of generality are thereby obviated in the meta-language in which these assignments are made.

The fact of the matter is that Prior does no more than issue an invitation to think about quantification in a manner to which we are ill accustomed. But this is not really an objection to his view. It is a struggle to provide even the contrary position that quantifiers inevitably harbour ontological commitment—that existential generalizations are inevitably equivalent to existence claims—with an argument in its favour. Reflecting upon the use of "I hurt him somehow" Prior remarks, "we might also say 'I hurt him in some way', and argue that by so speaking we are 'ontologically committed' to the real existence of 'ways'; but once again there is no *need* to do it this way, or to accept this suggestion" (1971: 37). When dealing with an issue of as great a generality as *generality* it should hardly come as a surprise that arguments that are discursive and convincing are difficult to come by. But this is a source of cold comfort if our concern is to establish whether by quantifying into predicative positions we thereby presuppose that predicative expressions are referring.[21]

19.2.3 Where are We?

Let us retrace the route that led to this sombre reflection. The disquotationalist about predication says that there is no more to be said about predication than is said by

---

[21] One difficulty that confronts Prior's conception of quantification is whether it blocks or hinders the provision of a systematic semantics of the kind that Tarski and Davidson have made familiar. Different advocates of the Prior view have taken contrary views concerning whether (*i*) anti-formalism blocks a recursive definition of truth for a language and (*ii*) it is necessary to provide such a semantics. See Williams (1981: 189–217) and Hugly and Sayward (1997: 241–316) for further discussion of this and related issues.

the instances of the schema (P) "F" applies to x iff x is F. Whether a predicate can be used in this way to provide an exhaustive account of its own application conditions depends upon whether there is some aspect of the use of predicates for which (P) cannot account. Quantification became an issue for us because of the connection that obtains between quantification and reference in the case of names; a quantifier that binds name position quantifies over the referents of names that are eligible to be inserted into this position. If a similar connection obtains in the case of predicates then (P) fails to capture everything there is to be said about predicates; it fails to capture the fact that predicates are referring expressions. However, even if it is admitted that devices of generality may bind positions in which predicative expressions occur, it does not follow that predicative expressions have reference. This is because it remains to be established that if predicative quantification is admitted such quantification is relevantly akin to the more familiar name kind that inevitably brings reference in its wake. Recognizing this reveals a gap in Quine's arguments *against* quantification into predicative position. For these arguments rely upon the assumption that predicate quantification—if it were admitted—would be just like quantification into name position. The strategies Quine employs suggest no means of plugging this gap that do not rely upon the prior acceptance of the thesis that predicates are referring expressions.

The neutralism and anti-formalism of Prior provide an alternative framework for thinking about quantification that denies a structural link between quantification and reference. By the lights of neutralism, a predicative quantifier is ontologically committing only if predicative expressions refer. Echoing the disquotational treatment of predication, his anti-formalism denies the necessity of assigning quantifiers a range of entities in order to account for the truth conditions of the sentences in which they occur; ultimately the role of quantifiers can only be explicated by *using* them.

If we find ourselves able to accept Prior's view—or at least the neutral component of it—then we must investigate whether predicates are referring expressions *before* settling whether predicative quantifiers range over a domain of entities. It remains unclear whether Prior's conception of quantification is acceptable. Nevertheless, the gap identified in Quine's arguments against predicate quantification indicates that there is a necessity anyway in establishing whether there are other reasons—that have nothing to do with quantification—for conceiving of predicates as referring expressions. It is therefore to an examination of the behaviour of predicates themselves, independently of their liaisons with quantifiers, to which we must turn.

19.3 IDENTITY AND IDENTIFICATION

Identity is expressed in English by those uses of "is" that are telescoped versions of "x is the same object as y". It is the occurrence of names in statements of identity that marks out names as paradigmatic cases of referring expressions. An appreciation of the significance of these constructions is owed to Frege. He laid down the requirement that if we are to understand an expression as referring to an object then we must be able to recognize the object as the same again: "If the symbol *a* is to designate an object for us, then we must have a criterion that decides in all cases whether *b* is the same as *a*, even if it is not always in our power to apply the criterion" (1884: §62). For if we lacked such a criterion of identity we would have no conception of *which* object the symbol "*a*" picked out. Indeed if we lacked altogether a conception of which object "*a*" picked out it would be questionable whether "*a*" was even being used by us *as* a name of an object. Our understanding of the fact that "*a*" is a referring expression is correspondingly bound up with our grasp of the conditions under which identity statements—that may also be called recognition statements—of the form "*a* is the same object as *b*" are true.

A grasp of the conditions under which "*a* is the same object as *b*" is true cannot, however, be arrived at independently of an appreciation of other contexts in which the proper names "*a*" and "*b*" occur. In the most basic cases these are typically constructions of the form "*x* is an *N*", where "*N*" marks the place for a common noun. These constructions are important because there is no asking after the identity of an object in abstraction from a specification of the *general kind* to which it belongs; what it takes for *a* to be the same object as *b* depends upon what kinds of object *a* and *b* are. So we cannot begin to set about answering the question "is *a* the same object as *b*?" unless we can already answer the question "same *what*?" We do so by using a common noun to say what *a* and *b* are.

Suppose that standing on the Embankment our companion points towards the Thames and says upon consecutive days "That is *a*" and "That is *b*". Whether *a* is the same object as *b* depends, for example, upon whether our companion is using "*a*" and "*b*" to pick out a flowing river or, alternatively, the droplets of water that happen to fill the river bed when the pointing gesture is made. Whether our companion is using "*a*" or "*b*" in one or other of these ways will thus depend upon his or her willingness to endorse such common noun constructions as "*a* is a river" and "*b* is a river". This is because a grasp of the noun "river" carries along with it a basis for identifying and distinguishing between objects of the river kind.

This is also why common nouns such as "river" or "person" that take the plural are often called count nouns. We may intelligibly be asked to count the number of rivers or persons there are. How many rivers? How many persons are there? Because correct counting requires that the same object not be counted twice these questions could not intelligibly be asked unless our grasp of "river" and "person" already provided a basis for identifying and distinguishing between the same and different rivers and persons. This contrasts with the case of adjectives. Like count nouns, adjectives carry with them a criterion of application; to grasp the significance of the adjective "red"—no less than to grasp the significance of the noun "river"—requires having a conception of the distinction between the things to which expression applies and those to which it does not. But, unlike count nouns, adjectives do not carry a criterion of identity with them. If asked "how many red things are there?" we do not even know where to start counting because a grasp of "red" does not settle where one red thing finishes off and another begins.[22]

The status of names as referring devices then is bound up with their occurrence in identity statements and interaction with common nouns. Are their corresponding grounds for attributing reference to predicative expressions? Obviously predicative expressions cannot themselves occur in the identity construction "x is the same object as y" or the common noun construction "x is an N"; predicative expressions are just the wrong grammatical shape to fit in the "x" and "y" positions that proper names occupy in these constructions. But are there analogous statements into which predicative expressions do grammatically fit that provide grounds for attributing a referential status to them?

Frege proposed that statements of co-extension among predicates be viewed as analogous to identity statements (see his 1892–5: 120–2). The relation of co-extension is expressed by constructions of the form "For every x, x is a Φ if and only if x is a Ψ", where "Φ" and "Ψ" mark positions that predicative expressions are grammatically eligible to fill. Statements of co-extension are analogous to identity statement in respect of the inference patterns they sustain. Where "a" and "b" are proper names and "F" a predicate, then from the identity statement "$a = b$" and "Fa" the sentence "Fb" may be inferred. Likewise, where "F" and "G" are predicates and "$M(\Phi)$" a second level predicate with an argument position for a first-level one, then from the co-extension "$\forall x\,(Fx \leftrightarrow Gx)$" and "$M(F)$" the sentence "$M(G)$" may be inferred.

Of course, this inference pattern breaks down where, for example, modal words, intentional verbs or quotation intervene. For example, it cannot be inferred from "a thing has a heart if and only if it has a kidney" and "John thought he had a heart" that "John thought he had a kidney." But the same vocabulary disrupts the former inference pattern too. For example, it cannot be inferred from "Hesperus is the same object as Phosphorus" and "John thought he saw Hesperus rise in the evening" that "John thought he saw Phosphorus rise in the evening." Nevertheless, insofar as some definite and principled circumscription can be made of the contexts that are extensional—i.e. contexts from which the disruptive vocabulary is excluded—the following analogy remains. Co-extensive predicates and co-referential names are intersubstitutable *salva veritate* in extensional contexts. It is because of this analogy between predicates and names that (in part) Frege felt compelled to construe predicates, like names, as referring expressions.

If the analogy is accepted—with the significance Frege read into it—further corroborative evidence for the claim that predicates are referring expressions may be found. Frege introduced the notion of reference in contradistinction to that of sense: whereas the referent of an expression is the item for which it stands, the sense of an expression is a particular way of thinking (a mode of presentation) of the referent. Frege introduced the notion of sense in order to account for the fact that identity statements in which different names occur are often not only true but also

---

[22] See Geach, 1962: 63–4 and Dummett, 1973: 73–6.

informative ("Hesperus is the same as Phosphorus"). Such statements are informative because in picking out the same object with different names we draw upon
different modes of presentation—different bodies of information—to amplify our
identification. In the same way a true but informative co-extension statement ("a
thing has a heart iff it has a kidney") may be viewed as a case in which different modes
of presentations associated with different predicates ("heart", "kidney") are used to
pick out the same underlying referent (Frege, 1891; Dummett, 1973: 209).

It may be objected that co-extension is too coarse-grained a relation to provide
a proper analogue of identity; that, in fact, we should be unwilling to identify the
referents of predicates unless the predicates in question are *necessarily* co-extensive.
Natural kind statements may be taken as a source of examples of predicates so
related. From this point of view "a thing is a horse iff it is a member of the
species *Equus caballus*" is necessarily true, a statement in which different modes of
presentations associated with "horse" and "*Equus caballus*" are used to pick out the
same underlying referent (Wiggins, 1984: 127–8). But even in the case of necessarily
co-extensive predicates it may be questioned whether the concepts thereby picked
out are really the same, albeit under different modes of presentation. The difficulty
we encounter here is not so much that of finding an analogue of identity for
predicates; it is rather that there appear too many analogous relations, more or less
fine-grained (co-extensive, necessarily co-extensive, structurally isomorphic . . .).

Yet whatever relation, however fine-grained, we light upon the same basic problem
remains. Let it be granted that there is the similarity that Frege makes out between
names and predicates—that predicates, like names, sustain in an extensional fragment of our language comparable principles of inference. But why think that this
formal analogy suffices to show that predicates are referring expressions? To say that
the predicates "*F*" and "*G*" are co-extensive is just to say that "*F*" and "*G*" are true
of the same things. There appears no necessity to construe "*F*" and "*G*" as referring
expressions in order to establish that they have the same extension; it appears only
necessary to determine that they are true of just the same range of objects. Why not,
indeed, turn Frege's way of thinking on its head and exploit the co-extensive occurrence of predicates to *explain away* what might otherwise have superficially appeared
to be instances of co-referring predicates? To say that two predicates have the same
reference is—from this point of view—to say nothing more than that they are co-
extensive (true of just the same individuals).

Let it be granted too that the uses of (e.g.) the predicative expressions "horse" and
"*Equus caballus*" draw upon different bodies of information. But what reason is there
to suppose that in drawing upon these different bodies of information we are exploiting different *modes of presentation* of the same referent? Why not say instead that the
predicates simply have different application conditions: that even though they apply
to the same individuals our understanding of what it takes for "horse" to apply to
an object is different from our understanding of what it takes for "*Equus caballus*"
to apply? A related difficulty afflicts Strawson's proposal that the criterion of application associated with the use of a predicate "*F*" serves as a criterion of identity for
the referent—the property or universal—that "*F*" picks out (see his 1976: 23). Say

this if you like. But why think of a predicate as any kind of referring expression in the first place? Indeed, why not take the equation of the criterion of application for a predicate with a criterion of identity for the universal it picks out as showing that the predicate is not a referring expression at all (a predicate only really has a criterion of application)? To this Strawson may respond that there is no need to treat his proposal in so reductionist a spirit (Strawson, 1979: 54). But equally, it may be stressed, there appears no need (so far) to treat his proposal in an inflationary spirit either.

The formal analogy that Frege makes between names and predicates therefore fails—at least in isolation—to establish that the latter, like the former, are referring expressions. Once again we are obliged to go looking for other reasons to construe predicates as referring expressions. By so construing predicates it may appear that an explanation is provided of the fact that different predicates apply to the same things. This appears especially plausible when different predicates are necessarily co-extensive; their extensions coincide in all possible worlds because they rigidly refer to the same property and therefore invariably apply to the same objects (whatever objects happen to instance the property in question). But while this explanation is plausible enough it is unclear what it really achieves for us. If the fact that two different predicates necessarily apply to the same objects cries out for explanation, the fact that two different modes of presentation necessarily present the same referent demands no less of an explanation.

What is it about our linguistic practice that makes it so overwhelmingly natural to construe names as referring devices? Doubtless it is (in part) the interaction of names with demonstratives ("this", "that"). We often learn to use a name "a" to refer to an ostensible object because someone points to the object in question and says, "This is a". By learning to judge whether "This is a"—what is sometimes called a 'recognition statement'—is true or false we learn to identify what "a" picks out. We do so because it is only by acquiring a grasp of the criterion of identity associated with the use of the name "a" that we are able to isolate what the demonstrative "this" is being used to pick out; if we do not, in the end, come upon this criterion we will be left at a loss as to what object "this" is being used to refer to.

Do predicates interact with demonstratives in comparable fashion so as to suggest that predicates are also referring expressions? It is certainly true that predicates and demonstratives do interact in a superficially similar way. We often come to learn to use a predicate "F" because someone points and says, "This is F". But Dummett sees an important contrast between the role of demonstrative in statements of this form—crude predications—and their role in recognition statements (1973: 232–3, 241, 406–8). Whereas in "This is a" the demonstrative is used to pick out the object to which "a" refers, the demonstrative in "This is F" is used only to pick out an object to which "F" applies. So learning how to use a predicate does not involve learning to identify something as the referent of the predicate. It just involves learning when to apply the predicate to an ostensible object, an object that is F. When the semantic contribution of names and predicates are so understood in relation to these "quite primitive linguistic performances" and "fundamental practices" the conclusion becomes inescapable, Dummett maintains, that there is nothing in the understanding of a predicate that corresponds to the identification of an object as the referent of a name (1973: 406).

The interpretation that Dummett imposes upon crude predications is, however, far from inescapable. One way in which the contrast Dummett has in mind between recognition statements and crude predications shows up is when repeated use is made of them to enable a hearer to catch onto their significance. When "This is a" is repeatedly and successfully used the demonstrative picks out the same object—what "a" refers to—again and again. By contrast, the repeated and successful use of "This is F" does not rely upon the demonstrative picking out of the same object again and again. The crude predication will succeed even if different objects are picked out each time a use of it is made. It is only required for the successful employment of the predication that the objects picked out are F. This difference arises because whereas Dummett interprets the copula in "this is a" as the "is" of identity—so that the recognition statement embodies the form "$x = a$"—the "is" in "this is F" is construed as the "is" of predication—so that the crude predication embodies the form "Fx". But this way of construing the difference between recognition statements and crude predications fails to take into account the possibility of ascribing an alternative form to "this is F".

Evidently a crude predication cannot be assigned the form "$x = a$" because, as we have already reflected the predicate letter "F" cannot grammatically figure in an identity statement. Nevertheless, as we have also reflected, predicate letters can figure in statements of co-extension. This suggests the form "$\forall x$ (this: $x \leftrightarrow Fx$)" for "This is F" where "this" occurs in predicate position and the copula expresses the "is" of co-extension. If such a predictival use of demonstratives could be made out this would provide the basis for an alternative interpretation of crude predications, an interpretation in which the referent of a predicate is picked out by a demonstrative just as the referent of a name is picked out by a demonstrative in a recognition statement.

Is it possible to use demonstratives in predicate position? It certainly is possible to place demonstratives in the position of adjectives and adverbs. Consider, for example, the predication "The rose is *this* colour" accompanied with a pointing gesture at a red book (Searle, 1970: 116). Or take the injunction "Don't talk like that." Is it not straightforward and natural to construe these demonstratives as devices of reference?

Dummett does not consider such varieties of demonstrative construction. However, he does argue independently of the grammatical propriety of these constructions that no predicate or predicative expression could perform the role of demonstrative. In order to press the analogy with recognition statements Dummett considers the possibility of a sentence of the form "For all x, $K(x)$ if and only if $P(x)$", a sentence where '$K(\xi)$' is intended to perform a role analogous to a demonstrative in a recognition statement. But what, asks Dummett, might the predicate "$K(\xi)$" be? He replies, "The only suggestion that comes to mind is that '$K(\xi)$' be a disjunction of predicates of the form '$\xi = a$'" (1973: 242). Such an analysis will fail if there are objects that lack names in the language. For then "$P(\xi)$" may be true of some object α unnamed in the language even though there fails to be a corresponding disjunct of "$K(\xi)$" of the form "$\xi = \alpha$". Dummett suggests that "we might just escape this objection by replacing the constituents "$\xi = a$" by predicates of the form "that is ξ", accompanied by a pointing gesture derived from recognition statements" (1973: 242–3). But, as Dummett next points out, this revised analysis will not help in the case of an infinite domain. Moreover, it has the absurd consequence anyway that a universal quantification involves reference to all the objects in the domain, a consequence that is absurd because "when I say that all men are mortal . . . I do not have in mind some African chief of whom I have never heard" (1973: 243).

The difficulties that Dummett places in the path of accepting a predicative device akin to a demonstrative relies upon the assumption that "$K(\xi)$" be analysable in terms of identity constructions manufactured from either names or demonstratives drawn from recognition statements (in terms of "$\xi = a$" or "that is ξ"). This is just to assume that it is ultimately through the channel of recognition statements that reference must flow. But what we have been entertaining is the possibility that crude predications and other forms of demonstrative construction provide an independent channel of reference to the world. In that case "$K(\xi)$" need not be analysable. It may demonstratively pick out its reference in the characteristic and *sui generis* way of predicative expressions. By learning to judge whether "For all x, $K(x)$ if and only if $P(x)$" is true or false we may thereby learn to identify what "$P(\xi)$" picks out by demarcating what "$K(\xi)$" refers to. Because Dummett assumes that "$K(\xi)$" must consist of ingredient expressions that refer in the manner characteristic of singular expressions his arguments fail to rule out the possibility of demonstrative identification of the referents of predicates.

While Dummett fails to rule out this possibility it nevertheless remains to be established that a referential construal of demonstratives in predicative position is imposed upon us. While it may be intelligible to interpret the crude predication "This is F" as making reference to what "F" picks out, it is no less natural to read this predication as Dummett does—as a predication of an ostensible object to which "F" applies. Of course there is no reason to suppose that crude predications must admit of only one analysis, that there is need to treat these different analyses as competing. Still the question remains: why take the referential construal of a crude predication seriously?

Yet even if it cannot be established that such a construal is imposed upon us, we should have been wary anyway of a proposal that links reference too closely to the possibility of demonstrative identification. There are just too many things inside and out of space and time to which names purport to refer to which we lack demonstrative access—objects and events in the distant past or future, numbers and other abstract objects, and so on. It can hardly be demanded that the referents of predicates be available for demonstrative identification when so many referents of names cannot be accessed in this way. But unfortunately this reflection still leaves us in the dark about whether or not predicates are referring expressions. And, sadly this is a state of affairs that is by now all too familiar.

But our troubles would be swept away if sense could be made of the idea that predicates might undergo grammatical transformation and thereby become eligible to fit into name position. Once transformed predicates would be able to figure directly in identity statements and be the subjects of common noun constructions and have their status as referring expressions confirmed that way. Because the transforms of predicates would thereby be shown to occur in explicitly referential position this would provide a basis for affirming that the predicates from which they are transformed occur in "implicitly referential position" (Strawson, 1960: 51).

It is the prevalence of nominalization in natural language—the transformation in which a verb or an adjective is turned into a noun—that makes this doctrine a plausible one. Nominalization allows us to transform (e.g.) the adjective "courageous" in "Wallace is courageous" into the noun "courage", a noun that is capable of figuring as the subject of the predication "courage is a virtue" or the object of "Wallace has courage." It is also the prevalence of nominalization in natural language that makes the traditional theory of universals so natural to adopt. According to this theory, universals are those things that can be referred by either a predicate ("resembles") or a name ("resemblance"). By contrast, particulars are things that can only be referred to by names ("Socrates"). It was a theory of just this kind that Strawson advanced in *Individuals* (see his 1959: 137–213). But the very coherence of this way of thinking—and the associated prospect of securing reference for predicates by transforming them into names—is cast into doubt by what Frege took to be an insight into the essential nature of reference itself.

19.4 FREGE ON REFERENCE

Frege arrived at this (purported) insight into reference by generalizing from the case of names. Proper names refer, or purport to refer to objects; "Russell" refers to a philosopher, "16" to a number and so on. But, in addition to proper names, Frege recognized a class of complex names that also pick out objects, for example, "the teacher of Wittgenstein" and "4^2". What is noteworthy is that complex names pick out objects because they have a structure; they refer by virtue of containing proper parts that also refer. For example, "the teacher of Wittgenstein" picks out Russell because "Wittgenstein" refers to one of his pupils. Frege identified a fundamental principle of substitution governing the contribution of the naming parts of a complex name to the reference of the whole: if a constituent name of a complex name is substituted for another with the same reference then the reference of the whole remains unchanged. Thus the substitution of "2 + 2" for the co-referential numeral "4" in "4^2" results in a complex name "$(2 + 2)^2$" that also refers to 16. From this principle of substitution Frege generalized. Noting that names occur in sentences too, Frege famously, or infamously, proposed that sentences be taken as complex names of truth-values. In this way he arrived at a principle of substitution governing the contribution of the naming parts of a sentence to the reference of the whole: "If our supposition that the reference of a sentence is its truth-value is correct, the latter must remain unchanged when a part of the sentence is replaced by another word with the same reference" (1892a: 64).

What Frege then took to be an insight was this: that substitution exerts an essential control on reference; if two expressions have the same reference then they must be intersubstitutable *salva veritate* (without change of truth-value). Call the substitution principle controlling reference that Frege endorses the "Reference Principle".[23] At first sight the Reference Principle may appear obvious or trivial. But it is far from toothless. It led Frege to deny that an occurrence of an expression inside the scope of modal operators, intentional verbs or quotation marks—what are often called intensional contexts—has the same reference as an occurrence of the same expression outside their scope—in extensional contexts (1892a: 58–9). Even though "Hesperus" and "Phosphorus" are intersubstitutable in extensional contexts (". . . is a planet", ". . . is brightly visible") these expressions fail to be intersubstitutable *salva veritate* in intensional contexts ("John thought he saw . . . . rise in the morning"). Because sameness of reference presupposes intersubstitutability *salva veritate* Frege concluded that "Hesperus" and "Phosphorus" cannot have the same reference in extensional and intensional contexts. In order to render intelligible the failure of substitutability *salva veritate* inside the scope of an intentional verb Frege argued instead that occurrences of "Hesperus" and "Phosphorus" must, in contexts of this kind, refer to their different *senses* or *modes of presentation*

The Reference Principle also led Frege to deny that names and predicates are capable of co-referring. If the name "wisdom" and the predicate "is wise" co-refer then "wisdom" and "is wise" must—at least in the absence of modal operators, intentional verbs of quotation marks that generate non-extensional contexts—be intersubstitutable *salva veritate*. But they are not. The attempt to substitute "wisdom" for "is wise" in "Socrates is wise" so far from leaving the truth-value of the sentence unchanged results in a mere list of names ("Socrates wisdom"); names and predicates are not even intersubstitutable *salva congruitate*, never mind *salva veritate*. Frege concluded that names like "wisdom" and predicates like "is wise" have "an essentially different behaviour, as regards possible substitutions. . . i.e. the references of the two phrases are essentially different" (1891: 50).

If Frege is right to deploy the Reference Principle the way he does then it follows that the traditional theory of universals rests upon a mistake, the mistake of supposing that the universal picked out by a predicate ("resembles") may also be picked out by a name ("resemblance"). It also follows that the prevalence of nominalization in natural language can do nothing to lend support to the doctrine that predicates are referring expressions. Since they fail to be intersubstitutable the Reference Principle dictates that the grammatically singular transform of a predicate cannot co-refer with a predicate. As a consequence the grammatical outputs of the process of nominalization must be interpreted differently. Either (*i*) the transformation of a predicate into a grammatically singular expression is *merely* grammatical. In other words, a logically

---

[23] To denote the substitution principle that Frege endorses Wright employs the expression "Reference Principle" (see his 1998: 73). But this principle has also been dubbed, variously: "Principle of Interchangeability", "Frege's test for identity of reference", and "Principle of Interchange". See Carnap, 1947: 51, 98, 122, Geach, 1955: 227 and Furth, 1968: 12.

perspicuous representation of the sentences in which the nominalization occurs must show that they are merely idiomatic variations on sentences in which the predicate appears untransformed. Or (*ii*) the transformation is genuinely logical in which case a perspicuous representation must show that the nominalization performs a quite different role in the sentences it occurs in from the predicate from which it is derived. In that case the fact that the nominalization of a predicative expression refers (if it does) provides no support for the view that the predicative expression from which it is derived refers too.

19.4.1 The Concept *Horse* Paradox

Is Frege right to deploy the Reference Principle the way he does? Is the Principle even true? Before answering these questions it is important to trace another connection between the Reference Principle and the issue of predicate reference, a connection that casts in doubt the very idea that predicative expressions are referring.

Frege's thinking about predication was beset by the notorious Paradox of the Concept *Horse* (see his 1891). Frege maintained that predicates are referring expressions; he called the worldly items to which predicates referred 'concepts' and contrasted them with the worldly items picked out by names that he dubbed 'objects'. Because the Reference Principle prevents predicates from ever co-referring with names—they fail to be intersubstitutable—Frege was obliged to deny that concepts are ever to be picked out by names or objects by predicates. Frege therefore concluded that the worldly division between concepts and objects is an exclusive one: concepts can no more be objects than objects concepts because the referent of a predicate can no more be picked out by a name than the referent of a name by a predicate. But this conclusion has some puzzling consequences. According to Frege, the referent of the predicate "ξ is a horse" is a concept. But what concept is it? One might expect to answer, as Frege sometimes does, "the concept *horse*". But since "the concept *horse*" is a singular phrase—that fails to be intersubstitutable with "ξ is a horse"—it must pick out an object. Since no object is a concept it follows, paradoxically, that the concept *horse* is not a concept. Worse still the predicate "ξ is a concept" cannot even be satisfied by the referent of a predicate. Grammatical propriety requires of "ξ is a concept"—like "ξ is a horse"—that its argument position "ξ" be filled with a name, not a predicate. Since names only pick out objects it also follows, paradoxically, that the only grammatical completions of "ξ is a concept" are false sentences.

What is responsible for the Paradox of the Concept *horse* arising? According to one plausible treatment of the paradox, Frege was led astray by the misleading nomenclature of 'concepts'. This makes it appear as if concepts are objects because "concept" may be used to construct definite descriptions ("the concept *horse*")to pick concepts out, and first level predicates ("ξ is a concept") to say what the referents of predicates are like. However, it may be argued, a proper appreciation of the logical—rather than grammatical—role of "the concept *horse*" and "ξ is a concept" reveals otherwise: it is really first-level predicates that are being used to refer to concepts, second-level predicates to characterize them; there is consequently nothing in this way of talking to belie the predicative nature of the underlying concepts. Frege did not avail himself of this way out. Because of the presence of the definite article, Frege felt obliged to insist that the phrase "the concept *horse*" must be construed as a proper name that stands for an object, not a concept (1892: 45–6). But one might allow for different uses of "the" and construe contexts in which "the concept *horse*" occurs as involving the completion of a second-order predicate by a first-order one. Thus in "the concept *horse* applies to Shergar", it is the "the concept ... applies to Shergar" rather than "the concept *horse*" that forms a logical unit, the former completed by the first-level predicate "ξ is a horse" where the resulting whole just means "Shergar is a horse."[24] In a similar spirit "ξ is a concept" may also be construed as a second level predicate that may be completed with grammatical propriety by a first-level predicate. Since "ξ is a concept" is intended to characterize concepts in general—where a concept is conceived as the referent of (at least) every first-level predicate—the second-level predicate to which "ξ is a concept" is deemed equivalent must be such that *any* first level predicate may be inserted into its argument position so as to yield a *true* sentence. Assuming the Law of Excluded Middle, "Φ is something which everything either is or is not" is a plausible candidate; the result of completing the argument position "Φ" by a predicate is a sentence that says the law holds for the corresponding concept. Thus "the concept *horse* is a concept" may be construed as the completion of "Φ is something which everything either is or is not" by "ξ is a horse" where the resulting sentence is "a horse is something which everything either is or is not". Since neither the construal of contexts that embed "the concept *horse*" nor those that involve "ξ is a concept" belie the nature of what "ξ is a horse" picks out—by using a name to pick it out or a first-level predicate to say what it is like—paradox appears thereby to be avoided (Geach, 1951: 133; Dummett, 1973: 216–17).

Unfortunately this response does not go deep enough. For even when the terminology of concepts is abandoned altogether it remains questionable whether the very idea of assigning reference to predicates is even intelligible. I will call this residual difficulty that survives the abandonment of Frege's terminology the Reference Problem to distinguish it from the version of the Concept *Horse* Paradox lately considered. The Reference Problem arises in the following way.[25] If there is to be any intelligibility to the claim that a given category of expressions have reference then it must be possible to say of an expression in that category that (1) it has some referent or other—i.e. to make clear that the expression is not, in fact, empty—and (2) to specify what, in particular, the expression refers to. It is easy to see how these procedures may be undertaken with respect to the category of proper names. We can say (e.g.) of the name "Myomar" that it is not empty because, in fact, there is something

---

[24] See Dummett, 1951: 102 and Geach, 1955: 228. The suggestion that Frege is misled by the definite article into thinking that "the concept *horse*" denotes an object is developed more systematically in Parsons, 1986: 455–63.

[25] Different versions of this argument are to be found in Dummett, 1951: 101; Furth, 1968: 17–21; Searle, 1970: 102–3; Dudman, 1976: 78; Long, 1978: 79; and Wright, 1997: 74–5.

"Myomar" refers to. Moreover, we can specify what "Myomar" refers to, namely Burma.

(1*) $(\exists x)$ ("Myomar" refers to x)
(2*) "Myomar" refers to Burma

But when it comes to the category of predicative expressions the Reference Principle prevents our undertaking these procedures in any straightforward way. The Reference Principle dictates that it is only possible to refer to what an expression "X" picks out by employing another "Y", where the latter is intersubstitutable *salve veritate* with the former. It follows that "X" and "Y" must, at least, belong to the same syntactic category otherwise they would fail to be intersubstitutable altogether. But the predicative machinery we use to say that an expression has reference all appear to be two place predicates ("x refers to y", "x stands for y", "x picks out y", "x denotes y") that grammatical propriety requires to be completed by names or variables fit for binding name positions—the name of an expression in one position, and a first-order variable that includes what the expression stands for among its values or a name that refers to it directly. It follows that we can neither use this vocabulary to say that a predicate has reference nor to specify what the predicate picks out. Consider the following attempt to do so.

(3) $(\exists X)$ ("ξ is a horse" refers to ...)
(4) "ξ is a horse" refers to ...

The attempt to ascribe reference to or specify the referent of "ξ is a horse" using the familiar vocabulary of reference misfires because grammar prohibits our inserting a predicate constant or variable intersubstitutable with "ξ is a horse" into the blanks marked by " ...". So whatever expressions are used to fill the blanks they cannot—by the Reference Principle—co-refer with "ξ is a horse". And since the only other forms of vocabulary apparently available for ascribing reference to predicates (vocabulary such as "x stands for y") are subject to the same grammatical prohibitions it appears that reference cannot be intelligibly assigned to predicates.

19.4.2 Three Ways Out

How are we to respond to the Reference Problem? *Prima facie* this successor to the Concept *horse* paradox presents a stark dilemma. Either it must be denied that predicates are referring expressions, or, the Reference Principle must be given up. Embracing the latter horn of this dilemma hardly seems advisable. If we give up the Reference Principle altogether then it becomes doubtful whether we can hold on to what was a significant insight on Frege's part—that there *are* very many ordinary contexts in which we succeed in picking out an individual and where what we say about it is true or false irrespective of whatever name we may happen to use to pick that individual out ("If words are used in the ordinary way, what one intends to speak of is what they mean [*Bedeutung*]" Frege 1892a: 58). If, for example, it is true to say of Venus that it is a planet with a shorter period of revolution than the Earth, then it is true no matter whether we harness one or other of the co-referring devices "Hesperus" or "Phosphorus" that pick Venus out to the task of saying that this is so. In such contexts it is legitimate to infer from the truth of the statement "Hesperus is a planet with a shorter period of revolution than the Earth" that the statement "Phosphorus is a planet with a shorter period of revolution than the Earth" is also true. Evidently in *some* circumstances the Reference Principle does receive straightforward application and a philosophically convincing account of the matter should render intelligible why in some, but not other, circumstances this should be so. To simply deny the Reference Principle is to precipitately deny the prospects of providing a philosophical account of this kind.

Must we therefore take the former course and deny predicates reference altogether?[26] To think so would appear to be a premature overreaction to the Reference Problem. For a number of intriguing proposals have been made about the semantics of predicates that suggest a variety of different ways of respecting the Reference Principle while construing predicates (in some sense) as referring expressions. They include the claims that: (*i*) the notion of reference is ambiguous as between semantic levels; (*ii*) it is only a proper part of a predicate that refers; (*iii*) whereas names figure in the reference relation to objects, predicates figure in a different *sui generis* word–world relation to concepts.

Proposal (*i*): Dummett

Proposal (*i*) arises from reflection upon the Fregean doctrine of levels. According to that doctrine, it is senseless to attempt to say the very same thing about expressions of different levels. Consequently, it is senseless to attempt to say that first-level predicates, like 0 level names, are referring expressions. It follows that if there is a relation of reference between, say, first-level predicates and the worldly items they pick out, then this relation can be no more than—as Dummett puts it—"analogous" to the reference relation that obtains between names and the objects they pick out.[27] It is also a corollary of this position that there is no such thing as *the* Reference Principle. Instead there are many such principles, for each level a different principle governing the interchange of 'referring' expressions of that level (a different Reference Principle for names, for first-level predicates, and so on).

What evidence is there that the notion of reference is ambiguous in this way? Dummett finds relevant evidence in the double use of the pronouns "what" and

---

[26] This first horn of this dilemma is arguably embraced in Furth, 1968: 23–45. According to Furth, what is intelligibly to be grasped about the notion of reference is what may be formulated in terms of the contexts "has the same reference as" and "has a reference". From the point of view that Furth develops, what it means for two predicates to have the same reference is just that they are co-extensive; what it means to say that a predicate has reference is just that every completion of the predicate by a singular term that has a reference results in a sentence with a truth-value. Of course, this does not imply, nor does Furth take it to imply, that predicates have reference in the same sense that names do.

[27] See Dummett, 1973: 171, 182–3, 218, 253, 411. See also Parsons, 1986: 451.

"which" to construct relative clauses (1973: 213–14). Contrast, for example, "what you gave me yesterday" and "what I used to be and Peter has just become". According to Dummett, the former construction is first order, picking out an object, whereas the latter construction is higher-order. It is because relative clauses of the former kind are first-order that they may be used to pick out the referent of names. Thus, for example, the relative clause "what 'Mount Everest' stands for" may be used to pick out the referent of the name "Mount Everest". Why? Because "what 'Mount Everest' stands for" and "Mount Everest" are completely interchangeable expressions (witness the sample substitution "Mount Everest is a dangerous mountain", "What 'Mount Everest' stands for is a dangerous mountain"). So their referent, if they have one, must be the same. Analogously, relative clauses of the latter kind may be used to pick out the referents of predicates. Thus, for example, "what 'ξ is a horse' stands for" may be used to pick out the referent of the predicate "ξ is a horse" because, again, the expressions "what 'ξ is a horse' stands for" and "ξ is a horse" are completely interchangeable (consider "Shergar is a horse" and "Shergar is what 'ξ is a horse' stands for").[28] However, by contrast to "what 'Mount Everest' stands for", "what 'ξ is a horse' stands for" fails to be interchangeable, completely or otherwise, with any name whatsoever. So relative clauses of the form "what 'ξ is a horse' stands for" cannot refer in the same sense as relative clauses of the form "what 'Mount Everest' stands for". Consequently, Dummett maintains, we are able to see that there is a legitimate use of "—stands for . . . " (and its cognates) in connection with predicates that "displays its analogy with (and type-difference from) its use in connection with proper names" (1973: 254).

How then does Dummett propose to use "—stands for . . . " to say that a predicate has reference and specify its referent? To say that the name "Mount Everest" has reference Dummett offers the construction "There is something which "Mount Everest" stands for." Here the relative clause 'which "Mount Everest" stands for' is naturally read as a definite description of an object, the "something" that precedes it correspondingly interpreted as a device signifying first-order generality. Accordingly, "There is something which 'Mount Everest' stands for" is just a roundabout way of saying "There is such a thing as being Mount Everest", a statement that may be rendered symbolically, "For some x, x is Mount Everest" (where "is" signifies identity).

To say that the predicate "ξ is a horse" has a reference Dummett offers the analogous construction:

(5) There is something which "ξ is a horse" stands for

How is this statement to be understood? Since the relative clause 'which "ξ is a horse" stands for' is predictival the 'something' that precedes it must be interpreted

---

[28] Dummett develops here a suggestion of Frege's: 'we should really outlaw the expression "the meaning of the concept-word A", because the definite article before "meaning" points to an object and belies the predicative nature of a concept. It would be better to confine ourselves to saying "what the concept word A means", for this at any rate is to be used predicatively: "Jesus is, what the concepts word 'man' means' in the sense of 'Jesus is a man'"' (Frege, 1892-5: 122).

as a device expressing second-order generality. Accordingly, Dummett maintains, (5) is just a roundabout way of saying "There is such a thing as being a horse" that may be rendered symbolically, "For some Φ, for every x, Φx if and only if x is a horse." Since it is "impossible" to deny that there is such a thing as being a horse Dummett concludes that "the appearance of tendentiousness in the thesis that reference can be ascribed to predicates thus apparently wholly dissolves away" (1973: 218).

To specify the referents of predicates Dummett introduces a class of predicative expressions derived from predicates in the following way. If the main verb of a predicate is the copula then the corresponding predicative expression results from dropping the copula. For example, "a horse" is the predicative expression that corresponds to "ξ is a horse". If the main verb of a predicate is other than the copula then the predicative expression results from converting the main verb into the participial form of the same tense. For example, "running" is the predicative expression that corresponds to "ξ runs". According to Dummett, predicative expressions may be used to pick out the referents of their corresponding predicates. They do so when they are conjoined with relative clauses where "what" performs the role of a higher-order pronoun. Thus "a poet" picks out the referent of "ξ is poet" when the former expression is conjoined with the relative clause "what Blake was but Hayley was not" prefixed by the copula ("A poet is what Blake was but Hayley was not"). Similarly "a horse" may be used to specify the referent of "ξ is a horse" when the former expression is conjoined with the relative clause 'what "ξ is a horse" stands for' prefixed by the copula:

(6) A horse is what "ξ is a horse" stands for

The Reference Problem arose because—it appeared—that the only machinery available ("—stands for . . .") for saying that a predicate has reference or specifying its referents are all two place predicates that grammatical propriety requires to be completed by names or variables fit for binding name positions (recall (3) and (4)). So long as the Reference Principle is respected we appear, therefore, to be left in an impossible predicament, the predicament of being unable to say that a predicate has reference or to specify what the predicate picks out. Dummett's ingenious proposal promises to extricate us from this predicament. For, according to Dummett, there is a use of "stands for" that when harnessed to the machinery of higher-order quantification, pronouns and predicative expressions enables us to say that a predicate has reference and to specify its referents without employing names and lower-order variables to do so and thereby belying its predicative nature.

It is questionable, however, whether Dummett's proposal fulfils its brief. The worry is that the higher-order variables, relative clauses, and predicative expressions Dummett employs are no more interchangeable with predicates than names or name variables are.[29] Surface grammar prohibits not only the relative clause "what 'ξ is a

---

[29] See Dudman, 1976: 78–82; Sen, 1982: 100–1; Wiggins, 1984: 132; Russinoff, 1992: 81–2; and Wright, 1998: 80–1.

horse' stands for" but also the predicative expression "a horse" being interchanged with the predicate "ξ is a horse" ("Shergar is a horse", "Shergar what 'ξ is a horse' stands for", "Shergar a horse"). They fail to be interchangeable because the relative clause and predicative expression, by contrast to the predicate, lack a copula. Predicative expressions that are participial conversions of a verb other than the copula are no more interchangeable with the predicates from which they are derived ("Shergar runs", "Shergar running"). Another failure of substitution casts doubt upon the use of higher-order quantifiers to say that a predicate has reference. If it is correct to say that there is something which "ξ is a horse" stands for then it ought to be possible to specify what "ξ is a horse" stands for. We ought to be able to construct a sentence of the form: "There is something (namely...) which 'ξ is a horse' stands for." But the natural fillings for the "namely..." clause are gerundive expressions like "being a horse"—expressions to which Dummett makes appeal—that are no more interchangeable with predicates than predicative expressions ("Shergar being a horse").

Proposal (ii): Wiggins

Proposal (*ii*) arises from an appreciation of what are perceived to be the shortcomings of Dummett's account. First consider the class of cases where a predicative expression is derived from a predicate whose main verb is the copula. In such cases the failure of interchange between the predicative expression ("a horse") and its corresponding predicate ("is a horse") appears to establish that—*contra* Dummett—these expressions do not co-refer. Nevertheless, it also appears that the predicative expressions of the relevant class *are* referring expressions. For—as Wiggins points out—the positions of these predicative expressions are accessible to a species of quantification we understand fairly well in ordinary English. We understand that if the statement "Shergar is a horse" is true then the statement "there is something Shergar is" is also true. In this latter statement the quantifier "there is something" binds not the entire predicate position occupied by "is a horse" but rather the position of the predicative expression "a horse" *inside* the predicate. Consequently the copula—that, while adjacent to, nevertheless lies outside the position occupied by "a horse"—is left unbound at the end of the latter statement when the position of the predicative expression in the former statement is bound. Moreover, it also appears that we are able to specify *what* is quantified over by the binding of the position of predicative expression in "Shergar is a horse." We do so by attaching a "namely..." clause to the corresponding quantified statement; witness, "There is something Shergar is, *namely a horse.*"

According to Wiggins the same quantificational procedures may be seen at work when attention is switched from predicates whose main verb is the copula to other predicates. In such cases it is not the predicative expression—conceived à la Dummett—that results from converting the verb into its participial form that is subjected to the rigours of quantification. It is rather the expression that results from shedding the inflections that convert the verb into its finite form; witness the transition from "John walks" to "there is something John does, *namely walk*". Wiggins concludes that while predicates do not refer, parts of them do—the parts that result from, where relevant, the subtraction of the copula or the finite form of the verb ("(a) man", "(a) horse", "(an) admirer of Hegel", "wise", "run", "walk", "sit", "work", "sleep")(1984: 132–4). So while, for Wiggins, "ξ is a horse" does not refer, it is nevertheless possible to say that a part of this predicate has reference and to specify its referent:

(7) There is something "a horse" stands for
(8) A horse is what "a horse" stands for

It is important to emphasize two questionable aspects of Wiggins' proposal. First, it assumes that expressions that occur in positions open to quantification are inevitably referring. But we have already seen this to be a questionable assumption (Section 19.2 above). For what our earlier discussion of quantification and reference showed was that it is necessary to establish whether a category of expressions are referring *before* settling whether these expressions range over an associated domain of entities. But Wiggins' proposal does nothing to establish whether "a horse" or "walk" are referring expressions independently of their occurring in positions accessible to quantification; he assumes rather that "a horse" and "walk" are referring expressions *because* they may be subjected to the rigours of quantification. Consequently Wiggins' proposal fails to establish that parts of predicates are referring expressions even if predicates are not.

Second, it is essential to Wiggins' proposal that predicates and their grammatical parts ("a horse", "run", and so on) belong to different semantic categories. It is because Wiggins conceives them to do so that he is able to deny that predicates have reference—thereby distancing Dummett's proposal from his own—while affirming that parts of predicates are referring expressions. But if the distinction between a predicate and its parts is merely grammatical then not only do Wiggins' reasons for doubting the reference of predicates become questionable but also the reasons that have been given for rejecting Dummett's proposal that predicative expressions may be employed to pick out the referents of predicates.

We have already had occasion to consider the Fregean suggestion that the copula is a mere auxiliary device without content of its own that does no more than convert a phrase into a verbal phrase where grammar demands one (Section 9.2.1 above). From this point of view, as Dummett remarks, the copula is akin to the pronoun 'it' when used to supply a grammatical subject even though the sense of the sentence in which it occurs requires none (consider, for example, the role of "it" in "it is raining") (1973: 214). If the copula (or the finite form of a main verb other than a copula) has no more significance than that of a grammatical tick then the failures of substitution that obtain between a predicate and a predicative expression are entirely superficial; such failures of substitution hardly establish that predicates and predicative expressions cannot co-refer. Similarly, if these grammatical features are entirely superficial then the failures of substitution between predicates and their grammatical parts hardly establish the predicates and their proper parts cannot co-refer either.

In that case: (*a*) the criticisms that have been made of Dummett's proposal lapse; (*b*) the differences that separate proposal (*ii*) (Wiggins) from proposal (*i*) (Dummett) transpire to be merely grammatical. Of course, it requires an argument to show that this is so—that the copula, or the finite form a main verb, are without logical significance. But it cannot be assumed that they bear logical significance either. Moreover, the arguments presented in favour of this assumption have already been seen to be weak—for what appears to be logically significant about the structure of predicates is not the copula, nor the finite form of the main verb other than the copula, but the presence of argument positions (see Section 19.2.1 above). It consequently remains unclear whether, or how, it is to be established that proposal (*ii*) is distinct from proposal (*i*), or that proposal (*i*) is undermined by substitution failures.

Proposal (iii): Wright

Proposal (*iii*) promises to lift us free of entanglement with the issues that bedevil the assessment of proposals (*i*) and (*ii*). According to Wright, predicates do not refer; nevertheless, he declares, predicates figure in an alternative word–world relation to the worldly items they pick out.[30] Predicates do not refer because, Wright holds, the Reference Principle rules out the possibility of a singular expression picking out the referent of a predicate; for if such cross-reference were possible then the Reference Principle would demand the inter-substitution of these expressions, thereby reducing a sentence to a list. Consequently the Reference Principle rules out the possibility of an intelligible thought of the form ' "is a horse' refers___" being framed; for Wright holds, *contra* Dummett, that "—refers to___" is a verb that is required by grammatical propriety to be completed by singular expressions to form a (singular) sentence. Wright takes this as a *reductio* of the assumption that the relation between predicates and the worldly items they pick out is reference, i.e. the relation expressed by the verb "—refers to___" that obtains between names and the objects they pick out. It follows that predicates and the worldly items—call them properties—that predicates pick out must figure in a different word–world relation. Wright dubs this relation 'ascription'. So whereas it is the role of a name in a (singular) sentence to refer to an object, it is, Wright claims, the role of a predicate to 'ascribe' a property. Correspondingly, whereas the inter-substitution of names is governed by the Reference Principle, the inter-substitution of predicates is governed, Wright claims, by the Ascription Principle. This principle says, "co-ascriptive expressions will be cross-substitutable *salva veritate* in extensional contexts, and *salva congruitate* in general" (Wright, 1998: 87).

What are the advantages of proposal (*iii*) purported to be? That, as we have seen, (α) it enables us to maintain a conception of predicates as standing in a semantically significant word–world relation, a conception that is not liable to *reductio* via

---

[30] See Wright, 1998: 84–90. Related versions of this proposal may be found in Searle, 1970: 97–102 and Sen, 1982: 104. By contrast to both Sen and Wright, Searle goes on to develop proposal (*iii*) in a nominalistic spirit, conceiving of the properties ascribed by predicates as "parasitic on predicate expressions" (1970: 119–21).

the Reference Principle. That (β) it is a conception of predicates that allows us to explicitly state the semantics of individual predicates. Of course, proposal (*iii*) denies that predicates are referring expressions. So, by the lights of this proposal, it is neither possible to state that predicates have reference nor to specify their referents. Nevertheless, it is possible to state that predicates have ascription and to specify their ascripta. For even though predicates cannot intelligibly refer to but only ascribe properties, this puts "no obstacle in the way of *reference* to the relevant ascripta by the use of relevant singular terms" (1998: 87). In other words, even though names and predicates cannot co-refer (or co-ascribe), the worldly items that predicates ascribe may also be referred to by singular terms. So even though ascription is expressed by a verb "*x* ascribes *y*" that grammatical propriety requires to be completed by singular expressions to form a sentence, this does not prevent us from using this verb to state that predicates have ascription and specify their ascripta. For first-order bound variables and singular terms may be employed to quantify over, and refer to, the very properties that predicates ascribe:

(9) $\exists x$ ("is a horse" ascribes x)
(10) "is a horse" ascribes the property of being a horse

What are the disadvantages of proposal (*iii*)? The most significant, perhaps, is that it is open to the complaint that ascription *is* reference in all but name, and that proposal (*iii*) does not resolve but merely masks by re-labelling the difficulties that the Reference Principle poses for the intelligible assignment of reference to predicates. Wright responds to this concern by making appeal to what he takes to be common sense intuitions about names, predicates and their contrasting roles. What does it mean for a predicate to stand in the relation of ascription? Wright answers: "for its sense so to relate it to that property . . . that it may be used in concatenation with an appropriate singular term to say of the bearer of that term that it has the property . . . in question" (1998: 88). That relation, Wright declares, is "pre-theoretically, every bit as clear as the ordinary notion of reference as applied to singular terms"; moreover "It is also pre-theoretically utterly intuitive" that so-conceived ascription is not the relation that obtains between singular terms like "the property of being a horse" and the properties to which they refer. But, *contra* Wright, a more sober assessment of the deliverances of common sense suggests otherwise.

What does seem to be "mere common sense to one innocent of Frege's thought about the matter" is that whereas names are used to pick out objects, predicates are used to describe the objects thereby picked out. But from the fact that predicates are used to describe the objects picked out by names it does not follow—at least not without further ado—that when a predicate "*F*" is used to describe some object *x*, there is inevitably some other thing *y* to which *F* is also related (*viz.* the ascriptum of "*F*"). Of course, it does not follow either that there is no such *y*—that *F* does not also lie in a relevant relation to a property or concept that semantically underpins the capacity of "*F*" to describe *x* (see Section 19.1 above). But common sense does not itself settle whether this is so. Common sense underdetermines whether predicates require a semantics that relates them only to the objects they are used to describe, or whether predicates must also stand in a further distinctive relation (reference or ascription) to properties or concepts in order to fulfil their descriptive function.

It remains the case, however, that ascription, as Wright conceives of it, *is* distinct from reference, at least if reference is the relation that obtains between a name and its bearer. For, according to Wright, ascription is the relation expressed by the open sentence (S): "ξ is fitted to be used, in concatenation with an appropriate singular term, to say of the bearer of that term that it falls under the concept Φ" (1998: 89). Evidently (S) cannot be satisfied by a name and the object it picks out—for a name cannot be used, in concatenation with a singular term, to say anything whatsoever. It follows that the intelligible avenue for the expression of the thought that ascription is no more than reference in disguise is that ascription is a composite relation—roughly speaking, a composite of the reference relation between predicates and properties, and the functional relation between predicates and singular terms that enables predicates to be used to describe the objects picked out by singular terms. However, Wright dismisses the suggestion that ascription is a composite relation, demanding "an argument that this is so—that it is a definite mistake to treat ascription as a *sui generis* form of relation between an expression and a concept" (1998: 89). He goes on to express scepticism that such an argument will be forthcoming, an argument that isolates a common ingredient in the way predicates and singular terms relate to their associated properties/concepts and objects without rubbing out the all too obvious differences that obtain between predicates and singular terms. But it is entirely unclear what warrants Wright's scepticism here. For Wright's own description of ascription is composite: (S) not only incorporates *reference* to the concept Φ ascribed by the predicate ξ (for some Φ and ξ) but also points up the functional *difference* between predicates and singular terms with respect to describing the bearers of singular terms. Wright therefore owes an argument on behalf of proposal (*iii*) that ascription is, despite appearances, a *sui generis* form of relation and that it is a definite mistake to treat ascription otherwise.

We began this section with a dilemma: either predicates fail to have reference or the Reference Principle must be given up. Three proposals that attempt in different ways to evade this dilemma have been considered. Enough has now been said to indicate that each of these proposals faces significant difficulties of its own, although it remains to be established that any can be ruled out of court. Nevertheless each of these proposals assumes that there is a theoretical necessity to uphold the Reference Principle in full generality. However in the next section I will argue there is no such necessity. The Reference Problem results from a misconception about the Reference Principle. Once we see that the Reference Problem results from such a misconception, it will become evident that Frege did nothing to establish that predicates and their corresponding nominalizations cannot co-refer.

19.4.3 Suspending the Reference Principle

The Reference Principle was introduced in the following terms: co-referential expressions are intersubstitutable *salva veritate*. So stated the principle is open to familiar counter-examples. For example, as we have seen, "Hesperus" and "Phosphorus" are co-referential but still fail to be intersubstitutable *salva veritate* inside the scope of an intentional verb like "believes" or "knows". Modal operators and contexts of direct quotation generate other familiar counter-examples. To preserve the Reference Principle it is therefore necessary to restrict the principle so as to exclude the troublesome contexts that generate counter-examples to it—to exclude so-called 'intensional' contexts in which there is no guarantee that the substitution of co-referential expressions will preserve truth-value. In order for this restriction to be justified—rather than an *ad hoc* manoeuvre to preserve an otherwise appealing principle—it is also necessary to offer an account of what the features of these contexts are that result in the intelligible suspension of the Reference Principle.

What these features are will vary from case to case. In the case of a statement involving an intentional verb it is plausible, as Frege proposed, that the truth-value of the whole is a function not of the usual referent of a singular term but of the sense or mode of presentation of its usual referent. In other cases different accounts will be fitting. This is nicely illustrated by an example of Quine's (1953d: 139–40). Even though the statement "Giorgione was so-called because of his size" is true, and "Giorgione" and "Barbarelli" are co-referring, it still does not follow that "Barbarelli was so-called because of his size" is also true. In this case the failure of substitution is accounted for by the fact that the context "*x* was so-called because of his size" is not only a function of the reference of "Giorgione"/"Barbarelli". As Quine puts the point, "Failure of substitutivity reveals merely that the occurrence to be supplanted is not *purely referential*, that is, that the statement depends not only on the object but on the form of the name" (1953d: 140).

Even though the details may vary of what accounts for the suspension of the Reference Principle in a given intensional context, it has nevertheless become orthodoxy to assume that intentional verbs, modal operators, devices of quotation and the like are between them responsible for what failures of substitutivity *salva veritate* among co-referring expressions there are. So it has become orthodoxy to assume that absent the presence of the familiar forms of intensional vocabulary that routinely disrupt substitution between co-referring expressions, the Reference Principle will hold sway. But it appears that the successes that have been made in explaining away some (important) counter-examples to the Reference Principle have blinded us to the possibility of others. For there are other failures of substitution among co-referential expressions even in what are routinely taken to be extensional contexts—i.e. even in the absence of what are usually taken to be intensional devices. Once these counter-examples are understood aright it becomes questionable whether Frege was ever justified in deploying the Reference Principle to show that names and predicates are incapable of cross-reference.

One significant source of counter-examples to the Reference Principle is furnished by the failures of substitution that occur between relational predicates and their converses. If we consider the fact in virtue of which it is true that some *A* is before *B* then, as Russell once remarked "it seems plain that this fact consists of *A* and *B* in succession, and that whether we describe it by saying "*A* is before *B*" or by saying "*B* is after

A" is merely a matter of language" (Russell, 1913: 85). There are, in other words, not two independent chunks of reality, one responsible for the truth of "A is before B", another responsible for the truth of "B is after A". It is for this reason that the facts of temporal succession may be fully stated employing just one of these expressions. Russell thus arrived at the conclusion that the predicate "x is before y" and its converse "x is after y" must pick out the same relation.[31] But even though these predicates are co-referential they cannot, as Russell recognized, be substituted for one another *salva veritate*. Substituting the former predicate for the latter in,

(1) A is before B

generates the statement,

(2) A is after B

a substitution that is hardly guaranteed to preserve truth-value. This is a failure of substitutivity *salva veritate* that occurs in the absence of intentional verbs, modal operators, devices of quotation etc. But it does not follow that "x is before y" and "x is after y" are not referring expressions. For the more modest conclusion to draw is simply that these predicates do not *merely* refer to the relation they pick out; the positions in which they occur are not *purely* referential.

Following Russell let us employ "succession" as a "neutral" expression for this relation (1913: 88). It is essential to an understanding of the contribution the expressions "x is before y" and "x is after y" make to the contexts in which they occur that they not only pick out the succession relation but do so in different ways to which these contexts are sensitive.[32] How so? In general there is a rule associated with the use of each n-place predicate R_n that determines how the n objects referred to by the singular terms flanking the position of a predicate in a sentence are to be correlated with the argument positions of the n-place relation R_n picks out. Thus, in particular, there is a rule associated with "x is before y" that determines that the object picked out by a left-flanking singular term in a given sentence is to be correlated with one argument position (p_1) of the succession relation while the object picked out by the corresponding right-flanking name is to be correlated with the other (p_2). But, by contrast, "x is after y" is associated with the converse rule according to which the object picked out by the right-flanking singular term in a given sentence is to be correlated with p_1 and the object picked out by the corresponding left-flanking singular term is to be correlated with p_2. It is because "x is before y" and "x is after y" not only pick out the relation of succession but also come associated with converse rules about how the objects referred to by their flanking singular terms are to be correlated to the argument positions of the succession relation that they fail to be intersubstitutable *salva veritate*.

---

[31] It is arguable that the early Frege was also wedded to this conception of relational predicates and their converses (1879: §3). See Williamson, 1985 and Fine, 2000 for related arguments in favour of Russell's conclusion.

[32] See Russell, 1913: 88 and Williamson, 1985: 257.

Such failures of substitution are not restricted to relational predicates and their converses. Consider, for example, "x is between y and z" and "x and y are end points of a line on which z lies". Since the latter predicate simply spells out what the former means it follows—by Russell's reasoning—that the latter refers to the relation that the former picks out. Nevertheless, it is because these predicates are associated with different rules for correlating objects with argument positions that these predicates fail to be intersubstitutable.

We are presented then with a significant class of cases where it appears entirely intelligible that the Reference Principle should have been suspended, suspended because the expressions in question are not merely referential; in such cases there is no reason to suppose that because relational predicates fail to be intersubstitutable *salva veritate* that they also fail to co-refer. What's more, a consideration of these cases also casts doubt upon Frege's employment of the Reference Principle to show that names and predicates do not co-refer. [33]

Relational predicates impose a structure upon the contexts in which they occur; they do so because they are associated with rules for correlating the referents of flanking singular terms with the argument positions of relations. By contrast, expressions that occur in name position impose no such structure; they are associated with no rules of this kind. For this reason names and relational predicates cannot be inter-substituted. Does it follow that names and relational predicates cannot co-refer? No. For what has already been said about relational predicates allows for the intelligible suspension of the Reference Principle in such cases. Relational predicates, we have suggested, perform two distinct semantic roles: (*i*) they refer to a relation; (*ii*) they correlate objects with argument positions. It has been argued that failures of intersubstitution

---

[33] Fitzpatrick (1960) suggests that the following example (due to Geach, 1969: 91–2) provides a counter-instance to the Reference Principle: suppose (1) The first man who ever stole a book from Sneads made a lot of money by selling it and (2) Robinson is the first man whoever stole a book from Sneads. Yet despite the fact that "Robinson" and "the first man who ever stole a book from Sneads" are co-referring (on the assumption that definite descriptions are referring expressions) the substitution of the former for the latter in (1) generates the nonsense: (3) Robinson made a lot of money by selling it. This is nonsense because "it" no longer has the antecedent "a book" which it had in (1). Geach denied that this example constitutes an exception to the reference principle, dismissing this suggestion on the grounds that the "usually recognized exceptions" to the reference principle arise "when we replace one designation by another in direct or indirect quotations, in modal contexts, or with intentional verbs like wants" (1961: 93–4). But this seems to be an overreaction to the case in hand. The more modest conclusion to draw is that the definite descriptions "the first man . . ." is not *merely* a referential expression. Wolterstorff provides another counter-example involving definite descriptions, noting that while co-referential "'John'" and 'the name "John"' fail to be intersubstitutable in the context 'We gave him the name "John"' generating, when the latter is substituted for the former, the nonsense construction, 'We gave him the name the name "John"' (see his1970: 70–1). Wolterstorff concludes that, "the following principle should not be accepted. If two expressions designate the same thing, then in substituting the one for the other in some context one never changes sense into nonsense" (1970: 71). Oliver (2005) offers a different range of counter-examples to the Reference Principle, involving centrally, cases in which definite descriptions fail to be intersubstitutable with proper names that occur in apposition to pre-modifying adjectives. Thus consider the nonsense that is produced by substituting "the referent of 'Russell'" for 'Russell' in "Clever Russell solved Frege's Paradox": "Clever the referent of 'Russell' solved Frege's Paradox."

between co-referring predicates are rendered intelligible by noting that relational predicates that agree with regard to (i) may nevertheless differ with respect to (ii). Recognizing that relational predicates are multifunctional in this way provides insight into the failures of substitution that obtain between names and relational predicates. It is because, for example, "succession" embodies the first, but not the second, of these functions that "succession" cannot intelligibly be substituted into contexts where the predicate "x is before y" occurs.

This account of substitution failures among names and relational predicates does not, however, extend straightaway to substitution failures among names and *non*-relational predicates. Monadic predicates such as "x is wise", no less than names, do not have rules for correlating different objects picked out by flanking singular terms with different argument positions of a relation. It is therefore an entirely conventional matter—one without semantic significance—whether a name is written to the right or left of a monadic predicate sign. For this reason what appears in English as "Socrates is wise" may be accurately represented in the formal language of predicate calculus as "Fa". Nevertheless, there is a rule associated with the use of a monadic predicate (e.g.) "x is wise", a rule according to which the object picked out by the singular term—whether right or left-flanking—is correlated with the argument position of the property or concept "x is wise" picks out. By contrast there is no such rule associated with a corresponding singular expression (e.g.) "being wise" that—intuitively at least—picks this property out. So even a monadic predicate imposes a structure in this limiting sense. This is signalled by the fact that when predicates undergo the process of nominalization, transforming "x is wise" into "being wise", "x is between y and z" into "between" and so on, the argument positions of the corresponding predicate expressions disappear (or, at least, are syntactically bound). Consequently there is no route back from the isolated inspection of a nominalized predicate that occurs in name position to an appreciation of the structure imposed by the corresponding predicate (whether the structure of "x is between y and z" or "x is wise") upon the sentences in which it occurs. This just highlights the fact that expressions that occur in name position do not carry the same semantically relevant structural information as expressions that occur in predicate position; this structural information is lost once a predicate is nominalized. But rather than showing that names and predicates do not co-refer, this fact provides the basis of a general explanation of why names and predicates may fail to be intersubstitutable *salva veritate* even though they co-refer. It is because the contexts in which predicates occur are sensitive to the structural information predicates carry—information that co-referring nominalizations have given up—that the latter expressions fail to be intersubstitutable with the former.

The failures of substitution that occur between names and predicates need not then betoken the absence of co-reference between these expressions. It need merely be the consequence of the intelligible and legitimate suspension of the Reference Principle in certain cases. Allowing for co-reference between names and predicates may, however, appear to carry with it an unacceptable cost—namely a commitment to a property-theoretic version of Russell's paradox.[34] For if the property expressed by the predicate "*x* is not predicable of itself" may be picked out by a corresponding singular term (viz. "being not-predicable of oneself") then it appears that either this property must be predicable of itself, or not. But to suppose either that this property is, or that it is not, predicable of itself leads to contradiction. But it does not follow from this contradiction that names and predicates do not co-refer. It need only follow, as Russell immediately acknowledged, that the gerundive expression "being not-predicable of oneself" and the corresponding predicate "*x* is not predicable of itself" fail to pick out a property. This may lead one to question whether it is the role of predicates to refer at all. But the fact that *some* predicates are determined by logic to be incapable of referring hardly settles that *no* predicates refer. After all, we do not take the fact that some names do not refer to establish that no names refer. Indeed the possibility that a predicate might fail to pick out a property—that some predicates should be empty—is just what should be expected if it is the ordinary function of predicates, at least in more favourable conditions, to refer.

19.4 CONCLUSION

What has been established by the foregoing discussion? We have a negative result. When the Reference Principle is understood aright—when it is understood what range of intelligible exceptions the principle properly admits—then it becomes apparent that the Reference Principle cannot be employed to show that names and predicates are incapable of co-reference. In particular the principle cannot be employed to show that predicates and their derived nominalizations are incapable of co-reference. But, alas, this still leaves us without a positive result. We are still without reason for affirming that predicates and nominalizations co-refer and are therefore hardly in a position to affirm that predicates are referring expressions *because* their nominalizations pick out (say) properties.

Preceding sections argued that we have no more reason to affirm that predicates are referring expressions because of their interaction with quantifiers, demonstratives and other particles. The fact of the matter is that we are neither in a position to rule in, nor to rule out, a referential construal of predicates and related predicative expressions. This state of affairs is to be lamented. It is true that twentieth century philosophy of language gave rise to an extraordinary variety of sophisticated proposals that have greatly illuminated our understanding of a number of otherwise perplexing constructions—treatments of definite descriptions, demonstratives and adverbs stand out. One might even go so far as to say that these proposals mark the high water mark of analytic philosophy. But until an understanding is achieved

---

[34] See Russell, 1903: §101 and Geach, 1955: 228–9. It is noteworthy that versions of this paradox afflict both proposals (*ii*) and (*iii*) above. See Wiggins, 1984: 134 and Wright, 1998: 90. Only proposal (*i*) evades this paradox since it retains the structure of the Fregean hierarchy. See Dummett, 1973: 254.

of predication—that most basic and pervasive of linguistic constructions—what is essential to language will remain obscured from us.

References

Armstrong, D. M. (1978). *Nominalism and Realism: Universals and Scientific Realism, Volume 1*. Cambridge: Cambridge University Press.

_____ (1980). "Against 'Ostrich' Nominalism: A Reply to Michael Devitt", *Pacific Philosophical Quarterly*, 61, pp. 440–9.

Boolos, G. (1975). "On Second-Order Logic", *Journal of Philosophy*, 72, 509–27.

Davidson, D. (1969). "True to the Facts", *Journal of Philosophy*, pp. 66, 748–64; reprinted in Davidson 1984, pp. 37–54.

_____ (1977). "On the Method of Truth in Metaphysics", *Midwest Studies in Philosophy 2: Studies in the Philosophy of Language*, pp. 244–54; reprinted in Davidson 1984, pp. 199–214.

_____ (1984). *Truth and Interpretation*. Oxford: Clarendon Press.

Devitt, M. (1980). "'Ostrich Nominalism' or 'Mirage Realism'?", *Pacific Philosophical Quarterly*, 61, pp. 433–9.

Dudman, V. H. (1972). "The Concept Horse: Critical Notice of G. Frege *Nachgelassene Schriften*", *Australasian Journal of Philosophy*, 50, pp. 67–75.

_____ (1976). "*Bedeutung* for Predicates", in M. Schirn (ed) *Studies on Frege III* (Stuttgart-Bad Cannstatt: Frommann-Holzboog), pp. 71–84.

Dummett, M. (1973). *Frege: Philosophy of Language*. London: Duckworth.

_____ (1978). *Truth and Other Enigmas*. London: Duckworth.

_____ (1981). *The Interpretation of Frege's Philosophy*. London: Duckworth.

Field, H. (1972). "Tarski's Theory of Truth", *Journal of Philosophy*, 69, pp. 347–75.

Fine, K. (2000). "Neutral Relations", *Philosophical Review*, 109, pp. 1–33.

FitzPatrick, P. (1961). " 'Heterological' and Namely-Riders", *Analysis*, 22, pp. 18–22.

Frege, G. (1879). *Begriffschrift, eine der arithmetischen nachgebildete Formelsprache des reinen Denkens* (Halle: Nerbert); partially transl. in Geach and Black 1980, pp. 1–20.

_____ (1884). *Die Grundlagen der Arithmetik. Eine logisch-mathematische Untersuching über den Begriff der Zahl* (Breslau: Koebner); reprinted as *The Foundation of Arithmetic* trans. by J. L. Austin (Oxford: Blackwell, 1950).

_____ (1891). *Function und Begriff*, Hermann Pohle: Jena; trans. as "Function and Concept", in Geach and Black 1980: 21–41.

_____ (1892). "Über Begriff and Gegenstand", *Vierteljahrsschrift für wissenschaftliche Philosophie* 16, pp. 195–205; trans. as "On Concept and Object", in Geach and Black 1980, pp. 42–55.

_____ (1892a). "Über Sinn und Bedeutung", Zeitschrift *für Philosophie und philosophische Kritik*, 100, pp. 25–50; trans. as "On Sense and Meaning", in Geach and Black 1980: pp. 56–78.

_____ (1892–5). "Comments on Sense and Meaning", in Frege 1979: pp. 118–25.

_____ (1906). "Introduction to Logic", in Frege 1979: pp. 185–96.

_____ (1979). *Posthumous Writings*. Edited by H. Hermes, F. Kambartel and F. Kaulbach. Trans. by P. Long and R. White. Oxford: Blackwell.

Geach, P. T. (1951). "On What There Is", *Proceedings of the Aristotelian Society Supplementary Volume* 25, pp. 125–36.

Geach, P. T. (1955). "Class and Concept", *Philosophical Review*, 64, pp. 561–70; reprinted in Geach 1972, pp. 226–35.

____ (1960). "Ryle on Namely-Riders", *Analysis*, 21; reprinted in Geach 1972, pp. 88–92

____ (1961). "Namely-Riders Again", *Analysis*, 22; reprinted in Geach 1972, pp. 92–5.

Geach, P. T. (1962). *Reference and Generality*. Ithaca: Cornell University Press.

____ (1972). *Logic Matters*. Oxford: Basil Blackwell.

____ (1974). "Names and Identity", in S. Guttenplan (ed) *Mind and Language* (Oxford: Oxford University Press), pp. 139–58.

____ (1980). "Strawson on Subject and Predicate", in Van Straaten (ed.), pp. 174–88.

Geach, P. and M. Black (eds.) (1980). *Translations from the Philosophical Writings of Gottlob Frege*. Oxford: Basil Blackwell, 3rd edn.

Hochberg, H. (1978). "Nominalism, General Terms and Predication", *The Monist*, 71; reprinted in his *Logic, Ontology and Language* (München Wein: Philosophia Verlag, 1984), pp. 133–48.

Hugly, P. and Sayward, C. (1997). *Intensionality and Truth: An Essay on the Philosophy of A.N. Prior*. London: Kluwer Academic Publishers.

Long, P. (1978). "Are Predicates and Relational Expressions Incomplete?", *Philosophical Review*, 78, 90–8.

MacBride, F. (2003). "Speaking with Shadows: A Study of Neo-Logicism", *British Journal for the Philosophy of Science*, 54, pp. 103–63.

____ (2005). "Properties and Predicates: An Examination of P. K. Sen's Theory of Universals", in A. Chakrabarty and P. F. Strawson (eds.) *Universals, Qualities, Concepts: New Essays on Meaning of Predicates* (Aldershot: Ashgate), pp. 67–90.

Marcus, R. (1972). "Quantification and Ontology", *Noûs*, 6, pp. 240–50; reprinted in Marcus 1993, pp. 76–87.

____ (1978). "Nominalism and the Substitutional Quantifier", *The Monist*, 71, pp. 351–362; reprinted in Marcus 1993, pp. 112–26.

____ (1993). *Modalities: Philosophical Essays*. New York: Oxford University Press.

Moore, G. E. (1898). "The Nature of Judgement", *Mind*, pp. 176–93.

Oliver, A. (2005). "The Reference Principle", *Analysis*, 65, pp. 177–81.

Parsons, T. (1986). "Why Frege Should Not Have Said 'The Concept *Horse* is Not a Concept'", *History of Philosophy Quarterly*, 3, pp. 449–65.

Prior, A. N. (1971). *Objects of Thought*. Edited by P. T. Geach and A. Kenny. Oxford: Oxford University Press.

Quine, W. V. O. (1939). "Designation and Existence", *Journal of Philosophy*, 36, pp. 701–9.

____ (1947). "On Universals", *Journal of Symbolic Logic*, 12, pp. 74–84.

____ (1948). "On What There Is", *Review of Metaphysics*, 2, pp. 21–38; reprinted in Quine 1953, pp. 1–19.

____ (1953). *From a Logical Point of View*. Cambridge, Mass.: Harvard University Press.

____ (1953b). "Logic and the Reification of Universals", in Quine, 1953, pp 102–29.

____ (1953c). "Notes on the Theory of Reference", in Quine, 1953, pp. 130–8.

____ (1953d). "Reference and Modality", in Quine, 1953, pp. 139–59

____ (1960). *Word and Object*. Harvard: Harvard University Press.

____ (1969a). "Ontological Relativity", *Journal of Philosophy*, 65, pp. 185–212; reprinted in his 1969c, pp. 26–68.

____ (1969b). "Existence and Quantification", in his 1969c, pp. 91–113.

____ (1969c). *Ontological Relativity and Other Essays*. New York: Columbia University Press.

____ (1970). *Philosophy of Logic*. Englewood Cliff, N.J.: Prentice-Hall Inc.

____ (1980). "The Variable and its Place in Reference", in Z. Van Straaten (ed.), pp. 164–73.

Ramsey, F. P. (1925). "Universals", *Mind*, 34, pp. 401–17; reprinted in his *Philosophical Papers*, edited by D. H. Mellor (Cambridge: Cambridge University Press), pp. 8–30.

Russell, B. (1903). *The Principles of Mathematics*. London: George Allen and Unwin Ltd.

—— (1912). *The Problems of Philosophy*. Oxford: Oxford University Press.

—— (1913). *Theory of Knowledge: The 1913 Manuscript*, edited by E. R. Eames I collaboration with K. Blackwell (London: Routledge, 1992).

Russinoff, S. (1992). "Frege and Dummett on the Problem with the Concept *Horse*", *Noûs*, 26, pp. 63–78.

Searle, J. R. (1970). *Speech Acts: An Essay in the Philosophy of Language*. Cambridge: Cambridge University Press.

Sellars, W. (1960). "Grammar and Existence: A Preface to Ontology", *Mind*, 69, pp. 499–533; reprinted in his *Science, Perception and Reality* (London: Routledge and Kegan Paul, 1963), pp. 247–81.

Sen, P. K. (1982). "Universals and Concepts", in P. K. Sen (ed.) *Logical Form, Predication and Identity*, Jadvapur Studies in Philosophy, vol. 4 (Delhi: Macmillan); reprinted in his *Reference and Truth* (Delhi: Indian Council of Philosophical Research, 1991), pp. 82–110.

Shapiro, S. (1991). *Foundations without Foundationalism: A Case for Second-Order Logic*. Oxford: Clarendon Press.

Strawson, P. F. (1959). *Individuals*. London: Methuen.

—— (1961). "Singular Terms and Predication", *Journal of Philosophy*, 58, pp. 393–412.

—— (1974). *Subject and Predicate in Logic and Grammar*. London: Methuen.

—— (1974b). "Positions for Quantifiers", in M. K. Munitz and P. Ungers (eds.) *Semantics and Philosophy* (New York: New York University Press); reprinted in Strawson 1997, pp. 65–84.

—— (1976). "Entity and Identity", in H. D. Lewis (ed.) *Contemporary British Philosophy*, Fourth Series (London: George Allen and Unwin), 193–219; reprinted in Strawson 1997, pp. 21–51.

—— (1979). "Universals", in *Midwest Studies in Philosophy, Vol. 14: Studies in Metaphysics*; reprinted in Strawson 1997, pp. 52–63.

—— (1987). "Concepts and Properties", *Philosophical Quarterly*, 37, pp. 402–6; reprinted in Strawson 1997, pp. 85–91.

—— (1997). *Entity and Identity And Other Essays*. Oxford: Clarendon Press.

Van Straaten, Z. (1980). *Philosophical Subjects: Essays Presented to P.F. Strawson*. Oxford: Clarendon Press.

Wiggins, D. (1984). "The Sense and Reference of Predicates: A Running Repair to Frege's Doctrine and a Plea for the Copula", *Philosophical Quarterly*, 34, pp. 126–42.

Williams, C. J. F. (1981). *What is Existence?* Oxford: Clarendon Press.

Williamson, T. (1985). "Converse Relations", *Philosophical Review*, 94, pp. 249–62.

Wittgenstein, L. (1922). *Tractatus Logico-Philosophicus*. Trans. by C. K. Ogden. London: Routledge and Kegan Paul Ltd.

Wolterstorff, N. (1970). *Universals: An Essay on Ontology*. Chicago: University of Chicago Press.

Wright, C. (1998). "Why Frege Did Not Deserve His *Granum Salis*: A Note on the Paradox of "The Concept Horse" and the Ascription of Bedeutungen to Predicates", *Grazer Philosophische Studien*, 55, pp. 239–63; reprinted in B. Hale and C. Wright *The Reason's Proper Study* (Oxford: Oxford University Press, 2001), pp. 72–90.

CHAPTER 20

RIGIDITY

DAVID SOSA

20.1 WHAT IS RIGIDITY?

FOR an expression to be *rigid* means (abstracting from some variations[1]) that it *refers* to one and the same thing *with respect to* any *possible situation*.[2] But how is this in turn to be understood?

An example will help us work through the definition. Take a word like "Aristotle." That word is a proper name; and proper names are a clear case of a type of word that refers. "Aristotle" refers to a particular person, the last great philosopher of antiquity; in general, a name *refers* to the thing of which it is the name.

Now, consider the idea of a *possible situation*. We can imagine other ways things might have been, situations in which things are different from the way they actually are. For instance, we can imagine a situation in which Aristotle was not a philosopher. Perhaps he remained in Stagira and never studied with Plato at the Academy. Or perhaps he never returned from tutoring Alexander, or never founded the Lyceum. These situations are not actual—they do not obtain (or hold): in fact, Aristotle *was* a philosopher, *did* study with Plato at the Academy, *did* return from tutoring Alexander, and *did* found the Lyceum. But they are still possible situations:

Thanks to Josh Dever for valuable comments.

[1] Kripke (1980), p. 21 n. 21, distinguishes *de jure* from *de facto* rigidity and later, p. 48, distinguishes *strong* rigidity. See Brock (2004), pp. 283–5, for distinction of *vacuous, nonvacuous, obstinate, persistent, tenacious,* and *insular* rigidity.

[2] Kripke (1980). See, e.g., pp. 6, 10, and 48.

it might have happened that Aristotle's life differed in any of those ways. The world as it actually is of course is also a possible situation.

Now, to continue working through the definition of rigidity, we need to make sense of referring *with respect to*. It is tempting, for example, but mistaken, to understand a word's referring with respect to a possible situation as its being used, *in* that situation, to refer to something. To dramatize this error, consider the possible situation in which Aristotle was given a different name. In that situation, "Aristotle" would not be used to refer to Aristotle. Is this a situation with respect to which "Aristotle" does not refer to the same thing as it does with respect to the actual world? In the actual world, "Aristotle" refers to Aristotle. But in the possible situation we are considering, he was given a different name. So people in that situation wouldn't call him "Aristotle." It may look like "Aristotle" does not refer with respect to that situation to the same thing as it actually does.

But if I were to ask you *who* in that possible situation people wouldn't be calling by the name "Aristotle," who it is in that situation that was given a different name, you could do no better than to say "Aristotle." With respect to the situation in question, it would be *Aristotle* that wouldn't be called by that name. Even with respect to a situation in which Aristotle was given a different name, still "Aristotle" refers to Aristotle with respect to that situation. For a word to refer to a thing with respect to a situation is not a matter of its being used in that situation to refer to that thing.

For an expression to refer to a thing with respect to a situation is rather a matter of its *specifying* that situation in a certain way, as in some sense involving that thing, where this specification takes place in the actual situation, in which the expression is used. So we can use a word like "Aristotle" to specify a possible situation in which, for example, Aristotle is not a philosopher. When you do that, you have described a situation in which a particular person—the person who in fact was last among the great philosophers of antiquity—is not a philosopher. Because "Aristotle" refers with respect to that situation to the same person it refers to here—and indeed appears to refer to that same person with respect to any situation—"Aristotle" appears to be a rigid term, a rigid designator.

To feel a contrast, consider the expression "the last great philosopher of antiquity." That expression is a *definite description* that appears to pick out Aristotle, just as "Aristotle" does. And we can use the definite description too in specifying a situation. You might be asked, for example, to consider a situation in which the last great philosopher of antiquity is not Aristotle. In that case, it seems, the expression "the last great philosopher of antiquity" is *not* used to specify the situation as one involving Aristotle. "The last great philosopher of antiquity" seems to function in a very different way. The situation has been characterized as one in which something was last among the great philosophers of antiquity and something has been said about whoever that is in that situation; but there's a sense in which no particular thing has been specified *as* last among the great philosophers of antiquity. It has been made explicit, for example, that it is not Aristotle. If "the last great philosopher of antiquity" referred to the same person with respect to that situation as it actually refers to, then no possible situation will have been specified: it would be a would-be situation in which Aristotle was not himself. So whatever "the last great philosopher of antiquity" refers to with respect to this situation in which the last great philosopher is not Aristotle, it is not Aristotle. Thus, it seems, that expression does not refer to the same thing with respect to any possible situation: it actually refers to Aristotle, but with respect to the possible situation imagined it does not. So it is apparently not a rigid expression, according to the definition.

Rigidity is a feature of an expression just in case it refers to one and the same thing with respect to any possible situation. And we have seen examples of a type of expression that appears to be rigid and a type that appears not to be rigid. Proper names, such as "Aristotle," appear to be rigid. And definite descriptions such as "the last great philosopher of antiquity" appear not to be rigid.

20.2 WHY IS RIGIDITY IMPORTANT?

In his seminal book *Naming and Necessity* (1980), Saul Kripke claimed that because names are rigid designators and definite descriptions are not, therefore a certain traditional view of the *meaning* of names is mistaken. According to this traditional view (which Kripke, alluding to two important philosophers with whom the view has been associated, calls the "Frege–Russell" view), words are about things *indirectly*, in virtue of being associated with some sort of *descriptive content* where the referent is described by that content.

The traditional view was originally developed, largely by Frege, in order to deal with a puzzle, Frege's Puzzle: how can a sentence of the form "*a* is *b*," if true, differ in meaning from one of the form "*a* is *a*"?[3] If *a* is identical to *b*, then what the first sentence asserts is the identity of an object to itself. But the second sentence too asserts the self-identity of that same object. The two sentences seem to have the same truth condition, at least. And the meaning of a sentence might well be thought to amount to the claim it makes on the world, to what it takes for the sentence to be true, to its truth condition. Thought of that way, the meaning of the two sentences would have to be the same.

But of course even when *a* is identical to *b*, one might not know that (one might even deny it). And so one might sincerely utter something of the form "*a* is *a*" while rejecting the corresponding form "*a* is *b*." And here the puzzle sharpens: if the sentences mean the same, why should there be this sort of difference? If we assume that believing that *a* is *a* is a matter of some sort of *acceptance* (some positive epistemic attitude) with respect to the meaning of the sentence "*a* is *a*," then we already do believe that *a* is identical to *b*—since in believing that *a* is *a*, we already accept the meaning of the sentence "*a* is *b*" too (it is the same meaning as that of "*a* is *a*").

One way to understand Frege's solution is as denying that the meaning of a sentence amounts simply to its truth condition. Crucially, he rejects the idea that the

---

[3] Salmon (1986) is an excellent discussion of Frege's Puzzle.

meaning of an expression amounts to the contribution it makes to the truth conditions of sentences of which the expression is a part.[4] For Frege, words that have the same reference—and so in that sense contribute the same item to the truth conditions of sentences in which they appear—might nevertheless have different meanings. Consider the following example.

One of Cicero's other names comes into English as "Tully." But one might not know, it seems, might not even believe, might even disbelieve, that Cicero is Tully—perhaps you think Tully is someone else (as it were). Now suppose the meaning of a proper name is just its referent. Then the meaning of "Cicero is Tully" is just that of "Cicero is Cicero": there seems to be no possible situation with respect to which one of these is true and the other is not. Accordingly, if you believe that Cicero is Cicero, and thus accept the meaning of the sentence "Cicero is Cicero," then you have already accepted the meaning of the sentence "Cicero is Tully." And if to believe that Cicero is Tully is just to accept the meaning of that sentence, then you already believe that Cicero is Tully. But this now seems problematic: remember, one might not believe that Cicero is Tully.

In response, Frege denies that the meaning of the sentence "Cicero is Cicero" is just that of the sentence "Cicero is Tully." According to him, although the names in those sentences have the same referent (the same *bedeutung*, in his usage), 'Cicero' and 'Tully' must not have the same sense (the same *sinn*). And Frege associates what we might call the meaning of an expression with its sense, which he takes to determine—but not be determined by—its reference.

When Frege developed his views, some of what he said suggested that the senses of expressions might be thought of as descriptive. Examples he gave[5] used descriptive contents as the sort of senses speakers might associate with names. This combined nicely several years later with a view promulgated by Russell[6] about the meaning of sentences containing definite descriptions. The upshot was the conception mentioned above of the meaning of names and descriptions, according to which their meaning is fundamentally descriptive and according to which they refer (or "denote") as they do indirectly, in virtue of a particular thing's satisfying the relevant descriptive content. Russell went so far as to say, at one point, that ordinary proper names are simply "abbreviated" definite descriptions.[7]

It should now be clear how such a view would be challenged by the position that names are rigid and definite descriptions are not. If any name is supposed to have the same meaning as a definite description, then how can it be that names are rigid and descriptions are not? Whether a name refers to one and the same thing with respect to any possible situation (in which that thing exists) would now seem to depend on whether the definite description with which it is to be synonymous does so as well. But definite descriptions seem, except perhaps for special cases (in which the descriptive content involves distinctive and essential features of the object denoted), not to refer to the same thing with respect to different possible situations. And names

---

[4] See Frege (1960), p. 57.   [5] Frege (1960), p. 58fn.   [6] Russell (1905).
[7] Russell (1919).

seem to be, quite generally, rigid. The traditional "Frege–Russell" view of names thus appears to be challenged.

20.3 COMPLICATION

Although the discussion so far may seem straightforward, a doubt can be raised: take the last great philosopher of antiquity and consider a possible situation in which he is not a philosopher at all. Consider, that is, a situation in which the last great philosopher of antiquity is not a philosopher. That does not seem problematic. Indeed it seems to involve precisely considering a possible situation in which Aristotle is not a philosopher. After all, Aristotle is the last great philosopher of antiquity. So any possible situation involving the last great philosopher of antiquity involves Aristotle. If you go on to consider a possible situation in which, say, the last great philosopher antiquity *is* a philosopher but is not a great one, or in which he is great but is not last among the great philosophers of antiquity, it seems you must consider situations in which that same person—again, Aristotle—is a philosopher but not a great one, or is great but is not last among the great philosophers of antiquity. It begins to seem as if "the last great philosopher of antiquity" may be rigid after all: the expression seems to refer to one and the same thing with respect to any situation.

The simple point is that we *can* use definite descriptions, like "the last great philosopher of antiquity," to specify possible situations directly as involving particular individuals. It is true, of course, that we can also use definite descriptions, as we did earlier in initially working through the definition of rigidity, in a very different way. In that other use, the description characterizes the situation as one in which something is last among the great philosophers of antiquity; but there's a sense in which no particular thing has been specified *as* last among the great philosophers of antiquity. Definite descriptions can be used *attributively*, to characterize situations as such that some thing (or other, as it were) in the situation satisfies certain conditions. Or they can be used *referentially*, to specify situations directly as involving a particular thing.[8]

What does this point show about the traditional "Frege–Russell" theory of the meaning of proper names? That traditional view was challenged, recall, by the fact that names appear to be rigid designators while definite descriptions seem not to be in general rigid. The point noted here suggests that whether or not a definite description is rigid is a matter of use. If the meaning of a description does not disqualify it from being used rigidly, then it is not impossible for the meaning of a name to be the same as that of a description. It is not impossible for a name to have as its meaning simply a descriptive content.

---

[8] I co-opt the terms of a distinction made by Donnellan (1966). In his distinction a referential use of a definite description can refer to an item that does not satisfy the description. Here, a referential use can refer to an item with respect to a situation even if the item does not, in that situation, satisfy the description: it must however satisfy the description in the situation in which the description is used.

Importantly, if we are trying to block the use of the rigidity considerations from rebutting the traditional view of the meaning of proper names, we will have to show how rigid uses of definite descriptions are *literal* uses. Suppose, for example, it is not literally true that in a possible situation in which Aristotle is a philosopher, the last great philosopher is a philosopher in that situation. In other words, suppose it in no sense *follows* from the fact that in a possible situation Aristotle is a philosopher that the last great philosopher of antiquity is a philosopher in that situation. Then the fact that we can use "the last great philosopher of antiquity" to specify a situation directly as involving Aristotle, the fact for example that we can intelligibly consider a possible situation, so specified, in which the last great philosopher is not a philosopher, will not counter the argument that proper names cannot have the meaning of a definite description. The phenomenon in question would emerge as *merely* pragmatic, a matter of using an expression to convey a meaning that the expression itself does not have.[9]

If this is right, then investigation of rigidity has set us a task: provide an account of (the syntax and semantics of) names and definite descriptions, or of sentences that contain them, that will accommodate the phenomena we've noted. Interestingly, Russell's own theory of descriptions appears to have the resources to do just that.

20.4 RUSSELL'S THEORY

An important aspect of Russell's theory is that definite descriptions and the names by which they are abbreviated are not, in an important sense, *terms*. In the language of classical first-order logic, terms, such as individual constants, can combine with predicate symbols to constitute a well-formed formula—into which a simple sentence of a natural language such as English could be translated. But Russell's theory has the consequence that simple sentences such as "Aristotle thinks" would not be translated into the logical symbolism as "Fa." According to Russell, we should not ask for the meaning of a name or definite description taken in isolation: in isolation such expressions have no complete meaning. Rather, "Aristotle" and "the last great philosopher of antiquity" are incomplete symbols, requiring a context in order to contribute to the meaning of the more complex expression—the sentence—of which it will then form a part.

Russell develops this idea by giving a "contextual definition" for definite descriptions: he defines those expressions only *in context*. In short, he provides a method for determining the meaning of any *sentence* of which a definite description is a part. For simple sentences the method is relatively clear: for a sentence such as

(1) The King of France is bald,

the theory yields as truth conditions something of the following form.

---

[9] Kripke (1977) objects to one reading of Donnellan (1966) in something like this way.

(2) Exactly one thing is King of France and it is bald.

And in general, for any sentence of the form "The F is G," Russell's theory will render it, informally, as: *Exactly one thing is* F *and it is* G. Given that he believes names abbreviate definite descriptions, Russell would also render any sentence that you might have been tempted to translate as "*Ga*" as if, rather, the name you are tempted to replace by the constant term "*a*" were really a description such as "the *F*." So for "Aristotle thinks" you would get something like this: *Exactly one thing is* F *and it thinks,* where 'F' would express the descriptive content abbreviated by the name "Aristotle."

But Russell's method also predicts that certain sentences will be ambiguous. The theory is critically indeterminate in giving truth conditions for complex sentences in which there is more than one nested context in which the description appears. Consider for example

(3) The King of France is not bald.

That sentence can be interpreted *either* as embedding the description "The King of France" within the sentential context "_is bald," which in turn appears within the scope of the sentential operator "not," *or* as embedding that description within the sentential context "_is not bald," in which the "not" modifies the predicate "is bald." Accordingly, the contextual definition Russell has given can be applied to yield either:

(4) It is not the case that exactly one thing is King of France and is bald,

or

(5) Exactly one thing is King of France and it is not bald.

In the example considered here, because there is no King of France, the ambiguity makes a difference to truth-value: (4) is true and (5) is false. Russell (i) was aware of this ambiguity, (ii) proposed a syntactic convention that could disambiguate any formal language, and (iii) proved that, in any case, unless nothing was uniquely described by the description's content, both of the resulting interpretations of the original ambiguous sentence would have the same truth-value.[10] Russell says that in (5) the description (as it occurs in (3)) has been interpreted as having a *primary* occurrence, in contrast to the *secondary* occurrence it has been interpreted as having in (4). In a more contemporary terminology, we say that in (5) the description is taking *wide scope* and that in (4) it takes *narrow* scope (relative to the "not").

But Russell did not explicitly consider *modal* questions—issues about what could be or could have been, for example—in this connection. And although a syntactic convention may serve to disambiguate any formal language, there remains the issue of how to render the form of sentences of a natural language such as English. In the case of a sentence such as "The last great philosopher of antiquity might have remained in Stagira," there are (ignoring the further complexities arising because of

---

[10] Russell (1903).

the presence of the name "Stagira") two interpretations consistent with the contextual definition Russell gives:

(6) Exactly one thing is last among the great philosophers of antiquity and it could have remained in Stagira.

And,

(7) It could have been that exactly one thing were last among the great philosophers of antiquity and remained in Stagira.

In other words, modal expressions create a scope ambiguity similar to that we saw in the case of "not," though in this case the matter does not effectively reduce to whether the description is uniquely satisfied. Here, it seems, what's at issue is precisely whether the possible situation being described, in which something remains in Stagira, is being specified directly as involving Aristotle, or whether it is being characterized in the very different way, as containing something that is last among the great philosophers of antiquity (whoever it might be in that possible situation).

The idea that the scope ambiguity to which Russell's theory of descriptions gives rise might be used to resist Kripke's attempted refutation of the "Frege–Russell" theory of the meaning of proper names was initially developed by Dummett in the 1970's.[11] And in a preface to *Naming and Necessity*, Kripke responded by urging that the relevant intuitions can be marshaled without using any complex sentence.[12] We can, Kripke insists, observe an important semantic difference in the evaluation of such complex sentences as "It might have been that Aristotle was fond of dogs" and "It might have been that the last great philosopher of antiquity was fond of dogs." But in any case, Kripke claims, the same important semantic difference can equally be observed with respect to simple sentences

(8) Aristotle is fond of dogs

and

(9) The last great philosopher of antiquity is fond of dogs.

Consider (8). And now assess its truth-value with respect to a possible situation— let's call the situation 'S'—in which Aristotle is not a philosopher, a circumstance that only augments his enthusiasm for dogs, but in which the person that is in S last among the great philosophers of antiquity does not love dogs. Now, Kripke asks, isn't it clear that with respect to such a situation, even the simple sentences (8) and (9) vary in truth-value? Isn't it clear that with respect to S, (8) is true and (9) is not true? Didn't we indeed describe the situation precisely in such a way as to make (8) true and (9) false? Accordingly, since the variation in truth-value is between the simple sentences (8) and (9), and since Russell's theory does not predict any ambiguity in the interpretation of either of those sentences, it seems we cannot use scope

[11] Dummett (1973); Dummett (1981). See also Loar (1976); Yu (1980); and Sosa (2001); and cf. Hudson and Tye (1980).
[12] Kripke (1980), especially pp. 11–12.

considerations to resist Kripke's argument against the "Frege–Russell" theory of names. Again, the phenomenon of rigidity appears to exclude the view that an ordinary proper name has the meaning of a definite description.

20.5 USE AND DISAMBIGUATION

But recall now the simple point we noted earlier: there's nothing unintelligible about considering, for example, what else might have been true if the last great philosopher of antiquity had remained in Stagira and never become a philosopher. Recalling this point may lead us to a different understanding of the situation concerning (8) and (9) above.

Consider again situation S. What is involved in that situation? We specified S as a situation in which Aristotle is not a philosopher, a circumstance that does not dampen his enthusiasm for dogs, but in which the person that is in that situation last among the great philosophers of antiquity does not love dogs. But we might also, or instead, have described the situation—the very same situation—as one in which the last great philosopher of antiquity is not a philosopher, a circumstance that does not dampen his enthusiasm for dogs. And now it is not so clear that (9) is not true with respect to that situation. In fact, we have now used something very like (9) in describing S.

On one way of looking at the situation then, whether or not (8) and (9) vary in truth-value with respect to one or another situation is an ambiguous question. For "the last great philosopher of antiquity is fond of dogs" to be true with respect to S is just for "with respect to S, the last great philosopher is fond of dogs" to be true. And this latter sentence, we have seen, harbors, according to Russell's theory, an ambiguity of scope: We can *use* the definite description in (9) either *attributively*, to characterize S generally, or *referentially*, to specify the situation directly as involving a particular individual. And it does not seem that either use is non-literal.

Of course, (9) itself is unambiguous. Using it to specify or characterize a possible situation, however, introduces the need for precision: in specifying S with (9), do we mean to claim that the last great philosopher of antiquity is, in S, fond of dogs or do we mean rather that in S, the last great philosopher of antiquity (whoever he is, as it were) is fond of dogs? (9) can be used, *in specifying S*, in either way, compatibly with the semantics given by Russell's contextual definition.

For the "Frege–Russell" theory to be refuted, there has to be a possible situation with respect to which (8) is true and (9) is not. It may seem obvious that there is such a situation: S above. But whether S is a situation with respect to which (9) is not true depends on the status of the following claim:

(10) "The last great philosopher of antiquity is fond of dogs" is true with respect to S.

And this claim, it's reasonable to hold, is true just in case

(11) With respect to S, the last great philosopher of antiquity is fond of dogs

is true. Whether (11) is true, in turn, depends on the relative scopes of the modal operator and the definite description. And finally, which relative scopes the terms should be understood to have depends on how the description was used in specifying the possible situation.

What would be true in the possible situation in which the last great philosopher of antiquity is not a philosopher? Well, we can suppose that someone else would have been last among the great philosophers of antiquity instead. So we can say that if the last great philosopher of antiquity hadn't been a philosopher, then someone else would have been the last great philosopher of antiquity instead. Accordingly, it seems, Russell's theory cannot only *accommodate* rigidity, it can systematically *explain* the phenomenon. The relevant intuitions correspond to an ambiguity resulting from the interaction of descriptions and operators, given a thesis about the relation between material mode and formal mode formulations—a thesis about the relation between " 'Aristotle was fond of dogs' is true with respect to S" and "With respect to S, Aristotle was fond of dogs."[13]

So in noting that whether or not a definite description is rigid is a matter of use, we have not undermined the "Frege–Russell" view according to which the meaning of a proper name is just that of a description. For neither the rigid, referential, use nor the non-rigid, attributive use is non-literal. The variation in use is the product of a latent ambiguity in the semantics of the sentence used, an ambiguity that emerges in modal contexts: each use corresponds to a possible disambiguation. And the ambiguity in question is indeed predicted, plausibly, by Russell's theory.

20.6 ANOTHER ALTERNATIVE[14]

It's important to note that the so-called "Frege–Russell" theory can be defended from Kripke's modal argument in another way. Remember that the main problem for the theory is that names appear to be rigid while definite descriptions appear not in general to be. On the other hand, it does seem possible systematically to convert a non-rigid definite description into a rigid one: simply add the word "actually" (or a cognate) appropriately. So, compare "the last great philosopher of antiquity" with "the person who is actually the last great philosopher of antiquity." It seems plausible that, notwithstanding any scope issues, the latter refers to one and the same thing with respect to any possible situation. That is, if I ask you to consider a world in which the person who is actually the last great philosopher of antiquity does not go to study with Plato at the Academy, then, it seems, I have asked you (in other words) to consider a possible situation in which Aristotle does not go to study with Plato at the Academy.

---

[13] See Sosa (2001), p. 5.

[14] For further alternatives, not to be discussed here, see Kaplan (1978) and Recanati (1993).

If we think in general of expressions like "the actual *F*," as uttered in a given possible world A, as picking out, with respect to any possible world *w*, the individual that, in A, is *F*, then, it seems, such expressions will be rigid. They will refer, with respect to any possible situation, to one and the same thing. And indeed, the standard semantics for "actually" (and its cognates) has just that consequence. It appears that names could after all be synonymous with definite descriptions, only with definite descriptions that are *rigidified* in virtue of involving such an actuality operator.[15]

As with the defense of the Frege–Russell theory based on considerations of scope, above, this defense of the theory is controversial.[16] Indeed, it is almost orthodoxy in philosophy of language that neither defense is successful. Though I myself think the theory continues to hold some promise, one should consider sentences such as the following:

(12) If Gore had won the election, the actual president would be more environmentalist.

Intuitively, this sentence is ambiguous. Is it claiming that losing the election would have swung Bush in a more environmentalist political direction? Or is it claiming rather, in effect, that Gore is more environmentalist than Bush (presupposing that if Gore had won, he would be the actual president—and *I* don't mean by this: presupposing that he would then be Bush!)? In fact, *contra* the standard semantics for "actually," the second interpretation seems the more natural reading. "Actually" seems to have a literal use in which expressions such as "the actual *F*," as uttered in a given possible world A, denote, with respect to any possible world *w*, the individual that, *in* w, is *F*. A literal use of "the actual president" as part of an utterance of (12) by us is apt to denote the individual that, in the possible situation in which Gore wins, is president. So the rigidified description approach will need to accommodate the fact that "actual" (like "current," and "local," for example) has a more variable semantic value than might at first be evident. This issue is not insuperable: to begin with, a suitable disambiguation could simply be stipulated.

20.7 GENERAL TERMS

Following, in this respect, the history of discussion in this area, I have focused on the issue of rigidity as it concerns names. Because ordinary proper names, such as "Aristotle," are such a clear case of a type of expression that refers, and because the issue of rigidity has normally been treated in connection with the rigidity of ordinary proper names, it is best to develop the relevant considerations in that context. But Kripke also argued that other types of expression—natural kind terms (*e.g.* 'water,' 'tiger,' and 'gold'), phenomenon terms (*e.g.* 'heat' and 'lightning'), and ("suitably elaborated") color terms and other predicates (*e.g.* 'red' and 'hot')—exhibit the same

---

[15] See Stanley (1997).   [16] See, e.g., Soames (2002), pp. 39–49.

sort of rigidity profile as do proper names.[17] So the question arises, how should one characterize rigidity in application to general terms?

One obvious starting point would be to think of a general term's *extension*—the things to which it applies—as analogous to a name's referent. Accordingly, a general term would count as rigid just in case it had the same extension with respect to any possible situation. An immediate issue for this sort of approach is that it seems to erase any real distinction between rigid general terms and non-rigid such terms. For most any general term (that applies to things that exist contingently), it seems, there will be possible situations with respect to which it applies to things to which it does not actually apply. In other words, for most any general term, there will be possible situations with respect to which it will have an extension that is different from the extension it actually has.

Take a term like 'water.' Kripke argued that 'water' is, like 'Cicero,' a rigid term. And he took that rigidity to be significant in the necessary truth of the "theoretical identification" sentence 'water is H_2O'.[18] But of course there might have been more water than there actually is. With respect to such possible situations, 'water' would refer to that additional stuff. But, it seems, because that water does not actually exist, the word does not actually refer to it. Thus, on this view we have taken as a starting point, 'water' comes out as non-rigid.

Consider as another alternative the feature shared by things to which a general term applies (and in virtue of which the term applies to them). Suppose we thought of that as the relevant analog, for general terms, of a name's referent. Here again, however, there is the risk of erasing any distinction between rigid and non-rigid general terms. For most any general term can seem to be associated with a feature in virtue of which it applies to things it does. And even with respect to other possible situations, it seems, the term applies to the (perhaps different) things it does in virtue of those things having that same feature. Even paradigmatically non-rigid general terms seem to be cases in point.

Take a term like 'philosopher.' Such a term is naturally thought to be non-rigid. The term is not a 'natural-kind' term and it does not refer to a natural phenomenon or to a color. But even with respect to possible situations in which the last great philosopher of antiquity does not go into philosophy, and so with respect to which the general term 'philosopher' does not apply to Aristotle, it seems the feature he lacks in that world, and which lacking determines that 'philosopher' does not apply to him with respect to that situation, is the same feature as would be picked out with respect to any other possible situation (in some of which, of course he would not lack it): *being a philosopher.* So on this alternative view, it may seem as though any general term comes out as rigid, and any significant distinction between rigid and non-rigid general terms appears to be erased.[19]

---

[17] Kripke (1980), p. 134.

[18] See Gallois (1986) and Ramachandran (1992) for issues about such identifications.

[19] Salmon (forthcoming) resists this conclusion.

How to proceed from these initial considerations is still controversial.[20] An option we have not explored here is to think of a general term as rigid if anything that has the feature expressed by the term has that feature *essentially*. (Of course, this would seem to conflict with the adjectival cases—'red' and 'hot'—mentioned by Kripke.) Ultimately, the fundamental challenge[21] is to articulate a notion of rigidity for general terms which maintains the significant different—and the significance of that difference for the distinctive necessity of "theoretical identifications"—between rigid and non-rigid general terms.

REFERENCES

Brock, S. (2004). "The Ubiquitous Problem of Empty Names", *Journal of Philosophy*, 101: 277–98.

Donnellan, K. (1966). "Reference and Definite Descriptions", *Philosophical Review*, 75: 281–304.

_____ (1979). "The Contingent *A Priori* and Rigid Designators", in French *et al.* (eds.), *Contemporary Perspectives in the Philosophy of Language* (Minneapolis: University of Minnesota Press), pp. 45–60.

_____ (1983). "Kripke and Putnam on Natural Kind Terms", in Ginet, C. and Shoemaker, S. (eds.), *Knowledge and Minds* (Oxford: Oxford University Press), pp. 84–104.

Dummett, M. (1973). *Frege: Philosophy of Language* (London: Duckworth).

_____ (1981). *The Interpretation of Frege's Philosophy* (London: Duckworth).

Frege, G. (1960). "On Sense and Reference", in Geach, P. and Black, M. (eds.), *Translations from the Philosophical Writings of Gottlob Frege*, 2nd edn (Oxford: Blackwell Publishers), pp. 56–78.

Gallois, A. (1986). "Rigid Designation and the Contingency of Identity", *Mind*, 95: 57–76.

Hudson and Tye (1980). "Proper Names and Definite Descriptions with Widest Possible Scope", *Analysis*, 40: 63–4.

Kaplan, D. (1978). "Dthat", in P. Cole (ed.) *Syntax and Semantics 9: Pragmatics* (New York: Academic Press), pp. 221–43.

Kripke, S. (1979). "Speaker's Reference and Semantic Reference", in French *et al.* (eds.), *Contemporary Perspectives in the Philosophy of Language* (Minneapolis: University of Minnesota Press), pp. 6–27.

_____ (1980). *Naming and Necessity*, 2nd edn (Cambridge, Mass.: Harvard University Press).

Laporte, J. (2000). "Rigidity and Kind", *Philosophical Studies*, 97: 293–316.

Loar, B. (1976). "The Semantics of Singular Terms", *Philosophical Studies*, 30: 353–77.

López de Sa, D. (2001). "Theoretical Identifications and Rigidity for Predicates", in José Miguel Sagüillo *et al.* (eds.), *Formal Theories and Empirical Theories* (Santiago de Compostela: Universidad de Santiago de Compostela), pp. 611–21.

Nelson, M. (2002). "Descriptivism Defended," *Noûs*, 36: 408–36.

Ramachandran, M. (1992). "On Restricting Rigidity," *Mind*, 101: 141–4.

Recanati, F. (1993). *Direct Reference* (Oxford: Blackwell Publishers).

Russell, B. (1903). *The Principles of Mathematics* (London: George Allen and Unwin).

[20] See, e.g., Salmon (forthcoming), Soames (2002); LaPorte (2000); Schwartz (2002); and López de Sa (2001).

[21] As summarized by Soames (2002), p. 263.

—— (1905). "On Denoting," *Mind*, 14: 479–93.

—— (1919). *Introduction to Mathematical Philosophy* (London: George Allen and Unwin).

Salmon, N. (1981). *Reference and Essence* (Princeton: Princeton University Press).

—— (1986). *Frege's Puzzle* (Atascadero: Ridgeview).

—— (forthcoming). "Are General Terms Rigid", *Linguistics and Philosophy*.

Schwartz, S. (2002). "Kinds, General Terms, and Rigidity: A Reply to LaPorte", *Philosophical Studies*, 109: 265–77.

Soames, S. (2002). *Beyond Rigidity* (Oxford: Oxford University Press).

Sosa, D. (2001). "Rigidity in the Scope of Russell's Theory", *Noûs*, 35: 1–38.

Stanley, J. (1997). "Names and Rigid Designation", in Hale, R. and Wright, C. (eds.), *A Companion to the Philosophy of Language* (Oxford: Blackwell Publishers), pp. 555–85.

Yu, P. (1980). "The Modal Argument Against Description Theories of Names", *Analysis*, 40: 208–9.

CHAPTER 21

NAMES AND NATURAL KIND TERMS

DAVID BRAUN

NAMES and natural kind terms have long been a major focus of debates about meaning and reference. This article discusses some of the theories and arguments that have appeared in those debates.

It is remarkably difficult to say what *names* are (more exactly, *proper* names) without making controversial theoretical assumptions. I shall not attempt to do so here. I shall instead rely on paradigm examples that nearly all theorists would agree are proper names, for instance, 'Aristotle', 'Mark Twain', 'London', 'Venus', and 'Pegasus'. All of the proper names that I shall discuss are singular nouns that have no syntactic structure. Most of them refer to objects (for instance, people, cities, and planets), but some, such as 'Pegasus', apparently do not.[1]

Thanks to Kent Bach, John Bennett, Ben Caplan, Leslianne LaVallee, Ernest Lepore, Gail Mauner, Panu Raatikainen, Jennifer Saul, and Theodore Sider for helpful comments and discussions.

[1] One might initially think that an expression is a proper name iff it is a singular noun that lacks syntactic structure. But this proposal has at least three problems. First, it incorrectly entails that certain simple indexicals, such as 'I' and 'you', are proper names. We could try to correct this by requiring that names not be indexicals, but the resulting characterization would be controversial, for some theorists hold that names themselves are indexicals. (These theorists say that 'John' is an expression that refers to different people in different contexts; its referent in any context is constrained to be some individual that bears the name 'John'. Other theorists think that proper names like 'John' are ambiguous in some way similar to 'bank'. This is the view that is adopted in the text, partly for convenience.) Second, some proper names, such as 'the Nile', may have genuine syntactic structure: notice that modifiers can be inserted between 'the' and 'Nile', as in 'the beautiful blue Nile'. Also, the singular nouns 'Mount Everest',

Natural kind terms are expressions that refer to, or are in some way semantically associated with, *natural kinds*, such as biological taxa, natural substances, and natural phenomena. Saul Kripke's (1980) examples of natural kind terms include 'water', 'gold', 'cat', 'tiger', 'whale', 'heat', 'hot', 'loud', 'red', and 'pain'. By '*non*-natural kind terms' most philosophers mean terms that are semantically associated either with *artifactual* kinds (such as 'gin', 'pencil', 'sonata', 'financial', and 'sale') or with *metaphysically heterogeneous* kinds (such as 'grue' and 'nonhuman').

I begin below with proper names and the question 'What is the meaning of a proper name?' I turn to natural kind terms later.

21.1 THE MILLIAN THEORY OF PROPER NAMES

One particularly simple theory of meaning for proper names says that *the meaning of a proper name is the object to which it refers.*[2] This theory is now strongly associated with John Stuart Mill (1843), and is often called the *Millian Theory* of proper names or *Millianism.*[3] Many modern philosophical discussions of proper names have been concerned either with criticizing the Millian Theory and finding a replacement for it, or with defending the Millian Theory from objections.

Millianism is often combined with a certain traditional theory about the meanings of sentences. According to this theory, declarative sentences *express propositions*, and the meaning of a declarative sentence is the proposition it expresses. Distinct sentences can express the same proposition: for example, 'Cologne is pretty' and 'Köln ist schön' (in German) both express the proposition that Cologne is pretty. When a person assertively utters a sentence, she asserts the proposition that the sentence expresses. People also bear various attitudes towards propositions, such as belief, disbelief, and doubt. Propositions have truth-values; the truth-value of a sentence is that of the proposition it expresses. Some versions of this view say that propositions have constituent structures that resemble the constituent structures of sentences. On such views, if sentence S expresses proposition P, then the ultimate constituents

'10 January 2001', 'Queen Elizabeth II', and 'Professor Michael Dummett' should perhaps be counted as proper names, but they may have semantically significant syntactic structures. Third, some apparent proper names are not syntactically singular. For instance, 'the Pittsburgh Pirates' is a proper name for a baseball team, but it is not syntactically singular, for the sentence 'The Pittsburgh Pirates *is* winning the game' is ungrammatical.

[2] More accurately: the meaning of a proper name, *if any*, is the object to which it refers, *if any*. Contemporary philosophers of language distinguish between many different sorts of meaning, including linguistic meaning, character, propositional content, intension, and extension, to name a few. (See the entries on FORMAL SEMANTICS.) Millianism is a theory about the propositional contents of names. I ignore all other sorts of meaning from here on. I also ignore tense and context-sensitivity.

[3] This theory is almost certainly ancient in origin. It is sometimes called 'the theory of direct reference', following Kaplan (1989).

of P are the meanings of the words that appear in S. For example, 'Venus shines' expresses a proposition whose constituents are the meanings of 'Venus' and 'shines'. The combination of this traditional theory with Millianism entails that 'Venus shines' expresses a proposition that has the planet Venus itself as a constituent. This is a *singular* proposition, that is, a proposition that has an individual as a constituent. It can be represented with the ordered pair ⟨Venus, shining⟩. I shall use 'Millianism' to refer to this combined theory in most of what follows.

21.2 OBJECTIONS TO THE MILLIAN THEORY

There are four objections to Millianism that have often motivated philosophers to reject it. These objections appear in the work of Gottlob Frege (1893/1952) and are sometimes known as *Frege's Puzzles* (see the entry on FREGE AND SEMANTICS).

The first is the *Objection from Cognitive Significance*. The names 'Mark Twain' and 'Samuel Clemens' refer to the same person. Therefore, if Millianism is correct, they have the same meaning. Sentences (1) and (2) differ only in that (2) contains the name 'Samuel Clemens' in a position where (1) contains 'Mark Twain'.

(1) Mark Twain is Mark Twain.
(2) Mark Twain is Samuel Clemens.

Therefore, if Millianism is true, sentences (1) and (2) mean the same thing, and express the same proposition. However, (2) is informative whereas (1) is not: as Frege put it, (2) can contain a valuable extension of our knowledge, but (1) cannot. Furthermore, a rational, competent speaker could understand both and yet think that (1) is true and (2) is false. Finally, (1) is analytic and *a priori*, whereas (2) is synthetic and *a posteriori*. (More accurately, the propositions that sentences (1) and (2) express are *a priori* and *a posteriori*, respectively.) In short, these sentences differ in *cognitive significance*. But if they expressed the same proposition, they would not differ in cognitive significance. Therefore, Millianism is incorrect.

Frege used identity sentences to state his objection, but a parallel objection can be formulated without them (Salmon, 1986). For instance, Millianism entails that (3) and (4) express the same proposition.

(3) If Mark Twain is an author, then Mark Twain is an author.
(4) If Mark Twain is an author, then Samuel Clemens is an author.

Yet (3) is uninformative, *a priori*, and analytic, whereas (4) is informative, *a posteriori*, and synthetic. A closely related objection concerning cognitive significance can be stated using (5) and (6).

(5) Mark Twain wrote *Huckleberry Finn*.
(6) Samuel Clemens wrote *Huckleberry Finn*.

(5) and (6) are both synthetic, *a posteriori*, and informative, yet they still differ in cognitive significance, in the following sense: a competent, rational speaker who understands both could think that (5) is true and (6) is false.

The second major argument against Millianism is the *Objection from Belief Ascriptions*. Consider belief ascriptions (7) and (8).

(7) Mary believes that Mark Twain is Mark Twain.
(8) Mary believes that Mark Twain is Samuel Clemens.

These belief ascriptions are exactly alike, except that (8) contains the name 'Samuel Clemens' in a position where (7) contains 'Mark Twain'. Therefore, if Millianism is correct, then (7) and (8) express the same proposition and cannot differ in truth-value. But (7) could be true while (8) is false. Therefore, the Millian Theory is incorrect. Notice that this objection relies on the claim that (7) and (8) can differ in *truth-value*, whereas the previous objection relied on the claim that (1) and (2) differ in *cognitive significance*.

The third major argument is the *Objection from Meaningful Sentences Containing Non-Referring Names*. The name 'Pegasus' does not refer. Therefore, Millianism entails that it is meaningless. Thus, if Millianism is correct, then sentence (9) contains a meaningless word.

(9) Pegasus flies.

But if (9) contains a meaningless word, then (9) as a whole is meaningless. Therefore, if Millianism is correct, then sentence (9) is meaningless. But (9) is clearly meaningful.

The final argument, the *Objection from Negative Existentials*, is closely related to the previous argument. Consider (10).

(10) Pegasus does not exist.

If the Millian Theory is correct, then 'Pegasus' and sentence (10) are meaningless. If (10) is meaningless, then it is not true. But (10) is true. Therefore, the Millian Theory is incorrect. Notice that the preceding objection relies on the claim that (9) is *meaningful*, whereas this objection relies on the claim that (10) is *true*.

21.3 DESCRIPTION THEORIES OF PROPER NAMES

The problems with Millianism have motivated many philosophers to accept *Description Theories of Proper Names* (also known as *Descriptivist Theories*). These philosophers include Frege (1893/1952), Bertrand Russell (1911), Ludwig Wittgenstein (1953), John Searle (1958), and Peter Strawson (1959).[4] The basic idea of these theories is that the meanings of proper names are the same as those of

---

[4] It is controversial whether Frege accepted a Description Theory; see the entry on FREGE AND SEMANTICS. Nevertheless, in what follows I shall assume that the Fregean *sense* of a proper name is, or determines, a descriptive meaning of a sort like that described below.

certain definite descriptions. One particularly simple Description Theory says that a speaker associates a definite description with each name that she uses. The speaker will provide the description she associates with name N if she is asked "Who, or what, is N?" or "Who do you mean by 'N'?" [5] The description "defines" the name and determines its reference, in her idiolect. For example, when some people are asked 'Who is Aristotle?' they consistently answer 'The ancient philosopher who wrote the *Nicomachean Ethics*'. The sentence 'Aristotle was smart' expresses, in such a speaker's idiolect, the proposition that the ancient philosopher who wrote the *Nicomachean Ethics* was smart. The referent of her utterances of 'Aristotle' is the referent of the definite description.

Other Description Theories differ from this simple one in important respects, but many satisfy the following theory *schema*.

A Schema for Description Theories of Meaning for Proper Names

If S is a speaker, and N is a proper name in S's language L, then there is exactly one property P such that:

(1) P satisfies condition C.
(2) S authoritatively associates P with N.
(3) N refers in L to object O iff O is the one and only thing that is P.
(4) If F is a predicate that expresses property P in English (or in some language L' that is an extension of English), then N in L is synonymous with the definite description "the F" in English (or L').

Clause (1) allows Description Theorists to place substantive conditions, or constraints, on property P. Some sort of constraint is necessary to assure that description theories avoid the objections that plague Millianism. Suppose, for instance, that a Description Theory said that the property associated with 'Twain' in every English speaker's language is *being identical with Twain* and that the property associated with 'Clemens' is *being identical with Clemens*. These properties are the same, and so this theory would entail that the names 'Twain' and 'Clemens' have the same meaning in every English speaker's language. Certain other *relational properties* (properties whose instantiation consists in standing in relations to other individuals) must also be ruled out. For instance, similar problems would arise if 'Twain' were associated with *being the author most admired by George Orwell* and 'Clemens' with *being the author most admired by Eric Blair*, for Orwell is identical with Blair, and so these are the same property. Clause (1) is schematic because Description Theorists differ about the constraints that they wish to place on property P. Theorists with strong Fregean leanings might hope to avoid the above problems by insisting that property P be a purely general, non-relational property. Russell (1910) would allow P to be a relational property, but would hope to avoid problems with cognitive significance by requiring that the relata be objects with which speaker S is *directly acquainted*,

---

[5] I use double quotes in place of corner quotes throughout this article.

for instance, S herself and her current experiences, and the properties and relations exemplified by her current experiences.

Clause (2) uses the notion of *authoritative association*. A typical user of the name 'Twain' believes that Twain (and the referent of 'Twain') is human, is an American, is a writer, and so on. In that loose sense, typical users of 'Twain' *associate* many properties with it. But Description Theorists hold that for every speaker and name there is a single associated property that has a certain *authority* for the speaker. This is the property that determines the reference and meaning of the name for the speaker. Suppose, for instance, that S consciously introduces the name N into her language by saying or thinking "I shall use 'N' as an abbreviation for 'the P' ", and suppose her subsequent uses of N are guided by this stipulation.[6] Then Description Theorists would say that S authoritatively associates P with N. But most Description Theorists think that such a ceremony is not necessary for authoritative association. Many hold that one or more of the following are at least strong indicators that S authoritatively associates P with N. (a) Whenever S utters "N is Q", S entertains and intends to communicate the proposition that the P is Q. (b) Whenever S is asked "Who is N?", S answers "N is the P" (or "N, if he exists, is the P").[7] (c) S takes the question "Does N exist?" to be settled once S knows whether there is a unique thing that has P.

Most Description Theorists think that different people who speak the same public language (e.g. English) authoritatively associate different properties with the same proper name. Therefore, most Description Theorists think of language L as the speaker's *idiolect*.[8]

Clause (3) specifies how the *referent* of the name in S's idiolect is *determined* (or *fixed*, as Kripke, 1980, puts it): it is the object that uniquely satisfies the authoritatively associated property. Clause (4) adds something further: it specifies the *meaning* of the name in S's idiolect, by requiring that N be *synonymous* with a definite description. It mentions extensions of English, and cross-linguistic synonymy, because many Description Theorists hold that property P may be inexpressible in both ordinary English and the speaker's language L (except by using the name N).

Early advocates of Description Theories (such as Frege and Russell) seemed to assume that the property that a speaker authoritatively associates with a name is rather simple, for instance, a property that specifies a famous deed of the name's

---

[6] For the sake of simplicity, I often assume in this paragraph (and the remainder of this section) that the relevant speaker's public language is English. I also freely abuse the distinction between use and mention.

[7] A speaker might introduce N as an abbreviation for "the P", even if she thinks that there is nothing that is uniquely P and so thinks that "the P" is non-referring. (Thanks to Leslianne LaVallee for this point.) Kripke (1980) overlooks or ignores this possibility in his critique of Description Theories.

[8] See the entry on LANGUAGES AND IDIOLECTS. Some description theorists seem to allow L to be a public language (e.g., English), apparently because they think that every proper name has a single descriptive meaning in a given public language. These theorists seem to hold that the descriptive meaning of a name in a public language is determined by the beliefs of all the speakers of that language who use the name. Such theorists conceive of the authoritative association relation differently from other description theorists. See Searle (1958), Strawson (1959), and, for discussion, Evans (1973). See also nn. 12 and 13.

referent, or a property that specifies the appearance of the referent to the speaker. Subsequent Description Theorists (such as Wittgenstein, Strawson, and Searle) have doubted this. These theorists point out that speakers usually do not introduce names into their languages in formal ceremonies using simple definite descriptions. Speakers also tend to answer the question "Who is N?" differently on different occasions. Moreover, speakers tend *not* to think that questions of the form "Does N exist?" are conclusively settled once it is determined whether there is an object that uniquely has one of these simple properties. These considerations lead some Description Theorists to hold what are sometimes called *Cluster Description Theories*. According to these theories, the property that a speaker authoritatively associates with a name is (typically) a property of the form *being a thing that satisfies a majority of the properties $P_1, P_2, P_3, \ldots P_n$ when these properties are weighted in way W*. Call this a *cluster property* and a description that expresses it a *cluster description*. Cluster Description Theorists do not think that speakers consciously use cluster descriptions to introduce names into their languages or that they will produce one when asked "Who is N?". Rather, they think that the cluster property that S authoritatively associates with N is determined by more complex relations among S, N, and $P_1 - P_n$, for instance, S's disposition to think that the sentence "N exists" is true in various scenarios in which there is an object that has P_1 and P_2, but not P_3, or has P_2 and P_3, but not P_1, and so on.[9]

Description Theories seem to deal well with Frege's objections to Millianism. Suppose typical speakers authoritatively associate different properties with the names 'Mark Twain' and 'Samuel Clemens'. Suppose, for example, that a given speaker authoritatively associates the property of being an author of *Huckleberry Finn* with 'Mark Twain', and authoritatively associates the property of being a person who published U.S. Grant's autobiography with 'Samuel Clemens'. Then sentences (1) and (2) express the same propositions as (1D) and (2D) in that speaker's language.[10]

(1) Mark Twain is Mark Twain.

(2) Mark Twain is Samuel Clemens.

(1D) The author of *Huckleberry Finn* is the author of *Huckleberry Finn*.

(2D) The author of *Huckleberry Finn* is the person who published U. S. Grant's autobiography.

---

[9] The Cluster Description Theories described above entail that the referent of N has a certain disjunctive property, *being a thing that is Q_1 or Q_2 or $\ldots$ or Q_n*, where each Q_i is a conjunction of properties in $P_1 - P_n$ such that having Q_i is sufficient for having a majority of $P_1 - P_n$, when these are weighted in way W. (For instance, the referent of N has the property of being either (P_1 and P_2) or (P_2 and P_3 and P_4) or ….) Therefore, some Description Theories hold that the meaning of a proper name N is a complex disjunctive property of the above sort. The main advantage of this alternative is that it does not entail that the meaning of a proper name partly concerns an arcane weighting of properties. I shall count these as Cluster Description Theories.

[10] (1D) and (2D) contain the proper names 'U. S. Grant' and '*Huckleberry Finn*'. On most Description Theories, these names have descriptive meanings in nearly all idiolects. I ignore this in what follows (similarly for all other proper names that appear in definite descriptions).

Thus, (1) and (2) express different propositions in the speaker's language, and so the sentences can differ in informativeness, *a priority*, and analyticity, in her language, and the speaker could rationally think that they differ in truth-value. Moreover, the 'that'-clauses of (7) and (8), in her language, refer to different propositions.

(7) Mary believes that Mark Twain is Mark Twain.
(8) Mary believes that Mark Twain is Samuel Clemens.

Therefore, (7) and (8) attribute belief in different propositions to Mary, and so can differ in truth-value. Suppose this same speaker authoritatively associates the property of being a winged horse with the name 'Pegasus'. Then sentences (9) and (10) are synonymous with (9D) and (10D) in her language.

(9) Pegasus flies.
(10) Pegasus does not exist.
(9D) The winged horse flies.
(10D) The winged horse does not exist.

Thus sentences (9) and (10) are both meaningful in the speaker's language, and sentence (10) is true.[11]

Some Description Theorists deny that proper names are *synonymous* with definite descriptions, but hold that proper names have their *references fixed* by description. They accept a theory that satisfies clauses (1)–(3), but not clause (4). Let us call the schema obtained by deleting clause (4) *A Schema for Description Theories of Reference-Fixing for Proper Names*.[12] A theory of this latter sort does *not* attempt to describe the *meanings* of proper names. In fact, a Millian can accept a Description Theory of reference-fixing for proper names: such a Millian would hold that the *meaning* of a proper name is simply its referent, but would hold that the reference of the name is fixed by some description. Theorists who accept a Description Theory of Reference-Fixing, but who reject Description Theories of Meaning, cannot respond to Frege's Puzzles in the ways described above. They need alternative responses.[13]

---

[11] Sentences containing non-referring definite descriptions raise complications for many semantic theories. Russell, for instance, would hold that (10D) is ambiguous, and is true on one disambiguation and false on another. Frege might say that in (10D) 'the winged horse' refers to its customary sense (descriptive meaning). See Salmon (1989, 1998) for discussion.

[12] Mere reference-fixing theorists differ from full-blown meaning theorists about the nature of the authoritative association relation. Suppose predicate F expresses property P for two speakers. Suppose one of them stipulates that N will be an abbreviation for "the F" in her language, while the other uses "the F" to fix the reference, but not the meaning, of N in his language. Then both speakers will, in some sense, authoritatively associate P with N, but the nature of the association will be different in the two cases.

[13] It is unclear whether some Cluster Description Theorists are mere reference-fixers or full-blown meaning theorists. See Strawson (1959), Searle (1958, 1983), and Jackson (1998b), and, for discussion, Kripke (1980) and Evans (1973). Some of these theorists seemingly hold that the relevant reference-fixing property does *not* vary from speaker to speaker within a single linguistic community. Rather, there is a single reference-fixing property that is determined by the beliefs of the community's members. See also n. 8.

21.4 OBJECTIONS TO DESCRIPTION THEORIES

Keith Donnellan (1972), Saul Kripke (1977, 1980), and David Kaplan (1973, 1989) have presented three influential types of objection to Description Theories of meaning and reference-fixing: modal, epistemic, and semantic.[14]

21.4.1 Modal Objections

The modal objections are mainly due to Kripke. Let Sue be an English speaker whose language includes the name 'Mark Twain'. Description Theories entail that there is some property that she authoritatively associates with the name. Suppose that when she is asked 'Who is Mark Twain?' she consistently answers 'Mark Twain is the author of *Huckleberry Finn*.' Then simple Description Theories say that she authoritatively associates the property of being an author of *Huckleberry Finn* with the name. So these theories entail that the name is synonymous in Sue's idiolect with the description 'the author of *Huckleberry Finn*' and that sentences (11) and (12) are synonymous in her idiolect.

(11) If Mark Twain exists, then Mark Twain is an author *Huckleberry Finn*.

(12) If the author of *Huckleberry Finn* exists, then the author of *Huckleberry Finn* is an author of *Huckleberry Finn*.

(12) expresses a necessary truth, in Sue's idiolect. So, if (11) is synonymous with (12), in her idiolect, then (11) also expresses a necessary truth, in her idiolect. But (11) does not express a necessary truth in Sue's idiolect, if she is a typical speaker. For Sue (if she is typical) will concede that Mark Twain could have been dropped on his head as an infant, and consequently suffered brain damage, and never have written anything. She will (if she is typical) persist in this judgment after long reflection, and so will judge that (11) is not a necessary truth. Thus (11) is not a necessary truth in her idiolect, and simple Description Theories of the above sort are false.

A similar objection can be stated using sentences that contain modal phrases. Make the same assumptions about Sue as above, and consider sentences (11N) and (12N).

(11N) Necessarily: if Mark Twain exists, then Mark Twain is an author *Huckleberry Finn*.

(12N) Necessarily: if the author of *Huckleberry Finn* exists, then the author of *Huckleberry Finn* is an author of *Huckleberry Finn*.

(The colons indicate that 'necessarily' takes *wide scope* over the definite descriptions in the sentences: see the entry on RIGIDITY). It seems that, on simple Description Theories, (11N) and (12N) should be synonymous in Sue's idiolect. (12N) is clearly

---

[14] There is another important objection to Description Theories of Meaning that I do not have space to describe in detail here. It claims that if Description Theories were correct, then most belief ascriptions would be false, roughly because different people authoritatively associate different properties with the same proper name. See Kripke (1979, section I), and Richard (1990, ch. 2).

true in Sue's idiolect, but the above considerations seem to show that (11N) is false in her idiolect.

A similar objection can be posed for Cluster Description Theories. Let us suppose that Sue sincerely says 'Twain was human, was American, was an author of *Huckleberry Finn*,...', where the ellipsis is filled in with various other predicates. Suppose that, by close questioning, we discover that she thinks that certain of the properties expressed by the predicates are "more important" to Twain than others. Then a Cluster Description Theorist might hold that the property that she authoritatively associates with 'Twain' is the property of being a thing that has a majority of the properties being-human, being-American, being-an-author-of-*Huckleberry Finn*,... when these are weighted in way W. If so, then a Cluster Description Theory would entail that (13) and (14) are synonymous in Sue's idiolect.

(13) If Mark Twain exists, then Mark Twain is a thing that has a majority of the properties being-human, being-American, being-an-author-of-*Huckleberry Finn*,... when these are weighted in way W.

(14) If the thing that has a majority of the properties being-human, being-American, being-an-author-of-*Huckleberry Finn*,... when these are weighted in way W exists, then the thing that has a majority of the properties being-human, being-American, being-an-author-of-*Huckleberry Finn*,... when these are weighted in way W is a thing that has a majority of the properties being-human, being-American, being-an-author-of-*Huckleberry Finn*,... when these are weighted in way W.

(14) expresses a necessary truth, in Sue's idiolect. The above Cluster Description Theory thus entails that (13) also expresses a necessary truth in her idiolect. But, if Sue is typical, there will be plenty of evidence against this claim. Sue, if she is typical, would concede that Twain could have failed to be American (his mother could have moved to Canada just before he was born), could have been dropped on his head while an infant and not written anything, and so on. Thus she is likely to concede that he could have failed to have a majority of the properties that she attributes to Twain. Therefore, (13) does not express a necessary truth in her idiolect, and so the above Cluster Description Theory is false.[15]

Considerations like those above led Kripke (1980) to claim that ordinary proper names are *rigid designators*. A singular term T (for instance, a proper name or definite description) *refers to object O at possible world W* iff O is the object that is (semantically) relevant for determining the truth-value at W of sentences containing T. A singular term T is a *rigid designator* iff T refers to the same object with respect to all possible worlds.[16] For instance, 'The Stagirite teacher of Alexander is a philosopher' is true at a given world W iff the thing in W (whatever it may be) that is both Stagir-

---

[15] The objection can easily be modified to target Cluster Description Theories that use complex disjunctive properties instead of weightings. See n. 9.

[16] Kripke (1977, 1980) gives various definitions of 'rigid designator'. The one in the text is the simplest. See Salmon (1981) for a taxonomy of types of rigid designator. See also Kaplan (1989) and Stanley (1997). For more on the use of possible worlds in semantics, see the entry on FORMAL SEMANTICS.

ite and a teacher of Alexander in W is also a philosopher in W. The relevant person is Aristotle in some worlds, but someone else in others. Thus, 'the Stagirite teacher of Alexander' does not refer to the same object with respect to all worlds, and so is not a rigid designator. By contrast, 'Aristotle is a philosopher' is true at a world W iff Aristotle (*our* Aristotle, so to speak) is a philosopher at W. Thus, Aristotle is the referent of 'Aristotle' at all possible worlds, and so 'Aristotle' is a rigid designator. Kripke claimed that, in general, the definite descriptions that ordinary speakers associate with proper names are not rigid designators, and so cannot be synonymous with those names. (For more details, see Salmon, 1981; Stanley, 1997; and the entry on RIGIDITY.)

The modal objections target Description Theories of *meaning* that claim that proper names are *synonymous* with definite descriptions. They are ineffective against Description Theories of *Reference-Fixing* that deny synonymy, for these theories do not imply that (11) is necessary if (12) is, or that (13) is necessary if (14) is.

21.4.2 Epistemic Objections

The epistemic objections are due to Kripke. Return to Sue and the earlier simple Description Theory. According to this simple Description Theory, (11) and (12) are synonymous in Sue's idiolect. Therefore, they express the same proposition. (12) expresses a logical truth, in Sue's idiolect. That proposition is knowable *a priori*, without any appeal to empirical evidence. Moreover, it can *easily* be known to be true by reflection. Thus, if (11) expressed the same proposition as (12) in Sue's idiolect, then it would be an *a priori* knowable logical truth that could easily be known to be true simply by reflection. But Sue cannot know the proposition expressed by (11) in her idiolect by reflection alone, without any appeal to empirical evidence. Moreover, Sue, if she is typical, would not claim that (11) is logically true, or "true by definition". She would surely think that she needs empirical evidence to bolster her claim to know that (11) is true. Thus, the simple Description Theory is incorrect. A similar argument, with appropriate changes, can be mounted against the earlier Cluster Description Theory: (14) expresses a proposition, in Sue's idiolect, that can be known *a priori*, whereas (13) does not.

The objection is directed at theories that claim that proper names are *synonymous* with definite descriptions. Kripke says that a similar argument is effective against Description Theories of Reference-Fixing that deny synonymy. Suppose that Ellen deliberately fixes the reference of 'Twain' using the description 'the author of *Huckleberry Finn*', but does not take the name to be synonymous with the description. Kripke claims that any speaker who fixes the reference of 'Twain' in this way can easily know *a priori* the proposition expressed by (11) in her idiolect. Call this 'Kripke's *a priority* claim'. If Kripke's *a priority* claim is correct, then on Description Theories of Reference-Fixing, Ellen could easily come to know the proposition expressed by (11) in her idiolect by reflection alone. But she could not. In fact, if she is typical, she would think that she needs empirical evidence to know that (11) is true. Thus, Kripke concludes, Description Theories of Reference-Fixing are incorrect. It is controversial whether epistemic arguments of this sort are sound, for many philosophers disagree with Kripke's *a priority* claim (see, for instance, Donnellan, 1979 and Salmon, 1986).

21.4.3 Semantic Objections

The final type of objection is semantic, and is due to Donnellan and Kripke. (Devitt and Sterelny (1999) call these 'arguments from ignorance and error'.) Suppose that Bobby learns the name 'Christopher Columbus' in grade school in a normal way. When asked 'Who is Christopher Columbus?' he consistently answers 'The first European to land in America.' So suppose that he authoritatively associates the property of being the first European to land in America with the name 'Christopher Columbus'. Then, according to simple Description Theories, the name in his language refers to the first European to land in America. But this person (if there is one) is probably a Norse sailor. Clearly the name 'Christopher Columbus' does not refer, in Bobby's language, to any such Norse sailor. Thus simple Description Theories are false. Cluster Description Theories seem to fare just as badly with examples like this one, for the other properties that Bobby associates with the name may also be ones that Columbus fails to have. For instance, Bobby may say 'Columbus was Spanish, and sailed the ocean blue in 1392, . . .'. In short, a speaker may have a name N in his language that refers to object O, though the beliefs that he would express by uttering sentences containing N are seriously erroneous. Description Theories of Meaning and Reference-Fixing incorrectly entail, in such cases, that N fails to refer or that N refers to an object that is not the real referent of the name. This objection casts serious doubt on clause (3) of the Description Theory Schema.

A related semantic objection casts doubt on both clause (2) and clause (3). Suppose that Paul acquires the name 'Richard Feynman' by overhearing someone say 'Richard Feynman is a physicist'. When asked 'Who is Richard Feynman?', he answers 'A physicist.' At first glance, it seems that the only property that Paul could authoritatively associate with the name 'Richard Feynman' is the property of being a physicist. But Paul, like most normal people, does not believe that there is one and only one physicist. This raises a problem for clause (2), for it is doubtful that he *authoritatively* associates any property with the name. Furthermore, contrary to clause (3), the name 'Richard Feynman' in his idiolect refers to Feynman, even though he does not associate a property with the name that uniquely picks out Feynman.

The semantic objections work equally well against both Description Theories of Meaning and Description Theories of Reference-Fixing, for the problematic consequences follow merely from their common claim about reference-fixing.

21.4.4 Responses

Defenders of Description Theories have vigorously responded to the above objections. In response to the modal objections, some defenders have claimed that proper names take *wide scope* with respect to modal operators, such as 'necessarily' (Dummett, 1981; Sosa, 2001). On this view, (11N) is synonymous not with (12N), but with (12N*).

(12N*) The author of *Huckleberry Finn*$_i$ is such that: necessarily, if he$_i$ exists, then he$_i$ is an author of *Huckleberry* Finn.

But (12N*) is false, just like (11N). However, this view does not provide an immediate response to the modal objection that relied on the *non*-modal sentences (11) and (12). For further discussion, see Stanley (1997), Sosa (2001), Soames (2002), and the entry on RIGIDITY. Other defenders of Description Theories have claimed that proper names are synonymous with *rigid* descriptions, such as 'the thing that *actually* authored *Huckleberry Finn*'. For discussion, see Salmon (1981), Soames (2002), and the entry on RIGIDITY.

Description Theorists' replies to the epistemic objections are often closely connected with their replies to the semantic objections (see below). Some claim that when the *correct* description is used, the resulting sentence expresses, in the speaker's language, an *a priori* knowable proposition. A Description Theorist of *Reference-Fixing* who denies synonymy could claim that his view does not imply that the speaker can know *a priori* the proposition expressed by the sentence in her idiolect.

Defenders of Description Theories have argued that the semantic objections incorrectly specify the relevant reference-fixing property. For instance, Description Theorists might claim that Bobby's reference-fixing property for 'Christopher Columbus' is not the property of being the first European to land in America. Rather, it is the property of being a thing that the person from whom Bobby got the name referred to with the name 'Columbus'. Or, even more likely, it is some cluster property that involves the preceding property and many others. These defenders say, in effect, that the semantic objections rely on faulty assumptions about the authoritative association relation: the reference-fixing property that a speaker authoritatively associates with a name cannot be discovered simply by asking the speaker "Who is N?" For further discussion, see Searle (1983), Lewis (1984), Kroon (1987), Jackson (1998b), and Soames (2002).

21.5 THE CAUSAL THEORY OF REFERENCE

In addition to arguing *against* Description Theories of Meaning and Reference, Kripke, Donnellan, Kaplan, Devitt (1981) and others argued *in favor* of an alternative theory of reference that is often called the *Causal Theory of Reference* (or 'the Historical Explanation Theory' or 'the Causal–Historical Theory'). On this theory, an utterance of a name refers to an object in virtue of standing in a certain causal relation to the object: for example, our present utterances of 'Aristotle' refer to Aristotle because our utterances are causally connected to Aristotle in the right way. According to typical versions of this theory, there is a causal chain that begins with Aristotle's parents' dubbing him with the ancient Greek equivalent of 'Aristotle'. The chain continues with various other people acquiring the name, mostly by hearing others use the name and intending to use the name in the same way. As long as the receiving speakers intend to use the name in the same way as those that preceded them, the right sort of causal relation is maintained, and their utterances of the name refer to Aristotle. Thus, utterances of 'Aristotle' by people in the chain refer to Aristotle even if those people know very little about the referent, or have seriously erroneous beliefs about the referent.

Although the Causal Theory paints a picture of reference-fixing that many philosophers find attractive, some cases present apparent problems for it. There seem to be cases in which a name is passed along a causal chain in the way prescribed by the Causal Theory, but in which the name shifts its reference from one object to another. For instance, Evans (1973) claims that the name 'Madagascar' shifted in reference from a region of mainland Africa to an island near Africa's coast, though every speaker in the chain intended to use the name in the same way as his predecessors. There may also be a causal chain of the above sort connecting our utterances of 'Santa Claus' to a historical saint, even though our utterances do not refer to that saint (Kripke, 1980). These cases show, at the very least, that the causal relation that allegedly fixes reference is quite complex.

The problems with the Causal Theory have little evidential bearing on Millianism, for the theories are concerned with two different questions. One question is 'What is the meaning of a proper name?' Another question is 'What makes it the case that a given proper name has whatever meaning it has, or refers to whatever object it refers to?' Millianism is an answer to the first question. It does not try to describe how reference occurs; it simply takes for granted that proper names refer. Consequently, Millianism is consistent with a very wide range of theories of reference-fixing, including, for instance, Description Theories of Reference-Fixing, the Causal Theory, the Divine Command Theory of Reference (the view that reference is an irreducible relation that holds between a name and an object because God commands it), and the Supervenience Theory (the view that facts about reference supervene on the physical facts, but perhaps in a way that cannot be finitely described). The Causal Theory, on the other hand, is concerned with the second question. It attempts to describe how the reference of a proper name is determined by other facts. It does not try to specify the meaning of a proper name. In fact, the Causal Theory is consistent with non-Millian theories of meaning, for instance, the theory that the meaning of a proper name consists of the referent together with the name itself. Description Theories of Meaning are unusual, in that they not only specify the meaning of a proper name (roughly, a property), but also describe what makes it the case that a proper name refers to an object (the object satisfies the property) and what makes it the case that a name means what it does (authoritative association). This may explain why some critics of Description Theories of Meaning have felt obligated to give an alternative theory of reference-fixing for proper names. For further discussion, see Kaplan (1989) and Stalnaker (1997).

21.6 TWO SPECIAL DESCRIPTION THEORIES AND SOME NON-MILLIAN, NON-DESCRIPTIVE ALTERNATIVES

There are two special Description Theories that are worth mentioning separately. The first is the *Metalinguistic Theory* (Bach, 1981; Katz, 1994). According to one version of this theory, a proper name N is synonymous with a definite description of the form "the bearer of 'N' ". This theory takes the bearing relation for granted (just as Millianism takes the referring relation for granted). The second special Description Theory is the *Causal-Description Theory* (Lewis, 1984; Kroon, 1987; Jackson, 1998b). According to one theory of this type, an utterance U of proper name N is synonymous with a description of the form "the thing to which U bears relation R", where R is the causal relation that fixes the reference of utterances of N.

Some philosophers have argued for theories that are neither Millian nor descriptive. For instance, Devitt (1996) has proposed that the meaning of a proper name N that refers to O is the property of referring to O via C, where C is a causal chain involving tokens of N. On this view, 'Twain' and 'Clemens' have different meanings because they refer in virtue of different causal chains, one involving tokens of 'Twain', the other involving tokens of 'Clemens'. Devitt furthermore holds that speakers need not have even tacit beliefs about these causal chains. In that sense, speakers need not know the meanings of the names they understand.

There are various theories that hold that the meaning of a proper name either is, or can be represented by, an ordered pair consisting of the referent and something else that figures importantly in how the speaker thinks of the referent. For instance, one such theory says that the meaning of 'Twain' consists of Twain himself and some property that the speaker ascribes to the referent, such as the property of being human (Geach, 1962). Other such theories hold that the meaning of 'Twain' for a speaker consists of (or can be represented by) the ordered pair of Twain and either (i) the name 'Twain', or (ii) the speaker's *mental* name for Twain, or (iii) the speaker's *mental file* on Twain, or (iv) the conceptual, inferential, or causal role of the name in the speaker's thought processes. (See Field, 1977; Evans, 1982; Forbes, 1990; and the entry on CONCEPTUAL ROLE SEMANTICS.)

The above theories may be vulnerable to modal and epistemic objections, depending on details. More importantly, many of these theories entail that distinct names rarely or never have the same meaning. (Some entail that distinct *utterances* of a single name cannot have the same meaning.) This consequence suggests that many seemingly true assertion ascriptions are false. Consider, for instance, the Metalinguistic Theory. Suppose that the monolingual German speaker Karl utters 'Köln ist schön'. Then an English speaker can truly say 'Karl said that Cologne is pretty.' But according to the Metalinguistic Theory, the English ascription says that Karl said that the bearer of 'Cologne' is pretty. Yet Karl said no such thing.

Analogous criticisms can be made of the other theories.[17] For discussion, see Salmon (1986), Richard (1990), and Soames (2002).

According to some versions of *Two-Dimensional Semantics*, every proper name has *two* meanings, one of which is (roughly) a uniquely identifying property and the other of which is the individual that satisfies the property.[18] These theories may be vulnerable to versions of the preceding objections to Description Theories. For discussion and criticisms, see Jackson (1998a), Stalnaker (2001), Chalmers (2002), Byrne and Pryor (2004), Soames (2004, 2005), and the entry on TWO-DIMENSIONAL SEMANTICS.

21.7 THE MILLIAN THEORY RECONSIDERED

The apparent problems with non-Millian theories (particularly with Description Theories) have led some philosophers to reconsider the objections to Millianism. Many modern Millian replies to the objections rely on two ideas: the theory of *mediated belief*, and the distinction between *semantics and pragmatics* (Salmon, 1986; Soames, 2002; and Braun, 1998).

According to many defenders of Millianism, the binary belief relation is mediated by a third type of entity, for instance, a sentence, a mental state, or a mental representation. One believes a proposition by accepting a sentence, or being in a mental state, or having a mental representation function in one's mind in the right way. These mediating entities are *ways of taking propositions* or *propositional guises*. An agent can believe a single proposition in two distinct ways, or under two distinct guises. For instance, a person who thinks that (1) and (2) are both true believes the proposition that Twain/Clemens is Twain/Clemens in two distinct ways.

(1) Mark Twain is Mark Twain.
(2) Mark Twain is Samuel Clemens.

But a rational agent can believe the identity proposition in one way without believing it in another way. Such an agent might think that (1) is true but be unsure about (2). A rational agent can even believe the identity proposition in one way, and also believe the *negation* of that proposition in a suitably different way. Such a rational agent could think that (1) is true and (2) is false. Furthermore, some Millians hold that the proposition expressed by (2) is *a priori* and uninformative, but that this proposition may appear to lack those properties when it is entertained in a way that corresponds to sentence (2). This is one Millian response to the Objection from Cognitive Significance.

---

[17] Mere reference-fixing versions of these theories may not be vulnerable to this criticism, but they also do not provide immediate solutions to Frege's Puzzles.

[18] More accurately, the advocates of these theories say that every proper name has two *propositional contents*, each of which is an *intension*. See n. 2 and the entry on TWO-DIMENSIONAL SEMANTICS.

Many Millians also emphasize the distinction between (i) the proposition that a sentence expresses as a matter of *semantics*, or meaning, and (ii) the propositions that utterances of the sentence "suggest", or conversationally implicate, or *pragmatically convey* in some way. (See the entry on THE DISTINCTION BETWEEN SEMANTICS AND PRAGMATICS.) An alternative Millian response to the Objection from Cognitive Significance says that utterances of (1) and (2) pragmatically convey different propositions, even though they semantically express the same proposition. For instance, an utterance of (2) might pragmatically convey the proposition that the author of *Huckleberry Finn* is the publisher of U.S. Grant's autobiography. A rational speaker could disbelieve this pragmatically conveyed proposition, and so mistakenly think that (2) itself is false.

The Objection from Belief Ascriptions is the subject of a large literature (see OPACITY). Some Millian responses to it use the same ideas as the preceding responses. Some Millians (Salmon, 1986; Braun, 1998) hold that (7) and (8) semantically express the same proposition, but a rational agent can believe this proposition in one way (a way corresponding to (7)), while believing the negation of this proposition in another way (a way corresponding to (8)).

(7) Mary believes that Mark Twain is Mark Twain.

(8) Mary believes that Mark Twain is Samuel Clemens.

Some Millians also (or instead) think that utterances of these sentences typically differ in the propositions they pragmatically convey (Salmon, 1986; Soames, 2002). For instance, an utterance of (7) conveys the true proposition that Mary would assent to sentence (1), whereas (8) conveys the false proposition that Mary would assent to sentence (2). This might lead a speaker to think that (8) can differ in truth-value from (7). Other Millians (who might be more accurately called "quasi-Millians") think that, although (1) and (2) semantically express the same proposition, (7) and (8) semantically express distinct propositions that can differ in truth-value. This occurs because the 'that'-clauses of (7) and (8) refer to amalgams of (i) the proposition expressed by (1) and (2) and (ii) certain representations, for instance, the words in the 'that'-clauses, or Mary's mental representations. See Richard (1990) for a representative theory of this sort.

In response to the Objection from Meaningful Sentences Containing Non-referring Names, some Millians, such as Salmon (1998), argue that the name 'Pegasus' refers to a mythical object. Thus on this view, 'Pegasus' is meaningful and so is sentence (9).

(9) Pegasus flies.

Other Millians (Braun, 2005) maintain that 'Pegasus' fails to refer, but that sentence (9) nevertheless expresses a *gappy* proposition, a proposition that has an unfilled position where an individual referent would normally appear. The mythical-object response entails that Pegasus exists and that (10) is false.

(10) Pegasus does not exist.

On the gappy proposition response, (10) expresses a gappy proposition that is either true or truth-value-less.

The Millian responses to Frege's Puzzles are far from universally accepted. The theories of meaning and reference-fixing for proper names continue to be topics of intense investigation and debate.

21.8 NATURAL KIND TERMS

As I pointed out earlier, Kripke says that all of the following expressions are natural kind terms: 'water', 'gold', 'cat', 'tiger', 'whale', 'heat', 'hot', 'loud', 'red', and 'pain'. I noted that the distinction between natural and non-natural kind *terms* relies on a distinction between natural and non-natural *kinds*. Thus, the distinction between natural and non-natural kind terms is more metaphysical than linguistic. Viewed linguistically, Kripke's natural kinds terms are quite diverse. Some are nouns, whereas others are adjectives. Some can be used as a singular term (for instance, 'red' in 'Red is a color') whereas others cannot ('cat'). Of the nouns, some are count nouns ('tiger'), while others are mass nouns ('water'). But nearly all of them are *general terms* (or 'general names', as Mill called them): they can be correctly applied to more than one object, when they are used *predicatively*. (Predicative uses often involve the copula and/or the determiner 'a', as in 'is hot' and 'is a tiger'.) I begin below with the semantics of kind terms in general. I consider later whether the semantics of natural kind terms is in any interesting way distinct from that of non-natural kind terms.

Millianism says that the meaning of a proper name is its referent. An obvious analogous view for kind terms is the view that the meaning of a kind term is its *extension*, where the *extension* of a kind term is the set of objects to which it correctly applies, in predicative uses. Call this view *Extensionalism*. Extensionalism faces serious difficulties with pairs of kind terms that have the same extension and yet differ in meaning. For instance, it is often said that the common nouns 'renate' (animal having a kidney) and 'cordate' (animal having a heart) are co-extensive. Whether or not this is so, the terms clearly differ in meaning. One indication of this is that the sentence 'Necessarily, all renates are renates' is true, whereas the sentence 'Necessarily, all renates are cordates' is false. *Complex* kind terms provide further counterexamples to Extensionalism. For instance, the common noun phrases 'person who was President of the USA in March 2002' and 'person who was governor of Texas in 1998' have the same extension (the set whose sole member is George W. Bush), but differ in meaning.

An obvious alternative to Extensionalism is the view that the meaning of a simple kind term is a *property*. Thus the meaning of 'round' is the property of being round, the meaning of 'renate' is the property of being a renate, the meaning of 'cordate' is the property of being a cordate, and so on. Such a theory can be extended to complex kind terms in several ways (Salmon, 1981, 1986; Soames, 2002). This theory escapes the above problems with Extensionalism, for the preceding kind terms express distinct properties.

According to traditional *Description Theories of Meaning for Kind Terms*, many syntactically simple kind terms are synonymous with complex descriptive phrases (Mill, 1843). These theories are in many ways similar to Description Theories of proper names. On a simple theory of this type, speakers associate complex descriptive phrases with many simple adjectives and common nouns. A speaker will provide the descriptive phrase that she associates with a simple kind term K if she is asked "What is a K?" or "What do you mean by 'K'?". The speaker takes this descriptive phrase to "define" the kind term, and to determine which objects fall under it, and to determine whether "There are K's" is true. In that sense, she authoritatively associates the property expressed by the complex descriptive phrase with the simple kind term. For example, a speaker who is asked 'What is a tiger?' might answer 'a carnivorous cat-like animal with a tawny coat and transverse black stripes'. The sentence 'All tigers live in Asia' expresses, in such a speaker's idiolect, the proposition that all carnivorous cat-like animals with tawny coats and transverse black stripes live in Asia. The extension of 'tiger' in her idiolect is the set of objects that are carnivorous cat-like animals with tawny coats and transverse black stripes. The sentence 'There are tigers' is true iff this set has members.

Like Description Theories of proper names, Description Theories of kind terms come in many versions. Yet many satisfy the following theory schema.

A Schema for Description Theories of Meaning for Kind Terms

If S is a speaker, and K is a simple kind term of type T in S's language L, then there is exactly one property P such that:

(1) P satisfies condition C.
(2) S authoritatively associates P with K.
(3) O is a member of the extension of K in L iff O has property P.
(4) If D is a complex descriptive phrase that expresses P in English (or in some extension of English L'), then K in L is synonymous with D in English (or L').

Description Theorists claim that many simple kind terms are synonymous with complex descriptive phrases that provide substantive *analyses* of those terms. But Description Theorists admit that this is not the case for all simple kind terms— some express simple properties and are unanalyzable. For instance, some theorists might say that 'red', 'round', and other observational terms are not analyzable; other theorists would say the same about some other class of simple kind terms. Thus, the above Schema is restricted in its application to simple kind terms of type T, where T is a schematic constraint on kind terms about which description theorists may disagree. Clause (1) is also schematic and allows different theorists to place different constraints on property P. Theorists with Russellian leanings might allow P to be a relational property that involves individuals with whom the speaker is directly acquainted. Theorists with Fregean leanings might insist that P be purely general.

Clauses (1)–(3) provide a theory of how the extension of a kind term is fixed. Clause (4) specifies the meaning of such a kind term. Let us say that the schema that includes (1)–(3), but excludes clause (4), is *A Schema for Description Theories of **Extension-Fixing** for Kind Terms*. There are *cluster* versions of Description Theories of Meaning and Extension-Fixing for Kind Terms, just as there are for proper names. On such a view, a simple kind term's extension is fixed, and perhaps its meaning is expressed, by a complex phrase of the form *has a majority of properties $P_1, P_2, P_3, \ldots P_n$ when these properties are weighted in way W*.

Description Theories are initially attractive for several reasons. As mentioned before, when speakers are asked "What do you mean by 'K'?", they usually provide complex descriptions. Moreover, it may initially seem that a speaker does not understand a term, or is not competent with it, unless she can provide such a description. Finally, it might initially seem that sentences such as 'Tigers are large, cat-like animals with orange and black stripes' express necessary, *a priori*, and analytic truths, or at least come close to doing so. Description Theories of Kind Terms easily explain these judgments.

21.9 OBJECTIONS TO DESCRIPTION THEORIES OF KIND TERMS

The objections to Description Theories of Kind Terms are similar to the preceding objections to Description Theories of Proper Names. They are due primarily to Kripke (1980) and Putnam (1975). I concentrate below on simple Description Theories concerning simple kind terms, and assume that it is obvious how to modify them so as to target cluster theories.

Suppose that 'tiger' is a kind term in Sue's language. The Description Theory says that she authoritatively associates some (complex) property with it. Assume that when Sue is asked 'What is a tiger?' she answers 'A tiger is a carnivorous cat-like animal with a tawny coat and transverse black stripes.' So, on simple Description Theories, she authoritatively associates the property expressed by the complex descriptive phrase with the term 'tiger'. Thus, (15) and (16) are synonymous in her language.

(15) A thing is a tiger if and only if it is a carnivorous cat-like animal with a tawny coat and transverse black stripes.

(16) A thing is a carnivorous cat-like animal with a tawny coat and transverse black stripes if and only if it is a carnivorous cat-like animal with a tawny coat and transverse black stripes.

This theory is vulnerable to a modal objection. Sentence (16) obviously expresses a necessary truth in Sue's language. But (15) does not: it is (metaphysically) possible for there to be some species of animal whose members look like tigers but whose members differ radically in important internal respects from tigers. Members of this species may be incapable of interbreeding with tigers; they may even be reptilian. They are not tigers. Sue would surely concede all of this, if she is a typical speaker. Thus, (15) does not express a necessary truth in her language, contrary to the Description Theory.

The theory is also vulnerable to epistemic objections. Sentence (16) expresses a proposition that can be known *a priori*. Thus, the Description Theory entails that sentence (15) does also. But the proposition expressed by (15) in Sue's language is not knowable *a priori*. Empirical evidence is needed in order to be justified in believing that every animal that has a "tigerish" appearance is a genuine tiger (and Sue would concede this, if she is typical).

The preceding objections make use of Description Theories' claim that the kind term 'tiger' is *synonymous* with the complex descriptive phrase. Description Theories of *Extension-Fixing* are not vulnerable to the modal objection. It is controversial whether such theories are vulnerable to the epistemic objection. (The controversies are similar to those surrounding Description Theories of proper names.) But the following semantic objections are intended to show that even Description Theories of Extension-Fixing for kind terms are incorrect.

Consider Sue again, and assume that she acquired the term 'tiger' in a normal way, and that (as before) she associates the above complex descriptive phrase with 'tiger'. Suppose that, deep in the jungles of some unexplored region of Earth, there is a species of animal whose members look like tigers, but whose members cannot interbreed with tigers, and differ radically in important internal respects from tigers. Suppose, for instance, that they are reptilian rather than mammalian. Such animals would not fall in the extension of 'tiger' in Sue's language, contrary to Description Theories of Extension-Fixing.

Other arguments from ignorance and error also seem to be effective against extension-fixing theories. Suppose that Bobby acquires the term 'dinosaur' by seeing pictures of them and hearing that they lived millions of years ago. If asked 'What is a dinosaur?' he might say, 'A dinosaur is a large lizard that lived millions of years ago.' Dinosaurs, however, are not lizards. Thus, according to Description Theories, the extension of 'dinosaur' in Bobby's language does not include any dinosaurs. But surely it does. Suppose that Doug is a desert-dweller who has never seen an elm or a beech, but hears some visitors discussing them. He associates the same description with each term, 'a large tree'. Nevertheless, if he utters 'No elm is a beech', he expresses a truth. Thus, it seems that the two expressions have different extensions in his language, contrary to Description Theories (Putnam, 1975).

The *Twin Earth Objection* is another semantic objection due to Putnam (1975). Suppose that there is a distant planet that is a duplicate of Earth in many respects, except that the clear, drinkable liquid that falls from the sky and fills the lakes and streams on Twin Earth is not H_2O, but another compound, XYZ. Suppose that Oscar on Earth and Twin Oscar on Twin Earth are molecule-for-molecule duplicates of each other. Then, it seems, Oscar and Twin Oscar associate the same descriptions and properties with the word 'water'. Yet the extension of 'water' for Oscar is the set of all portions of water (i.e. H_2O), whereas the extension of 'water' for Twin Oscar is the set of all portions of XYZ.

Defenders of Description Theories of Kind Terms have given replies to the above objections that are similar to the previous replies to objections to Description Theories of Proper Names. To defend Description Theories from modal objections, some add rigidifying devices to complex descriptive phrases, for instance, 'member of the species whose *actual* members are carnivorous cat-like animals with tawny coats and transverse black stripes'. Some claim that the sentences containing the correct extension-fixing descriptions do express *a priori* knowable propositions. Most importantly, many defenders claim that the alleged counterexamples do not give the correct extension-fixing description for a given kind term and speaker. In Sue's case, the correct extension-fixing description may include reference to herself, as in 'the type of animal I saw at the zoo yesterday', or may include reference to experts' judgments, as in 'animals called 'tigers' by biologists'. Probably, the correct description is a complicated cluster description that includes these descriptions and more. In any case, the correct extension-fixing description cannot be elicited from a speaker simply by asking her 'What is a tiger?'. For discussion, see Searle (1983), Lewis (1984), Jackson (1998b), and Soames (2005).

21.10 Natural Kind Terms, Non-Natural Kind Terms, Rigid Designation, and the Causal Theory of Reference

Most of Kripke's and Putnam's objections focus on Description Theories of *natural* kind terms, but many of them work equally well against Description Theories of *non*-natural kind terms. Suppose, for instance, that Sue uses the term 'pencil' and associates with it the property of being a cylindrical writing instrument with a metallic lead core. On Description Theories, ordinary pencils, which have non-metallic graphite cores, do not fall in the extension of her utterances of 'pencil'. Yet it seems that Sue utters a truth when she grasps an ordinary pencil and says 'This is a pencil'. Thus, Description Theories of non-natural kind terms are as implausible as Description Theories of natural kind terms. For further discussion, see Putnam (1975), Burge (1979), Donnellan (1983), and Devitt and Sterelny (1999).

In light of the arguments against Extensionalism and Description Theories, one might reasonably conclude that the meaning of *any* simple kind term, whether natural or non-natural, is a simple non-descriptive property. The meaning of 'tiger' is the property of being a tiger, and the extension of the term is the set of things that have that property. Similarly, the meaning of 'pencil' is the property of being a pencil, and its extension is the set of pencils. Call this the *Property Theory* of kind terms.[19] On

---

[19] An advocate of the Property Theory could allow that the *extension* of a kind term is a property when it is used as a singular term, as is 'red' in 'Red is a color'. See Soames (2002).

this view, the semantics of simple *non*-natural kind terms is just like that of simple natural kind terms.

Kripke (1980) and Putnam (1975) claim that natural kind terms are rigid designators. This claim conflicts with the Property Theory, given three assumptions: (i) a kind term is a rigid designator iff it has the same reference with respect to all possible worlds, (ii) the reference of a kind term at a possible world is its extension at that world, (iii) the extensions of most natural kind terms vary from possible world to possible world. Kripke and Putnam apparently reject (ii): they hold that natural kind terms refer, not to their extensions, but to natural kinds. For instance, 'tiger' refers to the species *Felis Tigris*, 'water' to the substance *Water*, and so on. Each simple natural kind term refers to the same natural kind with respect to all possible worlds, and so is a rigid designator, even if the extension of the term varies from world to world. (See the entry on RIGIDITY.) Suppose, in addition, that the *meanings* of these simple natural kind terms are just the kinds to which they refer.[20] Then predicative uses of kind terms can be analyzed in terms of kind membership: 'All tigers are animals' is (roughly) synonymous with 'All members of *Felis Tigris* are members of *Animalia*'. Call this the *Kind Designation* theory. There are two main differences between it and the Property Theory. First, the Kind Designation Theory says that simple kind terms rigidly refer to kinds, whereas the Property Theory says that kind terms non-rigidly refer to extensions (sets). Second, the Kind Designation Theory says that the *meaning* of a simple kind term is the kind to which it refers, whereas the Property Theory says that the meaning is a property.[21]

The Kind Designation theory can easily be extended to non-natural kind terms (Salmon, 1981, 2003; Soames, 2002). The expression 'pencil' refers to the kind *Pencil*, with respect to all possible worlds. Thus, 'pencil' is a rigid designator. If the *meaning* of 'pencil' is the kind to which it refers, then predicative uses can be analyzed in terms of membership: 'All pencils are yellow' is (roughly) synonymous with 'All members of *Pencil* are members of *Yellow*'. Thus, there is nothing distinctive about the semantics of natural kind terms on either the Property Theory or the Kind Designation Theory.

The Property Theory and the Kind Designation Theory are consistent with many different theories concerning the *fixation* or *determination* of meaning, reference, and extension for kind terms (just as Millianism is consistent with many different

[20] This claim conflicts with Putnam's (1975) theory of meaning (see Salmon, 1981). Kripke (1980) does not present a theory of *meaning* for natural kind terms.

[21] Kinds and properties appear, at first glance, to be distinct types of entity, for objects *have* (or exemplify) properties, but are *members* of kinds. (This apparent difference may be misleading, but I cannot address this metaphysical issue here.) Advocates of the Kind Designation Theory can allow that some *complex* kind terms are *non*-rigid designators: for instance, 'the species that Sue esteems above all others' may refer to *Felis Tigris* in one world and to *Cynomys Ludovicianus* (the prairie dog) in another. Other complex kind terms rigidly refer, for instance, 'the species that *actually* Sue esteems above all others'. For discussion, see Salmon, 1981; Soames, 2002; and Salmon 2003. Some advocates of the Kind Designation Theory might also wish to distinguish between *reference* and *designation*: they may claim that simple kind terms rigidly *designate* kinds (just as proper names rigidly designate objects), but non-rigidly *refer* to extensions.

theories of reference-fixing for proper names). Kripke (1980) and Putnam (1975) argue for a Causal Theory of Reference for *natural* kind terms. (See also Salmon, 1981 and Soames, 2002.) On this theory, a person who introduces a natural kind term typically does so by observing a sample of the kind, and fixing the reference of the term with a description like "the TK of which *this* sample is a member", where TK is a term for a Type of Kind, for instance, 'species' or 'chemical substance'. If a subsequent speaker hears the introduced kind term, then he can use it to refer to the same kind, as long as he intends to use the term in the same way as his predecessors, even if he is quite mistaken about the kind's properties. Ordinary users defer to expert users when deciding whether an item falls in a term's extension (this is part of what Putnam calls 'the division of linguistic labor'), but even experts can make mistakes. If the meaning of a simple natural kind term is just the kind to which it refers, then the reference-fixing process also fixes the meaning.

The Causal Theory of Reference for natural kind terms may be even more problematic than the Causal Theory of Reference for proper names see (Devitt, 1981; Wilson, 1982; Devitt and Sterelney, 1999; Soames, 2002). But if it is correct, then much of it could be extended to *non*-natural kind terms. (For discussion, see Lewis, 1984; Devitt and Sterelny, 1999, and Soames, 2002.) It remains controversial whether natural and non-natural kind terms differ in how their meanings, references, and extensions are determined.

REFERENCES

Bach, Kent (1981). "What's In a Name?" *Australasian Journal of Philosophy*, 59: 371–386.

Braun, David (1998). "Understanding Belief Reports." *Philosophical Review*, 107: 555–595.

—— (2005). "Empty Names, Fictional Names, Mythical Names." *Noûs*, 39: 596–631.

Burge, Tyler (1979). "Individualism and the Mental." *Midwest Studies in Philosophy*, 4: 73–121.

Byrne, Alex and Pryor, James (2004). "Bad Intensions." In Garcia-Carpintero and Macià (2004).

Chalmers, David (2002). "On Sense and Intension." *Philosophical Perspectives*, 16: 135–82.

Devitt, Michael (1981). *Designation*. New York: Columbia University Press.

—— (1996). *Coming to Our Senses*. Cambridge: Cambridge University Press.

Devitt, Michael and Sterelny, Kim (1999). *Language and Reality*, 2nd edn. Cambridge, MA: MIT Press.

Donnellan, Keith (1972). "Names and Identifying Descriptions." In Donald Davidson and Gilbert Harman (eds.), *Semantics of Natural Language*, pp. 356–79. Dordrecht: Reidel.

—— (1979). "The Contingent *A Priori* and Rigid Designators." In P. French, T. Uehling, and H. Wettstein (eds.), *Contemporary Perspectives in the Philosophy of Language*, pp. 45–60. Minneapolis: University of Minnesota Press.

—— (1983). "Kripke and Putnam on Natural Kind Terms." In Carl Ginet and Sydney Shoemaker (eds.), *Knowledge and Mind: Philosophical Essays*. Oxford: Oxford University Press.

Dummett, Michael (1981). *The Interpretation of Frege's Philosophy*. London: Duckworth.

Evans, Gareth (1973). "The Causal Theory of Names." *Proceedings of the Aristotelian Society*, Supplementary Volume 47, pp. 187–208.

Evans, Gareth (1982). *The Varieties of Reference*. Oxford: Oxford University Press.

Field, Hartry (1977). "Logic, Meaning, and Conceptual Role." *Journal of Philosophy*, 74: 379–409.

Forbes, Graeme (1990). "The Indispensability of *Sinn*." *Philosophical Review*, 99: 535–64.

Frege, Gottlob (1952). "On Sense and Reference." In P. Geach and M. Black (trans.), *Translations from the Philosophical Writings*. Oxford: Blackwell. Originally published as "Über Sinn und Bedeutung," *Zeitschrift für Philosophie und Philosophische Kritik*, 100 (1893): 25–50.

Garcia-Carpintero, M., and Macià, J. (2004). *The Two-Dimensional Framework: Foundations and Applications*. Oxford: Oxford University Press.

Geach, Peter (1962). *Reference and Generality*. Ithaca, NY: Cornell University Press.

Hale, Bob and Wright, Crispin (eds.) (1997). *A Companion to the Philosophy of Language*. Oxford: Blackwell.

Jackson, Frank (1998a). *From Metaphysics to Ethics: A Defence of Conceptual Analysis*. New York: Oxford University Press.

____ (1998b). "Reference and Description Revisited." *Philosophical Perspectives*, 12: 201–18.

Kaplan, David (1973). "Bob and Carol and Ted and Alice." In J. Hintikka, J. Moravcsik, and P. Suppes (eds.), *Approaches to Natural Language*, 490–518. Dordrecht: Reidel.

____ (1989). "Demonstratives" and "Afterthoughts". In Joseph Almog, John Perry, and Howard Wettstein (eds.), *Themes from Kaplan*, pp. 481–614. Oxford: Oxford University Press.

Katz, Jerrold J. (1994). "Names Without Bearers." *Philosophical Review*, 103: 1–39.

Kripke, Saul (1977). "Identity and Necessity." In Stephen Schwartz (ed.), *Naming, Necessity, and Natural Kinds*, pp. 66–101. Ithaca, NY: Cornell University Press.

____ (1980). *Naming and Necessity*. Cambridge, MA: Harvard University Press.

____ (1979). "A Puzzle About Belief." In A. Margalit (ed.), *Meaning and Use*, 239–283. Dordrecht: Reidel.

Kroon, Frederick (1987). "Causal Descriptivism." *Australasian Journal of Philosophy*, 65: 1–17.

Lewis, David (1984). "Putnam's Paradox." *Australasian Journal of Philosophy*, 62: 221–36.

Mill, John Stuart (1843). *A System of Logic*. New York: Harper Brothers.

Putnam, Hilary (1975). "The Meaning of 'Meaning'." In Keith Gunderson (ed.), *Language, Mind, and Knowledge*, pp. 131–93. Minneapolis: University of Minnesota Press.

Richard, Mark (1990). *Propositional Attitudes*. Cambridge: Cambridge University Press.

Russell, Bertrand (1910). "Knowledge by Acquaintance and by Description." *Proceedings of the Aristotelian Society*, 11: 108–28.

Salmon, Nathan (1981). *Reference and Essence*. Princeton, NJ: Princeton University Press.

____ (1986). *Frege's Puzzle*. Cambridge, MA: MIT Press.

____ (1989). "Reference and Information Content: Names and Descriptions." In D. Gabbay and F. Guenther (eds.), *Handbook of Philosophical Logic, Vol. IV*, 409–61. Dordrecht: D. Reidel.

____ (1998). "Nonexistence." *Noûs*, 32: 277–319.

____ (2003). "Naming, Necessity, and Beyond." *Mind*, 112: 447–92.

Searle, John (1958). "Proper Names." *Mind*, 67: 166–73.

____ (1983). *Intentionality*. Cambridge: Cambridge University Press.

Soames, Scott (1987). "Direct Reference, Propositional Attitudes, and Semantic Content." *Philosophical Topics*, 15, pp. 47–87.

____ (2002). *Beyond Rigidity: The Unfinished Semantic Agenda of Naming and Necessity*. Oxford: Oxford University Press.

____ (2004). "Kripke, the Necessary A Posteriori, and the Two-Dimensionalist Heresy." In Garcia-Carpintero and Macià (2004).

—— (2005). *Reference and Description: the Case Against Two-Dimensionalism.* Princeton, NJ: Princeton University Press.

Sosa, David (2001). "Rigidity in the Scope of Russell's Theory." *Noûs*, 35: 1–38.

Stalnaker, Robert (1997). "Reference and Necessity." In Hale and Wright (1997), pp. 534–54.

—— (2001). "On Considering a Possible World as Actual." *Proceedings of the Aristotelian Society*, Supplementary Volume 75, pp. 141–56.

Stanley, Jason (1997). "Names and Rigid Designation." In Hale and Wright (1997), pp. 555–85.

Strawson, Peter (1959). *Individuals.* London: Methuen.

Wilson, Mark (1982). "Predicate Meets Property." *Philosophical Review*, 91: 549–89.

Wittgenstein, Ludwig (1953). *Philosophical Investigations* (trans. G. E. M. Anscombe). London: MacMillan.

CHAPTER 22

WHAT DOES IT TAKE TO REFER?

KENT BACH

Referring is not something an expression does; it is something that
someone can use an expression to do.

P. F. Strawson (1950)

EVEN though it's based on a bad argument, there's something to Strawson's dictum.
He might have likened 'referring expression' to phrases like 'eating utensil' and
'dining room': just as utensils don't eat and dining rooms don't dine, so, he
might have argued, expressions don't refer. Actually, that wasn't his argument.
Rather, Strawson exploited the fact that almost any referring expression, whether
an indexical, demonstrative, proper name, or definite description, can be used to
refer to different things in different contexts. This fact, he argued, is enough to
show that what refers are speakers, not expressions. He didn't reckon here the
perfectly coherent view that an expression's reference can vary with context. So, he
concluded, what varies from context to context is not what a given expression refers
to but what a speaker uses it to refer to. Strawson went on to suggest that there
are several dimensions of difference between various sorts of referring expressions:
degree of dependence on context, degree of "descriptive meaning," and being
governed by a general convention vs. an expression-specific one. But despite these
differences, he insisted that regardless of kind, referring expressions don't themselves
refer—speakers use them to refer.

Strawson's dictum flies in the face of common philosophical lore. It is generally
assumed, and occasionally argued, that there is indeed a class of referring

expressions—indexicals, demonstratives, and proper names—and that they aren't just eminently capable of being used to refer, which nobody can deny, but that they themselves refer, albeit relative to contexts. There is general consensus that at least some expressions do this, but there is considerable dispute about which ones. It is rare to find a philosopher who includes indefinite descriptions among referring expressions, but some are liberal enough to include definite descriptions. Some reject definites but include demonstrative descriptions (complex demonstratives) on their list. Some balk at descriptions of any kind referring but have no qualms about proper names. Some have doubts about proper names referring, but readily include indexicals and simple demonstratives. Yet I can't recall anyone directly responding to Strawson's argument. Instead, what I've observed is that philosophers slide down a verbal slippery slope.

Suppose Madonna says, referring to Britney Spears, "She is ambitious."
Slippery Slide
Madonna is using 'she' to refer to Britney.
Madonna's use (or utterance) of 'she' refers to Britney.
The token of 'she' produced by Madonna refers to Britney.
'She', as used by Madonna, refers to Britney.
'She', relative to the context of its use by Madonna, refers to Britney.

The slide goes from a person using a term to refer to a use referring (as if uses refer) to a reference by a token to reference by a term relative to a use to reference by a term relative to a context.[1]

   With this slippery slide in mind, from now on (except when discussing others' views) instead of using 'referring expression' I'll use the marginally better phrase 'singular term' for expressions that can be used to refer. This phrase is only marginally better because there is also a tradition to use 'singular term' for the natural-language counterparts of individual constants in logic. This tradition excludes definite descriptions from counting as singular terms, at least from the perspective of anyone who has learned the lesson of Russell's (1905) theory of descriptions (however problematic the details of his formulation of it), but using 'singular term' at least has the advantage that I won't have to say that some referring expressions don't refer. By 'reference' I will mean singular reference only (I will not be considering whether general

---

[1] In my view, only the last notion, context-relative reference by an expression, has a genuine place in linguistic semantics. In particular, I think utterance reference is a bastard notion, as is the notion of utterance content considered as semantic. The only respect in which an utterance has content over and above the semantic content (relative to the context) of the uttered sentence is as an intentional act performed by a speaker. In that respect, the content of an utterance is really the content of the speaker's communicative intention in making the utterance. Focusing on the normal case of successful communication, where the listener gets the speaker's communicative intention right, can make it seem as though an utterance has content in its own right, independently of that intention. But this is illusory, as is evident whenever communication fails. In that case, in which the speaker means one thing and his audience thinks he means something else, there is what the speaker means (and what he could reasonably mean) and what his listener takes him to mean (and what she could reasonably take him to mean), but there is no independent utterance content. For further discussion, see Bach, 2005: sec. 1.

terms refer and, if so, to what), and when I describe a use as non-referential, I will not mean that reference fails but that there is no attempt to refer.[2]

In this chapter, I will be making a number of points about reference, both speaker reference and linguistic (or semantic) reference. The bottom line is simple: reference ain't easy—at least not nearly as easy as commonly supposed. Or so it seems to me. Much of what speakers do that passes for reference is really something else, and much of what passes for linguistic reference is really nothing more than speaker reference. But here's a running disclaimer: I do not pretend that the data, observations, or even the arguments presented here are conclusive. I do think they support what might fairly be regarded as default hypotheses about speaker reference and linguistic reference. So if you think these hypotheses are wrong, you need to show that. You need to argue against them and to find a way to accommodate or explain away the data and the observations.

We'll take up speaker reference first. Referring is one of the basic things we do with words, and it would be a good idea to understand what that involves and requires before worrying about the linguistic means by which this is done. Then we'll focus on expressions that are used to refer. Rather than start with intuitions about the semantic values or propositional contributions of various singular terms and proceed from there, we're going to start with common uses of singular terms. By going from speaker reference to linguistic reference, we'll be in a position to raise questions about the semantics of singular terms that take these various uses into account. Here are the main points to be made:

Speaker Reference

s0 Speaker reference is a four-place relation, between a speaker, an expression, an audience, and a referent: you use an expression to refer someone to something.
s1 To be in a position to refer to something (or to understand a reference to it) requires being able to have singular thoughts about it, and that requires perceiving it, being informed of it, or (having perceived or been informed of it) remembering it.
s2 To refer an audience to something involves conveying a singular proposition about it.

---

[2] Although our topic is singular reference, there is a broad sense in which every expression refers (or at least every expression that has a semantic value that contributes to the propositional content of sentences in which it occurs). There is also the question of which expressions have such semantic values or, to put it differently, which syntactic units are semantic units. The most famous instance of this question concerns definite descriptions. Russell's answer was that they are not semantic units. Although he granted that definite descriptions have denotations of sorts, according to his theory of descriptions they "disappear on analysis" and are therefore semantically inert. This does not follow from the fact (or alleged fact, if Graff (2001) is correct) that they are quantifier phrases, because quantifier phrases can be, and nowadays often are, treated as semantic units whose semantic values are properties of properties (with the determiners they contain having two-place relations between properties as their semantic values). In any case, the phrase 'referring expression' is ordinarily limited to any expression whose propositional contribution is its referent (if it has one).

S3 In using a certain expression to refer someone to something, you are trying to get them, via the fact that you are using that expression, to think of it as what you intend them to think of.

S4 We generally choose the least informative sort of expression whose use will enable the hearer to identify the individual we wish to refer to, but this is not a matter of convention.

S5 Even though definite descriptions are not referring expressions, often the only way to refer to something is by using a definite description.

S6 Just as an object can be described without being referred to, so a singular proposition can be described without being grasped.

S7 Descriptive 'reference', or singling out, is not genuine reference.

S8 With a specific use of an indefinite description, one is not referring but merely alluding to something.

Linguistic (semantic) Reference and Singular Terms

L0 If an expression refers, it does so directly, by introducing its referent into the proposition semantically expressed by sentences in which it occurs (so 'direct reference' is redundant).

L1 So-called singular terms or referring expressions—indexicals, demonstratives (both simple and complex), proper names, and definite descriptions—can all be used in non-referential ways too.

L2 A given singular term seems to mean the same thing whether it is used referentially or not, and an adequate semantic theory should explain this or else explain it away.

L3 When meaning doesn't fix reference, generally "context" doesn't either.

L4 The speaker's referential intention determines speaker reference, but it does not determine semantic reference, except in a pickwickian way.

L5 There is no such thing as descriptive "reference-fixing" (not because something isn't fixed, but because it isn't reference).

22.1 SPEAKER REFERENCE

Here's a platitude for you. We commonly talk about particular persons, places, or things. We refer to them and ascribe properties to them. In so doing, we are able to accommodate the fact that an individual can change over time (as to properties, relations, and parts), that our conception of it can also change over time, that we can be mistaken in our conception of it, and that different people's conceptions of the same individual can differ. This suggests something less platitudinous: the feat it describes is possible because in thinking of and in referring to an individual we are not constrained to represent it as that which has certain properties. This may smack of direct reference but, as we will see shortly, it is really indicative of something else. First we need to consider what it is to refer to something.

s0) Speaker reference is a four-place relation, between a speaker, an expression, an audience, and a referent: you use an expression to refer someone to something

What referring is depends on whether expressions do it or speakers do it. The reference relation between singular terms and individuals (objects, persons, times, places, etc.) is a two-place relation.[3] However complicated the explanation for what makes it the case that a certain term refers to a certain thing, the relation itself is between the term and the thing. If 'Mt. Everest' refers to Mt. Everest, this is a simple relation between a linguistic expression and a thing, regardless of what explains the fact that this relation obtains. On the other hand, when a speaker uses an expression to refer, the relation in question is a four-place relation: a *speaker* uses an *expression* to refer his *audience* to an *individual.* Communication is essentially an interpersonal affair, and reference by a speaker is part and parcel of an act of communication.[4] So whereas expressions just refer to things, speakers don't just refer but use expressions to refer audiences to things.

I am claiming, then, that speaker reference is essentially an audience-directed affair.[5] One might object and suggest there is another, more basic sort of speaker reference that has nothing directly to do with an audience. This more basic sort involves a specifically *semantic* intention regarding a singular term (except for "pure" indexicals like 'I' and 'today') that endows it with its reference. For example, in using 'that' to refer to a certain thing, the speaker intends 'that' to stand for that thing then and, *in addition,* intends his audience to recognize that it does. So this view implies that speakers have two referential intentions, one semantic and one pragmatic (communicative). One primarily concerns the referring expression, and the other concerns how the audience is to interpret it.

---

[3] One could argue that linguistic reference is not really a two-place relation, in that (some) expressions, namely indexicals and demonstratives, refer only relative to a context, so that the same expression can have different referents in different contexts, and, further, that it is only as belonging to a particular language that an expression refers, so that the same expression could have different referents in different languages. In reply one could argue, first, that even if linguistic reference is context-relative, this shows only the relation that obtains between an expression and its referent is context-bound, not that it is really a three-term relation, and, second, that the same expression cannot literally occur in more than one language (that expressions are individuated partly by the languages they belong to). I think that nothing substantive hinges on either question—both seem merely terminological.

[4] The view I am alluding to, inspired largely by Austin (1962), Strawson (1964), and Grice (in the papers on meaning and conversation collected in his 1989 volume), was expounded and defended in Bach and Harnish, 1979 and is sketched in Bach, 2004a.

[5] Evans takes a similar view. He conceives of referring as part of communicating, and thinks that "communication is essentially a mode of the transmission of knowledge" (1982: 312), whereby the addressee comes to know of the individual to which the speaker refers.

Though consistent with the deep-seated tendency to treat singular terms used to refer as themselves referring, this view implausibly multiplies intentions beyond necessity. Moreover, it overlooks the fact that in choosing a singular term to use, the speaker does so with the audience in mind. One chooses it to enable one's audience to think of or focus on the intended object. So I question whether speakers have referential intentions that are not part of their communicative intentions. As I see it, a speaker has one referential intention that is essentially audience-directed, an intention to use a certain expression to refer his audience to a certain thing. Indeed, part of what enables them to think of or focus on what one intends them to is the pragmatic fact that one is using that expression. This information is not carried by the expression itself, not even in a context-relative way (see Point L3).

There is a different and psychologically more plausible way of thinking of the connection between a person's demonstrative thought (a thought he would express using a demonstrative) and the linguistic means by which he expresses the thought. Say you look at a lamp near you and think a singular thought that you would express by uttering "That is bright." The connection between your having this thought and its linguistic manifestation is not a matter of intention but a matter of expression. You think of the lamp by way of a percept, which functions as a mental indexical, and you use a demonstrative to express that constituent of your thought. But your thought does not *itself* have a demonstrative constituent; it has merely an indexical one. That is, there is nothing by means of which you are calling your *own* attention to the object you're attending to. You're just attending to it. You don't think of the lamp as "that" but, rather, think of it under the percept involved in your attending to it. The fact that you are inclined to express your thought by uttering "That is bright" does not show that you have any independent intention to use 'that' for the lamp, apart from your communicative intention to refer your audience to it. What happens, rather, is that you form an intention to refer to a certain thing and choose an expression whose use by you, under the circumstances, will enable your audience to figure out that this is what you intend to refer to (see Points S3 and S4 below).

S1) To be in a position to refer to something (or to understand a reference to it) requires being able to have singular thoughts about it, and that requires perceiving it, being informed of it, or (having perceived or been informed of it) remembering it

Obviously you can't refer to something unless you're in a position to refer to it. So what does that involve? Here I will sketch but not defend a view on singular thought, according to which we have singular thoughts about objects we are perceiving, have perceived, or have been informed of (Bach, 1987/1994: ch. 1). We do so by means of non-descriptive, '*de re* modes of presentation', which connect us, whether immediately or remotely, to an object. The connection is causal—historical, but the connection involves a chain of representations originating with a perception of the object. Which object one is thinking of is determined relationally, not satisfaction-ally. That is, the object one's thought is about is a matter not of satisfying a certain description but of being in a certain relation to that very thought (token). We cannot form a singular thought about an individual we can "think of" only under a descrip-tion. So, for example, we cannot think of the first child born in the 22nd century because we are not suitably connected to that individual (see Point s7). We cannot think of *it* but merely that there will exist a unique individual of a certain sort. Our thought "about" that child is general in content, not singular. We cannot think of the first child born in the fourth century BC either. However, we can think of Aristotle, because we are connected to him through a long chain of communication. We can think of him even though we could not have recognized him, just as I can think of the bird that just flew by my window. Being able to think of an individual does not require being able to identify that individual by means of a uniquely characterizing description.[6]

So on my conception of singular thought, there must be a representational connection, however remote and many-linked, between thought and object. A more restrictive view, though not nearly as restrictive as Russell's (1917, 1918), limits this connection to personal acquaintance (via perception and perception-based memory), and disallows singular thoughts about unfamiliar objects. A more liberal view would allow singular thought via uniquely identifying descriptions of special sorts. In any case, although I am assuming the above conception of singular thought, the questions to be asked and the distinctions to be drawn, such as the distinction between referring to something and merely alluding to or merely singling out something, do not essentially depend on that conception (of course, how one uses these distinctions to divide cases does depend on one's conception). I'll mainly rely on the assumption that one can have singular thoughts about at least some objects one has not perceived and that only certain relations one can bear to an object put one in a position to have singular thoughts about it.

s2) To refer an audience to something involves conveying a singular proposition about it

If the expression (normally a noun phrase) one uses to refer to something itself refers to that thing, that expression must introduce an object into what is semantically

---

[6] There is the further question of whether a singular proposition can comprise the complete content of a singular thought. Schiffer (1978) argued that it cannot. In my view, *de re* modes of presentation are also involved (Bach, 1987/94: ch. 1). Moreover, I have argued that a belief ascription whose 'that'-clause expresses a singular proposition does not fully individuate the belief being ascribed (Bach, 1997, 2000). I point out that, for example, the one 'that'-clause (assuming it expresses a singular proposition) in the two ascriptions, 'Peter believes that Paderewski had musical talent' and 'Peter disbelieves that Paderewski had musical talent', does not fully characterize something that Peter both believes and disbelieves. And, as I say, every case is potentially a Paderewski case.

expressed by the sentence in which it occurs. If that sentence semantically expresses a proposition (it might not—see Bach 1994), it expresses a singular proposition with respect to that object.[7] The referent of that expression is a constituent of that proposition. But whether or not that expression itself refers, when a speaker uses it to refer he uses it to indicate which thing he is speaking about. If he is making an assertive utterance, he is asserting a singular proposition about that object.

What does it take to refer to an individual?[8] In particular, can you refer to something if, as Russell would say, you "know it only by description"? Suppose you use a description and believe there to be a unique individual that satisfies the description, but you are not in a position to think of that individual. Can you refer to that individual anyway? If descriptions are quantificational and the propositions semantically expressed by sentences containing them are general, it would seem that you can't use such a sentence to convey a singular proposition involving whichever individual satisfies the description (see Point S7). For example, if you said, "The Sultan of Brunei is fabulously wealthy" but had no idea who the sultan of Brunei is, you would be stating a general proposition, albeit one that is made true by a fact about a particular individual (to wit, Haji Hassanal Bolkiah Mu'izzaddin Waddaulah). Of course, your audience, if they were in a position to think of that individual and thought that you were too, might mistakenly take you to be conveying a singular proposition, but that's another matter. Here's a different situation. Suppose you are in a position to think of a certain individual, but you do not wish to indicate which individual that is. You might say, for example, "A special person is coming to visit." You intend your audience to realize that you have a certain individual in mind, but you do not intend them to figure out who it is. Indeed, you intend them not to. You are not referring but merely *alluding* to that individual (see Point S8). In my view, neither alluding to an individual nor singling one out descriptively count as referring to it—you are not expressing a singular proposition about it.

S3) In using a certain expression to refer someone to something, you are trying to get them, via the fact that you are using that expression, to think of it as what you intend them to think of

In using a noun phrase to refer to a certain individual, your aim is to get your audience to think of that individual by way of identifying that individual as the one you are thinking of, hence referring to. How referring works and what it involves depends on whether the referent is already the subject of discussion, is at least an object of the audience's attention, is at least capable of being called immediately to their attention,

---

[7] Note that a proposition, e.g. the proposition that I eat anchovies, can be singular with respect to one argument place and general with respect to another.

[8] Our discussion here is limited to reference to spatio-temporal things.

is at least familiar to them, or is not even familiar to them. Which situation obtains constrains what sort of singular term you need to use to enable them to think of, or at least to direct or keep their attention on, the object you intend to be referring to. Also, what it takes to refer your audience to something depends on whether it has a name and whether you and they know its name. Reference succeeds only if your audience identifies the individual you are talking about *as* the individual you intend to be talking about. Your audience must think of the right thing in the right way, of the individual intended in the way intended. If your audience identifies the individual in some other way, that's a matter of luck, not of successful communication. It is rather like having a justified true belief that p without knowing that p.

There are different ways in which a speaker can fail to refer. In the case just considered, there is a certain thing he intends to refer to, but his listener does not identify the intended individual (in the intended way). More interesting is the case in which the speaker intends to refer to something but there is no such thing. In that case there is no singular proposition about that individual to be expressed or conveyed. The speaker can have a referential intention, and his audience can recognize that he has such an intention, but nothing counts as getting it right. The speaker's referential intention cannot be fulfilled, and full communication cannot be achieved. Since there is nothing for the hearer to identify, and no singular proposition for her to entertain, the best the hearer can do is recognize that the speaker intends to convey a singular proposition of a certain sort. The speaker has the right sort of intention, to be speaking of some particular thing, but there is no thing for him to succeed in referring to.

A different situation arises when the speaker merely makes as if to refer to something, perhaps to deceive the hearer ("See that spider over there?") or perhaps to play along with the hearer's mistaken belief in the existence of something ("Bigfoot was seen in Montana last night"). In this case, although the speaker does not intend to refer to something, he does intend to be taken to be. He can succeed in that if he is taken to be referring to the individual the hearer mistakenly believes in. But since there is no such thing, there is no singular proposition to be grasped.

s4) We generally choose the least informative sort of expression whose use will enable the hearer to identify the individual we wish to refer to, but this is not a matter of convention

Suppose you want to refer to your boss. In some circumstances, it may be enough to use the pronoun 'she' (or 'he', as the case may be). The only semantic constraint on what 'she' can be used to refer to is that the referent be female (ships and countries excepted). So its use provides only the information that the intended referent is female. If it is to be used successfully to refer the hearer to a certain female, there must be some female that your audience can reasonably suppose you intend to be referring to. If out of the blue you said, "She is insufferable," intending with 'she' to refer to your boss, you could not reasonably expect to be taken to be referring to her. However, if she were already salient, say by being visually prominent or by having just been mentioned, or you made her salient in some way, say by pointing to her office or to a picture of her, then using 'she' would suffice. In other circumstances, you would have to use some more elaborate expression. For example, to distinguish her from other women in a group you could use 'that woman', with stress on 'that' and an accompanying demonstration. Or, assuming your audience knows her by name, you could refer to her by name. Otherwise, you would have to use a definite description, say 'my boss'.

This example suggests that a speaker, in choosing an expression to use to refer the hearer to the individual he has in mind, is in effect answering the following question: given the circumstances of utterance, the history and direction of the conversation, and the mutual knowledge between me and my audience, how informative an expression do I need to use to enable them to identify the individual I have in mind? Note that informativeness here can depend not only the semantic information encoded by the expression but on the information carried by the fact that *it* is being used.

Some linguists have suggested that which sort of expression is most appropriately used depends, as a matter of convention, on the degree of "accessibility" (or "givenness" or "familiarity") of the intended referent. For example, Gundel, Hedberg, and Zacharski (1993) distinguish being in focus (being the unique item under discussion or current center of mutual attention), being activated (being an item under discussion or being an object of mutual awareness), being familiar (being mutually known), and being uniquely identifiable (satisfying a definite description). They suggest that different degrees of accessibility are not merely associated with but, as a matter of linguistic convention, are encoded by different types of singular terms. Perhaps they suggest this because, taking their accessibility scale to concern the cognitive status of representations in the mind of the hearer, they think this status has to be linguistically marked if it is to play a cognitive role. As I see it, however, this scale concerns the mutual (between speaker and hearer) cognitive status of the intended referent. After all, in using an expression to refer the speaker aims to ensure that the hearer thinks of the very object the speaker is thinking of, and what matters is that the expression used to refer, and the fact that the speaker is using it, provide the hearer with enough information to figure out what he is intended to take the speaker to be thinking of, hence to think of it himself. The parsimonious alternative to Gundel *et al.*'s conventionalist view is that the different degrees of accessibility associated with different types of singular terms are not encoded at all; rather, the correlation is a by-product of the interaction between semantic information that *is* encoded by these expressions and general facts about rational communication. On this, the null hypothesis, it is *because* different expressions are more or less informative that the things they can be used to refer to must be less or more accessible. That is, the more accessible the referent is, the less information needs to be carried by the expression used to refer to it to enable the hearer to identify it.

Notice that not only is it enough to use the least informative sort of expression needed to enable your audience to identify the individual you have in mind, it is normally misleading to use a more informative one (or at least odd, as when Michael Jordan would refer to himself as "Michael Jordan"). So, in general, when you can use an indexical to refer to something, you should. And when you can use a short definite or demonstrative description to refer to something rather than use a long one, you should. For example, in talking to a student, normally you would refer to yourself with 'I'. Only if your capacity as, say, his adviser needed to be stressed, would you use 'your adviser' to refer to yourself. Normally you would only use it to refer to someone else. Similarly, you wouldn't refer to the previous day by its date or even as 'last Thursday' when you could use 'yesterday'. To refer to something that has just been mentioned, you would use 'it' if nothing else is also salient. Otherwise, you would use a definite description, say 'the car', but not 'the car that Jones rented last week to drive to Lake Tahoe', even if, indeed especially if, it had just been said that Jones rented a car the previous week to drive to Lake Tahoe. In telling a story about a particular person, it is always sufficient, once the individual is introduced, to use a personal pronoun—provided, of course, that no other individual of the same gender has been introduced in the meantime. There are stylistic or other literary reasons to use their name or a definite description every so often, but unless it is obvious that this is the name or a description of the individual in question, it would be inferred that reference is being made to some other individual. This inference would be made on the charitable assumption that one is not being needlessly informative (and violating Grice's (1989: 26) second maxim of quantity).

The basic point here is that to refer to something you need to use an available singular term that is as informative as necessary but no more.

s5) Even though definite descriptions are not referring expressions, often the only way to refer to something is by using a definite description

If Russell's theory of descriptions is basically right, which I think it is (see Bach, 2004b), then definite descriptions are the paradigm of singular terms that can be used to refer but are not linguistically (semantically) referential.[9] So we should not be overly impressed by the fact that a given class of singular terms is commonly used referentially.

Suppose you want to refer to some thing (or someone). Suppose it is not perceptually present, has not just come up in the conversation, and is not otherwise salient. Suppose that it does not have a name or that you are unaware of its name or think

---

[9] It is odd that Kripke (1977), in defending Russell's theory against the claim that Donnellan's (1966) distinction has semantic significance, contrasts "speaker's reference" with a definite description's "semantic reference." But by this he can only mean the description's denotation, the individual that uniquely satisfies it. See Point 10 below.

your audience is unaware. Then you cannot use an indexical, a demonstrative (pronoun or phrase), or a proper name to refer to it. If you want to refer to it, what are you going to do? Unless you can find it or a picture or some other non-linguistic representation of it to point to, you need to use a linguistic expression, some sort of singular noun phrase (what else?), to call it to your audience's attention. You must choose one that will provide your audience with enough information to figure out, partly on the supposition that you intend them to figure out, which object you're talking about. Your only recourse is to use a definite description.

This raises the question, when you use a description, how does your audience know that you are referring to something and expressing a singular proposition, rather than making a general statement and expressing a kind of existential proposition? Although the presence of a description does not signal that you are referring—semantically, descriptions are not referring expressions—what you are saying might not be the sort of thing that you could assert on general grounds, that is, as not based on knowledge of some particular individual (see Ludlow and Neale, 1991). This will certainly be true whenever it is mutually evident which individual satisfies the description in question and what is being said regarding the individual that satisfies the description can only be supposed to be based on evidence about that individual. For example, if Claire says to me, "The decanter is broken," I can't not take her to be talking about the actual decanter of ours. On the other hand, if before we decided on a decanter she said, "The decanter had better not cost more than $100," clearly she would be making a general statement pertaining to whichever decanter we buy. Also, its being mutually evident which individual satisfies a description will generally be sufficient for a referential use, since there will usually be no reason for the hearer not to be taken as making a singular statement about that individual. This applies especially to descriptions of occupiers of social positions or practical roles, such as 'the boss' or 'the freezer'. Moreover, if the description is incomplete, as in these cases, and there is no mutually salient or obviously distinctive completion in sight, then the hearer, at least if he and the speaker are mutually familiar with the boss or freezer in question, can only take the description to be used referentially.[10] But if 'the F' is incomplete and it is obvious that the hearer is unfamiliar with the relevant F, then a (referential) use of 'the F' must be preceded by an introduction of the relevant F.

Now according to Russell's theory, a sentence of the form 'The F is G' semantically expresses a general (uniqueness) proposition. So if you utter such a sentence but use the description referentially, what you *say* is a general proposition but what you *mean* is a singular one.[11] But how and why does the hearer take you to be doing that? For

[10] Why *mutually* salient or familiar? Obviously it is not enough for the intended referent to be salient or familiar merely to the speaker, if it is not salient or familiar to the audience and if this is not evident to the speaker (etc.). So, in general, when I say that something is salient or familiar, I will mean that it is mutually so.

[11] Here and throughout I am assuming a distinction between saying and meaning or stating, a distinction that I have tried elsewhere to vindicate (Bach, 2001). It corresponds to Austin's distinction between locutionary and illocutionary acts. This distinction is often blurred, e.g. by Donnellan (1966),

example, if you uttered 'The plumber is pernicious,' I would take you to be asserting not a general proposition but a singular one, about the plumber. Why would I do that? Well, I am acquainted with the plumber and presumably so are you. Besides, that a certain individual is a plumber has nothing to do with his being pernicious. To suppose that it does would be to take you to be stating something for which you have no evidence (you would be violating Grice's (1989: 27) second maxim of quality). So I have no reason to suppose, as if you were unfamiliar with the plumber, that you are making a general statement, the content of which is independent of who the plumber is. So I have positive reason to think that you have in mind, and intend me to think you have in mind, a certain individual who satisfies the description you are using.

If you are using the description to refer and I am taking you to be doing so, we must have ways of thinking of the individual in question, the plumber, in some other way than as the plumber. Presumably we both remember him by way of a memory image derived from seeing him. In thinking of him via that image, you take him to be the plumber and use the description 'the plumber' to identify him for me, which triggers my memory of him. We both think of him, via our respective memories of him, as being the plumber. This fits with how Mill describes the functioning of a proper name in thought as an "unmeaning mark which we connect in our minds with the idea of the object, in order that whenever the mark meets our eyes or occurs to our thoughts, we may think of that individual object" (1872: 22). Though not "unmeaning," a definite description can play a similar role. In using a description referentially, you are using it in lieu of a sign for the object.

s6) Just as an object can be described without being referred to, so a singular proposition can be described without being grasped

It is one thing to entertain a singular proposition and another thing merely to know that there exists a certain such proposition. Russell's famous discussion of Bismarck illustrates how this can be. He operates with a notoriously restrictive notion of acquaintance, but this is not really essential to the distinction he is drawing. I agree with Russell that we cannot have singular thoughts about individuals we "know only by description," but I will not assume that the ones we can have singular thoughts about are limited to those with which we are acquainted in his highly restrictive sense. We can have singular thoughts about individuals we are perceiving, have perceived, or have been informed of and remember. So although Russell's choice of example (Bismarck) would have to be changed to be made consistent with a much more liberal notion of acquaintance, I will use it to illustrate his distinction.

Russell contrasts the situation of Bismarck himself, who "might have used the name ['Bismarck'] directly to designate [himself] . . . to ma[k]e a judgment about

---

whenever he suggests that in using a description referentially rather than attributively, one is *saying* something different, allegedly because the content of the description does not enter into what is said.

himself" having himself as a constituent (1917: 209), with *our* situation in respect to him:

> when we make a statement about something known only by description, we often intend to make our statement, not in the form involving the description, but about the actual thing described. That is, when we say anything about Bismarck, we should like, if we could, to make the judgment which Bismarck alone can make, namely, the judgment of which he himself is a constituent. [But] in this we are necessarily defeated. ... What enables us to communicate in spite of the varying descriptions we employ is that we know there is a true proposition concerning the actual Bismarck and that, however we may vary the description (as long as the description is correct), the proposition described is still the same. This proposition, which is described and is known to be true, is what interests us; but we are not acquainted with the proposition itself, and do not know it, though we know it is true. (1917: 210–11)

The proposition that "interests us" is a singular proposition, but we cannot actually entertain it—we can know it only by description, that is, by entertaining a general (uniqueness) proposition which, if true, is made true by a fact involving Bismarck. But this general proposition does not itself involve Bismarck, and would be thinkable even if Bismarck never existed.[12]

s7) Descriptive 'reference', or singling out, is not genuine reference

In summing up his account of the referential—attributive distinction, Keith Donnellan concedes that there is a kind of reference, reference in a "very weak sense," associated with the attributive use of a definite description (1966: 304). Since he is contrasting that use with the referential use, this is something of a token concession. Reference in this very weak sense is too weak to count as genuine reference, for one is "referring" to whatever happens to satisfy the description, and one would be "referring" to something else were it to have satisfied the description instead. This is clear in modal contexts, such as in (1):

(1) The next president, though probably a man, could be a woman.

---

[12] The difference in type of proposition is clear from Russell's observations about the use of the indefinite description 'a man':

What do I really assert when I assert "I met a man"? Let us assume, for the moment, that my assertion is true, and that in fact I met Jones. It is clear that what I assert is *not* "I met Jones." I may say "I met a man, but it was not Jones"; in that case, though I lie, I do not contradict myself, as I should do if when I say I met a man I really mean that I met Jones. It is clear also that the person to whom I am speaking can understand what I say, even if he is a foreigner and has never heard of Jones. But we may go further: not only Jones, but no actual man, enters into my statement. This becomes obvious when the statement is false, since there is no more reason why Jones should be supposed to enter into the statement than why anyone else should. Indeed, the statement would remain significant, though it could not possibly be true, even if there were no man at all. (1919: 167–8)

The speaker is not likely to be asserting of some one potential president that he or she will probably be a man but could be a woman, say if he had a sex-change operation before her inauguration. Here the description is taken to fall within the scope of 'could'. The speaker is allowing for different possible presidents, some male, some female, only one of whom will actually be the next president. Surely this is not reference, not even in a very weak sense.

David Kaplan seems to think otherwise. He suggests that one can use a description to refer to something even if one is not in a position to have a singular thought about it or, as he would say, not "en rapport" with it. In his view, "a special form of knowledge of an object is neither required nor presupposed in order that a person may entertain as object of thought a singular proposition involving that object" (1989a: 536). As he asks rhetorically, "If pointing can be taken as a form of describing, why not take describing as a form of pointing?" (1979: 392). Well, there's a reason why not.

Consider, for example, whether one can refer to the first child born in the 22nd century. Assume that this description will eventually be satisfied (uniquely), and suppose that one wishes to assert that this child will be bald. Then there is a singular proposition involving that child, to the effect that it will be bald.[13] However, this is not the proposition as semantically expressed by (2),

(2) The first child to be born in the 22nd century will be bald.

This sentence expresses a general (uniqueness) proposition. Even so, in uttering this sentence can one use the description 'the first child to be born in the 22nd century' referentially, to refer to that child? Kaplan thinks there is nothing to prevent this, that it is a perfectly good example of pointing by means of describing. However, what enables one to form an intention to refer to the individual who happens to satisfy that description? If one is prepared to assert (2), presumably one is prepared to do so without regard to who the actual such child will be—one's grounds are general, not singular. For example, one might believe that the first child born in the 22nd century is likely to be born in China and that Chinese children born around then will all be bald, thanks to China's unrestrained use of nuclear power. But this only goes to show that one's use of the description is likely to be taken to be attributive. Unless one were known to be a powerful clairvoyant, one could not plausibly be supposed to have singular grounds for making the statement. Yet Kaplan thinks that one could intend to use the description referentially anyway, to whoever actually will be the first child born in the 22nd century. It seems, however, that one is in the same predicament as the one Russell thought anyone other than Bismarck would be in if he wanted to refer to Bismarck.

---

[13] A singular proposition is not only object-involving but also object-dependent, in that it would not exist if its object-constituent did not exist (at some time or other). So a singular proposition exists contingently. This does not imply that it exists only when its object-constituent exists. Existing contingently does not make singular propositions temporal.

Would it help to have the tacit modal intention of using the description rigidly, or even to insert the word 'actual' into the description? Referring to something involves expressing a singular proposition about it, but rigidifying the description or including the word 'actual' would not make its use referential.[14] Even though the only individual whose properties are relevant to the truth or falsity of the proposition being expressed (even if that proposition is modal) is the actual F (if it exists), in this still that proposition is general, not singular. This proposition may in some sense be object-dependent, but it is not object-involving. The property of being the actual F may enter into the proposition, but the actual F does not.

The fact that there is something that satisfies a certain definite description does not mean that one can refer to it. One can use a description to identify or, as I will say, *single out* something without actually *referring* to it. For if a different individual satisfied the description or you were discussing a hypothetical situation in which that would be the case, you would have singled out that individual instead. Nevertheless, you can use the description just as though you were introducing the thing that satisfies it into the discourse. You can, for example, use pronouns to "refer" back to it. You can say, "The first child to be born in the 22ⁿᵈ century will be bald. It will be too poor to use Rogaine." Giving it a name won't help. You could dub this child 'Newman-1', but this would not enable you to refer to it or to entertain singular propositions involving it. In this, as Russell would have said, "we are necessarily defeated."

It might be objected that in characterizing descriptive "reference" as singling out and not as referring to an object, I am not making a substantive claim but am merely engaging in terminological legislation. I would reply that anyone who insists on calling this *reference* should either show that a singular proposition is expressed or explain why, when one conveys a general, object-independent proposition, this should still count as referring. One possible reason is taxonomic: if we are to maintain that indexicals and demonstratives are inherently referring expressions and not merely expressions that are normally used to refer, we would have to count merely singling out an object, even if we are not in a position to have singular thoughts about it, as actually referring to it. Then, for example, using 'he' or 'that child' to single out the first child born in the 22ⁿᵈ century would count as referring to it.[15] But the question is whether this *should* count as real referring. As we will see (see Point L1 below), the mere fact that philosophers are in the habit of calling indexicals and demonstratives "referring expressions," as if that's what they inherently are, does not justify cultivating this habit.

---

[14] Kaplan even proposes some notation, of putting the description in brackets and preceding it with his 'dthat' operator, which is supposed to yield a term that directly refers, in this case to whoever actually will be the first child born in the 22ⁿᵈ century and enables a speaker explicitly to refer to that child. Kaplan seems to think this ability can be created with the stroke of a pen. However, as Point L5 will suggest, it is not clear how the user of such a phrase could thereby refer to, and form singular thoughts about that individual.

[15] Indeed, one can use such expressions without even singling out an individual, as in, "If a child eats a radioactive Mars bar, he/that child will be bald."

s8) With a specific use of an indefinite description, one is not referring but merely alluding to something

Indefinite descriptions can be used non-specifically, referentially, or specifically.[16] In the very common non-specific (or purely quantificational) use, there is no indication that the speaker has any particular thing in mind; one is expressing a general proposition. With the referential use, which is relatively rare, as it is with quantificational phrases generally, one does express a singular proposition (see Ludlow and Neale, 1991: 176–80), but this is about an individual that is already the focus of mutual attention. Here I will consider the specific use of indefinite descriptions.

What is distinctive about the *specific* use is that the speaker communicates *that* he has a certain individual in mind, but he is not communicating *which* individual it is, and he doesn't intend you to identify it. Suppose a man says to his wife,

(3) An old girlfriend will call today.

Unless he thinks this is the sort of day for a call from an old girlfriend, presumably he has a particular one in mind. He could have made this clear by including the word 'certain' (or 'particular'), as in "A certain old girlfriend will call today."[17] He could even elaborate on why he is not specifying which old girlfriend it is by continuing "An old girlfriend will call today" with "but I can't tell you who" or "but only to discuss Russell."

In a specific use, the speaker indicates that he is in a position to refer to a certain individual, but is not actually doing so. He is not identifying or trying to enable the hearer to identify that individual—he is merely *alluding* to her. He has a certain singular proposition in mind but is not trying to convey it. So what must the hearer do in order to understand the utterance? It would seem that she must merely recognize that the speaker has some singular proposition in mind, about a certain individual of the mentioned sort, in this case an old girlfriend.

It might be objected that a specific use of an indefinite description is a limiting case of a referential use, not mere allusion but what might be called 'unspecified'

---

[16] They can also be used predicatively, as when one refers to an object and describes it as a such-and-such, as when you say of the thing in your hand, 'This is a pomegranate.' It is arguable that this is not really a quantificational use but a distinctively predicative use, no different in kind from saying, 'This is red'. It is merely because phrases containing singular common nouns require (in English) an article that one cannot say, 'This is pomegranate' (one could say the equivalent of this in Russian). Graff (2001) has argued that *all* uses of indefinite descriptions are actually predicative, and boldly extends her arguments to definite descriptions. Her account also covers generic uses of definite and indefinite descriptions, as in 'The tiger has stripes' and 'A philosopher is not in it for the money.'

[17] I do not mean to suggest that 'a certain F' is always used to indicate that the speaker has a particular unspecified individual in mind. He might have in mind merely some unexpressed restriction on 'F'. For example, one might say, 'A certain contestant will go home happy', without specifying that whoever wins the contest in question will go home happy. Similarly, an utterance of the quantified 'Every author loves a certain book' could be made true if every author loves, say, the first book he wrote.

reference. After all, can't the hearer, recognizing that the speaker has some individual in mind, at least think of that individual under the description 'the individual the speaker has in mind'? But, as we have already seen, descriptive 'reference' is not genuine reference. Besides, the speaker is not really referring the hearer to that individual and, in particular, does not intend her to think of the individual he has in mind under the description 'the individual you (the speaker) have in mind' or in any similar way. He is merely indicating that he has a certain unspecified individual in mind. That is, he is not referring but merely alluding to that individual.

To appreciate why this is, consider a situation in which the speaker has in mind one F among many and proceeds to say something not true of that individual. Suppose a group of unsavory men crash a party late at night and start a fight. Later an elderly partygoer utters (4) to the police,

(4) A big hoodlum had a concealed weapon.

She has a particular hoodlum in mind when she says this, but does not specify which one. Obviously the words 'a big hoodlum' do not refer to the hoodlum she had in mind, for if some big hoodlum had a concealed weapon but she was mistaken about which one, (4) would still be true. So (4) semantically expresses a general proposition. Even so, since the elderly partygoer does have a certain hoodlum in mind, is she using this indefinite description to refer to that hoodlum? Even if what she said is a general proposition, is what she meant a singular proposition, about the hoodlum she had in mind? No, because the police could understand her perfectly well without having any idea which hoodlum she has in mind. They understand merely that she has a certain hoodlum in mind, the one she is alluding to. It seems, then, that alluding is not a kind of referring.

Summing Up So Far

According to the picture sketched here, being in a position to refer to something requires being able to have singular thoughts about it. That requires perceiving it, being informed of it, or, having perceived or been informed of it, remembering it. Thinking of it under a description is not enough. Succeeding in referring one's audience to something requires them to form a singular thought about it (they must also take it to be the thing one is talking about). From this perspective, much of what speakers do that passes for referring really isn't. This is evident once we distinguish referring to something from merely alluding to something or just singling something out descriptively. In referring to something one conveys a singular proposition having that thing as a constituent. When one alludes to something, one does have a singular proposition in mind, and this may be evident to one's audience, but one is not conveying that proposition. And singling something out descriptively involves conveying merely a general, uniqueness proposition.

It is worth mentioning a couple of other things speakers do that sometimes pass for referring. First there is so-called "discourse reference," illustrated here:

(5) Russell met a man today. He/The man was bald.

Here an unbound pronoun or, alternatively, a definite description, is used anaphorically on an indefinite description. Now if the speaker is in no position to refer to the man Russell met that day, he can't very well use 'he' or 'the man' to refer to that man.[18] The most he can intend to convey is the general proposition that Russell met that day a man who was bald.[19] Even so, many semanticists would describe this man, even if there is no such man, as a "discourse referent." I am not suggesting that these semanticists seriously believe that discourse referents are real referents, but this only makes it puzzling why they use that locution.[20]

Then there is the case of so-called fictional "reference." This is far too big a topic to take up here, but it needs to be mentioned because it is sometimes regarded as genuine reference. Here we must distinguish "reference" in a fiction from reference outside the fiction to fictional entities. If Nathan Salmon (1998) is right in suggesting that fictional entities, such as characters in a play, are real, albeit abstract entities, then *we* can genuinely refer to them. However, authors of fictions are not purporting to refer to abstract entities but to persons, places, and things. So "reference" in a fiction, except when it is to real persons, places, and things, is not genuine reference but pseudo-reference. Authors don't really refer to such things but merely pretend to.[21]

If many things speakers do that can seem to be acts of referring are really something else, what about expressions speakers use to refer? In light of the fact that expressions can be used to refer even if they themselves do not, what does it take for an expression to refer? And what sorts of expressions can do it?

---

[18] In other words, each link in an 'anaphoric chain' (Chastain, 1975) is treated as having a discourse referent, even if intuitively it does not refer. It should not be supposed, as Chastain (1975) and many others have, that when the links in the chain (the expressions anaphoric on the indefinite description) are used to refer, the indefinite description itself refers.

[19] For a plausible account of such examples, see King, 1987.

[20] The notion of discourse referent has inspired a great deal of theorizing in semantics, including discourse representation theory (DRT) and so-called dynamic semantics. Here is how Lauri Karttunen introduced the phrase: "Let us say that the appearance of an indefinite noun phrase establishes a *discourse referent* just in case it justifies the occurrence of a coreferential pronoun or a definite noun phrase later in the text. . . . We maintain *that the problem of coreference within a discourse is a linguistic problem and can be studied independently of any general theory of extra-linguistic reference*" (1976, 366; my emphasis). However, what Karttunen regards as *co*reference need not be reference at all. A chain of "reference" isn't a chain of *reference* unless it is anchored in an actual ("extra-linguistic") referent. The pronoun in a sentence like (5) is not used as a referential term. It is used as a surrogate for a definite description, which if present in place of the pronoun would not be referential. It is what Stephen Neale (1990: ch. 5) calls a "D-type pronoun." Neale develops a detailed account of how D-type pronouns work in a wide variety of cases. The basic idea is that the pronoun is used elliptically for a definite description recoverable from the matrix of the antecedent indefinite description (see Bach 1987/1994, 258–61).

[21] Although fictional "reference" is a special sort of speech act (as is telling a story), there is nothing special about fictional language itself. That is, words do not have special meanings, roles, or references just because they occur in fictional discourse (Bach, 1987/94: 214–18).

22.2 LINGUISTIC (SEMANTIC) REFERENCE AND SINGULAR TERMS

Strawson's dictum was that expressions don't refer, speakers do. The basis for it had nothing to do with Russell's strange contention that the only "logically proper" names of ordinary language, of English in particular, are the demonstratives 'this' and 'that,' but only as used to refer to one's current sense-data, and the pronoun 'I' (1917: 216). Russell based this contention on his highly restrictive doctrine of acquaintance, according to which the only particulars one can be acquainted with are one's current sense-data and oneself. Everything else one can know only by description. Accordingly, Russell denied that ordinary proper names, like 'Plato' and 'Pluto', are logically proper names. That is, ordinary proper names cannot be understood on the model of individual constants of formal logic, which are Millian in the sense that their meanings are their references.

Combining Strawson's dictum with Russell's contention yields an extremely restrictive answer to the question of which expressions are capable of referring. I will defend this answer, but on different grounds than Strawson's and Russell's. Strawson's grounds were that virtually any expression that can be used to refer to one thing in one context can be used to refer to something else in another context. Even if that is correct, it is not a good reason for denying that expressions refer. It's a good reason only for denying that they refer independently of context. Perhaps many expressions do refer, but do so only relative to a context. So Strawson's dictum needs the support of a better argument. Here's a very simple one: almost any term that can be used to refer can also be used not to refer, and without any difference in meaning. This argument may seem too simple to be credible, but it does call into question philosophers' knee-jerk tendency to view singular terms on the model of individual constants in formal logic. As for Russell's contention, we don't need to accept his highly restrictive conception of acquaintance to insist that for an expression to refer to something it must introduce that thing into propositions semantically expressed by sentences in which it occurs. But what does it take for an expression to do that?

L0) If an expression refers, it does so directly, by introducing its referent into the proposition semantically expressed by sentences in which it occurs (so 'direct reference' is redundant)

Contrary to Frege, Russell insisted that the relation of a description to what it denotes is fundamentally different from the relation of a name to what it refers to. Whereas a genuine, "logically proper" name introduces its referent into the proposition, a description introduces a certain quantificational structure, not its denotation. The denotation of a description is thus semantically inert—the semantic role of a description does not depend on what, if anything, it denotes. But a genuine name "directly designat[es] an individual which is its meaning" (1919: 174). Notice Russell's use here of the adverb 'directly' in characterizing how names designate their objects, just as Kaplan (1989a) characterizes indexicals and demonstratives as "directly referential." However, given the distinction between denotation and reference, the occurrence of 'directly' in 'directly referential' is redundant; and 'indirectly referential' would be an oxymoron. So if we distinguish reference from denotation as two different species of what Kripke calls "designation," then all expressions that (semantically) refer are rigid designators and all denoting expressions are non-rigid designators, except those, like 'the smallest prime', that are rigid *de facto,* that is, rigid for non-semantic reasons (Kripke, 1980: 21). This leaves open which expressions fall into which category.

L1) So-called singular terms or referring expressions— indexicals, demonstratives (both simple and complex), proper names, and definite descriptions—can all be used in non-referential ways too

To repeat the platitude from the beginning of Section 22.1, we commonly talk about particular persons, places, or things, and in so doing we are able to accommodate the fact that they can change over time, that our conceptions of them can also change over time, that we can be mistaken about them, and that different people's conceptions of them can differ. Moreover, it seems that all this is possible if in thinking of and in referring to an individual we are not constrained to represent it as having certain properties. This was Mill's idea about proper names. In his view, their function is not to convey general information but "to enable individuals to be made the subject of discourse"; names are "attached to the objects themselves, and are not dependent on . . . any attribute of the object" (1872: 20). Similarly, according to Russell, a proper name, at least when "used directly," serves "merely to indicate what we are speaking about; [the name] is no part of the fact asserted . . . : it is merely part of the symbolism by which we express our thought" (1919: 175). In contrast, because the object a definite description describes "is not part of the proposition [expressed by a sentence] in which [the description] occurs" (170). Nevertheless, Russell allowed that proper names can not only be "used as names" but also "as descriptions," adding that "there is nothing in the phraseology to show whether they are being used in this way or as names" (175).

Interestingly, Russell's distinction regarding uses of names is much the same as Donnellan's famous distinction regarding uses of definite descriptions. If the property expressed by the description's matrix (the 'F' in 'the F') enters "essentially" into the statement made, the description is used attributively;[22] when a speaker uses a description referentially, this is "to enable his audience to pick out whom or what he is talking about and states something about that person or thing" (1966: 285). Donnellan's distinction clearly corresponds to Russell's. Whereas an attributive use of a definite description involves stating (if the utterance is assertive) a general proposition, as with the use of a proper name "as a description," a referential use involves stating a singular proposition, just as when a proper name is used "as a name." And just as Russell comments that "there is nothing in the phraseology" to indicate in which way a name is being used, so Donnellan observes that "a definite description occurring in one and the same sentence may, on different occasions of its use, function in either way" (281).

If Russell and Donnellan are right, respectively, about proper names and definite descriptions, then expressions of both sorts can be used referentially (as a name, to indicate what we are speaking about) or attributively (as a description). This leaves open whether either sort of expression is semantically ambiguous (or maybe underdeterminate) or whether, in each case, one use corresponds to the semantics of the expression and the other use is accountable pragmatically from that use.[23] For Russell a definite description, whichever way it is used, is inherently a quantifier phrase, whereas a "logically proper" name is a referring term.[24] Evidently Donnellan was unsure whether to regard the referential—attributive distinction as indicating a semantic ambiguity or merely a pragmatic one. However, it seems highly implausible that a given description-containing sentence should be semantically ambiguous, expressing a singular or a general proposition depending on whether the description is being used referentially or attributively. And very few philosophers are so moved by the referential–attributive distinction as to defend this rather implausible ambiguity.[25]

---

[22] Unless otherwise indicated, when discussing definite descriptions I will assume that the description occurs in a simple sentence of the form 'the F is G'. On Russell's theory, the type of general proposition is what Strawson called a "uniquely existential" or what I call simply a "uniqueness" proposition.

[23] Alternatively, an expression could be semantically unspecified with respect to each use—each is compatible with, but neither is determined by, the meaning of the expression. Recanati (1993: ch. 15) and Bezuidenhout (1997) take this line with definite descriptions. They deny that descriptions are semantically ambiguous but do not treat one use as literal and explain the other pragmatically. They do this because intuitively they find referential uses to be no less literal than attributive ones. Accordingly, they suggest that the existence of both uses is symptomatic of semantic underdetermination or what Recanati calls, borrowing a phrase from Donnellan, "pragmatic ambiguity" (perhaps this is what Donnellan had in mind by that phrase). However, from this it implausibly follows that a sentence like 'The discoverer of X-rays was bald' does not express a determinate proposition. If we wish to maintain that such a sentence does express a determinate proposition, and does so univocally, the obvious choice is a general proposition, in which case the description functions as a quantifier phrase and only its attributive use is the strictly literal one.

[24] Of course Russell held that ordinary proper names are 'disguised' or 'truncated' descriptions, in which case they too, contrary to appearances, are quantificational.

[25] For a recent defense of "referential descriptions," see Devitt, 2004. I reply to his main arguments in the final section of Bach, 2004b.

Proper Names

Philosophers have hardly noticed Russell's observation about the dual use of proper names. Like it or not, proper names have non-referential uses, including not only attributive but even predicative uses, as we'll soon see. But first consider Russell's rationale for his very narrow view regarding what singular terms qualify as logically proper names, on which ordinary proper names do not qualify. He insisted that a logically proper name can refer only to an object of acquaintance, in his idiosyncratically narrow sense that there can be absolutely no doubt about the existence of the object. Although Russell is often ridiculed for his highly restrictive conception of acquaintance, it is interesting to note that he also had a more plausible, logical reason for his view about ordinary proper names. Consider that in standard, first-order logic the role of proper names is played by individual constants and that existence is represented by the existential quantifier. So there is no direct way to use that notation to say that a certain object exists, say the one assigned the name 'n'. In standard logic, we can't straightforwardly say that n exists. We have to resort to using a formula like '$\exists x(x = n)$', which is to say that there exists something identical to n. And, when there is no such thing as n, we can't use the negation of a formula of that form, '$\sim \exists x(x = n)$', to express the truth that there isn't anything to which n is identical, because standard first-order logic disallows empty names. Free logic allows this, but either it has to represent existence as a predicate or else invoke some dubious distinction, such as that between existence and being. Anyway, the point here is that Russell had a logical motivation for insisting that a genuine name be one, which is guaranteed (epistemically) to have a referent.

By not treating ordinary proper names as genuine names, Russell's view avoids the familiar problems, which he and Frege had discovered, for the Millian view. These include the problems of existential statements (both positive and negative), empty names, identity sentences, and propositional attitude ascriptions. They arise because the Millian view treats proper names as purely referential, on the model of individual constants in logic. Frege's solution was to suppose that while names do refer, they have descriptive senses (at least his examples suggest that the senses of names are descriptive, whereas Russell supposed that they do not semantically refer but have descriptive semantic contents). Millians who address these problems (Braun, 1993, 1998, 2005; Salmon, 1998, and Soames, 2002) have to engage in some fancy footwork, involving appeals to pragmatics and/or psychology, to handle them in a way that comports with their Millianism.[26] I won't examine their treatments of these problems nor propose an alternative here (see Bach, 2002), but I mention these problems just to underscore Russell's insight that it is not that easy for proper names to be purely referential and that he had a reason other than his restrictive doctrine of acquaintance for supposing that ordinary proper names are not logically proper names.

---

[26] Soames is not a strict Millian, since he attributes additional descriptive content to proper names of certain sorts. I do not believe that this has any bearing on any points made here.

Millians have confronted the well-known Frege/Russell problems, but they have neglected a different problem for their view. It arises from the fact that names can be used as predicates (Burge, 1973; Lockwood, 1975), as in (6) and (7).

(6) Leningrad became St. Petersburg in 1991.
(7) As of 1964, Muhammad Ali was no longer Cassius Clay.

(6) does not say that Leningrad became identical to St. Petersburg in 1991, and (7) does not say that as of 1964, Muhammad Ali was no longer identical to Cassius Clay. Also, Millians neglect the fact that names can be pluralized and combined with quantifiers, as in (8) and (9).

(8) Many Kennedys have died tragically.
(9) There are hundreds of O'Learys in Dublin.

The problem is that these uses seem to be perfectly literal. This is a problem for Millianism because it treats proper names on the model of individual constants. Indeed, these examples suggest that proper names are more like other nominals than is commonly supposed. In general, nominals occur with determiners (as in 'the man', 'an animal', 'few tigers', 'all reptiles,' and 'some water'), and so-called bare nominals, such as 'reptiles' and 'water', are treated by syntacticians as constituents of noun phrases with covert determiners. In fact, noun phrases are now generally classified as determiner phrases, which include a position for a determiner even if there is no overt one. As some of the above examples illustrate, proper names can occur with overt determiners, but even singular proper names (in the context of a sentence) are constituents of noun phrases, despite generally occurring, at least in English, without an overt determiner (in some languages, such as Italian and German, singular proper names are often used with the definite article).

Also, the Millian model has trouble with attitude ascriptions like these:

(10) Nimrod thinks that Michael Jackson is the greatest basketball player ever.
(11) Bozo thinks that Michael Jackson is Michael Jordan.

The contents of these ascriptions, in their most likely uses, do not accord with Millianism. In uttering (10) a speaker would probably not be attributing to Nimrod a belief about Michael Jackson. And it is unlikely that a speaker uttering (11) would be using 'Michael Jordan' to refer to Michael Jordan, much less to attribute to Bozo a belief in the false identity proposition which, according to Millianism, is semantically expressed by 'Michael Jackson is Michael Jordan'. The Millian's only way around these examples would be to argue, implausibly it seems to me, that when used in the ways described, these sentences are not being used literally.

I could go into much greater detail, but examples like (6)–(11) suffice to suggest that proper names can be used non-referentially yet literally.[27] At the very least,

---

[27] No doubt my own intuitions are as theory-driven as Millians', for in my view, which I defend in Bach, 2002, a proper name expresses the property of bearing that very name. This was not Mill's view, of course, but, interestingly enough, he did write, "When we refer to persons or things by name, we do not convey "any information about them, *except that those are their names*" (1872: 22; my emphasis).

Millians need to show that these are not literal uses or else that proper names are systematically ambiguous as between referential and non-referential uses.

A further consideration is that proper names seem to be able to function as variable binders in just the same way as noun phrases that are clearly quantificational. Compare the following two sentences, in which the relation between the pronoun and the noun phrase that syntactically binds it seems to be the same:

(12) Bob_1 hates his_1 boss.
(13) Every $employee_1$ hates his_1 boss.

It might seem that the pronoun 'his_1' is a referentially dependent anaphor when bound by a singular term like a proper name and is a variable when bound by a quantificational phrase. However, it is difficult to see what the relevant difference could be (for a detailed argument to this effect, see Neale, 2005). Notice further that there are readings of the following sentences in which the proper name is coordinate with a quantifier phrase, as in (14) and (15), or occurs as part of a quantifier phrase, as in (21), that binds the pronoun:

(14) [Bob and every other $employee]_1$ hates his_1 boss.
(15) [Bob and most other $employees]_1$ hate $their_1$ boss.
(16) [Only $Bob]_1$ hates his_1 boss.

Against the suggestion that a proper name is a variable binder it could be argued, I suppose, that in (14) and (15) it is the entire phrase in which the proper name occurs that binds the pronoun, but consider the following example, involving verb-phrase ellipsis:

(17) Bob hates his boss, and so does every other employee.

If the pronoun is not a bound variable, then (17) could only mean that every other employee hates Bob's boss. It could not have a reading on which it says that every other employee hates his respective boss.

Indexicals

Indexicals can also be used non-referentially but literally.[28] The most obvious example is when they are anaphoric on but not bound by an indefinite description

---

[28] As promised by his title, "The Multiple Uses of Indexicals," Quentin Smith (1989) identifies various unorthodox ways in which indexicals can be used. Accordingly, he rejects the view, such as Kaplan's theory of character, according to which reference is determined as a simple function of context. No simple rule can directly account for this variety of uses. However, he still thinks that each use is rule-governed and proposes that for each indexical there is a "meta-rule" that determines, as function of a context, which reference-determining rule is operative (at least in cases where the indexical is used to refer). Unfortunately, his statement of these meta-rules is too sketchy and schematic to be very helpful. Moreover, he makes no attempt to show that all the uses he identifies for a given indexical are literal uses. It seems that some are not, in which case there is no need for a rule of the sort he imagines covering them. On the other hand, since indexicals can be used literally but non-referringly, if there is such a meta-rule, it would have to take those uses into account, in which case it would not be limited to determining, as function of a context, which *reference*-determining rule is operative. However, it is not clear that there is any rule that determines semantic content as a function of context (see Point 13 below).

or other quantifier phrase and are used as short for a definite description recoverable from the nominal contained in that phrase:

(18) Russell met *a man* today. *He* was bald.

(19) *A plumber* bought a lottery ticket yesterday, and *he* won $1,000,000.

(20) If there were *a mermaid* there, Merlin would have seen *her*.

(21) Every farmer owns *a donkey*. He feeds *it* popcorn.

Here are two more examples, involving simple and complex demonstratives:

(22) I thought I saw a dagger, but *it* was only a hallucination.

(23) Everyone who survives a heart attack never forgets *that moment*.

King (2001) has investigated various non-referential uses of complex demonstratives and develops a unitary semantic account on which both their referential and non-referential uses can be understood as literal.

What about so-called descriptive uses of indexicals, as documented by Nunberg (1993, 2004; see also Recanati, 1993: ch. 16), as well as quantificational uses? Here are some examples:

(24) [Answering the phone after 10 rings] I thought *you* were a telemarketer.

(25) Any time *she* gives you her phone number, she's interested.

(26) [bumper sticker] If *you* can read this, you're getting too close.

(27) *He* who hesitates is lost.

(28) Never put off to *tomorrow* what you can do *today*.

These uses are clearly not referential, but are they literal? If so, an adequate semantic account of each of these indexicals, unless it posits outright ambiguity, would have to characterize their meanings in a way that is compatible with their having both non-referential and referential uses. Perhaps, however, it is arguable that these uses are not literal.[29] But they are not needed to make our case—the non-referential uses of the indexicals and demonstratives in (18)–(23) seem clearly to be literal and do not suggest any semantic ambiguity.

L2) A given singular term seems to mean the same thing whether it is used referentially or not, and an adequate semantic theory should explain this or else explain it away

Philosophers may disagree about which particular sorts of expressions are capable of referring, but there is general consensus that at least some deserve the label 'referring expression'. For example, it is widely supposed that proper names, indexicals, and demonstratives are referring expressions, with allowances made for reference failure if not for non-referential uses. It is almost as widely supposed that definite

---

[29] In his commentary on an earlier version of this paper (APA Pacific Division, March 26, 2004), Jeff King offered compelling reasons to suppose that these uses are not literal, and thus require a partly pragmatic explanation.

descriptions are not referring expressions, even though they can be used to refer, and are, rather, quantifier phrases. A more controversial case is that of complex demonstratives, which have the form of quantifier phrases but often seem to behave like referring expressions.[30] So what should we say about Strawson's dictum? Do some expressions, at least in some of their uses, qualify as referring expressions and not merely as expressions that can be used to refer? Or was he right to insist that referring is not something an expression does and is merely something that speakers can use expressions to do?

If Strawson was right, it was not for the right reasons. He relied heavily on the fact that an alleged referring expression can be used to refer to different things on different occasions and took that to be sufficient for his conclusion. He did not consider the possibility that, à la Kaplan, an expression can have different referents with respect to different contexts. So, for example, relative to a context 'I' would seem to refer to whoever uses it, and 'now' would seem to refer to the time at which it is used (but see Smith, 1989 and Predelli, 1998). Even so, the question remains, given that some expressions, notably definite descriptions, which are clearly not referring expressions can be used to refer, why suppose that expressions of *any* sort that can be used to refer can be so used only because they themselves (semantically) refer?
Here's an embarrassingly simple argument:

ESA

(1) Virtually any expression that can be used to refer can also be used literally but not referentially.
(2) No variation in meaning (semantic ambiguity or underspecification, indexicality, or vagueness) explains this fact.
(3) So the meaning of such an expression is compatible with its being used non-referentially.
(4) So virtually any expression that can be used to refer is not inherently referential.[31]

It remains to be seen who this argument embarrasses. If it is a bad argument, even if put more rigorously than stated here, it should embarrass me. However, whether good or bad, it should embarrass anyone who endorses an account according to which expressions of a given type are referring expressions and who does not address

[30] Being of the form 'that F', these may also be called 'demonstrative descriptions'. See Braun 1994 for a critical comparison of various referential and non-referential approaches and their respective accounts of the semantic role of the 'F' in 'that F'. See King, 2001 for a thoroughgoing defense of the claim that complex demonstratives are quantifier phrases.

[31] Two qualifications here. First, to say that an expression is used to refer does not entail that it is successfully used to refer. For example, a use of the description 'the dagger I see before me' could count as referential even if there is no dagger before the speaker. Also, premise 1 in the ESA says '*virtually* any expression' to allow for the case of 'I', 'today', and a few others ("pure" indexicals). 'You' might be added to that list, despite the fact that it has an impersonal use, for it is not generally true that the second-person pronoun has an impersonal use. For example, French has 'on' rather than an impersonal 'tu' or 'vous', and German has 'man' rather than an impersonal 'du' or 'sie'. Also, I wouldn't argue that 'he' and 'she' have non-referential uses because they are colloquially used as count nouns ("It's a she!").

the case of non-referential uses of those expressions, much less reconcile their pet account with those uses. Referentialists about definite descriptions are the only ones who regularly face up to the fact that the expressions they're concerned with have non-referential uses. They may have to resort to the claim that definite descriptions are systematically ambiguous, indexical somehow, or semantically underspecified, but at least they confront the problem. Referentialists about indexicals, demonstratives, and proper names try to survive on a lean diet of examples and, to stay on their diet, keep non-referential uses out of sight. Direct-reference theorists about indexicals and demonstratives rarely consider descriptive uses of those expressions, and when they do treat of such uses, tend to engage in special pleading to avoid abandoning their referentialist predilections. Similarly, Millians, who think of proper names on the model of individual constants do not bother reckoning with predicative uses of proper names. They implicitly dismiss predicative uses as marginal cases. Long ago Tyler Burge (1973) deplored such an attitude, with its "appeal to 'special' uses whenever proper names do not play the role of individual constants," as "flimsy and theoretically deficient" (1973/97: 605). Much preferable is a unified account of names, one that handles their various uses instead of marginalizing those uses which, according to one's pet theory, count as deviant.

As the examples in the last section illustrate, indexicals seem to have literal uses that do not fall into the referentialist paradigm. These uses do not seem to be explained by some special sort of semantic ambiguity or underspecification. So how can they be explained? The ESA suggests that whatever their explanation, a purely referentialist account can't provide it.

L3) When meaning doesn't fix reference, generally "context" doesn't either

At the outset I mentioned a verbal slippery slide that seems to lead philosophers from the trivial claim that singular terms can be used to refer to the conclusion that these terms are semantically referring expressions. Here's another verbal slippery slide I've noticed. It starts from the platitude that what an expression can be used to refer to can vary from one context to another or, in the case of an ambiguous expression, that what an expression can be used to mean can so vary. People slide from contextual variability to context relativity to context sensitivity to context dependence to contextual determination. This leads people to conclude that context somehow manages to "provide" or "supply" semantic values to expressions, resolve ambiguities, and work other semantic miracles. That's why I call this an appeal to "context *ex machina*" (the title of Bach, 2005). Context does have a role to play in semantics, but its role is limited. There are a few expressions that really do refer as a function of context, but in general it's not the context that does the trick. Later (Point L4) I defend the obvious alternative, that the speaker's referential intention does the trick, and that it is a mistake to treat the speaker's intention as part of context, as just another contextual parameter.

Indexicals and demonstratives are often casually described as "context-sensitive" or "context-dependent." Taken literally, this means that the reference of such a term is determined by its linguistic meaning as a function of a contextual variable (call this the *semantic* context). But is the reference of indexicals and demonstratives really context-dependent in this sense? It is not obvious that indexicals in general, including demonstratives, should be assimilated to the special case of "pure" indexicals. The reference of pure indexicals, such as 'I' and 'today', may be determined by their linguistic meanings as a function of specific contextual variables (this is context in the narrow, semantic sense), but other indexicals—and demonstratives—are different. Their meanings merely impose constraints on how they can be used to refer (Bach, 1987/94: 186–92), and context doesn't finish the job. That's why John Perry describes their reference as "discretionary" rather than "automatic," as depending on the speaker's intention, not just on "meaning and public contextual facts" (2001: 58–59). That is, the speaker's intention is not just another contextual variable, not just one more element of what Kaplan calls "character" (1989a: 505). If this is correct, then demonstrative and most indexicals suffer from a *character deficiency*.[32] Context does not determine reference, in the sense of *constituting* it, of making it the case that the reference is so-and-so; rather, it is something for the speaker to exploit to enable the listener to determine the intended reference, in the sense of *ascertaining* it. Accordingly, although it is often casually remarked that what a speaker says in uttering a given sentence "depends on context," is "determined" or "provided" by context, or is otherwise a "matter of context," this is not literally true.[33]

What Perry describes as "public contextual facts" is not context in the narrow, semantic sense but context in a broad, cognitive, or evidential sense. It is the mutually salient common ground, and includes the current state of the conversation (what

---

[32] In the case of demonstratives, Kaplan points out the need for "completing demonstrations and recognizes some of the problems this poses for his framework of character and content. David Braun (1996) has made the best effort I know of to solve these problems broadly within that framework, but it requires an additional level of meaning and requires that demonstrations be explicitly represented. Leaving aside non-referring uses of demonstratives, it is not clear to me how Braun's account can be extended to handle referring uses of demonstratives that do not involve demonstrations or cases in which what is referred to is not what is demonstrated, as in many of Nunberg's (1993) well-known examples (see also Borg, 2001). Nunberg (2004) now disavows describing these as cases of "deferred reference."

[33] Points similar to those of this paragraph are made incisively by Schiffer (except that he invokes the notion of token reference):

Meaning-as-character may initially seem plausible when the focus is on a word such as 'I', but it loses plausibility when the focus is on other pronouns and demonstratives? What "contextual factors" determine the referent of the pronoun 'she' in a context of utterances? . . . Evidently, the meaning of 'she' (very roughly speaking) merely constrains the speaker to refer to a female. We do not even have to say that it constrains the speaker to refer to a contextually salient female, since the speaker cannot intend to refer to a particular female unless he expects the hearer to recognize to which female he is referring, and the expectation of such recognition itself entails that the speaker takes the referent to have an appropriate salience. What fixes the referent of a token of 'she' are the speaker's referential intentions in producing that token, and therefore in order for Kaplan to accommodate 'she', he would have to say that a speaker's referential intentions constitute one more component of those n-tuples that he construes as 'contexts'. The trouble with this is that there is no work for Kaplanian contexts to do once one recognizes speakers' referential intentions. The referent of a pronoun or demonstrative is always determined by the speaker's referential intention. (Schiffer, 2005: sec. 2)

has just been said, what has just been referred to, etc.), the physical setting (if the conversants are face-to-face), salient mutual knowledge between the conversants, and relevant common background knowledge. Its role is epistemic not constitutive, pragmatic not semantic. Because it can constrain what a hearer can reasonably take a speaker to mean in saying what he says, it can constrain what the speaker could reasonably mean in saying what he says. But it is incapable of determining what the speaker actually does mean. That is a matter of the speaker's referential intention and his communicative intention as a whole, however reasonable or unreasonable it may be.

To appreciate this point, first consider an example involving ambiguity. Suppose a dinner host utters the ambiguous sentence 'The chicken is ready to eat.' Presumably she is not saying and does not mean that a certain chicken (one of the guests!) is hungry. Even so, given the ambiguity of the sentence, she could, however bizarrely, say and mean that. Context doesn't make it the case that she does not. But, of course, she could not reasonably expect such a communicative intention to be recognized. Now consider an example involving demonstrative reference. Suppose you see a group of ducks sitting quietly by a pond and one duck starts quacking furiously. You say, "That duck is excited." I naturally take you to be referring to the duck that's quacking. But is it the context that makes it the case that this is the duck that you are referring to? Not at all. For all I know, and contrary to what I can reasonably suppose, you could be referring to a quiet duck that you recognize by its distinctive color. I won't identify which duck you're referring to, and you haven't done enough to enable me to, but still you could be trying to refer to that duck, however ineffectually. So if 'that duck' refers (relative to this context), what does it refer to? To the quacking duck or to the distinctively colored duck? Given the story I have just told, it is clear which duck you intend to be referring to (the distinctively colored one) and which duck I take you to be referring to (the quacking one). But is there any determinate fact of the matter as to which duck 'that duck' refers to? I don't think so, and I don't think there is any reason to expect so.

So philosophers can casually describe context as "providing" or "supplying" the references of demonstratives and discretionary indexicals, but these expressions do not refer as a function of the contextual variables given by their meanings, that is, narrow, semantic context. But broad, cognitive context does not determine reference either, in the sense of making it the case that the expression has a certain reference. It merely enables the audience to figure out the reference. That's why I say that demonstratives and discretionary indexicals suffer from a "character deficiency"—they do not refer as a function of context. It is only in an attenuated sense that these expressions can be called 'referring' expressions. Besides, as we have seen, they have clearly non-referential but perfectly literal uses, e.g. as proxies for definite descriptions and as something like bound variables. That's why it's a real challenge to give a fully general account of the meaning of indexicals. I wish I could meet that challenge here and do something like King (2001) has done for complex demonstratives.

l4) The speaker's referential intention determines speaker reference, but it does not determine semantic reference, except in a pickwickian way

The fact that the speaker's intention picks up the slack in determining reference might suggest that the specification of the meaning of a discretionary indexical or a demonstrative contains a parameter for the speaker's intention. However, I am unaware of any direct argument for that. There is talk about how the reference of indexicals and demonstratives is "determined by context" but no argument as to why the speaker's referential intention should count as part of the context. I think there's reason to think that it shouldn't. If context were defined so broadly as to include anything other than linguistic meaning that is relevant to determining what a speaker means, then of course the speaker's intention would be part of the context. But if the context is to play the explanatory role claimed of it, it must be something that is the same for the speaker as it is for his audience, and obviously the role of the speaker's intention is not the same for both. Context can constrain what the speaker can succeed in communicating given what he says, but it cannot constrain what he intends to communicate in choosing what to say. Of course, in implementing his intention, the speaker needs to select words whose utterance in the context will enable the hearer to figure out what he is trying to communicate, but that is a different matter.

To illustrate the role of speakers' intentions, let's look at some simple examples involving pronouns used to make anaphoric reference.[34] Compare (29a) and (29b):

(29) a. A cop arrested a robber. He was wearing a badge.
    b. A cop arrested a robber. He was wearing a mask.

It is natural to suppose that in (29a) 'he' refers to the cop and in (29b) to the robber. It is natural all right, but not inevitable. The speaker of (29a) could be using 'he' to refer to the robber, and the speaker of (29b) could be using it to refer to the cop. Such speakers would probably not be understood correctly, at least not without enough stage setting to override commonsense knowledge about cops and robbers, but that would be a pragmatic mistake. Nevertheless, the fact that 'he' can be so used indicates that it is the speaker's intention, not the context, which determines that in (29a) it refers to the cop and in (29b) to the robber. The same point applies to these examples with two pronouns used anaphorically:

(30) a. A cop arrested a robber. He took away his gun.
    b. A cop arrested a robber. He used his gun.
    c. A cop arrested a robber. He dropped his gun.
    d. A cop arrested a robber. He took away his gun and escaped.

In (30a), presumably 'he' would be used to refer to the cop and 'his' to the robber, whereas in (30b) both would be used to refer to the cop, in (30c) both would be

---

[34] Our examples are limited to non-reflexive pronouns, which can also be used to make deictic reference. Linguists reserve the term 'anaphor' for reflexives and reciprocals.

used to refer to the robber, and in (30d) 'he' would be used to the robber and 'his' to the cop. However, given the different uses of the pronouns in what is essentially the same linguistic environment, clearly it is the speaker's intention, not the context, that explains these differences in reference. It is a different, pragmatic matter how the audience resolves these anaphoric references; the broad, communicative context does not literally determine them but merely provides the extralinguistic information that enables the audience to figure them out.

Similar points apply to demonstrative reference. Reference is not determined by acts of demonstration or by any other features of the context of utterance. Rather, these features are exploited by the audience to ascertain the reference, partly on the basis of being so intended. Indeed, they are exploited by the speaker in choosing what expression to utter to carry out his referential intention, since, as part of his communicative intention, he intends his audience to take into account the fact that he intends them to recognize his intention. His referential intention determines the reference, but this is not to suggest that it succeeds by magic or is somehow self-fulfilling. You cannot utter any old thing and gesture in any old way and expect to be taken to be referring to whatever you have in mind. You do not say something and then, as though by an inner decree (an intention), determine what you are using the expression to refer to. You do not just have something in mind and hope your audience is a good mind reader. Rather, you decide to refer to something and try to select an expression whose utterance will enable your audience, under the circumstances, to identify that object (see Point S4). If you utter 'that duck' and the duck you intend to be referring to is the only one around or is maximally salient in some way, you won't have to do anything more to enable your audience to identify it. Otherwise, you will need to point at it and make it salient, hence make it obviously the one you intend to be referring to.[35]

Here are a few more examples. Suppose you point at a Ferrari and say, "That belongs to me." Presumably you're referring to that particular car. Suppose you say instead, "That's my favorite color." Presumably you're referring to the color of that car. Suppose you say instead, "That's my favorite sports car." Presumably you're referring to that type of car, Ferrari, or perhaps that particular model, say a Spider. In each case, what enables your audience to figure out what you're referring to is

---

[35] It might seem that the property of being salient, which has figured in our discussion of the pragmatics of reference, somehow figures in the meaning of demonstrative phrases. For example, on John Perry's account of the content of a demonstrative phrase, the "basic content of [an utterance of 'that ϕ'] is the identifying condition, being the salient ϕ to which the speaker of [that utterance of 'that ϕ'] directs attention" (2001: 77). But why suppose the role of salience is anything more than pragmatic? A speaker who wishes to use a simple demonstrative or demonstrative phrase to refer to something needs to make sure that the intended referent is salient not because the meaning of 'that' requires this but because otherwise his audience would not be able to figure out what he is referring to. If he uses the demonstrative to (try to) refer to something that isn't salient, he is not misusing the word 'that', in the sense of using it to mean something it doesn't mean (as he would if, say, he thought 'honorary' meant what 'honorable' means). Rather, he would be committing the pragmatic mistake of trying to refer to something that his listener would have no reason to take him to be referring to. It would be like correctly using arcane words knowing full well that one's audience was unfamiliar with them. Obviously it is not part of the meaning of arcane words that they be uttered only to people who understand them.

the content of the predicate. In each case, that's what you can expect them to take into account in figuring this out, and they can reasonably assume that this is what you expect. But nothing prevents you from intending to refer to something else. For example, you could be referring to that particular car when you say, "That's my favorite sports car" (you might have a big car collection that includes many sports cars). And, you could be referring, however incoherently, to that model of Ferrari when you say, "That's my favorite color." In this last case, you'd have to say something much more elaborate in order to succeed in communicating what you mean. With a personal pronoun or a complex demonstrative, more remote references are possible. You could say "He/That guy spends all his money on cars" and be referring to the owner of that Ferrari, or you could say, "She/That woman is going to leave him" and be referring to his wife. In each of these cases, it is not literally the context but the speaker's referential intention that determines the reference. And, as I have been suggesting, it's only in an attenuated sense that the expression used to refer, whether a demonstrative or a personal pronoun, does the referring.

Now I have been supposing all along that speaker reference is essentially an audience-directed affair, that you use an expression to refer someone to something. This was Point s0, that speaker reference is a four-place relation, between a speaker, an expression, an audience, and a referent. One might agree that a referential intention in that sense, which is inherently pragmatic, does not determine semantic reference, but insist that speakers have specifically semantic intentions that do. After all, it might be argued, when a speaker utters a sentence containing a lexical or a structural ambiguity, it is the speaker's intention that resolves the ambiguity. For example, if someone utters, "My lawyer is lying on the bench" or "The turkey is ready to eat," how it is to be taken is a matter of the speaker's intention. So why not suppose that when we use a demonstrative word or phrase, a discretionary indexical, or a proper name belonging to more than one individual, we use it with an intention that genuinely gives it a reference relative to that context?[36]

The short answer is that it's one thing to select from properties that an expression or a string of words already has and quite another thing to endow an expression with a new property. (Indeed, in the former case it is arguable, on the assumption that linguistic items are form-meaning pairs, that the relevant linguistic intention is simply to utter a certain sentence, rather than another, like-sounding one.) To appreciate the difference, imagine that you utter a sentence containing a common expression you intend to use in a new, unprecedented way. Say you utter "My dog has a deleterious tail" and mean that your dog has a curly tail. Even though this is what you mean, your intention to use 'deleterious' to mean curly does not endow 'deleterious' with a new meaning. Even if your audience figures out what you mean, in much the way they would if you used a word unfamiliar to them, 'deleterious' doesn't acquire a new meaning. The situation is more like that of using an expression metaphorically, where you say one thing and mean something else instead, except that the literal

---

[36] Jason Stanley posed this objection in his commentary on an earlier version of this paper (APA Pacific Division, March 26, 2004).

meaning plays no role in enabling the audience to figure out what the speaker means. In both cases, the audience has to figure out that the expression is not being used in a normal way, but in the case of 'deleterious' its conventional meaning is merely a distraction.

Now I am not suggesting that using an expression (such as a demonstrative) to refer to something is just like using a familiar word in an unfamiliar way. Obviously, a referential use of a demonstrative is consistent with its meaning. The relevant similarity is that in both cases the putative property of the expression plays no role. So if you say, referring to your desk lamp, "That is black," your audience does not figure that you are using 'that' to refer to your lamp by way of determining that 'that' refers to it. Rather, they figure out what you could plausibly intend and reasonably expect them to be using 'that' to refer to. So even if, contrary to what I am suggesting, 'that' does refer to the lamp, this would play no role in how your audience recognizes what you're using 'that' to refer to. Except perhaps for the case of pure indexicals, semantic reference by singular terms is an otiose property. Attributing this property to singular terms across the board commits a version of what Barwise and Perry call the "fallacy of misplaced information," that is, "that all the information in an utterance must come from its interpretation" (1983, 34), and ignores the essentially pragmatic fact that the speaker is making the utterance.

I am well aware of our deep-seated inclination to think of demonstratives and singular terms generally as expressions that refer. This inclination is especially strong in the context of modal logic, formal semantics, and model theory, where it's customary to speak of "assignments" and not worry about where they come from. We think this way when proving that a certain proposition is possibly true, that a certain proposition is necessarily true, that one proposition entails another, etc., but what is the rationale for this way of thinking when theorizing about natural language and its use? I don't deny that for formal purposes one can assign referents to singular terms, but this is a matter of pure stipulation. However, the singular terms of natural language, with the possible exception of pure indexicals, all have literal but non-referential uses and at least some of these uses are perfectly literal. So however deep-seated our tendency to think that singular terms refer and are not merely used to refer, there is still a need for an argument for why we need the notion of reference made by a singular term and for why we can't make do with the notion of reference made by a speaker in using it. What do we need the former notion for? What is added by saying not merely that the speaker is using 'that', for example, to refer to something but also that the word 'that', as used by the speaker, refers to it?

L5) There is no such thing as descriptive "reference-fixing" (not because something isn't fixed, but because it isn't reference)

This point is a corollary of an earlier one, Point s7, that descriptive singling out does not count as real referring. Using a description like 'the planet that is perturbing

Uranus' to "fix" the reference of 'Neptune' to a certain planet, or using a description like 'the serial killer terrifying the people of London' to "fix" the reference of 'Jack the Ripper', where the description is treated as rigidified, is to do nothing more than to make the names equivalent to rigidified descriptions. It does not enable such a name to introduce the individual described into propositions semantically expressed by sentences in which the name occurs. I am not denying that, when the names 'Neptune' and 'Jack the Ripper' were introduced, there were singular propositions containing Neptune or Jack the Ripper. I am merely denying that sentences containing those names expressed such propositions. I am not denying that Neptune was given the name 'Neptune' or that Jack the Ripper, whoever he was, was given the name 'Jack the Ripper'. In denying that so-called "descriptive reference-fixing" manages to fix reference, I am denying that these names functioned as referring terms.

To see why, consider Kaplan's liberal view (questioned in Point s7) that "a special form of knowledge of an object is neither required nor presupposed in order that a person may entertain as object of thought a singular proposition involving that object" (1989a, 536) and how it inspired his introduction of the 'dthat' operator: "My liberality with respect to the introduction of directly referring terms by means of 'dthat' ... allow[s] an arbitrary definite description to give us the object" (1989a: 560), such as the first child to be born in the 22nd century, as in (31).[37]

(31) Dthat [the first child to be born in the 22nd century] will be bald.

As Kaplan explains, "the content of the associated description is no part of the content of the dthat-term" (1989b: 579); it is "off the record (i.e. off the *content* record)" (1989b: 581). So 'dthat' is not merely a rigidifier (like 'actual') but a device of direct reference.[38] What gets into the proposition is the actual object (if there is one) that uniquely satisfies the description, not the description itself (i.e. the property expressed by its matrix).[39]

Kaplan's liberality about direct reference imposes no constraint (beyond the requirement of unique satisfaction) on the definite description to which 'dthat' can be applied to yield a "directly referential" term. This corresponds to his rejection of any epistemological constraint on what a speaker can "directly refer" to: "a special form of knowledge of an object is neither required nor presupposed in order that a person may entertain as object of thought a singular proposition involving that object" (1989a: 536). No wonder he supposes that any definite description can be turned into a directly referential term, so that a sentence containing the 'dthat' phrase

---

[37] Since I am discussing Kaplan, I will here use his term 'direct' to modify 'reference', although, it is redundant (see Point s0). An expression, like a definite description, that merely denotes an object does not *refer* to that object, in the sense that the object is not a constituent of propositions expressed by sentences in which the expression occurs.

[38] As Kaplan explains (1989b: 579–82), certain things he had previously said, and even his formal system (in Kaplan, 1989a), could have suggested that 'dthat' is an operator on definite descriptions that allows the content of the associated description to be included in the content of the whole phrase. This would make 'dthat' a rigidifier but not a device of direct reference.

[39] To stipulate that any phrase of the form 'dthat [the F]' refers "directly" does not, of course, mean that it is guaranteed a referent. It means only that the referent, if there is one, is a constituent of the singular proposition (if there is one) expressed by a sentence in which the phrase occurs.

expresses a singular proposition about the actual object (if there is one) that uniquely satisfies the description. Kaplan seems to think that simply having the 'dthat' phrase at hand enables one to refer to, and form singular thoughts about, that object, as if this ability could be created with the stroke of a pen.

For Kaplan, then, the 'dthat' operator can turn any definite description into an indexical. In his view, "ignorance of the referent does not defeat the directly referential character of indexicals" (1989a: 536). Similarly, a proper name like 'Newman-1' can directly refer to something epistemically inaccessible, such as the first child born in the 22nd century. Now I grant that there's nothing to prevent us, early in the 21st century, from dubbing this child (assuming there is one) 'Newman-1', but I would deny that this act of dubbing thereby enables us to form singular thoughts about Newman-1. There is a singular proposition about Newman-1 that he is bald, but we are not in a position to entertain it. We can stipulate that if some child other than the child actually the first to be born in the 22nd century had been born first, the name 'Newman-1' would not have belonged to him, thereby ensuring that the name is rigid, but making it rigid does not make it directly referential. An act of dubbing can't do that.

The closest that "descriptive reference-fixing" comes to enabling a name to refer is turn the name into the equivalent of a rigidified definite description. But this doesn't mean that sentences containing the name express singular propositions. Even though rigidification, by means of a description of the form 'the actual F', makes sure that the only individual whose properties are relevant to the truth or falsity of the proposition expressed (even if that proposition is modal) is the actual satisfier of the description, still that is a general, not a singular proposition. This proposition may in some sense be object-dependent, but it is not object-involving. The property of being the actual F may enter into the proposition, but the actual F does not.

22.3 THE BOTTOM LINE

Referring is not as easy as is commonly supposed. Much of what speakers do that passes for referring really isn't but is merely alluding or describing. And it is far from clear that so-called referring expressions (aside from the few pure indexicals) really refer, except in a pickwickian sense. But I must repeat my running disclaimer: I do not pretend that the data, observations, or even the arguments presented here, especially what I dubbed the "Embarrassing Simple Argument," are conclusive. I do think they support what might fairly be regarded as default hypotheses about speaker reference and linguistic reference, for example, that a demonstrative has the same meaning whether or not it is used referentially and is used literally either way. The ESA poses the challenge of refuting these hypotheses. So if you think these hypotheses are wrong, you need to show that. You need to argue against them and to find a way to accommodate or explain away the data and observations. You can't just appeal to intuitions about truth or falsity of certain sentences in various circumstances unless you make a case that this is what the intuitions are really responsive to. And you can't make that slippery slide from speaker reference to linguistic or semantic reference by blindly attributing referential properties to uses of linguistic expressions or to tokens of them. It is one thing for a speaker, when using an expression in a certain way, to express a thought about a certain object and quite another for the expression to stand for that object, even relative to the context. Pure indexicals may do this, but other singular terms do not, or at least we have not seen any reason to suppose that they do, however deep-seated our tendency to think that they do.

References

Austin, J. L. (1962). *How to Do Things with Words.* Oxford: Oxford University Press.

Bach, Kent (1987/1994). *Thought and Reference*, pbk. edn, revised with postscript. Oxford: Oxford University Press.

—— (1994). "Conversational Impliciture," *Mind and Language*, 9: 124–62.

—— (1999). "The Semantics–Pragmatics Distinction: What it is and Why it Matters," in K. Turner (ed.). *The Semantics–Pragmatics Interface from Different Points of View.* Oxford: Elsevier, 65–84.

—— (2000). "A Puzzle about Belief Reports," in K. Jaszczolt, *The Pragmatics of Propositional Attitude Reports.* Oxford: Elsevier, 99–109.

—— (2001). "You Don't Say?," *Synthese*, 128: 15–44.

—— (2002). "Giorgione Was So-called Because of His Name," *Philosophical Perspectives*, 16: 73–103.

—— (2004a). "Speech Acts and Pragmatics," in L. Horn and G. Ward (eds.), *The Handbook of Pragmatics.* Oxford: Blackwell, 463–487.

—— (2004b). "Descriptions: Points of Reference," in A. Bezuidenhout and M. Reimer (eds.), *Descriptions and Beyond.* Oxford: Oxford University Press, 189–229.

—— (2005). "Context *ex Machina*," in Z. Szabó (ed.), *Semantics vs. Pragmatics.* Oxford: Oxford University Press, 15–44.

Bach, Kent and Robert M. Harnish (1979). *Linguistic Communication and Speech Acts.* Cambridge, MA: MIT Press.

Barwise, Jon and John Perry (1983). *Situations and Attitudes.* Cambridge, MA: MIT Press.

Bezuidenhout, Anne (1997). "Pragmatics, Semantic Underdetermination, and the Referential–Attributive Distinction," *Mind*, 106: 375–410.

Borg, Emma (2002). "Pointing at Jack, Talking about Jill: Understanding Deferred Uses of Demonstratives and Pronouns," *Mind and Language*, 17: 489–512.

Braun, David (1993). "Empty Names," *Noûs*, 27: 449–69.

—— (1994). "Structured Characters and Complex Demonstratives," *Philosophical Studies*, 74: 193–219.

—— (1996). "Demonstratives and Their Linguistic Meanings," *Noûs*, 30: 145–73.

—— (1998). "Understanding Belief Reports," *Philosophical Review*, 107: 555–95.

—— (2005). "Empty Names, Fictional Names, and Mythical Names," *Noûs*, 39: 596–631.

Burge, Tyler (1973). "Reference and Proper Names," *Journal of Philosophy*, 70: 425–39; reprinted in Peter Ludlow (ed.), *Readings in The Philosophy of Language.* Cambridge, MA: MIT Press, 593–608.

Chastain, Charles (1975). "Reference and Context," in K. Gunderson (ed.), *Minnesota Studies in the Philosophy of Science, vol. 7, Language, Mind, and Knowledge*, Minneapolis: University of Minnesota Press, 194–269.

Devitt, Michael. (2004). "The Case for Referential Descriptions," in A. Bezuidenhout and M. Reimer (eds.), *Descriptions and Beyond*. Oxford: Oxford University Press, 280–305.

Donnellan, Keith (1966). "Reference and Definite Descriptions," *Philosophical Review*, 75: 281–304.

Evans, Gareth (1982). *The Varieties of Reference*. Oxford: Oxford University Press.

Graff, Delia (2001). "Description as Predicates," *Philosophical Studies*, 102: 1–42.

Grice, Paul (1989). *Studies in the Way of Words*. Cambridge, MA: Harvard University Press.

Gundel, Jeanette, Nancy Hedberg, and Ron Zacharski (1993). "Cognitive Status and the Form of Referring Expressions in Discourse," *Language*, 69: 274–307.

Kaplan, David (1979). "Dthat," in P. French, Theodore Uehling, and H. Wettstein (eds.), *Contemporary Perspectives in the Philosophy of Language*. Minneapolis: University of Minnesota Press, 383–400.

——— (1989a). "Demonstratives," in J. Almog, J. Perry, and H. Wettstein (eds.), *Themes from Kaplan*. Oxford: Oxford University Press, 481–563.

——— (1989b). "Afterthoughts," in J. Almog, J. Perry, and H. Wettstein (eds.), *Themes from Kaplan*. Oxford: Oxford University Press, 565–614.

Karttunen, Lauri (1976). "Discourse Referents," in J. D. McCawley (ed.), *Syntax and Semantics 7*. New York: Academic Press, 363–86.

King, Jeffrey (1987). "Pronouns, Descriptions, and the Semantics of Discourse," *Philosophical Studies*, 51: 341–63.

——— (2001). *Complex Demonstratives: A Quantificational Account*. Cambridge, MA: MIT Press.

Kripke, Saul (1977). "Speaker's Reference and Semantic Reference," *Midwest Studies in Philosophy*, 2: 255–76.

——— (1980). *Naming and Necessity*. Cambridge, MA: Harvard University Press.

Ludlow, Peter and Stephen Neale (1991). "Indefinite Descriptions: In Defense of Russell," *Linguistics and Philosophy*, 14: 171–202.

Lockwood, Michael (1975). "On Predicating Proper Names," *Philosophical Review*, 84: 471–98.

Mill, John Stuart (1872). *A System of Logic*, definitive 8th edn. 1949 reprint. London: Longmans, Green and Company.

Neale, Stephen (1990). *Descriptions*. Cambridge, MA: MIT Press.

——— (2005). "Pragmatics and Binding," in Z. Szabó (ed.), *Semantics vs. Pragmatics*. Oxford: Oxford University Press, 165–285.

Nunberg, Geoffrey (1993). "Indexicality and Deixis," *Linguistics and Philosophy*, 16: 1–43.

——— (2004). "Descriptive Indexicals and Indexical Descriptions," in A. Bezuidenhout and M. Reimer (eds.). *Descriptions and Beyond*. Oxford: Oxford University Press, 261–79.

Perry, John (2001). *Reference and Reflexivity*. Stanford: CSLI Publications.

Predelli, Stefano (1998). "I am not here now," *Analysis*, 58: 107–15.

Recanati, François (1993). *Direct Reference: From Language to Thought*. Oxford: Blackwell.

Russell, Bertrand (1905). "On Denoting," *Mind*, 14: 479–93.

——— (1917/1957). "Knowledge by Acquaintance and Knowledge by Description," in *Mysticism and Logic*, pbk. edn. Garden City, NY: Doubleday Anchor, 202–24.

——— (1918/1956). "The Philosophy of Logical Atomism," in *Logic and Knowledge*. London: George Allen and Unwin, 175–281.

——— (1919). "Descriptions," ch. 16 of *Introduction to Mathematical Philosophy*. London: George Allen and Unwin, 167–80.

Salmon, Nathan (1986). *Frege's Puzzle*, Cambridge, MA: MIT Press.

——— (1998). "Nonexistence," *Noûs*, 32: 277–319.

Schiffer, Stephen (1977). "Naming and Knowing," *Midwest Studies*, 2: 28–41.

Schiffer, Stephen (2005). "Russell's Theory of Descriptions," *Mind*, 114.

Smith, Quentin (1989). "The Multiple Uses of Indexicals," *Synthese*, 78: 167–91.

Soames, Scott (2002). *Beyond Rigidity*. Oxford: Oxford University Press.

Strawson, P. F. (1950). "On Referring," *Mind*, 59: 320–44.

—— (1964). "Intention and Convention in Speech Acts," *Philosophical Review*, 73: 439–60.

PART V

SEMANTIC THEORY

....

FORMAL SEMANTICS

....

JEFFREY C. KING

SEMANTICS is the discipline that studies linguistic meaning generally, and the qualification 'formal' indicates something about the sorts of techniques used in investigating linguistic meaning. More specifically, formal semantics is the discipline that employs techniques from symbolic logic, mathematics, and mathematical logic to produce precisely characterized theories of meaning for natural languages (i.e. naturally occurring languages such as English, Urdu, etc.) or artificial languages (i.e. first-order predicate logic, computer programming languages etc.).

Formal semantics as we know it first arose in the twentieth century. It was made possible by certain developments in logic during that period. What follows will chronicle those developments and how they led to the development of formal semantics. This will provide the reader with a preliminary understanding of the discipline.

Though the works of Gottlob Frege, Bertrand Russell, and Ludwig Wittgenstein in the late 1800s and early 1900s were important precursors, the development of formal semantics really begins with the work of the Polish logician Alfred Tarski on the notion of truth. During and immediately prior to the late 1920s and early 1930s, the time when Tarski produced his seminal work on truth, a movement called *logical positivism* was beginning to dominate scientifically minded philosophy. Scientifically minded philosophers and logicians of the time thought that the use of techniques from mathematics and symbolic logic in philosophy was the way to move the discipline forward. The logical positivists generally very much shared this vision

---

Throughout I adopt the slightly different use–mention conventions of the figures I discuss without comment. No confusion should result.

of philosophy. However, they also thought that much traditional philosophy was nonsense, and they had formulated criteria of meaningfulness according to which much traditional work in philosophy failed to satisfy these criteria and so was meaningless (Carnap, 1932). As a result of this outlook, the positivists were extremely suspicious of the use of any terms in philosophy that appeared to attempt to make reference to things that in some sense were beyond human experience. Thus, talk of "things in themselves", "the absolute", and so on were dismissed as gibberish. Talk of truth made the positivists nervous as well, perhaps because it seemed to them to presuppose some mind independent reality that in principle could extend beyond human experience and that served as that which makes true things true.

Tarski's work on truth needs to be viewed in this context. Tarski (1935) takes as its goal the definition of 'true sentence' for a range of formal languages. It should be mentioned that Tarski thought that it was not possible to coherently define the notion of 'true sentence' for natural languages such as German or Polish. Because such languages contain, or allow for the introduction of, names for its own sentences, and contain the expression 'true sentence' as well as other semantic vocabulary ('names', 'denotes' etc.), these languages allow the formulation of the liar paradox (and others as well). Thus, Tarski regarded such languages as logically inconsistent and thought that as a result there could be no correct definition of 'true sentence' for such languages.

Tarski (1935) produced a definition of 'true sentence' for what he called *the languages of the calculus of classes*. This language is a first-order language containing two sentential connectives (the negation sign, disjunction), a universal quantifier, and a two-place predicate ('I') whose meaning is 'is included in'. Considered as the language under study, the language for which 'true sentence' will be defined, we call this the *object language*. The *sentences* of this language are the well-formed formulas lacking free occurrences of variables.[1] The *metalanguage*, the language in which we construct the definition of truth, Tarski did not attempt to formalize, though he did clearly describe its important features. The crucial point is that for every sentence S of the object language, the metalanguage contained a name (or structural description—a linguistic description of the sentence of the object language in the vocabulary of the metalanguage) of S and a translation of S. Tarski's famous *convention T* stated that an adequate definition of 'true sentence' for a language must have as consequences all sentences obtained from 'x is true iff p' by substituting for 'x' a structural description of a sentence of the object language and for 'p' the translation of this sentence in the metalanguage. Tarski notes that for languages with infinite numbers of sentences, the idea suggests itself of defining 'true sentence' by recursion, (i.e. one defines 'true sentence' for the simplest sentences, and then shows how whether a complex sentence is true depends on whether the simpler sentences it is made up of are true). One would consider all the ways complex sentences can be built out of simpler ones, and then specify how the truth or falsity of a complex

---

[1] An occurrence of a variable α in a formula ϕ is *bound* if it occurs in ϕ in a formula of the form $(\alpha)\psi$ (recall that the language under consideration contains only the universal quantifier). Otherwise it is *free*.

sentence depends on the truth or falsity of its component sentences. The problem is that some sentences are not built up out of *sentences*, but rather formulae with free variables, to which the notion of truth simpliciter is not applicable (.e.g. the sentence '$(x_1)Ix_1x_1$' is built out of the well-formed formula with free variables 'Ix_1x_1', and the latter is not true or false simpliciter, but only true or false *relative to an assignment of values to the variable 'x_1'*). As a result, Tarski suggests defining another semantic notion that is applicable to all well-formed formulae and that can be used to define truth directly. This is the notion of *satisfaction*. To define it, Tarski considered infinite sequences f of objects, in the present case classes. As indicated, in Tarski's object language, 'I' is the two-place predicate meaning 'is included in' and individual variables were subscripted as follows : 'x_1', 'x_2', etc. (actually, Tarski used one, two, etc. *strokes* as subscripts, but the present notation is more readable). Tarski stipulated that the nth element of the sequence f be associated with the variable 'x_n'. Let f_n be the nth element of the sequence f. Now, consider a formulae containing free variables, such as:

(1) Ix_1x_2

Tarski's definition of satisfaction has it that f satisfies 1 iff (the class) f_1 is included in f_2. For a disjunctive formula, a sequence satisfies it iff it satisfies one of the disjuncts, (satisfaction of negations of formulae works in the obvious analogous way). Finally, a sequence f satisfies a universally quantified formula whose quantifier's variable is 'x_n' iff for every sequence f' like f except that f'_n might not be the same as f_n, f' satisfies the formula resulting from stripping off the universal quantifier being treated whose variable is 'x_n'.

For sentences, Tarski's definition of satisfaction has the consequence that either every sequence satisfies it or none does (since there are no free variables in sentences, it doesn't matter what a sequence assigns to variables). Thus, one can immediately define a 'true sentence' (of the language in question) as one that is satisfied by every sequence. Tarski goes on to note that his definition satisfies convention T and that 'true sentence' on his definition has a variety of properties that one would expect it to have. Finally, he discusses defining 'true sentence' for a variety of other languages.

It should be noted that Tarski (1935) did not define the now more familiar 'true sentence relative to a model M'. He held the meaning of the non-logical symbols ('I') fixed (it means 'is included in') and so simply defined 'true sentence' (for that language). Because assigning the conditions under which sentences of a language are true and false to those sentences has come to be viewed as the central task of formal semantics, it is hard to overstate the significance of the fact that Tarski showed for the first time how to do this for a range of formal languages.

Rudolf Carnap was very much aware of Tarski's work, and very much influenced by it. Carnap's 1947 *Meaning and Necessity* was the first work that, using Tarski's techniques, provided formal semantics for languages that go beyond first-order logic in including devices akin to some of the more problematic devices present in natural languages, including expressions for expressing modality ('Necessarily') and verbs of propositional attitude ('believes').

Carnap (1942, 1947) explicitly undertook the task of providing what he called a "semantical analysis" of meaning. Carnap's work here is naturally seen as a clear precursor to what we now consider formal semantics since he appeared to be attempting to precisely capture the pretheoretical notion of the meaning of an expression by employing techniques drawn from logic (or perhaps provide what he called an *explication* of the notion of the meaning of an expression—this is replacing an unclear pretheoretical notion by an exact notion that serves the same purpose). Carnap (1947) considers three formal languages[2] as well as "the English word language". Carnap is concerned to show in outline how to rigorously assign to certain expressions of these languages entities that can be precisely characterized and that constitute the meaning of the expressions. I shall focus here on the formal language Carnap calls S_1 since it is the simplest language he considers and it is the most easily explained. I shall only consider very simple sentences of S_1 and shall not describe the whole language. S_1 contains the individual constants 's' and 'w', which translate into English as the names 'Walter Scott' and 'Waverly' (the name of a book), respectively. It also contains predicates including 'Hx' and 'Axy', which translate into English as 'x is human' and 'x wrote y', respectively. Finally, S_1 contains devices for combining sentences to form larger sentences, including 'v' which roughly translates into English as 'or'. So if S and S' are sentences of S_1, then SvS' is also a sentence which would translate into English as S_e or S_e', where S_e and S_e' are the English translations of S' and S', respectively. Turning now to Carnap's "formal semantics" for S_1, Carnap calls the statements specifying the above (fixed) meanings for individual constants and predicates *rules of designation*. Using these, Carnap, following Tarski, gives a definition of 'true (sentence) in S_1'. As with Tarski's definition, Carnap's holds the meanings of non-logical symbols fixed (as specified in the rules of designation).

Next, Carnap defines what he calls a *state description* in S_1. The *atomic sentences* of S_1 are the (syntactically) simplest sentences of S_1. A predicate with one-place, e.g. 'H', followed by a single individual constant, e.g. 's', is an atomic sentence (e.g. 'Hs'). Similarly, a two-place predicate like 'A' followed by two individual constants is an atomic sentence (e.g. 'Asw'). In general, a predicate with n places followed by n individual constants is an atomic sentence. Now a state description in S_1 is a set of sentences such that for each atomic sentence, it contains that sentence or its negation. Intuitively, a state description is a complete description of a possible state of the universe, at least as far as the properties expressed by the predicates and the individuals designated by the individual constants of S_1 are concerned. In effect, a state description (in S_1) describes a state of the universe in which all the sentences in the set that is the state description are true.

Carnap then defines what it is for a sentence of S_1 to *hold in a state description of S_1*. For example, an atomic sentence holds in a state description iff it is a member of the state description (because the state description is intuitively saying that in that

---

[2] S_1: the predicate calculus (with lamda abstracts and definite descriptions); S_2: the predicate calculus enriched with modal operators; and S_3: the predicate calculus enriched with an infinite number of individual expressions of standard form 'o', 'o'', 'o''' (which function as singular terms syntactically).

possible way the universe might be, the atomic sentence is true). Where S and S' are sentences, a sentence of the form SvS' holds in a state description iff S holds in it or S' holds in it. Carnap calls the state descriptions in which a given sentence holds, its *range*. Hence the rules specifying the conditions under which an atomic sentence, a disjunction or a universal quantification holds in a state description Carnap calls *rules of ranges*. Carnap thinks that the rules of designation and rules of ranges give the interpretations or meanings of the sentences of S_1. For they tell us in what possible circumstances a sentence would be true. It should be noted that the connection to the definition of truth is that there is one state description D that represents the actual world. A sentence is true (according to the definition of 'true sentence of S_1') iff it holds in D.

Using these notions Carnap defines what it is for a sentence to be L-true in S_1: a sentence of S_1 is L-true in S_1 iff it holds in every state description. An L-true sentence holds in every way the universe might have been since state descriptions are descriptions of all the ways the universe might have been. Carnap took L-truth to be an *explication* (see p. 8) of the inexact notions of necessary or logical truth. Carnap also defines other L-notions, most importantly L-equivalence (two sentences are equivalent iff they have the same truth-value; they are L-equivalent iff they hold in the same state descriptions).

Finally, Carnap generalizes the notion of L-equivalence so that not just sentences but individual constants, predicates, sentential connectives, variables and quantifiers can be L-equivalent to other individual constants, predicates, etc. Further, these generalizations allow that expressions in different "semantical systems" (roughly, formal languages) can be L-equivalent. Carnap then uses the notions of equivalence and L-equivalence to introduce the notions of *having the same extension* and *having the same intension* as follows. Two expressions have the same extension iff they are equivalent. They have the same intension iff they are L-equivalent. This doesn't tell us what extensions and intensions of various expressions are, but it constrains the answer to this question. Whatever extensions are, equivalent expressions must have the same one. Whatever intensions are, L-equivalent expressions must have the same one. Carnap thought that the most natural and obvious entities satisfying these conditions on extensions for individual constants, predicates, and sentences were (respectively), the individuals they designate, the individuals the predicates apply to and their truth-values. In the case of intensions, he thought that the intensions of individual constants, predicates and sentences were individual concepts, properties, and propositions, respectively.

Carnap seemed to think that the intension and extension of an expression comprised its meaning (or perhaps that the precise notions of intension and extension explicated the vague, ordinary notion of meaning). Earlier, I noted that Carnap also thought that the rules of designation and rules of ranges (which, given the state description that describes the actual world, serve to characterize truth) together assigned meanings to sentences. That doesn't conflict with the present claim regarding intensions and extensions, since the crucial notion in defining sameness of extension (which tells us what extensions have to be like) is the *truth* of a certain sentence and the crucial notion in defining sameness of intension is the *L-truth* of a certain sentence (i.e. the sentence holding in every state description). So for sentences, their intensions and extensions can be thought of as a sort of summary of their truth conditions and what state descriptions they hold in.[3]

Equipped with the generalized relation of L-equivalence, which can now hold between expressions of all syntactic categories and between expressions of different languages, Carnap characterizes what it is for complex expressions to be *intensionally isomorphic*. Crudely put, two expressions are intensionally isomorphic iff they are built up in the same way out of L-equivalent expressions. Carnap thought that the notion of intensional isomorphism could be used to give a semantics for verbs of propositional attitude such as 'believes'. Carnap thought that even if two sentences D and D' were L-equivalent, "John believes that D" and "John believes that D'" could differ in truth-value (he imagines D being a simple sentence that is a logical truth and D' being a very complex sentence that is a logical truth). Thus, for such sentences to be incapable of diverging in truth-values, the relation between D and D' must be tighter than L-equivalence. Carnap suggested that the semantics for a sentence like 'John believes that D' could be given as follows (p. 53):

15-1. 'There is a sentence S_i in the semantical system S' such that (a) S_i is intensionally isomorphic to 'D' and (b) John is disposed to an affirmative response to S_i.'

Church (1950) offered what many take to be a devastating criticism of this account. But many philosophers were influenced by Carnap's idea that the objects of belief are structured entities built up in the same way out of entities with the same intensions. See especially Lewis (1970) and Cresswell (1985).

Carnap also gave a semantics for the symbol 'N', which syntactically fronts a for-mula to yield a new formula. 'N' is added to Carnap's first-order logic S_1 and the result he calls S_2. Carnap says that 'N' is a sign for logical necessity. When it fronts a sentence '...' of S_2, 'N(...)' is true iff '...' is L-true.[4] However, Carnap's S_3 also allows for quantification over 'N' into a formula with free variables. Carnap shows that in his system, the following formulae are equivalent (where '..x..' is a formula containing only free occurrences of 'x'):

(x)N(..x..)
N((x)(..x..))

Meaning and Necessity was an important work in the history of formal semantics, in that it offered formal semantic analyses of recalcitrant expressions like 'It is necessary that' and 'believes'. Though the details of Carnap's proposals have been

---

[3] It should be mentioned that Carnap had an unusual attitude towards intensions and extensions. At the end of Carnap (1947), he writes:

The formulations in terms of 'extension' and 'intension', 'class', 'property', etc., seem to refer to two kinds of entities in each type. We have seen, however, that, in fact, no such duplication of entities is presupposed by our method and that those formulations involve only a convenient duplication of modes of speech. (p. 202)

I won't attempt to determine precisely what Carnap meant by this.

[4] p. 175.

abandoned, his proposals were influential and elements of his accounts have been preserved in the accounts of others.

Though, as we saw, Carnap formulated a semantics for a system of quantified modal logic, it was the work of Kripke and others (most notably, Hintikka, 1961; Kanger, 1957, and Montague, 1960) that secured the semantic foundations of quantified modal logic. Since much of subsequent formal semantics makes use of the tools introduced for the semantics of modal logic, we shall discuss it in some detail. We focus here on the formulations in Kripke (1963b). Consider a standard first-order logic with sentential connectives $\sim$, & and $\square$ (the first and third one-place, the second two-place), individual variables (with or without subscripts) x,y,z,...; n-place predicates P^n, Q^n, ... (0 place predicate letters are *propositional variables*), and a universal quantifier (for any variable x_i, (x_i)). A *model structure* is a triple $\langle G,K,R \rangle$, where K is a set, G ε K and R is a *reflexive relation* on K (i.e. for all H ε K, H R H). Intuitively, G is the "actual world" and the members of K are all the possible worlds. R is a relation between worlds and is usually now called the *accessibility relation*. Intuitively, if HR H' (H' is accessible from H), then what is *true* in H' is *possible* in H. Again intuitively, the worlds accessible from a given world are those that are possible relative to it. Putting conditions on R gives one model structures appropriate to different modal logics. If R is merely reflexive, as required above, we get an *M* model structure. If R is reflexive and *transitive* (i.e. for any H, H', H" ε K, if H R H' and H' R H", then H R H"), we get an *S4* model structure. Finally, if R is reflexive, transitive and *symmetric* (i.e. for any H, H' ε K, if H R H', then H' R H), we get an *S5* model structure.

Recall that for Carnap, state-descriptions (certain sets of atomic formulae or their negations) represented possible worlds. Here in Kripke's (1963b) semantics possible worlds are taken as primitive elements in the model structures. (By contrast, in Kripke (1959) possible worlds are identified with functions that map variables to individuals, propositional variables to T or F and n-place predicates to sets of n-tuples. Kripke (1963a) discusses the reason for this change.)

A *quantificational model structure* is a model structure $\langle G,K,R \rangle$, together with a function ψ that assigns to every H in K a set of individuals called *the domain of H*. Intuitively this represents the individuals existing in the possible world H. Of course, this allows different worlds (members of K) to have different domains of individuals. This formally captures the intuitive idea that some individuals that exist might not have, and that there might have been individuals that there aren't.

Given a quantificational model structure, the set U is the union of ψ(H) for all H in K. Intuitively, this is the set of all possible individuals. That is, any individual in the domain of any world is in U. U^m is the set of all n-tuples whose elements are in U. A *quantificational model* on a quantificational model structure $\langle G,K,R \rangle$ is a function φ that maps a zero-place predicate and a member of K to T or F; and for n>0, an n-place predicate and a member of K to a subset of U^n. We extend φ by induction to assign truth-values to all formulae/world pairs *relative to a function assigning members of U to variables* (i.e. the function assigns a possible individual to each variable):

(1) *Propositional Variable*: Let f be a function assigning elements of U to all individual variables. Let P be a propositional variable. Then for any H in K, $\varphi(P, H) = T$ relative to f iff $\varphi(P, H) = T$; otherwise $\varphi(P, H) = F$ relative to f.

(2) *Atomic*: Let f be as in 1. For any H in K, $\varphi(P^n x_1, \ldots, x_n, H) = T$ relative to f iff $\langle f(x_1), \ldots, f(x_n) \rangle \varepsilon \, \varphi(P^n, H)$; otherwise $\varphi(P^n x_1, \ldots, x_n, H) = F$ relative to f.

(It should be emphasized that 2 allows that an atomic formula can have a truth-value at a world relative to an assignment to its variables, where some or all of its variables get assigned things not in the domain of the world, since f assigns elements of U to free variables; and φ assigns subsets of U^m to P^n at a world!)

(3) *Truth functional connectives*: Let f be as in 1. Let A and B be formulae. For any H in K, $\varphi(A\&B, H) = T$ relative to f iff $\varphi(A, H) = T$ relative to f and $\varphi(B, H) = T$ relative to f; otherwise $\varphi(A\&B, H) = F$ relative to f. (Similarly for $\sim$)

(4) Let f be as in 1. $\varphi(\Box A, H) = T$ relative to f iff $\varphi(A, H') = T$ relative to f for all H' ε K such that H R H'; otherwise $\varphi(\Box A, H) = F$ relative to f.

(According to 4, whether a formula $\Box A$ is true at a world (relative to f) depends only on whether A is true at all worlds *accessible* from the original world.)

(5) *Quantifiers*: Let f be as in 1. Let $A(x, y_1, \ldots y_n)$ be a formula containing only the free variables $x, y_1, \ldots, y_n$. For any H in K, and any function g (assigning elements of U to variables), suppose $\varphi(A(x, y_1, \ldots, y_n), H)$ *relative to g* is defined. Then $\varphi((x) A(x, y_1, \ldots y_n), H) = T$ relative to f iff for every f' such that $f'(x) \, \varepsilon \, \psi(H)$ and f' differs from f at most in that f'(x) is not f(x), $\varphi(A(x, y_1, \ldots y_n), H) = T$ relative to f'; otherwise, $\varphi((x)A(x, y_1, \ldots y_n), H) = F$ relative to f.

(The fact that in 5 we consider only functions f' such that $f'(x) \, \varepsilon \, \psi(H)$ means that quantifiers range over only the objects that exist at the world where the quantified sentence is being evaluated.)

The reason Kripke's semantics for modal logic is so important from the standpoint of semantics of natural language is that it contained the crucial ideas that were developed into what is now called *possible worlds semantics*, (though these ideas are traceable to Carnap (1947), they are essentially formally implemented in Kripke (1963b) in the way they are now standardly implemented). To see this, consider again a model on a quantificational model structure, forgetting for the moment about functions f that make assignments to variables and that the domains of members of K can vary. This essentially amounts to considering a model on a *propositional* model structure. A *model* φ on a (M/S4/S5) model structure $\langle G, K, R \rangle$ assigns to a propositional variable (a zero-place predicate—an atomic formula without any variables) and a member of K either T or F. Now consider a particular propositional variable P. Consider the function f_P defined as follows:

For any H in K, $f_P(H) = T$ iff $\varphi(P, H) = T$; otherwise $f_P(H) = F$

f_P is a function from worlds to truth-values. Many people had thought that the proposition expressed by a sentence should determine whether the sentence is true or false, given a way the universe might have been. Kripke's semantics, and specifically the ability to trivially define functions like f_P above using his models, suggested to philosophers and logicians that propositions be *identified* with functions like f_P. So propositions are simply functions from world to truth-values and so f_P is the proposition expressed by P (relative to φ and $\langle G, K, R \rangle$). Similarly, one can use Kripke models to define functions from possible worlds to extensions of other expressions as well. Thus, for example, n-place predicates can be associated with functions from possible worlds to sets of n-tuples. For example, 'loves' could be associated with a function from worlds to sets of pairs $\langle a,b \rangle$, where a loves b at the world in question. These functions from possible worlds to extensions have come to be called *intensions*. Possible worlds semantics essentially amounts to assigning intensions to linguistic expressions, which in turn determine their extensions at possible worlds.

Apparently because of the ease with which one can define intensions from Kripke's models, Montague (1960b) credits Kripke with being the first to employ intensions so understood. At any rate, the idea of applying possible worlds semantics to natural language was very much in the air in the 1960s as a result of the work of Kripke and others. Two influential works that did just this were Lewis (1970) and Montague (1973). Because Montague (1973) arguably has been the more influential of the two, it is discussed here.

Montague wanted to give a formal semantics for a fragment of English that included various expressions that were problematic for semanticists including verbs of propositional attitude such as 'believes', so-called intensional transitive verbs such as 'seeks', modal operators such as 'necessarily' and others.

Montague (1973) specifies a syntax for a fragment of English that includes the above expressions, and that allows for the formation of prepositional phrases as well as relative clauses. Since the fragment allows the formation of relative clauses, it also allows for the formation of complex noun phrases such as 'woman such that she loves every man'. So Montague's English fragment contains sentences such as:

(2) John seeks a unicorn.
(3) Mary talks about a unicorn.
(4) Every man such that he talks loves a woman such that she walks.
(5) Mary believes that a unicorn is in the park.
(6) Necessarily, every man is a man.

Many sentences of Montague's fragment had distinct syntactic analyses that would be given different semantic interpretations. So, for example, on one analysis of 4, the final step in its construction is to put the expression 'Every man such that he talks' in subject position. This is assigned the reading of the sentence on which the sentence is true if every talking man loves some walking woman, with talking men possibly loving different walking women. (4) has another analysis on which the last step in its construction is adding 'a woman such that she walks'. This analysis gets assigned a reading that requires for its truth that there be some walking woman, say Stephanie, that every talking man loves. Hence it is really syntactic analyses of sentences that get assigned semantic interpretations.

Montague assigns (syntactic analyses of) sentences of the English fragment semantic interpretations by translating them into sentences of a typed intensional logic, which are themselves given semantic interpretations. The expressions of Montague's English fragment were grouped by categories, which corresponded to traditional grammatical categories but were characterized in terms of the basic categories e ("entity expression"—an expression for an individual—there were no basic expressions of this sort in Montague's fragment) and t (truth-value expression—declarative sentence—there were no basic expressions of this sort in Montague's fragment).[5] These categories of English expressions were correlated with types of Montague's intensional logic, so that an English expression of a given category got translated into an expression of the corresponding type in intensional logic. For the sake of brevity, we shall here simply describe the sorts of semantic interpretations given to English expressions in various syntactic categories. To see why these expressions received the interpretations they did, consider sentence (2) above. One might think that transitive verbs would have as their extensions (at a world) sets of pairs of individuals. For example, the extension of 'loves' at a world would be a set of pairs of individuals such that the first loves the second. But sentence (2) (on one of its readings) shows that this cannot be right: that sentence can be true (at a world) even if there are no unicorns. So 'seeks' cannot have as its extension at a world a set of pairs of individuals.[6] The extension of 'seeks' must somehow be more abstract.

To deal with this and related problems, Montague assigned to expressions semantic interpretations that seem more complex and abstract than they need be. Michael Bennett (1974) suggested a simplification of Montague's view, though the simplification didn't allow Montague's own solution to certain puzzles.[7] Because it will be simpler to do so, I will describe the semantic interpretations of various English expressions that result from Bennett's simplifications.

Common nouns and intransitive verbs get assigned sets of individuals as their extensions (relative to a world and time—I will henceforth suppress this). This reflects the fact that e.g. intransitive verbs don't exhibit the odd behavior exhibited by the object position of 'seeks'.[8] Quantifiers, expressions such as 'every man', get

---

[5] There were no basic expressions of category e, because these would have been expressions that designated individuals. But the best candidates for basic expressions of this type, names like 'Chris', Montague treated as designating the set of Chris's properties instead of Chris (in Bennett's simplified version of Montague's view—see below) so that they would function in the same way as other noun phrases such as 'every man'. There were no basic expressions of category t, because these would be syntactically simple expressions that designate truth-values, that is, sentences. And English arguably has no syntactically simple sentences.

[6] Unless we fooled around with our metaphysics e.g. by allowing things that don't exist at a world to nonetheless stand in relations at that world.

[7] In particular, it didn't allow for Montague's explanation as to why 'The temperature is ninety' and 'The temperature rises' don't entail 'Ninety rises'. But there is some doubt as to whether Montague's explanation is correct. See Dowty, Wall and Peters (1981) for discussion, especially pp.184–90 and Appendix III.

[8] Actually, Montague himself thought the common noun 'temperature' and the intransitive verb 'rises' did exhibit such odd behavior. See previous note.

assigned as extensions sets of properties of individuals (intuitively, 'every man' has as its extension the set of properties possessed by every man). 'Necessarily' gets assigned as its extension a set of propositions (those that are necessary). Verbs of propositional attitude get assigned as extensions functions from propositions to sets of individuals (in the case of 'believes', the function maps a proposition to the set of individuals who believe it). Finally, transitive verbs get assigned as extensions functions from properties of properties of individuals (i.e. functions from worlds/time pairs to functions from world/time pairs to sets of individuals) to sets of individuals. In the case of (2) above, the sentence will be true at a world/time pair iff the function that is the extension of 'seeks' maps the property of being a property had by some unicorn to a set of individuals that contains John. Thus, (2) can be true even though there are no unicorns. (In order that 'John seeks a unicorn' and 'John seeks a hydra' be allowed to differ in truth-value at a world/time pair, this treatment assumes that at some world/time pairs, unicorns and hydras possess properties. This would be doubted by many contemporary philosophers, since they think that unicorns and hydras are impossible creatures and so don't exist in any possible worlds. See Kripke (1980) for discussion.) I have described the extensions (at world/time pairs) Montague's approach assigned to English expressions of various categories, but he also assigned intensions to those expressions: these, of course, were functions from world/time pairs to the sorts of extensions described.

In order to handle transitive verbs such as 'eat' that don't exhibit the characteristic behavior of 'seek' (i.e. if you eat a unicorn, unicorns must exist and you must have eaten a specific one), Montague required certain formulas to be true in all interpretations of his intensional logic that served as interpretations of English (indirectly, by being interpretations of formulae of intensional logic that English sentences (really, syntactic analyses) get translated into). This insured that any interpretation that makes 'John ate a fish' true (at a world and time) is one in which the individual John stands in a relation (eating) to a specific fish.

Montague's work showed that techniques borrowed from symbolic logic could be used to give sophisticated semantic accounts of significant fragments of English, even when those fragments included intensional transitive verbs, verbs of propositional attitude and modal expressions. Many linguists and philosophers interested in semantics were quickly convinced that this was the way to pursue the subject.

As indicated, Montague had assigned intensions, functions from world and times to extensions, to English expressions. Call these things that are the arguments of intensions, here world/time pairs, *indices*. Obviously, indices were world/time pairs because the extensions of expressions varied over worlds and times for Montague. That is, worlds and times partly determine the extensions of expressions. When it was realized that other factors, such as who is speaking, who is being addressed, where the utterance was taking place and so on, also determine the extensions of expressions (such as 'I', 'you', 'here' etc.), it was thought that these elements too should be included in indices. Thus indices grew into n-tuples of (at least) a world, a speaker, an addressee, a time, a location and so on. Lewis (1970) is a good example of a semantics with such enlarged indices.

However, Hans Kamp (1971) discovered a problem with such semantic approaches involving a single index with many *features* (world, speaker, time, etc.). Operators work by shifting features of indices. Assume that indices are world/time pairs as they were for Montague and suppose we have a past tense operator 'P' that works as follows (Montague (1973) had a past operator in his intensional logic):

Pϕ is true at $\langle w,t \rangle$ iff ϕ is true at $\langle w,t' \rangle$ for some t' prior to t.

where ϕ is a formula, w a world and t a time.

Now suppose your language also contains a contextually sensitive expression that is sensitive to time of utterance, such as 'now'. When you embed such an expression under a past operator, problems result. So consider the sentence

(7) Two weeks ago, Sarah didn't think she would be seeing the Pope now.

Assuming 'two weeks ago' is a past tense operator, 7 is true at a world w and time t iff

(7a) Sarah didn't think she would be seeing the Pope now.

is true at w and t', where t' is two weeks prior to t. But then 'now' will take as its value t' and 7 will end up being true at w,t iff two weeks prior to t, Sarah didn't think she would be seeing the Pope *then*. But these aren't the correct truth conditions for 7. 'Now' must refer to the time of utterance of 7, not a time two weeks prior to t.

To solve this problem, Kamp noted that in a language like this containing feature of index shifting operators ('P') and a contextually sensitive expression that is sensitive to the same feature ('now', which is sensitive to time), one needs two separate indices: one to have its feature shifted by the operator and one to have its feature unshifted for the contextually sensitive expression to exploit. Thus, in the above example, we would assign sentences extensions relative to *two* temporal indices. The argument here depends on the assumption that expressions like 'two weeks ago' are features of index shifting operators, and this is a claim many philosophers and linguists currently doubt, (see King (2003) for discussion). But the same argument could be made using modal operators and the contextually sensitive expression 'actual'.

Though the need for double indexing was widely accepted on the basis of Kamp's work, it was David Kaplan (1989) who was responsible for clarifying the significance of the two indices and what each represented. Kaplan (1989) (much of which was written in the early 1970s and a version of which was circulated for years in mimeograph form) formulates a semantic theory of two kinds of contextually sensitive words: *pure indexicals* ('I', 'today', etc.) and *demonstratives* ('he' (in its use as a demonstrative pronoun), 'this', 'that'). The difference between the two is that in order for an utterance of the latter to refer to something in a context, the speaker must supplement her utterance in some way (perhaps by pointing as she utters 'he') whereas this is not required for the former. Kaplan argued that one index, the one that provides the value for a contextually sensitive expression, represents the *context of utterance*. Thus, this index must contain features to be the semantic values (relative to the context) of contextually sensitive expressions. Because of 'I', 'now', 'actually' and 'here', the context of utterance must contain at least a speaker, a time, a world and a location. A sentence like 'I am eating now' when taken relative to a context, say the context with me as speaker, May 26, 2005 at 2:00 p.m. PST as the time, and Mammoth Mountain as the location, has values assigned to 'I' and 'now'. The sentence as a whole has a *content*, what is said by the sentence in that context. In the present case, this content would be roughly that Jeffrey King is eating on May 26, 2005 at 2:00 p.m. PST.

The other index is the index at which we evaluate (sentence) contents for truth or falsity. Kaplan calls this a *circumstance of evaluation*. Let's suppose a circumstance of evaluation is just a possible world. Then we can take the content expressed by 'I am hungry now' in the above context and evaluate it at different circumstances/possible worlds. It is true at those circumstances in which I am eating on May 26, 2005 at 2:00 p.m. PST.

The distinction between context of utterance and circumstance of evaluation corresponds to a distinction between two kinds of meaning possessed by expressions. On the one hand, the sentence 'I am eating now' has the same meaning whenever uttered, and this meaning determines the content of a sentence when taken in a context. This meaning, which Kaplan called *character*, determines a function from contexts to contents. The second kind of meaning an expression has is its content when taken in a context, as we saw above. For sentences, content determines a function from circumstances of evaluation to truth-values.

Kaplan's distinction between context of utterance and circumstance of evaluation on the one hand and character and content on the other has been virtually universally accepted.

Kaplan also argued that demonstratives and pure indexicals are *devices of direct reference*. If we think of the content of a sentence (relative to context), a *proposition*, as a structured entity with the contents of the words in the sentence (in that context) as constituents, Kaplan's view was that indexicals and demonstratives contributed to these propositions their referents in contexts. In other words, the content of a pure indexical or demonstrative in a context is whatever it refers to in that context. This view of Kaplan's has also been widely influential, (though see King, 2001 for a dissenting view in the case of *complex demonstratives*).

Developments in formal semantics of a rather different sort began in the mid to late 1970s. Robert Stalnaker, following Paul Grice, had been interested in the question of how information can get conveyed by participants in a conversation even though the information is not the semantic content of any sentence uttered in the conversation. In Stalnaker (1978), Stalnaker gave an account of how context of utterance and the content of a sentence relative to that context mutually influence each other. On the one hand, as we have seen, context provides semantic values of contextually sensitive expressions and so partly determines the content of sentences in context. On the other hand, Stalnaker thought that which possibilities (possible worlds) are "live options" at a given point in a conversation is a central feature of the context of utterance at that point in the conversation. Stalnaker called the set of these possibilities the *context set*. Now Stalnaker proposed that what happens when a sentence is asserted and accepted in a conversation is that it cuts down the context set. For example, suppose that at a certain point in a certain conversation among the live options for the purposes of the conversation at that point are some possible worlds in which I will be in Santa Monica this coming July, some according to which I will be in Paris in July, etc. That is, at this point in the conversation it is a "live option" that I will be in Paris in July, or Santa Monica or . . . . I then assert 'I will be in Argentina this July'. If my assertion is accepted, then all possible worlds that had been in the context set according to which I am in places other than Argentina in July are eliminated from the context set. By using this simple idea to motivate the claim that speakers obey certain principles in making assertions in conversations, Stalnaker is able provide interesting explanations of a variety of phenomena.

Stalnaker (1978), along with Lewis (1979), was among the first to attempt to provide precise models of "conversational dynamics": the way in which utterances of successive sentences can interact with each other and the context of the conversation in order to convey information and affect the context. Stalnaker took his work to be work in pragmatics (which Stalnaker takes to be the study of the relation between linguistic expressions and contexts of use) and not semantics. However, it was not long before philosophers and linguists formulated *semantic* theories that attempted to capture dynamic features of conversation.

Irene Heim (1982) and Hans Kamp (1981) independently formulated very similar semantic theories that were designed to apply to multi sentence discourses and so to capture certain features of conversational dynamics. Kamp's theory is generally called *Discourse Representation Theory (DRT)* and Heim's version is either called the same thing or *File Change Semantics (FTS)*. Here we employ Kamp's formulation. To illustrate aspects of the theory, we will consider how it applies to a case of simple *discourse anaphora* such as the following (though the reader should understand that the theory is much more complex and applies to many more phenomena than our discussion indicates):

(8) Steph owns a truck. She loves it.

(assume 'she' has 'Steph' as its antecedent and 'it', 'a truck').

Kamp associates with a discourse a *discourse representation structure (DRS)*. The DRS associated with the first sentence of 8 alone would look roughly as follows:

$x_1 \quad x_2$
$x_1 = $ Steph
truck(x_2)
x_1 owns x_2

Notice that the indefinite 'a truck' contributes to the DRS a predicate and a variable (and does not express existential quantification, as many philosophers would suppose it does). The DRS for the discourse as a whole would just be an extension of the above as follows:

$x_1 \quad x_2$
$x_1 = $ Steph
truck(x_2)

x_1 owns x_2
x_1 loves x_2

One then gives a semantics for the DRSs, which in turn gives a semantics for the original discourse. Crudely put, this DRS (and hence the original discourse) is true (in a model M) iff there is an assignment to the variables of the DRS that results in all the "conditions" in it ('$x_1 =$ Steph', etc.) being true (in M). This is so iff according to M, Steph owns and loves a truck. Note that it is the requirement that *there be* an assignment to free variables making all the sentences of the DRS true that results in the indefinite 'a truck' here having existential force. So the indefinite 'a truck' contributes a free variable (and predicate) to the DRS and free variables in DRSs undergo default existential quantification.

In Heim/Kamp type theories it is the DRSs that capture conversational dynamics. That is, DRSs are built up and changed as the new sentences of the discourse are treated. But once one has the DRS for an entire discourse, the semantics itself is traditional and "static". Because of this (and other features of DRT), some semanticists were eager to develop semantic theories in which dynamic elements of conversation were captured in the semantics itself. Groenendijk and M. Stokhof (1991) was among the first attempts at such a theory. Theories of this sort are often called *dynamic semantics*. Groenendijk and Stokhof (1991) provides a dynamic semantics for a system of first-order predicate logic and treats English indirectly by considering the translations of English sentences into their logic. They call the logic they formulate (with a dynamic semantics) *dynamic predicate logic (DPL)*. The leading idea of the approach is to identify the meaning of an expression with pairs of inputs and outputs. On a traditional approach to the semantics of expressions in logic, we can think of the meanings (in models) of formulae of first-order logic as being the sets of assignments to variables that satisfy the formulae. So for example, the meaning of 'Fx' in a model M is the set of all assignments such that they assign to 'x' something in the extension of 'F' in the model M. Dynamic logic holds instead that the meaning of a formula in first-order logic is a set of *pairs* of assignments: the first, the input assignment; the second, the output assignment. For "externally dynamic" expressions (e.g. conjunction, existential quantifiers), these can differ and the result is that interpreting these expression can affect how subsequent expressions get interpreted. For since the output assignments can be different from the input assignments for these dynamic expressions, and since the output of these expressions may be the input to subsequent expressions, the interpretation of those subsequent expressions may be affected. A bit more concretely, let's look at how DPL would treat an English discourse such as (9), which is in crucial respects like (8) above:

(9) A man loves Lori. He is rich.

In DPL, in contrast with DRT, indefinites such as 'a man' are treated as existential quantifiers. Further, DPL treats consecutive sentences in discourses as being conjoined. So we can think of (9) as follows:

(9a) $(\exists x)$ (man x & x loves Lori) & x is rich

Here the anaphoric pronoun 'He' is translated into DPL as the variable 'x', the same variable that is the variable of its quantifier antecedent. This represents the anaphoric connection between 'He' and 'A man' in (9). A crucial point is that the anaphoric pronoun/variable in (9a) is not within the syntactic scope of its quantifier antecedent. This corresponds to the fact that in DPL, the syntactic scopes of quantifiers are confined to the sentences in which they occur (as most think is true of quantifiers in natural language).

Now the fact mentioned above, that existential quantifiers are externally dynamic and so interpreting such a quantifier can affect the interpretation of expressions outside its scope, together with the fact(s) that conjunction is "internally" (and externally) dynamic, which allows the interpretation of the first conjunct to affect the interpretation of the second, results in the following two formulas being equivalent in DPL even when 'ψ' contains free occurrences of 'x':

$(\exists x)(\phi) \ \& \ \psi$ and $(\exists x)(\phi \ \& \ \psi)$

So if we consider again our example of 9 and its "representation" in DPL (9a):

(9a) $(\exists x)$ (man x & x loves Lori) & x is rich

this ends up being equivalent to

(9b) $(\exists x)$ (man x & x loves Lori & x is rich)

and so the sentences of the discourse (9) are true iff some rich man loves Lori. Since conjunction is externally dynamic, we can keep adding sentences with anaphoric pronouns to similar affect. Thus in a discourse such as

(9c) A man loves Lori. He is rich. He is famous.

the sentences are all true iff some rich famous man loves Lori.

There is currently much research being done within the framework of dynamic semantics, particularly among linguists. Muskens, van Benthem and Visser (1997) provide a good general overview.

We have not here attempted to give anything like an exhaustive treatment of important work in formal semantics, and so the reader should be aware that important topics (e.g. generalized quantifiers, conditionals) and approaches (two dimensional semantics) have not been covered. The hope has been to sketch the development of the field from the 1940s to the present day. This should give the reader a reasonable overview and grasp of what the field is about.

References

Ayer, A. J. (1959). *Logical Positivism*, A. J. Ayer (ed.), The Free Press, New York.

Bennett, Michael (1974). *Some Extensions of a Montague Fragment*, UCLA PhD dissertation.

Carnap, Rudolf (1932). 'Uberwindung der Metaphysik durch Logische Analyse der Sprache' *Erkenntnis* Vol II; translated into English under the title 'The Elimination of Metaphysics Through the Logical Analysis of Language' and reprinted in Ayer (1959).

_____ (1942). *Introduction to Semantics*, Harvard University Press, Cambridge, MA.

_____ (1947). *Meaning and Necessity*, The University of Chicago Press, Chicago, IL.

Church, Alonzo (1950). 'On Carnap's Analysis of Statements of Assertion and Belief', *Analysis*, 10: 97–9.

Cresswell, M. J. (1985). *Structured Meanings*, MIT Press, Cambridge, MA.

Dowty, D., R. Wall and S. Peters (1981). *Introduction to Montague Semantics*, D. Reidel, Dordrecht, Holland.

Groenendijk, J. and M. Stokhof (1991). 'Dynamic Predicate Logic', *Linguistics and Philosophy*, 14: 39–100.

Heim, Irene, (1982). *The Semantics of Definite and Indefinite Noun Phrases*, Doctoral Thesis, University of Massachusetts, Amherst.

Hintikka, Jaakko (1961). 'Modality and Quantification', *Theoria*, 27: 110–28.

Kamp, Hans (1971). "Formal Properties of 'Now' ", *Theoria*, 37: 227–73.

_____ (1981). 'A Theory of Truth and Semantic Representation', *Formal Methods in the Study of Language*, Groenendijk, Janssen, Stokhof (eds.), Mathematical Centre, Amsterdam.

Kanger, Stig (1957). *Provability in Logic*, Stockholm, Almqvist and Wicksell.

Kaplan, David (1989). 'Demonstratives', in *Themes from Kaplan*, Almog, Perry, Wettstein (eds.), Oxford University Press.

King, Jeffrey C. (2001). *Complex Demonstratives: A Quantificational Account*, MIT Press, Cambridge, MA.

_____ (2003). 'Tense, Modality and Semantic Values' *Philosophical Perspectives Volume 17, Philosophy of Language*, J. Hawthorne (ed.), 195–245.

Kripke, Saul (1959). 'A Completeness Theorem in Modal Logic', *The Journal of Symbolic Logic*, 24, 1: 1–14.

_____ (1963a). 'Semantical Analysis of Modal Logic I Normal Modal Propositional Calculi', *Zeitshcrift fur Mathematsiche Logik und Grundlagen der Mathematik*, 9, 67–96.

_____ (1963b). 'Semantical Considerations on Modal Logic', reprinted in *Reference and Modality*, Leonard Linsky (ed.), 1971, Oxford University Press.

_____ (1980). *Naming and Necessity*, Harvard University Press, Cambridge, MA.

Lewis, David (1970). 'General Semantics', *Synthese*, 22: 18–67.

_____ (1979). 'Scorekeeping in a Language Game', *Journal of Philosophical Logic*, 8: 339–59.

Montague, Richard (1960a). 'Logical Necessity, Physical Necessity, Ethics and Quantifiers', reprinted in *Formal Philosophy*, 1974, Richmond Thomason (ed.), Yale University Press, New Haven, CT.

_____ (1960b). 'On the Nature of Certain Philosophical Entities', reprinted in *Formal Philosophy*, 1974, Richmond Thomason (ed.), Yale University Press, New Haven, CT.

_____ (1973). 'The Proper Treatment of Quantification in Ordinary English', reprinted in *Formal Philosophy*, 1974, Richmond Thomason (ed.), Yale University Press, New Haven, CT.

Stalnaker, Robert (1978). 'Assertion', *Syntax and Semantics 9*, Peter Cole (ed), Academic Press, New York; reprinted in *Context and Content*, 1999, Robert Stalnaker, Oxford University Press, pp. 78–95.

Tarski, Alfred (1935). 'Der Wahrheitsbegriff in den formalisierten Sprachen', *Studia Philosophica*, I, 261–405. Translated into English and published under the title 'The Concept of Truth in Formalized Languages' in Tarski (1956).

_____ 1956. *Logic, Semantics and Metamathematics*, Oxford University Press.

C H A P T E R   2 4

....

TWO-DIMENSIONAL SEMANTICS

....

DAVID J. CHALMERS

TWO-dimensional approaches to semantics, broadly understood, recognize two "dimensions" of the meaning or content of linguistic items. On these approaches, expressions and their utterances are associated with two different sorts of semantic values, which play different explanatory roles. Typically, one semantic value is associated with reference and ordinary truth-conditions, while the other is associated with the way that reference and truth-conditions depend on the external world. The second sort of semantic value is often held to play a distinctive role in analyzing matters of cognitive significance and/or context-dependence.

In this broad sense, even Frege's theory of sense and reference might qualify as a sort of two-dimensional approach. More commonly, two-dimensional approaches are understood more narrowly to be a species of possible-worlds semantics, on which each dimension is understood in terms of possible worlds and related modal notions.

In possible-world semantics, linguistic expressions and/or their utterances are first associated with an *extension*. The extension of a sentence is its truth-value: for example, the extension of 'Plato was a philosopher' is true. The extension of a singular term is its referent: for example, the extension of 'Don Bradman' is Bradman. The extension of a general term is the class of individuals that fall under the term: for example, the extension of 'cat' is the class of cats. Other expressions work similarly.

One can then associate expressions with an *intension*, which is a function from possible worlds to extensions. The intension of a sentence is a function that is true at a possible world if and only if the sentence is true there: the intension of 'Plato was a philosopher' is true at all worlds where Plato was a philosopher. The intension of a singular term maps a possible world to the referent of a term in that possible world: the intension of 'Don Bradman' picks out whoever is Bradman in a world. The intension of a general term maps a possible world to the class of individuals that fall under the term in that world: the intension of 'cat' maps a possible world to the class of cats in that world.

It can easily happen that two expressions have the same extension but different intensions. For example, Quine's terms 'cordate' (creature with a heart) and 'renate' (creature with a kidney) pick out the same class of individuals in the actual world, so they have the same extension. But there are many possible worlds where they pick out different classes (any possible world in which there are creatures with hearts but no kidneys, for example), so they have different intensions. When two expressions have the same extension and a different intension in this way, the difference in intension usually corresponds to an intuitive difference in meaning. So it is natural to suggest that an expression's intension is at least an aspect of its meaning.

Carnap (1947) suggested that an intension behaves in many respects like a Fregean sense, the aspect of an expression's meaning that corresponds to its cognitive significance. For example, it is cognitively significant that all renates are cordates and vice-versa (this was a non-trivial empirical discovery about the world), so that 'renate' and 'cordate' should have different Fregean senses. One might naturally suggest that this difference in sense is captured more concretely by a difference in intension, and that this pattern generalizes. For example, one might suppose that when two singular terms are cognitively equivalent (so that '$a = a$' is trivial or at least knowable a priori, for example), then their extension will coincide in all possible worlds, so that they will have the same intension. And one might suppose that when two such terms are cognitively distinct (so that '$a = b$' is knowable only empirically, for example), then their extensions will differ in some possible world, so that they will have different intensions. If this were the case, the distinction between intension and extension could be seen as a sort of vindication of a Fregean distinction between sense and reference.

However, the work of Kripke (1980) is widely taken to show that no such vindication is possible. According to Kripke, there are many statements that are knowable only empirically, but which are true in all possible worlds. For example, it is an empirical discovery that Hesperus is Phosphorus, but there is no possible world in which Hesperus is not Phosphorus (or vice-versa), as both Hesperus and Phosphorus are identical to the planet Venus in all possible worlds. If so, then 'Hesperus' and 'Phosphorus' have the same intension (one that picks out the planet Venus in all possible worlds), even though the two terms are cognitively distinct. The same goes for pairs of terms such as 'water' and 'H_2O': it is an empirical discovery that water is H_2O, but according to Kripke, both 'water' and 'H_2O' have the same intension (picking out H_2O in all possible worlds). Something similar even applies to terms such as 'I' and 'David Chalmers', at least as used by me on a specific occasion: 'I am David Chalmers' expresses non-trivial empirical knowledge, but Kripke's analysis entails that I am David Chalmers in all worlds, so that my utterances of these expressions have the same intension. If this is correct, then intensions are strongly dissociated from cognitive significance.

Still, there is a strong intuition that the members of these pairs ('Hesperus' and 'Phosphorus', 'water' and 'H_2O', 'I' and 'David Chalmers') differ in some aspect of meaning. Further, there remains a strong intuition that there is *some* way the world could turn out so that these terms would refer to different things. For example, it seems to be at least *epistemically* possible (in some broad sense) that these terms might fail to co-refer. On the face of it, cognitive differences between the terms is connected in some fashion to the existence of these possibilities. So it is natural to continue to use an analysis in terms of possibility and necessity to capture aspects of these cognitive differences. This is perhaps the guiding idea behind two-dimensional semantics.

Two-dimensional approaches to semantics start from the observation that the extension and even the intension of many of our expressions depend in some fashion on the external world. As things have turned out, my terms 'water' and 'H_2O' have the same extension, and have the same (Kripkean) intension. But there are ways things could have turned out so that the two terms could have had a different extension, and a different intension. So there is a sense in which for a term like 'water', the term's extension and its Kripkean intension depend on the character of our world. Given that *this* world is actual, it turns out that 'water' refers to H_2O, and its Kripkean intension picks out H_2O in all possible worlds. But if another world had been actual (e.g. Putnam's Twin Earth world in which XYZ is the clear liquid in the oceans), 'water' might have referred to something quite different (e.g. XYZ), and it might have had an entirely different Kripkean intension (e.g. one that picks out XYZ in all worlds).

This suggests a natural formalization. If an expression's (Kripkean) intension itself depends on the character of the world, then we can represent this dependence by a function from worlds to intensions. As intensions are themselves functions from worlds to extensions, this naturally suggests a two-dimensional structure. We can represent this structure diagramatically as shown in Table 24.1.

This diagram expresses an aspect of the two-dimensional structure associated with the term 'water'. It is intended to express the intuitive idea that if the H_2O-world turns out to be actual (as it has), then 'water' will have a Kripkean intension that picks out H_2O in all worlds; but if the XYZ-world turns out to be actual (as it has not), then 'water' will have a Kripkean intension that picks out XYZ in all worlds. Intuitively, the worlds in the column on the left represent ways the actual world can turn out

Table 24.1

	H_2O-world	XYZ-world	...
H_2O-world	H_2O	H_2O	...
XYZ-world	XYZ	XYZ	...
...	...	...	...

(these are sometimes thought of more precisely as possible contexts of utterances, and are sometimes thought of as epistemic possibilities), while the worlds across the top reflect counterfactual ways that a world could have been (these are sometimes thought of more precisely as possible circumstances of evaluation, and sometimes thought of as metaphysical possibilities). It is sometimes said that worlds on the left column (one world per row), making up the "first dimension" of the matrix, correspond to different worlds *considered as actual*; while the worlds in the top row (one world per column), making up the "second dimension" of the matrix, correspond to different worlds *considered as counterfactual*.

This two-dimensional matrix can be seen as a *two-dimensional intension*: a function from ordered pairs of worlds to extensions. Such a function is equivalent to a function from worlds to intensions, and seen this way can be regarded as capturing the intuitive idea that a term's intension depends on the character of the actual world. One can also recover the intuitive idea that a term's *extension* depends on the character of the actual world by examining the "diagonal" of this matrix, i.e. the cells that correspond to the same world considered as actual and as counterfactual. In the example above: where the H_2O-world is considered as actual and as counterfactual, then 'water' picks out H_2O, while if the XYZ-world is considered as actual and as counterfactual, then 'water' picks out XYZ. We can say that an expression's "diagonal intension" is a function mapping a world w to the term's extension when w is taken as both actual and as counterfactual. So the diagonal intension of 'water' maps the H_2O-world to H_2O, the XYZ-world to XYZ, and so on.

We can then see how pairs of terms with the same extension and the same Kripkean intension might nevertheless have different two-dimensional intensions, and different diagonal intensions. For example, 'water' and 'H_2O' have the same Kripkean intension, but it is plausible that if the XYZ-world had turned out to be actual, they would have had different Kripkean intensions: 'water' would have had an intension that picked out XYZ in all worlds, while 'H_2O' still would have had an intension that picked out H_2O in all worlds. If so, then these terms have different two-dimensional intensions and different diagonal intensions.

One can make a case that something similar applies with 'Hesperus' and 'Phosphorus', and with 'I' and 'David Chalmers': the members of each pair have a different two-dimensional intension and a different diagonal intension. If so, then this begins to suggest that there is some sort of connection between an expression's two-dimensional intension (or perhaps its diagonal intension) and its cognitive significance. One might even speculate that an expression's diagonal intension behaves in some respects like a Fregean sense, in a way that might vindicate Carnap's project.

At this point it must be acknowledged that things are not so simple. A number of different two-dimensional approaches to semantics have been developed in the literature, by Kaplan (1979, 1989); Stalnaker (1978); Chalmers (1996, 2002a, 2004); and Jackson (1998), among others; and closely related two-dimensional analysis of modal notions have been put forward by Evans (1977) and by Davies and Humberstone (1981). These approaches differ greatly in the way that they make the intuitive ideas above precise. They differ, for example, in just what they take the "worlds" in the left column to be, and they differ in their analysis of how a term's intension and/or extension depends on the character of the actual world. As a result, different approaches associate these terms with quite different sorts of two-dimensional semantic values, and these semantic values have quite different connections to cognitive significance.

In what follows, I will first go over the two-dimensional approaches pioneered in the 1970s by Kaplan, Stalnaker, Evans, and Davies and Humberstone.[1] Each of these approaches can be seen as sharing some of the formal structure described above, but with quite different conceptual underpinnings. Each of the approaches asserts some sort of connection between two-dimensional semantic values and apriority, but the connection is usually limited in scope, applying to indexicals (Kaplan) and to descriptive names (Evans), and 'actually' involving expressions (Davies and Humberstone), while Stalnaker's later work rejects a connection to apriority altogether. I will then describe the more general two-dimensional approach to semantics developed in the 1990s by Chalmers, Jackson, and others. This approach associated two-dimensional semantic values with expressions of all kinds, and asserts a strong general connection between these semantic values and the domain of apriority and cognitive significance. I will close by briefly describing some applications of the framework, and by considering and responding to a number of objections.

24.1 Early Two-Dimensional Approaches

24.1.1 Kaplan: Character and Content

Perhaps the best-known broadly two-dimensional approach is Kaplan's analysis of the character and content of indexicals (Kaplan, 1979, 1989). According to Kaplan, his work is partly grounded in work in tense logic by Kamp (1971) and Vlach (1973), which gives a sort of two-dimensional analysis of the behavior of 'now'. Kaplan applies his analysis to indexicals such as 'I', 'here', and 'now', as well as to demonstratives such as 'this' and 'that'. Kaplan's analysis is well-known, so I will describe it only briefly here.

For Kaplan, the "worlds" involved in the first dimension are *contexts of utterance*: these can be seen as at least involving the specification of a speaker and a time and place of utterance, within a world. The "worlds" involved on the second dimension are *circumstances of evaluation*: these are ordinary possible worlds at which the truth of an utterance is to be evaluated.

---

[1] More detailed discussions of all of these two-dimensional frameworks and their interrelations can be found in two recent collections: the March 2004 special issue of *Philosophical Studies* on "The Two-Dimensional Framework and its Applications", and the book *Two-Dimensional Semantics* (Garcia-Carpintero and Macia, 2006). See especially Chalmers, 2006; Davies, 2004; and Stalnaker, 2004, and also the discussion in Soames, 2005.

Consider an expression such as:

(1) I am hungry now

According to Kaplan's analysis, when this expression is uttered by Joe at time t_1, it expresses a proposition that is true if and only if Joe is hungry at t_1. We can call this proposition expressed the *content* of the utterance. This content can naturally be represented as an intension that is true at all and only those worlds (those circumstances of evaluation) in which Joe is hungry. (Kaplan regards propositions as structured entities rather than intensions, but the difference does not matter much here.) In a different context—say, a context with Diana speaking at t_2—an utterance of the same expression will have a different content. This content will be a proposition that is true at a world if and only if Diana is hungry at t_2 in that world.

The *character* of an expression is a function from contexts to contents, mapping a context of utterance to the content of that expression in that context. (If content is seen as an intension, then character is a sort of two-dimensional intension.) So the character of 'I am hungry' maps the first context above to the proposition that Joe is hungry at t_1, and the second context above to the proposition that Diana is hungry at t_2. Extending this idea to subsentential indexical terms, we can say that the character of 'I' maps the first context to Joe and the second context to Diana; more generally, it maps any context into the speaker in that context. Similarly, the character of 'now' maps any context into the time specified in that context.

The above definition of character is still somewhat imprecise, and many tricky issues come up in giving a precise definition. But to a rough first approximation, one can say that the character of an expression maps a context to the content that the expression would have if uttered in that context. There is more to say than this (especially as Kaplan intends his analysis to apply even to contexts in which there is no token of the relevant utterance), but this is enough for now. In general, character is associated with an expression type rather than with an expression token, although this matter is complicated somewhat by the case of demonstratives such as 'this' and 'that', whose character may vary between different utterances.

On Kaplan's analysis, the character of indexicals such as 'I', 'now', and 'here', as well as the character of demonstratives such as 'this' and 'that', reflects their cognitive significance. For example, 'I am here now' has a propositional content that is true in only some worlds, but its character yields a proposition that is true in all contexts of utterance. (Kaplan does not "diagonalize" character into an intension, but it would be easy enough to do so. If one did so, then 'I am here now' would be associated with a diagonal intension that is necessarily true.) So the character rather than the content seems to reflect the fact that the sentence can be known *a priori* (or near enough). Likewise, when a true utterance of 'this is that' is cognitively significant, the occurrences of 'this' and 'that' will refer to the same object, but their characters will differ. So at least in these domains, character behaves a little like a Fregean sense.

This behavior does not extend to other expressions, however. For example, Kaplan holds that names refer to the same individual in any context of utterance. On this view, co-extensive names such as 'Mark Twain' and 'Samuel Clemens' will have exactly the same character, and an identity such as 'Mark Twain is Samuel Clemens' will have a character that yields a true proposition in every context, even though the identity appears to be *a posteriori* and cognitively significant. Something similar applies to natural kind terms such as 'water'. So on Kaplan's analysis, names and natural kind terms have a "constant character" that is dissociated from their cognitive roles.

One can diagnose the situation by noting that character is most closely tied to the patterns of context-dependence associated with an expression, rather than to the expression's cognitive significance. In the case of indexicals, the patterns of context-dependence of an expression are themselves closely associated with the expression's cognitive significance. But for many other expressions, such as names and natural kind terms, cognitive significance is strongly dissociated from patterns of context-dependence. (The same goes for numerous ordinary context-dependent expressions, such as 'tall'.) As a result, in the general case, Kaplan's framework is better suited to the analysis of the context-dependence of expressions than to an analysis of their cognitive significance.

24.1.2 Stalnaker: Diagonal Proposition and Proposition Expressed

Stalnaker's analysis starts with the idea that although sentences such as 'Hesperus is Phosphorus' express necessary truths, they are sometimes used to convey contingent information about the world. Stalnaker (1978) analyzes this contingent information as the *diagonal proposition* associated with an utterance.

On Stalnaker's analysis, the *proposition expressed* by an utterance is a standard intension, or a set of possible worlds. So the proposition expressed by an ordinary utterance of 'Hesperus is Phosphorus' is the set of worlds in which Hesperus is Phosphorus, which is the set of all worlds (leaving aside questions about existence). Stalnaker defines the *propositional concept* associated with an utterance as a function from possible worlds to propositions, mapping a world to the proposition that that utterance would express in that world. He then defines the *diagonal proposition* associated with an utterance as a function that maps a possible world to the truth-value of that utterance when used in that possible world.

Stalnaker individuates utterances in such a way that a given utterance could have been used with an entirely different meaning. For example, an utterance of 'Hesperus is Phosphorus' could have been used to express the proposition that Mark Twain is George Bush, in a world w in which 'Hesperus' is used as a name for Twain and 'Phosphorus' is used as a name for Bush. It follows that while the propositional concept of my utterance maps the *actual* world to the proposition that Hesperus is Phosphorus, it maps world w to the proposition that Twain is Bush (which is itself presumably the empty set of worlds). The diagonal proposition of my utterance maps the actual world to the truth-value of the former proposition in the actual world (true), and maps world w to the truth-value of the latter proposition in w (false). So although my utterance of 'Hesperus is Phosphorus' expresses a necessary proposition in the ordinary sense, it is associated with a contingent diagonal proposition.

Stalnaker's propositional concept is a sort of two-dimensional intension, and his diagonal proposition is the associated diagonal intension. Like Kaplan, Stalnaker's framework can be seen as capturing a certain way in which the content of an utterance depends on the context in which it is uttered. But while Kaplan's analysis is in effect restricted to contexts in which the expression retains its original meaning, Stalnaker's analysis ranges over contexts in which the expression is used with entirely different meanings. As a result, Stalnaker characterizes his use of the two-dimensional framework as a "metasemantic" use: unlike Kaplan's character, diagonal propositions are not really part of the meaning of an utterance, but rather capture something about how meaning is determined by the external world.

Stalnaker uses this framework mainly to analyze the information conveyed by assertions. In a context where the hearer knows the full meanings of the terms used in an utterance (e.g. if they know that 'Hesperus' and 'Phosphorus' both refer to Venus), and where this knowledge is common ground between speaker and hearer, then the utterance will convey its original propositional content. But if the hearer does not know the meanings of the terms, then the utterance will convey a different content. In particular, it will convey the diagonal proposition of the utterance: here, the proposition that 'Hesperus is Phosphorus' expresses a truth. If the common ground between speaker and hearer includes partial knowledge of meaning—say, the knowledge that 'Hesperus' is used to refer to the evening star and that 'Phosphorus' is used to refer to the morning star—then worlds outside this common ground are in effect excluded by presuppositions, and the diagonal proposition will in effect be equivalent to the proposition that the morning star is the evening star (at least across the relevant range of worlds). So in such a context, an assertion of 'Hesperus is Phosphorus' will convey the information that the morning star is the evening star.

In his 1978 paper, Stalnaker says that if one defines an operator '†' such that '†P' is true iff P has a necessary diagonal proposition, then '†' is equivalent to the "a priori truth" operator. In later work (e.g. Stalnaker, 2004), however, he retracts that claim. It is easy to see why. Even paradigmatic a priori claims such as '1 + 1 = 2' do not have a necessary diagonal proposition: the diagonal proposition of '1 + 1 = 2' is false at a world where '1' refers to 3 and '2' refers to 7, for example. It is true that a statement such as 'Hesperus is the evening star', which is arguably an a priori truth, will have a diagonal proposition that is true in all worlds in a class that is restricted as in the previous paragraph (by imposing the restriction that 'Hesperus' is used to refer to the evening star). But in this case, it is the restriction that is doing all the work in connecting the diagonal proposition to a priori truth.

Because of this, there is no strong connection between diagonal propositions and a priori truth. There is sometimes a connection between an utterance's diagonal proposition and its cognitive significance, but this connection arises only in certain contexts where certain special restrictions due to limited knowledge of meaning are in force. Because of this, Stalnaker's diagonal propositions cannot be used to ground a two-dimensional approach to the cognitive significance of linguistic items in general.

Instead, they are most useful for analyzing what is conveyed by utterances when there is limited knowledge of meaning in place.

24.1.3 Evans: Deep Necessity and Superficial Necessity

Evans' analysis (Evans 1977) is focused on *descriptive names*: names whose reference is fixed by a description. His main example is the name 'Julius', which is stipulated to be a name for whoever invented the zip, if anyone uniquely invented it (I will omit references to uniqueness in what follows, but they should be tacitly understood). He considers the following sentence:

(2) If anyone invented the zip, Julius invented the zip.

If one follows Kripke, then (2) expresses a contingent proposition. 'Julius' picks out the actual inventor (William C. Whitworth) in all worlds, so the proposition is false in all worlds where someone other than Whitworth invented the zip.

According to Evans, however, this sort of contingency is superficial. (2) is *superficially contingent*, in that the claim 'It might have been the case that someone other than Julius invented the zip' is true. Superficial necessity and contingency of a sentence turns on how it embeds within modal operators: S is superficially necessary iff 'It is necessary that S' is true. But Evans suggests that in a deeper sense, (2) is necessary. He holds that the sentence is necessary because it expresses a necessary *content*. On Evans' view, there is a semantic rule connecting 'Julius' with the invention of the zip, and this semantic rule makes it the case that the content of (2) is necessarily true.

Evans' framework has two modal operators, rather than two intensions. The framework does have two semantic values: the proposition expressed by a sentence, which is something like the familiar proposition that is true in all worlds where Whitworth invented the zip, and the content of the sentence, which behaves as characterized above. Neither propositions nor contents are characterized as intensions, but it is easy enough to define intensions in the vicinity. We can say that the *superficial intension* of S is the set of worlds in which the proposition expressed by S is true: roughly, the set of worlds w such that 'if w had obtained, S would have been the case' is true. We can say that the *deep intension* of S is the set of worlds in which the content of S is true. In these terms, (2) has a superficial intension that is false at some worlds, but a deep intension that is true at all worlds.

In the case of descriptive names such as 'Julius', deep necessity (as opposed to superficial necessity) seems closely connected to apriority, and deep intensions are closely connected to an expression's cognitive role. It is tempting to extend this connection beyond the case of descriptive names, but Evans does not discuss other expressions, and it is not entirely clear how an extension would go. A more precise analysis of Evans' notion of deep necessity would require a more precise understanding of his notion of "content", which serves as something of an unanalyzed primitive in his 1978 article.

From other work, it seems clear that Evans thinks in the case of ordinary proper names (as opposed to descriptive names), there is a semantic rule that ties a name to its referent, so that the referent is part of the content. Correspondingly, it seems that Evans held that identities involving ordinary proper names have a content that is necessary, so that an identity such as 'Mark Twain is Samuel Clemens' is not only superficially necessary but deeply necessary. If this is right, then the two names involved will have the same deep intension. So in these cases (and probably in analogous cases involving natural kind terms), deep necessity and deep intensions are not as strongly connected to cognitive significance or to apriority as in the case of descriptive names.

24.1.4 Davies and Humberstone: 'Fixedly Actually' and 'Necessarily'

The two-dimensional framework of Davies and Humberstone (1981) is based on an analysis of the operator 'actually' (A). AP is true in a world w iff P is true in the actual world. Davies and Humberstone note that 'P iff AP' is contingent but knowable *a priori*. They suggest that although the sentence is contingent, there is an intuitive sense in which it is necessary: intuitively, no matter which world turns out to be the actual world, 'P iff AP' will be true. Likewise, for a contingent empirical truth P, AP will be necessary, but there is an intuitive sense in which it is contingent: intuitively, there are some worlds such that if those worlds had been actual, then AP would have been false.

   This intuition can be formalized by introducing a "floating" actual world into a possible-worlds model. Instead of simply designating a fixed world as the actual world, we take actuality to be a feature that can attach to different worlds. We can then evaluate sentences in a world w, where a world w' is taken to be actual ("considered as actual"). Or equivalently, we can evaluate sentences at pairs of worlds (w', w), where the first world represents the world that is designated as actual, and the second world represents the world in which the sentence is evaluated (relative to the designation of the first world as actual).[2]

   Doubly indexed evaluation behaves as follows. A sentence P without modal operators is true at (w', w) iff P is true at w according to ordinary singly indexed evaluation. $\Box P$ is true at (w', w) iff P is true at (w', v) for all v (i.e. iff P is true at all worlds relative to w' considered as actual). AP is true at (w', w) iff P is true at (w', w') (i.e. iff P is true at w' when w' is considered as actual). In conjunction with the obvious semantics for truth-functional logical operators, this suffices to recursively define doubly indexed evaluation of sentences in modal propositional logic (including '$\Box$' and 'A') in terms of standard singly indexed evaluation of atomic sentences.

   Davies and Humberstone then introduce the further operator "fixedly" (F), which can be defined as follows: FP is true at (w', w) iff P is true at (v, w) for all v (i.e. iff P is true at w relative to all worlds considered as actual). The "fixedly actually" operator

---

[2] For simplicity of presentation, I depart from Davies and Humberstone's own formalization, but the formalization here gives equivalent results.

FA is consequently such that *FAP* is true at (w', w) iff *AP* is true at (v, w) for all v, i.e. iff *P* is true at (v, v) for all v. So *FAP* is true iff *P* is true at all worlds w when w itself is considered as actual.

The two crucial modal operators here are $\square$ and *FA*. We can say that *P* is necessary when $\square P$ is true (i.e. when *P* is true at all worlds when our world is considered as actual), and that *P* is FA-necessary when *FAP* is true (i.e. when *P* is true at all worlds w when w is considered as actual). Let us say that *P* is A-involving iff *P* contains an instance of *A* or of *F*. It is easy to see that when *P* is not A-involving, *P* will be FA-necessary iff it is necessary. But when *P* is A-involving, the two may come apart. In particular, the sentence '*P* iff *AP*' is not necessary, but it is FA-necessary. Likewise, for a contingent atomic truth *P*, *AP* is necessary, but it is FA-contingent. So Davies and Humberstone suggest that FA-necessity captures the intuitive sense in which these two sentences are necessary and contingent respectively.

Davies and Humberstone also extend the discussion to Evans' case of descriptive names. They observe that descriptive names such as 'Julius' behave very much like A-involving descriptions of the form 'The actual inventor of the zip'. For example, just as 'Julius invented the zip' seems contingent and *a priori*, 'The actual inventor of the zip invented the zip' seems contingent and *a priori*. Furthermore, it is easy to see that when formalized in modal predicate logic, sentences of the latter form are not necessary but are FA-necessary. This mirrors Evans' claim that 'Julius (if he exists) invented the zip' is not superficially necessary but is deeply necessary. Davies and Humberstone suggest the natural hypothesis that descriptive names are in fact abbreviated A-involving descriptions, and that Evans' deep necessity is just FA-necessity.

Davies and Humberstone speculate that all contingent *a priori* sentences may be (perhaps tacitly) A-involving sentences that are contingent and FA-necessary.[3] They also suggest that some necessary *a posteriori* sentences are A-involving sentences that are necessary and FA-contingent: for example, 'The actual *F* is *G*' (where 'the *F* is *G*' is contingent) and analogous claims involving descriptive names. They speculate tentatively that natural kind terms (such as 'water') might be seen as abbreviated A-involving descriptions (such as 'the actual waterish stuff around here'), in which case necessary *a posteriori* identities such as 'water is H_2O' may also be necessary and FA-contingent. However, they do not extend the claim to all necessary *a posteriori* sentences. In particular, they hold that ordinary proper names are not A-involving, so that identities involving ordinary proper names (such as 'John is Tom') are FA-necessary iff they are necessary. It follows from this that necessary *a posteriori* identities involving these names are FA-necessary, rather than FA-contingent.

Davies and Humberstone do not posit two semantic values to go along with their two modal operators, but one could naturally do so. We can say that the standard intension of *P* is true at w iff *P* is true at w when our world is considered as actual (i.e. iff *P* is true at (a, w), where a is the actual world), and that the FA-intension of *P*

---

[3] This claim will be true only if all contingent *a priori* sentences are A-involving. For some reasons for doubt about this (involving indexical contingent *a priori* sentences, for example), see Chalmers, 2006.

is true w iff P is true at w when w is considered as actual (i.e. iff P is true at (w, w)). We can also define the two-dimensional intension of P in the obvious way; then the FA-intension will be equivalent to the "diagonal" of the two-dimensional intension.

As defined here, FA-intensions are closely tied to apriority for some sentences: especially for A-involving sentences, and for tacitly A-involving sentences such as those involving descriptive names and perhaps natural kind terms (if these are indeed tacitly A-involving). If the "actually" operator were the *only* source of the necessary *a posteriori* and the contingent *a priori*, then there would be a strong general tie between FA-intensions and apriority. But if there are other sources of the necessary *a posteriori* and the contingent *a priori* (such as ordinary proper names and indexicals), then in these cases, FA-intensions will not be closely tied to apriority at all.

24.2 TWO-DIMENSIONALISM

The two-dimensional approaches discussed above all introduce "first-dimensional" semantic values or modal notions that are more strongly connected to apriority and to cognitive significance than are the more familiar "second-dimensional" semantic values and modal notions. But in each of these approaches, the connection is somewhat attenuated. In the case of Kaplan's character, the connection only applies in the case of indexicals. In the case of Evans it is asserted only for descriptive names. In the case of Davies and Humberstone, it holds only for A-involving expressions and tacitly A-involving expressions such as descriptive names and perhaps some natural kind terms. In the case of Stalnaker, it applies only under certain strong restrictions on the domain of a diagonal proposition, or not at all.

In recent years, a number of philosophers (e.g. Chalmers, 1996, 2002, 2004 and Jackson, 1998, 2004; see also Braddon-Mitchell, 2004; Lewis, 1993; and Wong, 1996) have advocated a two-dimensional approach on which first-dimensional semantic values are connected to apriority and cognitive significance in a much stronger and more general way. On this approach, the framework applies not just to indexicals and descriptive names, but to expressions of all sorts. Proponents hold that any expression (or at least, any expression token of the sort that is a candidate for having an extension) can be associated with an intension that is strongly tied to the role of the expression in reasoning and in thought. The term *two-dimensionalism* is usually used for views of this sort.

24.2.1 The Core Claims of Two-Dimensionalism

Five core claims of two-dimensionalism are as follows.

(T1) Every expression token (of the sort that is a candidate to have an extension) is associated with a primary intension, a secondary intension, and a two-dimensional intension. A primary intension is a function from scenarios to extensions. A secondary intension is a function from possible worlds to extensions.

A two-dimensional intension is a function from ordered pairs of scenarios and worlds to extensions.

(T2) When the extension of a complex expression token depends compositionally on the extensions of its parts, the value of each of its intensions at an index (world, scenario, or ordered pair) depends in the same way on the values of the corresponding intensions of its parts at that index.

(T3) The extension of an expression token coincides with the value of its primary intension at the scenario of utterance and with the value of the secondary intension at the world of utterance.

(T4) A sentence token S is metaphysically necessary iff the secondary intension of S is true at all worlds.

(T5) A sentence token S is *a priori* (epistemically necessary) iff the primary intension of S is true at all scenarios.

In what follows I will first clarify and motivate these principles, without precisely defining all of the key notions or making a case for their truth. In later sections, I will discuss how the relevant notions (especially the notion of a primary intension) can be defined, in such a way that the principles might be true. These principles should not be taken to provide an exhaustive characterization of two-dimensionalism, but they lie at the core of the view.

Start with claim (T1). Here, a scenario is something akin to a possible world, but it need not be a possible world. In the most common two-dimensionalist treatments, a scenario is a *centered world*: an ordered triple of a possible world along with an individual and a time in that world. Other treatments of scenarios are possible (see Chalmers, 2004), but I will use this understanding here.

An expression's secondary intension (or what Jackson calls its C-intension) is just its familiar post-Kripkean intension, picking out the extension of the expression in counterfactual worlds. For example, the secondary intension of a token of 'I' as used by speaker X picks out X in all worlds. The secondary intension of 'water' picks out H_2O in all worlds. The secondary intension of 'Julius' picks out William C. Whitworth in all worlds. And so on.

An expression's primary intension works quite differently. I will defer a full characterization, but some examples will give a rough idea. The primary intension of a token of 'I', evaluated at a centered world, picks out the designated individual at the "center" of that world. (So the primary intension of my use of 'I', evaluated at a world centered on Napoleon, picks out Napoleon, rather than David Chalmers.) The primary intension of a token of 'water', very roughly, picks out the clear, drinkable liquid with which the individual at the center is acquainted. (So the primary intension of my use of 'I', evaluated at a "Twin Earth" world centered on a subject surrounded by XYZ in the oceans and lakes, picks out XYZ, rather than H_2O.) The primary intension of a token of 'Julius' picks out whoever invented the zip in a given world. (So the primary intension of 'Julius', evaluated at a world where Tiny Tim invented the zip, picks out Tiny Tim, rather than William C. Whitworth.) And so on.

Thesis (T1) also holds that expression tokens can be associated with a *two-dimensional intension*: roughly, a function from (scenario, world) pairs to extensions.

We can then say that at least on the centered worlds understanding, the primary intension coincides with the "diagonal" of the two-dimensional intension (i.e. the value of S's primary intension at a centered world w coincides with the value of S's two-dimensional intension at the pair (w, w^*), where w^* is the possible-world element of w). Likewise, the secondary intension coincides with the "row" of the two-dimensional intension determined by the scenario of an utterance (i.e. the value of S's secondary intension at a world w coincides with the value of S's two-dimensional intension at (a, w), where a is the scenario of utterance). However, for most purposes the two-dimensional intension of an expression is somewhat less important than its primary and secondary intension, and the two-dimensionalist need not hold that an expression's primary and secondary intension are derivative from its two-dimensional intension.

Thesis (T2) says that the primary and secondary intensions of a complex expression depend on the primary and secondary intensions of its parts according to the natural compositional semantics. For example, the primary intension of 'I am Julius' will be true at a scenario if the individual at the center of that scenario is the inventor of the zip in that scenario.

Thesis (T3) states a natural connection between the intensions and the extension of an expression token. This thesis requires that for every utterance, just as there is one world that is the world of the utterance, there is also one scenario that is the scenario of the utterance. If scenarios are understood as centered worlds, this will be a world centered on the speaker and the time of the utterance. When evaluated at the scenario and world of utterance, the primary and secondary intensions (respectively) of an expression token will coincide with the extension of the expression token. At other worlds and scenarios, however, the values of these intensions may diverge from the original extension, and from each other.

Turning to claims (T4) and (T5): Here, we can say that S is *a priori* when it expresses a thought that can be justified independently of experiences. S is metaphysically necessary when it is true with respect to all counterfactual worlds (under the standard Kripkean evaluation). Thesis (T4) is a consequence of the standard understanding of metaphysical necessity and the corresponding intensions. Thesis (T5) is intended to be an analog of thesis (T4) in the epistemic domain.

Thesis (T5) is the distinctive claim of two-dimensionalism. It asserts a very strong and general connection between primary intensions and apriority, one much stronger than obtains with the other two-dimensional frameworks discussed earlier. It is possible that a two-dimensionalist might grant some limited exceptions to thesis (T5) (say, for certain complex mathematical statements that are true but unknowable) while still remaining recognizably two-dimensionalist. But it is crucial to the two-dimensionalist position that typical *a posteriori* identities involving proper names or natural kind terms, such as 'Mark Twain is Samuel Clemens' or 'water is H_2O', have a primary intension that is false in some scenario.

Consequences of the previous theses include the following:

(T6) A sentence token S is necessary *a posteriori* iff the secondary intension of S is true at all worlds but the primary intension of S is false at some scenario.

(T7) A sentence token S is contingent *a priori* iff the primary intension of S is true at all scenarios but the secondary intension of S is false at some world.

So two-dimensionalism proposes a unified analysis of the necessary *a posteriori*: all such sentences have a necessary secondary intension but a contingent primary intension. Likewise, it proposes a unified analysis of the contingent *a priori*: all such sentences have a necessary primary intension but a contingent secondary intension.

From the previous theses, one can also draw the following conclusions about the primary and secondary intensions of both sentential and subsentential expressions. Here 'A' and 'B' are arbitrary expressions of the same type, and '$A \equiv B$' is a sentence that is true iff 'A' and 'B' have the same extension. For example, if A and B are singular terms, '$A \equiv B$' is just the identity statement '$A = B$', while if A and B are sentences, '$A \equiv B$' is the biconditional 'A iff B'.

(T8) '$A \equiv B$' is metaphysically necessary iff A and B have the same secondary intension.

(T9) '$A \equiv B$' is *a priori* (epistemically necessary) iff A and B have the same primary intension.

It follows that for *a posteriori* necessary identities involving proper names, such as 'Mark Twain is Samuel Clemens', the two names involved will have the same secondary intensions, but different primary intensions. Something similar applies to kind identities such as 'water is H_2O'. If this is correct, then primary intensions behave in these cases in a manner somewhat reminiscent of a Fregean sense.

24.2.2 Epistemic Two-Dimensionalism

For these claims, especially claim (T5), to be grounded, we need to have a better idea of what primary intensions are. Clearly, they must differ from characters, diagonal propositions, deep intensions, and FA-intensions, at least as these are understood by their proponents. Here, I will outline one approach (the approach I favor) to understanding primary intensions. This approach, which we might call *epistemic two-dimensionalism*, is elaborated in much greater detail in other works (Chalmers, 2002a, 2002b, 2004, 2006; Chalmers and Jackson, 2001).

According to epistemic two-dimensionalism, the connection between primary intension and epistemic notions such as apriority requires that primary intensions should be characterized in epistemic terms from the start. On this approach, the scenarios that are in the domain of a primary intension do not represent contexts of utterance. Rather, they represent *epistemic possibilities*: highly specific hypotheses about the character of our world that are not ruled out *a priori*. The value of an expression's primary intension at a scenario reflects a speaker's rational judgments involving the expression, under the hypothesis that the epistemic possibility in question actually obtains.

For example, 'water is not H_2O' is epistemically possible, in the sense that its truth is not ruled out *a priori*. Correspondingly, it is epistemically possible that our world is the XYZ-world (or at least, that it is qualitatively just like the XYZ-world). And if we suppose that our world is the XYZ-world (that is, that the liquid in the oceans and lakes is XYZ, and so on), then we should rationally endorse the claim 'water is XYZ', and we should rationally reject the claim 'water is H_2O'. So the primary intension of 'water is H_2O' is false at the XYZ-world, and the primary intension of 'water is XYZ' is true there.

Likewise, 'Mark Twain is not Samuel Clemens' is epistemically possible, in the sense that it is not ruled out *a priori*. Correspondingly, it is epistemically possible that our world is a world w where one person wrote the books such as *Tom Sawyer* that we associate with the name 'Mark Twain', and a quite distinct person is causally connected to our use of the term 'Samuel Clemens'. If we suppose that w is our world, then we should rationally endorse the claim 'Mark Twain is not Samuel Clemens'. So the primary intension of 'Mark Twain is Samuel Clemens' is false at w.

According to two-dimensionalism, something similar applies to any Kripkean *a posteriori* necessity. For any such sentence S, the negation of S is epistemically possible. And it is plausible that for any such S, there is a world w such that if we suppose that our world is qualitatively like w, we should rationally reject S. If so, then the primary intension of S is false at w. If this pattern generalizes to all *a posteriori* necessary sentences, then any such sentence has a primary intension that is false at some scenario, as thesis (T6) above suggests.

Here, primary intensions are characterized in thoroughly epistemic terms. It should be noted that the claims above are in no tension with the Kripkean claims that 'water is H_2O' is metaphysically necessary, or that 'water' picks out H_2O in all worlds. Even Kripke allows that 'water is not H_2O' is *epistemically* possible. And it is a familiar Kripkean point that there can be an epistemic necessitation between two statements A and B even when there is no metaphysical necessitation between them (witness 'X is the source of heat sensations' and 'X is heat'). We simply have to strongly distinguish this sort of epistemic evaluation of sentences in worlds (which turns on epistemic necessitation) from the usual sort of counterfactual evaluation (which turns on metaphysical necessitation). Primary intensions are grounded in the former; secondary intensions are grounded in the latter.

24.2.3 Defining Primary Intensions

It remains to define primary intensions more precisely. To generalize from the above, we might suggest that the primary intension of a sentence S is true at a scenario w iff the hypothesis that w is actual should lead us to rationally endorse S. Somewhat more carefully, we can say that the primary intension of S is true at a scenario w iff D epistemically necessitates S, where D is a canonical specification of w. It remains to clarify the notion of a scenario, a canonical specification, and epistemic necessitation.

Scenarios are highly specific epistemic possibilities. On the centered-worlds version of epistemic two-dimensionalism, scenarios are identified with centered worlds. It is also possible to develop a version of epistemic two-dimensionalism where scenarios are more strongly dissociated from ordinary possible worlds (see Chalmers,

2004; forthcoming a), and instead are characterized in more purely epistemic terms (for example, as maximal epistemically consistent sets of sentences in an idealized language). But I will focus on the centered-worlds understanding here.

For any possible world w, it is epistemically possible that w is actual; or at least, it is epistemically possible that a world qualitatively identical to w is actual. (More precisely: it is epistemically possible that D is the case, where D is a complete qualitative characterization of w. More on this notion shortly.) But epistemic possibilities are more fine-grained than possible worlds. For example, the information that the actual world is qualitatively like a possible world w is epistemically consistent with various different epistemic possible claims about one's self-location: for example, it is consistent with the claims 'It is now 2004' and 'It is now 2005'.

To handle these claims about self-location, we model epistemic possibilities using centered worlds. The individual and the time marked at the "center" of a centered world serve as a "you are here" marker, which serves to settle these claims about self-location. For a given thinker, the hypothesis that a given centered world w is actual can be seen as the hypothesis: 'D is the case, I am F, and the current time is G', where D is a complete qualitative characterization of w, and F and G are qualitative descriptions that pick out the individual and the time at the center of w. We can think of this conjunctive claim as a *canonical specification* of the centered world in question.

In the foregoing, a qualitative vocabulary is, to a first approximation, a vocabulary that is free of terms (such as names and natural kind terms) that give rise to Kripkean *a posteriori* necessities and *a priori* contingencies. (Restricting world-descriptions to a vocabulary of this sort avoids obvious problems that would arise if we allowed, for example, 'water is H_2O' into the description of the XYZ-world. For more on the characterization of qualitative, or "semantically neutral", vocabulary, see Chalmers, 2004.) A complete qualitative characterization of w is a qualitative statement D such that (i) D is true of w, and (ii) if E is a qualitative statement that is true of w, then D necessitates E.

We also need to define epistemic necessitation. To a first approximation, we can say that D epistemically necessitates S iff accepting D should lead one to rationally endorse S (without needing further empirical information, given idealized reflection). On a refined definition, we can say that D epistemically necessitates S iff a conditional of the form '$D \supset S$' is *a priori*. The refined definition is arguably better in some difficult cases, but for many purposes, the first approximation will suffice.

Because they are defined in epistemic terms, there is an inbuilt connection between primary intensions and the epistemic domain. In particular, there will be a strong connection to apriority. When a sentence token S is *a priori*, then it will be epistemically necessitated by any sentence whatsoever (this is especially clear for the second understanding of epistemic necessitation above), so its primary intension will be true in all scenarios. When a sentence token S is not *a priori*, then its negation will be epistemically possible, and S will be false relative to some highly specific epistemic possibility. As long as there is a scenario for every epistemic possibility, then the primary intension of S will be false in some scenario. (On the centered worlds understanding of scenarios, the existence of a scenario for every epistemic possibility is a substantive but plausible claim; see Chalmers, 2002c and 2004.) If so, then thesis (T5) will be correct.

One can define the secondary intension of a sentence in a similar, if more familiar, way. The secondary intension of S is true at a world w iff D metaphysically necessitates S, where D is a canonical specification of w. Here a canonical specification can be characterized much as before as a complete specification, although here it is not necessary to impose the restriction to qualitative specifications. Metaphysical necessitation could be taken as basic, or perhaps better, we can define it in terms of subjunctive conditionals: D metaphysically necessitates S when a subjunctive conditional of the form 'if D had been the case, S would have been the case' is true.

One can likewise define the two-dimensional intension of a sentence. The two-dimensional intension of S is true at (v, w) iff D epistemically necessitates that D' metaphysically necessitates S, where D is a canonical description of the scenario v and D' is a canonical specification of the world w. If we understand epistemic necessitation in terms of *a priori* material conditionals and metaphysical necessitation in terms of subjunctive conditionals, this will be the case iff '$D \supset (D' \Rightarrow S)$' is *a priori*, where the outer conditional is material and the inner conditional is subjunctive.

This discussion of the intensions of sentences can be extended to the intensions of subsentential expressions in a reasonably straightforward way. For details, see Chalmers, 2004.

24.2.4 The Roots of Epistemic Two-Dimensionalism

The epistemic two-dimensional framework is grounded in a thesis about the *scrutability* of reference and truth: once a subject is given enough information about the character of the actual world, then they are in a position to make rational judgments about what their expressions refer to and whether their utterances are true. For example, once we are given enough information about the appearance, behavior, composition, and distribution of various substances in our environment, as well as about their relations to ourselves, then we are in a position to conclude (without needing further empirical information) that water is H_2O. And if instead we were given quite different information, characterizing our environment as a "Twin Earth" environment, then we would be in a position to conclude that water is XYZ.

Of course, if we allow the "enough information" to include arbitrary truths, such as 'water is H_2O', the scrutability claim will be trivial. But we can impose significant restrictions on the information without compromising the plausibility of the thesis. For example, one can argue that even if we restrict ourselves to truths that do not use the term 'water' or cognates, it remains the case that given enough truths of this kind, we are in a position to know the truth of 'water is H_2O' (see Chalmers and Jackson, 2001). The same goes for many or most other terms, plausibly including most names or natural kind terms.

The upshot is that there is some reasonably restricted vocabulary V, such that for arbitrary statements T, then once we know enough V-truths we will be in a position to know (without needing further empirical information) the truth-value of T. Just how restricted such a vocabulary can be is an open question. Chalmers and Jackson (2001) argue that $PQTI$, a conjunction of microphysical, phenomenal, and indexical truths along with a "that's all" truth, can serve as a basis. But this claim is not required here. All that is required for present purposes is that some qualitative vocabulary, conjoined with indexical terms such as 'I' and 'now', is sufficient.[4]

This suggests that for any true sentence token S, there is a V-truth D such that D epistemically necessitates S, in that a subject given the information that D will be in a position to rationally endorse S (given ideal rational reflection). Furthermore, it appears that in principle, no further empirical information is needed to make this judgment; if such information were required, we could simply include it (or equivalent qualitative information) in D to start with. This strongly suggests that there is a non-empirical warrant for the transition from D to S. In particular, one can make the case that in these cases, the material conditional '$D \supset S$' will be *a priori*. (This case is made at length by Chalmers and Jackson, 2001). If this is correct, then D epistemically necessitates S in the second, stronger sense given above.

The scrutability claim does not apply only to the actual world. It is plausible that for all sorts of scenarios, if we are given the information that the scenario is actual, then we are in a position to make a rational judgment about the truth-value of arbitrary sentences. For example, if we are given a complete qualitative characterization of the bodies visible in the sky at various times, with the feature that no body is visible both in the morning sky and the evening sky, then we should rationally reject the claim 'Hesperus is Phosphorus'. This sort of judgment is part of the *inferential role* associated with our use of the terms 'Hesperus' and 'Phosphorus'. The point is general: for any expression that we use, then given sufficient information about the actual world, certain judgments using the expression will be irrational, and certain other judgments using the expression will be rational. It is arguable that the expressions of any language user will have this sort of normative inferential role. This is just part of what being a language user involves.

It is this sort of inferential role that grounds the primary intension of an arbitrary expression (as used by an arbitrary speaker). A given sentence token will be associated with a raft of conditional rational judgments, across a wide variety of scenarios. This raft of conditional judgments corresponds to the sentence's primary intension. Something very similar applies to subsentential expressions: for a singular term, for example, there will be a raft of conditional rational judgments using the expression across a wide variety of scenarios, and these can be used to define the extension of

---

[4] As before, a qualitative vocabulary is one that excludes terms, such as names and natural kind terms that give rise to Kripkean *a posteriori* necessities. A qualitative vocabulary may include all sorts of high-level expressions: 'friend', 'philosopher', 'action', 'believe', and 'square', for example. It will not designate individuals by using names: instead it will make existential claims of the form 'there exist such-and-such individuals with such-and-such qualitative properties'. Some theoretical terms (perhaps including microphysical terms) may be excluded, but information conveyed using these terms can instead be conveyed by the familiar Ramsey-sentence method, characterizing a network of entities and properties with appropriate causal/nomic connections to each other and to the observational and the phenomenal. For familiar reasons, no important information is lost by doing this.

the expression relative to those scenarios (see Chalmers, 2004). So we will have sub-stantial primary intensions for a wide range of sentential and subsential expression tokens.

It should be noted that nothing here requires that the expressions in question be definable in simpler terms (such as in qualitative terms), or that they be equivalent to descriptions (even to rigidified or "actually" involving descriptions). The inferential roles in question will exist whether or not the term is definable and whether or not it is equivalent to a description (for more on this, see Chalmers and Jackson, 2001 and Chalmers, 2002a).

These claims are quite compatible with Kripke's epistemological argument that terms such as 'Gödel' are not equivalent to descriptions. In effect, Kripke describes a scenario w where someone called 'Schmidt' proved the incompleteness of arith-metic, and then it was stolen by someone called 'Gödel' who moved to Princeton, and so on. Kripke's argument might be put by saying that (i) w is not ruled out *a priori*, and (ii) if we accept that w obtains, we should reject the claim 'Gödel proved the incompleteness of arithmetic', so (iii) 'Gödel proved the incompleteness of arith-metic' is not *a priori*. A two-dimensionalist will put this by saying that the primary intension of 'Gödel proved the incompleteness of arithmetic' is false at w, so that the primary intension of 'Gödel' differs from that of 'the prover of the incompleteness of arithmetic'. If Kripke's argument generalizes to other descriptions, it will follow that the primary intension of Gödel is not equivalent to the primary intension of any such description. But nothing here begins to suggest that 'Gödel' lacks a primary intension.

Although the primary intension of an expression may not be equivalent to that of a description, one can often at least approximately characterize an expression's primary intension using a description. For example, one might roughly characterize the primary intension of a typical use of 'water' by saying that in a centered world w, it picks out the dominant clear, drinkable liquid with which the individual at the center of w is acquainted. And one might roughly characterize the primary inten-sion of 'Gödel' by saying that it picks out that individual who was called 'Gödel' by those from whom the individual at the center acquired the name. But these char-acterizations will usually be imperfect, and it will be possible to find Kripke-style counterexamples to them. Ultimately a primary intension is not grounded in any description, but rather is grounded in an expression's inferential role.

24.2.5 Two-Dimensionalism and Semantic Pluralism

Two-dimensionalism is naturally combined with a *semantic pluralism*, according to which expressions and utterances can be associated with many different semantic (or quasi-semantic) values, by many different semantic (or quasi-semantic) relations. On this view, there should be no question about whether the primary intension or the secondary intension is *the* content of an utterance. Both can be systematically asso-ciated with utterances, and both can play some of the roles that we want contents to play. Furthermore, there will certainly be explanatory roles that neither of them play, so two-dimensionalism should not be seen as offering an exhaustive account of the content of an utterance. Rather, it is characterizing some aspects of utterance content, aspects that can play a useful role in the epistemic and modal domains.

Likewise, there should be no question about which of the two-dimensional frameworks described in this paper is the "correct" framework. Each framework offers a different quasi-semantic relation that associates expressions with two-dimensional semantic values, and each of these may play an explanatory role in different domains. Each has different properties. Most obviously, primary intensions have a stronger connection to apriority and cognitive significance than the semantic values described earlier. Unlike characters, deep intensions, and FA-intensions, the primary intension associated with an *a posteriori* identity such as 'Mark Twain is Samuel Clemens' will be contingent. Unlike diagonal propositions, the primary intension of an *a priori* sentence such as '2 + 2 = 4' will be necessary.

These differences arise from the differences in the way the semantic relations are defined. Unlike characters and diagonal propositions, primary intensions are not defined in terms of context-dependence. Unlike deep intensions, they are not defined in terms of a prior notion of content. Unlike FA-intensions; they are not defined in terms of the behavior of an 'actually' operator. Rather, they are defined in epistemic terms.

Because they are defined in epistemic terms, primary intensions can often vary between tokens of an expression type. This will happen most obviously for context-dependent terms such as 'tall', for which tokens in different contexts will be associated with different inferential roles. Primary intensions may also vary between different tokens of the same name (especially by different speakers), for different tokens of the same demonstrative (e.g. 'this' or 'that'), and perhaps also for different tokens of the same natural kind term. It follows that in these cases, a primary intension does not constitute an expression's linguistic meaning, where this is understood as what is common to all tokens of an expression type, or as what is required for any competent use of the expression. Instead, a primary intension can be seen as a kind of utterance content.

Even if they are not always part of linguistic meaning, primary intensions are nevertheless a sort of truth-conditional content. The primary intension of an utterance yields a condition under which the utterance will be true. For example, the primary intension of 'there is water in the glass' will be true at some scenarios and false at others, and the utterance will be true iff the primary intension is true at the scenario of the utterance (roughly, if the glass picked out by the individual at the center of the scenario contains the dominant watery stuff in the environment around the center). This can be seen as an *epistemic* truth-condition for the utterance, specifying how the truth of the utterance depends (epistemically) on which epistemically possible scenario turns out to be actual. This contrasts with the "metaphysical" truth-condition corresponding to the secondary intension, which might be seen as specifying how the truth of the utterance depends (metaphysically) on which metaphysically possible world is actual. Again, there is no need to decide the question of which of these is *the* truth-condition associated with an utterance.

Are primary intensions a sort of semantic content? This depends on how we understand the notion of semantic content. If we stipulate that the semantic content of an utterance is truth-conditional content, then primary intensions are a variety of semantic content. On the other hand, if we stipulate that semantic content is linguistic meaning in the sense above, or that semantic content is always associated with expression types and not tokens, then primary intensions are not in general part of semantic content (though they may be part of semantic content for some expressions, such as some indexicals and qualitative expressions). In any case, once we are clear on the various properties of these intensions, nothing important to the framework turns on the terminological question of whether they count as "semantic".

A semantic pluralist can allow that for some explanatory purposes, it may be useful to modify two-dimensionalist semantic values in some respects. For example, one might define the *structured* primary intension of a complex expression as a structured entity involving the primary intensions of the simple expressions involved in the expression's logical form. One might likewise define structured secondary and two-dimensional intensions. Given compositionality, a structured primary intension will determine an unstructured primary intension (and likewise for the other intensions), but the reverse need not be the case. This means that structured primary intensions are more fine-grained than unstructured primary intensions: for example, all *a priori* truths will have the same unstructured primary intension (one that is true at all scenarios), but they will have different structured primary intensions. The fine-grainedness of structured intensions makes a difference for certain purposes, described below.

What are *propositions*, according to two-dimensionalism? Some two-dimensionalists (e.g. Jackson, 1998) hold that propositions are sets of possible worlds, in which case a given utterance expresses two propositions (a primary proposition and a secondary proposition). This view is naturally combined with the view that there are no necessary *a posteriori* propositions: necessary *a posteriori* sentences have a primary proposition that is contingent and knowable only *a posteriori*, and a secondary proposition that is necessary and knowable *a priori*. Other two-dimensionalists may hold that propositions have more structure than this. For example, one could hold that propositions are structured entities involving both the primary and secondary intensions (and/or perhaps the two-dimensional intension) of the simple expressions involved. A two-dimensionalist of this sort may allow that there are necessary *a posteriori* propositions.

A semantic pluralist view tends to suggest that there are numerous entities which can play some of the explanatory roles that propositions are supposed to play, and that there is no need to settle which of these best deserves the label 'proposition'. My own view is that if one were forced to identify propositions with one sort of entity that can be modeled in the framework, there would be a good case for choosing structured two-dimensional entities of some sort (perhaps those discussed as candidates for Fregean senses, below). But one might also allow that at least for some purposes, propositions should be seen as entities more fine-grained than any two-dimensional objects, so that propositions can be associated with intensions without themselves being intensions. In any case, core two-dimensionalism as characterized above is compatible with a wide range of views here.

24.3 APPLICATIONS OF TWO-DIMENSIONALISM

I will briefly sketch some applications of the two-dimensionalism outlined in the previous section.

(i) *Fregean sense* (Chalmers, 2002a): Thesis (T9) above says that two expressions A and B have the same primary intensions iff '$A \equiv B$' is epistemically necessary. This is reminiscent of the Fregean claim that two singular terms A and B have the same sense iff '$A = B$' is cognitively insignificant. It suggests that primary intensions can play at least some of the roles of a Fregean sense, individuating expressions by their epistemic role. Of course there are some differences. For example, primary intensions are not as fine-grained as Fregean senses: *a priori* equivalent expressions (such as '7 + 3' and '10') will have different Fregean senses, but they have the same primary intension (though they will usually have different structured primary intensions). Further, there are differences between primary intensions and Fregean senses in the case of indexicals: for example, uses of 'I' by different speakers have the same primary intension, whereas Frege held that they have different senses. Relatedly, where Frege held that sense determines reference, primary intensions do not determine extensions in a strong sense (although they may still determine extension relative to context), as two expressions may have the same primary intensions and different extensions. Still, we may nevertheless think of primary intensions as a broadly Fregean aspect of an expression's content.

One can also use the two-dimensional framework to define semantic values that behave even more like Fregean senses. (Here I go beyond the discussion in Chalmers, 2002a.) We might stipulate that the sense of a simple expression token is an ordered pair of its primary intension and its extension, and that the sense of a complex expression token is a structured complex made up of the senses of its parts. Now, most pairs of *a priori* equivalent expressions, such as '7 + 3' and '10' will have different senses. (The only potential exceptions will arise if there are *a priori* equivalent but cognitively distinct simple expressions, which is not obvious.) Furthermore, uses of 'I' by different speakers will have different senses. And now, sense determines reference in the strong sense. So entities of this sort might be seen as very much akin to Fregean senses, and we might think of the structured entity associated with a sentence token as akin to a Fregean thought.

(ii) *Contents of thoughts* (Chalmers, 2002b). One can extend the framework above so that primary and secondary intensions are not just associated with sentences but with thoughts, where these are understood as occurrent mental states. For example, my thought *water is H_2O* will have a contingent primary intension (false in the XYZ-scenario) but a necessary secondary intension. One can then argue that a thought's primary intension is a sort of *narrow content*: content that is shared between intrinsically identical thinkers. For example, when Oscar on Earth and Twin Oscar on Twin Earth say 'water is wet', the thoughts they express will have different secondary intensions (so secondary intensions are a sort of "wide content"), but they will have the same primary intension.

(iii) *Belief ascriptions* (Chalmers, 2002b): One can use this framework to analyze ascriptions of belief and other propositional attitudes. As a first attempt, one might suggest that an ascription '*S* believes that *P*' is true iff the referent of *S* has a belief with the primary intension of '*P*' (in the mouth of the ascriber), or a belief with the secondary intension of '*P*' (in the mouth of the ascriber). Neither of these suggestions works: the first is falsified by cases such as 'John believes that I am hungry', while the second is falsified by cases such as 'Lois believes that Clark Kent can fly'. However, more sophisticated analyses are possible. For example, Chalmers, 2002b suggests

An utterance of '*S* believes that *P*' is true iff the referent of *S* has a belief with the structured secondary intension of '*P*' (in the mouth of the ascriber) and with an appropriate structured primary intension.

Here, "appropriate" functions to pick out a range of primary intensions (allowing, for example, that the Pierre can satisfy a 'London'-involving ascription even if he uses the term with a different primary intension), where this range may depend on the context of utterance. (Structured intensions are needed in order that independent "appropriateness" constraints may be imposed separately on each element of a belief.) This analysis is closely related to "hidden-indexical" analyses of belief ascriptions, with primary intensions playing the role of "modes of presentation".

One can also use primary intensions to give an analysis of *de re* attitude ascriptions, in the style of Kaplan, 1968.

A *de re* attitude ascription '*S* believes of *X* that it is *F*' is true iff *S* has a belief with the secondary intension of '*X* is *F*', and which picks out the referent of *X* under a *de re*-appropriate primary intension.

Here, the conditions on a *de re*-appropriate primary intension may again be context-independent, but to a first approximation we can think of such an intension as one that is acquaintance-entailing: necessarily, if a subject *S* has a state with a *de re*-appropriate primary intension that picks out extension *E*, then *S* will be acquainted with *E*.

(iv) *Indicative conditionals* (Weatherson, 2001): We can also use epistemic two-dimensionalism to give a possible-worlds-style analysis of the intuitive acceptability-conditions of indicative conditionals that is analogous to the familiar Lewis–Stalnaker analysis of subjunctive conditionals.

A token of an indicative conditional 'If *P*, then *Q*' is acceptable iff the epistemically closest scenario satisfying the primary intension of '*P*' (in the mouth of the speaker) also satisfies the primary intension of '*Q*'.

Of course an elaboration of this account requires an elaboration of what epistemic closeness amounts to. But given that the familiar Ramsey Test for the acceptability of an indicative conditionals is defined in epistemic terms (if one conditionally accepts P, should one rationally conclude Q?), and given that primary intensions are defined in very similar terms, it is not surprising that there is a close relation.

(v) *Conceivability and possibility* (Chalmers, 2002): If thesis (T5) is correct, it licenses a certain sort of move from conceivability to possibility. Let us say that S is conceivable when it is epistemically possible: that is, when S is not ruled out *a priori*. If (T5) is correct, then when S is conceivable, the primary intension of S will be true at some scenario. If scenarios are centered worlds, then there will be some centered (metaphysically possible) world w satisfying the primary intension of S. This does not entail that S is metaphysically possible, but it nevertheless allows us to draw conclusions about metaphysically possible worlds from premises about conceivability. Reasoning of this sort is central to some uses of conceivability arguments in the philosophy of mind (e.g. in Chalmers, 1996).

24.4 Objections
to Two-Dimensionalism

A number of objections to two-dimensionalism have been made in the literature. Some objections (the first nine considered here) rest on the attribution of views to which two-dimensionalism is not committed. They might be considered objections to certain versions of two-dimensionalism, but they do not apply to the epistemic two-dimensionalism that I have outlined. Other objections (the next two considered here) show that the claims of two-dimensionalism must be restricted in certain respects. Still others (the last three considered here) raise substantive issues whose adjudication is an ongoing project.

What is held constant? (Block and Stalnaker, 1999): Evaluation of primary intensions turns on claims about what a term such as 'water' would have picked out in counterfactual circumstances. But this raises the question of what is held constant across worlds in counting an expression as a token of 'water'. If only orthography is held constant, then many tokens of 'water is watery' will be false; if reference is held constant, then no token of 'water is H_2O' will be false. So to yield the desired results, a two-dimensionalist must hold constant some intermediate sort of content, such as Fregean or descriptive or narrow content. But it is question-begging for a two-dimensionalist to presuppose such a notion of content.

Response: Evaluation of primary intensions does not turn on metalinguistic claims about what a term would have picked out in counterfactual circumstances. One could define an expression's *contextual intension* as a mapping from worlds containing a token of the expression to the extension of that token in that world. The question of what is held constant would then become relevant: one would obtain different sorts of contextual intensions depending on just what one counts as a relevant token. But primary intensions are not like this. They simply turn on the epistemic properties of an expression in the actual world. For example, it is epistemically possible (not ruled out *a priori*) that there are no utterances, and so the primary intension of 'There are no utterances' will be true in an utterance-free world (whereas the contextual intension of 'There are no utterances' will not be defined there). Because properties of counterfactual tokens are irrelevant to the evaluation of primary intensions (except in some special cases), the problem of "what is held constant" does not arise.

Twin Earth intuitions are irrelevant (Soames, 2005). Intuitions about the reference of 'water' as used on Twin Earth are irrelevant to the meaning of our term 'water', as the term 'water' on Twin Earth has a different meaning.

Response: Again, evaluation of primary intensions does not depend on the referents of homonymous terms in counterfactual worlds. Rather, it depends on certain epistemic properties associated with uses of 'water' in our world. For example, if we are given the information that the liquid in the oceans and lakes is and has always been XYZ, we should conclude that water is XYZ. This is a fact about the inferential role associated with uses of *our* term 'water'. Epistemic two-dimensionalism uses this inferential role to analyze an aspect of the content of these uses of the term.

Names and natural-kind terms are not indexicals (Nimtz and Beckermann, forthcoming; Soames, 2005): Two-dimensionalism entails that terms such as 'water' are really disguised indexicals that can pick out different referents in different contexts. But such terms are not indexicals. Any utterance of the English term 'water', in any context, picks out H_2O.

Response: Epistemic two-dimensionalism does not entail that names and natural kind terms are disguised indexicals, and it is consistent with the claim that any utterance of the English term 'water' refers to H_2O. If primary intensions were Kaplanian characters or contextual intensions, then the claim that 'water' refers to H_2O in any context would be inconsistent with the two-dimensionalist claim that the primary intension of 'water' picks out XYZ in the Twin Earth world. But primary intensions are not Kaplanian characters or contextual intensions. To ground the desired behavior of primary intensions, the two-dimensionalist simply requires the plausible claim that it is *epistemically* possible (i.e. not ruled out *a priori*) that water is XYZ. This claim is consistent with the claim that (given that 'water' actually refers to H_2O), all metaphysically possible tokens of the English term 'water' refer to H_2O.

Names are not rigidified descriptions (Soames, 2005). Two-dimensionalism entails that names and natural kind terms are disguised rigidified descriptions (of the form 'the actual ϕ', for some ϕ). But Kripke's epistemic arguments show that names are not rigidified descriptions, as do considerations about the way that names and descriptions behave in belief ascriptions.

Response: Two-dimensionalism does not entail that names and natural kind terms are rigidified descriptions. We have noted already that Kripke's epistemic arguments are accommodated by the observation that primary intensions cannot always be encapsulated into a description. Furthermore, as noted above, it is consistent with two-dimensionalism to hold that names and natural kind terms, unlike rigidified descriptions, have the same referent in any context of utterance. It is also consistent with two-dimensionalism to hold that the primary intension of a name or natural kind term may vary between speakers. The account of belief ascriptions given above does not entail that names will behave like rigidified descriptions in belief contexts, and handles the relevant data straightforwardly.

Speakers lack identifying knowledge (Byrne and Pryor, 2005; Schiffer, 2003). Two-dimensionalism requires that every name N (at least as used by a speaker) be associated with a "uniqueness property" ϕ (such that at most one individual has ϕ), and requires that the speaker have *a priori* "identifying knowledge" of the form 'N is ϕ'. But speakers in general lack this sort of knowledge.

Response: Two-dimensionalism does not require that speakers possess identifying knowledge. It is true that primary intensions can be associated with uniqueness properties (or better, uniqueness relations, because of the role of centering). But speakers need not have beliefs about these uniqueness properties (expressible in the form 'N is ϕ'). Epistemic two-dimensionalism simply requires that speakers have a *conditional ability* to determine the referent of N (or better, to determine the truth-value of claims using N), given relevant information about the character of the actual world and given idealized rational reflection. This conditional ability need not be grounded in the possession of identifying knowledge. Furthermore, the invocation of rational reflection makes this a normative claim that idealizes away from cognitive limitations of the speaker. For example, even if a child cannot actually identify a referent across all circumstances, there may still be idealized inferential norms on how they should update their relevant beliefs given relevant information about the world. These norms are all that is required.

Ordinary expressions are not ambiguous (Bealer, 2002; Marconi, 2005): Two-dimensionalism explains the difference in truth-value between

(3) It is metaphysically necessary that water is H_2O.
(4) It is epistemically necessary that water is H_2O.

by saying that 'water' expresses its primary intension in the first context and its secondary intension in the second context. But this entails implausibly that 'water' is ambiguous. Further, this view cannot handle combined contexts, such as 'It is metaphysically necessary but not epistemically necessary that water is H_2O'.

Response: Two-dimensionalism does not hold that ordinary expressions are ambiguous. 'Water' has exactly the same content in both (3) and (4) above: in both contexts (and in all contexts) it has both a primary intension and a secondary intension (or equivalently, it has a complex semantic value involving both a primary and a secondary intension). This does not entail that 'water' is ambiguous, any more than the distinction between character and content entails that indexicals are ambiguous. The distinction between (3) and (4) is handled instead by the difference between the modal operators. The semantics of these operators are such that 'It is metaphysically necessary that S' is true when S has a necessary secondary intension, while 'It is epistemically necessary that S' is true when S has a necessary primary intension. Combined contexts are handled in the obvious combined way.

Two-dimensionalism cannot handle belief ascriptions (Soames, 2005): It is natural for two-dimensionalists to hold that '*x* believes that *S*' is true when the subject has a belief whose primary intension is the primary intension of *S*. But this view gives the wrong result in a number of cases, and no better two-dimensionalist treatment of belief ascriptions is available.

Response: The view of belief ascriptions mentioned above is considered and rejected in Chalmers (1995, 2002), and to the best of my knowledge no two-dimensionalist endorses the view. The account of belief ascriptions described in Section 24.4, straightforwardly handles most of the puzzle cases developed by Soames (see Chalmers, 2004 for details). Soames raises some further puzzle cases for this account involving the relationship between ordinary belief ascriptions and *de re* belief ascriptions, but the account of *de re* belief ascriptions sketched above (and also given in Chalmers, 2002) handles these cases straightforwardly.

Two-dimensionalism requires global descriptivism (Stalnaker, 2003, 2004): Two-dimensionalism holds that the primary intension of an utterance or a belief is determined by the internal state of the speaker or believer. This requires an internalist "metasemantic" theory, showing how intentional content is determined by internal state. The main candidate for such a theory is the "global descriptivism" of Lewis (1984), holding that the content of our utterances and beliefs is determined by whatever assignment of content yields the "best fit" between the beliefs and the world. But global descriptivism is false.

Response: Two-dimensionalism does not require global descriptivism. Of course there is not yet any satisfactory theory of the basis of intentionality, but there are many possible internalist alternatives. For example, one might hold that the primary intension of a mental state is determined in part by its internal functional role, and in part by associated phenomenal states (where the latter may be especially relevant for phenomenal and perceptual concepts).

The wrong sentences are a priori: Two-dimensionalism requires the claim that sentences such as 'Hesperus (if it exists) is Phosphorus' are not *a priori*, while sentences such as 'Julius (if he exists) invented the zip' are *a priori*. But these claims are incorrect: the former expresses a trivial singular proposition that can be justified *a priori*, while the latter expresses a non-trivial singular proposition that cannot be justified *a priori*.

Response: If one stipulated that apriority of a name-involving sentence is to be understood in terms of the *a priori* knowability of an associated singular proposition, these (controversial and counterintuitive) claims would be correct. But the two-dimensionalist takes this as good reason to reject the stipulation, or at least stipulates a different understanding of apriority for the purposes of the framework. For these purposes, an utterance can be said to be *a priori* when it expresses a belief (or at least an occurrent thought) that can be justified non-empirically, yielding *a priori* knowledge. There is an obvious epistemic difference between beliefs expressed by typical occurrences of 'Hesperus is Hesperus' and 'Hesperus is Phosphorus': no amount of non-empirical reasoning can convert the latter belief into *a priori* knowledge, but the former is easily justified *a priori*. (Note that on this definition of apriority, two different beliefs might be related to the same singular propositional content while differing in their epistemic status: the epistemic status attaches primarily to belief tokens, not to belief types or to propositional contents.) This epistemic difference at the level of thought can be used to ground the relevant claims about the apriority of utterances. More generally, the primary intensions of utterances are grounded in the (normative) cognitive role of associated thoughts.

Primary intensions are not linguistic meaning: Different speakers can use the same name ('Fred') or natural kind term ('water') with quite different cognitive roles, and with distinct patterns of epistemic evaluation. If so, the same expression will have different primary intensions for different speakers. So an expression's primary intension is not part of its linguistic meaning, where this is understood as meaning that is associated with an expression type simply by virtue of the conventions of a language.

Response: This point is correct: primary intensions are not always part of linguistic meaning. For example, it can happen that an identity statement (e.g. 'Bill Smith is William Smith') can be cognitively insignificant for one speaker (e.g. his wife, who uses the two names interchangeably) but not for another (e.g. a colleague who uses the names in quite different domains without knowing that they are coextensive). If so, then the primary intensions of the names will coincide for one speaker but not for another, so that the primary intension of at least one of them must vary across speakers. Primary intensions can also vary for context-dependent terms such as 'tall' and 'heavy'. The moral is that for maximal generality, primary intensions should be associated with expression tokens (or with utterances of expression types) rather than with expression types.

Primary intensions are insufficiently fine-grained. Cognitively distinct expressions may have the same primary intensions. When expressions are equivalent *a priori*, their primary intensions will coincide. For example, logical and mathematical truths all have the same primary intension (true in all scenarios), and have the same secondary intension too. But these clearly differ in meaning and in cognitive significance. So two-dimensional semantic values do not exhaust meaning (or utterance content), and are not as fine-grained as Fregean senses.

Response: A two-dimensionalist can accommodate many of the relevant cases here by invoking structured intensions. This will distinguish between different logical and mathematical truths, for example. The only residual problem will arise if there are pairs of simple expressions that are equivalent *a priori* but that are cognitively distinct. It is not obvious that there are such pairs, but if there are, there is more to meaning than primary intensions. We might say that primary intensions individuate expressions by their *idealized* cognitive significance, and so do not capture differences in *non-idealized* cognitive significance. One might try to capture these differences by moving to intensions that are defined over a space of finer-grained epistemic possibilities. Or a two-dimensionalist might simply allow that in addition to intensions, expressions are associated with finer-grained semantic values that lie behind and determine these intensions. But in any case, this point is no threat to the two-dimensionalist who is a semantic pluralist. Primary and secondary intensions are not all there is to meaning, but nevertheless utterances can be associated with primary and secondary intensions, in a way that can play the various explanatory roles described above.

There are epistemic possibilities that correspond to no centered world (Yablo, 1999, 2002). A key two-dimensionalist claim holds that when S is not ruled out *a priori*, then there is some centered world at which the primary intension of S is true. This may be so for typical Kripkean *a posteriori* necessities such as 'water is not H_2O', but there are other sentences for which the claim is false. For example, it may be that the existence (or non-existence) of a god is necessary without being *a priori*. If so, 'There is no god' (or 'There is a god') is not ruled out *a priori*, but it is necessarily false. There appears to be no relevant difference between primary and secondary intensions here, so the primary intension is true in no possible world. Something similar applies if the laws of nature in our world are the laws of all possible worlds. If these views are correct, then the space of epistemic possibilities outstrips the space of metaphysical possibilities in a way that falsifies the two-dimensionalist claim.

Response: All of these purported counterexamples rest on controversial claims about modality or apriority, and I have argued (Chalmers, 1999, 2004) that none of them succeed. Furthermore, there is good reason to believe that the concept of metaphysical modality itself has roots in the epistemic domain, so that there cannot be "strong necessities" that exhibit this sort of disconnect between epistemic and metaphysical modalities. Still, the existence or non-existence of strong necessities is a delicate and controversial issue. An alternative version of two-dimensionalism remains neutral on this issue by understanding scenarios not as centered metaphysically possible worlds, but instead as maximal epistemic possibilities (corresponding roughly to maximal epistemically consistent sets of sentences). Then even if no metaphysically possible world verifies 'There is no god', some maximal epistemic possibility will verify 'There is no god', so there will be a scenario at which the primary intension of this sentence will be true. Understood in this neutral way, two-dimensionalism does not ground inferences from conceivability to metaphysical possibility (those inferences will turn on a further claim about the relationship between scenarios and metaphysically possible worlds), but it can still play much the same role as before in the epistemic and semantic domains.

Complete canonical descriptions are not available (Schroeter, 2004): Epistemic two-dimensionalism requires that there be qualitative descriptions of a given scenario that are complete in that they epistemically determine the truth-value of arbitrary judgments. But there may be some features of the world, such as intrinsic physical features, which cannot be captured in a qualitative description.

Response: It is not clear whether there are intrinsic properties that cannot be captured in a qualitative description, but if there are, this will be irrelevant to epistemically determining the truth-value of any of our sentences. When information about these features is needed to epistemically determine the truth-value of a sentence in a scenario, a qualitative characterization of the features (e.g. an existential or a Ramsey-sentence characterization) will suffice. (Such a characterization may not suffice for metaphysical determination, and for evaluating truth-values of sentences in counter-factual worlds according to their secondary intensions. But qualitative descriptions are only needed for primary intensions.) The minimal size of a vocabulary that can epistemically determine the truth of all sentences is an important open question, but there is good reason to believe that some qualitative (and indexical) vocabulary suffices. It should also be noted that if we take the purely epistemic approach to scenarios described in the previous response, a restriction to qualitative vocabulary is not needed, and so the issue here does not arise.

Objections to the role of apriority (Block and Stalnaker, 1999; Yablo, 2002). It is true that there is an epistemic relation between information about the world and claims about reference: for example, given the information that we are in the H_2O-world (appropriately characterized) we should conclude that water is H_2O, and given the information that we are in the XYZ-world, we should conclude that water is XYZ. And it is true that we can makes these conditional inferences from the armchair, without needing to perform further investigation of the environment. But neverthe-less, these inferences are not justified *a priori*. The inferences are justified in part by background empirical knowledge of the world (Block and Stalnaker) or by "peeking" at our own judgments (Yablo). As a result, primary intensions are not connected to apriority as strongly as the two-dimensionalist supposes.

Response: Chalmers and Jackson (2001) argue that these connections are in fact *a priori*: although empirical facts about the world can play a causal role in determ-ining the relevant patterns of inference, there is good reason to believe that they do not play a justifying role (Chalmers (2002) responds to Yablo). It is also worth noting that even a skeptic about apriority can use the epistemic two-dimensional frame-work. Even if the relevant inferential connections are not *a priori*, one can still use them to define primary intensions, and the resulting primary intensions will still behave much as they are supposed to (assigning a necessary intension to 'Hesperus is Hesperus' but not to 'Hesperus is Phosphorus', for example). The connection between primary intensions and apriority will be lost, but primary intensions will still be strongly connected to the epistemic domain.

REFERENCES

Bealer, G. (2002). Modal Epistemology and the Rationalist Renaissance. In T. Gendler and J. Hawthorne (eds.), *Conceivability and Possibility*. Oxford: Oxford University Press.

Block, N. and Stalnaker, R. (1999). Conceptual Analysis, Dualism, and the Explanatory Gap. *Philosophical Review*, 108: 1–46.

Braddon-Mitchell, D. 2004. Masters of our Meaning. *Philosophical Studies*, 188: 133–52.

Byrne, A. and Pryor, J. (2006). Bad Intensions. In M. Garcia-Carpintero and J. Macia, (eds.), *Two-Dimensional Semantics*. Oxford: Oxford University Press.

Carnap, R. (1947). *Meaning and Necessity*. Chicago: University of Chicago Press.

Chalmers, D. J. (1995). The Components of Content. Manuscript. [consc.net/papers/content95.html]

——— (1996). *The Conscious Mind: In Search of a Fundamental Theory*. Oxford: Oxford University Press.

____ (1999). Materialism and the Metaphysics of Modality. *Philosophy and Phenomenological Research*, 59: 473–96 [consc.net/papers/modality.html]

____ (2002a). On Sense and Intension. [consc.net/papers/intension.html]

____ (2002b). The Components of Content (revised version). In *Philosophy of Mind: Classical and Contemporary Readings*. Oxford: Oxford University Press. [consc.net/papers/content. html]

____ (2002c). Does Conceivability Entail Possibility? In T. Gendler and J. Hawthorne (eds.), *Conceivability, and Possibility*. Oxford: Oxford University Press. [consc.net/papers/ conceivability.html]

____ (2004). Epistemic Two-Dimensional Semantics, *Philosophical Studies*, 118: 153–226.

____ (2006). The Foundations of Two-Dimensional Semantics. In M. Garcia-Carpintero and J. Macia, (eds.), *Two-Dimensional Semantics*. Oxford: Oxford University Press. [consc.net/ papers/foundations.html]

____ (forthcoming). The Nature of Epistemic Space. [consc.net/papers/espace.html]

Chalmers, D. J. and Jackson, F. (2001). Conceptual Analysis and Reductive Explanation. *Philosophical Review*, 110: 315–61 [consc.net/papers/analysis.html]

Davies, M. and Humberstone, I. L. (1981). Two Notions of Necessity. *Philosophical Studies*, 58: 1–30.

Evans, G. (1977). Reference and Contingency. *The Monist*, 62: 161–89.

Frege, G. (1892). Über Sinn und Bedeutung. Translated in P. Geach and M. Black (eds.), *Translations from the Philosophical Writings of Gottlob Frege*. Oxford: Blackwell, 1952.

Garcia-Carpintero, M. and Macia, J. (eds.) (2006). *Two-Dimensional Semantics*. Oxford: Oxford University Press.

Jackson F. (1998). *From Metaphysics to Ethics: A Defense of Conceptual Analysis*. Oxford: Oxford University Press.

Kamp, H. (1971). Formal Properties of 'Now'. *Theoria*, 37: 227–273.

Kaplan, D. (1968). Quantifying in. *Synthese*, 19: 178–214.

____ (1979). Dthat. In P. Cole (ed.), *Syntax and Semantics*. New York: Academic Press.

____ (1989). Demonstratives. In J. Almog, J. Perry, and H. Wettstein (eds.), *Themes from Kaplan*. Oxford: Oxford University Press.

Kripke, S. A. (1980). *Naming and Necessity*. Cambridge, MA: Harvard University Press.

Lewis, D. (1984). Putnam's Paradox. *Australasian Journal of Philosophy*, 62: 221–37.

____ (1994). Reduction of Mind. In S. Guttenplan (ed.), *Companion to the Philosophy of Mind*. Oxford: Blackwell.

Marconi, D. (2005). Two-Dimensional Semantics and the Articulation Problem. *Synthese*, 143(3): 321–49.

Nimtz, C. and Beckermann, A. (forthcoming). Why 'Water' is not an Indexical.

Putnam, H. (1975). The Meaning of 'Meaning'. In K. Gunderson (ed.), *Language, Mind, and Knowledge*. Minneapolis: University of Minnesota Press.

Schiffer, S. (2003). Two-Dimensional Semantics and Propositional Attitude Content. In *The Things We Mean*. Oxford: Oxford University Press.

Schroeter, L. (2004). The Rationalist Foundations of Chalmers' Two-Dimensional Semantics. *Philosophical Studies*, 18: 227–55.

Soames, S. (2005). *Reference and Description: The Case Against Two-Dimensionalism*. Princeton, NJ.: Princeton University Press.

Stalnaker, R. (1978). Assertion. In P. Cole (ed.), *Syntax and Semantics: Pragmatics, Vol. 9*. New York: Academic Press.

Stalnaker, R. (2003). Conceptual Truth and Metaphysical Necessity. In *Ways a World Might Be: Metaphysical and Anti-Metaphysical Essays*. Oxford: Oxford University Press.

_____ (2004). Assertion Revisited: On the Interpretation of Two-Dimensional Modal Semantics. *Philosophical Studies*, 118: 299–322.

Vlach, F. (1973). Now and Then: A Formal Study in the Logic of Tense Anaphora. PhD dissertation, UCLA.

Weatherson, B. (2001). Indicatives and Subjunctives. *Philosophical Quarterly*, 51: 200–216.

Wong, K.-Y. 1996. Sentence-Relativity and the Necessary A Posteriori. *Philosophical Studies*, 83: 53–91.

Yablo, S. (1999). Concepts and Consciousness. *Philosophy and Phenomenological Research*, 59: 455–63.

_____ (2000). Textbook Kripkeanism and the Open Texture of Concepts. *Pacific Philosophical Quarterly*, 81: 98–122.

_____ (2002). Coulda, Woulda, Shoulda. In T. Gendler and J. Hawthorne (eds.), *Conceivability and Possibility*. Oxford: Oxford University Press.

CHAPTER 25

DEFLATIONISM

DORIT BAR-ON AND KEITH SIMMONS

THERE is a core metaphysical claim shared by all deflationists: truth is not a genuine, substantive property. But anyone who denies that truth is a genuine property must still make sense of our pervasive truth *talk*. In addressing questions about the meaning and function of 'true', deflationists engage in a *linguistic* or *semantic* project, a project that typically goes hand-in-hand with a deflationary account of the *concept* of truth. A thoroughgoing deflationary account of truth will go beyond the negative metaphysical claim about truth and the positive linguistic account of the word 'true': it will also maintain that the concept of truth is a 'thin' concept that bears no substantive conceptual connections to other concepts to which it is traditionally tied.

These deflationary claims can seem startling. Consider the fundamental role that truth plays in the tradition. As a dyadic relation that obtains, or fails to obtain, between our thoughts and utterances on the one hand and the world on the other, it is a basic component of the familiar triangle of mind, language, and world. It is a crucial measure of the success of our mental and verbal acts, something to aim for in our transactions with the world. It exhibits deep connections to a host of basic notions in our conceptual scheme: meaning, belief, assertion, validity, verification, explanation, practical success, and more besides. It is central to the very characterization of central philosophical debates about, for example, scientific realism, non-cognitivism in ethics, paradox, and vagueness. Once truth is deflated, the philosophical landscape is transformed.

25.1 VARIETIES OF DEFLATIONISM

25.1.1 Disquotationalism

According to disquotationalism, a view championed by Quine (1970: esp. 10–13) and more recently by Field (1994), there is no more to the truth of, say, the sentence 'aardvarks amble' than is given by the disquotation of its quote name. One can think of the so-called *T-sentence*

'aardvarks amble' is true if and only if aardvarks amble

as a partial definition of 'true': the biconditional defines 'true' with respect to the sentence 'aardvarks amble'. And all such T-sentences together constitute an exhaustive and complete definition of 'true'.[1]

The idea behind the disquotational view is sometimes put this way: to say that a sentence is true is really just an indirect way of saying the sentence itself. To say that the sentence 'snow is white' is true is just an indirect way of saying that snow is white. This prompts the question: why not dispense with the truth predicate in favor of direct talk about the world? The disquotationalist will respond by pointing to generalizations like "Every sentence of the form 'p or not p' is true", and truth ascriptions such as "What Joe said is true." In the former case, we could dispense with the truth predicate here if we could produce an infinite conjunction of sentences of the form 'p or not p': "Aardvarks amble or aardvarks do not amble, and bison bathe or bison don't bathe, and . . . ". But we cannot produce such an infinite conjunction, and instead we achieve the desired effect by generalizing over sentences, and then bringing those sentences back down to earth by means of the truth predicate.[2] In cases like "What Joe said is true", the target utterance is picked out by means other than a quote-name. Indeed, the ascription may be *blind*: the speaker may not know what Joe said, but have every confidence in Joe's truthfulness. In these cases, 'true' serves to express an infinite disjunction:

What Joe said = 's$_1$' and s$_1$, or
What Joe said = 's$_2$' and s$_2$, or
. . . . ,

where 's$_1$', 's$_2$', . . . are quote-names of the sentences of Joe's language. So the disquotationalist takes the truth predicate to be a logical device: a device for disquotation, and for expressing infinite conjunctions and disjunctions.

It is clear that according to the disquotationalist, there is no robust *property* of truth. The term 'true' is not a typical property-ascribing predicate like 'triangular' or 'ripe'. Consider a natural disquotational definition of 'true' for a given language:

(DisquT)   x is true iff (x = 's$_1$' & s$_1$) or (x = 's$_2$' & s$_2$) or . . . ,

where 's$_1$', 's$_2$', . . . abbreviate sentences of the language.[3] Tarski's T-sentences ('s$_1$' is true iff s$_1$, 's$_2$' is true iff s$_2$, ...) are easy logical consequences of DisquT. (So the definition satisfies Tarski's condition of material adequacy on a definition of truth.)

---

[1] The phrase "partial definition" is Tarski's (see Tarski (1930–1: 155) and (1944: 50)). But it is far from clear that Tarski's semantic conception of truth is deflationary. See Simmons (forthcoming (a)) for more on this.

[2] See Quine (1970: 11).

[3] DisquT is suggested by remarks in Leeds (1978: 121–31, and fn.10), and versions of it are presented explicitly in Field (1986: 58); Resnik (1990: 412); and David (1994), ch.4 and p.107.

If we substitute for 'x' the sentence abbreviated by 's$_1$', we will find that 's$_1$' is true iff s$_1$. Similarly, 's$_2$' is true iff s$_2$. The truth of s$_1$ and the truth of s$_2$ have no more in common than the sentences s$_1$ and s$_2$. There is no property of truth that they share.

And there is no more to our understanding of the *concept* of truth than an understanding of the disquotational role of the truth-predicate. Since the concept of truth is a 'thin' concept in this sense, then it can make no substantive contribution to our understanding of assertion, meaning, belief, or any other concept in this cluster. Explanations of these notions that make use of the truth-predicate can avail themselves only of its role as a logical device of disquotation.

In this vein, Field observes that it may *seem* as though we need to appeal to truth to characterize the realist doctrine that "there might be (. . .) sentences of our languages that are true that we will never have reason to believe" (where the realist is contrasted with the antirealist, who identifies truth with some notion of justifiability). However, Field claims that the role of truth in such a characterization is "purely logical" (1994:). But for our finite limitations, the realist doctrine *could* be expressed without the use of a truth-predicate via an infinite disjunction, where each disjunct is of the form "*p* and we will never have reason to believe *p*." And Field thinks that the appeal to truth in general claims, for example that there is "a 'norm' of asserting and believing the truth", is merely disquotational (*ibid.*). The idea is that such general claims are in effect abbreviations for infinite conjunctions.

25.1.2 Minimalism

In contrast to disquotationalism, Horwich's *minimal theory of truth* takes propositions, rather than sentences or utterances, to be the primary truth-bearers.[4] The axioms of Horwich's minimal theory are all the infinitely many instances of the equivalence schema

The proposition that p is true if and only if p,

such as

The proposition that snow is white is true if and only if snow is white.

According to Horwich, these axioms together constitute a complete theory of truth; no more needs to be added. The denominalizing function of 'true' embodied in the axioms exhausts what there is to be said by way of explaining truth. Like the disquotationalist, Horwich claims that "the truth predicate exists solely for the sake of a certain logical need", that is, to express what otherwise could only be expressed by infinite conjunctions and disjunctions (1990: 2–6).

The minimal theory, says Horwich, has the virtue of simplicity, providing an account of truth in isolation from affiliated phenomena such as verification, practical success, reference, meaning, validity and assertion; it is "*a theory of truth that is a*

---

[4] Horwich (1990) and (1998a).

theory of nothing else" (1990: 26). By the same token, if we do resort to truth-talk in our explication of other concepts, we cannot expect the notion of truth to contribute to our understanding of these concepts beyond what is afforded by the minimal theory, since

all of the facts whose expression involves the truth predicate may be explained . . . by assuming no more about truth than instances of the equivalence schema.   (1990: 24)

For example, consider the following "fact about truth":

(1) True beliefs engender successful action. [5]

On its face, (1) seems to forge substantial links between truth, belief and action. But according to Horwich, this appearance is misleading. We need only a minimal account of truth to explain the role of truth in this thesis. Horwich considers the following instance:

If all Bill wants is to have a beer, and he thinks that merely by nodding he will get one, then, if his belief is true, he will get what he wants.

At one point in his explanation, Horwich makes "the familiar psychological assumption" that if one has a desire, and believes that a certain action will satisfy that desire, one will perform the action.[6] That is, conceptual connections are assumed between belief, desire and action. But *all* that is assumed about truth in Horwich's explanation is its denominalizing role. In the course of the explanation, we move from "The proposition that if Bill nods then Bill has a beer is true" to "If Bill nods then Bill has a beer"; and a little later we move from "Bill has a beer" to "The proposition that Bill has a beer is true". These are the only steps where truth has a role to play, and it is the role given to it by the equivalence schema. (A disquotational analysis will run parallel, in terms of truth's disquotational role.)

This style of explanation, says Horwich, may be universalized to show how in general true beliefs lead to successful action. And beyond that, it extends to all other facts involving 'true'. We can, presumably, learn more about the concepts of belief, desire and action by an improved understanding of their inter-relations. But no such improvement is possible in the case of truth: the equivalence schema exhausts all that the notion of truth can contribute to our understanding of any other concept. In this sense, truth is isolated from other concepts. This is so as much for the disquotationalist as it is for Horwich.

25.1.3 The Redundancy Theory

According to the disquotationalist and Horwich, 'true' is a genuine predicate which has a distinctive use. But according to a more radical version of deflationism, the redundancy theory of truth, the term 'true' is entirely dispensable. Ramsey writes:

---

[5] This is considered by Horwich (1990: 23–4).   [6] See (5), Horwich (1990: 24).

[I]t is evident that 'It is true that Caesar was murdered' means no more than that Caesar was murdered.   (Ramsey 1927: 106)

Truth is less easily eliminated from generalizations like 'Everything the Pope says is true', but, unlike Horwich[7] and the disquotationalists, Ramsey maintains that it can be done:

[S]uppose we put it thus 'For all p, if he asserts p, p is true', then we see that the propositional function p is true is simply the same as p, as e.g. its value 'Caesar was murdered is true' is the same as 'Caesar was murdered'.   (*Ibid.*)

Ramsey dismisses any problem about what it is for a proposition or judgment to be true—just make the judgment. For Ramsey, the real question is what is involved in making a judgment in the first place. Ramsey's essentially behavioristic approach to belief and judgment makes connections to various concepts, including *use* and *commitment*; but as far as truth is concerned, there is no place in this account for anything but the thinnest concept of truth.

25.1.4 The Prosentential Theory of Truth

For Ramsey, 'true' is an eliminable predicate. For the prosententialist, 'true' is not even a predicate.[8] Consider the discourse:

MARY Chicago is large
JOHN If that is true, it probably has a large airport.

In John's utterance, the expression 'that is true' is a *prosentence*, which shares its content with its antecedent, namely 'Chicago is large'. Prosentences are analogous to pronouns: just as 'She stopped' differs from 'Jane stopped' in its explicit dependence on a token of 'Jane' as its anaphoric antecedent, so the prosentence 'That is true' differs from 'Chicago is large' because the former is dependent on the latter as its anaphoric antecedent. But there is no difference of semantic content between the prosentence and its anaphoric antecedent. The occurrence of 'that is true' in John's utterance exemplifies a *prosentence of laziness*: John avoids the repetition of 'Chicago is large' by way of a prosentence with the same content. There are also *quantificational prosentences*. For example, the generalization 'Everything the Pope says is true' is analyzed along the following lines: 'For anything one can say, if the Pope says it, it is true'. Here 'it is true' is a quantificational prosentence, anaphorically tied to each of the Pope's utterances. Every instance of the generalization (say, 'Given "$2 + 2 = 4$", if the Pope says it then it is true')—is taken to contain a lazy prosentence, and treated accordingly. Most occurrences of 'true' are quantificational, despite surface appearances. For example, 'The first sentence Bismarck uttered in 1865 is true' is construed as a quantified conditional of the form 'For any sentence, if it is the first sentence Bismarck uttered in 1865, then it is true', where 'it is true'

---

[7] See Section 25.3 below.
[8] "Truth, to coin a phrase, isn't a real predicate." (Grover *et al.* (1975: 97)).

is a prosentence of quantification. Whether lazy or quantificational, the prosentence itself has no internal semantic structure, and so 'true' is a syncategorematic fragment of prosentences. On the prosentential view, 'true' does not survive as a discrete term that could denote a property of truth or express a concept of truth.[9]

25.1.5 Illocutionary Deflationism

Agreeing with Ramsey that the forms 'p' and 'the proposition that p is true' are equivalent in content, Ayer goes on to isolate a distinctive *illocutionary* role for 'true':

> [T]o say that a proposition is true is just to assert it, and to say that it is false is just to assert its contradictory. And this indicates that the terms 'true' and 'false' connote nothing, but function in the sentence simply as marks of assertion and denial.   (1946: 88–9)

Strawson's variant of the redundancy theory identifies a performative role for 'true': we use 'true' not to describe sentences or propositions, but rather to perform speech acts such as endorsing, agreeing, and conceding.[10] Given an illocutionary account of truth, there is no property or concept of truth to be investigated; as Ayer puts it, "there can be no sense in asking us to analyze the concept of 'truth' " (*ibid.*).

25.2 IS DEFLATIONISM SELF-DEFEATING?

It is sometimes argued that deflationism is self-defeating. One version of the argument is alluded to by Horwich: if we grant that 'true' is a "perfectly good English predicate" and further that "one might well take this to be a conclusive criterion of standing for a property of *some* sort" (1990: 38), then it might seem that the deflationist's distinctive metaphysical claim, that truth is not a property, is undermined. This argument seems to have little force. It has none against the prosentential theory, according to which 'true' is not a predicate. Though for the redundancy theorist and the illocutionary deflationist 'true' is a predicate, its application to a sentence (or proposition) says nothing *about* the sentence, but either says just what the original sentence says or adds illocutionary force. As for the disquotationalist's treatment of 'true', we saw above that it does not yield a property shared by all truths. For his part, Horwich takes 'true' to attribute not a "*complex* or *naturalistic* property" but a "*logical* property"—tied, presumably, to the denominalizing role of 'true'.[11]

---

[9] Brandom has proposed a disquotational or "unnominalizing" variant of the prosentential theory according to which 'is true' takes a nominalization and yields a prosentence whose anaphoric antecedent is the sentence tokening picked out by the nominalization (1994: 303–5). Still, whether 'true' is a prosentence-forming operator or a syncategorematic part of a prosentence, it is clearly not a property-denoting or a concept-expressing predicate.

[10] Strawson (1949).

[11] See (1990: 38–9). Horwich credits Field with the suggestion that truth is a logical property, and does not say more about it.

Boghossian has argued that the deflationist's very claim about truth is self
-defeating.[12] Consider the deflationist thesis, couched in terms of reference:

(1) The predicate 'true' does not refer to a property.

Boghossian distinguishes between deflationary and robust conceptions of reference.
On a deflationary understanding of 'refers', a term refers to a property provided it has
the syntax of a predicate and has a role in the language; on a robust understanding,
'refers' expresses some sort of objective relation between predicates and language-
independent properties. With respect to (1), Boghossian argues that the notion of
predicate-reference must be *robust*, since the deflationist is denying that there is any
substantive objective relation between 'true' and some language-independent property. Boghossian puts it this way:

The denial that a given predicate refers to, or expresses, a property, only makes sense
on a *robust* construal of *predicate reference*; on a deflationary construal, there is, simply,
no space for denying, of a significant, predicative expression, that it expresses a property.
(1990: 181)

So in particular (1) presupposes a robust notion of reference. Boghossian goes on to
say that there's a platitude connecting reference and truth, namely, that

'x is P' is true if and only if the object denoted by 'x' has the property expressed by 'P'.
(p. 181)

So since truth is tied in this way to a robust concept of reference, truth itself is robust;
that is, the deflationary conception of truth expressed by (1) presupposes a robust
notion of truth. Boghossian concludes: "So the denial that truth is robust attempted
in (1) can succeed only if it fails." (1990: 181)

However, observe that (1) formulates deflationism about truth in *semantic*
terms—in terms of reference. But a deflationist about semantic notions need not
be forced to accept such a formulation. The deflationist may make her negative
metaphysical claim—that truth is not a substantial property—without employing a
robust notion of reference. And the leading deflationary accounts of 'true', as we have
seen, make no use at all of the notion of reference. The deflationist's metaphysical
and linguistic (and conceptual) theses may be expressed independently of any robust
notion of reference.[13]

25.3 PROBLEMS OF STATEABILITY

Whether or not deflationism is self-defeating, there are difficulties in the very formulation of certain deflationary theories. Consider disquotationalism. We can present

---

[12] Boghossian (1990: esp. 178 ff.).
[13] Parallel remarks apply to Boghossian's formulation of deflationism about reference:

The expression 'refers to a property' does not itself refer to a property.

A sensible deflationist about reference will not use the notion of reference to articulate her position. She
might give the familiar disquotational, list-like account, and say that there's no more to 'refers' than that.

disquotationalism either via the infinitary definition DisquT, or as an axiomatic theory, where the infinitely many axioms are the T-sentences (which do not form a recursively enumerable set).

The infinitary nature of these accounts may give us pause. We might well be suspicious of a theory that cannot be finitely or recursively stated. Further, if a proper understanding of 'true' consists in an understanding of DisquT or the T-sentences, then this understanding would require "massive conceptual resources", to use a phrase of Gupta's (1993)—we would have to understand *every* sentence of English (or whatever the target language may be).

Can a finite formulation be found? We might turn to this finitely stated schematic definition:

x is a true sentence iff $\exists p(x = \text{'p'} \& p)$.

Obvious problems arise if we interpret the quantifier objectually. (There is the problem of quantification into quotes. And the string 'x = "p" & p' is grammatically ill-formed, since the variable 'p', taken as an objectual variable, cannot serve as a conjunct.) But the move to a substitutional reading is threatened by circularity: substitutional quantification is typically characterized in terms of truth (more specifically, in terms of true substitution instances).[14]

A disquotationalist might abandon a direct definition of truth in favor of a recursive account, according to which 'true' is defined Tarski-style in terms of the more basic notions of reference and satisfaction. Given a language with a finite stock of names and predicates, reference may be disquotationally defined by a finite list of sentences of the form ' "a" refers to a', and satisfaction by a finite list of sentences of the form 'x satisfies "F" iff x is F'. In this way, reference and satisfaction are finitely defined—and so truth is finitely defined. But such a recursive disquotationalist is restricted to languages whose sentences have the appropriate kind of logical form. And there is an array of truths that are notoriously hard to fit into the Tarskian mold: belief attributions, counterfactuals, modal assertions, statements of probability, and so on.[15]

In short, there is a question about the very *statement* of the disquotational theory. The same question can be raised about Horwich's minimal theory of truth, since it too is infinitary in nature. Horwich *accepts* that the theory cannot be explicitly formulated, for two reasons: first, the axioms that we could formulate are infinite in number and so cannot be written down; and second, there are some propositions we cannot express, and so their corresponding axioms are also inexpressible.[16] Moreover, Horwich rejects the idea of a formulation of the minimal theory in terms of a single principle

For any x, x is true if and only if Σp (x = the proposition that p & p)

---

[14] One suggestion (made for example in Field, 1986: 56 ff) is to understand substitutional quantification as an abbreviation for infinite disjunctions and conjunctions, but this it seems just sends us back to the infinitary account above.

[15] See David (1994: esp. 107–24) for an extended discussion of disquotationalism and finite stateability.

[16] Horwich (1990: 21–2).

where the existential quantifier is understood substitutionally, again because substitutional quantification is standardly defined in terms of truth.[17]

But if neither disquotationalism nor minimalism can be finitely stated, if all we can formulate is a finite subset of the infinitely many individual axioms, then it seems that any formulation of these theories will be irremediably partial. Moreover, the theories describe only the conditions under which a finite subset of *particular* sentences or propositions are true—the theories are piecemeal, and do not include any universal generalizations about truth. Consequently, Gupta has argued, minimalism is unable to explain our acceptance of such generalizations as 'Only propositions are true'. (And since the theory doesn't tell us what isn't true, it doesn't rule out, for example, the absurdity that the Moon is true.) An adequate explanation of a generalization about truth would require its derivation from the minimal theory—but it is a logical fact that there can be no derivation of a universal generalization from the set of the *particular* propositions that comprise the minimal theory.[18]

Hill has taken Gupta's objection to heart and proposed a finitely axiomatized version of minimalism.[19] Hill's *simple substitutional theory of truth* is composed of just one axiom, a universal generalization:

(S) For any object x, x is true if and only if Σp(x = the proposition that p, and p).[20]

The substitutional quantifier here cannot of course be characterized in terms of truth. Hill's characterization proceeds in terms of rules of inference, modeled on the elimination and introduction rules for the standard objectual quantifiers.[21] Thus the substitutional quantifiers are defined by describing their logical behavior. Despite being composed of just one axiom, Hill's theory yields as logical consequences all instances of 'The proposition that p is true if and only if p', and generalizations about truth such as 'Only propositions are true'.[22]

---

[17] See Horwich (1990: 27). Horwich also resists the move to substitutional quantification because he takes the minimal notion of truth to provide a simple alternative to the "cumbersome" apparatus of substitutional quantification (1990: 31–4).

[18] Gupta, 1993.

[19] Hill (2002: 16 ff.).

[20] See Hill (2002: 22). 'Σ' stands for the substitutional existential quantifier. In Hill's formulation, "proposition" is replaced by "thought".

[21] For example, one form of the Existential Introduction rule is this:

$$(\ldots T \ldots)$$
$$\text{---------------}$$
$$(\Sigma p)(\ldots p \ldots)$$

where T is a particular, determinate proposition, and (...T...) is the particular, determinate proposition that comes from replacing all free occurrences of the propositional variable p in the open proposition (...p...) with T (see Hill, 2002: 18–22).

[22] See Hill (2002: 22), and Appendices I and II of chapter 2, pp. 33–7. For a critical discussion of Hill (2002), see Simmons (forthcoming (b)).

25.4 PROBLEMS OF SCOPE

Suppose that on the authority of others I believe that Dmitri is always right, though I speak no Russian. I say, with apparent understanding, 'What Dmitri says is true'. But according to disquotationalism, understanding what I have said is just a matter of understanding what Dmitri said; and since I cannot understand what Dmitri said, I cannot understand what I have said.

Disquotationalists typically restrict the scope of their theory to the sentences of a given natural language such as English.[23] And since an English speaker will not understand every sentence of English, some disquotationalists recognize the need to go further and restrict the theory to the sentences of a given speaker's idiolect (those sentences that the speaker understands). According to Field, for example, a person can meaningfully apply 'true' only to utterances she understands; Field suggests, as a heuristic, that when I say a sentence is true, I am saying that it is true-as-I-understand-it. Field characterizes *pure disquotational truth* in terms of a strong equivalence: my claim that utterance u is true (that is, true-as-I-understand-it) is *cognitively equivalent* to u (as I understand it). So the T-sentence

(S) 'Aardvarks amble' is true iff aardvarks amble

expresses a cognitive equivalence—according to Field, a T-sentence holds "of conceptual necessity", and enjoys an "axiomatic status" (1994: 258, 267).

Relativized to a speaker's idiolect, DisquT and the T-sentences will not outrun the speaker's conceptual resources. But the restriction to idiolect is very strong. One may feel that we are a long way from our commonsensical notion of truth. After all, I do apply 'true' to sentences beyond those of my actual idiolect. I do it when I say "Most of what Socrates said was true", even though I have little or no understanding of ancient Greek. I do it when I allow that there are true sentences of my language (English) that I do not understand. And I do it when I express my modal intuition that 'snow is white' might have meant that grass is red—indeed, this intuition might well suggest that the T-sentence (S) is only contingently true, and not a cognitive equivalence or conceptual necessity.

According to Field, we should be methodological deflationists, taking pure disquotational truth to be the fundamental truth concept as long as this adequately serves our practical and theoretical purposes. The present concern is that pure disquotational truth is too restricted to serve these purposes. The challenge, then, is to find a way of supplementing the basic notion of pure disquotational truth by other notions of truth that remain suitably deflationary and allay the concern.[24]

---

[23] There is another reason for this restriction. According to the disquotationalist, if penguins waddle then 'Penguins waddle' is true (this is just the right to left direction of the T-sentence). But the linguistic item 'Penguins waddle' may be a false sentence of some language other than English. For related discussion, see Section 25.6 (a) below.

[24] To accommodate our modal intuitions that our sentences could have had different meanings, Field introduces the notion of "quasi-deflationary truth". And to deal with the application of 'true' to foreign

In sharp contrast to disquotationalism, Horwich's minimalism does not restrict the scope of 'true' to a particular language or idiolect: 'true' applies to *all* propositions, expressed in *any* language. To accommodate propositions that are not yet expressible, Horwich supposes that every proposition is expressed by a sentence in some *possible* language. Horwich also assumes that whatever can be expressed in some possible language can be said in some possible extension of English. So in order to encompass all propositions we need only consider possible extensions of English.[25] Acceptable substituends for the occurrences of 'p' in the schema 'The proposition that p is true iff p' are sentences of English, actual *and possible*. So Horwich's minimal theory is composed of infinitely many axioms, infinitely many of which we cannot formulate or understand. We could hardly be further removed from the restriction to speakers' idiolects. Clearly, understanding 'true' cannot be a matter of understanding all the axioms of the minimal theory. According to Horwich, our understanding of 'true' consists in the disposition to accept *a priori* any instantiation of the schema 'The proposition that p is true if and only if p'.[26] This disposition provides the best explanation of our overall use of the term 'true'. So, by appeal to the use theory of meaning, Horwich maintains that the meaning of 'true' is constituted by this disposition. This provides the truth predicate with a fixed meaning, even when it is applied to propositions that we cannot formulate or understand. And an understanding of 'true' does not require massive conceptual resources.[27]

We can now see how Horwich addresses the issues that confronted the disquotationalist. Sentences beyond a speaker's idiolect present no special problem, because 'true' applies to all propositions, and in particular to all those expressed in foreign languages. And there seems less room for controversy about the modal status of

(P)   The proposition that aardvarks amble is true iff aardvarks amble.

It seems plausible that (P) is necessary, since propositions wear their meanings on their sleeves, or perhaps *are* meanings.

25.5 PRESUPPOSITIONLESS TRUTH?

Horwich says, as we saw, that minimalism is a theory of truth and nothing else. Hill writes:

If minimalism is correct, then there is no particular set of concepts that one must acquire prior to acquiring the concept of truth ... ... minimalism represents the concept of truth as autonomous and presuppositionless.   (Hill, 2002: 4)

sentences, he introduces as one option the notion of "extended disquotational truth". But these notions still seem too restricted. With respect to "quasi-deflationary truth", the truth conditions that sentences may counterfactually receive are limited to those enjoyed by the sentences of my actual idiolect. And with respect to "extended disquotational truth", 'true' does not extend to a foreign sentence unless it is synonymous with a sentence of my idiolect.

[25] See Horwich (1990: 20, fn.4).   [26] Horwich (1990: 36).
[27] This might be seen as a response to the objection that Gupta presents (1993/9: 297ff).

According to Michael Williams:

[W]hen we have pointed to certain formal features of the truth-predicate (notably its 'dis-quotational' feature) and explained why it is useful to have a predicate like this (e.g. as a device for asserting infinite conjunctions), we have said just about everything there is to be said about truth.   (Williams 1988: 424)

So it may seem that deflationism provides a "presuppositionless" account of truth. As Hill puts it: "[a] theory that explains truth and other semantic concepts in terms of a logical device is paradigmatically deflationary" (2002: 23). No weighty semantic, linguistic or psychological notions figure in the deflationary story, or so it may seem.

But consider again the axioms of Horwich's minimal theory. They comprise all the instances of the schema

The proposition that p is true if and only if p.

Instances of this schematic generalization are obtained by replacing the two occur-rences of 'p' by tokens of an actual or possible English sentence. We may feel some discomfort here: the tokens are placed in two quite different contexts. The first token forms part of a referring term, the term 'the proposition that p'. The second consti-tutes the right hand side of the biconditional. With Davidson, we may wonder how these two appearances are connected.[28] At any rate, it is clear that certain conditions must be placed on such an instantiation. We can list four:

  (i)   each 'p' is replaced with tokens of an (actual or possible) English sentence,
  (ii) these tokens are given the same meaning or interpretation,
  (iii) under that interpretation they express a proposition,

and

  (iv) the terms 'that' and 'proposition' are given their English meanings.

Since a fully explicit formulation of the minimal theory must include these conditions, the very statement of Horwich's minimal theory is shot through with semantical concepts and talk of sentence-tokens. This may raise two concerns. First, since talk of sentence-tokens is unavoidable anyway, might it not be advisable to work with sentence tokens (or token utterances) all along? Why not be more economical and adopt the schema

'p' is true iff p,

constrained by conditions (i) and (ii)? This avoids the appeal to propositions, which will come as a relief to anyone who finds them suspect or mysterious.[29]

The second concern is prompted by the observation that when we specify the axioms of the minimal theory we must employ a number of semantical concepts: the notion of a *language* (specifically, English), the notion of an *interpretation*, the rela-tion of *expressing*, and, of course, the notion of a *proposition*. Since the formulation

---

[28]   See Davidson (1996/9: 317–19). For more critical discussion of minimalism, see Davidson (1990).
[29]   The thought is encouraged by Horwich's own claim that the minimal theory of truth for propositions is easily inter-derivable with a minimal theory of truth for utterances. (See Horwich (1990:103–8)).

of the minimal theory of truth itself requires these notions, it is no longer at all clear that the minimal theory of truth is as innocent of involvement with semantic and linguistic notions—as "presuppositionless"—as its proponents claim.[30] The difficulty here is not unique to minimalists. Though disquotationalists do not trade in propositions and the expressing relation, they too cannot dispense with semantic notions in a fully explicit statement of their account. Given the disquotational schema

'p' is true if and only if p,

conditions (i) and (ii) must be specified in order to obtain appropriate instances.

25.6 TRUTH AND OTHER CONCEPTS

If the notion of *meaning* and its cognates are needed for the formulation of minimalism and disquotationalism, then truth appears not be the autonomous, presuppositionless notion the deflationist says it is. And deflationists face a further challenge here: to explain the notion of meaning independently of the notion of truth, on pain of circularity. This is a stiff challenge, for it is a widespread view that the meaning of a sentence is given, at least in part, by its *truth*-conditions. The challenge generalizes to other notions, since truth is standardly tied to other central concepts and philosophical claims—consider, for example, the claim that *to assert is to present as true*, or the claim that *evaluative statements are not truth-apt*.

Now deflationists typically focus their attention on sentences like 'Fermat's last theorem is true', 'What John said yesterday is true', and 'Everything Gandhi said is true' (or the propositions expressed by these sentences). These sentences do not directly present the evaluated sentences, unlike ' "Penguins waddle" is true'; instead, the evaluated sentences are indirectly referred to, or belong to a domain that is quantified over. In all these cases, truth applies to sentences (or the propositions they express), whether they are directly presented, referred to indirectly, or quantified over. Call such applications of the concept of truth *first-order*.

Deflationists tend to be concerned almost exclusively with first-order uses of truth. But there are other uses of the concept of truth that are not first-order—uses that are more reflective or theoretical or *second-order*. When we say "Meaning is given by truth-conditions" or "To assert is to present as true" or "Evaluative statements are not truth-apt", we are not calling any specific sentence true, nor are we making oblique reference to some set of sentences and saying of its members that they are true. Rather, we are identifying conceptual connections between truth and other notions. Truth appears to have a substantive explanatory role in these cases, an important role in the explanation of assertion, meaning, evaluative statements. But according to deflationists, this appearance is illusory. For the minimalist and the disquotationalist, the role of 'true' is strictly limited to its disquotational

---

[30] Similar remarks can be made about Hill's simple substitutionalism. See Simmons (forthcoming (b)).

or denominalizing function—recall Horwich's treatment of *True beliefs engender successful action*, or Field's characterization of the realist doctrine. And if 'true' is redundant, or a syncategorematic ingredient of prosentences, or merely adds illocutionary force, it will be quite unsuited to articulate substantial conceptual connections. Can the deflationist maintain the thesis that, despite appearances, truth is explanatorily inert? We consider three cases: meaning, assertion, and truth-aptness.

(a) *Meaning* Since Davidson (1967), it has been widely accepted that at least part of what constitutes the meaning of a sentence is its *truth condition*. The condition under which 'Worms wriggle' is true—the worldly condition of wriggling worms—is at least in part constitutive of the meaning of the sentence. Davidson proposed that a theory of meaning for a language L could be given by a Tarskian truth theory for L, which yields as theorems biconditionals of the form

s is true iff p,

where 's' is a mentioned sentence of L and 'p' is a used sentence of the theorist's language that specifies s's truth-condition. In the special case of a theory of meaning for, say, English that is given *in* English, the theorems will be the T-sentences of English. Thus, for the sentence 'Worms wriggle' the meaning-giving theorem will be its T-sentence:

'Worms wriggle' is true iff worms wriggle.

Deflationism is often taken to be incompatible with a Davidsonian truth-condition theory of meaning. Following Dummett (1959), several authors identify a vicious circularity in the attempt to use Tarskian T-sentences as meaning-giving while at the same time holding that the T-sentences exhaust all there is to say about the concept of truth.[31] If, as deflationists claim, the truth predicate is just a logical device, and speaking of the truth of a sentence S is just a way of saying what S says, then the meaning of 'S is true' is parasitic on the meaning of S. But then it would seem circular to specify the meaning of 'S' in terms of the condition under which S is true. Or, as Horwich puts it, "knowledge of the truth condition of a sentence cannot simultaneously constitute *both* our knowledge of its meaning *and* our grasp of *truth* for the sentence" (1990: 71). Field goes as far as to characterize the main idea behind deflationism as the idea that "what plays a central role in meaning and content not include truth conditions" (Field, 1994: 253).

Both deflationists and truth condition theorists make theoretical use of the Tarskian truth schema. But the status they assign to its instances is very different. For the Davidsonian, the T-sentence itself is *informative*, because it reveals a key meaning property of the sentence, namely its truth condition. And it is *contingent*, since the quoted sentence might have had a different truth-condition (and thus a different

---

[31] For discussions of the incompatibility claim and the circularity objection, see Soames (1984, 1999); Etchemendy (1988); Horwich (1990); Gupta (1993/9); Brandom (1994); Rumfitt (1995); and Horisk (forthcoming).

meaning). For the deflationist, T-sentences are neither informative nor contingent, but are necessary and *a priori*; together they constitute a *definition* of 'true'.

However, the deflationist must recognize at least this much contingency in the use of the T-schema. Appending 'is true' to the sentence 'Worms wriggle' may be just another way of speaking of the wriggling of worms, but only *given what that sentence means*. In a world where crickets chirp and worms wriggle, and where 'Worms wriggle' means what our English sentence 'Crickets croak' now means, the T-sentence ' "Worms wriggle" is true iff worms wriggle' (as understood by *us*) is false, since the mentioned sentence on the left hand side is false at that world, while the used sentence on the right hand side is still true.[32] To ensure that the truth schema only has instances that are necessarily true, one must find a way to guarantee that the quoted sentence on the left hand side has a fixed meaning across possible worlds. Thus, we should think of the right-to-left direction of the T-biconditional as follows:

> Given that 'Worms wriggle' means that worms wriggle, if worms wriggle, then 'Worms wriggle' is true.

But this means that we must recognize meaning as an 'independent variable' that factors into the T-schema. 'Worms wriggle' is true, given how the world is, *and given what the sentence means.*

This raises familiar questions. If the notion of meaning is an ingredient of the deflationary account, then how can truth be presuppositionless? And further, how is meaning to be explained independently of truth? A deflationist could try replacing the notion of a truth condition with that of a verification condition or assertibility condition, or with the notion of convention-governed use, or communicative intentions; and she could adopt a conceptual role semantics or an inferential role semantics.[33]

However, it can be argued that meaning and truth cannot be separated in the way the deflationist envisages. The deflationist must agree that whether a sentence can be properly called 'true' depends on the meaning it has, as well as on the way the world is. But then meaning is (at least) whatever determines truth-value, given how the world is. On a broad, not specifically Davidsonian, understanding of 'truth condition', this is just what a truth condition is. So, if we follow Lewis (1972), and take it that "meaning is what meaning does", then the meaning of a sentence must at least include the condition of its truth, whatever else it may include.[34] Put in epistemological terms, meaning is at least whatever the speaker needs to know in order to determine the truth value of a sentence, given complete knowledge of nonlinguistic worldly facts. This simple argument presents a persistent challenge to the deflationist: show how meaning does what it does, without appeal to the broad notion of a truth condition.

---

[32] Depending on how sentences are individuated, "Worms wriggle" may even be false in our world, if there is a language in which it actually means something different from its English meaning.

[33] See e.g. Horwich (1990), (1998a) and (1998b); Brandom (1994); and Field (1994).

[34] The argument is briefly presented in Lewis (1972). For an interpretation and discussion of Lewis's argument, as well as possible deflationist objections, see Bar-On *et al.* (1999).

Suppose, for example, that the meaning of a sentence is taken to be its conceptual role, and that our grasp of that role does not in any way involve a grasp of the condition in which the sentence would be true. Then it becomes mysterious how a speaker's understanding of a sentence allows her to assign a truth-value to the sentence, once she knows all the nonlinguistic facts. Moreover, well-known 'twin-earth' arguments seem to suggest that knowledge of non-truth-related features of a sentence (e.g. its conceptual role) are never sufficient for knowing whether the sentence is true or false, even when one knows all the relevant nonlinguistic facts.[35] The intuitive truth-conditionalist idea is that, since meaning at least involves truth conditions, and understanding a sentence involves knowing its truth condition, there will be no mystery. For knowing the truth-condition of 'Worms wriggle' is knowing precisely *which* condition is relevant to deciding the sentence's truth-value. Here, then is the objection to the deflationist: a deflationary theory of truth cannot explain meaning in terms of the notion of a truth condition—but meaning cannot be explained in any other way.

(b) *Assertion* According to Frege and others, assertion and assertoric force is to be understood in terms of truth: to assert that *p* is to *present p as true*.[36] Frege's view of assertion is a natural one. There are many speech-acts I can perform that involve a given proposition: I can suppose it, propose it, float it, question it. Frege plausibly claims that the distinguishing mark of assertion—what sets it apart from other speech-acts—is the fact that when I assert something, I present a certain proposition *as true*.

So here is the challenge to the deflationist: to explain how to achieve a proper theoretical understanding of what it is to assert that *p* without help from the concept of truth. How might the deflationist respond? Consider disquotationalism or minimalism. According to these deflationary views, the function of 'true' is exhausted by its disquotational or denominalizing role. Now consider the thesis that to assert is to present as true. The thesis involves the use of the truth-predicate; in Horwich's terms, it is a fact about truth that needs to be explained. With the denominalizing role of 'true' in mind, a deflationist might claim that the thesis that *to assert that p is to present p as true* is equivalent to the thesis that *to assert that p is to present p*. This commits us to the claim that to present *p* as true is just to present *p*; for example, to present as true the proposition that aardvarks amble is just to present the proposition that aardvarks amble. But this claim is false, for there are many ways to present a proposition. I can present a proposition as worthy of your consideration, or as a conjecture, or as a remote possibility, or as outrageous—and I can also present it as true. Presenting as true is just one way of presenting. So it seems that we cannot disquote away truth from the locution "present as true".

---

[35]   For an argument, see ch. 10 of Lycan (1984).

[36]   Frege distinguishes between judging and the mere entertaining of a thought, and correlatively, between the act of assertion and the mere expression or articulation of a thought. At one place he writes: "Once we have grasped a thought, we can recognize it as true (make a judgement) and give expression to our recognition of its truth (make an assertion)" (1979: 185).
See also (1979: 139) for one of many passages in the same vein.

Illocutionary deflationists such as Ayer will take a different tack. They will agree that there is an undeniable connection between assertion and truth, but that it is misleading to present the connection in terms of the slogan *to assert is to present as true*. Better to reverse the order: *to present as true is to assert*. Assertion is not to be characterized in terms of truth; rather, our use of the predicate 'true' is to be characterized in terms of assertion. To predicate 'true' of a sentence (or a thought, or a proposition) *is just to assert the sentence (thought, proposition)*. The illocutionary deflationist will take on board the equivalence thesis, and agree that the *content* of ' "Aardvarks amble" is true' is no different from that of 'Aardvarks amble'. But though 'true' does not add content, it does introduce assertoric force.

But there is a difficulty with this illocutionary account, a difficulty articulated by Frege. At first glance, it may seem surprising that Frege should oppose illocutionary deflationism. Frege does emphasize the illocutionary aspect or role of truth, and he regards truth as belonging to the same family of concepts as assertion and judgment. Moreover, Frege famously endorses the equivalence thesis, that 'p' and ' "p" is true' are equivalent in content—predicating 'true' makes no difference to content.[37] But according to Frege, 'true' also makes no difference to the force with which the thought is expressed. Frege says:

If I assert "it is true that sea-water is salt", I assert the same thing as if I assert "sea-water is salt". This enables us to recognize that the assertion is not to be found in the word 'true'..."   (1979: 251)

If one's deflationary view of 'true' is based on the equivalence thesis, then, according to Frege, 'true' cannot be the mark of assertion. Indeed, Frege says that "there is no word or sign in language whose function is simply to assert something" (1979: 185).

Frege is explicitly opposed to illocutionary deflationism, and for good reason. If one accepts the equivalence thesis, there seems to be no difference between asserting that *p* and asserting that *p* is true. Further, the locution '*p* is true' can occur as the antecedent of a conditional, where it cannot be produced with assertoric force. Further still, I can say 'It is true that aardvarks amble' with a variety of different illocutionary forces—I can be supposing, conjecturing, pretending, or acting.[38] As Frege puts it:

In order to put something forward as true, we do not need a special predicate: we need only the assertoric force with which the sentence is uttered.   (Frege, 1979: 233)

So Frege explicitly rejects illocutionary deflationism. It is also noteworthy that Frege's remarks about truth seem inhospitable to conceptual deflationism: truth is "primitive and simple" (*Ibid.*) and "the goal of scientific endeavour" (1979: 2).

---

[37] Frege writes: "[T]he sentence 'I smell the scent of violets' has just the same content as the sentence 'It is true that I smell the scent of violets'" (1956/99: 88). In general, "... the sense of the word 'true' is such that it does not make any essential contribution to the thought" (1979: 251).

[38] Frege writes : "[I]n the mouth of an actor upon the stage, even the sentence 'The thought that 5 is a prime number is true' contains only a thought, and indeed the same thought as the simple '5 is a prime number'." (1892/1960: 60).

Clearly we must distinguish what Frege says about the word 'true', and what he says about truth. Science aims at the truth, and "logic is the science of the most general laws of truth" (1979: 128)—but it does not follow that science or logic is concerned with the word 'true':

[W]hat logic is really concerned with is not contained in the word 'true' at all but in the assertoric force with which a sentence is uttered.   (1979: 252)

We can learn a lesson from Frege: deflationism about the word 'true' is one thing, deflationism about the concept of truth quite another. According to Frege, 'true' adds neither content nor illocutionary force. But for all that Frege is not a conceptual deflationist. One can be deflationary about first-order uses of 'true' without being deflationary about second-order uses. A deflationary treatment of first-order uses of 'true' need not bring conceptual deflationism in its train. If Frege is right, truth is implicated in the assertoric force with which a sentence is uttered. The Fregean point is precisely that presenting *as true* (that is, asserting) is not a matter of ascribing a property to a sentence or thought, but rather is a special kind of doing or act, different from conjecturing, or surmising, or assuming, etc. So when we explain assertion, we ourselves use a truth-locution and employ the concept of truth. Thus, even if we grant, as does Frege, that first-order uses of 'true' submit to the equivalence thesis, we may need to employ the concept of truth for explanatory purposes. As we have seen, Frege is not at all shy about using truth-locutions in an explanatory way in connection with assertion, logic and science. He does *not* accept a deflationary view of the *concept* of truth.

It is not clear where Frege stands on the metaphysical issue regarding truth.[39] But it is possible to endorse metaphysical deflationism together with a deflationary view about first-order uses of 'true', while still rejecting conceptual deflationism. Brandom is a prosententialist about 'true' (see note 9 above), and he denies that there is a property of truth (1994: 325–7). But Brandom equates asserting with *taking-true* or *putting forward as true*. A theory of asserting is a theory of taking-true. In Brandom's phrase, truth here is "what one is taking, treating, or putting forward a claim *as*" when one asserts (1994: 202). At this point, then, a deflationist would need a suitably deflationary account of *taking as true* and the associated concept of truth. But Brandom's account is not deflationary. Rather, Brandom seeks an account of truth that proceeds from the attitude of taking-true: "once one understands what it is to take or treat something as true, one will have understood as well the concept of truth" (1994: 291). What are we doing when we assert or put forward a sentence as true? Brandom's general answer is that we are undertaking a certain kind of commitment.[40]

---

[39] On the one hand, many of his remarks suggest that he thinks we get nowhere in our understanding of truth by pairing the predicate 'is true' with some property that all and only true items share. On the other hand, Frege's talk of truth as "something primitive and simple" may suggest that he is reifying truth as a special, irreducible property.

[40] The commitment may be explained in terms of Sellars' notion of a "game of giving and asking for reasons". It is a necessary condition of assertional commitments that they play the dual role of justifier and subject of demand for justification; assertions "are fundamentally fodder for inferences" (1994: 168).

Brandom's pragmatic account of asserting or taking as true goes forward in terms of commitments, inferences, entitlements, and justificatory responsibilities—and this account is clearly not deflationary.[41]

(c) *Truth-aptness* Recall that disquotationalism can be presented either via DisquT or axiomatically via the T-sentences. Which sentences should be admitted into DisquT or the T-sentences? Clearly not imperatives such as 'Shut the door!' or interrogatives such as 'Is the door closed?' These sentences are not *truth-apt*; for example, the T-sentence ' "Shut the door!" is true if and only if shut the door!' makes no sense. So it seems that the notion of truth-aptness must appear in the very statement of disquotationalism: either DisquT or the list of T-sentences must be accompanied by the restriction *'where 's_1', 's_2', . . . abbreviate truth-apt sentences of English'*. This raises two concerns for the disquotationalist. First, is truth-aptness a rich concept that does not belong in a deflationary, presuppositionless account of truth? Second, is the notion of truth-aptness itself dependent on the concept of truth? After all, it might seem natural to characterize a truth-apt sentence as one that is either true or false.[42] If so, then disquotationalism appears to be circular. These are not concerns for the minimalist, since propositions are truth-apt by their very nature.

As a first step, the disquotationalist might embrace *syntacticism*, according to which a sentence is truth-apt if it displays the appropriate syntax. If a sentence is declarative in form—if it can be embedded in conditionals, negation, propositional attitude constructions, and so on—then it is truth-apt.[43] This would certainly exclude imperatives and interrogatives and other inappropriate grammatical forms. But it is clear that declarative syntax is not sufficient for truth-aptness. Suppose that in a logic class I write the sentence 'Fred has flat feet' on the board (perhaps in order to introduce the symbolization 'Fa').[44] The sentence is declarative, but, lacking any context to render it true or false, it is not truth-apt. Or consider a tongue-twister, say 'She sells sea-shells by the sea-shore'[45]—again, this is declarative but not truth-apt. So more than declarative form is needed.[46]

Wright and Boghossian have proposed the strengthening of syntacticism to *disciplined syntacticism*. For a sentence to be truth-apt, it must not only be declarative, but it must also be part of a discourse that is *disciplined*, a discourse where "there are firmly acknowledged standards of proper and improper use of its ingredient

---

[41] Brandom's willingness to place the notion of taking as true and its cognates in so central a position might suggest that he would reject deflationism about the concept of truth; on the other hand he embraces deflationism without any apparent reservation. Interpretation aside, we are urging that Brandom's account of assertion is incompatible with being deflationist about the concept of truth. For more on assertion and deflationism, see Bar-On and Simmons (forthcoming).

[42] This is the way it is characterized by Jackson *et al.* For example: "Non-cognitivism in ethics holds that ethical sentences are not in the business of being either true nor false—for short, they are not truth-apt" (1994: 287).

[43] Syntacticism is mentioned, but not endorsed, by Jackson *et al.* (1994: 291–3).

[44] The example is from Jackson *et al.* (1994), p. 293.

[45] The example is from Porubcansky, 2004.

[46] Notice also that if we embrace syntacticism, we settle immediately issues that surely cannot be settled so quickly: non-cognitivism about ethical statements would be false, and performatives—such as 'I name this ship "Queen Mary II" '—would count as true.

sentences" (Wright, 1992: 29).[47] This is a *minimal* account of truth-aptness, according to Wright, because the truth-aptness of a sentence depends only on surface features: the syntactical form of the sentence (its having "all the overt trappings of assertoric content" (Wright, 1992: 29)), and the disciplined character of the discourse. If these surface features of the sentence and the discourse are present, then the sentence is truth-apt: "if things are in all these surface respects as if assertions are being made, then so they are" (Wright, 1992: 29). So, for example, evaluative statements—such as 'Pre-emptive wars are wrong'—are truth-apt, because the requisite surface features are present. The statement is declarative in form, and evaluative discourse is disciplined—if I change my mind about the statement 'Pre-emptive wars are wrong', I will do so within a framework of standards governing the proper use of the sentence. Ethical expressivists will protest that such evaluative statements are not truth-apt, that they are neither true nor false. Appearances are deceptive, they will say: evaluative sentences do have declarative form, they do have the "trappings of assertoric content", and there are norms governing the proper use of such sentences—yet they are not really truth-apt. But according to disciplined syntacticism, only the appearances matter where truth-aptness is concerned—and it is in this way that disciplined syntacticism is minimal.

Does disciplined syntacticism help the disquotationalist about truth? Clearly, requiring the sentences 's$_1$', 's$_2$', ... to be declarative in form does not introduce the kind of rich concept that might compromise the disquotational account. But the requirement of discipline might seem more troublesome: if the very statement of disquotationalism incorporates the requirement that 's$_1$', 's$_2$', ... be governed by norms of correct use, by "acknowledged standards of proper and improper use", then that might seem to put into question the supposedly presuppositionless character of disquotational truth. Moreover, there are standards of proper use for tongue-twisters and logic examples and other kinds of sentences that are not truth-apt—what is special about the norms or standards governing the use of *truth-apt* sentences? In the same breath in which he speaks of discipline and norms, Wright speaks of assertoric content and the making of assertions. Now, it may be natural enough to treat truth-aptness in terms of assertion, along the lines of "A sentence is truth apt if it can be used to make an assertion." But this treatment seems unavailable to the disquotationalist. Surely disquotationalists will not want to articulate their deflationary theory in terms that include such a rich notion as assertion, especially one which is, as we saw in the previous section, so intimately tied to truth.

There is reason anyway to doubt that disciplined syntacticism provides an adequate account of truth aptness. It can be argued that declarative syntax is not *necessary* for truth-aptness (we have already seen that it is not sufficient).[48] Asked under oath whether he murdered Jones, Smith may reply: "No". If he didn't murder Jones, then what Smith says is true. If he did murder Jones, then what Smith says is false, and

---

[47] As Boghossian puts it, the sentence must be "significant", or, more fully, must "possess a role within the language: its use must be appropriately disciplined by norms of correct utterance" (1990: 163).

[48] Here we are indebted to Porubcansky, 2004.

he has committed perjury. On seeing a Ferrari, I may say: "Expensive car that". Or asked what I bought at the store, I may say: "Two red apples". If it is an expensive car, and if I did buy two red apples, then what I said is true. Our utterances, Smith's and mine, appear to be truth-apt, but they are not declarative in form.[49] We may distinguish between three senses of 'sentence': $sentence_{syntactic}$ (an expression with a certain structure), $sentence_{semantic}$ (an expression which expresses a proposition), and $sentence_{pragmatic}$ (an expression which can by itself be used to perform a certain speech act).[50] Arguably what I said about the car counts as a $sentence_{semantic}$, and what I said about apples counts as a $sentence_{pragmatic}$. Similarly with Smith's sentence. But none of our utterances counts as a $sentence_{syntactic}$. Declarative syntax is unnecessary for truth aptness.[51]

Sentences like Smith's 'No' and my 'Two red apples' pose a problem not only for disciplined syntacticism, but for the disquotationalist too. Though apparently truth apt, these sentences cannot figure in DisquT or the T-sentences—obviously, ' "No" is true if and only if no' is not well-formed. And the problem is compounded by perfectly ordinary truth ascriptions referring to these sentences—for example: "What Smith said in court today was true". Here the disquotationalist faces a dilemma. If 'No' is admitted as truth-apt, then the definiens of DisquT will contain 'What Smith said in court = "No" and no', which is ill-formed. If 'No' is excluded on the grounds that it is not declarative, then we have a run-of-the-mill truth-ascription that the disquotational theory cannot handle.

Perhaps the disquotationalist will point out that Smith's utterance is associated with a declarative sentence, namely 'I did not murder Jones' (and mine with 'That's an expensive car' and 'I bought two red apples'.) What is the nature of this association? One might characterize it in terms of *expressing the same proposition*, or *making the same assertion*. This suggests the following strategy. Accept that there are truth-apt sentences that are not declarative. Do not, however, admit them into DisquT or the T-sentences—admit instead their associated declarative sentences. This removes

---

[49] One would be hard-pressed to say that our utterances, despite appearances, are really declarative. The claim is not supported by evidence in linguistics. For example, syntactically elliptical sentences, like 'Alex does too', cannot usually initiate a discourse. But the sentence fragment 'Two red apples' can—for example, to buy apples from a fruit peddler. (See Stainton, 2000: 448). See Stainton's article for more on sentences and sentence fragments.

[50] Here we follow Stainton, 2000. These three ways of understanding 'sentence' is further refined by Stainton, but the present formulation is sufficient for our purposes.

[51] Jackson, Oppy and Smith argue that disciplined syntacticism does not go far enough (see also Smith, 1994). They contend that it ignores a platitudinous connection between truth-aptness and belief: a sentence counts as truth-apt only if it can be used to give the content of a belief. And since, in their view, any adequate analysis of a concept should comprise all the platitudes about a concept (and nothing more), the connection between truth-aptness and belief cannot be omitted. Their preferred account of truth-aptness, though richer than disciplined syntacticism, will be minimal in the sense that it makes no controversial assumptions—it is composed only of platitudes. It seems, however, that this platitude-respecting minimalism cannot be endorsed by the disqotationalist, or by deflationists generally. As Jackson, Oppy, and Smith themselves point out, platitudes can be substantive. On their account of truth-aptness, in order to show that a sentence is truth-apt it needs to be shown: "that the state an agent is in when she is disposed to utter a sentence . . . bears the relations to information, action and rationality required for the state to count as a belief. This is a substantial matter" (p.296).

the threat of ill-formed instantiations. But now the disquotationalist's restriction is either "*where 's₁', 's₂', ... is a declarative sentence that expresses a proposition*" or "*where 's₁', 's₂', ... is a declarative sentence that makes an assertion*". And the familiar problem is back: disquotational truth is supposed to be a mere logical device, not a concept whose explication requires substantive semantic concepts such as *assertion* or *expressing a proposition*.

Finally, there is a family of sentences that fail to be truth apt in a specially dramatic way. Liar sentences, such as 'This sentence is false', cannot be admitted into the truth-schema, *on pain of contradiction*. It is often presumed that the Liar is as much a problem for the substantivist about truth—the correspondence theorist, for example—as it is for the deflationist.[52] But it can be argued that the correspondence theorist has resources to deal with the Liar that the deflationist does not.[53] For example, the correspondence theorist can accommodate truth value gaps, along the following lines: a sentence is true iff it corresponds to a state of affairs that obtains, false iff it corresponds to a state of affairs that does not obtain, and neither true nor false if it fails to correspond to any state of affairs. But if truth is given by DisquT, and falsity by

DisquF   x is false iff $(x = $ 's₁'$ \& \sim s_1)$ or $(x = $ 's₂'$ \& \sim s_2)$ or ...,

then it follows easily that a sentence s_k is neither true nor false only if it is outside the scope of these definitions (since otherwise we can derive $\sim s_k$ and $\sim\sim s_k$). So it seems there is no room for a sentence to be neither true nor false, except in the attenuated sense that Julius Caesar is neither true nor false. As regards minimalism, Horwich himself notes that the move to propositions seems to close off any appeal to gaps.[54]

But suppose that the disquotationalist can somehow accommodate truth value gaps. Then it might seem that Liar sentences need not compromise DisquT. For where 'L' is a liar sentence, its associated T-sentence

'L' is true iff L

can be counted as true, given that both sides are gappy. Even the truth of Liar sentences, it may seem, is a matter of disquotation. However, the disquotationalist cannot take this tack. We are taking L to be gappy—so the right hand side of the biconditional is gappy. But the left hand side is false: it is false that 'L' is true.[55] This is an instance of a more general problem: given a gappy sentence (whether a Liar sentence, or a vague sentence, perhaps, or some other), the corresponding T-sentence is untrue. In order to maintain the truth of such a T-sentence, we might introduce a *weak* notion of truth, where ' "P" is true' always has the same semantic status as 'P'.[56] (In particular, if 'P' is gappy, so is ' "P" is true'.) The revision theory of truth is a theory of this weak notion.[57] But the disquotationalist cannot ignore the

[52] See, for example, David (1994: 7, 70, 191), and Horwich (1990: 42).
[53] For an extended treatment of deflationary truth and the Liar, see Simmons (1999).
[54] Horwich (1990: 80).   [55] Compare an argument of Dummett's (1959/78: 4).
[56] Gupta and Belnap present this distinction in 1993: 22, citing Yablo, 1985.
[57] See Gupta and Belnap, 1993: 22, 29, and fn52 on p.29.

strong notion of truth, where if we say of a gappy sentence that it's true, we have said something false.[58] A successful deflationism must deflate all truth, weak and strong.

REFERENCES

Bar-On, Dorit, Horisk, Claire, and Lycan, William (1999). 'Deflationism, Meaning and Truth Conditions', *Philosophical Studies*, 101: 1–28.

Bar-On, Dorit, and Simmons, Keith, (forthcoming). 'The Use of Force Against Deflationism: Assertion and Truth'. *Truth and Speech Acts: Studies in the Philosophy of Language*, D. Greimann and G. Siegwart (eds.), Routledge.

Blackburn, Simon, and Simmons, Keith, eds. (1999). *Truth*. Oxford: Oxford University Press.

Boghossian, Paul (1990). 'The Status of Content'. *Philosophical Review*, 99: 157–84.

Brandom, Robert (1994). *Making It Explicit*. Cambridge, Mass.: Harvard University Press.

David, Marian (1994). *Correspondence and Disquotation*. New York: Oxford University Press.

Davidson, Donald (1996/9). 'The Folly of Trying to Define Truth'. *Journal of Philosophy*, 93: 263–79; repr. in Blackburn and Simmons (eds.) 308–22.

——— (1990). 'The Structure and Content of Truth'. *Journal of Philosophy*, 87: 279–328.

Dummett, Michael (1959/78). "Truth". *Proceedings of the Aristotelian Society*, 59: 141–62. Repr. with a postscript in *Truth and Other Enigmas*. Cambridge, Mass.: Harvard University Press, 1–24; page references are to this reprint.

Etchemendy, Jon (1988). 'Tarski on Truth and Logical Consequence'. *Journal of Symbolic Logic*, 53: 51–79.

Field, Hartry (1986). 'The Deflationary Conception of Truth' in G. MacDonald and C. Wright, eds. *Fact, Science and Morality: Essays on A. J. Ayer's* Language, Truth and Logic. Oxford: Blackwell, 55–117.

——— (1999). 'Deflationist Views of Meaning and Content', reprinted in Blackburn and Simmons, 1999, 351–91.

Frege, G. (1892/1960). 'On Sense and Reference'. Translated in Geach, P., and Black, M., eds., 56–78.

——— (1956/99). 'The Thought: A Logical Inquiry'. *Mind*, 65: 289–311 Repr. in Blackburn and Simmons, 1999: 85–105; page references are to this reprint.

——— (1979). *Posthumous Writings*. Oxford: Basil Blackwell.

Grover, D., Camp, J., and Belnap, N. (1975). 'A Prosentential Theory of Truth'. *Philosophical Studies*, 27: 73–125.

Gupta, Anil (1993). 'Minimalism'. In James E. Tomberlin (ed.), *Philosophical Perspectives* vii, *Language and Logic*. Atascadero: Ridgeview Press, 359–69.

——— (1993/9). 'A Critique of Deflationism'. *Philosophical Topics*, 21/2: 57–81. Repr. in Blackburn and Simmons (eds.), 282–307; page references are to this reprint.

Gupta, Anil and Belnap, Nuel (1993). *The Revision Theory of Truth*. Cambridge, Mass.: MIT Press.

Hill, Christopher (2002). *Thought and World*. Cambridge: Cambridge University Press.

Horisk, Claire (forthcoming). 'What Should Deflationism Be When it Grows Up?', *Philosophical Studies*.

Horwich, Paul (1990). *Truth*. Blackwell, Oxford.

——— (1998a). *Truth*. 2nd edn. Blackwell, Oxford.

---

[58] In Simmons (1999), it is argued that the correspondence theory is better equipped than deflationism to deal with strong truth and related strengthened liar paradoxes.

Horwich, Paul (1998b). *Meaning*. Oxford: Oxford University Press.

Jackson, Frank, Oppy, Graham, and Smith, Michael (1994). 'Minimalism and Truth Aptness'. *Mind*, 103 (411): 287–302.

Leeds, Stephen (1978). 'Theories of Reference and Truth,' *Erkenntnis*, 13: 111–129.

Lewis, David (1972). 'General Semantics'. In Davidson, D. and Harman, G., eds., *Semantics of Natural Language*. Dordrecht: D. Reidel.

Lycan, William (1984). *Logical Form in Natural Language*. Cambridge, MA: Bradford Books/MIT Press.

Porubcansky, David (2004). 'Deflationism and Truth Aptness', MA thesis, UNC Chapel Hill.

Quine, W. V. (1970). *Philosophy of Logic*. Prentice Hall: Englewood Cliffs.

Resnik, Michael (1990). 'Immanent Truth'. *Mind* 99 (1990), 405–24.

Rumfitt, Ian (1995). 'Truth Conditions and Communication'. *Mind*, 4: 827–59.

Simmons, Keith (1999). 'Deflationary Truth and the Liar'. *Journal of Philosophical Logic*, 28: 455–88.

——— (forthcoming (a)). 'Tarski's Logic'. *The Handbook of the History and Philosophy of Logic*, vol. 3, J. Woods and D. Gabbay, eds. North-Holland.

——— (forthcoming (b)). 'Deflationism and the Autonomy of Truth', *Philosophy and Phenomenological Research*.

Smith, Michael (1994). "Why Expressivists about Value Should Love Minimalism about Truth". *Analysis*, 54: 1–12.

Soames, Scott (1984). 'What is a Theory of Truth?' *Journal of Philosophy*, 81(8): 411–29.

——— (1999). *Understanding Truth*. Oxford: Oxford University Press.

Stainton, Robert (2000). 'The Meaning of "Sentences"'. *Noûs*, 34(3): 441–54.

Strawson, P. F. (1949). 'Truth'. *Analysis*, 9: 83–97.

Tarski, Alfred (1930–1/1983). 'The Concept of Truth in Formalized Languages', first published in Polish. In *Logic, Semantics, Metamathematics* (2nd edn.), trans. J. H. Woodger. Indianapolis: Hackett, 152–278.

——— (1944). 'The Semantic Conception of Truth and the Foundations of Semantics', *Philosophical and Phenomenological Research*, 4: 342–60. Repr. in Blackburn and Simmons (eds.), 1999, 115–43; page references are to this reprint.

Yablo, Stephen (1985). 'Truth and Reflection', *Journal of Philosophical Logic*, 14: 297–349.

PART VI

··

LINGUISTIC
PHENOMENA

··

CHAPTER 26

COMPOSITIONALITY

JOSH DEVER

THE following English sentence has never before been produced:

Having recently exhumed the vicar's nephew, the stockbroker wistfully contemplated a large wheel of pungent blue cheese.

Nevertheless, any competent speaker will know what it means. What explains our ability to understand sentences we have never before encountered? One natural hypothesis is that those novel sentences are built up out of familiar parts, put together in familiar ways. This hypothesis requires the backing hypothesis that English has a *compositional semantic theory*:

(Compositionality) A language is *compositional* if the meaning of each of its complex expressions are derived from the meanings of its simple expressions.[1]

The backing hypothesis can seem obviously true. A sentence, after all, just *is* a collection of words; how could its meaning not be determined by the meanings of its constituent words?

   Further examples, however, suggest that English may not have a compositional semantics. Consider the phrase 'large wheel of pungent blue cheese' from the above sentence. If English is compositional, then the meaning of this phrase should be determined by the meanings of its parts. But getting the meaning of 'large cheese' (to simplify a bit) out of the meanings of 'large' and 'cheese' is not straightforward. Appropriate standards of largeness vary depending on the type of object in question. What's large for a cheese may be quite small for a person.[2] It's thus hard to see how the right reading for 'large cheese' could be derived by combining independent

---

[1] This is only a rough sketch of compositionality; see Section 26.1 for a more careful formulation of the principle.

[2] The Octuple Gloucester of Pynchon (1997) notwithstanding.

meanings for 'large' and 'cheese'. Another way of putting the problem: saying that Sveto is a large man cannot amount to saying that he is large and he is a man, because he can be a large man and a sumo wrestler without also being a large sumo wrestler.[3]

On the other hand, while these examples of *non-intersective adjectives* raise problems for compositionality, those problems are not obviously insuperable. While the meaning of 'large cheese' cannot be built from the meanings of 'large' and 'cheese' in one way—through conjunction, or set intersection—it can be in another way. Suppose that:

$$[[\text{cheese}]] = \{x : x \text{ is a cheese}\}$$

$$[[\text{large}]] = f, f(X) = \{x \in X : x \text{ is larger than the average size of } X\}$$

Then the meaning of 'large cheese' can be derived from $[[\text{large}]]$ and $[[\text{cheese}]]$ through functional application, which yields the set of all cheeses above average in size. The same procedure allows Sveto to be a large man without thereby also being a large sumo wrestler. Compositionality is achieved, at the price of a slight complication of the lexical semantics.

Other difficult cases for compositionality abound, as do attempts to deal with those difficulties. The question of whether natural languages have compositional semantics continues to attract considerable interest, as do questions about the reasons for wanting compositionality, the consequences of compositionality, and the very formulation of the principle of compositionality. This overview begins, in Section 26.1, by developing a precise definition of compositionality. In Section 26.2 some technical consequences of that definition are explored. Section 26.3 examines two compositionally problematic semantic phenomena, and proposed compositional treatments thereof. Section 26.4 closes by asking why one might *want* a compositional meaning theory, and attempting to explain the philosophical significance of compositionality.

26.1 What is Compositionality?

Compositionality is a tool for limiting what can be relevant to determining the meaning of a complex expression. As such, it represents the simultaneous imposition of two constraints:

(Semantic Closure) Only semantic information can go into the determination of the semantic value of a complex expression.

(Semantic Locality) Only information derived from parts of a complex expression can go into the determination of the semantic value of that expression.

---

[3] The reasoning proceeds as follows:
1. Sveto is a large man and a sumo wrestler.
2. Therefore, Sveto is large and a man and a sumo wrestler (by the proposed analysis of 'large X').
3. Therefore, Sveto is large and a sumo wrestler and a man (by the commutivity of 'and').
4. Therefore, Sveto is large and a sumo wrestler (by 'and' elimination).
5. Therefore, Sveto is a large sumo wrestler (again by the proposed analysis of 'large X').

Semantic Closure prevents, for example, the meaning of:

(1) Lois Lane believes that Superman can fly.

from being determined in part by the *word* 'Superman' (its phonetic, morphological, historical-causal[4] properties, etc.), rather than the *meaning* of the word 'Superman' (whatever that meaning turns out to be).[5] Semantic Locality, on the other hand, prevents the meaning of the occurrence of 'Superman can fly' in (1) from being a function of (perhaps among other things) the meaning of 'believes'. Combining Semantic Closure and Semantic Locality yields Compositionality—the requirement that the meaning of a complex expression be determined by the meanings of its parts.

Making this requirement more precise requires clarifying the notion of *determination*. Two versions of determination dominate discussion of compositionality: the *functional* analysis and the *substitutional* analysis.[6]

26.1.1 Compositionality as Functionality

The heart of the functional conception of compositionality is the requirement that the meaning of a complex expression be a function of the meanings of the parts of that syntactic expression and their mode of composition. We give a rather complex implementation of this simple idea. Suppose that, for any language **L**, we have function $[[\cdot]]_L$ mapping from **L** to some set **M** of meanings and a collection of (syntactic formation) functions $\delta_n : \mathbf{L}^{m_n} \mapsto \mathbf{L}$.[7] Then we say:

A meaning theory $[[\cdot]]$ for language **L** is compositional relative to (i) a class $\mathbf{L}^+$ of extensions of **L**, (ii) a parthood relation $\sqsubseteq_{L_i}$ for each $L_i \in \mathbf{L}^+$, where the parthood relations for the extensions in $\mathbf{L}^+$ agree on **L**, (iii) a level of structural analysis $\{\delta_{n_\epsilon}(\theta_\epsilon^1, \ldots, \theta_\epsilon^{m_\epsilon}) | \epsilon \in \mathbb{L}_i\}$ for each $L_i \in \mathbf{L}^+$, where the θ_ϵ^i's are $\sqsubseteq_{L_i}$-parts of ϵ, and where the levels of structural analysis agree on **L**, and (iv) a class G^+ of functions if for each $L_i \in \mathbf{L}^+$ there is some function $G_i \in G^+$ such that for all $\epsilon \in \mathbb{L}_i$, $[[\epsilon]]_{L_i} = G(\langle \delta_\epsilon^2, [[\theta_\epsilon^1]]_{L_i}, \ldots, [[\epsilon_\epsilon^{m_\epsilon}]]_{L_i}\rangle)$, and the G_i's agree on **L**.

We thus have a four-fold relativized notion of compositionality—a language can be compositional relative to a parthood relation, a level of structural analysis, a collection of possible extensions of the language, and a range of admissible meaning

---

[4] See the conception of words defended in Kaplan (1990).

[5] Assuming, of course, that the word 'Superman', or its phonetic, morphological, historical-causal, etc. properties are not part of the semantics of 'Superman'.

[6] See Szabo (2000b) and Szabo (2000a) for an excellent discussion of these two notions of compositionality. Szabo formulates compositionality as a supervenience principle, and then employs Kim's distinction between weak and strong supervenience (see Kim (1983)) to argue for a strengthened conception of compositionality. The current discussion treats compositionality as a weak supervenience principle, and discusses some of Szabo's arguments for the move to strong supervenience. See Dever (2003) for further discussion of Szabo's use of supervenience.

[7] In order to maximize generality, no constraint is placed on the set **M**. Thus, for example, in a bilevel Fregean semantic theory compositionality constraints could be imposed separately on each level, by taking **M** first to be the set of referents and second to be the set of senses. Semantic compositionality thus falls into a genre of mereological reducibility.

composition functions. Each dimension of relativization responds to a shortcoming of or objection to the simple heart of the functional conception:

1. The parthood relation ⊑ will typically be given by the syntactic theory, but need not be.[8] A syntactic theory may deliver multiple candidate parthood relations, though—do we require compositionality at the level of deep structure or of surface structure? At LF or PF, or some combination of the two, in a minimalist syntax? Relativization to a choice of ⊑ allows the core theory of compositionality to avoid the need to take a stand on such questions.

2. A complex expression can typically be given syntactic analysis at varying levels of detail. Suppose:

(2) Some philosopher fears Socrates
receives the rather flat-footed syntactic analysis:

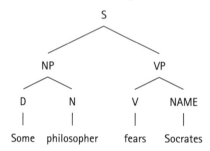

At one level of analysis, (2) is the result of applying a syntactic function δ_1 to parts $[_{NP} [_D$ some$] [_N$ philosopher $]]$ and $[_{VP} [_V$ fears $] [_{NAME}$ Socrates $]]$. At another, finer-grained level, it results from applying a different function δ_2 to the parts $[_D$ some$]$, $[_N$ philosopher $]$, $[_V$ fears $]$, and $[_{NAME}$ Socrates $]$.[9] By selecting the level of syntactic analysis, we can distinguish between:

(Strong Compositionality) L is *strongly compositional* if every expression has a coarsest non-trivial syntactic analysis, and the meaning of every expression is a function of the meanings of the meanings of its parts and their mode of combination, under that coarsest analysis.[10]

(Weak Compositionality) L is *weakly compositional* if every expression has a finest syntactic analysis, and the meaning of every expression is a function of the meanings of the meanings of its parts and their mode of combination, under that finest analysis.

Suppose, for example, that the semantic value of a definite description were its denotation. Then a strongly compositional theory would be committed to the equivalence of:

---

[8] Note that any language is compositional under *some* parthood relation. Minimally, we want ⊑ not to be reflexive.

[9] I assume throughout that every expression receives only unambiguous parthood analyses, even if analyses are available at multiple levels of grain. See Pelletier (1999) for an argument that ambiguity blocks the possibility of compositional semantics, Fernando (1997) and Fernando (2001) for attempts to show how ambiguity and compositionality can be combined, and Westerstahl for mathematical examination of notions of compositionality designed to take ambiguity into account.

[10] This definition is equivalent to Larson (1995)'s notion of strong compositionality.

(3) In 1983, the President of the United States was named Ronald.

(4) In 1983, the son of George Herbert Walker Bush was named Ronald.

since [[the President of the United States]] = [[the son of George Herbert Walker Bush]] = George Walker Bush, and since the behaviour of the sentence must be determined by the semantic values of its immediate constituents. A weakly compositional theory, however, could appeal to semantic differences among the components of the definite descriptions ('President', 'George Herbert Walker Bush', etc.) to ground a semantic difference between (3) and (4).[11]

A language which is compositional at one level of analysis is compositional under any finer-grained level of analysis; hence strong compositionality is indeed stronger than weak compositionality.

3. An immediate consequence of a simple functional analysis of compositionality is that if a language contains no synonyms, it is trivially compositional.[12] This fact makes functional compositionality appear undesirably weak. Consider the language *Lenglish*—a synonym-free fragment of English, with the idiosyncracy that, given any expression ϵ occurring in a sentence containing the letter K, $[[\epsilon]] = T$. Lenglish should be wildly noncompositional, but it meets the simple functional requirement.

The undesirable result can be avoided through a richer conception of *function*. The above assumes that $[[\cdot]]$ is given in extension, but the nature of our semantic competence suggests that meaning functions are in fact given in intension. Semantic mastery of a language extends to the ability to determine what the meanings of complex expressions of the language *would be*, were they to include (at least some) newly introduced lexical items of specified meaning. We thus model the desired intensionality by considering a class of extensions of the base language. Lenglish fails of compositionality in natural extensions containing synonyms.[13]

4. Suppose (following an objection raised by Szabo in Szabo (2000b) and Szabo (2000a), we form a language L' identical to English, except that the meanings of the sentences:

(5) Elephants are gray.

(6) Julius Caesar was murdered on the ides of March

are swapped. If English is (functionally) compositional, so is L', via composition of the English meaning function with a simple permutation function. We might,

---

[11] Since (3) and (4) are clearly not equivalent, strong compositional theories have reason not to use denotation as the semantic value of a definite description.

[12] See Westerstahl (1998) for a brief note of this fact, and Szabo (2000b) for an argument that it shows that the functional approach does not capture the principle of compositionality.

[13] Every language will be noncompositional relative to some class of extensions, so the crucial point is what classes of extensions matter to compositionality considerations. Speakers' semantic mastery provides one natural class of extensions—consisting of extensions in which new lexical items are introduced in existing syntactic categories, with meanings appropriate for those categories, and integrate into complex expressions in accordance with the intensionally given meaning functions of the core language—but whether this class is the right one to consider depends on why one is interested in compositionality.

however, want to call L' noncompositional, perhaps feeling the meaning of 'Julius Caesar was murdered on the ides of March' simply cannot be built out of the meanings of 'elephant' and 'gray' and a few simple syntactic rules. While you may be able to make an omelette from eggs and milk using one recipe (language) and a crème brûlée from the same ingredients using another recipe, there is no recipe for making roast venison from those ingredients—eggs and milk simply don't combine in that way, no matter what you do with them. Similarly, perhaps there's just no way to combine large African land mammals and shades of gray to produce a claim about the murder of a Roman general.

We thus require that the function G, determining the meaning of a complex expression from the meanings of its parts, be drawn from a class G^+ of permissible functions, and relativize the definition of compositionality to a choice of G^+. By making G^+ small, a quite strong notion of compositionality can be determined. If G^+ contains only the technique of functional application, so that $G(\langle \delta, [\![\epsilon_1]\!], [\![\epsilon_2]\!]\rangle)) = [\![\epsilon_1]\!]([\![\epsilon_2]\!])$, where $G \in G^+$, then the corresponding compositionality constraint requires semantics to be done in a Montagovian style. If G^+ contains only functions which extend mereological fusion, the result is what Szabo in Szabo (2000a) calls *strong parallelism*—the view, endorsed by Frege for senses, that the meaning of a complex contains the meanings of its parts as parts.[14]

The functional conception of compositionality is frequently connected to the idea of a *homomorphism*. Assuming that the parthood relation $\sqsubseteq$ reflects a collection Δ of syntactic constructions, compositionality acts as a requirement that semantic interpretation closely track syntactic form. Suppose that complex expressions in **L** are built up via applications of two syntactic rules: one of predication of a verb phrase to a subject, and one of adjectival modification of a subject. Then there ought to be two corresponding semantic rules: one determining the meaning of a sentence from the meanings of its component verb phrase and subject, and one determining the meaning of a complex subject from the meanings of its component adjective and subject. More generally, the relation between syntax and semantics is given by what Bach (1976) calls the *rule to rule hypothesis*:

(R-R) Given **L** with syntactic rules Δ and meaning function μ, there is a set $\Gamma = \{\gamma_\delta : \delta \in \Delta\}$ of functions such that if $\epsilon \in \mathbb{L}$ is the result of applying some δ to some $\epsilon_1, \ldots \epsilon_n$, then $\mu(\epsilon) = \gamma_\delta(\mu(\epsilon_1), \ldots, \mu(\epsilon_n))$.

Taking the syntax and the semantics of **L** as algebras (of expressions in one case, of meanings in the other) generated by operations (syntactic construction rules in the one case, semantic composition procedures in the other case), the rule-to-rule hypothesis requires that there be a homomorphism between the two algebras preserving the structure imposed by the operations of each.[15]

---

[14] See, for example, Frege (1997), 127.
[15] See Montague (1970), Janssen (1986), Hendriks (1993), Zadrozny (1994), Janssen (1997), and Westerstahl (1998) for examples of this approach.

Compositionality in the simple functional sense of the previous section and in the homomorphism sense are trivially equivalent constraints. Suppose L is compositional in the homomorphism sense. Define $G(\langle \delta, \mu(\epsilon_1), \ldots, \mu(\epsilon_n) \rangle) = \gamma_\delta(\mu(\epsilon_1), \ldots, \mu(\epsilon_n))$, and G is a composition function for all of L. If, on the other hand, L has a composition function G, then define, for each $\delta \in \Delta$, $\gamma_\delta(\mu(\epsilon_1), \ldots, \mu(\epsilon_n)) = G(\langle \delta, \mu(\epsilon_1), \ldots, \mu(\epsilon_n) \rangle)$.[16]

26.1.2 Compositionality as Substitutability

Suppose Lex Luthor believes Superman is harmed by Kryptonite, but does not believe Clark Kent is harmed by Kryptonite. Then if [[Superman]] = [[Clark Kent]], compositionality has a problem. The two sentences:

(7) Lex Luthor believes Superman is harmed by Kryptonite.
(8) Lex Luthor believes Clark Kent is harmed by Kryptonite.

have different truth-values, and hence on almost any semantic theory also have different meanings. But, other than the substitution of 'Clark Kent' for 'Superman', they are made of the same parts in the same way,[17] and the two parts 'Superman' and 'Clark Kent' have the same meaning. Thus the two sentences are made in the same way of parts of the same meaning, and ought, if compositionality holds, to be synonymous. A language in which they are not synonymous, then, cannot be a compositional one.[18]

More generally, suppose language L has two expressions ϵ_1 and ϵ_2 with the same meanings, and two complex expressions E_1 and E_2 which differ only in that some occurrences of ϵ_1 in E_1 have been replaced with occurrences of ϵ_2 in E_2, and which are such that $\mu(E_1) \neq \mu(E_2)$. Then E_1 and E_2 are constructed in the same way out of parts with the same meaning, and since they are not synonymous, L is not compositional. This suggests the following alternative definition of compositionality:

A meaning theory $[[\cdot]]$ for language L is compositional iff for all complex expressions ϵ_1, ϵ_2 such that $\epsilon_1 = \delta(\eta_1, \ldots, \eta_n)$ and $\epsilon_2 = \delta(\theta_1, \ldots, \theta_n)$, where for each i $[[\eta_i]] = [[\theta_i]]$, we have $[[\epsilon_1]] = [[\epsilon_2]]$.

A language is compositional, that is, if substitution of synonyms always preserves synonymy.[19]

---

[16] See Theorem 4 of Hodges (2001) for a more precise statement of this result.
[17] This can be denied. Triadic theories of attitude verbs typically take sentences like (7) and (8) to contain additional semantic information (some sort of guise or mode of presentation) which is not syntactically overt, and which differs between (these occurrences of) the two sentences.
[18] Partly for this reason Millians are under pressure to accept that proper names intersubstitute *salva significatio* in propositional attitude contexts.
[19] Some care is needed in specifying what counts as the substitution of synonyms. Szabo (Szabo (2000b), 16–18) gives the example of the prima facie synonymous sentences:

(9) Plato was bald.
(10) Baldness was an attribute of Plato.

Like the functional definition of compositionality, the substitutional definition can be relativized to a parthood relation, a level of structural analysis, and a collection of possible extensions of the language. Relativization to a range of admissible meaning functions, however, comes less naturally to the substitutional definition. Abstracting away from the various dimensions of relativization, the functional and substitutional definitions turn out to be equivalent:

Functionalism implies substitutionalism: Suppose L is compositional in the functional sense, and let $\Sigma(\alpha)$, $\Sigma(\beta)$ differ only by substitution of α with the synonymous β. Some function G gives the meanings of both $\Sigma(\alpha)$ and $\Sigma(\beta)$ from the meanings of their parts and their syntactic structure. But by assumption, each has the same syntactic structure, and each has parts of the same meaning, so G must assign to each the same meaning. Thus substitution of synonyms preserves synonymy.

Substitutionalism implies functionalism: Suppose L is compositional in the substitutional sense. Suppose L were not compositional in the functional sense. Then there would be some syntactic rule and some collection of part meanings such that two different expressions formed from those part meanings had different meanings. Let $\Sigma(\alpha)$ and $\Sigma(\beta)$ be two such expressions.[20] Then α and β have the same meaning, but $\Sigma(\alpha)$ and $\Sigma(\beta)$ do not, violating substitutional compositionality. Thus L is compositional in the functional sense.[21]

26.2 THE MATHEMATICS
OF COMPOSITIONALITY

With a precise definition of compositionality in hand, we consider the implications of that definition. Before turning to the empirical, in §3 below, we begin with some *a priori* issues. First we examine arguments suggesting that compositionality is a surprisingly weak constraint, one that any meaning theory can meet. Next we turn to an argument in the other direction, one claiming that compositionality is a surprisingly strong constraint—one which (under minimal assumptions) fixes the meanings of all subsentential expressions in a language.

which do not always preserve meaning when one is replaced for the other, as in:

(11)   The philosopher whose most eminent pupil was Plato was bald.
(12)   The philosopher whose must eminent pupil was baldness was an attribute of Plato.

If the substitutional conception of compositionality is to be a reasonable one, it must not count (12) as a substitution instance of (11) with (9) swapped for (10). Substitution thus cannot be simple replacement of strings of words, but must respect syntactic structure.

[20]   This step illicitly supposes that the two expressions differ only by intersubstitution of a *single* pair of synonymous parts. A more careful approach would either define substitutionalism to allow replacement of arbitrary numbers of synonymous parts, or add additional assumptions in the manner of Hodges (2001) to guarantee that large-scale substitutions could be achieved by a sequence of single-pair substitutions.

[21]   See Hodges (2001), Theorem 4, for more precise versions of each direction of this proof.

26.2.1 The Weakness of Compositionality

Given the substitutional construal of compositionality, it is a simple matter to construct a noncompositional meaning theory—simply assign the same meaning to two lexical items, and different meanings to two complex expressions differing only via intersubstitution of the now-synonymous lexical items. Despite the ready availability of non-compositional semantic theories, some recent work has claimed that compositionality is a trivial requirement, typically in the sense that all possible languages *can be made* compositional. Making a language compositional involves changing its meaning function in some way to achieve compositionality; care is needed here to distinguish between adapting an existing meaning theory and giving a wholly new meaning theory (the latter of which can, of course, always be done compositionality). Since compositionality requires that three factors—the meanings of atoms, the meanings of complexes, and the parthood relation between atoms and complexes—be properly aligned, there are correspondingly three ways of making a meaning theory compositional. We set out one of these three ways in detail, and then sketch the thought behind the other two.

1. **Tinkering with the Bottom:** Let L be an arbitrary language, consisting of a set $\mathbb{L}$ of expressions closed under the syntactic operation of concatenation.[22] Suppose $[[\cdot]]$ is a meaning function, assigning members of $\mathbb{L}$ to various meanings. $[[\cdot]]$ can be wholly arbitrary, and as noncompositional as desired. Nevertheless, Zadrozny, in Zadrozny (1994), claims that L can be given a compositional analysis, and that, more generally:

   We can prove a theorem stating that any semantics can be encoded as a compositional semantics, which means that, essentially, the standard definition of compositionality is formally vacuous. (Zadrozny (1994), 329)

   How is this possible? Consider a small example using a minimally noncompositional language. Let L contain atomic elements a, b, and c, and the following meaning theory:

$$[[a]] = 1$$
$$[[b]] = 1$$
$$[[c]] = 2$$
$$[[a \frown c]] = 3$$
$$[[b \frown c]] = 4$$

   L thus fails the substitution test, and is not compositional. Zadrozny, however, gives us a procedure for producing a compositional meaning function μ "which agrees with the function $[\,[[\cdot]]\,]$" (Zadrozny (1994), 330). Zadrozny's μ function

---

[22] I follow Zadrozny (1994) in imposing an inessential restriction to languages with only a single syntactic operation.

satisfies the following two constraints:

$$\text{For all } \epsilon, \mu(\epsilon)(\epsilon) = [[\epsilon]]$$
$$\text{For all } \epsilon, \eta, \mu(\epsilon \frown \eta) = \mu(\epsilon)(\mu(\eta))$$

The first constraint gives the promised agreement with $[[\cdot]]$, while the second gives compositionality. Finding μ is then a matter of solving a system of equations:

$$\mu(a) = \{\langle a, 1 \rangle, \langle \mu(c), \mu(a \frown c) \rangle\}$$
$$\mu(b) = \{\langle b, 1 \rangle, \langle \mu(c), \mu(b \frown c) \rangle\}$$
$$\mu(c) = \{\langle c, 2 \rangle\}$$
$$\mu(a \frown c) = \{\langle a \frown c, 3 \rangle\}$$
$$\mu(b \frown c) = \{\langle b \frown c, 4 \rangle\}$$

The two unsolved terms resolve to:

$$\mu(a) = \{\langle a, 1 \rangle, \langle \{\langle c, 2 \rangle\}, \{\langle a \frown c, 3 \rangle\}\rangle\}$$
$$\mu(b) = \{\langle b, 1 \rangle, \langle \{\langle c, 2 \rangle\}, \{\langle b \frown c, 4 \rangle\}\rangle\}$$

The resulting μ meets both the agreement and the compositionality constraints. More generally, μ is constructed from $[[\cdot]]$ by solving the set of simultaneous equations given by $\mu(\epsilon) = \{\langle \epsilon, [[\epsilon]]\rangle\} \cup \{\langle \mu(\eta), \mu(\epsilon \frown \eta)\rangle\} : \epsilon \frown \eta \in \mathbb{L}\}$.[23]

The compositional μ function matches the noncompositional $[[\cdot]]$ function in that μ, when applied to an expression ϵ produces not the $[[\cdot]]$-meaning of ϵ, but another function which, when *it* is applied to ϵ, produces $[[\epsilon]]$. Thus, in the above example, $\mu(\epsilon) \neq [[\epsilon]]$ for every expression in the language. The resulting sense of "agreement" is thin, and fails to preserve synonymies—$[[a]] = [[b]]$, but $\mu(a) \neq \mu(b)$. In fact, the construction of μ guarantees that no distinct terms of a language L have the same μ-meaning. But if μ allows no synonymies, then it is trivially compositional by way of satisfying the substitution test. Once this point is seen, it becomes obvious that there are many ways of building a μ which (a) is compositional and (b) allows extraction of $[[\cdot]]$-meanings. For example:

Define $\mu(\epsilon) = \{\langle \eta, [[\eta]]\rangle : \eta \in \mathbb{L}\}$ for all $\epsilon \in \mathbb{L}$. Then the μ-meaning of each term in the language encodes the $[[\cdot]]$-meanings of every term and compositionality is trivial.

Define $\mu(\epsilon) = \langle [[\epsilon]], \epsilon \rangle$. Encoding of $[[\cdot]]$-meanings is obvious, and compositionality is guaranteed because no expressions are μ-synonymous.[24]

If part meanings can be set *however* one pleases (and requiring that some pretheoretic part meanings be *somehow or other* encoded in the theoretically dictated part meanings represents no significant deviation from perfect freedom), then

---

[23] A solution is always available in the set theory AFA, with an anti-foundation axiom (see, e.g. Aczel (1987) for formal details on AFA). The use of AFA is essential for Zadrozny's result—the system of equations lack a solution in ZFC if L has two elements which can be concatenated in either order—but the generalizations of Zadrozny's result discussed below do not require AFA.

[24] See Dever (1999) for more details on alternative ways of producing Zadrozny's result.

achieving compositionality is no trick. Apparently noncompositional behaviour at higher levels can be finessed by 'value loading' lexical items with information about the desired semantic behaviour of complexes formed out of them.[25] If, however, the meaning function must meet significant constraints on the meanings of the atoms, then this route to cheap compositionality is blocked.[26,27]

2. **Tinkering with the Top**: Consider a syntax L, complete with atomic and complex expressions and a parthood relation between the two. Suppose you are given meanings for all of L's atomic expressions, but are told that the meanings of the complex expressions are entirely up to you, and then are asked to give a compositional meaning theory for all of L. Under these conditions, your task is trivial. Since compositionality requires properly aligning part meanings and complex meanings via parthood structure, and since one variable in this equation has been left unconstrained, solutions abound. For example, you could assign the same meaning to every complex expression, guaranteeing satisfaction of the substitution principle. Given complete freedom to set the meanings of complexes, those meanings can always be made functions of any meanings of atomic expressions. Complete freedom to tinker at the top, then, gives a clear case in which compositionality places no constraint on meanings—as before, compositionality is a tug-of-war between the meanings of parts and the meanings of complexes, and if one side lets go the rope, the war is easily won. The formal point is straightforward, but it also threatens to be uninteresting. One cannot, in general, construct a useful semantic theory via utter indifference to the meanings of complex expressions.

Because pre-theoretic views on the meanings of sentences are typically more robust than those on the meanings of individual words, tinkering with the top is not a common strategy for achieving compositionality. Arguably Horwich's claim that 'the compositionality of meaning places no constraint at all on how the meaning properties of *words* are constituted' (Horwich (1998), 154) rests on such tinkering, backed by a minimalist view of sentence meaning evidenced in comments such as 'once one has worked out how a certain sentence is constructed from primitive elements, and provided one knows the meanings of those elements, then, automatically and without further ado, one qualifies as understanding the sentence' (Horwich (1998), 155). The more common interpretation, however, is that Horwich fails to account for the

---

[25] Thus, for example, if even a single lexical item is left wholly unconstrained in its meaning, then a semantic theory can be given such that all sentences which have that lexical item as a part behave compositionally, just by having that item carry case-by-case instructions on what each sentence is to mean. Value loading, of coarse, need not be so crude, and is not always inappropriate in a semantic theory. The proposal in the introduction for treating 'large' as a function from $\overline{N}$ extensions to extensions is a more refined version of value-loading, with 'large' carrying upward instructions on how to interact with different modified nouns.

[26] One obvious example: if the meaning function is required to respect pretheoretic judgements of synonymy, then compositionality is impossible if the distribution of such pretheoretic judgements violates the substitution principle.

[27] See Dever (1999), Janssen (1997) Kazmi (1998), and Westerstahl (1998) for additional discussion of Zadrozny.

role of the variable mode of composition in determining the meaning of the sentence.[28]

3. **Tinkering in Between:** Let L be a language with expressions $\mathbb{L}$ and a fixed meaning function μ. If the parthood relation $\sqsubseteq$ is subject to no pretheoretic constraints, then it can always be chosen so as to make L compositional.[29] Most trivially, this can be done by setting $\sqsubseteq$ to be the identity relation on $\mathbb{L}^2$. Alternatively, $\sqsubseteq$ can be chosen in any way such that no two expressions have the same parts. Pretheoretic judgements about parthood can be partially respected: suppose that associated with each expression ϵ are two sets $\sqsubseteq_\epsilon^+$ and $\sqsubseteq_\epsilon^-$ of expressions which, pretheoretically, are and are not (respectively) parts of ϵ. If, for all $\epsilon \in \mathbb{L}$, $|\{\eta : \sqsubseteq_\epsilon^+ = \sqsubseteq_\eta^+ \wedge \sqsubseteq_\epsilon^- = \sqsubseteq_\eta^-| \leq |\mathbb{L}| - |\sqsubseteq_\epsilon^+ \cup \sqsubseteq_\epsilon^-|$, then the pretheoretically given constraints on parthood can always be extended to a parthood relation $\sqsubseteq$ making the language compositional. If L is allowed to contain an arbitrary set of expressions whose $\sqsubseteq$-behaviour is unconstrained by pretheoretic judgements (corresponding, perhaps, to theoretical entities of syntax), then $\sqsubseteq$ can *always* be chosen to make L compositional.

Compositionality marks the convergence of three components of a semantic theory: the assignment of meaning to the parts, the assignment of meaning to the complexes, and the parthood relation between parts and complexes. It is thus only as stringent a requirement as the prior constraints on these three components are robust. Should any of the three be arbitrary (i.e. available for free choice by the theory constructor), then the satisfaction of compositionality is no task. If the intended use of the principle of compositionality is as a tool to *choose among* a range of otherwise acceptable semantic theories, then that range of theories needs to be dictated by rich views, from whatever source, on what sentences mean, what words mean, and what the grammar of the language is.

26.2.2 The Strength of Compositionality

Having seen the weakness of the compositionality constraint in the ways in which it can be trivially satisfied, we now examine the strength of that constraint by setting out a surprising consequence of it due to Hodges (Hodges (1997)).[30] Suppose we have a set $\mathbb{L}$ of expressions, and two meaning functions μ_1 and μ_2 whose domains are

---

[28] For more detailed criticisms of Horwich's views on trivial compositionality, see Fodor (2001) and Heck (2003).

[29] See Janssen (1997) and Janssen (1986). Janssen proves the stronger result that if the parthood relation is recursively enumerable and the meaning theory m is computable, then the composition function is also computable.

[30] The following discussion is a simplified presentation of Hodges' results. The main point of simplification is that I ride roughshod throughout over Hodges' distinction between *compositional* and *1-compositional*. The two are equivalent under the assumption that the meaning functions meet a condition Hodges calls being *Husserlian*. I thus simply presuppose (rather unjustly, given Hodges' care in highlighting the importance of the condition) that all meaning functions are involved are Husserlian.

(possibly improper) subsets of $\mathbb{L}$. μ_1 and μ_2 can thus be thought of as specifying two languages whose expressions are drawn from, but may not exhaust, $\mathbb{L}$. Then μ_2 is a *Fregean cover* of μ_1 if the following two conditions are met:

1. If $\mu_2(\epsilon) = \mu_2(\tau)$ then $\Sigma(\epsilon)$ is in the domain of μ_1 iff $\Sigma(\tau)$ is, and if both are, then $\mu_1(\Sigma(\epsilon)) = \mu_1(\Sigma(\tau))$. ($\mu_2$-synonyms are μ_1-intersubstitutable; hence μ_1 is 'almost' compositional; μ_1-meanings of complexes are functions of μ_2-meanings of parts.)

2. If $\mu_2(\epsilon) \neq \mu_2(\tau)$, then either:

   There is some Σ such that $\Sigma(\epsilon)$ is μ_1-meaningful and $\Sigma(\tau)$ is not, or vice-versa. or:

   There is some Σ such that $\Sigma(\epsilon)$ and $\Sigma(\tau)$ are both μ_1-meaningful but $\mu_1(\Sigma(\epsilon)) \neq \mu_1(\Sigma(\tau))$

   Terms differ in μ_2-meaning only if complex terms which differ only by substitution of the starting terms themselves differ in μ_1-behaviour; this is intended to be a version of Frege's Context Principle:

   never to ask for the meaning of a word in isolation, but only in the context of a proposition. (Frege, (1980), x)[31]

A Fregean cover of a meaning function μ is another meaning function which assigns two expressions different meanings when and only when intersubstitution instances of those two expressions differ in μ-meaning. Suppose, for example, that μ assigns meanings to all of the sentences in $\mathbb{L}$. A Fregean cover of μ whose domain included subsentential expressions of $\mathbb{L}$ would treat subsentential meanings as driven by the need to *account* for the sentential data, assigning different subsentential meanings only when there was a corresponding difference in sentential behaviour.

Fregean covers are always compositional. Suppose μ_2 is a Fregean cover of μ_1. Then if μ_2 violates the substitution principle, $\mu(\epsilon) = \mu_2(\tau)$ and $\mu_2(\Sigma(\epsilon)) \neq \mu_2(\Sigma(\tau))$ for some ϵ, τ, and Σ. But then, since μ_2 is a Fregean cover, there must be some larger context Ω such that $\mu_1(\Omega(\Sigma(\epsilon)) \neq \mu_1(\Omega(\Sigma(\tau))$ (or one of the two is not in the domain of μ_1). But terms synonymous under a Fregean cover must be intersubstitutable according to the covered meaning function, so this is a contradiction. Thus μ_2 is compositional.

Every meaning function has a Fregean cover. Let μ_1 be an arbitrary meaning function on a subset D_1 of language $\mathbb{L}$. Call ϵ and τ *co-categorical* if $\Sigma(\epsilon)$ is μ_1-meaningful iff $\Sigma(\tau)$ is. Then define μ_2 as follows:

$\mu_2(\epsilon) = \{\tau : \tau$ and ϵ are co-categorical for μ_1 and $\mu_1(\Sigma(\epsilon)) = \mu_1(\Sigma(\tau))$ whenever $\Sigma(\epsilon)$ is in $D_1\}$

---

[31] The context principle is frequently taken to be in tension with, the principle of compositionality, because it suggests that meanings of wholes are prior to meanings of parts, and thereby threatens to make nonsense of the compositional idea that meanings of wholes are built out of meanings of parts. See Dummett (1973), 3-5 for one influential attempt to reconcile Frege's apparent commitment to both context and compositionality, and Pelletier (2001) and Janssen (2001) for more recent discussions.

Then μ_2 is a Fregean cover for μ_1:

Suppose $\mu_2(\epsilon) = \mu_2(\tau)$, and $\Sigma(\epsilon)$ is in D_1. $\epsilon \in \mu_2(\epsilon) = \mu_2(\tau)$, so ϵ and τ are co-categorical. Thus $\Sigma(\tau)$ is in D_1. By construction, $\mu_1(\Sigma(\epsilon)) = \mu_1(\Sigma(\tau))$.
Suppose $\mu_2(\epsilon) \neq \mu_2(\tau)$. Then there is some $\eta \in \mu_2(\epsilon)$ but not $\eta \in \mu_2(\tau)$ (or vice-versa). Then either η and τ are not co-categorical for μ_1, or there is some Σ such that $\mu_1(\Sigma(\tau)) \neq \mu_1(\Sigma(\eta))$.

— If the former, then ϵ and τ are not co-categorical for μ_1 and there is some Σ such that $\Sigma(\epsilon)$ and $\Sigma(\tau)$ are not both μ_1-meaningful.
— If the latter, then since $\mu_1(\Sigma(\eta)) = \mu_1(\Sigma(\epsilon))$, we have $\mu_1(\Sigma(\epsilon)) \neq \mu_1(\Sigma(\tau))$.

In either case, μ_2 meets the requirements for a Fregean cover.

A Fregean cover for a given μ, however, need bear little similarity to μ. Suppose μ is a meaning function defined on a subset of the closure of a, b, c, and d under concatenation, fully characterized by:

$\mu(a \frown b) = 1$ 　　 $\mu(a \frown d) = 2$ 　　 $\mu(c \frown b) = 2$
$\mu(c \frown d) = 1$ 　　 $\mu((a \frown b) \frown b) = 3$ 　　 $\mu((a \frown b) \frown d) = 3$
$\mu((a \frown d) \frown b) = 4$ 　 $\mu((a \frown d) \frown d) = 5$ 　 $\mu((c \frown b) \frown b) = 4$
$\mu((c \frown b) \frown d) = 5$ 　 $\mu((c \frown d) \frown b) = 3$ 　 $\mu((c \frown d) \frown d) = 5$

Constructing a Fregean cover for μ defined on the closure of μ's domain under the part-hood relation yields:

$\mu_1(a) = \{a\}$ 　　 $\mu_1(b) = \{b\}$
$\mu_1(c) = \{c\}$ 　　 $\mu_1(d) = \{d\}$
$\mu_1(a \frown b) = \{a \frown b\}$ 　　 $\mu_1(a \frown d) = \{a \frown d, c \frown b\}$
$\mu_1(c \frown b) = \{a \frown d, c \frown b\}$ 　 $\mu_1(c \frown d) = \{c \frown d\}$
$\mu_1((a \frown b) \frown b) = \{(a \frown b) \frown b, (a \frown b) \frown d, (c \frown d) \frown b\}$
$\mu((a \frown b) \frown d) = \{(a \frown b) \frown b, (a \frown b) \frown d, (c \frown d) \frown b\}$
$\mu_1((a \frown d) \frown b) = \{(a \frown d) \frown b, (c \frown b) \frown b\}$
$\mu((a \frown d) \frown d) = \{(a \frown d) \frown d, (c \frown b) \frown d, (c \frown d) \frown d\}$
$\mu_1((c \frown b) \frown b) = \{(a \frown d) \frown b, (c \frown b) \frown b\}$
$\mu((c \frown b) \frown d) = \{(a \frown d) \frown d, (c \frown b) \frown d, (c \frown d) \frown d\}$
$\mu_1((c \frown d) \frown b) = \{(a \frown b) \frown b, (a \frown b) \frown d, (c \frown d) \frown b\}$
$\mu((c \frown d) \frown d) = \{(a \frown d) \frown d, (c \frown b) \frown d, (c \frown d) \frown d\}$

The crucial point is the pattern of synonymies, so any meaning function (on the requisite domain) which makes synonymous the groups $a \frown d$ and $c \frown b$; $(a \frown b) \frown b$, $(a \frown b) \frown d$, and $(c \frown d) \frown b$; $(a \frown d) \frown b$ and $(c \frown b) \frown b$; and $(a \frown d) \frown d$, $(c \frown b) \frown d)$, and $(c \frown d) \frown d$ is a Fregean cover of μ. But the synonymies of the Fregean cover needn't be the same as those of the covered function: μ_1 denies the synonymy that μ asserts between $a \frown b$ and $c \frown d$.

However, if μ is compositional, then the relation between it and its Fregean covers is more intimate. We then have Hodges':

(Theorem 2) Suppose μ_1 is a meaning function on some subset D_1 of $\mathbb{L}$. Then μ_1 is compositional if and only if there is a Fregean cover μ_2 on $D_2 = \{\epsilon \in \mathbb{L} : \exists \eta \in D_1 \epsilon \sqsubseteq \eta\}$ such that for all $\epsilon \in D_1, \mu_2(\epsilon) = \mu_1(\epsilon)$.

Proof: Left to right: Let μ be an arbitrary Fregean cover of μ_1. Suppose ϵ and τ are μ_1-synonymous. Since μ_1 is compositional, $\Sigma(\epsilon)$ and $\Sigma(\tau)$ are μ_1-synonymous for all Σ, and any Fregean cover must also treat ϵ and τ as synonymous. If ϵ and τ are not μ_1-synonymous, then μ cannot treat them as synonyms either, given the second clause of the definition of Fregean cover, with Σ the null context.[32] Thus μ must have exactly the same synonymies as μ_1 on D_1. Now define:

$$\mu_2(\epsilon) = \begin{cases} \mu_1(\epsilon) & \epsilon \in D_1 \\ \mu(\epsilon) & \text{otherwise} \end{cases}$$

μ_2 is then a Fregean cover of μ_1 agreeing with μ_1 on D_1. Right to left: Since μ_2 is a Fregean cover, it is compositional. Hence it satisfies the substitution constraint. Since $\mu_1 \subseteq \mu_2$, μ_1 also satisfies the substitution constraint, and is compositional. $\therefore$

Suppose a semanticist seeks a meaning theory for language L. Perhaps he is given meanings for all of the sentences of L, and needs an assignment of meanings to individual lexical items compatible with the given sentential meanings. General worries about the underdetermination of theory by data might have led us to suspect that there would be many ways for the semanticist to complete his task. However, Theorem 2 shows that if L is compositional on the sentential level[33] and the semanticist wants the lexical meanings to be well-fitted to the sentential meanings (in the sense of satisfying the Context Principle), then there is, up to equivalence, only a single meaning function available, and a compositional one. The puzzle of semantics has an almost unique solution.[34]

On reflection, however, Hodges' result is less surprising, and hence also less significant, than it might at first seem. A commitment to constructing meaning theories in accord with the Context Principle carries with it a commitment to distributing meanings among expressions in exactly one pattern—not making so few distinctions in meaning as to violate compositionality, and not making so many distinctions in meaning as to differentiate expressions which contribute in the same way to complex expressions. Inevitably, then, meaning theories constructed in accord with the Context Principle are unique up to equivalence. If the starting fragment is compositional, then it fits into the semantic agenda dictated by the Context Principle, so the final pattern of synonymies contains the starting pattern as a fragment. But our goals in semantic theorizing may outstrip the commitments of the Context Principle. Suppose, for example, that, in attempting to extract ontological commitments from our semantic practice, we come to wonder whether the lexical item 'gavagai' should be understood as meaning *rabbit* or *undetached rabbit part*. Given meanings for all of the sentences, adherence to the Context Principle dictates what 'gavagai' is synonymous with, but does not tell us what it means. The mere synonymy information does nothing to settle the ontology acquired via the use of the term 'gavagai'. Clearly, many conceptions of semantic theory will regard this only as the barest of starts toward construction of an adequate theory.

---

[32] A Fregean cover can only break, not introduce synonymies.

[33] This is a non-trivial requirement if sentences can contain sentences as proper parts.

[34] See Werning (2004) for an application of Hodges' result along these lines.

26.3 SOME PROBLEM CASES
FOR COMPOSITIONALITY

While the results of Section 26.2.1 show that when semantic theories are sufficiently unconstrained, compositionality can be cheaply obtained, the question remains whether a *satisfactory* semantic theory for a natural language, one properly responsive to natural constraints on semantic and syntactic facts, can be given compositional form. In this section we consider two problem cases for the construction of compositional semantics, examining the data which resist a compositional treatment and then considering ways of overcoming that resistance. The goal is not to settle the question of whether natural languages have compositional semantics, or even the smaller questions of whether the particular phenomena discussed here have a compositional semantics, but rather to see how questions of compositionality influence semantic theorizing.[35]

26.3.1 What the Hell

The Problem: Compare the following two sentences:

(13) Who bought that book?
(14) Who the hell bought that book?[36]

The two are roughly synonymous. While the addition of 'the hell' alters the rhetorical impact of (14) (perhaps encouraging the conversational implicature that it is surprising that the book was bought), the core semantic value of each is a request for information about the identity of a book buyer. Whatever the semantic contribution of 'the hell', it must be compatible with the close semantic proximity of (13) and (14).

However, 'who' and 'who the hell', or, more generally, 'wh-' and 'wh- the hell' expressions, diverge in meaning in other contexts. Thus:[37]

- The minimal variant of adding a modal auxiliary causes a difference to emerge:
  (15) Who would buy that book?

---

[35] The literature abounds in problem cases for compositionality and treatments thereof. In addition to the issues addressed below, see among many others discussion of compositionality and: independence-friendly logics in Hintikka, Hodges (1997), Hodges (1997), Hodges (1998), Hodges (2001); prototype theory in Fodor (1998) (ch. 5), Fodor (1996), Fodor (1991), Kamp (1995), Osheron (1988), Smith (1999); idioms in Katz (1963), Katz (1973), Nunberg (1994), Westerstahl (1999); 'unless' in Higginbotham (1986), Pelletier (1994), Fintel (1991); propositional attitude cases in innumerable places, but especially Salmon (1986) (ch. 4), Schiffer (1987) (ch. 8), Kripke (1988), Crimmins (1998); 'any' and other negative polarity items in Lakoff (1969), Ladusaw (1979), Carlson (1981), Linebarger (1987), Krifka (1995); anaphora in Kamp (1984), Groenendijk (1991), and Jacobson (2000). Janssen (2001) also contains an overview of several compositionally problematic semantic phenomena.

[36] These two examples are drawn from Dikken (2001). The behaviour of 'the hell' phrases was first noted in Pesetsky (1987).

[37] The first three of these examples are drawn from Dikken (2001); the last draws from Dikken (2001) and Pesetsky (1987).

(16) Who the hell would buy that book?

The first of these is most naturally read as a request for information, but the second is most naturally, and perhaps obligatorily, read as an indirect assertion that nobody would buy that book.[38]

- When the original examples are embedded in an indirect question, a difference in grammaticality emerges:

  — I know who bought that book.
  — * I know who the hell bought that book.

'Who the hell' phrases are grammatical only in negative contexts, whether overt:

  — I don't know who the hell bought that book.

in the antecedent of a conditional:

  — If anyone knows who the hell bought that book, please tell me.

or in the scope of so-called *adversative attitude verbs*:[39]

  — John refused to tell me who the hell bought that book.

- 'The hell' blocks certain scope readings of sentences with multiple quantifiers. Thus:

  — What did everyone buy for Max?

is ambiguous between a reading on which 'everyone' takes wide scope, and people make separate purchases for Max, and a reading on which 'everyone' takes narrow scope, and there is some one thing bought by everyone for Max. However:

  — What the hell did everyone buy for Max?

allows only the second of these two readings.

- 'Wh- the hell' phrases, unlike normal 'wh-' phrases, cannot enter into anaphoric attachment. Thus:

  — Someone$_i$ walked in the park, but I don't know who$_i$.

is acceptable, but:

  — * Someone$_i$ walked in the park, but I don't know who the hell$_i$.

is not. Similarly, 'which' phrases, which require an anaphoric link to a contextually provided range of salient objects, do not allow 'the hell' modification:

  — * Which the hell book did you read that in?

---

[38] Dikken (2001) claims that only the indirect assertion reading of (16) is available, but I find the data less univocal. The pressure toward the indirect assertion reading, in my judgement, increases with the strength of the attached vulgarity. In order to keep this volume suitable for a family audience, I have used 'the hell' throughout, but the reader is encouraged to substitute as his imagination allows.

[39] See Ladusaw (1979).

The puzzle for compositional semantics is to show how 'the hell' can systematically contribute to the meanings of larger expressions in a way that allows its impact to be minimal, if anything at all, in (14), but much greater in the other cases set out above.[40]

A Solution:[41] A simple 'who' question can have its interpretation influenced by linking the range of admissible answers to a contextually provided domain. Thus consider the following dialogue:

(17) A: Various friends of mine voted for each of the different presidential candidates in the 2000 election.

  B: Really? Who voted for David McReynolds?

B's question is not answered by specifying an arbitrary McReynolds voter (and does not require listing *all* such voters); rather, it calls for a (or all) McReynolds voter *among A's friends*. In another context, however, 'Who voted for David McReynolds?' can receive an unlinked reading, in which it calls for the total list of McReynolds voters.

Suppose the semantic function of 'the hell' is to require that the range of admissible answers to a wh-question include *novel answers*—ones not already provided as possible by contextual linkages of the sort just discussed. When a wh-question is an unlinked one, as on one natural reading of (13), adding 'the hell' has no effect, because when unlinked, all answers are novel. But when the wh-question is a linked one, adding 'the hell' has a semantic impact. Thus consider:

(18) A: Various friends of mine voted for each of the different presidential candidates in the 2000 election.

  B: Really? Who the hell voted for David McReynolds?

This dialogue, unlike the first, creates the implicature that B expects all of A's friends not to have voted for McReynolds. If the effect of adding 'the hell' is to insist on the admissibility of novel answers (here, people other than those B counts as A's friends), this new implicature is to be expected. The various effects of 'the hell' noted above now fall out:

- 'Wh- the hell' phrases refuse anaphoric linkage because that linkage dictates the range over which the wh- phrase ranges, which contradicts the novelty requirement imposed by 'the hell'.[42] 'Which' phrases, which *always* require anaphoric/contextual linkage, can thus never combine with 'the hell'.

- A question of the form 'Who would buy that book?' takes as answer pairs of people and possible situations.[43] Given the broad total range of possible situations, such a

---

[40] A compositional semantics need account for the failures of *grammaticality* such as '* I know who the hell bought that book' and '* Which the hell book did you read that in' only if the syntax is not thoroughly autonomous. It is tempting to think that grammatical failures due to failures of anaphoric linkage, at least, have a semantic explanation.

[41] The following solution is a simplified and modified version of the proposal of Dikken (2001). Any shortcomings of it are due to the present alterations.

[42] Although note the acceptability of:
  — Someone walked in the park, but I don't know who the hell it was.

[43] Thus: 'Albert, if it has a chapter on direct reference', 'Louisa, if autographed copies are available', etc.

question is typically linked to a contextually provided range of admissible situations.[44] Adding 'the hell' to form 'Who the hell would buy that book?' requires the admissibility of novel answers, and thus defeats any contextually provided restriction on admissible situations. But once all possible situations are provided, the question becomes trivialized: anyone would, in some situation, buy the book. The asking of trivial questions, though, is pragmatically proscribed, and an alternative communicative explanation is favoured, such as the explanation that the speaker is emphasizing the remoteness of any situation in which the book is bought.

• The requirement of novelty imposed by 'the hell' is impossible to fulfill when the 'wh- the hell' phrase is simply imbedded in an operator of positive epistemic commitment. To say that I know who the hell bought the book is to undermine, by my knowledge, the requisite novelty of the admissible book buyers. Similarly an epistemically positive operator in the antecedent of a conditional, such as the earlier:

— If anyone knows who the hell bought the book, please tell me.

creates no conflict with the novelty requirement, since the function of the antecedent is to entertain hypothetical situations. Operators of negative epistemic commitment, such as 'refused to tell', for similar reasons allow 'the hell' modification. The novelty requirement thus explains the distributional facts noted above.

• The novelty requirement makes 'wh- the hell' phrases *negative polarity items*, where various sorts of negation license the introduction of novelties. Suppose that negative polarity items are subject to:

(Immediate Scope Constraint) A negative polarity item can appear only in the immediate scope of its licensing negative item.[45]

Consider again:

— What the hell did everyone buy for Max?

and assume that the licensing item is the marker of interrogative force. If 'every one' is raised to give it scope over 'what the hell', it intervenes between 'what the hell' and its licenser, violating the Immediate Scope Constraint. The unavailability of a reading wide-scoped for 'everyone' is thus explained.

26.3.2 Many Scandinavians

The Problem: Fourteen Scandinavians have won the Nobel prize in literature.[46] Since there have been only 99 Nobel laureates in literature, and since Scandinavians are only about 0.5% of the world's population, the following claim looks acceptable:

---

[44] Thus ruling out answers such as 'Brian, if we threaten to kidnap his dog if he doesn't'.
[45] See Linebarger (1987) for formulation and defense of the Immediate Scope Constraint.
[46] Björnstjerne Björnson, Selma Lagerlöf, Verner von Heidenstam, Karl Gjellerup, Henrik Pontoppidan, Knut Hamsun, Sigrid Undset, Erik Karlfeldt, Frans Eemil Sillanpää, Johannes Jensen, Pär Lagerkvist, Nelly Sachs, Eyvind Johnson, and Harry Martinson. This observation and the subsequent problematic sentence (19) are both due to Westerstahl (1985). The intervening years have not been kind to the recognition of Scandinavian literature, and the number remains 14.

(19) Many Scandinavians have won the Nobel prize in Literature.

On reflection, however, the acceptability of (19) is puzzling. Fourteen, after all, is not by most natural standards *many*. Consider the oddity of:

(20) Many Scandinavians have emigrated to the United States. Fourteen, in fact.

The acceptability of (19) seems to derive from having fourteen qualify not as *many Scandinavians*, but rather as *many winners of the Nobel prize in literature*, and thus from reading (19) as:

(21) Many winners of the Nobel prize in literature have been Scandinavian.

A similar apparent 'swapping of positions' can be found in sentences with adverbs of quantification:[47]

(22) Scandinavians often win the Nobel prize in literature. (The Nobel prize in literature is often won by Scandinavians.)

and in sentences with generics:[48]

(23) Scandinavians win the Nobel prize in literature, but Americans win the Nobel prize in economics. (The Nobel prize in literature is won (generically) by Scandanavians, but the Nobel prize in economics is won (generically) by Americans.)

Some other determiners, such as 'few' and 'several', exhibit similar behaviour. These cases look like violations of the semantic locality component of compositionality: 'many' in imposing its cardinality constraint requires semantic interaction with the syntactically distant verb phrase.[49]

A Solution: We concentrate on addressing the problem in its 'many' form, deferring integration of these suggestions with theories of adverbs of quantification and generics. In some cases, the semantic role of 'many' in a sentence of the form 'Many X's Y' is merely to require that the number of X's that Y is above some minimum threshold cardinality κ.[50] This sort of 'many' can be given a straightforward compositional semantics:

$$[\![\text{many}]\!] = f : \wp(D) \mapsto \wp(\wp(D)), f(X) = \{Y : |X \cap Y| \geq \kappa\}$$

$$[\![[_S [_{DP} \text{many } X][_{VP} Y]]]\!] = \textbf{true iff } [\![Y]\!] \in [\![\text{many}]\!]([\![X]\!])$$

'Many' applied to a noun phrase thus yields a collection of sets, each of which contains many of the satisfiers of the noun phrase. If any of those sets is the extension

---

[47] See de Swart (1991) and Cohen (2001).

[48] See Cohen (1996) and Cohen (2001).

[49] The apparent position swapping can be taken as suggesting that 'many' is *symmetric*, in the sense that 'Many X's Y' and 'Many Y's X' are equivalent. From the perspective of compositionality, however, the observation that 'many' is symmetric (if correct) merely restates the problem—how *can* 'many' be symmetric, given that symmetry requires giving equal semantic footing to the immediate complement of 'many' and a syntactically distant verb phrase?

[50] The required number of Y-ing X's will surely be vague, but the idealization to a specific κ is harmless here.

of the verb phrase, the sentence is true. 'Many' is symmetric on this 'cardinality' semantics, in the sense that 'Many X's Y' is equivalent to 'Many Y's X', which would allow for position swapping without alteration of truth-value, but no plausible value for κ accounts for the truth of (19).

In other cases, though, the impact of 'many' seems more subtle than a simple cardinality constraint. Compare the following:

(24) Many philosophers of mathematics have read Russell and Whitehead's *Principia Mathematica*.
(25) Many Brazilians have read Russell and Whitehead's *Principia Mathematica*.

Suppose that among the 2000 philosophers of mathematics, 800 have read the *Principia*, and that among the 180 million Brazilians, again 800 have read the *Principia*. Then (24) looks true and (25) false, which is impossible if 'many' simply imposes a cardinality constraint. This suggests the following alternative reading of 'many':

$$[[many]] = f : \wp(D) \mapsto \wp(\wp(D)), f(X) = \{Y : |X \cap Y| \geq \rho|X|\}$$
$$[[[_S [_{DP} many\, X][_{VP} Y]]]] = \textbf{true iff } [[Y]] \in [[many]]([[X]])$$

where ρ sets the threshold percentage for *manyness*. Symmetry is now lost, since the complement noun phrase to 'many' has the privileged role of providing the number of objects a percentage of which must satisfy the verb phrase. This second, 'proportionate' reading thus also gives the wrong analysis of (19).

On both the cardinality and the proportionate analyses, if the number of X's who Y is the same as the number of Z's who W, then many X's Y if and only if many Z's W. However, some examples fail to fit this pattern:

(26) Many penguins live in Antarctica.
(27) Many penguins live in my bedroom.

Twelve penguins in a bedroom suffices for *many*, but will hardly do for a whole continent. Here 'many' means something like *more than one would expect*, where expectations are set (in part) by the verb phrase. This 'expectation' semantics can be roughly characterized by requiring that X's Y at a rate greater than the general rate of Y-ing:

$$[[many]] = f : \wp(D) \mapsto \wp(\wp(D)), f(X) = \{Y : |X \cap Y| \geq \frac{|X| \cdot |Y|}{|D|}\}$$
$$[[[_S [_{DP} many\, X][_{VP} Y]]]] = \textbf{true iff } [[Y]] \in [[many]]([[X]])$$

This is a crude measure of expectation, but it suffices for a start. The resulting semantics is symmetric, like the cardinality semantics, and gives the desired result for (19), since Nobel laureates in literature are represented among Scandinavians at a higher rate than that at which they appear in the general population.

The 'expectation' semantics uses 'value loading' to get the right truth conditions for (19) in a compositional manner, by granting 'many' a parameterized sensitivity to the verb phrase interpretation which is 'passed up' until semantic composition meets that part of the sentence. However, it fails to explain why the 'position swapped' reading of (19) seems *preferable* to the straight reading, given that it makes the two equivalent. It also yields undesirable results in closely related cases. Nobel laureates in literature appear in the general population at a rate of about one in every 60 million.[51] Thus St. Lucia, with its population of some 200,000 and a single Nobel laureate in literature,[52] dramatically exceeds the expectation threshold. But the claim:

(28) Many St. Lucians have won the Nobel prize in literature.

seems false. One laureate out of the 99 is too few, no matter how few the St. Lucians are. This result is predicted if the 'proportionate' semantics is applied to the position swapped:

(29) Many winners of the Nobel prize in literature have been from St. Lucia.

But the position swapping is then again a problem for compositionality. Two possible moves at this point:

- Combine the 'proportionate' semantics with a syntactic story swapping the argument positions of 'many' sentences prior to semantic analysis. Thus (19), at the level of semantic analysis, would *be* 'Many winners of the Nobel prize in literature have been Scandinavian', which would then combine with the 'proportionate' semantics to yield to desired result. However, note that quantification over empty classes is typically pragmatically disfavoured; hence the peculiarity of:

(30) Many Freedonians have won the Nobel prize in literature.

But as Cohen (2001) observes, a sentence like:

(31) Many Scandinavians have won the Nobel prize in silly walks.

seems simply false, rather than pragmatically disfavoured, despite the fact that the syntactic swapping story would make the class quantified over the empty class of Nobel laureates in silly walks.

- Give a 'reverse proportionate' semantics, by altering the class a minimal percentage of which needs to behave as required:

— $[\![\text{many}]\!] = f : \wp(D) \mapsto \wp(\wp(D)), f(X) = \{Y : |X \cap Y| \geq \rho|Y|\}$

(19), under this approach, requires a certain minimal percentage of the Nobel laureates in literature to be Scandinavian.[53] However, we must now explain why 'many' allows both proportionate and reverse proportionate semantics, while 'most' allows only the proportionate semantics:

— $[\![\text{most}]\!] = f : \wp(D) \mapsto \wp(\wp(D)), f(X) = \{Y : |X \cap Y| \geq \frac{|X|}{2}\}$
— $*[\![\text{most}]\!] = f : \wp(D) \mapsto \wp(\wp(D)), f(X) = \{Y : |X \cap Y| \geq \frac{|Y|}{2}\}$

---

[51] I idealize here by assuming all Nobel laureates in literature are currently alive.
[52] Derek Walcott
[53] Note that this approach allows (28) to be false.

26.4 WHY MIGHT ONE WANT COMPOSITIONALITY?

The examples of the previous section show that the question of whether English and other natural languages have compositional semantics is a difficult one to answer. What remains to be seen is why that question is one worth answering. In this final section, we turn to reasons for caring about compositionality. Three types of reasons will be considered:

1. Claims that natural languages are observably compositional, and hence that a semantic theory faithful to the data must take a compositional form.
2. Claims that compositionality is a consequence of or has as a consequence some other property which is of independent interest, and hence that compositionality is a derivatively desirable feature of a semantc theory, via its connection with that other property.
3. Claims that compositionality is a methodological principle for semantic theorizing, or a consequence of proper semantic methodology.

26.4.1 Observational Compositionality

Enough has been said already to dispel the attraction of the following naive line of reasoning:

A natural language like English *must* be compositional. For it to be compositional is for the meanings of its sentences to be functions of the meanings of their component words and their syntactic arrangement. But a sentence just *is* its component words and their syntactic arrangement, so there is nothing else that its meaning could be a function of.

This argument fails twice: once in its blindness to the possibility that the meaning of a sentence depends on *non-semantic* features of its constituent words (failure of semantic closure), and again in its blindness to the possibility that the meaning of a sentence depends on features (semantic or otherwise) of things which are not parts of it (failure of semantic locality). Commission of the second failure is encouraged by thinking of a semantic theory as assigning meanings to expression *types*, since doing so isolates the type from contexts of its instantiation, and thereby makes it difficult to identify factors relevant to its meaning outside its own parts. However, an adequate meaning theory is available on the type level only if the tokens are compositional in their semantic behaviour, so presupposing a type-level semantic theory begs the question.

More sophisticated variants on the naive argument, however, are available. Thus Fodor and Lepore (Fodor (2001)) cite two aspects of our experience with language:

Apparent Compositionality (AC): Practically all competent speakers of a natural language who understand all the parts of an expression ϵ also understand ϵ.

Apparent Reverse Compositionality (ARC): Practically all competent speakers of a natural language who understand an expression ε also understand all parts of ε.

AC and ARC, Fodor and Lepore argue, are straightforwardly observable semantic facts. But they are best explained by the assumption that natural languages are compositional (in fact, strongly parallel), so by inference to the best explanation we should endorse that assumption.

AC and ARC are intended to be observable features of natural languages, but it is in fact not obvious that either is true. One can, for example, know the meaning of 'squid' and of 'chair', but still find the complex expression 'squid chair' obscure. However, its meaning might become clear (and clear in different ways) when imbedded in a larger context. Similarly with reverse compositionality—one can understand:

(32) Greta Garbo possessed a certain *je ne sais quoi.*

without knowing that 'je' means *I*, and one can understand 'telephone' without knowing that 'tele' means *far.*[54]

Even granting AC and ARC, compositionality may not be the best explanation. Suppose a speaker of English, familiar with the meanings of 'dogs' and 'bark', understands the sentence 'dogs bark'. Compositionality follows only if the meanings of 'dogs' and 'bark', together with syntax, are the only facts reliably available to the speaker. But, of course, they are not. Minimally, the speaker also has facts about the morphology and phonology of the words 'dogs' and 'bark', combined with facts about the context of utterance, and these facts may be pivotal in sentential interpretation. We know that *some* collection of information made available in communicative utterances suffices for understanding; the argument from AC could thus succeed only when bolstered by a further argument that only a compositional language could explain the very phenomenon of language learnability. ACR follows from the innocuous assumption that speakers of a language typically understand most of the words in that language, which in turn follows from the assumption that meanings of words are often partially determinative of meanings of sentences, which (finally) falls short of the compositional requirement that meanings of words are always fully determinative of meanings of sentences.[55]

Compositionality might also be argued for inductively, on the grounds that successful semantic theories have tended to be compositional. This line of argument is at most as strong as its inductive evidence base, and the examples of Section 26.3, as

---

[54] Are such expressions idioms? (See Fodor (1998).) Such a defense of ACR requires minimally a standard of idiomaticity other than the trivializing one that idioms are expressions one can understand without understanding the meanings of their parts.

[55] Note that even if ACR is strengthened to state that speakers understand meanings of words *by virtue* of understanding meanings of sentences containing those words, compositionality still does not follow. The strengthened ACR remains compatible with the assumption that word meanings plus other factors determine sentence meanings and with the assumption that speakers are nascently aware of the semantic processes by which they calculate sentence meanings, even if the sentence meanings themselves weed out some of the richness of those processes.

well as many others, cast substantial doubt on that base. Also, if semanticists tend to prefer compositional theories for reasons other than theoretical adequacy, then the sample space may be illegitimately biased toward such theories, with many potentially successful non-compositional theories never given sufficient consideration. The *form* of the inductive argument, however, is unobjectionable, and if the worries about the evidence quality can be addressed, it can ground a rational confidence in the compositionality of natural languages.

26.4.2 Consequentialist Compositionality

Suppose the compositionality of a language L is not a directly observable or inducible feature, but that there is some other feature X which L observably or inducibly possesses, or which we would like L to possess. X might be *first-order*, or *hyperintensional*, or *of subject–predicate form*, or *systematic*, or *bivalent*, or *admitting of adherence to the Gricean maxims*, or any number of other features. If compositionality can be shown to be inferentially related to feature X, a reason for wanting compositionality then emerges. Two versions of this argument style are available:

1. If compositionality is a necessary condition for feature X, then the presence of X in L guarantees the compositionality of L.
2. If compositionality is a sufficient condition for feature X, then the presence of X in L offers no guarantee that L is compositionality, but compositionality may still serve as a plausible explanation of the X-ness of L, allowing for an inference to the best explanation of the compositionality of L.

In the ideal case, compositionality is both necessary and sufficient for X, but features so closely inferentially related to compositionality, but nevertheless independently verifiable in L, are hard to come by. Both styles of argument are legitimate, but care should be taken to distinguish the two. Both styles of argument can be thought of as consequentialist—compositionality is endorsed either because of its consequences, or because of what it is a consequence of, rather than on its own merits. The crucial question in evaluating consequentialist arguments thus becomes the tightness of the inferential relation between compositionality and the chosen X.

We will focus on one instance of a consequentialist argument for compositionality—the *learnability argument*. This overview of compositionality began with an example of a novel sentence which was immediately comprehensible to any competent speaker of English. All natural languages have an infinite number of grammatical and meaningful sentences, and *a fortiori* an infinite number of such sentences never encountered by a given speaker. Nevertheless, linguistic competence gives one the capacity to understand all of these sentences. This feature of linguistic competence stands in need of an explanation. A newborn lacks the capacity to understand any sentences; some five years later, after taking in a finite body of information, he has gained the capacity to understand an infinite number of sentences. How can this infinite capacity be finitely learnable?

Frege famously answers this question as follows:

It is astonishing what language can do. With a few syllables it can express an incalculable number of thoughts, so that even a thought grasped by a terrestrial being for the very first time can be put into a form of words which will be understood by somebody to whom the thought is entirely new. This would be impossible, were we not able to distinguish parts in the thought corresponding to the parts of a sentence, so that the structure of the sentence serves as an image of the structure of the thought.   (Frege (1963), 1)

English has a finite vocabulary, and a finite collection of syntactic rules for forming complex expressions. These features of English are thus finitely learnable. If English is compositional, Frege suggests, this finite information accounts, via recursive reapplication, for our infinite linguistic capacity. Thus we have reason to think that English is compositional. Frege puts the argument in terms of the *necessity* of compositionality for learnability; an analogous argument could also be framed in terms of sufficiency.

The learnability argument is that most frequently cited in discussions of compositionality. Textbooks on formal semantics, for example, typically introduce compositionality via the learnability argument. Consider two examples:

We presumably understand a sentence like:

(1) I saw a pink whale in the parking lot.

because we know what the single words in it mean (what *pink* and *whale* mean, for example) and we have an algorithm of some kind for combining them. Thus part of the task of semantics must be to say something about what word meaning might be and something about the algorithms for combining those word meanings to arrive at phrasal and sentential meanings.   (Chierchia (1990), 6)

and:

If there were no direct relation between lexical and sentential meaning, of course, the meaning of each sentence would have to be listed. Since the number of sentences that make up a language is infinite, this would mean that no human being would be able to determine the meanings of all the sentences of any language due to the finite resources of the brain. This is absurd, of course, and just as sentences are defined recursively by syntactic rules, taking words (or morphemes) as their basis, so their meanings should also be defined recursively from the meanings ascribed to the lexemes they contain.   (Cann (1993), 3)

Nevertheless, learnability provides no good reason for taking natural languages to be compositional. For a language to be learnable, it is necessary and sufficient that it have a computable meaning function. If the meaning function for L is computable, then it gives a procedure, graspable by beings like us, by which meanings of complex expressions can be determined. L is thus learnable if computable. If, on the other hand, L has no computable meaning function, then any procedure, graspable by beings like us, for determining meanings of complex expressions fails to determine the meanings of some expressions of L. L is thus unlearnable if uncomputable.

However, computability and compositionality turn out to float quite free of one another:

A language can be compositional without being computable. Let L have concatenation as its only syntactic operation, and have expressions taking natural numbers as meanings. Let M be an arbitrary noncomputable function on $\mathbb{N}$. If $[\![\alpha \frown \beta]\!] = M([\![\alpha]\!], [\![\beta]\!])$, then L is compositional, but $[\![\cdot]\!]$ is not computable. Compositionality does not make for computability unless the mode of composition is itself computable.

A language can be computable without being compositional. Let L have concatenation as its only syntactic operation, and have expressions taking natural numbers as meanings. Suppose that the meaning of $\alpha \frown \beta$, when it appears in the context $\gamma \frown (\alpha \frown \beta)$, is $[\![\alpha]\!] + [\![\beta]\!] + [\![\gamma]\!]$. $[\![\cdot]\!]$ is then computable, but the computation proceeds in a noncompositional way, violating semantic locality. Computability does not make for compositionality unless the mode of computation appeals only to compositionally available features.

Compositionality is thus neither necessary nor sufficient for computability. The two features are wholly orthogonal, and no evidence for the presence of the one can be derived from the presence of the other. Learnability is a feature which goes to the computational complexity of meaning functions, but compositionality is a feature of the topology of meaning functions. Without further assumptions, the one tells us nothing about the other.[56]

26.4.3 Methodological Compositionality

When compositionality is not motivated using the learnability argument, it is most often introduced as a *methodological principle* governing semantic theorizing. Call Φ a methodological principle for an activity A if Φ either is, or is a logical consequence of, a claim whose truth is a constitutive feature of performance of A. Suppose, for example, that for the construction of a theory to count as the construction of a *semantic* theory, the theory constructed must obey the Context Principle. Perhaps this is the case, as Frege suggests in Frege (1980), because it is constitutive of a semantic theory to characterize objective features, independent of merely psychological facts about individual speakers, in virtue of which linguistic expressions convey information, and only with the Context Principle is it possible to avoid psychologism in characterizing the meanings of expressions whose meanings are not concrete particulars.[57] Perhaps it is the case, as Peregrin (2003) suggests, because a semantic theory requires an ontology of meanings, an ontology of meanings requires a principle of individuation of meanings, and the Context Principle provides the only available such principle. In either case, the Context Principle is a methodological principle of semantic theorizing, and given that, as seen in Lemma 1 of Section 26.2.2, the

---

[56] Szabo, in chapter 3 of Szabo, (2000b), gives an extended and insightful critique of the learnability argument, drawing attention to additional assumptions about the relation between linguistic understanding and meanings as provided by semantic theories, without which assumptions the learnability argument cannot get started.

[57] Thus: Only by adhering to [the Context Principle] can we, as I believe, avoid a physical view of number without slipping into a psychological view of it (Frege (1980), §106).

Context Principle entails compositionality, compositionality is also a methodological principle.

This overview closes with a brief consideration of another attempted methodological justification of compositionality. Why do individual words of a language have meaning? If the goal of a semantic theory is to account for meanings at some terminal level (say, the level of whole sentences), then word meanings seem superfluous. Perhaps the productivity of language requires that sentence meanings be derived systematically from some prior information base, but there is no reason why this information base need be either semantic or lexical. If word meanings (plus syntax) determine sentence meaning, and words determine word meanings, and orthographic structure determines word, then orthographic structure (plus syntax) determines sentence meaning, despite the fact that orthographic structure is not semantically invested.

Consider the following example.[58] Sentences of 'donkey anaphora', such as the classic:

(33) If a farmer owns a donkey, he beats it.

present two challenge to compositionality. First, an account of the anaphoric pronouns must be given without violating semantic locality. Second, an explanation of the semantic shift in the indefinites from existential in the null context to universal in the embedded context must be provided. Kamp's Discourse Representation Theory (DRT) (introduced in Kamp (1984)) aims at a natural treatment of natural language anaphora. DRT treats indefinite descriptions, such as 'a farmer' as introducing *discourse referents* into a discussion, and uses as a tool of semantic analysis discourse representation structures (DRS's), which consist of a combination of discourse referents and conditions imposed on those discourse referents. For example, (33) receives the following DRS:

(34)

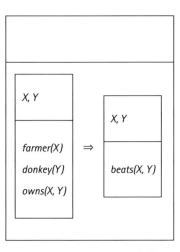

---

[58] Other familiar examples of the same phenomenon: Frege's desire for a compositional treatment of propositional attitudes leads to an ontology of senses; Davidson's compositional solution to adverbial modification leads to an ontology of events.

The two indefinites 'a farmer' and 'a donkey' introduce the two discourse referents, and the conditions '*farmer*(X)', '*donkey*(Y)', and '*owns*(X, Y)' are then imposed on them. The subsequent anaphoric pronouns pick up on these discourse referents, and impose the further condition *beat*(X, Y) on them. A DRS is true relative to a model if there is an assignment to the discourse referents satisfying the conditions. The accumulation in a single DRS of discourse referents and constraints from multiple clauses then guarantees that anaphorically linked phrases receive the same interpretation. When two DRS's are linked by a conditional, semantic interpretation requires that every variable assignment satisfying the conditions of the first DRS can be extended to an assignment satisfying the conditions of the second DRS. Indefinites in the antecedents of conditions thus have universal force.

While the matter is not perfectly straightforward, DRT is typically taken to be a non-compositional semantic theory.[59] Construction of a DRS for a sentence with anaphoric pronouns depends crucially on the way that DRS's have been constructed for sentences elsewhere in the conversational context, and the mode of quantification of DRS variables cannot be determined locally, shifting from existential in null contexts to universal in conditional contexts.[60] Non-compositionality might come as no surprise here, of course, given that the target phenomenon of cross-sentential anaphora seems in its very nature to involve violations of semantic locality.

Dynamic predicate logic (DPL) (see Groenendijk (1991)) restores compositionality while capturing the key insights of DRT. A compositional treatment of anaphora is achieved by making a fundamental alteration in the kind of semantic values assigned. Whereas static quantified logics assign sentences satisfaction conditions, DPL assigns *input-output pairs*. A sentence of DPL does not simply *receive* an assignment and evaluate relative to it; it can, instead, *change* an assignment. Thinking of variable assignments as specifications of context indicating which objects are conversationally salient, the dynamic insight of DPL is that sentences can affect, as well as be affected by, context.

Syntactically, DPL is a standard first-order language. Semantically, DPL assigns to sentences sets of ordered pairs of variable assignments, thought of as input-output pairs. Atomic sentences have no dynamic effects; they merely pass assignments satisfying a descriptive condition:

$$[[\Pi\tau_1 \ldots \tau_n]] = \{\langle g, h \rangle : g = h \wedge g \models \Pi\tau_1 \ldots \tau_n\}^{61}$$

Existential quantifiers and quantifiers, however, are dynamic. An existentially quantified sentence expands the set of assignments to include all individuals meeting the

---

[59] If DRS's are part of the *semantic* analysis, then DRT is straightforwardly non-compositional. If, on the other hand, DRS's are a *syntactic* prologue to semantic analysis, along the lines of logical form, then DRT is plausibly compositional, albeit with an idiosyncratic syntax.

[60] Non-compositionality shows up in the inability to replace a sentence in a discourse with a logically equivalent one, as in:

(35) * Not every man doesn't own a donkey. He beats it.

[61] where $\models$ is classical truth-in-a model.

existentially quantified condition:

$$[[\exists x\phi]] = \{\langle g, h\rangle : \exists k : k[x]g \wedge \langle k, h\rangle\epsilon\ [[\phi]]\}$$

$k[x]g$ asserts that k differs from g at most in the assignment to x. Conditionals are *internally* dynamic—the output assignment h must equal the input assignment g, but an input passes through to become an output only if every possible output of it, passed through the antecedent, produces some output when passed through the consequent:

$$[[\phi \to \psi]] = \{\langle g, h\rangle : g = h \wedge \forall k(\langle h, k\rangle\epsilon\ [[\phi]] \to \exists j\langle k, j\rangle\epsilon\ [[\psi]])\}$$

Thus consider:

(36) $\exists xFx \to Gx$[62]

Suppose we start with an assignment g assigning Napoleon to x (thus x represents a discourse referent in the DRT sense, and Napoleon is a live option for the real identity of that discourse referent). When that assignment hits the conditional, the existential quantifier $\exists x$ temporarily erases this information, allowing g to be replaced by any assignment which agrees with it in all non-x positions and which assigns an F to the x position. These assignments then input to Gx, with x now representing possible identities of the discourse referent introduced by the existential quantifier (indefinite) of $\exists xFx$. Gx acts as a test on these assignments, passing them through unchanged if their x value is G. If some internally altered assignment passes through, then then g is output, unchanged, from the conditional. Thus g emerges unchanged if and only if every F is G. DPL hence produces the desired universal interpretation of (33).

The DPL semantics are compositional: every constituent of a formula is locally semantically evaluated. The requirement, felt in DRT, for information about the prior communicative context, is eliminated by having each sentence in its semantic interpretation specify how it interacts with context; thus (a) the way in which early sentences in a discourse alter its context is built into their semantic interpretation and (b) the way in which a later sentence in the discourse reacts to any given changed context is built into *its* semantic interpretation. Simple context-sensitivity of language can seem a threat to compositionality; one way of eluding that threat is to shift from thinking of expression meanings as wholly context-free entities to treating them as functions from contexts to traditional meanings. Dynamic context sensitivity represents a further shift, and it can in turn be responded to with another shift in our conception of basic semantic value—now as a tool of updating context through language.[63] This pattern suggests another methodological argument for compositionality, one based on protecting the philosophical role of subsentential semantics.

Suppose that lexical meanings play the role of revealing the ontological commitments inchoately present in our linguistic practice. Fulfillment of this role requires that the structure of the linguistic practice be faithfully mirrored in lexical meanings. Here we find a role for compositionality. Compositionality demands a certain

---

[62] Where, importantly, the scope of the existential quantifier is limited to the antecedent.

[63] For more on the dynamic perspective, see (e.g.) Veltman (1996).

integration of the meanings of sentences and words (given background assumptions about the syntactic relation between the two). Suppose, for example, that intensional contexts are distinguished from extensional ones by the inability to substitute *salva veritate* therein terms identical at one, extensional, level of meaning. Given compositionality, this failure of intersubstitutability signals the presence of a further, intensional, dimension of meaning possessed by those terms, and a corresponding sensitivity to that dimension of meaning on the part of the intensional operators. Without compositionality, however, failures of intersubstitutability are without special significance, and do not reveal anything about the semantics of the terms involved. Thus it is only with compositionality that a meaningful distinction between the extensional and the intensional can be made, and thus that modal commitments can be localized in particular parts of our linguistic practice (counterfactuals, deontic expressions, epistemic contexts, and so on). Without compositionality, semantic features of the linguistic practice can 'float free', not appearing anywhere in the lexicon but emerging non-compositionally as lexical items are combined. Compositionally thus enforces a variety of honesty in semantic theory construction. If the role of words is to allow ontological taxonomizing of the world, this honesty, and hence compositionality, is essential.

References

Aczel, Peter (1987). *Lectures on Non-Well-Founded Sets.* CSLI Lecture.

Bach, Emmon (1976). An Extension of Classical Transformational Grammar. In *Problems in Linguistic Metatheory: Proceedings of the 1976 Conference.* Michigan State University Press.

Cann, Ronnie (1993) *Formal Semantics: An Introduction.* Cambridge University Press.

Carlson Gregory, (1981) Distribution of Free Choice 'Any'. *Chicago Linguistic Society*, 17: 8–23.

Chierchia, Gennaro and Sally McConnell-Ginet (1990). *Meaning and Grammar: An Introduction to Semantics.* The MIT Press.

Cohen Ariel (1996). *Think Generic: The Meaning and Use of Generic Sentences.* Ph.D thesis, Carnegie-Mellon University.

____ (2001). Relative Readings of Many, Often, and Generics. *Natural Language Semantics*, 9: 41–67.

Crimmins, Mark (1998). Hesperus and Phosphorus: Sense, Pretense, and Reference. *The Philosophical Review*, 107: 1–47.

de Swart, H. (1991). *Adverbs of Quantification: A Generalized Quantifier Approach.* Ph.D thesis, Groningen University.

den Dikken, Marcel and Anastasia Giannakidou (2001). From Hell to Polarity: "Agressively Non-d-Linked" wh-Phrases as Polarity Items. *Linguistic Inquiry*, 33: 31–61.

Dever, Josh (1999). Compositionality as Methodology. *Linguistics and Philosophy*, 22: 311–26.

____ (2003). Review of Zoltan Gendler Szabo, Problems of Compositionality. *The Philosophical Review*, 112: 254–58.

Dummett, Michael (1973). *Frege: Philosophy of Language.* Harvard University Press.

Fernando, Tim (1997). Ambiguity Under Changing Contexts. *Linguistics and Philosophy*, 20: 575–606.

Fernando, Tim (2001). Ambiguous Discourse in a Compositional Context. *Journal of Logic, Language, and Information*, 10: 63–86.

Fodor, Jerry (1998). *Concepts: Where Cognitive Science Went Wrong*. Oxford University Press.

——— (1998). *In Critical Condition: Polemical Essays on Cognitive Science and the Philosophy of Mind*. The MIT Press.

Fodor, Jerry and Ernest Lepore (1991). Why Meaning (Probably) isn't Conceptual Role. *Mind and Language*, 6: 328–42.

——— (1996). The Pet Fish and the Red Herring: Why Concepts Aren't Prototypes. *Cognition*, 58: 243–76.

——— (2001). Why Compositionality Won't Go Away: Reflections On Horwich's 'Deflationary' Theory. *Ratio*.

Frege, Gottlob (1963). Compound Thoughts. *Mind*, 72: 1–17.

——— (1980). *The Foundations of Arithmetic*.

——— (1997). Letter to Jourdain, Jan. 1914. In Michael Beaney, ed., *The Frege Reader*. Blackwell Publishers.

Groenendijk, Jeroen and Martin Stokhof (1991). Dynamic Predicate Logic. *Linguistics and Philosophy*, 14: 39–100.

Heck, Richard (2003). Is Compositionality a Trivial Requirement?

Hendriks, Hermann (1993). *Studied Flexibility: Categories and Types in Syntax and Semantics*. Ph.D thesis, University of Amsterdam.

Higginbotham, James (1986). Linguistic Theory and Davidson's Program in Semantics. In Ernest Lepore, ed., *Truth and Interpretation: Perspectives on the Philosophy of Donald Davidson*. Blackwell.

Hintikka, Jaako and Gabriel Sandu. Game-Theoretical Semantics. In *Handbook of Logic and Language*.

Hodges, Wilfrid (1997). Compositional Semantics for a Game of Imperfect Information. *Journal of the IPGL*, 5: 539–63.

——— (1997). Some Strange Quantifiers. In *Structures in Logic and Computer Science*. Springer-Verlag.

——— (1998). Compositionality is not the Problem. *Logic and Logical Philosophy*, 6: 7–33.

——— (2001). Formal Features of Compositionality. *Journal of Logic, Language, and Information*, 10: 7–28.

Horwich, Paul (1998). *Meaning*. Oxford University Press.

Jacobson, Pauline (2000). Paycheck Pronouns, Bach-Peters Sentences, and Variable-Free Semantics. *Natural Language Semantics*, 8: 77–155.

Janssen, Theo (1986). *Foundations and Applications of Montague Grammar*, volume 19 of *CWI Tracts*. Center for Mathematics and Computer Science, Amsterdam.

——— (1997). Compositionality. In Johan van Benthem and Alice ter Meulen, eds., *Handbook of Logic and Language*. The MIT Press.

——— (2001). Frege, Contextuality and Compositionality. *Journal of Logic, Language, and Information*, 10: 115–36.

Kamp, Hans (1984). A Theory of Truth and Semantic Representation. In Jeroen Groenendijk, Theo Janssen, and Martin Stokhof, eds., *Truth, Interpretation, and Information: Selected Papers From the Third Amsterdam Colloquium*. Foris.

Kamp, Hans and Barbara Partee (1995). Prototype Theory and Compositionality. *Cognition*.

Kaplan, David (1990). Words. *Aristotelian Society Supplement*, 64: 93–119.

Katz, Jerrold (1973). Compositionality, Idiomaticity, and Lexical Substitution. In *A Festschrift for Morris Halle*. Holt, Rinehart, and Wilson.

Katz, Jerrold and Paul Postal (1963). Semantic Interpretation of Idioms and Sentences containing them. *Quarterly Progress Report of the MIT Research Laboratory of Electronics*, 70: 275–82.

Kazmi, Ali and Francis Jeffrey Pelletier (1998). Is Compositionality Formally Vacuous? *Linguistics and Philosophy*, 21: 629–33.

Kim, Jaegwon (1983). Concepts of Supervenience. In Jaegwon Kim, ed., *Supervenience and Mind*. Cambridge University Press.

Krifka, Manfred (1995). The Semantics and Pragmatics of Polarity Items. *Linguistic Analysis*, 25: 209–57.

Kripke, Saul (1988). A Puzzle about Belief. In Nathan Salmon and Scott Soames, eds., *Propositions and Attitudes*. Oxford University Press.

Ladusaw, William (1979). *Polarity Sensitivity as Inherent Scope Relations*. Ph.D thesis, University of Texas at Austin.

Lakoff, Robin (1969). Some Reasons Why There Can't be Any Some–Any Rule. *Language*, 45.

Larson, Richard and Gabriel Segal (1995). *Knowledge of Meaning: An Introduction to Semantic Theory*. The MIT Press.

Linebarger, Marcia (1987). Negative Polarity and Grammatical Representation. *Linguistics and Philosophy*, 10: 325–87.

Montague, Richard (1970). Universal Grammar. *Theoria*, 36: 373–98.

Geoffrey, Nunberg, Ivan Sag, and Thomas Wasow (1994). Idioms. *Language*, 70: 491–538.

Osheron, Daniel and Edward Smith (1988). Conceptual Combination with Prototype Concepts. In *Readings in Cognitive Science*. Morgan Kaufman Publishers.

Pelletier, Francis Jeff (1994). On an Argument Against Semantic Compositionality. In Dag Prawitz and Dag Westerstahl, eds., *Logic and the Philosophy of Science in Uppsala*. Kluwer.

—— (1999). Semantic Compositionality: Free Algebras and the Argument from Ambiguity. In M. Faller, S. Kaufmann, and M. Pauly, eds., *Proceedings of Seventh CSLI Workshop on Logic, Language, and Computation*. CSLI Publications.

—— (2001). Did Frege Believe Frege's Principle? *Journal of Logic, Language, and Information*, 10: 87–114.

Peregrin, Jaroslav (2003). Is Compositionality an Empirical Matter?

Pesetsky, David (1987). Wh-in-situ: Movement and Unselective Binding. In *The Representation of (In)definiteness*. The MIT Press.

Pynchon, Thomas (1997). *Mason and Dixon*. Henry Holt and Company.

Salmon, Nathan (1986). *Frege's Puzzle*. The MIT Press.

Schiffer, Stephen (1987). *Remnants of Meaning*. The MIT Press.

Smith, Edward Daniel Osherman, Lance Rips, and Margaret Keane (1999). Combining Prototypes: A Selective Modification Model. In Eric Margolis and Stephen Laurence, eds., *Concepts: Core Readings*. The MIT Press.

Szabo, Zoltan Gendler (2000a). Compositionality as Supervenience. *Linguistics and Philosophy*, 23: 475–505.

—— (2000b). *Problems of Compositionality*. Garland Publishing, Inc.

Veltman, Frank (1996). Defaults in Update Semantics. *Journal of Philosophical Logic*, 25: 221–61.

von Fintel, Kai (1991). Exceptive Conditionals: The Meaning of 'Unless'. *NELS*, 22: 135–48.

Werning, Markus (2004). Compositionality, Context, Categories, and the Indeterminacy of Translation. *Erkenntnis*, 60: 145–78.

Westerstahl, Dag. Compositionality and Ambiguity.

—— (1985). Logical Constants in Quantifier Languages. *Linguistics and Philosophy*, 8: 387–413.

Westerstahl, Dag. (1998). On Mathematical Proofs of the Vacuity of Compositionality. *Linguistics and Philosophy*, 21: 635–43.

_____ (1999). Idioms and Compositionality.

Zadrozny, Wlodek (1994). From Compositional to Systematic Sematics. *Linguistics and Philosophy*, 17: 329–342.

CHAPTER 27

OPACITY

MARK RICHARD

TRUTH is often indifferent to which of an object's names we use. The sentence *Gauguin twice visited Martinique*, for example, remains true when we replace the name 'Gauguin' with any other way of singling out the painter. But for some ways of putting words together, this sort of thing can make a difference. Quotation marks, for example: *'Gauguin' begins with a 'G'* is true; *'Paul Gauguin' begins with a 'G'* is not.[1] When a construction is like quotation in this regard—within the construction, replacing one way of picking out an object with another has the potential to effect a change like that from truth to falsehood—it is said to be *opaque*.

There seems to be a lot of opacity in our language. Quotation is opaque. The modal idioms are apparently opaque (it's necessary that Gauguin is Gauguin, but not that he's the best known artist to have painted in Tahiti). Propositional attitude ascriptions seem opaque (though Gauguin married Mette Gad, many know that Gauguin painted in Tahiti but don't know that Mette Gad's husband painted there), as do the environments created by verbs such as 'seeks' and 'fears'. The tenses—at least when construed as operators on sentences—also look opaque. And there are a variety of constructions where substituting one way of referring to an object for another can lead from truth to ungrammaticality ('723 is odd' vs. '72three is odd') or to nonsense (if 'the price of a Lexus is $45,000 and rising' is true, then 'the price of a Lexus is rising' is true, but '$45,000 is rising' is, at best, silly).

Opacity raises a number of issues—first and foremost, whether there *is* such a thing. Notoriously, Davidson claimed that opacity must be an illusion, for the "apparent invalidity" of the rule that one can replace one term with a co-referential one without effecting truth "can only be apparent."[2] Part of Davidson's motivation,

---

[1] I use italicization as a device of quasi-quotation.

[2] Davidson (1969), reprinted in Davidson (1984), 93. (Subsequent references to Davidson specify 1984's pagination.)

one suspects, is that acknowledging (non-quotational) opacity commits us to a picture of language on which expressions have a sort of meaning not to be explained in terms of reference, satisfaction, or truth. For suppose the (non-quotational) position of t in the sentence S(t) is opaque. Then for some t and t' picking out the same object, S(t) and S(t') differ in truth value. But presumably a sentence's semantic properties are determined compositionally—by the semantic properties of its parts and its syntax. So there must be some semantic property of t and t'—at least when they occur in this position in a sentence—not determined simply by what those terms refer to.

If we follow Davidson, we have a lot of explaining away to do—how could the appearance of opacity be illusory? If we don't follow him, there are still questions to be answered. Is opacity a unified phenomenon, so that whenever a construction is opaque, the explanation for its opacity is the same? *Does* opacity along with compositionality require semantic theories to posit "non-extensional" semantic values, i.e. things other than ordinary objects and set theoretic constructions there from? Are opaque constructions in some sense anomalous? Quine, for example, has argued that contrary appearances not withstanding, opacity prevents quantifiers from quantifying: Though it may seem as if a quantifier outside of an opaque context can bind a variable within, as in

There is a man such that John suspects that he is a spy,

this, Quine claims, cannot occur.

In what follows, I concentrate on the question of whether there is any opacity to be found in natural language, examining various reasons one might have for denying that apparent opacity is genuine.

27.1 WHAT, EXACTLY, IS OPACITY?

Philosophical use of 'opaque' traces back to Quine, and so we begin with his account of it. In some works (Quine, 1943, for example), Quine speaks of a "purely designative" or "purely referential" *occurrence* of a singular term; such occurrences are ones on which the term "is used solely to designate its object." The contrast is between occurrences such as that of 'Gauguin' in

Gauguin was born in Paris,

and its occurrence in

The sentence 'Gauguin was born in Paris' starts with a 'g',

which is not "purely referential". Elsewhere, Quine speaks of a singular term's *position* or *context* being purely referential, such positions being ones where a term is "used simply to specify its object." The difference, presumably, is that if referentiality or opacity is a property of occurrences, it could in principle be a one-off affair, with

t in $S(t)$ occurring opaquely, t' in $S(t')$ not so occurring; if opacity is a property of a locus or position, it won't be one-off in this way.[3]

Let us think of opacity as a property of positions in sentences. The idea that a term might be used "simply to specify its object" cries out for explanation. But we needn't try to explain it, as Quine gives a criterion for purely referential positions: they are ones open to the *substitutivity of identity*. When $S(t)$ is a sentence, the position of t is so open if, no matter what terms t' and t'' we might pick, the truth of

$$t' = t'' \text{ and } S(t')$$

guarantees the truth of

$$S(t'').$$

Positions which aren't so open are said to be *opaque*.

On Quine's (latter) views, opacity traces in one way or another to the productive mechanisms of the language—the language's *constructions*, as Quine (1970) calls them. Sometimes, Quine speaks of certain constructions "turning a position open to substitutivity" into one which is not. If we think of quotation as something like a grammatical rule—*to form a name of a symbol, put it in quotes*—we think of it as a construction in this sense, and an opaque one at that—opaque in the sense that it has the power to turn positions in a sentence open to substitutivity into ones that aren't.

As Quine (1960) notes, opacity is a special case of what is sometimes called *non-extensionality*. Say that the extension of a singular term is what it is used to refer to or denote; the extension of a predicate, the collection of things of which it is true; the extension of a sentence, its truth value. In many cases, the extension of a complex expression is determined by its syntax and the extensions of its parts. For example, the extensions of the sentences *t was an impressionist* and *t' was an impressionist* cannot differ if the extensions of the terms t and t' don't; the extensions of *the N who married Jean* and *the N' who married Jean* can't vary if the extensions of the N and N' don't. When the extensions of $\ldots e \ldots$ and $\ldots e' \ldots$ cannot differ unless the extensions of e and e' do, the locus of e in $\ldots e \ldots$ is *extensional*; otherwise it is non-extensional. An opaque construction is one in which the locus of some singular term is non-extensional.

Whether a construction counts as opaque turns on what counts as a singular term. For Quine a singular term is an expression whose use "names or purports to name just one object" (Quine, 1960, 90), as opposed to general terms which can, in principle, be true of many objects. The intent, and Quine's practice, is to lump definite

---

[3] Convention. Something of the form

(a) S(t)

is a proxy for expressions (generally, but not invariably, sentences) in which t occurs; the occurrence of t in (a) represents that occurrence (or some specific one, if t occurs several times). We then understand

(b) S(t')

as proxy for the expression just like (that for which) (a) (is proxy), save that the relevant occurrence of t has been replaced by t'. Analogously for things like $\ldots e \ldots$ and $\ldots e' \ldots$.

descriptions (e.g. 'the man who painted *Nafea faa ipoipo*'), possessives ('Med's husband'), and functional terms ('2-1') with demonstratives, indexicals, pronouns, and proper names.

Expressions can, of course, play the role of a singular term in some occurrences but not others. Consider, for example, the individual variables of logic and the English pronouns 'he', 'she', and 'it'. A variable taken relative to an assignment of objects to the variables certainly refers. But, of course, bound uses of variables aren't used to name or designate anything. Even if we assume an assignment to have been fixed, there is something deeply wrong with the argument

$x = y$
$\forall x \exists y(x \neq y \ \& \ Fx)$
So, $\forall x \exists y(y \neq y \ \& \ Fx)$.

But the problem is not that the prefix '$\forall x \exists y$' generates opacity, thus rendering the substitution of 'y' for 'x' invalid. The same remarks apply to 'he' and 'him', which are paradigmatic of singular terms when accompanied by a demonstration, but are not referring or purporting to in sentences such as 'every boy admires the woman who raised him'. Likewise for phrases with bound variables or anaphoric pronouns, such as 'the woman who raised him' as used in the (natural reading of) the last sentence, or 'the first student who comes to my office the next day' in 'Whenever I give a test, the first student who comes to my office the next day complains about it.'

There is a use of 'singular term' on which bound variables and anaphoric pronouns count as singular terms. There is no harm in using 'singular term' in this way, but if we do, we need to find a new label for the class of expressions whose substitution failure signals the advent of opacity.

Quine, as observed above, took anything which "purports to designate" a single object to be a singular term. Many deny that such a grouping is a semantic natural kind. There is something like a consensus that definite descriptions, but not proper names, indexicals or simple demonstratives pattern semantically with phrases such as 'every painter', 'several French impressionists', and 'most critics who have written about Gauguin'. These latter expressions are *quantifiers*, combinations of a *determiner* ('every', 'several', 'most', etc.) and a (possibly complex) noun. Nouns, like verb phrases, are taken to have sets of objects as extensions; determiners are understood to pick out relations between sets. Thus, for example,

Every A Bs is true iff every object in A's extension is in B's;
Some A Bs is true iff some object in A's extension is in B's;
Most As B is true iff most objects in A's extension are in B's.

A quantifier such as *every A* or *most As* has as its extension a property of sets, one gotten in the obvious way from the extension of its determiner and the extension of A. Treating descriptions as quantifiers is straightforward: we simply add to the list

The A Bs is true iff there's exactly one object in A's extension and it's in B's extension.

The idea that descriptions aren't really singular terms is, of course, Russell's. So is the idea that a "genuine" singular term has a semantics quite different from those of quantifiers. According to Russell, a real singular term—a "logically proper name", as he sometimes called such—is an expression which makes no contribution to what is said by a sentence in which it is used beyond the object for which it stands. Notoriously, Russell denied that most "ordinary" proper names were genuine terms in this sense—most uses of names, Russell held, were "truncated definite descriptions": when a speaker uses an ordinary name n in a sentence $S(n)$, there is typically a description d (one which, in some sense, the speaker associates with that use of d) such that what the speaker said with $S(n)$ is something expressed by a literal use of $S(d)$.[4]

The current consensus is that Russell was simply wrong to think that there is no difference between the semantics of natural language's descriptions and its ("ordinary") proper names, demonstratives, and indexicals. No matter how they are construed, the sentences

T1. Between 1950 and 1970, George W. Bush wasn't old enough to be President.

N1. It is necessary that George W. Bush is George W. Bush

are true; they remain so if occurrences of 'George W. Bush' are replaced by any other proper name of Bush, or demonstrative or indexical referring to Bush. In general, exchanging one name of (demonstrative or indexical referring to) an object for another within the scope of a tense or modal has no effect on truth value. This sort of thing isn't true of the sentences

T2. Between 1950 and 1970, the President of the US wasn't old enough to be President.

N2. It is necessary that the President of the US is George W. Bush,

which have readings (on which 'between 1950 and 1970' and 'necessary' govern the rest of the material in the sentence) on which they are obviously false.[5]

Does this and kindred facts show that the tenses and modalities actually aren't opaque, because descriptions aren't "really" singular terms? Does it instead show that the class of singular terms is a heterogenous mess? It isn't clear whether the questions are to be answered by discovery or stipulation. Relevant, however, are our remarks above about expressions which shouldn't be taken to be singular terms (for the purposes of defining opacity) because they are or contain expressions functioning as do the bound variables.

Suppose—as many theorists now think—that the tenses and associated constructions are best understood as quantifiers over temporal entities—instants, intervals, temporally located events, something of the sort. On a natural development of this view:

(a) expressions (like verbs and nouns) which have argument structure contain a temporal argument place; 'mayor', for example, regiments as *mayor* (x,t);

---

[4] Russell 1905 is the classic statement of Russell's views of descriptions. The idea of "logically proper names" surfaces in Russell (1903) and (1905). Russell (1911) exposits the truncation idea.

[5] Is there anyone reading this essay unaware that the classic sources for these observations about proper names and demonstrative 2nd indexicals are Kripke (1980) and Kaplan (1989)?

(b) roughly put, a tense auxillary or expression such as 'it was the case' regiments as a restricted quantifier over some temporal entity, binding free temporal variables in its scope. So 'was' might regiment as *for some t′ earlier than t*; 'was mayor' would regiment as *for some t′ earlier than t, mayor (x, t′)*;

(c) Taken relative to a time I, the semantic properties of an unembedded expression are determined by assigning I to those temporal variables which occur freely in e. So 'Tom was mayor', which would regiment as *for some t′ earlier than t, mayor(tom, t′)*, will be true at I iff Tom was mayor at some time before I.

And now consider a putative illustration of opacity induced by 'between 1950 and 1970':

A1.   Between 1950 and 1970, George W. Bush wasn't old enough to be President.

A2.   George W. Bush is the US President.

A3.   Between 1950 and 1970, the US President wasn't old enough to be President.

These sentences are supposed to exhibit the ability of 'Between 1950 and 1970' ability to generate opacity, since giving the expression scope over all it surveys makes A1 and A2 true, A3 false. But how are these to be regimented, if the temporal indicator is a quantifier? Compact regimentations go:

A1′.   [Every t: t between 1950 and 1970] $\neg O(g,t)$

A2′.   [the x: P(x,t)] $g = x$

A3′.   [Every t: t between 1950 and 1970] [the x: P(x,t)] $\neg O(x,t)$

The fact that A1′ and A2′ may be true without A3′ being so just does **not** show that the temporal quantifier induces opacity. Whether or not we choose to call (the regimentation of) 'the US President' as used in A3 (in A3′) a singular term, it is not a singular term in the sense relevant to opacity. 'the US President' as regimented in A3′ contains a bound temporal variable; the English phrase is to be understood as containing such a variable. 'the US President', as used in (A3), no more refers or purports to refer than do any of the 'x's in 'there is an x such that x = x'. We have opacity when there are singular terms which co-refer and which are such that substituting one for the other in a position takes us from truth to falsity. The current case isn't a case in which we substitute one singular term for another, since when we embed 'the US President' under the tense, it stops even purporting to refer.

Of course exactly the same thing is true of the tense auxillaries when tense is treated quantificationally. If a use of 'the President was democratic' is properly regimented as

[for some t′ : t′ before t] [the x: P(x,t′)] Dx

it is just a mistake to think the fact that Bush is the President and Bush was never a Democrat shows that the tenses induce opacity.

In my opinion, the very same considerations show that the *modalities* are **not** sources of opacity. It is after all somewhat unbelievable, given their syntactic parallelism, that the tense auxiliaries should have one sort of semantics—they are quantifiers—and the modal auxiliaries a completely different sort—they provide properties of what's said by a sentence. If the tenses quantify over times, the modals like 'could' and 'must' surely quantify over possible situations of some sort. Since the semantics of "operators" like 'it must be that', 'it's possible that' are surely absorbed from those of the modal auxiliaries, the conclusion to draw is that to find genuine opacity in natural language, we must look in places other than the tenses and modalities.

All this was occasioned by the question of whether definite descriptions ought to count as singular terms for the purposes of defining opacity. So far as I can see, the only plausible candidates for constructions whose opacity would be evidenced by substitution failures of descriptions but not of names are the tenses and modalities.[6] But substitution of descriptions within tense or modality *isn't* evidence of opacity. So it doesn't really make any difference—save, perhaps, a difference of simplification—as to whether we think of descriptions, for the purposes of discussions of opacity, as terms or not.

27.2 Is There Really Such a Thing as Opacity? (Part I)

On Russell's conception of a name, a name contributes its referent and nothing else to what is said when the name is used; its referent exhausts its semantics. That ordinary names, demonstratives, or indexicals are names in this sense is, of course, controversial. But suppose that all names and singular terms *were* like this. What, if anything, would be left of opacity in natural language? Well, there would still be quotation. But ignore quotational contexts. If names are Russellian, then wherever a name is used, it contributes only its referent to what is said by the sentence in which it is used.[7] So replacing a name used in a sentence with a co-referential one does not effect any semantically relevant fact about the sentence. So such exchange doesn't effect what the sentence says. But what a sentence says determines its truth conditions. So exchanging one name of an object for another can't effect truth. But then there is no opacity, save that supplied by quotation, in natural language.

So, at any rate, one might argue. Let us consider the argument in more detail. We can assume that a semantic theory is something whose purpose is to systematically assign, to a suitably parameterized sentence, either truth conditions or "what the sentence says" relative to the parameters. Call the relevant parameters contexts. They will include something like the assignments of first-order logic to variables,

---

[6] This is of course controversial. Those who take names to be "directly referential" or "Millian" will say that co-referential names are substitutable within the context of 'believes' *salva veritate*, while descriptions are not.

[7] Henceforth, I assume that descriptions have been excluded from the range of the *t*'s in the definition of opacity.

machinery to assign referents to context sensitive expressions, and perhaps other things as well.

Assume further that semantic theories have the sort of structure familiar from the work of David Kaplan. In particular, they assign to simple expressions *meanings*, which are or determine rules which take the theory's contexts and return what we will call *semantic values*. The theory inductively defines sentence truth (relative to a context, at a world) via an induction on the syntactic complexity of a sentence; the input to the induction is nothing more than sentence syntax and the semantic values of simple expressions.

If this is how a semantic theory is structured—and so far as I know, pretty much every attempt at a theory that is currently taken at all seriously can be seen as having such a structure—it is straightforward to say what it is for an expression to have the semantics of one of Russell's "genuine names": The expression has a meaning which, relative to any context (at which it delivers any value at all), delivers an individual as the name's semantic value.[8]

With these assumptions, the argument rehearsed above can be put so. Since a semantic theory assigns truth conditions to sentences via an induction based on syntactic form and the semantic values of simple expressions, it will assign such values in accord with the following principle of compositionality:

C: Let S:...e...be a sentence in which the expression e is used (not quoted); let S':...e'...be the result of replacing e in S with the expression e'. Relative to any context c, if the semantic value of e in c is the same as that of e' in c, then the truth conditions of S in c are the same as those of S' in c.

But from this, the assumption

R: Every singular term is Russellian (and so, in any context, has its referent as semantic value),

and the definition

O: A language displays (non-quotational) opacity only if it contains some sentences S and S', differing only by (non-quotational) occurrences of terms t and t', such that, for some context c, t and t' are co-referential in c, but S and S' differ in truth value relative to c,

it follows that no language displays (non-quotational) opacity. Part of the interest of this argument is that it has seemed to many that in a locus such as that marked by the dots in '.... is sad', it makes no difference, as to what is said, what name of an object one uses. If so, one thinks, then co-referential names (in our current broad sense of 'name') will have the same semantic value in the sense of 'semantic value' used above. So the argument looks like it might in fact show that non-quotational opacity does

---

[8]   The term of art is, of course, 'directly referential expression'; see Kaplan (1989). I am ignoring various facts—such as the fact that a sentence with an empty name can apparently say something, and replacing an empty name with another empty name typically changes what's said—which complicate matters in ways not relevant here.

not exist, at least given the starting point that substituting 'Twain' for 'Clemens' in 'Twain is sad' makes no difference to the sentence's semantic value.

On reflection, it seems unlikely the argument shows any such thing. Let us suppose that, in virtue of their meaning, uses of the sentences 'Twain is sad', 'Clemens is sad', 'I am sad' (as used by Clemens), and 'he is sad' (used when Twain is demonstrated) all convey the same information, that a certain person, Twain, is sad. Then, in some important sense, uses of the sentences say the same thing. So, we may conclude, in these sentences the names of Twain make the same contribution to what is said, in some important sense of 'what is said'.

Why suppose that this semantic value—which we may identify with Twain—is contributed by a name of Twain *no matter where the name occurs*? We *might*, after all, say that in certain contexts, most notably those provided by quotation marks, the semantic value of 'Twain' is not the man Twain, but the *word* 'Twain'. When the name 'Twain' occurs within the scope of a complementizer such as 'that' or 'whether', we *might* hold that its semantic value shifts. If we say this, it is perfectly possible to say that while

Twain is sad
Clemens is sad

say the same thing, this no more implies that

(T) Mark thinks that Twain is sad
(C) Mark thinks that Clemens is sad

say the same thing then it implies that

'Twain' begins with 't'
'Clemens' begins with 't'

do. For embedding a name within a complementizer such as 'that' may shift the name's semantic value: perhaps the name there contributes *both* its referent and some "way of thinking" thereof, or just a "way of thinking" of the referent, or both its referent *and* itself (so that in some sense a name is both used and mentioned in a complement clause), or just itself, or something else.

If we say this, we have rejected the compositionality principle C as resting on a false presupposition, that (even after relativizing to a context) expressions have a single semantic value. We are also in effect proposing an alternative view of what it is for an expression to be a Russellian term: Such a term is an expression which *outside of certain linguistic contexts* (such as quotation and complementizers) is used simply to identify an object (and thus, outside of such contexts, provides only an object to the process that determines what a sentence says). Without some additional argument, that C is to be preferred to a relativized compositionality principle, or that a name cannot shift its contribution to what is said as its location in a sentence shifts, the argument we have been considering (that "non-quotational opacity" is impossible) gets no purchase.

27.3 OPACITY AND QUANTIFICATION

The idea that the semantic properties of an expression might shift on its embedding is due to Frege.[9] In "On Sense and Reference", Frege suggests that all meaningful expressions refer, and that reference is determined compositionally. Frege reconciles this with the (to him obvious) idea that sentences like (T) and (C) may diverge in truth value by saying that, on embedding under 'believes' or 'says', expressions refer to their "ordinary senses" and express "indirect senses."

Frege's view might be offered as a way of "saving" language from the specter of opacity. Our working definition of opacity is this: A construction $C(...)$ is opaque iff there are terms t and t' which refer to the same thing and such that $C(t)$ and $C(t')$ differ in extension. But if the reference of a term depends on where it occurs, the definition needs to specify where we are to assess the terms for reference. If we think that terms somehow acquire a reference independently of where they occur (which they may shift or shed when embedded) we could assess reference independently of occurrence; or we could assess it in the context of the (unembedded) identity $t = t'$; or we could assess it within the context $C(...)$. If we take this last path and tell Frege's tale about sentences about the attitudes, the possible divergence of truth value (T) and (C) does not imply that *believes that* is opaque.

Of course, to define 'opacity' in this way doesn't make it the case that natural language does not "suffer" from opacity in a perfectly straightforward sense. It *is* plausible that proper names are conventional means for referring to an object, that when those names do not find themselves below a word like 'believes' or 'says' their task, first and foremost, is to introduce said object so that something can be said about it. This gives a fairly clear sense to the idea that such terms have reference independently of where they occur in a sentence; if we use 'refer' in this way in defining 'opaque', natural language does "suffer" from opacity.

Prima facie, Frege's view that reference shifts under embedding is untenable as a view about natural language semantics. For it seems to make it impossible to understand how the quantifier 'someone' in

(O) Someone just entered the house, and John believes that he is a spy.

can control the pronoun 'he'. Such control is, after all, modeled to a first approximation by variable binding in first-order languages. In such languages, variables have the semantics of names, save that a variable names an object relative to an assignment, a function mapping the variables onto the objects over which the language quantifies. A sentence of the form *for some x, Fx* is true just in case there is some assignment on which *Fx* is true.

---

[9] It has recently been developed in an interesting way by Jim Higginbotham; see, for example Higginbotham (1986), in which the idea that semantic values must be relativized to linguistic locus is discussed.

The only semantically relevant fact about a variable (relative to an assignment) seems to be what it names; variables, one might say, have reference but no sense. Thus, if 'believes' in

(O′) ∃x(x just entered the house, and John believes that x is a spy)

has a Fregean semantics, the sentence as a whole appears uninterpretable: within the scope of 'believes', on Frege's view, an expression refers to its sense, but the variable, under assignment, doesn't have a sense.

One could have assignments assign to the variables a sense and thereby a reference; the reference would be the variable's referent in "normal" contexts, the sense would be referent in embeddings such as that of the variable in (O′). If we do this, then (O′) is interpretable on a Fregean account of 'believes': If, for example, the sense and reference of 'Orcutt' make the sentence

(O″) Orcutt just entered the house, and John believes that Orcutt is a spy

true, then (O′) will be true. However, this semantics invalidates the principle—sometimes called Leibniz's Law—that the universal closure of any sentence of the form

(L) If x is identical with y, then if . . . x . . . , then . . . y . . .

is true. (Here, . . . x . . . and . . . y . . . are any well formed sentences exactly alike, save that some free occurrence(s) of x in the first are replaced by free occurrences of 'y' in the second.) For example, suppose that the sense and reference of the names 'Orcutt' and 'Harry' are such that the sentence

(I) Ortcutt is identical with Harry, John believes that Orcutt is a spy, but John doesn't believe that Harry is a spy

is true. Assigning the sense/reference of 'Orctutt' to 'x' and that of 'Harry' to 'y' then falsifies

(I′) If x is identical y, then if John believes that x is a spy, then John believes that y is a spy.

So (I)'s universal closure is false. If, as it has been said, the truth of Leibniz's Law is a "fundamental constraint" which a language must satisfy if it has quantification to begin with, this is unacceptable.[10]

If one likes Frege's story about 'believes', one might say that it is simply impossible to "quantify into" opaque contexts, at least using the quantifiers provided by natural (and familiar artificial) languages. And this has been said, most notably by Quine.[11] Quine ingeniously saves the phenomenon—the apparent sense and possible truth of sentences like (O)—by suggesting that 'believes' actually takes a *pair* of arguments, which name an intensional entity (a proposition, a property, a n-ary relation) and a (possibly null) sequence of individuals. Quantifiers which on the surface appear to

---

[10] See Cartwright (1979). I have argued elsewhere (Richard, 1987) that Leibniz's Law is not a "fundamental constraint" on (objectual) quantification, but the issue is orthogonal to our current concerns.
[11] See, for instance, Quine (1951).

bind a variable in the opaque name of a proposition in fact, Quine says, bind variables in the non-opaque name of a sequence. On this story, to say that Warren believes that Tim has resigned is to say that Warren is related by belief to the proposition that Tim has resigned and the empty sequence; to say there is someone such that Warren believes that he has resigned is to say that for some x, Warren is related by belief to the property of resigning and the sequence ⟨x⟩; to say that there are two philosophers whom Warren believes are engaged is to say that there are philosophers x and y such that belief relates Warren to the relation of engagement and the sequence ⟨x,y⟩; etc.[12]

There is a sort of syntactic extravagance in this proposal—one looks in vain for evidence in the surface structure of (O) of multiple arguments for 'believes'. But according to Quine, something like this *must* be right if sentences like (O) are sensible, for, says Quine, it is *impossible* for a quantifier outside an opaque construction to bind a variable within! But while Quine has often insisted upon this, it is hard to find a compelling argument for it in his work. David Kaplan ingeniously reconstructs Quine (1943) as arguing for this conclusion roughly so:

An occurrence of a variable can be bound by a quantifier only if the variable, in that occurrence, has no semantic role but to provide or designate an object.

If a construction $C(\ldots)$ is opaque, then (as there will be a pair of terms t and t' such that $C(t)$ and $C(t')$ differ in truth value), occurrences of terms within that construction have some semantic role other than or beyond the role of providing or designating an object.

So, an occurrence of a variable within an opaque construction can't be bound by a quantifier (outside of the construction).

The second premises *is* tempting. How, after all, could (T) and (C) differ in truth value unless 'Twain' and 'Clemens' make differing contributions when they appear after 'believes' to the process of determining a truth value? They can't. So, one thinks, terms in the position of 'Twain' in (T) contribute something besides an object. So, generalizing from this case, in any opaque occurrence terms are making more of a contribution than their referent. The problem, as Kaplan points out, is that all that follows from these considerations is that *some* occurrences of terms in the relevant position are doing more than just contributing an object. Perhaps a proper name following the verb 'believes' *always* contributes something beyond a referent to determining truth. It doesn't follow that a variable *ever* contributes anything more than an object.

Some of Quine's writings suggest that there is something about existential generalization:

(EG) (a) $C(t)$

So, (b) there is something such that C(it)

which makes quantifying into an opaque context impossible.[13] On one way of understanding Quine's worry, it goes so: (EG) is a valid pattern of inference: if something

---

[12] See Quine (1956) and the remarkable discussion thereof in Kaplan (1986).

Quine's favored account of 'believes' has it naming a relation to a linguistic entity (a closed sentence, a n-place open sentence) and an appropriate sequence. Nothing hangs on which version we focus on here.

[13] A representative passage is found in Section II of Quine (1951).

of the form of (b) makes sense to begin with, it follows from (a). And if (b) makes sense, then so does (d), which thus must follow from (c):

(c) ¬ C(t)

So, (d) there is something such that ¬ C(it).

But if the position of *t* in (a) is opaque, there will be a pair of terms *t* and *t′* such that

t = t′, and C(t), but ¬C(t′)

is true. So, if we can validly existentially generalize on *t* and *t′*, the sentence

There are two objects x and y such that x=y, and ¬ C(x), but C(y)

will be true. But on any standard understanding of the locution 'there are two objects', this can't be true

This much is surely true: if EG is valid without restriction in a language, none of the language's constructions induce opacity. EG is not valid *without* restriction in English, at least not if characterized in the ham handed way it's characterized above. As Quine is fond of pointing out, one can't validly infer *there is something such that 'it' begins with a consonant* from *'Gaugan' begins with a consonant*.

Now why should we suppose that (b) *must* follow from (a), (d) from (c), if the quantifier in (b) is able to bind the 'it'? One might argue so. If (b) *is* sensible, then the C(...) functions as a predicate, as something which can be true or false of an object. It must, since *there is something such that C(... it ...)* is true just in case there is something of which C(...) is true. But then (a) is the application of the predicate C(...) to the name *t*. Such an application is true iff the predicate is true of the object named by *t*. But if the predicate is true of what *t* names, it's true of something, so (b) is true. Ditto for (c) and (d). So EG *is* valid without restriction, provided if (b) is interpretable, the transition from (a) to (b) is valid.[14]

The argument seems to presuppose that if in some appearances a form of words functions as a predicate—as something which contributes satisfaction conditions to what a sentence says—then in every appearance the form functions as a predicate contributing the very same satisfaction conditions. If we don't assume that, the argument falls apart: for why then suppose that C(...) contributes the same satisfaction conditions to (a) and (c) as it does to (b) and (d)? Why think that the predicate C(...) so much as *occurs* in (a) or (c)?[15] It is true, of course, that we ought

(EG) is sometimes identified with an inference which requires, in addition to the premises C(t) the premises *t exists*. I'll ignore this complication.

[14] Worries related to, though not quite identical with, this argument appear in Sider (1995) and Spencer (2001).

[15] Our notation for (a)—'C(t)'—of course makes this idea almost irresistible. But suppose that a sentence such as 'John believes that Bob is sad' is generated thus: one applies the complementizer 'that' to the sentence 'Bob is sad', and then combines the resulting term with the verb 'believes' and term 'John'. Then the idea is far from obvious. We can of course *form* a predicate from this sentence by replacing names with variables. If things go well, the result may have a meaning. But—especially because in replacing the name 'Bob' with a referential variable, we are (from a broadly Fregean perspective) replacing an expression with a reference and a sense with one which has only a reference, there is no

to expect there to be a close connection between the ways $C(\dots)$ functions in all these sentences. But there can be such connections without the way it functions in the sentences being *exactly* the same.

To make the point vivid, let us consider how Frege himself, with a small modification of his view, could have given an account of quantifying into the complement of 'believes'. The modification necessary is to allow that within a complement phrase words not only refer to their senses but to their ordinary references. After 'believes', the word 'Bob' doesn't just refer to **Bob** (I'll use boldfacing for the next few paragraphs to manufacture names of the senses of words), it refers to ⟨**Bob**, Bob⟩; instead of referring to **is sad**, 'is sad' refers to ⟨**is sad**, the set of the sad⟩. A closed complement phrase—i.e. one without free variables—then refers to a complex composed of the (ordinary) senses and referents of its words, a sort of combination of a Fregean thought and a Russellian proposition.[16] 'that Bob is sad', for example, refers to ⟨⟨**Bob**, Bob⟩, ⟨**is sad**, the set of the sad⟩⟩. These are to be taken as what one believes, asserts, and so on. We call them FRT's, since they are an amalgam of what Frege and Russell took to be thoughts. A sentence such as 'John believes that Bob is sad', one would then say, is true just in case its subject is related by belief to the FRT named by the complement clause, so that the sentence just mentioned is true iff John—well, believes the FRT that Bob is sad.[17]

Now, suppose we want to turn 'John believes that Bob is sad' into a predicate by replacing its names with variables—to turn it into 'x believes that y is sad'. Let us assume that the variables are to be understood (a bit anachronistically, since we are putting words in Frege's mouth) in the way Tarski taught us to think of them, as supplying an object (but not a sense) relative to an assignment. What would the predicate mean?

Well, what would the complement 'that y is sad' determine, taken by itself? The complement supplies all of an FRT save what would be supplied by a name with sense and reference. So there are two equivalent stories about what it determines. Most directly, it determines an FRT with a "hole", or, rather, two holes in it: ⟨⟨__, __⟩, ⟨**is sad**, the set of the sad⟩⟩. Equivalently, it determines the *set* of all those FRTs which are completions of the holey one. What would 'that y is sad' determine, relative to an assignment of Bob to the variable 'y'? Again, there are two equivalent answers: it determines the holey FRT, but with Bob filling the second hole: ⟨⟨__, Bob⟩, ⟨**is sad**, the set of the sad⟩⟩. Equivalently, it determines the class of FRTs which are completions of this—and thus have the last hole filled in with something that presents Bob.

What, then, would it mean to say that John and Bob stood in the relation expressed by 'x believes that y is sad'? It seems obvious: John would have to believe one of the FRTs determined by 'that y is sad', when Bob is assigned to 'y'. That is, speaking

---

reason to think that the meaning of the original sentence is to be identified with the result of combining the meaning of the predicate and of the names we removed to form that predicate.

[16] One would want the reference of predicates and quantifiers to be "more intensional", identifying the reference, for example, of 'is sad' with the property of being sad, or with some function mapping worlds to their sad denizens. Let's not worry about this here.

[17] See the next note for a minor adjustment.

more generally, the predicate will be true of ⟨u.v⟩ just in case there is *some* way w of thinking of v such that, among the objects of μ's belief, is the FRT ⟨⟨w, v⟩, ⟨is sad, the set of the sad⟩⟩. These are the satisfaction conditions of the predicate. The satisfaction conditions of 'it's not the case that x believes that y is sad' are, of course, just the complement of these conditions: it's true just in case there is *no* way w of thinking of v such that among the objects of μ's belief is the FRT ⟨⟨w, v⟩, ⟨is sad, the set of the sad⟩⟩.[18]

If we are (modified) Fregeans, we will say that 'Bob' in 'believes that Bob is sad' is doing double duty: it is referring to Bob *and* it is providing a way of thinking of him. We will, that is, say that the position of 'Bob' here is a paradigm of opacity. If the 'y' in 'believes that y is sad' is a variable of the familiar sort, it is simply incapable of doing this sort of double duty: a variable (under assignment) has reference, but no sense. If we take 'believes's meaning to be determined by its role in sentences like 'John believes that Bob is sad', we will say that the verb is looking for something—a way of thinking of something—that the variable is simply incapable of providing.

This doesn't mean that quantifying in is uninterpretable. It is, after all, simply obvious what the truth conditions of 'John thinks of Bob that he is sad' should be on a Fregean view—they should involve existential quantification over ways of thinking. It is hardly a leap from a neo-Fregean understanding of 'John believes that Bob is sad' to this understanding of 'there is someone whom John believes to be sad'—anyone with a wit of sense could and would have this understanding of the latter once they understood the former.

Notice that the satisfaction conditions we have given to sentences involving quantifying in predict that while the inference

John believes that Bob is sad
So, there is someone, Bob, such that John believes that he is sad

is valid, the inference

John doesn't believe that Bob is sad
So, there is someone, Bob, such that John doesn't believe that he is sad

is not valid. The premiss tells us that John doesn't believe a *particular* FRT of the form ⟨⟨w, Bob⟩, ⟨is sad, the set of the sad⟩⟩; the conclusion tells us that John doesn't believe *any* such FTR. The upshot, as I see it, is that Quine's argument involving (EG) is fallacious, and there is nothing incoherent, impossible, or particularly unlikely about a quantifier outside of an opaque construction binding a variable within it.[19]

---

[18] A small detail. Things look smoothest if complement clauses name *sets* of FRTs. 'that John is sad' names, relative to any assignment to the variables, the unit set of the relevant FRT; 'that y is sad' gets assigned, relative to an assignment f to the variables, the set of FRTs of the form ⟨⟨w, f(y)⟩, ⟨is sad, the sad things⟩⟩, w a way of thinking of f(y). We may then say that *t believes that S* is true relative to an assignment f provided what *t* names relative to f bears belief to some member of what *that S* determines relative thereto.

[19] I tell a story about complements and attitude verbs that in some ways resembles the tale just told in Richard (1990).

Let me tie what I have been doing in the last few paragraphs more closely to Frege's actual views. We should distinguish the spirit of those views from the letter of their development. Frege's leading insight, as I see it, is simply that a word doesn't have to function in *exactly* the same way in every linguistic environment in which it may find itself. One can agree with this—pretty banal—claim without holding, as Frege in fact did, that while 'the Earth' refers to the Earth in 'The Earth moves', it doesn't refer to the Earth in 'Galileo said that the Earth moves'. Why not—more plausibly—simply say that in the latter sentence 'the Earth' not only refers to the Earth, but does some other things as well? One doesn't even have to say that 'the Earth' "changes its meaning" upon being embedded under 'says'. The meaning of a word or phrase is (presumably something like) its conventionally associated semantic role, the powers and potentials we all expect one another to associate with it and to deploy in its use. What earthly reason could there be to think that such a meaning can't be a package of powers and potentials, some of which are only invoked in some linguistic environments?

27.4 Is There Really such a Thing as Opacity? (Part II)

Davidson famously complains at the end of 'On Saying That' that

If we could recover our pre-Fregean semantic innocence, I think it would seem to us plainly incredible that the words 'the earth moved', uttered after the words 'Galileo said that', mean anything different, or refer to anything else, than is their wont when they come in other environments.[20]

Davidson, it seems to me, is partly right and partly wrong. He is right that it is plainly incredible that words after 'said that' stop referring to that to which they usually refer. But why is it plainly incredible to think that they are doing something else as well? Doesn't it seem as obvious as the beard on Frege's chin that they *are* doing something *in addition* to what is their wont in other environments?

There are opaque constructions which are unlike the verbs of attitude in these ways. When someone utters the sentence

'the Earth' contains eight characters and a space

it seems they *don't* refer to the Earth. While the move from 'Galileo said that the Earth moves' to 'Of the Earth, Galileo said that it moves' is harmless, the move from the sentence just displayed to 'Regarding the Earth, 'it' contains eight characters and a space' is lunatic.

Quotation seems a pretty straightforward phenomenon. Given a word or a phrase, we can form a name of it by enclosing it in quotes; what more can there be to say

---

[20] Davidson (1969), 108.

about the syntax or semantics of quotation? Given that this is the right thing to say, quotation produces opacity, if we think of opaque constructions as those which applied to expressions with the same *unembedded* extensions produce expressions with divergent extensions. But this is because the meaning (ordinary or otherwise) of an expression is just *irrelevant* to the meaning of its quotation name. It is not that the filling of a quotation name is doing something new or novel when quoted; it's not doing anything at all. And there's no mystery about this—the one sentence rule of the syntax and semantics of quotation just given tells us how all this comes to pass.

Davidson objects to a kindred account of quotation names given by Tarski. According to Tarski

Quotation-mark names may be treated like single words of a language, and thus like syntactically simple expressions. The single constituents of these names—the quotation marks and the expressions standing between them—fulfill the same function as the letters and complexes of letters in single words. Hence, they can possess no independent meaning. Every quotation name is thus a constant individual name . . . and in fact a name of the same nature as the proper name of a man.[21]

Davidson says this can't be right. We know something that allows us (limitations of time and attention set to the side) to understand the sentences of our language. Since we are finite, what we know must be finitely statable. But, says Davidson, on a view such as Tarski's

nothing would be lost if for each quotation-mark name we were to substitute some unrelated name, for that is the character of quotation names [i.e. they are without significant structure] . . . .There are an infinite number of quotation-mark names. [Since on Tarski's theory such names are without structure] [i]t follows that a theory of truth could not be made to cover generally sentences containing quotation.[22]

Davidson in fact thinks that in a straightforward sense quotation doesn't involve opacity. Quotation marks, according to Davidson, function as demonstratives; uttering

(G) 'Gauguin was born in Paris' starts with 'g'

is doing something very similar to what one does in uttering

(G′) He [pointing to Gauguin] was born in Paris,

as the role of the quotation marks is to indicate their filling. A use of (G) is analogous to the use of 'That sentence begins with this' in

(G″) Gauguin was born in Paris. That sentence begins with this: g.

If this is right, then 'Gauguin' no more occurs in (G) than Gauguin occurs in (G′).

If Davidson's objections to Tarskian accounts of quotation were plausible, we would need to take this view of his up. But, in my opinion, the objections are not very plausible. Tarski's idea, presumably, was that a quotation name was "of the

---

[21] Tarski (1936), 159–60.   [22] Davidson (1979), 83.

same nature as a proper name" in the sense that semantics is to assign to such names their referents "directly"—that is, without determining those referents on the basis of the meanings or referents of those names' parts. But the rule *the quotation of an expression names that expression* does this quite nicely, handling infinitely many names all at once. Davidson's suggestion that on Tarski's view "nothing would be lost" by replacing such a rule with an infinite set of rules ("*'Arthur Danto'*" *names* *'Arthur Danto';* "*'Pierre Melville'*" *names 'Pierre Melville';* . . . .) is just wrong—what would be lost is the axiomatizability of semantics!

Davidson's thought was presumably that if a quotation name is "of the same nature" as a proper name, it can't have *any* structure whatsoever, beyond the "structure" induced by the fact that a name is a sequence of characters. But why should Tarski have to say that? Quotation names have no semantically significant structure; it does not follow that they lack other sorts of structure. Following Quine, call the syntactic processes which construct complex expressions from simpler ones *constructions*. Constructions typically have semantic significance, in the sense that associated with a construction is a function which maps the meanings (or extensions) of the expressions it operates on to the meaning (extension) of its output. Thus, the output of a construction typically has a certain kind of structure, "semantically significant" structure. But there's no need for *every* construction of a language to endow expressions with this sort of structure. The purpose of some constructions—quotation, for example—might be "merely lexical", to introduce words into the lexicon. So long as *something* interprets the words so introduced (and the interpretation gets done in a finite manner) what objection can there be to the idea that there are such constructions?[23]

I said above that the syntax and semantics of quotation is given by the simple rule *Given a word or a phrase, we can form a name of it by enclosing it in quotes.* This can't be all there is to quotation. We can form quotation names of gibberish ("'eghi dor hasty gop'"), of foreign words in foreign alphabets ("'λωγωζ'"), of arbitrary symbols ("'☎'"). Some say we can form the name of a squiggle—a thing which is not of a type—by enclosing it in quotes. Given this, one might think, there must be something to Davidson's complaint. For there is no limit to the number of things which might be quoted to manufacture quotation names. And there doesn't seem to be any effective way of describing this material, either. So wasn't Davidson right to think that a Tarskian account of quotation is untenable?[24]

I think not. Before explaining why, let me take a brief detour to discuss types, tokens, and grammar. I have been implicitly assuming that what a grammar for a language tells us is what the expression *types* of the language are. It thereby tells us, of course, what the expression tokens of a language are as well, as those tokens are tokens of the language's sentence types. A grammar is usually thought of as generating expressions (types) from a primitive set (of types), the language's lexicon. The generating mechanisms—constructions, as we have been calling them—can be

---

[23] These ideas about quotation are developed in Richard (1986).
[24] Davidson (1979) pushes some of these worries; LePore (1998) raises the squiggle problem.

thought of as functions which map (ordered series of) expressions to expressions. Usually, the output of such mechanisms will be (the types of) expressions standing in a certain structural relation; in the simplest languages, such as those studied in logic, these relations sometimes boil down to nothing more than concatenation. Thus, a rule like *If S and T are sentences, so is SvT* is to be understood as telling us that for any two sentence types S and T, there is a sentence type—a property of inscriptions—which is had by an inscription iff it is the result of concatenating a token of S to the left of a token of 'v' and concatenating all that to the left of a token of T. It is usually assumed that for each construction there is a rule which assigns a meaning, or extension, or semantic value (or whatever we choose to call what semantics assigns to expressions) on the basis of the semantic meanings (extensions . . .) of its parts. For the above, the rule might be phrased so: The truth value (0 or 1) of a sentence of the form *SvT* is the maximum of the truth values of S and T.

Now let me set the issue of quotation names of things like squiggles—which not being parts of a language or other symbol system, do not possess the sort of type of the things named by standard quotation names—to the side for a moment. Then the thrust of the objections made two paragraphs above comes to this: there are indefinitely—for all we know, infinitely—many simple symbols which have quotation names in English. There are certainly an infinity of quotable symbol sequences. (Henceforth, use 'symbol' so that such sequences are symbols.) There is no reason to think that there is any means of generating these symbols that we English speakers have a handle on. But we must know something which implies that each such quotation name is a name of English. For we know the language we speak, in the sense that there is something we know which determines what the sentences of that language are. We are finite, so this something must be finitely statable. But given that the simple symbols with quotation names can't be generated by anything we know, there is no way to say in finitely many words what the quotation names of English are—at least not it we adopt the sort of account sketched above.[25]

The objection goes awry when it suggests we know no rule that generates all possible quote names. Why, after all, can't we simply say

(Q1)   For any symbol (type) s, a quotation mark followed by s followed by another quotation mark is a name of s

This is finite. It implies that for *any* symbol our language contains a name of it.

He who lodges the objection two paragraphs back presumably assumes (something along of the lines of the claim) that if E is an expression of English of type T, then an adequate grammar for English must, all by itself, entail something of the form *e is an expression of type T of English*, where e is a term which picks out E and in some way describes or enables one to describe how E looks when correctly written. But it is hard to see why we ought to demand this of a grammar. Perhaps it will be said that only a

---

[25] Even if there are only finitely many simple symbols in the universe, the problem remains, for we must grant that however we know what we know about quotation names, it is not through having internalized a very, very large list.

grammar with this property would be something, knowledge of which is adequate for linguistic competence.

But why suppose that? Competence in English in using quotation names seems to consist in being able to recognize quotation names of English expressions (and nonsense strings of such), and knowing that quite generally when one quotes a symbol one forms a name of it. One doesn't have to know *a priori* what the range of symbols which might be quoted is; this is extra-linguistic information that we acquire as we learn about the world and its symbol systems. Let us agree with the generative grammarian that an adequate grammar is in some sense a transcription of what the competent speaker has internalized about her language, a transcription of that which she invokes in production and comprehension thereof. No one thinks that production and comprehension involves *nothing* beyond grammatical knowledge—one must register and make use of facts about the situation in which one finds oneself. What good reason can be provided for denying that among these "extra-linguistic" facts are facts about what things, outside of the symbols of one's own language, are quotable symbols?

This leaves us with the objection based on the possibility of using quotation to name things like random squiggles which have no type which makes them part of a symbol system. On this use of quotation marks, it seems, enclosing a token in quotes yields a name of that very token. Assume that no such token is a type. Why can't we say that this use of quotation is of a piece with the use we have been discussing? To say this is to say that the rule (Q1) tells some, but not all, of the story about quotation; the rest of the story is told by

(Q2) For any inscription (token) s, a quotation mark followed by s followed by another quotation mark is a name of s.

Once both (Q1) and (Q2) are acknowledged as governing the use of quotation, there are two ways to interpret something like

(D) 'dog' is a word,

for its first word could be understood as a name of the word type 'dog' or as a name of the very token inscribed above. On the first interpretation, we understand (D) as generated using (Q1); on the second, using (Q2). This, of course, is just what one would expect, if one thinks that inscription of a quotation name can be inscription which names either the type of its filling or the filling itself.[26]

---

[26] Doesn't the story I told above, about a grammar's productive mechanisms being (n-ary) maps from types to types, needs some modification once we adopt this story? After all, (Q2) doesn't take a type as input, but a token.

One could modify the story, but it doesn't seem necessary. (Q1) can be understood as encoding the function which (for example) maps the type *dog*—the type which is realized by inscribing realizations of the types *d*, *o*, and *g*—to the type 'dog'—that is, the type realized by inscribing realizations of the quote mark, *d*, *o*, *g*, and the quote mark. (Q2) can be understood as encoding a function which maps "singular types"—properties of being identical with a particular token—to types. Applied to the (property of being identical to) token d of 'dog' displayed in the token (D) above, this function yields the property of being realized by inscribing d with quotes surrounding it.

$$* * *$$

I have looked at some of the places opacity is usually said to occur in natural language—within tense and modality; inside ascriptions of belief and other attitudes; inside of quotation marks. Though I have had something to say about the syntax and semantics of such constructions, I have been as much concerned with the reasons one might have for saying or denying that a particular construction is opaque.

It seems to me that there is *some* opacity in natural language—though its locus is not exactly what it is usually thought to be, at least if I am right about tense and modality. It is not clear that all opacity is on a par—what renders a quotation name opaque seems fundamentally different from what renders a complement opaque. At least this is so if what I have said in the last two sections is on track.

Indeed, the two cases—attitude ascription, quotation—seem so different that one is tempted to say that they shouldn't be labeled in the same way. It is one thing to put a word in an environment where semantic properties beyond (ordinary) reference help shape the meaning of that of which the word is a part; it seems quite another to put the word in an environment where its meaning is simply irrelevant to the meaning of the containing whole. Whether we would do better to introduce a new taxonomy here is a question left to the Linnaeuses of semantics.

References

Cartwright, Richard (1979). "Indiscernability Principles", in *Midwest Studies in Philosophy IV*, French *et al*, eds., University of Minnesota Press.

Davidson, Donald (1969). "On Saying That", in Davidson (1984).

_____ (1979). "Quotation", in Davidson (1984).

_____ (1984). *Inquiries into Truth and Interpretation*, Oxford University Press.

Higginbotham, James (1986). 'Linguistic Theory and Davidson's Program in Semantics', in LePore (1986).

Kaplan, David (1986). "Opacity", in *The Philosophy of W. V. Quine*, Schilpp (ed.), 1986, Open Court.

_____ (1989). 'Demonstratives', in *Themes from Kaplan*, Almog, Perry, Wettstein (eds.), Oxford University Press.

Kripke, Saul (1980). *Naming and Necessity*, Harvard University Press, Cambridge, MA.

Lepore, Ernie (1998). "The Scope and Limits of Quotation", *Mind*.

_____ ed. (1986). *Truth and Interpretation: Perspectives on the Philosophy of Donald Davidson*, Blackwell, Oxford.

Quine, W. V. (1943). "Notes on Existence and Necessity", *The Journal of Philosophy*.

_____ (1951). "Reference and Modality", reprinted in slightly altered form in Quine 1961.

_____ (1956). "Quantifiers and Propositional Attitudes", *The Journal of Philosophy*.

_____ (1960). *Word and Object*, MIT Press.

_____ (1961). *From a Logical Point of View*, Harvard University Press.

_____ (1970). *Philosophy of Logic*, Prentice Hall.

Richard, Mark (1986). "Grammar, Quotation, and Opacity", *Linguistics and Philosophy*.

_____ (1987). "Quantification and Leibniz's Law", *The Philosophical Review*.

_____ (1990). *Propositional Attitudes*, Cambridge University Press.

Russell, Bertrand (1903). *Principles of Mathematics*, Allen and Unwin.

Russell, Bertrand (1905). "On Denoting", *Mind*.

_____ (1911). "Knowledge by Acquaintance and Knowledge by Description", *Proceedings of the Aristotelian Society*, 11.

Sider, Ted (1995). "Three Problems for Richard's Theory of Belief Ascription", *Canadian Journal of Philosophy*.

Spencer, Cara (2001). 'Belief and the Principle of Identity', *Synthese*.

Tarski, Alfred (1935). 'Der Wahrheitsbegriff in den formalisierten Sprachen', *Studia Philosophica*, I. Translated into English and published under the title 'The Concept of Truth in Formalized Languages' in Tarski (1956).

_____ (1956). *Logic, Semantics and Metamathematics*, Oxford University Press.

C H A P T E R   2 8

....

TENSE

....

PETER LUDLOW

AT first blush, the analysis of tense seems like a fairly straightforward enterprise. There are supposedly a handful of tenses (past, future, past perfect etc.), these are visible syntactic features of our language (for example the inflectional tense morphology of our language), and the task is to get clear on their semantics. As we will see, matters are not nearly so simple.

There is already a problem about whether tense is merely a feature of our language and thoughts or whether tense might be a property of aspects of the external world. A common refrain has it that language is tensed and that the world is not, and to think otherwise is just a category mistake. The problem is that this refrain may well have things upside down. Most languages of the world have nothing resembling standard Indo-European tense morphology. Other languages rely upon elements like aspect, evidentials,[1] and modals to talk about temporal features of the world. Even in English it seems doubtful that we have a genuine future tense (clearly 'will' is a modal in 'I will eat'), and our past tense morpheme '-ed' looks for all the world like an aspectual marker (presumably indicating perfect aspect). Now of course we are good at identifying the ways in which different languages express past, future, etc., but there is no common feature of the *syntax* of these languages that we are picking up on (since they express temporal notions in radically different ways). Talking about tensed thoughts only removes the problem by one step, since, unless we adopt a Cartesian theory of psychology, we will want to know what makes a particular mental state *tensed* if not some feature of the world that it represents. In the face of these

---

[1] Evidentials are grammatical elements that encode the source of the information. So for example imagine that English had a suffix '-foo' which when appended to a verb indicated that the event in question was seen with one's own eyes (as opposed to via testimony or inference). Then if I say 'John walkfoo', I am saying that I saw John walk with my own eyes. The past tense is presumably inferred from the nature of perceptual reports. Many languages use elements like this in complimentary distribution with past tense morphology.

considerations, one begins to suspect that there are temporal features of the world and that different languages of the world devise different strategies for talking about those features. If this is right, then natural language tense may only enter into the picture when we consider how language hooks up with the tensed features of the world.

We have different ways of expressing temporal notions, but there is also the pressing question of what exactly we are talking about when we express these temporal notions. We may be talking about features of the world, but what features? On one view, we are just talking about a series of tenselessly existing events ordered by the earlier-than/later-than relation. On the other view, we are talking about some important temporal features of the world (for example a tensed fact—like the fact that it rained yesterday—that currently obtains). Philosophers and semanticists who hold the former view are often called "detensers"; those who hold the latter view are typically called "tensers." This distinction is subtle, but it also lies at the root of the distinction between the two main approaches to tense in philosophy and the semantics of natural language. Accordingly, we will need to spend a bit of time trying to get clear on this distinction before we move on to the alternative conceptions of tense themselves.

28.1 TENSE, TENSERS, AND DETENSERS

For better or for worse most semanticists and philosophers are detensers—they believe that the proper analysis of temporal language is to hold that there are no fundamentally tensed semantic primitives and that the semantics of temporal language is best given in a metalanguage from which tense has been stripped away.

The odd thing about this standard treatment of tense in the semantics of natural language is it would not count as a *tense logic* in the sense of Burgess (2003); the treatment is rather a "regimentation" of tense. To illustrate, on such an approach an utterance of (1) might have an analysis like (1').

(1) John ate
(1') if S is an utterance of 'John ate' by speaker s in context c, and R is an implicit reference event picked out by s in c, then S is true iff the event of John's eating temporally overlaps with R and R is earlier than S

A close neighbor of this analysis would swap talk of events for talk of times:

(1") if u is an utterance of 'John ate' at time S, for speaker s, and R is an implicit reference to a temporal interval picked out by s, then u is true iff John's eating is at time E, E is contained in R, and R is earlier than S

That isn't what happens in a tense logic in the sense that Burgess has in mind—a tense logic in that sense takes tense to be ineliminable. So for example, the semantics of a past tense morpheme PAST in conjunction with a sentence S, would be something like the following:

(1''') 'PAST[S John eats]' is true iff '[S there is an eating by John]' was true

Notice that on the right hand side of the biconditional we have our tensed predicate 'was true'. Another way to think about the different approaches is that tensers think that propositions (or in any case the bearers of truth) shift in truth-value over time (you might take this to be definitional of their being tensed), while detensers put a time index in propositions and argue that propositions are anchored to a time (John ate at time t) in such a way that the propositions are eternal.

In the untensed case—(1')—tense is a relational predicate holding between an utterance (or utterance time) and an event (or event time). In the tensed case—(1''')—tense is a kind of monadic indexical predicate holding of a proposition. Semantically, its analysis would involve a Fregean indexical sense which might be displayed in the metalanguage by expressions like 'was true' and 'will be true'. A defense of the tenser's position thus requires a plausible defense of the Fregean analysis of indexicals, as well as a response to challenges that tense is not an indexical period (much less an indexical predicate).

28.2 TWO THEORIES OF TENSE

More formally, the two approaches to tense that I have discussed thus far look something like the following.

28.2.1 Theory A (A Semantics of Tense with a *Tensed Metalanguage*)

For this theory we assume a simple syntax in which tense morphemes detach from the verbal stem and move (via operator raising) to a position where they can take the entire clause (or some semantic value computed from the clause—perhaps a proposition) as an argument. Let's call the resulting structure a "Tense Phrase" or "TP", and suppose that the syntactic structures that are handed to the semantics include the following. (From here out we are adopting the conceit that tense is a genuine syntactic category—obviously this leads to worries in the cross-linguistic context as well as in English given the concerns raised above).

(2) a. [TP PAST S]
   b. [TP FUT S]

Turning to our semantics, let's use the symbolism '$[]\alpha[]$' to indicate a proposition that is related—in way to be specified—to the syntactic form α (presumably a clause).[2] Tense morphemes can be thought of as predicates taking these propositional objects as their arguments.

---

[2] One possibility would be that this proposition-like object is an interpreted logical form (ILF) in the sense of Larson and Ludlow (1993) that is recursively constructed from the clause and the semantic values of its constituents.

We now distinguish *inherent verbal tense* from *morphological tense*. According to theory A, most if not all verbs have inherent present tense which is reflected in their base axioms (e.g. Val($\langle$x,y$\rangle$, *hits*) iff x hits y). Morphological tense is another matter. Morphological tenses (like '-ed') are not inherent parts of the verbs with which they appear but are operators that take the proposition-like objects as their arguments.
Morphological Tense:

(3) a. Val(T, [TP PAST S], σ) iff
       []S[] was true

    b. Val(T, [TP FUT S], σ) iff
       []S[] will be true

The question naturally arises as to how we should treat complex tenses like the future perfect, past perfect (pluperfect) etc. One idea, apparently endorsed by Prior (1969), was to nest the morphological tenses to get the appropriate complex tense. The syntax for sentences containing complex tenses would accordingly be as follows (in a bit we will discuss the limitations of this proposal).
future perfect:

(4) [S FUT[S PAST [S]]]

past perfect:

(5) [S PAST[S PAST [S]]]

future in the future:

(6) [S FUT[S FUT[S]]]

In theory A, temporal adverbs (*today, yesterday, now*, etc.) are naturally treated disquotationally:

(7) a. Val(x, [ADV *today*], σ) iff
       x is true today

    b. Val(x, [ADV *yesterday*], σ) iff
       x held (was true) yesterday

Note that most of these may also be reducible to a single primitive tensed predicate:

(8) Val(x, [ADV *yesterday*], σ) iff x held the day before the day occurring now

By itself Theory A does not constitute a tense logic, but merely a semantics that might be given for the sort of tense logic envisioned by Prior. Prior himself was basically unconcerned with giving a semantics in this sense, and focused on the logical rules that might support logical inferences from, for example, 'I am eating' to 'I will have eaten'. For Prior these inferences were not supported by the semantics, but rather by the syntax of the tense logic. It is a rather different picture from current practice in the semantics of natural language, which incorporates what we can call a B-theoretic approach to the semantics of tense. In the resulting picture logical inferences involving natural language tense are supported by the semantics.

28.2.2 Theory B (A Semantics of Tense with a *Detensed* Metalanguage)

This approach to tense was pioneered by Reichenbach (1947), but has been adopted in some form or other by most semanticists, including Guenther (1979); Hinrichs(1986, 1988); Hornstein (1981, 1990); Vickner (1985); Kamp and Reyle (1993). On this approach, we need to introduce three temporal points, S, R, and E, understood as follows.

S: is the utterance event (utterance time)
E: is the matrix event (time the event takes place)
R: is a reference event (reference time)

The various tenses are then a function of the relative ordering of these events on a time line (the primitive temporal relation will simply be the linear ordering relation earlier-than/later-than). Here is a possible way of representing the tenses.

(9)

> *Present*:⟨--E,S--⟩
> *Past*:⟨--E---S--⟩
> *Future*:⟨--S---E--⟩
> *Pluperfect*:⟨--E---R---S--⟩
> *Future perfect*:⟨--S---E---R--⟩
> *Future in Future*:⟨--S---R---E--⟩
> *Future in the Past*:⟨--R---S---E--⟩ or ⟨--R---E---S--⟩

We can introduce this basic idea into a T-theory for natural language in the following way. We introduce a six place predicate Val(A, B, S, R, E, σ), which can be read as "A is the semantic value of B at time of utterance S, reference time R, event time E, and assignment σ." The various tenses then receive a semantics like the following.

(10) a. Val(e, PAST, S, R, E, σ) iff
R/E is earlier than S and At(e, E)

b. Val(e, PRES, S, R, E, σ) iff
S, R, and E temporally overlap and At(e, E)

c. Val(e, FUT, S, R, E, σ) iff
S is earlier than R/E and At(e, E)

d. Val(e, PRES PERFECT, S, R, E, σ) iff
E is earlier than S/R and At(e, E)

e. Val(e, PAST PERFECT, S, R, E, σ) iff
E is earlier than R, R is earlier than S and At(e, E)

f. Val(e, FUT PERFECT, S, R, E, σ) iff
S is earlier than E, E is earlier than R and At(e, E)

Unlike the A-theory of tense we cannot simply disquote the temporal adverbs; they are not B-theoretically legitimate. One needs to replace them with talk of events and our primitive earlier-than/later-than relation. The following is a possibility.

(11) a. Val(e, *yesterday*, S, R, E, σ) iff E is a day earlier than S and At(e, E)

　　　b. Val(e, *today*, S, R, E, σ) iff S and E are the same day and At(e, E)

　　　c. Val(e, *tomorrow*, S, R, E, σ) iff R is a day later than S and At(e, E)

On the other hand, basic temporal relations like 'before' and 'after' basically can receive a disquotational analysis.

(12) a. Val (T,[$_S$ S1 *before* S2], S, R, E, σ) iff
　　　　　Val (T, S1, S, R1, E1, σ) and Val (T, S2, S, R2, E2, σ) and E1 is earlier than E2

　　　b. Val (T,[$_S$ S1 *after* S2], S, R, E, σ) iff
　　　　　Val(T, S1, S, R1, E1, σ) and Val(T, S2, S, R2, E2, σ) and E1 is later than E2

　　　c. Val(T,[$_S$ S1 *while* S2], S, R, E, σ) iff
　　　　　Val(T, S1, S, R1, E1, σ) and Val(T, S2, S, R2, E2, σ) and E2 temporally contains E1

Returning to the inference from 'I am eating' to 'I will have eaten', the inference can be accounted for directly from the semantics just given. If I am now eating, then for any future reference event R that we chose, my eating will be earlier than R.

28.3 THE CASE FOR REGIMENTATION

If Semanticists have favored Theory B (the detensed semantics of tense), it is not without reason. In this section we will canvass a number of objections that have been raised against attempts to give a semantics of tense in a tensed metalanguage.

28.3.1 The Non-public Nature of Tensed Theorems

The first and most obvious objection to a tensed metalanguage is that if (as commonly assumed) meanings are to be public objects that persons grasp when they understand a sentence, and further that different people can grasp the same meaning at different times, then the result seems to be allegedly incoherent truth conditions like the following.

(13) 'John is hungry now' is true iff John is hungry now

After all, not only am I capable of grasping the meaning of an utterance of 'John is hungry now' right now, but if I do grasp the meaning then I am quite capable of grasping its meaning tomorrow, and so are many other individuals. But what I grasp tomorrow won't be that John is hungry now, so I'll need a different theorem to grasp it tomorrow.

　　Suppose that we take the natural step and think of tense—the tenser's version, not the detenser's version—as being a kind of indexical sense of the type broadly advocated by in Frege (1956). Then the objection just given is, in effect, the objection that Perry (1977) advanced in his paper "Frege on Demonstratives," when he objected to the Fregean idea that indexicals like 'today' have an indexical sense. If you want to say that the sense/meaning can be grasped at different times by different people (and Frege (1956) did seem to want this), then truth conditions like the above won't do. According to many philosophers, a theory of meaning—or at least a semantic theory—should concern itself with that component of understanding that is stable across users and times. We can get at this component with a theorem like the following.

(14) At utterance u, by speaker s, at time t of 'John is hungry now' is true iff John is
      hungry at t

For the detenser this is a plausible story about the truth conditions of the utterance, since it is faithful to the part of the meaning that is stable among all temporal perspectives.

On the other hand, as we will see, philosophers like Prior (1959) argued that this sort of theorem is grossly inadequate, for it doesn't correctly characterize the difference in meaning between 'John is hungry now' and 'John is hungry at 7:00 p.m. on July 3, 2004'. If we are unaware of the time, knowing the former sentence to be true might stir us to take John to dinner, whereas only knowing the latter to be true may not affect our actions in the same way.

We will return to this topic when we give the case for the tenser, and while we will see that the strategic position of the tenser is not impossible, it is certainly very difficult. If contents must be public and shared then it is really very difficult to see how the project of the tenser can even get off the ground. Before we get that far, however, we need to consider some other objections to tensism, including an important objection due to McTaggart (1908, 1927), and a class of problems having to do with the phenomenon of temporal anaphora.

28.3.2 McTaggart's Paradox

In a famous argument that drove much of the twentieth century research on time, McTaggart offered a two-pronged argument for the incoherence ("unreality" of time in McTaggart's language) by showing that it led to contradiction. The idea was to show first that the A-theory conception of time was not reducible to the B-theory conception (in effect, that temporal language could not be detensed), and second that the A-theory is incoherent. Philosophers in the ninety years thence have agreed that McTaggart had this half wrong—they just disagreed about which half he got wrong. A-theorists (tensers) think he was wrong about the incoherence of the A-theory; B-theorists (detensers) think he was wrong about A-series being ineliminable ("more fundamental"). For now, we need only concern ourselves with the alleged incoherence of the A-series.

We begin with the assumption that objects (including propositions and events) cannot have incompatible properties. For example no event could be entirely in the future and entirely in the past. But, according to McTaggart, that is precisely what the A-theorist is committed to. Take the event of your reading this paper, and let's call that event E. According to McTaggart, we are now committed to the following:

(M1) future(E) & present(E) & past(E)

But wait! The A-theorist now wants to object that this is obviously false—that E's being past present and future don't all hold now, but at different times, in effect we are really only committed to (A1).

(A1) E is future/past/present at different times

Here McTaggart makes a clever move in the dialectic, holding that proposition (A1) sneaks in a B-theory notion of "different times".
At this point the A-theorist might decide to avoid talk of "times" (which does look like a bit of B-theoretic vocabulary) and opt for a formulation that is more A-theory kosher. So the correct reformulation of (M1) might be as follows.

(A2) future(E) has been true & past(E) will be true & present(E) is true

But McTaggart won't buy this, claiming that it constitutes more A-theoretic subterfuge. (A2) is using talk of times in disguise.

From McTaggart (1927 par. 331) But what is meant by "has been" and "will be"? And what is meant by "is," when, as here, it is used with a temporal meaning, and not simply for predication? When we say that X has been Y, we are asserting X to be Y at a moment of past time. When we say that X will be Y, we are asserting X to be Y at a moment of future time. When we say that X is Y (in the temporal sense of "is"), we are asserting X to be Y at a moment of present time.

What is the A-theorist to say in response to this? Well, Prior contended that it wasn't the A-theorist that is caught in the regress, but the B-theorist, who, at every level must attempt to translate a perfectly acceptable A-theoretic formulation into something that traffics in B-theoretic vocabulary:

We are presented, to begin with (in step 1), with a statement which is plainly wrong (that every event *is* past, present, and future). This is corrected to something which is plainly right (that every event either *is* future and *will be* present and past, or *has been* future and *is* present and *will be* past, or *has been* future and present and *is* past). This is then expanded (in step 2) to something which, in the meaning intended, is wrong. It is then corrected to something a little more complicated which is right. This is then expanded (in step 3) to something which is wrong, and we are told that if we correct this in the obvious way, we shall have to expand it into something which is again wrong, and if we are not happy to stop there, or at any similar point, we shall have to go on *ad infinitum*. Even if we are somehow compelled to move forward in this way, we only get contradictions half the time, and it is not obvious why we should get these rather than their running mates as the correct stopping-points.   (1967: 5–6)

So who is on the treadmill? For now we should perhaps shelve this debate because it has the makings of a stalemate, and turn to a second issue that appears to involve more pedestrian linguistic concerns, but which arguably lies at the core of the McTaggart argument. Before we get to that, however, one might be attracted to another solution to the McTaggart paradox: why not be a tensing B-theorist?

Here is the idea: Go with the B-theorist and allow that there is a series of events that are ordered by the earlier-than/later-than relation, but then hold that these positions can also be tensed! The idea is that the tenses (and temporal indexicals like 'now') "move along" the B-theory time line. The philosophical consensus since Williams (1951) is that this view is incoherent. If "now" "moves" along the time line, then of course that movement must take place in time—but we were supposed to be giving an analysis of time. It looks like one needs to opt for a second order time in which temporal indexicals can move from the past into the future. But then it is easy enough to replicate the problem at the second level, forcing us to an infinite hierarchy of "times". And then we can construct sentences that mix up the levels, and the problems go on and on. Oddly, it seems that tensers are forced into being presentists—holding that only the present is real and that the future and past are not real. (Prior, for example, accepted this conclusion quite happily, but if correct it implies that tensers inherit all the philosophical problems of presentism. We don't have space to review these here, but see Sider (2003) for a nice survey of the difficulties.)

28.3.3 The Problem of Temporal Anaphora

Anaphora has to do with the use of pronouns and pronominal-like elements to "refer to" or less tendentiously, "pick up" some antecedent that is either explicitly or implicitly in the discourse. For example, the pronoun 'he' is an anaphor in the following two sentences: "A man came in the room. He sat down." In addition to anaphors that pick up individuals like the man who came into the room, some anaphoric elements appear to pick up times or earlier events, as in the following example from Partee (1973, 1984):

(15) John turned off the stove

As Partee observed, it is not enough to give this an analysis like that in (15') or even (15"),

(15') 'John turns off the stove' was true
(15") 'There is an event of John turning off the stove' was true

The problem with both of these analyses is that they are not explicit enough. An utterance of (15) is presumably not a claim that John turned off the stove once in his life—it is a claim that he did it at some relevant time or temporal interval (like this morning before he left the house or after he made the meatloaf). The Theory A analysis of tense doesn't appear to have the resources to deal with this.

A related problem for Theory A is its analysis of the complex tenses. Consider a sentence like (16).

(16) I had eaten

The problem is that simply nesting the tenses as in

(16') [S PAST [S PAST ['I eat']]]

collapses into the simple past. To see this, consider the case where time is discrete, and call the smallest unit of time a "chronon". Then (16') merely says that my eating took place more than one chronon ago. If time is non-discrete, then (16') effectively collapses into the simple past.

What is missing, of course, are the temporal reference points advocated by Reichenbach, and these, in effect, are simply temporal anaphors! If tensers can't avail themselves of temporal points or past and future events then they have a problem. (And remember, if they try to simply add the points or events they will become tensing B-theorists—an unstable position.)

And the situation only gets worse from here. We have apparent reference to temporal intervals as in (17),

(17) Abelard lived in the Middle Ages. It was an interesting time

and we also have cases of temporal anaphora built into the noun phrases, as in the following example from Enç (1986, 1987), uttered after the hostages were freed.

(18) The hostages came to the White House

If this wasn't complicated enough, we have the Sequence of Tense phenomenon (discussed in Abush, 1988; Ogihara, 1996; Higginbotham, 2002) in which it appears that an embedded tensed verb can shift the time of the event under discussion further into the past.

(19) Mary said that Biff was ill

Higginbotham (2002) has argued that these cases in effect sink the Theory A proposal discussed above, since no theory that treats tense as an operator that is evaluated only at the utterance time can get the relevant shifted reading. In effect, according to Higginbotham, these cases show that tense is not an indexical like 'now' or 'today' which never allow a shifted reading (except in certain literary contexts like narrative present).

In the same vein, there are the Double Aspect Readings (Abush, 1991; Giorgi and Pianesi, 1997: ch. 6) in which it appears that the embedded clause ('Mary was pregnant') could well have a present tense reading.

(20) Bill said that Mary was pregnant

And the list of problems goes on. In the face of all this what is the case for being a tenser, and can these objections be answered? Well, perhaps.

28.4 The Case for being a Tenser and the Modal Profile Problem

28.4.1 The Case for being a Tenser

In spite of the objections canvassed above, we *do* have a *prima facie* case for thinking the semantics of tense might require something in addition to the time being picked out—let's call this extra something, if it exists, *indexical content*. Suppose that I am sitting in my office one day, painfully aware that I have an important meeting with the President of the University at 3:00 o'clock. I might even utter (21) under my breath as I shuffle papers and take care of academic administrative minutia.

(21) I have a meeting with the President at 3:00 o'clock.

As I dither about in my office, I realize that the clock on my wall hasn't moved off of 2:30 in a while. Puzzled I check the clock on my computer. It says that it is 3:00. I double-check the time on-line. I conclude that it is in fact 3:00 o'clock and I utter (22).

(22) Oh no, I have a meeting with the President now!

I immediately get up and race to the President's office.

Arguably, my utterance of (22) reflects a piece of knowledge that my utterance of (21) does not and this additional piece of knowledge played a roll in my actions. The thought which I expressed by my utterance of (21) was not enough to get me up out of my chair. It was only by coming to have the thought that I express by my utterance of (22) that I formed the intention to run over to the president's office immediately.

Obviously there is something more to my utterance of (22) than there is to my utterance of (21) but the big question is whether this "something more" is something *semantic. Fregeans* think that it is. That is, the semantics must reflect the difference in cognitive significance between my utterance of (21) and my utterance of (22). Accordingly, or so says the Fregean, the semantics must give different truth conditions to my utterances of (21) and (22), perhaps (to a first approximation) along the following lines.

(21-F1) An utterance u, at 3:00 o'clock of 'I have a meeting with the President at 3:00 o'clock' is true iff [the individual picked out by the sense of 'I' in u] has a meeting at 3:00 o'clock.

(22-F1) An utterance u, at 3:00 o'clock of 'I have a meeting with the President now' is true iff [the individual picked out by the sense of 'I' in u] has a meeting at [the time picked out by the sense of 'now' in u].

For *referentialists* like Kaplan (1977, 1990); Soames (1986, 2002); and (in an early incarnation) Perry (1979), the problem with (21-F1) and (22-F1) are not that they load too little information into the semantics, but rather that they load *too much* into the semantics. Referentialists think that this extra bit of indexical content does not make it into the truth conditions. On their view, the truth conditions for (21) and (22) would fundamentally look the same:

(21-R) An utterance u, by s, at t, where t = 3 : 00 o'clock of 'I have a meeting with the President at 3:00 o'clock' is true iff s has a meeting with the President at t.

(22-R) An utterance u, by s, at t, where t = 3 : 00 o'clock of 'I have a meeting with the President now' is true iff s has a meeting with the President at t.[3]

What about the difference in cognitive significance between (21) and (22)? As noted earlier, Wettstein (1986) argued that it is a mistake to think that the something extra is semantical. On such a view there is semantics and there is psychology, and it is just "sloppy thinking" (Kaplan, 1990) to mix the two. But what is the harm of mixing them? Plenty, according to the referentialists, and the central problem has to do with the modal profile of these utterances.

28.4.2 The Modal Profile Problem

As Kaplan (1977) stressed, if the indexical content of a demonstrative (or indexical) makes it into the truth conditions, then what are we to say about examples like the following?

(23) You are the person I'm addressing with this utterance

We surely don't want (23) to have an analysis like (24), because (24) appears to be a necessary truth while (23) does not.

(24) The person I'm addressing with this utterance is the person I'm addressing with this utterance.

Clearly there are counterfactual environments where someone else might have been standing before me when I make my utterance, so (23) is only contingently true. But (24) does not appear to allow this possibility; it appears to be a necessary truth.

Thus our dilemma: If we include the extra bit in our semantics—if we make it part of the truth conditions—we mess up the modal profile of the sentence. If we leave out the extra bit, we don't seem to have a way of accounting for cognitive significance. Now of course referentialists will say that this is not a problem because the issue of cognitive significance can be dealt with in other ways, and the Fregean will say that this is not a problem because there are fancier stories to tell about the modal profile of utterances containing indexicals.

The tenser wants to take the second horn of the dilemma, perhaps, taking heart in the following remark from Higginbotham (1995; 248): "The quirks of modality should not . . . be allowed to undermine the thesis that what we say and think is literally and robustly expressed by the words that we use."

---

[3] Here I am assuming that variables do not display sense content. If Heck (2002) is right this assumption may not be so innocent.

But what then of the modal profile of indexical sentences? In recent work both Perry and Higginbotham have explored the possibility of using "modal discards" to keep some notion of indexical content while saving the modal profile.

28.4.3 Modal Discards

If we want some form of indexical content, but find that it gets us into trouble when we evaluate the sentence in other possible worlds, why not suppose that the indexical content that we use to express tense in the semantics is simply discarded when we evaluate the sentence in other possible worlds? One way to develop this idea would be to say that there are multiple semantic contents (for example a referential content and some additional content to accommodate indexical facts) and specify that only the former is relevant to the evaluation of the sentence in other possible worlds.

Both Higginbotham (1995) and Perry (2001) have suggested versions of this strategy. Perry, for example, suggests that utterances have at least three kinds of content:

The *indexical content* (sometimes he calls this *content-M*) of an utterance corresponds to the truth-conditions of the utterance given the facts that fix the language of the utterance, the words involved, their syntax and their *meaning.*

The *referential content* (sometimes he calls this *content-C* and sometimes the *official content*) of an utterance corresponds to the truth-conditions given all of these factors, plus the facts about the *context* of the utterance that are needed to fix the designation of indexicals.

The *designational content* (sometimes he calls this *content-D*) of an utterance corresponds to the truth-conditions given all of these factors, plus the additional facts that are needed to fix the *designation* of the terms that remain (definite descriptions in particular, but also possessives, etc.).

It will be useful to say a bit more about the natures of indexical content and referential content (designational content won't concern us here). Referential content (or "official content") consists in the content that referentialists find kosher. So, for example, the official content of (22) is as given in (22-R). Indexical content is *not* what is given in (22-F1). Both Perry and Higginbotham enlist a modified version of Reichenbach's token-reflexive theory of content. On Perry's formulation the token-reflexive content of (22) would be something akin to (22-X) (Higginbotham's formulation is a bit more robust, as we will see shortly).

(22-X) This utterance u, at 3:00 o'clock of 'I have a meeting with the President now' is true iff the utterer of u has a meeting with the President at the time u is uttered.

This formulation departs from Reichenbach's in that it is not the utterance *tokens* that are constituents of the descriptions in (22-X), but rather the utterances themselves—we will follow Perry's usage and simply call this type of content *reflexive.*

Of course the Kaplanesque worries about the modal profile of (22-F1) carry over mutatis mutandis to (22-X), and we didn't even need Kaplan to tell us this, the point was made by Casteñada (1967; 87):

Reichenbach, for instance, claims that the word "I" means the same as "the person who utters this token." This claim is, however, false. A statement formulated through a normal use of the sentence "I am uttering nothing" is contingent: if a person utters this sentence he falsifies the corresponding statement, but surely the statement might, even in such a case, have been true. On the other hand, the statements formulated by "The person uttering this token is uttering nothing" are self-contradictory: even if no one asserts them, they simply cannot be true.

So (22-X) apparently can't be the content of (22) either.

Returning to the idea of modal discards, since we have (at least) two kinds of contents, we can rely upon the reflexive content to give us an account of the cognitive significance of the utterance, but we don't need to keep the reflexive content around all the time. In fact, when we want to consider the modal profile of a sentence (i.e. when we want to evaluate it in a counterfactual situation) we can simply discard (ignore) the reflexive content and rely on the referential content. This is the sense in which we can have our cake and eat it too. We can account for both the cognitive significance and the modal profile of an utterance if we simply get clear that these involve different contents of the same utterance!

There are some further complications to this story, but it is perhaps more urgent for us to consider whether the reflexive contents offered by Perry and Higginbotham are adequate to the task at hand, or whether we need to introduce some additional sense content to adequately give a semantics of tense. The tenser will argue that the reflexive content deployed by Perry is inadequate, and that the notion of reflexive content proposed by Higginbotham is perhaps adequate, but only so far as it ends up smuggling a form of sense content—presumably tense itself—back into the analysis.

28.4.4 Is Reflexive Content too Thin?

Perry and Higginbotham provide us with a way of having our cake and eating it too, but the question asked by the tenser is whether there is enough cake here. Perhaps reflexive content is not enough and we need something more robust—like indexical sense. If the tenser is correct and some form of indexical sense is required, the strategy of modal discards can still be utilized; senses can be discarded just as easily as reflexive contents can.

The question is, what's wrong with reflexive content? Why is it too thin? Consider again the classic case for tense from Prior.

(25) I am thankful that my root canal is over with.

According to Perry's theory, for an utterance u, of (25), at time t, by Ludlow, we have a reflexive content akin to the following,

(25-X) The utterer of u is thankful that the event of his root canal is earlier than the time of u.

and a referential content as in (5-R).

(25-R) Ludlow is glad that the event of his root canal is earlier than u (at time t).

The first thought is, well, are (25-X) and (25-R) really something to be glad about? That is, why should I care about the relative ordering of my utterance and my root canal? One might respond that this objection has no force, because at a minimum my utterance of (25), by having (or being associated with) the reflexive content in (25-X) temporally situates me with the time of that very utterance and therefore places me well after the root canal.

But of course it can and has been argued that the contents expressed by (25-R) and (25-X) do no such thing, either individually or in concert. Famously, Prior, in his "thank goodness" paper concluded (p. 17) with the claim that token-reflexive theories do not capture what I express with my utterance of (25). The question is, why did Prior consider reflexive content (or at least Reichenbach's token-reflexive content) to be inadequate?

For a B-theorist,[4] my location just is my space–time worm and while that includes my utterance of (25) as a temporal segment, there are still big chunks of my space–time worm that are eternally situated earlier than that root canal. The only thing that an utterance actually claims to be safely situated later than the root canal is the utterance itself (utterance *event*, for Perry) and the part of my space–time worm that follows the utterance. The problem is that we still want to know why *that* utterance and the corresponding part of my space–time worm are supposed to be special and why I should be glad about the fact that *that* utterance and worm segment are a safe temporal distance from the unpleasant event. Isn't it important that the root canal be *past*?

The question is particularly pressing for Perry given his own remarks on the close connection between the contents posited by semantic theory and the explanations of our actions.

I cannot accept that a semantic theory can be correct that does not provide us with an appropriate interface between what sentences mean, and how we use them to communicate beliefs in order to motivate and explain action. A theory of linguistic meaning should provide us with an understanding of the properties sentences have that lead us to produce them under different circumstances, and react as we do to their utterance by others. (2001; 8)

Perry also offers the following "cognitive constraint on semantics":

If there is some aspect of meaning, by which an utterance u of S and an utterance u′ of S′ differ, so that a rational person who understood both S and S′ might accept u but not u′, then a fully adequate semantics should say what it is.   (2001: 9)

Given such a constraint, how can Perry reject the idea that tense should be part of the semantics? Wouldn't the consistent strategy be to try and augment the theory with additional content so as to account for Prior's "thank goodness" case? Here is a possible amendment: just add a new kind of content to the mix.

---

[4] Canonical examples would be Mellor (1981) and Sider (2001).

The *sense content* (we can call this the *content-S*) of an utterance corresponds to the mode of presentation or sense displayed by truth-conditions of the utterance.

This would result in a very ecumenical theory. We would now have the "official" referential content, the reflexive content, and Fregean sense content among others.

One might think that Perry's reflexive content is more austere than it needs to be—indeed, more austere than past token-reflexive accounts have been. Would the analysis of tense go more smoothly if we jazzed up the reflexive content of (25)? For example, we could take Higginbotham's proposal to be that the reflexive content of (25) is actually much closer to (25-XX).

(25-XX) The utterer of this utterance u is thankful that the event of his root canal is earlier than the time of u—*this very utterance*!

That is, maybe it would help if we added some reflexivity in the way that we describe u. Perry avoided this strategy, and it is pretty clear why. The problem comes in with the way we go about identifying (reflexively) an utterance. In (25-XX), for example, we used the phrase 'this very utterance'. Question: just how innocent is that indexical 'this'?

Arguably, the answer to the question is that the appearance of the indexical in the metalanguage is not innocent at all, for it amounts to smuggling in a closet disquotational treatment of indexicals. For Evans (1982); Rumfitt (1993); and Ludlow (1999), deploying indexicals in the metalanguage is precisely how one would want to proceed, but for reflexive content advocates like Perry as well as for direct reference theorists, that is basically giving away the store.

It is true enough that the kinds of indexicals being deployed in the metalanguage (e.g. 'this') may be different than those found in the utterance of the object language sentence (we have, in the case of (25-XX), traded in a 'now' for a 'this'), but the 'this' being deployed in the metalanguage doesn't look much like the indexical we use when pointing to nearby objects; we aren't pointing at anything, there is no act of indicating, and we don't appear to have any relevant referential intention. What is going on when we use 'this' in (25-XX)? As suggested in Ludlow (1999), it seems as though in cases like (25-XX), when one says 'this very utterance' one is really saying 'the utterance happening now', or more accurately, 'the utterance I am producing now' or perhaps 'the present utterance'.

In effect, the Higginbotham proposal, depending on how it is spelled out, may just be a form of indexical sense content (for tense) in sheep's clothing. In this case we may well ask why not shed the sheep's clothing and explicitly introduce a notion of indexical sense in our analysis of tense.

It is pretty clear why Perry would be allergic to such a move, given his worries about indexical senses that we briefly touched on in Section 28.3.1. Presumably his cognitive constraint on semantics is not strong enough to trump his worries about deploying Fregean senses in the service of indexicals like tense. But are those worries really that well founded?

28.4.5   Making Sense of Temporal Indexical Sense

Earlier we said that a good way to think about tense would be as a kind of temporal indexical sense similar to what Frege had envisioned for expressions like 'today' and 'yesterday'. In Section 28.3.4 we saw that Higginbotham has used phenomena like Sequence of Tense to challenge the similarity between indexicals and genuine tenses (leaving open the possibility that indexical sense would be viable for indexical expressions like 'today' if not for past and future tenses). We will return to the Higginbotham objection shortly, but first we need to consider arguments that the very idea of an indexical sense is incoherent even for expressions like 'today' (and thus also for tenses), offer some possible replies, and then we will try to sketch a possible way of displaying indexical sense within a semantic theory.

To set up the discussion properly, it will be useful to begin with an outline of the Fregean project as laid out in Heck (2002).

According to Heck, Frege was committed to the following doctrines.

(1a)   There can be different Thoughts that "concern the same object" and ascribe the same property to it. For example, the Thought that Superman flies and the Thought that Clark Kent flies are different, even though Superman is Clark Kent.

(2a)   Sentences of the form 'N believes that a is F' and 'N believes that b is F' can have different truth-values, even if 'a' and 'b' refer to the same object.

(3)   Sense determines reference[5]

(4)   The sense of a sentence is what one grasps in understanding it.

(5)   The sense of a sentence is a Thought.

In Heck's view not all of these doctrines can be maintained. In particular, we shall have to abandon the idea, implicit in doctrine (4) that there is a single thought associated with the understanding of a sentential utterance. To see why, we might begin with the following passage from Frege (1956).

If someone wants to say the same today as he expressed yesterday using the word 'today', he must replace this word by 'yesterday'. Although the thought is the same, the verbal expression must be different so that the sense, which would otherwise be affected by the differing times of utterance, is readjusted. The case is the same with words like 'here' and 'there'. In all such cases the mere wording, as it is given in writing, is not the complete expression of the thought, but the knowledge of certain accompanying conditions of utterance, which are used as means of expressing the thought, are needed for its correct apprehension. The pointing of fingers, hand movements, glances may belong here too. The same utterance containing the word 'I' will express different thoughts in the mouths of different men, of which some may be true, others false.

---

[5]   Heck(2002: 3) allows that this may be understood in a weak way: "On the weakest interpretation of (3), it speaks of 'determination' only in a mathematical sense: it claims only that senses are related many—one to references."

Perry (1977) argued that Frege gets into trouble by trying to identify the sense of a sentence (utterance) with a thought. Why? Well, because 'yesterday' and 'today' presumably have different senses, and it therefore follows that 'Today is a fine day' and 'Yesterday is a fine day' must have different senses (since they are *composed* of different senses). But if I can express the same thought today with an utterance of 'yesterday is a fine day' than I expressed yesterday with an utterance of 'today is a fine day' then thoughts cannot be associated with senses. Clearly. Different senses are deployed in expressing the same thought so thoughts are not in a one-to-one correspondence with the senses of sentences.

It seems that Frege has to give something up. He can either give up the one-to-one identification of senses with thoughts, or he can give up the idea that the two utterances can express the same thought. Evans (1981) argued that there is no dilemma for the Fregean here:

there is no headlong collision between Frege's suggestion that grasping the same thought on different days may require different things of us, and the fundamental criterion of difference of thoughts which rests upon the principle that it is not possible coherently to take different attitudes towards the same thought. For that principle, properly stated, precludes the possibility of coherently taking different attitudes towards the same thought *at the same time*.

Evans appeared to be saying that thoughts are to be identified with senses—but with different senses at different times. This strategy loosens up the link between senses and thoughts by identifying thoughts with different senses at different times (and more generally in different contexts).

An alternative strategy, which some philosophers have attributed to Evans, would be to hold that indexical expressions like 'today' can be used to express or display senses, but that they do not express the same sense on each occasion of use. This second strategy holds the sense associated with a thought constant, but allows that different indexical *expressions* can display the same sense (albeit on different occasions of use). Both strategies appear to ameliorate the worry articulated by Perry. Or do they?

Neither of these strategies is capable of salvaging the Fregean project in its entirety. To see why, however, we need to begin introducing the details of these proposals. We can follow Evans in thinking of senses as being displayed by the theorems of a T-theory in the sense of Davidson (1967).

Here is the idea: given a T-theory for a language L, we want to be careful to distinguish (a) what the truth conditions literally state, (b) the way in which the truth conditions are represented, and finally, (c) the sense displayed by the truth conditions so represented.

To see how this works, consider the following example, pertaining to names, discussed by McDowell (1980) and Lepore and Loewer (1987). The idea is that while theorems (26) and (27) in some sense state the same truth conditions, they do so in different ways, so that they "display" different senses.

(26) 'Cicero is bald' is true iff Cicero is bald

(27) 'Cicero is bald' is true iff Tully is bald

What one wants from an adequate T-theory is that it gives the truth conditions in such a way that the senses of the object language sentences are correctly displayed in the metalanguage.

Matters are a little more involved when we move to the introduction of indexicals in the metalanguage. Following Rumfitt (1993) and Ludlow (1999) we can simply disquotationally enter the indexical expression into the right hand side of a biconditional. So, for example, we might have axioms and theorems like the following.

(28) Val(x, 'I') iff x = I

(29) Val(T, 'I walk']) iff I walk

Of course, as we noted in Section 28.3.1, this *appears* hopelessly naive. If we deployed such an axiom wouldn't we get absurd results when interpreting the utterances of others? For example, if someone says "I walk", it is no good for me to have a T-theory which interprets that utterance as saying that *I* walk. But that appears to be what a theorem like (29) delivers.

Likewise in the temporal case if someone leaves me a voice mail on Monday saying "Little Rupert went to the dentist today," if I only retrieve the voice mail today (several days later) it is no good for me to interpret this as saying that Little Rupert went to the dentist *today*. So presumably axioms like the following for temporal indexicals are also problematic.

(30) Val(x, 'today') iff x is true today

Or so goes the objection. However, tensers (and fans of indexical sense generally) are in a position to reject this claim. In the first place, if we are talking about language (I-language) in the sense of Chomsky (1986), and if, as some have suggested, the primary use of I-language is not communication but thought, then axioms like the above are entirely appropriate for I-language tokenings. Such axioms are also entirely suitable for the interpretation of any speech which we *produce* or intend to produce. The only drawback for such axioms appears to be in the interpretation of the utterances of others.

It is possible to argue that even if we are concerned with interpretation of other individuals, it is far from clear that these kinds of axioms are inadequate. For example, it is a plausible position to maintain that when we interpret the remarks of another, we amend the axioms of our T-theory to account for the position of the speaker. Accordingly, we might have conditionalized axioms like the following, where S is a sentential clause modified by the adverb 'today'.

(31) if yesterday s left a message m, having the form 'S is true today', then in m 'S is true today' is true iff S was true yesterday

This sort of paraphrase might allow us to track the indexical utterances of others from different spatial and temporal vantage points.

The idea was that a single thought having a single sense would have to be represented in different ways from different spatiotemporal perspectives. Applying this idea to T-theorems, the idea was that the way the theorem is represented helps determine what sense is displayed, but that the particular representation cannot be identified with the sense, for that sense must be displayed in different ways at different times.

The problem for this proposal comes in when something happens that causes us to "lose track" of how a particular sense should be displayed. In the above case we were able to keep track of the sense of (31) because we knew that the message was left yesterday, but we are not always in a position to know when the message was left, and we may be mistaken about when it was left. This brings us to cases like Rip van Winkle, post cards, voice mail messages and the like. As Kaplan (1977) noted, these cases present serious difficulties for stand-alone sense based accounts of indexicals.[6] Consider first the case of Rip van Winkle, who goes to sleep one day saying to himself "today was a fine day." When he awakes 20 years later, he may want to express what he expressed by the utterance that he made before he fell asleep. He may try to do this by saying 'yesterday was a nice day', but in doing so Rip fails to express what he did with his original utterance because he has lost track of the relative temporal position of his original utterance.

For Evans (speaking of beliefs rather than utterances here) this was a bullet that we should bite:

I see no more strangeness in the idea that a man who loses track of time cannot retain beliefs than in the idea that a man who loses track of an object cannot retain the beliefs about it with which he began.   (1981; 87n-88n)

This is not a particularly attractive move by Evans. Unless we assume some technical notion of "recollection", Rip certainly does recall his earlier belief (and what he expressed) in some interesting sense.

The tenser needn't bite this bullet, however, if they follow Heck's lead and reject the idea that there is something like "the [unique] Thought" that is expressed by an utterance. Perhaps a more plausible picture emerges if one supposes that "a given utterance can differ in cognitive value for two speakers without their being unable to communicate successfully." There may be limits to the variation that successful communication can tolerate: "speakers cannot associate with an utterance just any Thought that determines the right singular proposition . . . and still understand it." If we want to hang on to plank (4) of the Fregean project, then speakers will have to deploy demonstrative thoughts (senses) to understand the utterance, however "no one of the different Thoughts different speakers might permissibly associate with an utterance is plausibly taken to be its meaning: none of them is privileged over the others."

Notice that having a demonstrative thought is still crucial for understanding the utterance. So for example, while Rip may not be able to express what he expressed

---

[6] See also Perry (1997) for discussion of these cases.

with his original utterance via the sense he deployed before he slept, he may well express its content (or one of its contents) by deploying another sense. When he wakes up, he might express it uttering the words "that was a fine day", thereby deploying a new demonstrative sense.

Heck's point is that it is a mistake to suppose that there is a single thing that one must thereby grasp or which constitutes the one thought expressed by an utterance. These thoughts must, of course, be related in some interesting way, but we should resist the pull to say that there must therefore be The Meaning of the utterance.

But why do we want to find something to call the meaning? What we (relatively) uncontroversially have are speakers who associate Thoughts with utterances and restrictions upon how the different Thoughts they associate with a given utterance must be related if they are to communicate successfully: to put it differently, we have the fact that utterances have cognitive value for speakers, and we have communicative norms determining how the cognitive values a given utterance has for different speakers must be related if we are to understand them.   (p. 31)

In effect, there is plenty of space for the tenser to maneuver in response to the challenge in Section 28.3.1. As noted earlier, the position is a difficult one to defend, but there are clear defense strategies available. Admittedly, however, the strategies in question are certainly not consistent with the more popular theories of indexicals.

Even if we are satisfied that an answer can be found to the class of objections sketched in 28.3.1, this still leaves the objections in 28.3.2 (the McTaggart objection) and the objections in 28.3.3 (involving the problem of temporal anaphora). We will take up these objections in reverse order because it is reasonable to think that the McTaggart objection is, at bottom, just a version of the problem of temporal anaphora.

28.5 CAN THE A-THEORY HANDLE TEMPORAL ANAPHORA?

What is the tenser to say about the problem of temporal anaphora? In this section we will canvass two different approaches. One involves the introduction of temporal anaphora in the form of a robust syntactic proposal. The second approach suggests that something like E-type temporal anaphora can be had for relatively little cost if we simply reinterpret current work in Discourse Representation Theory.

28.5.1 E-Type Temporal Anaphora

Ludlow (1999) suggested that the whole problem of temporal anaphora could be avoided if we could introduce a notion of anaphora that was not dependent upon reference—in particular the notion of E-type anaphora introduced by Evans (1977).

In the case of nominal anaphora, Evans suggested that in a sentence like (32), the pronoun "stood proxy" for a description as in (32'). He then gave a stock Russellian analysis of the proxy description, according to which it was a denoting expression and not a referring expression.

(32) A man came in. *He* tripped over the chair.
(33) A man came in. *The man who came in* tripped over the chair.

We can also argue that a similar strategy could be introduced to handle temporal anaphora as well. Instead of a description, the temporal anaphor would be standing proxy for an implicit temporal conjunction. For example, consider again Partee's example with the temporal anaphor explicitly introduced as in (33).

(33) John turned off the stove then

Partee suggested that the anaphor 'then' must *refer* to a moment or period of time, however, it is also possible that 'then' is standing proxy for a temporal conjunction. For example, *then* could be "standing proxy" for 'when I left the house', or 'when you told me to'. In effect it had a structure like that in (34).

(34) [S [S PAST [S John turn off the stove]] [S when . . .]]

More generally, the idea was that temporal anaphors stand proxy for expressions of the following forms: "when [s...]", "before [s...]", "after [s...]", "while [s...]", "during [s...]".

   On such a story, a complex tense like past perfect would not involve nested operators at all, but would involve temporal conjunctions. For example, a past perfect sentence like 'I had eaten' would have a logical form like the following,

(35) PAST['I am eating'] before PAST [. . .]

where the second implicit clause would be filled in by contextual information. The resulting semantics for this sentence would be along the following lines (ignoring the introduction of propositions and syntactic details).

(36) 'PAST['I am eating'] before PAST[. . .]' is true iff 'I am eating' was true before '[. . . (filled in by context) . . .]' was true

The other examples that appear to involve temporal anaphora would be resolved in like manner. For example in the Enc case of the hostages who came to the White House, the tenser can introduce an implicit clause into the noun phrase.

(37) [NP [NP The hostages] [S (who were captured in the US Embassy during the Iranian revolution)]] came to the White House

The sequence of tense case which Higginbotham considered to be fatal to the tenser can be handled by positing separate temporal conjunctions for both the upper and lower events and adopting an analysis that dates back to Dowty (1982) in which there really isn't a shifted tense but simply different temporal markers (one which we take to be further in the past by virtue of discourse pragmatics) selected by the context.

(38) [S Mary said that [S′ Biff was ill (when) PAST[. . .]] when PAST[__]]

More puzzling are the so called Double Aspect Reading cases in which the internal event is considered to at least overlap the present (an utterance of 'Bill said that Mary was pregnant' could certainly be taken to communicate that she is now pregnant). The puzzle comes from the fact that the embedded clause has an apparent past tense as in (39).

(31) [S Bill said that [S′ Mary was pregnant (when) PAST[. . .]] when PAST[__]]

But arguably here the present tense reading comes when the elided material in the embedded clause includes an event that, given our real world knowledge of pregnancies, probably persists. In effect, the "shiftiness" is not a function of grammar at all but is driven by pragmatic elements in the discourse.

To see the plausibility of this line of thought, suppose that pregnancies lasted only one nanosecond. Then an utterance of 'Bill said that Mary was pregnant' could hardly be understood with Mary's pregnancy in the present. But given our common knowledge that pregnancies endure for some time, we certainly can utter such a sentence, implicating and expecting our audience to infer that Mary is still pregnant.

Similar considerations apply to the past-shifted reading of 'Mary said that Bill was ill'. The shifted reading is arguably due to the fact that we infer from discourse cues that Biff's illness was prior to Mary's utterance. To see this, consider first the case where Mary has no long term memory and at the time of conversation had no access to records or testimony, we both know this, and I report thus: 'Mary said that Biff was ill'. In this case the shifted reading looks to be impossible to get. Alternatively, if illnesses always lasted for 9 months, we might well infer that Biff was *currently* ill. If Mary was stuck in the past and only reported things that were a week old, then we would *only* get the past shifted reading. We know the dangers of overplaying the pragmatics card, but in this case it is hard to locate either evidence or arguments that might trump it on behalf of the thesis that this is clearly a syntactic (or semantic) phenomenon.

Even if the reading in question *is* a syntactic or semantic phenomenon and not a function of the pragmatics it is far from clear that the indexical analysis of tense is threatened. Indeed the analysis of the past perfect in Ludlow (1999) and given in Theory A above shows that grammatically triggered shifted readings are entirely compatible with an analysis of tense as indexical sense. Consider the analysis in (38').

(38') [S Mary said that [S′ Biff was ill (before) PAST[. . .]] when PAST[. . .]]

Here the inherent tenses and the morphological tenses are all monadic indexical predicates, but a shifted reading is still forced by the additional relational tense 'before'. Is 'before' also indexical? It would be hard to test this, but there is no reason to say that it isn't. Even if it *is* non-indexical the inherent and morphological tenses *are* indexical, so it is hard to see the force of the Sequence of Tense objection against an indexical analysis of tense (and by an extension, an analysis of tense as indexical sense).

The upshot of all this is that the E-type anaphora strategy can use implicit temporal conjunctions to mimic most analyses utilizing reference times or past and future events. This strategy does however require introducing a number of irreducible semantic primitives, including the following monadic and binary basic tenses.

(T1) Val(x, *PAST*, σ) iff x was true

(T2) Val(x, *FUT*, σ) iff x will be true

(T3) Val(T, [$_S$ TP1 *when* TP2], σ) iff
        Val(T, TP1, σ) when Val(T, TP2, σ)

(T4) Val(T, [$_S$ TP1 *before* TP2], σ) iff
        Val(T, TP1, σ) before Val(T, TP2, σ)

(T5) Val(T, [$_S$ TP1 *after* TP2], σ) iff
        Val(T, TP1, σ) after Val(T, TP2, σ)

Is it legitimate to introduce this many primitives in the semantics? Probably: it is a major tenant of tensism that primitive temporal properties and relations cannot be eliminated. Is it reasonable to introduce the invisible syntactic structure? That is less clear, and one might hope for a solution that avoids it.

28.5.2 Reinterpreting Discourse Representation Theory

The standard way of treating temporal anaphora (e.g. in Kamp and Reyle, 1993 and Asher, 1993) is to think of temporal anaphors as being "anchors" in a cross-discourse representation structure. As the discourse proceeds, the anchors can be exploited via various devices of temporal reference or they may also be used as the R positions in the Reichenbachian analysis of complex tenses. Now this analysis is typically thought of as one in which the anchors are either bound variables or terms of reference, so the effect is a kind of *de re* quantification over (or reference to) times. However, that is just one way of interpreting the anchors in discourse representation structures.

Another way of thinking about the anchors and variable positions in a discourse representation structure is that they are not individual constants or variables in the sense of standard first order logic, but are rather pointers to data structures that are being assembled as the discourse proceeds. A helpful way to think of them would be along the lines of the files proposed in the file change semantics of Heim (1982: ch. 3). On that proposal the introduction of term (presumably even a temporal object) leads to the opening of a file which is updated as the discourse proceeds.

If we begin to think of the variables and terms in a discourse representation structure in this way then we can begin to see a way that the structures can be understood in a presentist friendly—and hence tenser friendly—way: simply think of the variables as place-holders for structural information about an event description R, and evaluate the information inside the scope of the relevant tensed operators.

In effect, this proposal would have the same logic as the proposed E-type temporal anaphora up above, but without the contentious syntactic thesis that there are implicit temporal conjunctions. Syntactically we would merely have the same variable positions posited in standard theories of Discourse Representation Theories. If we think of the data structures as being accessed and interpreted each time the variable is encountered, then they will be interpreted within the scope of the tense operators and the result should be a presentist/tenser-compatible theory of temporal anaphora.

28.5.3 McTaggart Reconsidered

Earlier it was suggested that the McTaggart objection was really a species of the problem of temporal anaphora. To see why this might be, consider the argument again, but now replacing talk of events with talk of sentences.

(40) FUT(S) & PRES(S) & PAST(S)

The paradox requires ignoring the implicit temporal anaphor that goes with each clause. For example, we could argue that in natural language we never say that an event is future simpliciter, but rather that it is future at some temporal marker. Using implicit when clauses to illustrate this point (but keeping in mind that we may be free to replace them as suggested in Section 28.5.2) we can say that a simple future claim like (41) actually has the structure in (41').

(41) FUT[S]
(41') FUT[S] when FUT[.....]

The semantics then interprets this as in (41*).

(41*) []S[] will be true when [][.....] [] will be true

Now returning to the PAST(S) from (40), we see that when its temporal anaphor is made explicit, we don't have the bare (42), but rather something with the semantics in (42*).

(42) PAST[S]
(42*) []S[] was true when [][.....] [] was true

And the idea is that these will be distinct temporal markers (or distinct temporal conjunctions). In effect, the first intuition of the tenser/presentist was the correct one. The tenser wants to say that the event or sentence in question is true at different times. What the E-type temporal anaphora story shows is that the tenser/presentist has a perfectly innocent notion of time-talk that she can appeal to. In the end, the McTaggart objection rests upon the assumption that the presentist/tenser has no viable form of temporal anaphora. This assumption can certainly be challenged.

28.6 CONCLUSION

While most approaches to the semantics of tense have attempted to regiment tense away in a tenseless metalanguage, a good case can be made that this is not without cost (the same case could be made for regimentation of modality and other aspects of natural language as well). On the other hand, it is pretty clear that attempts to treat tense in a tensed metalanguage introduce serious complications. It is probably not so important which of these positions is correct at this point (we may be some distance from resolving that question), as it is that we understand the costs of the respective positions. Perhaps, by having a firm enough grasp on *both* approaches we afford ourselves a deeper insight into the nature of tense itself.

REFERENCES

Abusch, D. (1997). "The Sequence of Tense and Temporal De Re", *Linguistics and Philosophy*, 20: 1–50.

――― (1991). "The Present Under Past as De Re Interpretation". In D. Bates (ed.) *Proceedings of the Tenth West Coast Conference on Formal Linguistics*. Stanford: CSLI Publications (distributed by University of Chicago Press), 1–14.

Asher, N. (1993). *Reference to Abstract Objects in Discourse*. Dordrecht: Kluwer.

Burgess, J. (2003). "Basic Tense Logic", in D. Gabbay and F. Guenthner (eds.) *The Handbook of Philosophical Logic*, Second Edition. Dordrecht: Kluwer.

Casteñada, H.-N. (1967). "Indicators and Quasi-Indicators", *American Philosophical Quarterly*, 4: 85–100.

Chomsky, N. (1986). *Knowledge of Language*. New York: Praeger.

Davidson, D. (1967a). "Truth and Meaning", *Synthese*, 17: 304–23. Reprinted in *Inquiries Into Truth & Interpretation*. Oxford: Oxford University Press, 1984.

――― (1967b). "The Logical Form of Action Sentences". In *Essays on Actions and Events*. Oxford: Oxford University Press, 1980.

Dowty, D. (1982). "Tenses, Time Adverbs, and Compositional Semantic Theory". *Linguistics and Philosophy*, 5: 23–55.

Enç, M. (1986). "Towards a Referential Analysis of Temporal Expressions". *Linguistics and Philosophy*, 9: 405–26.

――― (1987). "Anchoring Conditions for Tense". *Linguistic Inquiry*, 18: 633–57.

Evans, G. (1977). "Pronouns, Quantifiers, and Relative Clauses (I)", *Canadian Journal of Philosophy*, 7: 467–536. Reprinted in Evans (1985).

――― (1981). "Understanding Demonstratives", from H. Parret and J. Bouveresse (eds.), *Meaning and Understanding*, Berlin: W. de Gruyter. Reprinted in *Collected Papers*. Oxford: Oxford University Press.

――― (1982). *The Varieties of Reference*. Oxford: Oxford University Press.

Frege, G. (1956). "The Thought", trans. A. M. and Marcelle Quinton, *Mind*, 65: 289–311.

Giorgi, A., and F. Pianesi (1997). *Tense and Aspect: From Semantics to Morphosyntax*. Oxford: Oxford University Press.

Guenthner, F. (1979). "Time Schemes, Tense Logic, and the Analysis of English Tenses". In. F. Guenthner and S. Schmidt (eds.), *Formal Semantics and Pragmatics for Natural Languages*. Dordrecht: D. Reidel, pp. 201–22.

Heck, R. (2002). "Do Demonstratives have Senses?" *Philosophers' Imprint*, 2, (2), <www.philosophersimprint.org/002002/>.

Higginbotham, J. (1995). "Tensed Thoughts", *Mind and Language*, 10: 226–49.

――― (2002). "Why is Sequence of Tense Obligatory". In G. Preyer and G. Peter (eds.) *Logical Form and Language*. Oxford: Oxford University Press, 207–27.

Hinrichs, E. (1986). "Temporal Anaphora in Discourses of English", *Linguistics and Philosophy*, 9: 63–82.

—— (1988). "Tense, Quantifiers, and Contexts", *Computational Linguistics*, 14: 3–14.

Kamp, H. (1984). "A Theory of Truth and Semantic Representation". In Groendijk *et al.* (eds.) *Truth, Interpretation, and Information*. Dordrecht: Foris.

Kamp, H., and U. Reyle (1993). *From Discourse to Logic*. Dordrecht: Kluwer Academic Publishers.

Kaplan, D. (1977). "Demonstratives", manuscript UCLA. Reprinted in J. Almog *et al.* (eds.), *Themes from Kaplan*. Ithaca: Cornell University Press, 1989.

—— (1979). "On the Logic of Demonstratives". *The Journal of Philosophical Logic*, 8: 81–98.

—— (1990). "Thoughts on Demonstratives". In Yourgrau (1990), 34–49.

Larson, R., and P. Ludlow (1993). "Interpreted Logical Forms." *Synthese*, 95: 305–56.

Ludlow, P. (1999). *Semantics, Tense and Time: an Essay in the Metaphysics of Natural Language*. Cambridge: MIT Press.

McTaggart, J. (1908). "The Unreality of Time", *Mind*, 68: 457–74.

—— (1927). *The Nature of Existence*. Vol. 2, Cambridge: Cambridge University Press.

Mellor, D. H. (1981). *Real Time*. Cambridge: MIT Press.

Partee, B. (1973). "Some Structural Analogies Between Tenses and Pronouns in English", *The Journal of Philosophy*, 70: 601–9.

—— (1984). "Nominal and Temporal Anaphora", *Linguistics and Philosophy*, 7: 243–86.

Perry, J. (1977). "Frege on Demonstratives", *Philosophical Review*, 86: 474–97.

—— (1979). "The Problem of the Essential Indexical". *Nous*, 13: 3–21.

—— (1997). "Rip van Winkle and other Characters", *The European Review of Philosophy*, 2: 13–40. Reprinted in Perry (2000).

—— (2001). *Reference and Reflexivity*. Stanford: CSLI Publications.

Prior, A. N. (1959). 1959. "Thank Goodness That's Over". *Philosophy*, 34: 12–17.

—— (1967). *Past, Present and Future*. Oxford: Oxford University Press.

—— (1968). *Time and Tense*. Oxford: Oxford University Press.

Reichenbach, H. (1947). *Elements of Symbolic Logic*. New York: Macmillan.

Rumfitt, I. (1993). "Content and Context: The Paratactic Theory Revisited and Revised", *Mind*, 102: 429–53.

Sider, T. (2001). *Four-Dimensionalism*. Oxford: Oxford University Press.

Smart, J. J. C. (1963). *Philosophy and Scientific Realism*. London: Routledge and Kegan Paul.

—— (1966). "The River of Time". In A. Flew (ed.) *Essays in Conceptual Analysis*. London: Routledge and Kegan Paul.

Vickner, S. (1985). "Reichenbach Revisited: One, Two, or Three Temporal Relations". *Acta Linguistica Hafniensia*, 19: 81–98.

Wettstein, H. (1986). "Has Semantics Rested on a Mistake?" *Journal of Philosophy*, 83; 185–209.

Williams, D. C. (1951). "The Myth of Passage", *The Journal of Philosophy*, 48; 457–72.

CHAPTER 29

....

PLURALS

....

BARRY SCHEIN

Plurals are essential where what is said of what the plural refers to in (1) cannot be said of any one of what it refers to (2).

(1) The oven fires clustered.
    The custards clumped.

(2) *The oven fires each clustered.
    *The custards each clumped.

    *An oven fire clustered.
    *A custard clumped.

Extension of the logical language to deliver plural reference and the logical relations that constitute knowledge of the singular and plural acquires empirical bite just in case it conforms with increasing precision to the syntax of the natural language and affords explanation of what speakers know about the distribution and meaning of plural expressions in their language.

As for the syntax of natural language, this discussion, being none too precise, is guided throughout by just two considerations and their immediate consequences, discussed at greater length in Section 29.0. The first, morpheme univocality, is that a morpheme despite its various syntactic and morphological contexts has a single meaning that supports all its occurrences: bare nouns (*fire, custard*), the article *the*, quantifiers (*some, any, all, most*), partitive *of*, and any others that transgress the

Many thanks for discussion including admonition to Marta Abrusan, Rajesh Bhatt, Dan Blair, Bridget Copley, Marcelo Ferreira, Elena Guerzoni, Martin Hackl, Elena Herburger, Jim Higginbotham, Norbert Hornstein, Kathrin Koslicki, Utpal Lahiri, Richard Larson, Peter Ludlow, Roumi Pancheva, Paul Pietroski, Agustín Rayo, Daniel Rothschild, Philippe Schlenker, Roger Schwarzschild, Anna Szabolcsi, and Eytan Zweig.

boundaries of singular, plural and mass terms are never on these grounds to be treated as ambiguous among two or three homophones. Similarly, the morpheme *cluster*, occurring in different parts of speech, in both verb and noun in (3), is univocal too (see Parsons, 1990).

(3) The fires clustered in two clusters.

The second consideration is the conservation of lexical classes: any morphemes that belong by all grammatical reckoning to the same lexical class, *zero* and *two*, as an example with portent, do so and therefore share the same logical syntax.

Assuming what has just been observed, that the language presents phrases $\Phi[\xi]$, such as *clustered*$[\xi]$, complex or simple, for which a plural idiom is essential, Section 29.1 develops an apparatus for plural reference—plural (and mass) definite and indefinite descriptions and the partitive construction. Much of what constitutes a speaker's knowledge of singular and plural is reflected in inferences within the language of the partitive construction relating singular and plural expressions. A discussion of nominal syntax and morphology and the axioms supporting inference within the object language precedes statement of its semantics and what is to be said about plural reference itself. Section 29.2 goes on to survey the language that makes plurals essential: the inventory of primitive plural vocabulary, the composition of singular or plural expressions into complex phrases $\Phi[\xi]$ that in turn demand plural ξ, and the combinatorial interactions between plural quantification and the other phrases that lie within simple sentences. These interactions conclude in Section 29.2.2.4 and Section 29.2.3 in a revision of basic clause structure.

29.0.1 The Many and the None

The logical syntax of (4)–(9) does not diverge from that of (10)–(15) under any plausible parse of the natural language.[1] In so far as sentences such as (4)–(9) are true, (4), given the definite description [the ξ: *nonselfidentical custards*$[\xi]$]],[2,3] entails (16).

(4) The nonselfidentical custards are zero in number.
     The moons of Venus are zero in number.[4]
(5) The nonselfidentical custard is as perfectly round as the nonselfidentical flan.
(6) The at most one person still alive with a face like that descends from a tribe of Brooklyn.
(7) The hairs on Humpty Dumpty's head are sparse.

---

[1] Rejecting, for example, that (4) could be a negation entailing the negations of sentences like (10), as in: $\neg[\exists n: n > 0]$ the nonselfidentical custards are n in number.
[2] The definite description as quantifier rather than referring term is expedient; nothing hinges on it.
[3] $\Phi[v_i, v_j]$, *nonselfidentical*$[\xi]$ and the like to indicate a formula of arbitrary complexity in the free variables indicated. $\Phi(v_i, v_j)$, of(ξ,ζ), Fx, Gxy, etc. for primitive predicates and relations.
[4] "If I say 'Venus has 0 moons,' there simply does not exist any moon or agglomeration of moons for anything to be asserted of; but, what happens is that a property is assigned to the *concept* 'moon of Venus,' namely that of including nothing under it." (Frege, 1884, §46)

(8) The hair on Humpty Dumpty's head is sparse.

(9) The zero or more solutions to this equation are all unidentified prime numbers.

(10) The custards are twelve in number.

(11) The custard is as perfectly round as the flan.

(12) The person with that face descends from a tribe of Brooklyn.

(13) The hairs on Rapunzel's head are luxuriant.

(14) The hair on Rapunzel's head is luxuriant.

(15) The three solutions to this equation are all unidentified prime numbers.

(16) $\exists \xi \; zero[\xi]$

Given the truth of (4)–(6), nothing in the meaning of the article *the* or the plural, mass or singular morphemes proper entails a non-zero measure in either number or amount of what the description refers to, and neither does the existential quantification in (16) or the evaluation of the variable ξ of plural reference. Plural expressions refer fluently to the many and the none.

What has been observed in definite descriptions holds as well of the variables and morphology engaged in distributive quantification if (20)–(24) parse along the lines of (17)–(19):

(17) [Any ξ: *nonselfidentical custards*$[\xi]$] ... *zero*$[\xi]$ ...

(18) [Any ξ: *nonselfidentical custard*$[\xi]$] ... *zero*$[\xi]$ ...

(19) [Any ξ: (sg.)*of the nonselfidentical custard(s)*$[\xi]$] ... *zero*$[\xi]$ ...

(20) a. Any nonselfidentical custards are zero in number.
  b. F Any nonselfidentical custards are one or more in number.

(21) a. Any of the nonselfidentical custards are zero in number.
  b. F Any of the nonselfidentical custards are one or more in number.

(22) a. Any nonselfidentical custard is zero desserts.
  b. F Any nonselfidentical custard is one or more desserts.

(23) a. Any of the nonselfidentical custards is zero desserts.
  b. F Any of the nonselfidentical custards is one dessert.

(24) a. Any of the nonselfidentical custard is zero desserts.
  b. F Any of the nonselfidentical custard is one or more desserts.

Here too, given that (20)a–(24)a are true and (20)b–(24)b are not, nothing in the evaluation of the variable ξ, whether taken to be plural, (20)–(21), singular (22)–(23), or mass (23)/(24) entails a non-zero measure nor does the meaning of the singular, plural or mass morpheme or the partitive construction entail that what satisfies the restriction has a non-zero measure.

Both definite descriptions ((25) and (26)) and distributive quantifiers ((27) and (28)) talk glibly about the none as what no one can be ((25), (27)) and as what no several can be ((26), (28)) using essential plurals:

(25) The custards each of which is not identical to itself are zero in number.
  [The ξ: *custards*$[\xi]$ & [Each ς: *of*$[\varsigma, \xi]$]$\neg \varsigma = \varsigma$] ... *zero*$[\xi]$ ...

(26) The custards that outnumber themselves are zero in number.
      [The ξ: *custards*$[\xi]$ & *outnumber themselves*$[\xi]$] . . . *zero*$[\xi]$ . . .
(27) Any custards each of which is not identical to itself are zero in number.
      (F Any custards each of which is not identical to itself are one or more in number.)
      [Any ξ: *custards*$[\xi]$]&[Each ς: *of*$[\varsigma, \xi]$]$\neg\varsigma = \varsigma$] . . . $n[\xi]$ . . .
(28) Any custards that outnumber themselves are zero in number.
      (F Any custards that outnumber themselves are one or more in number.)
      [Any ξ: *custards*$[\xi]$]& *outnumber themselves*$[\xi]$] . . . $n[\xi]$ . . .

If the definite descriptions parse as shown, (26) entails (29), and yet it should not of course imply that the zero outnumber themselves:

(29) $\exists\xi$(*custards*$[\xi]$ & *outnumber themselves*$[\xi]$] & *zero*$[\xi]$)

Something intervenes between the devices that refer to the none and the descriptive content that describes it not. Let it be stipulated that restriction to a quantifier subjects descriptive content to the operator defined in (31):

(30) [the ξ: I$\Phi[\xi]$]], [any ξ: $\Phi[\xi]$]]
(31) I$\Phi[\xi]$ $\leftrightarrow_{df}$ $\exists x$ *x is one of* ξ $\rightarrow$ $\Phi[\xi]$[5]

Although '(*custards*$[\xi]$ & *outnumber themselves*$[\xi]$)' fails to be true of any ξ, 'I([*custards*$[\xi]$ & *outnumber themselves*$[\xi]$)' is true of the none.

Elsewhere, as in (32)–(36), an appearance to the contrary—that what satisfies the restriction has a non-zero measure—betrays a separate, unspoken measure, *any (one (or more))* *(of the) custards*, so that custards zero in number do not falsify (32)b–(36)b.[6]

---

[5] The partitive construction is defined below.
[6] Note that it is not enough that a speaker of *any (of the) F(s)* . . . be taken to implicate or presuppose that there are Fs unless taken to know that there are no Fs. While it serves talk about nonselfidentical custard that its existence is thereby never implicated, presupposed or entailed in (20)–(24), in (32)b–(36)b domain restriction to existent custard remains necessary for the truth of these sentences, even if custard's existence is presupposed or implicated.

The pragmatics of contextual restriction left unexplained, it nevertheless remains in light of (4)–(9) and (20)–(24) that a relentless habit to favor talk about the existent is no sign of the meaning of *the*, -sg, -pl, or *of* or the evaluation of variables. Admittedly, pragmatics is asked to bear a heavy burden, since the facts of (32)b–(36)b reflect no slight preference for the interpretation reported. Speakers seem blind to the alternative attested in (20)–(24), which, were they aware of it when turning to (32)b–(36)b, should suggest to them an interpretation that is false. If not pragmatics alone, perhaps syntax steps in to require a prenominal measure phrase and semantics to stipulate that the silent kind means non-zero, or perhaps there is an explicit convention that all domains of quantification are restricted to the existent, the "realis" and non-modal unless explicit mention directs otherwise, or perhaps the force of such a convention is derived from a syntax and semantics that relates the evaluation of a quantifier's restriction to the tense and modality of its host sentence. Relevant to the division of labor between pragmatics and syntax & semantics, quantifier phrases diverge in their existential commitments when no measure phrase is pronounced:

  (i) The nonselfidentical custards are zero in number.
 (ii) Any nonselfidentical custards are zero in number.
(iii) *Some nonselfidentical custards are zero in number.
 (iv) Some zero or more nonselfidentical custards are in fact (always) zero in number.

(32) a. #Any custards are zero or more in number.
    b. Any custards are one or more in number.
(33) a. #Any of the custards are zero or more in number.
    b. Any of the custards are one or more in number.
(34) a. #Any custard is zero or one dessert.
    b. Any custard is one dessert.
(35) a. #Any of the custards is zero or one desserts.
    b. Any of the custards is one dessert.
(36) a. #Any of the custard is zero or more desserts.
    b. Any of the custard is one or more desserts.

It would of course defeat the point of a measure phrase if it fell within the scope of the operator defined in (31), which recommends its position in (37), a position corroborated in Section 29.1.2.2.

(37) $[\text{the } \xi\colon (\mu\ P)\ \mathbf{I}\Phi[\xi]], [\text{any } \xi\colon (\mu P)\ \mathbf{I}\Phi[\xi]]$

29.0.2 *one* and *zero or more* vs. *one or more* and *zero or more*

Nothing in this reference to the none should however be mistaken to imply that the primitive 'custard' is as promiscuous as the phrasal '$\mathbf{I}custards[\xi]$' in being true of it. One might after all cherish a concept of custard that fails to be true of the none no matter how meager the diet. To put it concretely in more familiar language, the phrase that is an immediate constituent of the definite description may be a second-order description, itself true of the none, projected as in (38) from a first-order property that is not:

(38) $\mathbf{I}custards[X] \leftrightarrow \forall x(Xx \rightarrow \text{custard}(x))$
    'They are custards $\leftrightarrow$ Any one of them is custard.'

A primitive concept of custard, one that is first-order and thus true only of what there is, enters a description of the none such as '$\mathbf{I}nonselfidentical\ custards[\xi]$' only by a logical construction. If the primitive concept is first-order and singular, '$\mathbf{I}custards[\xi]$' is derived as in (38) or to the same effect through the intervention of a partitive relation discussed further below:

(39) $\mathbf{I}custards[\xi] \leftrightarrow \forall x(x \text{ is one of } \xi \rightarrow \text{custard}(x))$

Either way, (38) or (39), singular reference is primitive and plural reference to the many and the none is derived. Alternatively, while reference to the none remains a second-order construction (40), it could be that the primitive, first-order concept itself subsumes plural reference, to the many as well as the one, despite certain knowledge that many concepts such as *custard* are distributive, as in (41):

(40) $\mathbf{I}custards[\xi] \leftrightarrow \exists x\, x \text{ is one of } \xi \rightarrow \text{custard}(\xi)$

(41) custard(ξ) $\leftrightarrow$ $\forall x$(x *is one of* ξ $\rightarrow$ custard(x))
        custard(ξ) $\rightarrow$ $\exists x$ x *is one of* ξ

It just so happens, as everyone knows who knows what custard is, that things are custards just in case each of them is. The primitive, first-order concept 'custard(ξ)' privileges singular reference no more than it privileges dual or triple reference, all of which rather require supplement to the primitive concept:

(42) custard.sg[ξ] $\leftrightarrow_{df}$ custard(ξ) & sg[ξ]

$\cdots$

        custard.n[ξ] $\leftrightarrow_{df}$ custard(ξ) & n[ξ]

A contest between (39) and (41) looks to be a sterile one unless appreciated in full generality to characterize the primitive conceptual vocabulary. On the larger scale, indifference to the contrast between singular and plural reference may matter. Singular reference is concept-dependent: often a fire is many scattered fires, but never is a custard several scattered custards. Moreover, a judgment that there is one fire where there are two, or that there is one musical passage where there are two, reflects arcane knowledge of the subject and may itself be context-dependent and interest-relative:

(43) $\Gamma_{fire}[x, y]$ $\vdash$ (fire(x) & fire(y) & $x \neq y$) $\rightarrow$ $\exists z$($z \neq x$ & $z \neq y$ & fire(z))
(44) $\Gamma_{custard}[x, y]$ $\vdash$ (custard(x) & custard(y) & $x \neq y$) $\rightarrow$ $\exists z$($z \neq x$ & $z \neq y$ & custard(z))

Yet, as arcane as it may be to know what constitutes a fire, a custard or a musical passage, once singular reference is fixed, so it seems is plural reference. Perhaps plural reference is so easily extended to arbitrary concepts because there is indeed so little to it beyond a partitive relation '*is one of* ' or some other logical construction and thus so little to know to extend it. If, on the other hand, plural reference is intrinsic to primitive concepts in general, the arcane knowledge attested about a concept's singular reference is merely one of its many aspects:

(45) $\Gamma_{fire}[\xi, \zeta]$ $\vdash$ (fire(ξ) & sg[ξ] & fire(ζ) & sg[ζ] & $\xi \neq \zeta$) $\rightarrow$ $\exists\varsigma$($\varsigma \neq \xi$ & $\varsigma \neq \zeta$ & fire(ς) & sg[ς])
(46) $\Gamma_{custard}[\xi, \zeta]$ $\vdash$ (custard(ξ) & sg[ξ] & custard(ζ) & sg[ζ] & $\xi \neq \zeta$) $\rightarrow$ $\exists\varsigma$($\varsigma \neq \xi$ & $\varsigma \neq \zeta$ & custard(ς) & sg[ς])

Among the primitive concepts, there could be those that fail one or the other direction of the biconditional in (41), e.g.:

(47) custard'(ξ) $\rightarrow$ $\forall x$(x *is one of* ξ $\rightarrow$ custard'(x)) &
        $\neg\forall\xi$($\forall x$(x *is one of* ξ $\rightarrow$ custard'(x)) $\rightarrow$ custard'(ξ))

And, among these, one could imagine that things each of which is a custard' are some custard's only under conditions that are as arcane but still different from those that assemble a single custard'. Or worse, that the conditions constituting three custard's from three each of which is a custard' are yet again different from those constituting two custard's from two each of which is a custard'. The world of singular and plural reference is then again remade anew with fire and musical passages. If speakers are not as diffident in their grasp of plural reference as these remarks imply they should be, it implies that some further taxonomy or classification informs them—perhaps, those primitive concepts expressed by a primitive morpheme eligible to be a noun are with few exceptions distributive, and, in marked contrast, the concepts of primitive plural reference expressed by natural language determiners, cardinality predicates and many a verb are known not to be. It could then be allowed that the asymmetry between singular and plural reference, the extensibility and near logicality of the latter—that the concept-, context-, and interest- dependence of singular reference does not find its match in plural reference—argues only for more theory rather than for first-order primitives that are only singular. If so, it remains largely an empirical question the extent to which plural reference reaches into the primitive vocabulary, requiring investigation piecemeal through the language.[7]

29.0.3 Morphological Preliminaries

Singular, count nominals, plural nominals and mass nominals share a common vocabulary of primitive lexical items, *custard*, *fire*. The denotation of any of these must be consistent with its occurrences in singular, plural and mass expressions, which are themselves related by analytic truths such as (48)–(51):

(48) Any/all custard is custard.
(49) Any a/Every custard is custard.
(50) Any custards are custard.
(51) Any a/Every custard is one or more custards.
(52) That ((one) custard) is (a) custard.

The same primitive 'custard(ξ)', denoting whatever it denotes, occurs throughout, modified by singular(.sg)-, plural(.pl)- or mass(.$\emptyset$)- term morphology. The sentences of (52), varying the occurrence of count and mass terms, can nevertheless be true of the very same thing.

All that will be said later about the reference of count terms and plural terms and about their inferential behavior is extensible to novel vocabulary whenever a new item is dressed in the appropriate nominal morphology. Generalization to novel vocabulary itself demands a parse of the natural language that factors out the bare nouns and makes explicit their morphological modification. The analytical truths (48)–(51) relating count and mass terms then suggest that the bare 'custard' that pluralizes is the same lexical item expressing the same concept as the bare 'custard' that massifies.[8]

---

[7] I hedged that it is "largely" an empirical question. A natural language with primitive plural reference that does not go beyond a designated relation '*is one of*' may be fit into monadic second order logic and enjoys whatever conceptual advantages can be claimed for that achievement.

[8] I ignore accidents that some lexical nouns do not occur as both count and mass terms—*All bonfire is bonfire*—and hold such a sentence to be analytically true too. See Sharvy 1978 and Borer 2005. If, on the contrary, the gaps are not accidental, it will suffice for the argument to follow that English and other natural languages contain at least some nouns that occur as both count and mass and that the class of such nouns be extensible.

As with nouns, the lexical quantifiers, articles and partitive *of* that occur across singular, plural and mass terms are not themselves specified as singular, plural or mass:

(53) Any (one) custard is dessert. (*cf.* Any tart is pastry.)
(54) Any (three) custards are dessert.
(55) Any (one) of the custards is dessert.
(56) Any (three) of the custards are dessert.
(57) Any of the custard is dessert. (*cf.* Any of the sugar dissolves in water.)

It is thus left to the quantifier's restriction to enforce singular, plural, or mass reference as in [*any* ξ: *custard*.sg[ξ]], [*any* ξ: *custard*.pl[ξ]], or [*any* ξ: *custard*.$\emptyset$[ξ]]. With little else to tell (58) and (59) apart, the partitive construction is itself taken to sort out singular ξ in (58) from non-singular ξ in (59). Both (58) and (59) contain the same lexical item, the partitive *of*, which in (58) is further modified by (unspoken) singular morphology:

(58) Any of the custards is a custard.
      [*any* ξ: sg.*of the custards*[ξ]] *is a custard*[ξ]
(59) F Any of the custards are a custard.
      [*any* ξ: *of the custards*[ξ]] *are a custard*[ξ]

Continuing flat-footed to treat the morphology the same wherever it is encountered, the singular quantification in mass terms, both simple and partitive, translates as:[9]

(60) Any of the pastry is one or more pastries.
      [*any* ξ: sg.*of the pastry*[ξ]] *is one or more pastries*[ξ]
(61) F Any of the pastry is a pastry.
      [*any* ξ: sg.*of the pastry*[ξ]] *is a pastry*[ξ]
(62) Any/all pastry is one or more pastries.
      [*any* ξ: *pastry*.sg[ξ]] *is one or more pastries*[ξ]
(63) F Any/all pastry is a pastry. (cf. F Any/all patisserie is a pastry.)
      [*any* ξ: *pastry*.sg[ξ]] *is a pastry*[ξ]
(64) None of the pastry is more than some pastries.
      [*None* ξ: sg.*of the pastry*[ξ]] *is more than some pastries*[ξ]
(65) F None of the pastry is more than one pastry.
      [*None* ξ: sg.*of the pastry*[ξ]] *is more than one pastry*[ξ]
(66) No pastry is more than some pastries.
      [*No* ξ: *pastry*.sg[ξ]] *is more than some pastries*[ξ]
(67) F No pastry is more than one pastry. (cf. F No patisserie is more than one pastry.)
      [*No* ξ: *pastry*.sg[ξ]] *is more than one pastry*[ξ]

If the least of pastry is a single pastry, one might have anticipated that (61) and (65) would be true. Apparently, however, any quantity of pastry *is* pastry, in the singular,[9]

---

9 *v.* Burge, 1972; Koslicki, 1997, 1999, 2005, in preparation and the references cited therein.

and therefore one or perhaps more pastries rather than a single one. But, if what be pastry is further restricted to what are pastries, anything singular is just a pastry, and thus (68) and (69) contrast minimally with (61) and (65):

(68) Any of the pastries is a pastry.
   [*any* ξ: sg.*of the pastries*[ξ]] *is a pastry*[ξ]
(69) None of the pastries is more than one pastry.
   [*None* ξ: sg.*of the pastries*[ξ]] *is more than one pastry*[ξ][1011]

Consonant with these remarks, both mass terms and singular, count terms are taken to share the same singular morphology and are now to be parsed accordingly:

(70) custard.pl.sg[ξ].   [Every ξ: custard.pl.sg[ξ]], *every custard*.
   custard.pl[ξ].   [All ξ: custard.pl[ξ]], *all custards*.
   custard.Ø.sg[ξ].   [All ξ: custard.Ø.sg[ξ]], *all custard*.

Singular morphology therefore does not imply a countable domain, which is indicated rather by the presence of the plural morpheme so-called,[12] nor does it imply non-zero measure, as remarked above in (4), (5), (6), (8), (22) and (24) (although it will imply measurement no greater than one).

29.1 KNOWLEDGE OF SINGULAR AND PLURAL

29.1.1 Inference in the Object Language

To know of an *F* is to know of one or more *F*s, and often, what is true of every one of the *F*s is true of every *F*, and conversely, what is true of every *F* is true of every one of the *F*s. At least so much is distilled from distributivity inferences like (71)–(80). *Extensibility*, as reflected in a speaker's willingness to extend these inferences to arbitrary substitutions for *F* (under conditions noted below), including novel vocabulary, and even to affirm them for *F* of uncertain meaning, is bedrock for a speaker's knowledge of singular and plural.[13]

---

[10] Schein, 2005, n. 12 discusses the possibility that number agreement for singular count terms and mass terms is accidentally homophonous.

[11] Schein, 2005, n. 13, for further remarks on the (cross-linguistic) univocality of closed-class vocabulary, *the*, *of* and quantifiers, and on alternative paraphrases for the partitive relation.

[12] See Sharvy, 1978; Borer, 2005 and references therein. If mass reference simply suppresses the conditions for count reference without imposing any special conditions of its own, there might not be a mass term morpheme -Ø, a mass noun being indicated only by the absence of count morphology. On the semantics of the count/mass distinction and the surrounding metaphysics, see Koslicki, 1997, 1999, 2005, in preparation and the references cited therein.

[13] Boolos, 1984, 1985ab; Higginbotham, 1998, 2000; Lewis, 1991; Schein, 1993: ch. 2.

Distributivity

(71) a. A fire expired. ⊢ (Some) one of the fires expired.

    b. (Some) one of the fires expired. ⊢ A fire expired.

(72) a. Every one of the custards hides a jewel. ⊢ Every custard hides a jewel.

    b. Every custard hides a jewel. ⊢ Every one of the custards hides a jewel.

(73) a. None of the puff pastries is more puff than pastry. ⊢ No puff pastry is more puff than pastry.

    b. No puff pastry is more puff than pastry. ⊢ None of the puff pastries is more puff than pastry.

(74) Many a fire of the fires from heaven scorches the earth. ⊢ Many a fire from heaven scorches the earth.

Many a fire from heaven scorches the earth. ⊢ Many a fire of the fires from heaven scorches the earth.

(75) Many fires of the fires from heaven scorch the earth. ⊢ Many fires from heaven scorch the earth.

Many fires from heaven scorch the earth. ⊢ Many fires of the fires from heaven scorch the earth.

Plural Partitivity

(76) a. Some fires expired. ⊢ Some of the fires expired.

    b. Some of the fires expired. ⊢ Some fires expired.

(77) a. Any of the custards hide a jewel. ⊢ Any custards hide a jewel.

    b. Any custards hide a jewel. ⊢ Any of the custards hide a jewel.

(78) a. None of the puff pastries are more puff than pastry. ⊢ No puff pastries are more puff than pastry.

    b. No puff pastries are more puff than pastry. ⊢ None of the puff pastries are more puff than pastry.

(79) Most any of the butter pastries is all butter. ⊢ Most any butter pastry is all butter.

Most any butter pastry is all butter. ⊢ Most any of the butter pastries is all butter.

(80) Most of the butter pastries are all butter. ⊢ Most butter pastries are all butter.

Most butter pastries are all butter. ⊢ Most of the butter pastries are all butter.

Note that the patterns in (81) instantiated by (71)a–(73)a and (76)a–(78)a are valid just in case (82) holds, and those in (83) instantiated by (71)b–(73)b and (76)b–(78)b, just in case (84) holds:

(81) $[\text{Some }\xi\colon \Phi[\xi]]\Psi[\xi] \vdash [\text{Some }\xi\colon \Phi'[\xi]]\Psi[\xi]$

    $[\text{Every }\xi\colon \Phi'[\xi]]\Psi[\xi] \vdash [\text{Every }\xi\colon \Phi[\xi]]\Psi[\xi]$

    $[\text{Any }\xi\colon \Phi'[\xi]]\Psi[\xi] \vdash [\text{Any }\xi\colon \Phi[\xi]]\Psi[\xi]$

    $[\text{No }\xi\colon \Phi'[\xi]]\Psi[\xi] \vdash [\text{No }\xi\colon \Phi[\xi]]\Psi[\xi]$

(82) $\Phi[\xi] \rightarrow \Phi'[\xi]$

(83) $[\text{Some }\xi\colon \Phi'[\xi]]\,\Psi[\xi] \vdash [\text{Some }\xi\colon \Phi[\xi]]\,\Psi[\xi]$
　　　$[\text{Every }\xi\colon \Phi[\xi]]\,\Psi[\xi] \vdash [\text{Every }x\colon \Phi'[\xi]]\,\Psi[\xi]$
　　　$[\text{Any }\xi\colon \Phi[\xi]]\,\Psi[\xi] \vdash [\text{Any }x\colon \Phi'[\xi]]\,\Psi[\xi]$
　　　$[\text{No }\xi\colon \Phi[\xi]]\,\Psi[\xi] \vdash [\text{No }\xi\colon \Phi'[\xi]]\,\Psi[\xi]$

(84) $\Phi'[\xi] \rightarrow \Phi[\xi]$

The speaker reasoning all directions in (71)–(73) thus requires (85):

(85) $\Phi[\xi] \leftrightarrow \Phi'[\xi]$

With non-monotonic quantifiers, *many* in (74)–(75) and *most* in (79)–(80), a single inference in either direction of its own demands the biconditional (85). Accepting the distributivity inferences of (71)–(80) thus commits speakers to the instances of (85) relating singular and plural as in (86), and plural to plural partitive as in (87), which become (88) and (89), assuming a common syntax and semantics for the partitive *of* and suppressing grammatical variation. Constitution principles are those like (88) and (89) that constitute *via* a partitive construction the plural reference of the plural definite description from the denotation of the singular and plural predicates.

(86) *one of the custards*$[\xi] \leftrightarrow custard[\xi]$
　　　a fire of the fires from heaven$[\xi] \leftrightarrow fire\,from\,heaven[\xi]$
　　　any of the butter pastries$[\xi] \leftrightarrow any\,butter\,pastry[\xi]$

(87) *some of the custards*$[\xi] \leftrightarrow custards[\xi]$
　　　fires of the fires from heaven$[\xi] \leftrightarrow fires\,from\,heaven[\xi]$
　　　of the butter pastries$[\xi] \leftrightarrow butter\,pastries[\xi]$

Singular constitution principles for plural terms

(88) *of the custards*$[\xi] \leftrightarrow custard[\xi]$
　　　of the fires from heaven$[\xi] \leftrightarrow fire\,from\,heaven[\xi]$
　　　of the butter pastries$[\xi] \leftrightarrow butter\,pastry[\xi]$

Plural constitution principles for plural terms

(89) *of the custards*$[\xi] \leftrightarrow custards[\xi]$
　　　of the fires from heaven$[\xi] \leftrightarrow fires\,from\,heaven[\xi]$
　　　of the butter pastries$[\xi] \leftrightarrow butter\,pastries[\xi]$

An account of plurals in natural language promises an analysis of the constitution principles (88) and (89) that derive the elementary inferences of distributivity and plural partitivity in (71)–(80). Given that the constitution principles are as numerous as substitutions for F are unbounded, these principles must derive from some generalization about the object language. The correct generalizations are not (90) and (91) that any plural definite description instantiates valid constitution principles:

(90) $\nvdash (\forall\Phi)^{14}\,(of\,the\,\Phi.pl[\xi] \leftrightarrow \Phi[\xi])$
(91) $\nvdash (\forall\Phi)\,(of\,the\,\Phi.pl[\xi] \leftrightarrow \Phi.pl[\xi])$

---

14 '$(\forall\Phi)$', '$(\exists\Phi)$', quantifiers in parentheses to indicate substitutional quantification.

The generalizations must rather be restricted as warranted by (92)–(108) to those descriptions that do not themselves contain essential tokens of plural terms:

(92) (Some) one of the custards that blanketed a buffet was served in a cup.
      ⊬ A custard that blanketed a buffet was served in a cup.
(93) Every custard that blanketed a buffet was served in a cup.
      ⊬ Every one of the custards that blanketed a buffet was served in a cup.
(94) No custard that blanketed a buffet was served in a cup.
      ⊬ None of the custards that blanketed a buffet was served in a cup.
(95) ⊬ *of the custards that blanketed a buffet*[ξ] → *custard that blanketed a buffet*[ξ]

(96) Some of the custards that blanketed a buffet were served in a cup.
      ⊬ Some custards that blanketed a buffet were served in a cup.
(97) Any custards that blanketed a buffet were served in a cup.
      ⊬ Any of the custards that blanketed a buffet were served in a cup.
(98) No custards that blanketed a buffet were served in a cup.
      ⊬ None of the custards that blanketed a buffet were served in a cup.
(99) ⊬ *of the custards that blanketed a buffet*[ξ] → *custards that blanketed a buffet* [ξ]

A custard that is one of the custards that blanket a buffet, a description that is essentially about some custards, is not itself a custard that blankets a buffet. Similarly, some of the custards that blanket a buffet need not themselves blanket a buffet.

Plying a more subtle observation about plural definite description,[15] the converse inferences are also seen to fail. All of what the description *the custards that blanket exactly one buffet* refers to, if it refers at all, is some custards that blanket exactly one buffet. With two buffets blanketed in custards, definite reference fails: to refer to the custards on just a single buffet, one and not the other, fails to include the custards on the other buffet that do themselves blanket exactly one buffet; yet, to refer to all the custards is not to refer to custards that blanket exactly one. A failure of definite reference undermines converses of (96)–(99):

(100) Thirty custards that blanketed exactly one buffet were served in a cup.
       ⊬ Thirty of the custards that blanketed exactly one buffet were served in a cup.
(101) Every thirty of the custards that blanketed exactly one buffet were served in a cup.
       ⊬ Every thirty custards that blanketed exactly one buffet were served in a cup.
(102) None of the custards that blanketed exactly one buffet were served in a cup.
       ⊬ No custards that blanketed exactly one buffet were served in a cup.
(103) ⊬ *custards that blanketed exactly one buffet*[ξ] → *of the custards that blanketed exactly one buffet*[ξ]

The converses of (92)–(95) are also unsound, provided one is careful not to equivocate on the meaning of the definite description:

15 Sharvy, 1980; Cartwright, 1996.

(104) A custard that blanketed exactly one buffet was served in a cup.
       ⊬ (Some) one of the custards that blanketed exactly one buffet was served in
       a cup.
(105) Every one of the custards that blanketed exactly one buffet was served in a cup.
       ⊬ Every custard that blanketed exactly one buffet was served in a cup.
(106) None of the custards that blanketed exactly one buffet was served in a cup.
       ⊬ No custard that blanketed exactly one buffet was served in a cup.
(107) ⊬ *custard that blanketed exactly one buffet*[ξ] → *of the custards that blanketed
       exactly one buffet*[ξ]
(108) ⊢ *custard that blanketed exactly one buffet*[ξ] → *of the custards that* each
       blanketed exactly one buffet[ξ]

In imagining a premise made true by a giant custard draped across the buffet, one
should not then take the plural definite description to tacitly contain a distributive
quantifier, *the custards that* each *blanketed exactly one buffet*, for which the constitution principle (108) and associated inferences are indeed valid. Note that in formulating a generalization to cover the valid constitution principles, it is to be explained
how the insertion of 'each' manages to classify the description that contains it among
those in which plural terms do not occur essentially, resulting in the contrast between
(107) and (108).

Joining the distributivity of count terms are analogue inferences of dissectivity
among mass terms, (109)–(112), analogous constitution principles in (113) and analogue restrictions on their generalization (114)–(121).

Dissectivity

(109) a. (Some) fire expired. ⊢ Some of the fire expired.
      b. Some of the fire expired. ⊢ (Some) fire expired.
(110) a. Any of the custard[16] hides a jewel. ⊢ Any custard hides a jewel.
      b. Any custard hides a jewel. ⊢ Any of the custard hides a jewel.
(111) a. None of the puff pastry is more puff than pastry. ⊢ No puff pastry is more
         puff than pastry.
      b. No puff pastry is more puff than pastry. ⊢ None of the puff pastry is more
         puff than pastry.

(112) Most of the butter pastry is all butter. ⊢ Most butter pastry is all butter.
      Most butter pastry is all butter. ⊢ Most of the butter pastry is all butter.

Constitution for Mass Terms

(113) *of the fire*[ξ] ↔ *fire*[ξ]
      of the custard[ξ] ↔ *custard*[ξ]
      of the puff pastry[ξ] ↔ *puff pastry*[ξ]

---

[16] Any of the custard *is* custard, and thus unlike any part of the custard, egg protein, that is not custard.
v. Burge, 1972; Koslicki, 1997, 1999, 2005, in preparation.

(114) Some of the puff pastry that blanketed a buffet was more puff than pastry.

     ⊬ (Some) puff pastry that blanketed a buffet was more puff than pastry.

(115) Any fire that dotted Carmel had a cool spot.

     ⊬ Any of the fire that dotted Carmel had a cool spot.

(116) No custard that fills a hundred pastries is without a jewel hidden somewhere inside.

     ⊬ None of the custard that fills a hundred pastries is without a jewel hidden somewhere inside.

(117) ⊬ *of the puff pastry that blanketed a buffet*$[\xi]$ → *puff pastry that blanketed a buffet*$[\xi]$

     ⊬ *of the fire that dotted Carmel*$[\xi]$ → *fire that dotted Carmel*$[\xi]$

     ⊬ *of the custard that fills a hundred pastries*$[\xi]$ → *custard that fills a hundred pastries*$[\xi]$

(118) (Some) puff pastry that blanketed exactly one buffet was more puff than pastry.

     ⊬ Some of the puff pastry that blanketed exactly one buffet was more puff than pastry.

(119) Any of the fire that dotted exactly one estate in Carmel had a cool spot.

     ⊬ Any fire that dotted exactly one estate in Carmel had a cool spot.

(120) None of the custard that fills a hundred pastries but no more is without a jewel hidden somewhere inside.

     ⊬ No custard that fills a hundred pastries but no more is without a jewel hidden somewhere inside.

(121) ⊬ *puff pastry that blanketed exactly one buffet*$[\xi]$ → *of the puff pastry that blanketed exactly one buffet*$[\xi]$

     ⊬ *fire that dotted exactly one estate in Carmel*$[\xi]$ → *of the fire that dotted exactly one estate in Carmel*$[\xi]$

     ⊬ *custard that fills a hundred pastries but no more*$[\xi]$ → *of the custard that fills a hundred pastries but no more*$[\xi]$

Since distributivity, plural partitivity, dissectivity, constitution and (48)–(52) are all extensible to novel *F*, it compels a parse that factors out the recurrent *F* and makes explicit its morphological modification. In particular, the constitution principles become (122)–(124), instantiating NP with the same *F* throughout.

(122) *of the* NP.pl$[\xi]$ ↔ NP.pl.sg$[\xi]$

     of the fire.pl$[\xi]$ ↔ *fire*.pl.sg$[\xi]$

     of the custard.pl$[\xi]$ ↔ *custard*.pl.sg$[\xi]$

     of the butter pastry.pl$[\xi]$ ↔ *butter pastry*.pl.sg$[\xi]$

(123) *of the* NP.pl$[\xi]$ ↔ NP.pl$[\xi]$

     of the custards$[\xi]$ ↔ *custards*$[\xi]$

     of the fires$[\xi]$ ↔ *fires*$[\xi]$

     of the butter pastries$[\xi]$ ↔ *butter pastries*$[\xi]$

(124) *of the* NP.Ø[ξ] $\leftrightarrow$ NP.Ø[ξ]
   *of the fire.*Ø[ξ] $\leftrightarrow$ *fire.*Ø[ξ]
   *of the custard.*Ø[ξ] $\leftrightarrow$ *custard.*Ø[ξ]
   *of the puff pastry.*Ø[ξ] $\leftrightarrow$ *puff pastry.*Ø[ξ]

So refined, the problem of plurals in natural language becomes the question of what in the speaker's knowledge of the syntax and semantics of singular, plural and mass terms validates the constitution principles (122)–(124) and with them the corresponding inferences of distributivity, plural partitivity and dissectivity. No answer is forthcoming without deciding on a syntax and semantics for the singular, plural and mass-term morphemes, the definite article *the* and the partitive construction embedding *of.*

29.1.2 The Language of the Partitive Construction[17]

Suppose expressions of the form *of the* NP.pl[ξ] and *of the* NP.Ø[ξ] as they occur in the object language, the natural language on display in (71)–(80) and (109)–(112), contain expression of a relation to whatever the definite description denotes. A speaker in accepting (122)–(124) affirms instances of (125)–(127):

(125) [*the* ς: NP.pl[ς]] sg.*of*[ξ, ς] $\leftrightarrow$ NP.pl.sg[ξ]
   [*the* ς: *custard*.pl[ς]] sg.*of*[ξ, ς] $\leftrightarrow$ sg.*custard*.pl[ξ]
(126) [*the* ς: NP.pl[ς]] *of*[ξ, ς] $\leftrightarrow$ NP.pl[ξ]
   [*the* ς: *custard*.pl[ς]] *of*[ξ, ς] $\leftrightarrow$ *custard*.pl[ξ]
(127) [*the* ς: NP.Ø[ς]]sg.*of*[ξ, ς] $\leftrightarrow$ NP.Ø[ξ]
   [*the* ς: *custard*.Ø[ς]]sg.*of*[ξ, ς] $\leftrightarrow$ *custard*.Ø[ξ]

The partitive relations thus exposed, the non-singular relation and its restriction to a singular first argument are related by valid inferences of the form in (128) and (129), which rely on speakers knowing (130):

(128) Any of the custards is one or more of the flans. $\vdash$ Any of the custards are one or more of the flans.
(129) Some of the custards are none of the flans. $\vdash$ Not every one of the custards is one of the flans.
   (Some) *n* of the custards are not *n* of the flans. $\vdash$ Not every one of the custards is one of the flans.
(130) $\forall\varsigma\forall\gamma\forall\xi$(sg.*of*[$\xi$, ς] $\rightarrow$ sg.*of*[ξ, γ]) $\rightarrow$ $\forall\xi$(*of*[ξ, ς] $\rightarrow$ *of*[ξ, γ]))

Similarly, the converse inferences rely on the converse to (130) in (133):

(131) Any of the custards are one or more of the flans. $\vdash$ Any of the custards is one or more of the flans.

---

[17] *v.* Higginbotham, 1998, 2000; Hossack, 2000; Linnebo, 2003, 2004; McKay, forthcoming: ch. 6, Oliver and Smiley, 2001; Rayo, 2002; Simons, 1982, 1987; Yi 2005.

(132) Not every one of the custards is one of the flans. δ Some of the custards are none of the flans.

Not every one of the custards is one of the flans. δ (Some) *n* of the custards are not *n* of the flans.

(133) ∀ς∀γ (∀ξ(*of*[ξ, ς] → *of*[ξ, γ]) → ∀ξ(sg.*of*[ξ, ς] → sg.*of*[ξ, γ]))

Speakers also know the non-singular partitive relation to be reflexive (135) in affirming all instances of (134):

(134) (Some) *n* of the *n* Fs are the Fs.
(135) ∀ξ *of*[ξ,ξ]   (reflexivity)

With reflexivity, (130) and (133) entail (136) and, in turn, the transitivity of the non-singular partitive relation:

(136) ∀ς∀γ (∀ξ(sg.*of*[ξ, ς] ↔ sg.*of*[ξ, γ]) ↔ *of*[ς, γ])
(137) ∀ς∀γ (∀ξ(*of*[ξ, ς] → *of*[ξ, γ]) ↔ *of*[ς, γ]) (transitivity)

The non-singular partitive relation is also known to be antisymmetric (139), as reflected in speakers' acceptance of all instances of (138):

(138) Any of the Fs are Gs.
Any of the Gs are Fs.
⊢ The Fs are the Gs.
(139) ∀ξ∀ς((*of*[ξ, ς] & *of*[ς, ξ]) → ξ = ς) (antisymmetry)

Antisymmetry and (136) derive a principle of extensionality for the singular partitive relation:

(140) ∀ς∀γ(∀ξ(sg.*of*[ξ, ς] ↔ sg.*of*[ξ, γ]) ↔ ς = γ) (extensionality)

Extensionality holds of the partitive construction occurring in the distributive quantifiers of (71)–(79), whatever may be meant by 'sg.*of*[ξ,ς]'. But, unpacking it as in (141) will afford a common syntax and semantics for the singular morpheme here and elsewhere:

(141) sg.*of*[ξ,ς] *for* (sg[ξ] & *of*[ξ,ς])
(142) sg.Φ [ξ,ς] *for* (sg[ξ] & Φ[ξ,ς])
sg.Φ [ξ] *for* (sg[ξ] & Φ[ξ])

As far as a speaker's inferential behavior goes as reflected in constitution principles and inferences of distributivity, plural partitivity and dissectivity, the morphological and syntactic analysis has bottomed out. It could leave speakers in command of a primitive constitution relation around which the partitive constructions are constructed, *of*[ξ,ς] for 'of(ξ,ς)'. It could also be said of the singular morpheme that it expresses a primitive concept of singularities and that a speaker's grasp of that concept conforms to the principle of extensionality and other principles canvassed above. Instead, joining the literature,[18] the singular morpheme is defined in terms of the non-singular partitive construction.

29.1.2.1 A Primitive Partitive Relation 'of(ξ,ς)' is a Partial Order with Zero

(143) $\forall\xi$	$\text{of}(\xi,\xi)$	(reflexivity)
(144) $\forall\xi\forall\varsigma$	$((\text{of}(\xi,\varsigma)\,\&\,\text{of}(\varsigma,\xi))\to\xi=\varsigma)$	(antisymmetry)
(145) $\forall\varsigma\forall\gamma$	$(\forall\xi(\text{of}(\xi,\varsigma)\to\text{of}(\xi,\gamma))\leftrightarrow\text{of}(\varsigma,\gamma))$	(transitivity)
(146) $\exists\xi\forall\varsigma$	$(\text{of}(\xi,\varsigma)\,\&\,(\text{of}(\varsigma,\xi)\to\xi=\varsigma))$	(zero)

Some zero or more ξ be singular just in case nothing else non-zero is of them:

(147) $\text{sg}[\xi]\leftrightarrow_{df}\forall\varsigma\forall\gamma(\neg\text{of}(\varsigma,\gamma)\to(\text{of}(\varsigma,\xi)\to\text{of}(\xi,\varsigma)))$[19]

Recall Section 29.0.1 that zero is singular—(5), (6), (22), (23) (and, also non-singular (4), (9), (20)–(22), (24)). A domain restricted to the non-zero as in (32)–(36) is restriction to the existent:

(148) $\text{E}[\xi]\leftrightarrow_{df}\exists\varsigma\neg\,\text{of}(\xi,\varsigma)$

As above, the singular and non-singular partitive relations are related by extensionality, which can be formulated with equivalent results either as (149) or (150):

(extensionality)

(149) $\forall\varsigma\forall\gamma\,(\forall\xi((\text{sg}[\xi]\,\&\,\text{of}(\xi,\varsigma))\leftrightarrow(\text{sg}[\xi]\,\&\,\text{of}(\xi,\gamma)))\leftrightarrow\varsigma=\gamma)$. That is,
      $\forall\varsigma\forall\gamma\,(\forall\xi(\text{sg.of}[\xi,\varsigma]\leftrightarrow\text{sg.of}[\xi,\gamma])\leftrightarrow\varsigma=\gamma)$
(150) $\forall\varsigma\forall\gamma\,(\forall\xi((\text{sg}[\xi]\,\&\,\text{E}[\xi]\,\&\,\text{of}(\xi,\varsigma))\leftrightarrow(\text{sg}[\xi]\,\&\,\text{E}[\xi]\,\&\,\text{of}(\xi,\gamma)))\leftrightarrow\varsigma=\gamma)$.
      That is,
      $\forall\varsigma\forall\gamma\,(\forall\xi(\text{sg.E.of}[\xi,\varsigma]\leftrightarrow\text{sg.E.of}[\xi,\gamma])\leftrightarrow\varsigma=\gamma)$

As (150) invites, a partitive construction can be viewed as overt expression of the predication relation that holds between a singular, first-order predicate and anything it denotes, translating as in (151):

(151) 'Xx' for '$\text{sg.E.of}[x,X]$' where uppercase and lowercase variables belong to the same sort in the language of the partitive construction.

In a first-order language where any primitive noun is singular, including those underlying mass terms such as *fire*, any X be fire if and only if $\exists xXx\,\&\,\forall x(Xx\to\text{fire}(x))$. Any quantity of fire, on this view, is a first-order object of fire. Although it may cheat an intuition that the concept *fire* is pre-individuative, the view is common to all accounts searching out a common semantics for mass and count terms.[20] In the

---

[18] Linnebo, 2004; Link, 1983, 1987; Rayo, 2002; McKay forthcoming, ch. 6; Simons, 1982, 1987; Yi, 2005: $\text{sg}[\xi]\leftrightarrow_{df}\forall\varsigma\forall\gamma(\text{of}[\varsigma,\xi]\to\text{of}[\xi,\varsigma])$.
[19] *Cf.* n. 18.
[20] *v.* Burge, 1972; Koslicki, 1997, 1999, 2005, in preparation and the references cited therein.

language of the partitive construction, absent the assumption of a first-order syntax with singular variables, it is declared outright that if there exist anything at all—some fire, for example—(at least) some of it is singular:

(152) $\forall \xi (E[\xi] \rightarrow \exists \varsigma (sg[\varsigma] \& E[\varsigma] \& of(\varsigma, \xi)))$

29.1.2.2 Definite Description

The partitive relation becomes the basis for a translation of definite descriptions in which the same lexical item, the article *the*, appears in singular, plural and mass definite descriptions, as desired. Define first the iota operator as in (153):[21]

(153) $[\iota \xi: \Phi[\xi]]\Psi[\xi] \leftrightarrow_{df} [\exists \xi: \Phi[\xi] \& \forall \varsigma (\Phi[\varsigma] \rightarrow of(\varsigma, \xi)) \& \forall \gamma (\forall \varsigma (\Phi[\varsigma] \rightarrow of(\varsigma, \gamma)) \rightarrow of(\xi, \gamma))]\Psi[\xi]$

Many definite descriptions, *the* Φ, are adequately translated without further comment assuming 'the' to be the pronunciation of the iota operator. In *the custard(s) that blanketed exactly one buffet*, the condition that $\Phi[\xi]$, that the custard(s) referred to be custard that blanketed exactly one buffet, induces reference to fail if the custard(s) referred to blanketed two buffets. Yet, the condition that $\forall \varsigma (\Phi[\varsigma] \rightarrow of(\varsigma, \xi))$ requires that any custard(s) that blanketed exactly one buffet be some of what is referred to, and thus if two buffets are blanketed in custard, reference again fails if any of it is excluded.[22]

The definite description in (154) containing a prenominal measure phrase fails to refer, as above, if there are two buffets blanketed in custards—even if one buffet holds 365 and the other 248. In this respect, the prenominal measure phrase agrees with the non-restrictive modifier in (156) rather than the restriction in (155), and the translation is (158) rather than (157):[23]

(154) The 365 custards that blanketed exactly one buffet were served in a cup.
(155) The custards that blanketed exactly one buffet and numbered 365 were served in a cup.
(156) The custards that blanketed exactly one buffet, which numbered 365, were served in a cup.
(157) $*[the \xi: \mu P \Phi[\xi]]\Psi[\xi] for [\iota \xi: \mu P[\xi] \& \Phi[\xi]]\Psi[\xi]$
(158) $[the \xi: \mu P \Phi[\xi]]\Psi[\xi] for [\iota \xi: \Phi[\xi] \& [\iota \xi: \Phi[\xi]]\mu P[\xi]]\Psi[\xi]$

---

[21] Sharvy, 1980; Cartwright, 1996.
[22] The final condition that $\forall \gamma (\forall \varsigma (\Phi[\varsigma] \rightarrow of(\varsigma, \gamma)) \rightarrow of(\xi, \gamma))$ is that what is referred to be the least such to meet the antecedent conditions. Let there be just one buffet blanketed in custard(s). The definite description should refer to this custard alone and not to this custard and in addition some blancmange.
[23] Already for a construction as elementary as *More than 365 custards blanketed the buffet*, Hackl (2001, 2003ab) proves that the quantification conceals full-blown comparative clauses of degree. Presumably that syntax and semantics should be fit into *The more than 365 custards blanketed the buffet*, disappointing any expectation that a measure phrase will compose as simply as in (157). In the light of this result, (158) is at best provisional even if equivalent to the target meaning.

29.1.3 Constitution and Comprehension

With definite descriptions in place, it can be verified that the constitution principles (125)–(127) are equivalent to (159)–(161),[24] which take on the form of conditional comprehension principles:

Conditional Singular–Plural Comprehension

(159) $\exists\xi NP.sg[\xi] \rightarrow \exists\varsigma\forall\xi(sg.of[\xi, \varsigma] \leftrightarrow NP.sg[\xi])$

Conditional Plural-Plural Comprehension

(160) $\exists\xi NP.pl[\xi] \rightarrow \exists\varsigma\forall\xi(of[\xi, \varsigma] \leftrightarrow NP.pl[\xi])$

Conditional Mass-term Comprehension

(161) $\exists\xi\ NP.\emptyset[\xi] \rightarrow \exists\varsigma\forall\xi(of[\xi, \varsigma] \leftrightarrow NP.\emptyset[\xi])$

The cited inferences of distributivity, plural partitivity and dissectivity are nothing stronger; but, the zero that (146) stipulates and *the nonselfidentical custard(s)* and the like refer to warrant unconditional comprehension principles. If, as supposed in section 29.0.1 (*v.*(31)), the quantifiers' restrictions—plural '**1**(nonselfidentical[ξ] & custard.pl[ξ])', singular '**1**(nonselfidentical[ξ] & custard.pl.sg[ξ])' (*v.* (5), (6), (22)) and mass '**1**(nonselfidentical[ξ] & custard.$\emptyset$[ξ])'—are true of zero ξ, the conditions of (160)–(161) are satisfied so that:

Singular–Plural Comprehension Principles

(162) $\exists\varsigma\forall\xi(sg.of[\xi, \varsigma] \leftrightarrow NP.sg[\xi])$

Plural-Plural Comprehension Principles

(163) $\exists\varsigma\forall\xi(of[\xi, \varsigma] \leftrightarrow NP.pl[\xi])$

Mass-term Comprehension Principles

(164) $\exists\varsigma\forall\xi(sg.of[\xi, \varsigma] \leftrightarrow NP.\emptyset[\xi])$

These comprehension principles and their related constitution principles, as numerous as the valid substitutions for NP, are to be derived from a generalization to a single restricted comprehension axiom:

Restricted Comprehension Axiom

(165) $\vdash (\forall\Phi[\xi])\exists\varsigma\forall\xi(sg.E.of[\xi, \varsigma] \leftrightarrow sg.E.\Phi[\xi]))$

---

[24] *v.* Schein, 1993: 29 ff.

As soon as a universal quantifier over phrases of the object language is introduced, the axiom's formulation is constrained by Russell's paradox.[25]

29.1.3.1 Restricted Comprehension

Russell's paradox constrains generalization, excluding unrestricted comprehension axioms, such as (166)–(169), instantiating as shown any formula Φ free in a single variable. Substituting the negation of the reflexive of the constitution relation, whatever that may be, results in contradiction:[26]

(166) $\nvdash (\forall\Phi[\xi])\exists\varsigma\forall\xi(of[\xi,\varsigma] \leftrightarrow \Phi[\xi])$. Contradiction substituting '$\neg of[\xi,\xi]$' for $\Phi[\xi]$.

(167) $\nvdash (\forall\Phi[\xi])\exists\varsigma\forall\xi(sg.of[\xi,\varsigma] \leftrightarrow \Phi[\xi])$. Contradiction substituting '$\neg sg.of[\xi,\xi]$' for $\Phi[\xi]$.

(168) $\nvdash (\forall\Phi[\xi])\exists\varsigma\forall\xi(E.of[\xi,\varsigma] \leftrightarrow \Phi[\xi])$. Contradiction substituting '$\neg E.of[\xi,\xi]$' for $\Phi[\xi]$.

(169) $\nvdash (\forall\Phi[\xi])\exists\varsigma\forall\xi(sg.E.of[\xi,\varsigma] \leftrightarrow \Phi[\xi])$. Contradiction substituting '$\neg sg.E.of[\xi,\xi]$' for $\Phi[\xi]$.

In contrast, restricted comprehension (170)[27] escapes. Substitution of the Russell predicate '$\neg sg.E. of[\xi,\xi]$' in (171) benignly entails that there is what is zero in number or more than one.

Restricted Comprehension Axiom

(170) $\vdash (\forall\Phi[\xi])\exists\varsigma\forall\xi(sg.E.of[\xi,\varsigma] \leftrightarrow sg.E.\Phi[\xi]))$

$$
\begin{aligned}
(171)\,(170) &\vdash \exists\varsigma\forall\xi(sg.E.of[\xi,\varsigma] \leftrightarrow sg.E.(\neg sg.E.of)[\xi,\xi])) \\
&\vdash sg.E.of[\varsigma,\varsigma] \leftrightarrow sg.E.(\neg sg.E.of)[\varsigma,\varsigma]) \\
&\vdash (sg[\varsigma]\ \&\ E[\varsigma]\ \&\ of(\varsigma,\varsigma)) \leftrightarrow (sg[\varsigma]\ \&\ E[\varsigma]\ \&\ \neg(sg[\varsigma]\ \&\ \\
&\quad E[\varsigma]\ \&\ of(\varsigma,\varsigma))) \\
&\vdash (sg[\varsigma]\ \&\ E[\varsigma]) \leftrightarrow (sg[\varsigma]\ \&\ E[\varsigma]\ \&\ \neg(sg[\varsigma]\ \&\ E[\varsigma])) \\
&\vdash \exists\varsigma\neg(sg[\varsigma]\ \&\ E[\varsigma])
\end{aligned}
$$

As presented, the restriction includes restriction to the existent. Since Φ may be any formula of the object language in one free variable, consider the substitution of '$\neg\xi = \xi$' into an axiom unrestricted to the existent:

(172) $\vdash (\forall\Phi[\xi])\,\exists\varsigma\forall\xi(sg.of[\xi,\varsigma] \leftrightarrow sg.\Phi[\xi]))$

(173)\,(172) $\vdash \exists\varsigma\forall\xi(sg.of[\xi,\varsigma] \leftrightarrow (sg[\xi]\ \&\ \neg\xi = \xi))$

---

[25] For the details deriving the comprehension and constitution principles from (165), see Schein, 2005, § 1.3.0. Axiom (165) has abstracted away from the nominal morphology, from the plural and mass morphemes in particular, and these need to be re-introduced as discussed in § 1.3.0 in any derivation of the comprehension and constitution principles.

[26] Boolos 1984, 1985ab, and also, among others, Cartwright, 1994; Higginbotham, 1998, 2000; Higginbotham and Schein, 1989; Lewis, 1991; Oliver and Smiley, 2001; Pietroski, 2003; Rayo, 2002; Schein, 1993: ch. 2; Williamson, 2003.

[27] Schein, 1993: 35.

$$\vdash \exists\varsigma\forall\xi\neg sg.of\,[\xi,\varsigma]$$
$$\vdash \exists\varsigma\forall\xi(\neg sg[\xi] \vee \neg of(\xi,\varsigma)))$$

It will contradict that the zero ((146)) are singular and of everything. The same substitution into an axiom restricted to the existent entails harmlessly that the zero are not existent:

(174) (170) $\vdash \exists\varsigma\forall\xi(sg.E.of\,[\xi,\varsigma] \leftrightarrow (sg[\xi] \,\&\, E[\xi] \,\&\, \neg\xi = \xi))$
$$\vdash \exists\varsigma\forall\xi\neg sg.E.of\,[\varsigma,\varsigma]$$
$$\vdash \exists\varsigma\forall\xi(\neg sg[\xi] \vee \neg E[\xi] \vee \neg of(\xi,\varsigma)))$$

The restricted comprehension axiom (170) reprises in the language of the partitive construction second-order comprehension (175),[28] the validity of which is deductively equivalent to second-order logic itself (Boolos 1985b):[29]

Second-Order Comprehension Axiom

(175) $\vdash (\forall\Phi)\,\exists X\forall x(Xx \leftrightarrow \Phi[x])$, where Φ is any formula free in only the first-order variable x.

Apart from a reconciliation with Russell's paradox, restricted comprehension serves sound empirical purpose too. Recall that the inferences of distributivity, plural partitivity, and dissectivity, their constitution principles and the comprehension axiom from which they all derive must be restricted as warranted by (92)–(108) to those descriptions that do not themselves contain essential tokens of plural terms. For arbitrary Φ in any one free variable, its restriction to ⌜sg.E. $\Phi[\xi]$⌝ forms a description that contains no essential plural terms or their mass term analogues.

   In affirming the constitution principle (176) and denying (177), a speaker discriminates between formally identical plural definite descriptions, neither of which contains restriction to the singular:

(176) *of the glazed custards*$[\xi] \leftrightarrow$ *a glazed custard*$[\xi]$
(177) *of the clustered custards*$[\xi] \leftrightarrow$ *a clustered custard*$[\xi]$

Restricted comprehension (170) merely guarantees that there are zero or more things each of which is as the singular description on the right-hand side of (176) or (177)

28 *v.* Hossack, 2000; Linnebo, 2004; McKay, forthcoming, ch. 6.
29 Linnebo 2004; McKay, forthcoming; Oliver and Smiley, 2001; Rayo, 2002; and Yi, 2005 deplore singularist (*v.* Section 29.1.4.1) theories of plural reference, theories that deploy only one sort of variable, the value of which is a singular object, in part because consistency in such a theory is achieved only by restricting comprehension and thus withdrawing from quantifying over everything there is, a defect that Boolos (1984, 1985ab)) remedies basing plural reference on second-order logic (*v.* also Lewis, 1991; Cartwright, 1994; Linnebo, 2003, 2004; Pietroski, 2003; Williamson, 2003). Linnebo, 2004; McKay, forthcoming; Oliver and Smiley, 2001; Rayo, 2002; and Yi, 2005, graduate to plural variables that refer plurally while their language retains only one sort of variable and in this respect closely resembles the language of the partitive construction, including a constitution relation similar to *of*. Because one-sorted, the proposed plural language is as much at risk from Russell's paradox as the deplored singularist accounts and so comprehension must be restricted just the same (*cf.* McKay, forthcoming, ch. 6). Higginbotham (1998, 2000) and Linnebo (2003, 2004) also favor plural terms *sui generis* rather than second-order expressions but advance a two-sorted logical syntax.

describes it, without securing, as it should not in light of (177), that these things are the referents of the corresponding plural description unrestricted to the singular. What distinguishes *glazed custards* from *clustered custards* is that the former is distributive. It applies to some things just in case it applies to each of them:

(178) $Distributive(\Phi) \leftrightarrow_{df} \forall \xi(\Phi[\xi] \leftrightarrow \forall \zeta(\text{sg.E.}of[\zeta,\xi] \rightarrow \Phi[\zeta]))$

A definite description finds its reference in the things that satisfy a possibly non-distributive description and includes all such things. It of course does not follow that just *any* thing among what has just been referred to also satisfies that description. An affirmed constitution principle is the speaker's knowledge that the description is distributive and subject to comprehension. Classification of a complex Φ as distributive is itself a deduction, assisted in part by considerations such as (179) and (180):

(179) $Distributive(\Phi)$ & $Distributive(\Psi) \rightarrow Distributive(\ulcorner \Phi[\xi] \,\&\, \Psi[\xi] \urcorner)$
(180) $Distributive(\ulcorner [\forall \zeta : \text{sg.E.}of[\zeta,\xi]]\Phi[\zeta] \urcorner)$

29.1.4 Semantics

For the semantics of an object language with plural expressions, it cannot be wrong for the metalanguage to include all the resources of its object language, the use of plural expressions in particular, its crucial clauses (181)–(184) quantifying in the plural over things and speaking in the plural of assignments of an object to a variable (Boolos 1985a and others):

(181) $\Sigma(\langle \alpha, \xi \rangle) \leftrightarrow_{def} (\text{sg}[\alpha] \,\&\, \text{E}[\alpha] \,\&\, \text{sg}[\xi] \,\&\, \text{variable}(\xi) \,\&\, of(\langle \alpha, \xi \rangle, \Sigma))$
(182) $\Sigma \approx_{\xi} \Sigma' \leftrightarrow_{def} \forall \zeta(\zeta \neq \xi \rightarrow \forall X(\Sigma(\langle X, \zeta \rangle) \leftrightarrow \Sigma'(\langle X, \zeta \rangle)))$
(183) $\Sigma satisfy \ulcorner [\exists \xi : \Phi] \Psi \urcorner \leftrightarrow$
    $[\exists X : \exists \Sigma'(\Sigma \approx_{\xi} \Sigma' \,\&\, \forall Y(\Sigma'(\langle Y, \xi \rangle) \leftrightarrow \text{sg.E.}of[Y,X]) \,\&\, \Sigma' satisfy \, \Phi)]$
      $\exists \Sigma'(\Sigma \approx_{\xi} \Sigma' \,\&\, \forall Y(\Sigma'(\langle Y, \xi \rangle) \leftrightarrow \text{sg.E.}of[Y, X]) \,\&\, \Sigma' satisfy \Psi)$
(184) $\Sigma satisfy \ulcorner of(\xi, \zeta) \urcorner \leftrightarrow$
    $\exists X \exists Y(\forall Z(\Sigma(\langle Z, \xi \rangle) \leftrightarrow \text{sg.E.}of[Z,X]) \,\&\, \forall Z(\Sigma(\langle Z, \zeta \rangle) \leftrightarrow \text{sg.E.}of[Z,Y]) \,\&\,$
    $of(X,Y))$

How could one spurn a semantics that aims at disquotational truths such as (185) and reproach the theorist's use of a plural 'some custards' on the right-hand side to interpret the plural *some custards* on the left-hand side taken from her own language?

(185) *Some custards are dessert* is true $\leftrightarrow$ Some custards are dessert.

Yet, along the way, regimentation in terms of a partitive relation 'of' and the nominal morphology as defined above spins off some empirical claims about the natural language in use that are not as innocent as the disquotations aimed at. Any subject who assents to (186) commits herself to (187):

(186) Two custards are dessert.
(187) $\exists \xi \neg \text{sg}[\xi]$

Acquiring a free-standing word as in (188) with the meaning of the negated singular morpheme, she can be expected to assent to (189) and (190), which are, as fits her usage, indeed true under the proposed analysis.

(188) *non-singular*$[\xi]$ $\leftrightarrow_{df}$ $\neg$sg$[\xi]$
(189) Two custards are non-singular.
(190) Some things are non-singular.
       There are non-singulars.
(191) *Something is non-singular.
       *There is a non-singular.

As soon, however, as she slips from (190) to (191), she utters a falsehood. It is to suffer a linguistic illusion, so the analysis claims, to believe that (190) entails (191) or for the theorist to think that (190) and (191) are indifferent paraphrases of (187). Likewise, the literal meaning of (192) does not contradict (187) or deny the existence of what *the two custards* or any other plural expression refers to, and illusion to hear it otherwise.

(192) Nothing is (a) non-singular.
       There is no non-singular.

The margins of this illusion are exposed when juxtaposed to alternative paraphrases for '$\neg$sg$[\xi]$' and for (187). Introduce to the subject a verb: to *non-singularize* is to be non-singular, so that (193) is fair translation of (187).

(193) There are the things that non-singularize.
       The things that non-singularize exist.
(194) *Any of the things that non-singularize non-singularizes.

With some prompting, the subject recognizes that (194) is false, like any of (92)–(108) or like (196) that would apply an essentially plural description to a singular object:

(195) There are the things that are more than one.
       The things that are more than one exist.
(196) *Any of the things that are more than one is more than one.
(197) Everything is one of the things that are more than one.

There is, in effect, no difference in meaning between *be more than one* and *non-singularize* or *be non-singular*. And, yet, although the noun in (199) is declared synonymous and (199) supposed therefore to be as transparently false as (194) or (196) is, (199) comes across as true as "any of the whatevers is a whatever":

(198) There are the non-singulars.
       The non-singulars exist.
(199) Any of the non-singulars is a non-singular.

Unlike verbs and relative clauses, frequent vehicles for expressing the essentially plural, the speaker who accepts (199) easily has assumed that nouns are for the most part distributive expressions ((178)).[30]

The natural language has proven to be more precise—or, precious—than common usage is always aware of, but without obvious hindrance to its expressive power. The theorist speaker finds words, if not one way then another, to accurately speak her mind that (187) $\exists \xi \; \neg sg[\xi]$. Moreover, despite the regimentation of singular and plural reference and the restriction on comprehension, there is implied no confinement on what she may quantify over. If she uses *everything*, a singular quantifier, she may use it intending without contextual restriction to quantify over absolutely everything[31] there *is* and everything she thinks there *is*. Of course it is not the case that any two things that there *are* is something that there *is*, affording a contrast between (200) and (201), although any of them is indeed something that there is and any of them is among the things she quantifies over.

(200) Some things that there are are somehow related.

(201) *Something that there is somehow related.

It seems benign for the analysis to deny that any things that there are is something that there is, at least to the extent that it does not violate any deeply held pre-theoretic judgment to the contrary, even without instruction from Russell's paradox. A more controversial implication of the analysis is its dark view of any alleged identity between the one and the many:

(202) The cards are one deck.

(203) The trees are one copse.

No doubt (202) and (203) are true sentences of English, but the analysis then requires that the copula occur here not as an expression of identity or predication but as a non-logical relation expressing coincidence.

29.1.4.1 *Against Singularism*

Singularism is the mistaken view that the semantics of any language can be developed in a metalanguage with only singular reference so that an object language that contains both singular and plural expression is projected in the metalanguage onto that fragment of itself that contains only singular expression.[32] In showing that all plural talk is mere disguise reducible to a formally more restricted singular idiom,

---

[30] Nouns, adjectives and abstractions on clauses in a single variable belong to the same logical type but are not always interchangeable. A speaker's presumption that a noun is distributive or even an adjective (allowing her to infer (191) from (190)) may reflect grammatical conditions on what the meaning of a noun or adjective can be. Perhaps, '$\neg sg[\xi]$' is ungrammatical as a noun or adjective, neither being distributive nor enough like the small class of adjectives and nouns such as *neighbor, relative, associate* that are systematic exceptions.

[31] *v.* Boolos, 1984, 1985ab; Lewis, 1991: 68, Cartwright, 1994; McGee, 2000; Williamson, 2003.

[32] The term is from Lewis, 1991: 65 ff. The objection to singularism is from Boolos, 1984, 1985ab; and discussed subsequently in, among others, Cartwright, 1994; Higginbotham, 1998, 2000; Higginbotham

singularism would have been a significant discovery, unlike the banal achievement (Section 29.1.4.) of giving a semantics for plural expressions in a language that uses them. An obstacle for the singularist view (adapted from Rayo and Yablo, 2001: 75), typical of those canvassed in the literature, is how to keep the disquotational truths of (204) from becoming the self-defeating contradictions of (205) when the object language is interpreted without benefit of plural expressions in the metalanguage:

(204) "Some things are too many to be *a* thing" is true iff some things are too many to be a thing.
    "Some things are not *a* thing" is true iff some things are not a thing.

(205) "Some things are too many to be *a* thing" is true iff a thing [viz., the thing that those some things are] is too many to be a thing.
    "Some things are not *a* thing" is true iff a thing is not a thing.

In this setting, if the theory that entails (187) is not to entail the contradiction that *a* thing is non-singular (*cf.* (191)) or that *a* thing non-singularizes, (187) had better not find its way into the object language.[33] The theorist's conviction that (187), which formerly may have provoked some mistranslation and linguistic illusion, lapses here into the ineffable. As in the language with a homophonic semantics Section 29.1.4., it cannot be asserted within a language for which a singularist semantics has been defined that there is a non-singular thing, a plural object, but singularism has no other conveyance for (187).

29.1.4.2 *The Semantic Type of Singular, Plural and Mass (In)definite Descriptions*

A plural or mass definite description is used as an expression of direct or demonstrative reference to the same extent as a singular counterpart, and thus no classification of their semantic types should divorce them. That direct or demonstrative reference defies paraphrase in words is sometimes taken as evidence that expressions of direct or demonstrative reference are terms or arguments rather than predicates.[34] Yet, *one* in (206) is unmistakably a predicate, both syntactically and semantically (the red and

---

and Schein, 1989; Lewis, 1991; Oliver and Smiley, 2001; Pietroski, 2003; Rayo, 2002; Schein, 1993: ch. 2; Williamson, 2003.

The singularist thesis that a plural term refers to *a* plural object is in Russell, 1903 and ever after in among others, Barker, 1992; Burge, 1977; L. Carlson, 1982; Cormack and Kempson, 1981; Davies, 1989; Higginbotham, 1980; Landman, 1989ab, 1995, 2000; Lasersohn, 1988, 1990, 1995; Link, 1983, 1993; Lønning, 1987; Scha, 1981; Schwarzschild, 1991, 1996.

[33] *v.* Schein, 1993: 33 ff.

[34] Higginbotham (1998, 2000) appears to invoke such considerations when he says that there seems to be nothing predicational about the plural demonstrative when the speaker waves his hand at some boys, saying 'They built a boat yesterday'. Even if the speaker thinks 'They—the only things in that corner of the room that could have built a boat—built a boat yesterday', he cannot be taken to have intended to communicate this thought or to be disappointed if the hearer understands instead 'They—the only things that this schmuck could be referring to without telling me what he is referring to—built a boat yesterday'.

the blue being only a few individuals among the ones), and hardly less immune to paraphrase than its demonstrative antecedent:

(206) These are indescribable, and the three red ones and the one blue one will taste that same indescribable taste everybody remembers.

If the demonstrative contributes nothing more than its reference to (206)'s meaning, then so too does the predicate *one* contribute nothing more than what it denotes. Arguments that the name *Aristotle* bears direct reference to Aristotle apply, as Burge (1973) points out,[35] with equal force to the relation between any of the Aristotles and *Aristotle* as it occurs in *the three Aristotles* or *those Aristotles*, where it is plainly a predicate. As with the simple name, nothing 'predicational' is felt to intervene between such an austere predicate and what it denotes. An impression of direct reference offers no insight into the logical form of the phrase bearing it—Fido–*Fido* or Fido–$[\iota$ x: *Fido*$(x)]$. Burge's remarks about the logical syntax of direct reference are next joined by a Fregean point. If in the constant presence of mutually occlusive objects, demonstrative reference to *these* or *those* goes unresolved and their number unknown unless resolved under some concept,[36] it must be that whenever definite reference succeeds, speaker and hearer have grasped just such a concept, even if words should fail to paraphrase and nothing 'predicational' seems under introspection to be involved. Just imagine failures, where the hearer is at a loss for the concept intended, as when gesturing to an assortment, the speaker says (207) or (208):[37]

(207) These have been arranged in an attractive pattern for you and you alone.
(208) As many as I could arrange, I arranged in an attractive pattern just for you.

Every use of a demonstrative, *these, those, they* and so on, is *these* NP, *those* NP, *the-*NP, and every use of a quantifier *all, most, some, as many as* Φ is *all* NP, *most* NP,

---

Verbs too are acquired demonstratively, without intervention from anything 'predicational', as when a clarinet sounds in demonstration of a nonce verb *to chalumeau* or John Cleese displays the meaning of *to Silly-Walk* relying on the learner's exquisite but inarticulate sense for sound and gesture to grasp the subtleties of chalumeau-ing and Silly-Walking.

[35] See Platts (1979) and Larson and Segal (1995) for further discussion.

[36] "... if I place a pile of playing cards in [someone's] hands with the words: find the number of these, this does not tell him whether I wish to know the number of cards, or of complete packs of cards, or even, say, of honor cards at skat. To have given him the pile in his hands is not yet to have given him completely the object he is to investigate; I must add some further word—cards, or packs, or honors." (Frege, 1884, §22)

[37] To expose the (subdoxastic) concepts that resolve demonstrative reference,

(i)   They are (all) separated from each other.
(ii) □□   □□
      □□   □□

judge (i) against contexts that present to the subject figures such as (ii), varying the parameters familiar from experiments in gestalt perception, e.g., ratio of enclosed area to interstitial area, ratio of the area of individual enclosures to area of aggregate enclosure, ratio of aggregate enclosed area to interstitial area, ratio of aggregate area to the number aggregate, absolute number aggregated, geometric regularity of individual enclosures, similarity and scaling, heterogeneity, symmetry and axial orientation and alignment, color, shading, (partial) occlusion, animation with rigid vs. elastic motion. In a forced choice between truth and falsity, what things does the subject seize upon to judge whether *they* are separated or not, and does the individuation of *them* track the same conditions as object recognition in general?

some NP, *as many* NP *as* Φ, even if NP is unspoken, where any demonstration (to a point in space) or any counting must be supplemented with a concept in order to settle reference on some intended objects.

A related observation is that quantifying-in elicits the predicative *de re*, assuming the restriction in restricted quantification to be a predicate, Φ in (209):

(209) [Q: Φ]Ψ

(210) a. [the ξ: ... [Q: ξ]Ψ ...] ...
  b. [the ξ: ...] ... [Q: ξ]Ψ ...

An honest casino is invaded one night without the house's knowledge by underage gamblers. Sentences (211)–(214) can make true *de re* reports that ascribe neither knowledge of a felony nor knowledge of a game that is anything but fair, certainly with winners and losers but without anyone's winnings certain in advance:

(211) The casino operator knew that some patrons that night that unknown to him were underage must win and some lose. (adapted from Bricker, 1989)
(212) Them, with the false IDs around their necks, the casino operator knew that some must win and some lose.
(213) The gamblers such that the casino operator knew that some must win and some lose were underage.
(214) [ιξ: underage gamblers[ξ]]the casino operator knew that must [some ς: ξ[ς]]ς win and [some ς: ξ[ς]]ς lose.

As in (214), the logical form for these sentences quantifies in the restrictions to the quantifier *some*, a predicate construed *de re*, and in (212)–(214), the antecedent for this predicate is a plural expression. If plural definite descriptions are univocal in their semantic type, and plural definite descriptions *sometimes* quantify in the restrictions to quantifiers, then the variables of plural quantification, ξ in (210) and (214), *always* belong to the same type, the type of predicates.[38]

29.1.4.3 *Monadic Second-Order Logic and the Language of the Partitive Construction*

If the logical form of natural language quantification presents as in (215) two predicates Φ and Ψ, one might expect, absent special pleading, that speakers evaluate quantifying in the one and the other in roughly the same way, especially if the quantifier is symmetric, as *some* is in (216) and (217):

(215) [Q: Φ] Ψ
(216) (∃Φ) ... [some: Φ] Ψ
(217) (∃Ψ) ... [some: Φ] Ψ

As above, sentence (218) quantifies in the restriction to *some*, and thus its logical form realizes (216). If now (220) is taken to realize (217) (as in effect when stipulating

---

[38] Schein 2005, n. 46 for further discussion.

that (220) paraphrases second-order logic '∃X∃xXx') quantifying in *some*'s matrix predicate, we should arrive at a pair of sentences that speakers should judge rather alike:

(218) There are some things such that some are things.
(219) There are the things such that some are things.

(220) There is something that some things are. (*cf*.∃X∃xXx)
(221) There are the things that some things are.

Yet, as in Williamson (2003), the resemblance fades as soon as these sentences are embedded in modal contexts:

(222) Something that possibly some things are, some things are.
(223) The things that possibly some things are, some things are.

(224) Some things such that possibly some are things, some things are (them).
(225) The things such that possibly some are things, some things are (them).

(226) Some things such that possibly some are things, some are things.
(227) The things such that possibly some are things, some (of them) are things.

Quantifying into the matrix predicate of *some things*, sentence (223) is plainly false in that the possibility of some things being wealthy, beautiful and wise does not entail that some things are. In contrast, a necessary truth of metaphysical identity results, (225) or (227), if instead one quantifies in the restriction to *some*. If one sticks to the logical translation proposed, the report is allegedly of a contrast in truth between (228) (translating (225)) and (229) (translating (227)):

(228) [the ζ: ◇[some ξ: things[ξ]] ζ[ξ]][some ξ: things[ξ]] ζ[ξ]
(229) [the ζ: ◇[some ξ: ζ[ξ]] things[ξ]][some ξ: ζ[ξ]] things[ξ]

Something has been lost in translation since (228) and (229) cannot contrast in truth. A dilemma has been exposed: if, uncontroversially, natural language quantification is as in (215), then which of (218)/(219) or (220)/(221), if either, realizes (monadic) second-order quantification, quantifying in a predicate, Φ or Ψ respectively?

Without faulting the parse in (215) or denying the implied symmetry between (216) and (217), translation should scorn less the grammar of sentences (220) and (221). These sentences, after all, quantify in the complement to a tensed copula. They therefore do not realize (217), which may in fact go unattested in natural language, and rather quantify in not Ψ but a phrasal position properly contained within Ψ. The dilemma is resolved: quantifying in a quantifier's restriction and also plural quantification, in so far as it belongs to the same type as argued in Section 29.1.4.2, realizes quantifying in a monadic predicate, i.e., monadic second-order quantification. In contrast, sentences such as (220) and (221), quantifying in the complement of a tensed copula, exemplify either quantifying in at least a dyadic relation (between objects and times or states (and perhaps worlds))[39] or substitutional quantification

---

[39] *v*. Rayo and Yablo, 2001.

over verb-phrasal complements, the latter suggestion cognizant of the fact that speakers seem to have under consideration when asserting (230) a list of alternative descriptions of what the psychiatrist might be:

(230) There is something that the old psychiatrist never was and may never yet be to anyone that consults him—attentive and interested more in her problems than his fee.

Substitutional quantification is undefeated by the obvious truth of (231) and the fact that the takings of arbitrary objects outnumber the phrases of any natural language:

(231) Take any objects you like, there is something that they and only they are. (Rayo and Yablo 2001)

For, among those phrases are those that embed anaphoric expressions, already attested in (230), so that a verifying continuation of (231) is (232):

(232) Take any objects you like, there is something that they and only they are—namely, "some of *them*".

Some discussions genuflecting to Frege treat (monadic) second-order logic as if it were given to be anything more than a calculus in search of an interpretation, as if it were given that if '$\exists X \exists x Xx$' (or (217)) means anything at all, it means what (220) means. Speakers' reliable intuitions about the meaning of (220) are then mistaken as insight into the meaning of '$\exists X \exists x Xx$' and second-order logic in general, even though '$\exists X \exists x Xx$' is lame as an analysis of (220) and introspection about (220) is not introspection about any such logical form. Shunting aside (220)–(223) as either substitutional or polyadic second-order quantification, it is rather quantifying in a quantifier's restriction (216) that realizes in natural language monadic second-order quantification. Then, since plural quantifiers quantify in quantifier restrictions, plural quantification is monadic second-order quantification.

In quantifying in monadic predicates, *of* may be deployed in the interpretation of their predication relation (*v.* (151); Boolos 1984, 1985ab; Higginbotham 1998, 2000; Hossack 2000):

(233) Σ *satisfy* $\ulcorner V_i v_j \urcorner \leftrightarrow$
$\exists X \exists Y (\forall Z (\Sigma(\langle Z, v_j \rangle) \leftrightarrow \text{sg.E.of}[Z, X]) \ \& \quad \forall Z (\Sigma(\langle Z, V_j \rangle) \leftrightarrow \text{sg.E.of}[Z, Y])$
$\& \text{sg.E.of}[X, Y])$

Thus, the partitive construction and predication are just two sides, pronounced and unpronounced, of the same coin.[40] Occurrences in the object language of $\ulcorner V_i v_j \urcorner$ (*v.* (211)–(214), (224)–(227)) could all be replaced (*v.* (151)) with $\ulcorner \text{sg.E.of}[v_j, V_i] \urcorner$ provided that the partitive goes unpronounced here. Correlatively, it could be denied

---

[40] See Hossack, 2000; Linnebo, 2004; Rayo, 2002 on the equi-interpretability of monadic second-order logic and what I have called the language of the partitive construction.

that *of* tokens a relation in the object language and is rather the pronunciation of the concatenation indicating predication:[41]

---

[41] Better than (233), why not a more disquotational (1) or (2), "learn[ing] to use the higher-order languages as our home language (Williamson, 2003)", and thus in effect deriving (3) rather than (4)?

(1) Σ *satisfy* $\ulcorner V_i v_j \urcorner \leftrightarrow$
   $\exists X \exists y (\forall z (\Sigma (\langle z, v_j \rangle) \leftrightarrow z = y) \ \& \ \forall z (\Sigma (\langle z, V_j \rangle) \leftrightarrow Xz) \& Xy)$

(2) Σ *satisfy* $\ulcorner V_i v_j \urcorner \leftrightarrow$
   $\exists X \exists y (\forall Z (\Sigma (\langle Z, v_j \rangle) \leftrightarrow sg.E.of[Z, y]) \ \& \ \forall Z (\Sigma (\langle Z, V_j \rangle) \leftrightarrow sg.E.of[Z, X]) \& Xy)$

(3) '$\exists X \exists x Xx$' is true if and only if Something somethings.

(4) '$\exists X \exists x Xx$' is true if and only if Something is one of some things.

If the theorist's language does not itself quantify in matrix predicates, some other locution must be recruited in the metalanguage to explain the semantics of the second-order quantification that occurs in the object language, recruiting a locution that is felt to be readily available, as in (4) (*v.* Boolos, 1984, 1985ab; Higginbotham, 1998, 2000), or extending the theorist's language as in (3). The latter would be more faithful to the language under analysis except for the suspicion that (3) is coherent only in so far as it translates into (4)—a suspicion that the theorist cannot really make herself at home in the higher-order language. Even philosophers who agree with Boolos in rejecting the tradition that joins at the hip second-order logic and Frege-speak about concepts may feel compelled to apologize for his use of the locution 'is one of' in (4), caught as they are between what makes sense and how they think a faithful semantics for second-order logic should read, namely, as in (3). I think however that fealty to (3) and mistrust of (4) are overrated. Surely a disquotational and homophonic semantics, wearing its own infallibility, should be treasured whenever it can be had. Yet if it seems to the theorist who doubts her understanding of (3) that her language will not support it, she is no worse off here than she is elsewhere in much of her linguistic analysis. Whenever she meets a bound morpheme, such as *re-* in English, and attempts a semantics for '*re-V*', she retreats to a circumlocution such as "do V-ing again" displaying little of the syntax of that fragment of the object language under analysis. She cannot make free use of *re-* on the RHS. It is a bound morpheme after all. At the same time, it would be silly to conclude from circumlocution in the semantics that *re-* is other than a bound morpheme. It has the syntax that it has. A semantics in English for a language with a bound causative morpheme illustrates the point as well. No doubt the causative morpheme in the object language has neither the syntax nor exact meaning of *cause* in English, and the English theorist's best efforts to convey the notion of direct causation that the bound morpheme expresses are not also an effort to revise the syntax of the object language which cannot be simulated in English. A speaker of the object language who attempts the semantics for her own language will also be driven to circumlocution for the semantics of her bound causative morpheme, as was the English theorist facing *re-*. As it turns out, the language of the partitive construction relies on a charitable view of circumlocution too. The reader may have accepted without challenge that *of* as it occurs in the partitive construction is a dyadic relation; but, its semantics is not disquotational and homophonic, to the extent that (5) and (6) are no better than (3):

(5) '$sg.E.of[\xi, \varsigma]$' is true of $\langle$it, them$\rangle$ if and only if it ofs them.

(6) '$sg.E.of[\xi, \varsigma]$' is true of $\langle$it, them$\rangle$ if and only if it is of them.

Rather, the semantics in (7) resorts to a circumlocution with a rather complex syntax including quantification (*Cf. It is one of these and one of those. It is one and no more than one of them. One of them, it is*), notwithstanding the self-deception of occasionally writing *is-one-of*:

(7) '$sg.E.of[\xi, \varsigma]$' is true of $\langle$it, them$\rangle$ if and only if it is one of them.

Yet, no one who offers (7) commits herself to revising the syntax of object language *One of them* as if it should become 'One who is one of them' to reflect the quantificational structure of her circumlocution in the semantics for *of*. The syntax of *One of them* remains whatever grammar and inference in the object language requires of it. Likewise, should grammar or logic prompt parsing a natural language construction as an expression of second-order logic, circumlocution in its semantics, Boolos' use in (4) of the locution 'is one of ', is no grounds to rescind that analysis.

(234) 'sg.E.of$[\xi,\zeta]$' for '$\zeta(\xi)$'.
        'E.of$[\xi,\zeta]$' for '$\exists x \xi(x)$ & $\forall x(\xi(x) \rightarrow \zeta(x))$'
        'of$[\xi,\zeta]$' for '$\forall x(\xi(x) \rightarrow \zeta(x))$'

The language of the partitive construction has resumed in a syntax of monosortal variables the essential features of monadic second-order logic. Like predicative variables, variables in the language of the partitive construction stand in indifferently for count predicates and mass predicates. Like predicates, they may denote nothing at all, and thus the language of the partitive construction supports an analogue of unconditional second-order comprehension:

Unconditional, Restricted Comprehension Axiom

(170) $\vdash$ $(\forall \Phi)$ $\exists \zeta \forall \xi$(sg.E.*of*$[\xi,\zeta]$ $\leftrightarrow$ sg.E.$\Phi[\xi]$)), where Φ is any formula free in only ξ.

(Unconditional) Second-Order Comprehension Axiom

(175) $\vdash$ $(\forall \Phi)$ $\exists X \forall x(Xx \leftrightarrow \Phi[x])$, where Φ is any formula free in only the first-order variable x.

Furthermore, the semantic type of the direct object of the partitive construction is the same as that which restricts a quantifier, that is, the semantic type of predicates, one presumes. Boolos' (1985a) semantics for monadic second-order logic extended here to the language of the partitive construction shows, conforming to his nominalism, that there is reference to the none just in case there is no reference to anything that there is, without reference to a concept or to a null object. A language with only one sort of variable is threatened by Russell's paradox, prompting a comprehension axiom that is restricted, which in this case is not without empirical justification (Section 29.1.3.1.) and implies no restriction on the expressive power of the language provided its semantics is not singularist (Section 29.1.4.1). The choice posed between a language with one sort of variable and another with two seems to me to be decided in part by one's view of a single morpheme, 'sg'. If one holds that it has a meaning, sg$[\xi]$, true or false of some ξ, it is hard to imagine how it could not apply

---

The analysis in the text favors taking the natural language at its superficial word. Thus the natural language contains both second-order quantification, attested at least when quantifying in a quantifier's restriction, and quantification into the partitive relation *of*. In the natural language, then, one finds a synonymy (*v.* (151)) between predication and the partitive construction:

(8) $V_i v_j \leftrightarrow$ sg.E.of$[v_j, V_i]$

Deduction within the language of the partitive construction, whether deductions in the object language or deductions of the semantic theory couched in that language, relies both on a logic for *of* (*cf.* Hossack, 2000; Linnebo, 2004; McKay, forthcoming: ch. 6; Rayo, 2002; Yi, forthcoming) governing the use of that lexical item in inference and on monadic second-order logic governing plural quantification elsewhere. Regimentation, translation from the language of the partitive construction into the language of second-order logic and from the language of second-order logic into the language of the partitive construction, demonstrates the deductive equivalence of second-order logic and the logic of the partitive construction (*v.* (170) and (175)).

to ξ that could not also be the direct objects of the partitive relation, as supposed, for example, by the definition (147), thus allowing that $\ulcorner \xi \urcorner$ is a variable of plural reference:

(147) $\text{sg}[\xi] \leftrightarrow_{\text{df}} \forall\varsigma\forall\gamma(\neg\text{of}(\varsigma,\gamma) \rightarrow (\text{of}(\varsigma,\xi) \rightarrow \text{of}(\xi,\varsigma)))$

But, if singular variables do not occur in conjunction with the singular morpheme, where else would they? It seems that two-sorted variables are better suited to the claim that the singular morpheme does not mean anything at all and is rather the auditory analogue of graphical lowercase indicating a first-order variable, a suggestion which semanticists in the business of finding meaning everywhere might recoil from. Note that if the language of the partitive construction has only the one sort of variable and its type is that of predicates, it is then a language without any first-order variables. To be is to be some zero or more things satisfying $\ulcorner E[\xi] \& \Phi[\xi] \urcorner$ for some formula Φ.

29.2 Essential Plurals in Natural Language

Essential plurals occur as the second argument to *of* but not as argument to the primitive concept *custard*, which is distributive, and they occur again in many complex phrases as above in (1),(3),(4)–(15), and (92)–(108). What is the inventory of primitive vocabulary with essentially plural arguments, from which derive their essential occurrences in complex phrases?

In the limit, *of* is the only one, (or, there aren't any if monadic second-order logic is both object and meta-language. *v.* n. 41). Appearances to the contrary would be rescued by what has been called changing-the-subject (Oliver and Smiley 2001) and the surrogate method (Rayo 2002), which exposes a hidden parameter to explain away any illusion to the contrary.

29.2.1 Cardinality Predicates and Relations

One might have thought, for example, that the predicate *zero*$[\xi]$ expressing a primitive 'zero(ξ)' is an example *par excellence* of the primitive second-order (*v.* n. 4). But, *zero*$[\xi]$ can be taken to pronounce a relation, *card*$[0, \xi]$, to a first-order object, the number 0, and that relation may in turn be analyzed without recourse to any primitive relation to plurals or to concepts other than that expressed by *of* (235)–(236) or equivalently analyzed entirely within the analogue (monadic) second-order logic (237)–(238):

(235) *injective*$[\theta] \leftrightarrow_{\text{df}} \forall\xi\forall\zeta\forall\nu(((\text{sg.E.of}[\langle\nu,\xi\rangle, \theta]\&\text{sg.E.of}[\langle\nu, \zeta\rangle, \theta]) \rightarrow \xi = \zeta) \& ((\text{sg.E.of}[\langle\xi, \nu\rangle, \theta]\&\text{sg.E.of}[\langle\zeta, \nu\rangle, \theta]) \rightarrow \xi = \zeta))$

$card[\zeta, \xi] \leftrightarrow_{df} [\exists\theta: injective[\theta]]\forall\varsigma(\text{sg.E.of}[\varsigma, \xi] \leftrightarrow \exists v(\text{sg.E.of}[v, \zeta] \&$
$\quad \text{sg.E.of}[\langle v, \varsigma\rangle, \theta]))$

(236) $card[n, \xi] \leftrightarrow_{df} [\iota\eta: \forall v(\text{sg.E.of}[v, \eta] \rightarrow (N(v) \& v < n))] card[\eta, \xi]$

(237) $injective[\theta] \leftrightarrow_{df} \forall x\forall y\forall z(((\theta(\langle x, y\rangle) \& \theta(\langle x, z\rangle)) \rightarrow y = z) \& ((\theta(\langle y, x\rangle) \&$
$\quad \theta(\langle z, x\rangle)) \rightarrow y = z))$

$card[Z, X] \leftrightarrow_{df} [\exists\theta: injective[\theta]]\forall x(Xx \leftrightarrow \exists z(Zz \& \theta(\langle z, x\rangle)))$

(238) $card[n, X] \leftrightarrow_{df} [\iota Z: N(n) \& \forall z(Zz \rightarrow (N(z) \& z < n))] card[Z, X]$

A relation θ is *injective*, that is, one-to-one, just in case anything it relates it relates to exactly one thing, and anything that is related by it is related by it to exactly one thing. Some Xs and Some Ys have the same cardinality, $card[X,Y]$, just in case there is an injective relation between them. Cardinal equivalence as defined in (235)/(237) provides the resources to express in (240) an equivalent of (239) if one is feckless enough to ignore the syntax of (239)'s comparative construction:

(239) The ordinals are as many as the cardinals.

(240) $[The\ X: ordinals[X]][\exists Y: of(Y, X)][the\ Z: cardinals[Z]]card[Y,Z]$

The special case of equivalence to a number is then defined in (236)/(238): some Xs have the same cardinality as some number n, $card[n,X]$, just in case they have the same cardinality as the numbers less than n. With the cardinal predicate construed as a relation, (241) comes out as true without further comment:

(241) The moons of Venus are zero in number.
$\quad$ [The ξ: ❙ moons of Venus[ξ]] $card[0, \xi]$

If not relational, $zero[\xi]$ is indeed a primitive second-order property, a comment on the concept *the moons of Venus*, as Frege thought. In particular, its meaning cannot otherwise be constructed from plural, arithmetic predicates that are first-order, those that hold only of what there is or are (*v.* Section 29.0.2):

(242) *First-Order*(Φ) $\leftrightarrow_{df} \forall\xi(\Phi[\xi] \rightarrow E[\xi])$

The first-order arithmetic predicates would be those that count more than zero, whether primitive properties, '1(ξ)', '2(ξ)', ..., or relations '$card[1, \xi]$', '$card[2,\xi]$', ...

The point to be observed is that the meaning of $zero[\xi]$ cannot be, as if it were 'No-number', that no first-order arithmetic predicate holds of ξ:

(243) F The cardinals are zero in number.
$\quad$ [The ξ: ❙ cardinals[ξ]] $card[0, \xi]$

(244) *[The ξ: ❙ cardinals[ξ]]$\neg\exists n\ card[n, \xi]$
$\quad$ * [The ξ: ❙ cardinals[ξ]]$\neg\exists N\ N[\xi]$

For, on such a construal, sentence (243), which is plainly false and comes out as such interpreted according to (235)/(237), would be rendered true as in (244) since the cardinals indeed have no cardinality. In desperation, it could be claimed that *zero in number* is a colorful way of denying existence, without genuine arithmetic content or understanding of what 'zero' contributes, while *one in number, two in number* and so on are still alleged to express first-order properties.[42] If however the pretense of linguistic analysis is not abandoned, a common semantics for *zero in number, one in number, two in number* and so on requires either a relational analysis to numbers or a full Fregean embrace of the higher-order.

With numbers and relational cardinality in hand, whatever useful remarks are to be made about natural language quantifiers in terms of cardinality can be made within the language of the partitive construction (or within monadic second-order logic).[43]

29.2.2 Eventish

Whatever is said about determiners and quantifiers, it plays no role in the occurrence of essential plurals in (1),(3),(4)–(15), and (92)–(108), which look instead to the vocabulary of simple clauses, verbs, prepositions, and verbal morphology. If clause structure as antecedently established in Parsons, 1990, and much linguistic research since reflects a neo-Davidsonian decomposition demanded by the proper treatment of variable polyadicity, adverbial modification, nominalization, causativization, tense and aspect and so on, the primitive vocabulary of simple clauses comprises sub-atomic thematic relations and event concepts. These, for reasons unrelated to plurals and plural reference, happen to provide a hidden parameter referring to events. It may be that this parameter is sufficient to dissolve the appearance of primitive plural reference beyond *of*. If not, primitive plural reference beyond *of* amounts to discovering it among one of the thematic relations or event concepts that neo-Davidsonian analysis takes to comprise the primitive vocabulary.

If *of* is the only primitive with an essentially plural argument, all of the predicates in (1) must exploit the hidden parameter, so that *cluster* is not 'cluster(ξ)' but rather *cluster*[e,ξ], expressing some complex relation that all and only the ξs each bear to the revealed e, as for example in (245) (or (246), its analogue in monadic second-order logic (Higginbotham and Schein, 1989; Schein 1993)):

(245) *cluster*[e, ξ] $\leftrightarrow$ cluster(e) & $\forall\zeta$ (sg.E.of[ζ, ξ] $\leftrightarrow$ Theme(e, ζ))

(246) *cluster*[e, X] $\leftrightarrow$ cluster(e) & $\forall x(Xx \leftrightarrow$ Theme(e, x))

As soon as such an analysis is advanced for (1), the observation that the same morpheme *cluster* occurs twice in (247) and that (247) entails (248) leads straightaway to plural reference with respect to the unspoken parameter in (248), plural reference to some clusters or some clusterings, which is as essential to (248)'s meaning as plural reference to the fires.

(247) The fires clustered in two clusters (and not in one).

(248) The fires clustered.

---

[42] Yi (1999b) alleges that *being two* is a first-order property.

[43] For a development of this last point, see Schein, 2005 § 2.1.

If indeed *of* is the only primitive with an essentially plural argument, it intervenes in logical form with every instance of plural reference so that (248)'s predicate is the complex relation in (251) (or, (254)). Every one of the fires is in one of the clusters and anything in any of the clusters is one of the fires:

(249) *cluster*$[\varepsilon] \leftrightarrow \forall\delta(\text{sg.E.of}[\delta, \varepsilon] \rightarrow \text{cluster}(\delta))$ (*cf*.(38))

(250) Theme$[\varepsilon, \xi] \leftrightarrow \forall\zeta(\text{sg.E.of}[\zeta, \xi] \leftrightarrow \exists\delta(\text{sg.E.of}[\delta, \varepsilon] \& \text{Theme}(\delta, \zeta)))$

(251) $[_{\text{VP}}cluster][\varepsilon, \xi] \leftrightarrow cluster[\varepsilon] \& \text{Theme}[\varepsilon, \xi]$

(252) *cluster*$[E] \leftrightarrow \forall e(Ee \rightarrow \text{cluster}(e))$

(253) Theme$[E, X] \leftrightarrow \forall x(Xx \leftrightarrow \exists e(Ee \& \text{Theme}(e, x)))$ (Pietroski 2003: 282)

(254) $[_{\text{VP}}cluster][E, X] \leftrightarrow cluster[E] \& \text{Theme}[E, X]$

29.2.2.1 *Plural Reference and Event Quantification*

Plural reference and plural quantification interact with the clause structure that the neo-Davidsonian analysis presents them with and thus corroborate that the decomposition is writ across the syntax.[44]

29.2.2.1.1 *Geach–Kaplan Reciprocal Sentences*

In a discussion that surveys various complex phrases demanding essential plurals, Boolos (1984) proves that the Geach–Kaplan sentence in (255) requires a formalization with essentially plural reference to some critics, and the formalization considered is (256):

(255) Some critics admire only each other.

(256) $\exists X(\exists x Xx \& \forall x \forall y(Axy \rightarrow (x \neq y \& Xy)))$

As a comment on the logical structure of natural language sentences, it applies with equal force to the reciprocal construction in (257) the translation of which should, parallel to (256), solve for 'Axy'. Substituting '$\text{suffocate}(x,y)$' as in (258) however mistranslates the sentence, which is true under conditions where no cockroach can be said to have suffocated any other.

(257) Some cockroaches suffocated only each other.

(258) $*\exists X(\exists x Xx \& \forall x \forall y(\text{suffocate}(x, y) \rightarrow (x \neq y \& Xy)))$

Imagine some cockroaches in a bottle with a diminished supply of air at the cusp of catastrophe. They would have all made it had not another cockroach joined them, making them one too many to survive.[45] At issue, ignoring the contribution of *only* to

---

[44] Decomposition in the syntax of the object language is defended on grounds unrelated to plurals in Hornstein, 2002 and Kratzer, 1996.

[45] More examples—

(1) The zebra mussels are choking each other in the drainpipe.

(2) The bamboo shoots smother each other.

(3) The politicians stifle each other.

(4) The motors overheated each other.

the proof that (255) is non-firstorderizable, is that (259) does not mean the same as any of either (260) or (261):

(259) Some cockroaches suffocated each other.
(260) Some cockroaches each suffocated the others.
          Some cockroaches each suffocated some of the others.
(261) Some cockroaches suffocated, each suffocating the others.
          Some cockroaches suffocated, each suffocating some of the others.

Neither (257) nor (259) is accurately translated when *each* ('$\forall x$' in (258)) includes in its scope the verb (Langendoen, 1978). What each cockroach does is something less than a suffocation, rather an acting against as in (262), where altogether the cockroaches acting against each other results in or amounts to their suffocation:

(262) Some cockroaches suffocated (themselves), each acting against (some of) the other(s).

The reciprocal construction in (259) proves to be a reduced version of the adverbial clause in (262) (Schein, 2001/2003), conforming to the syntax and semantics of adverbial modification. As of this writing, the only game in town (since Parsons, 1990) treats this adverbial modification as a relation between the events (or states) described by the adverbial clause and those described by the modified, matrix clause:

(263) [Some *X*: cockroaches][ιE: each *of* them$_X$ acting against (some of) the other(s))] [$\exists E'$: $R[E, E']$] suffocated[E'] (themselves).

In contrast to (261), the reduced adverbial clause in (257)/(259) omits the verb describing suffocations and includes only the subatomic vocabulary of thematic relations, substituting in effect 'Agent(e,x) & Patient(e,y)' for 'Axy' in (256). Only a few considerations lead up to this conclusion: 'each' in *each other* is a universal distributive quantifier (as the discussion of the Geach–Kaplan sentence assumes), its scope cannot in the case of (257)/(259) include the verb, and yet, whatever is its scope forms a phrase with *each* that modifies *suffocate*. Note that the reduced adverbial clause translating the reciprocal construction separates thematic relations from the verb, corroborating that these are constituents separate from the verb in accord with the neo-Davidsonian analysis of variable polyadicity.

29.2.2.1.2 *Separation Within Simple Clauses*

Apart from the reciprocal construction of the Geach–Kaplan sentence, which turns out to hide a second, adverbial clause, within simple clauses, separation is discovered in the interaction of plurals and quantifiers (Schein 1993: ch. 4). In (265), the terms decomposing the verb phrase, 'Theme[e,X]' and '$cover(e')$', apply to different events, and they are separated by elements from elsewhere in the sentence: the quantifiers *two workbenches* and *each* include within their scope '$cover(e')$' but not 'Theme[e,X]'.

(264) Three hundred quilt patches covered over two workbenches each with two bedspreads.

(265) $\exists e([\exists X : 300\ quilt\ patches]\ \text{Theme}[e, X]\ \&\ [\exists Y : two\ workbenches]\ [Each\ y : Yy]$
    $[\exists e' : e' \leq e](cover(e')\ \&\ \text{Goal}[e', y]\ \&\ [\exists Z : two\ bedspreads]\ with[e', Z])$

The separation of 'Theme$[e,X]$' and '$cover(e')$' is essential to the extent that sentences like (264) have interpretations that can be represented only by the likes of (265). A tedious argument shows that no other logical syntax will do (Schein, 1993: ch. 4),[46] but it is easy enough to imagine conditions for the truth of (264) that are congenial to (265). Imagine that four bedspreads, draped as described, are made altogether from a total of three hundred quilt patches. The three hundred patches together cover the workbenches but do not all go into the bedspreads on any one bench. Moreover, some of the individual patches have themselves been torn between this or that bedspread. There is in this case a large event, e in (265), where exactly three hundred patches covered workbenches with bedspreads, and nothing more precise can be said about how the patches were disposed of, just that this large event comprises two smaller events, e' in (265), in each of which a workbench is covered by patches making up two bedspreads.[47] The sentence (264) can be taken to assert that two workbenches were each covered over with two bedspreads while leaving vague the distribution of the quilt patches. It is this combination of distributivity between *two workbenches each* and *two bedspreads* with the vague distribution of the quilt patches that makes the separation of thematic relations in (265) essential in this and many like examples.[48]

29.2.2.2 Plural Event Quantification

The Davidsonian analysis prefixes to every clause an existential quantifier over events, which must itself be plural quantification, as remarked in Section 29.2.2, if the same morpheme *cluster* occurs twice in (247), and (247) entails (248):

(247) The fires clustered in two clusters (and not in one).
(248) The fires clustered.

---

[46] See Schein, 2005, n. 58 for an extended restatement and discussion of the argument.

[47] The logical form (265) simplifies and slights an important aspect of the meaning of (264), which for present purposes we can ignore. The two workbenches' being each covered with two bedspreads is not merely part of the three hundred patches' covering but completely coincides with it. *v.* Schein, 1993: 146 ff.

[48] It is a puzzle to reconcile in (i) apparent collective reference to the same vaudevillians dancing and singing with the scope of *no more than three ballads*. . .

(i) No vaudevillians$_i$ danced together to no more than three ballads that they$_i$ sang together.
(ii) *[No x: vaudevillian(x)][$\exists X$: Xx & vaudevillians[X]] . . . together[X] . . .   [no more than three ballads that X sang together[X]] . . .

Sentence (i) is not the vacuous falsehood in (ii) that no vaudevillian is among some who dance and sing together no more than three ballads. Of course, (ii) is falsified by any vaudevillian, e.g., Fanny Brice, for whom there is at least one other whom she has not appeared on stage with, Al Jolson. Rather, (i) means that no vaudevillian has no more than three ballads that he sang and danced to together with other vaudevillians, which would be true if vaudevillians were many years on the circuit with the same troupe performing the same routines. The puzzle is how to extract this meaning from a translation of (i) that conforms to its syntax. For further argument for the separation of thematic relations in the logical syntax of the object language, see Schein, 1993: ch. 8.

(266) $\exists E([\text{The } X : fires[X]]\text{Theme}[E, X] \& cluster[E])$

Likewise, when the current Broadway season finds twenty composers divided among seven, rival and cutthroat productions, what they do is hardly *a* collaboration but several, which verify plural quantification over events in (267):[49]

(267) Twenty composers collaborated on seven shows. (Gillon, 1987)
(268) $\exists E([\exists X : 20[X] \, composers[X]]\text{Agent}[E, X] \& collaborate[E] \&$
$[\exists Y : 7[Y]shows[Y]] \, on[E, Y])$

Plural quantification over events is evident in the logic as well. First consider (269) on the reading indicated:

(269) Twenty truckers loaded up one or more trucks.
'Whenever there was a loading up of one or more trucks, 20 truckers were the loaders'.
$[\forall e: load \; up \; of \; one \; or \; more \; trucks[e]] \; [\exists X : 20[X] \, truckers[X]]\text{Agent}[e, X]$

There is no felt implication that it was the same 20 truckers in every event, and thus the relevant domain of events is not closed under fusion. Otherwise, the fusion of all loadings up of one or more trucks would itself be a loading up of one or more trucks, and they could each involve twenty truckers only if they were the same twenty.

(270) These 10 truckers loaded up one or more trucks.
<u>Those 10 truckers loaded up one or more trucks.</u>
The 20 truckers loaded up one or more trucks.

On the other hand, (270) is valid; and unlike the universal, distributive quantifier in (269), the sentences in (270) must not lead with a singular 'there was an event of 10 truckers. . .' and 'there was another event of 10 truckers'. Even if there is one loading by these 10 truckers and another by those 10 truckers, there is no certainty that the domain contains their fusion, a single event of loading by the twenty truckers. Rather, these sentences start off in the plural, 'there were some events . . .', and the inference in (270) follows as a matter of logic: There were loadings by these 10 truckers and loadings by those 10 truckers, and so there were loadings by the 20 truckers. (Schein 1993: 107 ff.) In light of such elementary examples, there is little to the Davidsonian design unless its foundation is plural quantification over events (Schein, 1993, 2002, 2001/2003).

Plural quantification over events displays characteristics of plural, *count* quantification.

(271) The vegetables are too heavy for the laboratory scale and too light for the bathroom scale.
(Schwarzschild, 1991, 1996)

---

[49] Again, the argument assumes that the same morpheme *collaborate* is involved in judgments involving its nominalization that there is not a *collaboration* and in assertions involving the verb that so-and-so *collaborate* (Parsons, 1990).

(272) The vegetables weigh one kilogram.

As Gillon, 1990 and Schwarzschild, 1991, 1996, point out, sentences (271) and (272) weigh the vegetables individually or as a single collection but in no other configurations unless the context individuates them, as when it becomes understood that the vegetables have been divided among several trials each of which is to weigh the contents of a basket of vegetables. In such a context, (271) acquires the additional interpretation that the vegetables in each trial, the contents of a basket, are too heavy for one scale and too light for the other, and (272), that the vegetables divide among trials that turn out each to have been weighing one kilogram. Schwarzschild (1996: 82f., 92f.) also offers a spatial analogue. Speakers do not hesitate to judge (273) true of (274), parsing the scene into a running parallel that relates the rectangles' horizontals and another that relates their verticals, the logical structure of (273) and (267) being the same in this respect.

(273) The sides of R1 run parallel to the sides of R2. (Scha 1984)
(274)

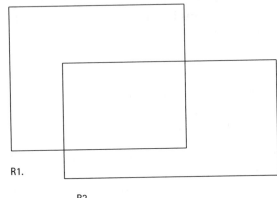

R1.

R2.

Yet, the same logical structure fails to provide (275) with an interpretation true in (276) or (277), where speakers would sooner go blind than parse these scenes into the runnings parallel necessary to make the sentence true:

(275) The double lines run parallel to the single lines.
(276)

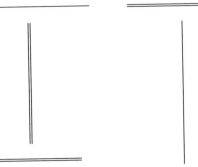

(277)

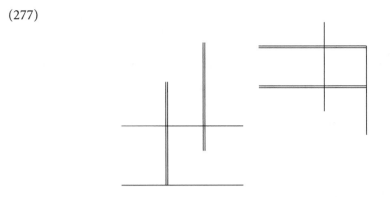

If the truth of sentences such as (273) and (275) (as well as (271) and (272)) depend on the conditions under which events or states are individuated, it does these sentences no harm for them to contain a term in which this dependence is explicit. It is rather further evidence of plural quantification over what are individuated.

29.2.2.3 Coordination and Thematic Relations

Plural quantification over events is endemic, and the verbs *cluster*[E] and *collaborate*[E] that have appeared in the sentences of Section 29.2.2.2 apply distributively to the events E. In support of the sense and logic of these sentences, it is necessary and sufficient that their thematic relations be cumulative (278), as they would be in consequence of their first-order, distributive definition in (250)/(253):

(278) *Cumulative*(θ) $\leftrightarrow_{df}$
$(\forall e(Ee \leftrightarrow (E_1e \lor E_2e)) \& \forall x(Xx \leftrightarrow (X_1x \lor X_2x))) \to ((\theta[E_1, X_1] \&$
$\theta[E_2, X_2]) \to \theta[E, X])$

(252) *cluster*[E] $\leftrightarrow \forall e(Ee \to$ cluster(e))

(253) Theme[E, X] $\leftrightarrow \forall x(Xx \leftrightarrow \exists e(Ee \& \text{Theme}(e, x)))$

These verbs and thematic relations manage well enough without primitive plural arguments (except as argument to partitive *of*); but, cumulativity in these sentences could also be served if the expressions tokened in (266) and (268) are themselves the result of a distributivity operator applied to yet more primitive thematic relations (or verbs) for which plural reference is for some reason held to be essential (*v.* Landman, 1995, 2000):[50]

(279) Theme[E, X] $\leftrightarrow_{df} \forall X'(\text{sg.E.of}[X', X] \leftrightarrow \exists E'(\text{sg.E.of}[E', E] \& \text{sg}[X'] \&$
Theme(E', X'))) (*cf.*(250), (253))

In this section, an empirical consideration is introduced in favor of a strengthened argument against essentially plural thematic relations: everywhere they occur, they occur distributively, and thus there can be no context that shows a plural to be essential for thematic relations.

---

[50] For discussion of Landman's (1995, 2000) reasons and a reply, see Schein, 2005, n. 62.

To this end, thematic relations under coordination looks to constrain their meaning. It has long been known (Perlmutter and Ross, 1970; Jackendoff, 1977; McCawley, 1981) that apparent reduction in a coordination acquires essentially plural interpretations for Ψ in (280) that are absent from the unreduced counterpart. The first sentence of (281) describes a collective flooding and blanketing of a thousand fields of grain that the second sentence does not. Similarly, the reduced coordination in (282) allows it to comment on attitudes towards a collective proposition about student and professor.

(280) Φ_1 *and* $\Phi_2\Psi$ $\nLeftrightarrow$ $\Phi_1\Psi$ *and* $\Phi_2\Psi$

(281)   The surging waters flooded and the hailstones blanketed a thousand fields of barley and rye (between them). $\nLeftrightarrow$ The surging waters flooded a thousand fields of barley and rye (between them) and the hailstones blanketed a thousand fields of barley and rye (between them).

(282)   Not many a student proposed and not many a professor (of his) accepted that they should collaborate even more than they already have. $\nLeftrightarrow$
Not many a student proposed accepted that they should collaborate even more than they already have, and not many a professor (of his) accepted that they should collaborate even more than they already have.

Despite reduction, it is uncontroversial that *and* in (281) and (282) is a sentential connective, with each conjunct containing a tensed verb, and it has long been an open problem how the phrases Ψ acquire their collectivizing force in this setting of sentential coordination.[51] Nevertheless, this setting extends to the following, where adverbs within each conjunct (and iterated in (285)) indicate sentential coordination, even though the reduction has cut deeper eliding the verb:

(283)   Robin by this morning and Hillary by last night have drunk more bordeaux between them than the region produces in a week.

(284)   Saul (while) hooting and David (while) hollering are drowning out the lecture heckling each other.

(285)   Marvin this afternoon from Great Neck and Bernice this evening from Syosset are schlepping the hors d'oeuvres to Leonard's in a rented Mercedes.

But, if there must be unspoken predicates for these adverbs to modify, there is then no reason to deny that they also occur unmodified in (286)–(288) (the adverbs themselves never being obligatory) within clauses conjoined by that same sentential connective *and*.

(286)   Robin and Hillary have drunk more bordeaux between them than the region produces in a week.

(287)   Saul and David are drowning out the lecture heckling each other.

(288)   Marvin and Bernice are schlepping the hors d'oeuvres to Leonard's in a rented Mercedes.

---

[51] See Schein (in preparation) for further discussion and a proposal.

Whatever derives the collectivizing interpretations for (283)–(285) and for (289)–(291) below (and for reduced sentential coordinations in general as in (281) and (282)) cannot help but derive it for (286)–(288) and (292)–(294) just the same. Sentences such as (286)–(288) are thus poor excuse to plead an ambiguity, defining *ad hoc* an *and* joining two terms to form another referring plurally, an orphan left helpless when sentential coordination is explicit or anywhere else a coordination other than of terms collectivizes, such as when generalized quantifiers seem to conjoin in (292)–(294).

(289)   No philosopher today and no linguist yesterday have drunk more bordeaux between them than the region produces in a week.

(290)   No linguist (while) hooting and no philosopher (while) hollering are drowning out the lecture heckling each other.

(291)   No caterer this afternoon from Great Neck and no florist this evening from Syosset are bringing (as scheduled) the hors d'oeuvres and centerpieces we ordered from them months ago.

(292)   No philosopher and no linguist have drunk more bordeaux between them than the region produces in a week.

(293)   No linguist and no philosopher are drowning out the lecture heckling each other.

(294)   No caterer and no florist are bringing (as scheduled) the hors d'oeuvres and centerpieces we ordered from them months ago.

If adverbs, *today, yesterday, from Great Neck*, etc., describe events, the unspoken predicates in (283)–(285) and (289)–(291) express how the subjects of each conjunct participate in the events described, that is, a thematic relation. It is safe to assume that the unspoken content will be the same thematic relation in both conjuncts:

(295) $\exists E(\text{Agent}[E, X] \ \& \ yesterday[E]) \ and \ \exists E(\text{Agent}[E, Y] \ \& \ today[E]) \ \& \ldots$

Since what is today is not yesterday and what is this afternoon from Great Neck is not this evening from Syosset, the events described by each conjunct are distinct events that only the subject participates in. Yet, the point of these sentences is to know what the subjects did severally by their joint effect. There are some events among which their agents are distributed each in her own as the adverbs impose, and these amount to drinking more bordeaux than the region produces, to drowning out a lecture or to catering the banquet. Distributivity with respect to thematic relation is apparently no impediment to the collectivizing interpretation of larger phrases.

With this in mind, consider a plausible empirical generalization that there is nothing that can be said of the *n* Bs that could not also be said of b_1 and . . . and b_n, replacing the plural term with a coordination of names for the individuals referred to (whenever there are such names):[52]

---

[52] It is faith in this generalization that prompts everybody else to say that 'b_1 and . . . and b_n' is an expression with the same reference as 'the *n* Bs' and to invent an operator *and* yielding this result. Schein, 2005 § 2.2.3 discusses the generalization's apparent counterexamples.

(296) *The* n *Bs* $\Phi \Rightarrow b_1$ and ... and $b_n \Phi$.

The Beatles harmonized. $\Rightarrow$ John, Paul, George and Ringo harmonized.

(297) $[The\ X: n[X]\ Bs[X]]\ \exists \Theta[E, X]\ \&\ \Phi \Rightarrow [\iota x:\ b_1[x]]\ \exists E\,\theta[E, x]\ and...and$
$[\iota x: b_n[x]]\ \exists E\,\theta[E, x]\ \&\ \Phi$

That is as much as to say that there is nothing that can be said of the *n Bs* that cannot be said of some events in which they participate distributively as in (297). Given this generalization, it is necessary that the thematic relations in use are always distributive, and if so, there can never be need to recognize a primitive thematic relation with an (essentially) plural argument relating the *n Bs* to events.

29.2.2.4 *Clause Structure and Relations between Events*

The individuals' actions in (298) and (299) are all different—none of the hooting, hollering, rasping, warbling, twanging and bellowing is the same event as any of the others—and none of the individuals' actions is sufficient to drown out the lecture or harmonize.

(298) Saul hooting and David hollering drowned out the lecture.

(299) John rasping C, Paul warbling E♭, George twanging G and Ringo bellowing B♭ harmonized in c minor.

Some relation, mereological, topological, or causal, mediates between the individuals' actions and the larger events to convey that they amounted to a drowning out or harmonizing:

(300) $\exists E(Agent[E, X]\ \&\ hooting[E])\ and\ \exists E(Agent[E, Y]\ \&\ hollering[E])\ \&\ R[E, E']$
$\&\ drown\ out\ the\ lecture[E']$[53]

The logical form of (300) is further revision to the citation (neo-) Davidsonian forms. The thematic relations and verbs are no longer applied to the same event or events (*cf.* Section 29.2.2.1.2.). Logical form applies them to distinct events, and the sentence is held together with the introduction of further relations between sentences, '$R[E, E']$' in (300). Alongside coordinate structures like (298) and (299), plural quantification over events and the underlying distributivity of thematic relations combine on their own to present an empirical problem the solution of which corroborates the revision in the logical syntax of simple clauses.

According to Broadway tradition, the casts of rival shows retire after every performance to Patsy Grimaldi's where they hold separate court, darting poisonous glances and feigning indifference at other tables. The composers who have collaborated on a show share a ritual of toasts and pizza, so that tonight at Patsy Grimaldi's with 17 composers from rival shows present and the kitchen turning out 23 pizzas (Schein, 1993: 126 ff.; Schein, 2002):

---

[53] The formula suppresses the device of cross-reference; but, I have in mind descriptive anaphora: *There was some hooting, there was some hollering, and (all)* **that** *drowned out the lecture.* (Schein, in preparation).

(301) a. 17 composers share 23 pizzas.
　　　b. 17 composers share at the show's table 23 pizzas.
　　　c. 17 composers share, every composer breaking pizza with every other composer, 23 pizzas.

The composers are divided among several tables at which every composer shares with every other and across which there is no such conviviality. That is, (301) is true only to the extent that several sharing*s* verify it, as many as there are tables.

(302) Agent$[E, X]$ & *share*$[E]$ & Patient$[E, Y]$

As the composers are neatly divided among these, a distributive thematic relation describes accurately their participation in the sharings. The pizza however is ordered and served by the slice, and it happens that this evening none of the twenty-three pizzas is consumed at any one of the tables. Even so, (301) remains true and indifferent to these pizza particulars, but (302) is false interpreting 'Patient$[E,Y]$' distributively ((*cf.* (250), (253)), (279)) to imply that any *a* pizza is consumed at *an* event of sharing. The truth of (301) looks to argue that 'Patient$[E,Y]$' expresses a relation between plural arguments, the sharings and the pizzas, that cannot be reduced to a first-order, distributive relation. But, the argument above resumes—The twenty three pizzas may be referred to severally and their participation qualified by adverbs:

(303) a. 17 composers share the first pizza first, the second pizza second,... and the 23rd pizza 23rd.
　　　b. 17 composers have shared at their (own) show's table the first pizza first, the second pizza second,... and the 23rd pizza 23rd.
　　　c. 17 composers share, every composer breaking pizza with every other composer, the first pizza first, the second pizza second,... and the 23rd pizza 23rd.

If Grimaldi's sells off one pizza before starting in on the next, (303) is true *ceteris paribus*, even though distributivity has been imposed on the thematic relation relating pizzas to events. The thematic relation relates pizzas to events distributively, but pizzas cannot be related to the sharings distributively. Revising therefore the syntax of simple clauses, the events distributively related to the pizzas are not the sharings, which have been distributively related to the composers:

(304) Agent$[E_1, X]$ & *share*$[E_1]$ & Overlap$[E_1, E_2]$ & Patient$[E_2, Y]$
(305) Overlap$[E_i, E_j]$ $\leftrightarrow_{df}$ $\forall e_i(E_i e_i \leftrightarrow \exists e_j(E_j e_j$ & Overlap$(e_j, e_i)))$

Rather, what the agents do E_1 and what happens to patients E_2 is mediated by some other relation (Schein 1993, 2002, in preparation), mereological coincidence or overlap in this case, which is itself distributive ((305)) and projected from the primitive, first-order mereological relation.[54]

---

[54] Overlap(x, x)
　　Overlap(x, y) $\leftrightarrow$ Overlap(y, x)

These observations may be revisited at every position for plural predication (306) prompting the revision in (307) to basic clause structure that applies thematic relations to their own events and holds the sentence together with further relations such as 'Cause$[E,E']$' and 'Overlap$[E,E']$':

(306) Lenny toasting, Kurt praising, ..., and George dishing it out share the first pizza first,.., and the 23rd pizza 23rd.
(307) Agent$[E_1, X]$ & Cause$[E_1, E_2]$ & $share[E_2]$ & Overlap$[E_2, E_3]$ & Patient$[E_3, Y]$

29.2.3 Russelling Eventish[55]

According to the neo-Davidsonian analysis, event quantification and thematic relations to the events quantified over occur in the logical form of every sentence in natural language, simple or complex. For at least some events and some thematic relations, events do not bear thematic relations to themselves:

(308) The fires expand.
(309) The fires cluster.

When (308) and (309) are true, some events, a clustering or clusterings and an expansion or expansions, are such that their only themes are the fires, and thus these events are not their own themes.

(310) The events that are not their own themes expand (in their own space and time).
(311) The events that are not their own themes cluster.

Given some such events, (310) is trivially true; and, reflecting on how they are gotten from truths like (308) and (309), it is also clear that there are enough of them for (311), even for a single, dense cluster of them. Yet, according to the neo-Davidsonian analysis, the sentences are true just in case there are some events, some expansions in (310) and a clustering in (311), that the events that are not their own themes are themes of. Russell's paradox threatens (Oliver and Smiley, 2001; Rayo, 2002; Yi 1999: 186 n. 34): If the expansions are among their own themes, then they must be among the events the subject refers to, that is, among events that are not their own themes. On the other hand, if the expansions are not events that are their own themes, they are among the events the subject refers to and hence their own themes. Implying a clustering in (311) similarly tilts the neo-Davidsonian analysis towards contradiction. With a commitment to sentence-verifying events and thematic relations, paradox will threaten as soon as the object language contains plural definite descriptions deploying thematic relations or their equivalent to refer to events that

$x \leq y \leftrightarrow \forall z(\text{Overlap}(z, x) \rightarrow \text{Overlap}(z, y))$
$x = y \leftrightarrow (x \leq y \,\&\, y \leq x)$
$\text{Overlap}(x, y) \leftrightarrow \exists z \forall u(\text{Overlap}(u, z) \leftrightarrow (\text{Overlap}(u, x) \,\&\, \text{Overlap}(u, y)))$ (meet)
$\exists z \forall u(\text{Overlap}(u, z) \leftrightarrow (\text{Overlap}(u, x) \lor \text{Overlap}(u, y)))$ (join)

55 Thanks to Paul Pietroski and Philippe Schlenker for critical discussion, March 2002.

are not so related to themselves. The paradox presents itself whether the (existential) event quantification is thought of as plural (310) or as singular (311), and it threatens a neo-Davidsonian analysis no matter what view of plural reference and predication accompanies it. In a blunt response, one may despair of the neo-Davidsonian analysis and exorcise events altogether as in (312) and (314) (*v.* Oliver and Smiley, 2001; Rayo, 2002; Yi, 1999) and thereby forfeit, in (314) for example, adverbial modification, tense and aspect, nominalization and any other grammatical construction explained by reference to events (Parsons, 1990):

(312) [The ξ: fires(ξ)] expand(ξ).
(313) [The ξ: fires(ξ)] cluster(ξ).
(314) The fires first clustered slowly along the ridgeline in several clusters and have been expanding rapidly across the leeward side while flaring out on the windward side.

Language scientists and engineers lie in wait with their reply:

"And here I go by the semanticists' First Amendment:
    The right to solve Russell's Paradox some other time shall not be restricted." (Landman, 2000: 79)

To formalize the argument in pursuit of a way out, recall (315) and (316). Some convenient shorthand abbreviating the singular is introduced in (317)–(319):[56]

(315) cluster[E] $\leftrightarrow$ $\forall e(Ee \rightarrow$ cluster(e))
(316) Theme[E, X] $\leftrightarrow$ $\forall x(Xx \leftrightarrow \exists e(Ee$ & Theme(e, x)))
(317) cluster[e] $\leftrightarrow$ cluster(e)
(318) Theme[e, X] $\leftrightarrow$ $\forall x(Xx \leftrightarrow$ Theme(e, x))
(319) Theme[e, x] $\leftrightarrow$ $\forall y(y = x \leftrightarrow$ Theme(e, y))

Recall that thematic relations as tokened in logical form, $\theta[E, X]$, are always exhaustive: according to (316), X are *the* themes of the *E*s.
    Some translations of (310) and (311) end in paradox, and some do not. Suppose the subject refers specifically to the events that are not among their own themes, [the X: ¬[$\exists Y$: of(X,Y)] Theme[X,Y]]:

(320) $\exists E$[the X : ¬[$\exists Y$: of(X, Y)] Theme[X, Y]] Theme[E, X] expand[E]

Let **X** be the events the subject refers to, and **E**, the expansions, so that, given the truth of (320), Theme[**E,X**]. If, on the one hand, of(**E,X**), then by description, ¬[$\exists Y$: of(**E**,Y)] Theme[**E**,Y], in particular, ¬(of(**E,X**) & Theme[**E,X**]) and therefore, ¬ Theme[**E,X**], a contradiction. If, on the other hand, ¬of(**E,X**), then by description [$\exists Y$: of(**E**,Y)] Theme[**E**,Y], from which, by the exhaustivity of thematic relations, of(**E,X**), contradiction again. Since nothing in this argument rests on **E** being

---

[56] The monosortal language of the partitive construction could be used just as well at the cost of further eyestrain.

non-singular, the same translation of the subject will also pitch (311) into paradox:

(321) $\exists e$ [the $X: \neg[\exists Y: \text{of}(X, Y)]$ Theme$[X, Y]]$ Theme$[e, X]$ cluster$[e]$

Suppose next that the events that are not their own themes are the events each of which is not one of its own themes, [the $X: [\forall x: Xx]\neg[\exists X: Xx]$Theme$[x,X]]$. As translation of (311), consider:

(322) $\exists e$ [the $X: [\forall x: Xx]\neg[\exists X: Xx]$ Theme$[x, X]]$ Theme$[e, X]$ cluster$[e]$

Let **X** be the events the subject refers to, and **e**, the clustering. If, on the one hand, **Xe**, then by description $\neg[\exists X: Xe]$ Theme$[e,X]$, implying in contradiction that $\neg$**Xe**. If on the other hand $\neg$**Xe**, then by description $[\exists X: Xe]$ Theme$[e,X]$, from which exhaustivity implies that **Xe**, contradiction again.

In contrast, this same translation of the subject seems benign in talk about plural expansions:

(323) $\exists E$ [the $X: [\forall x: Xx]\neg[\exists X: Xx]$ Theme$[x, X]]$ Theme$[E, X]$ expand$[E]$

Let **X** be the events the subject refers to, and **E**, the expansions. If, first, $\neg$of(**E,X**), then by description, for some **e**, an **E**, $[\exists X: Xe]$Theme$[e,X]$, which, by the exhaustivity and distributivity of thematic relations, implies **Xe**, which in turn by description implies in contradiction that $\neg[\exists X: Xe]$Theme$[e,X]$. If, on the other hand, of(**E,X**), then any **e** of **E** meets the description, '$\neg[\exists X: Xe]$Theme$[e,X]$', that it is not among its very own themes. Given that it is one of the themes **X** of **E**, it is implied without apparent contradiction only that **e** is a theme of some of the other **E** rather than of itself.

A fully distributive interpretation of the subject's description, referring to the events each of which is not its own theme, [the $X: [\forall x: Xx]\neg$Theme$[x,x]]$, allows translation of both (310) and (311) to escape:

(324) $\exists e$ [the $X: [\forall x: Xx]\neg$Theme$[x, x]]$ Theme$[e, X]$ cluster$[e]$

If (324) is true, the clustering **e** cannot be its own theme, since it is asserted that many events, all those that are not their own themes, are in fact the themes of **e**. By the same token, since **e** is not its own theme, it is among the things the subject refers to, and so **e** is properly among the themes of **e**, without contradiction. Similarly, there is no contradiction in the expansions being among their own themes, as each other's for example, while none is its own:

(325) $\exists E$ [the $X: [\forall x: Xx]\neg$Theme$[x, x]]$ Theme$[E, X]$ expand$[E]$

The paradox latent in (310) and (311) is joined when a malicious interpreter fixes on certain interpretations of the subject or finds further disambiguating language and knows that (310) and (311) so construed or elaborated are true.

If there is a malicious interpreter, the way out from paradox for her insists on the revision to basic clause structure from Section 29.2.2.4. No sentence of her language, despite her gloss on the subject, parses the matrix as in (320)–(325). A further relation between events intrudes as in (326)–(328):

(326) $\exists E_1 \exists E_2[\text{the } X: \neg[\exists Y: \text{ of}(X,Y)] \text{ Theme}[X,Y]] \text{ Theme}[E_1,X] \text{ Overlap}[E_1,E_2]$
        $\text{expand}[E_2]$

(327) $\exists E_1 \exists e_2[\text{the } X: \neg[\exists Y: \text{ of}(X,Y)] \text{ Theme}[X,Y]] \text{ Theme}[E_1,X] \text{ Overlap}[E_1,e_2]$
        $\text{cluster}[e_2]$

(328) $\exists E_1 \exists e_2[\text{the } X: [\forall x: Xx]\neg[\exists X: Xx] \text{ Theme}[x, X]] \text{ Theme}[E_1,X]$
        $\text{Overlap}[E_1, e_2] \text{ cluster}[e_2]$

Intending with (311) to refer to the events each of which is not one of its own themes, she means (328), which is taken to be true. Let e_2 be the clustering, and $\mathbf{X}$, the events the subject refers to. If $\mathbf{X}e_2$, then $\neg\text{Theme}[e_2,\mathbf{X}]$ and $\exists E_1(\text{Overlap}[E_1, e_2] \, \& \, \text{Theme}[E_1,\mathbf{X}])$, from which follows only that $\exists E_1(\text{Theme}[E_1,\mathbf{X}] \, \& \, e_2 \neq E_1)$, without paradox. If instead $\neg\mathbf{X}e_2$, then $[\exists X: Xe_2] \text{ Theme}[e_2,X]$ and $\exists E_1(\text{Overlap}[E_1,e_2] \, \& \, \text{Theme}[E_1,\mathbf{X}])$, with even less risk.

Similarly, intending with (310) to refer as in (326) to the events that are not among their own themes, let $\mathbf{E}_2$ be the expansions and $\mathbf{X}$, the events the subject refers to. If $\text{of}(\mathbf{E}_2,\mathbf{X})$, then $\neg[\exists Y: \text{of}(\mathbf{E}_2,Y)]\text{Theme}[\mathbf{E}_2,Y]$, in particular, $\neg(\text{of}(\mathbf{E}_2,\mathbf{X})$ $\& \, \text{Theme}[\mathbf{E}_2,\mathbf{X}])$ and therefore, $\neg\text{Theme}[\mathbf{E}_2,\mathbf{X}]$, which comports without apparent contradiction with the requirement that for some E_1, $\text{Overlap}[E_1,\mathbf{E}_2] \, \& \, \text{Theme}[E_1,\mathbf{X}]$ provided that $E_1 \neq \mathbf{E}_2$.

Seeking out paradox, the malicious interpreter will reach for greater havoc taking up into her description the new relations provided to the matrix clause and referring instead to the events that are not among those that even overlap their themes. As far as I can tell, translation does not come any closer to paradox:

(329) $\exists E_1 \exists E_2[\text{the } X: \neg[\exists Y: \text{of}(X,Y)]\exists E_1 (\text{Theme}[E_1,Y] \text{ Overlap}[E_1,X])]$

        $\text{Theme}[E_1,X]\text{Overlap}[E_1,E_2] \text{ expand}[E_2]$

(330) $\exists E_1 \exists e_2 [\text{the } X: \neg[\exists Y: \text{of}(X,Y)]\exists E_1 (\text{Theme}[E_1,Y] \text{ Overlap}[E_1,X])]$

        $\text{Theme}[E_1,X] \text{ Overlap}[E_1,e_2] \text{ cluster}[e_2]$

(331) $\exists E_1 \exists e_2 [\text{the } X: [\forall x: Xx]\neg[\exists X: Xx]\exists E_1 (\text{Theme}[E_1,X] \text{ Overlap}[E_1,x])]$

        $\text{Theme}[E_1,X] \text{ Overlap}[E_1,e_2] \text{ cluster}[e_2]$

Presuming (329) to be the logical form of a true sentence like (310), let $\mathbf{E}_2$ be the expansions and $\mathbf{X}$, the events the subject refers to. If $\text{of}(\mathbf{E}_2,\mathbf{X})$, then $\neg[\exists Y: \text{of}(\mathbf{E}_2,Y)]$ $\exists E_1 (\text{Theme}[E_1,Y] \text{ Overlap}[E_1,\mathbf{E}_2])$, in particular, $\neg(\text{of}(\mathbf{E}_2,\mathbf{X}) \, \& \, \exists E_1(\text{Theme}[E_1,\mathbf{X}]$ $\text{Overlap}[E_1,\mathbf{E}_2]))$ and therefore $\neg\exists E_1(\text{Theme}[E_1,\mathbf{X}] \text{ Overlap}[E_1,\mathbf{E}_2])$, contradicting (329). On the other hand, if $\neg\text{of}(\mathbf{E}_2,\mathbf{X})$, then (i) $[\exists Y: \text{of}(\mathbf{E}_2,Y)]\exists E_1(\text{Theme}[E_1,Y]$ $\text{Overlap} [E_1,\mathbf{E}_2])$ and yet, given (329), (ii) $\exists E_1(\text{Theme}[E_1,\mathbf{X}] \text{ Overlap}[E_1,\mathbf{E}_2])$. But, again, there is no apparent conflict with exhaustivity (or, distributivity) provided that the events coincident with $\mathbf{E}_2$ of which $\mathbf{X}$ are the themes (according to (ii)) are not the same ones as those coincident with $\mathbf{E}_2$ the themes of which $\mathbf{E}_2$ are among (according to (i)). Recall ((301)) that events the themes of which are pizza slices may very well coincide with events the themes of which are different, pizzas whole. As again these remarks do not rely on $\mathbf{E}_2$ being non-singular, they also show (330) *mutatis mutandis* to be a benign translation of (311) about a single clustering.

If the subject is taken instead to refer (semi-)distributively as in (331) to the events each of which does not overlap its own themes, paradox is equally remote. Let X be the events the subject refers to, and e_2, the clustering. If Xe_2, then by description $\neg[\exists X: Xe_2] \exists E_1 (\text{Theme}[E_1,X] \text{ Overlap}[E_1,e_2])$, implying in particular that $\neg\exists E_1 (\text{Theme}[E_1,\mathbf{X}] \text{ Overlap}[E_1,e_2])$, contradicting (331). But, if $\neg Xe_2$, then (i) $[\exists X: Xe_2] \exists E_1(\text{Theme}[E_1,X] \text{ Overlap}[E_1,e_2])$, and yet, given (331), (ii) $\exists E_1(\text{Theme}[E_1,\mathbf{X}] \text{ Overlap}[E_1,e_2])$. Both conditions (i) and (ii) are met when the events with themes X and coincident with e_2 are distinct from the events coincident with e_2 of which e_2 is itself a theme.

In summary, granted the truth of (310) and (311), the malicious interpreter finds paradoxical translations just in case the neo-Davidsonian clause is unrevised as in (332); translation eludes paradox under the revised clause structure (333).

(332) ... Theme$[E, X]$ expand$[E]$ ...

   ... Theme$[e, X]$ cluster$[e]$ ...

(333) ... Theme$[E_1, X]$ Overlap$[E_1, E_2]$ expand$[E_2]$ ...

   ... Theme$[E_1, X]$ Overlap$[E_1, e_2]$ cluster$[e_2]$ ...

If so, the divorce between linguistics and philosophy looming earlier can be rescheduled pending further inquiry (perhaps into alleged events that are themes in events coincident with themselves). In the meantime, Russell's paradox joins the empirical considerations of Section 29.2.2.4 in urging a particular articulation of the neo-Davidsonian clause.[57]

REFERENCES

Chris Barker (1992). Group Terms in English: Representing Groups as Atoms. *Journal of Semantics*, 9: 69–93.

George Boolos (1984). To be is to be a Value of a Variable (or to be Some Values of some Variables. *Journal of Philosophy*, 81.8: 43–449. Reprinted in Boolos, 1998: 54–72.

_____ (1985a). Nominalist Platonism. *Philosophical Review*, 94.3: 327–44. Reprinted in Boolos 1998: 73–87.

_____ (1985b). Reading the *Begriffschrift*. *Mind*, 94.375: 331–44. Reprinted in Boolos 1998: 155–70.

_____ (1998). *Logic, Logic and Logic*. Cambridge: Harvard University Press.

Hagit Borer (2005). *Structuring Sense: Volume I—In Name Only*. Oxford: Oxford University Press.

Philip Bricker (1989). Quantified Modal Logic and the Plural *de re*. *Midwest Studies in Philosophy*, 14: 372–94.

Tyler Burge (1972). Truth and Mass Terms. *Journal of Philosophy*, 69.10: 263–82.

_____ (1973). Reference and Proper Names. *Journal of Philosophy*, 70: 425–39. Reprinted in Peter Ludlow, ed., *Readings in the Philosophy of Language*, Cambridge: MIT Press, 1997, 593–608.

_____ (1977). A Theory of Aggregates. *Noûs*, 11: 97–117.

---

[57] Schein in preparation, for further discussion.

Lauri Carlson (1982). Plural Quantifiers and Informational Independence. *Acta Philosophica Fennica*, 35: 163–74.

Helen Cartwright (1996). Some of a Plurality. In James E. Tomberlin, ed. *Philosophical Perspectives*, 10: 137–57. Blackwell.

Richard Cartwright (1994). Speaking of Everything. *Noûs*, 28: 1–20.

Annabel Cormack and Ruth Kempson (1981). Ambiguity and Quantification. *Linguistics and Philosophy*, 4: 259–309.

Martin Davies (1989). *Two Examiners Marked Six Scripts*: Interpretations of Numerically Quantified Sentences. *Linguistics and Philosophy*, 12: 293–323.

Gottlob Frege (1884). *Die Grundlagen der Arithmetik*. Breslau: Koebner. Trans. J. L. Austin. 1980. *The Foundations of Arithmetic*. Evanston: Northwestern University Press.

Brendan Gillon (1987). The Readings of Plural Noun Phrases in English. *Linguistics and Philosophy*, 10.

____ (1990). Plural Noun Phrases and their Readings: A Reply to Lasersohn. *Linguistics and Philosophy*, 13: 477–85.

Martin Hackl (2001). *Comparative Quantifiers*. PhD diss. MIT.

____ (2003a). On the Internal Composition of Comparative Quantifiers: Some Semantics and some Processing. ms. Pomona College.

____ (2003b). On the Decomposition of *Most, More* and *Fewer*: Cross-Linguistic Evidence and Evidence from Eye-Tracking. ms. Pomona College.

James Higginbotham (1980). Reciprocal Interpretation. *Journal of Linguistic Research*, 1.2: 97–117.

____ (1998). On Higher-Order Logic and Natural Language. In Timothy Smiley, ed., *Philosophical Logic*. Proceedings of the British Academy, 95: 1–27. Oxford: Oxford University Press.

____ (2000). On Second-Order Logic and Natural Language. In Gila Sher and Richard Tieszen, ed., *Between Intuition and Logic: Essays in Honor of Charles Parsons*. Cambridge, UK: Cambridge University Press.

James Higginbotham and Barry Schein (1989). Plurals. In Juli Carter and Rose-Marie Déchaine (eds.), *Proceedings of the North Eastern Linguistics Society 19*, Cornell University, Amherst, MA: Graduate Linguistics Students Association, University of Massachusetts, pp. 161–75.

Norbert Hornstein (2002). A Grammatical Argument for a neo-Davidsonian Semantics. In Gerhard Preyer and Georg Peter, (eds.), *Logical Form and Language*. Oxford: Oxford University Press. pp. 345–64.

Keith Hossack (2000). Plurals and Complexes. *British Journal for the Philosophy of Science*, 51: 411–43.

Ray Jackendoff (1977). *X' Syntax: A Study of Phrase Structure*. Linguistic Inquiry Monograph No. 2. Cambridge: MIT Press.

Kathrin Koslicki (1997). Isolation and Non-Arbitrary Division: Frege's Two Criteria for Counting. *Synthese*, 112.3: 403–30.

____ (1999). The Semantics of Mass-Predicates. *Noûs*, 33.1: 46–91.

____ (2005). Nouns, Mass and Count. Forthcoming in *Encyclopedia of Philosophy* 2nd edn., ed. Donald M. Borchert, Macmillan Reference, USA.

Angelika Kratzer (1996). Severing the External Argument from the Verb, in Johan Rooryck and Laurie Zaring (eds.), *Phrase Structure and the Lexicon*, pp. 109–37. Dordrecht: Kluwer.

Fred Landman (1989a). Groups I. *Linguistics and Philosophy*, 12.5.

____ (1989b). Groups II. *Linguistics and Philosophy*, 12.6.

____ (1995). Plurality. In *Handbook of Semantics*, ed. Shalom Lappin. 425–57. Cambridge, MA: Blackwell.

_____ (2000). *Events and Plurality: The Jerusalem Lectures.* Dordrecht: Kluwer Academic.

D. Terence Langendoen (1978). The Logic of Reciprocity. *Linguistic Inquiry,* 9.2: 177–97.

Richard Larson and Gabriel Segal (1995). *Knowledge of Meaning: An Introduction to Semantic Theory.* Cambridge: MIT Press.

Peter Lasersohn (1988). *A Semantics for Groups and Events.* Ohio State University PhD diss.

_____ (1990). Group Action and Spatio-Temporal Proximity. *Linguistics and Philosophy,* 14.2: 179–206.

_____ (1990). On the Readings of Plural Noun Phrases. *Linguistic Inquiry,* 20.1: 14–144.

_____ (1995). *Plurality, Conjunction and Events.* Kluwer.

David Lewis (1991). *Parts of Classes.* Oxford: Blackwell.

Godehard Link (1983). The Logical Analysis of Plurals and Mass Terms: A Lattice–Theoretic Approach. In Rainer Bäuerle, Christoph Schwarze and Arnim von Stechow, eds., *Meaning, Use and Interpretation of Language,* pp. 302–23. Berlin: Walter de Gruyter.

_____ (1993). Plural. In Dieter Wunderlich and Arnim von Stechow (eds.), *Handbook of Semantics.* Berlin: de Gruyter.

Øystein Linnebo (2003). Plural Quantification Exposed. *Noûs,* 37: 71–92.

_____ (2004). Plural Quantification. *Stanford Encyclopedia of Philosophy.* Plato.stanford.edu

Giuseppe Longobardi (2005). Toward a Unified Grammar of Reference. *Zeitschrift für Sprachwissenschaft* 24: 5–24.

J. T. Lønning (1987). Collective Readings of Definite and Indefinite Noun Phrases. In P. Gärdenfors, ed., *Generalized Quantifiers: Linguistic and Logical Approaches.* Studies in Linguistics and Philosophy, 31, D. Reidel, Boston.

James. D. McCawley (1981). *Everything that Linguists have Always Wanted to Know about Logic: But were Ashamed to Ask.* Chicago: University of Chicago Press.

Vann McGee (2000). Everything. In Gila Sher and Richard Tieszen (ed.), *Between Intuition and Logic: Essays in Honor of Charles Parsons.* Cambridge, UK: Cambridge University Press.

Thomas McKay (forthcoming). *Plurals and Non-Distributive Predication.* Oxford: Oxford University Press.

Friederike Moltmann (1997). *Parts and Wholes in Semantics.* Oxford: Oxford University Press.

Alex Oliver and Timothy Smiley (2001). Strategies for a logic of plurals. *The Philosophical Quarterly,* 51.204: 289–306.

Terence Parsons (1990). *Events in the Semantics of English: A Study in Subatomic Semantics.* Cambridge: MIT Press.

David M. Perlmutter and John Robert Ross (1970). Relative Clauses with Split Antecedents. *Linguistic Inquiry* 1.3: 350.

Paul M. Pietroski (2002). Function and concatenation. In Gerhard Preyer and Georg Peter (eds.), *Logical Form and Language.* 91–117. Oxford: Clarendon Press.

_____ (2003). Quantification and second-order monadicity. *Philosophical Perspectives,* 17.1: 259–98.

Mark Platts (1979). *Ways of Meaning: An Introduction to a Philosophy of Language.* London: Routledge and Kegan Paul.

Arthur Prior (1971). *Objects of Thought.* Oxford: Oxford University Press.

Agustín Rayo (2002). Word and objects. *Noûs,* 36.3: 436–64.

Agustín Rayo and Stephen Yablo (2001). Nominalism through De-Nominalization. *Noûs,* 35.1: 74–92.

Bertrand Russell (1938). *The Principles of Mathematics.* 2nd edn. NY: W.W. Norton. 1st edn. 1903.

Remko Scha (1981). Distributive, collective and cumulative quantification. Reprinted in J. Groenendijk *et al.,* (eds.), *Truth, Interpretation and Information,* GRASS 2, Dordrecht: Foris, 1984. pp. 141–158.

Barry Schein (1993). *Plurals and Events.* Current Studies in Linguistics No. 23. Cambridge: MIT Press.

____ (2001). Adverbial, Descriptive Reciprocals. Abridged in Rachel Hastings, Brenda Jackson and Zsofia Zvolenszky (eds.), *Proceedings of Semantics and Linguistic Theory XI.* Ithaca: CLC Publications, pp. 404–30. Unabridged in *Philosophical Linguistics, Philosophical Perspectives,* 17.1: 333–67, 2003.

____ (2002). Events and the Semantic Content of Thematic Relations. In Gerhard Preyer and Georg Peter, eds., *Logical Form and Language.* Oxford: Oxford University Press. pp. 263–344.

____ (2005). Plurals. Expanded Electronic Version. www-rcf.usc.edu/~schein/Plurals2005 .pdf.

____ (in preparation) *Conjunction Reduction Redux.*

Roger Schwarzschild (1991). *On the Meaning of Definite Plural Noun Phrases.* PhD. UMass. Amherst.

____ (1996). *Pluralities.* Kluwer.

Richard Sharvy (1978). Maybe English has no Count Nouns: Notes on Chinese Semantics. *Studies in Language,* 2.3: 345–65.

____ (1980). A More General Theory of Definite Descriptions. *Philosophical Review,* 89.4: 607–24.

Peter Simons (1982). Number and Manifolds. In Smith (ed.), 1982, pp. 160–98.

____ (1982). Plural Reference and Set Theory. In Barry Smith (ed.), *Parts and Moments: Studies in Logic and Formal Ontology.* pp. 199–256. Munich: Philadelphia.

____ (1987). *Parts, a Study in Metaphysics.* Oxford: Clarendon Press.

Timothy Williamson (2003). Everything. *Philosophical Perspectives,* 17.1: 415–65.

Byeong-uk Yi (1999). Is Two a Property? *Journal of Philosophy,* 96.4: 163–90.

____ (2002). *Understanding the Many.* Studies in Philosophy. Outstanding Dissertations. New York: Routledge.

____ (2005). The Logic and Meaning of Plurals. Part I. *Journal of Philosophical Logic.* 34: 459–506.

....

THE PRAGMATICS
OF THE LOGICAL
CONSTANTS

....

DOROTHY EDGINGTON

FROM one point of view, this seems something of a non-subject: the logical con-stants are technical terms, invented and precisely defined by logicians for the purpose of producing rigorous formal proofs. Mathematics virtually exhausts the domain of deductive reasoning of any complexity, and it is there that the benefits of this refined form of language are felt. Pragmatic issues may arise—issues concerning the point of making a certain statement—for there will be more or less perspicuous and illumin-ating ways of presenting proofs in this language, and we may be puzzled or misled when we wonder why the mathematician is taking some particular step. But this is hardly a compulsory topic in the philosophy of language. From this perspective, it looks as if I am about to fill a welcome gap in the literature.

From another point of view, the 'logical forms' identified in formal logic have much to teach us about the semantic structure of natural languages, and hence about the language-user's ability readily to produce and to understand new sentences. The logical constants are crucial elements in logical form. The question arises whether or how well, on the logician's account of their meanings, they match their nearest ordinary-language equivalents—words such as 'and', 'or', 'not', 'if', 'all', and 'some'. Paul Grice famously argued that they do match: apparent discrepancies are not indicative of differences in meaning, but are to be explained, pragmatically, in terms of rational principles governing conversation. They would arise, and would be explicable, even for speakers of 'logician's English', who, by stipulation, use the words with the logician's meanings.

Although he did not use the term 'pragmatics', Grice breathed new life into this subject, and changed the way we think of it. Traditionally, semantics concerns the meanings of words and sentences, pragmatics concerns people's use of words and sentences. But this is hardly a perspicuous distinction, if it is a distinction at all: words mean what people use them to mean; and, it would seem, if I want to communicate that p, I shall do so by using a string of words which means that p. What Grice showed is that when one says something, one inevitably communicates more than is attributable to the meanings of the words one uses, for the hearer properly makes inferences not just from the content of what you said, but from the fact that you said it. For instance, there are a great many people of whom it could be truly said that they haven't been to prison yet, but if I make that remark about someone, you are likely to infer that he is a shady character, and there was some likelihood that he would have been to prison by now, otherwise it is inexplicable why I should make the remark. Thus, the heart of pragmatics is what gets communicated *beyond* what one's words literally mean; and there is a subject here, however explicit our words.

Controversy remains surrounding the semantics-pragmatics distinction. Consider words whose reference depends on the context in which they are used, like 'I', 'she', 'that man' and 'yesterday'. Is the business of establishing their reference on a particular occasion a matter of semantics or pragmatics? On the older conception, it is pragmatics. If this is so, semantics alone does not yield a truth-evaluable content, in the presence of such words. On the Grice-inspired conception, it is semantics: the meanings of these words determine, in a context, or at least serve as a guide to their reference, on which the truth or falsity of the sentence in which they occur turns. Their meanings can be represented as a function from contexts to denotations. Pragmatics comes in after a truth-evaluable thought has been expressed. This issue might be dismissed as terminological, but it hinges on views about where the theoretically important line is to be drawn. On the Grice-inspired view, reference-fixing is part of semantics because semantics delivers the proposition expressed by one's words, a proposition which concerns the objects the singular terms refer to. On opposing views, semantics rarely delivers propositions: the meanings of the words uttered, together with syntax, even together with assignments of references to pronouns and the like, underdetermine the proposition expressed, and pragmatics is involved; so nothing is gained by insisting that reference-fixing is semantics. At its most general, the issue here is how much of our ability to communicate rests on specifically linguistic knowledge, and how large a role is played by background knowledge, common sense and inference to the best explanation, all of which play a role in the pragmatics of communication.

30.1 LOGICAL FORM AND THE LOGICAL CONSTANTS

Here is a relatively modest conception of logical form. Formal logic is the study of patterns of valid argument. It discerns a common structure or form in arguments with different subject matter, and pronounces on whether any argument of that form is valid. For example, from 'Either John or Mary will chair the meeting' and 'John will not chair the meeting' we may deduce that Mary will chair the meeting; and from 'Sue caught either the four o'clock train or the five o'clock train' and 'Sue did not catch the four o'clock train' we may deduce that she caught the five o'clock train. Despite the different subject matter, each exemplifies a common pattern of argument: either A or B; not A; from which we may deduce that B. (Note that we play around a little with the structure of the original sentences to discern their 'logical form', so that 'or' comes between whole sentences and 'not' precedes a whole sentence: we construe the first sentence as equivalent to 'Either John will chair the meeting or Mary will chair the meeting', the second as 'It is not the case that John will chair the meeting', etc.)

Of course we do not abstract entirely from the content of the sentences in the original arguments: the form still contains the words, common to both arguments, 'either . . . or' and 'not'. These are examples of logical constants: constants because we keep their meaning fixed, when abstracting away from the rest of the content to exhibit the form of an argument; logical because these words are the crucial words on which the validity of many arguments hinge.

Logical constants are therefore correlative to the notion of logical form. From this modest perspective, there is no need to think that there is a unique, absolute logical form of a sentence. We may wish to isolate different patterns of valid argument for different purposes. (Not all valid arguments are formally valid: 'It's round; so it isn't square' is a valid argument.) Hence there is no definitive list of logical constants. But there is a standard list, due to the fact that we have a standard logic, largely due to Gottlob Frege (1879), and vastly more powerful than any previous system of logic.

First there are the sentence connectives, or sentential operators: expressions which, when applied to a declarative sentence or to two such sentences, yield another, more complex sentence. Given two sentences A and B (e.g. 'Ann is in Paris' and 'Bob is in Paris), we can form the sentences 'A and B', 'A or B' and 'If A, B'. And given the sentence A we can form the sentence 'It is not the case that A.' We shall abbreviate these '$A\&B$', '$A \lor B$' '$A \supset B$' and '$\neg A$'. The meanings of the sentence-connectives, as they are used in standard logic, are usually displayed in truth tables, which show how these words generate a sentence with certain truth conditions, given the truth conditions of the sentences to which they apply:

A	B	$\neg A$	$A\&B$	$A \vee B$	$A \supset B$
T	T	F	T	T	T
T	F	F	F	T	F
F	T	T	F	T	T
F	F	T	F	F	T

There are four possible combinations of truth-values for the two sentences, displayed on the left. The columns on the right tell us that $\neg A$ is true if A is false, false if A is true; '$A\&B$' is true if A and B are both true, otherwise it is false; '$A \vee B$' is false if A and B are both false, otherwise it is true; '$A \supset B$' is false if A is true and B is false; otherwise (so standard logic tells us) it is true. If understanding a sentence is knowing the conditions under which it is true, the above table shows how an understanding of the complex sentence is derived from an understanding of the component sentences, and the particular logical constant with which it is constructed.

Then there are the quantifiers, 'all' and 'some' (and equivalent expressions). Here, for good reason, Frege departed further from the syntax of natural languages. Take a sentence which contains one or more occurrences of a particular singular term, say 'Tom': 'Tom is tired'; 'Tom is tired and hungry (i.e. Tom is tired and Tom is hungry)', 'If Tom has been travelling all day, he (Tom) is tired and hungry.' Remove the singular term, 'Tom', marking the places from which it has been removed by 'x', and you have a one-place predicate: 'x is tired', 'x is tired and x is hungry', 'If x has been travelling all day then x is tired and x is hungry.' We can now express the thought that somebody satisfies the predicate, or everybody satisfies the predicate: $(\exists x)(x$ is tired$)$, $(\exists x)(x$ is tired $\& x$ is hungry$)$; $(\forall x)(x$ has been travelling all day $\supset x$ is tired and x is hungry$)$. (I assume for simplicity that the quantifiers range over people.) This syntactic machinery pays dividends when we consider sentences containing more than one quantifier. 'Everybody loves somebody', on its most natural reading, is formed by applying the universal quantifier to the one-place predicate $(\exists y)(x$ loves $y)$, (x being the space from which a singular term has been removed), to form $(\forall x)(\exists y)(x$ loves $y)$. 'Somebody is loved by everybody', on its most natural reading, is formed by applying the existential quantifier to the one-place predicate $(\forall y)(y$ loves $x)$, to form $(\exists x)(\forall y)(y$ loves $x)$. The syntax makes clear how the sentence is built from its parts, and enables us to employ simple rules governing the role of quantifiers in inferences.

Of course, there are very many other words or phrases which, when applied to a sentence, or two sentences, yield a sentence: it is possible that, probable that, surprising that, relevant that, known that A; A because B, A before B, A despite B, ... There are many other quantifiers, including 'most', 'many' 'few'. Some of these occur in interesting patterns of argument. For examples, from 'Most Fs are G' and 'All Gs are H' it follows that most Fs are H; but from 'All Fs are G' and 'Most Gs are H' it does not follow that most Fs are H. Counterexample: all kiwis are birds; most birds fly; therefore most kiwis fly. From 'It is possible that $A\&B$' it follows that it is possible that A, and it is possible that B; but from 'It is possible that A' and 'It is possible that B' it does not follow that it is possible that $A\&B$. Counterexample: exercise.

The focus of standard logic is partly explained by the overriding purpose of its founders: that of providing a system of logic adequate for mathematical reasoning. The treatment of the quantifiers, making multiple generality perspicuous, was the great advance. Mathematics does not need to make modal, temporal or causal distinctions, nor does it have much use for quantifiers such as 'most', 'many' and 'few'. Thus, for more general purposes, we may wish to extend standard logic in a number of directions. In modal logic we add the logical constants 'It is possible that' and 'It is necessary that', symbolized $\Diamond$ and $\Box$. Their meanings cannot be given on the model of the truth table, for the truth-value of 'A' does not always determine the truth-value of '$\Diamond A$' or '$\Box A$'. Saul Kripke (1963) showed how to provide a semantics for modal logic, by invoking a set of possible worlds, and interpreting sentences as true (or false) at a world w. Cutting a long story short, '$\Box A$' is true at w iff A is true at all worlds, and '$\Diamond A$' is true at w iff A is true at some world. Thus we have the beginnings of intensional logic, as opposed to Frege's extensional logic.[1]

As mentioned above, there is a more ambitious project based on the idea of logical form: it is taken as the model for the semantic structure of natural language. The 'deep structure' does not match perfectly the superficial grammatical structure of our sentences, but it is nevertheless the key to our ability to produce and to understand sentences we have never heard before. There are two variants of this project. One, associated with Donald Davidson (1967, 1973), departs as little as possible from the resources of standard logic, and in any case is committed to keeping the modes of combination extensional. The other takes modal logic as its model: the proposition expressed by a sentence may be thought of as a function from possible worlds to truth-values, determined by possible-world-relative interpretations of the parts of the sentence. This approach is associated with Richard Montague (1974); David Lewis (1970); Robert Stalnaker (1999); David Kaplan (1989); and Saul Kripke (1980), among others. One of the best-known applications of the latter approach is to the semantics of conditionals.

A symptom of the difference between the logician's and the semanticist's interest in logical form is one's attitude to the fact that some logical constants are definable in terms of others. In setting up a system of deductive reasoning, a premium is attached to reducing the number of primitive logical constants. Frege had $\supset$, $\neg$ and $\forall$ as primitive, with '$A\&B$' and '$A \vee B$' defined as short for '$\neg(A \supset \neg B)$' and '$\neg A \supset B$' respectively, and '$(\exists x)\phi x$' as short for '$\neg(\forall x)\neg\phi x$'. Alternatively, '$A \vee B$' and '$A \supset B$' can be defined as '$\neg(\neg A\&\neg B)$' and '$\neg(A\&\neg B)$' respectively; or '$A\&B$' and '$A \supset B$' can be defined as '$\neg(\neg A \vee \neg B)$' and '$\neg A \vee B$' respectively. Indeed one can go further and reduce all four sentence-connectives to a single connective, 'neither A nor B', or alternatively to 'not both A and B'. Write the former '$A|B$'. '$\neg A$' becomes '$A|A$'. 'A or B' becomes 'Not: neither A nor B', i.e. $(A|B)|(A|B)$. The discovery of this reduction excited Russell, who, in the preface to the second edition of *Principia Mathematica*, calls it 'the most definite improvement resulting

---

[1] Extensional logic is truth-functional: the truth-value of a complex sentence is determined by the truth-values of its components.

from work in mathematical logic in the past fourteen years' (1927, p. xiii); and also inspired Wittgenstein in the *Tractatus* (§5.5ff). But (Wittgenstein notwithstanding) the reductions are of no interest from the point of view of semantic structure, for they make sentences in the primitive vocabulary barely decipherable by ordinary mortals. There is no case for saying that the thought 'A or B' really has the form 'Not: not A & not B', or the thought 'A and B' really has the form 'It's not the case that if A, not B', etc.; and there is plenty of case for not saying that the 'Stroke' gives the real structure of our thoughts and utterances of conjunctions, disjunctions, negations and conditionals.

30.2 DISCREPANCIES

The founders of modern logic were ready to admit that they were departing from ordinary language, in the kinds of linguistic structure they proposed for employment in deductive reasoning, often appealing, by way of analogy, to the need for specialized, technical terms in science. Thus Frege:

> In determining the sense of scientific expressions we cannot undertake to concur exactly with the usage of ordinary life; this, indeed, is unsuited to scientific purposes, where we feel the need for more precise definition.   (1923, in Frege, 1977: 64)

and

> Just here I see the greatest difficulty for philosophy: the instrument it finds available for its work, namely ordinary language, is little suited to the purpose, for its formation was governed by requirements wholly different from those of philosophy. So also logic is first of all obliged to fashion a usable instrument from those already to hand. And for this purpose it initially finds but little in the way of usable instruments available.   (*Ibid.*: 69)

And Russell:

> Any attempt to be precise and accurate requires modification of common speech both as regards vocabulary and as regards syntax. . . . In philosophy it is syntax, even more than vocabulary, that needs to be corrected.   (1959: 242)

And Tarski (1944: 122) speaks of 'the hope that languages with specified structure could finally replace everyday language in scientific discourse'.

And yet, it is impossible to read 'On Denoting' or 'On Sense and Reference' without taking Russell and Frege to be providing insights into the workings of natural language. Very well, they were idealizing, but in such a way that was meant to throw light on how natural language, at its best, at least approximately, functions. Frege's essay cited above begins

> It is astonishing what language can do. With a few syllables it can express an incalculable number of thoughts, so that even a thought grasped by a terrestrial being for the very first time can be put into words which will be understood by someone to whom the thought is entirely new. This would be impossible were we not able to distinguish parts in the thought

corresponding to parts in the sentence, so that the structure of the sentence serves as an image of the structure of the thought.   (*Ibid.*: 56)

Value judgements aside, P. F, Strawson, in *Introduction to Logical Theory* (1952), agrees about the discrepancies:

The fact is that in ordinary speech and writing, clauses and sentences do not contribute to the truth conditions of things said . . . in any such simple way as that pictured by the truth tables, . . . but in far more subtle, various and complex ways. But it is precisely the simplicity of the way in which, by the definition of a truth-function, clauses joined by these connectives contribute to the truth-conditions of sentences resulting from the junctions, which makes possible the stylized, mechanical neatness of the logical system. It will not do to reproach the logician for his divorce from linguistic realities, any more than it will do to reproach the abstract painter for not being a representational artist; but one may justly reproach him if he *claims* to be a representational artist.   (*Ibid.*: 81)

About conjunctions, Strawson claimed that

'They got married and had a child' or 'He set to work and found a job' are by no means logically equivalent to 'They had a child and got married' or 'He found a job and set to work'   (80)

and comments

We do not string together at random any assertions we consider true; we bring them together, in spoken or written sentences or paragraphs, only when there is some further reason for the *rapprochement*, e.g. when they record successive episodes in a single narrative. And that for the sake of which we conjoin may confer upon the sentences embodying the conjunction logical features at variance with the rules for '&'. Thus we have seen that a statement of the form 'p and q' may carry the implication of temporal order incompatible with that carried by the corresponding statement 'q and p'.   (81)

On disjunctions, he considers 'Either we catch this bus or we shall have to walk all the way home' and says

Obviously, we should not regard our catching the bus as a sufficient condition for the truth of [this] statement; if it turns out that the bus we caught was not the last one, we should say that the man who had made the statement had been wrong. The truth of one of the alternates is no more a sufficient condition of the truth of the alternative statement than the falsity of the antecedent is a sufficient condition for the truth of the hypothetical statement.   (90)

And on conditionals he says

The standard or primary use of an 'if . . . then . . .' statement [is] where, not knowing whether some statement which could be made by the use of a sentence corresponding in a certain way to the first clause of the hypothetical is true or not, or believing it to be false, we nevertheless consider that a step in reasoning from that statement to a statement related in a similar manner to the second clause would be a sound or reasonable step. (83)

30.3 CONVERSATIONAL IMPLICATURE

In his William James Lectures, delivered at Harvard in 1967, entitled 'Logic and Conversation', Grice argued that phenomena such as those adduced by Strawson do not demonstrate a difference in meaning between the natural-language words and the logical symbols. They can be pragmatically explained, in terms of something's being a reasonable thing to say: 'I wish . . . to maintain that the common assumption of the contestants [the 'formalists' and 'informalists'] . . . is a . . . mistake, and that the mistake arises from inadequate attention to the nature and importance of the conditions governing conversation' (1989: 24).

Grice had two targets in his lectures. One was the prevalent habit, in the ordinary-language philosophy of the recent past, of asking 'Would one *say* such-and-such, in such-and-such circumstances?', and drawing consequences about the nature of the concepts involved. He cites a catalogue of examples. The fact that one wouldn't *say* 'It looks red to me', when looking under normal conditions at a clearly red object, does not show that the 'looks' statement isn't true in these circumstances. The use of this non-committal form of words, rather than simply saying 'It's red', is to be expected only if there is some reason to doubt the stronger statement. But that is to be explained in terms of the propriety of a conversational remark, not in terms of a peculiarly limited applicability of the 'looks' vocabulary. A similar point is made about Ryle's claim that 'in their ordinary employment "voluntary" and "involuntary" are used . . . as adjectives applying to actions which ought not to be done'. Outside this context, we must beware of 'an unwitting extension of the ordinary use of "voluntary" and "involuntary" on the part of philosophers' (1949: 69).

Speaking is a rational activity, and one needs reasons for saying something, beyond taking it to be true. Hearers make inferences not just from the content of what is said, but from the fact that you said it. And if you violate the principles governing conversation, you can mislead your audience without saying anything false. Grice invented the term 'implicature'[2] for what is 'implicated' by the fact that you say something, beyond the content of what is said. The kind of implicature with which he is primarily concerned he calls 'conversational implicature' (which he distinguishes from 'conventional implicature' carried by certain words like 'but', 'moreover', 'nevertheless'). He lists a number of maxims of conversational practice, classified under the categories, Quantity, Quality, Relation and Manner:

Quantity: (1) Make your contribution as informative as is required (for the current purposes of the exchange). (2) Do not make your contribution more informative than is required.

Quality: Try to make your contribution one that is true, i.e. (1) do not say what you believe to be false; (2) do not say that for which you lack adequate evidence.

---

[2] The term has since made its way into the English language: it is given in *The Chambers Dictionary*, 2003 edition, in Grice's sense, with an example of his kind (with no mention of philosophy or linguistics, or of Grice).

Relation: Be relevant.

Manner: Be perspicuous. (1) Avoid obscurity of expression. (2) Avoid ambiguity. (3) Be brief (avoid unnecessary prolixity). (4) Be orderly.

It is presumably 'Be orderly' which is meant to explain the perceived difference between 'She got married and had a baby' and 'She had a baby and got married' which, if Grice is right, must share a truth-value, though they carry different implicatures. But the maxim that does most explanatory work, in both the philosophical examples and the case of the logical constants, is the first Maxim of Quantity: make your contribution as informative as is required. Violation of this maxim is misleading. I am asked how many people attended my lecture. I say 'Less than a hundred'. Three people attended. I (knowingly) spoke truly, but left you with the wrong impression, as you assume I gave as good an estimate as I could. The same applies if I say 'I just saw part of the butler's body in the cellar' when I saw the butler going about his everyday business there. Closer to our topic, I am asked where John is. I know he is in the pub, and I know that he never goes near libraries. I say 'He is either in the pub or the library.' I speak truly but mislead you into thinking that this is all the information I have. And an example of a negated conjunction (Lewis, 1976: 143): 'You won't eat those and live', I say of some wholesome and delicious mushrooms, knowing that you will now leave them alone, deferring to my expertise. You don't eat them, so what I said was true (as I had good reason to believe it would be), but I misled you.

How is one to decide whether something is a conversational implicature rather than part of the content of what is said? A feature of conversational implicature is that it is cancellable, either explicitly: 'They went to France and Spain; I don't mean to imply that they went in that order', or contextually: 'I did my BA in London and my A-levels in Manchester.'[3] If the temporal order were part of the meaning of the conjunction, it would not be cancellable: to say 'They went to France and then to Spain; I don't mean to imply that they did so in that order' is as incoherent as 'My car is red; I don't mean to imply that it is coloured.' With disjunctions, it is normally a violation of the Maxim of Quantity to assert a disjunction when you are in a position to assert one of the disjuncts, but in special circumstances one may say 'The prize is in either the garden or the attic. I'm not going to tell you which.'

Against the claim that the constants sometimes have their truth-functional sense, and sometimes a stronger sense, Grice states his Modified Occam's Razor: senses are not to be multiplied beyond necessity. This also implies that senses are to be kept weak rather than strong, thin rather than thick, for thick senses would not apply to all cases. The fact that we typically assert a disjunction on grounds which do not license the assertion of either disjunct is adequately accounted for by its truth-functional sense together with general principles governing conversation, and this explanation is to be preferred to postulation of further senses of 'or'.

---

[3] This example comes from Robyn Carston (2002: 233). General knowledge (at least in Britain) of the order in which one does A-levels and BAs dissipates any oddity in the reversal of the temporal order.

What are we to make of Strawson's claim, concerning 'Either we catch this bus or we shall have to walk all the way home', that 'obviously', we should not regard our catching the bus as sufficient condition for its truth, and 'if it turns out that the bus we caught was not the last one, we should say that the man who had made the statement had been wrong'? This last remark is rather rash: he has identified the most obvious reason for making this statement, but by no means the only one. Perhaps we are likely to meet someone we wish to avoid if we take a later bus. Perhaps we are on a strict exercise regime: if we catch this bus, we'll make it to the gym, but if we don't, walking home is the only way of fulfilling the requirements. Perhaps we were given money for the bus in order to be home in time for dinner, and if we miss this bus, we shall be too late for dinner, and shall be obliged to return the money. Naturally, one is expected to have some reason for what one says, but people can have different reasons for the same thing, and the question arises: what are all these reasons *for*? The truth table gives the answer: they are reasons for the claim that one or the other of the disjuncts is true.

Also, one can be right by luck, or wrong by bad luck. My reasons may be quite spurious for saying that John is either in Oxford or in London, but if it turns out by some fluke that he is in Oxford, I was right.

Grice cites further evidence of the truth-functional meaning of 'or': 'It is not the case that either A or B' seems just to say that neither A nor B; and 'to say "Suppose that A or B" seems to be to invite someone to suppose merely that one of the two disjuncts is true' (1989: 45–6).[4] Thus he commits himself to the view that when a compound sentence is embedded in a longer sentence—for instance, when it is negated, or occurs as one disjunct of a disjunction or as the antecedent of a conditional—it is only its truth-functional meaning which contributes to the meaning of the longer sentence. This commitment is central to the defence of the truth-functional account: the point of the truth table for '&' (say) is not only to give the truth conditions of conjunctions standing alone, but also to show how conjunctions contribute to the meaning of longer sentences. This commitment has been the source of much criticism, as we shall see in Section 30.5

Grice devotes most attention to the case of the indicative conditional. According to the logic books, 'If A, B' is equivalent to 'Either not A, or B', so defence of the truth-functional conditional follows the same lines as the defence of truth-functional disjunction: it would be a violation of principles governing conversation, and hence misleading, to assert 'If A, B' knowing just that $\neg A$, or just that B; for in these circumstances one could make the briefer, more informative statement: $\neg A$; or alternatively B. Just as it would be misleading but true to say 'He's either in the pub or the library' knowing that he is in the pub and never goes near libraries, so for 'If he's not in the pub he's in the library', in the same circumstances. Similarly if I say 'You won't eat those and live', knowing that you won't eat them, and knowing that they are wholesome, I mislead but do not lie, and the same goes for 'If you eat those you will die', or

---

[4] We shall see later (Section 30.5.5) that there is a problem about disjunctive suppositions and disjunctive antecedents.

better, 'If you eat those, they will kill you.' Provided you don't eat them—and I have reason to think you won't—what I said was true, but misleading.

Grice argues for the cancellability of the implicature as follows. I say 'I know just where Smith is and what he is doing, but all I will tell you is that if he is in the library he is working.' No one would be surprised, he says, if it turned out that my basis for saying this was that I had just looked in the library and found him working. But that is the relatively easy case: many non-truth-functionalists will agree with the top two lines of the truth table, i.e. agree that a conditional is true if its antecedent and consequent are true. If it turned out that I had just seen Smith on the football pitch, and moreover I know that he visits libraries only to read newspapers, not many would agree that my conditional remark was true.

Grice is aware of this difficulty, and points to a disanalogy between disjunctions and conditionals. *Pace* Strawson, it is natural to see a disjunction as confirmed—verified, established—by the discovery that one of its disjuncts is true. Yet no one takes the discovery that the antecedent is false as establishing that a conditional is true (1989: 63). No one would take the fact that you don't eat the mushrooms as establishing the truth of my remark 'If you eat them they will kill you.' This is more than a difficulty: it looks like a direct refutation of the claim that our use of conditionals conforms to the truth function.

He points out another 'serious difficulty' (1989: 80): 'It is not the case that if *A*, *B*' does not seem to mean the same as the negation of the truth-functional conditional, which is equivalent to '*A*&¬*B*'. Of an unseen geometrical figure, I may say 'It's not the case that if it's a pentagon it has six sides.' But I am not willing to say that it is a pentagon and does not have six sides: for all I know, it is not a pentagon (in which case the truth-functional 'Pentagon ⊃ six sides' is true). Grice goes on to examine various ways the assertion of the negation of a conditional might be interpreted: the assertion of a contrary conditional; the denial that the conditional is assertible. This is all very well, but it is hard to square with the thesis being advanced: that the truth functions are correct accounts of the meanings of 'if' and 'it is not the case that'.

30.4 PRAGMATICS AND THE CONDITIONAL

30.4.1

Missing from Grice's discussion is any very powerful reason why we should think that the truth function gives the meaning of 'if', as opposed to a simplified, near-relative of 'if' the advantage of whose clarity outweighs the oddities it engenders, at least in mathematical reasoning. (He merely offers a highly artificial example of a conventional Bridge bid which is supposed to mean 'If I have a red king, I also have a black king.') There *are* powerful reasons for thinking that 'if' is truth-functional. There are facts about our acceptance of conditionals which (it seems) only the truth-functional account (henceforth TF) can explain. Any rival account of the truth conditions of conditionals gives them stronger truth conditions: it is not enough that the truth function is satisfied; something more is required. Yet, when all I know of relevance is either A or B, I will readily infer that if not A, B. Return to the case where I am told 'The prize is either in the garden or the attic; I'm not going to tell you which.' Assuming my informant to be reliable and honest, I head for the garden thinking 'If it's not in the garden, it's in the attic.' Nothing more than the (truth-functional) disjunction is required. It is very hard to see how this can be explained on the hypothesis that conditionals have stronger truth conditions, for then the disjunction does not entail the conditional, so how could knowing just the disjunction be enough to license the conditional?

On the other hand, as we have seen, there are equally compelling reasons for stronger, non-truth-functional truth conditions (henceforth NTF). We may both believe that the Tories won't win, yet disagree about what will happen if they do. Believing that $\neg A$ leaves one free to reject 'If A, B'. This seems to imply that the conditional may be either true or false when its antecedent is false: something further is required for its truth. Whichever horn of this dilemma one opts for, pragmatics must be appealed to to dispel the attraction of the other.

There is a third alternative, due originally to F. P. Ramsey (1929), and developed by Ernest Adams (1975). Conditionals do not express propositions. A conditional statement does not make a claim about how things are, true or false as the case may be. They are essentially hypothetical judgements. When we make a conditional judgement, we suppose that A, and make a hypothetical judgement about B, under that supposition. Two propositions are involved, but they play different roles—one as the content of a supposition, one as the content of a hypothetical belief or assertion, under the supposition—and they do not combine into a single proposition which is believed or asserted. I have defended this 'suppositional theory' (henceforth Supp) elsewhere (e.g. Edgington 2001, 2003), and will not give a detailed defence here, but it needs some exposition because it plays a role in some of the pragmatic strategies that have been adopted for conditionals.

Uncertain conditional judgements are at the heart of Ramsey's and Adams's work. Our uncertain judgements are assumed, idealizing somewhat, to conform to the rules of probability, and there we find a valuable conditional concept, that of a conditional probability—the probability of B on the supposition that A, written $p(B|A)$. Supposing that A amounts to setting aside the possibility that $\neg A$, and focusing on the possibilities A&B and A&$\neg$B. If you think that A&B is about ten times more likely than A&$\neg$B, you think it is about 10 to 1 that B if A.

Uncertain judgements present further problems for TF. Suppose you think it unlikely that A, i.e. likely that $\neg A$. Then, for any B, you must, if consistent, think it likely that at least one of the propositions $\{\neg A, B\}$ is true, i.e. likely that $\neg A \lor B$, i.e. likely that $A \supset B$: TF implies that all conditionals with unlikely antecedents are likely to be true. This is intolerable. We need to be able to distinguish between believable and unbelievable conditionals whose antecedents we judge to be unlikely: 'I don't think I'll need to get in touch, but if I do, I'll need a phone number'; not: 'I don't think I'll need to get in touch, but if I do, I'll manage by telepathy.'

Supp solves the dilemma with which this section begins. If I know *just* that $A \lor B$ (I don't know which), then, on the supposition that $\neg A$, I must conclude that B. Here Supp agrees with the TF. On the other hand, the fact that I think it likely that $\neg A$, leaves me free to judge $A\&B$ less likely than $A\&\neg B$, and so to reject 'If A, B'. For example, suppose I think it is about 90 per cent likely that Sue won't be offered the job, 9 per cent likely that she will be offered and accept, one per cent likely that she will be offered and decline. The conditional probability that she will decline, on the supposition that she is offered the job, is 10 per cent. Here Supp agrees with NTF, that one may consistently disbelieve A, and disbelieve 'If A, B'. For TF, this is not possible. It is 91 per cent likely that (Either she won't be offered the job, or she will be offered it and decline). Hence, the probability of (Offered $\supset$ Decline) is 91 per cent.

30.4.2

David Lewis (1976) proved that there is no proposition A^*B the probability of whose truth can be systematically equated with $p(B|A)$, thus underlining the fact that Supp does not treat conditionals as propositions. While finding Supp attractive, he was not prepared to give up truth conditions for conditionals. He argued that indicative conditionals have truth-functional truth conditions but, for Grice's reasons, are assertible only if the conditional probability of consequent given antecedent is high. He appealed to the Gricean maxim 'assert the stronger rather than the weaker (when you have sufficient grounds for the stronger, and when the stronger is relevant)'. We then get some algebra—not totally impenetrable qua algebra, but somewhat obscure why it is the right bit of algebra for the purpose—to show that we must subtract a factor which involves $p(\neg A)$ from $p(A \supset B)$ to get a measure of the assertibility of 'If A, B'—lo and behold, $p(B|A)$ (*Ibid.* 142–3).

However, there is no way of using Gricean considerations to show that conditionals are assertible when one has a high probability for B given A. Indeed, Gricean considerations show that thesis to be false. Supp is primarily a theory of conditional belief, not of assertibility; and Gricean principles show that not everything you are in a position to believe is a reasonable thing to say. Consider this case: you believe A and B. Then it will usually be misleading for you to say 'If A, B', for this is weaker than what you are in a position to say. For instance, you are asked who is coming to the party. You know that Ann is coming, and you know that Bob is coming, and you also know that there is no relevant connection between these two facts. It is misleading to say 'Bob is coming if Ann is.' But a high $p(A\&B)$ guarantees a high $p(B|A)$. Here the suppositional part is, as it were, idle: suppose that Ann is coming (I already know she is); under that supposition, is Bob coming? Yes. This is an acceptable but boring conditional belief, on a par with the belief that Ann or Bob is coming when I know that they are both coming, but not a reasonable thing to say.

Another case: I believe that the match will be cancelled, because all the players are ill. I believe that whether or not it rains, the match will be cancelled: if it rains, the match will be cancelled, and if it doesn't rain, the match will be cancelled. But I would mislead, for Gricean reasons, by saying, if asked whether the match will be played, 'If it rains, the match will be cancelled.'[5]

Grice identified a real phenomenon. I don't think he succeeds in his defence of TF, but everyone's theory of conditionals or of anything else must allow that there are cases where one has grounds for believing something which, in a normal conversational context, would not be a reasonable remark to make.

30.4.3

Frank Jackson (1979, 1980–1, 1987) argues in a different way that the truth-functional truth conditions are correct, but 'If A, B' is assertible when $p(B|A)$ is high.[6] But have we not, a couple of paragraphs back, refuted that thesis? No, because Jackson means something different by 'assertible'. He uses a different spelling: 'assertable' for the notion which is sensitive to Gricean considerations about what is a reasonable thing to say in conversation, 'assertible' for his notion, which abstracts from these considerations. Something is assertible, for Jackson, if (a) the speaker gives it a high probability of truth and (b) the speaker is not violating any rules concerning terms carrying conventional implicatures. 'If', he claims, carries a conventional implicature, as do words like 'but', 'even', 'nevertheless'. These words do not contribute to the truth-conditional content of what is said. Their role is to aid the transfer of information from speaker to hearer. They do not change the content of what is being transferred.

What then is the conventional implicature associated with 'if'? In saying 'If A, B', the speaker not only communicates her belief that $A \supset B$, i.e. $\neg A \vee B$, but also signals that this belief is 'robust' with respect to the antecedent A. In his earliest writings, this means that the speaker signals that she would not give up her belief in $(A \supset B)$ were she to learn that A (call this robustness$_1$). Therefore, she doesn't believe $(A \supset B)$ just because she believes that $\neg A$; for if that were the case, and she learned that A, she would change her mind about the conditional. Robustness makes asserted conditionals fit to be used in inferring by modus ponens, for they survive the learning of A, hence enabling the inference to B.

He claimed that this is equivalent to having a high degree of belief in $A \supset B$ given A, i.e. that it obtains when $p((A \supset B)|A)$ is high, i.e. $p((\neg A \vee B)|A)$ is high, i.e. $p(B|A)$ is high (call this robustness$_2$).

Unfortunately, as Jackson soon learned, these two characterizations of robustness are not equivalent. The most famous kind of counterexample to the alleged equivalence is due to Richmond Thomason, reported by Bas van Fraassen (1980: 503). There are many things we are likely never to know; consequently, there are many things I'm prepared to assert of the form 'If A, I'll never find out (or, no one will ever

---

[5] Note that I don't believe *every* conditional whose consequent is 'the match will be cancelled': I don't believe 'If all the players make a very speedy recovery, the match will be cancelled'.

[6] Lewis (1986: 152–6) came to accept Jackson's account as preferable to his own.

know).' For example, if there was a chaffinch on this lawn a hundred years ago today, I'll never find out (or no one will ever know). I have a high probability for the consequent on the assumption of the antecedent. But were I, surprisingly, to learn that the antecedent is true (say, by coming across a bird-watcher's diary that inspires total confidence), I would not come to believe that I will never find out that it is true! On the contrary, I will reject my previous conditional belief.[7]

So Jackson's official account of conditionals uses robustness$_2$: a conditional is true iff $(A \supset B)$ and assertible iff, in addition, $p((A \supset B|A)$, i.e. $p(B|A)$ is high.

My main complaint against Grice's defence of TF is this: Grice laudably showed that reasons for believing something are insufficient reasons for saying it. But in the case of conditionals, in a large class of cases, people don't believe them, indeed, disbelieve them, although the truth-functional truth condition is satisfied. On the face of it, the same objection applies to Jackson: he is committed to the view that 'If A, B' is probably true whenever A is probably false. So someone who thinks it unlikely that the Tories will win, must think it likely to be true that if they win they will nationalize the car industry. But that is not the way we think. If you and I agree that the Tories won't win, that leaves us free to disagree about what will happen if they do win. And this is a non-optional, important part of our mental life.

Jackson is well aware of this objection (1980–1: 132–3; 1987: 39–40). Here another strand in his thinking emerges. It is an error theory (or once he has freed us from error, a 'convenient fiction' theory). We speak and think as if there were a proposition $A * B$ such that $p(A * B) = p(B|A)$. But Lewis and others have proved that there is not.

I find this hard to square with the official theory. Return to the example of Sue, of whom we think that it is 90 per cent likely that she will not be offered the job, 9 per cent likely that she will be offered and accept, one per cent likely that she will be offered and decline. According to Jackson's official theory we think it's 91 per cent likely to be true that if she is offered the job she will decline; but this is not assertible, in the sense in which 'Even Gödel understood first-order logic' is not assertible. According to the error theory, we think it is 10 per cent likely to be true that if she is offered she will decline, but this is an illusion (or a pretence). The theories seem to say incompatible things about how likely we think it is that a conditional is true.

The charge of incompatibility could be avoided if it is maintained that what we are really up to when we assert conditionals is deeply hidden from consciousness. Admittedly, controversy amongst philosophers shows that the correct account of these matters is not manifestly obvious. Still, a theory which maintains that competent, intelligent folk systematically and incorrigibly make wrong judgements in a large class of cases, is hard to swallow. It also makes the official theory wonderfully immune to counterexamples. It's no good objecting that no one who thinks that the Republicans won't win thinks 'If the Republicans win, they will double income tax'

---

[7] This is not the only kind of counterexample to the equation of robustness$_1$ and robustness$_2$. I discuss others in Edgington (1995) and Edgington (forthcoming).

is probably true, albeit unassertible: of course not, says Jackson, they are under the illusion that it is probably false.

The error theory comes into its own in Jackson's discussion of the validity of inferences: 'I am committed to gross misperceptions of validity in the case of inferences involving indicative conditionals' (1987: 48). Conventional implicatures, he claims, get in the way of our perception of validity. We confuse truth-preservation with assertibility preservation. Once more, the theory is immune to counterexamples in the form of arguments we take to be invalid which are valid on the truth-functional reading of 'if'.

Jackson must hold that we *should* judge 'If the Republicans win, they will double income tax' to be probably true, albeit unassertible, when it is improbable that they will win. But it is quite unclear why we should—would we better off if we judged all conditionals with improbable antecedents to be probably true? The error theory involves less error than the official theory: it gives the right answer to how likely we think it is that Sue will decline if she is offered the job, rather than describing this as a proposition which is 91 per cent probable but 10 per cent assertible. If there is an error, it is a harmless one of too liberal a use of the words 'true' and 'false', to which it would be pedantic to object. And a little rephrasing or re-punctuation eliminates the error: 'you mean that it's likely to be false that she will decline, on the assumption that she is offered the job?'

30.4.4

Let us now turn to Stalnaker's influential NTF theory. Stalnaker (1968) was the first to offer a possible-worlds semantics for conditionals, and it was motivated by Ramsey's thought that we assess conditionals by supposing the antecedent—adding it hypothetically to our stock of knowledge—and assessing the consequent under that supposition:

Now that we have found an answer to the question 'How do we decide whether or not to believe a conditional statement?' [Ramsey's answer] the problem is to make the transition from belief conditions to truth conditions. . . . The concept of a *possible world* is just what we need to make the transition, since a possible world is the analogue of a stock of hypothetical beliefs. The following is a first approximation to the account I shall propose: Consider a possible world in which A is true and otherwise differs minimally from the actual world. 'If A, then B' is true (false) just in case B is true (false) in that possible world. (1968: 33–4)

Stalnaker treats both indicative and subjunctive conditionals along these lines:

'If A, B' is true at w iff B is true at F(A, w)

where F is a 'selection function' which selects, for any proposition A and any world w, a world w' which is the 'closest' world to w at which A is true. But there are pragmatic constraints on the selection function—i.e. on which A-worlds count as closest to the actual world or to any other world—which differ for the two kinds of conditionals.

The pragmatic constraint for indicative conditionals is set in the framework of conversational dynamics. At any stage in a conversation, many things are taken for granted between speaker and hearer, i.e. many possibilities are taken as already ruled out. The remaining possibilities are live. Call the set of worlds which have not been ruled out—the live possibilities—the context set. For indicative conditionals, antecedents are typically live possibilities, and we focus on that case. The pragmatic constraint for indicative conditionals is that when A is compatible with the context set, the closest A-world is a member of the context set; that is, the closest A-world is a member of the set of live possibilities, not already ruled out.

The proposition expressed by 'If A, B' is the set of worlds w such that the closest A-world to w is a B-world. The ordering of worlds depends on the conversational setting. As different possibilities are live in different conversational settings, it is almost inevitable that a different proposition is expressed by 'If A, B' in different conversational settings.

Let us transpose this to the one-person case: I am talking to myself, i.e. thinking. I suppose that A (which is a live possibility for me). The pragmatic constraint requires that the closest A-world is one compatible with what I take for granted—take myself to know. It is epistemically possible for me. Provided you and I have different bodies of information, the proposition I think when I think 'If A, B' will differ from the one you think when you think something you would express be the same words: the constraints on closeness differ; what counts as 'closest' for me may not be 'closest' for you.

Stalnaker uses this machinery to explain why, although $A \lor B$ does not entail 'If $\neg A$, B', in a context in which we take for granted that $A \lor B$, but don't take for granted that A, 'If $\neg A$, B' is true. There are no $\neg A \& \neg B$-worlds compatible with what we take for granted, but there are some $\neg A$-worlds compatible with what we take for granted. Worlds compatible with what we take for granted, in this context, count as closer than worlds incompatible with what we take for granted. So, in this context, the closest $\neg A$-world must be a B-world.

Start with a context in which we don't take for granted that $A \lor B$, and we are wondering whether, if $\neg A$, B. Here is a list of the possibilities. I write the Stalnaker conditional '$A > B$'.

	$\neg A$	B	$\neg A > B$
1.	T	T	T
2.	T	F	F
3.	F	T	T
4.	F	T	F
5.	F	F	T
6.	F	F	F

Lines 3–6 manifest the non-truth-functionality of '>': when the antecedent is false, that leaves open whether or not the closest antecedent-world is a B-world.

Now we learn that $A \lor B$, nothing stronger. That rules out line 2, and nothing else. For TF and for Supp, that is enough to conclude that if $\neg A$, B. But for NTF, it would seem, it is not enough, for there remain the possibilities 4 and 6 in which $\neg A > B$ is false.

Stalnaker avoids this consequence: once line 2 has been eliminated, we are in a new context, our selection function is based on a new closeness-relation between worlds. We have to select a $\neg A$-world which is compatible with what we take for granted, so it is bound to be a B-world, because there are now no $\neg A \& \neg B$-worlds compatible with what we take for granted. We have not discovered to be true the proposition, if $\neg A$, B, that we were previously uncertain about. There is now a new proposition expressed by the same words, which we know to be true.

This amount of sensitivity to what we take for granted seems to me implausible. One usually distinguishes quite sharply the content of what is said from the epistemic attitude one takes to that content. Someone conjectures that if Ann isn't home, Bob is. We are entirely agnostic about this. Then we discover that at least one them is home (nothing stronger). It seems more natural to say that we have now discovered to be true what we were previously uncertain of (or from Supp's perspective, that we now have a different attitude to the same conditional thought, that B on the supposition that $\neg A$). It does not seem as though the content of our conditional thought has changed.

Also, Stalnaker's argument is restricted to the special case where we take the $\neg A \& \neg B$-possibilities to be ruled out. Consider a case when, starting out agnostic, we become close to certain, but not certain, that $A \lor B$: say we become about 95 per cent certain that $A \lor B$ but are about 50 per cent certain that A. According to Supp, we are entitled to be quite close to certain that if $\neg A$, B: 90 per cent certain, in fact.[8] In this case, no possibilities have been ruled out. There are $\neg A \& \neg B$-worlds as well as $\neg A \& B$-worlds which are permissible candidates for being nearest. The pragmatic constraint is inoperative. Stalnaker has not told us why we should think it likely, in this case, that the nearest $\neg A$-world is a B-world.

Uncertain conditional judgements create difficulties for all propositional theories. It is easy to construct probabilistic counterexamples to TF; and it is easy for the Lewisian variant of Stalnaker's theory that says '$A > B$' is true iff B is true in *all* closest A-worlds. But it is rather harder for Stalnaker's own theory. Here is a putative counterexample.[9] We have no idea how much fuel, if any, there is in the car. Ann is going to drive it along a straight road which is 100 miles long. She will go at constant speed and her car will use fuel at a uniform rate. If the tank is full, she will go exactly 100 miles then stop. If it's empty, she won't start. Otherwise, if her tank is x per cent full she will travel x miles then stop. Bob gives equal credence to the propositions 'She'll stop in the first mile', 'She'll stop in the second mile' and so on.

Now consider the conditionals:

(1) If she stops before half way, she will stop in the 1st mile.

(50) If she stops before half way, she will stop in the 50th mile.

---

[8] If $p(A \lor B) = 95\%$ and $p(A) = 50\%$, $p(\neg A \& B) = 45\%$. $p(\neg A \& \neg B) = 5\%$. So, on the assumption that $\neg A$, it's 45:5, or 9:1, that B.

[9] I owe this example to my student, James Studd, who used it for a different purpose.

According to Supp, these all get the same probability: each gets 2 per cent. This seems reasonable.

Write Stalnaker's truth condition thus:

'$A > B$' is true iff either $A\&B$, or $\neg A$ & the closest A-world is a B-world.

The following assumption is very plausible: consider a world w in which Ann goes more than half way. A world in which she stops in the 50th mile is more similar to w than a world in which she doesn't stop in the 50th mile is similar to w. After all, it is spatially and temporally more similar, more similar in terms of the amount of fuel in the tank, more similar in its likely causes and consequences, etc.

There are two ways in which (1) can be true: (a) she stops in the first mile. (1 per cent likely); (b) she doesn't stop before half way, and in the closest world in which she does stop before half-way, she stops in the first mile. By our assumption, (b) is certainly false. So (1) gets one per cent probability.

There are two ways in which (50) can be true: (a) she stops in the 50th mile (1 per-cent likely); (b) she doesn't stop before half way, and the closest world in which she does stop before half way is one in which she stops in the 50th mile. By our assumption, (b) is true iff she doesn't stop before half way, and so is 50 per cent likely. So (50) gets a probability of 51 per cent.

Thus, Stalnaker's theory appears to give wrong results for uncertain conditional judgements.

30.4.5

Finally a remark about disjunctions in the antecedents of conditionals: 'If either A or B, then C' seems to have two readings. On the first reading, it is equivalent to 'If A, C, and if B, C.' For example, 'If I get Mary or John as a tutor, I'll pass' seems to be equivalent to 'If I get Mary as a tutor, I'll pass; and if I get John as a tutor, I'll pass.' In Supp's terms, this reading goes: suppose that A, or alternatively suppose that B; either way, C. In Stalnaker's terms it is something like 'Select the nearest A-world, or alternatively select the nearest B-world; either way, the world you select is a C-world.

The second reading: make one single supposition, that '$A \vee B$' is true. For instance, there are two candidates in the election, X and Y. I probably won't vote, but if I vote for either of them, X or Y, I'll vote for X. We don't want this remark to entail 'If I vote for Y, I'll vote for X.' Or, someone says she thinks that John is in France or Italy' and I say, 'Well, if he's in France or Italy, he's in Rome: that's the only place in France or Italy he ever goes.' Supposing it's true that he's in France or Italy, he's in Rome. The nearest world in which it's true that he's in France or Italy is one in which he is in Rome. This reading doesn't entail 'If he's in France he's in Rome.'

The first reading seems the commoner, and leads to an apparent problem about the substitution of logically equivalent propositions in antecedents. I'm pretty sure the match is not wet and other conditions conducive to lighting obtain. 'If you strike the match it will light', I say. The antecedent is equivalent to 'You strike it and it's wet, or you strike it and it's not wet.' But 'If you strike and it's wet, or if you strike it and it's not wet, it will light' sounds wrong! On the first reading, we don't really have a disjunctive antecedent at all; you're given the choice of two antecedents from each of which the consequent follows.

On TF, we do have $(A \lor B) \supset C$ equivalent to $(A \supset C)\&(B \supset C)$. So, on TF, 'If you strike it, it will light' is equivalent to 'If you strike it and it's wet, it will light, and if you strike it and it's not wet, it will light.' This is not an advantage: since Adams's and Stalnaker's work, we have appreciated the fact that strengthening of the antecedent is not valid for conditionals: 'If you strike it, it will light' does not commit me to 'If you strike it and it's wet, it will light.' The conditional probability of consequent given antecedent can be high for the first and low for the second. The nearest possible world in which the antecedent is true is one in which the consequent is true for the first, and not the second.

30.5 RADICAL PRAGMATICS: CONJUNCTION AND NEGATION

A number of philosophers and linguists now give pragmatics a larger role in communication than that emphasized by Grice: they argue that the meaning of a sentence uttered (even given assignments of references to pronouns and demonstratives) typically underdetermines the proposition expressed.[10] Linguistic knowledge needs to be supplemented by pragmatic inference for any communication to take place. One school of thought of this kind is the Relevance Theory of Dan Sperber and Deirdre Wilson (1986/95). See Relevance Theory—New Directions and Developments. As well as Grice's implicatures, their theory employs the notion of an 'explicature': the proposition actually expressed, which is derived from the linguistic meaning of the sentence uttered, supplemented by pragmatics. A work in this framework which pays attention to some logical constants is Robyn Carston's *Thoughts and Utterances* (2002). Chapters 3 and 4 are on the pragmatics of 'and'-conjunction, and the pragmatics of negation, respectively.

On 'and', Carston agrees with Grice that pairs of sentences such as 'He took off his boots and got into bed' and 'He got into bed and took off his boots' do not differ in linguistic meaning. But that is not to say that utterances of these sentences express the same proposition. The proposition expressed depends on pragmatics as well as linguistic meaning, and typically involves a temporal ordering of the events.

She points out the variety of relations that may be conveyed by conjunctions, other than mere temporal sequence:

> He handed her the scalpel and she made an incision.
> We spent the day in town and I went to Harrods.

---

[10] Among philosophers who take this line are Kent Bach (2005); Stephen Neale (2005); François Recanati (1989); Charles Travis (1997). Needless to say, there are significant disagreements between them.

She shot him in the head and he died instantly.

He left her and she took to the bottle.

He was short-sighted and mistook her for a hatstand.

She went to the yoga class and found it very calming.

I forgot to hide the cake and the children ate it.

Although all these are asymmetric[11], they cannot all be paraphrased with 'and then'. It is extremely implausible that 'and' is multiply ambiguous. Firstly, there is no expectation that lexical ambiguity will carry over to other languages. Secondly, if, in each of these examples, we eliminate 'and' in favour of a full stop between two sentences, the same message will be conveyed; and it can hardly be claimed that the full stop is multiply ambiguous![12] Thirdly, the natural reading is cancellable, if highly artificially: 'She shot him in the head and he died instantly, but not as a result of her shot' is not a contradiction in terms; nor is 'I forgot to hide the cake and the children ate it; but they would have found it and eaten it even if I had hidden it.' And as we have already seen, reversal of the temporal order is permissible when the order of events is presumed to be already known: 'I did my BA in London and my A-levels in Manchester'; 'The plant died and it was Mary who forgot to water it'; and

A: Did John break the vase?

B: Well, it broke and he dropped it.

Like Grice, Carston favours 'minimal univocal semantics with pragmatic enrichment', but unlike Grice, she claims that the pragmatic enrichment is needed to generate the explicit content of what is communicated. The main reason for this claim is that the pragmatic enrichment is preserved when the conjunction is embedded in longer sentences. She cites a principle formulated by Recanati (1989: 91)

A pragmatically determined aspect of meaning is part of [the content of] what is said (and, therefore, not a conversational implicature) if—and perhaps only if—it falls within the scope of logical operators such as negation and conditionals.

Consider

(1) If he took to drink and she left him, it serves him right.

(2) If she left him and he took to drink, he deserves some sympathy.

(3) Either she got married and had a baby, or she had a baby and got married, I don't know which.

(4) It is better to drive home and drink three beers than to drink three beers and drive home. (Wilson, 1975: 151)

(5) She didn't make a lot of money and go to live in Bermuda; she went to live in Bermuda and made a lot of money.

---

[11] After a list like this it is worth reminding ourselves that there are plenty of conjunctions which do not concern sequences of events or episodes, and are symmetric: 'John is a teacher and Mary is an artist.'

[12] Interestingly, as Carston points out, the full stop and the 'and' are not always interchangeable: the former allows for some relations between sentences not permitted by the latter. For instance, 'He broke his leg. He fell off a step ladder' is fine, the latter sentence being an explanation of the first. But the two sentences conjoined in that order by 'and' yields a sentence which is bizarre, would demand a very special context, and would not convey that the second was an explanation of the first.

If Grice is right, and '*A&B*' expresses the same proposition as '*B&A*' none of the above examples make much sense. I could accept both (1) and (2) despite the fact that their consequents conflict (the consequent of (1) could just as well be 'he deserves no sympathy'). (3) is of the form '*A* or *A*, I don't know which'; (4) says that *A* is better than *A*; (5) says 'Not *A*; *A*'.[13]

Assume for the time being that the thesis of pragmatic enrichment of content is correct. What then is the 'minimal univocal semantics' for 'and'? Is it given by the truth table? Carston does not think so, for this would involve a mixture of levels: at the minimal semantic level, one does not usually have any truth-evaluable propositions to feed into the truth function. She comes to no definite conclusion about the lexical meaning of 'and'—if any: she considers and does not reject the possibility that it has no lexical meaning at all (256; 257). I don't see how this can be right: it may be eliminable in favour of a full stop when it is the main connective, but it plays an essential role in the embedded clauses found in (1)–(5) above. She also considers the possibility that it functions as an instruction to treat the sentences it connects as a single unit for semantic processing (*Ibid.*). Maybe so, but this must be true of sentence-connectives in general, and not peculiar to 'and'.

I see no compelling reason to deny that semantically, 'and' is truth-functional. Granting pragmatic enrichment, it is the sentences 'and' connects which get enriched: 'He took off his boots and got into bed (a little later).' 'He handed her the scalpel and she (then) made an incision (with the scalpel).' 'We spent the day in town and I went to Harrods (during that day).' 'She shot him in the head and (as a result of the former) he died instantly.' Recall that the same effects are generated by a full stop between two sentences. It is not specially the 'and' which does the enriching, but general pragmatic principles governing the assignment of times to the events described, with causal and other implications added on as appropriate. And even if it were specially the 'and' that does the enriching, its semantic meaning could still be that it operates truth-functionally on the pragmatically enriched content of the sentences it connects.

When Carston turns to negation, this is the kind of conclusion she reaches concerning so-called 'metalinguistic negation', exemplified by

We didn't see hippopotamuses. We saw hippopotami.
She's not pleased at the outcome; she's thrilled to bits.

Here she argues, against numerous opponents, that we need not postulate a nonstandard use of negation. Rather, we pragmatically enrich the sentences negated: they express something like 'It's not the case that what we saw are properly called "hippotamuses"'; and ' "Pleased" would not be an appropriate way of describing her.' Thus she saves the thesis that negation is semantically univocal, and indeed, truth-functional. I suggest that if this move is permissible for negation, it is permissible for conjunction also: enrich the sentences conjoined without tampering with the meaning of the conjoining device, 'and'.

---

[13] This difficulty for Grice was first pointed out by Cohen (1971).

Before returning to conjunction, I shall make a brief comment on the other main problem discussed in Carston's chapter on negation: the 'scope ambiguity' in sentences such as 'All the children haven't passed the exam', 'Fred didn't scrub the potatoes with sand-paper in the bath-tub at midnight' and the notorious 'The present King of France is not bald.' Here she agrees with Grice (1970/1989) : semantically, negation has wide scope, and narrow-scope readings are pragmatic enrichments, appropriate when some part of the remark is taken for granted, as common ground, not up for question. In many remarks of the form 'The F is not G' it will be taken as uncontroversial that there is a unique salient F, and so what is being denied is that it is G. But this is pragmatic rather than semantic: 'The King of France is not bald: there is no King of France' is quite in order.

Now it is convenient for Grice and Carston that the wide-scope reading is the weak reading, in the cases they discuss, and hence ripe for pragmatic enrichment. But not all scope ambiguities involving negation have this structure. Consider this example:

The Head of Department will never be an octogenarian.

This could be a comment on the limited life expectancy of Ann, the present Head of Department; or it could be a comment on the fact that rules require that whoever is Head retire before the age of eighty. The two readings are logically independent. Neither reading (out of context) is to be preferred to the other. They have roughly the forms:

Concerning the present Head of Department, there is not a future time t at which she will be an octogenarian.

It is not the case that there is a future time t at which the Head of Department at t is an octogenarian.

Hence I am inclined to the more traditional view that these sentences are semantically ambiguous because they are syntactically ambiguous, represented by different logical forms.

Return to conjunctions. It is not uncontroversial that we must treat the temporal implications of conjunctions purely as a matter of pragmatics. In examples like 'John came in and sat down', Jeffrey King and Jason Stanley (2005) claim that 'according to most twenty-first-century syntactic theories' (144) each verb has a time indication in its logical form: John came in at t and sat down at t'. Certainly, context is required to determine what the time references are. But this is a standard case of reference-fixing, a proper part of semantics. They quote a general maxim, formulated by Barbara Partee (1984: 254) 'there is a past reference time r-p specified at the start of the discourse, and . . . the introduction of new event sentences moves the reference time forward'. On the basis of this, t' is later than t. Admittedly, this is described as a pragmatic maxim, for it establishes a norm, from which there may be exceptions; but this is pragmatics only to the extent that pragmatic procedures are engaged in establishing the reference of pronouns like 'she' or demonstratives like 'that man'. This is an instance of a bold, general thesis defended by Stanley (2000: 391): all context-dependence which affects truth conditions results from fixing the values of contextually sensitive elements in the real structure of natural language sentences. King and Stanley offer an analysis of the more complex example (4), along the same lines (146).

If temporal factors can be treated along familiar semantic lines, what about the conjunctions which seem to impute causal connections? These seem less entrenched, riding on the back of the temporal factors. One could not deny that causation was involved by saying 'It's not the case that he pushed her and she fell.' Often, it would seem, they could be treated as conversational implicatures. The difficulty is that the causal implication seems to survive embedding in the antecedents of conditionals, as in (1) and (2) above. Here Stanley adopts Stalnaker's theory of indicative conditionals: we are speaking of a 'close possible world' in which the antecedent is true. Closeness is a contextually sensitive matter. The temporal relations are built into the semantics. And it may well be that the relevant 'close' possible worlds to consider are those in which not only temporal but also causal relations hold. Similarly on the suppositional theory: consider 'Suppose that he pushed her and she fell'; I could go on to say that it doesn't necessarily follow that the push caused the fall. Nevertheless, that would typically be thought to be much the most likely way the supposition would be true, and affect what one took the likely consequences of the supposition to be.

Despite her defence of univocal, truth-functional negation, Carston hints at a conception of semantics very different from the classical conception. She voices the suspicion that the origin of classical semantics in logic has distorted our theories of linguistic processing. She quotes with approval Pieter Seuren (2000: 289) who says 'The logical properties of the sentences of natural languages are best seen as epiphenomenal on the semantic and cognitive processing of the sentences in question. They emerge when semantic processes and properties are looked at from the point of view of preservation of truth through sequences of sentences, which is the defining question of logic, not of semantics.' And she says 'The truth relation holds between thoughts and states of affairs, so between propositions expressed by utterances (semantic/pragmatic hybrids) and states of affairs. Then, it is systems of thought, rather than linguistic systems, for which a truth calculus, that is, a logic, should be devised. If this is right, there is no obvious reason to suppose . . . that what natural-language connectives . . . encode is identical to the context-free, truth-based properties of the logical operators' (257).

In his inaugural lecture, 'Meaning and Truth' (1969), Strawson speaks of the 'Homeric struggle' between the formal semanticists and the theorists of communication intention (5). On the question of how much of linguistic communication can be explained by semantics as opposed to pragmatics, the battles continue. As far as the sentential logical constants are concerned, no great damage has been done to the logician's treatment of 'and', 'or' and 'not'. But the logician's 'if' is a technical concept. The advantages of its simplicity and clarity arguably outweigh its defects in mathematical reasoning. Outside mathematics, especially because uncertain conditional judgements matter, its use would be intolerable. Pragmatics is a valuable discipline, but one must beware of its overuse to prop up indefensible semantic theories.

REFERENCES

Adams, Ernest (1975). *The Logic of Conditionals*. Dordrecht: Reidel.

Bach, Kent (2005). 'Context *ex machina*' in Szabo (ed.), 15–44.

Carston, Robyn (2002). *Thoughts and Utterances: the Pragmatics of Explicit Communication*. Oxford: Blackwell.

Cohen, L. J. (1971). 'Some Remarks on Grice's view about the Logical Particles of Natural Language' in Bar-Hillel, Y. (ed.) *Pragmatics of Natural Language*, 50–68. Dordrecht: Reidel.

Davidson, Donald (1967). 'Truth and Meaning'. *Synthese*, 17: 304–23, reprinted in Davidson (1984), 17–36.

_____ (1973). 'In Defence of Convention T' in Davidson (1984), 65–75.

_____ (1984). *Inquiries into Truth and Interpretation*. Oxford: Clarendon Press, 1984.

Edgington, Dorothy (1995). 'Conditionals and the Ramsey Test'. *Proceedings of the Aristotelian Society Supplementary Volume*, 69: 67–86.

_____ (2001). 'Conditionals': *Stanford Encyclopedia of Philosophy*. http://plato.stanford.edu/entries/conditionals.

_____ (2003). 'What if? Questions about Conditionals'. *Mind and Language* 18: 380–401.

_____ (forthcoming). 'Conditionals, Truth and Assertion' in Ian Ravenscroft (ed.) *Essays in Honour of Frank Jackson*. Oxford: Oxford University Press.

Frege, Gottlob (1879). *Begriffschrift* in Jean van Heijenoort (ed.) *Frege and Gödel: Two Fundamental Texts in Mathematical Logic*. Cambridge MA: Harvard University Press, 1970.

_____ (1923). 'Compound Thoughts' in Frege, *Logical Investigations*. Oxford: Blackwell, 1977.

Grice, Paul (1970). 'Presupposition and Conversational Implicature', in Grice (1989): 269–282.

_____ (1989). *Studies in the Way of Words*. Cambridge MA: Harvard University Press,

Jackson, Frank (1979). 'On Assertion and Indicative Conditionals'. *Philosophical Review*, 88: 565–89. Reprinted in Jackson (ed.) *Conditionals*.

_____ (1980–1). 'Conditionals and Possibilia'. *Proceedings of the Aristotelian Society*, 81: 125–37.

_____ (1987). *Conditionals*. Oxford: Blackwell.

_____ (1991). (ed.) *Conditionals*. Oxford: Oxford University Press.

Kaplan, David (1989). 'Demonstratives' in J. Almog, J. Perry and H. Wettstein (eds.), *Themes from Kaplan*, 481–563. New York: Oxford University Press.

King, Jeffrey and Stanley, Jason (2005). 'Semantics, Pragmatics and the Role of Semantic Content', in Szabo (ed.): 111–64.

Kripke, Saul (1963). 'Semantic Considerations on Modal Logics'. *Acta Philosophica Fennica*, 83–94.

_____ (1980). *Naming and Necessity*. Oxford: Blackwell.

Lewis, David (1970). 'General Semantics'. *Synthese*, 22: 18–67.

_____ (1976). 'Conditional Probabilities and Probabilities of Conditionals'. *Philosophical Review* 85: 297–315, reprinted in Lewis, *Philosophical Papers*, vol. 2 (Oxford University Press 1986). Page references to this volume.

Montague, Richard (1974). *Formal Philosophy*. Yale University Press.

Neale, Stephen (2005). 'Pragmatism and Binding' in Szabo (ed.): 165–285.

Ramsey, F. P. (1929). 'General Propositions and Causality', in his *Philosophical Papers* ed. by D. H. Mellor. Cambridge: Cambridge University Press.

Russell, Bertrand (1959). 'Mr Strawson on Referring'. *Mind*. Reprinted in Russell, *My Philosophical Development*. London: George Allen and Unwin 1959, 238–245. Page reference to this volume.

Partee, Barbara (1984). 'Nominal and Temporal Anaphora'. *Linguistics and Philosophy*, 7: 243–86.

Ryle, Gilbert (1949). *The Concept of Mind*. London: Hutchinson.

Seuren, P. (2000). 'Presupposition, Negation and Trivalence'. *Journal of Linguistics*, 36: 1–37.

Sperber, Dan and Wilson, Deirdre (1986). *Relevance: Communication and Cognition*. Cambridge, MA: Harvard University Press. (2nd edn 1995, Oxford: Blackwell).

Stalnaker, Robert (1968). 'A Theory of Conditionals'. *Studies in Logical Theory, American Philosophical Quarterly, Monograph* 2 (Oxford: Blackwell): 980112. Reprinted in Jackson (ed.) 1991: 28–45. Page references to the reprint.

―― (1975). 'Indicative Conditionals'. *Philosophia*, 5: 269–86, reprinted in Jackson (ed.) 1991, 136–54.

―― (1999). *Context and Content*. Oxford: Oxford University Press.

Stanley, Jason (2000). 'Context and Logical Form'. *Linguistics and Philosophy*, 23 4: 391–434.

Strawson, P. F. (1952). *Introduction to Logical Theory*. London: Methuen.

―― (1969). 'Meaning and Truth'. Inaugural lecture. Oxford: Oxford University Press.

Szabo, Zoltan Gendler (ed.) (2005). *Semantics versus Pragmatics*. Oxford: Oxford University Press.

Tarski, Alfred (1944). 'The Semantic Conception of Truth and the Foundations of Semantics'. *Philosophy and Phenomenological Research*, 4, reprinted in S. Blackburn and K. Simmons (eds.), *Truth*. Oxford, 1999, 115–43.

Travis, Charles (1997). 'Pragmatics' in B. Hale and C. Wright (eds.), *A Companion to the Philosophy of Language*. Oxford, Blackwell: 87–107.

van Fraassen, Bas (1980). Review of Brian Ellis, *Rational Belief Systems*. *Canadian Journal of Philosophy*, 10: 497–511.

Wilson, Deirdre (1975). *Presupposition and non-truth-conditional semantics*. New York: Academic Press.

Wittgenstein, Ludwig (1922). *Tractatus Logic-Philosophicus*. London: Routledge and Kegan Paul.

CHAPTER 31
....

QUANTIFIERS

....

MICHAEL GLANZBERG

QUANTIFIED terms are terms of generality. They also provide some of our prime examples of the phenomenon of scope. The distinction between singular and general terms, as well as the ways that general terms enter into scope relations, are certainly fundamental to our understanding of language. Yet when we turn to natural language, we encounter a huge and apparently messy collection of general terms; not just *every* and *some*, but *most, few, between five and ten*, and many others. Natural-language sentences also display a complex range of scope phenomena; unlike first-order logic, which clearly and simply demarcates scope in its notation.

In spite of all this complexity, the study of quantification in natural language has made remarkable progress. Starting with a seminal trio of papers from the early 1980s, Barwise and Cooper (1981), Higginbotham and May (1981), and Keenan and Stavi (1986), quantification in natural language has been investigated extensively by philosophers, logicians, and linguists. The result has been an elegant and far-reaching theory. This chapter will present a survey of some of the important components of this theory. Section 31.1 will present the core of the theory of generalized quantifiers. This theory explores the range of expressions of generality in natural language, and studies some of their logical properties. Section 31.2 will turn to issues of how quantifiers enter into scope relations. Here there is less unanimity than in the theory of generalized quantifiers. Two basic approaches, representative of the main theories in the literature, will be sketched and compared. Finally, Section 31.3 will turn briefly to the general question of what a quantifier is.

Thanks to the members of the Syntax Project at the University of Toronto, and to Ernie Lepore, for comments on earlier drafts.

31.1 GENERALITY IN NATURAL LANGUAGE

The first of our topics is the notion of quantified expressions as expressions of generality. We have already observed that natural languages present us with a wide range of such expressions. We thus confront a number of questions, both foundational and descriptive: what are the semantics of expressions of generality, what sorts of basic semantic properties do they have, and what expressions of generality appear in natural language?

One of the accomplishments of research over the last twenty-five years is to give interesting answers to these questions. Though many problems remain open, a great deal about the basic semantic properties of natural-language quantifiers is known. This is encapsulated in what is often called *generalized quantifier theory*. This section will be devoted to the core of this theory. It should be noted at the outset that generalized quantifier theory is a large and well-developed topic, and there is too much in it to cover in any exhaustive way. There are, fortunately, two very good more specialized surveys to which interested readers may turn for more details and more references: Keenan and Westerståhl (1997) and Westerståhl (1989).

31.1.1 Denotations for Quantifier Expressions?

Consider two sentences:

(1) a. Bill weighs 180 lbs.
   b. Everything weighs 180 lbs.

The beginning of a story about the semantics of (1a) is easy to see. The subject expression *Bill* picks out an individual, and the predicate *weighs 180 lbs.* predicates some property of that individual. The sentence is true if and only if the individual has the property.

But what of (1b)? The property of weighing 180 lbs. remains the same, but what is it being predicated of? Is there some *denotation* for the expression *everything*? More generally, we might ask what contribution *everything* makes to the truth conditions of (1b). Can we identify some entity, the *semantic value* of *everything*, which captures this contribution? (I shall use the terms *denotation* and *semantic value* interchangeably.)

It is fairly obvious that no individual can be the denotation of an expression of generality like *everything*. That would be a strange individual indeed, both some particular individual and at the same time 'everything'. But it might seem appealing to make the semantic value of such an expression something like a property. For instance, we might propose that the contribution of *everything* to (1b) is the property of being among everything.

There are a number of problems with this idea. One might raise metaphysical concerns about properties, or about whether properties can be the denotations of terms the way individuals can be the denotations of names (hence, the more neutral term *semantic value* might be more apt). But there are also some more immediate semantic problems which make this proposal fail. First, it leaves mysterious how the truth conditions of a sentence like (1b) could be determined. If both the subject *everything* and the predicate *weighs 180 lbs.* contribute properties, we lack an account of how to combine them to determine a truth value.

We might attempt to solve this problem, but it looks like we would simply get the wrong results for some cases. Here is an idea: suppose we say a sentence like (1b) is true if the things which fall under the property given by *everything* also fall under the property given by *weighs 180 lbs.* This seems to work for (1b). But the same idea would get the wrong answers for:

(2) Nothing weighs 180 lbs.

Presumably our idea would associate with *nothing* the property of being among nothing, i.e. an empty property. But then everything which falls under this property also bears the property of weighing 180 lbs., vacuously. So, our idea predicts that (2) is true. This is just wrong. (For more extensive arguments along these lines, see Heim and Kratzer (1998).)

The solution is to treat the semantic values of expressions of generality not as properties of individuals, but as *properties of properties*, i.e. as *second-level properties*. This idea essentially comes from Frege (1879, 1891, 1893). (Frege himself would have insisted that quantifiers are what he called *second-level concepts*, but we do not need to worry about Frege's particular notion of concept to make the basic point.) Let us first think of this in the more familiar terms of first-order logic. A sentence like $\forall x F(x)$, according to the Fregean view, tells us that the property of being F is such that everything falls under it. Thus, the contribution of $\forall$ is the second-level property which holds of first-level properties under which every individual falls.

We can think of *everything* in (1b) as working the same way. It contributes the second-level property of being a property under which everything falls. The sentence says that the property of weighing 180 lbs. has this feature, which is false. Likewise, we get the right answer for (2). In (2), *nothing* contributes the second-level property of being a property under which nothing falls. The sentence says that the property of weighing 180 lbs. has this feature, which is false.

31.1.2 Generalized Quantifiers

For our purposes, we do not need to worry in any serious way about the nature of properties. They apply to individuals, and in doing so make a certain kind of contribution to the truth or falsehood of a sentence. To make this vivid, we can represent them by *sets*. This is to ignore the intensional aspects of properties, but they will not be at issue here. For our purposes, treating properties as sets is a harmless theoretical simplification.[1]

---

[1] I am generally assuming that semantic values are sets, and that they are *extensional*. Much of what follows is independent of these assumptions, though there are a number of applications in the literature for which it is crucial that predicate semantic values have *cardinalities*.

If we represent properties by sets, then second-level properties are sets of sets. This allows us to put the fundamental observation of Section 31.1.1 as a thesis about the semantic values of quantifier expressions:

(3) The semantic values of quantifier expressions are sets of sets.

This thesis, though it will be refined in some ways as we progress, is the core of the theory of quantifiers we will develop.

We need a little more detail to make this thesis precise. We will generally start with some background *universe of discourse M*. The semantic value of a predicate is then thought of as a *subset* of M (which we think of a representing something like a property). A quantified expression like *everything* or $\forall$ has as semantic value a set of subsets of M. *Everything* has as value the set of subsets of M which include all of M, i.e. are the entire universe. Likewise *something* or $\exists$ has as value the set of subsets of M which are non-empty.

Once we see quantifiers as sets of sets, we can quickly observe that being non-empty and being the entire universe are merely two among many. Set theory provides many such sets of sets, and some of them prove of interest in logic. So, for instance, relative to a fixed universe M, we can define:

(4) a. $(\mathbf{Q}_R)_M = \{X \subseteq M| \, |X| > |M \backslash X|\}$
    b. $(\mathbf{Q}_\alpha)_M = \{X \subseteq M| \, |X| \geq \aleph_\alpha\}$

($|X|$ is the cardinality of a set X. In many cases, where we have some set which is to be thought of as the semantic value of an expression, I shall put the set in **bold**; so $(\mathbf{Q}_R)_M$ interprets Q_R relative to a universe M. As I mentioned above, I shall use 'semantic value' and 'denotation' interchangeably.)

Sets of sets like those defined in (4) are often called *generalized quantifiers* or *Mostowski quantifiers*, in honor of their first extensive study by Mostowski (1957). Mostowski quantifiers can be added to the usual first-order logic. $Q_\alpha x F(x)$ says that the extension of F has cardinality $\geq \aleph_\alpha$. $(\mathbf{Q}_R)_M$ is the Rescher quantifier (Rescher, 1962). For a finite universe M, $Q_R x F(x)$ says that the extension of F is more than half the size of M. Mostowski quantifiers thus allow us to supplement our usual first-order logic to express more than $\forall$ and $\exists$. The basic idea of quantifier expressions denoting sets of sets allows us also to express such properties as being of a certain cardinality, and being more than half.

One fairly technical distinction needs to be made before we close this subsection. We defined Mostowski quantifiers for a fixed universe M. These are what are usually called *local* generalized quantifiers. *Global* generalized quantifiers are simply functions from sets M to local generalized quantifiers on M. So, for instance, for each M, $(\mathbf{Q}_R)_M$ is the local Rescher quantifier on M. Q_R, the global Rescher quantifier, is the function which takes M to $(\mathbf{Q}_R)_M$. For the most part, we will ignore this rather technical distinction, but it will matter in a few important places.

31.1.3 Generalized Quantifiers in Natural Language

Though the kind of generalization of $\forall$ and $\exists$ given by Mostowski quantifiers is a major step, it is not enough to accurately explain natural language quantifiers. For instance, in a way the Rescher quantifier Q_R expresses *most*, but not the way natural language does. Consider:

(5) a. Most students attended the party.
  b. Most birds fly.
  c. Most people have ten fingers.

These do not do what Q_R does. Q_R compares the size of a predicate extension with the size of the entire universe. These, on the other hand, compare the size of one sub-set of the universe with another. The first, for instance, says that the set of students who came to the party is larger than the set of students who did not come to the party.

In (5), we see quantifiers comparing one set to another, relating the denotation of one predicate with the denotation of a second predicate. We see a fundamentally *binary* structure. This binary structure is quite widespread in natural language. We see, for instance:

(6) a. Few students attended the party.
  b. Both students attended the party.
  c. Enough students attended the party.

Each of these involves an expression of generality (*few, both, enough*) relating two predicates (*students, attended the party*).

We also see the same binary pattern of expression of generality relating two predicates in many more constructions, as:

(7) a. Between five and ten students attended the party.
  b. At least ten students attended the party.
  c. All but five students attended the party.
  d. More male than female students attended the party.
  e. John's mother attended the party.
  f. More of John's than Mary's friends attended the party.

In fact, though we treated *everything* and *something* as like the unary $\forall$ and $\exists$ in Section 31.1, the English *every* and *some* really display this binary structure as well:

(8) a. Every student attended the party.
  b. Some students attended the party.

(These examples are modeled on the much more extensive list in Keenan and Stavi (1986).)

The binary pattern in natural-language expressions of generality is no accident. It reflects a fundamental feature of the syntax of natural languages. Simplifying somewhat, we can observe that sentences break down into combinations of noun phrases (NPs) and verb phrases (VPs). Noun phrases also break down, into combinations of *determiners* (DETs) and common nouns (CNs) (or more complex construction with adjectival modifiers like *small brown dog*). Quantifier expressions of the sorts we see in (6)–(8) occupy the determiner positions in subject noun phrases. The basic structure we see in all those examples follows the pattern:

(9)

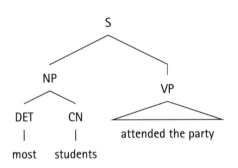

This structure is not only a matter of syntax. It is *semantically significant*. Examples like (5) show that we need to see the CN position as semantically significant to capture the meaning of expressions like *most*.[2]

To do this, we need a modest extension of the idea of a Mostowskian generalized quantifier. That idea took Frege's suggestion that quantifiers are second-level properties and formalized it as the idea that quantifiers are sets of sets. To capture the binary structure of natural-language expressions of generality, we need to work not with sets of sets, but with *relations* between sets. In (9), we see that the semantic value of the determiner *most* should relate the value of the CN *students* and the VP *attended the party*. As we are assuming CNs like *students* and VPs like *attended the party* have sets as their semantic values, the determiner *most* must have a relation between sets as its semantic value. This is our next thesis:

(10) The semantic values of many quantifier expressions (determiners) in natural languages are relations between sets.

This is often called the *relational theory of determiner denotations*.

The relational theory of determiner denotations allows us to explicitly define a wide range of natural-language quantifiers. As with Mostowski quantifiers, we start with a universe M. We now define relations between subsets of M. For instance, for each M and $X, Y \subseteq M$:

(11) a. $\textbf{every}_M(X, Y) \leftrightarrow X \subseteq Y$
   b. $\textbf{most}_M(X, Y) \leftrightarrow |X \cap Y| > |X \backslash Y|$

---

[2] There are a number of syntactic issues I am putting aside here. See any current syntax text, or the handbook discussions of Bernstein (2001) and Longobardi (2001). For some interesting cross-linguistic work, see Baker (2003), Matthewson (2001), and the papers in Bach *et al.* (1995).

    c. **neither**$_M(X, Y) \leftrightarrow |X| = 2 \wedge X \cap Y = \emptyset$

    d. **at least 10**$_M(X, Y) \leftrightarrow |X \cap Y| \geq 10$

Similar definitions can be given for other quantifiers, including those in (6) and (7).

It will be useful to have some notation to keep track of whether we are talking about relational quantifiers like those in (11), or unary ones like those in (4). A Mostowski quantifier, which takes one set input, is classified as type $\langle 1 \rangle$. The quantifiers we have just looked at are classified as type $\langle 1, 1 \rangle$, taking two set inputs. The number 1 signifies that each input is a set (so the quantifier is *monadic*). As in Section 31.1.2, technically we want to distinguish *local* from *global* quantifiers. So our official definitions are:

(12) a. A (local) type $\langle 1, 1 \rangle$ quantifier on M is a relation $\mathbf{Q}_M(X, Y)$ on sets $X, Y \subseteq M$.

    b. A (global) type $\langle 1, 1 \rangle$ quantifier is a function from universes M to local quantifiers $\mathbf{Q}_M$.

As before, the difference between local and global quantifiers will matter in a few places; but not many.

We thus see that natural-language *determiners* can be interpreted as type $\langle 1, 1 \rangle$ quantifiers. Full NPs (combining a determiner with a CN, like *most students*) can be understood as these quantifiers with one argument fixed, which are then type $\langle 1 \rangle$ quantifiers.[3]

31.1.4 Restricted Quantifiers

Type $\langle 1, 1 \rangle$ quantifiers appear to be *restricted* quantifiers. Whereas $\forall$ and $\exists$, and other type $\langle 1 \rangle$ quantifiers, range over the entire universe, a quantifier like **most** seems to range over its first input, corresponding to the CN position in a noun phrase. In (6), for instance, we think of **most** as ranging over the set **students**. Intuitively, this means that the truth or falsehood of *Most students attended the party* should depend only on what happens in the set **students**, and nothing else about the universe of discourse.

It does turn out that natural language quantifiers display important features of restricted quantification. However, the reason is more complex than the mere presence of an extra input position corresponding to a CN. It is entirely possible to define type $\langle 1, 1 \rangle$ quantifiers which are not restricted. For instance:

(13) **more**$_M^{\langle 1, 1 \rangle}(X, Y) \leftrightarrow |X| > |Y|$

This does not behave as if its domain is restricted to X, in cases where Y and X do not overlap. So, **more**$_M^{\langle 1, 1 \rangle}$(**animals, humans**) holds if there are more animals than humans, which has as much to do with the number of non-humans as humans. (This

---

[3] Terminology varies on whether determiners or full NPs are called 'quantifiers'; for instance, Barwise and Cooper (1981) reserve the term 'quantifier' for NP denotations, i.e. type $\langle 1 \rangle$ quantifiers.

is a perfectly good type $\langle 1, 1 \rangle$ quantifier, but as we will see in a moment, it may not correspond to any natural language expression.)

The core feature which makes natural language quantifiers behave like restricted quantifiers is exhibited by the following pattern:

(14) a. i. Every student attended the party.
　　　 ii. Every student is a student who attended the party.
　　 b. i. Few students attended the party.
　　　 ii. Few students are students who attended the party.
　　 c. i. Most students attended the party.
　　　 ii. Most students are students who attended the party.

In each of these, (i) and (ii) are equivalent. The corresponding feature for $\mathbf{more}_M^{\langle 1,1 \rangle}$ would be $|X| > |Y| \leftrightarrow |X| > |X \cap Y|$, which is easily falsified.

The pattern we see in (14) but not in (13) is called *conservativity*:[4]

(15) (CONS) For each $X, Y \subseteq M$, $\mathbf{Q}_M(X, Y) \leftrightarrow \mathbf{Q}_M(X, X \cap Y)$.

Conservativity expresses the idea of *restrictedness*. For instance, in (14c), it tells us that the truth of *Most students attended the party* depends only on the member of the set **students**.

One of the striking facts about natural languages, observed in Barwise and Cooper (1981) and Keenan and Stavi (1986), is that all natural-language determiner denotations satisfy CONS. It appears that all natural-language quantification is restricted quantification. This is not a conceptual or a logical matter. Examples like (13) clearly violate CONS; hence, there are perfectly intelligible non-conservative quantifiers. Rather, it appears to be an empirical fact about human languages that though logically speaking they could have non-conservative determiner denotations, they do not. We thus have a proposed *linguistic universal*: a non-trivial empirical restriction on possible natural languages.

As an empirical claim, one of the substantial issues about conservativity is whether it really does hold universally. Much of the discussion has focused on a number of potential counter-examples. Some of them remain controversial, but the consensus in the literature is that the universal holds. Let me give a couple of examples. Why is $\mathbf{more}_M^{\langle 1,1 \rangle}$ not a counter-example? Because this quantifier does not appear to be the denotation of a natural-language determiner. It might have seemed to be the denotation of *more*, but this is not so. The determiner *more* appears to be a *two-place* determiner, figuring in constructions like:

(16) More students than professors attended the party.

More than is conservative. (Quantifiers taking more than two arguments have been investigated by Beghelli (1994) and Keenan and Moss (1984). See Keenan and Westerståhl (1997) for additional discussion.)

---

[4] This same property was called the 'lives on' property by Barwise and Cooper (1981) and 'intersectivity' by Higginbotham and May (1981). I believe the terminology 'conservativity' is due to Keenan and Stavi (1986).

Another much-discussed case is *only*. It may appear to be an easy example of the failure of conservativity. Consider:

(17) Only dogs bark.

A natural reading of this sentence makes it true if and only if the set of barking things is included in the set of dogs. This suggests a highly simplified semantics for *only*:

(18) $\mathbf{only}_M(X, Y) \leftrightarrow Y \subseteq X$

This is simplified in many ways, but it makes the failure of conservativity vivid. $Y \subseteq X \leftrightarrow (Y \cap X) \subseteq X$ only holds when $Y \subseteq X$. Hence, any false sentence suffices to show that conservativity fails.

Even so, there is good reason to think that *only* is not a determiner. It appears outside of noun phrases, as in:

(19) John only talked to Susan.

It also appears in places we do not see determiners in English noun phrases:

(20) a. Only the Provost/John talked to Susan.
     b. Only between five and ten students came to the party.

We have good reason to think that *only* is not a counter-example to conservativity because it is not a determiner.[5]

It appears that all natural-language determiner denotations are conservative, and so the linguistic universal of conservativity holds. A moment ago, I identified conservativity as the reason natural-language quantification appears to be restricted quantification. However, there is a minor complication to this claim, due to differences between local and global quantifiers. (This is one of those points where this technical distinction does matter.)

Conservativity tells us that for a given M and $X, Y \subseteq M$, whether $\mathbf{Q}_M(X, Y)$ holds depends only on X. But this does not guarantee that some change in M which has no effect on X cannot matter. Intuitively, for a restricted quantifier, we expect that it cannot. Intuitively, we think that the only thing that can matter to a restricted quantifier is X, period. This is a property of *global* quantifiers. It tells us that as far as a global restricted quantifier $\mathbf{Q}$ is concerned, $\mathbf{Q}_M(X, Y)$ is just the same as $\mathbf{Q}_X(X, Y)$. This stronger notion of restrictedness is given by the principle:

(21) (UNIV) For each M and $X, Y \subseteq M$, $\mathbf{Q}_M(X, Y) \leftrightarrow \mathbf{Q}_X(X, X \cap Y)$.

('UNIV' for 'universe-restricting'. Note the subscript on the right-hand side is X.)

The difference between CONS and UNIV is relatively small, but not entirely trivial. It was observed by van Benthem (1983, 1986) that UNIV is equivalent to CONS together with the property EXT (for 'extension'):

(22) (EXT) For each $X, Y \subseteq M \subseteq M'$, $\mathbf{Q}_M(X, Y) \leftrightarrow \mathbf{Q}_{M'}(X, Y)$.

---

[5] For more on *only*, see Herburger (2000) and Rooth (1985, 1996). Related to expressions like *only* are adverbs of quantification, such as *always* and *never*. For discussion of these, see Lewis (1975) and von Fintel (1994).

As observed by Westerståhl (1985b, 1989), EXT expresses the idea that quantifiers do not change their meanings on different domains. This, plus CONS, captures the strong intuitive idea of restrictedness.

A moment ago I glossed the proposed universal of conservativity as one that told us that all natural-language quantification is restricted. In light of our observation that restrictedness is really expressed by UNIV, and that CONS might leave out EXT, we should also ask if it is a linguistic universal that all natural-language determiner denotations satisfy EXT (and hence UNIV) as well.

It appears that they do. As with CONS, logic easily provides us with quantifiers that violate EXT. One example given by Westerståhl (1985b) is:

(23) $\mathbf{many^*}_M(X, Y) \leftrightarrow |X \cap Y| > 1/3 \cdot |M|$

As with CONS, there appear to be reasons to reject this as a genuine counter-example, as there appear to be reasons to deny that **many*** is the denotation of a natural-language determiner. One reason is that *many* appears to be context-dependent, in that what counts as many is heavily influenced by context. Depending on how this sort of context-dependence is handled, it may be argued that *many* has a very different sort of meaning than **many***. If it does, we have no reason to think that *many* violates EXT or CONS. Of course, we still need to see how to interpret *many* properly. This remains a controversial issue, and I shall not pursue it in any more detail. See Westerståhl (1985b) for extensive discussion.[6]

Though there remains some controversy, especially in cases like *many*, the proposed linguistic universal that all natural-language determiner denotations satisfy CONS and EXT enjoys a great deal of support. It thus appears plausible that all natural-language quantification really is restricted quantification.

In introductory logic classes, we are shown how to build certain restricted quantifiers out of unrestricted ones. *Every student attended the party* can be analyzed as $\forall x(student(x) \rightarrow attended\,the\,party(x))$. This shows us how to define the $\langle 1, 1 \rangle$ restricted quantifier $\mathbf{every}_M(X, Y)$ in terms of the type $\langle 1 \rangle$ unrestricted quantifier $\forall$. We have now seen that natural-language determiners denote type $\langle 1, 1 \rangle$ quantifiers, and they are restricted quantifiers. This raises the question of whether they can all be defined in terms of type $\langle 1 \rangle$ quantifiers.

The answer is they cannot. It is a somewhat technical matter in logic, but it is known that $\mathbf{most}_M$ defined in (11) cannot be defined by any combination of type $\langle 1 \rangle$ quantifiers. (There is a modest complication here, involving issues to be discussed in Section 31.1.6. I shall return to this briefly in Section 31.1.8.)

---

[6] The context-dependence proposed for determiners like *many* is in the meaning of the determiner, not in the restriction of its domain. For discussions of how context restricts the domains of quantifiers, see Cappelen and Lepore (2002); Stanley and Szabó (2000) (with comments by Bach (2000) and Neale (2000)); von Fintel (1994); and Westerståhl (1985a). I am skipping over the issue, related to paradoxes, of whether all quantifiers, including such apparently unrestricted ones as *everything*, wind up with some non-trivial contextual domain restriction. This is discussed in Glanzberg (2004) and Williamson (2004).

31.1.5 How many Quantifiers are There?

The simple answer to this question is a lot. If we take a universe M of size n, there are 2^{4^n} type $\langle 1, 1 \rangle$ (local) quantifiers on M.

Conservativity does more than capture (most of) our intuitive idea of restricted quantification. It also has a significant effect on how many quantifiers there are, and more generally, what the space of quantifiers is like. First of all, there are fewer conservative quantifiers: there are 2^{3^n} type $\langle 1, 1 \rangle$ quantifiers satisfying CONS on a universe of size n (cf. van Benthem, 1984).

Perhaps more importantly, the space of conservative quantifiers is much more orderly than its size might make it seem. Conservative quantifiers are all built up in stages. We start with a small collection of basic determiner denotations. In particular, we can start with just $\mathbf{every}_M$ and $\mathbf{some}_M$ (as type $\langle 1, 1 \rangle$ quantifiers). We then build more quantifiers by a couple of systematic procedures. One is to combine quantifiers we already have by operations of *Boolean combination*. This gives us quantifiers like **all or some**$_M$. We also build more quantifiers by further restricting the domains of quantifiers we already have. This will allow us to build **some yellow**$_M$. More generally, if we have built $\mathbf{Q}_M(X, Y)$, we may then build $\mathbf{Q}_M(X \cap C, Y)$ for $C \subseteq M$. This amounts to closure under (intersective) adjectival restriction in an NP. Call this closure under *predicate restriction*.

One of the striking features of the space of conservative quantifiers is that it includes *exactly* the quantifiers that we can build this way. This is the *conservativity theorem* due initially to Keenan and Stavi (1986), further investigated by Keenan (1993) and van Benthem (1983, 1986). Let us give it a more precise statement. Let M be a fixed *finite* universe. Call the collection of conservative type $\langle 1, 1 \rangle$ quantifiers on M by $CONS_M$. Call the collection of quantifiers we build up from our base set $D - GEN$. More formally, $D - GEN$ is the set of quantifiers on M containing $\mathbf{every}_M$ and $\mathbf{some}_M$ and *closed* under Boolean combination and predicate restriction. The conservativity theorem tells us:

(24) $CONS_M = D - GEN_M$

(This is a *local* theorem. The proof carries out different constructions for different size M.)

It is an appealing speculation that this might explain why the linguistic universal of conservativity holds. Natural languages might build up their stock of quantifiers in much the way $D - GEN_M$ is built up. Whether this explanation holds good or not, it does point out that the space of conservative quantifiers is not 'too big'. For any finite universe M and any given quantifier in $CONS_M$, we can follow the proof of the conservativity theorem to build a natural language expression which denotes it (granted, one that can be quite long and syntactically complex). This is the *Finite Effability Theorem* of Keenan and Stavi (1986):

(25) For a finite M, each element of $CONS_M$ is expressed by a determiner of English.

Thus, the conservativity property makes for a much more tractable space of determiner denotations, built up in a systematic way which is closely tied to constructions we can carry out in natural language.

31.1.6 Logicality

We began this section with the idea that quantifiers are expressions of generality. Though we have seen a wide range of determiner denotations which fall within *CONS* and *EXT*, we have yet to give any statement of what makes them general. Intuitively, expressions like *most students* do not pick out any particular individual, but pick out 'most of the students, whomever they may be'. This contrasts, for instance, with proper names or demonstratives, which pick out a particular individual, not just whichever individuals meet some conditions.

One way to articulate the notion of generality is that it requires the truth of a sentence to be independent of exactly which individuals are involved in interpreting a given quantifier. This can be captured formally by the constraint of *permutation invariance*:

(26) (PERM) Let π be a permutation of M (i.e. a bijection from M to itself). Then $\mathbf{Q}_M(X, Y) \leftrightarrow \mathbf{Q}_M(\pi[X], \pi[Y])$.

PERM guarantees that changing the individuals we are talking about does not change the truth of what we are saying, so long as the individuals satisfy the right properties.

Technically speaking, PERM is a local condition. It works with a fixed universe M. A global version can be stated:

(27) (ISOM) For any M and M', if $\iota : M \to M'$ is a bijection, then $\mathbf{Q}_M(X, Y) \leftrightarrow \mathbf{Q}_{M'}(\iota[X], \iota[Y])$.

ISOM states the property of *isomorphism invariance*, which captures the idea of changing the individuals we are talking about, not just within a universe M, but across different universes. The mathematical literature on quantifiers commonly assumes ISOM, and it is built into the definitions of quantifiers in Lindström (1966) and Mostowski (1957).[7]

Though ISOM is the standard condition in the literature, and technically somewhat stronger than PERM, the difference between the two conditions is not that great. Westerståhl (1985b, 1989) observed that if we assume EXT, the domain of quantification ceases to matter, and ISOM and PERM are equivalent.

Following van Benthem (1983, 1986), one sometimes sees quantifiers satisfying CONS, EXT, and ISOM called *logical quantifiers*. There is a rich and extensive

---

[7] The condition is called 'ISOM', as ι induces an isomorphism between the structures $\mathfrak{M} = \langle M, X, Y \rangle$ and $\mathfrak{M}' = \langle M', \iota[X], \iota[Y] \rangle$. In essence, as Lindström (1966) observed, a type $\langle 1, 1 \rangle$ generalized quantifier is a class of structures of the form $\langle M, X, Y \rangle$; if it satisfies ISOM, we have a class of structures closed under isomorphism.

mathematical theory of the logical quantifiers. For an introduction, see van Benthem (1986) or Westerståhl (1989).

ISOM (or PERM) does appear to capture the idea that quantifiers are *general*, and so not about any objects in particular. It is a further question whether this makes them genuinely *logical constants*, as the label 'logical quantifier' suggests. The idea that some sort of permutation-invariance is a key feature of logical notions has been proposed by Mautner (1946) and Tarski (1986). A vigorous defense of the logicality of ISOM quantifiers is given in Sher (1991).

31.1.7 Quantifiers and Noun Phrases

We have seen that, noting a few controversial potential exceptions, natural-language determiner denotations satisfy CONS and EXT. Intuitively, we might also want to say that the expressions we identify as *quantifiers* also satisfy ISOM (or PERM). It is a tempting generalization that natural-language quantifiers are the *logical quantifiers*.

However, there are some clear cases treated by generalized quantifier theory which do not satisfy ISOM, and so are not logical quantifiers. We have already seen one. The possessive construction *John's* in (7) violates ISOM. So do some syntactically complex constructions like *every__except John* when treated as determiners.

Perhaps a more pressing case is that of proper names. We *can* treat proper names as generalized quantifiers. Suppose *John* denotes an individual j. We can build a type ⟨1⟩ generalized quantifier to interpret the NP *John* following Montague (1973). Let $John_M = \{X \subseteq M \mid j \in X\}$. This is a quantifier violating ISOM.

There are two ways to respond to these cases. One is to give up on ISOM as a feature of quantifiers in natural language. This leaves the generalization that determiners denote type ⟨1, 1⟩ quantifiers satisfying CONS and EXT, but not necessarily ISOM. These determiners build type ⟨1⟩ quantifiers satisfying CONS and EXT when combined with a CN denotation, so we might make the further generalization that all NPs denote type ⟨1⟩ generalized quantifiers, once we have given up on ISOM.

Another response is to keep the generalization that all natural-language quantifiers satisfy ISOM, and attempt to explain away the apparent violations. (If we count constructions like *every__except John* as determiners, we should specify only quantifiers denoted by syntactically simple determiners.) In the type ⟨1⟩ case, we can easily observe that though it is possible to treat *John* as a generalized quantifier, it can also be treated as simply denoting an individual. There are good reasons to take this simpler route (cf. Partee, 1986). (Indeed, much of the philosophical literature on names would not even consider any other option!) Thus, an apparently non-ISOM quantifier in natural language may not be a quantifier at all. Likewise, in the type ⟨1, 1⟩ case, we might find analyses of possessive constructions which do not treat them as syntactically on par with simple determiners, or do not treat them as determiners at all. (See Barker (1995) for an extensive discussion of the syntax and semantics of possessives.)

If we offer this second response, we can defend a strong hypothesis: quantifiers in natural language are the denotations of determiners (or perhaps the syntactically simple determiners), and they are logical generalized quantifiers satisfying CONS, EXT, and ISOM. In light of non-ISOM examples like proper names, this hypothesis predicts an important difference between genuine quantified noun phrases, built up out of determiners denoting ISOM quantifiers, and other noun phrases like proper names or possessive constructions.

If this strong hypothesis is correct, there are real differences between quantified NPs and other NPs. We could provide further support for the hypothesis by finding ways in which quantified NPs behave differently from other NPs. The more differences we can see in the ways quantified and non-quantified NPs behave, the more reason we have to accept an analysis which makes them fundamentally different.

In fact, there are ways in which quantified and non-quantified NPs behave differently. One way is brought out by what are called *weak crossover* cases. Compare:

(28) a. *His$_i$ mother loves every boy$_i$.
    b. *His$_i$ mother loves Mary's brother$_i$.
    c. His$_i$ mother loves John$_i$.

(The subscripts here are to indicate that the desired reading has *his* bound by or coreferring with the subsequent expression it is co-indexed with.) A number of authors have noted that we get unacceptability in weak crossover environments with ISOM quantified noun phrases, but not with non-ISOM or non-quantified ones. We thus have a difference in behavior between quantified and non-quantified NPs, and so we have evidence for the strong hypothesis (cf. Higginbotham and May, 1981; Larson and Segal, 1995; Lasnik and Stowell, 1991). (Readers of the logic literature should be aware that regardless of their status in natural language, most logicians take generalized quantifiers to satisfy ISOM by definition.)

31.1.8 Glimpses Beyond

We now have seen the beginnings of generalized quantifier theory, but only the beginnings. The surveys of Keenan and Westerståhl (1997) and Westerståhl (1989) discuss a number of extensions of the theory, and applications of generalized quantifier theory in linguistics.

Among the results they discuss is one that shows that the quantifier **most** defined in (11) cannot be defined by any combination of ISOM type $\langle 1 \rangle$ quantifiers. This shows that we really do need at least type $\langle 1, 1 \rangle$ quantifiers (cf. Väänänen, 1997). They also investigate the delicate issue of whether we need to go beyond $\langle 1, 1 \rangle$. We saw that *more* should be interpreted as taking *three* arguments. Whether we will also need to consider what are called *polyadic* quantifiers, which take *relations* rather than sets as inputs, remains an active area of research (cf. Hella *et al.*, 1996; Higginbotham and May, 1981; Keenan, 1992; May, 1989; Moltmann, 1996; van Benthem, 1989; Westerståhl, 1994).

31.2 QUANTIFICATION AND SCOPE

The relational theory of determiner denotations, which we examined all too briefly in Section 31.1, explains some of the important properties of the semantic values of determiners. But it does not do very much to explain how determiners interact with the rest of semantics. As an example of where quantifiers fit into semantic theory, I shall present some ideas about how quantifiers take scope in natural language. In an example like *Every student likes some professor*, for instance, it is clear that the sentence can be read as having *every student* take scope over *some professor*, or vice versa. The theory of generalized quantifiers by itself does not explain how this can happen. Indeed, as we will see, the theory of generalized quantifiers by itself already runs into trouble explaining how the parts of a sentence like this can combine. Seeing how they can, and how they can in ways that allow for multiple scope readings, will show us something about how quantifiers work.

Perhaps more so than the theory of generalized quantifiers, this area remains controversial. There are a number of good textbook presentations of the basic material, including Heim and Kratzer (1998) and Larson and Segal (1995). (I follow the former quite closely here.) But there is also some significant disagreement in the literature. To illustrate this disagreement, I shall discuss two representative examples of approaches to quantifier scope. I shall need some machinery to do so, which is built up in Sections 31.2.1 to 31.2.4. The actual discussion of scope is in Section 31.2.5.

31.2.1 Quantifiers and Semantic Types

The account of generalized quantifiers as relations between sets pays no attention to the order in which a quantifier's arguments are 'processed'. For studying the properties of determiners, this has proved a useful idealization. But if we are to consider how quantifiers interact with the rest of semantics, we will need to be more careful about how they combine with other semantic values.

A glance at the sentence structure in (9) tells us that the compositional semantics of determiners should first have the determiner's value combine with the value of the CN, resulting in an NP semantic value. It is the NP value which combines with the VP value to determine the value of the sentence. We should first build the value of *most students*, and then see how that combines with the value of *attended the party*.

To capture this, it will be useful to reformulate our description of a quantifier somewhat. Generally, we will turn our attention from sets, and sets of sets, to *functions*. Recall that a set of elements of M can be thought of as a function from M to *truth values*. The members of the set are the elements on which the function returns the value true. A set of sets (i.e. a type $\langle 1 \rangle$ quantifier) can be thought of as a function which takes functions (giving sets) as inputs and outputs truth values.

It will be useful to have some notation to keep track of the inputs and outputs of functions. One way to do this is to use *type theory*. Type theory is a highly general theory of functions. In order to try to avoid confusion between types in the sense of quantifier types and this type theory, I shall sometimes call the latter *semantic type theory*.

Semantic type theory starts with two basic types: t is the type (set) of truth values, which we may take to have two elements $\top$ and $\bot$; e is the type (set) of individuals, which we may take to be some fixed universe M. The theory then builds up functions out of these. The type (e, t) is the type of functions from individuals to truth values, i.e. it is a notation for $\wp(M)$, the set of subsets of M. A quantifier-type $\langle 1 \rangle$ quantifier (a set of sets) is a function of type $((e, t), t)$, taking as input functions representing sets, and having truth values as outputs. Generally, for any two types a and b, (a, b) is the type of functions from a to b.[8]

Using the apparatus of semantic types, we can put our definition of quantifier-type $\langle 1, 1 \rangle$ quantifiers in terms of functions. Definition (12) makes a type $\langle 1, 1 \rangle$ quantifier Q_M a relation between sets. We might think of this as a function on two arguments X and Y. But our semantic type theory only has functions of one argument. To handle functions of multiple arguments, we simply process the arguments in sequence.[9] We first input X, and output the function $Q_M(X)$. This is a function from Y to truth values, which has output $\top$ iff $Q_M(X, Y)$ is true. Our notation helps make this clear. A quantifier-type $\langle 1, 1 \rangle$ quantifier is of semantic-type $((e, t), ((e, t), t))$. It takes as input a set (element of type (e, t)), and returns a function of type $((e, t), t)$. This is a function which takes another set as input, and outputs a truth value. (From now on, we will work with a fixed universe M, giving type e, and only consider local quantifiers on M.)

Semantic type theory gives us a useful notation for keeping track of complex functions. It also gives us a useful way to keep track of the kinds (the types) of semantic values various expressions should have. We will continue with our assumption that the values of VPs and CNs are sets of individuals, i.e. are of type (e, t). We will also continue with the extensional perspective, which gives sentences semantic values of type t. (This is of course, an idealization.) We will also assume that non-quantified NPs are of type e, in accord with the strong hypothesis of Section 31.1.7 supposed. As we have just seen, quantified NPs have semantic values of type $((e, t), t)$. Determiners have values of type $((e, t), ((e, t), t))$. (I shall often abuse notation and say that e.g. determiners *are* of type $((e, t), ((e, t), t))$.)

This analysis of determiner denotations is essentially the relational one of Section 31.1, except that it takes into account the order in which inputs are processed. For the most part, I shall treat semantic type theory simply as a notational device. Most of what we will do with semantic type theory can be done without it as well. (There is one point at which this will not be the case, in Section 31.2.4.)

---

[8] I am writing semantic types with round brackets, such as (a, b). Much of the literature writes semantic types with angle brackets, but these are already being used for quantifier types.

[9] This is what is sometimes called 'Currying' a binary relation, in honor of the logician Haskell B. Curry.

31.2.2 Quantifiers in Object Position

Our semantic analysis starts with the idea that determiners are of type $((e, t), ((e, t), t))$, CNs are of type (e, t), and VPs are of type (e, t). Describing these semantic values in terms of semantic types also allows us to explain how they combine according to the structure of a sentence, to yield the semantic value of the sentence (of type t). For instance, in sentences like (9), the DET value takes as argument the CN value, and yields a quantified NP value, of type $((e, t), t)$. This takes as input the VP value, and the result is of type t, i.e. a truth value, as desired.

If we look at little more widely, however, we run into problems of composition. Transitive verbs with quantifiers in object position provide one sort of problem. A transitive verb will be of type $(e, (e, t))$, taking two type e arguments (in sequence). But consider an example like:

(29) a. John offended every student.
     b.

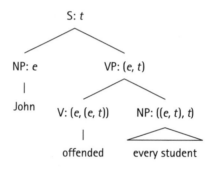

The entries for the VP simply do not match. *Offended* is of type $(e, (e, t))$. But the quantified NP *every student* is of type $((e, t), t)$. Neither can be the argument for the other. If, as the basic type-theoretic perspective supposes, semantic composition is composition of function and argument, we have no way to combine them. The notation of semantic types makes this problem vivid, but it is not special to semantic type theory. One way or another, the quantified NP *every student* should denote something like a second-level property, set of sets, or elements of type $((e, t), t)$, while the V offended should denote a two-place first-level property, or element of type $(e, (e, t))$. The problem is we have no way to combine these denotations.

The theory of generalized quantifiers, as a theory of determiner denotations, does not help us to solve this problem.[10] Instead, some more apparatus is needed, either in the semantics or in the syntax. There are two basic approaches to solving this problem. One involves significant claims about *logical form*. The other makes some corresponding claims about *semantic types*.

---

[10] There is one drastic generalized quantifier theory option we might take, which would be to appeal to polyadic quantifiers of the sort hinted at in Section 31.1.8, following Keenan (1992).

31.2.3 Logical Form and Variable Binding

One approach to the problem of quantifiers in object position, perhaps the dominant one, is to posit underlying logical forms for sentences which are in some ways closer to the ones used in the standard formalisms of logic.

The problem of quantifiers in object position does not arise in first-order logic. It does not because Frege in effect solved it. In first-order logic, we would represent (29) as:

(30) $\forall x(student(x) \rightarrow offended(John, x))$.

The solution implicit here has nothing to do with unrestricted versus restricted quantifiers. We could do just as well if we could produce a structure that looks something like:

(31) Every student$_x$ (John offended x).

What solves the problem is the apparatus of quantifiers and variables. We put a variable in the predicate, and *bind* it with the quantifier. In terms of the structure of (29), the idea is to replace the quantified NP *every student* in the VP with a variable of type e. This variable would function as the argument of the type $(e,(e, t))$ verb, and also be *bound* by the quantifier from outside the VP. This is in effect what we see in (31).

To explain how this can work in our framework of semantic types, we need to look a little further at how variables work. Let x be a variable of type e. If x is free, we can treat it like the pronoun *it*. It has its value fixed by context, but otherwise acts like a referring expression. It is like any other expression of type e, except for needing context to fix its value.

Because of this, an overly simple implementation of the idea in (31) does not work. We might propose simply to replace *every student* in the VP with a variable x of type e, and write the quantified NP *every student* all the way to the left. This would give something like:

(32)

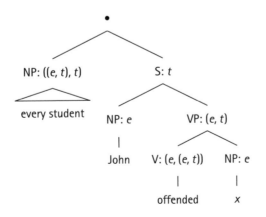

But we still have a mismatch of types, and the structure cannot be interpreted. The variable x is simply an expression of type e. It does combine with the V *offended*. Running up the tree, all looks well up to the S node, which is of type t as it should be. But then we have a problem. This cannot combine with the NP node of type $((e, t), t)$.

What we left out of this overly simple implementation is what is supposed to be shown by the subscript in *every student$_x$*. To get the structure we had in mind in (31), we need to cash out the idea that *every student$_x$* really *binds x* in the VP. Insofar as x is just another expression of type e, we have no explanation of how it might be bound by a quantifier. Writing the subscript on the quantifier is just notation: we need to explain the idea this notation is supposed to show us. We need some explanation of how binding works.

In the type-theoretic setting, binding is done by the apparatus of λ-*abstraction*. λ is the operation that creates *functions* in the framework of semantic types. Consider the semantic value **offended** x of the S node in (32). This is of type t because x is treated as another type e expression, which contributed its value to **offended** x and then is done. We want it not to contribute its value there, but rather to mark an *input* place, resulting in a function which takes an input into the x place, and gives an appropriate output. This is the function $\lambda x.$**John offended** x. This function is an element of type (e, t), i.e. a function which takes a type e input in the x position, and outputs a type t value.

λ *binds* a variable position, resulting in a function. Building a function by binding a variable with a λ is usually called λ-*abstraction*. (For more discussion of the mathematics of λs, see Gamut (1991) or Hindley and Seldin (1986).) In full generality, if β is an element of type b and y is a *variable* of type a, then $\lambda y.\beta$ is an element of type (a, b). λ-abstraction allows us to build functions, and so allows us to construct elements of complex types like (a, b).

To get something that works like (31), we need to add λ-abstraction. With it, we can resolve the mismatch between types we see in (29) along the following lines:

(33)

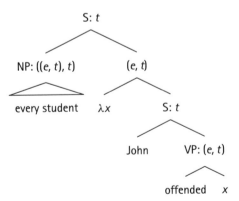

Adding the variable in VP produces an element **John offended** x of type t. λ-abstraction then yields the desired element $\lambda x.$**John offended** x of type (e, t). This can now properly combine with the denotation of the quantified noun phrase.[11]

The use of λ-abstraction in (33) explains what we intuitively represented by the subscript x on *every student*$_x$ in (31). We wanted to make clear that the quantified NP *every student* binds the x position. This is explicitly done by the λ-node in (33). More fully, the λ-note binds the x position, in such a way as to make an input for the quantified NP of the right sort.

The role of λ-abstraction highlights a point about generalized quantifier theory. Generalized quantifier theory as discussed in Section 31.1 is not a theory of variable binding. Describing relations between sets does not explain how they figure into variable binding. On the approach I am sketching here, variable binding is done by λ-abstraction, which produces semantic values of appropriate type to be inputs into generalized quantifiers. There are other ways to treat variable binding, but the moral is that generalized quantifier theory does not do this job.

The structure of (33) represents a very rough proposal for the *logical form* of (29); the fully worked out version is that of Heim and Kratzer (1998). This is a significant proposal. The claim is not merely that a formalism like (31) makes the logical dependencies of a sentence clear. Rather, it is that the semantic interpretation of a sentence of natural language is derived from a structure like (33). Thus, logical form is posited as a genuine level of linguistic representation. This is a substantial empirical claim. For more thorough discussion of this notion of logical form, see "Logical Form and LF" in this volume.[12]

It should be noted that once we have forms looking like (31), it is possible to treat binding in a more Tarskian way, without relying on the apparatus of λ-abstraction and types. As I mentioned a moment ago, some account of binding is needed, but there are versions not using λs. One example is the more Davidsonian treatment of Larson and Segal (1995). There are some general methodological questions about the use of higher types in semantics, but the basic idea of treating quantifiers in object position by way of a substantial level of logical form is not particularly sensitive to them.[13]

31.2.4 Type Shifting

This section is somewhat more technically demanding than the rest of the paper. Readers wanting to avoid long λ-terms might want to skip to Section 31.2.5, which can be read without this one.

---

[11] Technically, we should say that we add syntactic elements which are interpreted as variables and λs. See Büring (2004) and Heim and Kratzer (1998) for more discussion of the syntax and semantics of these particular structures.

[12] Following May (1977, 1985), many linguists think of logical form as the result of *movement processes* which move quantifiers from their *in situ* positions to positions more or less like the ones in (33). A survey of ideas about logical form in syntactic theory is given in Huang (1995).

[13] Lepore (1983) and Pietroski (2002) offer critiques of type-based semantics from a broadly Davidsonian viewpoint. Another view of logical form and its role in semantics, more explicitly Davidsonian than the one I am sketching here, is presented in Higginbotham (1985).

The approach to resolving the problem of quantifiers in object position I briefly sketched in Section 31.2.3 relies on some substantial ideas about logical form. It posits underlying logical forms which look substantially different from the surface forms of sentences, as we saw in (33). There is another way to handle quantifiers in object position, and more generally, to think about issues of binding. Rather than positing a distinct level of *logical form*, the other approach posits more complex modes of *composition* in the semantics.

In this section, I shall very briefly indicate some of the ideas that go into this other approach. This is not to offer any kind of objection to the logical-form-based approach, nor to suggest which approach is right. It is only to show that formally speaking, there are other options.

Suppose we change the type of a quantified NP from $((e, t), t)$ to $((e,(e, t)),(e, t))$. Then we can interpret (29) directly:

(34)

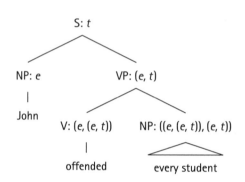

The values of the V and NP compose by the NP value taking the V value as an argument.

How can we change something's type? In this case, the transformation from $((e, t), t)$ to $((e,(e, t)), (e, t))$ is more natural than it might seem. It is an instance of what is known as the *Geach Rule* (cf. Geach, 1972):

(35) $(b, c) \Rightarrow ((a, b), (a, c))$

This can be thought of as introducing an additional mode of composition, over and above function application. It is essentially *function composition*:

(36) a. i. $(a, b) + (b, c) \Rightarrow (a, c)$
    ii. $\alpha_{(a,b)} + \beta_{(b,c)} \Rightarrow (\beta \circ \alpha)_{(a,c)}$
  b. i. $(e, (e, t)) + ((e, t), t) \Rightarrow (e, t)$
    ii. $\gamma_{(e,(e,t))} + \delta_{((e,t),t)} \Rightarrow (\delta \circ \gamma)_{(e,t)}$

(36) displays the scheme of function composition, according to which we apply one function α followed by another β. (36b) shows the specific case of (36a) in which we are interested.

(35) adds an operation of function composition by adding a type-shifting operator. It can be spelled out by:

(37) $Geach_a(\beta_{(b,c)}) = (\lambda X_{(a,b)}\lambda y_a[\beta_{(b,c)}(X_{(a,b)}(y_a))])_{((a,b),(a,c))}$

For $\mathbf{Q}_{((e,t),t)}$ of type $((e, t), t)$, $Geach_e(\mathbf{Q}_{((e,t),t)}) = \lambda v_{(e,(e,t))}\lambda x_e[\mathbf{Q}_{((e,t),t)}(v_{(e,(e,t))}(x_e)))]$. So, for instance $(Geach_e(\textbf{every student}))(\textbf{offended}) = \textbf{every student} \circ \textbf{offended}$. This is now of the right type to combine with **John**. Thus, applying the Geach rule solves the problem of quantifiers in object position.

The operator *Geach* carries out λ-abstraction, as we see in (37). Thus again in this framework, the essential function of having a quantifier interact with the right position in a VP in the right way is done by λ-abstraction. This is a beginning of a theory of binding which does not invoke logical forms different from the surface forms of sentences. For more development along these lines, see Barker (forthcoming); Hendriks (1993); Jacobson (1999); and Steedman (2000); as well as the earlier Cooper (1983).[14]

The basic idea of the type-shifting approach exemplified here is to think of expressions as *polymorphic*. They inhabit multiple types at once. We think of expressions as entered into the lexicon with their minimal type, which can then be *shifted* by type-shifting rules, like the Geach rule. This makes expressions in a way ambiguous. (See Partee (1986); Partee and Rooth (1983); and the extensive discussion in van Benthem (1991).)

Whereas the logical form approach made relatively minor use of type theory, the type-shifting approach leans very heavily on it. Type-shifting approaches do not posit additional levels of linguistic representation, over and above the more or less overt surface structure of the sentence, but they do make use of some powerful mathematics. It is a significant question, both empirical and methodological, which approach is right.

31.2.5 Scope Relations

The problem of quantifiers in object position barely hints at the complexity of the semantics of quantification. To give a slightly richer example, I shall finally turn to some aspects of quantifier scope relations.

One important feature of quantifiers in natural language is that they can generate scope ambiguities. Recall, as every student of first-order logic learns, *Everyone likes someone* has two first-order representations:

(38) Everyone likes someone.
  a. $\forall x \exists y L(x, y)$
  b. $\exists y \forall x L(x, y)$

The second is usually called the *inverse scope reading*, as it inverts the surface order of the quantifiers. Another, more complicated inverse scope example is that of inverse linking (May, 1977):

---

[14] Much of this literature works in the framework of categorial grammar, and attempts to develop 'variable-free' accounts of binding phenomena. The background mathematics for this work is combinatory logic, which is a close cousin of the λ-calculus I have employed here. See Hindley and Seldin (1986) for extensive comparisons.

(39) Someone from every city despises it.

May observed that in this sort of case, the inverse scope reading is the only natural one (or perhaps the only one available).

The logical form approach has no fundamental problem with the existence of inverse scope readings. Basically, the logical form approach treats quantifier scope much the way it is treated in first-order logic, modified to employ generalized quantifiers and the account of binding outlined in Section 31.2.3. Direct and inverse scope readings are simply the result of different mappings of a sentence to logical forms, corresponding to different orders in which the quantifiers are 'moved' from their *in situ* positions to positions further to the left and higher in the tree. For instance, the inverse scope reading of (38) is given by:

(40)

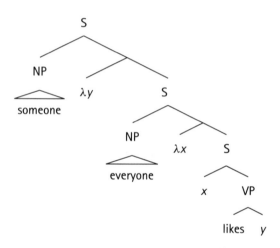

If we adopt the logical form theory, quantifier scoping is taken care of by the same apparatus which handled quantifiers in object position.[15]

This is an elegant result, and part of a battery of arguments often marshaled to show the existence of a level of logical form (cf. May, 1985). Scope ambiguity is explained by holding that in fact sentences like (38) have *two* distinct logical forms—two distinct linguistic structures. At logical form, scope ambiguity is structural ambiguity.

Type-shifting approaches have to do more work to handle inverse scope. The Geach rule described in Section 31.2.4 is not sufficient. One approach to scope via type shifting is to introduce two type-shifting operators which raise the types of the arguments of a transitive verb from e to $((e, t), t)$, allowing the verb to combine with two quantifiers. The *order* in which these operators are applied determines the scope relations between the quantifiers, much as the order in which the quantifiers

---

[15] The syntax of scope is a rich area of linguistics. The basics can be found in many syntax books. For a recent survey, see Szabolcsi (2001).

Though many logical form theories take the syntax of logical form to determine scope, May (1985, 1989) considers a theory in which it does not completely do so.

are moved does on the logical form approach. Hendriks (1993) shows that these operators can be derived from a single type-shifting principle, but I shall leave the rather technical details to him.[16]

Both approaches thus *can* handle inverse scope (though I have suppressed more detail in the type-shifting approach). Which one is right is a substantial question, both methodological and empirical. We face general questions about the apparatus of type shifting and linguistic levels like logical form. We also face empirical issues about which theories can explain the full range of data related to scope and binding. Perhaps the preponderance of current research (at least, research close to syntax) takes place in some version of the logical form approach, but see Jacobson (2002) for a spirited defense of the type-shifting approach.

Though both approaches can handle basic scope inversion cases like (38), the phenomena related to scope in natural language are in fact quite complex. I shall close this section by mentioning a few of the many issues that a full theory of quantifier scope must face.

Though in many cases quantifiers can enter into arbitrary scope relations, there are some well-known situations where they cannot. For instance, quantifiers cannot scope out of relative clauses. Consider (Rodman, 1976):

(41) Guinevere has a bone that is in every corner of the house.

This cannot be given the (more plausible) interpretation in which *every corner of the house* has wide scope. This fact is often cited as evidence in support of logical form theories, which seek to explain it by general syntactic principles, but see Hendriks (1993) for a discussion in type-shifting terms.

Different languages display different scope interactions. Aoun and Li (1993) note sentences which are ambiguous in English but not in Chinese, including the simple:

(42) Every man loves a woman.

(The example is credited to Huang.) It is also known that not all quantifiers exhibit the same scope potentials, even in one language. Beghelli and Stowell (1997) and Szabolcsi (1997) note that inverse scope readings do not appear to be available in:

(43) a. Three referees read few abstracts.
     b. Every man read more than three books.

Aoun and Li (1993) and Beghelli and Stowell (1997) and Szabolcsi (1997) use this data to support their own developments of the logical form approach (cf. Takahashi, 2003). There are also much-discussed difficult issues about the scope of *the* and *a*. See Heim (1991) and van Eijck and Kamp (1997) for surveys.

---

[16] There are systems which produce inverse scope readings with type-shifting operations more closely related to the Geach rule, like the elegant Lambek calculus with permutation of van Benthem (1991). Unfortunately, this system over-generates scope ambiguities, predicting one in *John loves Paris*, as Hendriks (1993) shows. A more refined theory along van Benthem's lines is given a textbook presentation in Carpenter (1997).

31.3 What is a Quantifier?

Can we now say what quantifiers are? Perhaps. Generalized quantifier theory, and the relational theory of determiner denotations which goes with it, offer an answer. The strong hypothesis we considered in Section 31.1.7 holds that natural-language quantifiers are logical generalized quantifiers, satisfying the constraints CONS, EXT, and ISOM. These are expressed by determiners, which combine with CNs to build quantified noun phrases. A somewhat weaker hypothesis holds that natural-language quantifiers need not be ISOM, but must be CONS and EXT. Section 31.1.7 offered some reasons to prefer the stronger hypothesis.

In a way, this tells us what quantifiers *are* in remarkably specific terms. But the moral of Section 31.2 is that it does not tell us all that much about how quantifiers *work*. The examples there show us that to understand *quantification* in natural language is to understand more than what quantifiers are; it is also to understand significant aspects of semantics, and the ways semantics interacts with syntax. Being a quantifier is a property with significant semantic and grammatical implications.

References

Aoun, J. and Li, Y.-H. A. (1993). *Syntax of Scope* (Cambridge: MIT Press).

Bach, E., Jelinek, E., Kratzer, A., and Partee, B. H. (eds.) (1995). *Quantification in Natural Languages* (Dordrecht: Kluwer).

Bach, K. (2000). 'Quantification, Qualification, and Context: A Reply to Stanley and Szabó', *Mind and Language*, 15: 262–83.

Baker, M. C. (2003). *Lexical Categories* (Cambridge: Cambridge University Press).

Barker, C. (1995). *Possessive Descriptions* (Stanford: CSLI Publications).

——— (forthcoming). 'Remarks on Jacobson 1999: Crossover as a Local Constraint', *Linguistics and Philosophy*.

Barwise, J. and Cooper, R. (1981). 'Generalized Quantifiers and Natural Language', *Linguistics and Philosophy*, 4: 159–219.

Beghelli, F. (1994). 'Structured Quantifiers', in M. Kanazawa and C. J. Piñón (eds.), *Dynamics, Polarity, and Quantification* (Stanford: CSLI Publications), 119–45.

Beghelli, F. and Stowell, T. (1997). 'Distributivity and Negation: The Syntax of *Each* and *Every*', in A. Szabolcsi (ed.), *Ways of Scope Taking* (Dordrecht: Kluwer), 71–107.

Bernstein, J. B. (2001). 'The DP Hypothesis: Identifying Clausal Properties in the Nominal Domain', in M. Baltin and C. Collins (eds.), *Handbook of Contemporary Syntactic Theory* (Oxford: Blackwell), 536–61.

Büring, D. (2004). *Binding Theory* (Cambridge: Cambridge University Press).

Cappelen, H. and Lepore, E. (2002). 'Insensitive Quantifiers', in J. Keim Campbell, M. O'Rourke, and D. Shier (eds.), *Meaning and Truth: Investigations in Philosophical Semantics* (New York: Seven Bridges Press), 197–213.

Carpenter, B. (1997). *Type-Logical Semantics* (Cambridge: MIT Press).

Cooper, R. (1983). *Quantification and Syntactic Theory* (Dordrecht: Reidel).

Frege, G. (1879). *Begriffsschrift, eine der arithmetischen nachgebildete Formelsprache des reinen Denkens* (Halle: Nebert). References are to the translation as "Begriffsschrift, a Formal

Language, Modeled upon that of Arithmetic, for Pure Thought" by S. Bauer-Mengelberg in van Heijenoort (1967).

_____ (1891). *Function und Begriff* (Jena: Pohle). References are to the translation as "Function and Concept" by P. Geach in Frege (1984).

_____ (1893). *Grundgesetze der Arithmetik*, vol. I (Jena: Pohle). References are to the partial translation as "The Basic Laws of Arithmetic" by M. Furth, University of California Press, Berkeley, 1964.

_____ (1984). *Collected Papers on Mathematics, Logic, and Philosophy* (Oxford: Basil Blackwell). Edited by B. McGuinness.

Gamut, L. T. F. (1991). *Logic, Language, and Meaning*, vol. 2 (Chicago: University of Chicago Press). 'Gamut' is a pseudonym for J. van Benthem, J. Groenendijk, D. de Jongh, M. Stokhof, and H. Verkuyl.

Geach, P. (1972). 'A Program for Syntax', in D. Davidson and G. Harman (eds.), *Semantics of Natural Language* (Dordrecht: Reidel), 483–97.

Glanzberg, M. (2004). 'Quantification and Realism', *Philosophy and Phenomenological Research*, 69: 541–72.

Heim, I. (1991). 'Artikel und Definitheit', in A. von Stechow and D. Wunderlich (eds.), *Semantics: An International Handbook of Contemporary Research* (Berlin: de Gruyter), 487–535.

Heim, I. and Kratzer, A. (1998). *Semantics in Generative Grammar* (Oxford: Blackwell).

Hella, L., Luosto, K., and Väänänen, J. (1996). 'The Hierarchy Theorem for Generalized Quantifiers', *Journal of Symbolic Logic*, 61: 802–17.

Hendriks, H. (1993). *Studied Flexibility* (Amsterdam: ILLC Publications).

Herburger, E. (2000). *What Counts* (Cambridge: MIT Press).

Higginbotham, J. (1985). 'On Semantics', *Linguistic Inquiry*, 16: 547–93.

Higginbotham, J. and May, R. (1981). 'Questions, Quantifiers and Crossing', *Linguistics Review*, 1: 41–79.

Hindley, J. R. and Seldin, J. P. (1986). *Introduction to Combinators and λ-Calculus* (Cambridge: Cambridge University Press).

Huang, C.-T. J. (1995). 'Logical Form', in G. Webelhuth (ed.), *Government and Binding Theory and the Minimalist Program* (Oxford: Blackwell), 127–75.

Jacobson, P. (1999). 'Towards a Variable-Free Semantics', *Linguistics and Philosophy*, 22: 117–84.

_____ (2002). 'The (Dis)organization of Grammar: 25 Years', *Linguistics and Philosophy*, 25: 601–26.

Keenan, E. L. (1992). 'Beyond the Frege Boundary', *Linguistics and Philosophy*, 15: 199–221.

_____ (1993). 'Natural Language, Sortal Reducibility and Generalized Quantifiers', *Journal of Symbolic Logic*, 58: 314–25.

Keenan, E. L. and Moss, L. S. (1984). 'Generalized Quantifiers and the Expressive Power of Natural Language', in J. van Benthem and A. ter Meulen (eds.), *Generalized Quantifiers in Natural Language* (Dordrecht: Foris), 73–124.

Keenan, E. L. and Stavi, J. (1986). 'A Semantic Characterization of Natural Language Determiners', *Linguistics and Philosophy*, 9: 253–326. Versions of this paper were circulated in the early 1980s.

Keenan, E. L. and Westerståhl, D. (1997). 'Generalized Quantifiers in Linguistics and Logic', in J. van Benthem and A. ter Meulen (eds.), *Handbook of Logic and Language* (Cambridge: MIT Press), 837–93.

Larson, R. and Segal, G. (1995). *Knowledge of Meaning* (Cambridge: MIT Press).

Lasnik, H. and Stowell, T. (1991). 'Weakest Crossover', *Linguistic Inquiry*, 22: 687–720.

Lepore, E. (1983). 'What Model-Theoretic Semantics Cannot Do', *Synthese*, 54: 167–87.

Lewis, D. (1975). 'Adverbs of Quantification', in E. L. Keenan (ed.), *Formal Semantics of Natural Language* (Cambridge: Cambridge University Press), 3–15.

Lindström, P. (1966). 'First Order Predicate Logic with Generalized Quantifiers', *Theoria*, 32: 186–95.

Longobardi, G. (2001). 'The Structure of DPs: Some Principles, Parameters, and Problems', in M. Baltin and C. Collins (eds.), *Handbook of Contemporary Syntactic Theory* (Oxford: Blackwell), 562–603.

Matthewson, L. (2001). 'Quantification and the Nature of Crosslinguistic Variation', *Natural Language Semantics*, 9: 145–89.

Mautner, F. I. (1946). 'An Extension of Klein's Erlanger Program: Logic as Invariant Theory', *American Journal of Mathematics*, 68: 345–84.

May, R. (1977). *The Grammar of Quantification*, Ph.D. dissertation, MIT.

_____ (1985). *Logical Form: Its Structure and Derivation* (Cambridge: MIT Press).

_____ (1989). 'Interpreting Logical Form', *Linguistics and Philosophy*, 12: 387–435.

Moltmann, F. (1996). 'Resumptive Quantifiers in Exception Sentences', in M. Kanazawa, C. Piñón, and H. de Swart (eds.), *Quantifiers, Deduction, and Context* (Stanford: CSLI Publications), 139–70.

Montague, R. (1973). 'The Proper Treatment of Quantification in Ordinary English', in J. Hintikka, J. Moravcsik, and P. Suppes (eds.), *Approaches to Natural Language* (Dordrecht: Reidel), 221–42. Reprinted in Montague (1974).

_____ (1974). *Formal Philosophy* (New Haven: Yale University Press). Edited by R. Thomason.

Mostowski, A. (1957). 'On a Generalization of Quantifiers', *Fundamenta Mathematicae*, 44: 12–36.

Neale, S. (2000). 'On Being Explicit: Comments on Stanley and Szabó, and on Bach', *Mind and Language*, 15: 284–94.

Partee, B. H. (1986). 'Noun Phrase Interpretation and Type-Shifting Principles', in J. Groenendijk, D. de Jongh, and M. Stokhof (eds.), *Studies in Discourse Representation Theory and the Theory of Generalized Quantifiers* (Dordrecht: Foris), 115–43.

Partee, B. H. and Rooth, M. (1983). 'Generalized Conjunction and Type Ambiguity', in R. Bäuerle, C. Schwarze, and A. von Stechow (eds.), *Meaning, Use and the Interpretation of Language* (Berlin: de Gruyter), 361–93.

Pietroski, P. M. (2002). 'Function and Concatenation', in G. Preyer and G. Peter (eds.), *Logical Form and Language* (Oxford: Oxford University Press), 91–117.

Rescher, N. (1962). 'Plurality-Quantification: Abstract', *Journal of Symbolic Logic*, 27: 373–4.

Rodman, R. (1976). 'Scope Phenomena, 'Movement Transformations,' and Relative Clauses', in B. H. Partee (ed.), *Montague Grammar* (New York: Academic Press), 165–76.

Rooth, M. (1985). *Association with Focus*, Ph.D. dissertation, University of Massachusetts at Amherst.

_____ (1996). 'Focus', in S. Lappin (ed.), *Handbook of Contemporary Semantic Theory* (Oxford: Blackwell), 271–97.

Sher, G. (1991). *The Bounds of Logic: A Generalized Viewpoint* (Cambridge: MIT Press).

Stanley, J. and Szabó, Z. G. (2000). 'On Quantifier Domain Restriction', *Mind and Language*, 15: 219–61.

Steedman, M. (2000). *The Syntactic Process* (Cambridge: MIT Press).

Szabolcsi, A. (1997). 'Strategies for Scope Taking', in A. Szabolcsi (ed.), *Ways of Scope Taking* (Dordrecht: Kluwer), 109–54.

_____ (2001). 'The Syntax of Scope', in M. Baltin and C. Collins (eds.), *Handbook of Contemporary Syntactic Theory* (Oxford: Blackwell), 607–33.

Takahashi, S. (2003). 'More than Two Quantifiers', *NELS*, 33: 405–24.

Tarski, A. (1986). 'What Are Logical Notions?', *History and Philosophy of Logic*, 7: 143–54. Posthumous publication of a lecture given in 1966, ed. J. Corcoran.

Väänänen, J. A. (1997). 'Unary Quantifiers on Finite Models', *Journal of Logic, Language, and Information*, 6: 275–304.

van Benthem, J. (1983). 'Determiners and Logic', *Linguistics and Philosophy*, 6: 447–78.

—— (1984). 'Questions about Quantifiers', *Journal of Symbolic Logic*, 49: 443–66.

—— (1986). *Essays in Logical Semantics* (Dordrecht: Reidel). Includes revised versions of van Benthem (1983) and van Benthem (1984).

—— (1989). 'Polyadic Quantifiers', *Linguistics and Philosophy*, 12: 437–64.

—— (1991). *Language in Action* (Amsterdam: North-Holland).

van Eijck, J. and Kamp, H. (1997). 'Representing Discourse in Context', in J. van Benthem and A. ter Meulen (eds.), *Handbook of Logic and Language* (Cambridge: MIT Press), 179–237.

van Heijenoort, J. (ed.) (1967). *From Frege to Gödel: A Source Book in Mathematical Logic, 1879–1931* (Cambridge: Harvard University Press).

von Fintel, K. (1994). *Restrictions on Quantifier Domains*, Ph.D. dissertation, University of Massachusetts at Amherst.

Westerståhl, D. (1985a). 'Determiners and Context Sets', in J. van Benthem and A. ter Meulen (eds.), *Generalized Quantifiers in Natural Language* (Dordrecht: Foris), 45–71.

—— (1985b). 'Logical Constants in Quantifier Languages', *Linguistics and Philosophy*, 8: 387–413.

—— (1989). 'Quantifiers in Formal and Natural Languages', in D. Gabbay and F. Guenthner (eds.), *Handbook of Philosophical Logic*, vol. IV (Dordrecht: Kluwer), 1–131.

—— (1994). 'Iterated Quantifiers', in M. Kanazawa and C. J. Piñón (eds.), *Dynamics, Polarity, and Quantification* (Stanford: CSLI Publications), 173–209.

Williamson, T. (2004). 'Everything', *Philosophical Perspectives*, 17: 415–65.

CHAPTER 32

LOGICAL FORM AND LF

PAUL PIETROSKI

WE can use sentences to present arguments, some of which are valid. This suggests that premises and conclusions, like sentences, have structure. This in turn raises questions about how logical structure is related to grammar, and how grammatical structure is related to thought and truth.

32.1 PATTERNS OF REASON AND TRADITIONAL GRAMMAR

Consider the argument indicated with (1).

(1) Chris swam if Pat was asleep, and Pat was asleep; so Chris swam.

An ancient thought is that endlessly many such arguments have the following form: Q if P, and P; so Q. The conclusion is evidently part of the first premise, which has the second premise as another part. Let us say that the variables, represented in bold, range over *propositions*. This leaves it open what these potential premises/conclusions are: sentences, statements, states of affairs, or whatever. But presumably, propositions can be evaluated for truth or falsity; they can be endorsed or rejected. And sentences can be used to indicate (or "express") them. In ordinary conversation, the context partly determines which proposition (if any) is indicated. A speaker s might use 'I am tired' at time t to express one proposition, and use it at time t' to express another, while speaker s' uses the same sentence at t to express a third proposition. Context sensitivity, of various kinds, is ubiquitous in natural language. But if only for simplicity, let's assume that we can speak of the proposition indicated in a given context with a declarative sentence.[1]

Even given that propositions can be complex, it is not obvious that all valid inferences are valid by virtue of propositional structure. But this thought has served as an ideal for the study of logic, at least since Aristotle's treatment of syllogisms like (2).

(2) Every politician is deceitful, and every senator is a politician; so
     every senator is deceitful.

The first premise—that every politician is deceitful—seems to have several parts, each of which is a part of the second premise or the conclusion. And conditionals of the form 'Every P is D, and every S is a P, then every S is D' are sure to be true. (So the corresponding argument schema is valid.) Similarly: if no P is D, and some S is a P, then some S is not D. The variables, represented here in italics, are intended to range over certain parts of propositions. Nouns like 'politician' and adjectives like 'deceitful' are general terms, since they can apply to more than one individual. If propositions contain corresponding predicates, then even "simple" propositions (with no propositional parts) exhibit logical structure. And the network of inferential relations revealed by syllogistic logic suggests that many propositions contain a quantificational element (indicated with words like 'every', 'some', or 'no') along with two predicates.

On some views, discussed below, the conclusion of (3) also has this form.

(3) Every planet is bright, and Venus is a planet; so Venus is bright.

Though one can describe the validity of (3), less tendentiously, in terms of the following schema: every P is D, and n is a P; so n is D; where the lower-case variable ranges over proposition-parts of the sort indicated by names. This highlights the intuitive division of declarative sentences into subjects and predicates: 'Every planet/is bright', 'Venus/is bright', 'Some politician/swam', etc. And on Aristotle's view, propositions are like sentences in this respect. With regard to the proposition that Venus is bright, he would have said that bright(ness) belongs to—or in modern terms, is predicated of—Venus; in the proposition that every politician is deceitful, deceitfulness is predicated of every politician. Using slightly different terminology, later theorists said that simple propositions have categorical form: subject-copula-predicate; where a copula, indicated with a word like 'is' or 'was', links a subject (which can consist of a quantifier and predicate) to a predicate.[2] A sentence like 'Every politician swam' can be paraphrased, as in 'Every politician was an individual who did some swimming'. So perhaps the categorical form of the indicated proposition is not fully reflected

---

[1] Eventually, we may have to relax this assumption. Is any *one* proposition indicated with a sentence containing a vague predicate? Is *any* proposition indicated with a sentence containing a demonstrative if nothing is demonstrated? Another complication is that in speaking of an argument or inference, one might be talking about a verbal or mental *process*. But it will be simpler to characterize episodes of (in)valid reasoning in terms of propositions, even if talk of propositions should ultimately be understood in terms of intentional activities.

[2] In English, an article is often required, as in 'Every senator is *a* politician'. But let's assume that this particular feature of English does not reflect propositional structure.

with the first sentence. Maybe 'swam' abbreviates 'was one who did some swimming', much as 'bachelor' is arguably short for 'unmarried marriageable man'.

The proposition that *every planet is bright if Venus is bright* seems to be a compound of categorical propositions. And the proposition that *not only every planet is bright* apparently extends a categorical proposition, via elements indicated with 'not' and 'only'. Medieval logicians explored, with great ingenuity, the hypothesis that all propositions are composed of categorical propositions and a small number of so-called syncategorematic elements. Many viewed this project, in part, as an attempt to uncover principles of a mental language common to all thinkers. From this perspective, one expects a few differences between propositional structure and the manifest structure of spoken sentences. For example, Ockham held that a mental language would not need Latin's declensions. And the ancient Greeks were aware of sophisms like 'Since that dog is a father, and that dog is yours, that dog is your father', which contrasts with the superficially parallel but impeccable inference, 'Since that dog is a mutt, and that mutt is yours, that dog is your mutt.' Still, the assumption was that spoken sentences reflect the most important aspects of propositional form, including subject–predicate structure. The connection between logic and grammar was thought to run deep. But there were known problems.

32.2 MOTIVATIONS FOR REVISION

Some valid schemata, like (4), are reducible to others.

(4) Some *P* is not *D*, and every *S* is *D*; so not every *P* is an *S*.

If some *P* is not *D*, then trivially, not every *P* is *D*. So if it is also true that every *S* is *D*, it must be false that every *P* is an *S*; otherwise, every *P* is *D*. This fully general reasoning tells us that each instance of (4) is valid. And one suspects that there are relatively few *basic* inferential patterns. Perhaps 'Q if P, and P; so Q' is so obvious that logicians should take it as axiomatic. But how many inference patterns are plausibly regarded as logically fundamental?

Medieval logicians made great strides in reducing syllogistic logic to two principles, *dictum de omni* and *dictum de nullo*. Often, perhaps even typically, replacing a predicate with a less restrictive predicate corresponds to a valid inference. Suppose that Rex is a brown dog. Then Rex is a dog. Replacing 'brown dog' with the less restrictive 'dog' yields a valid inference in environments like 'Rex is __'. (And if 'animal' is even less restrictive, then every dog is an animal, and it follows that Rex is an animal.) But sometimes, as in cases involving negation, the direction of valid inference is reversed. In the environment 'Rex is not __', replacing 'dog' with 'brown dog' yields a valid inference; if Rex is not a dog, then Rex is not a brown dog. It turns out that many valid inference forms, including Aristotle's original examples, can be captured in these simple terms. Nonetheless, traditional logic/grammar was inadequate.

Prima facie, propositions involving relations do not have categorical form. One can paraphrase 'Juliet kissed Romeo' with 'Juliet was a kisser of Romeo'. But 'kisser of Romeo' differs, in ways that matter to inference, from predicates like 'politician'. If some kisser of Romeo died, it follows that someone was kissed; whereas the proposition that some politician died has no parallel logical consequence to the effect that the someone was __-ed. Correlatively, if Juliet kissed Romeo, it follows that Juliet kissed someone. The proposition that Juliet kissed someone is of interest, even if we express it with 'Juliet was a kisser of someone', because a quantifier appears *within* the predicate. And complex predicates of this sort were problematic.

If 'respects some doctor' and 'respects some senator' indicate non-relational proposition-parts, like 'is tall' and 'is ugly', then the argument indicated with (5)

(5) Some patient respects some doctor, and every doctor is a senator;
    so some patient respects some senator

has the following form: Some P is T, and every D is an S; so some P is U. But this schema is not valid. Evidently, 'respects some doctor' and 'respects some senator' are logically related, in ways that 'is tall' and 'is ugly' are not. If we allow for propositions with relational components, introducing a variable 'R' ranging over relations, we can formulate valid schemata like the following: some $P\ R$ some D, and every D is an S; so some $P\ R$ some S. But this is a poor candidate for a basic inference pattern. And the problem remains. Inference (6) is valid.

(6) Every patient who met every doctor is tall, and
    some patient who met every doctor respects every senator;
    so some patient who respects every senator is tall.

But many inferences of the form 'Every P is T, and some $P\ R$ every S; so some U is T' are not. One can abstract a valid schema that covers (6), letting parentheses indicate a relative clause: every $P(R1$ every $D)$ is T, and some $P(R1$ every $D)\ R2$ every S; so some $P(R2$ every $S)$ is T. But there can be still further quantificational structure within the predicates. And so on. It seems that quantifiers can be logically significant constituents of predicates, and not just devices for creating proposition-frames into which monadic predicates can be inserted.

Relative clauses posed further questions. If every patient respects some doctor, then every old patient respects some doctor. This is expected if the phrase 'every (old) patient' is governed by *dictum de nullo*: the direction of valid inference is from 'patient' to 'old patient'. But in (7)–(8),

(7) No lawyer who saw every patient respects some doctor
(8) No lawyer who saw every old patient respects some doctor

the valid inference is from 'old patient' to 'patient'. One can say that the typical direction of implication, from more to less restrictive predicates, has been "reversed twice" in (7)–(8). But one wants a detailed account of propositional structure that explains why and how this is so.[3]

---

[3] For further discussion, see Ludlow (2002); Kneale and Kneale (1962).

32.3 FUNCTIONS AND FORMAL LANGUAGES

Frege (1879, 1892a) showed how to resolve these difficulties and more. But on his view, propositions have "function–argument" structure, as opposed to subject-predicate structure. Frege's system of logic, the single greatest contribution to the subject, required a substantial distinction between logical form and grammatical form as traditionally conceived. This had an enormous impact on subsequent discussions of thought and its relation to language.

We can represent the successor function, with a variable ranging over integers, as follows: $S(x) = x + 1$. This function takes integers as arguments; and the value of the function, given a certain argument, is the successor of that argument. Correspondingly, we can say that the arithmetic expression 'S(3)' exhibits function–argument structure, and that the "Semantic Value" (*Bedeutung*) of this complex expression is the number four—i.e. the value of the relevant function given the relevant argument. Likewise, the division function can be represented as a mapping from ordered pairs of numbers to quotients: $Q(x, y) = x/y$. And we can say that the Semantic Value of 'Q(8, 4)' is the number two. Functions can also be specified conditionally. Consider the function that maps every even integer onto itself, and every odd integer onto its successor: $C(x) = x$ if x is even, and $x + 1$ otherwise; $C(1) = 2$, $C(2) = 2$, $C(3) = 4$, *etc.* By itself, however, no function has a value. Frege's metaphor, encouraged by his claim that we can indicate functions with expressions like 'S( ) = ( ) + 1', is that a function is saturated by arguments of the right sort.[4]

On Frege's view, 'Mary sang' indicates a proposition with the following structure: Sang(Mary), with 'Mary' indicating the argument. Frege thought of the relevant function as a conditional mapping from individuals in a given domain to truth-values: $Sang(x) = t$ if x sang, and f otherwise; where 't' and 'f' stand for values such that for each individual x, $Sang(x) = t$ iff x sang, and $Sang(x) = f$ iff x did not sing. The proposition that John admired Mary was said to have a functional component, indicated by the transitive verb, saturated by an ordered pair of arguments: Admired(John, Mary); where $Admired(x, y) = t$ if x admired y, and f otherwise. According to Frege, the proposition that Mary was admired by John has the same function–argument structure, even though 'Mary' is the subject of the passive sentence. And his treatment of quantified propositions departs radically from previous conceptions of logical form.

Let F be the function indicated by 'sang', so that Mary sang iff $F(Mary) = t$. Someone sang iff some individual x is such that $F(x) = t$. Using a modern variant of

---

[4] Variable letters like 'x' and 'y' are typographically convenient. But we can index "gaps" as follows: $Q[( )_i, ( )_j] = ( )_i/( )_j$. We could also replace the subscripts with lines that link gaps. But the idea, however we encode it, is that a proposition has at least one constituent saturated by the requisite number of arguments. One can think of an unsaturated proposition-part as the result of abstracting away from the arguments in a particular proposition. Frege was here influenced by Kant's discussion of judgment, and the ancient observation that merely combining two things does not make the combination truth-evaluable; predicates evidently play a special role in "unifying" propositions.

Frege's notation, someone sang iff $\exists x[\text{Sang}(x)]$; where the quantifier '$\exists$' binds the variable '$x$'. Every individual in the domain sang iff F maps each individual onto $\mathbf{t}$; in formal notation, $\forall x[\text{Sang}(x)]$. A quantifier binds each occurrence of its variable, as in '$\exists x[D(x)\&C(x)]$', which reflects the logical form of 'someone is deceitful and clever'. With regard to the proposition that some politician is deceitful, traditional grammar suggests the division 'Some politician/is deceitful'. But for Frege, the logically relevant division is between the existential quantifier and the rest: $\exists x[P(x)\&D(x)]$; someone is both a politician and deceitful. With regard to the proposition that every politician is deceitful, Frege again says that the logically important division is between the quantifier and its scope: $\forall x[P(x) \to D(x)]$; everyone is such that if he is a politician then he is deceitful. But in this case, the quantifier combines with a conditional predicate, suggesting that grammar is doubly misleading. The phrase 'every politician' does not indicate a constituent of the proposition. Grammar also masks a logical difference between the existential and universally quantified propositions: predicates are related conjunctively in the former, but conditionally in the latter.

Moreover, on Frege's view, two quantifiers can bind two unsaturated positions associated with a function that takes a pair of arguments. So the proposition that everyone trusts everyone has a very non-categorical form: $\forall x \forall y[T(x, y)]$. Given that 'John' and 'Mary' indicate arguments, it follows that John trusts everyone, and that everyone trusts Mary—$\forall y[T(j, y)]$ and $\forall x[T(x, m)]$. And it follows from all three propositions that John trusts Mary: $T(j, m)$. Frege's rules of inference capture this. A variable bound by a universal quantifier can be replaced with a name, and a name can be replaced with a variable bound by an existential quantifier: $\forall x(\ldots x \ldots)$, so $\ldots n \ldots$; and $\ldots n \ldots$, so $\exists x(\ldots x \ldots)$. Given that John trusts Mary, it follows that someone trusts Mary, and that John trusts someone: $T(j, m)$; so $\exists x[T(x, m)]$, and $\exists x[T(j, x)]$. And it follows from all three propositions that someone trusts someone: $\exists x \exists y[T(x, y)]$. A single quantifier can bind multiple argument positions, as in '$\exists x[T(x, x)]$'; but this means that someone trusts herself.

Mixed quantification introduces an interesting wrinkle. The propositions indicated with '$\exists x \forall y[T(x, y)]$' and '$\forall y \exists x[T(x, y)]$' differ. We can paraphrase the first as 'there is someone who trusts everyone' and the second as 'everyone is trusted by someone or other'. The second follows from the first, but not *vice-versa*. This suggests that 'Someone trusts everyone' can be used to indicate two different propositions. According to Frege, this is further evidence that natural language is not suited to the task of representing propositions perspicuously. Natural language is good for efficient human communication. But he suggested that natural language is like the eye, while a good formal language can be like a microscope that reveals structure not otherwise observable. On this view, propositional form is revealed by the structure of a sentence in an ideal formal language, a *Begriffsschrift* (Concept-Script); where the sentences of such a language exhibit function–argument structures, as opposed to subject–predicate structures.

The real power of Frege's logic is most evident in his discussion of the Dedekind–Peano axioms for arithmetic, and in particular, how the proposition that every number has a successor is logically related to more basic truths.[5] But here, it will be enough to consider (9)–(10) and the corresponding Fregean analyses.

(9)   Every patient respects some doctor
(9a) $\forall x\{P(x) \rightarrow \exists y[D(y) \& R(x, y)]\}$
(10) Every old patient respects some doctor
(10a) $\forall x\{[O(x) \& P(x)] \rightarrow \exists y[D(y) \& R(x, y)]\}$

In Frege's logic, (10a) follows from (9a), as desired. But one can also account for why the proposition indicated with (7) follows from the one indicated with (8).

(7)   No lawyer who saw every patient respects some doctor
(7a) $\neg \exists x\{Lx \& \forall y[P(y) \rightarrow S(x, y)] \& \exists z[D(z) \& R(x, z)]\}$
(8)   No lawyer who saw every old patient respects some doctor
(8a) $\neg \exists x\{Lx \& \forall y\{[O(y) \& P(y)] \rightarrow S(x, y)\} \& \exists z[D(z) \& R(x, z)]\}$

In this way, one can handle a wide range of inferences that had puzzled logicians since Aristotle.

Frege originally spoke as though propositional constituents just were the relevant functions and (ordered n-tuples of) entities that such functions map to truth-values. But he refined this view in light of his distinction between *Sinn* and *Bedeutung*: the *Sinn* of an expression was said to be a "way of presenting" the corresponding *Bedeutung*, which would be an entity, truth-value, or function. We can think of 'Hesperus' as an expression that presents the evening star (Venus) as such, while 'Phosphorus' presents the morning star (also Venus) in a different way. Likewise, we can think of 'is bright' as an expression that presents a certain function in a certain way, and 'Hesperus is bright' as a sentence that presents its truth-value in a certain way—i.e. as the value of the function in question given the argument in question (**t** if Hesperus is bright, and **f** otherwise). From this perspective, propositions are sentential ways of presenting truth-values. Frege could thus distinguish the proposition that Hesperus is bright from the proposition that Phosphorus is bright, even though these propositions are alike with regard to the relevant function and argument.[6] Likewise, he could distinguish the trivial claim that Hesperus is Hesperus from the nontrivial claim that Hesperus is Phosphorus. This is an attractive view. For intuitively, ancient astronomers were correct not to regard the inference 'Hesperus is Hesperus, so Hesperus is Phosphorus' as an instance of the valid schema '**P**, so **P**'. But this raised questions about what the *Sinn* of an expression really is, what "presentation" could amount to, and what to say about a name with no *Bedeutung*.

---

[5] Zalta (2003) provides a helpful introduction and preparation for Demopolous (1994).
[6] This in turn led Frege (1892b) to say that psychological reports, like 'Mary thinks that Venus is bright', are also misleading with respect to the forms of the indicated propositions; cf. Soames (1987, 1995).

32.4 DESCRIPTIONS AND ANALYSIS

It can seem obvious that names and descriptions, like 'John' and 'the tall boy from Canada', indicate arguments as opposed to functions. So one might think that the logical form of any proposition indicated with 'The tall boy from Canada sang' is simply 'Sang(b)', where 'b' stands for the individual in question. But this makes the linguistic elements of the description logically irrelevant. And if the tall boy from Canada sang, then a boy from Canada sang; hence, a boy sang. Moreover, 'the' apparently implies uniqueness in a way that 'some' does not.[7]

Russell (1919) held that such implications reflect logical form. On his view, a proposition expressed with 'The boy sang' has the following structure: $\exists x\{Boy(x)\& \forall y[Boy(y) \to y = x]\&Sang(x)\}$. As we'll see, the middle conjunct is just a way of expressing uniqueness with Fregean tools, and it can be rewritten without affecting the main point. According to Russell, even if a speaker refers to a certain boy when saying 'The boy sang', that boy is not a constituent of the proposition indicated: the proposition has the form of an existential quantification, not the form of a function saturated by (an argument that is) the boy referred to; and in this respect, 'the boy' is like 'some boy'. Though on Russell's view, not even 'the' indicates a propositional constituent. This extended Frege's idea that natural language is misleading.

As Russell stressed, a description can be meaningful without describing anything. While France is kingless, 'The present king of France is bald' can be used to indicate a proposition. Call this proposition '**Frank**'. If **Frank** consists of the function indicated with 'Bald( )', saturated by an entity indicated with 'The present king of France', there must *be* such an entity. But appeal to nonexistent kings, or ways of presenting them, is dubious at best. Russell held instead that **Frank** is a quantificational proposition of the form '$\exists x\{K(x)\& \forall y[K(y) \to y = x]\& B(x)\}$'. In which case, the following reasoning is spurious: since **Frank** is true or false, the present king of France is bald or not; so there is a king of France, who is either bald or not. On Russell's view, **Frank** is false, given that $\exists\neg x[K(x)]$. It hardly follows that $\exists x\{K(x)\&[B(x) \vee\neg B(x)]\}$. But the ambiguity of natural language may lead us to *confuse* the true negation of **Frank** with the following false claim: $\exists x\{K(x)\& \forall y[K(y) \to y = x]\&\neg B(x)\}$. According to Russell, puzzles about "nonexistence" can be resolved without dubious metaphysics, given the right views about logical form. (This invited the thought, developed by Wittgenstein [1921] and others, that other philosophical puzzles might dissolve if we properly understood the logical forms of our claims.)

Russell also held that we are directly acquainted with the constituents of propositions we entertain. But at least typically, we are not directly acquainted with the mind-independent bearers of proper names. This led Russell to say that typical names are disguised descriptions, not labels for propositional constituents. On this view,

---

[7] Of course, one can say 'The boy sang' without denying that universe contains more than one boy. But likewise, in ordinary conversation, one can say 'Everything is in the trunk' without denying that the universe contains some things not in the trunk. And intuitively, a speaker who uses 'the boy' does imply that there is exactly one contextually relevant boy.

'Hesperus' is semantically associated with a complex predicate—say, for illustration, a predicate of the form '$E(x) \& S(x)$'. In which case, 'Hesperus is bright' indicates a proposition of the form '$\exists x\{[E(x) \& S(x)] \& \forall y\{[E(y) \& S(y)] \rightarrow y = x\} \& B(x)\}$'. It follows that Hesperus exists iff $\exists x\{[E(x) \& S(x)] \& \forall y\{[E(y) \& S(y)] \rightarrow y = x\}\}$; and this would be challenged by Kripke (1980). But Russell offered an attractive account of why the proposition that Hesperus is bright differs from the proposition that Phosphorus is bright. He could say that 'Phosphorus is bright' indicates a proposition of the form '$\exists x\{[M(x) \& S(x)] \& \forall y\{[M(y) \& S(y)] \rightarrow y = x]\} \& B(x)\}$'; where '$E(x)$' and '$M(x)$' indicate different functions, specified (respectively) in terms of evenings and mornings. This leaves room for the discovery that '$E(x) \& S(x)$' and '$M(x) \& S(x)$' both indicate functions that map Venus and nothing else to the truth-value t.

32.5 REGIMENTATION AND QUANTIFICATION

Positing unexpected logical forms thus seemed to have explanatory payoffs. This invited attempts to provide analyses of propositions, and accounts of the "conventions" governing natural language, with the aim of saying how sentences could be used to indicate propositions. The logical positivists held that the conventional meaning of a declarative sentence is (ideally) a procedure for determining the truth or falsity of that sentence. But they had little success in formulating rules that were plausible both as descriptions of how ordinary speakers understand natural language, and bases for the envisioned analyses. And until Montague (1970), discussed briefly below, there was no real progress in showing how to systematically associate quantificational constructions of natural language with Fregean logical forms.

Carnap (1950) developed a sophisticated position according to which philosophers could (and should) articulate alternative sets of conventions for associating sentences of a language with propositions. Within each such language, the conventions would determine what follows from what. But one would have to decide, on broadly pragmatic grounds, which interpreted language was best for certain purposes. On this view, questions about "the" logical form of an ordinary sentence are in part questions about which conventions one should adopt. This was, in many ways, an attractive view. But it also raised a worry. Perhaps the structural mismatches between sentences of a natural language and sentences of a *Begriffsschrift* are so severe that we cannot systematically associate the former with the latter.

Quine (1951, 1960) combined behaviorist psychology with a conception of logical form similar to Carnap's. The result was an influential view according to which: there is no fact of the matter about which proposition a speaker indicates with a sentence of natural language, because talk of propositions is at best a way of talking about how we should regiment our verbal behavior for purposes of scientific inquiry; claims about logical form are in this sense evaluative; and such claims are not determined by the totality of facts concerning our dispositions to use language. From this perspective, mismatches between logical and grammatical form are expected. Quine also held that decisions about how to associate natural and formal sentences should be made holistically. As he sometimes put it, the "unit of translation" is an entire language, not a particular sentence. On this view, one can regiment a sentence S of natural language with a structurally mismatching sentence μ of a formal language—even if it seems (locally) implausible that S is used to indicate the proposition associated with μ—so long as the association between S and μ is part of a more general system of regimentation that is at least as good as any alternative.

For present purposes, we can abstract from debates about whether this is plausible. But one aspect of Quine's thought, about the kind of regimented language we should use, proved especially important for discussions of logical form. Recall that Frege's *Begriffsschrift* was designed to capture the Dedekind–Peano axioms for arithmetic, including the axiom of induction. This required quantification into positions occupiable by predicates. In current notation, Frege allowed for formulae like '$(Fa \& Fb) \rightarrow \exists X(Xa \& Xb)$' and '$\forall x \forall y[x = y \leftrightarrow \forall X(Xx \leftrightarrow Xy)]$'. And he took second-order quantification to be quantification over functions. On this construal, '$\exists X(Xa \& Xb)$' is true iff: there is a function that maps the individual a and the individual b onto the truth-value t. Frege also assumed that each predicate indicates a function such that for each individual x, the function maps x to t iff x satisfies the predicate. This generated Russell's Paradox, given predicates like 'is not an element of itself'. And for various reasons, Quine and others advocated restriction to the *first-order* fragment of Frege's logic, disallowing quantification into positions occupied by predicates.[8] From this perspective, we should replace '$(Fa \& Fb) \rightarrow \exists X(Xa \& Xb)$' with first-order quantification over sets, as in '$(Fa \& Fb) \rightarrow \exists s \forall x\{[x \epsilon s \leftrightarrow Fx] \& a \epsilon s \& b \epsilon s)\}$'; where this conditional is a non-logical hypothesis. Insisting on first-order regimentation now seems tendentious; see Boolos (1998). But it fueled the idea that logical form can diverge wildly from grammatical form, since first-order regimentations of natural sentences are often highly artificial (and in some cases, unavailable).

Another strand of thought in analytic philosophy—pressed by Wittgenstein (1953) and developed by others, including Strawson and Austin—also suggested that a single sentence could be used (on different occasions) to express different kinds of propositions. Strawson (1950) argued that *pace* Russell, a speaker could use an instance of 'The F is G' to express a singular proposition about a specific individual: namely, the F in the context at hand. According to Strawson, sentences themselves do not indicate propositions; and speakers can use 'The boy is tall' to express a proposition with the contextually relevant boy as a constituent. Donnellan (1966) went on to argue that a speaker could even use an instance of 'The F is G' to express a singular proposition about an individual that is not an F. Such considerations suggested that relations between natural language sentences and propositions are

[8] Gödel had proved the completeness of first-order predicate calculus, thus providing a purely formal criterion for what followed from what in that language. Quine (150, 1970) also held that second-order quantification illicitly treated predicates as names for sets, thereby spoiling Frege's conception of propositions as unified by virtue of having unsaturated predicational constituents that are satisfied by things denoted by names.

(at best) very complex and mediated by speakers' intentions.[9] This bolstered the Quine–Carnap idea that questions about the structure of premises and conclusions are really questions about how we *should* talk, when trying to describe the world, much as logic itself seems to be concerned with how we *should* reason. From this perspective, the connections between logic and grammar seemed rather shallow.

On the other hand, more recent work on quantifiers suggests that the divergence had been exaggerated, in part because of how Frege's idea of variable-binding was originally implemented. Consider again the proposition that some boy sang, and the proposed logical division: $\exists x[\text{Boy}(x) \ \& \ \text{Sang}(x)]$. This is one way to regiment the English sentence. But one can also offer a "logical paraphrase" that parallels the grammatical division between 'some boy' and 'sang': for some individual x such that x is a boy, x sang. One can formalize this by using restricted quantifiers, which incorporate restrictions on the domain over which bound variables range. For example, 'x:Boy(x)' is an existential quantifier that binds a variable ranging over boys in the relevant domain. So '$\exists x$:Boy(x)[Sang(x)]' means that some boy sang. And logic provides no reason for preferring '$\exists x[\text{Boy}(x) \ \& \ \text{Sang}(x)]$'.

Universal quantifiers can be restricted, as in '$\forall x$:Boy(x)[Sang(x)]', interpreted as follows: for every individual x such that Boy(x), x sang; that is, every boy sang. Restrictors can also be complex, as in 'Some tall boy sang' or 'Every boy who respects Mary sang', rendered as '$\exists x$:Tall(x) & Boy(x)[Sang(x)]' and '$\forall x$:Boy(x) & Respects(x, m)[Sang(x)]'. So it seems that the inferential difference between 'Some boy sang' and 'Every boy sang' lies entirely with the propositional contributions of 'Some' and 'Every' after all—not with the different contributions of '&' and '→'. Words like 'someone', and the grammatical requirement that 'every' be followed by a noun (phrase), reflect the fact that natural language employs restricted quantifiers. Expressions like 'every boy' are composed of a determiner and a noun. So one can think of determiners like 'every' as words that can combine with an ordered pair of predicates to form a sentence, much as transitive verbs can combine with an ordered pair of names to form a sentence. And this analogy, between determiners and transitive verbs, has a semantic correlate.

On Frege's view, the function indicated by 'loves' maps the ordered pair $\langle x, y \rangle$ to the truth-value **t** iff x loves y. Here, 'y' corresponds to the verb's *internal* argument (or direct object), which combines with the verb to form a phrase, as in 'loves Juliet'; 'x' corresponds to the verb's *external* argument. In 'Every boy sang', 'boy' is the internal argument of 'Every', since 'Every boy' is a phrase, and we can think of 'sang' as the external argument. So following Frege, let 'X' and 'Y' be second-order variables ranging over functions, from individuals to truth-values. Then we can say that the function indicated by 'Every' maps the ordered pair $\langle X, Y \rangle$ to **t** iff the extension of X

---

[9] See also Grice (1975). Fodor (1975, 1978) combines a version of this view with the idea that propositions are sentences of a mental language that may well differ structurally from the languages humans use to communicate.

includes the extension of Y. Likewise, the function indicated by 'Some' maps $\langle X, Y \rangle$ to **t** iff the extension of X *intersects with* the extension of Y.[10]

This suggests an alternative to Russell's treatment of 'The'; see Montague (1970). We can rewrite '$\exists x\{Boy(x)$ & $\forall y[Boy(y) \rightarrow x = y]$ & $Sang(x)\}$' as '$\exists x{:}Boy(x)[Sang(x)]$ & $|Boy| = 1$', interpreted as follows: for some individual x such that x is a boy, x sang, and exactly one (relevant) individual is a boy. Neither 'the boy' nor 'the' corresponds to a constituent of this formalism. But one can depart farther from Russell's notation, while stressing that 'The' is relevantly like 'Some'. One can analyze 'The boy sang' as '$!x{:}Boy(x)[Sang(x)]$', specifying the propositional contribution of '!' as follows: $!x{:} Y(x)\ [X(x)] = $ **t** iff the extensions of X and Y intersect, and Y maps exactly one (relevant) individual to **t**. This preserves Russell's central claim. Even if a speaker refers to a boy in saying 'The boy sang', that boy is not a constituent of the quantificational proposition indicated with '$!x{:}Boy(x)[Sang(x)]$'; see Neale (1990) for discussion. But far from showing that logical form diverges from grammatical form, the second-order restricted-quantifier notation suggests that in this case, propositional structure parallels sentential structure.

32.6 TRANSFORMATIONAL GRAMMAR

Still, the subject/predicate structure of 'Mary/trusts every doctor' diverges from the restricted quantifier formula '$\forall y{:}Doctor(y)[Trusts(Mary, y)]$'. We can rewrite '$Trusts(Mary, y)$' as '$[Trusts(y)](Mary)$', reflecting the fact that 'trusts' combines with a direct object. But this does not affect the main point. Grammatically, 'trusts' and 'every doctor' form a phrase. Though with respect to logical form, 'trusts' combines with 'Mary' and a variable to form a complex predicate that is in turn an external argument of the higher-order predicate 'every'. Similar remarks apply to 'Some boy trusts every doctor' and '$\exists[x{:}Boy(x)][\forall y{:}Doctor(y)]\{Trusts(x, y)\}$'. So it seems that mismatches remain, in the very places that troubled medieval logicians—quantificational direct objects, and other examples of complex predicates with quantificational constituents.

Montague (1970) showed that these mismatches do not preclude systematic association of natural language sentences with the corresponding propositional structures. He specified an algorithm that pairs each natural language sentence containing one or more quantificational expressions with appropriate sentences of a *Begriffsschrift*. This was a significant advance, establishing that one can fruitfully employ Frege's formal tools in the study of natural language. Montague still held that the syntax of natural language was misleading for purposes of (what he took to be) real semantics. But even this was becoming less clear.

---

[10] See Pietroski (2003) for a variant, drawing on Boolos (1998) and Schein (1993), that avoids Russell's Paradox.

In thinking about the relation of logic to grammar, one must not assume a naive conception of the latter. For example, the grammatical form of a sentence need not be determined by the linear order of its words. Using brackets to indicate phrasal structure, we can distinguish sentence (11) from the homophonous sentence (12).

(11) {Mary [saw [the [boy [with binoculars]]]]}
(12) {Mary [[saw [the boy]] [with binoculars]]}

The direct object of (11) is 'the boy with binoculars', while in (12), 'saw the boy' is modified by an adverbial phrase. Presumably, only (11) implies that the boy had binoculars, and only (12) implies that Mary used binoculars to see the boy.

More generally, the study of natural language suggests a rich, non-obvious conception of grammatical form; see especially Chomsky (1957, 1965, 1981, 1986, 1995). A leading idea of modern linguistics is that at least some grammatical structures are transformations of others. Expressions often appear to be *displaced* from positions canonically associated with certain grammatical relations. For example, the word 'who' in (13) seems to be associated with the internal (direct object) argument position of 'saw'.

(13) Mary wondered who John saw

Correspondingly, (13) can be glossed as 'Mary wondered which person is such that John saw that person'. This invites the hypothesis that (13) reflects a transformation of the "Deep Structure" (13D) into the "Surface Structure" (13S),

(13D) {Mary [wondered {John [saw who]}]}
(13S) {Mary [wondered [who$_i$ {John [saw (_)$_i$]}]]}

with indices indicating a structural relation between the coindexed positions. In (13D), the embedded clause has the same form as 'John saw Bill'. But in (13S), 'who' occupies another position. Similar remarks apply to 'Who did John see' and other question-words (like 'why', 'what', 'when', and 'how').

One might also explain the synonymy of (14) and (15) by positing a common deep structure, (14D):

(14) John seems to like Mary
(15) It seems John likes Mary
(14D) {Seems {John [likes Mary]}}
(14S) {John$_i$ [seems {(_)$_i$ [to like Mary]}]}

If every English sentence needs a grammatical subject, (14D) must be modified: either by displacing 'John', as in (14S); or by inserting a pleonastic subject, as in (15). Note that in (15), 'It' does not indicate any thing; compare 'There' in 'There is something in the garden'. Appeal to displacement also lets one distinguish the superficially parallel sentences (16) and (17).

(16) John is easy to please
(17) John is eager to please

If (16) is true, John is easily pleased; using a pleonastic subject, it is easy (for some-one) to please John. But if (17) is true, John is eager that he please someone or other. This asymmetry is effaced by representations like 'Easy-to-please(John)' and 'Eager-to-please(John)'. The contrast is made manifest, however, with (16S) and (17S);

(16s) {John$_i$ [is easy {e [to please (_)$_i$]}]}}
(17s) {John$_i$[is eager {(_)$_i$ [to please e]}]}}

where 'e' indicates an unpronounced argument position. This reflects the idea that the "surface subject" of a sentence may be understood as the direct object of a verb embedded within the main predicate, as in (16S). Such hypotheses about grammat-ical structure require defense. But Chomsky and others have long argued that such hypotheses are needed to account for many facts. As an illustration of the *kind* of data that is relevant, note that (18–20) are perfectly fine expressions of English, while (21) is not.

(18) The boy who sang was happy
(19) Was the boy who sang happy
(20) The boy who was happy sang
(21) *Was the boy who happy sang

This suggests that an auxiliary verb cannot be displaced from some positions. We can encode this hypothesis by saying that (19S) is the result of a permissible transforma-tion, while (21S) is not.

(19s) Was$_i${[the [boy [who sang]]][(_)$_i$ happy]}
(21s) *Was$_i${[the [boy [who [(_)$_i$ happy]]]] sang}

The ill-formedness of (21) is striking, since one can sensibly ask whether or not the boy who was happy sang. Likewise, one can also ask whether or not (22) is true. But (23) is not the yes/no question corresponding to (22).

(22) The boy who was lost kept crying
(23) Was the boy who lost kept crying

Rather, (23) is the yes/no question corresponding to 'The boy who lost was kept cry-ing'. We can explain this "negative fact," concerning what (23) *cannot* mean, assum-ing that 'was' *cannot* be displaced from the relative clause in (22): *Was$_i$ {[the [boy [who [(_)$_i$ lost]]]] [kept crying]}. For in that case, (23) must be understood as structured in (23S).

(23s) *Was$_i$ {[the [boy [who lost]]][(_)$_i$ kept crying]}

Such explanations appeal to substantive constraints on transformations. The idea was that a sentence has a deep structure (DS), which reflects semantically relev-ant relations between verbs and their arguments, and a surface structure (SS) that may include displaced (or pleonastic) elements; and in some cases, pronunciation might depend on still further transformations of SS, resulting in a distinct "phon-ological form" (PF). Linguists posited various constraints on these levels of gram-matical structure, and the transformations that relate them. Though as the theory was elaborated and refined under empirical pressure, various apparently relevant facts still went unexplained. This suggested another level of grammatical structure, called 'LF' (intimating 'logical form'), obtained by a different kind of transformation on SS.

The hypothesized transformation, which targeted the kinds of expressions that indicate (restricted) quantifiers, mapped structures like (24s) onto structures like (24L).

(24s) {Pat [trusts [every doctor]]}
(24L) {[every doctor]$_i$ {Pat [trusts (_)$_i$] }}

Clearly, (24L) does not reflect the pronounced word order in English. But the idea was that PF determines pronunciation, while LF was said to be the level at which the scope of a natural language quantifier is determined; see May (1985). If we think of 'every' as a second-order transitive predicate, which can combine with two predicates like 'doctor' and 'Pat trusts___' to form a complete sentence, we should expect that at some level of analysis, the sentence 'Pat trusts every doctor' has the structure indicated in (24L). And mapping (24L) to the logical form '[∀x:Doctor(x)]{Trusts(Pat, x)}' is trivial. Likewise, one can hypothesize that (25s) may be mapped onto (25L) or (25L'),

(25s) {[some boy][trusts [every doctor]]}
(25L) {[some boy]$_i$ {[every doctor]$_j$ {(_)$_i$ [trusts (_)$_j$] }}}
(25L') {[every doctor]$_j$ {[some boy]$_i$ {(_)$_i$ [trusts (_)$_j$] }}}

which are easily mapped onto '[∃x:Boy(x)][∀y:Doctor(y)]{Trusts(x, y)}' and '[∀y:Doctor(y)][∃x:Boy(x)]{Trusts(x, y)}'. This assimilates quantifier scope ambiguity to the structural ambiguity of examples like 'Mary saw the boy with binoculars'.

More generally, many apparent examples of grammar/logic mismatches were rediagnosed as mismatches between different aspects of *grammatical* structure—between those aspects that determine pronunciation, and those that determine interpretation. In one sense, this is fully in keeping with the idea that in natural language, "surface appearances" are often misleading with regard to propositional structure. But it makes room for the idea that grammatical and logical form converge, in ways that can be discovered through investigation, once we move beyond traditional subject–predicate conceptions of structure with regard to both logic and grammar.

There is independent evidence for "covert quantifier raising"—displacement of quantificational expressions from their audible positions, as in (24L); see Huang (1995), Hornstein (1995). Consider the French translation of 'Who did John see', 'Jean a vu qui'. If we assume that qui ('who') is displaced at LF, we can explain why the question-word is understood in both French and English like a quantifier binding a variable: which person x is such that John saw x? Similarly, example (26) from Chinese is transliterated as in (27).

(26) Zhangsan zhidao Lisi mai-te sheme
(27) Zhangsan know Lisi bought what

But (26) is ambiguous, between the interrogative (27a) and the complex declarative (27b).

(27a) Which thing is such that Zhangsan knows Lisi bought it
(27b) Zhangsan knows which thing (is such that) Lisi bought (it)

This suggests covert displacement of the quantificational question-word in Chinese; see Huang (1982, 1995). And note that (28) has the reading indicated in (28a) but not the reading indicated in (28b), suggesting that 'every patient' gets displaced, but only so far.

(28) It is false that Chris saw every patient
(28a) $\neg \forall x$:Patient(x)[Saw(Chris, x)]
(28b) $\forall x$:Patient$(x)\neg$[Saw(Chris, x)]

Likewise, (13) cannot mean that for every patient x, no lawyer who saw x respects some doctor.

(13) No lawyer who saw every patient respects some doctor

As we have already seen, English seems to abhor "fronting" certain elements from within an embedded relative clause. This invites the hypothesis that quantifier displacement is subject to a similar constraint, and hence, that quantifiers are often displaced. Indeed, many linguists (following Chomsky [1995, 2000]) would now posit only two levels of grammatical structure, PF and LF—the thought being that constraints on DS and SS can be eschewed in favor of a simpler theory that only posits constraints on how expressions can be combined in the course of constructing complex expressions that can be pronounced and interpreted. If this development of earlier theories proves correct, then (some future analog of) LF may be *the* semantically relevant level of grammatical structure. But in any case, there is a large body of work suggesting that many logical properties of quantifiers, names, and pronouns are reflected in properties of LF.

For example, linguists have discovered modern grammatical correlates of *dictum de nullo* environments. The word 'ever' can be used in sentences like (29)–(31). But there is something wrong with (32)–(34).

(29) No senator ever lied
(30) No senator who ever lied got away with it
(31) Every senator who ever lied got away with it
(32) *Every senator ever lied
(33) *Some senator ever lied
(34) *Some senator who ever lied got away with it

To a first approximation, certain expressions like 'ever' can appear only in phrases that licence inferences from more restrictive to less restrictive predicates. (Idiomatic alternatives to 'any'—like 'a plug nickel', roughly synonymous with 'any money'—exhibit this pattern: Nobody/*Somebody would pay a plug nickel for that horse.) Such discoveries, of which there have been many, confirm the Aristotelian and medieval suspicion that logical properties and grammatical properties are deeply related after all.[11]

There is, to be sure, an important conceptual distinction between the theoretical notion of LF and the traditional notion of logical form. There is no guarantee that structural features of natural language sentences will mirror the structural features of propositions. But this leaves room for a range of empirical hypothesis about how grammar is related to logic. For example, even if the LF of a sentence S underdetermines the logical form of the proposition a speaker expresses with S (on a given occasion of use), perhaps the LF provides a "scaffolding" that is somehow elaborated in particular contexts—with little or no *mismatch* between sentential and propositional architecture. If some such view is correct, it would avoid some unpleasant questions prompted by earlier Fregean views: how can sentences be used (reliably) to indicate propositions with very different structures; and if grammar is deeply misleading, why think that our intuitions concerning impeccability of inferences provide good evidence for which propositions follow from which? These are, however, issues that remain very much unsettled.

32.7 SEMANTIC STRUCTURE AND EVENTS

Prima facie, 'Every tall sailor respects some doctor' and 'Some short boy likes every politician' exhibit common modes of linguistic combination. So especially in light of transformational grammars, a natural hypothesis is that the meaning of each sentence is somehow fixed by these modes of combination, given the word meanings. It may be hard to see how this hypothesis could be true, given pervasive mismatches between logical and grammatical form. But it is also hard to see how the hypothesis could be false, given that children typically acquire the capacity to understand the endlessly many expressions of the languages spoken around them. A great deal of recent work has focussed on these issues, concerning the connections between logical form and apparent compositionality of natural language.

It was implicit in Frege that each sentence of an ideal language has a compositionally determined truth-condition. Frege did not specify an algorithm that would associate each sentence of his *Begriffsschrift* with its truth-condition. But Tarski (1933) showed how to do this for the first-order predicate calculus, focussing on the interesting cases of multiple quantification. This made it possible to capture, with precision, the idea that an inference is valid in the predicate calculus iff: every interpretation that makes the premises true makes the conclusion true, holding fixed the interpretations of symbols like '∃' and '¬'. Davidson (1967a) conjectured that there are similar "theories of truth" for natural languages; see Higginbotham (1985) for development within an explicitly Chomskyan framework. And Montague, also

---

[11] See Ladusaw (1981), and Ludlow (2002) for further discussion and references.

inspired by Tarski, showed how to start dealing with quantificational predicates. Sentences like 'Pat thinks that Hesperus is Phosphorus' present difficulties; though Davidson (1968) offered an influential suggestion. And while many apparent objections to the conjecture remain, Davidson's (1967b) proposal concerning examples like (35–38) proved especially fruitful.

(35) Juliet kissed Romeo quickly at midnight.
(36) Juliet kissed Romeo quickly.
(37) Juliet kissed Romeo at midnight.
(38) Juliet kissed Romeo.

If (35) is true, so are (36)–(38); and if (36) or (37) is true, so is (38). The inferences are impeccable. But if we treat 'kissed quickly at midnight' as an unstructured transitive predicate like 'kissed', we treat the inference from (35) to (38) as having the form '$K^*(x, y)$, so $K(x, y)$'. And invalid inferences, like 'Juliet kicked Romeo, so Juliet kissed Romeo', share this form. Put another way, one wants to know *why* conditionals like following are tautologous: if Juliet kissed Romeo in a certain manner at a certain time, then Juliet kissed Romeo. Davidson argued that sentences like (35)–(38) mask important semantic structure. He proposed that such sentences are understood in terms of quantification over events, as suggested by paraphrases like 'There was a kissing of Romeo by Juliet' and 'There was a quick kissing of Romeo by Juliet, and it happened at midnight'. The details are less important here than the idea that a sentence like (35) might be understood as a quantificational claim, structured along the following lines:

∃[Agent(e, Juliet) & Kissing(e) & Patient(e, Romeo) & Quick(e) & At(e, midnight)].

This raises the possibility that theories of meaning/understanding for natural languages will associate sentences (whose grammatical structures are not obvious) with "semantic structures" that are not obvious.[12] Perhaps in the end, talk of logical forms is best construed as talk of the structure(s) that speakers impose on words in order to understand natural language systematically; see Lepore and Ludwig (2002); Ludwig (2003). From this perspective, which remains tendentious, the phenomenon of valid inference is at least largely a reflection of semantic compositionality.

At this point, many issues become relevant to discussions of logical form. Given any sentence of natural language, one can ask interesting questions about its grammatical structure and what it can(not) be used to say. More generally, how should we characterize sentential meanings? (In terms of truth theories? In first-order terms?) What should we say about the various paradoxes? Are claims about the "semantic structure" of a sentence fundamentally descriptive claims about speakers (or their communities, or their languages)? Or is there an important sense in which claims about semantic structure are normative claims? Are facts about language acquisition germane to hypotheses about propositional structure? But it seems clear that the traditional questions—what kinds of structures do propositions and sentences exhibit,

---

[12] Whether or not such theories take the form of an algorithm for *transforming* sentences of natural language into sentences of a mental (or invented ideal) language.

and how do human beings relate thought to speech—must be addressed in terms of increasingly sophisticated conceptions of logic and grammar.

REFERENCES

Boolos, G. (1998). *Logic, Logic, and Logic.* Cambridge, MA: Harvard University Press.
Carnap, R. (1950). Empiricism, Semantics, and Ontology. Reprinted in *Meaning and Necessity*, 2nd edn. (Chicago: University of Chicago Press, 1956).
Chomsky, N. (1957). *Syntactic Structures.* The Hague: Mouton.
—— (1965). *Aspects of the Theory of Syntax.* Cambridge, MA: MIT Press.
—— (1981). *Lectures on Government and Binding.* Dordrecht: Foris.
—— (1986). *Knowledge of Language* (New York: Praeger).
—— (1995). *The Minimalist Program.* Cambridge, MA: MIT Press.
Davidson, D. (1967a). Truth and Meaning. *Synthese*, 17: 304–23.
—— (1967b). The Logical Form of Action Sentences. In N. Rescher (ed.) *The Logic of Decision and Action* (Pittsburgh: University of Pittsburgh Press).
—— (1968). On Saying That. *Synthese* 19: 130–46.
Demopolous, W, (ed.) (1994). *Frege's Philosophy of Mathematics.* Cambridge, MA: Harvard.
Donnellan, K. (1966). Reference and Definite Descriptions. *Philosophical Review*, 75: 281–304.
Frege, G. (1879). *Begriffsschrift.* Halle: Louis Nebert. English translation in J. van Heijenoort (ed.), *From Frege to Gödel: A Source Book in Mathematical Logic, 1879–1931* (Cambridge, MA: Harvard University Press, 1967).
—— (1892a). Function and Concept. In Geach and Black (1980).
—— (1892b). Sense and Reference. In Geach and Black (1980).
Fodor, J. (1975). *The Language of Thought.* New York: Crowell.
Fodor, J. (1978). *Propositional Attitudes. The Monist*, 61: 501–23.
Geach, P. and Black, M. (1980). *Translations from the Philosophical Writings of Gottlob Frege* (Oxford: Blackwell).
Grice, H. Paul. Logic and Conversation (1975). In *Syntax and Semantics, vol. 3*, eds. P. Cole and J. Morgan. New York: Academic Press.
Higginbotham, J. (1985). On Semantics. *Linguistic Inquiry*, 16: 547–93.
Hornstein, N. (1995). *Logical Form: From GB to Minimalism.* Oxford: Blackwell.
Huang, J. (1995). Logical Form. In Webelhuth, G. (ed.) *Government and Binding Theory and the Minimalist Program: Principles and Parameters in Syntactic Theory* (Oxford: Blackwell).
Kneale, W. and Kneale, M. (1962). *The Development of Logic.* Oxford: Oxford University Press, 1962 (reprinted 1984).
Kripke, Saul. *Naming and Necessity.* Cambridge, MA: Harvard University Press, (1980).
Ladusaw, W. (1981). On the Notion *Affective* in the Analysis of Negative Polarity Items. *Journal of Linguistic Research*, 1: 1–16.
Lepore, E. and Ludwig, K.. (2002). What is Logical Form. In Preyer and Peters 2002.
Ludwig, K. (2003). *Contemporary Philosophy in Focus: on Davidson* (Cambridge: Cambridge University Press).
Ludlow, P. (2002). LF and Natural Logic. In Preyer and Peters 2002.
May, R. (1985). *Logical Form: Its Structure and Derivation.* Cambridge, MA: MIT Press.
Montague, R. (1970). English as a Formal Language. Reprinted in his collected essays, *Formal Philosophy* (New Haven: Yale University Press, 1974).
Pietroski, P. (2003). Quantification and Second-Order Monadicity. *Philosophical Perspectives*, 17: 259–98.

Preyer, G. and Peters, G. (eds.) (2002). *Logical Form and Language*. Oxford: Oxford University Press.

Quine, W. V. O. (1950). *Methods of Logic*. New York: Henry Holt.

____ (1951). Two Dogmas of Empiricism. *Philosophical Review*, 60: 20–43.

____ (1960). *Word and Object*. Cambridge MA: MIT Press.

____ (1970). *Philosophy of Logic*. Englewood Cliffs, NJ: Prentice Hall.

Russell, Bertrand (1919). *Introduction to Mathematical Philosophy*. London: George Allen and Unwin.

Soames, S. (1987). Direct Reference, Propositional Attitudes, and Semantic Content. *Philosophical Topics*, 15: 47–87.

____ (1995). Beyond Singular Propositions. *Canadian Journal of Philosophy*, 25: 515–50.

Strawson, P. (1950). On Referring. *Mind*, 59: 320–44.

Tarski, A. (1933). The Concept of Truth in Formalized Languages. Reprinted in *Logic, Semantics, Metamathematics* (tr. J. H. Woodger, 2nd edn. ed. J Corcoran). Indianapolis: Hacket.

Wittgenstein, G. *Tractatus Logico-Philosophicus*, trans. D. Pears and B. McGuinness London: Routledge and Kegan Paul, (1921).

____ *Philosophical Investigations*. New York: Macmillan, (1953).

Zalta, Edward Frege (logic, theorem, and foundations for arithmetic). *The Stanford Encyclopedia of Philosophy* (Fall 2003 edn.). Available from http://plato.stanford.edu/archives/fall2003/entries/frege-logic.

PART VII

VARIETIES OF SPEECH ACT

CHAPTER 33

METAPHOR

MARGA REIMER
AND ELISABETH CAMP

33.1 WHAT IS METAPHOR?: A TENTATIVE CHARACTERIZATION

METAPHOR has traditionally been construed as a linguistic phenomenon: as something produced and understood by speakers of natural language. So understood, metaphors are naturally viewed as linguistic expressions of a particular type, or as linguistic expressions used in a particular type of way. We adopt this linguistic conception of metaphor in what follows. In doing so, we do not intend to rule out the possibility of non-linguistic forms of metaphor. Many theorists think that non-linguistic objects (such as paintings or dance performances) or conceptual structures (like *love as a journey* or *argument as war*)[1] should also be treated as metaphors. Indeed, the idea that metaphors are in the first instance conceptual phenomena, and linguistic devices only derivatively, is the dominant view in what is now the dominant area of metaphor research: cognitive science.[2] In construing metaphor as linguistic, we merely intend to impose appropriate constraints on a discussion whose focus is the understanding and analysis of metaphor within contemporary philosophy of language.

Given this starting point, what can be said about metaphor that is not controversial? Very little, as it turns out. Metaphor is a trope or figure of speech, where a 'figure

We would like to thank Richard Moran, William Lycan, Emma Borg, Ram Neta, Mike Harnish, and Barry Smith for helpful comments on earlier drafts of this article.

[1] For an extensive discussion of these and other 'conceptual metaphors', see Lakoff and Johnson (1980, 1999) and Lakoff (1993).

[2] See e.g. the *Center for the Cognitive Science of Metaphor Online*: (http://philosophy.uoregon.edu/metaphor/metaphor.htm)

of speech' is a *non-literal* use of language. This class also includes irony, metonymy, synecdoche, hyperbole, and meiosis.[3] What distinguishes metaphor from these other tropes? One standard definition of metaphor is as *a figure of speech in which one thing is represented (or spoken of) as something else*. This construal of metaphor comports well with many examples of metaphor drawn from classic literary works. Consider, for instance, "Juliet is the sun" (Shakespeare), "Time is the devourer of all things" (Ovid), or "Poverty is the sister of beggary" (Aristophanes). In the first, a girl, Juliet, is spoken of as the sun; in the second, time is spoken of as a ferocious beast; in the third, poverty is spoken of as a sister (and thus as a person).

Some philosophers, in an effort to explain metaphor's characteristic rhetorical force, have elaborated on this standard construal in terms of "representing-as." Thus, Monroe Beardsley (1967) identifies two features working in tandem within a metaphor. On the one hand, a metaphor produces a *conceptual tension* between the concept that is expressed by the metaphorical term and the concept(s) that we normally and intuitively apply to the subject. So, for example, there is a 'tension' or mismatch between representing Juliet as the sun and as a girl, or between representing poverty as a sibling and as an economic state. Often (though, as we will see, not always) this 'tension' renders the metaphorical sentence logically absurd if construed literally. For this reason, Nelson Goodman (1968) characterizes the conceptual tension to which Beardsley refers as involving a kind of "calculated category mistake." A metaphor, he says, "projects" a set of "labels" belonging to one realm of objects (e.g. celestial bodies) upon another realm to which those labels do not ordinarily apply (e.g. human beings).

On the other hand, Beardsley points out, in spite of their apparent absurdity metaphors are generally quite *intelligible* and even profound. So, for example, Romeo's metaphor seems to serve as an effective means for communicating his feelings about Juliet (such as being dazzled by her), to evoke similar attitudes in others, and to claim that she possesses certain properties (such as being beautiful and life-giving). Beardsley (1962) claims that metaphors are able to do this because the sentence's inherent conceptual tension imposes a "metaphorical twist" on the relevant term, forcing it to refer to features with which it is normally merely associated.

These characterizations of metaphor do have a certain intuitive appeal, but they themselves employ metaphorical language ("conceptual tension", "label", "projection") in crucial explanatory roles, and so fail to provide fully explicit and satisfactory theories of metaphor. As we will see in what follows, this is quite typical. But it may also be unavoidable: as will also become clear, metaphor is itself a vague and elusive phenomenon.

---

[3] In irony, the intended meaning is in some sense the 'contrary' of the words uttered, as when one says of a job that has clearly been poorly done, 'Good job!' In metonymy, a single characteristic or entity is used to identify a more complex, related entity, as when 'The White House' is used to refer to the President. Synecdoche is a kind of metonymy in which part of something is used to represent the whole, as in 'All hands on deck.' Hyperbole involves exaggeration, meiosis understatement. When I say 'These Tucson summers are killing me', I am engaging in hyperbole; when I say of a wild party that things 'got just a bit out of hand', I am engaging in meiosis.

33.2 Metaphor and Contemporary Analytic Philosophy

Armed with this intuitive idea of what metaphor involves, let's consider metaphor's place within analytic philosophy, broadly construed. We will then sharpen our focus and consider how it has been treated by contemporary philosophers of language.

Although the last thirty years have seen an explosion of interest in metaphor within analytic philosophy, the topic had previously been eschewed by analytic philosophers. Indeed, until Max Black's seminal (1962) paper "Metaphor", it was virtually ignored. This was due largely to the dominance of logical positivism during the preceding decades. Logical positivists viewed metaphor as without cognitive significance, because they assumed that metaphors lacked the crucial criterion for meaningfulness: *verification conditions*. Thus, consider Shakespeare's famous line from *MacBeth* (V.v. 24–26): "Life's but a walking Shadow, a poor player that struts and frets his hour upon the stage, and then is heard no more." It seems that nothing could possibly count as observational evidence for (or against) this claim, because life, as an abstract entity, cannot in principle cast a shadow, let alone a shadow that walks. We therefore have no idea what sort of situation, if observed, would demonstrate that the sentence was true. From the fact that metaphors apparently fail to specify verification conditions, logical positivists concluded that metaphorical speech lacks cognitive content altogether; instead, it merely serves to arouse feelings and images in its hearers.

Metaphor was thus mentioned by mid-century analytic philosophers only in order to be set aside as irrelevant because unimportant to truth and knowledge. However, with the publication of Black's paper advocating an "interaction" theory of metaphor's irreducible "cognitive content", analytic philosophers began to turn their attention to metaphor in earnest. In the 1970s and 1980s a flood of scholarly papers on metaphor were published, along with many anthologies devoted to metaphor. Several of the latter contained contributions not only by philosophers of language, but also by literary theorists, philosophers of science, linguists, psychologists, and cognitive scientists.[4] The interest in metaphor among contemporary analytic philosophers, and philosophers of language in particular, remains strong today. This is no doubt due to a continued interest in natural, as opposed to formal or artificial, languages.

Philosophers of language have traditionally been interested in issues concerning meaning and truth. And so, when they have turned their attention to metaphor, they have naturally focused on these same issues. Before we turn to these particular topics, though, we should note that virtually every area of analytic philosophy, broadly construed, has paid at least some serious (if relatively limited) attention to metaphor.

Thus, within aesthetics, theorists have endeavored to understand the special sort of 'aptness' and beauty that certain metaphors exhibit: the way in which a good

[4] See, for instance, Sacks (1978); Ortony (1979 a); and Johnson (1981).
[5] See Hills (1997); Hills cites the phrase from Stevens (1950). See also Isenberg (1973).

metaphor can be, as Wallace Stevens writes, "the cry of its occasion".[5] This feature is particularly palpable when metaphors are used to capture aspects of subjective experience that elude expression in literal terms.[6] In philosophy of religion, there is interest in the appropriate principles for interpreting religious texts, such as the Bible, metaphorically.[7] Some theologians and philosophers of religion believe that the nature of religious truth is such that it can only be conveyed metaphorically.[8] Epistemologists have considered the nature and utility of analogical reasoning, which many cognitive psychologists believe to be crucially involved in the interpretation of metaphor.[9] Metaphysicians have been interested in the possibly metaphorical status of crucial but theoretically troublesome terms, such as "existence" and "possible worlds."[10] Similarly, in philosophy of mathematics, there is talk of the metaphorical status of mathematical concepts and truths.[11] Finally, within philosophy of science, questions about the epistemic status of scientific models have been linked to the status of metaphors, which seem to bear important structural similarities to models.[12]

33.3 FOUR CENTRAL QUESTIONS

Let us now turn our attention to the understanding and treatment of metaphor within contemporary philosophy of language. Of the many questions concerning metaphor that have been addressed within this area of philosophy, four stand out as especially central. These are: (i) what are metaphors? (ii) what is the nature of metaphorical meaning? (iii) how do metaphors work? and (iv) what is the nature of metaphorical truth? While these questions can be formulated independently, they are logically connected insofar as the response given to any one constrains possible responses to at least some of the others.

In addressing these questions, many philosophers have followed Black's (1962) methodological lead by first isolating a few uncontroversial cases of metaphor.[13] These examples in effect provide an extensional definition of "metaphor", from which, it is hoped, an explicit definition can eventually be derived. The benefit of this approach is that it gives us an intuitive, if vague, sense for how metaphor differs both from literal language and from other figures of speech. The drawback is that not all theorists begin with the same sorts of examples. Some focus on relatively familiar, conversational metaphors like "You are the cream in my coffee", or "I destroyed my opponent's argument", while others attend to more novel, poetic metaphors such as "A geometrical proof is a mousetrap", or "Christ was a chronometer." Employing

---

[6] See Camp (forthcoming a).   [7] See Tracy (1978)

[8] See Soskice (1987), McFague (1982).

[9] See Gentner (1989); Gentner et al. (2001); Holyoak and Thagard (1995).

[10] See Yablo (1996, 1998); and Walton (2000).

[11] See Yablo (forthcoming, 2003, 2002) and Lakoff and Nunez (1997).

[12] See Hesse (1966, 1993); Kuhn (1979); Boyd (1979); Brown (2003); see also Godfrey-Smith (2002) for an analysis of the role played by the metaphor of genetic 'coding' in scientific investigation and theory.

[13] This group includes both Davidson (1978) and Searle (1979); see Hills (1997) for some discussion of how one might attempt to reconcile extensional and theoretical definitions.

such different examples as paradigm cases raises the risk that the different parties will simply talk past one another. The alternative, which is to provide a theoretical definition at the outset, is equally problematic, simply because there are so few uncontroversial assumptions about metaphor.

We now spell out our four central questions in more detail. In the next section, we'll examine how various theories of metaphor have attempted to answer them.

(i) What are Metaphors?

Specifically, how does metaphorical language differ from literal language and from other figures of speech? Philosophers have traditionally assumed that there is an important in-principle difference between literal and figurative language, that figurative language is essentially "marked" or distinctive, and that the figurative is in some sense a "deviant" exploitation of the literal. These assumptions have recently come under scrutiny. Thus, for instance, Sadock (1979) and Rumelhart (1979) have questioned whether there is a genuine difference in kind between literal and metaphorical language. Those working in the tradition of Relevance Theory (e.g. Carston and Powell (this volume), Carston (2002), Beznidenhout (2001), Recanati (2004, 2001) Sperber and Wilson (1986);) treat metaphor as a form of 'loose talk', in which the speaker's intended meaning more or less closely resembles semantically encoded meaning;[14] on this view, the difference between literal and metaphorical meaning is merely a matter of degree not a difference in kind. Finally, theorists like Goodman (1968); Searle (1979); and Nunberg (2002) have rejected or at least downplayed the classical distinctions among different forms of figurative language. Instead, they treat metaphor, simile, metonymy, synecdoche (and sometimes other forms of figurative and non-literal language as well) as a single unified phenomenon.

(ii) What is the Nature of Metaphorical Meaning?

Answers to this question are tied to assumptions about what counts as "meaning" more generally. Many philosophers believe that metaphorical meaning is of the same propositional kind as literal meaning; the difference between literal and metaphorical meaning (if any) lies in how that propositional content is expressed. Thus, Grice (1975) and Searle (1979), argue that metaphor is like other forms of indirect speech in expressing a distinctive *speaker* meaning while contextualists claim that metaphorical meaning is a form of *utterance* meaning or "what is said", and semanticists, such as Starn (2000) and Hills (1997) maintain that metaphorical meaning is a form of semantic meaning *per se*. Other philosophers, such as Black (1962) and Kittay (1987), reject the assumption that metaphorical meaning is fundamentally of the same kind as literal meaning: they argue that metaphors have a special, irreducible and essentially non-propositional cognitive "meaning" or "significance". Still others, like Davidson (1978) and Rorty (1987), agree that metaphors' effects are

---

[14] In the Continental tradition, philosophers from Nietzsche (1886/1966) to Jacques Derrida (1988) have also challenged the idea that an in-principle distinction can be drawn between literal and metaphorical language.

non-propositional, but they conclude from this that metaphors have no distinctive meaning at all (apart from any literal meaning), on the grounds that the only genuine candidates for "meaning" are truth-conditional, propositional contents.

(iii) How do Metaphors Work?

That is, how do metaphors manage to mean what they do? This is perhaps the central 'problem' of metaphor, for the ease with which we are often able to interpret metaphors, even subtle and complex ones, is rather puzzling on its face. In the case of literal utterances, the interpretative process is presumably compositional. The hearer computes the utterance meaning on the basis of his or her grasp of individual word meanings (where this includes fixing the values of any contextually-sensitive terms) and syntax. Presumably something more is needed in the interpretation of metaphor, or else metaphorical meaning would just *be* literal meaning. What 'more' could this be?

Some have thought that the words themselves have special metaphorical meanings which combine compositionally in the usual fashion, or that metaphorical meaning results from some alteration in the process of composition itself. Thus, Beardsley (1962). Cohen and Margalit (1972), and Levin (1977) all argued that the process of attempted composition somehow "twists" the literal meaning into a metaphorical one. More recently, Stern (2000) argues that metaphor is represented by a contextually-sensitive operator at the level of logical form, while contextualists argue that metaphorical meaning involves the same sort of pragmatic adjustment of word meaning as we find with 'enrichment' and 'loosening'; on these latter views, composition proceeds in the usual way, albeit with non-literal inputs. Those who treat metaphorical meaning as a form of indirect speech, like Grice (1975) and Searle (1979), tend to assume that metaphorical meaning is computed by employing global pragmatic conversational principles *after* the process of literal composition is completed. Finally, those who reject the notion that metaphorical meaning is propositional assume that metaphorical interpretation and meaning have little to do with composition at all, and point to other sorts of cognitive processes instead.

(iv) What is the Nature of Metaphorical Truth?

Are metaphors associated with a distinctive brand of truth? Here, the logical connection with the earlier questions is perhaps most obvious. If the meaning of a metaphor is simply the proposition(s) the speaker intends to communicate, and if these propositions can be given literal expression, then presumably literal and metaphorical truth are presumably identical in kind. If, on the other hand, metaphors are not in the business of communicating propositions at all, but rather serve to evoke certain distinctive responses to certain sorts of situations, then the relevant brand of truth, if any, must be quite different: perhaps something more akin to "revealingness", "comportment", nor "insight."[15] Finally, it might be the case that metaphors do serve to communicate contents which can be true or false in the usual sense, but that for one reason or another these contents are not capable of literal expression.[16]

[15] See Heidegger (1975), Cooper (1993).   [16] See Camp (forthcoming a).

33.4 FOUR INFLUENTIAL THEORIES

Many theories of metaphor have been proposed and defended by philosophers of language since the publication of Black's "interaction" theory. Most attempt to answer questions (i) through (iv), even if only indirectly. In this section, we survey four influential theories; this survey is intended to be representative rather than exhaustive.

(i) Simile Theories

Simile theories are the oldest and, until fairly recently, the most widely held theories of metaphor.[17] Aristotle seems to have been the first to suggest[18] that metaphors are 'compressed' or 'abbreviated' similes. On any such theory, the meaning of a metaphor is identified with that of the corresponding simile: where "A is B" is the metaphor (e.g. "Love is a journey"), its meaning is given by the sentence "A is like B" (e.g. "Love is like a journey"). On such a view, the interpretation of a metaphor is a matter of interpreting the corresponding simile, and the truth of the metaphor is thus reduced to that of the simile.

The simile theory has both intuitive and methodological motivations. First, it often seems as though some sort of comparison is made, or at least adumbrated, in metaphor. Consider Hermann Melville's (1856) "I had somehow slept off the fumes of vanity." Although no comparison is made explicitly here, it is nonetheless clear that Melville is drawing our attention to similarities between the toxicity of fumes and the personality flaw of vanity. Second, the simile theory appears to account for our conflicting intuitions about metaphors' truth values. "Juliet is the sun" is false if interpreted literally: Juliet is clearly not a gaseous ball of fire ninety-three million miles from earth. But the simile that gives the sentence's metaphorical meaning— "Juliet is *like* the sun"—is arguably true.

The most obvious methodological motivation for the theory lies in the reductive nature of its central claim, that metaphor is a form of simile. At a minimum, the theory reduces two problems to one: we now need only to explain how similes themselves work. Further, if the meanings of similes are unproblematic because literal, then the 'problem' of metaphor has been resolved altogether: we have analyzed metaphorical meaning and truth in terms of literal meaning and truth.

Despite these virtues, the simile theory has been criticized on a number of counts.[19] First, not all metaphors are so readily translatable into simile form, if at all. William Lycan (1999) makes the point nicely with the Shakespearean metaphor "When the

---

[17] We should also mention the so-called 'substitution theory' of metaphor, according to which a metaphor is merely a substitute for some other expression which, used literally, would have expressed the same content. This view is no longer widely held, if it is held at all. For some criticisms, see Black (1962).

[18] We use 'suggest' here advisedly, as not all theorists agree that Aristotle actually endorsed this theory; see Johnson (1981).

[19] See Black (1962); Beardsley (1967); Davidson (1978); Searle (1979); and Tirrell (1991).

blood burns, how prodigal the soul/Lends the tongue vows."[20] Concerning the simile that this metaphor is alleged to abbreviate, Lycan (1999, p. 217) writes:

A first pass might be: When *x*, which is like a person's blood, does something that resembles burning, how prodigally *y*, which is like a person's soul, does something similar to lending some things that are vowlike to *z*, which resembles a person's tongue.

He then remarks dryly, "We are not much wiser."

Second, the simile analysis appears to represent metaphor as superficial and uninformative. Many philosophers have claimed that similes themselves are trivial, on the grounds that everything is like everything else in some respect or other.[21] Yet metaphors often appear to be informative and even profound. Third, and perhaps most importantly, the similarities that we most naturally cite in explaining what a metaphor's corresponding simile means are often themselves figurative. Consider the opening lines of Sylvia Plath's (1961) poem "Mirror": "I am silver and exact/I have no preconceptions." Presumably the protagonist is here describing herself metaphorically as a mirror; on the simile theory she thus means that she is like a mirror. One natural elaboration of what this simile means is that she *reflects* the world around her, but the key word "reflects" here is itself obviously metaphorical. We seem to have fallen into a vicious explanatory circle.

In response to the second and third of these worries, Robert Fogelin (1988) has proposed a figurative version of the simile theory. According to Fogelin, statements of similarity should be understood in terms of the notion of "salience": the respect(s) in which *A* is said to be like *B* depend on which of *B*'s features are salient in that context of utterance.[22] What is distinctive about similes as *figurative* statements of similarity, and in turn about the metaphors that abbreviate them, is how those salient features are determined. Consider the metaphor "Churchill was a bulldog." According to Fogelin, in using this metaphor we compare Churchill to a bulldog; but in order to understand this comparison we must "trim the feature space" of bulldogs in terms of Churchill's salient features.[23] More specifically: the hearer rules out a literal interpretation of the implicit simile on the grounds that Churchill shares none of the usual and obviously salient features of bulldogs. The hearer nonetheless charitably assumes that the alleged similarity does obtain, and so he ignores the salient features of bulldogs that render the literal comparison false, such as having floppy ears and wet noses. He searches instead for features of bulldogs that match up with the salient features of Churchill. Presumably, these include 'character traits' like resoluteness and stubbornness; they might also include physical traits like having a thick neck and jowly face. The metaphor "Churchill was a bulldog" claims that Churchill is like a bulldog in these respects.

---

[20] Shakespeare, *Hamlet*, I.iii.116–17.
[21] See e.g. Goodman (1972); Davidson (1978); and Searle (1979).
[22] In this Fogelin follows Tversky's influential theory of similarity; see also Ontony (1979b). Those who reject the claim that metaphors just are elliptical similes can also appeal to a process of comparison in order to determine how the metaphor's meaning, or cognitive effects, are produced.
[23] Fogelin (1988), p. 91.   [24] See Ortony (1979 b); Searle (1979).

Fogelin's theory nicely defuses one of the main objections against the literal simile theory: that it could not explain the informativeness and profundity of metaphor. While "Juliet is like the sun" is literally false, according to Fogelin, it is true and even profound when interpreted figuratively, because it raises to salience certain features that Juliet does share with the sun, and that we might not otherwise notice. It also goes some way toward addressing the third worry—that appealing to similes to analyze metaphor is unhelpful, because the similes are themselves figurative—by giving an analysis of figurative similes. However, it is doubtful that all figurative similes can be adequately analyzed in terms of features which the two objects in question are believed to actually share, as Fogelin assumes.[24] So, for instance, "Sally is a block of ice" is intuitively true just in case Sally is like ice in being cold. But there's no obvious single property, of coldness, which applies to both frozen water and personal temperaments in the same way, and so it's not clear how to analyze the simile further into features that are in fact shared. Similarly, the sense in which Juliet is like the sun intuitively depends in part on a higher-order analogy between the properties of being bright and being beautiful, rather than upon a concrete feature possessed by both Juliet and the sun.[25] Finally, Fogelin's view is clearly still vulnerable to the first objection above, that not all metaphors can be translated into simile form.

(ii) Interaction Theories

As we mentioned, one of the earliest modern alternatives to the simile theory was the "interaction" view. This view was first advocated by the literary theorist I.A. Richards (1936), and was subsequently developed by the philosopher Max Black (1962). Such theories have two central claims: (i) that metaphors have an irreducible "cognitive content", and (ii) that this cognitive content (or "meaning") is produced by the "interaction" of different cognitive systems. Interactionists generally claim that the "cognitive contents" of metaphors can be true, even though they are not amenable to literal expression.

According to Black, in a metaphor of the form "A is B", the "system of associated commonplaces" for B "interacts with" or "filters" our thoughts about the 'system' associated with A, thereby generating a metaphorical meaning for the whole sentence. Consider one of Black's examples: "Man is a wolf." The properties of being a predator, traveling in packs, and being fierce and ruthless are all commonplaces associated with "wolf." These properties are therefore instrumental to comprehending the metaphor: they serve as the "filter" for thinking about mankind, by emphasizing just those commonplaces associated with "man" that fit with them. The metaphor's "cognitive content" or meaning is the distinctive way of thinking about mankind that this filtering produces. Notice here that "commonplaces" need not be true. For instance, the commonplace that wolves are ruthless is part of the relevant system even though wolves, as creatures, non-moral arguably cannot be ruthless. Likewise, the other commonplaces

---

[25] In this case, we can construct a higher-order property which Juliet and the sun do share: the property of possessing a property which bears a certain relation R to other properties. But then we seem to be back in the situation of postulating uninformative analyses of the sort criticized by Lycan above.

mentioned above would remain relevant even if it turned out that wolves are in fact docile herbivores who tend to travel in pairs. What matters is not the actual properties of the objects denoted, or even the properties that speakers and hearers *believe* those objects to possess, but rather what the denoting expressions "call to mind."[26]

The interaction theory's central motivation is to account for the fact that metaphors powerful cognitive tools: can be such devices that enable us to better understand the world in which we live. It thus coheres nicely with the view, advocated by Thomas Kuhn (1979) and Richard Boyd (1979) among others, that scientific models appear to increase scientists' understanding of the universe. The interaction theory also comports well with the view, popular among certain cognitive scientists, that ordinary thought and reason are largely, and irreducibly, metaphorical.[27] For the interactionist regards any attempt to reduce metaphorical meaning to literal meaning as misguided.

Perhaps not surprisingly, though, the interaction theory as presented by Black has seemed too vague to be of great theoretical value. Part of the problem is, once again, that Black analyzes metaphor itself in terms of other metaphors like "association", "interaction", and "filtering". Nevertheless, some theorists have managed to develop Black's central claim—that metaphors have an irreducible cognitive content—in more theoretically tractable terms. Kittay (1987), for instance, appeals to "semantic field" theory to flesh out the contents of the two interacting systems'.

Rather different criticisms have been launched by Donald Davidson (1978) and Fogelin (1988). Davidson claims that there is no clear theoretical value to positing special metaphorical "meanings" or "cognitive contents".[28] As he puts it, to say that metaphorical meaning explains how metaphor works is "like explaining why a pill puts you to sleep by saying it has a dormative power"[29]: we have simply found a new, fancier way to describe the phenomenon under investigation, but we have made no real explanatory progress. A second objection of Davidson's concerns Black's claim that metaphors are not amenable to precise literal paraphrase. If so, asks Davidson, why should we suppose that there is any meaning there to begin with? If metaphors have a "cognitive content" beyond the literal, then why should it be so difficult, even impossible, to capture that content in literal language? Finally, Fogelin points out that not all cases of metaphor are so easily explained in terms of conceptual "interaction". Consider John Keats's (1819) metaphor: "O for a beaker full of the warm south." One would be hard pressed to specify the "cognitive systems" whose "interaction" makes this such an effective use of language. More generally, Black's view works best for metaphors that consist of a general kind term predicated of an individual or kind, but not all metaphors take this form.[30]

---

[26] "Commonplaces" can still call features to mind even if they are not believed to be true of the objects denoted by the relevant term. For instance, even if both the speaker and hearer know that gorillas are in fact gentle creatures, the stereotype that gorillas are nasty and violent can play a role in determining the metaphor's "cognitive content".

[27] See Lakoff and Johnson (1980, 1999) and Lakoff (1993).

[28] For Black's reply to Davidson, see his (1978); see also Kittay (1987).

[29] Davidson (1978), p. 31.

[30] See White (1996) for criticism of 'predicational' models of metaphor, like Black's, and presentation of an alternative view on which metaphor involves interaction between two sentence-frames.

Philosophers suspicious of the special, irreducible "cognitive contents" posited by interactionists have developed several alternatives, the best known of which are Gricean and non-cognitivist theories. We'll consider these in turn.

(iii) Gricean Theories

Gricean theories of metaphor are in the first instance theories of metaphorical *interpretation*. Their central claim is that a metaphor just is understanding what a speaker intends to communicate by means of it, where communication is analyzed in Gricean terms.[31] Roughly, successful communication consists in the hearer's recognizing the speaker's intention to get the hearer to recognize what she is trying to communicate to him. Insofar as a metaphor can be said to have a meaning, this is identified with what the speaker intends to communicate; the sentence uttered has only its literal meaning. A metaphor's truth value is reduced to that of what the speaker intends to communicate.

Since John Searle is the best-known advocate of a broadly Gricean theory of metaphor,[32] we will consider his view. According to Searle (1979, pp. 76–8):

The problem of explaining how metaphors work is a special case of the general problem of explaining how speaker meaning and sentence or word meaning come apart . . . Our task in constructing a theory of metaphor is to try to state the principles which relate literal sentence meaning to metaphorical [speaker's] utterance meaning.

Searle divides the interpretative process into three stages. First, the hearer must decide whether to look for a non-literal, and specifically for a metaphorical, interpretation. Such a search is typically undertaken because a literal interpretation would render the utterance in some sense defective. Second, once the hearer decides to interpret the utterance metaphorically, she employs a set of principles to generate meanings that the speaker might intend by her utterance. Searle offers eight principles by which the uttered phrase can "call to mind" a different meaning "in ways that are specific to metaphor,"[33] focusing on the simple case in which the speaker says something of the form 'S is P' and means something of the form 'S is R'. The principles include Rs being a salient feature of P-things, either by definition or by contingent fact; P-things may also be typically believed to be R, although both speaker and hearer know them not in fact to be R; or it may be a "fact about our sensibility", whether culturally or naturally determined, that we just do perceive a connection between being P and being R; or the condition of being P may be like the condition of being R. Third, having generated a set of possible meanings by these principles, the hearer must identify which element in that set is most likely to be the speaker's intended meaning. Thus, the fact that pigs are stereotypically thought to be dirty, sloppy, and willing to eat anything that's placed before them seems more

---

[31] For more on the Gricean account of meaning, see the papers in this volume by Borg and Gendler Szabo.

[32] See Grice (1975) for a brief sketch of such a view; see also Martinich (1984).

[33] Searle (1979), p. 85.

likely to be relevant to interpreting "Sam is a pig" than the facts that pigs have cloven hoofs, that they are non-ruminants, or that they are intelligent, social animals; the hearer therefore concludes that the speaker meant that Sam is dirty, sloppy, and gluttonous.

The motivation for a Gricean account is three-fold. First, it captures the intuition that metaphors are meaningful, that they have a "cognitive content" other than their literal content. Second, it does this without violating what Grice (1975) called "Modified Occam's Razor." This methodological principle is simply Occam's Razor applied to linguistic meanings: *Don't multiply senses beyond necessity.* The Gricean account respects this principle because it explains metaphors' meanings by appealing only to literal sentence meaning plus general interpretive principles. And third, a Gricean theory embeds the explanation of metaphor within a well-developed and independently motivated theory of linguistic communication that accommodates a variety of cases where sentence meaning and speaker meaning come apart.

Criticisms of Gricean theories of metaphor are varied. First, on many Gricean accounts, the hearer must first identify the utterance as somehow defective if interpreted literally: only then is the search for an alternative, non-literal interpretation triggered.[34] However, not all utterances used metaphorically are defective, in any sense of the term.[35] A sentence like "No man is an island" exhibits no grammatical deviance; it is literally true, albeit trivially so. Utterances of sentences like "The rock is becoming brittle with age" or "Anchorage is a cold city" could plausibly be true and informative when construed literally, given an appropriate context of utterance. And a "twice true" metaphor like "Jesus was a carpenter" could count as both literally and metaphorically true and informative within a single context of utterance. It seems that a speaker could even plausibly intend to communicate both contents simultaneously, and that both interpretations could be conversationally relevant.[36] So there need be no deviance either in the sentence itself or in the utterance of it.

Second, some empirical evidence suggests that the literal meaning of a sentence used metaphorically needn't actually be processed in order for the metaphor to be understood.[37] If this is correct, then it seems that a Gricean theory could at most serve as a rational reconstruction, rather than a factual description, of the interpretive process.[38] Third, even considered as rational reconstructions, Gricean accounts typically say so little about the process by which hearers could have arrived at the intended interpretation that they both lack empirical predictive power, and indeed, fail even to identify any theoretically distinctive feature of metaphor. For instance, although Searle's stated aim is to specify the distinctive principles by which metaphorical utterances "call to mind" the speaker's meaning, his eight principles are so

---

[34] However, Searle explicitly allows that metaphorical interpretations may be triggered without any defectiveness, for instance when we are on the lookout for them while reading a Romantic poem (p. 105).

[35] See Reddy (1969); Cohen (1975); and Tirrell (1991).

[36] See Hills (1997) for discussion of such metaphors, which he calls "twice apt."

[37] See Rumelhart (1979); Gibbs (1994); Giora (2002); but see Blasko and Connine (1993) and Bowdle and Gentner (2005) for evidence that novel metaphors do take longer to process than literal statements.

[38] This seems to be how both grice and Searle intend their views to be understood.

broad that they threaten to encompass nearly every instance of non-literal meaning. The main interpretive burden therefore shifts to the third stage, at which the set of possible metaphorical meanings is narrowed to the intended one. But the operative interpretive principles at this stage are supposed to be those that govern pragmatic reasoning generally, and so they cannot be used to distinguish metaphor from other sorts of non-literal and indirect meaning. (In a similar fashion, Relevance theorists claim that metaphorical meanings "interpretively resemble" the literal meaning of the uttered sentence, so that words get used to express "*ad hoc*" concepts; but they don't say anything more about *how* the metaphorical meaning must resemble the literal meaning. Without such a specification, though, nearly any utterance will count as metaphorical.)[39]

Fourth, on a Gricean theory, the speaker's communicative intentions exhaust the metaphor's meaning. Yet a metaphor's import often seems to go beyond what the speaker explicitly anticipated, especially for novel, poetic metaphors. Finally, Griceans generally assume that metaphorical meaning, like speaker meaning more generally, is fully propositional in form and fully capable of literal expression. The Gricean theory thus seems doomed to leave out what is most interesting about metaphor: its complex cognitive and affective "import", which seems to be inherently inexpressible in literal terms.[40]

(iv) Non-cognitivist Theories

In light of the difficulties we've encountered so far, some contemporary philosophers of language have questioned the widely-held view that metaphors are, in any substantive sense, meaningful. These philosophers—"non-cognitivists"—do not question metaphor's *effectiveness*, only the means by which its effects are achieved. The central claim of such theorists is that a sentence used metaphorically has no distinctive cognitive content aside from its literal content. Non-cognitivists thus resemble Griceans in denying that the words uttered themselves have any special meaning. They depart from Griceans, though, in also denying that there is any determinate propositional thought which the speaker intends to communicate by means of those words. These negative claims are typically coupled with a positive view about how metaphor does manage to "work its wonders" after all. Thus, Davidson (1978) offers what might be termed a "causal theory" of metaphor.[41] On his view, "a metaphor

---

[39] Contextualists, especially those in the tradition of Relevance Theory, are also committed to an account along the lines sketched by Grice: they too treat metaphor as a pragmatic phenomenon, where metaphorical meaning is a function of the speaker's communicative intentions. However, they differ from Grice and Searle in at least two important respects. First, they do intend their theory as an empirical hypothesis about actual processing. And second, they reject the three-stage model of interpretation, arguing instead that comprehension proceeds directly to the intended interpretation. In this respect metaphor is taken to be quite different from implicature, and is thought to belong within 'what is said' instead. See e.g. Bezuidenhout (2001) and Recanati (2001); see also Camp (2006) for criticism.

[40] See Camp (2003) for defense of a broadly Gricean theory on which at least some metaphorical utterances can be intended to communicate complex representations which are not fully and explicitly appreciated by the speaker, and which may not be expressible in literal terms.

[41] See Rorty (1987) for discussion of metaphor's merely causal status on this view.

makes us attend to some likeness, often a novel or surprising likeness, between two or more things", by making us "see one thing as another".[42]

Despite its undeniable counter-intuitiveness, non-cognitivism is not without motivation. First, it accounts for the facts that many metaphors don't easily admit of literal paraphrase, and that their "import" seems to be different in kind from that of typical literal utterances. Second, it is remarkably economical: it purports to explain how metaphor works without appealing to special word meanings or even Gricean speaker meanings. According to Davidson, a metaphor is like a bump on the head, or a drug: one can employ it to cause certain effects in one's audience, including noticing surprising similarities between objects, but this should not lead us to suppose that the metaphor, the bump or the drug itself *means* those effects, or even that the agent meant that effect *by* her action. Third, Davidson argues, the analogy with similes actually supports non-cognitivism. We are much less tempted to suppose that similes have a special meaning beyond their literal meaning: "Juliet is like the sun" means that Juliet is like the sun, nothing more, nothing less. Of course, the *point* of uttering the simile would not be merely to express that proposition, but rather to draw the hearer's attention to similarities between Juliet and the sun. But we needn't then suppose that the speaker means to claim *that* those similarities are there to be noticed.[43]

The non-cognitivist theory has been criticized on a variety of grounds.[44] Most obviously, the theory flies in the face of the intuition that metaphors are cognitively significant: that they can be understood or misunderstood, that they figure in our reasoning and thought, and that they can be true or false. Moreover, as Merrie Bergmann (1982) and others have pointed out, a non-cognitivist view misses the role that metaphors play in assertion and counter-assertion. If I call Bill a vulture, and you deny this, then it seems clear that *something* has been asserted and denied, and that this 'something' is not the claim that Bill is a certain kind of bird.[45]

Finally, as several philosophers[46] have pointed out, the non-cognitivist view appears to be incompatible with the phenomenon of dead metaphors. Dead metaphors are expressions which have lost their metaphorical import through frequent use and so no longer invite creative interpretation. Their former metaphorical import has 'hardened' into a new literal meaning. Thus, the expression "burned up", as in "He was all burned up about his impending divorce", is a dead metaphor, whose second literal meaning is just *extremely angry*. As Davidson puts it, the expression no longer conjures up "fire in the eyes or smoke coming out of the ears".[47] This poses a difficulty for the non-cognitivist because it seems as if dead metaphors could only acquire their secondary literal meanings if they were previously used to communicate those very meanings. And this would seem to conflict with the basic non-cognitivist commitment: that speakers do not mean anything by metaphors.[48]

---

[42] Davidson (1978), pp. 31, 45.   [43] Here, there is clear disagreement with Fogelin (1988).
[44] See Moran (1989, and 1997) for these and other objections.
[45] See Hills (1997) and Bezuidenhout (2001) for further discussion of this point.
[46] See Goodman (1978); Moran (1989); and Reimer (1996).
[47] Davidson (1978), p. 36.   [48] But see Reimer (2001) for a defense of Davidson.

33.5 CURRENT AND FUTURE TRENDS

The most active research into metaphor is currently located in cognitive science.[49] The focus here is typically on issues such as metaphor's influence on thought and action, and the role of metaphor in cognitive development and linguistic competence.[50] There is generally less emphasis on metaphor as a form of expression in natural language. Thus, for instance, George Lakoff and his colleagues are most interested in metaphor as a cognitive tool for extending concepts' initial applications to new realms. They argue that we metaphorically transfer basic physical concepts like *up* and *over* to other domains: to the social, emotional, scientific, and even mathematical domains. These metaphorical mappings render certain ways of speaking and acting natural (e.g. "He's moving *up* in the world", "I'm feeling quite *up* today"). What we would normally classify as metaphorical language should, on this view, be analyzed instead as a direct, explicit representation of a metaphorical way of thinking.[51]

The future of metaphor research within the philosophy of language itself is less clear. One hope is that philosophers of language will work with, or at least along-side, researchers in other disciplines, so that their theories can be informed and even shaped by the varied observations garnered from these other disciplines. In partic-ular, many of the theories discussed above invoke the notions of "salience" and "similarity" in one way or another, but have little to say about what these involve. Researchers in linguistics, cognitive science, psychology, and neurobiology are devel-oping such notions, in work on metaphor and on other areas.[52]

To see how philosophical theories of metaphor could be informed by other dis-ciplines, we need only return to the four questions we discussed above as central concerns for philosophers of language:

  (i) What are metaphors?
 (ii) What is the nature of metaphorical meaning?
(iii) How do metaphors work?
 (iv) What is the nature of metaphorical truth?

Interest in these questions is by no means confined to philosophy of language. Literary theorists are interested, among other things, in distinguishing metaphor from other figures, such as simile and irony, and thereby address (i). Cognitive scientists do so as well, by proposing that metaphors be viewed primarily as mental representations and only derivatively as linguistic phenomena. Philosophers and historians of science argue, along with cognitive scientists, that metaphors are significant cognitive tools, and in this way they address (ii). Cognitive psychologists and psycholinguists have done empirical research on the processing of metaphor and of language generally, thus shedding light on (iii). Interest in (iv) is perhaps more fully limited to philosophy *per se*, but metaphysicians, philosophers of mathematics, and even some historians of science have been concerned to explore the possibility of a substantive sort of truth

---

[51] See Lakoff (1993); Lakoff and Turner (1989).
[49] See e.g. Gibbs and Steen (1999).   [50] See e.g. Happé (1995); Langdon *et al.* (2001).
[52] See e.g. Gentner *et al.* (2001), Barsalou (1993, 1983), Holyoak and Thagard (1995), Fauconnier and Turner (1998).

which is not literal. It should thus be clear that philosophers of language can learn much about metaphor from the research efforts of those outside of their own area.

At the same time, an increasing focus on various forms of context-sensitivity within philosophy of language and linguistics has led to the development of new explanatory tools and strategies. "Hidden indexicals" (Stanley, 2000), "unarticulated constituents" (Perry, 1986), and "free enrichment" (Recanati, 1995) have all been postulated as mechanisms for bridging the gap between what might seem to be a sentence's semantically encoded content and the content that is expressed by an utterance of it on a given occasion (see Carston and Powell, this volume, for discussion). These same mechanisms have recently begun to be deployed in explaining metaphor as well. Josef Stern (2000) has argued that metaphors function like demonstrative terms.[53] Kendall Walton (1993) and David Hills (1997) have argued that metaphorical meaning crucially depends upon "pretense" or "make-believe", both about word use and about the schema of objects invoked.[54] And Anne Bezuidenhout (2001), François Recanati (2001), and Carston (2002) have all advocated treating metaphor as a form of pragmatic "direct expression".[55] Perhaps this influx of new ideas will lead to a fruitful reconfiguration of the established options, much as occurred around the time of Davidson's and Searle's seminal publications in the late 1970s.

REFERENCES

Barsalou, L. (1993). "Flexibility, Structure, and Linguistic Vagary in Concepts: Manifestations of a Compositional System of Perceptual Symbols," in A.C. Collins, S.E. Gathercole, and M.A. Conway (eds.), *Theories of Memory* (Hillsdale, NJ: Lawrence Erlbaum Associates).

_____ (1983): "Ad Hoc Categories," *Memory and Cognition* 11, 211–227.

Beardsley, M. (1967). "Metaphor", in *The Encyclopedia of Philosophy*, vol. 5, ed. P. Edwards (New York: Macmillan).

Beardsley, M. (1962). "The Metaphorical Twist", *Philosophy and Phenomenological Research*, 22:3: 293–307.

Bergmann, M. (1982). "Metaphorical Assertions", *Philosophical Review*, 91: 225–245.

Bezuidenhout, A. (2001). "Metaphor and What is Said: A Defense of a Direct Expression View of Metaphor", *Midwest Studies in Philosophy*, 25: 156–86.

Black, M. (1978). "How Metaphors Work: A Reply to Donald Davidson", in *On Metaphor*, ed. S. Sacks (Chicago: University of Chicago Press).

_____ (1962). "Metaphor", in *Models and Metaphors* (Ithaca: Cornell University Press).

Blasko, D. and C. Connine (1993). "Effects of Familiarity and Aptness on Metaphor Processing," *Journal of Experimental Psychology*: Learning, Memory and Cognition, 19: 295–308.

Bowdle, B. and D. Gentner (2005). "The Career of Metaphor", *Psychological Review*, 112:1: 193–216

[53] See Camp (2005) for criticism of Stern's analysis. See also Leezenberg (2001) for an alternative semantic view which, like Stern's, employs a Kaplanian logic of indexical terms.

[54] See also Nogales (1999) for a semantic view of metaphor on which interpretation proceeds through "reconceptualization" based on prototypical features rather than through pretense.

[55] See Camp (2006) for one response to arguments for treating metaphor as a form of "direct expression."

Boyd, R. (1979). "Metaphor and Theory Change: What is 'Metaphor' a Metaphor For?" in *Metaphor and Thought*, ed. A. Ortony (Cambridge: Cambridge University Press).

Brown, T. (2003). *Making Truth: Metaphor in Science* (Urbana and Chicago: University of Illinois Press).

Camp, E. (2006). "Contextualism, Metaphor, and What is Said", *Mind and Language*, 21:3: 280–309.

—— (2005). "Josef Stern, *Metaphor in Context*", *Noûs*, 39:4: 715–731.

—— (forthcoming). "Metaphor and That Certain 'Je Ne Sais Quoi' ", *Philosophical Studies*.

—— (2003). *Saying and Seeing-as: The Linguistic Uses and Cognitive Effects of Metaphor*, dissertation, University of California, Berkeley.

Carston, R. (2002). *Thoughts and Utterances: The Pragmatics of Explicit Communication* (Oxford: Blackwell Publishers).

Cohen, L. J. and A. Margalit (1972). "The Role of Inductive Reasoning in the Interpretation of Metaphor", in *Semantics of Natural Language*, ed. D. Davidson and G. Harman (Dordrecht: D. Reidel).

Cohen, T. (1975). "Figurative Speech and Figurative Acts", *Journal of Philosophy*, 71: 669–84.

Cooper, D. (1993). "Truth and Metaphor", in *Metaphor and Knowledge: Knowledge and Language*, vol. III, ed. F. R. Ankersmit and J. J. A. Mooij (Dordrecht: Kluwer Academic Publishers).

Davidson, D. (1978). "What Metaphors Mean", in *On Metaphor*, ed. S. Sacks. (Chicago: University of Chicago Press).

Derrida, J. (1988). *Limited, Inc.* (Evanston, IL: Northwestern University Press).

Fauconnier, G. and M. Turner (1998). "Conceptual Integration Networks", *Cognitive Science*, 22: 133–87.

Fogelin, R. (1988). *Figuratively Speaking* (New Haven: Yale).

Gentner, D. (1989). "The Mechanisms of Analogical Learning", in *Similarity and Analogical Reasoning*, ed. A. Ortony and S. Vosniadou (Cambridge: Cambridge University Press).

—— B. Bowdle, P. Wolff, and C. Boronat (2001). "Metaphor is Like Analogy", in *The Analogical Mind: Perspectives from Cognitive Science*, ed. D. Gentner, K. J. Holyoak and B. N. Kokinov, (Cambridge, MA: MIT Press).

Gibbs, R. (1994). *The Poetics of Mind: Figurative Thought, Language, and Understanding* (Cambridge: Cambridge University Press).

—— and Steen, G. (1999). *Metaphor in Cognitive Linguistics* (Amsterdam: John Benjamin Publishers).

Giora, R. (2002). "Literal v. Figurative Language: Different or Equal?" *Journal of Pragmatics*, 34: 487–506.

Godfrey-Smith, P. (2002). "On Genetic Information and Genetic Coding", in *In the Scope of Logic, Methodology, and the Philosophy of Science*, vol. II ed. P. Gardenfors, J. Wolenski and K. Kajania-Placek (Dordrecht: Kluwer).

Goodman, N. (1978). "Metaphor as Moonlighting", in *On Metaphor*, ed. S. Sacks. (Chicago: University of Chicago Press).

—— (1972). "Seven Structures on Similarity", in *Problems and Projects* (New York: Babbs-Merrill).

—— (1968). *Languages of Art: An Approach to a Theory of Symbols* (Indianapolis: Hackett).

Grice, H. P. (1975). "Logic and Conversation", *Speech Acts: Syntax and Semantics* vol. 3, ed. P. Cole and J. L. Morgan. (New York: Academic Press).

Happé, F. G. E. (1995). "Understanding Minds and Metaphors: Insights from the Study of Figurative Language in Autism", *Metaphor and Symbolic Activity*, 10: 275–95.

Heidegger, M. (1975) "The Origin of the Work of Art", in *Poetry, Language and Thought*, trans. A. Hofstadter (New York: Harper).

Hesse, M. (1993). "Models, Metaphors and Truth", in *Metaphor and Knowledge: Knowledge and Language*, vol. III, ed. F. R. Ankersmit and J. J. A. Mooij (Dordrecht: Kluwer Academic Publishers).

———— (1966). "The Explanatory Function of Metaphors", in M. Hesse, *Models and Analogies in Science* (Notre Dame, Quebec: Notre Dame University Press), 157–77.

Hills, D. (1997). "Aptness and Truth in Verbal Metaphor", *Philosophical Topics*, 25:1, 117–53.

Holyoak, K. and P. Thagard (1995). *Mental Leaps: Analogy in Creative Thought* (Cambridge, MA: MIT Press).

Isenberg, A. (1973). "On Defining Metaphor", in *Aesthetics and The Theory of Criticism: Selected Essays of Arnold Isenberg*, ed. W. Callagan, L. Cauman, and C. Hempel (Chicago: University of Chicago Press).

Johnson, M. (1981), ed.: *Philosophical Perspectives on Metaphor* (Minneapolis: University of Minneapolis Press).

Keats, J. (1819). "Ode to a Nightingale", reprinted in *The Complete Poetical Works and Letters of John Keats* (New York: Houghton Mifflin and Co., 1899).

Kittay, E. (1987). *Metaphor: Its Cognitive Force and Linguistic Structure* (Oxford: Oxford University Press).

Kuhn, T. (1979). "Metaphor in Science", in *Metaphor and Thought*, ed. A. Ortony (Cambridge: Cambridge University Press).

Lakoff, G. (1993). "The Contemporary Theory of Metaphor", in *Metaphor and Thought*. 2nd edn., ed. A. Ortony, (Cambridge: Cambridge University Press), 202–51.

Lakoff, G. and M. Johnson (1999). *Philosophy In The Flesh: The Embodied Mind and Its Challenge to Western Thought* (New York: Basic Books).

———— (1980). *Metaphors We Live By* (Chicago: University of Chicago Press).

———— and R. Nunez (1997). "The Metaphorical Structure of Mathematics: Sketching Out Cognitive Foundations for a Mind-Based Mathematics", in *Mathematical Reasoning: Analogies, Metaphors, and Images*, ed. L. English (Hillsdale, N. J.: Erlbaum).

———— and M. Turner (1989). *More than Cool Reason: A Field Guide to Poetic Metaphor* (Chicago: University of Chicago Press).

Langdon, R., M. Davies and M. Coltheart (2002). "Understanding Minds and Understanding Communicated Meanings in Schizophrenia", *Mind and Language*, 17:1/2: 68–104.

Leezenberg, M. (2001). *Contexts of Metaphor*. Current Research in the Semantics/Pragmatics Interface, vol. 7 (Oxford: Elsevier Science).

Levin, S. (1977). *The Semantics of Metaphor* (Baltimore: Johns Hopkins University Press).

Lycan, W. (1999). *Philosophy of Language: A Contemporary Introduction* (London and New York: Routledge).

Martinich, A. P. (1984). "A Theory for Metaphor", *Journal of Literary Semantics*, 13: 35–56.

McFague, S. (1982). *Metaphorical Theology: Models Of God In Religious Language* (Philadelphia: Fortress Press).

Melville, H. (1856). "Bartleby the Scrivener", in *The Piazza Tales* (New York: Dix, Edwards, and Co.).

Moran, R. (1997). "Metaphor", in *A Companion to Philosophy of Language* ed. C. Wright and R. Hale (Oxford: Basil Blackwell).

———— (1989). "Seeing and Believing: Metaphor, Image, and Force", *Critical Inquiry*, 16: 87–112.

Nietzsche, F. (1886/1966). *Beyond Good and Evil*, trans. Walter Kaufmann (New York: Vintage).

Nogales, P. (1999). *Metaphorically Speaking* (Stanford, CA: CSLI Publications).

Nunberg, G. (2002). "The Pragmatics of Deferred Interpretation", in *The Blackwell Encyclopedia of Pragmatics*, ed. L. Horn and G. Ward (Oxford: Blackwell Publishers).

Ortony, A. (1979 a), ed.: *Metaphor and Thought* (Cambridge: Cambridge University Press); 2nd edn. (1993).

—— (1979 b). "Beyond Literal Similarity", *Psychological Review*, 87: 161–80.

Perry J. (1986). "Thought without Representation", *Proceedings of the Aristotelian Society*, 60: 137–51.

Plath, S (1961). "Mirror", reprinted in *Collected Poems* (London: Faber and Faber, 2002).

Recanati, F. (2004). *Literal Meaning* (Cambridge: Cambridge University Press).

—— (2001). "Literal/Nonliteral", *Midwest Studies in Philosophy*, 25: 264–74.

—— (1995). "The Alleged Priority of Literal Interpretation", *Cognitive Science*, 19: 207–32.

Reddy, M. J. (1969). "A Semantic Approach to Metaphor", in *Papers from the Fifth Regional Meeting of the Chicago Linguistics Society*, ed. R. I. Binnick *et al.* (Department of Linguistics, University of Chicago).

Reimer, M. (2001). "Davidson on Metaphor", *Midwest Studies in Philosophy*, 25: 142–55.

—— (1996). "The Problem of Dead Metaphors", *Philosophical Studies*, 82:1: 13–25.

Richards, I. A. (1936). *The Philosophy of Rhetoric* (Oxford: Oxford University Press).

Rorty, R. (1987). "Unfamiliar Noises I: Hesse and Davidson on Metaphor", *Proceedings of the Aristotelian Society* (supp. volume 61): 283–96.

Rumelhart D. (1979). "Some Problems With the Notion of Literal Meaning", in *Metaphor and Thought*, ed. A. Ortony (Cambridge: Cambridge University Press).

Sacks, S. (1978). *On Metaphor* (Chicago: University of Chicago Press).

Searle, J. (1979). "Metaphor", in *Metaphor and Thought*, ed. A. Ortony (Cambridge: Cambridge University Press).

Sadock, J. (1979). "Figurative Speech and Linguistics", in *Metaphor and Thought*, ed. A. Ortony (Cambridge: Cambridge University Press).

Soskice, J. M. (1987). *Metaphor and Religious Language* (Oxford: Clarendon Press).

Sperber, D. and D. Wilson (1986). "Loose Talk", *Proceedings of the Aristotelian Society*, 86: 153–71.

Stanley, J. (2000). "Context and Logical Form", *Linguistics and Philosophy*, 23: 391–434.

Stern, J. (2000). *Metaphor in Context* (Cambridge, MA: MIT Press).

Stevens, W. (1950). "An Ordinary Evening in New Haven", in *The Auroras of Autumn* (New York: Knopf).

Tirrell, L. (1991). "Reductive and Nonreductive Simile Theories of Metaphor", *Journal of Philosophy*, 88:7: 337–58.

Tracy D. (1978). "Metaphor and Religion: The Test Case of Christian Texts", in *On Metaphor*, ed. Sheldon Sacks (Chicago: University of Chicago Press).

Tversky, A. (1977). "Features of Similarity", *Psychological Review*, 84:4: 327–52.

Walton, K. (1993). "Metaphor and Prop-oriented Make-Believe", *European Journal of Philosophy*, 1: 39–57.

White, Roger (1996). *The Structure of Metaphor: The Way the Language of Metaphor Works* (Oxford: Blackwell Publishers).

Yablo, S. (forthcoming). "The Myth of the Seven", in *Fictionalist Approaches to Metaphysics*, ed. M. Kalderon (Oxford: Oxford University Press).

—— (2003). "Abstract Objects: A Case Study", in *Philosophical Issues on Realism and Relativism* ed. E. Sosa and E. Villanueva (Oxford: Blackwell).

—— (2002). "Go Figure: A Path Through Fictionalism", *Midwest Studies in Philosophy*, 25: 72–102.

—— (1998). "Does Ontology Rest on a Mistake?" *Proceedings of the Aristotelian Society*, (supp. vol. 72): 229–61.

—— (1996). "How in the World?" *Philosophical Topics*, 24: 255–86.

CHAPTER 34

....

SEMANTICS FOR NONDECLARATIVES

....

DANIEL BOISVERT AND
KIRK LUDWIG

THE major sentential moods of English[1] are the declarative ('Time is short'),
imperative ('Leave the room'), and interrogative ('Where are we going?').[2] The
minor moods include the exclamative ('Congratulations!', 'What gall he has!'), and
the optative ('May the world know peace', 'Would that we were free').[3] Molecular
sentences whose component sentences are in the same mood we classify under the
heading of the component sentences. Thus, 'Eat your peas and keep your mouth
shut' and 'Eat your peas or keep your mouth shut' are imperative, 'Do you want steak

---

[1] English is our object language, but the morals of the discussion will be general.

[2] Our interest here is in sentential rather than verbal mood (Jesperson, 1924). The subjunctive,
conditional, indicative, etc., are verbal moods, determined by the morphology of their main verbs.
Differences in verbal mood, as between indicative and subjunctive, do not track differences in type
of satisfaction condition, and so don't differ along the dimension that declaratives, imperatives, and
interrogatives do. Sometimes the interrogative and imperative moods are ascribed to subordinate clauses
in sentences of indirect discourse or attitude reports when these are about questions or commands, or the
like. They are, in line with traditional grammar, called indirect questions and commands. Thus, in 'Bill
told him to leave', the complement is said to be in the imperative mood (Pendlebury, 1986). While it is
natural that the complements of indirect discourse reports should differ depending on the type of speech
act reported ('Bill told him I was tired' vs. 'Bill told him to leave'), this is not adequate reason to postulate
the same semantic device. The complement in 'Bill told him to leave' clearly does not have the same role
as an imperative, and we see no reason to think the same semantic device is in use. See (Harnish, 1994:
427–9).

[3] The other minor moods can be understood in terms of those we will discuss. See (Harnish, 1994).

or would you rather not eat anything?' is interrogative, and 'Time is short and I am tired' is declarative. Molecular sentences which embed sentences of different moods, such as 'If you are ready, let's go' and 'Leave me alone or would you like a knuckle sandwich?', we call mixed mood sentences.[4]

The tradition in philosophy of language has focused mainly on declaratives, which are true or false on an occasion of utterance. Attempts to understand sentence meaning have focused on how words with their meanings combine to determine the truth conditions of the sentences they form. A complete account of this for a language for declarative sentences would provide a compositional semantics for that portion of the language, that is, an account of how we understand complex expressions, and ultimately sentences, on the basis of understanding their significant parts and modes of combination.

Non-declarative sentences, including mixed mood sentences, pose a problem for standard truth-conditional approaches to providing a compositional semantics for natural languages, for utterances of them are *prima facie* not truth evaluable. Thus, the truth-conditional approach to sentence meaning appears at the least incomplete.

Broadly speaking there are two approaches to the semantics of non-declaratives. One is to assimilate non-declaratives to declaratives and to insist that, despite appearances, their semantics can be represented adequately in terms of truth conditions. The other is to accept that non-declaratives do not have truth conditions, but rather fulfillment conditions, a generalization of the notion of truth conditions, and to show how fulfillment conditions can be understood in terms of the same semantic machinery that enables us to understand how the truth conditions of declarative sentences are determined.

We begin by distinguishing force and mood. Then we lay out desiderata on a successful account. We sketch as background the program of truth-theoretic semantics. Next, we survey assimilation approaches and argue that they are inadequate. Then we show how the fulfillment-conditional approach can be applied to imperatives, interrogatives, molecular sentences containing them, and quantification into mood markers. Next, we consider briefly the recent set of propositions approach to the semantics of interrogatives and exclamatives. Finally, we show how to integrate exclamatives and optatives into a framework similar to the fulfillment approach.

34.1 MOOD AND FORCE

The contribution of sentential mood to sentence meaning must be distinguished from the illocutionary force with which sentences can be uttered.

Illocutionary force is a feature of a token utterance, a speech act. A speech act has illocutionary force when the speaker has some specific linguistic purpose in performing it. The force of an utterance will vary along a number of different dimensions,

---

[4] We assume an adequate syntactic analysis of the sentential moods to concentrate on their semantics.

such as point (an assertion vs. a question), strength (a request vs. an order), and style (announcing vs. confiding). The most important dimension along which speech acts vary is the point of the utterance, henceforth, 'illocutionary point' (Austin, 1962; Bach and Harnish, 1982; Searle, 1969; Searle, 1979; Searle and Vanderveken, 1985). Each sort of speech act has a particular illocutionary point; for example, to inquire, prohibit, report, advise, warn, suggest, thank, congratulate, admit, announce, etc. Utterances which have an illocutionary point are "illocutionary acts."[5] While there are many distinct kinds of illocutionary acts, they can be grouped into a smaller number of more general categories. We will generally follow Searle's taxonomy (1979), which uses illocutionary point as the primary means of differentiating speech acts.[6] Searle argues for five basic kinds of illocutionary act. *Assertives* (e.g. the statement, report, or suggestion that the moon is full) describe the world, and are correct or incorrect. *Directives* (e.g. a request or order to buy some milk) direct one's audience to bring it about that something is so, and are complied with or not. *Expressives* (e.g. a congratulations or thanks) express emotions or attitudes, and are sincere or insincere. *Commissives* (e.g. a promise or blood oath) commit the speaker to doing something, and are carried out or not. Finally, *declaratives* (e.g. a christening or a firing) make something the case, and they take or fail to take hold. (We underline 'declarative' when referring to an illocutionary act kind.) Declaratives are typically used for assertives; imperatives for generalized directives, interrogatives for requests for information; and exclamatives and optatives for expressive speech acts. *Declaratives* in the present tense active, such as 'You are fired' and 'You're out', are used typically in issuing declaratives. Performative sentences like 'I (hereby) promise to pay up' are often used to issue commissives. A performative sentence is a declarative sentence in the first person present tense active, or second person present tense passive, whose main verb expresses a speech act type which is or can be modified with an adverb such as 'hereby' or 'by so saying'.[7] These features are summarized in Table 34.1.[8]

Assertives, directives, commissives, and declaratives have satisfaction conditions, which come in two varieties: those with word-to-world direction of fit, and those with world-to-word direction of fit.[9] Assertives have word-to-world direction of fit, since their point is to make the words match the world; directives and commissives have world-to-word direction of fit, since their point is to make the world match the words. Declaratives have at least world-to-word direction of fit since their point is to bring the world to match their contents (the point of firing someone is to make it the case), and arguably, in some cases, word-to-world direction of fit as well (the umpire calling a strike both settles the matter and reports the facts). Each has its sincerity

---

[5] Illocutionary acts (He told me not to do it) should be distinguished from locutionary acts, i.e. acts performed by saying something (He said, 'Don't do it'), and perlocutionary acts, acts characterized in terms of consequences of saying something (He stopped me). See (Hornsby, 2006), in this volume, for more on these distinctions.

[6] For other taxonomies, see (Alston, 2000; Austin, 1962; Bach and Harnish, 1982).

[7] See (Austin, 1961, p. 382; 1962, p. 320).

[8] See (Searle, 1979).   [9] (Anscombe, 1963).

Table 34.1

Illocutionary Act	Illocutionary Point	Typically Performed with
Assertives	To describe the world	Declaratives
Directives	To direct one's hearer to perform a certain kind of act	Imperatives and Interrogatives
Expressives	To express the speaker's emotion or attitude	Exclamatives and Optatives
Commissives	To commit the speaker to doing something	Declaratives in the first person present tense whose main verb expresses the type of commissive, e.g. 'I promise I'll call'
Declaratives	To make it the case that p	Declaratives expressing that p

condition: belief in what is described for assertives, desire for what is directed for directives, intention to do what one commits oneself to doing for commissives, and intention to bring about what is declared (or at least a desire for it) for declaratives, and perhaps also belief in hybrid cases like that of the umpire.[10] In contrast, expressives have no direction of fit. Their purpose is to express psychological states, but not to state that one has them. They are sincere or insincere.

Directives and expressives are of special interest to us. A directive is complied with provided that the audience does what is directed with the intention of carrying it out. If someone takes out the trash by accident, or without regard to an order, he has not thereby obeyed an order to take it out. Lacking direction of fit, expressives admit of no evaluation parallel to that for other speech act types. We can at best speak of their sincerity or lack of it, as when someone congratulates you on your recent promotion, though his heart is sore. Speech acts can have false presuppositions. They are then p-infelicitous, we'll say. Thanking someone by mistake for his wonderful wedding gift misfires because of a false presupposition. But this is not a parallel for satisfaction conditions. Not all expressives have presuppositions like this (an utterance of "Hurrah!" or "Ouch!"), so p-felicity will not cover all cases. Furthermore, in other cases p-felicity is not a form of satisfaction. Directives and interrogatives can also have presuppositions. The question whether someone has got over his boot fetish presupposes he has one. Clearly the falsity of the presupposition would prevent the question from being correctly answerable. But its truth does not suffice for its being answered.

The five moods we distinguished above are features of sentences. We will call the syntactic features by which the moods are distinguished their mood markers.

Clearly there is a close connection between the mood of an unembedded sentence and the typical force of a use of it. Declaratives are specially suited for use in performing assertives, likewise imperatives for use in issuing directives, interrogatives

---

[10] In this we depart from Searle who holds that declaratives have no sincerity condition.

for use in asking questions, and exclamatives and optatives for use in performing expressives. However, it is important to distinguish between mood and force. Mood is a syntactic property of a sentence; force is a property of an utterance act. It makes no sense to talk of the semantics of force. An account of the semantics of a language focuses on its expression types. The force of an utterance is not an expression type, nor a property of an expression type. An utterance may have an illocutionary point, and, hence, a force, though it is not the production of any expression token in any language. Likewise, it makes no sense to speak of the illocutionary force of declaratives, interrogatives, imperatives, exclamatives or optatives, since these are sentences and not speech acts. This distinction is shown in the fact that a sentence in any mood may be used to perform any type of speech act. 'My coffee cup is empty' may be used to direct someone to fill the cup. 'Do you realize what trouble you're in?' may be used to assert that someone is in trouble. 'Tell me what time it is, please' may be used to ask a question. 'I will be there without fail', may be used to make a promise. 'In my opinion he is safe' may be used, by an umpire, to declare a runner safe. 'What a fool he is!' may be used to make an assertion and 'Isn't he the cutest thing?' may be used to perform an expressive.

   A central question in the semantics of non-declaratives is how to explain the close relation between mood and force: what is the semantic contribution of the mood markers, and how is this connected with their aptness for performing certain types of illocutionary acts?

34.2 DESIDERATA ON A SUCCESSFUL ACCOUNT

An adequate semantic account of the sentential moods must meet the following desiderata:

(1) It must explain the connection between sentential mood and suitability for the performance of certain sorts of speech acts.

(2) It must treat the moods as making the same general type of semantic contribution. This is an imprecise requirement, because we want variations in the contributions to explain differences, while understanding them as the same type of device. A clear violation, though, would be to treat only some of the moods as semantically significant.

(3) It must be compositional. It must exhibit our understanding of sentences in any mood as resting on understanding their significant components and mode of composition.

(4) It must account for our intuition that uses of non-declarative sentences are not truth evaluable.

(5) It must assign the right intuitive force to serious literal utterances of atomic and molecular sentences, and particularly mixed-mood sentences.

(6) It must explain quantifying into mood markers, as in 'Invest every penny you earn.' A condition on meeting (6) is that an account meet (5), since 'Invest every penny you earn' is equivalent to 'For every x, if x is a penny you earn, invest x.'

(7) It should explain the distribution patterns found for sentences in non-declarative moods, for example, why imperatives are never used in the antecedents of conditionals.[11]

34.3 TRUTH-CONDITIONAL SEMANTICS

Truth-theoretic semantics provides a compositional semantics for a language by providing an interpretive truth theory for it.[12] An interpretive truth theory employs axioms that use metalanguage predicates that interpret the object language expressions for which they give satisfaction conditions or truth conditions. In giving an interpretive truth theory for French (the object language) in English (the metalanguage) we use 'red' to give the satisfaction conditions of 'rouge'. Similarly for productive terms, 'and', 'or', 'if ... then', etc., and quantifiers, 'all', 'some', etc. For a non-context sensitive language, an interpretive truth theory would enable us to prove biconditionals of the form (T), where 's' is replaced by a structural description of an object language sentence and 'p' by a metalanguage sentence translating it ('iff' $=_{df}$ 'if and only if').

(T) s is true iff p.

Given this, we can replace 'is true iff' with 'means that' preserving truth. Such a theory meets Tarski's Convention T, and the theorem is an interpretive T-sentence. The simplest proof of an interpretive T-sentence reveals how understanding the sentence rests on understanding its significant parts and their mode of combination.

For a context-sensitive language, axioms and theorems must quantify over contextual parameters relevant to understanding context sensitive expressions—tensed verbs, and words like 'I', 'here', 'now', etc. For present purposes, we relativize semantic predicates to utterances of expressions. Thus, 'satisfies(u)' and 'true(u)' are read as 'satisfied relative to u' and 'true relative to u'. These do not mean 'satisfied as uttered in u' or 'true as uttered in u', for we will analyze what is uttered in terms of expressions themselves not uttered, but evaluated relative to the utterance. We introduce also 'means(u)', read as 'means relative to u'. For convenience we suppress explicit relativization to the object language. We designate the speaker of u as S(u) and its time as $t(u)$, treated as directly referring terms. A speech act u performed using an expression φ (perhaps as embedded in a longer expression) is $u(\varphi)$. Metalanguage predicates have an explicit argument place for time, and so are context insensitive (see (Lepore and Ludwig 2003a)).

---

[11] See (Harnish, 2001, Boisvert, 1999) for a discussion of the patterns that are not admissible.
[12] See (Lepore and Ludwig, 2003b, 2005; Ludwig, 2002).

Consider a simple informal truth theory for a context sensitive fragment of English, with the names 'Caesar', 'Brutus', the predicates 'x is honorable', 'x stabbed y', the first person pronoun 'I', the connectives 'and', 'not', the universal quantifier 'For all x', variables 'x', 'x_1', ..., 'y', 'y_1', ..., and parentheses for grouping. Sentences are formed in the obvious way. We use functions from variables to objects as satisfiers. We define 'f' is an 'x'-variant of f' as 'f' differs from f at most in what it assigns to 'x''.

A1. For any u('Caesar'), ref('Caesar', u) = Caesar.

A2. For any u('Brutus'), ref('Brutus', u) = Brutus

A3. For any u('I'), ref('I', u) = S(u).

A4. For any referring term α, for any u ($\ulcorner\alpha$ is honorable$\urcorner$), for any function f, f satisfies(u) $\ulcorner\alpha$ is honorable$\urcorner$ iff ref(α,u) is($t(u)$) honorable.

A5. For any referring terms α, β, for any u ($\ulcorner\alpha$ stabbed $\beta\urcorner$), for any function f, f satisfies(u) $\ulcorner\alpha$ stabbed $\beta\urcorner$ iff for some time t' earlier than $t(u)$, ref(α,u) stabs(t') ref(β,u).

A6. For any u('x is honorable'), for any function f, f satisfies(u) 'x is honorable' iff f('x') is($t(u)$) honorable.

A7. For any u('x stabbed y'), for any function f, f satisfies(u) 'x stabbed y' iff for some time t' earlier than $t(u)$, f('x') stabs(t') f('y').

A8. For any sentences φ, ψ, for any u($\ulcorner(\varphi$ and $\psi)\urcorner$), for any function f, f satisfies(u) $\ulcorner(\varphi$ and $\psi)\urcorner$ iff f satisfies(u) φ and f satisfies(u) ψ.

A9. For any sentence φ, for any u(φ), for any function f, f satisfies(u) $\ulcorner$not $\varphi\urcorner$ iff it is not the case that f satisfies(u) φ.

A10. For any formula φ, for any u($\ulcorner$For all x, $\varphi\urcorner$), for any function f, f satisfies(u) $\ulcorner$For all x, $\varphi\urcorner$ iff every 'x'-variant f' of f is such that f' satisfies(u) φ.

A11. For any φ, for any u(φ), φ is true(u) iff every function f satisfies(u) φ.

The axioms of this theory are interpretive. From this simple theory we can prove, e.g. the theorems:

For any u('I am honorable'), 'I am honorable' is true(u) iff S(u) is($t(u)$) honorable.

For any u('Brutus stabbed Caesar'), 'Brutus stabbed Caesar' is true(u) iff there is a time t' earlier than $t(u)$ such that Brutus stabs(t') Caesar.

In each of these we can replace 'is true(u) iff' with 'means(u) that' preserving truth.

34.4 TRUTH-CONDITIONAL ACCOUNTS

(a) The Force Indicator Account

A traditional view is that mood is an illocutionary force indicating device.[13] On this view, sentential mood *conventionally* indicates which *direct* illocutionary act type is

---

[13] Frege's distinction between judgment and content in *Begriffsschrift* (Frege 1997 (1879)) is the source of this view. See also (Frege 1997 (1892), p. 161; 1997 (1918), p. 329). Expressions and developments of this idea can be found in (Austin, 1961; Bach and Harnish, 1982; Davies, 1981, ch. 1; Dummett, 1973, ch. 10; 1993; Hare, 1952; 1970; Hornsby, 1986; McDowell, 1976; Searle, 1969, p. 54; Stenius, 1967). See (Harnish, 2001) on Frege's views.

being performed, though illocutionary acts of any type may be performed *indirectly* via a sentence in any mood. An indirect illocutionary act is an illocutionary act that is performed on the basis of performing another, and a direct illocutionary act one that is not indirect.[14] On this view, then, the declarative mood is a conventional device that serves to indicate that the speaker is performing a direct assertive; the imperative mood is a conventional device that serves to indicate that the speaker is performing a direct directive; and so on. The sentence is analyzed into a sentence radical,[15] which has truth conditions, and a mood marker that indicates the force with which it is uttered, and is treated as an operator on the radical. Thus, (1)–(3) are analyzed as in (4)–(6), where the sentence radical is indicated by the declarative core and the force-indicator is represented in curly brackets. The declarative core is the sentence itself in the case of a declarative, and it is the declarative from which the interrogative or imperative is derived in the case of interrogatives and imperatives respectively. Different varieties of interrogatives would have mood markers with distinct functions.

(1) We are ready.
(2) Are you awake?
(3) Take your time.
(4) {Assertive} <we are ready>
(5) {Question: yes-no} <you are awake>
(6) {Directive} <you will take your time>

This is an attractive view, for it assigns a clear semantic function to the sentential moods, and treats all of them in the same way. At first glance, it appears to satisfy at least desiderata (1)–(4).

The mood markers on this view would be only *prima facie* force indicator devices. Not every utterance of an imperative or declarative in English is *ipso facto* a directive or assertive. The speaker must intend the utterance to have that force. Uttering 'John is indefatigable' in response to a question about how to pronounce it is not an assertion, just as utterances of imperatives, declaratives and interrogatives, etc., when reading, or acting in a play, are not directives, assertions or questions, for the requisite intention is missing.

As attractive as this view is, however, it fails to give the right results when we consider molecular sentences. Consider (7)–(11).

(7) If the war goes badly, the President's approval rating will drop.
(8) If you're going to the store, buy some milk.
(9) If you'll be in later, would you like to have lunch?
(10) Don't cheat or you'll get a failing grade for the course.
(11) Is it a secret or can you tell me who it is?

In (7), uses of the antecedent and the consequent are not assertions, nor is there any conventional suggestion that, being in the declarative mood, they are to be

---

[14] For more on the distinction between direct and indirect illocutionary acts, see (Searle, 1979) and Hornsby in this volume.

[15] See (Stenius, 1967), who derives the notion from Wittgenstein. It is also introduced in (Hare, 1952, p. 18) as the *phrastic*.

interpreted as indicating that the speaker is making assertions with them. This under-cuts the view that mood functions as a simple force indicating device. One might respond that only the mood of the conditional sentence as a whole is semantically significant, there being a convention according to which the mood of embedded sen-tences becomes semantically inert. However, this fails for the other examples. In (8) and (9), the antecedents are declaratives, while the consequents are an imperative and interrogative respectively. These are not used to make true or false statements. But (8) is not used to issue a simple directive, nor (9) to ask a simple question. (8) is used to issue a conditional directive, and (9) to ask a conditional question. Thus, for (8), if the addressee is not going to the store, he need not do anything. If he is going to the store, then the utterance is satisfied only if he buys some milk as an intentional result of it. Thus, (8) is not in the declarative or imperative mood, and (9) likewise is neither declarative nor interrogative. Similarly, (10) is neither a declarative nor an imperative, and is not used either to make a statement or to issue a simple directive. In (11), no simple question is asked. (11) does not mean the same as 'Is it the case that (it is a secret or you can tell me who it is)?', since the latter can be answered simply 'yes' or 'no', while the former is answered with either 'Yes, it is a secret' or 'No, it is not a secret', or 'Yes, I can tell you' or 'No, I cannot tell you.'

The moods of the component sentences make a semantic difference to how we interpret them. They are not semantically inert, or (8) would have the same conven-tional meaning as 'If you are going to the store, you will buy some milk', an utterance of which would be true or false. Similarly for the other examples. If the moods are semantically active in these embedded contexts, however, the force indicator account cannot be correct. For on that account, (9), for example, would involve an assertion with the content of its antecedent, and a question with the content of its consequent.

Thus, the connection between the semantic contribution of mood and the force of an utterance must be more indirect than that suggested by the force indicator approach. Undoubtedly the mood of an unembedded sentence is apt for its use to perform a speech act of a certain sort. But the use of sentences of various moods in embedded contexts, where it would be inappropriate to use it with the associated force, and where that force cannot be attached to the whole sentence, but where the mood is semantically significant, shows that mood is not a simple force indication device. The force indicator approach thus fails when we come to desiderata 5 and 6.[16]

(b) The Performative Paraphrase Account[17]

The performative paraphrase approach integrates the imperative and interrogative moods into the truth-conditional approach by treating them as syntactic devices that

[16] See (Belnap, 1990; Huntley, 1984; Wilson and Sperber, 1988) for similar criticisms.
[17] Most famously championed by (Lewis, 1975, sec. 4), (Hamblin, 1987, ch. 3) has traced the proposal back to Husserl (Husserl, 2001 (1913), pp. 837, 847), but it appears also in Austin (Austin, 1961; 1962, p. 32), though with the complication that explicit performatives are not treated as used to perform assertives. See also (Katz and Postal, 1964, pp. 74–89). There are other, less plausible reductive accounts, e.g., that 'Go home' means 'I want you to go home.' See (Beardsley, 1944; Hamblin, 1958; Hare, 1949) for critical discussion of various other reductive accounts.

are interpreted like corresponding explicit performatives. For example, (2) and (3), repeated here, are interpreted as (12) and (13).

(2) Are you awake?

(3) Take your time.

(12) I hereby ask you whether you are awake.

(13) I hereby direct you to take your time.

The semantic function of the moods is thus to encode a performative. Imperatives and interrogatives are treated semantically as declaratives that achieve their special effect by using verbs for the speech acts they are used to perform. Asking a question using an interrogative or giving an order using an imperative is a matter of asserting that one is asking or ordering a certain thing. The question or order is an indirect speech act, carried by the primary speech act of asserting that one is asking a question or giving an order.[18] *Prima facie*, the approach meets desiderata 1 and 3.

It fails to meet the rest of the desiderata, however. First, unlike literal utterances of (12) and (13), literal utterances of (2) and (3) are intuitively not true or false. Furthermore, an utterance of (12) entails that someone has asked someone whether he is awake, and an utterance of (13) entails that someone has directed someone to take his time, but utterances of (2) and (3) do not. In response to (12) it would be appropriate to assert (14) but not in response to (2); in response to (13) it would be appropriate to assert (15), but not in response to (3).

(14) I wish you wouldn't.

(15) You are not in a position to do so.

Likewise, it doesn't make sense to respond to an utterance of (2) or (3) with 'That's a lie', though it does in response to (12) and (13). Furthermore, (12) and (13) can be used simply to state something, but (2) and (3) cannot. For example, in teaching someone sign language, I may sign a question and remark at the same time, 'I hereby ask you whether you are awake', by way of explanation. The signing constitutes asking a question, but not the remark about it. Thus, the performative paraphrase approach fails to meet desideratum 4.[19]

It also fails to meet desideratum 5. It treats (8) as equivalent to (16), but utterances of these are clearly not equivalent.

(8) If you're going to the store, buy some milk.

(16) If you're going to the store, I hereby direct you to buy some milk.

(8) is used to issue a conditional directive. (16) cannot be so used. The consequent of (16) is either true or false when uttered. If true, then a simple directive is issued, though none is issued in uttering (8). If the consequent is false, then no directive is issued, conditional or otherwise, by (16). This cannot be remedied by interpreting (8) as (17).

---

[18] Here we follow (Bach, 1975; Bach and Harnish, 1982, ch. 10.1). See also (McGinn, 1977, p. 305). In any case, this is the line that has to be taken if the current approach is to be amenable to a truth-theoretic approach.

[19] See (McGinn, 1977; Segal, 1991) for similar criticisms.

(17) I direct that if you go to the store, you will buy some milk.

No simple directive is issued by (8). However, the intended use of (17) issues a simple directive, which could be fulfilled if its intended audience fails to go the store as a result of being directed to make it the case that if he goes to the store, he buys some milk; and this is clearly not what is intended by (8). Thus, the approach fails to meet desiderata 5 and therefore 6.

Finally, if this approach were correct, we would have to treat declaratives similarly, since, on this view, declaratives just as much as imperatives and interrogatives are typically used to perform a specific kind of speech act, and this is to be associated with the declarative mood setter. However, this requires a declarative sentence, such as (1), repeated here, to be interpreted as (18).

(1) We are ready
(18) I hereby assert that we are ready.

However, (18) can be true when (1) is not.[20] Also, this leads immediately to an infinite regress, since (18) is itself a declarative sentence. This can be blocked only at the cost of not treating all the moods similarly, violating desideratum 2. Thus, interrogatives and imperatives are not paraphrases of the corresponding performative sentences.

(c) The Paratactic Account

Davidson's paratactic analysis of non-declarative sentences (Davidson, 2001 (1979)) is similar to the performative paraphrase approach, but Davidson argues that it avoids some of its difficulties while retaining its virtues. Davidson's suggestion derives from reflection on explicit performatives in light of his treatment of indirect discourse (Davidson, 2001 (1968)). Consider the explicit performative (19). Davidson's analysis of indirect discourse represents (19) as semantically equivalent to two separate sentences, as in (20).

(19) I assert that the moon is full.
(20) I assert that. The moon is full.

The second sentence is referred to by the first. Since the first says that the speaker asserts the second, the first is true iff the speaker, in uttering the second sentence, asserts it. This view explains the use of the performative as a device to indicate the speaker's intention to his audience. This account of explicit performatives suggests an analogous treatment for non-declaratives. Declaratives, Davidson says, we can leave alone, on the grounds that "we have found no intelligible use for an assertion sign" (Davidson, 2001 (1979), p. 119). Imperatives and interrogatives we treat as declaratives plus an imperative or interrogative mood marker. The declarative sentence is the declarative core of the imperative or interrogative. Each is assigned truth conditions. Thus, the declarative core of (21) is 'You will put on your hat'.

---

[20] See (Harnish, 1994, pp. 417–18).

(21) Put on your hat.

The mood marker in (21) is the truncation of the declarative core, the result of leaving out the subject term and modal auxiliary. The declarative core has its usual truth conditions. The mood marker is true "if and only if the utterance of the indicative core is imperatival in force" (p. 21). In short, the proposal is that an utterance of a sentence like (21) is understood to be two direct speech acts, one involving as content the declarative core of the sentence and the other involving a claim about the utterance of the declarative core. This account contains an element of parataxis in that the sentence uttered is semantically, though not syntactically, decomposable into two distinct utterance acts each possessing independent truth conditions. The account thus aims to meet desiderata 1, 3 and 4.

There is some unclarity attaching to how to integrate this account into a truth-theoretic semantics, but putting this aside, the proposal faces most of the difficulties of the performative paraphrase approach. First, Davidson's aim to explain the lack of truth value of utterances of non-declaratives as the result of its being semantically two utterances which are not the utterance of a conjunction does not blunt the force of the objection that utterances of non-declaratives are not truth evaluable. While the sequence of utterances of 'I am tired' and 'I am thirsty' is neither true nor false, each of the component utterances *are*. If the utterer of (22) is both tired and thirsty, he has uttered two truths.

(22) I am tired. I am thirsty.

Thus, Davidson is committed to saying that in literally uttering (21) one has said two things which are truth valued. If someone utters (21) thereby commanding you to put on your hat, and you do, Davidson's account entails that he has said two true things, and asserted at least one. However, intuitively, the speaker has not said anything which is true or false, and has not asserted anything. Thus, the account fails to meet desideratum 4 after all. And like the performative paraphrase account, it suggests that there are things that follow from utterances of non-declaratives which intuitively do not.

The paratactic account likewise fails when applied to embedded imperatives and interrogatives. (8), repeated here, would be represented as in (23).

(8) If you're going to the store, buy some milk.
(23) If you go to the store, my next utterance is a command. You will buy some milk.

However, the status of my utterance of 'You will buy some milk' is determined by my intentions when I utter it. Thus, it is a command if I intend it to be so, regardless of whether you go to the store; in that case it is a simple directive. But no simple directive is issued with (8). Thus if the consequent in the conditional in (23) were true as uttered, it would get the import of (8) wrong. But if the consequent is false, it fails to capture that (8) is complied with provided that the auditor does not go to the store or, if he does, he buys some milk as a result of the conditional directive received. As before, it is no help to represent (8) as (24), an utterance of which could be satisfied by deliberately not going to the store as a result of its being issued; an utterance of (8) issues no order which could be obeyed by staying at home.

(24) My next utterance is a command. If you go to the store, you will buy some milk.

Thus, the paratactic account fails to meet desiderata 5 and so 6.

Finally, the paratactic account, like the performative paraphrase approach, treats the declarative and non-declarative moods differently. However, as in the case of the performative account, this seems unmotivated and counterintuitive. Just as interrogatives are apt for asking questions, so declaratives are apt for making assertions. Thus, part of what was to be explained is left unexplained, violating desideratum 2.[21]

34.5 Fulfillment-Conditional Accounts

A fulfillment-conditional account does not attempt to assign truth conditions to imperatives and interrogatives.[22] It rather treats them as receiving their own type of satisfaction conditions, distinct from, but analogous to, truth conditions. This section develops the basic approach. The next section sketches how to extend it to handle quantifying into mood setters. This discussion is based on (Ludwig, 1997), though it contains some refinements of the work presented there.

(a) Basic Approach

Imperatives and interrogatives are incorporated into a generalization of truth-theoretic semantics that gives the truth theory a central role to play, but still allows that imperatives and interrogatives in use are neither true nor false. Imperatives and interrogatives, like declaratives, are given bivalent evaluations, relativized to appropriate contexts. Rather than being true or false, imperatives are *obeyed* and interrogatives are *answered* relative to a speech act u. We introduce 'obeyed(u)' and 'answered(u)' respectively as technical terms parallel to 'true(u)'. 'obeyed' and 'answered' are borrowed from the terminology for evaluating speech acts of the sort typically performed using imperatives and interrogatives. However, they are not predicates of speech acts, but of ordered pairs of sentences and speech acts. They bear to the terms that are applied to speech acts the same relation that 'x is true(u)' bears to 'is true' as used of speech acts.

---

[21] See (Bierwisch, 1980, 10–11; Dummett, 1993; Ludwig, 1997, §5; Segal, 1991, 106) for further criticisms.

[22] The first developed fulfillment approach that we are aware of is (McGinn, 1977). See also (Lappin, 1982), though his account is given for speech acts rather than sentences, and (Segal, 1991). See (Ludwig, 1997) for a discussion of the limitations of these approaches. See also (Harnish, 1994: 431–7).

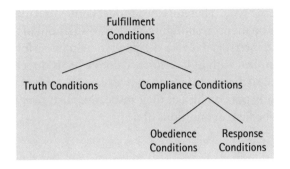

Fig. 34.1

Context relative "obedience conditions" are assigned to imperatives, and "response conditions" to interrogatives. Both are forms of compliance conditions. Compliance conditions and truth conditions, in turn, are treated as different forms of fulfillment conditions, as illustrated in Figure 34.1.

A fulfillment theory is introduced which aims to issue in theorems of the form [F] where 'φ' is replaced by a structural description of an object language sentence, and 'p' is replaced by a formula of the metalanguage.

[F]   For any $u(\varphi)$, φ is fulfilled(u) iff p

For atomic φ, the predicate 'is fulfilled(u)' is defined in terms of the truth, obedience, and response predicates.

(25)   For all atomic ϕ, for any $u(\varphi)$, ϕ is fulfilled(u) iff
    if ϕ is a declarative, then ϕ is true(u);
    if ϕ is an imperative, then ϕ is obeyed(u);
    if ϕ is an interrogative, then ϕ is answered(u).

Fulfillment conditions for molecular sentences are given using the usual recursive clauses, until reaching components to which (25) can be applied. The key to exhibiting the truth theory as central to the fulfillment theory lies in showing how to define 'obeyed(u)' and 'answered(u)' in terms of 'true(u)'. Then given an interpretive truth theory, for a declarative sentence we can replace 'is fulfilled(u) iff' in canonical theorems with 'means(u) that', for imperatives with the parallel 'directs(u) that', and for interrogatives with 'asks(u) that', preserving truth.

The explanation for the connection between the declarative mood and aptness for performing assertives is that declarative sentences, relative to a context, like assertives, are evaluated as true or false. Identifying the force of an utterance depends upon identifying the speaker's linguistic intentions. Given knowledge that a sentence used in a context has certain truth conditions, the default assumption in a communicative context will be that the speaker intends to be performing a speech act of a type which has the same mode of evaluation and the same content, that is, an assertive. Similarly, we have a straightforward explanation of the connection between the imperative and interrogative sentences and their use to issue directives provided we assign them a semantic evaluation of the same type. Therefore, we model context relativized obedience and response conditions on the corresponding bivalent evaluations of the kinds of directive that imperatives and interrogatives are designed to help us perform.[23]

A directive is complied with iff its audience does what is directed as an intentional result of having been so directed. An imperative like (21) is obeyed relative to u iff the audience subsequently puts on his (or their respective) hat(s) as an intentional result of recognizing the obedience conditions of u.

(21) Put on your hat

To generalize, some notation will be useful. Let Core(φ) be a function that takes an imperative or interrogative to its declarative core. Let $A(u)$ be a function from a speech act u to its audience. Obedience conditions for imperatives are as follows.

(I) For any imperative φ, for any $u(\varphi)$, φ is obeyed (u) iff $A(u)$ makes it the case that Core(φ) is true(u) with the intention of fulfilling u.[24]

Core(φ) yields a future tense sentence, so the forward looking character of imperatives is built into (I). $A(u)$ accommodates audiences consisting of one or more individuals. Though in general substitution of coreferential or coextensive terms in the complement of 'makes it the case' is not valid, it will be valid for all the substitutions made on the basis of a correct truth theory for the language, since if 'P' is made true in L by something, then if the truth of 'P' in L requires the truth of 'Q' in L, then 'Q' is made true in L by the same thing. 'makes it the case' is a tenseless, timeless metalanguage predicate; 'x makes it the case that p' is satisfied for a value of 'x' if at some time, it brings it about that p; the requirement that this be done with the intention of fulfilling the utterance of the relevant imperative guarantees it occurs afterwards.

Applying (I) to (21) with respect to utterance act U, where $t(U) = T$, $A(U) =$ ref('you', U) = A, assuming a singular audience, yields (26) (' $>$ ' $=_{df}$ 'is later than').

(26) 'Put on your hat' is obeyed(U) iff A makes it the case that [the $x : x$ is(T) a hat and x belongs(T) to A][there is a $t' : t' > T$] (A puts(t') on x with the intention of fulfilling U).

If the audience is plural, (26) must be modified by replacing 'A makes it the case that' with 'for each y such that y is one of A, y makes it the case that', and then subsequent appearances of 'A' with 'y'. Note that an utterance u of (21) will be obeyed(u) or not regardless of whether it is an illocutionary act, just as an utterance of 'The moon is full' will be true or false regardless of whether it is an illocutionary act.

One might object that, since the right hand side of the biconditional contains a declarative sentence, or sentence form, specifying the truth conditions for some

---

[23] Cf. (Segal, 1991, p. 117).

[24] Harnish's 1994 account (p. 431) likewise takes its cue from the satisfaction conditions of the related speech acts, though he does not assign fulfillment conditions recursively or extend the account to mixed-mood sentences or quantifying into mood setters, or to 'how' and 'why' questions. Criticisms of aspects of this can be found in (Wilson and Sperber, 1988, pp. 80–3); see (Ludwig, 1997, nts. 18, 24) for a response.

declarative sentence, we have after all represented this imperative as having truth conditions. This is a mistake, however. Different sorts of propositional attitudes likewise admit of different sorts of satisfaction conditions—for example, beliefs are true or false, but desires are satisfied or unsatisfied. We have no choice but to use declarative sentences to specify their satisfaction conditions. It does not follow that desires, like beliefs, are true or false. Thus, while any specification of a condition that determines which of two bivalent evaluations something receives will be a specification of a truth condition for some sentence, it need not be that whenever such a condition is specified it functions as a condition for something's being true or false.

Interrogatives are in the same line of business as imperatives, but are more specialized. We use the same template to provide response conditions for interrogatives as for imperatives. Different varieties of interrogative, however, require different response conditions. The basic varieties are yes-no questions ('Do you know where you are going to?'), how and why questions ('How did he do it?', 'Why did he bother?'), and wh-questions, which are distinguished by being formed from open rather than closed sentences ('Which of them is guilty', 'What time is it?', 'How many people were there?').

[YN] For any yes/no-interrogative φ, for any $u(\varphi)$, φ is answered(u) iff $A(u)$ makes it the case that $\ulcorner$you will say that Core(φ)$\urcorner$ is true(u) with the intention of fulfilling u or $A(u)$ makes it the case that $\ulcorner$you will say that Neg(Core(φ))$\urcorner$ is true(u) with the intention of fulfilling u.[25]

[WHY] For any why-interrogative φ, for any $u(\varphi)$, φ is answered(u) iff $A(u)$ makes it the case that $\ulcorner$you will explain why Core(φ)$\urcorner$ is true(u) with the intention of fulfilling u.

[HOW] For any how-interrogative φ, for any $u(\varphi)$, φ is answered(u) iff $A(u)$ makes it the case that $\ulcorner$you will explain how Core(φ))$\urcorner$ is true(u) with the intention of fulfilling u.

[WH] For any wh-interrogative φ, for any $u(\varphi)$, φ is answered(u) iff $A(u)$ makes it the case that [there is a θ: θ is a completion of Core(φ)]($\ulcorner$you will say $\theta\urcorner$ is true(u)) with the intention of fulfilling u.

In the case of [WH], the quantification over completions cannot be discharged. Rather, to see whether someone has answered a wh-question, we must wait for a response and see whether it satisfies the existential condition.

This approach handles the problem of mixed-mood sentences (excepting for now those involving exclamatives or optatives). In applying the fulfillment theory to (27), we will first employ a standard recursion clause as in (28). Then we employ the appropriate clauses of (25) for the antecedent and consequent to get (29).

---

[25] We assume that a question has been answered provided that someone provides a response of the appropriate form, whether or not it is correct. However, it is easy to modify the account to require a correct answer, by requiring that the speaker respond to Y/N(p) with 'p' if 'p' is true and 'not-p' if 'p' is false. For how and why questions the issue comes down to whether we require correct explanation, and for wh-interrogatives to whether we require the auditor to respond with a completion of the core which is true. These changes would make a difference to extension of the generalized relation of logical consequence discussed in the last paragraph of this section. An intermediate position would be to require the speaker to provide what he believes to be the correct answer.

(27) If you are tired, go to bed.

(28) For any φ, ψ, for any $u(\ulcorner$If φ, $\psi\urcorner)$, $\ulcorner$If φ, $\psi\urcorner$ is fulfilled(u) iff if φ is fulfilled(u), ψ is fulfilled(u).

(29) 'If you are tired, go to bed' is fulfilled(u) iff if 'you are tired' is true(u), then 'go to bed' is obeyed(u).

If a speaker addresses an audience A using (27) in U, and $t(U) = T$, we have (30).

(30) 'If you are tired, go to bed' is fulfilled(U) iff if A is(T) tired, then A makes it the case that [there is a $t' : t' > T$](A goes(t') to bed with the intention of fulfilling U).

This does not collapse into either the requirement to make the conditional true (or no requirement on the addressee at all) or simply the requirement that would be expressed by a standalone use of the consequent. (For discussion see (Ludwig, 1997)). Crucially, though declaratives, imperatives, and interrogatives receive a semantic evaluation that parallels the semantic evaluations of assertives and directives, they can have these conditions of evaluation without being uttered with any force.[26] This approach therefore satisfies desiderata (1)–(5). The next section shows how to extend it to satisfy 6.

As we have noted, not all semantically possible mixed mood combinations are found in natural languages. Desideratum 7 requires an account of non-declaratives to explain this. There are good reasons to think that these restrictions have largely to do with such constructions being useless for any practical purpose, despite our being able to assign to them a coherent semantics.[27] For example, given the semantics above, a conditional with an imperative in the antecedent is pointless since it places no constraints on the person addressed. However, there will not be space here to explore how this account can meet this last desideratum.

(b) Extension to Handle Quantifying-In

To extend the theory to open sentences, we introduce two additional satisfaction predicates, 'satisfies^{I}' and 'satisfies^{Q}' for imperatives and interrogatives respectively, which are recursively defined in terms of the satisfaction predicate for declarative sentence forms, which is the bare predicate 'satisfies' ('imperatives', 'interrogatives' and 'declaratives' are used to cover open sentences of these forms, as well as closed sentences). A general satisfaction predicate, 'satisfies^{F}' is introduced, with the usual recursive clauses for connectives and quantifiers. The application of 'satisfies^{F}' to atomic open sentences is defined in terms of those for the more specific varieties of satisfaction, as in (31).

---

[26] We thus differ with Davidson on whether "the concept of force is part of the meaning of mood" (Davidson, 2001 (1979), p. 121). If we are right, it is not, and a condition on handling embedded mood markers is that it is not. As we have said, the connection with force is less direct.

[27] See (Boisvert, 1999) for a defense of this claim.

(31) For all functions f, all atomic formulas φ, for all $u(\varphi)$, f satisfies$^F(u)$ φ iff
        if φ is declarative, then f satisfies(u) φ;
        if φ is imperative, then f satisfies$^I(u)\varphi$;
        if φ is interrogative, then f satisfies$^Q(u)\varphi$.

The satisfaction conditions for imperative and interrogative formulas are modeled on the fulfillment conditions given in the previous section, as illustrated with respect to the clause for imperatives [I-sat].

[I-sat] If φ is imperative, f satisfies$^I(u)\varphi$ iff $A(u)$ makes it the case that f satisfies(u)
        Core(φ) with the intention of fulfilling u.

For interrogatives, 'satisfaction^Q' is defined in terms of satisfaction conditions appropriate for each particular kind of interrogative, as in (32).

(32) For all functions f, for any interrogatives φ, for any $u(\varphi)$, f satisfies$^Q(u)$ iff
        if φ is a yes-no interrogative, then ...;
        if φ is a why interrogative, then ...;
        if φ is a how interrogative, then ...;
        if φ is a wh-interrogative, then ....

The satisfaction conditions for each variety are patterned after the response conditions given in the previous section. For example, in the case of wh-interrogatives, we have [WH-sat].

[WH-sat] If φ is a wh-interrogative, then f satisfies$^Q(u)\varphi$ iff $A(u)$ makes it the case
        that [there is a $\psi : \psi$ is a completion of Core(φ)]$(f$ satisfies(u) ⌜you will
        say ψ⌝) with the intention of fulfilling u.

Then 'is fulfilled(u)' is defined in terms of satisfaction^F by all functions. Consider the application of [I-sat] to (33), a regimented version of 'Invest every penny you earn', which yields (34), and then (35), and (36) — ignoring tense.

(33) [Every x: x is a penny you earn](invest x).

(34) For any function f, f satisfies$^F(u)$ '[Every x: x is a penny you earn](invest x)' iff
        every 'x'-variant f' of f such that f' satisfies 'x is a penny you earn' is such that f'
        satisfies^I 'invest x'.

(35) For any function f, f satisfies$^F(u)$ '[Every x: x is a penny you earn](invest x)' iff
        every 'x'-variant f' of f such that $f'('x')$ is a penny and ref('you', u) earns $f'('x')$
        is such that $A(u)$ makes it the case that f' satisfies(u) Core('invest x') with the
        intention of fulfilling u.

(36) For any function f, f satisfies$^F(u)$ '[Every x: x is a penny you earn](invest x)'
        iff every 'x'-variant f' of f such that $f'('x')$ is a penny, and ref(u, 'you') earns
        $f'('x')$ is such that $A(u)$ makes it the case that Ref(u, 'you') invests $f'('x')$ with
        the intention of fulfilling u.

This completes the sketch of the extension of the approach to a language with quantifiers.[28]

---

[28] See (Ludwig, 1997) for further details, complications and alternatives.

The fulfillment approach provides a basis for extending the usual logical notions from declaratives to imperatives and interrogatives. A sentence, relative to a context, "holds logically" provided that it is fulfilled on all reinterpretations of its non-logical features, where we treat its sentential mood as a logical feature of it. A sentence s is a logical consequence of another s', relative to a context, provided that every interpretation on which s' is fulfilled is one on which s is fulfilled. For example, this approach straightforwardly explains why uses of 'Go' and 'Do not go' at the same time and directed at the same auditor are logically inconsistent: they cannot be simultaneously obeyed relative to the context on any reinterpretation of their non-logical terms. It also makes perfectly good sense of the idea that an imperative can have as a consequence a declarative, for any time at which 'Go home' is directed at someone S, if that is fulfilled relative to the context, so will be 'S will go home'. Importantly, this is not an inference from the *truth* of a premise to the *truth* of conclusion, but from the *fulfillment* of the one to the *fulfillment* of the other.[29]

34.6 THE SET OF PROPOSITIONS APPROACH TO INTERROGATIVES AND EXCLAMATIVES

We take a brief look at the set of answers approach to the semantics of interrogatives and its extension to exclamatives. On this approach, the semantics of interrogatives is provided in terms of what they denote or express, namely, a set of propositions that constitute a (possibly complete) answer or a correct (possibly complete) answer to the interrogative. This set of *answers* is called the *question* the interrogative denotes or expresses. Thus, as 'question' and 'answer' are used in this approach, neither a *question* nor an *answer* is a speech act or a sentence. There are a variety of views about what *answers* should be (Groenendijk and Stokhof, 1997; Hamblin, 1973; Higginbotham, 1993; 1996; Higginbotham and May, 1981; Karttunen, 1977). For our purposes, these differences are not important. The set of propositions approach is motivated by the desire to provide a unified account of direct and so-called indirect questions. (37) is taken to be a direct question and the complement of (38), 'whether she was tired', is taken to be an indirect question. The indirect question is said (for example) to denote what the direct question expresses, namely, its *answer*. This is taken to be parallel to the Fregean account of the relation of direct statements and indirect statements as in (39) and (40). (39) expresses the proposition that the complement of (40) denotes.

(37) Is she tired?
(38) He asked whether she was tired.

---

[29] (Hare, 1989, p. 24) denies the inference is valid. See (Harnish, forthcoming) for related discussion. See (Williams, 1963) for an argument against a logic of imperatives. Also: (Rescher, 1966; Ross, 1944; Sosa, 1967).

(39) She is tired.

(40) He said that she was tired.

There is evidently some relation between the complement of (38) and the interrogative (37). But the motivation to say that they share sentential mood in the sense in which that is relevant to the distinction between semantic functions of the moods of 'You will go home', 'Will you go home?' and 'Go home', is not clear. One question that arises is whether 'whether' and 'that' should be treated as part of the verb rather than complement (Harnish, 1994, pp, 426–9); 'asked that' and 'asked whether' evidently express different speech act types, though they share 'asked'. In that case, the mood of the complement in (38) and (40) are the same. But independently of this, this approach fails to connect the interrogative mood to its use in asking questions. As (Stainton, 1999) points out, that an expression denotes or expresses a certain set of propositions would not make it especially apt for use in asking questions. For example, '{the proposition that you are awake, the proposition that you are not awake}' is not particularly apt for asking whether you are awake. Thus, the set of *answers* approach fails to answer adequately one of the central questions of the semantics of sentential mood, which is a precondition for meeting most of our desiderata.

The set of answers approach to interrogatives has been extended to certain kinds of exclamatives, motivated by the close syntactic similarities between certain exclamative clauses and interrogatives, such as that between (41) and (42).

(41) How cute he is!

(42) How cute is he?

Some accounts take the denotation of (41) to be identical to that the set of answers approach would assign to (42) (Gutierrez-Rexach, 1996), while some would allow for slight differences between the respective denotations (Collins, 2004; Michaelis and Lambrecht, 1996; Portner and Zanuttini, 2000; 2005; Zanuttini and Portner, 2000; 2003). One difficulty for this approach is that many exclamatives lack propositional content, e.g. 'Wow!', 'Ouch!', 'Hooray!', 'Congratulations!', 'What a year!' Thus, it cannot serve as a general account of the semantics of the exclamative mood. But its Achilles heel is that it shares with the set of answers approach to interrogatives it is based on the failure to connect exclamatives to their aptness for use in performing expressives.[30] Indeed, in assigning the same set of propositions to (41) and (42), the difference in *mood* is left altogether out of account.

34.7 EXCLAMATIVES AND OPTATIVES

The fulfillment condition approach cannot be used for exclamatives and optatives, since they are not used to perform speech acts with direction of fit, and many do

---

[30] Zanuttini and Portner's account is an exception. They attempt to account for the connection by holding that exclamative clauses have a semantic feature they call "widening." See (Zanuttini and Portner, 2003).

not have propositional content. Nevertheless, we can apply the central insight of that approach to provide a semantic account of exclamatives and optatives. That was to look to the characteristic mode of evaluation of the sort of speech act which the declarative, imperative and interrogative moods are specially suited to perform.

(a) Sincerity Conditions

Exclamatives and optatives are particularly suited for performing expressives, which are not satisfied or unsatisfied, but are rather sincere or insincere. We shall then take exclamatives and optatives to have sincerity conditions. The assignment of sincerity conditions as the primary mode of evaluation in turn explains why they are specially suited for use in performing expressives.

Standardly an expressive's sincerity condition is identified as the having of the psychological state that it expresses. Thus, a literal unembedded use of 'Yippee!' is an expressive that is sincere only if the speaker is excited at the time of utterance and insincere otherwise. That is, the expressive is sincere iff the speaker has the psychological state he represents himself, in virtue of his utterance, as having. It would be natural then to identify the sincerity condition of an exclamative or optative as having the psychological state that would be expressed by a standalone use of it.

This won't work, however, for exclamatives and optatives that can appear in the consequent of conditionals, as in (43) and (44).

(43) If you cleaned up the mess, thanks.
(44) If you won the lottery, congratulations.

We typically use such conditionals when we are unsure whether it is appropriate to thank or to congratulate our auditor, where the antecedent expresses a condition on that. If the antecedent is true, we are taken to have thanked, or congratulated, the person addressed, but otherwise not.[31]

These conditionals cannot be evaluated as sincere or as fulfilled, since they mix moods which cut across these sorts of evaluations. We will call them apt or not apt. If the antecedent of (43) is false, then the conditional is apt. But what if the antecedent is true?

Someone who uses (43) is unsure whether the person addressed meets a condition for it to be appropriate to feel grateful to him, thanks being an expression of gratitude. It might be thought that, if he is sincere, then at least he must be grateful to the person who cleaned up the mess, and just unsure about whether the addressee, under the present mode of presentation, is that person. But he may utter (43) with the thought that you may have cleaned it up since he discovered it, but without being sure that it has been cleaned up at all. If so, he cannot even be said to be grateful to

---

[31] There are other sorts of mixed mood exclamatives and optatives, but we focus on just the conditional. The considerations here will generalize to other permissible combinations. The contexts in which exclamatives and optatives are comfortable are limited, but we do not pursue the question why here.

the person who cleaned up the mess, for this implies he believes someone did. But he may use (43) appropriately. It follows that a use can be apt though the speaker is not grateful to the person addressed under any mode of presentation. Aptness conditions for the conditional should be assigned recursively in terms of the appropriate conditions for antecedent and consequent.[32] This rules out assigning aptness conditions on the basis of taking gratitude toward the person addressed as the sincerity condition for 'thanks'. For then the aptness of the conditional with a true antecedent will depend upon the speaker being grateful to the addressee. But this is not a requirement on the conditional being apt.

The sincerity condition for 'thanks' for both standalone and embedded uses can be identified by asking when an utterance of (43) with a true antecedent is not apt. To thank someone is to express (in the speech act sense) gratitude. Gratitude involves the thought that something which occurred is beneficial to one, the belief someone is responsible for it, and then a resulting feeling of goodwill toward the person responsible and a disposition to do something in return. Intuitively, someone who utters (43) without the commitment to come to feel goodwill toward the person addressed on the condition that he cleaned up the mess, and the disposition to return a benefit, utters it insincerely. We can then identify the sincerity condition with this commitment to feel goodwill toward the addressee and to be disposed to do something in return on the condition that he has benefited one.

This commitment is not a general disposition to feel gratitude toward people who benefit one. The commitment involved is of the same sort as that involved in conditional intending. If one plans to do something provided that some condition obtains, then one has settled on intending upon learning the condition obtains, without further deliberative reflection. This is the form of commitment which underlies conditional promises. It is the same sort of commitment which underlies conditional thanking or congratulating. One is settled on and rationally committed to having the appropriate attitude without further reflection, the appropriate conditions being met.

If commitment rather than the attitude one is committed to is the appropriate sincerity condition for standalone uses of 'thanks', then one might expect to find cases in which someone is sincere but lacks the relevant attitude in a standalone use. However, if the commitment is to have the state, appropriate conditions being met toward a particular object, it is not clear there is room for commitment in a standalone case without the attitude. For a standalone use would typically be motivated by the thought that someone is one's benefactor. The commitment then would straight off lead to the state.[33] Perhaps, though, one could say 'Thank you' to someone, being unsure that he is one's benefactor, but being committed to being grateful should it be confirmed. In this case, one would not be counted as insincere. This would be a standalone use in which being grateful and being sincere come apart in the right way.

---

[32] One could argue for a change in the function of such exclamatives in embedded contexts. But other things being equal a uniform account is to be preferred.

[33] Being committed to having it is not incompatible with having it, for having a disposition is not incompatible with its exercise.

We suggest then that the sincerity condition for those exclamatives which can appear in the then-clause in conditionals is commitment, in the sense discussed above, to have a certain psychological state, the one expressed by its literal use. This is to be distinguished from the commitment to having the state that arises from taking responsibility for having it in making a sincere literal use of an exclamative, for this commitment one has even if insincere.

For exclamatives which cannot appear in conditionals, there is no pull to treat the sincerity condition as commitment. And commitment modeled on the commitment involved in conditional intention seems to require that there be certain conditions independent of the state itself which have a bearing on the rational appropriateness of the state. Thus, for exclamatives such as 'ouch!', it is not clear that we can make sense of a sincerity condition that amounts to rational commitment to have a state on a certain condition for its appropriateness being met. Therefore, we do not extend the suggestion to all exclamatives. Exclamatives like 'ouch' are treated as sincere, then, iff the speaker has the state expressed.

Aptness conditions are not a subcategory of fulfillment conditions, and fulfillment conditions are not a subcategory of aptness conditions. We could then introduce a more general category of success conditions of which fulfillment and aptness conditions are kinds.

We assign sincerity conditions first to standalone exclamatives and optatives. Exclamatives can be structured or unstructured. Optatives invariably have structure. In assigning sincerity conditions we need to take into account both the type and the contribution of its structure to what is expressed. For illustration, consider (45)–(48).[34]

(45) Terrific!

(46) Terrific car!

(47) What a car!

(48) Oh, that I could be with you!

Literal, unembedded utterances of (45)–(47) express some highly positive affective attitude, excitement, say. While optatives are usually said to express a wish or hope that p, where 'p' gives the propositional content of the optative, this falls short of what is required. Just wishing or hoping to be rich would not license saying, 'Would that I were rich!' We will take them to express rather strong regret that not-p. In the case of (48), a speaker would express regret that he or she was not with the person addressed. The regret expressed in literal utterances of optatives distinguishes them from exclamatives, which may be used to express a variety of attitudes, including regret.

A use of (48) has a propositional object. Literal felicitous uses of (46) and (47) appear to have at least intentional objects. The speaker, if serious, expresses excitement about some car he has in mind. In (46) the noun phrase following 'terrific' tells us what object the speaker has in mind. A use of (45) seems to require that an object

---

[34] All of these seem to admit embedding: if you won the race, terrific! If you won the race in that car, terrific car too! If you are going to the stars, oh, that I could be with you!

be selected in the context for felicitous use. While exclamatives may be used to just express excitement, the fact that it is appropriate to ask 'What is terrific?' in response to (45) suggests that a proper use requires an object.

Let $O(u)$ be a function whose value for an utterance of an exclamative or optative is its object, that is, what the speaker has in mind. Let $\text{pred}(x)$ take a noun or noun phrase and yield a corresponding predicate, for example, pred('a car') = 'x is a car'. Let $\text{form}(\varphi)$ take sentences of the form 'What' $^\frown$ NP to 'That is' $^\frown$ NP. For example, form('What a car!') = 'That is a car'. Let $\text{neg}(\varphi)$ take a sentence in the subjunctive and yield the negation of its present tense form. For example, neg('I could be there with you') = 'I cannot be there with you'.

Now let us state a general condition (49) for 'terrific!' that handles examples (45) and (46), where we allow the null string as a value of 'NP' and stipulate that every x satisfies the null string.

(49) For any noun phrase NP, for any u('terrific' $^\frown$ NP $^\frown$ '!'), for any $x = O(u)$, 'terrific' $^\frown$ NP $^\frown$ '!' is sincere(u) iff $S(u)$ is committed to being excited about x and x satisfies pred(NP).

For (47) we have (50). To handle (48) and similar constructions, we have (51).

(50) For any noun phrase NP, for any u('What' $^\frown$ NP $^\frown$ '!'), for any $O(u)$ x, 'What' $^\frown$ NP $^\frown$ '!' is sincere(u) iff $S(u)$ is committed to being excited about x and x satisfies pred(NP).

(51) For any subjunctive sentence ϕ, for any $u(\phi)$, 'Oh'/'Would' $^\frown$ 'that' $^\frown$ ϕ is sincere(u) iff $S(u)$ is committed to its being the case that $S(u)$ satisfies(u) 'x strongly regrets that' $^\frown$ neg(ϕ)

Note that in (49) and (50) we have invoked a satisfaction relation between individual objects and one-place predicates, rather than between functions and predicates. A condition on (45)–(47) being sincere is that there be an object corresponding to what the speaker has in mind. A speaker of (46) might be thought sincere even when hallucinating a car. But the attitude he is to commit to having is a de re attitude. Without an object, he can neither have the attitude, nor a commitment to it, both requiring the object for their characterization.

(b) Conditionals

The extension to conditionals is straightforward. We'll talk of aptness conditions for use of these sorts of conditionals, classify for convenience conditionals with exclamatives in the consequent as exclamatives, and those with optatives in the consequent as optatives, and say that atomic exclamatives and optatives are apt relative to a speech act u iff they are sincere(u). We'll say that a declarative is apt(u) iff it is true(u). We assign aptness conditions to the conditionals recursively. Instantiating (52) to (43), and a speech act u, we get (53).

(52) For any φ, ψ, for any $u(\ulcorner \text{if } \varphi, \psi \urcorner)$, $\ulcorner \text{If } \varphi, \psi \urcorner$ is apt(u) iff if φ is apt(u) then ψ is apt(u)

(53) 'If you cleaned up the mess, thanks!' is apt(u) iff if 'you cleaned up the mess' is true(u), then 'thanks!' is sincere(u).

Suppose A is the speaker of U, and B is the person addressed. The clause for 'thanks' will be (54). The result is (55) (ignoring tense).

(54) For any u('thanks'), 'thanks' is sincere(u) iff S(u) is committed to being grateful to the addressee of u.

(55) 'If you cleaned up the mess, thanks' is apt(U) iff if B cleaned up the mess, then A is committed to being grateful to B.

This yields the right result, for when B has cleaned up the mess, and A is prepared to be grateful to whoever cleaned up the mess, if anyone, A is thereby committed to being grateful to B. Thus, as is intuitively correct, the condition for the use of 'thanks' being apt is met. Furthermore, since for A to have thanked B is for A to have performed an utterance act, the success of which requires a commitment to being grateful to B, we also get the correct result that A has thanked B.[35]

(c) Quantifying into Exclamatives and Optatives

The extension to quantifying into exclamatives requires characterizing when an exclamative with a free variable is sincere *relative to a function*, as well as a speech act u. We illustrate using (57), which makes explicit the structure of (56). In (57), the relevant expression is 'congratulations to x on winning x's age-group'.

(56) Congratulations to each of the age-group winners on winning his age-group!
(57) [For each x: x is an age-group winner](congratulations to x on winning x's age-group!)

When offering congratulations, one expresses pleasure at someone's accomplishment. Sometimes we indicate this explicitly as in 'Congratulations to you on winning the race'. We will take it that whenever someone uses 'congratulations', there is an argument place for the addressee and for a property of the addressee, and that what is expressed is happiness toward the addressee having the property. The property itself may be individuated with respect to an individual. For example, one could congratulate Jim on marrying Jill, or congratulate Jill on winning her age-group in the race.

We first formulate relativized sincerity conditions for a fully explicit example, 'congratulations to x on x's winning x's age-group' in (58).

(58) For any function f, for any u('congratulations to x on winning x's age-group), 'congratulations to x on winning x's age-group' is sincere(u, f) iff S(u) is committed to being pleased about f satisfying 'x won x's age-group'.

---

[35] One might think that this is incorrect because if the antecedent is false, and the speaker is not grateful for the mess being cleaned up, then the utterance is not appropriate. But the sense of its being inappropriate in this case is due to there being no point in uttering the conditional when one knows that the antecedent is false. This is pragmatic inappropriateness rather than semantic infelicity.

Let us assume a function, from prepositional phrases of the sort which may appear after 'congratulations to x' and a variable, to open sentences containing the variable, pred(ϕ), yielding, for example, 'pred('winning the race', 'x')' = 'x won the race'. The function takes the nominalization of a predicate employing an action verb, V-ing (NP), to an open sentence with 'x' in the subject position and V as the main verb in the past tense with NP as an optional complement of the verb V. Then we generalize as in (59) (restricting PP to prepositional phrases which can follow 'congratulations').

(59) For any function f, for any prepositional phrase PP, for any u('congratulations to x'⌢PP), 'congratulations to x'⌢PP is sincere(u, f) iff S(u) is committed to being glad about f satisfying pred(PP, 'x').

If the relevant property is not explicit, we introduce a function from the speech act to a property, namely, the property the speaker of u is glad the addressee x has, which we will allow is possibly a property that involves in its individuation x himself, as in (60). We treat the function as having two argument places, one for the speech act and one for addressee to allow the property itself to vary with the value of 'x': prop(u, x).[36]

(60) For any function f, for any u('congratulations to x'), 'congratulations to x' is sincere(u, f) iff S(u) is committed to being glad about f('x') having prop(u, x).

In the case of a use of (56) or its proxy (57), a speaker would be most naturally interpreted as intending, for each x, to be glad that x has the property of *being the winner of x's age-group*. For someone then to sincerely utter (56), he would have to be committed to being glad of each winner of an age-group that that winner had the property of being the winner of his age-group. And that is the result which we intuitively want. This treatment can be extended to optatives.

34.8 SUMMARY AND CONCLUSION

Non-declaratives have presented a conundrum for traditional approaches to the theory of meaning, from Frege on. We have considered a number of different approaches to their semantics. The force indicator approach treats the moods as operators on sentence radicals that have truth conditions which indicate conventionally with what force they are to be taken. This line of approach traces back to Frege himself, and shows promise of meeting desiderata (1)–(4). It fails, however, in application to embedded sentences, where the mood clearly is semantically significant but does not serve to indicate the force with which the sentences are uttered. This approach thus fails to meet desiderata (5) and (6). This failure shows that the relation between mood, truth and force is less direct than the force indicator

---

[36] The resort to properties can be circumvented, but at the cost of complexity which would not provide additional illumination.

approach assumes. We considered also two approaches which in effect assimilate the moods to performatives, the explicit performative paraphrase approach, and Davidson's paratactic version of this. While these *prima facie* meet desiderata (1) and (3), they fail to satisfy (2) and (4)–(6). We argue that, in contrast to these approaches, the fulfillment-conditional approach is able to meet all of the desiderata (with a promissory note entered for (7)). It does this by making the relation between mood and force not that of a conventional indicator of the force of an utterance, but a conventional mark of the sort of satisfaction condition which it receives, which is modeled on the satisfaction conditions suitable for the sort of speech acts associated with their standalone uses. By assigning compliance conditions to imperatives and interrogatives which are determined recursively in terms of truth conditions, we were able to show that we can handle embedded occurrences in a straightforward way, and to extend the account to quantifying into mood markers. We have sketched how to extend the framework to the relatively neglected categories of exclamatives and optatives. Exclamatives and optatives are assigned sincerity conditions. For those that admit embedding we assign them sincerity conditions conceived of as rational commitments to have, given certain conditions, the attitudes expressed by serious literal standalone uses of them. This enabled us to assign a form of evaluation to unembedded uses that works also for embedded uses, and to extend the treatment to quantifying into exclamatives and optatives. In this way, we preserve the connection between mood and force without making it so intimate that it is difficult to see how to handle it in embedded contexts and in interaction with quantifiers.

References

Alston, W. P. (2000). *Illocutionary Acts and Sentence Meaning.* Ithaca, NY: Cornell University Press.

Anscombe, G. E. M. (1963). *Intention* (2nd edn.). Ithaca, NY: Cornell University Press.

Austin, J. L. (1961). Performative Utterances, *Philosophical Papers* (pp. 233–52). Oxford: Clarendon Press.

—— (1962). *How to Do Things with Words.* Cambridge, MA: Harvard University Press.

Bach, K. (1975). Performatives Are Statements Too. *Philosophical Studies*, 28: 229–36.

Bach, K., and Harnish, R. M. (1982). *Linguistic Communication and Speech Acts.* Cambridge: MIT Press.

Beardsley, E. L. (1944). Imperative Sentences in Relation to Indicatives. *Philosophical Review*, 53: 175–84.

Belnap, N. (1990). Declaratives Are Not Enough. *Philosophical Studies*, 59(1): 1–30.

Bierwisch, M. (1980). Semantic Structure and Illocutionary Force. In J. R. Searle, F. Kiefer, and M. Bierwisch (eds.), *Speech Act Theory and Pragmatics.* Dordrecht: D. Reidel.

Boisvert, D. (1999). *Pragmatics and Semantics of Mixed Sentential Mood Sentences.* Unpublished M. A. Thesis, University of Florida, Gainesville.

Collins, P. (2004). Clause Types. In B. Aarts, and A. McMahon (eds.), *The Handbook of English Linguistics.* Oxford: Blackwell.

Davidson, D. (2001 (1968)). On Saying That, *Inquiries into Truth and Interpretation* (pp. 93–108). Oxford: Clarendon Press.

―――― (2001 (1979)). Moods and Performances, *Inquiries into Truth and Interpretation* (pp. 109–22). Oxford: Oxford University Press.

Davies, M. (1981). *Meaning, Quantification, and Necessity*. London: Routledge and Kegan Paul.

Dummett, M. (1973). *Frege: Philosophy of Language*. Cambridge, MA: Harvard University Press.

―――― (1993). Mood, Force and Convention. In M. Dummett (ed.), *The Seas of Language* (pp. 202–23). Oxford: Oxford University Press.

Frege, G. (1997 (1879)). *Begriffsschrift* (Selections). In M. Beaney (ed.), *The Frege Reader* (pp. 47–78). Oxford: Blackwell.

―――― (1997 (1892)). On *Sinn* and *Bedeutung*. In M. Beaney (ed.), *The Frege Reader* (pp. 151–71). Oxford: Blackwell.

―――― (1997 (1918)). Thought. In M. Beaney (ed.), *The Frege Reader* (pp. 325–45). Oxford: Blackwell.

Groenendijk, J. A. G., and Stokhof, M. (1997). Questions. In J. V. Bentham, and A. T. Meulen (eds.), *Handbook of Logic and Language* (pp. 1055–124). Cambridge, MA: MIT Press.

Gutierrez-Rexach, J. (1996). The Semantics of Exclamatives. In E. Garrett, and F. Lee (eds.), *Syntax at Sunset: UCLA Working Papers in Linguistics* (pp. 146–62). Los Angeles: UCLA.

Hamblin, C. L. (1958). Questions. *Australasian Journal of Philosophy*, 36: 159–68.

―――― (1973). Questions in Montague English. *Foundations of Language*, 10 (1973): 41–53.

―――― (1987). *Imperatives*. Oxford: Basil Blackwell.

Hare, R. M. (1949). Imperative Sentences. *Mind*, 58: 21–39.

―――― (1952). *The Language of Morals*. Oxford: Clarendon Press.

―――― (1970). Meaning and Speech Acts. *Mind*, 79: 3–24.

―――― (1989). Some Subatomic Particles of Logic. *Mind*, 98: 23–37.

Harnish, R. (1994). Mood, Meaning and Speech Acts. In S. L. Tsohatzidis (ed.), *Foundations of Speech Act Theory*. London: Routledge.

―――― (2001). Frege on Mood and Force. In I. Kenesei, and R. M. Harnish (eds.), *Perspectives on Semantics, Pragmatics, and Discourse* (pp. 203–28). Philadelphia: John Benjamins.

―――― (Forthcoming). Mood and Inference, *Research in Language*. Stanford: CSLI.

Higginbotham, J. (1993). Interrogatives. In K. Hale, and S. J. Keyser (eds.), *The View From Building 20* (pp. 195–227). Cambridge, MA: MIT Press.

―――― (1996). The Semantics of Questions. In S. Lappin (ed.), *The Handbook of Contemporary Semantic Theory*. Cambridge: MIT Press.

Higginbotham, J., and May, R. (1981). Questions, Quantifiers and Crossing. *The Linguistic Review*, 1(41–80).

Hornsby, J. (1986). A Note on Non-Indicatives. *Mind*, 95: 92–9.

―――― (2006). Speech Acts. In B. Smith, and E. Lepore (eds.), *The Oxford Handbook of Philosophy of Language*. Oxford: Oxford University Press.

Huntley, M. (1984). The Semantics of English Imperatives. *Linguistics and Philosophy*, 7: 103–34.

Husserl, E. (2001 (1913)). *Logical Investigations*. London: Routledge.

Jesperson, O. (1924). *The Philosophy of Grammar*. London: Allen and Unwin.

Karttunen, L. (1977). The Syntax and Semantics of Questions. *Linguistics and Philosophy*, 1: 3–44.

Katz, J. J., and Postal, P. (1964). *An Integrated Theory of Linguistic Description*. Cambridge, MA: MIT Press.

Lappin, S. (1982). On the Pragmatics of Mood. *Linguistics and Philosophy*, 4: 559–78.

Lepore, E., and Ludwig, K. (2003a). Outline for a Truth Conditional Semantics for Tense. In Q. Smith, and A. Jokic (eds.), *Tense, Time and Reference* (pp. 49–105). Cambridge, MA: MIT Press.

——— (2003b). Truth and Meaning. In K. Ludwig (ed.), *Donald Davidson*. New York: Cambridge University Press.

——— (2005). *Donald Davidson: Truth, Meaning, Language and Reality*. New York: Oxford University Press.

Lewis, D. (1975). General Semantics. In D. Davidson, and G. Harman (eds.), *Semantics of Natural Language* (pp. 169–218). Boston: D. Reidel.

Ludwig, K. (1997). The Truth About Moods. *Protosociology*, 10: 19–66. Reprinted in *Concepts of Meaning: Framing an Integrated Theory of Linguistic Behavior*, Kluwer Academic Publishers, 2003.

——— (2002). What Is the Role of a Truth Theory in a Meaning Theory? In D. Shier, J. K. Campbell, and M. O'Rourke (eds.), *Meaning and Truth: Investigations in Philosophical Semantics* (pp. 142–63). New York: Seven Bridges Press.

McDowell, J. (1976). Truth Conditions, Bivalence and Verificationism. In J. McDowell, and G. Evans (eds.), *Truth and Meaning* (pp. 41–66). Oxford: Clarendon Press.

McGinn, C. (1977). Semantics for Nonindicative Sentences. *Philosophical Studies*, 32: 301–11.

Michaelis, L., and Lambrecht, K. (1996). The Exclamative Sentence Type in English, *Conceptual Structure, Discourse, and Language* (pp. 375–89). Stanford: CSLI.

Pendlebury, M. (1986). Against the Power of Force: Reflections on the Meaning of Mood. *Mind*, 95: 361–72.

Portner, P., and Zanuttini, R. (2000). The Force of Negation in Wh Exclamatives and Interrogatives. In L. R. Horn, and Y. Kato (eds.), *Studies in Negation and Polarity: Syntactic and Semantic Perspectives* (pp. 201–39). New York: Oxford University Press.

——— (2005). Nominal Exclamatives in English. In R. J. Stainton, and R. Elugardo (eds.), *Ellipsis and Non-Sentential Speech* (pp. 57–67). Dordrecht: Kluwer.

Rescher, N. (1966). *The Logic of Commands*. London: Routledge and Kegan Paul.

Ross, A. (1944). Imperatives and Logic. *Philosophy of Science*, 11: 30–46.

Searle, J. (1979). Indirect Speech Acts, *Expression and Meaning: Studies in the Theory of Speech Acts* (pp. 30–57). Cambridge: Cambridge University Press.

——— (1969). *Speech Acts: An Essay in the Philosophy of Language*. Cambridge: Cambridge University Press.

——— (1979). A Taxonomy of Illocutionary Acts, *Expression and Meaning*. Cambridge: Cambridge University Press.

——— and Vanderveken, D. (1985). *Foundations of Illocutionary Logic*. Cambridge: Cambridge University Press.

Segal, G. (1991). In the Mood for a Semantic Theory. *Proceedings of the Aristotelian Society*, 91: 103–18.

Sosa, E. (1967). The Semantics of Imperatives. *American Philosophical Quarterly*, 4: 57–64.

Stainton, R. J. (1999). Interrogatives and Sets of Answers. *Critica*, 31(91): 75–90.

Stenius, E. (1967). Mood and Language-Game. *Synthese*, 17: 254–74.

Williams, B. (1963). Imperative Inference. *Analysis Supplement*, 23: 30–6.

Wilson, D., and Sperber, D. (1988). Mood and Non-Declarative Sentences. In J. Dancy, J. M. E. Moravcsik, and C. C. W. Taylor (eds.), *Human Agency: Language, Duty and Value*. Stanford: Stanford University Press.

Zanuttini, R., and Portner, P. (2000). The Characterization of Exclamative Clauses in Paduan. *Language*, 76(1): 123–32.

——— (2003). Exclamative Clauses: At the Syntax–Semantics Interface. *Language*, 79: 39–81.

CHAPTER 35

SPEECH ACTS
AND
PERFORMATIVES

JENNIFER HORNSBY

> The total speech act in the total speech situation is the only actual phe-
> nomenon which, in the last resort, we are engaged in elucidating.
>
> J.L. Austin (1962: 147)

AT the start of *How to Do Things with Words*,[1] Austin spoke of a 'revolution' in
philosophy—a revolution instigated by claims to the effect that there are indicative sentences whose use is not to make statements of fact. His own claim was that
certain sentences—the performatives—disguise themselves as truth-evaluable but
aren't really such. By the end of the book, Austin allowed that performativity in some
sense is a feature of any speech; and he said that we need a 'general theory of speech
acts' (1962: 147).

This chapter aims to connect Austin's seminal notion of a speech act with developments in philosophy of language over the last forty odd years. It starts by considering
how speech acts might be conceived in Austin's general theory. Then it turns to the
illocutionary acts with which much philosophical writing on speech acts has been
concerned, and finally to the performatives which Austin's own treatment of speech
as action took off from.

---

[1] Austin, 1962. Austin delivered the lectures printed therein as the William James lectures at Harvard
University in 1955; earlier versions had been given in Oxford under the title 'Words and Deeds'.

35.1 Speech Acts and Linguistic Meaning

Austin believed that by considering sentences in abstraction from actual speech situations, theorists had privileged 'constative' (i.e. statement-making) uses of language and forgotten about the great variety of things that people do using words. Someone who utters words does lots of things; and this is to say that she performs many *speech acts*, constituting on any occasion some 'total speech act'. Here, for example, are just a few of the things that might have been done on the occasion of an utterance: *emitting such and such sounds, saying 'The train leaves at 12.07', telling X when the train leaves, reminding X that it's time to go, prompting X to put her coat on*. All these things are speech acts.[2]

Some of these acts might be done without the others: the act of reminding someone that it's time to go might be done by saying 'It's time to go', and without saying when the train leaves; saying 'The train leaves at 12.07' might be done in the course of contriving a plan, and without reminding anyone of anything; someone might tell someone when the train leaves by using words of some language other than English. Which speech acts are done along with which others obviously depends on the particularities of the occasion of utterance. Yet equally obviously there are some very definite limits on possible combinations. For example, in a very wide range of situations, a speaker of English who does this—come out with noises corresponding to 'The train leaves at 12.07'—also does this—assert something about the time of some train's departure.

35.1.1 Speech Acts as Classificatory

An illuminating description of the use of a language should have something to say about, very roughly, which speech acts are apt to go together, and what explains their going together when they do. A principled way of organizing speech acts would provide a framework into which the particularities of occasions on which one or another is done could potentially be fitted so as to provide for full and fully illuminating re-descriptions of utterances. What is needed is a theoretically motivated classification, which requires in the first place the isolation of important sorts of speech act.

The number of sorts that Austin distinguished by name in the first instance was six: phonetic, phatic, rhetic, locutionary, illocutionary, and perlocutionary. Here we can focus on just three of Austin's six, which, disregarding details, can be specified as follows (*Ibid.*: 92–3, 95):

---

[2] Austin himself used the term 'speech act' with less frequency but with greater generality [having application to a wider class of acts] than subsequent writers. Most contributors to the philosophical literature use 'speech act theory' having in mind something like the account of illocutionary acts that Searle, 1969, developed. See Hornsby, 1988, for an attempt at a definition of 'speech act' in line with Austin's very broad use.

PHATIC of uttering certain words, i.e. noises of certain types belonging to and uttered as belonging to a certain vocabulary in a certain construction

RHETIC of using one's words with a certain more or less definite sense and reference, i.e. linguistic meaning.

ILLOCUTIONARY done *in* doing an act of the rhetic sort, in virtue of which a certain force accrues to the use of the words.

This short list leaves out perlocutionary acts, which Austin defined in terms of speech's consequences, and which it seems an account of the workings of language proper might not need to be especially concerned with (see further Section 35.2.1). And it leaves out phonetic acts—the 'uttering of certain noises'—whose study belongs to specialists in phonetics. It also leaves out locutionary acts. Well, Austin said that he meant by 'locutionary act' simply 'the sum of the phonetic, phatic and rhetic' acts (*Ibid.*: 109). So we might employ Austin's word 'locutionary' not to name any sort of speech act, but instead to mark that portion of a description of the use of language which is concerned to relate phatic acts with rhetic acts. (Strawson, 1973, explores Austin on the subject of locutionary meaning, and reveals difficulties in finding a consistent interpretation of Austin's own terminology. My suggestion here is that we avoid 'locutionary act' for the time being and focus on Austin's own definition of 'rhetic act'. In due course, I shall follow others, and use 'locutionary act' as others do, to make a contrast with 'illocutionary act'.)

Austin himself said little about what a theory of locution should, or could, achieve: in this connexion, he spoke of 'sense and reference' and of the 'artificial abstraction' of 'traditional conceptions'. But we know that the locutionary portion of an overall account of language use will treat a specific language—English, Spanish, Pashto, or whatever—and that it must specify the linguistically meaningful ('rhetic') things that speakers of the language do when they produce particular sentences (when they do 'phatic' things). So a theory of locution for L, if it were stated quite in abstraction from speakers' use of L, would simply assign a meaning—to any of L's sentences ∗ ∗ ∗ ∗. And in order to incorporate such a theory (gestured at here with a schema) into a speech act account of L's use, it would only need to be laid down that:

Utterances in which the speaker's phatic act is producing ∗ ∗ ∗ ∗ are utterances in which the speaker's rhetic act is one whose meaning is that——.[3]

There are two very obvious reasons why this won't work as it stands. In the first place, sentences of natural languages typically contain indexical and demonstrative elements, and it isn't possible to say what rhetic acts may be done with sentences containing these except by specifying contexts for their utterance. Secondly, a theory that provides a general way of specifying rhetic acts must presumably fill '——',

---

[3] This formulation makes explicit a view of the individuation of action. Utterances are treated as particulars—as actions (each one 'fixed and physical' as Austin put it). The idea that there is a variety of speech acts on the occasion of a single utterance is then the idea that the utterance is the agent's doing one act, and is her doing another . . . For those who prefer to talk about redescription, it is the idea that the utterance (action) can be redescribed. (Different views about actions' individuation may be part of the explanation of differences in the use of 'speech act': cp. n.2 above.)

in any instance, with a sentence expressing something propositional; but that means that only indicative sentences would be accommodated: sentences in the interrogative, or imperative mood wouldn't belong.

Well, these two obvious points were of no particular concern to Austin. And theorists surely do take account of them; although of course there is much more to be said about how exactly they are to be accommodated. Thus even though Austin's writings may convey the impression that a speech act account of language use enforces some radical departures from a 'traditional' view of linguistic meaning, it can seem now as if a treatment of a language as (roughly) a meaningful system might be tailor-made for the locutionary portion of an overall account of the speech acts of users of that language. Those who advocate truth-conditional semantics, for instance, may claim that, so long as expressions' context-sensitivity is properly accommodated, a theory with theorems on the pattern of '* * * * is true if and only if—— ' can serve to effect pairings of speakers' phatic acts with their rhetic ones. And this now is just the upshot of a pairing of sentences with what are often called their propositional contents, now specified by *using* sentences. The proposal then may be that speech act theory proper belongs in the realm of pragmatics, where pragmatics for its part is concerned with illocutionary acts—i.e. with what speakers do in performing those rhetic acts that a purely semantic, truth-conditional theory for their language would predict. (To accommodate non-indicatives, a notion of 'rhetic' that includes more than indicative saying would need to be introduced [cp. Hornsby, 1986], or some other account be given.)

Some writing in the area of speech acts has been opposed to such a proposal (see Sections 35.1.2, 2.2, and end of 2.3), and some of it supportive (see Section 35.1.3).

35.1.2 The Changing Conditions of Speech

Opposition to this proposal comes from those concerned with context-sensitivity of a different sort from that which indexicals and demonstratives exhibit. One of Austin's examples was the sentence 'France is hexagonal'. Pointing out that its utterance would serve different purposes in different contexts, Austin said that this 'is good enough for a top-ranking general, perhaps, but not for a geographer'. Austin sometimes spoke as if 'true' and 'false' lacked any application in the case of such a sentence: 'It is just rough .. [and] not a true or false description [of France]'. If this was right, then we should have here further examples of sentences belonging in a category to which Austin put his performatives—sentences that can't be evaluated for truth. But there is a way of understanding Austin's point which avoids the idea that it is actually improper to predicate 'true' or 'false' of *utterances* of 'France is hexagonal.'[4] On this other understanding, whether a speaking of those words is true depends upon whether—*in all*

---

[4] And thus allows that the *sentence* is not true or false simply. Austin's own uses of 'utterance' and 'sentence' fails systematically to distinguish between these. For example, his claims about what he called performatives (see Section 35.3 below) are sometimes claims about sentences, sometimes about utterances of those sentences. I attempt to gloss over this here.

the particular circumstances, including, for instance, whether one is addressing a geographer—using 'hexagonal' of France is a fair and reasonable thing to do.

Charles Travis believes that context-sensitivity of this kind is a feature of nearly all natural-language predicates. In Travis's view, it cannot be stated once and for all what semantic properties words have: these vary from one speaking of them to another. By thinking about linguistic meaning from the standpoint of speech acts, Travis wants to expose difficulties for the idea that a language can be isolated as a semantic system divorced from the conditions of speech. (See e.g. Travis, 1994, 1996.) Here, then, we find one sort of departure from a view of a semantic theory for a language as in principle separable from a speech act account of its use. (Travis's is a thoroughgoing 'contextualist' position. See Recanati, 1994, for one account of the difference between contextualism and anti-contextualism.)

A different kind of departure was urged by Derrida (1972, 1977). Inasmuch as Austin and writers following him take linguistic meaning to go hand in hand with rhetic acts (or locutionary acts: see above), they often place restrictions on the utterances under consideration—so that language used by people who are joking, acting a part, or creating poetry is to be excluded and treated as parasitic on 'fully normal use'. In his 1977, Searle defended Austin against Derrida, saying that the theorist is obliged to work from 'standard cases' in which words are used according to reigning conventions. Derrida, 1972, however, had maintained that it is only a sort of conservatism that leads some theorists to set aside some uses of expressions as non-standard. According to him, such theorists overlook the dynamic aspect of a language: linguistic change may be effected in new contexts of use, so that contexts cannot be confined to those that are supposed to be standard.

Searle saw Derrida's intervention as a challenge from a different ('Continental') philosophical tradition. But Davidson, whose work certainly belongs in the 'analytical' tradition, would be at one with Derrida in denying that an idea of utterances conforming to linguistic conventions can be used to isolate speech acts in which words have standard meanings (see e.g. Davidson, 1982). Thus a speech act account of language use might be subversive of one aspect of a 'traditional' view of linguistic meaning without doing any damage to the conception of the distinction between semantics and pragmatics which Austin's classification seems naturally to lead to. At the very least, a speech act approach might be used in the formulation of disputed questions about the border between semantics and pragmatics. (For illuminating accounts of (a) different ways to draw the distinction; (b) the significance of Derrida's intervention; and (c) the exchange between Derrida and Searle, see (a) 'The Distinction between Semantics and Pragmatics' in this volume; (b) Moore, 2000 and (c) Richmond, 1996.)

35.1.3 Beyond the Rhetic: Force, Indirect Speech Acts, Implicature

Austin emphasized the variety of illocutionary things that could be done with a single sentence on different occasions—or the different 'forces' it might be used with. To take an example found in Austin and in Strawson (1964: 444), 'Don't go' may be used now as an order, now as a request, now as an entreaty—where ordering, requesting and entreating are different things that can be done *in* uttering those words, or different *forces* that might attach to one or another utterance of those words.

Austin sometimes wrote as if any particular utterance corresponded to the speaker's doing of exactly one locutionary thing and exactly one illocutionary thing. But actually what a speaker conveys with an utterance is very often not captured by specifying a single illocutionary act she does. Much of the literature under the head of speech act theory has aimed to accommodate this.

Recognizing that more than one illocutionary thing may be done with an utterance, Searle introduced the idea of an *indirect* speech act. 'For example a speaker may utter the sentence "Can you reach the salt?" and mean it not merely as a question but as a request to pass the salt' (1975 [1979: 30]). Here an illocutionary act of requesting the salt is performed indirectly—by way of performing an illocutionary act of questioning. This works, according to Searle, because the hearer will be in a position to infer that the speaker has some purpose beyond discovering whether the salt is in the hearer's reach. A nice example, in which quite different indirect speech acts would be performed depending on the circumstances, was given by Sperber and Wilson B replies to A's 'Would you like some coffee?' with 'Coffee would keep me awake.' According as the circumstances are such that what A knows about B is that she would prefer to remain wakeful *or* that she hopes soon to go to sleep, B will indirectly have accepted *or* indirectly refused the offer of coffee. (Treatments of different kinds may be offered of these examples: see 'Relevance Theory—New Directions and Developments' in this volume.)

Notable among many philosophers' examples of indirect speech acts is an apparent discrepancy between the grammatical mood of the sentence used and the illocutionary force of the speech act indirectly performed: an interrogative sentence is used to make a statement, or an indicative to issue a command, for example. But there need not be such a discrepancy for the content of a speaker's illocutionary act to diverge from the content of her rhetic act. Indeed the phenomenon of a speaker conveying to her hearer something different from what is meant by the words she uses is utterly pervasive. Grice's theory of conversational implicature provides an account of the phenomenon. It gives a systematic way of thinking about the inferences that linguistic communication involves, by treating the use of language as a cooperative enterprise. At its most general, Grice's claim is that a speaker S conversationally implicates that which she must be assumed to believe given (a) what S 'strictly and literally says', (b) what S and her audience know to be known by S and her audience, and (c) that S is co-operating. Since speakers must often be assumed to believe much more than what they 'strictly and literally say', they often convey much more to their interlocutors than what they strictly and literally say.

Grice's 'strict and literal saying' may seem to invoke Austin's notion of the *rhetic* on the present construal of this. But when indirect speech acts are encompassed by conversational implicature, speakers are seen as *getting across* that which their utterances strictly and literally say: it is in getting across 'the literal meaning' that a speaker 'indirectly' gets her real message across. In such cases, then, there is something the speaker does—namely state something to another—which is not merely rhetic but whose content is just the content of her rhetic act. These can be distinguished from cases (also covered by conversational implicature) in which the content of a speaker's rhetic act is *not* something she intends to convey. The latter are cases of 'non-literal-ness' in the terminology of Bach and Harnish, 1979. For example, a speaker says that a certain book weighs a ton, intending to convey that it is very heavy. There are fur-ther cases where non-literalness is not in question, and where the speaker's rhetic act is inexplicit and at most a starting point for the determination of what they con-vey. (For a treatment of these cases—of 'conversational impliciture'—and resulting additions to the Gricean framework, see Bach, 1994a and 1994b.)

Grice's introduction of conversational implicature shows that an account of what *speakers* mean may be thought of as supplementary to an account of what is meant by the *sentences* they use. So whereas Austin's emphasis on (as he saw them) non-truth-evaluable indicative sentences suggests that he thought that a speech-act approach would make difficulties for truth-conditional semantics, it seems now that, on the contrary, speech-act notions might take over where truth-conditional semantics leaves off.

There is a great deal more to be said, however. In addition to conversational impli-catures, Grice postulates conventional implicatures, in order to deal with a compon-ent of sentences' content which appears to be rule-based but not truth-conditional. To consider a single example: 'and' and 'but' differ in meaning (in some sense) but are equivalent in point of truth-affectingness; and one may take this on board by see-ing the difference between them as a difference in what speakers who use them con-ventionally implicate. Here again, then, we find the idea of using a speech-act notion to mop up some of the facts about what speakers mean which truth-conditional semantic theories of their languages cannot explain on their own. But it is a real ques-tion whether any worked-out implementation of this idea is acceptable—a question to which Barker, 2003 returns a negative answer.

(See Grice, 1967, for the two kinds of implicature. The idea of conversational implicature shows that an ability to contribute to conversations is an element of people's linguistic competence; and speech acts have been treated in the frame-work of discourse [see e.g. Edmondson, 1981; Merin, 1994] and dialogue [see e.g. Vanderveken, 2000].)

35.2 ILLOCUTION

Austin thought that the study of language had been too much focussed on *words* at the expense of failing to take into account what speakers *do*. Put in other terms, he thought that the emphasis had been too much on locution at the expense of illoc-ution. Austin's warnings against eliding the illocutionary—against allowing it to be swallowed up either by the locutionary or by the perlocutionary (1962:103)—were directed against those who believed that one could deal with language by dealing with 'sense and reference', and that anything else alluded to extra-linguistic consequences of language use. But despite his placing emphasis on it, and despite his struggling to isolate it, Austin himself had rather little to say about the illocutionary, beyond associating it with conventions. Subsequent theorists have engaged in attempts to characterize, or analyse, what it is for an act to be illocutionary.

35.2.1 Illocution and Communication

Strawson (1964) showed that Austin's doctrine of the conventional nature of illocutionary acts does not hold generally. In order to characterize the illocutionary, Strawson used a notion of a speaker's non-naturally meaning something by an utterance, which he took from Grice. The analysis that Strawson worked with had it that in order for S to mean something by an utterance, S must intend (at least) three things: (i) to produce by that utterance a certain response in an audience A; (ii) that A recognize intention (i); and (iii) that this recognition function as part of A's reason for the response.

Supplements to such a treatment of speaker meaning have been made in an attempt to avoid certain counterexamples. The result is analyses of tremendous complexity, which portray speakers as possessing multiple iterated intentions. (See Schiffer, 1972, and for useful commentary Avramides, 1989.) Many have objected to the complexity as artificial, and psychologically implausible. (See e.g. Blackburn, 1984: 116; Harman, 1986: 87–8.) But this does nothing to detract from Strawson's reason for invoking a Gricean notion of speaker-meaning in connection with illocution. Grice's idea was that there are audience-directed intentions whose fulfilment constitutes a piece of communication. Strawson's idea was that performing an illocutionary act was a kind of communication. Now speaker's communicative intentions, rather than being thought of as the iterative intentions which Strawson set off from, may be thought of as reflexive in character, as indeed Grice himself originally thought of them (1957: 383). Then an illocutionary act is conceived as one whose fulfilment consists in its recognition. (See Bach and Harnish, 1979 for the first statement of this idea; for variations, see McDowell, 1980; Hornsby, 1994.)

Many people have found reflexive intentions problematic. Bach, 1987 diagnosed their fears of paradox as based in a misunderstanding about what an account of reflexive intentions need involve. When reflexive intentions are introduced into an account of the illocutionary, not only are spuriously complex iterated intentions avoided, but also it becomes relatively clear why acts whose performance is the fulfilment of such intentions should not be counted as *perlocutionary* in Austin's sense. Austin defined perlocutionary acts in terms of effects or consequences. And it can seem as if one was told about something perlocutionary when a speaker's getting something across is said to be a matter of her producing a response or of her getting of an audience to recognize something (see Searle, 1969: 47; Recanati, 1987: 181 ff.).

But when the intended response on the part of the audience is recognition only of the very intention that generates the response, then the response counts simply as *understanding* the speaker. Austin called such a response 'uptake', and he would not have counted it among perlocutionary effects. Uptake, if it is an effect of speech, is an effect of a special sort, which embodies the special overtness of linguistic communication. Illocutionary acts, then, are communicative acts.

Alston, 2000, has given a fully developed account of illocution of his own, which brings out the normative dimension of language use. He characterizes a speaker's doing something illocutionary in terms of their assuming responsibility for the obtaining of a state of affairs related to the proposition they express. What distinguishes illocutionary act concepts from others that are intelligible in such terms, says Alston, is 'the fact that they also include the condition that U utters the sentence with the intention of getting the addressee to realize that U is [assuming responsibility ..]'. Alston claims that the intention here is a communicative one, and he rejects accounts of communication based in perlocutionary intentions. But it may be objected that *someone's realizing that S is assuming responsibility for a state of affairs* is not simply a matter of 'uptake': it actually looks very like a perlocutionary effect. (The matter is complicated: Alston distinguishes between performing some illocutionary act and achieving recognition of which illocutionary act one has performed.)

35.2.2 Illocution and Meaning

Alston calls upon illocutionary speech acts in order to deal with the semantic side of language. He takes illocutionary acts to be those reported in typical indirect discourse locutions in which both an illocutionary force and some propositional content are specified: 'She warned me that it might fall off', for instance. In Alston's account, propositional content isn't introduced at the level of sentences, but enters the theoretical scene only when a potential illocutionary act is associated with a sentence. Thus there is no place in Alston's picture for the kind of abstraction that rhetic acts (as understood in §1.1 above) represent: a sentence's meaning is to be thought of as deriving from its potential for use in the performance of illocutionary acts.

The claim that meaning is *illocutionary act potential* is one that Alston has defended for a long time (see Alston, 1963). His recent, fully worked-out account (in Alston, 2000) enables a very definite content to be attached to the much-voiced slogan 'Meaning is use'. But the account may be thought to face problems. One problem is the accommodation of non-literalness (see ends of Sections 35.1.2 and 1.3 above). Another is the treatment of word meaning. Alston allows that sentences' meanings are determinable from the meanings of their constituents, and thus that sentence meaning must be treated compositionally. But it can seem as if any steps that Alston might take in the direction of compositional theories would require using a notion of *reference*, so that meaning would be detached from illocution and the special features of Alston's approach would thereby be subverted. Alston objects to compositional

theories that leave reference unexplained (*Ibid.*: 288–300). But some of his opponents will wish to treat reference as a primitive relation, or as one whose explication is
independent of specific speech act notions.

Brandom 1994 gives an account of referential relations in terms ultimately of inferential relations among claims. The leading idea of his 'inferentialism' is that any sentence's semantic content is determined by the norms that govern inferences to and
from it. Brandom is not usually considered a speech act theorist (perhaps because he
does not use Austinian terminology, and perhaps because his account touches on
such a range of topics in metaphysics and epistemology as well as in philosophy of
language). But, like Alston, Brandom emphasizes the normative character of things
that people do using sentences; and, like Alston, he bases semantics on pragmatics.

35.2.3 Taxonomies of Illocutionary Acts

Illocutionary acts—communicative things that can be done with words—are plen-
tiful. (Austin said that a list of the English verbs that stand for illocutionary things
has 'the order of the third power of 10', 1962:149.) A taxonomy of illocutionary acts
brings these very various acts under broad heads—it furnishes determinables or genera of which particular speech acts are determinations or species.

Austin approached a taxonomy somewhat in the manner of a botanist impressed
by the variety of species. But as accounts of speech acts have been developed, others'
taxonomies have been caught up with one or another theoretical stance, and even
where authors' taxonomies coincide, they may be informed by differences in theoretical perspective. In Alston's, for instance, the genera of illocutionary acts can be
differentiated by reference (very roughly, and excepting assertions: see 2000: 130–4)
to patterns of commitment that a speaker may make. Alston's taxonomy departs
from Austin's own at the level of genera only insofar as Austin had a category of
behabitives, and no category of assertives. Alston's five genera, with a few species for
illustration, are as follows (*Ibid*: 34):

Assertives, e.g. *assert, allege, report, answer, deny, predict, complain.*
Directives, e.g. *ask, request, implore, tell, suggest, recommend, propose.*
Commissives, e.g. *promise, bet, guarantee, invite, offer.*
Expressives, e.g. *thank, apologize, commiserate, compliment, express—*, where—may be
enthusiasm, interest, relief, intention, delight.
Exercitives, e.g. *adjourn, appoint, pardon, name, hire, fire, approve.*

(See Allan, 1999 for a comparison of the taxonomies to be found in Austin *Ibid.*,
Vendler, 1972; Searle, 1969; Bach and Harnish, 1979; Allan, 1986.)

Searle's taxonomy (in his 1975) differs from this one in having a category of declaratives in place of exercitives. Searle uses his classification to further a kind of individualism that he promotes in the philosophy of mind. He has claimed (e.g. 1983:
9–10 and 174–9; 1986; 1991) that his five categories of illocution map onto kinds of
psychological attitude, and that a speaker's doing something illocutionary is a matter

of their expressing one or another of the five basic kinds of attitudes towards a proposition. Searle's arguments for necessary connections between types of attitude and types of expressed mental state have been questioned, however, e.g. by Tsohatzidis, 1994. (For a summary account of Searle's view, see his 1999: 146–52.)

Vanderveken's 1994 taxonomy uses Searle's categories (see Searle and Vanderveken, 1985). And it provides the foundation for a logical system, in which each of the five genera of act corresponds to a basic illocutionary point, from which all possible non-basic illocutionary acts are recursively derivable. Vanderveken's system, if it yielded a correct description, would show the need to transcend a purely truth-conditional account of sentences' propositional content. Vanderveken's claim is that a semantic theory, insofar as it is truth-conditional, can only be a sub-theory, for assertive speech acts, of a more general theory of satisfaction for speech acts with an arbitrary illocutionary force. So here, once again, we find speech act theory used to challenge an orthodox conception of semantic theory.

35.3 Performatives

Some sentences seem obviously fit to be used in stating whatever proposition it is that they express; and Austin called these *constatives*. But some sentences, even though they are indicative grammatically speaking, seem designed for a quite different use. Austin called these performatives.

35.3.1 Explicit Performatives

'Performative', as philosophers of language use it nowadays, is usually confined to what Austin came to call explicit performatives. Paradigm examples of explicit performatives are of the form:

I Φ—where, in any instance, 'Φ' is replaced by a verb in the simple (non-continuous) present tense, and '—' is replaced by a that-clause or sentence.

There are variant forms, inasmuch as (a) some speech-act verbs belong in different constructions, and (b) there are second- and third-person examples. Examples are: (a) 'I apologize', 'I implore you to —'; (b) 'You're fired', 'Passengers are hereby given notice —'. But always the main verb in a performative sentence is a word for what the speaker can be reported as having done in uttering the sentence. Thus when someone uses an explicit performative, something they do in using their words is explicit in the very words they use.

One of Austin's early examples of a performative was 'I name this ship the *Queen Elizabeth*'; a 'felicitious' utterance of this *is* a christening of a ship (*Ibid.*: 5). Another was 'Out' as said by an umpire in a cricket match; an utterance of this ensures that the batsman *is* out (*Ibid.*: 43). In these two cases, utterances of the sentence work as they do as the result of institutions, conventions or rules that are not themselves linguistic (see Urmson, 1978)[5]. It may be that Austin's characterization of the illocutionary as involving convention resulted from his focusing initially on examples like these. At any rate, it is now widely accepted that, save for these sorts of case, there need be nothing especially conventional about performatives, no more than there is anything especially conventional about illocution (see Section 35.1.2). (Searle, 1989, however, defends a role for convention in a general account of performatives.)

Austin made two claims about utterances of performatives: they aren't statements; they don't have truth-values. Because Austin assumed that the notions of *statement* and *truth* go hand in hand, he based the latter claim upon the former without disentangling the two. But these two claims should be kept separate: the former remains controversial (compare Schiffer, 1972 with Lewis, 1972); the latter is denied by almost everyone nowadays (see e.g. Lemmon, 1962; Warnock, 1973; Heal, 1974; Bach, 1975, Price 1979).

Those on Austin's side in denying that explicit performatives are used to make statements may point out that they appear to be cut out for a use that is incompatible with making a statement. If someone states that p, then usually it is possible to think of her as coming out with her words because she *already* believes, or takes herself to know, that p; by contrast, someone who says that she promises to return the book, usually intends to make it the case that, by speaking, she *will come to have* promised this.[6] The contrast made here, in order to suggest that performatives are not used for making statements, appears to require that they are assessable for truth. A speaker utters 'I Φ—' with the intention of bringing it about that they have Φ-d. In that case, where they succeed in what they intend, they have Φ-d. But if so, their utterance's success consists precisely in its truth. As Austin put it himself, 'Saying makes it so'.

Part of Austin's basis for his claim that performatives lack truth-values was an opposition he saw between the 'infelicity' of performatives and the falsity of statements. Consider, for example, the utterance of someone who, although they are in no position to enact a naming ceremony, comes out with 'I name this ship Potemkin'. It does not come naturally to call their utterance false, although the utterance certainly fails in some dimension. Still there are many ways in which utterances of *any* sort can go wrong apart from their not being true; so that explicit performatives' possible infelicity gives no immediate argument for their not being evaluable for truth. Austin could easily agree that someone who uses an explicit performative purports to do what they say they do. And surely the simplest explanation of their doing what they say they do—when all is well and they do what they purport to—will allow that

---

[5] Warnock 1973 subsumes such cases under his Mark 1 performatives, to distinguish them from others where specific extralinguistic conventions are not in play. Warnock's Mark 2 performatives are the explicit ones. But he acknowledges that the two Marks overlap, so that the notion of an explicit performative covers many of Austin's early examples, even if these examples are, as Urmson stresses, themselves of a special sort.

[6] This argument relies upon the use of a simple, non-continuous present tense in explicit performatives. It is much more plausible that 'I am Φ-ing [continuous present]' can be used to describe or state what one is doing than that 'I Φ [simple present]' can (as Austin was aware: *Ibid.*: 53). Cp. Jack, 1981.

what they say is *true*. (On this account, there is no need to say that a speaker of an explicit performative *states* anything. The idea of what the speaker *says* can be the idea of their *rhetic* act. The 'say' that one needs here, then, need not be the 'say' of everyday indirect speech reports, where it often appears to mean something close to 'state' or 'assert'.)

Austin's belief that performatives' grammatical character is misleading as to their true nature led him to call them 'masqueraders': performatives give the appearance of being usable for making truth-evaluable statements, he thinks, even though they aren't really usable so. Lewis, 1972, wanted to turn the tables, and to treat sentences which give the appearance of not being usable for making truth-evaluable statements as the masqueraders. In giving a semantic account of non-indicative sentences, Lewis subjects them to paraphrase, taking them to be equivalent to explicit performatives. If this treatment were right (and if explicit performatives are truth-evaluable, as Lewis in company with most philosophers believes), then truth-evaluability would be an utterly ubiquitous feature of utterances. But it is open to doubt whether Lewis's paraphrases are genuine. (See e.g. Hornsby, 1986; Alston, 2000: 301–3.)

35.3.2 Performativity

In Austin's book, the idea of a performative covers much more ground than utterances of explicit performatives. For example 'I shall be there', when used to make a promise, is, in Austin's terms, a 'primary' performative (*Ibid.*: 69; he sometimes says 'implicit performative' [32], sometimes 'primitive performative' [33]). Although a category of primary (or implicit or primitive) performatives is not recognized nowadays, of course the non-explicit performance of illocutionary acts—their performance without the use of words such as 'I promise...'—*is* recognized. Indeed the non-explicit performance of illocutionary acts is as ubiquitous as the use of language. Even with utterances of what Austin called constatives, an illocutionary act—namely stating (non-explicitly)—is typically performed. This is why Austin's initial distinction between constatives and performatives breaks down, as Austin himself acknowledged that it does.

What Austin acknowledged here is that every piece of language use is performative in his 'primary' sense. It is no wonder then that those who want to treat language as belonging in the sphere of human agency have taken over Austin's terms. Speech act theory has a continuing influence not only in philosophy and linguistics, but also, for example, in literary studies and in agent-based communication systems developed in computer science (e.g. Labrou *et al.* 1999). Moreover, as we started to see in Section 35.1.2 in connexion with Derrida, a political dimension has been introduced into the study of speech acts. In introducing such a dimension, various writers have extended speech act theory—principally in two directions, to be touched on briefly now before concluding.

Some speech acts require a certain social position for their performance. In certain examples this is rather obvious: a speaker needs to have authority of some kind or other if their utterance is to have the force of an order, for instance. But the ability to perform certain speech acts may also be affected in less obvious ways by a person's power or authority (cp. Richmond, 1996). And the idea that illocutionary success can depend upon how one is situated in relations of power has played a role in discussions of pornography (e.g. Dwyer, ed., 1995), of free speech e.g. (Hornsby and Langton, 1998), and of hate speech e.g. (Butler, 1997). In these treatments, speakers' possible illocutionary acts are sometimes brought under the head of 'performativity'.

In other writing, the idea of 'performativity' is given a more special sense, connected with the use of *explicit* performatives. In the sociology of economics, for example, it has been claimed that advancing theory may lead to the creation of the very institutions and behaviours that the theory purports to describe. Some of the utterances of economists are then labelled 'performatives': they are thought of as sharing with explicit performatives the property of making themselves true by being uttered. (See articles in Callon, ed., 1998, and Mackenzie and Millo, 2001.) The idea here—that saying, from the mouths of those with a particular influence, makes it so—has been urged in a variety of different connexions, not always with the 'performative' label. The idea gives rise to one understanding of 'social construction', for instance. (For a discussion of the idea in connexion with feminism, see Langton, 2000, 135–45.)

35.3.3 Conclusion

Political applications of speech act theory were surely far from Austin's mind when he spoke of a 'revolution' in philosophy. If speech act theory had indeed had a genuinely revolutionary influence, then the view that semantic notions should receive a speech act theoretic explication would have won the day. In fact, however, this view is at odds with current orthodoxy. (The view is however endorsed, for different reasons and to different effects, by Travis, Alston, Brandom, and Vanderveken: see above.)

Austin's own emphasis on non-truth-evaluability may suggest that he would be a staunch opponent of truth-conditional semantics. And certainly truth-conditional semantics is integral to the orthodoxy which present-day allies of Austin set themselves against. But we saw in Section 35.1 that things that Austin himself said actually appear to lead towards a proposal about the shape of an overall account of language use in keeping with this orthodoxy. And we should remember that the orthodoxy has taken shape since Austin wrote, and could not for him have been a definite target.[7]

However this may be, the idea of a speech act has surely found an enduring place in the study of the use of natural language. Work in speech act theory has encouraged philosophers of language to appreciate that truth is not the only dimension of assessment even of indicative utterances, and that 'context' in the broadest possible sense,

---

[7] When Austin speaks of 'sense and reference, i.e. linguistic meaning', he seems not to have envisaged truth-conditional semantics. He gave *telling me to get out* and *asking whether it was in Oxford or Cambridge* as examples of *rhetic* acts (1962: 95), suggesting that he took non-indicatives to present no special problem for an account of linguistic meaning. Yet those who endorse truth-conditional semantics must have something particular to say about non-indicatives, given that these are not truth-evaluable (or at most are only arguably so: see Lewis's treatment, end of Section 35.3.1 above).

embracing everything relevant to the shared understandings of speakers and hearers, is a determinant of the extremely various things that people do with words.[8]

References

Allan, Keith (1986). *Linguistic Meaning (Vols 1 and 2)*. London: Routledge and Kegan Paul.

―――― (1999). 'Meaning and Speech Acts'. http://www.arts.monash.edu.au/ling/speech_acts_allan.html

Alston, William P. (1963). 'Meaning and Use', *Philosophical Quarterly*, 13: 107–24.

―――― (2000). *Illocutionary Acts and Sentence Meaning*. Cornell, NY: Cornell University Press.

Austin, J. L. (1962). *How to Do Things with Words*. Oxford: Oxford University Press. Edited by J. O. Urmson.

Avramides, Anita (1987). *Meaning and Mind: An Examination of a Gricean Account of Language*. Cambridge, Mass.: MIT Press.

Bach, Kent (1975). 'Performatives are Statements too', *Philosophical Studies*, 28: 229–36. Reprinted slightly amended in Bach and Harnish, 1979: 203–8.

―――― (1987). 'On Communicative Intentions: A Reply to Recanati', *Mind and Language*, 2: 141–54.

―――― (1994a). 'Semantic Slack: What is Said and More', in Tsohatzidis ed. 1994: 267–291.

―――― (1994b). 'Conversational Impliciture', *Mind and Language*, 9: 124–62.

Bach, K. and Harnish R. M. 1979. *Linguistic Communication and Speech Acts*, Cambridge, Mass.: MIT Press.

―――― (1992). 'How Performatives Really Work', *Linguistics and Philosophy*, 15: 93–110.

Barker, Stephen (2003). 'Truth and Conventional Implicature', *Mind* 112: 1–33.

Berlin, I *et al.* (1973). *Essays on J. L. Austin*. Oxford: Clarendon Press.

Blackburn, Simon (1984). *Spreading the Word*. Oxford: Clarendon Press.

Brandom, Robert (1994). *Making it Explicit: Reasoning, Representing and Discursive Commitment*. Cambridge, Mass.: Harvard University Press.

Butler, Judith (1997). *Excitable Speech: A Politics of the Performative*. New York: Routledge.

Callon M. ed. (1998). *The Laws of the Markets*. Oxford: Blackwell.

Davidson, D. (1982). 'Communication and Convention'. Reprinted in Davidson 1984: 265–80.

―――― (1984). *Enquiries into Meaning and Truth*. Oxford: Oxford University Press.

Davidson, D. and Harman, G. eds. (1972). *Semantics of Natural Languages*. Dordrecht: Reidel.

Derrida, Jacques (1972) 'Signature Événement Contexte', in *Marges de la philosophie*. Paris: Les Editions de Minuit. English translation by Samuel Weber and Jeffrey Mehlman in *Glyph* 1: 172–97.

―――― (1977). 'Limited Inc a b c . . .'. English translation by Samuel Weber, *Glyph* 2. Baltimore: Johns Hopkins University Press.

Dwyer, Susan, ed. (1995). Part 4 of *The Problem of Pornography*. Montreal: Wadsworth Publishing Co.

Edmondson, Willis (1981). *Spoken Discourse: A Model for Analysis*. New York: Longman.

Grice, H. P. (1957). 'Meaning', *Philosophical Review*, 66: 377–88. Reprinted in Grice 1989.

---

[8] Speech act theory has ramified in the last fifty years, and many debates are hardly touched on in the present chapter. A view of some of these can be got from Tsohatzidis, ed., 1994, and Vanderveken and Kubo, eds., 2000.

Grice, H. P. (1967). 'Logic and Conversation'. William James lectures delivered at Harvard University. The first printed version is in Davidson and Harman, eds., 1972. The eventual version, with added material from 1987, is Part I of Grice 1989.

—— (1969). 'Utterer's Meaning and Intentions'. *Philosophical Review*, 78: 144–77. Reprinted in Grice 1989.

—— (1989). *Studies in the Way of Words*. Cambridge, Mass.: Harvard University Press.

Harman, Gilbert (1986). *Change in View*. Cambridge, Mass.: M.I.T. Press.

Heal, Jane (1974). 'Explicit Performative Utterances and Statements', *Philosophical Quarterly*, 24: 106–21.

Hornsby, Jennifer (1986). "A Note on Non-Indicatives", *Mind*, 95: 92–9.

—— (1988). "Things Done with Words", in *Language Duty and Value*, eds. J. Moravcsik, J. Dancy and C. C. W. Taylor, Stanford University Press, 27–46.

—— (1994). "Illocution and its Significance", in Tsohatzidis, ed., 1994: 187–207.

Hornsby J. and Langton R. (1998). 'Free Speech and Illocution', *Legal Theory*, 4.1: 21–37.

Jack, Julie (1981). 'Stating and Otherwise Subscribing', *Philosophia*, 10: 283–313.

Labrou, Y., Finin, T. and Peng, Y. (1999). 'Agent Communications Languages: The Current Landscape', *IEEE Intelligent Systems*, 14.2: 45–52.

Langton, R. (2000). 'Feminism in Epistemology', in *Feminism in Philosophy*, eds. M. Fricker and J. Hornsby (Cambridge: Cambridge University Press).

Lemmon, E. J. (1962). 'On Sentences Verifiable by their Use', *Analysis*, 22: 86–9.

Lewis, David K. (1972). 'General Semantics', in Davidson and Harman, 1972: 169–218. Reprinted with 'Postscripts' in *Philosophical Papers Volume 1*, Oxford: Oxford University Press, 1983: 189–232.

Mackenzie, D. A. and Millo, Y. (2003). 'Constructing a Market, Performing Theory: The Historical Sociology of a Financial Derivatives Exchange', *American Journal of Sociology* (forthcoming).

Merin, Arthur (1994). 'Algebra of Elementary Social Acts', in Tsohatzidis, ed., 1994: 234–63.

McDowell, John (1980). 'Meaning, Communication, and Knowledge', in *Philosophical Subjects: Essays Presented to P.F. Strawson*, ed. Zak van Straaten. London: Routledge and Kegan Paul. Reprinted in McDowell 1998, 29–50.

—— (1998). *Meaning, Knowledge, and Reality*. Cambridge, Mass: Harvard University Press.

Moore, A. W. (2000). 'Arguing with Derrida', *Ratio*, 13: 355–80. (Special issue: *Arguing with Derrida*, ed. S. Glendinning.)

Recanati, Francois (1986). 'On Defining Communicative Intentions', *Mind and Language* 1: 213–42.

—— (1987). *Meaning and Force*. Cambridge: Cambridge University Press. (Originally published in French as *Les Enoncés performatifs*. Editions de Minuit, Paris, 1981.)

—— (1994). 'Contextualism and Anti-contextualism in the Philosophy of Language', in Tsohatzidis ed. 1994: 156–66.

Richmond, Sarah (1996). 'Derrida and Analytical Philosophy: Speech Acts and their Force'. *European Journal of Philosophy*, 4:1: 38–62.

Schiffer, Stephen (1972). *Meaning*, Oxford: Clarendon Press.

Searle, John R. (1969). *Speech Acts: An Essay in the Philosophy of Language*. Cambridge: Cambridge University Press.

—— (1975). 'Indirect Speech Acts'. Reprinted in Searle 1979.

—— (1976). 'A Taxonomy of Illocutionary Acts'. *Language in Society*, 5: 1–23. Reprinted in Searle 1979.

—— (1977). 'Re-iterating the Differences: A Reply to Derrida'. *Glyph* 2: 198–208 Baltimore: Johns Hopkins University Press.

—— (1979). *Expression and Meaning: Studies in the Theory of Speech Acts*. Cambridge: Cambridge University Press.

—— (1983). *Intentionality: An Essay in the Philosophy of Mind*. Cambridge: Cambridge University Press.

—— (1986). 'Meaning, Communication and Representation', in *Philosophical Grounds of Rationality: Intentions, Categories, Ends*, eds. R. Grandy and R. Warner, Oxford: Oxford University Press.

—— (1989). 'How Performatives Work', *Linguistics and Philosophy*, 12: 535–58.

—— (1991). 'Response: Meaning, Intentionality, and Speech Acts', in *John Searle and his Critics*, eds. E. Lepore and R. Van Gulick, Oxford: Blackwell.

—— (1999). *Mind, Language and Society: Doing Philosophy in the Real World*. London: Weidenfeld and Nicholson.

Searle, J. R. and Vanderveken, D. (1985). *Foundations of Illocutionary Logic*, Cambridge University Press.

Strawson, P. F. (1964). 'Intention and Convention in Speech Acts', *Philosophical Review*, 73: 439–60.

—— (1973). 'Austin and Locutionary Meaning', in Berlin *et al.*, 1973: 69–89.

Travis, C. (1994). 'On Being Truth-Valued', in Tsohatzidis, ed., 1994: 167–86.

—— (1996). 'Meaning's Role in Truth', *Mind*, 105: 451–66.

Tsohatzidis, S. L. ed. (1994). *Foundations of Speech Act Theory: Philosophical and Linguistic Perspectives*. London: Routledge.

—— (1994). 'The Gap between Speech Acts and Mental States', in Tsohatzidis, ed., 1994: 220–33.

Urmson, J. O. (1977). 'Performative Utterances', *Midwest Studies in Philosophy*, 2: 120–7.

Vanderveken, D. (1994). 'A Complete Formulation of a Simple Logic of Elementary Illocutionary Acts', in Tsohatzidis, ed., 1994: 99–131.

—— (2001). 'Illocutionary Logic and Discourse Typology', *Revue Internationale de Philosophie*, 216: 243–55. (Special issue, edited by D. Vanderveken: *Searle with his Replies.*)

D. Vanderveken and S. Kubo, eds. (2001). *Essays in Speech Act Theory (Pragmatics and Beyond. New Series 77)*. Amsterdam Philadelphia: John Benjamins Pub. Co.

Vendler, Zeno (1972). *Res Cogitans*. Ithaca: Cornell University Press.

Warnock, G. J. (1973). 'Some Types of Performative Utterance', in Berlin *et al.*, 1973: 69–89.

PART VIII

THE EPISTEMOLOGY AND METAPHYSICS OF LANGUAGE

CHAPTER 36

....

MEANING AND
REFERENCE:
SOME CHOMSKIAN
THEMES

....

ROBERT J. STAINTON

THIS chapter introduces three arguments that share a single conclusion: that a comprehensive science of language cannot (and should not try to) describe relations of semantic reference, i.e. word–world relations. Spelling this out, if there is to be a genuine science of linguistic meaning (yielding theoretical insight into underlying realities, aiming for integration with other natural sciences), then a theory of meaning cannot involve assigning external, real-world, objects to names, nor sets of external objects to predicates, nor truth values (or world-bound thoughts) to sentences. Most of the chapter tries to explain and defend this broad conclusion. The chapter also presents, in a very limited way, a positive alternative to external-referent semantics for expressions. This alternative has two parts: first, that the meanings of words and sentences are mental instructions, not external things; second, as Strawson (1950) stressed, that it is people who refer (and who express thoughts) by using words and sentences, and word/sentence meanings play but a partial role in allowing speakers to talk about the world.

I am very grateful to Ash Asudeh, Alex Barber, Akeel Bilgrami, Andrew Botterell, Andy Brook, Ray Elugardo, Corinne Iten, Ernie Lepore, David Matheson, Julius Moravcsik, Paul Pietroski, Aryn Pyke, Jim McGilvray, Ray Jackendoff, and Catherine Wearing for comments on earlier drafts. Work on this chapter was supported financially by grants from the Canada Research Chairs program, the Ontario Ministry of Science, Energy and Technology, and the Social Science and Humanities Research Council of Canada.

Before turning to negative arguments and positive proposals, however, I want to clarify what the sources of the arguments are, and what view is being targeted.

36.0.1 The Source of the Arguments

The present chapter is not an attempt at Chomsky exegesis. Though many aspects of the arguments presented are explicitly due to Noam Chomsky, other parts of the argument(s) derive from the writings of other theorists, some thoroughly "Chomskian", some not: Akeel Bilgrami, Norbert Hornstein, Ray Jackendoff, James McGilvray, Julius Moravcsik, Paul Pietroski, and James Pustejovsky. For this reason alone, I describe the critical arguments and the positive alternative as exhibiting "Chomskian themes", rather than being exegeses of Chomsky's points. Of equal importance, the flow of the arguments—how the bits are put together into an overarching critique, and the formulation of the overall conclusion—are my own creations. Thus the arguments are at least twice removed from Noam Chomsky's writings.[1]

Having made the point that the topic is broadly Chomskian themes, let me say a bit more about what makes the themes "Chomskian". In brief, they all appeal, directly or indirectly, to *methodological naturalism*, "which holds that study of the mind is an inquiry into certain aspects of the natural world ... and that we should investigate these aspects of the world as we do any others, attempting to construct intelligible explanatory theories that provide insight and understanding of phenomena that are selected to advance the search into deeper principles" (Chomsky, 1993: 41). Three points about this orientation deserve emphasis. First, for the methodological naturalist, the object of study is a naturally occurring object, not an artificial construct. Second, she is seeking explanatory insight, not mere description (e.g. a systematic taxonomy is not enough). Third, the search for explanation is taken to imply, in turn, positing underlying realities, "deeper principles", that give rise to surface appearances; and to imply equally at least an attempt to connect up one's theories of language with other discoveries in the natural sciences. (Note: a genuine science of language, as understood here, involves the *aim* of *integration*; it need not involve *success* in *reduction*. These are quite different things.)

This methodological naturalist standpoint is taken to have several immediate and crucial implications. First, adopting methodological naturalism, the aim becomes not avowedly philosophical projects like "rational reconstruction", describing "knowledge which would suffice for interpreting", or defeating philosophical skepticism of some stripe, but rather the (familiar though terrifically difficult) project of empirically investigating, as best one can, the real (and frequently unobservable)

---

[1] Readers wishing to know what Chomsky himself thinks on these matters would do best simply to read him, especially the papers collected in Chomsky (2000a). McGilvray (1999) is also an excellent resource, which really does try to capture Chomsky's views and arguments, rather than merely presenting "Chomskian themes". See also Bezuidenhout, this volume. I should also make clear that, though the formulation of the conclusions is my own, as is the way the pieces of the arguments are put together, I am not presenting my own view on these matters.

features of a naturally occurring phenomenon, always looking forward to eventual integration with the core natural sciences.[2] Second, just as the sciences in general do not feel overly constrained by what "folk theorizing" suggests, or by how ordinary folks use words, for the Chomskian, linguistics and psychology are allowed to (indeed, they are expected to) put common sense conceptions aside, and to use terms in specialized ways, etc. Indeed, as Chomsky (1993: 25) rightly suggests, modern science gets going precisely when one is willing to be surprised by what are, from the perspective of common sense, "simple phenomena": e.g. that rocks fall, that people get sick and die, that a phrase is ambiguous, etc.[3] Third, since the sciences in general take their evidence wherever they can find it, there can be, for the methodological naturalist, no *a priori* restrictions on evidence in psychology or linguistics. On these grounds alone, much that has become conventional wisdom in the study of language—whether deriving from common sense talk, or from abstract philosophizing—has to be re-evaluated carefully.

If one studies the mind and language this way, taking preconceptions with a grain of salt, scientific inquiry into the salient natural object reveals—continues this line of thought—two less immediate implications. First, that the mature speaker/hearer's mind contains far more information than can be gleaned from the environment. This is the finding of the poverty of the stimulus. The most natural explanation of this finding, and the one that any unbiased scientist would immediately pursue, is that the human mind, including in particular the part of it responsible for language, benefits from a substantial innate endowment. A different though related hypothesis that emerges in this scientific endeavor is that the mind is divided, by nature, into a series of specialized faculties—rather than being, say, a homogenous "cognition/learning machine". This is the empirical hypothesis of modularity, with the language faculty being a case in point.[4] For the methodological naturalist, that some people find these latter results initially counterintuitive carries no real weight: after all, one should no more trust "intuitions" about brain structure and brain development than one should trust intuitions about the development and structure of the liver.

---

[2] See Chomsky, 1992a: 19, Chomsky, 1992b: 53 and Chomsky, 1994. For the idea of "knowledge that would suffice for interpretation", see Davidson, 1976, which builds on Foster 1976. For a very balanced comparison of this and other philosophical projects with Chomsky's naturalist one, see B. Smith, 1992. A trenchant critique of the former projects may be found in Antony 1997.

[3] This does not, of course, entail that Moore-style "common sense propositions"—e.g. "that there exist now both a sheet of paper and a human hand" (Moore, 1939: 165)—should be rejected as false. As will emerge below, the methodological naturalist perspective does not *conflict* with common sense views about particular matters; rather, it pursues a different path entirely. As Chomsky (1995b: 138–9) writes: "It is not that ordinary discourse fails to talk about the world, or that the particulars it describes do not exist, or that the accounts are too imprecise. Rather, the categories used and principles invoked need not have even loose counterparts in naturalistic inquiry".

[4] It's worth noting that Chomsky employs a different notion of 'module' than, say, Fodor, (1983) does. Also, some read Chomsky as merely *stipulating* that linguistics, in his sense, studies what he labels "I-language": the intensionally characterized rules internal to the individual language faculty. This understates his claims. Chomsky's point, I take it, is that an unbiased methodological naturalist will study I-language, rather than other possible constructs, because the I-language construct turns out to correspond to a real aspect of the natural world that emerges in careful inquiry, whereas other constructs do not. Again, see Bezuidenhout, this volume, for more.

It is this standpoint, here called "Chomskian", that will be seen to call into question, in several different ways, the idea that a comprehensive scientific semantics should be in the business of pairing public language words and sentences with external objects, sets of external objects, and world-bound thoughts.

36.0.2 The Intended Target: Word–World Relations in Semantics

Having clarified what fundamental commitment underlies the rejecting, let me now clarify the view to be rejected.

It may be the default view in philosophy of language that natural languages are, at least in key semantic respects, rather like the formal languages invented by mathematical logicians. (That the logical languages are invented, with their properties being explicitly stipulated, is meant to be an unimportant difference.) This is the first plank of the view to be rejected.

In logical languages, like those invented by Frege, Russell, and Tarski, there are primitive formal elements of a few basic kinds (e.g. constants, predicates, quantifiers); and there are lexical semantic rules, which assign an interpretation to each primitive.[5] What this typically involves, at a minimum, is that (primitive) constants are assigned individual objects, and (primitive) predicates are assigned sets of objects. In addition, there are syntactic rules for recursively composing parts of the symbolism into larger wholes; and, there are corresponding compositional semantic rules which determine an interpretation for each resulting complex, given the interpretation of its parts and how those parts are combined. In particular, in some of these logical languages, whole sentences are compositionally assigned truth values as their meanings.

On the view to be rejected, natural languages are supposed to share all of the core interpretational properties of the logical languages: natural language names like 'George Bush', 'London', and 'Aristotle' are assigned real-world objects; natural language predicates (e.g. adjectives and verbs) are assigned sets of real-world objects (e.g. 'sings' is assigned the set of things which actually sing); and sentences are compositionally assigned... Well, here matters get rather complicated. Different philosophical theories notoriously make rather different claims about what should be compositionally assigned to natural language sentences. Even restricting ourselves to indicative sentences, it obviously won't do to assign natural language sentences truth *values* as their interpretation, as is done in some formal languages, for two obvious

---

[5] I use the word 'assign', in describing both the invented logical languages and natural language, without intending any specific account of what the relation "being assigned to" amounts to. As Ernie Lepore (p.c.) reminded me, some semantic theorists think of assigning as involving something like a function whose input is a formal item and whose output is an external entity. That, very roughly, is how Frege, Carnap, and Montague conceived of 'assigning'. But others, including Davidson and Tarski, take a more deflationary view of what I'm here calling "assignment". Since what matters in what follows is the status of the relata, not the nature of the relation between them, I gloss over these differences here.

reasons. First, not all true sentences mean the same thing, nor do all false sentences mean the same thing: 'Five is larger than two' is not *synonymous* with 'France is in Europe', though both are true. So truth values are not finely grained enough to be meanings. Second, it's not obvious that sentences are even the right kind of thing to be true/false. Certainly many sentences are explicitly context sensitive: 'He bought that yesterday', for instance, is at best only true relative to an assignment of values for 'he', 'that', and 'yesterday'. Thus, this sentence just isn't the sort of entity to even have a truth value *tout court*. To overcome the first problem, one can take sentences to denote not truth values but propositions made up of objects and properties; or one can take them to have a truth value as referent, but a Fregean Thought as sense; or one can take the meaning of a sentence to be truth-*conditions*. Such are the treatments of natural language sentences proposed by the contemporary Russellian, Fregean, and Tarskian respectively. These distinctions about sentence meanings, though important for other purposes, can be glossed over here: in the present chapter, I will speak vaguely of indicative sentences "expressing thoughts". To overcome the second problem, that natural language sentences contain context-sensitive items like 'he', 'that', and 'yesterday', one can say that such sentences express not thoughts exactly, but "proto-thoughts": something which is true or false relative to a set of contextual parameters (time, place, speaker, addressee). Such, then, is the first plank of the view to be rejected.[6]

Typically added to this idea, in "mainstream" philosophy of language, is the assumption that languages are the common property of a whole community, such that the symbolic items (words, predicates, sentences) are all public property. Languages, on this view, exist independently of speakers; and, being a public entity, each speaker typically has only a partial grasp of his/her shared language. This is the second plank of the view to be rejected. (For more on the Chomskyan target, see Bezuidenhout, this volume.)

36.1 THE THREE NEGATIVE ARGUMENTS

36.1.1 The Radical "Argument from Ontology"

Having clarified what the target is, and what makes the critiques in question broadly "Chomskian", I turn to the negative arguments.

The view at issue invokes *relations* between public linguistic items on the one hand (names, predicates, sentences) and worldly items on the other (external objects, sets, world-bound thoughts). Obviously, then, the relata must be able to stand in the

---

[6] Famously, the philosopher-logicians who are taken to be the grandfathers of this tradition—i.e. Frege, Russell, and Tarski—explicitly disavowed the idea that natural languages, in all their messy detail, could be treated this way. It was their contemporary philosophical followers, most notably Davidson (1967) and Montague (1974), who took the analogy between logical and natural languages literally. Chomsky *et al.* emphatically agree with the grandfathers, and disagree with their contemporary heirs.

requisite relations, including in particular (something like) the denotation relation. But, patently, the relata can't do this job if they aren't real. The first negative argument questions whether they are.

The widespread idea, to be questioned here, is that there are *public* signs, of shared languages, available to have referents: words, phrases and sentences that belong to languages like English, Urdu, and Swahili. In what follows, I will introduce three worries about this idea, to give the flavor of the thing. (One could easily raise many more.)

The first problem has to do with individuation of words given variation. Crucially, as actual working linguists are wont to note, the way we divide up languages in common sense, and in much philosophical theorizing, does not actually correspond to any robust divide. One speaks of "Chinese" as a single language, despite the fact that its two largest "dialects", Mandarin and Cantonese, are not mutually intelligible. In contrast, we call Spanish, Portuguese, and Italian different languages, rather than speaking of several dialects of Romance, just as we treat Swedish and Danish as different languages—this despite the fact that they are much more similar to each other, and far closer to mutual intelligibility, than the "dialects of Chinese" are. The only semi-robust divide here is mutual intelligibility and, as noted, "languages" are not divided along those lines. One might reasonably reply that this worry can be overcome by thinking of words as belonging to dialects, not languages. But that won't really help, since what counts as a dialect is equally peculiar: Canadian English is supposed to be a single dialect, despite the many differences between speakers in urban centers and rural areas, and differences among the East, Central Canada, and the West; it also is supposed to be a different dialect than what is spoken in, say, Ohio. Clearly, we slice things as we do—both "languages" and "dialects"—not because of any robust linguistic divide, but because of colonial history, similar writing systems, shared canonical works of literature, present military might, arbitrary national boundaries, religious differences, and so on. That, and not "nature's joints", is what makes it the case that people "speak the same language/dialect". As Chomsky puts it, "This idea [of a common public language] is completely foreign to the empirical study of language... What are called "languages" or "dialects" in ordinary usage are complex amalgams determined by colors on maps, oceans, political institutions and so on, with obscure normative–teleological aspects" (1993: 18–19). (See also Chomsky, 1992b: 48; Chomsky, 1995b: 155 ff, and Bezuidenhout, this volume.) Instead of public languages/dialects, the real objects that one finds are (i) individual idiolects, (ii) sets of idiolects that share some non-obvious underlying parametric feature (e.g. having complements falling after heads), and (iii) the universally shared language faculty. None of these, however, corresponds even remotely to "public languages" like English and Urdu.

Now, to come to the problem of immediate interest here, if the boundaries around "languages" (or "dialects") don't reflect an objective difference in kind, what individuates *a word in a language*? What makes it the case, for instance, that distinct pronunciations are pronunciations "of the same word", if there aren't really objectively distinct languages? To take an example, why are 'fotoGRAFer' (said in Bombay) and 'foTAHgrafer' (said in Toronto) the same word, yet 'fotOgrafo' (said in Buenos Aires) is not the same word as the former two? We are wont to say that there are *two* words here—the "English" word and the "Spanish" word—not three words. But this won't do, if "English" isn't objectively real: after all, all three differ in pronunciation. For that matter, even within a single country, or a single part of a country, there can be many "different pronunciations of the same word". So, as noted, appeal to local dialects isn't likely to help either. For instance, even within the Eastern United States, there are many pronunciations of 'Harvard'. More than that, children don't pronounce things the same way adults do, women don't pronounce things the same as men, and so on. Given variation, there thus seems to be no good reason to count public words the way common sense wishes to: we can't put aside the differences on reasonable grounds.

A natural reply to this first problem about counting words is that a dialect, or a language, is the symbol system shared by community such-and-such. But this reply is quite unhelpful, for at least two reasons. First, a specific worry: it's not possible to individuate the right community except by appeal to shared language. In particular, as we saw above, mutual intelligibility won't allow us to distinguish groups along lines that correspond to "languages". What "the community" for whom 'fotoGRAFer' and 'foTAHgrafer' are supposedly one word really have in common, and what distinguishes this "community" from others, is that everyone in it speaks English! A broader worry is that communities are no more "robust" than languages turned out to be. So even if one could divide languages in terms of which communities used them, this still wouldn't yield the kind of robust divide that the methodological naturalist demands.

There is a second reason why it is hard to individuate "public language words", beyond the problem of individuation in the face of across-speaker variation. It has to do with how to count words even granting the existence of languages/dialects. To pick an example essentially at random, is there one word 'forge' which has multiple meanings: *create a fraudulent imitation, shape by heating in a fire and hammering*, and *furnace or hearth for melting or refining metal*? Or are there three words, one for each meaning?[7] And, even restricting ourselves to one of the meanings, are 'forged', 'forges', and 'forging' wholly different words, or are they merely variations on the same word? What about the tensed verb 'forged', as in 'He forged the document', the past participle, as in 'He has forged many documents' and the adjective as in 'A forged document'? Are they precisely the same word, wholly different words, or variations on a single word? Also, if there is just one word here, or variations on it, what *is* that word? Rather than calling out for discovery of something real, these seem matters of decision.

In light of these questions about individuation, both across and within a "dialect", one can readily doubt that there is any such thing as "words in English", "sentences

---

[7] And note the potential problem of circularity, if one does individuate words by their meanings. Meaning, recall, is supposed to derive from having two things stand in a relation. But now it turns out that one of the relata, on the "word" side, is individuated in terms of the other.

in Swahili", and so forth. To echo Quine, one might insist that there can be no entity without identity. But if there are no such objects, there patently cannot be a science of word–world relations that pairs "public words and sentences" with worldly objects, sets, and proto-thoughts.[8] (Granted, for all that's been said so far, there might be *other* things that can be paired with external objects: morphemes of an individual's mental lexicon, for instance. But this possibility offers little solace to the kind of theorist that Chomskians are targeting.)

I said that I would introduce three problems about words. The third one involves issues about language norms. Though almost universally used among "English speaking" children, 'broked', 'runned', 'swimmed' and so on are not "words in English".[9] Or again, despite its constant appearance in speech and writing, there isn't supposed to be a word in English that means *it is to be hoped that*, and is pronounced 'hopefully'. On the other hand, supposedly there is an English word pronounced 'ke-naw', because that's how Shakespeareans said 'know'; and there is, according to my Oxford dictionary, an English word 'peavey', even though almost no one would recognize it as such. These latter items aren't used, but they are "English words"; the former items are used, but aren't "English words". Clearly, what rules these words in or out is not how people *do* speak, but rather something about how they *should* speak. It's at least not obvious how there can really *be* such things, to stand in objective relations with external objects, sets thereof, and so on.

I pause to quickly summarize, before introducing a major objection to this line of argument. Because there is no objective way to individuate/count words (across or within a "dialect"), and because what makes something a shared, public word, if there really were any, would need to appeal to "ought" rather than "is", the Chomskian concludes that there aren't really any "public words". But then there cannot be a comprehensive science of language that pairs words (and sentences) with external things. Such is the radical argument from ontology.

A natural reaction to the claim that words (e.g. 'forged', 'photographer' and 'Harvard') are not real objects is perplexed disbelief that the claim has been seriously made. Surely it's just obvious that words exist. Besides, if an argument is needed, there is this: here we are discussing the various pronunciations *of the words 'Harvard' and 'photographer'*; and above it was said that the word 'peavey' exists because of norms. But how can something which doesn't exist have different

---

[8] For those familiar with Chomsky's (1986) terminology, the central point may be put like this: public language words/sentences are part of the E-language picture, and the methodological naturalist must eschew E-language as not a suitable candidate for scientific study. See Bezuidenhout, this volume, for discussion.

[9] This point relates to another one that Chomsky regularly raises. Public language approaches are at a loss to find a "thing" which children under, say, six years of age know. They don't yet "know English" (or Swahili, or Urdu, or. . .). Indeed, there is *no* "public language" which they know at this age. But then how, positively, are we to describe the state of their minds? It seems absurd that we can only make the negative claim: i.e. that they do not yet know English (or Swahili, or Urdu, or. . .), but are on the way to doing so. Note too, how well such children communicate. This puts the lie to the idea that having "a shared public language" is genuinely necessary for communication.

pronunciations—as the argument itself grants that 'Harvard' and 'photographer' do? And surely, if something exists because of norms, then it exists. (Indeed, we seem to infer the non-existence of words on the grounds that 'peavey' exists! That's patently absurd.) Our discussion thus seems to give rise to paradox. Given the obviousness of the existence of words, and the paradoxes that quickly arise from denying their existence, it's hard to see how it could be suggested, at least with a straight face, that public words do not really exist.

There are several replies to this natural worry. On the one hand, one can agree that these things are real enough, but go on to question whether there could be a *science* that treated of them. Where by 'a science' is meant, to repeat, rather more than "any inquiry that is both theoretical and empirical". As hinted at the outset, 'science' in the context of methodological naturalism means, at a minimum, seeking explanatory insight; which in turn entails positing underlying realities, and aiming for integration with the core natural sciences. Many things exist which are not subject to scientific investigation, in this sense. This concessive reply will be considered at length in the second negative argument. To anticipate briefly here, the core idea is that the standard for being a "real object" has been set too high in the discussion above. It's not just public languages and words, but corporations, songs, countries, universities, national dishes, hair styles, TV shows, etc., that won't really exist given this over-high standard. Indeed, it's arguable on similar grounds that none of us exist: to see why, think of the enormous puzzles about how to individuate persons. A natural alternative view, which doesn't set the standard so high, is that perfectly real objects can be quite hard to individuate/count, and can be norm-bound. They need not require a "robust divide", but can rather be objectively different only in degree, with human interests setting the kind-divide between them. One could thus allow that there is such a thing as English (and other public tongues), and that the nature of English and the words/sentences in it depend on a host of complex relations (political, military, historical, religious, etc.)—including even explicitly normative ones having to do with "correct speech". Adding, goes the reply, that this does not make English and its elements unreal. Personally, I think there is something very importantly right about this. Still, the key point that will re-emerge in negative argument two is that, even granting this, one is hard-pressed to rescue the idea that a genuine *science* of language can, or should try to, describe word–world relations. Indeed, the account proposed of what makes words and languages real—e.g. that their individuation rests on norms, quirky anthropocentric interests, and a complex mess of other things—pretty much ensures that they will *not* be scientifically tractable. More than that, if that's what makes something a "word", it's not even plausible that "public word" will be an *idealization* that will be of any use in science. As Chomsky puts the general point:

Such informal notions as Swedish-vs.-Danish, norms and conventions, or misuse of language are generally unproblematic under conditions of normal usage, as is "near New York" or "looks like Mary". But they can hardly be expected to enter into attempts to reach theoretical understanding. (1993: 20)

As I say, this concessive reply will be elaborated at length in the next section. But there are non-concessive replies too, which try to defend the radical version of the "argument from ontology" according to which one side of the supposed relations (i.e. the *public* words/sentences) just do not exist at all. Let me introduce a couple of those replies here. That there are no public words or languages strikes us as absurd, but—goes the first reply—that is because we are taken in by an illusion of some sort. Part of the concept of "public word", the argument would go, is that the things in question are "out there", the shared property of many. They are not inside the mind. Given this, the public word 'Harvard', the story would go, is "unreal" in roughly the same way that the sky, the daily sunset, perceived colour, and rainbows are not real *considered as external objects*. In all these cases, we project "out there" something that is really an amalgam of things going on inside the mind, and (non-obvious) things that are going on in the external world: "the structure of language is not "out in the world" but [is] rather a consequence of the mental organization of language users" (Jackendoff, 1987: 133). Ordinary people cannot fail to *think* of the sky, the sunset, blueness, and rainbows as mind-external objects, wholly out in the world, even after careful scientific training. But what scientific investigation teaches is that, appearances notwithstanding, they are partly in the individual mind. (Importantly, being open to taking these results seriously, thereby setting aside common sense, is part and parcel of being a methodological naturalist.)

The illusion that there really are public words, words "out there" that we share, is reinforced by the fact that people talk about words. An egregious case in point, as noted: the very argument against the existence of words apparently used as premises *claims about words*. But, coming to the second reply, that we talk about, say, 'Harvard', does not actually entail that there is a public word "out there" that we share. On the one hand, speakers regularly refer to things that simply do not exist: Santa, unicorns, the present King of France, etc.[10] On the other hand, even if there are some unquestionably real things that we refer to, when we speak of the word 'Harvard', there needn't be a single object which is *the* public word. A plausible alternative view is that there are many, many words 'Harvard'. For some purposes, we count all pronunciations as constituting "the word 'Harvard' "; for other purposes, we count only very few. And so on. We refer to different sets on different occasions, depending upon the context. The resulting sets are real, and they are intersubjective. Still, there isn't one thing, the word 'Harvard'. (See Bilgrami 2002 for this general line of thought.) Hence we can consistently talk about "the different pronunciations of 'Harvard' ", without committing ourselves to there being one unique thing, that publicly shared word, that can stand in a refers-to relation.

If the foregoing considerations work, then there cannot be a comprehensive scientific semantics that treats of relations between public words and external things. Indeed, what makes this the "radical variant" is that if this criticism is successful,

---

[10] Put metalinguistically, reports of speaker reference are referentially opaque in a way that expression reference, if it existed, would not be. See Bencivenga, 1983 for extended discussion; see also Jackendoff, 1987: 127 and Chomsky, 1995b: 150.

not only can there be no *comprehensive science* of word–world relations, there can be no truths *of any kind* that state relations between public words and worldly entities. (How could there be, if there aren't any public words?)

36.1.2 The Moderate "Argument from Ontology" (Science and Common Sense)

The first "argument from ontology" involved arguing that public words don't exist at all. The second "argument from ontology" accepts the reality of both relata. But it questions whether there can be a genuine *science* of the kind of common sense objects involved on both sides of the relation.[11]

Crucial to the argument will be the contrast between the world revealed to us by common sense, and that revealed by modern scientific inquiry. We therefore need a way to draw that distinction. The methodological naturalist thinks there is a way to draw it, given nativism and modularity: we can distinguish the world revealed by common sense from the world revealed by science *cognitively*, in terms of the kinds of concepts deployed.

The concepts of common sense, in the sense intended here:

- are not social artifacts, but are rather part of our biological endowment;
- more precisely, they are constructed from innately given semantic features—though only the elements out of which the concepts are constructed are innate (and universal), not the resulting wholes; (See Chomsky 2000b: 185.)
- are acquired (rather than *learned*), and they do not need to be taught—indeed, given the poverty of stimulus, it's unlikely that they *could* be learned by/taught to a creature lacking the requisite innate endowment;
- are at the disposal of every non-pathological human;
- bring with them a rich and complex internal structure that eschews elegance in favor of day-to-day practicality, especially for living in human company—precisely because they are built out of an innately given store of features;
- have, finally, and related to this last point, inherently built in implicit references to human hierarchies, rights/obligations, and our intentional states, rather than aiming for an objective description of the world, independent of us.

Scientific concepts, in sharp contrast, *are* social artifacts.[12] More than that, a useful scientific concept is often a hard-won achievement of many years of collective labor. Such concepts must be taught; and frequently enough they cannot be learned, even by non-pathological people. Their content is austere, rather than rich. And, far from

---

[11] That the issue is a *science* of public words, and public languages, is missed by some of Chomsky's critics. See, for example, Wiggins, 1997.

[12] I am unsure whether Chomsky himself would endorse what follows. He sometimes suggests that humans have a "science forming faculty", and if scientific concepts derive from it then they are not especially social after all. Since Chomsky exegesis is not my aim, however, I leave this issue aside here. (Thanks are due to Julius Moravcsik for drawing my attention to the issue.)

being tied to anthropocentric interests, the whole idea of a scientific concept is to capture how things "really are" independent of us.

It is telling, too, that science involves explicit reflection not just on the concepts it creates to describe and explain, but also on what counts as good evidence, justification, etc. Those standards of evaluation too are sanctioned by groups, over extended periods of time; they aren't just "given by nature". Sciences, and scientific concepts, are thus artifacts of a social practice, rather than being innately specified—which allows, as Chomsky (1993: 32) suggests, that science can afford to disregard common sense, and is happy to move beyond some of its tenets.

The overall picture can be summed up with the following long passage from Chomsky's *Language and Thought*:

> We have, by now, fairly substantial evidence that one of the components of the mind–brain is a language faculty, dedicated to language and its use—where by "language", now, we mean human language, not various metaphoric extensions of the term. Other components provide "common sense understanding" of the world and our place in it... Other components make it possible for humans to conduct scientific and mathematical inquiry, and sometimes to achieve remarkable insight: we may call them "the science-forming faculty", to dignify ignorance with a title. These could be quite different in character from those that yield "common sense understanding" in its various forms. It is an open empirical question, and no dogmatism is in order. The history of modern science perhaps suggests that the distinctions are not trivial; at least, that is one way to interpret the startling conflicts that have arisen between common sense understanding and what scientific inquiry reveals. (Chomsky 1993: 34–5)

Having contrasted science and common sense, we can now note that the concepts fall into two families, and add that each collectively provides a *perspective*.[13] What does the "scientific perspective" show us? Quarks, tectonic plates, genomes, and many other things. (To be clear, the scientific perspective does *not* merely reveal so-called "physical" objects; the mind–brain, at various levels of abstraction, can also be seen from this perspective. That, indeed, is just what linguistics is supposed to help reveal. And, of course, the common sense perspective does not merely reveal psychological states: it affords views of desks, house pets, tea, and toys.) Importantly, however, there is lots that the scientific perspective does *not* show us: it does not encompass normative categories like good wine, liveable cities, or well-prepared osso bucco; nor does it even encompass not-explicitly-normative yet mind-dependent things like clouds,[14] tea,[15] desks, sunsets, breakfast cereal, and hockey scores. In

---

[13] Chomsky (1993: 48) writes: "The information provided by lexical items and other expressions yields perspectives for thinking and speaking about the world..." Or again, "a lexical item provides us with a certain range of perspectives for viewing what we take to be things in the world, or what we conceive in other ways; these items are like filters or lenses providing ways of looking at things and thinking about the products of our minds" (Chomsky, 1992a: 36).

[14] On the natural assumption that whether a quantity of water in the atmosphere is a cloud depends upon mind-dependent relations—like being visible, in normal circumstances, to the naked eye of normal humans.

[15] As Chomsky has frequently noted, what is chemically the very same substance could be tea—if created by dipping a bag of tea leaves into a cup of hot water—or contaminated water—if created, say,

general, being objective and ignoring interest-relative distinctions, the "scientific perspective" cannot see entities whose individuation conditions inherently involve complex human interests and purposes. Those things are only "seen" through the in-born lens of natural language expressions and the sorts of sub-lexical concepts that help make up these expressions.[16]

The reason why the scientific perspective cannot "see" such objects is most easily illustrated with examples. Take London. Chomsky (1993: 22–3) writes:

We can regard London with or without regard to its population: from one point of view, it is the same city if its people desert it; from another, we can say that London came to have a harsher feel to it through the Thatcher years, a comment on how people act and live. Referring to London, we can be talking about a location, people who sometimes live there, the air above (but not too high), buildings, institutions, etc., in various combinations. A single occurrence of the term can serve all these functions simultaneously, as when I say that London is so unhappy, ugly, and polluted that it should be destroyed and rebuilt 100 miles away.

As Chomsky goes on to conclude, "No object in the world could have this collection of properties" (1993: 23). To be clear, it is not being claimed that London simply fails to exist. "London is not a fiction" (Chomsky, 1992a: 37). This is a key difference between the radical worry in the last section, about public words, and the present moderate worry. The issue this time is not whether the relata exist, but (as it were) what makes them exist: the worry is that the kind of socially constructed object that is London (and 'London'!), so highly dependent on human perspectives and interests as it is, cannot be seen by the peculiar instrument that is natural science. This, and not the very existence of London, is what seems doubtful. To generalize the point, imagine natural science looking for external world correlates of 'bargain', 'owner-ship', 'tenure', 'delicious', 'sacred', 'funny', 'notary public', 'nearby' or 'polite'. How can genuine science see any of these? The thing is, if many, or most, or even all common sense concepts are covertly like 'London' and the rest—and, given the contrast between scientific concepts and common sense concepts that emerged above, this is just what seems to be the case—then a scientific reference-based semantics is hopeless for the *vast majority* of lexical items in natural language.

Crucially for present purposes, granting that what common sense "sees" is perfectly real, we still arrive at the conclusion introduced at the outset: that a comprehensive science of language cannot (and should not try to) describe relations of semantic reference, i.e. word–world relations. That is because the things which manage to *be*, on this more moderate view—i.e. both words and ordinary objects—are

---

by the right combination of organic matter falling into a lake. Because "what is tea" reflects human interests in this way, science isn't in the business of contrasting tea from non-tea. See Chomsky, 1995b: 128 and Chomsky, 2000b: 189 for discussion.

[16] Some of the authors discussed here—e.g. Jackendoff and McGilvray—take an additional neo-Kantian step, and draw the metaphysical conclusion that there are two "worlds", one for each perspective. But this is not an immediate consequence of the present argument about the nature of scientific semantics. One can resist the metaphysical step, and stick to the epistemological claim that the scientific perspective can only "see" part of the one world. Either approach will yield the desired conclusion.

nevertheless not real *in the right sort of way*. Hence they cannot be "seen" from the scientific perspective. They are as "real" as governments, townships, by-laws, nearness, corporations, national dishes, and so on—which, as Heidegger and G. E. Moore rightly insisted, are as real as can be—but, like townships and nearness, they are invisible to the working scientist. In particular, then, they are invisible to the scientist of language, as such.

Before continuing, I should consider some natural objections. As a reminder, I have been trying to contrast two ways in which to look at the world: from the perspective of common sense, and from the perspective of modern science. I did so by contrasting two families of concepts, namely common sense concepts, and scientific concepts. I then suggested that, from the scientific perspective, there are many things which just cannot be seen—and hence that no science of language can describe them. Consider now four objections to this line of argument.

First, one might object that the distinctions between the kinds of concepts are being drawn, at least in part, along lines that a radical empiricist or cognitive holist would question. The reply to this is obvious. As hinted right at the outset, methodological naturalists consider radical empiricism, and also anti-modularity, to be empirical theses. They also consider modularity and a very significant innate endowment for language to be well supported on empirical grounds. So, the fact that the case against reference-based semantics may rest on such hypotheses will not detain them.

Second, one might reasonably complain that there will be a host of potential referents which the natural sciences *can* see, and which therefore could be described in a theory of word–world relations (assuming public words to exist). These are precisely the objects that the perspective of science specifically affords: quarks, tectonic plates, wh-traces, etc. Thus the foregoing argument does not on its own rule out a "linguistic science of reference" *for the vocabulary of the sciences*. (See Chomsky, 1992a: 42–3 and Chomsky, 1993: 27 ff for discussion.) Granted, one might not be able to have a comprehensive science of language; but a limited reference-based scientific semantics would still be possible. However, this is ruled out independently, given the Chomskian view that the proper object of study, for a science of language, is the human language faculty. That, after all, is the aspect of reality that we find, when we start to "investigate language" naturalistically. Now, the language faculty is the innately given part of the mind–brain which, in response to environmental triggers, settles into a steady state of linguistic competence *sometime before age five*; crucially, then, not everything one "learns about language", as we pre-theoretically say, belongs in the language faculty. In particular, Chomsky suggests that scientific vocabulary likely is *not* stored in the language faculty: it is learned, not acquired; it is austere, not rich; it is a construct, not an aspect of our biology. Thus, while there might conceivably be a science of reference for scientific terms, it would not be part of the science of natural language.[17]

---

[17] An interesting side effect of distinguishing common sense concepts from scientific ones is that one could follow Quine in holding that there is no analytic/synthetic distinction *for the concepts used in*

Third, one might doubt that science and common sense really do provide mutually exclusive and exhaustive perspectives. First, it's clearly true that the supposed gulf between science and common sense *seems* bridgeable in places, and this on at least three grounds: (a) there seem to be factual claims that straddle the divide: e.g. 'My cup of herbal tea boiled at 101.35 degrees centigrade'; (b) common sense reports can clearly serve as evidence for/against a scientific hypothesis: e.g. 'The Prime Minister died after eating one of those' or 'It turned red like a fire truck when we poured the liquid on it' can both support (or call into question) a genuine scientific hypothesis about the chemical make up of an unknown item; (c) it's arguable that there are whole disciplines which straddle the borderline: criminology, epidemiology, anthropology, medicine, horticulture, etc. Thus the difference may be not a difference of kind, but one of degree. (See Moravcsik, 1998: 127 for extended discussion.) This is a very important objection. It therefore merits a detailed rebuttal, comprising three related replies. The first reply is that there cannot be a *comprehensive* science of language unless that discipline can see all (or at least the vast majority) of objects that can bear names. Hence the conclusion stands even if the difference between what common sense can see, and what modern science can see, is a matter of degree, with intermediate cases along the way—as long as there are lots of things on the extreme end that science can't see. In short, the conclusion argued for doesn't really require the stronger premise that the distinction is exclusive and exhaustive. The second reply makes a related point about making do with a weaker premise. What the conclusion requires is not really the claim that "science simply cannot see common sense objects"; what it requires, instead, is merely that there is no *single* science which can see (almost) every common sense object—since a comprehensive science of language that described word–world relations would need to be just such a science. To imagine a comprehensive science of language that posits word–world relations is, for instance, to envisage a *single* genuine explanatory science that can "see" all of friends, yarmulkes, Tuesdays, symphonies, jokes, vagrants, bargains, and every other common sense object.[18] Put another way, the second reply is this: what is required, at a minimum, for a comprehensive scientific semantics that introduces word–world relations is *There exists a science x such that, for almost every y, x can see y*; but at best what is plausible is *For almost every y, there exists a science x, such that x can see y*. The third reply to this third objection is that even this weaker claim (which wouldn't actually avoid the conclusion in any case) gets much of its plausibility from loose terminology. To repeat, as the term

science (since those words really do get their meaning holistically, from their place in a world-describing theory), while nevertheless insisting that common sense concepts—built as they are from innately specified features—will license analytic truths. See Chomsky, 2000b: 186. For a discussion some of the epistemological implications of this way of slicing things, see Matheson and Stainton, (2002).

[18] Jackendoff draws a weaker (but still very interesting) conclusion, on related grounds. He argues that "language is about entities in *the world as construed by the language user/perceiver*" (1987: 128). (See also Jackendoff, 1991: 12.) As a result, word–world relations cannot be studied prior to, and independent of, psychological investigations about how humans categorize. In which case, external-referent semantics cannot be a genuine alternative to Jackendoff-style Conceptual Semantics, since the former implicitly presupposes the latter.

is being used here, not every systematic empirical inquiry counts as 'science': e.g. an exhaustive taxonomy of the Earth's beetles is not science, in the sense I have been discussing—not least because mere taxonomy does not seek out underlying explanatory realities. Noting this, it's not even clear that most common sense objects are "seen" by any genuine science after all, though it might well be plausible that some systematic empirical inquiry can see each such object.

Whereas the three previous objections were specific to the moderate argument from ontology—each attacking in a different way the proposed sharp and exhaustive contrast between the perspective of common sense and the perspective of modern science—the final objection, which is methodological in character, applies more globally to both arguments from ontology. The complaint here is that even *making* these two ontology based objections flies in the face, paradoxically enough, of what I described as the core tenet of the Chomskian approach to language, viz. methodological naturalism. From that perspective, the test of a theory is, surely, whether it can establish a rich body of empirically supported doctrine; and, the fourth objection continues, semantics has made great progress in those terms. There are thick textbooks full of results, journals packed with data and detailed debates, and so on. Thus, the fact that reference-based semantics might fail to meet certain arch ontological scruples should not cause us to reject it, since it is a thriving research program.

Actually, Chomsky himself agrees with the methodological point: questions of ontology *are*, for him, posterior to questions about explanatory and descriptive success (Chomsky, 2000b: 184). Presumably every methodological naturalist will agree. The objection still misfires, however, because it is based on the (thoroughly mistaken) idea that "Chomskians" reject semantics root and branch. It's not the entire sub-discipline of semantics that is being rejected, only a peculiar spin on it. And, continues the reply, the many existing results of semantics have little or nothing to do with the extraneous philosophical hypotheses that shared public words/sentences stand for real-world external objects, sets thereof, and world-bound thoughts.[19] Indeed, meaning broadly construed remains as central to Chomskian linguistic theorizing in 2003 as it was in 1955.[20] To give but one example, Chomsky's most recent Minimalist theorizing makes essential use of the principle of Full Interpretation, which requires (among other things) that only elements that have an interpretation can remain at the end of a derivation—this being the point where

---

[19] Some would say that, beyond leaving the key results of formal semantics standing, absolutely *nothing* is lost by linguistics, when it abandons the reference-based approach; moreover, much is gained. Thus Hornstein (1989) writes: "If semantics is concerned with truth conditions, and this is construed as correspondence, then I can see no reason for thinking that there is *any* link between semantics so defined and theories of linguistic interpretive competence. Moreover, this is all for the good as far as the latter enterprise is concerned, for semantic theories seem to require the ascription of powers and capacities to native speakers which are as mysterious as those capacities that we wish to explain. Syntactic theories, those types of theories that eschew language–world relations, are not similarly problematic. It is for this reason that syntactic theories are *methodologically* preferable". See also scattered remarks in Hornstein 1984.

[20] Neil Smith (1999: 163) quotes Chomsky as saying that "putting aside phonology, virtually everything I've done in the field since LSLT [*The Logical Structure of Linguistic Theory*] falls within semantics". See also Chomsky, 2000b: 174.

the string reaches the interface with Conceptual Structure. All other structure (e.g. nominative and accusative case marking, expletives, agreement features not bearing content) must be "checked", thereby being rendered "invisible", before this point. Thus meaning couldn't be *more* central to current linguistic theory. (See Radford, 1997: 170ff for introductory discussion, and Chomsky, 2001; Chomsky, 2000c; Chomsky, 1995a for the evolving details of Minimalism.) Moreover, as Pietroski (2003, 2005) points out, there is much of the same positive hard work for the sub-discipline of semantics to do, without reference and truth. First, this sub-discipline will explore semantic properties of expressions such as: what they can and cannot mean; whether they are ambiguous; if they are ambiguous, why, if they are not, why not; what referential dependencies must, can and cannot obtain; and so on. In fact, for all that has been said here, semantic theory could even retain the architecture of a Fregean or Tarskian theory, with both primitives and complexes, lexical and compositional rules, different semantic types, functions combining with arguments, compositional determination of whole-meanings from part meanings, and so on.[21] What is rejected is just the idea that the primitives stand for real world objects and sets outside the mind, and that sentences express world-bound thoughts (relative to a set of parameters). Thus, the two objections from ontology in no way force one to abandon the discipline of semantics, or its many results. (We will revisit the tasks of semantics at the end of the chapter, when discussing the positive alternative to reference-based semantics.)

36.1.3 The Failure of Compositional Referential Semantics

As presented here, the former two arguments have focused primarily on public *words* (e.g. 'Harvard', 'photographer') and external *objects* (e.g. London). But the Chomskian target is the whole tradition of treating natural languages as, in key respects, like the formal languages invented by logicians—and, as explained above, that tradition brings with it a not just about words and objects, but also views about predicates (e.g. verbs and adjectives) and sets, and sentences and truth. Traditionally, sentences are assigned "proto-thoughts": things which, given a particular setting for a fixed cluster of parameters (time, place, speaker, addressee), are true or false. And predicates are assigned sets of objects as their extension. These ideas are equally questionable, says the Chomskian—even putting aside the issues, raised above, of whether there *are* "public sentences" and "public predicates", and whether sets of common sense objects and proto-thoughts can be "seen" from the scientific perspective.

As noted at the outset, the mark of a Chomskian, as I here intend the term, is a commitment to methodological naturalism. Now, the methodological naturalist,

---

[21] See Jackendoff, 1983, 1991, 1996, 2002 for detailed examples of keeping much of this structure, but without external reference based semantics. It is worth stressing, however, that some of the authors discussed here remain highly skeptical about retaining this traditional superstructure, within a naturalist framework. See in particular Moravcsik 1998, who maintains that Fregean and Tarskian systems (i) need sharply defined word meanings, not permitting polysemy, and (ii) require that syntax mirror semantics—neither of which conditions, Moravcsik argues, hold for natural languages.

inquiring into language as an aspect of nature, will follow the canons of the sciences, and will seek out, as her object of inquiry, a real object—possibly differing in important ways from pre-theoretical conceptions—that is scientifically tractable. That object turned out to be the language faculty: that innately provided, specialized module of the mind–brain. For this reason, the methodological naturalist will approach semantics, like phonology and syntax, as part of the study of the language faculty. What will emerge below, however, is that it is not plausible that the language faculty, taken alone, can assign proto-thoughts to sentences, or sets of objects to verbs, adjectives, etc. Hence sentence meanings cannot be thoughts, nor even "thoughts relative to a set of parameters"; and predicate meanings cannot be sets of objects in the external world.[22]

Let's begin with sentences. The fundamental points here are made by Pietroski (2003, 2005), building on Chomsky (1977). On the one hand, there is no *empirical* reason for thinking that what the language faculty assigns to a sentence will be capable of being true or false, even given contextual parameters like time, place, speaker, hearer, etc. (There's lots of empirical reason for thinking that *people* can say, and think, things that are true or false; but that is another matter.) The only thing which drives one to this expectation is, at bottom, a dubious analogy between natural objects and artifacts whose properties are stipulated (e.g. the predicate calculus). For the methodological naturalist, that in itself is damning. On the other hand, there is lots of empirical evidence that the language faculty alone doesn't assign thoughts (or propositions, or truth conditions, or what have you). In particular, very many sentences either lack truth conditions altogether, or are assigned truth conditions only via the rich interaction of different mental faculties.

Consider, for instance, the following pair of sentences:

(1) Poems are written by fools like me
(2) Mountains are climbed by fools like me

Putting aside the difficult question of what a referential semantics would assign as meanings for the parts (e.g. what real-world object does the plural word 'poems' stand for?), it does seem that the same *kind* of meaning, whatever it is, would have to be assigned by the language faculty to 'poems' and 'mountains', and to 'are written' and 'are climbed'. Moreover, the same syntactic structure appears in both sentences. Thus, the prediction would be that, as far as the language faculty goes, (1) says about poems and being-written whatever (2) says about mountains and being-climbed. Yet, insofar as they assign a proto-thought at all, the proto-thought that an agent would typically associate with (1) requires that *all* poems are written by fools, while

---

[22] Looked at slightly differently, as Fodor (2001) has argued, if semantics has to yield "a thought expressed (give or take a bit)", then a compositional semantics for natural language is just not possible. What one should conclude, says the Chomskian, is not that natural languages lack compositional semantics, which is Fodor's conclusion, but rather that scientific semantics just shouldn't be in the business of assigning thoughts to sentences—nor even "thoughts give or take a bit". Instead, the linguistic meanings of whole sentences just are those things—whatever they turn out to be—which *are* compositionally determined from part-meanings plus syntax.

the proto-thought that an agent would typically associate with (2) does not require, for its truth, that *all* mountains are climbed by fools. Thus the truth conditions that language users tend to assign are importantly different. Nor is this an isolated example. Think, for instance, of how knowledge of the world impacts on what sense one assigns to 'may' in 'Marta may get cancer' versus 'Marta may smile if she wishes to.' In so far as one treats these as truth evaluable at all, one hears the first 'may' as expressing (epistemic or physical) *possibility*, and the latter 'may' as expressing *permissibility*. Moreover, this contrast in how 'may' is understood arises because, as a matter of fact, one isn't given permission to get cancer; and because it's too obvious to bear mention that it's (physically and epistemically) possible for a person to smile, if she wishes to. Or again, what the concatenation of a nominal and modifier contributes to meaning varies widely from case to case; in particular, the meaning of the nominal-modifier complex frequently reflects facts known about the world. For instance, compare 'Christmas cookie' ("made to be consumed at"), 'Girl guide cookie' ("sold by"), 'oatmeal cookie' ("made of"), 'yellow cookie' ("coloured"), 'fortune cookie' ("containing"), 'doggie cookie' ("made to be eaten by"), and 'Walmart cookie' ("sold at"). Given that concatenation doesn't always mean the same thing, if an agent is able to assign truth conditions at all to 'Phyllis ate a Boy Scout cookie', it is because the agent knows the relevant facts *about Boy Scouts*: e.g. that they are not an appropriate ingredient for a cookie, that there isn't a Boy Scout holiday, that Boy Scouts are too big to be inside a cookie, etc.

One might reply that language users are simply poor judges of what sentences mean: "the folk" mix up what the expression means with how it would be standardly used. For example, while language users do indeed assign quantificationally different truth conditions to the sentence types (1) and (2), they are wrong to do so. This is a fair point. Indeed, Chomskians themselves are wont to note that language users do not have direct insight into the syntax of their own idiolect: language users are apt on first hearing, for instance, to incorrectly judge that 'The horse raced past the barn fell' is ungrammatical. Still, if we ask the semantic theorist what the proto-thought expressed by (1) *is*, since by hypothesis it isn't that *all* poems are written by fools like me, it will become clear that the meaning that the language faculty taken alone assigns is not the sort of thing which, even relative to a set of parameters (speaker, addressee, time, place), is true or false. Similarly for 'Marta may get cancer' and 'Phyllis ate a Boy Scout cookie.' Whatever the context-invariant meaning of these sentences is, it's something *much* more abstract than a thought, or even a function from a restricted set of parameters to a thought.[23] Indeed, this attempted reply brings out even more clearly the deeper problem with trying to assign truth conditions to sentences. That deeper problem has to do with where the differences in truth conditions that agents assign—e.g. between (1) and (2)—derive from. Part

---

[23] The point is, of course, closely related to the idea—defended by Robyn Carston, Francois Récanati, John Searle, Dan Sperber and Deirdre Wilson, and Charles Travis—that there are "pragmatic determinants" of the truth conditions of speech acts. See Carston 2002 for detailed and illuminating discussion.

of the Chomskian point is precisely that the difference in the truth conditions that language users assign, in so far as they *do* assign truth conditions, derives from real world knowledge that people have—e.g. about poems versus mountains (i.e. that the former are all human creations, but the latter are not). Moreover, there is no other source of *truth* conditions: leave that real-world knowledge out and what is determined is too abstract to bear a truth value. Thus, in so far as we agents assign truth conditions to sentences at all, the truth conditions we assign are a massive interaction effect of different kinds of knowledge: knowledge afforded by the language faculty, yes, but also knowledge afforded by many other parts of the mind–brain. Not being solely an aspect of the language faculty, it follows that the truth conditions which people assign to sentences do not fall within the domain of the science of language. (See Borg, this volume, for a rather different view.)

Another kind of case raises problems for the idea that predicates (verbs, verb phrases, adjectives, adjective phrases, etc.) have sets of external objects as their content. Compare sentences (3) through (6):

(3) The house is green
(4) The ink is green
(5) The banana is green
(6) The stoplight is green

In each case, in so far as talk of "contributing sets" is appropriate at all, [$_{I'}$ is green] appears to be contributing a quite different set in the four cases. In (3), the house must be in the set of things which are green on the outside (though the house need not be *entirely* green on the outside). Similarly for (5), which requires only that the banana *peel* be green. In contrast (4) requires that the stuff (which right now looks black) be in the set of things which, when applied to paper and allowed to dry, will be green. As for (6), the science of colour tells us that the property exhibited by the stoplight is physically very different from that exhibited by the banana peel in (5): the stoplight being green involves not the reflection of light, but the emission of light. So, thought of as a physical set, the one which [$_I$is green] picks out in (6) is very different yet again. (See: Moravcsik 1998: 44–5 for similar remarks about 'is white'; Jackendoff, 1991: 44 on different senses for 'end'; and Jackendoff, 1983, 2002 and Pustejovsky, 1995 for a panoply of other examples.) *Part* of what appears to be going on here is this: which set of things is associated by speakers with one part of the sentence depends upon what they associate with the other parts. Here, the set that speakers associate with [$_{I'}$ is green] depends on the kind of thing that 'green' is thought of as applied to: houses, ink, bananas, etc. Worse, the variation in the set selected by the agent as the denotation for 'green', depends upon facts about how reasonable speakers would use the sentence—which in turn depends on factors like how likely it is for houses to be wholly and completely green, what ink is used for, etc. Once again, then, the denotation, in so far as language users assign one at all, is an enormous interaction effect, and does not depend solely upon the language faculty; so, there can be no science of language which assigns sets to predicates.

One natural reaction to this kind of example, an idea pursued by Jerry Fodor and Ernie Lepore in a series of articles, is to say that 'green' simply means *green* in (3) through (6)—adding that there are lots of different ways for things to be green. (See especially Fodor and Lepore, 1998.) The point is well taken. But green, so construed, now ceases to be a mind-independent property "out there in the world", to which words may simply attach. Of particular importance here, the set univocally denoted by 'green' becomes a set that no proper science could treat of—precisely because that collection of objects becomes wildly heterogeneous from a scientific perspective. What the house, the ink, the banana and the stop light have in common, in being green, is not something that any genuine science can see. To put the point differently, note that one might equally claim—and it isn't exactly false—that 'in' just means *in* as it occurs in 'a boy in trouble', 'a hole in her sock', 'a flaw in my argument', 'a detective in the novel', 'a C-sharp in the symphony', and so on. Even allowing that 'in' always means *in*, it clearly won't follow that there is scientifically tractable thing, "in-ness", denoted in all these cases. The worry is that the same holds for 'green', and the "green-set" univocally picked out by this word: if *that* is what 'green' stands for, we get a "single constant referent", but we cannot have an explanatory science that describes the word–world relation in the case of 'green'.

Once again, then, we have a reason for expecting that the science of language—which, for the methodological naturalist, is about the language faculty—cannot, and should not try to, assign as meanings the kind of thing that gets assigned in invented logical languages.

Actually, some would draw a stronger conclusion than the one I have been defending at length, viz. that a comprehensive *science of language* won't treat of word–world relations. Some might additionally conclude that, being a massive interaction effect of different causes, *no* genuine science will take the truth conditions we assign to sentences (or the sets we assign to predicates), as a thing to be explained—since genuine sciences are in the business of describing causal forces, not such highly complex particular effects.[24] To offer a comparison that Chomsky himself often gives, it is not the business of any science to describe the trajectory of a given falling leaf—even though it's quite true that scientific laws together contribute to how the leaf in fact fell. (Actually, there are two reasons why no science describes the falling of an individual leaf: first, it is non-tractable; second, it's just not interesting. I presume that the problem about any science assigning truth-conditions to sentences is the lack of tractability, not a lack of interest. But it might be both.) This may seem to go too far: surely it's altogether implausible that no science can capture such interaction effects. Part of the implausibility fades, however, when it's recalled that not every empirical enterprise that attempts to systematize is a genuine science; or anyway, it's not a science in the sense intended here. In the sense intended here, science involves explaining seemingly simple phenomena by postulating unobservables; and it involves the aim of

[24] Some of the authors listed at the outset explicitly disavow the idea that science, even "genuine explanatory science", is limited in this way. In particular, both Jackendoff (p.c.) and Moravcsik (1998, 2002) are much more sanguine than Chomsky is, about genuine sciences of complex interactions, including sciences of human creations.

integration with other "core natural sciences". It is, then, an open question whether the so-called "sciences of the complex", not to mention the "social sciences", really are *sciences* in the sense in question. No doubt the former uncover statistical patterns in the weather, ecosystems and the stock market, using sophisticated empirical methods; and the latter undoubtedly state empirically discovered rough generalizations about cultural products. And maybe similar techniques could be applied to the assignment of truth and satisfaction conditions. But this isn't enough. (To come at the point another way, it wouldn't be unreasonable to say that genuine natural science, in the sense in question here, is such a special enterprise, that it is a relatively recent arrival on the scene: it simply did not exist before the Renaissance. The question, then, is whether *that* "special enterprise" can be applied to massive interaction effects. Put this way, the extra worry, that goes beyond the main conclusion argued for in the article, is that this special enterprise cannot be so applied, so that, as a case in point, no science (of language, or of anything else) can treat of truth conditions for sentences or satisfaction conditions for predicates.)

36.2 REMARKS ON A POSITIVE ALTERNATIVE

So, what, from a methodological naturalist perspective, *does* the meaning of expression look like, if it isn't a matter of a word–world relationship? Well, meaning looks a lot like syntax. In particular, it looks like syntax *which has procedural implications.* Indeed, it isn't too far wrong to say that meaning is that aspect of natural language syntax which plays a causal role in the conceptual-intentional system (and ultimately, though in very unclear ways, in thought, and in the production of behavior). Though rather short on details, this broadly Chomskian idea can be fleshed out a little by making a comparison with phonetic features. Phonetic features are, for Chomsky and many other linguists, mental instructions, which are hooked up, in the first instance, with other representational systems—where something counts as an "instruction" because of its intricate form-based causal powers, not because it is contentful in the sense of standing for something in the external world; and where 'representation' is stripped of its philosophical "standing for" connotations. These latter representational systems ultimately contribute to moving tongue, lips, etc., thereby playing a crucial part in giving rise to speech sounds.[25] In the same sort of way, the meaning of an expression, on this approach, is a cluster of semantic features that similarly interface with (a rather different) mental system, the "conceptual and intentional system". And this and other systems play a part in actions by the agent. Chomsky writes:

---

[25] As Jackendoff, 2002, points out, these features are also instructions *from* the auditory system; and that system presumably cannot output motor instructions. So, identifying phonetic features with instructions to the sensorimotor system is clearly an oversimplification.

Each expression can be regarded as a collection of information for other systems of the mind–brain. The traditional assumption, back to Aristotle, is that the information falls into two categories, phonetic and semantic; information used, respectively, by sensorimotor systems and conceptual-intentional systems—the latter "systems of thought," to give a name to something poorly understood. (2002: 87)

(See Chomsky, 1997 for further discussion, and also Chomsky, 2000c: 90–1, where the notion of "instruction" in particular is discussed in a bit more detail.)

Crucially, semantics in this tradition can be nothing more than rules for mapping one mental representation to another, by well-defined tractable procedures. The science of language is thus restricted to describing the sub-personal, unconscious, automatic, cognitively impenetrable rules of the language faculty. Put in a nutshell, it is restricted to this because only this is formally tractable. The personal-level, conscious, reasoned and flexible *use* of language, to talk about the world, is excluded from the domain of science, properly so called.

Put this way, it can seem that semantics becomes extremely "thin", so that not much can be said about it. But that would be a mistaken impression. First, as McGilvray (1998) stresses, internalist semantics still faces the enormous task of finding out what the various "meaning features" are, and finding out which lexical items exhibit which features. (An especially nice example of how this task is pursued is Jackendoff, 1991.) Given the centrality of feature checking to Minimalism, hinted at above, lexical semantics of this kind is a very important task indeed. But there is also lots of work to do on the "compositional" side of semantics.

To give the flavor of how the semantics of syntactic complexes proceeds, consider two examples. (For many other early examples, see Jackendoff, 1983.) Compositional semantics, as reconceived, will still need to explain why, for example, whereas (7) is ambiguous (it can mean both *You want **who** to shoot?* and *You want to shoot **who**?*), sentence (8), with 'want' and 'to' contracted into 'wanna', is not ambiguous, and can only mean *You want to shoot **who**?*

(7) Who do you want to shoot?
(8) Who do you wanna shoot?

A partial explanation of this meaning-fact, simplifying greatly, goes as follows. Underlying (7) there are actually *two* syntactic structures, namely (9) and (10):

(9) Who$_1$ do you want t_1 to shoot?
(10) Who$_1$ do you want to shoot t_1

In contrast, only (10) underlies (8), because the trace t_1 in between 'want' and 'to shoot' in (9) blocks contraction: 'want t_1 to shoot' cannot become 'wanna shoot'. That is why (7) is ambiguous, but (8) is not. What remains to be said, to explain why (7) and (8) have the meaning they do, is to sort out why the two structures (9) and (10) mean what *they* do. This depends upon what the words mean, of course, which is the same in the two cases. It also depends upon what a trace co-indexed with 'who' contributes to meaning. It is this latter contribution which is different in (9) and (10), because of where the trace appears: because of the trace, in one case the direct object position is queried, in the other case it is the subject position that is queried. What's important for present purposes is not whether this explanation is correct, or complete; what matters is that specifying all of these things remains the job of semantics, even once external world reference and "proto-thoughts" are put aside.

To give another familiar kind of example, in (11) 'him' can be referentially dependent on 'Juan' (that is, put crudely, 'him' is allowed to, though it need not, take its meaning over from the name); but in (12) 'him' *cannot* be referentially dependent on 'Juan'.

(11) Juan$_1$ asked Maria to kill him$_1$ [Juan = him, is possible]
(12) *Juan$_1$ promised Maria to kill him$_1$ [Juan ≠ him]

This is a phenomenon that needs to be explained. A by-now traditional explanation, again simplifying for present purposes, goes like this.[26] First, the underlying structure of the two expressions is a bit more complex than what appears in (11) and (12). At a minimum, we need to add an unpronounced subject PRO for the embedded infinitival clause 'to kill him', and we need explicitly to bracket off this embedded clause:

(13) Juan$_1$ asked Maria$_2$ [$_S$ PRO$_2$ to kill him$_1$]   [Juan = him, is possible]
(14) Juan$_1$ promised Maria$_2$ [$_S$ PRO$_1$ to kill him$_1$]   [Juan ≠ him]

Now, continues the story, it is a semantic feature of the verb 'promise' that its subject gets co-indexed with the *subject* of the embedded clause that follows, here the sentence 'PRO to kill him'. Because of this lexical semantic fact about 'promise', the PRO subject of the embedded clause [$_S$ PRO to kill him$_1$], in (14), comes to share the index 1 both with 'Juan' and with 'him'. (This contrasts with 'ask', which is a verb whose *object* gets co-indexed with the subject of the embedded clause, as in (13); that is why the PRO subject of (13) shares the index 2 with 'Maria'.) But, as a result of a general restriction that needn't detain us here, in a simple sentence of the form 'SUBJECT kill him', 'him' *cannot* be referentially dependent on the subject phrase.[27] To see the pattern, note that 'him' cannot be referentially dependent on 'Juan', 'The man' or 'He' in (15)–(17):

(15) *Juan$_1$ killed him$_1$ [Juan ≠ him]
(16) *The man$_1$ killed him$_1$ [The man ≠ him]
(17) *He$_1$ killed him$_1$ [He ≠ him]

Given the semantic properties of 'promise', the co-reference principle that underlies (15)-(17), and the postulated element PRO in the embedded infinitival clause, the semantic fact that (12) cannot mean *Juan promised Maria to kill himself* is now partially explained. Again, what really matters for present purposes is not whether this

---

[26] In both of the compositional examples discussed here, the principles I appeal to are now thought to follow from deeper constraints. Indeed, in Minimalism all "rules" end up being typological artifacts of (i) lexical features, (ii) some very basic operations (e.g. Merge, Agree), (iii) overarching economy conditions (e.g. simplicity and locality), and (iv) output conditions imposed by the two interfaces. See Chomsky, 1995a, 2000c, 2001. I employ the older framework, however, because explanations in those terms are rather easier to present, and they exemplify equally well the *kind* of task that remains, even after reference-based semantics is abandoned.

[27] The general principle is Principle B of the Binding Theory: "A pronominal is free in its governing category" (Chomsky, 1981: 188).

explanation is precisely the right one; for present purposes, the key point is simply that this explanation draws on facts about the contrasting lexical semantic features of 'ask' and 'promise', on facts about structural constraints on co-indexing, and on facts about what co-indexing contributes to meaning. Here again, these are semantic issues that do not simply melt away with the rejection of reference-based semantics.[28]

In sum, as Pietroski (2005) concludes, "Trading in truth-values (and entities referred to)... does not change the basic questions. We still want to know, for any given sentence: what is its structure; what does it mean; and how is the former related to the latter?" Thus, semantics remains rich (and central to linguistic theorizing), and the sub-discipline of semantics still has much work to do in capturing the semantics properties of expressions—primitive and complex.[29]

But, it will be asked, if the science of language cannot ascribe real-world referents to words, and instead merely pairs linguistic representations with other linguistic expressions, and with inner representations of other kinds, how on earth does our talk manage to be about the world outside us? This is an exceedingly difficult question. The short answer is that, though words themselves don't refer,[30] *people* can refer using them. Nothing said above rules this out. Our speech acts and our thoughts are about the world—but not because of a relationship between particular natural language representations and particular outer things.[31] The long answer is... Well, no one knows what the long answer is.

In light of the short answer, one might hold out hope that there could be a science of *speaker reference*. Chomskians aren't optimistic about that, however: there cannot, they think, be a science that captures episodes of people referring either. First, speaker-reference is as much a massive interaction effect as speech episodes are in general—which entity the speaker manages to refer to, using 'he' or 'The woman from Spain', will clearly depend on a host of things. (Just as whether an expression "sounds right" will depend on many, many things beyond what the grammar states about the expression.) But, as hinted above, because of intractability (and sometimes because it's uninteresting), it may be that genuine sciences aren't in the business of

---

[28] Moreover, semantics as reconceived here will still explore relations *between* expressions, noting (and trying to explain) what logical entailments hold on the basis of meaning alone, which expressions are and are not synonymous, etc. Thus, to give but one example, semantics will try to explain why 'Saima persuaded Moonisah to leave' entails 'Moonisah formed the intention to leave'.

[29] David Lewis (1970: 190) famously complained that "Semantics with no treatment of truth conditions is not semantics". This slogan seems to have exerted enormous influence in philosophy of language. But, as Pietroski (2005) argues at length, at bottom Lewis is simply stipulating a usage for a technical term, 'semantics'. The methodological naturalist will eschew such stipulations, and will instead look for a real feature of the world to study. See also Jackendoff (1987: ch. 7) for related points about "Lewis's terminological imperialism" (1987: 130), and an early and extensive defense of internalist semantics in the face of Lewis' criticisms.

[30] To be clear, Chomsky does allow for *a* notion of reference for expressions. He labels it "relation R". But relation R does not introduce a relation between external entities and words; it is thoroughly internalist. See Chomsky, 1992a: 39 for discussion.

[31] Chomsky (1993: 22) does note that the use of 'refer' as applied to words is a technical coinage. However, as is clear from what has been said above, his reasons for saying that people refer, rather than having words refer, are not based on this minor detail about ordinary usage.

describing effects deriving from such multiple and varied causes; rather, genuine sciences are in the business of abstracting away to the causal forces that produce these effects. Thus, just as there is no science of which things "sound right", and no science of Chomsky's falling leaf, there may well be no science of what the person, in this particular circumstance, refers to. At least not in the sense of 'science' in play here. Second, and deeper, in so far as referring *is* something that the whole agent does, it is a conscious act of free will and reason. And, for Chomsky and some of his followers, that in itself puts it outside the scope of the sciences: for this reason alone, reference by speakers cannot be treated naturalistically either.[32]

However you slice it, then, meanings just *are* in the head. Or anyway, there can be no comprehensive science of language which studies "meanings" of the word–world variety: that kind of meaning-theory just isn't scientifically tractable. As Chomsky (1992a: 45) succinctly puts the conclusion, "Naturalistic inquiry will always fall short of intentionality."

REFERENCES

Antony, Louise (1997). "Meaning and Semantic Knowledge". *Aristotelian Society Supplementary Volume*, 71: 177–209.

Bencivenga, Ermanno (1983). "An Epistemic Theory of Reference", *The Journal of Philosophy*, 80: 785–803.

Bilgrami, Akeel (2002). "Chomsky and Philosophy". *Mind and Language*, 17: 290–302.

Carston, Robyn (2002). *Thoughts and Utterances*. Oxford: Blackwell.

Chomsky, Noam (2002). *On Nature and Language*. Cambridge, UK: Cambridge University Press.

——— (2001). "Derivation by Phase". In M. Kenstowicz (ed.) *Ken Hale: A Life in Language*. Cambridge, MA: MIT Press.

——— (2000a). *New Horizons in the Study of Language and Mind*. Cambridge, UK: Cambridge University Press.

——— (2000b). "Internalist Explorations". In Chomsky, 2000a.

——— (2000c). "Minimalist Inquiries: The Framework". In R. Martin, D. Michaels, and J. Uriagereka (eds.) *Step by Step: Essays on Minimalist Syntax in Honor of Howard Lasnik*. Cambridge, MA: MIT Press.

——— (1997). "New Horizons in the Study of Language". In Chomsky, 2000a.

——— (1995a). *The Minimalist Program*. Cambridge, MA: The MIT Press.

——— (1995b). "Language and Nature". *Mind*, 104: 1–61. Reprinted in Chomsky, 2000a.

——— (1994). "Naturalism and Dualism in the Study of Mind and Language". *International Journal of Philosophical Studies*, 2: 181–200. Reprinted in Chomsky, 2000a.

——— (1993). *Language and Thought*. London: Moyer Bell.

——— (1992a). "Explaining Language Use". *Philosophical Topics*, 20: 205–31. Reprinted in Chomsky 2000a.

---

[32] Chomsky writes: "It is not excluded that human science-forming capacities simply do not extend to this domain [i.e. how stimulus conditions given a cognitive state give rise to behavior (including the use of language)], or any domain involving the exercise of will, so that for humans, these questions will always be shrouded in mystery" (1975: 25). Also: "The phrase 'at will' points to an area beyond serious empirical inquiry" (Chomsky, 2002: 59).

_____ (1992b)."Language and Interpretation: Philosophical Reflections and Empirical Inquiry". In J. Earman (ed.) *Inference, Explanation and Other Frustrations: Essays in the Philosophy of Science*. Berkeley: University of California Press, pp. 99–128. Reprinted in Chomsky, 2000a.

_____ (1986). *Knowledge of Language*. New York: Praeger.

_____ (1981). *Lectures on Government and Binding*. Dordrecht: Foris.

_____ (1977). *Essays on Form and Interpretation*. New York: North Holland.

_____ (1975). *Reflections on Language*. New York: Pantheon Books.

Davidson, Donald (1984). *Inquiries into Truth and Interpretation*. Oxford: Oxford University Press.

_____ (1976). "Reply to Foster". In G. Evans and J. McDowell (eds.) *Truth and Meaning*. Oxford: Clarendon Press, pp. 33–41. Reprinted in Davidson, 1984.

_____ (1967). "Truth and Meaning" *Synthese*, 17: 304–323. Reprinted in Davidson, 1984.

Fodor, Jerry (2001). "Language, Thought and Compositionality". *Mind & Language*, 16: 1–15.

_____ (1983). *Modularity of Mind*. Cambridge, MA: MIT Press.

Fodor, Jerry & Ernie Lepore (2002). *The Compositionality Papers*. Oxford: Oxford University Press.

_____ (1998). "The Emptiness of the Lexicon: Reflections on Pustejovsky". *Linguistic Inquiry*, 29: 269–88. Reprinted in Fodor and Lepore, 2002.

Foster, John A. (1976). "Meaning and Truth Theory". In G. Evans and J. McDowell (eds.) *Truth and Meaning*. Oxford: Clarendon Press, pp. 1–32.

Hornstein, Norbert (1989). "Meaning and the Mental: The Problem of Semantics after Chomsky". In A. George (ed.) *Reflections on Chomsky*. Oxford: Blackwell, pp. 23–40.

_____ (1984). *Logic as Grammar*. Cambridge, MA: The MIT Press.

Jackendoff, Ray (2002). *Foundations of Language*. Oxford: Oxford University Press.

_____ (1996). "Semantics and Cognition". In S. Lappin (ed.) *The Handbook of Contemporary Semantic Theory*. Oxford: Blackwell, pp. 539–559.

_____ (1991). "Parts and Boundaries". *Cognition*, 41: 9–45.

_____ (1987). *Consciousness and the Computational Mind*. Cambridge, MA: The MIT Press.

_____ (1983). *Semantics and Cognition*. Cambridge, MA: The MIT Press.

Lewis, David (1970). "General Semantics". *Synthese*, 22: 18–67. Reprinted in *Philosophical Papers*, Volume 1. Oxford: Oxford University Press, pp. 189–229.

Pustejovsky, James (1995). *The Generative Lexicon*. Cambridge, MA: The MIT Press.

Matheson, David and Robert J. Stainton (2002). "Varieties of Empiricism". In Y. Bouchard (ed.) *Perspectives on Coherentism*. Aylmer, Quebec: Éditions du Scribe, pp. 99–113.

McGilvray, James (1999). *Chomsky: Language, Mind, and Politics*. Cambridge, UK: Polity Press.

_____ (1998). "Meanings Are Syntactically Individuated and Found in the Head" *Mind and Language*, 13: 225–80.

Montague, Richard (1974). *Formal Philosophy*. New Haven, CT: Yale University Press.

Moore, G. E. (1939). "Proof of an External World". *Proceedings of the British Academy*, 25: 273–300. Reprinted in T. Baldwin (ed.) (1993) *G.E. Moore: Selected Writings*. London: Routledge.

Moravcsik, Julius (2002). "Chomsky's New Horizons". *Mind and Language*, 17: 303–11.

_____ (1998). *Meaning, Creativity and The Partial Inscrutability of the Human Mind*. Stanford: CSLI.

Pietroski, Paul (2005). "Meaning before Truth". In G. Preyer and G. Peters (eds.) *Contextualism in Philosophy*. Oxford: Oxford University Press, pp. 255–302.

Pietroski, Paul (2003). "The Character of Natural Language Semantics". In A. Barber (ed.) *The Epistemology of Language*. Oxford: Oxford University Press, pp. 217–56.

Radford, Andrew (1997). *Syntactic Theory and the Structure of English*. Cambridge, UK: Cambridge University Press.

Smith, Barry C. (1992). "Understanding Language". *Proceedings of the Aristotelian Society*, 92: 109–41.

Smith, Neil (1999). *Chomsky: Ideas and Ideals*. Cambridge, UK: Cambridge University Press.

Strawson, Peter F. (1950). "On Referring" *Mind*, 59: 320–44. Reprinted in R. J. Stainton (ed.) *Perspectives in the Philosophy of Language*. Peterborough, ON: Broadview.

Wiggins, David (1997). "Languages as Social Objects". *Philosophy*, 72(282): 499–524.

CHAPTER 37

....

WHAT I KNOW
WHEN I KNOW
A LANGUAGE

....

BARRY C. SMITH

EVERY speaker of a language knows a bewildering variety of linguistic facts and will come to know many more. It is knowledge that connects sound and meaning. Questions about the nature of this knowledge cannot be separated from fundamental questions about the nature of language. The conception of language we should adopt depends on the part it plays in explaining our knowledge of language. This chapter explores options in accounting for language and our knowledge of language and defends the view that individuals' languages are constituted by the standing knowledge they carry from one speech situation to another.

The title of this chapter alludes, of course, to Michael Dummett's seminal paper, 'What Do I Know When I Know a Language?' in which he raises many fundamental questions for the philosopher of language. More than twenty-five years later, I hope we are at last beginning to see how to address some of the important foundational issues Dummett first brought to light. The chapter builds on issues first raised in Smith, 1992, 1998, and 2001. I should like to thank graduate students from the University of London and the University of California at Berkeley for their many helpful responses to this material; in particular Cheng-Hung Tsai, Julian Dutant, and April Jones. Thanks to Stephen Schiffer for discussion of his paper to which I responded at the GLOW conference in Geneva 2005 and to the audience at that session. And for their helpful conversations on many of these issues I should especially like to thank Paul Pietroski, Donald Davidson, John McDowell, John Searle, Jennifer Hudin, Stephen Neale, Guy Longworth, Peter Pagin, Kathrin Gluer, Asa Wikforss, Jim Higginbotham, Jason Stanley, Peter Ludlow, Georges Rey, Michael Devitt, Ernie Lepore, and John Collins.

37.1 Language as a Source
of Knowledge

Language enables us to acquire knowledge of the world and of other people. We learn what people think by what they say, and, in turn, we speak our minds to them. Words give us immediate entry to the minds of others. Just by using these words I can inform you or amuse you, excite you or insult you. I get straight through to your mind, perhaps uninvited. Similarly, your words have immediate and unexpected effects on my thinking. This is possible because we hear people's emission of sound as meaningful speech, and cannot but hear it that way when the words uttered are familiar. In this way, language establishes intimate connections between minds and shows how easily the sanctity of individual minds is violated.

In addition to being an interface between minds, language gives us much of our access to the wider world. Through what we are told and what we read we come to acquire a vast range of world knowledge. Language is our means of learning about science and culture, mathematics and history: information that makes up our much of our vision of the wider world. To gain access to this knowledge we must first have access to language. So what gives us access to language? Do we first need to know a language? Is this what equips us to produce and understand utterances?

These questions go to the heart of our ability to make intelligible sense of certain sounds people utter, and to give meaning to the sounds we utter. How are we able to attach linguistic form and significance to certain speech sounds we and other humans produce? Michael Dummett frames the philosophical issue as follows:

> The central task of the philosopher of language is to explain what *meaning* is, that is, what makes a language *language*. Consider two speakers engaged in conversation. To immediate inspection, all that is happening is that sounds of a certain kind issue from the mouths of each alternately. But we know that there is a deeper significance: they are expressing thoughts, putting forward arguments, stating conjectures, asking questions, etc. What the philosopher of language has to explain is what gives this character to the sounds they utter: what makes their utterances expressions of thought and all these other things?   (Dummett, 1978, p. 96)

The needed explanation has to cover a potential infinity of cases. For unless people live dull and repetitive lives, everyday they will produce and hear utterances of sentences they have never heard before. They will hear news, read interesting books, and engage in distracting conversations. What explains this capacity to share their states of minds linguistically in new but comprehensible ways? Whatever it is, the remarkable fact is that we understand utterances of sentences we have never heard before just as easily as we understand those which are already familiar, suggesting the same system is at work in our handling of both the novel sentence and the sentences already understood. What is this underlying system and how do we exploit it to form and recognize new sentences?

37.2 Language as an Object of Knowledge

After the passage just quoted, Dummett goes on to ask a key question: 'Is the significance of language to be explained in terms of a speaker's knowledge of his language?' (1978, p. 97). We want to know what gives certain sounds their linguistic character, and we also want to know how we are able to hear those sounds as the utterances of meaningful sentences (in indefinitely many cases). One approach would be to say why we were entitled to treat those sounds as the articulations of expressions from a particular language and how we were able to recognize them as belonging to that language. Another approach would be to suggest that it is our ability to hear those sounds as meaningful sentences that confers linguistic character on them. Either way, we are only able to pair up a potential infinity of sounds and meanings by knowing a language. We need to know indefinitely many sentences, and know for any sounds we hear, which sentences are being uttered. So the difference between merely hearing people issuing noises and hearing what they are saying resides in one's knowing the language being spoken. If so, we need to account for this knowledge—to account for its nature and what it gives us knowledge of—and how it enables us to hear and utter speech sounds as particular meaningful sentences and thus know the minds of others:

(i) What form does this knowledge take?
(ii) How do we acquire it?
(iii) How does it enable us to hear *sounds* as meaningful sentences?
(iv) How does it enable us to know what other people mean?

37.3 Two Conceptions of Language and Knowledge of Language

In addressing these questions it will be useful to consider two competing conceptions of language and our knowledge of language. On one traditional story, individuals in a linguistic community are able to use their language to express and convey their thoughts because of their participation in a common practice.[1] To understand other people's utterances, to hear what they are saying, one must know the meanings of the words and sentences they use. These will be the meanings those words and sentences have in the common practice, or public language. To know these meanings one must belong to that linguistic community and participate in its practices. But what enables

---

[1] See Dummett, 'What Do I Know When I Know a Language?', p. 102 and McDowell, 'In Defence of Modesty', especially p. 94, and 'Antirealism and the Epistemology of Understanding', p. 314, and pp. 332–3.

one as an individual to participate in those shared practices? What is the extent of the knowledge one thereby acquires? What does it give us knowledge of? And how exactly does it enable one to hear sounds as part of a public language? The traditional story is short on detailed answers to these questions. We are told that participation in a practice is a gradual matter; that 'Light dawns gradually over the whole';[2] that 'one hears more, in speech in a language, when one has learned the language';[3] that one cannot explain the linguistic significance of items by reference to anything outside our linguistic practices; that the meanings of words and sentences lie in open view to the surface of our practice but are only visible or audible to participants of that practice.

It is crucial to see that *the* language, or the common practice that displays and sustains it, has to extend beyond individual speakers, and beyond the actual point any speaker has reached since it must make room for the potential infinity of meaningful sentences yet to be encountered that count as part of the language. The expressive possibilities open to us are already mapped out by the language and must somehow be contained, or latent, in the practice. An individual's power of expression rests on how much of that language or practice has been mastered and how effectively it is put to use. The system underlying familiar and novel sentences is part of the workings of the language. Whatever gives us access to the language gives us access to that system. But what does give us access to the public language and how are individuals able to exploit the workings of the language for their own purposes? As Dummett points out, to understand a novel sentence we rely on our recognition of familiar words and the methods of sentence construction: for this we need knowledge of the meaning of words, of the grammatical means of combining them and some awareness of the significance of so combining them. It would be hard to overestimate what an achievement it is for a child to acquire this knowledge starting out by simply confronting sounds. Through language acquisition we succeed in putting our minds into our words in a way dictated by the requirements of the common language, so that others who do likewise can find out what we think.

A radical alternative sees the psychological states of speaker-hearers—their knowledge of language—as endowing speech sounds with the linguistic significance they have for us. Although we perceive sounds as linguistic items, on this view, the linguistic items are internal to the mind of a speaker-hearer (see '*Language as Internal*').[4] Knowledge of language is a state of the speaker-hearer that fixes which sounds count as expressions, which arrangement of expressions counts as grammatical, and what those expressions are taken to mean. It does not provide knowledge of anything external to the mind of speaker-hearer: it is not knowledge of an external system of linguistically significant sounds, or signs, speaker-hearers have to master. Instead, all there is in the world are sounds and marks: it is we who give them their linguistic form

---

[2] The phrase is of course Wittgenstein's from *On Certainty*, §141, and is appealed to by McDowell (1998a, p. 333).

[3] McDowell (1998a, p. 333)

[4] This is the view advocated by Noam Chomsky. As he has put it: 'language has no objective existence apart from its mental representation' in the mind of the speaker, (1972, p. 169 fn.).

and meaning. So it is not the sounds and signs people produce that constitute the subject matter of linguistics, but the *linguistic forms* people impose on those sounds and signs as a result of their internal states. It is because there are creatures like us, with the distinctive linguistic capacities we have, that signs and sounds come to be assigned a meaning and structure at all. On this view, the focus of linguistic inquiry shifts from the actual and potential behaviour of speakers to the internal organization of speakers' minds. The study of language becomes part of the study of mind, and so linguistics—the science of language—is seen as a branch of cognitive psychology.

As speakers, whether we are producing or perceiving speech sounds, it is we who supply whatever linguistic significance they have. The producer's awareness of the linguistic significance of the noises he emits is much like his awareness of his tapping out a tune for another with his fingers. The other may recognize the tune by the rhythmic tapping, or merely hear it as the drumming of fingers. But in the experience of the agent, the rhythm tapped out is an integral part of a whole musical score running through his head.[5] In a similar way, the speaker's psychological states give linguistic form and character to the sounds he experiences himself as producing. His utterances of sounds depend, for their particular linguistic character, on the precise psychological states that give rise to them, just as a bodily movement depends for its identity as an action on the states of mind of the agent performing it.[6]

Whatever experiences one has in producing speech sounds, comprehension of them by listeners is always due to what *they*, in turn, and in virtue of *their* internal apparatus, can make of the sounds uttered. Knowledge of language is a state that enables us to produce and understand a certain range of human speech sounds, as determined by our internal linguistic systems.[7] The difficulty for this account will be to explain how people succeed in communicating with one another, how language appears to put us immediately in touch with the minds of others, and why we often appear to speak the same language.

A correct view of language and our knowledge of language will need to account for our capacity to hear complex meaning in speech sounds and to invest sounds with such meanings; an account that explains our immediate readiness to produce and comprehend utterances of sentences we have never used or heard before. It will also have to explain how, by these means, we succeed in making our minds available to one another.

The traditional conception of language, and its accompanying view of knowledge of language, can be called, following Chomsky, an E-conception. 'E-language' was the term invented by Chomsky for languages conceived of as external, as sets of sentences extensionally characterized, and, we might add, as extended beyond the

---

[5] People are notoriously bad in their confidence judgements about how likely others are to recognize the tune they are tapping.

[6] This is not the view that linguistic productions are reducible to, or fully analysed in terms of, the intentional states such as beliefs and intentions. The mental states involved may be cognitive psychological states of the language faculty or, at any rate psychological states with dedicated linguistic contents.

[7] Chomsky conceives of a language: it is a 'way to speak and understand' rather than that which we make use of in speaking and understanding. See Chomsky, 1993, p. 49.

current reach of their speakers.[8] There are different notions of E-language. On a Platonist view, languages are abstract objects consisting of infinitely many sentences, each of which has at least one meaning in the language. Sentences of a language have a meaning for a speaker if and only if they are part of the language the speaker knows or uses.[9] The difficulty here will be to say what makes one rather than another of the infinitely possible languages the *actual language* of a given speaker, or community of speakers (see below).

By contrast, a social view of E-languages sees them as extrapolations from sets of common practices.[10] Rules enshrined in such public practices extend beyond the furthest reach of existing practice to determine which new combinations of words count as meaningful sentences of the language. In this way, rules dictate the precise contours of the language—the language spoken by those who participate in the practice.

The difficulty for the social view will be to say what counts as participation in a given practice as following rules for one rather than another language. Where the Platonist appeals to an infinity of *meaning facts*, the social theorist appeals to *meaning norms* governing infinitely many applications of the items found in the practice. (See 'Meaning, Rule-Following and Normativity'.) On either of these E conceptions, a language is independent of any individual speaker; on the Platonist version, language is independent of all speakers.

The alternative conception of language, and knowledge of language, takes languages to be individual and internal to the minds of speakers. Let us call it a Cognitive Conception to evoke cognitive–psychological conceptions of language grounded in the psychology of individual language users.[11] On this view languages have no existence independent of human cognition. A change in a speaker's cognitive organization can change his language. Selective loss of cognitive function can lead to loss of the language; and such permanent losses in all human language users would extinguish language altogether. The illusion of language continuing to exist in the absence of appropriately organized human minds would be due, perhaps, to the continued existence of recordings, written documents and signs that would no longer have linguistic significance for anyone.[12] One version of the Cognitive Conception, Chomsky's, admits of no epistemic relation between language and knowledge of language: what is meant by 'language' is just an I-language, a finite part of the speaker's mind/brain: a generative procedure for assigning structural descriptions to

---

[8] 'The standard approaches [in philosophy] to developing a more technical concept [of language] take a language to be a variety of what I called 'E-language', where 'E' is to suggest 'extensional' and 'externalised': for example, a characterization of language as a set of utterance types, or a set of (utterance, meaning) pairs, where meanings are construed in set-theoretic terms. This general approach, however, leads to innumerable problems and is best abandoned . . .' (Chomsky, *Mind and Language*, 1987, p. 179)

[9] Different varieties of Platonism have been advocated by George (1989); Higginbotham (1983); Katz (1990); Lewis, and Schiffer (1994).

[10] Advocates of this view include Dummett (1978); McDowell (1998); and Wiggins (1991)

[11] I avoid the use of 'I-conception' here with its association with I-languages since what Chomsky means by an I-language is a finite state of the mind/brain of a speaker; something that is definitely not an object of the speaker's knowledge.

[12] There is nothing enduring about our prose without anyone left to appreciate it.

expressions.[13] Language is just a means of speaking and understanding. It provides us with an infinite competence but the I-language itself is finite.[14] And since one's knowledge of language is just a state, amounting to possession of an I-language, it does not amount to knowledge *of* anything, certainly not to knowledge of the I-language. On Chomsky's view, nothing much remains of the ordinary notion of a language, nor of speakers' knowledge of language.

What this view downplays is a perfectly respectable notion of linguistic knowledge had by individual speakers. There is a vast amount of specific knowledge the speaker has and about which he is authoritative: including knowledge of what his words mean, knowledge of which arrangements of his words are sentences, and of how utterances of them can and cannot be understood.[15] Of course, knowledge involving sentences has to be derived since we don't carry around knowledge of individual sentences as part of our standing knowledge. Sentences are transient and ephemeral, no sooner produced than replaced by others, and there is evidence that in conversation we are not able to remember the sentences we have just heard even though we keep track of the conversation. Instead our standing knowledge provides the words and means by which we fashion indefinitely many sentences on the hoof and come to have knowledge of them. These are items of conscious knowledge that can be elicited by speaker's linguistic intuitions: judgements that give a speaker immediate and authoritative knowledge of linguistic facts. The states Chomsky is interested, however, are states that fix the facts of speakers' languages. But there is still a vast amount of conscious knowledge the speaker has about expressions of his language fixed by these states. It is an open question whether the states that give rise to the facts we know are themselves states of knowledge.

If so, we need a Cognitivist Conception that can do justice to the experience of the language user, to his having knowledge and being authoritative about what his words mean, about which arrangements of words are sentences, and about how utterances of them can and cannot be understood. To make room for such a view we need to make sense of there being *objects* for such pieces of speaker's knowledge to be about. And yet if the psychological states that determine *the facts* about one's language also *constitute* knowledge of language, how can they also be answerable to those facts as knowledge demands? Can there be something independent of the speaker for the speaker's intuitions to get right or wrong? Call this the problem of the Missing Object of Knowledge. It is about the putative object of knowledge our linguistic intuitions are thought to concern.

Speakers are authoritative, not infallible, in their native speaker intuitions. This authoritative knowledge is special because, although it purports to be about a range of objective facts (—the linguistic facts about one's language—), it is based on

---

[13] See Chomsky, 1987.

[14] See John Collins, 'Faculty Disputes' for a clear account of this point.

[15] A further question which I cannot address here is whether a speaker arrives at knowledge of the meaning of sentences or simply uses knowledge of word meaning and knowledge of syntax to constrain understanding of an utterance of that sentence in context. See 'The Distinction Between Semantics and Pragmatics'.

nothing more than what one takes one's words to mean, and which strings one takes to be grammatical. The problem, then, is to show how there can be a genuine subject matter for these judgements to concern—a range of objective facts about one's language—while at the same time accommodating authoritative knowledge of them. The objectivity of linguistics requires there to be objective facts to which a speaker's linguistic intuitions are answerable—there should be an intelligible gap between linguistic facts and our opinions about them. However, first-person authority requires the linguistic facts to be, pretty much, as we take them to be, for our linguistic intuitions to be largely correct, thus minimizing the gap between opinion and fact. This tension between the objectivity of linguistic facts and first-person authority of linguistic knowledge is a problem for the Cognitive Conception. Chomsky tries to reduce it by giving up claims to knowledge. But this is to deny not just the problem but the phenomena that give rise to it. In what follows, I will argue for a Cognitive Conception of language and knowledge of language that offers a solution to the Missing Object of Knowledge Problem, thereby safeguarding a genuine notion of speaker's knowledge.

Speakers' intuitions deliver information about the meaning of words and acceptability, or grammaticality, of word strings. We hear certain word strings as sentences, and where strings are ambiguous, what we hear is the utterance of one or other sentence.[16] We do not hear both readings of a string at once, or something neutral between the two. Our hearing a string as structured is why we hear it as the utterance of one sentence and not another. To do this we seem to draw on knowledge of word meaning and knowledge of grammar to extract key linguistic information from the string of words we hear uttered: we hear and interpret it as we do because of the joint exercise of these two kinds of knowledge. And although the product is experienced as a unified, conscious experience of what was said, we are not obliged to suppose that these two kinds of knowledge target the same aspects of linguistic reality. There is no reason to suppose there is a single locus of linguistic significance corresponding to what we are aware of in conscious speech. Meaning and structure play a joint role in creating linguistic objects but may occupy different locations in the world or the mind: they may be properties of quite different things.

There is an interesting puzzle when we compare our understanding of the notions of meaning and knowledge of meaning with our understand of the notions of grammar and our knowledge of grammar. In the case of grammar we know a great deal and we have developed well-attested theories of the syntax of natural languages that make detailed and specific claims about the structure of language. However, when we turn to our *knowledge* of syntax things are much less clear. Can speakers be credited with tacit knowledge of the syntactic properties described by theories of

---

[16] Strictly speaking, sentences are not ambiguous, only strings are ambiguous. A sentence has a structural organization, its constituents stand in grammatical relations to one another, it can be interpreted in a certain way. A string of words can have more than one internal organization, its elements can stand in different grammatical relations to one another and it can support different interpretations. Sentences type utterances. Utterances have tokens but sentences do not. Utterances can be ambiguous, sentences cannot.

their language? What is the nature of this knowledge? Despite well-advanced theories of syntax, accounts of our knowledge of syntax are problematic and controversial. However, when it comes to word meaning it is just the reverse. Our knowledge of word meaning is not in doubt: it is far from controversial to say that we know what a word means. If I ask you whether you know what 'pleached' means, you can immediately tell me. However, we have very little idea what a correct theory of word meaning would look like. We are not even sure what materials or primitives a theory of word meaning should employ. This puzzle alone should make us wonder whether meaning properties and syntactic properties are properties of the same thing.

Returning to Dummett's way of posing the problem, it is important to understand how knowledge of language *effects* the difference between hearing speech sounds as noises and hearing them as meaningful speech. For we have seen that there are two very different directions of explanation. Does that knowledge equip us to speak and understand *the* language spoken by those around us? Or does the presence of this kind of knowledge in human minds explain the very existence of language: is it knowledge in the minds of individual speakers that makes language *language*? As we shall see, this view comports best with empirical findings. But a fully satisfying account must meet several desiderata. We must respect the phenomenological datum that we hear more in the speech sounds when we have learned a language. We need an account of what knowledge of language gives us knowledge *of*. We need to respect the differences between knowledge of word meaning and knowledge of grammar. And we need to explain how our possessing such knowledge equips us to speak our minds and know the minds of others?

Let us start with our ability to experience sounds as speech. For before we can even talk about words, grammatical relations, and sentences we have to remember that speech episodes start as mere encounters with sounds, and that sounds by themselves are not identical with words, grammatical structures or sentences. The acoustic properties of speech and the linguistic material hearers perceive in it are not so easily aligned. Finding words in a sound stream is difficult for a learner of a foreign language. Grammatical relations occur in the gaps between the words in sentences. The syntactic arrangement of expressions is hierarchical and not linear or temporal. So the gap between words or syntax and sounds is vast. To understand how the gap is bridged we must begin by asking, as Dummett does, what gives the sounds people utter their linguistic form and character: the linguistic form and character they have *for us*.

37.4 Experiencing Sounds as Language

Acquisition of a first language should not be modelled on second language learning. Nonetheless, the experience of listening to speakers of an utterly foreign language is instructive. It reminds us that at one level all that goes on in the environment when we speak is the issuing of certain sounds. Even though this is not how speakers perceive the sounds of their language: to others they are just sounds. And far from being a philosophical distortion of the phenomena: we can actually perceive things this way in the foreign case. When listening to people speaking French or Japanese all that some people hear is a continuous sound stream with occasional pauses. Others will hear people engaging in intelligible speech. Speakers talk in a continuous flow of sounds, joining one sound to another and breaking off only when they need breath. So we have difficulty even recognizing the word boundaries in a foreign language since they do not correlate with breaks in the acoustic signal. Several properties we appear to perceive in speech do not correlate with acoustic properties of speech sounds at all. (We shall consider these below at 37.5.) So how does knowing a language enable us to perceive more in the speech sounds we listen to? How does knowing French or Japanese help us hear or see something that others miss?[17] In the case of a second language, we have good answers to questions (i) and (ii) in 37.2 about our knowledge of language. We can set out what the speaker has come to know by charting the explicit linguistic training he or she received in their laborious efforts to learn the language. But things are very different with a first language and these answers won't do. For a start, there is little evidence of explicit training in syntax. Some language learners receive no training of any kind at all. Secondly, it is obvious that in learning a second language one is relying on the fact that one already speaks a language and much of the learning is at first a matter of translation between one language and the other. It cannot be like this for the infant acquiring its first language.[18]

Although much more is experienced in speech sounds by those who know the language than by those who don't, the patterns the former 'perceive *in*' the sounds produced by speakers cannot be identified with, or taken to inhere in, the physical properties of the sound waves hearers encounter. The conscious auditory images of words, phrases or sentences, are inner mental objects, 'not physical phenomena inhering in sound waves' (Harris and Lindsay, 2003, p. 203). The same is true of most of the linguistic information we glean from speech. Such information consists of phonological patterns, word patterns, grammatical patterns, including hierarchical configurations of elements and dependencies between them, word meanings and logical scope. Information about such phenomena must be drawn upon in order to hear the sound stream as an unfolding sequence of meaningful words that makes up a particular sentence. But how can all the relevant information be extracted from the speech sounds one encounters? What is there in the much richer experience of one who knows the language is not *there* in the sounds emitted by the speaker:

[17] The seeing case is subsidiary if it is reading the language, though in the case of congenitally deaf language learners who use signing to communicate in the language, seeing may be the right modality from which to extent information about sentences.

[18] The idea that *we* 'translate' into thought is a non-starter. There is no such conscious experience in the home language: speech perception is fast and automatic and requires no conscious conversion of sounds first heard without any meaning. Nor do we have transparent access to the form and character of thought, so it is not clear how we would go about correlating an item of thought with a linguistic item. None of this rules out the idea of mechanisms that automatically map sounds or signs of the public medium into a language of thought. But explaining how this works is no easier than explaining how our knowledge of language makes possible our hearing of significant speech in the sounds we encounter. The two accounts may end up as notational variants.

'linguistic information is projected by means of articulations but is not embodied in them' (*Ibid.*, p. 203). The linguistic information read into, or onto, those sounds is simply part of 'the specifically human way with sounds' (*Ibid.*, p. 203).

However, according to John McDowell, what we perceive in speech, in virtue of having learned a language, is something lying open to view of the surface of linguistic practice. These are linguistic phenomena that we come to perceive as a result of acquiring knowledge of the language: a range of facts that were not previously perceptible and that come into view as we find our way into the language. But how does what goes on in us when we learn a language enable us to perceive these supposedly linguistic facts? McDowell thinks there is no way to explain language acquisition, or to account for what we know in terms available to people outside the practice. However, despite McDowell's self-imposed quietist embargo on giving explanations, he cannot resist giving hints about how the process might go. The acquisition of linguistic knowledge, he tells us, is a matter of drilling in certain behavioural routines, using sentences at first without fully understanding them.[19] So the question for him is:

How can drilling in a behavioural repertoire extend one's perceptual capacities—cause one to be directly aware of facts of which one would not otherwise be aware?   (McDowell, 1998a, p. 333)

McDowell admits that this is a very difficult question to answer but one could be forgiven for thinking that, on the contrary, it was impossible because it is the wrong question. No behavioural drilling could extend one's capacities for perceptual experience of meaningful sentences, nor could a repertoire of behavioural routines for the use of particular sentences yield any insight into why the learner extends his use and understanding of utterances, in potentially infinitely many ways, to some arrangements of words but not others.[20] McDowell suggests that we cannot explain how people arrive at their knowledge of sentence meaning in indefinitely many cases, but we can describe what contents people would hear assertoric utterances of those sentences as expressing.[21] We do this by means of a Tarskian truth-theory for the language of the linguistic community. The T-sentences will be homophonic but there

---

[19] See McDowell, 'Meaning. Communication and Knowledge', pp. 47–9.

[20] Chomsky's devastating 1959 critique of Skinner's account of verbal behaviour as conditioned learning showed how little of what was needed could be accomplished by a behaviourist account of language acquisition. Readers are advised to consult the details.

[21] See McDowell, 1998, p. 180. Note he does say, 'The ability to comprehend heard speech is an information-processing capacity, and the theory would describe it by articulating in detail the relation, which defines the capacity, between input information and output information', p. 179. However, to describe is not to explain and whatever mechanisms are responsible for this information processing capacity they do not amount to dealings with content. Later in the same article, McDowell tells us that; 'There is no merit in a conception of the mind that permits us to speculate about its states, conceived as states of a hypothesised mechanism, with a breezy lack of concern for facts about explicit awareness.' This way of thinking is described as 'philistine' and leads to darkness within. But one may wonder where the charge of philistinism belongs if there are explanations of linguistic intuitions to be had, by reference to underlying states, about why states of explicit awareness take the linguistic form and character they do and we refuse to avail ourselves of them and opt instead for mystery.

will be infinitely many of them and so the question remains how speakers in a linguistic practice succeed in conforming to the theory and arrive at indefinitely many pieces of knowledge described by the theory. The theory will identify constituent structure in sentences, and see the meaning of each sentence as having been assembled by the legitimate syntactic combining of meaningful parts. But talk of meaningful parts and wholes will be confined to the workings of the theory. Whenever we have such knowledge, however acquired, we simply perceive the meanings that lie open to view on the surface of our practice.

What precisely is the nature of the linguistic facts that become directly perceptually available to us as a result of learning the language? And what relations do such facts bear to the acoustic properties of the sounds uttered? McDowell says we hear the meaning in people's words? And while there is an authentic phenomenological insight here, we do hear meaning in *words*, but how do we hear *words* and *sentences* in the sounds people utter? It is necessary to identify the linguistic items we hear when we hear sounds as linguistically meaningful. Yet nothing in the phenomenological claim settles the issue of the location of the linguistic properties linguists describe. McDowell thinks of the words as out there, and he even supposes the same about syntax, as if it were to be found in the facts about behaviour we are presented with. He talks of a 'match between theoretical syntax and actual utterance-events' (1998, p. 146). The hard physical facts are thought to constrain 'the structural properties of physical utterance-events that permit the language to be given a syntactic description' (*Ibid.*). He tells us that a relation 'must hold between the structures assigned to sentences by the syntax with which the theory operates . . . and configurations observable in physical utterance-events' (*Ibid.*). But the overwhelming data from linguistics teach us to expect no such match between the syntax our best theories assign to sentences and the physical arrangements of uttered sounds (see Section 37.5 below). Words are only marginally easier to identify with particular ranges of sound. But if we reject McDowell's talk of a match between syntax and utterance-events, and reject the account of behavioural drilling in the use of whole, but at first unintelligible, sentences,[22] how do we come to have knowledge of the public language, and how does it help us secure the transition from facts about sound to facts about linguistic meaning?

According to McDowell, speaker-hearers directly perceive the linguistic facts displayed in the practice, however to know *the* language thereby displayed both speaker hearers and theorists of that language need a way to identity the relevant range of facts that belong to *the* language. What is that range of facts, and how do the relevant linguistic properties of words and sentences help speaker-hearers to identify them?

To say more about what enables us to experience a certain range of human sounds as part of *a language* we first need to say something more specific about what it is for something to be *a language*: to say more about what makes language *language*.

---

[22] This idea seems empirically flawed too. Children between the ages of 12 and 20 months are at the one-word and two-word stage. They show an understanding of these words and acquire many before they are able to use sentences. The use of sentences suddenly occurs at the syntax spurt at around 20–24 months.

At the very least, by *language* we mean a system for building complex structures combinatorially out of a stock of meaningful items—words or signs (in the case of a sign language)—and non-meaningful items—morpheme endings, phonemes, specific speech gestures. The structures humans build are recursive and potentially infinite in number despite employing only finitely many discrete elements and rules to generate them. While these syntactically complex combinatorial structures vary across human languages they do so within strict parametric limits, and have many properties in common.

The discrete infinity this system provides is built out of lexical items from a stock of between 50,000 and 120,000 items and appears to be species specific. Apes trained to use sign language or a keyboard may develop between a hundred and two hundred items at most and may combine them in two and three word combinations, without extending naturally and spontaneously to larger and larger combinations, as human children do. Moreover, chimpanzees do not go on acquiring vocabulary at the fast rate of the infant, nor is there sufficient evidence (in so far as they show elementary combining of symbols) of a capacity for *syntactic* combining of linguistic elements.

Whatever we should say of apes' word or symbol combining there is no evidence of the recursive structure building that characterizes the human linguistic capacity. Many animals show only sequence and signalling in fixed, alternating and repeated patterns. However, syntax requires hierarchical structuring. The requests, commands and assertions children make are syntactically structured. According to Hauser, Chomsky and Fitch (2002) the language faculty, narrowly conceived (FLN), is what equips us with the capacity for recursive structure building and should be distinguished from the faculty of language broadly conceived (FLB), involved in the totality of our linguistic communication. Hauser, Chomsky, and Fitch say:

most, if not all, of FLB is based on mechanisms shared with nonhuman animals . . . In contrast, we suggest that FLN—the computational mechanism of recursion—is recently evolved and unique to our species (p. 1573). We propose in this hypothesis that FLN comprises only the core computational mechanisms of recursion as they appear in narrow syntax and the mappings to the interfaces (p. 1573), the interfaces with mechanisms for speech perception and production, and the cognitive system for conceptual thinking and intention (p. 1573)

Could animals recruit recursion from elsewhere? There is evidence that many animals have numerosity and even some arithmetic but this is usually limited to between 4 and 6 items. Even monkeys taught to count up to 4 and do some subtraction and addition, do not naturally progress to 5 but have to be taught to deal with this new number all over again through repeated trials. They show no ability, of the sort the child has, to extend the series indefinitely; that is, they have no concept of successor.

Non-human primates do not have the capacity for language just characterized. What they do have is a variety of systems for (non-linguistic) communication. We are unique both in our handling of recursive structure and of our capacity to encode this in a limited range of speech sounds. And this ability to apprehend and integrate, so rapidly, the phonetic, syntactic and semantic information in virtue of which sounds events are recognized as linguistically significant speech is a staggering achievement and requires explanation. Nothing we are offered in terms of drilling in behavioural routines, or of matches between syntax and utterance-events begins to touch this problem or even to indicate how what is going on amounts to *linguistic* activity.

The perceptual experience of one who has learned the language is rich and complex but McDowell is missing much of the complexity involved, even in talk of our use of sentences. A sentence is a linguistic structured string of meaningful items (some with endings) that play certain grammatical roles in the sentence. The syntactic configurations will constrain in various ways the semantic interpretations we can give to a sentence, and how the sentence uttered will be perceived. Syntax plays a vital role in just which sentence is perceived and in what we take the uttered sounds to mean. How do we become apprised of these syntactic properties, how do we take them into account, and how does our knowledge of the language gained through participation in a common practice connect us with them?

What enables a child who at first hears only sounds to come to hear them as meaningful speech? How does it make the transition from one who lacks this capacity to someone who has it? And if it is distinctive linguistic knowledge, along with other cognitive, perceptual and motor skills, that explains our capacities to produce and comprehend meaningful speech, then a full explanation demands an account of the nature of that linguistic knowledge and what precisely it gives us knowledge *of*. We have been looking in vein for some way for the supposedly recruited public language to be used to make the difference between hearing what people say in speaking the language and merely hearing human noises but so far we have made no progress. Exploring an idea he ultimately rejects, Michael Dummett suggests:

The natural answer is what makes the difference is the fact that both speakers understand or know the language. Each has, so to speak, the same piece of internal (mental) equipment, which enables each to interpret the utterances of the other as an expression of thought, and to convert his own thoughts into sentences that the other can likewise understand. It thus seems as though the key to the explanation of the expressive power which makes a language a language is an individual speaker's mastery of the language; and this mastery . . . requires the notion of knowledge for its explication.   (Dummett, 1978, p. 97)

Dummett's suggestion looks at first to be offering a Cognitive Conception of language and our knowledge of language, but this is not what he intends. It is the language speaker-hearers know and share that explains their ability to express and convey indefinitely many things. Talk of internal equipment may be important for explaining how people keep in touch with, or keep track of, the language, but on this view it is still *the language itself* that is mastered and that affords the possibility of indefinitely many meaning possibilities. It is through mastery of the public language, albeit by means of a piece of internal equipment, (or for Dummett, the speaker's having certain practical and theoretical abilities) that the individual is able to take advantage of the expressive possibilities the language provides. Despite talk of internal mechanisms, speakers and hearers are still here seen as reaching for the same language, and the worry for Dummett is just how they can each be sure that the hypothesized mechanisms relate them to the same words and meanings. This picture has a powerful grip on our imaginations. What we are calling *the* language and *the* meanings of words is supposed to depend on the workings of a common language mastered by several individuals. But just how do they master the same public language? What is its nature and what does it provide? them with knowledge of? An what enables individuals to acquire knowledge of precisely that language and put it to use themselves?

37.5 ACQUIRING KNOWLEDGE
OF LANGUAGE

Given the complexity of language and our knowledge of it, there is little or no reason to suppose that children learn language by inductively generalizing from their linguistic experience. Such inductive explanations would have to show how exposure to others' use of language, first experienced as sound, leads the child to establish a highly complex and elaborate system for producing and understanding speech. Even if we had a ready explanation of how they recognize words from the sound stream itself, inductive explanations of their knowledge of syntax are implausible. Why, for instance, do learners never treat (1) and (2) as similar, despite having the same number of words of the same grammatical category in the same linear order?[23]

(1) John is easy to please
(2) John is eager to please

The fact that they don't can be shown by learners accepting the re-arrangement of (1) as (3), but never attempting the re-arrangement of (2) as (4).

(3) It is easy to please John
(4) *It is eager to please John

Also, why is it that no speaker interprets (8) in relation to (7) in the same way they interpret (6) in relation to (5)? Instead speakers suppose (8) means that John is too clever for anyone to catch him.

(5) John ate an apple
(6) John ate
(7) John is too clever to catch Peter
(8) John is too clever to catch

And why do no children attempt at first to form questions from statements by reversing the first two words of the sentence as in (11) when they have seen this done in cases like (9) and (10)?

(9) Peter is asleep

---

[23] The examples come from Chomsky (1965). [left justify]

(10) Is Peter asleep?
(11) *Man the is laughing?

Why *don't* they use the 'is' as the point around which to attempt the needed inversion? If they formed the generalization that the first 'is' mattered we would expect children to say (13) as the question form of (12). But they never do.

(12) The man who is laughing is silly
(13) *Is the man who laughing is silly?

We need to explain why *no* children attempt these most natural inductive generalizations. The negative facts about what speakers do *not* do are as important to explain here as the positive facts, if we are to formulate the correct explanatory generalizations. Notice too that children are not explicitly taught these regularities and yet as speaker-hearers they all conform to structure-dependent generalizations that must be given in terms of, not surface arrangements, but an underlying level of logical form (see 'Logical Form and LF). How would one learn generalizations about logical form from inductive generalizations over the surface forms from which they can depart so significantly?

Moreover, there are properties of grammatical structure common to all human languages, exemplified in the sentences produced by children around the ages of three or four years of age. Consider the Binding Principles that explain why we treat the pronoun 'him' and proper name 'John' as disjoint in reference in (14) and the reflexive pronoun or anaphor 'himself' as referentially dependent on 'John' in (15). By contrast, it is left open in (16) that 'John' and 'him' could take the same reference. That the position is not referentially dependent on 'John' can be seen in the unacceptable (17) where the anaphor cannot depend for it's referent on 'John'.

(14) [John shaved him]
(15) [John shaved himself]
(16) [[John's mother] shaved him]
(17) *[[John's mother] shaved himself]
(18) Peter said that [John shaved him]
(19) Peter said that [John shaved himself]

The asymmetric relations between the subject 'John' in the noun phrase (NP) and the object 'him' or 'himself' in the verb phrase (VP) in (14) and (15) ensures a syntactic configuration known as c-command.[24] An item in the syntax can referentially bind another when it c-commands it. Universal Principles of Binding tell us that:

(20) Principle A: An anaphor is bound in its domain
(21) Principle B: A pronoun is free in its domain

The domain of anaphors ('himself', 'herself', 'each other') and pronouns ('him' 'she', 'them') is indicated by bracketing in the above examples. In (16) and (17), the possessive noun 'John's' does not c-command the pronoun or the anaphor and cannot

---

[24] In tree-geometric terms, an expression α c-commands an expression β when the first branching node dominating α dominates β. For more on c-command and binding see Chomsky, 1995.

bind them. Notice, that a pronoun must not be 'too near' to its referential antecedent and an anaphor must not be 'too far away'. Hence, 'him' cannot be referentially bound by 'John' in (18) and 'himself' cannot be referentially bound by 'Peter' in (19). The semantic facts about how we use and understand (14) to (19) referentially are known to all speakers. They are also determined by configurational facts about syntactic structure. Were sentences not structured in an asymmetric and hierarchical NP-VP structure but simply linearly ordered as Noun–Verb–Noun we could not explain the abundant data: data that obtain in all human languages regardless of the surface order of subjects and verbs. Children all over the world in their early uses of sentences conform to these universal properties of structure despite the differences in the their experience, intelligence, and background culture.[25] How do all of them succeed, in pretty much the same time course, in closing the gap between what experience provides them with and the vastly greater knowledge they end up having about the speech sounds around them? The absence of any adequate explanation of how they do this on the basis of inductive learning strongly indicates that part of the cognitive system must be dedicated to arriving at this highly intricate form of knowledge on the basis of exposure to random and limited amounts of data.[26] As Noam Chomsky puts it:

The problem, then, is to determine the innate endowment that serves to bridge the gap between experience and knowledge attained.   (Chomsky, 1986)

The special, dedicated component that enables the normally functioning infant to acquire any of the possible human languages, on the basis of exposure to a course of experience, is the Language Faculty (narrowly described).[27] As mentioned above, it is a component of the mind/brain with which humans are uniquely endowed. And so far this is the only serious proposal we have about how humans acquire grammatical knowledge of their first language. The forlorn idea that we learn to do all this by analogy with the repetitive learning of a manual skill is a non-starter and does not merit serious discussion. There is no evidence that practice takes place or that mistakes of the kind expected in such training actually occur. What needs to be explained is why a speaker, who has had exposure to a limited set of utterances, can produce indefinitely many new ones and 'distinguish a certain set of "grammatical" utterances, among utterances [of sentences] that he has never heard and might never produce' and in doing so 'projects his past linguistic experience to include certain new utterances and excludes others'. (Chomsky, 1955, p. 61) Conformity to innate principles of grammar would explain how we do this, but not much else would.

[25] See Stephen Crain, 'Language Acquisition in the Absence of Experience' Behavioural and Brain Sciences, 1991.

[26] Limited success has been achieved in capturing individual patterns of structure or particular grammatical regularities through computational techniques for capturing statistical similarities across a large corpus (see Elman, *et al.*). But it is the bewildering number of patterns and highly interdependent regularities that have to be captured and so far the only way to encode such a system is through a finite set of highly interactive grammatical principles governing those structures that permit a certain flexibility within a strict parametric range.

[27] Empirical support for this view is to be found Chomsky, 1955, 1965, 1980, 1986.

Humans are the only creatures able to engage in such *linguistic* communication, because they alone are innately endowed with a language faculty that gives them the capacity to acquire any one of the possible human languages on exposure to a particular course of experience).[28],[29] These findings strongly suggest that the existence of languages is due to the existence of humans with minds like ours. If this is the case, language would not exist without us. However, the dependence of language on minds is not enough to establish claims about the location of linguistic phenomena and some philosophers remain wedded to the idea that languages exist external to, or even independently of, the minds of human language users, supposing that it is for these genetic reasons, or for some other non-linguistic reasons, that we may be the only creatures capable of accessing and exploiting the intricacies of languages.

Such philosophers still need to accommodate the facts about language that make language *language*. The essential properties of a language, those on which its identity as language depends—properties of syntactic structure, case and theta-role assignment, c-command, binding—are not brute properties of the physical sounds uttered, nor are they all properties experienced in our conscious reception of speech; although they can have precisely predictable effects on speakers' conscious linguistic intuitions.

An argument can now be given for a Cognitivist Conception of language and knowledge of language as follows. Structure is essential to language, to the very identity of sentences that count as part of our language, but we cannot locate these structural properties in the physical or phenomenal world of speaker-hearers. The other option is in a part of the mind, a special cognitive component, dedicated to handling language. According to the Cognitive Conception, the structural properties in question are sub-personally represented in the language faculty: a species-specific and largely innate component of the human mind. Note that these mental representations of linguistic structure play a content-involving causal role in shaping the first-person linguistic experience of the speaker-hearer, in giving one the linguistic experience one has. We can formulate hypotheses about the precise character of those syntactic representations by observing their impact on the form and character of a speaker-hearer's linguistic intuitions. What must her internalized grammar be like, we can ask, in order for her to find these arrangements of words acceptable but not those; for her to be able to interpret a sentence in this way but not in that. To arrive at specific hypotheses about the internalized grammar we reason counterfactually:

---

[28] Speakers come equipped with universal grammar, which prescribes a certain structural organization but leaves open certain permitted variations within strict parametric ranges. For example, Italians can use null subject sentences: sentences with a phonetically null subject position (e.g. __ha parlata/Gianni ha parlata), but English speakers cannot. Part of a child's acquisition and in which it does need information from its environment is to help it set the parameter for a null or non-null subject for its language. Much of syntactic acquisition is parameter setting, triggered by the child's linguistic environment.

[29] This is not to deny the fact that non-human animals have rich and complex systems of communication. It is simply to point out that they are non-linguistic. Humans are also capable of a good deal of non-linguistic communication, from a nod and a wink to raising one's eyebrows and looking at one's watch to signal to another it is time to go.

had the grammar been different, had it not respected a particular constraint then it would have been possible to hear certain utterances differently. For example, take the following ambiguous string:

(22) I saw her duck and swallow.

We can hear it in two different ways according to the readings shown in the following syntactic disambiguations:

(22a) I saw her [NP [N duck] and [N swallow]]
(22b) I saw her [VP [V duck] and [V swallow]]

But the question is why can't we hear it as four-ways ambiguous? We cannot even have the conscious experience of either of the two other readings. As theorists we can see they are logically possible:

(22c) ?I saw her [[N duck] and [V swallow]]
(22d) ?I saw her [[V duck] and [N swallow]]

but as speaker-hearers we cannot even consciously experience these ways of construing (22).[30] Why not? The explanation is that the internalized grammar that shapes and conditions our conscious experience of speech respects a co-ordination constraint. The co-ordination constraint says that we can conjoin expressions of the same syntactic category: e.g. NP and NP, VP and VP, PP and PP, S and S, etc, but not PP and VP, or VP and NP.[31] This is why we do not accept as grammatical, or intelligible, putative sentences like:

(23) *She coughed and the boy.

There is no reason why our grammars had to obey a co-ordination constraint but evidence from the conscious experience of speaker-hearers, elicited by their linguistic intuitions, confirm that the grammars that make up our linguistic competences do satisfy such a constraint. The methodology here shows why the conscious experiences of the language user—immediate and authoritative knowledge of language in the form of linguistic intuitions—do play a role in constructing explanatory adequate theories of our linguistic, and in particular, syntactic competence, pace Chomsky.[32]

Notice that the underlying states of our linguistic system are *content-involving* states. They *represent* the syntactic structure of sentences. They are not merely syntactic: formal symbols whose syntactic shape has a causal effect on our conscious states. When talking about syntax, philosophers are prone to make this vehicle-content conflation about such representations. Saying that we, or more accurately our language faculty, represents syntactic structure is not the same as saying that these are just syntactic representations, as though they had to take the syntactic structure of the sentence whose structure they represent. There is no reason why a

---

[30] My thanks to Emma Borg for pointing out this example.

[31] We may need to consider the syntactic category of a predicate to accommodate more difficult cases. The details can be finessed by a proper syntactic theory.

[32] See Chomsky, 2000.

representation of sentence structure has itself to have the *structure represented*, any more than a red idea has to be red. It is *what* those underlying representations represent, not the *way* they represent it, that plays the crucial role in fixing the linguistic character and content we experience in perceived speech.

What alternative is there to locating the essential properties of linguistic structure that make language *language* in the mind of speakers and listeners? The prospects for the traditional view of language as a social practice look bleak. It may be said that as participants in the practice we can just tell which strings of words are grammatical and which ones are not. But our being able to tell, to perceive which sentence was uttered, already takes into account what it is in us that shapes these perceptions and gives us our way of finding the utterance intelligible, permitting some interpretations and not others, hearing ambiguous strings one way and not another. In the case of the Cognitive Conception we have detailed explanations of why we hear some arrangements of words as grammatical sentences and others as not. On the social view we have none. It is also false to say that we don't need explanations because we can just tell which sentences are grammatical.[33] We are not infallible. When first asked whether sentence (24) is ambiguous most speakers will say no.

(24) I almost had my wallet stolen.

However, if we point out that they could have had their wallet stolen and were trying to steal it back when they we spotted and withdrew, or were in the process of having a third party try to steal it back from the thief when the attempt was foiled, we can see that (24) would do to report what happened. The sentence is three-ways ambiguous: I almost had my wallet stolen from me/for me/by me. An inverse case is the illusion of grammatical well-formedness:

(25) Many more people have been to Paris than I have.

At first most people will treat (25) as well formed and interpretable, but further reflection will show them there is nothing it could possibly mean.[34] Speakers' immediate intuitions are authoritative but not infallible. They can be corrected and the speaker can come to find out more about the character of *his* or *her* linguistic system.[35] We need an explanation of these facts and of the mistakes we make in performance. Such an explanation draws a distinction between competence and performance.

An alternative remains. For perhaps a Platonist E-conception could treat structural properties as part of the abstract realm. But now we need some account of how these properties of abstract objects have an impact on a speaker-hearer's intuitions and

---

[33] This would be like saying we do not need a theory of gravity since if you bring me objects I will tell you which ones fall.

[34] My thanks to Paul Pietroski for the use of this example.

[35] Even if it was possible to say we don't need explanations because as participants in the practice we know which arrangements of words are grammatical, since explanations *can* be given, this would be like saying to Newton, we don't need an account of gravity because if you bring me the objects I will tell you which ones fall. I take the moral is if genuine explanations are available we should avail ourselves of them.

how speaker-hearers conform to generalizations framed in terms of those structural properties. If languages are either social or platonic abstract objects, existing beyond individual speakers or outside space and time, there will have to be some finite fact about speakers' knowledge, or use of language, or some other property or practice, that relates them to one rather than another of these social, or abstract objects. The difficulty will be to say what makes one of these languages the actual language of a given speaker or a group, and just what is encompassed by that speaker's language. What language does the speaker speak and what is the precise extent of a speaker's language? So far we have had little by way of answers on the social E-conception of languages sustained by common practices. But Platonism provides a more robust idea of language, viewing it as a system of meaningful expressions existing independently of us: a system we must be related to in order to express and communicate our thoughts. The Platonist option makes it clear how languages can be characterized in full but it leaves the problem of what it is for speakers to use and understand these languages.[36]

In studying language the philosopher or linguist needs some way to delineate the whole language of a given speaker, or community, taking in the whole range of legitimate expressions in that language. This requires us to delineate all and only the meaningful and grammatical expressions of the language, even though all we have observed to date are the finitely many uses of the language speakers have displayed. How are we to extrapolate correctly beyond these observed uses to the case of as yet unused sentences, which speakers could, if presented with them, easily recognize as belonging to their language? How do we fix the full extent of a natural language?

37.5.1 Must the Study of Language Involve Reference to Speakers?

If we simply define languages without reference to speakers—as we do in purely formal languages—we can, using whatever formal means are at our disposal, construct infinitely many possible languages, each described in terms of an ordered pair $L = \langle \Sigma, M \rangle$ where Σ is the set of sentences and M is the set of meaning specifications, one for each of the sentences in Σ. (See M. Davies, 1981, pp. 5–6, D. Lewis 1983.) Assuming there is no ambiguity, we can treat L as a function from sentences in Σ to meaning-specifications in M, so $L(s) = p$, where p is the proposition that is the meaning of sentence s.

Each specified language L is conceived as an abstract object owing nothing to human nature. But the question is how (some of) these formally described languages can be the *natural languages* spoken by *actual speakers* or populations? If we assume

---

[36] A quick way with the Platonist options would be to point out we need an internal way to recapitulate the structures of the abstract domain in order to keep our sights fixed on one of these abstract objects. So why not settle for an account of the character of a speaker's representations in order to account for the properties of the speaker's language? We could then just slough-off the abstract structures, treating them as mere projections of the speaker's inner linguistic systems.

an exhaustive specification of the infinitely many combinations of sentence-meaning pairs, we can perhaps assume that the language of a given speaker or population is among the set of abstract objects of type $\langle \Sigma, M \rangle$. But which of the infinitely many possible languages is the *actual language* of a given set of speakers or speaker? This is the problem of defining the *actual language relation* between a speaker (or population) and a language L.[37]

A language L is the actual language of a given population P iff R(L,P)

The problem is to solve for R. What is the relation in question? If we can find out we will learn, it is supposed, in what way meaning and other linguistic properties supervene on the psychological states or social practices of language users.

The difficulty is that each language is itself infinitely large, permitting the construction of infinitely many well-formed meaningful sentences. But speakers will only ever produce finitely many utterances. How are we to know which of these infinitely large objects *is* the language spoken by a speaker, or set of speakers, if they can only ever exhibit finitely many uses of the language? The fragment they produce could be extended or enlarged in infinitely many different ways thus leaving it open which L is the language they are actually speaking.

(P)   What is it for a given language L to be the actual language a person uses?

However that relation is defined we will still want to an answer to the question:

(Λ)   What enables a person to understand indefinitely many sentences of his language?

Question (Λ) asks what equips us to do what we do linguistically? It is subtly different from the question:

(Ψ)   How do we actually produce and comprehend utterances?

which asks how we make use of our equipment to do what we do. Attempting answers to (Ψ) is a proper task for the psychology or psycholinguistics, while attempting answers to (Λ) is the proper task for generative linguistics. The linguist's question targets a particular conception of language and knowledge of language that proves theoretically fruitful and that diverges considerably from the Platonist's conception.

The Platonist philosopher of language has to say what secures the relation between a speaker and the language he speaks, where a language is itself a relation between infinitely many finite sentences and an infinite class of meanings. In that way we'll be able to say what is it for infinitely many sentences to mean something for a person since:

(S)   If L is x's actual language then what a sentence means for x is what it means in L.

---

[37] The problem was first discussed by David Lewis in response to challenge by Stephen Schiffer. I follow Schiffer, more or less in the presentation of the problem, though I reject his definitions of language that uses finite sequences of 'types of marks or sounds' as belonging to the set in the first member of the pairs. We cannot begin with sounds for the reasons that have just been rehearsed.

Fix the language the person is using, and since that language has infinitely many sentences with meanings the person has a language with infinitely many sentences that are meaningful *for him*. What of his knowledge of language? He will not be able to understand or know the meanings of any but a minority of the sentences of his language: nevertheless, if this is the language he uses then, according to Stephen Schiffer, he knows the language 'in the sense of knowing a language in which you ipso facto know the languages you use' (2005, p. 16). But what sense is that? Is knowledge of language to be equated with a person's use of language, or ability to use a language? This deflated (or deflationist) conception of linguistic knowledge converts the problem of accounting for our knowledge of language into the problem of explaining what it is for us to use a language. What is it about our use of language that secures the *actual language relation* to the abstract object L as the actual language we use?

In his paper 'Actual Language Relations', Schiffer considers a range of problems we face. The finite use of language doesn't seem to determine which infinite language we are using. For even if there was a practice of speakers uttering sentences of L with the meanings they have in L, this would only account for their conformity to L within a finite fragment of it. And given that there are infinitely many continuations of sentence-meaning pairs diverging beyond that point, all consistent with the sentence-meanings pairings in the fragment, what connects us to one rather than another of these languages? The problem is to understand how the used fragment of language can uniquely relate us to the unused part of our language. The problem is how to extend what we regard as the meanings and structures of the sentences used to the unused parts of the same language: what David Lewis calls *the meaning-without-use problem*.

A natural thought is that there are principles at work governing the grammaticality and meaning of the sentences in the used fragment that extend to sentences in the language as a whole. If we can discover the principles or rules governing the workings of the language fragment we can extrapolate to the properties of sentences in the whole of the language. To do so we need to figure out the rules of syntax and semantics that generate the sentences of the fragment that will also generate the rest of the sentences in L. This suggestion gives rise to L_G.

[L_G] L is the actual language of a given population P iff every adequate grammar that generates the fragment used by P is a grammar of L.

Lewis opted for this solution and after abandoning a number of attempts to solve the problem of the actual language relation in terms of conventions of trust and truthfulness. It requires extrapolation from the used fragment by a grammar for the whole language that covers that fragment:

First use *somehow* determines meaning for the fragment of the language that is actually used. There are rules of syntax and semantics that generate the right sentences with the right meanings within the used fragment. These rules also generate other, longer sentences, with meanings, outside the used fragment. Use determines some meanings, those meanings determine the rules, and the rule determine the rest of the meanings. Thus use determines meaning, in part directly and in part indirectly, for the entire language. ('Meaning without Use: Reply to Hawthorne', p. 149, italicsmine.)

But how do we know that *a* grammar that generates the sentences in the fragment is *the* grammar of the language as a whole and will continue generating only sentences of the language? Sensibly realizing that the finite facts of language use don't, and couldn't, determine the language we speak, Schiffer has come to accept that we must appeal to the linguist's conception of knowledge of language, which he describes as consisting in an internally represented grammar used in language processing. Only that will provide an explanatorily adequate grammar. The Chomskian idea is that the theorist's grammar G that generates L must be a grammar that generates the fragment used by P and must be a model of the internal grammar used by the speech processing mechanisms of speakers in P to produce and comprehend utterances in their language. The grammar (or the information it encodes) must be internally represented in the mind/brain of the speakers. Assuming that this grammar generates not only the linguistic forms and meaning of sentences in the used fragment, but also has the capacity to generate forms and meanings for all other possible expressions of our language, we can use the linguist's account of knowledge of language to connect the used and the unused part of the language so as to identify the infinitely large abstract object L that the speaker speaks.[38]

What is it for a sentence to mean something for a person, given that there are infinitely many meaningful sentences of the language? Knowing a language is thought to put infinitely many sentences at one's disposal and, if, following Schiffer, knowing a language is equated with (or deflated to) using a language, we can now ask what is it for a person x to use a language L with infinitely many sentences? Every sentence in L has a meaning (by the notion of language given), so if S means M in L and L is x's language then S means M in x's language. We relate the person to an infinity of meaningful sentences by showing why this is the language he uses. For L to be the language person x uses, is for the set of sentence-meanings pair meanings of L to match the infinity of linguistic forms and meanings generated by that person's internally represented grammar. The language generated by a speaker's internally represented grammar will be the language the speaker uses, the language the speaker knows 'in that sense of knowing a language in which you ipso facto know the languages you use'.[39]

Notice that if we take this way with the actual language relation we are unable to identify natural languages *without* mention of the psychological states or practices (or knowledge) of speakers. Shouldn't we then just look for an account of a speaker's language via an account of his or her knowledge of language?

Why give such a roundabout account of our knowledge of language and of the language known? By first invoking the notion of language as an abstract object we

---

[38] The search space is already constrained considerably by relating speakers to *sentences* rather than *sounds* as part of these abstract languages, and this will further constrain the semantic interpretations that human language users, whose language faculties are configured in accordance with the principles of universal grammar, will be able to give to those sentences, thus significantly reducing the possible pairings.

[39] Stephen Schiffer, 'Two Perspectives on Knowledge of Language', paper given at the GLOW Conference, Geneva, 2005, p. 16.

then have to define the actual language relation to relate a person to the language L he speaks. This is done via the forms and meanings generated by the person's internal grammar. These line up with the sentence-meaning pairs of L and us a result we then claim that what the person means by his use of language is what the corresponding items mean in the abstract object L. His knowledge of L is then taken to be knowledge "in that sense of knowing a language in which you ipso facto know the language you use". But why go this roundabout route when the linguist offers a more direct account by addressing (Λ) without reference to (P):

(a) What makes it the case that there are infinitely many meaningful sentences of a person's language?

(b') It is for the person's internal grammar to assign a form and meaning to each expression that features in his use and understanding of language.

Therefore:

(c') The language L the person uses and understands just is the set of expressions and sentences the internal equipment generates.

For the linguist, the order of determination is reversed. We fix the person's language, and the meaning of his sentences, by means of his knowledge of language. We specify the meanings and structures the person' internalized grammar assigns to his sentences. We don't start by specifying a language and try to work out the speaker's relation to it: we specify the language he knows by finding out which internalized grammar he has.

37.5.2 The Need to Study Speaker's Knowledge of Language

The problem created by treating languages as abstract objects—the problem of defining the actual language relation between languages and speakers—led us to conclude that the best (or perhaps the only) way to identify the actual language of a given speaker, or community of speakers, was via their knowledge of language or internalized grammar.

We have to delineate the whole language of a given speaker, or community, taking in the range of legitimate expressions in that language, and it is most likely that the only way to do this is to appeal to the knowledge speakers have of a language that equips them to produce or comprehend indefinitely many sentences. For this we need an account of what speakers know in advance of producing or encountering particular utterances that extends to new cases and enables them, effortlessly, to recognize such newly encountered expressions as part of their language.

The range of speech sounds we will produce or respond to, the meanings we attach to them, the structures we take them to have, all this depends entirely on our linguistic competence: it is the extent of our knowledge of language and so the extent of the language we know. So if we could find out precisely what range of linguistic knowledge people have and settle the boundaries of linguistic production and comprehension, we could find out what is and what is not part of *their* language. This would give us one important motive for studying speakers' knowledge of language as part of the study of language, of what makes language *language*.

A second, weaker motive for appealing to speakers' knowledge would simply be that once we have furnished an account of a given language we shall need some account of what it is for people to know that language. Notice, that this too provides an important epistemological constraint, since any account of a natural language that rendered it implausible that speakers should know the language in question would cast doubt on the cogency of the account as an account of *their* language.

A third, stronger motivation comes from viewing the relation between *language* and *knowledge of language* in terms of the latter constituting and exhausting the former. The range of speech sounds we can produce or respond to, the meanings we attach to them, the structures we take those expressions to have, depends entirely on and has no existence apart from our knowledge of language. In this way, the extent of our language is the extent of our knowledge of language. So if we could find out more precisely what range of expressions people had knowledge of—the scope of their potential linguistic production and comprehension—we would know what was and what was not part of *their* language.

Advocates of the second and third positions see it as an important adequacy constraint on a correct theoretical account of a given language that it respects the way that language is understood by its speakers. We could not ascribe grammatical or meaning properties to their language that diverged from the properties of the language as they understand it: their understanding of the language is fixed by their knowledge of meaning and grammar. The knowledge speakers have is our guide to the meanings of their words and sentences.

This view is advocated by Dummett, who claims that a theory of meaning for a language must be a theory of understanding: the understanding speakers have of that language. However Dummett stops short of the stronger, third position, advocated by Chomsky, that language is entirely constituted and exhausted by speaker's linguistic knowledge. For Dummett, the language known is a social language, shared by a community of language users. Individual speakers may have only a partial knowledge of their language, but it is important to see that there are no properties of the language that are beyond the epistemic reach of all speakers of the language.

On either Chomsky's or Dummett's view, the answer to the latter's key question: 'Is the significance of language to be explained in terms of a speaker's knowledge of his language?' (1978, p. 97) is yes. It is the only way to settle the matter. For it is what people know, linguistically speaking, that individuates the precise domain of the language they speak. The words and phrases they use, the significance they attach to them, the arrangements they take to be grammatical, all depend on their linguistic competence and this settles the identity of their languages. The hope is that by tracing out the full extent and character of a speaker's knowledge we should be able to fashion the precise contours of his or her language.[40]

---

[40] The tendency to think language extends beyond a speaker's knowledge of it, and to see the speaker as having partial knowledge of his (the) language depends on phenomena such as the existence of books,

To pursue such a strategy we need to know what we are out to study when we aim to investigate a *speaker's knowledge*. What is the nature of speakers' linguistic knowledge and how do we set about characterizing it accurately? And once we have answered this, what would such an account of a speaker's knowledge tell us about 'what makes language *language*' as Dummett puts it?

37.5.3 The Elusiveness of Speakers' Knowledge

The trouble is that it is unlikely to strike us as any easier to get at the facts of a speaker's knowledge than it is to study her language directly, and, in fact, it is apt to strike us as potentially a harder problem. How do we identify it? And isn't it more likely that it is via someone's use of language that we find out about their knowledge of language? The priority may seem to be exactly the reverse of what's being proposed. To overcome this we need a clear sense of how we capture facts about what speakers know linguistically.

But now the accessible evidence seems to be the expressions speakers use, how they use them, which combinations of them they find acceptable, and so on. And this is to suppose that we can identify the items of their knowledge before discovering anything about the nature of that knowledge. Doesn't this simply return us to the original problem of delineating someone's language with the detour through knowledge of language amounting to a redundant step?

37.5.4 Objection to Treating the Study of Language as the Study of Speakers' Knowledge of Language

One construal of this objection is faced by Dummett in 'What Do I Know When I Know a Language?'. If the only evidence of speaker's knowledge of language is the use he makes of words and sentences, then either there is a systematic description of that use or there isn't. If not, we can learn nothing of his linguistic understanding. On the other hand, if there is a systematic description of use then we don't need to appeal to a speaker's knowledge to account for the facts of his language. This dilemma is intended to show that knowledge plays no role in accounting for language.

A number of responses are available. Dummett resists the dilemma by arguing that no matter what regularities we can point to in linguistic use (in the course of giving a systematic description of someone's linguistic behaviour or practice), we cannot neglect the fact that language is a conscious rational activity, and we are aware of the regularities we make use of. After all, we don't just use language, we know how to use it, and use rests on understanding. For Dummett, it is no good just cataloguing regularities in the observable use of speech. The only regularities that can count as part of

and sign-posts and other static objects that exist independently of us. Whether all the properties we are inclined to attribute to them extend beyond us is another matter.

someone's language are the ones that speakers consciously choose and subscribe to. As Dummett puts it, we must distinguish,

between those regularities of which a language speaker, acting as a rational agent engaged in conscious, voluntary action, makes use from those that may be hidden from him and uncovered by a psychologist or neurologist: only those regularities of which, in speaking, he makes use characterize the language as a language   (Dummett 1993, p. 104)

This response very properly recognizes a conscious and first-personal dimension to human speech. But Dummett is surely wrong, on empirical or evidential grounds alone, to insist that the only generalizations or regularities that feature as part of our language are those of which we have conscious apprehension. That would be a hopeless move in the face of the generalizations linguistic theory gives rise to, and for which there is evidence in the conscious intuitive judgements (linguistic intuitions) of speakers. Consider the following:

(24) Mary expects to feed herself
(25) Mary expects the woman sitting up in bed to feed herself
(26) I wonder who Mary expects to feed herself

In (24), we take the reference of the reflexive pronoun to depend on the subject 'Mary'. The reflective pronoun appears to depend for its reference on the nearest noun-phrase that agrees with it in number and gender, as the Binding Principles require (cf. 'Mary expects to feed her' where the non-reflexive pronoun cannot depend on the nearest noun-phrase). Thus in (25), the reflexive pronoun depends referentially on the noun-phrase, 'the woman sitting up in bed'. However, in (26), the reflexive pronoun cannot be referentially dependent on 'Mary', and speakers never assume that it is, despite the very same expression (24) being contained in (26). Speakers know these facts but they do not know how they know them? The relevant generalizations governing this and countless other examples are that 'who', the subject of 'to feed' has moved and has left an NP trace or empty category after 'expects' and that NP referentially binds 'herself' as Principle A requires. Does the speaker make use of the regularities that explain these data? She certainly conforms to them. Does she consciously know the generalizations? The answer is obviously, no. But this does not mean that the psychologist or even less plausibly, the neurologist can explain the judgements we make in (24) to (26). The relevant generalizations are expressed in linguistic terms and cannot be expressed in neurological terms. The linguistic facts in question can only be explained in terms of the hierarchical structures of strings: structures assigned by the language faculty. These syntactic structures are derived from interacting principles governing the grammatical relations of the lexical items combined: we do not carry whole sentences around from one speech episode to another. Somehow we must deploy information about these structures, and so speakers have some way of conforming to, cognizing or heeding the principles of syntactic structure without being consciously aware of them. What is more, Dummett is mistaken in supposing that the consciously made generalizations will correctly predict the data about the speaker's own intuitions. Speakers reflecting on cases like (27) and (28) will usually predict that the use of the complentizer 'that' after 'believes' is optional. It can be put in or not.

(27) Bill believes that George is intelligent
(28) Bill believes George is intelligent

But this is not the case, as speakers themselves come to see in the unacceptability of (29):

(29) *Hillary believes that Bill to be intelligent

This is because of Exceptional Case Marking where 'believes' assigns accusative case to 'him' in structures like (30) and must be adjacent to it:

(30) Hillary believes him to be intelligent.

On this picture, the structure of language, on which the identity of language depends, is due to the internalized grammar, not consciously accessible to the speaker, but which is part of the language faculty. On Chomsky's cognitive conception of language there is *only* the internalized system or I-language:

a person who knows a language has mastered a particular way of interpreting expressions... the person has acquired a generative procedure g [I-language] which associates a structural description (SD) with every possible expression.   (Chomsky 1987, p. 179)

The identity of the language—the linguistic facts the theory of language aims to capture—depends on what goes on solely in the mind of language users. The cognitive states that embody this knowledge of linguistic structure becomes the domain of linguistic inquiry. A speaker's knowledge of language, conceived as some specialized internal cognitive state, becomes the object of inquiry, the proper domain of study in linguistics.

This is Chomsky's mentalist assumption about the status of the linguistic facts under discussion, which Chomsky sees as belonging wholly within the mind of the individual language user. According to this view, linguistic theory is not about linguistic behaviour or use: '... linguistic theory is mentalistic, since it is concerned with discovering a mental reality underlying actual behaviour.'   (Chomsky, 1965, p. 4)

This alternative response to Dummett's problem of documenting regularities in language use, relies on the argued for assumption there is no such project since the facts of natural language are not to be found in external or performance features of speakers' use, but in facts about speakers' minds—facts about the competence that consist in states of knowledge of language not always consciously accessible. These postulated states concern unobservable entities—levels of linguistic representation postulated by the theory that lie behind the behavioural data, giving it the form and character it has (cf. McDowell's talk of facts lying open to view of the surface of practice). The postulated entities are required to explain patterns in data, but they are not reducible to it. The states of knowledge should explain how we can be apprised of certain consciously apprehensible linguistic facts and of how we conform to the generalizations framed in terms of the underlying structures.

But why should we accept this wholesale move away from linguistic behaviour and use in linguistic theory and turn towards a cognitive domain of in-head psychological states?

Notice that Chomsky makes little of Dummett's appeal to language as a conscious, rational activity. According to Chomsky, 'consciousness forms a scattered and largely irrelevant subpart of the domain of cognitive states', it plays no role as far as the study of language is concerned. But this has been contested in examples like (22) above where data about speaker's conscious and immediate intuitions provides evidential grounds about how speakers can and cannot hear certain strings as structured, from which we draw conclusions about the underlying grammars. So we must modify Chomsky's picture to accommodate such phenomena. However, Chomsky's view of language as 'a system represented in the mind/brain of a particular individual' does provide a useful corrective to Dummett's view since it is not just (and sometimes not even) what the speaker consciously selects as regularities that constitutes his language. What matters is the phonological, lexical, and syntactic information mentally represented in the mind of the speaker. For Chomsky, this represented information exhausts the reality of language: 'language has no objective existence apart from its mental representation' (1972, p. 169, fn.). Here the concern is not with sets of sentences, nor with speech production and comprehension, or any other performance-related phenomena, but with the knowledge of language that makes all such phenomena possible.[41] Chomsky sees languages as epiphenomena. Linguistic theories are the study of I-language (internal, individual, functions in intension). It is the mental mechanisms responsible for our linguistic capacities that interest Chomsky, rather than the products of this capacity. For him, it is the particular configurations of the language faculty in each of us that determine the languages we speak: we can read off the language, or better, structure of the language, from the set of structures and meanings the I-language provides.

On this conception language is firmly located within the language faculty. Such a conception leaves no room to accommodate the *person*'s knowledge of the language he or she speaks. The account is strictly sub-personal, for facts about the internal configurations or cognitive mechanisms are not *first-personally* accessible. And yet we have first-personal and authoritative knowledge of what our words mean and which arrangements of those words are grammatical or deviant. So we must augment Chomsky's story to make room for a notion of a speaker's conscious and authoritative knowledge, as well as saying what it gives us knowledge of. In one sense Chomsky's cognitive conception of language may relieve us of the problem of relating speakers to the actual languages they speak; their languages are finite states of their mind/brains. But it doesn't relieve us of the epistemological burden of saying

---

[41] Language—a matter of linguistic competence—should be distinguished from speech—a matter of linguistic performance. Competence is just one cognitive factor among others responsible for speech production and comprehension. Other factors include memory, attention, perception, etc.

what it is for *a person* to know a language. (Waiting in the wings is the further problem of how we understand *other people's* languages, or what they are saying.) Must we accept even a modified Chomskian account of where our knowledge of language—and indeed the facts of our language—reside?

The move to mentalism in linguistic theory is based on powerful arguments designed to counter the mere suggestion that appeals to speakers' knowledge can be based solely on a characterization of language arrived at through the study of speakers' uses of their languages. The counter-arguments trade on a battery of empirical considerations about the impossibility of finding linguistic facts on the surface of speech.

Summarizing countlessly many pieces of empirical evidence of the sort mentioned above we see that:

the crucial properties of sentences are not revealed by thinking of them as they are outwardly presented to us, namely as strings of signs, but rather by their unobservable grammatical structure.   (Higginbotham, 1991, p. 555)

37.5.5 The Elusiveness of a Speaker's Language

These counter-arguments enable us to reject the all too hastily made assumption that the facts about speakers' languages are uncontroversially available to us as theorists. It is just this assumption that we have been questioning all along. What we want to know is how, from observing finite stretches of people's linguistic behaviour, characterized (at first) in non-question begging physical terms, as mere sounds or gestures, we can extract an account of the linguistic significance of those exchanges, revealing the meanings people attach to their expressions, the structures they assign them, leading us to extrapolate safely beyond any point so far reached, in just the right ways to compound words into sentences of their languages. As yet, we have seen no way to do that until we know something of what speakers know about the linguistic forms and meanings they attach to the sounds they use and respond to and what gives rise to this knowledge.

The Chomskian arguments also counter the McDowellian alternative: that of phenomenological presented linguistic facts, taken to be directly perceptually available on the surface of practice—though audible only to those who are part of the practice. No one disputes the phenomenological datum that in a language we understand we hear people's words as meaningful. But what we can and cannot hear, and why only these things, needs to be explained. As perceivers of meaningful speech, how do we arrive at these specific bits of knowledge of novel sentences in countlessly many cases. Part of that perceptual experience depends on one's knowledge of, and sensitivity to, syntactic structure described at a level remote from what is phenomenological accessible on the surface. The only empirically supportable—that is descriptively adequate—theories of grammar for natural languages are those that postulate underlying, or unobservable, structure as *the* structure of a sentence. But in doing so, we are postulating an structure that does not occur in the sounds or marks that make up the external or phenomenally accessible properties of speech. Just where, then, are we to locate the levels of linguistic structure that linguistic theory postulate to explain the patterns in the data? The only place is in the mind of the speaker: syntactic structure is the structure a speaker, or rather her linguistic system, imposes on or assigns to the sounds and signs she encounters in order to hear those sounds *as* meaningful sentences. Words are not words until the noises, or marks, by which we indicate them, are seen as carrying their full freight of semantic, syntactic and phonological properties. The same set of sounds can count as different linguistic expressions, belonging to different languages, or different sentences in the same language, depending on what structure the speaker/hearer assigns to them. It is the language faculty that assigns structure to the sounds people hear, it is the language faculty's contribution to speech events that makes up a large part of the domain of linguistic inquiry.

37.6 CAN MENTALISM BE RESISTED?

Despite overwhelming empirical evidence, mentalism in linguistics has been resisted and there are two sources of pressure. The first comes from Quine when considering the choice of grammar to characterize a speaker's language. This is the issue of the indeterminacy of grammar. But the indeterminacy in syntax is not so troubling, Quine claims, as the indeterminacy of meaning or translation, since there are no facts about syntax that we should find problematic. For Quine:

The business of syntax is the demarcation of strings of phonemes proper to the language. More than one battery of grammatical constructions and vocabulary will probably be capable of generating the same total output of strings, but in this freedom there is no indeterminacy analogous to that of translation. Indeterminacy of translation consists rather in conflict in the outputs themselves.   (Quine 1990, p. 49)

The difference between grammars is only verbal, according to Quine, or at most 'a choice of one syntactic structure rather than another for generating one and the same total output of [linguistic] strings.' (Quine 1990, p. 50) This contrasts, thinks Quine, with the case of meaning where two translation manuals for a given language can yield different results—different outputs—for given sentences of the object language, even though the two manuals are empirically equivalent, each being compatible with the same total set of behavioural observations.

But Quine's understanding of the purpose of grammar allows him to relegate differences between grammars to matters of the choice of delivery of the testable output, the empirical content, of the theories. The output of different grammars can be the same if they deliver (provide a means of recursively enumerating) the same set of well-formed strings. In this sense two incompatible grammars will be extensionally equivalent—generating the same set of strings—and empirically equivalent—accounting for all the same empirical evidence.

The trouble with this argument is that Quine's criterion of correctness is merely *observational adequacy*, i.e. that a grammar for a language L is correct if and only if it generates all and only the strings acceptable to speakers of L. (Such grammars only *weakly generate* strings, as Chomsky puts it.) Thus if a grammar G_1 and a grammar G_2 generates the same total output strings—the strings of the language acceptable to its speakers—there is no indeterminacy because the two theories (grammars) do not differ in their syntactic subject matter: the proper strings of the language.

This is not the notion of *descriptive* or *explanatory* adequacy that concerns the linguist. The output of grammars is not *strings* but *syntactically structured sentences*. Strings do not cut finely enough to say which, or how many, sentences belong to a speaker's language, since the same string can count as ambiguous and be assigned two sentences structures within one language, but not count us ambiguous and be assigned only one sentence structure in another. The two languages do not contain the same sentences. Grammars postulated by generative grammarians capturing generalizations about all human languages *strongly generate* strings by assigning them a *structural description*. None of these considerations are addressed by Quine, who simply doesn't engage with the real subject matter of linguistics: the properties that make language *language*.[42]

A second source of pressure against mentalism is the missing object of linguistic knowledge—after all how can the facts of language we study be identified with a speaker's knowledge of language? In what sense do speakers have knowledge of something if the linguistic facts they know are determined by the very states that are meant to provide knowledge of them? This is what we called the *Missing Object of Knowledge Problem*.

We do not find out about the speaker's knowledge of language by going via his language. The linguist studies the speaker's knowledge-of-language (a state of the speaker/hearer) and this tells her what a speaker is linguistically able to do: which expressions will count as well-formed, and which will not. This study yields the linguistic properties of all the expressions generated by the speaker's I-language: what we might be tempted to call the speaker's language or idiolect—even though it is not external to the states that constitutes the speaker's knowledge of language, and partly belongs to the language faculty.

If languages are no longer seen as 'out there' but are conceived as internal to speakers, what *is* the object of speakers' knowledge of language? It is not their I-language. The I-language a speaker using is discoverable by a theorist. So which object is *a person* to when he or she knows a language? There is less difficulty in conceiving a relation between speakers and their languages on this picture since in some sense people embody their languages: languages do not exist independently of them, and so there is no need for an elaborate account of the actual language relation. But we seem to have swapped one problem for another since now there appears to be nothing to relate them to: no *object* of knowledge. There is, however, still an important question about what notion of knowledge relates speakers to languages, and what we meant

---

[42] For a thorough treatment of these issues see Neale, (1987). [left justify]

here by the language they know. Chomsky has always insisted on departing from the ordinary notion of knowledge and has talked about a speaker *cognizing* his grammar or I-language.

37.6.1 What Notion of *Language* Should we Adopt?

It is one thing to give an account of Chomsky's notion of language and knowledge-of-language, it is another to decide whether it is philosophically adequate in addressing the issues with which we started. So now we must ask whether we should endorse the linguist's conception of what makes language *language*.

On the linguist's conception, where languages are not external objects, we do not represent them. We need initial experience (exposure to the data[43]) to trigger the settings of a narrow range of parameters, but we do not learn languages from our surroundings. Thus the complex structures we compute from selected lexical items, and that count as sentence structures, are not to be found in the data we are exposed to: they are *internal* to the speaker/hearer. That was the upshot of poverty of stimulus arguments.

Language in the sense of I-language are steady states of individuals' language faculties; faculties whose initial states are genetically determined in accordance with the principles of UG. I-languages are functions in intension, and internal states of the mind/brains of individuals. Our knowledge-of-language is just such a state. I-languages generate infinite pieces of knowledge but I-languages are not to be identified with what is infinitely generated: they are states of the speaker/hearer, and thus finite. So knowledge-of-language is a property of speakers rather than a relation to some independently existing object: it is not really knowledge *of* something independent of what we are calling the knowledge state itself. It *is* the state that (in part) enables speakers to produce and comprehend indefinitely many expressions. But now we need to ask: do we really have knowledge of language at all on the linguist's conception of language?

37.7 THE MISSING OBJECT OF KNOWLEDGE PROBLEM

It is one thing to say that speakers do not stand in a relation of representation or knowledge to their internal grammars, it is another to say that they do not have *knowledge of* a language. And yet without a notion of language as something independently known it is merely a *façon de parler* to talk of a person possessing *knowledge* of language. If knowledge-of-language is a state of the person and the

---

[43] Although what these data are is somewhat controversial and the subject of continuing empirical research.

language a person speaks is determined by that state, it is hardly knowledge that is at issue. For how can a genuine state of knowledge constitute the thing known?[44] Knowledge requires there to be a subject matter to be right or wrong about. And the trouble with the linguist's notion of knowledge-of-language is that it fixes the facts of the language rather than conforming to them. The problem in a nutshell is this: if the psychological states that constitute one's competence determine *the facts about one's language*, how can those psychological states be at the same time answerable to those facts in the way knowledge requires? They can't, of course, and this is the Missing Object of Knowledge Problem. But if there is nothing independent of the internal representations to be represented, there is nothing objective to know. So how can the linguist be getting at objective linguistic properties of expressions via the study of speaker's knowledge?

We seem forced to reject the idea of an object of knowledge on the Chomskian conception of knowledge-of-language, and this is exactly what John Collins confirms:

> There is, as it were, nothing to *get right*. Languages are not external objects we can go right or wrong about . . . It turns out, as part a matter of discovery, part methodology, that we do not *know* languages (better: I-languages).   (Collins, 2005, p. 514–16)[45]

But there is still room for genuine items of *linguistic* knowledge (and Collins acknowledges as much), like the *knowledge that* certain nominal expressions interpretatively depend on others in examples like (1)–(27).

Speakers know that the pronouns in (14) and (26) cannot be construed as referring to the same person the proper names refer to respectively in those sentences. In (15) the pronoun may bear the same interpretation as the proper name 'John' and so can the possessive pronoun in (16). The reflective pronoun (or anaphor) in (15) and (19) must be construed as indicating the same person as the preceding proper name, whereas it cannot in (17). A person's I-language will generate all these items of knowledge (in fact, infinitely many of them). And all I-languages will generate equivalent structures, since these exemplify universals of humanly acquired natural languages. But the known facts are determined entirely by the internal state. They are not facts 'about the language' so much as a reflection of it. The items themselves surely count as knowledge, but the knowledge-of-language that gives rise to them is not *knowledge-of* anything. How then can what we have just said about (14) to (19) count as knowledge? What is it knowledge *of*? If we cannot think of the products generated by a person's internal I-language as the person's language, how can we have *anything* that counts as knowledge of language, even in our intuitive judgements? And when we take our intuitive judgements in (1)–(27) to count as items of *knowledge that*, with the subject matter being the properties we have just described,

---

[44] Even psychological self-knowledge requires there to be a something known. In reflective or cogito-like cases the knowing and the known coincide but there is still a psychological state to have knowledge-of.

[45] Collins 2005 presents an exceptionally clear account of the linguist's conception of language along the lines discussed here.

how can the intuitive judgements that present such properties of sentences also be about them? If the linguistic judgements we form constitute their own subject matter, this raises the question of whether such judgements can concern objective facts, whether such judgements have objective correctness conditions. The problem is that the linguistic knowledge claims about (1)–(27) appear to assure their own success and depend on nothing but thinkers' being in the states of having made those claims. And unlike cases of psychological self-knowledge these knowledge claims do not even appear to be about the states of knowledge themselves.

What are we to make, then, of the ordinary point that as speakers we have indefinitely many pieces of individual knowledge about the words and sentences we use? Our production and comprehension of speech results in knowledge that someone is saying such and such by hearing that someone is saying such and such. These pieces of knowledge, the output of our linguistic system, operating in concert with many other cognitive systems, need to be respected. Yet the contemporary Chomskian linguist has no satisfactory way to do so.

37.8 A SOLUTION TO THE MISSING OBJECT OF KNOWLEDGE PROBLEM

How did the problem arise? For the cognitivist, a grammar provides a model of a speaker's knowledge-of-language. At the same time it describes facts about the structure of the speaker's language. It can do both simultaneously because a speaker's language is individuated by the knowledge-of-language that determines it. A speaker's knowledge-of-language fixes the language she speaks (and hence the properties of her language). So a linguistic theory that characterizes a person's knowledge-of-language can specify the properties of a person's language: the structured expressions produced and recognized. However, because the psychological states that constitute one's linguistic competence determine *the facts about one's language*, such states cannot at the same time be answerable to those facts.

So how can the person count as knowing the meanings and forms of the linguistic expressions generated?

The problem lies with the particular linguistic knowledge ascribed to speakers. Speakers typically do know, without evidence or inference, what they mean by their words and which configurations of their words are grammatical. However, their intuitive linguistic judgements are not *ipso facto* correct. Speakers are authoritative, not infallible, in their native speaker intuitions. This authoritative knowledge is special because, although it purports to be about a range of objective facts —the linguistic facts about one's language—, it is based on nothing more than what, *prima facie*, one takes one's words to mean, and what strings one takes to be grammatical. The problem, then, is to show how there can be a range of objective facts about language while accommodating authoritative knowledge of them. The objectivity of linguistics requires there to be objective facts to which a speaker's linguistic intuitions are answerable—there should be a gap between the linguistic facts studied and our opinions about them. On the other hand, first-person authority requires the linguistic facts to be, pretty much, as we take them to be,—for our linguistic intuitions to be largely correct. This tension between the objectivity and first-person authority of our knowledge of language is the real problem facing a Chomskian account. (For more see Smith 1998 and 2001)

The right way to secure the objectivity of linguistic knowledge is by finding a way to make room for a distinction between *how things seem*, linguistically, and *how they are*, even when the two coincide. We need not say that the linguistic facts are independent of the speaker's view of them. The Chomskian view that facts about languages are settled by facts about speakers' minds requires that linguistic phenomena are *dependent* on speakers' mental states. But the speaker's intuitions or judgements count as knowledge only if we say these intuitions are usually the reliable upshot of speakers' underlying states of competence. Thus the tension can be eased by paying more attention to the different levels in a speaker's linguistic knowledge. A speaker knows a vast amount about his language as a matter of ordinary conscious reflection, as examples like (1) to (27) demonstrates.

His occurrent and conscious knowledge of these, and a welter of other, facts depends on the systematic body of unconscious, standing knowledge that he carries from one occasion to another and which provides the means of generating structures from the lexicon. Each conscious item of linguistic knowledge about a particular string or expression is derived from more general knowledge governing the structure and content of the I-language. It is this underlying linguist's sense of knowledge-of-language, some of which is innate and shared by all language users, that fixes many of the facts an individual knows. The speaker may have no idea of the precise extent and nature of his standing knowledge; it is this knowledge the linguist is trying to model by means of a grammar. By contrast, when we say a speaker is authoritative about expressions in his language we are talking at the first-person level about his knowledge of particular linguistic facts such as which nominal expressions must be interpreted as referring to the same thing—facts accounted for by a descriptively adequate grammar. In cases of spontaneous linguistic intuitions, how the speaker takes things to be is usually how they are. But not always. The speaker can be out of step with his own linguistic system. However, the facts about the structure of his language will always be settled by reference to the underlying facts dictated by the I-language. And it is only when the effortless and groundless intuitive judgements speakers make flow from (in whatever way they do), and conform, to assignment of structure made by the underlying I-language that the speakers' intuitions count as knowledge. There will be cases where a string will appear, prima facie, meaningful to our immediate intuitions but on reflection will be uninterpretable, such as (25). And equally some strings will appear ungrammatical even though one's I-language can generate permissible structures, as reflection and some coaching with centre-embedding sentences like 'The girl the cat the dog bit scratched cried.', reveals.

What this shows is that our native speaker intuitions do *not* ensure their own success but when produced *in the right way*, so as to be in conformity with the underlying facts dictated by the I-language, they count as knowledge. In just those circumstances, how you take things to be linguistically *is* how they are. This preserves both authority and the claim to knowledge. But what is it knowledge of? What are we getting objectively right under these conditions? The answer will be something about the structure of our generative procedure or I-language. So although it may appear to us phenomenologically as though we were reacting to facts about the language, out there and external to us, in fact we are reacting to something within our own breasts and not consciously accessible to us at all. It is still psychological facts about the speaker that determine the linguistic properties of expressions but there is room for objective facts at the personal level, about which, our native speaker intuitions can be right or wrong. The full range of the facts we can know by this means makes up a substantial body of linguistic information about us as speakers—information the linguist has to account for—and there is some reason to call this linguistic knowledge, in the genuine philosophical sense of knowledge. It is both theoretically characterizable and first-personally available.

37.9 KNOWLEDGE OF WORD MEANING

Unlike our knowledge of grammar, there is no reason to think that our knowledge of word meaning is inaccessible or sub-personal. In fact, there are good empirical reasons to think it cannot be found in the language faculty, narrowly construed (see Hauser, Chomsky, and Fitch 2002).

We first learn words at the age of around 12 months, before we are able to use syntactic structure. We acquire words and their uses one by one, only later combining them in pairs. We do not move from two words, to three, to four, etc. But as mentioned above, we simply start using whole sentences in the 'syntax spurt' at around 20–24 months. This would appear to be the combination of a very different system with our facility to use sounds in a representational way prior to the onset of language. It is possible that word meanings have, prior to the syntax spurt, nothing to do with language, at least as the linguist understands it. What is needed, then, is an account of how we learn words, what meanings we give them, and how we use them to understand others.

Our knowledge of word meaning is conscious and first-personal. There is such an experience as the meaning of a word being all there at once, or of bringing the meaning of a word to mind as when one decides whether the use of a particular word is more apt than another. These experiences of meaning belong at the personal level. How do we acquire them and how can we use them to understand others? The quick answer, that can only be sketched here, is that we learn to have experiences with words in the context of learning words from others. The early conditions for word learning typically happen best under conditions of *joint attention* where the child and the parent are jointly attending to a commonly perceived object. The sharing of their experience of that object can be commemorated by introducing a sound label that saturates the experience. The resulting state will bring to mind, on each subsequent presentation, a recreation of the experience of a commonly perceived thing. These cases of early acquisition show us that when word meanings are introduced the experience of two subjects is co-ordinated and the involvement of an object and another person are not negligible. The traditional story may think of the child acquiring the meaning of the word from someone but more plausibly, the child is *endowing* or *investing* the sound with meaning.[46] These experiences set in place a way of focusing attention on a thing at a very early stage. The experiences of meaning will then attach to that word and subsequent uses of it and there will be no need for the child to entertain the idea that the word means anything different to anyone else. Were they to reflect, and there is no reason to expect them to do so, they would think: that's just what the word means. By hearing uses of the word accompanied by the understanding of the words they have, they come to attach semantic significance to what they hear others as saying. At first the meanings they hear other people's words as having are just the meanings the words have for them. This is the default case where we have no reason to suppose others are using words in a different way. This reliance by children on what *they* mean by the word will serve them well. In the default case, using words in the company of those from whom one learned them, or in sufficiently overlapping groups with whom one shares vocabulary communication will go well. It is a shock at first to a child in a foreign linguistic environment to discover that not everyone uses these sounds with the meanings they have for him. Eventually, there will be adjustments at a later and more sophisticated stage of learning. Also, it will be by dint of the grammatical and logical relations between words that the syntax spurt makes available that we come to acquire meanings of functional category words like 'of' and words less directly connected to the immediate environment.

The combination of these two systems—for word meaning and for syntax—brings about a dimension shift in the expressive power of the language user. Combining such knowledge is necessary for full language acquisition. But what we see is that the experience of meaning and the experience of hearing strings as structured respond to different parts of cognition and despite the experience of hearing what you say as there in the words uttered, the sources and objects of these two kinds of knowledge are quite different.

37.10 RELATIONS BETWEEN A THEORY OF LANGUAGE AND A SPEAKER'S KNOWLEDGE OF LANGUAGE

Competent speakers of a language L know which strings of words are grammatical sentences and know what those sentences mean. A correct theory for a language L

---

[46] See Davidson 2001 p.14. [left justify]

specifies the grammatical structure and meaning of each well-formed sentence of that language. What relation, if any, is there between the theory and the speaker's knowledge of a language? They both concern the same object: the language L used and understood by the speaker. The theory states what the speaker knows but not necessarily in the *form* in which the speaker knows it. Hence the speaker does not have knowledge (even unconscious or tacit) of the theory. Nevertheless, the correct theory of his language will be a theory of what the speaker knows, or of what determines all the facts he knows.

The theory will invoke certain linguistically relevant properties to describe the linguistic form and meaning of the expressions speakers use and recognize. What relation is there between speakers and these theoretically described properties? Is there some epistemic relation between the two that must be respected by any satisfactory theory of their language? Or can speakers be blind to the properties recorded by the theory? We have seen that the linguistic properties of structure uncovered by the theory of syntax are properties speakers must be sensitive to, or respect, in combining words into sentences. The structural properties of the strings they produce and respond to will be assigned by their underlying linguistic system and will have impact on their conscious experience of speech. In the case of word meaning, the best theory may have to make prior use of the meanings one hears words as having. There may be no other terms, and certainly no properties to be found in the language faculty, in terms of which to capture the meanings of words in the speaker's language. The meanings the speaker grasps are consciously experienced as part of the phenomenology of speaking and understanding. How close the theory gets to capturing the meanings of his terms depends on how close the theorist is in his understanding of those words to the speaker.

To end, there are two faulty assumptions in the study of language we are now in a position to give up. The first is Quine's behaviourist assumption, shared by many, that the task facing the child learning the language and the task facing the theorist may be the same. Quine is wrong on this point. As Chomsky's arguments show:

(i) the learner cannot learn a language L unless she knows P antecedently, (where P is some set of domain-specific constraints on the structure of possible human languages)

(ii) P is innately known (because it could not be learned on the basis of impoverished linguistic data available to the learner as the poverty of stimulus arguments show)

(iii) Universal Grammar aims to specify the domain-specific constraints P that speakers innately know and respect.

The linguist's task is to figure out the value for P. The learner's task is to construct a grammar (acquire any of the class of humanly possible natural languages) on the basis of knowing P and being exposed to the primary linguistic data. The tasks facing each are quite different.

Secondly, Dummett rejects the model of speaker and hearer having a similar piece of internal apparatus because it would make our understanding of others a matter of hypothesis about what is going on in the other, which is both risky and phenomenologically distorting. The phenomenology of understanding speech can be immediate precisely because no such hypothesis is entertained. What happens is that my internal equipment—my language faculty—automatically assigns a structure to what is perceived thus giving rise to my hearing a sentence as structured. That together with the default case in which the meanings I hear someone else's words as having are the meanings those words have for me, ensures that I arrive at an understanding of what I hear as a matter of the fast and mandatory workings of my linguistic capacities and conscious apprehension of meaning. The job of those capacities is to interpret the sound stream and present a product to consciousness: it is not to hypothesize about what is going on in some one else's mind. And when you use words with meanings similar to mine, words arranged according to the constraints grammar places on combining words of those categories in that order, the meaningful sentence I end up hearing is probably close enough to what you experienced in producing it for us to count as communicating. Beyond that, reflective interpretation may be needed to understand one another, but in the normal case nothing said here about knowledge of language shows understanding to be anything other than immediate, inner and relatively secure. But it is knowledge of different kinds with different sources that give shape and character to our use and understanding of language.

REFERENCES

Chomsky, N. (1955). *Syntactic Structures* (Mouton).
_____ (1980). 'Review of Skinner's *Verbal Behaviour*, 1959, reprinted in *Philosophy of Psychology*, Vol.1 edited by N. Block (Methuen).
_____ (1965). *Aspects of The Theory of Syntax* (MIT).
_____ (1972). *Language and Mind* (Harcourt, Brace, Johanovich).
_____ (1980). *Rules and Representations* (Blackwell).
_____ (1986). *Knowledge of Language* (Praeger)
_____ (1987). 'Reply to Alex George', *Mind and Language*.
_____ (1993). *Language and Thought* (Moyer Bell).
_____ (1995). *The Minimalist Program* (MIT).
_____ (2000). *New Horizons in the Study of Language and Mind* (Cambridge University Press).
Collins, J. (2004). 'Faculty Disputes' in *Mind and Language*.
Crain, S. (1991). 'Language Acquisition in the Absence of Experience' in *Behavioural and Brain Sciences*.
Davidson, D. (2001). 'Externalisms' in *Interpreting Davidson*, eds. P. Kotatko, P. Pagin, G. Segal (Stanford CSLI).
Davies, M. (1981). *Meaning, Quantification, Necessity* (Routledge).
Dummett, M. (1993). 'What Do I Know When I Know a Language' 1978 reprinted in his *Seas of Language* (Oxford University Press).
Elman, J., Bates, E., Johnson, M., Karmiloff-Smith, A., Parisi, D., Plunkett, K. (1996). *Rethinking Innateness: A Connectionist Perspective on Development*, (MIT Press).
Fodor, J. (1990). *In Critical Condition* (MIT).
George, A. (1989). 'Whose Language is it Anyway?' in *Philosophical Quarterly*.

Harris, J. and Lindsay, G. (2003). 'Vowel Patterns in Mind and Sound' in *Phonological Knowledge*, edited by Burton-Roberts, Carr & Docherty (Oxford University Press).

Hauser, M. D., Chomsky, N., and Fitch, W. T. (2002). 'The Faculty of Language: What is it, Who has it, and How did it Evolve?, *Science*, 298, 1569–79.

Higginbotham, J. (1983). 'The Psychological Reality of Grammar', in *How Many Questions*.

—— (1991). 'Remarks on the Metaphysics of Linguistics', in *Linguistics and Philosophy*.

Katz, J. (1990). *The Metaphysics of Meaning*, (Cambridge University Press).

Lewis, D. (1983). 'Language and Languages' in his *Collected Papers*, Vol. 1 (Oxford University Press).

—— (1995). 'Meaning without Use: a reply to Hawthorne' *Australasian Journal of Philosophy*.

McDowell, J. (1998a). 'Anti-realist Semantic and the Epistemology of Understanding' in his *Meaning, Knowledge and Reality*, (Harvard).

—— (1998b). 'In Defence of Modesty' in his *Meaning, Knowledge and Reality*, (Harvard).

—— (1998c). 'On the Sense and Reference of a Proper Name' in his *Meaning, Knowledge and Reality* (Harvard).

—— (1998d). 'Physicalism and Primitive Denotation: Field on Tarski' in his *Meaning, Knowledge and Reality* (Harvard).

Neale, S. (1987). 'Meaning, Grammar and Indeterminacy' *Dialectica*.

Quine, W. (1990). *The Pursuit of Truth* (Harvard).

Schiffer, S. (1994). 'Actual Language Relations' in *Philosophical Perspectives*, 9.

Schiffer, S. (2005). 'Two Perspectives on Knowledge of Language', Manuscript for GLOW.

Smith, B. C. (1992). 'Understanding Language', in *Proceedings of the Aristotelian Society*.

—— (1998). 'On Knowing One's Own Language', in *Knowing Our Own Minds*, eds. C. Wright, B. C. Smith and C. Macdonald (Oxford University Press).

—— (2001). 'Understanding Idiolects: a Reply to Barber in *Mind and Language*.

Wiggins, D. (1991). 'Language as a Social Object' in *Philosophy*.

Wittgenstein, L. (1969). *On Certainty* (Blackwell).

CHAPTER 38

REALISM AND ANTIREALISM

ALEXANDER MILLER

WHAT is the relevance of issues in the philosophy of language to debates in metaphysics between realists and their antirealist opponents? Michael Dummett argues that the philosophy of language—in particular, the theory of meaning—is the foundation of all philosophy and that the debate in metaphysics between realism and antirealism has to be prosecuted *within* the philosophy of language. Dummett prosecutes the debate by developing and attacking a position we can call "semantic realism". This chapter questions whether, once the conception of metaphysics as grounded in the philosophy of language has been jettisoned, Dummett's arguments against semantic realism can retain any relevance to the realist/antirealist debate. By focussing on realism about the external world as an example, we reach the conclusion that even without Dummett's conception of philosophy as grounded in the theory of meaning, his arguments against semantic realism do retain a limited but nevertheless genuine significance for the metaphysical debate. It emerges, though, that a certain key assumption, connecting the notions of linguistic understanding and knowledge, and necessary if Dummett's arguments are to have even this limited significance, is both underexplained and underdefended. The chapter concludes with some brief remarks on the cogency of the manifestation argument against semantic realism.

For comments and discussion I'm grateful to Michael Devitt, Frank Hindriks, Andy McGonigal, and Barry. C. Smith. Some of the material in this chapter was presented at a seminar at the University of Leeds in November 2002. I'm grateful to the audience on that occasion and in particular to Andy McGonigal for searching comments on the chapter in the pouring rain and long after the bell had rung for last orders.

38.1 SEMANTIC REALISM

Michael Dummett is famous (or better, infamous) for espousing a view of philosophy according to which:

[T]he theory of meaning is the fundamental part of philosophy which underlies all the others. Because philosophy has, as its first if not its only task, the analysis of meanings, and because, the deeper such analysis goes, the more it is dependent upon a correct general account of meaning, a model for what the understanding of an expression consists in, the theory of meaning, which is the search for such a model, is the foundation for all philosophy, and not epistemology as Descartes misled us into believing.   (1973: 669)

Dummett's view of the relationship between the philosophy of language and the debate in metaphysics between realism and antirealism follows directly from this picture: according to Dummett the realism issue makes no *literal* sense, and is at best a matter of *metaphor*, unless realism is couched in *semantic* terms. The following quotes are representative of Dummett's views:

[W]e have here two metaphors: the platonist compares the mathematician with the astronomer, the geographer or the explorer, the intuitionist compares him with the sculptor or the imaginative writer; and neither comparison seems very apt. The disagreement evidently relates to the amount of freedom that the mathematician has. Put this way, however, both seem partly right and partly wrong: the mathematician has great freedom in devising the concepts he introduces and in delineating the structure he chooses to study, but he cannot prove just whatever he decides it would be attractive to prove. How are we to make the disagreement into a definite one, and how can we then resolve it?   (1978: xxv)

[Any metaphysical view] is a picture which has in itself no substance otherwise than as a representation of the given conception of meaning.   (1977: 383)

Dummett also says that in evaluating realism, the greatest difficulty is

[T]o comprehend the content of the metaphysical doctrine. What does it mean to say that natural numbers are mental constructions, or that they are independently existing immutable and immaterial objects? What does it mean to ask whether or not past or future events are *there*? What does it mean to say, or deny, that material objects are logical constructions out of sense-data? In each case, we are presented with alternative pictures. The need to choose between these pictures seems very compelling; but the non-pictorial content of the pictures is unclear.   (1991: 10)

What, then, is the thesis in the philosophy of language that cashes out the literal content of the otherwise metaphorical dispute between realism and antirealism? According to Dummett the literal content of the realist view in a given area consists in adherence to *semantic realism* about that area.

What is semantic realism? In order to answer this we need the notions of *decidability* and *undecidability*:

P is an effectively decidable statement] only when P is a statement of such a kind that we could in a finite time bring ourselves into a position in which we were justified either in asserting or denying P.   (1978: 16)

An undecidable sentence is simply one whose sense is such that, though in certain effectively recognizable situations we acknowledge it as true, in others we acknowledge it as false, and yet in others no decision is possible, we possess no effective means for bringing about a situation which is one or the other of the first two kinds.   (1973: 468)

Thus, in the sense of "undecidable" used here, a sentence is undecidable if (a) we have no evidence either of its truth or its falsity and (b) we do not know a procedure which, if correctly implemented, is guaranteed after finitely many steps to put us in a position in which we have evidence that it is either true or false. Likewise, a sentence is decidable if either (a) we do have evidence either of its truth or its falsity or (b) we do know a procedure which, if correctly implemented, is guaranteed after finitely many steps to put us in a position in which we have evidence that it is either true or false. These characterizations of decidability and undecidability no doubt stand in need in clarification and defence, but for our present purposes it is sufficient to note that e.g. Goldbach's Conjecture—that every even number is the sum of two primes—is undecidable in the relevant sense. In mathematics, the notion of proof plays the role of evidence, and in this case we have no proof that the conjecture is true, no proof that there is a counterexample, and we do not know a procedure the correct implementation of which will guarantee us either a proof or a counterexample. We can also have undecidable statements about the external world, for example: there is intelligent life elsewhere in the universe. This is undecidable. We have no evidence that there is intelligent life elsewhere, and no evidence that there is not, nor do we know a procedure the correct implementation of which will guarantee us evidence one way or the other.

We should note that the claim that e.g. Goldbach's Conjecture is undecidable in the sense used here entails only that we do not *know* a procedure which will guarantee us either a proof or a counterexample. It does not entail that we know that Goldbach's Procedure *cannot* be proved or refuted: it is consistent with our definition of undecidability that we at some point have the good fortune to turn up a proof or a counterexample. Likewise, that "There is intelligent life elsewhere in the universe" is undecidable does not entail that we know that we will never have evidence concerning whether there is intelligent life elsewhere: it is consistent with our definition of undecidability that we have the good fortune to stumble across some evidence which points one way or the other. (Note, too, that we are working with notions of decidability and undecidability that are not equivalent to the notions in mathematical logic that go by the same names. In terms of these more familiar notions, to say that a universally quantified sentence is decidable is to say that there is either a proof or a counterexample. Dummett could not then say that Goldbach's Conjecture is undecidable. Dummett's antirealist holds that a statement is true just in case we are capable of recognizing its truth, and false just in case we are capable of recognizing its falsity. Given the assumptions that if we can't prove a statement we can't recognize it to be true and that if we can't refute a statement we can't recognize it to be false, it would follow from the undecidability of Goldbach's Conjecture that it is not true and not false (Shieh 1998: 326). This would be a clear violation of the principle of *Tertium Non Datur*, a principle to which Dummett is explicitly committed (Dummett

1978: xviii, xxx).The class of sentences over which, according to Dummett, the realist and the antirealist disagree would then have to be characterized, not as the class of undecidables, but as the class of statements *not known to be decidable*).[1]

We are now in a position to characterize semantic realism about a given area. Semantic realism consists of the following claim: our understanding of undecidable sentences about the area consists in our grasp of their truth-conditions. In such a case, the truth-conditions of the relevant sentences are *potentially evidence-transcendent*: we do not know a method, the correct application of which is guaranteed to yield evidence for those truth-conditions' obtaining or not, and we may never turn up evidence either way. So semantic realism about the external world, for example, is the view that *our understanding of at least some sentences about the external world consists in our grasp of their potentially evidence-transcendent truth-conditions.*

Dummett's fundamental claim concerning realism about a particular subject matter is that in so far as it has any literal content, it consists in adherence to semantic realism. This claim, and the conception of philosophy that goes along with it, have been widely rejected, by those sympathetic to Dummett as well as by those antipathetic to his philosophy.[2] We will not further concern ourselves with this issue in this chapter. Rather, our main concern will be with the relevance of arguments against semantic realism, in particular whether they retain any relevance once Dummett's conception of the theory of meaning's role within philosophy has been jettisoned. Dummett has two main arguments against semantic realism, the *acquisition argument* and the *manifestation argument*. In short, if our understanding of undecidable sentences is constituted by grasp of potentially evidence-transcendent truth-conditions, how could we have *acquired* that understanding, given that our training in the use of sentences is a training to respond to situations which we are, necessarily, capable of recognizing to obtain when they obtain? And if our understanding of undecidable sentences is constituted by grasp of potentially evidence-transcendent truth-conditions, how could we *manifest* that understanding in our *use* of those sentences, given that the situations to which we respond in our uses of those sentences are, necessarily, situations which we are capable of recognizing to obtain when they obtain?[3] In order to explore the relevance of these arguments, in the next section we will develop an austerely metaphysical (i.e. non-semantic) characterization of realism about the external world. In the section after that we will use this austerely metaphysical characterization to explore whether, once Dummett's conception of philosophy as grounded in the philosophy of language has been rejected, his arguments against semantic realism have any bearing on the plausibility or otherwise of realism about the external world.[4]

---

[1] For a good discussion of the terminological choices, and for arguments in favour of using the less familiar *epistemic* characterizations in giving an exposition of Dummett's views, see Shieh, 1998. See also appendix 1 in Weiss, 2002.

[2] See Devitt, 1991a; Blackburn, 1989, Wright Introduction to 1993; Hale, 1997; Miller, 2003a.

[3] For critical discussion of the acquisition argument and references to the relevant literature, see Miller, 2003b. For the manifestation argument, see Miller, 2002; and Gamble, 2003.

[4] What follows in Sections 38.2 and 38.3 is, I hope, an improvement on a cruder version of the same basic line of thought developed in Miller, 2003a.

38.2 Common-Sense Realism

Michael Devitt suggests the following characterization:

Common-Sense Realism: Tokens of most current observable common-sense and scientific physical types objectively exist independently of the mental.   (1991a: 24)

There are thus two dimensions to realism about the external world: the *existence* dimension and the *independence* dimension. The realist asserts that tables, chairs, cats, the moons of Jupiter, and so on, exist; and that these entities exist objectively and independently of the mental. The table I am writing on exists and is not con-stituted by "our knowledge, by our epistemic values, by our capacity to refer to it, by the synthesizing power of the mind, by our imposition of concepts, theories, or languages"(1991a: 15). Nor is it made up of sense-data or mental states, whether as characterized by Descartes or by modern materialism.

We can accept this characterization of realism about the external world, with one minor qualification. As stated, common-sense realism is consistent with the follow-ing scenario: tables, chairs, cats, the moons of Jupiter and so on, objectively exist independently of the mental; but in every case, and for every possible property which one of them might possess, their possessing (or failing to possess) that property is constituted by "our knowledge, by our epistemic values, by our capacity to refer to it, by the synthesising power of the mind, by our imposition of concepts, theor-ies, or languages". Thus, the table I am writing on objectively exists independently of the mental, but its colour, weight, shape, molecular constitution, etc. are all in some sense constituted by us. A position such as this is hardly worth describing as realism about the external world. So we need to strengthen Devitt's characterization in order to preclude this type of scenario. One way to do this would be as follows:

Common-Sense Realism: Tokens of most current observable common-sense and sci-entific physical types objectively exist independently of the mental, and they possess some of their properties objectively.

It is an interesting question how many of the properties we could allow to fail to be possessed objectively before realism is compromised: for instance, is a view which allows that the table's being black, but not its being square, is constituted by facts about how it strikes humans, worth describing as realism? We do not need to pursue this question here. Clearly, the more properties that fail to be possessed objectively, the weaker the version of realism. So our new characterization of common-sense realism is the weakest position that anyone worth calling a realist about the external world is committed to.[5] Call this the *austere metaphysical characterization* of realism about the external world.

---

[5] The point made here should not be confused with the one that Devitt considers when he says "We have said that the entities must be of common-sense and scientific types; but perhaps we ought to say also that they must have some of the properties which tokens of that type are believed to have"(1991a: 21). Devitt goes on to reject this addition to his characterization of realism, and we can grant him this for the sake of the argument. The point in the text is not that the realist has to say that the entities have

It is an interesting question whether we can say anything more about what is involved in an item's "possessing a property objectively". But rather than pursue this interesting question here, we can cash out the idea as follows:

Common-Sense Realism: Tokens of most current observable common-sense and scientific physical types objectively exist independently of the mental; they possess some properties which may pass altogether unnoticed by human consciousness; and their innermost nomological secrets may remain forever hidden from us.[6]

Note that this formulation of common-sense realism is no less austerely metaphysical than the formulation which led to it. As such, it should be entirely acceptable to Devitt. Henceforth, when we refer to the austere metaphysical characterization of realism about the external world, it is this final formulation that is intended. We can now ask the following questions. How exactly does the plausibility or implausibility of semantic realism, as characterized by Dummett, impact upon the plausibility or implausibility of realism about the external world, characterized as above in austerely metaphysical terms? If we had cogent arguments against semantic realism, what would this tell us about realism about the external world?

38.3 THE PLAUSIBILITY OF A REALISTIC WORLDVIEW

As we've seen, on the conception of philosophy advocated by Dummett, the theory of meaning is the foundation of all philosophy. An alternative to this conception is suggested by the rejection of "first philosophy" in favour of philosophy naturalized recommended by e.g. Devitt and Sterelny. According to them

Philosophy's most basic task is to reflect upon, and integrate, the results of investigations in the particular sciences to form a coherent overall view of the universe and our place in it (1987: 225).

In order to get clear on the relationship between the theory of meaning and metaphysics in this alternative naturalized conception of philosophy, let's introduce the idea of a *worldview*. What is a worldview? A worldview consists of at least a *metaphysics* (an account of what there is and its nature in general), an *epistemology* (an

---

some of the properties which they are believed to have, but rather that *whatever* properties they have, they have at least some of them objectively. Note also that the strengthening of Devitt's characterization suggested does not require us to adopt or argue for any particular position on the ontology of properties. Some of the things Devitt says suggest that he would take our proposed strengthening to be included tacitly in his characterization of realism. For example, he writes "an object has objective existence, in some sense, if it exists and *has its nature* whatever we believe, think, or can discover"(1991a: 15, emphasis added). If the reference to the object's nature is just a reference to (some of) its properties, then there is no disagreement between us.

[6] This final formulation of common-sense realism has been deliberately adapted to include Crispin Wright's formulation of what he calls the "modest" ingredient in realism (Wright, 1993: 1).

account of how we can possess knowledge of the objects and properties included in the metaphysics), and a *semantics* (an account of how we can talk and think about the objects and properties included in the metaphysics). A *plausible* worldview is a worldview in which each of the components is itself plausible, and in which the components are at least mutually compatible. A plausible realistic worldview, for our purposes, is a plausible worldview which has common-sense realism, characterized austerely as above, as its metaphysical component. An alternative to Dummett's conception of the relationship between the theory of meaning and metaphysics could be spelt out as follows: it is the job of philosophy to find a worldview in which the various elements, metaphysical, epistemological, and so on, are individually plausible and mutually integrated, and in carrying out this job no one of the various aspects, metaphysical, epistemological, semantic, and so on, has any *a priori* priority over the others.

Plausibly, a realist metaphysics which cannot be integrated into a plausible realistic worldview is to an extent rendered unattractive. An account of the nature of the world which renders it difficult to see how we could think, talk, or acquire knowledge about that world is to that extent less than fully satisfactory, although in accordance with the naturalized conception of philosophy the precise extent to which the realist metaphysics is rendered unsatisfactory or unattractive will be an *a posteriori* matter, depending on which adjustment (rejecting the metaphysical, semantic, or some other component of the worldview) renders it best placed to predict the future course of experience. There are thus two ways in which a realist metaphysics can be attacked: *directly*, via pointing out some inadequacy within the metaphysics itself, or *indirectly*, via an argument that it cannot be integrated into a plausible realistic worldview. A successful argument that a realist metaphysics cannot be integrated into a plausible realistic worldview would thus establish that metaphysics was to an extent unsatisfactory. *One way of viewing Dummett's arguments against semantic realism, a way that detaches them from his conception of the theory of meaning playing a foundational philosophical role, is to see them as providing an indirect attack of the latter sort on a certain sort of realistic worldview.*[7]

Take common-sense realism, as defined above, to constitute the metaphysical component of a realistic worldview. What about the semantic component? What constitutes the fact that a certain sentence means what it does, or that a certain speaker understands that sentence in the way that he does? One influential type of answer to these questions is given by the Truth-Conditional Conception of Meaning and Understanding (TCCMU). According to the TCCMU, a sentence's having the meaning that it has consists in its having a certain truth-condition, and a speaker's understanding that sentence in a particular way consists in his having grasped the relevant truth-condition.

---

[7] We write here as though adopting a naturalized conception of philosophy (with respect to the sciences and other disciplines) were of a piece with accepting a naturalized conception of the role of the theory of meaning within philosophy itself. Of course, this is strictly speaking incorrect as it would be possible in principle to hold to one but not the other. But this would surely be an odd coupling: so they are run together in the text. Nothing of any importance appears to hinge on this.

One way of viewing Dummett's arguments against semantic realism in line with the naturalized conception of philosophy would be to view them as attempting to establish, in the indirect manner just adumbrated, that common-sense realism cannot be conjoined with the TCCMU to form a plausible realistic worldview.

How so? Recall the characterization of realism about the external world from above:

Common-Sense Realism: Tokens of most current observable common-sense and scientific physical types objectively exist independently of the mental; and they possess some properties which may pass altogether unnoticed by human consciousness; and their innermost nomological secrets may remain forever hidden from us.

Suppose that the universe is one of the tokens covered in the first part of the characterization, and suppose that the property of containing extra-terrestrial intelligent life is one of the properties the universe's having or failing to have may pass altogether unnoticed by human consciousness. According to the TCCMU, our grasp of the sentence "There is intelligent life elsewhere in the universe" consists in our grasp of its truth-condition. But, as we have just seen, this truth-condition—there being intelligent life elsewhere in the universe—is one whose obtaining, or failing to obtain, may pass altogether unnoticed by human consciousness. Thus, it follows that our understanding of the sentence "There is intelligent life elsewhere in the universe" consists in grasp of a potentially evidence-transcendent truth-condition. In general, common-sense realism in combination with the TCCMU yields semantic realism. Thus, *a cogent argument against semantic realism would establish that common-sense realism could not be combined with the TCCMU to form (part of) a realistic worldview.*

What would follow if Dummett's arguments against semantic realism turned out to be compelling? In order to have a plausible worldview, we would have to either give up common-sense realism, or give up the TCCMU. Thus, if Dummett's arguments against semantic realism proved to be successful, the realist about the external world would face the challenge of embracing one of the following options:

(i) Keep common-sense realism by rejecting the TCCMU: understanding a sentence is not a matter of knowledge of truth-conditions or knowledge of any other sort of condition (Devitt 1991a, b, c, Devitt and Sterelny 1987).

(ii) Keep common-sense realism and the TCCMU, but defuse Dummett's arguments against semantic realism by rejecting his claim that we have to give an account of what the knowledge of truth-conditions adverted to in TCCMU consists in (Davidson 1983).[8]

(iii) Keep common-sense realism, the TCCMU, accept Dummett's claim that we have to give an account of what the knowledge adverted to in the TCCMU consists in, but argue that even so Dummett's arguments against semantic realism can still be defused (McDowell 1981, 1987).

---

[8] On Davidson, see Smith, 1992, pp. 17–24.

(iv) Keep common-sense realism by rejecting the TCCMU: understanding a sentence is now to be construed as grasp of a certain sort of assertibility condition (Edgington 1981).

Of course, Dummett himself is inclined towards the following, antirealist, option:

(v) Give up common-sense realism, but hold on to TCCMU subject to the condition that the notion of truth which it takes as central is not potentially evidence-transcendent (see in particular the preface to Dummett, 1978; also Wright, 1993, *passim*).

This taxonomy of the options perhaps sounds strange: how could finding an alternative to the TCCMU be a task for the *realist*, given Dummett's numerous claims in his early work that opposition to realism takes the form of proposing an assertibility-conditional alternative to TCCMU?[9] But there is actually nothing strange here. The alternative taxonomy suggested by Dummett's early work is tied up with the idea that realism is to be *identified* with the TCCMU, an idea which is, as we noted, widely rejected and which we are putting on one side for the purposes of this chapter. And the taxonomy we have proposed sits better with Dummett's considered opinion (and Wright's current view) that it is the *antirealist* who has the best claim to the TCCMU: according to Wright and the later Dummett there is nothing wrong with the TCCMU as such, it is just that the realist misconceives the notion of truth which figures therein. Once the notion of truth is viewed as essentially epistemically-constrained, there is no problem about adherence to the TCCMU.

In accordance with the naturalized conception of philosophy and of the role of the philosophy of language within philosophy, questions about the plausibility of theses in the philosophy of language can potentially impact upon issues in metaphysics. As Devitt puts it himself:

Knowledge is a seamless web, as Quine told us long ago. Everything in the web can make a difference to everything else   (Devitt, 1991c: 75)

Be that as it may, it is an *a posteriori* question whether, even given the failure of attempts to integrate the TCCMU within a realistic worldview, we should actually contemplate giving up common-sense realism. Devitt is surely on safe ground when he writes:

Realism is too strong a doctrine to be overthrown by current speculations about understanding.   (Devitt, 1991b: 286)

At least, he is on safe ground if he is suggesting that it is *highly unlikely* or *improbable* that we will find that, as a matter of *a posteriori* fact, our best working theory of the world involves rejecting common-sense realism and holding on to TCCMU rather than vice versa. This is all of a piece with the naturalized conceptions of philosophy and semantics. But Devitt may himself overstep the bounds of his own naturalized conception of philosophy when he writes:

---

[9] See e.g. the much-quoted remarks in the early paper "Truth" (Dummett 1978: 19).

If it proves very difficult to naturalise reference, then perhaps we should seek a nonreferential theory of mind and language. If we were completely desperate, perhaps we might contemplate giving up naturalism. What we should *never* countenance for a moment is the idea that 'we cut the world into objects when we introduce one or another scheme of description'. To accept that idea is not to rebuild the boat whilst staying afloat, it is to jump overboard.   (1993a: 52, Devitt's emphasis)

But the idea that we are constrained, *a priori*, never to end up with an idealist plank in the philosophical boat, or an idealist strand in the philosophical web, is completely at odds with the Neurathian and Quinean images of which Devitt here avails himself.

It is thus perhaps worthwhile pausing to reflect on the genuine but limited significance of Dummett's arguments against semantic realism. On our construal of the situation, Dummett's arguments against semantic realism, even if completely successful, would not establish the unacceptability of realism about the external world. They could do so only in conjunction with (1) a cogent argument to the effect that *there could be no alternative to the TCCMU* together with (2) the *a posteriori* result that giving up realism rather than the TCCMU would make for a theory better placed to predict accurately the future course of experience. Dummett nowhere attempts to provide an argument for (1), although he does attempt to rebut objections to the TCCMU and to raise objections for alternative semantic views such as causal theories of reference (e.g. Dummett, 1973, appendix to chapter 5). And Dummett's foundationalist conception of the place of the theory of meaning within philosophy prevents him from even seeing the need for (2). So the most that Dummett's arguments against semantic realism can establish is that the common-sense realist requires an alternative theory of meaning to the TCCMU in order to have a realistic worldview immune to the worry that it turn out as a matter of *a posteriori* fact that common-sense realism has to be jettisoned. Dummett's arguments, even if successful, simply leave the common-sense realist with the challenge of finding such an alternative. Again, in the absence of a general argument to the effect that such an alternative is impossible, even if Dummett's arguments against semantic realism are cogent there is simply no *refutation* of realism as such, merely the provision of a *challenge* which the realist is obliged to meet. And even if the realist cannot meet that challenge, it may well turn out that *a posteriori considerations* about theoretical success dictate that it is the TCCMU, and not common-sense realism, that has to be jettisoned.

This, then, is the proper conception of the relationship between realism about the external world and semantic realism. Realism about the external world together with the truth-conditional conception of understanding yields semantic realism, so if semantic realism is unacceptable, the realist about the external world faces the possibility that he may have to find an alternative to the truth-conditional conception if he is to have a plausible realistic worldview. Dummett's arguments against semantic realism thus have genuine, if limited significance, for the metaphysical debate between realism about the external world and its opponents. Importantly, this significance is independent of Dummett's view that the theory of meaning is the foundation of all philosophy. The rejection of that view thus does not endanger the limited but genuine importance of Dummett's arguments against semantic realism for the issue of realism about the external world.[10]

38.4 SEMANTICS AND PSYCHOLOGY

We have seen that if Dummett's arguments against semantic realism are cogent, the common-sense realist *may*, as a matter of *a posteriori* fact, have to contemplate giving up his realism in order to hold on to the TCCMU. As noted, this seems unlikely, although not impossible. However, Devitt and Sterelny would claim that Dummett's arguments do not even have the very limited sort of significance we outlined in the previous section, since they presuppose two claims that are, as a matter of fact, false. They write:

Philosophers have had a lot to say about linguistic competence. Implicitly, at least, they have been concerned with competence in the full semantic sense, for they have attended to truth and reference. Yet, interestingly enough, they have typically made two mistakes that are parallel to the two major mistakes of the linguists. First, they conflate the theory of competence with the theory of symbols. Second, they write as if that competence consisted in propositional knowledge of the language. (Devitt and Sterelny 1987: 147)

We will examine the second of these assumptions in Section 38.6. In this section we will see that, whatever independent interest attaches to the distinction between a theory of symbols and a theory of linguistic competence, it has no bearing on the question of the significance of Dummett's arguments against semantic realism, construed as in the section previous.

Of the conflation between a theory of symbols and a theory of competence, Devitt and Sterelny write:

[This] mistake is certainly made by Michael Dummett. It is reflected in his slogan, "a theory of meaning is a theory of understanding". (Devitt and Sterelny 1987: 147)

The mistake lies in not distinguishing clearly between, on the one hand, the semantic properties of linguistic symbols and, on the other, explaining the psychological properties of competent speakers and hearers. The position of Devitt and Sterelny on this issue could be summed up in the slogan "Semantics is not psychology".[11] We shall not enter here into the issue of whether this is correct as a piece of Dummett exegesis. Rather, we shall simply assume that it is true but show that it does not affect in any

---

[10] It is perhaps worth noting that Dummett himself, in his valedictory lecture "Realism and Antirealism"(1993, essay 20), suggests that his "antirealist" arguments actually have more modest pretensions than he originally led us to believe.

[11] Devitt and Sterelny thus ascribe to Dummett a view on the relationship between semantics and psychology that is identical to Chomsky's view on the relationship between linguistics and psychology. For an account of the slogan "a theory of meaning is a theory of understanding" on which Dummett's view departs significantly from Chomsky's, see Smith, 1992.

significant way the account in Section 38.4 of the limited but genuine significance of Dummett's arguments against semantic realism.

Recall that we characterized semantic realism as flowing from TCCMU together with common-sense realism. TCCMU we characterized as the view that a competent speaker's understanding of a sentence consists in his knowledge of its truth-condition. Now, semantic realism will seem like a misnomer if the description of TCCMU as a *semantic* theory, or as the *semantic* component of a worldview, is itself a misnomer. And this is what Devitt and Sterelny claim: the subject matter of semantics is linguistic expressions and their relations to extra-linguistic reality, and it is wrong to import psychological considerations, such as considerations concerning speakers' competence, into a semantic theory.

Suppose that Devitt and Sterelny are right. What consequences follow from this for our interpretation of the significance of Dummett's arguments against semantic realism? Our claim was that if Dummett's arguments against semantic realism are cogent, then we cannot rule out the possibility that *a posteriori* considerations lead to the rejection of a certain type of realist worldview via the rejection of common-sense realism and the retention of TCCMU. The same point holds, in a slightly different form, if we accept Devitt and Sterelny's extrusion of considerations concerning speakers' understanding from the subject matter of semantics.

Our realist worldview will now contain common-sense realism, as before, as a metaphysical component. It will contain a semantic component, this time to the effect that the meaning of a sentence is determined by its truth-condition. There is no mention of understanding, so it might seem to be the case that Dummett's arguments cannot have even the very limited significance outlined in the previous section. But this would be too hasty. A worldview is going to have to contain, in addition to a metaphysical component and a semantic component narrowly construed, a psychological component dealing with the psychological properties of competent speakers. Devitt and Sterelny cannot claim that psychology is not psychology: so now the significance of Dummett's arguments can be cashed out more or less as before. Call the psychological thesis that a speaker's understanding of a sentence consists in knowledge of its meaning the epistemic conception of understanding. Then, common-sense realism plus the truth-conditional theory of meaning (narrowly construed) plus the epistemic conception of understanding together entail semantic realism. So if Dummett's arguments against semantic realism are cogent, then we cannot rule out the possibility that *a posteriori* considerations lead to the rejection of a certain type of realist worldview only this time via the rejection of common-sense realism and the retention of the truth-conditional theory narrowly construed together with the epistemic conception of understanding. Even if Devitt and Sterelny are right to object to the characterization of TCCMU broadly construed as "semantic", this leaves the potential significance of Dummett's arguments completely unchanged, so long as we accept that a plausible worldview must contain a psychological component in addition to a semantic component narrowly construed.

This shows that the issue concerning the relationship between the theory of symbols and the theory of competence as broached by Devitt and Sterelny is really a non-issue so far as the significance of Dummett's arguments against semantic realism is concerned.[12] As we'll see in the next section, the real issue comes down to that of the epistemic conception of understanding. So we can now put the issue about the relationship between semantics and psychology to one side, and move to a consideration of the epistemic conception of understanding.

38.5 KNOWLEDGE AND UNDERSTANDING

If we put the idea that the meaning of a sentence is its truth-condition together with the epistemic conception of understanding, we get the view that a speaker's understanding of the sentences in his language consists in knowledge of their truth-conditions. This view is a key premise in the Dummettian arguments whose significance we have been considering. Without this view, the Dummettian arguments against semantic realism cannot even get started: if understanding a sentence isn't a matter of knowing its truth-condition, arguments to the effect that semantic realism cannot cope with the idea that competent speakers know the truth-conditions of certain sentences of their language will be neither here nor there. Given this, one would expect the antirealist literature to provide a battery of arguments in favour of the epistemic conception of understanding. Unfortunately, this is not the case: there appears to be no sustained and properly worked-out argument for the epistemic conception in the antirealist literature.[13] Instead, there are scattered remarks here and there reacting to arguments against the epistemic conception. We will limit ourselves in this section to a consideration of some of these remarks.

Firstly, consider Wright's general remark about Devitt's attack on the idea that understanding a sentence is a matter of *knowledge*:

If the more radical antirealist claims about the dubiety of a conception of verification-transcendent truth are correct—we, the theorists—have no business involving that 'notion' in any sort of theory, whether conceived as descriptive of the content of object-language speakers' understanding or not. There has been some curious muddle about this simple point in recent realist commentary [e.g. Devitt 1991a]. So perhaps it is worth emphasising the obvious: whether or not the theory of meaning is conceived—as Dummett always urges it must be—as a theory of speakers' understanding, the project is, trivially, constrained by the demand that the concepts which it uses must be in good order. Criticism of that particular ingredient in Dummett's philosophy of language, or highlighting of the non-sequitur involved in the transition from the claims 1) that the meaning of a sentence is what someone who understands it knows, and 2) that the meaning of a sentence

[12] Of course, the claim is not that the semantics-psychology issue is a non-issue *tout court*. For an interesting exchange on the issue see Laurence, 2003 and Devitt, 2003.

[13] To be fair to the antirealist, though, a reason for this may be that the epistemic conception of understanding is already adhered to by many realists (e.g. McDowell, Davidson, Edgington). But the point made in the text stands: in order for Dummett's arguments to get started, the realist has to construe understanding a sentence as consisting in knowledge of its truth-conditions. And a rigorous and compelling argument for this claim is still wanting.

is determined by its truth-conditions, to 3) one who understands a sentence knows its truth-conditions, is therefore entirely futile if what one is trying to do is to protect realist semantics from antirealist attack.   (Wright 1993: 238)

These remarks are puzzling, and appear to beg the question against Devitt. They ignore the fact that Dummett's arguments against the good-standing of the realist 'concept' of potentially evidence-transcendent truth proceed *via* the assumption that someone who understands a sentence knows its truth-conditions. This assumption figures as a *premise* in Dummett's arguments.[14] Those arguments, after all, claim that if speakers were credited with knowledge of a potentially evidence-transcendent concept of truth, it would be knowledge that they could not manifest and that they could not plausibly have acquired in the course of ordinary training in the practice of speaking a language. So how could undermining an argument for the idea that understanding is a matter of knowledge of truth-conditions be an 'entirely futile' exercise for the realist, given that, if successful, a key premise in the antirealist argument against realist semantics would have been undermined?

Similar points apply to Wright's remarks upon the potential import for the antirealist arguments of causal theories of reference and essentialist theories of the extensions of natural-kind terms. One might think such views are inimical to the epistemic conception of understanding that the antirealist arguments rely on because if such views are correct then "certain real (usually causal) relations between our words and the world may make an essential contribution to the content of utterances without in any way figuring in the knowledge of those who utter them" (1993: 34). Wright argues that in fact causal theories of reference have no bearing upon the question of the good standing of the realist conception of truth:

to suppose that the truth-conditions of statements involving e.g. singular terms or natural kinds may be determined, in part, by factors of which someone who understands those statements need not thereby be aware is—if indeed true—quite different from supposing that the truth-conditions so determined may be realised undetectably. So far as I can see, the first supposition provides no motive whatever for the second.   (1993: 34)

Again, this appears to miss the point. The causal theorist of reference doesn't attack Dummett by arguing that the causal theory implies that statements involving the relevant terms may be true undetectably. Rather, he argues that it appears to undermine the *premise* in the antirealist argument to the effect that understanding a sentence is a matter of knowledge of its truth-conditions. The point is presumably that since understanding a sentence involving a natural kind term, for example, is a matter of the obtaining of a causal relationship between one's uses of the term and instances of the relevant kind, and since one need not be aware of the relevant causal relationship, it is difficult to see why this state of understanding should nevertheless be described in terms of the possession of *knowledge*. The point is not intended to function as a premise in an argument *to* realism, as Wright seems to imply: rather, it is intended

---

[14] In the passage just quoted Wright is interpreting the dictum that a theory of meaning is a theory of understanding as the claim that the meaning of a sentence is known by someone who understands it.

to undermine one of the key premises in the argument *against* realism. Wright has to argue that even granted the causal theory of reference, it is still appropriate to think of speakers who understand sentences containing the relevant term as knowing the truth-conditions of those sentences.

Wright's most sustained discussion of the idea of speakers' knowledge appears in a paper dealing with the issue of speakers' implicit knowledge of a systematic formal semantic theory in the style of a Davidsonian theory of meaning for a natural language. If speakers could be credited with implicit knowledge of the axioms of such a theory we would have the beginnings of an explanation of how they are able to understand novel utterances: a speaker's understanding of a previously unencountered sentence would be equated with his implicit knowledge of the theorem that gives its meaning, and so could be viewed as derived from his implicit knowledge of its constituent expressions and their mode of syntactic combination in a way that mirrors the derivational route in the theory from semantic axioms giving the meanings of words to theorems giving the meanings of sentences. Wright develops an argument of Gareth Evans' to the effect that actual speakers cannot plausibly be credited with knowledge of axioms, before asking how his discussion of this issue bears on the realism/antirealism debate conceived along Dummettian lines:

The answer, it should now be clear, is: not at all. The antirealist claim is that nobody may reasonably be credited with knowledge of the truth-conditions of any of a very substantial class of statements ... The conclusion is then drawn that truth may not play the central role in a comprehensive theory of (statement) meaning—at least not when understood *a la mode realistique*. The justification for this conclusion is that the theory is supposed to represent the knowledge in which understanding of the sentences of a language consists, which it must be failing to do if it cannot do better than articulate that knowledge in terms of concepts which they cannot have. Now if the discussion of implicit knowledge ... had yielded the result that a theory of meaning simply cannot be concerned with the description of speakers' knowledge at all, then the antirealist critique of (realist) truth-conditional semantics could not take exactly this form. But ... what emerged as problematic was the idea of speakers' implicit knowledge of the content of the *axioms* of a theory of meaning—no reason emerged to doubt the propriety of crediting them with implicit knowledge of the content of the meaning delivering *theorems* (1993: 237–8).

In short:

There is no cause to regard the antirealist's basic negative case as making use of the idea of implicit knowledge in a way which seems to deserve mistrust.   (1993: 35)

Wright's remarks here are, strictly speaking, correct: the central worry about ascribing implicit knowledge of meaning-theoretic axioms to speakers appears not to threaten the ascription to those speakers of implicit knowledge of the theorems of a semantic theory.[15] But arguably, although correct, Wright's observation is not

---

[15] The worry is in effect that states of "knowledge" of the content of semantic axioms (unlike knowledge of semantic theorems) will be inferentially insulated in a way in which genuine states of knowledge are not. See Evans, 1981 and Miller, 1997.

enough to divorce entirely the question of knowledge of semantic axioms from the question of knowledge of semantic theorems. The residual worry concerns the *motivation* for the view that competent speakers know the theorems of a correct semantic theory for their language. The worry is that the central motivation for viewing speakers as possessing knowledge of the theorematic output of a semantic theory is that if one does so, and if one can view speakers as implicitly knowing the axioms of the theory, one will thereby be in a position to explain semantic creativity: the derivational route from axioms to theorems in the theory will shed light on how understanding of an unfamiliar sentence can result from an understanding of its familiar constituents and their mode of combination. It follows that even if the arguments against ascribing implicit knowledge of semantic axioms do not *rule out* the ascription of implicit knowledge of theorems, they undermine the main motivation for the latter sort of ascription: if speakers cannot be credited with implicit knowledge of semantic axioms, the explanation of semantic creativity adumbrated above will not be possible, so that that source of motivation for the idea that speakers have knowledge of the semantic theorems will simply lapse. So Wright's claim that the issue of knowledge of theorems is *independent* of the issue of knowledge of axioms is not quite right: without the ascription of implicit knowledge of axioms, the ascription of knowledge of theorems begins to appear theoretically idle.[16]

Dummett's remarks on the issue are by and large unhelpful and equivocal.[17] For example, he writes:

It is one of the merits of a theory of meaning which represents mastery of a language as the knowledge not of isolated, but of deductively interconnected propositions, that it makes due acknowledgement of the undoubted fact that a process of derivation of some kind is involved in the understanding of a sentence.   (1993: 13)

Passages like these suggest that Dummett harbours some substantial *explanatory* aspirations for a theory of meaning. A competent speaker of the language under consideration hears a sentence he has never heard before. He derives his understanding of the sentence from his understanding of its constituents and their mode of combination. If we could view the speaker as knowing the propositions expressed by the axioms of a theory of meaning for his language, we could explain this fact about comprehension: he derives his understanding of the novel utterance from his understanding of its constituents just as the theorem for the sentence in the theory of meaning is derived from its axioms. But this explanation will only work if

---

[16] Wright may reply that the ascription of knowledge of theorems may be motivated independently of ascribing implicit knowledge of axioms to speakers, via the imposition of what he calls the structural constraint (1993: 214). It is not clear that this can be placed at the service of the antirealist arguments against semantic realism: the structural constraint concerns the semantic knowledge possessed by an ideally rational speaker, while the antirealist arguments turn on claims about the knowledge possessed by ordinary, less than fully rational, speakers. In addition, see Miller 1997 for an argument to the effect that the imposition of the structural constraint is itself not motivated independently of the ascription of knowledge of semantic axioms to ordinary language speakers.

[17] In the next few pages, I draw on Miller 2003b.

the speaker *really does know* the propositions expressed by the theory's axioms. As Wright puts it:

For Dummett, the explanatory ambitions of a theory of meaning would seem to be entirely dependent upon the permissibility of thinking of speakers of its object language as knowing the propositions which its axioms codify and of their deriving their understanding of (novel) sentences in a manner mirrored by the derivation, in the theory, of the appropriate theorems.   (1993: 207)

Thus, implicit linguistic knowledge is conceived of as implicit propositional knowledge actually possessed by competent speakers.

The problem is that this explanatory ambition for the notion of implicit knowledge appears to be completely at odds with another strain in Dummett's thinking on the issue. For example:

Our problem is, therefore: What is it that a speaker knows when he knows a language, and what, in particular, does he thereby know about any given sentence of the language? Of course, what he has when he knows the language is practical knowledge, knowledge how to speak the language: but this is no objection to its representation as propositional knowledge; mastery of a procedure, of a conventional practice, can always be so represented, and, whenever the practice is complex, such a representation often provides the only convenient mode of analysis of it. Thus what we seek is a theoretical representation of a practical ability.   (1993: 36)

Richard Kirkham gives the following explanation of the view of linguistic competence in the background of quotations like these:

Language competence, according to Dummett, is a practical ability, so a theory of meaning must *model* (or *represent*, Dummett uses the two words interchangeably) this practical ability. The model is a set of propositions which *represent* what a competent speaker of the language knows. This does not mean that a competent speaker of the language has propositional knowledge of these propositions. Knowing a language is a knowing-how not a knowing-that. It is ability knowledge, not propositional knowledge .... But ability knowledge can be *represented* by propositions.   (Kirkham 1989: 212)

Kirkham gives a nice example to illustrate the idea that knowledge-how can be represented by knowledge-that. Jones knows how to touch type: he can type accurately without looking at the keyboard. But he does not have propositional knowledge of the layout of the keyboard: he does not know *that the "R" is immediately to the left of the "T"* and so on. This is shown by the fact that Jones cannot draw a map of the keyboard without looking at it (and we might add, would not be able to identify the correct such map if presented with it alongside a group of inaccurate maps). However, even though he does not know e.g. that the "R" is immediately to the left of the "T", this piece of propositional knowledge *represents* Jones's ability in so far as he acts *as if* he had it: he acts *as though* he knew that the "R" is immediately to the left of the "T". And the same goes for implicit knowledge of truth-conditions:

Dummett would label the sort of epistemic relationship I have with these propositions as "implicit knowledge", meaning I do not really know *them* at all, but it is as though I did. So, too, according to Dummett, linguistic competence is *implicit* knowledge. But . . . he means only that one could *represent* a competent speakers linguistic behaviour with a list of this set of propositions. He does *not* mean that the speaker *really* knows these propositions. (1989: 212)[18]

The notion of implicit knowledge in the background in those passages where Dummett appears to harbour explanatory ambitions for grasp of a theory of meaning thus appears to be inconsistent with the notion of implicit knowledge figuring in passages where the theory of meaning is characterized as a theoretical representation of speakers' practical abilities. Dummett's more recent musings on these matters do little to help dispel the fog. In the preface to his 1993 collected papers, he argues that we cannot view linguistic understanding as a pure practical ability which can only be represented by theoretical knowledge, because we need a more robust attribution of knowledge to speakers if we are to pay sufficient heed to the fact that

[L]inguistic utterances are (usually) rational acts, concerning which we may ask after the motives and intentions underlying them. (Dummett 1993: x)

In addition

[T]he classic examples of pure practical abilities, like the ability to swim, are those in which it is possible, before acquiring the ability, to have a fully adequate conception of what it is an ability to do. By contrast, there is a clear sense in which it is only by learning a language that one can come by a knowledge of what it is to speak that language, just as it is only by learning how to play chess that one can come by a knowledge of what it is to play chess. (*Ibid.*)

So linguistic understanding is not an example of a pure practical ability: it is not something that can only be modelled on theoretical knowledge, it really does, at least in part, consist in theoretical knowledge. Speaking of his earlier work on the question of linguistic understanding and implicit knowledge he writes:

I now think that knowledge of a language has a substantial theoretical component; better expressed, that the classification of knowledge into theoretical and practical (knowledge-that and knowledge-how) is far too crude to allow knowledge of a language to be located within it.   (*Ibid.*)

Unless more is said, it is hard not to see Dummett as susceptible to a worry that Devitt and Sterelny express regarding the idea that speakers have knowledge of a grammatical theory (G) for their language:

We are left quite uncertain of the nature of the claim that the speaker has knowledge of G. It sometimes seems to be suggested [by Chomsky] that this knowledge is of a third sort, neither knowledge-that nor knowledge-how . . . If this were so, knowledge of G would be sui generis and badly in need of an explanation that is never given.   (1987: 139)

---

[18] See Miller, 2003b for an argument to the effect that adherence to this latter conception of implicit knowledge can explain an asymmetry between the antirealist's manifestation and acquisition arguments regarding the import for those arguments of considerations concerning the compositionality of meaning.

The idea that a competent speaker's understanding of a declarative sentence consists in his knowledge of its truth-condition, widespread as it is among both realists and antirealists, is thus sorely in need of further explanation and defence. Until that explanation and defence is provided, we cannot be sure that Dummett's arguments against realism have even the limited significance attributed to them in Section 38.4 above.

38.6 THE ARGUMENT AGAINST SEMANTIC REALISM

In his most recent version of Dummett's manifestation argument, Crispin Wright represents the argument as pointing to a tension between three propositions:

(1) Understanding a declarative sentence is a matter of grasping its truth-conditions.
(2) Truth is essentially epistemically unconstrained: the truth of a sentence is a potentially evidence-transcendent matter.
(3) Understanding a sentence is a complex of *practical abilities* to use that sentence.

Wright's idea is that, given the uncontentious nature of (3), either (1) or (2) will have to be jettisoned.

As before, if there is no compelling argument to the effect that the defender of a realistic worldview has to accept (1), the argument will simply fail to get off the ground. In fact, Wright considers an argument to the effect that (1) is simply a consequence of a number of *platitudes*:

[T]he identification of statement-understanding with knowledge of truth-conditions is actually no more than the immediate consequence of a series of platitudes. Understanding a statement is knowing what it states; what it states will be that a certain state of affairs obtains; so one who understands a statement will know this and, hence, know what kind of state of affairs that would be. Plainly the obtaining of such a state of affairs will be both necessary and sufficient for the truth of the statement—since that such a state of affairs obtains is, to repeat, precisely what it states. Hence who understands a statement thereby has a concept of the state of affairs which is the truth-condition for it; and, presumably, conceives it as such. (1993: 19)[19]

It is unclear whether this argument is actually strong enough to compel us to accept (1), which is in effect the TCCMU.[20] But rather than pursue that question here, we will grant Wright the "platitudes argument" for (1) and investigate what implications this would have for the relevance of the antirealist argument and whether or not the version of the manifestation argument that he runs is cogent.

---

[19] See also Wright, 1993: 253. Wright attributes the argument to McDowell, 1981, 1987, and also finds the argument in Blackburn 1989.

[20] For one thing, the "platitudes" argument looks very similar to an argument of Dummett's criticized in detail by Devitt in his 1991a: 270–2. Wright doesn't explicitly consider Devitt's critique of this argument, though he does hint (1993: 238) that the argument Devitt criticizes is indeed a "non-sequitur".

Suppose that this argument for (1) is cogent. What would follow for the limited but genuine significance we discerned earlier for Dummett's arguments against semantic realism? Recall that if those arguments were cogent, we would be left in the following situation: it *may* turn out, courtesy of *a posteriori* considerations concerning the capacity of a worldview to anticipate successfully the future course of experience, that the metaphysical component of a realistic worldview (common-sense realism) has to be jettisoned. Now although this is unlikely—the *a posteriori* considerations more probably will sanction the rejection of the TCCMU rather than common-sense realism—it is still a genuine, if somewhat faint, possibility. But on the "platitudinous" construal of (1) and the TCCMU the manifestation argument no longer possesses even this limited significance for the plausibility of a realist worldview. The reason is that, as currently construed, the TCCMU, as a "platitude", simply has no genuine *explanatory* value. In jettisoning (1) and the TCCMU from our worldview we would not be depriving ourselves of *any* explanatory capital but merely of a certain *form of words*.[21] This cannot be said of common-sense realism: it may be platitudinous in the sense of being widely believed, but it is not platitudinous in the sense in which (1) as now understood is platitudinous. So in depriving ourselves of common-sense realism we would be depriving ourselves of genuine explanatory capital and much more than a mere form of words. Thus, on this construal of (1) and the TCCMU, arguments against semantic realism are bound not to have even the limited significance we attributed to them earlier.

In addition, we can question whether, on this current construal of the manifestation argument and the TCCMU, the argument has any force independently of the rejected conception of philosophy as grounded entirely in the theory of meaning. Consider a natural reply to the claim that (1) and (2) in the triad above are, when conjoined, in some tension with (3). One could reply that we can perfectly well hold on to (1) and (2) as well as (3), by noting that nothing in (1) and (2) rules out construing linguistic understanding of a type of statement as a complex of what Blackburn calls the "neighbourhood abilities", which include, in Wright's words "the ability to appraise (inconclusive) evidence for or against such statements, or to recognize that one has so far no such evidence; the ability to recognize the validity of inferences to and from such statements; and the ability to utilize such statements in the ascriptions of propositional attitude" (1993: 17). Wright replies to this natural suggestion as follows:

If it is indeed, for such reasons, a platitude that to understand a statement is to know its truth conditions, what follows is not that the antirealist doubts are platitudinously wrong

---

[21] The TCCMU, as now construed, could not even contribute to an explanation of speakers' capacity to understand novel utterances. See Wright, 1993: 208. Andy McGonigal has raised an interesting worry about the argument here. "The platitudes serve to characterise, in part, notions like linguistic understanding, knowledge and meaning. They are just putatively *a priori* truths about such concepts. Rejecting such platitudes, it seems to me, just entails rejecting those concepts. But those concepts are involved in lots of genuine explanations about why and how people act as they do". However, this appears to be an overreaction: rejecting the platitudes might call for some *revision* of the relevant concepts, but it is not clear that it would require their wholesale rejection.

but that realism, as a substantial theory of statement content, exceeds the platitude. And so, independently, it does. Someone, for instance, who understands "There is intelligent life elsewhere in the universe" will be credited, by the platitudinous reasoning, with a conception of a specific kind of state of affairs—there being intelligent life elsewhere in the universe—whose obtaining he conceives as necessary and sufficient for the truth of the statement. How do we proceed from there to foist on him a conception of how such a state of affairs can obtain *undetectably*? The platitudes may be allowed to reinstate "knowledge of truth-conditions" as a general description of the abilities which those who understand a statement thereby have; but they do nothing to justify the idea that the notion of truth which the reference therein to "truth conditions" invokes is the realist's objective truth. (1993: 18–19)

The key point to be noted here is the constraint that Wright imposes on realist answers that attempt to take us beyond the platitudes:

[H]ow, specifically, is the idea that statements of a certain kind can be unrecognisably true or false on display in our ordinary, evidential, inferential, explanatory and other practices with them? . . . Let us have a description . . . of what specifically, in the exercise of an understanding of such statements, manifests the fact that it consists in grasping a potentially evidence transcendent truth condition?   (Wright, 1993: 253–4)

Hale's reply, on behalf of the antirealist, involves imposing the same constraint:

Here it is crucial to remember that the truth-theorist to whose defence [the natural suggestion] is (or ought to be) contributing is a realist, who holds that grasp of the sense of a sentence consists, in the case where the sentence is not effectively decidable, in knowledge of its possibly evidence-transcendent truth-condition. The responses [the natural suggestion] mentions, however, are entirely consistent with the antirealist view that, in such cases, understanding the sentence consists in knowing the conditions for its warranted assertion. That is, such responses do not distinctively display grasp of *realist* truth-conditions for the sentence.   (Hale, 1997: 281)[23]

The argument proffered here by Wright and Hale seems to be that since *there is nothing in the full description of the neighbourhood abilities* that would require (2) in addition to (1), we have not yet been shown how to mesh (1) and (2) with (3). But one has to wonder why they think that *that* is the sort of place where we are constrained to look for a justification of (2). The most natural place to look for such a justification of the idea that the truth of "There is intelligent life elsewhere in the universe" is potentially evidence-transcendent would be in some story about the nature of the universe, its capacity to furnish us with evidential traces of intelligent life, and how those evidential traces might dissipate before they ever reach the earth.[24] Alternatively, we might question why the realist, in justifying (2), is constrained not to appeal to anything other than facts about our "evidential, inferential, explanatory and other practices" in attempting to go beyond the platitudinous version of the

---

[22]   The particular example used by Wright has been changed to suit our present purposes.
[23]   Hale is in fact responding to Strawson, 1977: Strawson's reply to the antirealist is quite clearly an example of what we've called "the natural suggestion" in the text. In the quote from Hale the "responses" mentioned are in effect exercises of neighbourhood abilities.
[24]   On this, see Loar, 1987.

claim that to understand a sentence is to know its truth-conditions. Why limit us to descriptions of *linguistic abilities or linguistic practices* in our attempt to justify the idea that there may be intelligent life elsewhere in the universe even though we have no guarantee of being able to find evidence either for or against its existence? *The answer can only be that both Wright and Hale tacitly assume that realism is an essentially semantic doctrine.* Only thus can the constraints they impose on the attempt to justify (2) be explained. *What this shows is that, advertisements to the contrary not-withstanding, the latest version of the manifestation argument proffered by defenders of Dummett like Wright and Hale, still depends for its force on the assumption that realism is an essentially semantic doctrine. And what could justify that claim except the idea that the theory of meaning is the foundation of all philosophy?*[25] Absent that assumption, the "natural reply" adumbrated above appears to disable completely this version of the manifestation argument.[26]

38.7 CONCLUSION

In conclusion we can note that given the TCCMU, Dummett's arguments against semantic realism can be viewed as having limited but nevertheless genuine significance for the viability of a realist worldview even given the rejection of Dummett's conception of philosophy as grounded in the theory of meaning (Sections 38.1–38.5); that the TCCMU as it stands is, however, in sore need of explanation and defence (Section 38.6); and that Dummett's main argument against semantic realism, the manifestation argument, is, at least in the latest form of that argument developed by Wright and Hale, unconvincing in the absence of the assumption that the theory of meaning is the foundation of all philosophy (Section 38.7). Overall, then, we can conclude that although the realist should not ignore Dummett's arguments, it seems unlikely that those arguments will ever justify jettisoning the metaphysical component of a realist worldview.

REFERENCES

Blackburn, S. (1989). "Manifesting Realism", *Midwest Studies in Philosophy*.
Davidson, D. (1984). *Inquiries Into Truth and Interpretation* (Oxford: Oxford University Press).

[25] This also shows that the argument is question-begging: the constraint seems to depend on construing reality as in some sense a construct of our linguistic practices. It thus *presupposes* antirealism to begin with, and so cannot provide a non question-begging argument against realism.

[26] For more on this issue, see Miller, 2002. It should be noted that the manifestation argument is only one—albeit the central one—of a number of antirealist arguments against semantic realism. Other arguments include the "acquisition argument" mentioned above in fn.3, as well as the "argument from rule-following" and the "argument from normativity". For the latter two arguments see Wright 1993, 23–9 and 257–61.

Devitt, M. (1991a). *Realism and Truth*, 2nd edn (Princeton: Princeton University Press).

____ (1991b). "Aberrations of the Realism Debate", *Philosophical Studies*, 61.

____ (1993c). "Realism Without Representation: A Response to Appiah", *Philosophical Studies*, 61.

____ (2003). "Linguistics is not Psychology", in A. Barber (ed.) *Epistemology of Language* (Oxford: Oxford University Press).

Devitt, M. and Sterelny, K. (1987). *Language and Reality* (Oxford: Blackwell).

Dummett, M. (1973). *Frege: Philosophy of Language* (London: Duckworth).

____ (1977). *Elements of Intuitionism* (Oxford: Oxford University Press).

____ (1978). *Truth and Other Enigmas* (London: Duckworth).

____ (1991). *The Logical Basis of Metaphysics* (Cambridge MA: Harvard University Press).

____ (1993). *The Seas of Language* (Oxford: Oxford University Press).

Edgington, D. (1981). "Meaning, Bivalence, and Realism", *Proceedings of the Aristotelian Society*, 81.

Evans, G. (1981). "Reply: Semantic Theory and Tacit Knowledge", in S. Holtzmann and C. Leich *Wittgenstein: To Follow a Rule* (London: RKP).

Gamble, D. (2003). "Manifestability and Semantic Realism", *Pacific Philosophical Quarterly*.

Hale, B. (1997). "Realism and its Oppositions", in B. Hale and C. Wright (eds.) *A Companion to the Philosophy of Language* (Oxford: Blackwell).

Kirkham, R. (1989). "What Dummett Says about Truth and Linguistic Competence", *Mind*, 98 (390).

Laurence, S. (2003). "Is Linguistics a Branch of Psychology?", in A. Barber (ed.) *Epistemology of Language* (Oxford: Oxford University Press).

Loar, B. (1987). "Truth Beyond All Verification", in B. Taylor (ed.) *Michael Dummett: Contributions to Philosophy* (Nijhoff: Dordrecht).

McDowell, J. (1981). "Anti-Realism and the Epistemology of Understanding", reprinted in his *Meaning, Knowledge and Reality* (Cambridge: Harvard University Press 1998).

____ (1987). "In Defence of Modesty", reprinted in his *Meaning, Knowledge and Reality*.

Miller, A. (1997). "Tacit Knowledge", in B. Hale and C. Wright (eds.) *A Companion to the Philosophy of Language* (Oxford: Blackwell).

____ (2002). "What is the Manifestation Argument?", *Pacific Philosophical Quarterly*, 83.

____ (2003a). "The Significance of Semantic Realism", *Synthese*.

____ (2003b). "What is the Acquisition Argument?", in A. Barber (ed.) *Epistemology of Language* (Oxford: Oxford University Press).

Shieh, S. (1998). "Undecidability in Antirealism", *Philosophia Mathematica*, 6.

Smith, B. (1992). "Understanding Language", *Proceedings of the Aristotelian Society*, 92.

Strawson, P. (1977). "Scruton and Wright on Anti-Realism", *Proceedings of the Aristotelian Society*, 78.

Weiss, B. (2002). *Michael Dummett* (London: Acumen).

Wright, C. (1993). *Realism, Meaning and Truth*, 2nd edn (Oxford: Blackwell).

CHAPTER 39

TRIANGULATION

KATHRIN GLÜER

TRIANGULATION, the *Encyclopedia Britannica* informs us, is a technique used in navigation, surveying, and civil engineering, for precise determination of a ship's or aircraft's position, and the direction of roads, tunnels, or other structures under construction. It is based on the laws of plane trigonometry, which state that, if one side and two angles of a triangle are known, the other two sides and angle can be readily calculated.[1] As an analogy, triangulation was introduced into the philosophy of mind and language in Donald Davidson's 1982 paper "Rational animals". The analogy is used to support the claim that linguistic communication not only suffices to show that a creature is a rational animal in the sense of having propositional thoughts, but that it is necessary as well: "rationality is a social trait. Only communicators have it" (1982: 105).[2]

As originally presented, the triangulation argument employs the premise that in order to have any propositional thought whatsoever, a creature needs to have the concept of objective truth. To have this concept, however, it must stand in certain relations of interaction not only with objects or events in the world but also with other creatures sufficiently like itself. The most simple such situation involves a 'triangle' of two creatures interacting with each other and an object or event in the world. This pre-cognitive, pre-linguistic situation is therefore *necessary* for thought, according to Davidson. Only when the interaction forming the base line of the triangle is linguistic in character is triangulation *sufficient* for thought, however:

If I were bolted to the earth, I would have no way of determining the distance from me of many objects. I would only know they were on some line drawn from me towards them.

---

[1] "triangulation", *Encyclopædia Britannica* from Encyclopædia Britannica Online.
[2] This conclusion is already drawn in Davidson, 1975, but there, the argument remains extremely sketchy. Triangulation is not mentioned.

I might interact successfully with objects, but I could have no way of giving content to the question where they were. Not being bolted down, I am free to triangulate. Our sense of objectivity is the consequence of another sort of triangulation, one that requires two creatures. Each interacts with an object, but what gives each the concept of the way things are objectively is the base line formed between the creatures by language. The fact that they share a concept of truth alone makes sense of the claim that they have beliefs, that they are able to assign objects a place in the public world.   (1982: 105)

The triangulation analogy has come to play a more and more central role in Davidson's latest work. The idea has undergone considerable development in the process and proven very powerful and prolific.

Most generally, triangulation is the key element in what could be characterized as Davidson's *'solitary content argument'*: According to him, propositional content, be it of thought or linguistic utterances, requires a social setting. No solitary creature can have thoughts or mean anything by language. Moreover, as we already saw, thought and language are interdependent; no creature can have one without the other. This position in the theory of content is then used to support *epistemological anti-foundationalism* and *anti-skepticism*: Davidson's triangular account of the conditions of thought rules out any kind of foundationalism regarding empirical knowledge. If it works, none of the basic kinds of knowledge—knowledge of the external world, of our own and of other minds—is conceptually or temporally prior to any of the others (cf. esp. 1991). Moreover, since having any thoughts at all requires all three kinds of knowledge, triangulation even allows us "to recognize that we could never be in a position to doubt our knowledge of other minds or of an external world. (...) [I]f we can think or question at all, we already know there are other people with minds like ours, and that we share a world with them" (1998: 55, see also 1990: 201).

In what follows, I shall concentrate on the solitary content argument. Davidson himself summarizes it as follows:

[T]he triangle I have indicated is essential to the existence, and hence to the emergence of thought. For without the triangle, there are two aspects of thought for which we cannot account. These two aspects are the objectivity of thought and the empirical content of thoughts about the external world.   (1997: 129)

In many of the relevant passages, the arguments for these two necessity claims are more or less run together. Here, however, I shall set out and assess them separately. Let's take the second line of argument first; it aims at showing that without triangulation, thoughts would not be about empirical *objects*. Here, triangulation is presented both as a condition on empirical reference and as a principle for the determination of empirical referents. I shall therefore call this 'the argument from content determination'. Then, we'll look at the line of arguments aimed at showing that without triangulation, thoughts would not be *objective*. Thoughts, that is, would not have objective truth conditions, would not be true or false independently of being thought. Triangulation here is presented as a condition on having truth conditions, but not as a principle for determining them: In order to have thoughts a creature needs to have the *concept* of objective truth, it needs to have a *sense of objectivity*, and according to Davidson, this is impossible without triangulation. I shall refer to this second line of argument as 'the argument from objectivity'.

39.1 THE ARGUMENT FROM CONTENT DETERMINATION

39.1.1 Ambiguities of Cause

Davidson subscribes to what he calls 'perceptual' externalism about propositional content. The basic idea is that the content of basic perceptual beliefs (and their expressions) is determined by what *typically causes* them. Perceptual table-thoughts, for instance, are typically, though not necessarily, caused by tables. But to determine the typical cause of a certain belief-state it is not sufficient to consider a single creature and its causal relations to objects and events in its environment, Davidson argues. A plausible externalism needs to combine a perceptual with a *social* element, it needs to bring a second creature into the picture, a creature sufficiently like the first.

The problem this is supposed to help with is solving for a certain "ambiguity of the concept of cause": "In the present case", Davidson explains,

the cause is doubly indeterminate: with respect to width, and with respect to distance. The first ambiguity concerns how much of the total cause of a belief is relevant to content. The brief answer is that it is the part or aspect of the total cause that typically causes relevantly similar responses. What makes the responses relevantly similar in turn is the fact that others find those responses similar (. . .). The second problem has to do with the ambiguity of the relevant stimulus, whether it is proximal (at the skin, say) or distal. What makes the distal stimulus the relevant determiner of content is again its social character; it is the cause that is shared.   (1997: 130)

A typical cause of an event or state e is an event of a kind F such that Fs typically or normally cause events or states of the same kind, E, as e. To determine such a cause, we therefore need to look at a number of situations in which Es are caused and see which elements these situations have in common. The second of Davidson's problems is that there might well be *more than one* typical cause for Es. There might be longer *sequences* or *chains of causes* typically leading to Es. The first problem, however, is to determine which chains to look at for relevant similarities. Given that our inquiry is into the very conditions of thought, we cannot even take the *caused kind E* for granted. Davidson likes to bring this out by considering an observer trying to determine whether some creature has any propositional thoughts at all. Simply looking at all the causal chains going 'through' our creature will not lead anywhere: "[s]ince any set of causes will have endless properties in common, we must look to some recurrent feature of the gatherer, some mark that he or she has classified cases as similar", Davidson explains, and he concludes: "This can only be some feature or aspect of the gatherer's reactions" (2001a: 4f). Reactions need to be similar in order to determine what a creature finds similar, what it is reacting to. But similar in what respect? Will not any set of reactions be similar in endless respects as well? There is no way, Davidson argues, to determine the relevant standard of similarity from the reactions of a single creature alone. We need a second creature, a creature that itself reacts to the reactions of the first and finds a number of them similar.[3] Such an observer can then go on to determine the typical cause of reactions of this kind.

This line of argument is far from unproblematic. In fact, it appears to lead into an infinite regress: If what someone finds similar is determined by someone else's finding his reactions similar this in turn requires that the second person's reactions are found similar by someone other than himself, too. Davidson is aware of this: "Our grounds for claiming that a person finds one wolf similar to another is the fact that the person responds in similar ways to wolves. This prompts the next question: what makes the reactions similar? The only answer is, someone else finds both wolves and the reactions of the first person similar. This of course only puts the basic question off once more" (1997a: 83). Nevertheless, the quoted passage continues, the triangular situation is necessary for thought. But how can we hold on to this claim if it leads into regress? An answer might be sought in the anti-reductivist nature of the Davidsonian account; we shall come back to that later.

Another puzzling element is the strong antirealism or idealism seemingly implied by these passages (cf. also 1991: 212); Davidson sounds as if the relevant similarity of responses would actually disappear with its observer.[4] But even observer-relative properties, we might feel like objecting, do not do that. According to the predominant view, 'secondary qualities', for instance colors, are specified by reference to their effects on certain observers. But if an object is red, it is so no matter whether actually observed or not. Moreover, this antirealism does not square well with statements Davidson makes elsewhere. If we disregard it, however, the conclusion that reactions need to be observed as similar, as opposed to merely being observably similar, would seem to lose its motivation. We shall have occasion to return to these worries, but let's put them aside for the time being and look at Davidson's second problem.

This is formulated as a problem about the 'location' of the stimulus, that is, the event or object that is *the* typical cause of a certain reaction *r*. 'Where' on the causal chain leading to the reaction is it? As remarked above, there might be a whole portion of the chain leading to *r* that typically does so. Take a visual table-belief: What determines the table as the typical cause as opposed to, for instance, certain patterns of visual stimulation? The second, after all, probably is an even more typical part of chains leading to such beliefs. Davidson:

If we consider a single creature by itself, its responses, no matter how complex, cannot show that it is reacting to, or thinking about, events a certain distance away rather than, say, on its skin.   (1992: 119)

---

[3] As far as I can see, Davidson nowhere explicitly requires reactions to be behavioral; given, however, that he claims that their similarity needs to be actually observed, behavioral reactions would seem the only plausible candidates.

[4] Cf. Pagin 2001: 203, Glüer 1999: 74.

The answer, again, is supposed to derive from the reactions of a second creature. As observers, we not only react to the first creature's reactions, we also react to some of the things that typically cause them. The question which of its typical causes determines the content of a perceptual belief can then be answered in the following way, here with a child as the first creature:

The relevant stimuli are the objects or events we naturally find similar (tables) which are correlated with responses from the child we find similar. It is a form of triangulation: one line goes from the child in the direction of the table, one line goes from us in the direction of the table, and the third line goes between us and the child. Where the lines from child to table and us to table converge, 'the' stimulus is located. Given our view of child and world, we can pick out 'the' cause of the child's responses. It is the common cause of our response and the child's response.   (1992: 119)

More precisely, the principle of content determination for perceptual belief Davidson advocates is this: "The stimulus that matters is the *nearest mutual cause*" (1998: 84, emph. mine). In the spatial terms of the trigonometrical analogy, the two creatures' reactions allow to triangulate their object as the 'closest' or 'nearest' mutual cause of these reactions.[5]

To sum up: Davidson argues that the interactions of a single creature with its environment alone do not determine what it is typically reacting to. Typical causes are determined only as the *'common causes'*, that is, as the nearest mutual typical causes of the reactions of at least two creatures interacting with the same object or event. Since this is a necessary condition for thought, externalism needs to be both perceptual and social: Causes determine content only in social settings, as common causes.

Notice, however, that the sense in which the triangular situation so far described is *social* is limited. So far, there is no requirement of *interaction* between the two creatures; all that is needed is that *one* of them observes the other. *This* is the form of triangulation that was at work already in radical interpretation, the Davidsonian scenario in which an interpreter tries to assign truth conditions to the sentences of a radically foreign language by finding correlations between sentences held true and observable circumstances in the environment of the speaker. Here, the interpreter triangulates the objects of basic perceptual beliefs by taking "the speaker to be responding to the same features of the world that he (the interpreter) would be responding to under similar circumstances" (1991: 211). This is not a matter of choice but the only way into the foreign language.

But what exactly can be derived from these considerations? At most, it seems to me, that, if there is thought, it is *possible* for a suitable observer to establish the relevant correlations. The presence or absence of a mere observer cannot plausibly be taken to make a difference to the states the observed creature is in. Even if it is us, the observers, that categorize events as relevant causes and similar responses, it would, as Davidson himself puts it elsewhere, "be foolish to deny that these divisions exist

---

[5] In terms of the *temporal* order of the causal chains leading to the reactions, it would be the *last* one that is an element of both chains.

in nature whether or not anyone entertains the thought" (1998: 80). Equally foolish would it be to deny the observer-independent existence of the content-determining correlations. Therefore, no conclusion to the need for an *actual* second creature seems warranted at this stage. Davidson, however, claims that thought and language are social in a much stronger sense than this; he holds that "[t]he possibility of thought as well as of communication depends (...) on the fact that two or more creatures are responding, more or less simultaneously, to input from a shared world, and *from each other*" (1997a: 83, emph. mine). Clearly, it is the presence of an actual second creature that is required, according to Davidson, and it needs to interact with the first one, not simply observe it.[6]

39.1.2 Reactions and Interactions

In an interactive triangle, there are two creatures reacting both to an object or event in the world and to each other's reactions. A mere observer assigns objects to reactions on the basis of what is salient to him—but that might not be what is salient to the observed creature itself. Davidson illustrates this with the example of a lioness stalking a gazelle:

If a second lioness joins the first in pursuit of the gazelle, I can eliminate such complete dependence on my own choice of salient object in this way: I class together the responses of lioness A with the responses of lioness B in the same places and at the same times. The focus of the shared causes is now what I take to be the salient object for both lionesses. I no longer have to depend on my own choice of the relevant stimulus of the lionesses' behavior. (2001a: 6f)

Even this picture falls short of interaction, however; what we see instead is that the second creature needs to be *sufficiently similar* to the first in terms of natural similarity responses in order to triangulate the objects of its reactions. Davidson continues as follows: "A *further element* enters when the lions cooperate to corner their prey. Each watches the other while both watch the gazelle, noting the other's reactions to the changes of direction" (2001a: 7, emph. mine). And: "[A]n interconnected triangle such as this (two lionesses, one gazelle) constitutes *a necessary condition for the existence of conceptualization, thought, and language*" (*Ibid.*, emph. mine). The necessity of interaction, that is, comes into view first when we consider the possibility of reactions expressing propositional thought.

---

[6] This claim has weaker and stronger readings, however: A strong reading would have it that it is only in social situations that any state is a thought with empirical content or any reaction expresses such a thought. This is clearly too strong, for surely we are able to talk to ourselves or think while alone. In a footnote to "The Second Person" (1992) Davidson attacks Chomsky for thinking "the pure Robinson Crusoe case possible". And he explains: "By the pure case, I mean a Robinson Crusoe who has never been in communication with others" (1992: 115, n. 11). This might indicate a weaker reading of the necessity of actual interaction according to which interaction is necessary *at some point*, for instance, it might be necessary for the *acquisition* of language and concepts. See below.

The question can be put like this: What do we need to add to mere reactions to objects in the world to make these reactions into expressions of (or evidence for our creature's having) thoughts about those objects? Davidson's answer, here in terms of a speaker:

The speaker must have the concept of the stimulus. Since (. . .) a table is identified only by the intersection of two (or more) sets of similarity responses (lines of thought, we might almost say), to have the concept of a table (. . .) is to recognize the existence of a triangle, one apex of which is oneself, the second apex another creature similar to oneself, and the third an object (. . .) located in a space thus made common.   (1992: 120f)

The argument seems to be this: Since the object a thought is about is determined by triangulation only, thinking of a particular object *eo ipso* is thinking of an object someone else is also thinking of. Moreover, it is thinking of that object *as* an object someone else is thinking about. And unless someone else is in fact thinking of the same thing, and the thinker is justified in thinking so, there is no determinate object of the thought. "[T]he basic triangle of two people and a common world is one of which we must be *aware* if we have any thoughts at all" (1998a: 86, emph. mine).

Let's call this the requirement of *knowledge of the triangle*. The considerations supporting this requirement are, again, far from unproblematic. Even if we lay our doubts about the necessity of the actual presence of the second creature aside for a moment, it is not clear why thinking of a table would be thinking of it *as* an object someone else is also thinking of. It is far from obvious that in order to think we need to know the conditions of thought (or the principles of content determination),[7] not to speak of knowing that they are fulfilled.[8] If the knowledge requirement can be motivated, however, it immediately turns into a requirement of *mutual* knowledge in the Davidsonian picture: If it is a condition on my thinking of a table, that I know that someone else is thinking of the same table, then this other person in his turn needs to know that someone else is thinking of this table. In a basic triangle of just two creatures we therefore need to know this of each other. How is that possible?

For two people to know of each other that they are so related, that their thoughts are so related, requires that they be in communication. Each of them must speak to the other and be understood by the other.   (1992: 121)

Actual linguistic interaction, therefore, is a condition on the possibility of thought and language, according to Davidson; both are essentially social, and there is no thought without language.

Remember, however, that our question was what needs to be added to mere reactions to objects in the world to make these reactions into (expressions of or evidence for) thought; the answer seems to be, bluntly put: language. Davidson acknowledges that this answer might seem unhelpful, indeed: "The reason this answer is not very

---

[7] This is a point often made in discussions concerning the compatibility of externalism and self-knowledge. See, for instance, Burge, 1988.

[8] Cf. Verheggen, 1997: 364, who asks why mere thinking that one is interacting with another creature would not suffice. See also Heil, 1992, ch. 6.

helpful is that it assumes what was to [be] explained: Of course if there is language there is thought, so it cannot be easier to explain the former than the latter" (2001a: 13). As an *account* of the conditions of thought or language, the triangulation scenario is patently circular; moreover, this is not really a circle that first comes to its close with the invocation of language at the very end of the story. Rather, the account seems to invoke *conceptual capacities* in characterizing the very element that makes it social in a strong sense: the interaction between the triangulating creatures. This becomes especially clear in the requirement of mutual *knowledge*. And there does not seem to be any way around this, no way, that is, of characterizing any kind of interaction *sufficient* for thought that would not invoke such capacities. Thus, Davidson for instance writes: "it is only when an observer *consciously correlates* the responses of another creature with objects and events in the observer's world that there is any basis for saying the creature is responding to those objects and events" (1991: 212, emph. mine). And an interactive triangle is sufficient for thought only if exercise of the same, clearly thought-like, conceptual capacities is required of the first creature itself. The circularity in question therefore cannot be avoided by merely shunning the last steps of the argument, by, for instance, arguing that the requirement of mutual knowledge does not hold, or by denying that only language can fulfill it. Rather, it seems to necessarily come with any attempt to answer the Davidsonian question: "What must be added to the basic triangle of two or more creatures interacting with each other through the mediation of the world *if that interaction is to support thought?*" (2001a: 13, emph. mine).

Davidson himself does not regard this circularity as damaging to his argument; he comments: "Nevertheless, it is useful to recognize the somewhat surprising fact that the social element that is essential to language is also essential to thought itself" (2001a: 13). The use of the triangulation analogy, he seems to be saying, does not lie in providing an account of the conditions of thought and language, at least not if by an account we mean something like *necessary and sufficient conditions*. Such an account is, according to Davidson, simply not forthcoming. Thought, language and the other intentional concepts cannot be reduced to anything else (cf. 1992: 120; 2001a: 13). It is, therefore, not surprising that as soon as we try to say what it is that must be added to the basic triangle that would *suffice* for thought we run in a circle.

However, being an anti-reductionist does *not* preclude one from having something interesting to say about the conditions of thought, not even in non-intentional terms. For even where necessary and sufficient conditions cannot be other than circular, the same does not hold for conditions that are *necessary, but not sufficient*. Even if triangular interaction that supports thought cannot be spelled out without circularity, triangular interaction that does *not* support thought can:

There is a prelinguistic, precognitive situation which seems to me to constitute a necessary condition for thought and language, a condition that can exist independently of thought, and can therefore precede it. (. . .) The basic situation is one that involves two or more creatures simultaneously in interaction with each other and with the world they share; it is what I call *triangulation*. It is the result of a threefold interaction, an interaction which is twofold from the point of view of each of the two agents: each is interacting simultaneously with the world and with the other agent. To put this in a slightly different way, each creature learns to correlate the reactions of other creatures with changes or objects in the world to which it also reacts. One sees this in its simplest form in a school of fish, where each fish reacts almost instantaneously to the motions of the others. This is apparently a reaction that is wired in. A learned reaction can be observed in certain monkeys which make three distinguishable sounds depending on whether they see a snake, an eagle, or a lion approaching; the other monkeys, perhaps without seeing the threat themselves, react to the warning sounds in ways appropriate to the different dangers, by climbing trees, running, or hiding. But on reflection we realize that the behavior of these primates, complex and purposeful as it is, cannot be due to propositional beliefs, desires, or intentions, nor does their mode of communication constitute a language.   (1997: 128)

A necessary condition on a creature's having thought and language that we can formulate in non-circular terms, is that of *the actual presence of and interaction with a second creature*, Davidson claims.[9]

But even if being an anti-reductionist does not preclude one from formulating interesting necessary conditions, it does not provide any *support* for the necessity of some particular condition. And, obviously, such support cannot be derived from conditions that are sufficient, but circular, either. So, the question is: Does Davidson provide sufficient support for the claim that thought and language are necessarily social? Support, that is, that does not derive from any circular, but sufficient condition? Pagin, when belaboring this point, is doubtful: "[A]s things actually stand in Davidson's account, we cannot understand *why* the second creature or person would be needed *except* by attributing thoughts, awareness and knowledge to the two creatures to begin with" (Pagin, 2001: 205).

What about animal triangulation, however? Assume, we grant Davidson that the lionesses, fish and even the monkeys in his examples do not have propositional thoughts. Still, a second lioness, fish or monkey is required to determine the objects of their non-cognitive reactions to objects in the world, according to Davidson. Does not this provide non-circular support for the claim that for cognitive reactions a second creature of the same kind is required, too?

There are a number of issues here. One is that Davidson claims that an *interactive* triangle is necessary for thought. It does not seem part of his argument, however, that a second lioness interacting with the first is necessary for determining the common causes of their reactions; as we saw above, he considers that possible as soon as we can observe two lionesses reacting simultaneously to the same gazelle; the lionesses interacting with each other, on the contrary, was considered as a further element on the road to thought, so to speak (cf. 2001a: 6f). This, however, would seem to

---

[9] It seems doubtful, however, that an analogous move really is open regarding the infinite regress started by requiring a second creature for the determination of relevant similarities among responses (see above, 39.1.1.). This regress clearly is of a vicious kind: The initial condition generates an infinity of conditions on similarity such that the fulfillment of the n+1st is *prior* to that of the nth. And there is no way to formulate the requirement that would not give rise to regress; in particular, the regress does not depend on presupposing thought. That the requirement of a second person leads to regress, therefore, does not allow for it's nevertheless being a necessary condition on similarity.

qualify the necessity of a second lioness, fish, or monkey. If no interaction is required to determine the objects of their reactions, the necessity of the actual presence of the second animal would be subject to exactly the same doubts as voiced above: The object does not have to be determined by actual causal chains intersecting, potential ones would seem to do equally well.

Another question is the following: Even if actual second monkeys were necessary, what would this teach us about the conditions of thought? If there is an irreducible gap between reactions like those of the monkeys and propositional thought and its expression, why would what is necessary for monkey reactions to have determinate objects also be necessary for propositional thought? Which relation between monkeys and sapient beings warrants this conclusion? It is natural and plausible to conceive of reactions like those of the monkeys as *an earlier stage in the evolution* of sepient beings. But does that support the necessity claim? Notice, that this is *not* a question about the modal force, if any, attaching to considerations of evolutionary priority. Even if we grant the evolutionary priority of the monkey reaction stage, both onto- and phylogenetically, we still lack good reason for thinking that what was necessary at an earlier stage remains so at a later.[10] This could only be changed, it seems to me, by a plausible story about how thought emerges from reactions like those of the monkeys, a story that would make essential use of second creatures in bridging the gap between monkeys and thoughts. But no such story can be expected, according to Davidson himself, and for conceptual reasons:

The difficulty in describing the emergence of mental phenomena is a conceptual problem (. . .). In both the evolution of thought in the history of mankind, and the evolution of thought in an individual, there is a stage at which there is no thought followed by a subsequent stage at which there is thought. To describe the emergence of thought would be to describe the process which leads from the first to the second of these stages. What we lack is a satisfactory vocabulary for describing the intermediate steps.   (1997: 127)

This concludes our discussion of Davidson's argument from content determination. Triangulation offers a powerful and suggestive analogy for the exploration of the conditions on and principles of externalist content determination. It seems doubtful, however, that the analogy really bears out the strong social necessity claim Davidson would like it to support. Content determination is only the first part of the triangulation arguments, though; it remains to consider the argument from objectivity.

39.2 THE ARGUMENT FROM OBJECTIVITY

If the argument from content determination strikes one as Quinean in character, one might like to characterize the argument from objectivity as more Wittgensteinian

---

[10] Notice, too, that this might seem to invert the intended direction of support when Davidson, for instance, says: "[T]he triangle I have indicated is essential to the existence, and *hence* to the emergence, of thought" (1997: 129, emph. mine).

in spirit.[11] It starts out from the following observation: "[T]hought is objective in the sense that it has a content which is true or false independent of the existence of the thought or the thinker" (1997: 129). That thought is objective in this sense should, despite the realist flavor of Davidson's formulation, be rather uncontroversial; basically, the claim is that propositional thought is something the concept of truth, however precisely it is to be understood, is essentially applicable to. Thoughts have truth conditions, and concepts have satisfaction conditions. Which applications of a given concept are true and which mistaken, however, is not determined by the thinker's believing them to be. The objectivity of thought minimally is the requirement that the concepts of truth and falsity have an application to thought and its expressions. According to Davidson, however, there is no 'space' for the application of these concepts outside or independent of a triangular setting: "The point isn't that consensus defines the concept of truth but that it creates the space for its application. If this is right, then thought as well as language is necessarily social" (1997: 129).

For one creature in isolation, the thought seems to be, it remains indeterminate which of its reactions, if any, constitute mistakes or even *deviate* from the others. Only a social setting provides a contrast necessary for determining any reaction as a deviation; if the reactions of two creatures to some kind of object or event normally agree, but on some particular occasion differ from each other, at least one of them deviates from the regularity in their joint behavior.[12] Such discrepancy is not sufficient to determine who is deviating, but, or so the space-metaphor suggests, it is necessary for applying the concept of deviation at all (cf. 2001a: 7). The argument from objectivity, thus tries to establish triangulation as a condition on thought's having determinate content, but not as a principle for determining truth conditions: "The point is not to identify the norm, but to make sense of there being a norm" (2001a: 7).

Possible deviation is not yet possible mistake, however:

[T]o have a belief it is not enough to discriminate among aspects of the world, to behave in different ways in different circumstances (. . .). Having a belief demands in addition appreciating the contrast between true belief and false, between appearance and reality, mere seeming and being. (. . .) Someone who has a belief about the world—or anything else—must grasp the concept of objective truth, of what is the case independently of what he or she thinks.   (1991: 209)

In order for the concept of *truth* to be applicable to thoughts, the argument goes, the thinker himself must have this concept. Davidson formulates what basically is the same requirement in a variety of ways; originally he put it in terms of the necessity of having the concept of *belief* for having any beliefs (1975; 1982). In other places,

---

[11] Pagin uses these characterizations in Pagin 2001, and Davidson repeatedly acknowledges Wittgensteinian inspirations. There are clear parallels between his argument and certain (community) readings of the so-called private language argument.

[12] This only holds on the assumption that there in fact is a joint regularity; otherwise, the discrepancy might equally well show that the creatures in question are not reacting to a common cause anymore—or have never been doing that.

the stress is on the concept of a *mistake*, of erring in one's beliefs. These concepts form a package, and without them, a creature cannot be said to have any beliefs at all, according to Davidson. And he concludes: "We must ask, therefore, after the *source of the concept of truth*" (1991: 209, emph. mine).

As in the argument from content determination, the perspective is, thus, shifted to the first person: It is not enough that there are two interacting creatures; rather, they need to be aware of each other's reactions and their possible divergence. Since mistakes are determined only on the basis of such divergence, having the concept of a mistake itself requires a social setting. Here, too, interaction is not supposed to be a sufficient condition for thought; the monkeys from the earlier example interact in this sense but they do not have propositional thought—exactly because, Davidson argues, their behavior does not justify the ascription of the *concepts* of truth and mistake to them. Again, only linguistic communication does: "A grasp of the concept of truth, of the distinction between thinking something is so and its being so, depends on the norm that can be provided only by interpersonal communication" (1994: 15).

That, from the perspective of the thinker himself, triangulation creates the 'space' for the application of the concepts of truth and mistake can mean at least two things, however. It can mean, either, that these concepts can be (truly) *applied* (to myself or others) only in triangular situations,[13] or it can mean that they can be *acquired* only in triangular situations.

There are many passages in Davidson suggesting that he, in fact, sees triangulation as a condition on the *acquisition* of the concepts of truth and mistake, for instance, the following one:

Thought, propositional thought, is objective in the sense that it has a content which is true or false independent of the existence of the thought or the thinker. Furthermore, this is a fact of which a thinker must be *aware*; one cannot believe something, or doubt it, without knowing that what one believes or doubts may be either true or false and that one may be wrong. *Where do we get the idea that we may be mistaken*, that things may not be as we think they are?   (1997: 129, emph. mine)

The suggestion then is that without the actual experience of discrepancy, and, possibly, correction, the acquisition of the concepts of truth and mistake is impossible.

As a point about the required causal history of the acquisition of these concepts, this might easily seem sheer empirical speculation. And even if it is empirically true that creatures like us do not develop rational minds in isolation—Kaspar Hauser cases might give some reason to think so—there is no evidence that this is due to missing experiences of divergent reactions. If this were their final resting point, the triangulation arguments would seem robbed of much of their intuitive force.[14]

---

[13]   Any use outside of social situations would have to be characterized as in some sense derivative from this original use.

[14]   Both Glüer (1999: 78) and Pagin (2001: 207) have charged Davidson with ultimately resting his case on sheer empirical speculation. Replying that there is a degree of empirical speculation in any argument short of logical proof does not really help here (cf. Davidson, 2001b). For even if we subscribe to this naturalist picture of philosophy, there clearly are degrees of empiricity and some claims clearly are too empirical to support much modal consideration.

On a more conceptual reading, however, the point of the argument from objectivity is that an isolated creature cannot (truly) apply the concepts of truth and mistake to anything, not even to what is going on in its own mind. This becomes possible only in a social setting:

If you and I can each correlate the other's responses with the occurrence of a shared stimulus, however, an entirely new element is introduced. Once the correlation is established it provides each of us with a ground for distinguishing the cases in which it fails. Failed natural inductions can now be taken as revealing a difference between getting it right and getting it wrong, going on as before, or deviating, having a grasp of the concepts of truth and falsity.   (1994: 15)

On this reading, the argument would seem open to much the same objections that were formulated for the argument from content determination. As witnessed by the passage just quoted, to be *sufficient* for thought, triangulation involves the very capacities it was to make possible and that leaves the necessity of those parts of the condition that can be formulated without circularity unsupported. Moreover, any 'norm' for truth and mistake determining these in relation to the reactions of fellow creatures would seem to determine them regardless of the actual presence or absence of those fellows.[15] While it might be true—and radical interpretation provides some reason to believe it is—that if a creature has language, and, thus, thought, triangular principles of content determination do apply, it thus remains doubtful that they apply *because of* the triangulation.

REFERENCES

Burge, T. (1988). "Individualism and Self-Knowledge", *Journal of Philosophy*, 85: 649–63.
Davidson, D. (1975). "Thought and Talk", in Davidson, 1984: 155–70.
_____ (1982). "Rational Animals", in Davidson, 2001: 95–106.
_____ (1984). *Inquiries into Truth and Interpretation*, Oxford: Clarendon Press.
_____ (1990). "Epistemology Externalized", in Davidson, 2001: 193–204.
_____ (1991). "Three Varieties of Knowledge", in Davidson, 2001: 205–220.
_____ (1994). "The Social Aspect of Language", in *The Philosophy of Michael Dummett*, eds. B. McGuiness, G. Oliveri, Dordrecht: Kluwer, 1–16.
_____ (1997). "The Emergence of Thought", in Davidson, 2001: 123–92.
_____ (1997a). "Indeterminacy and Antirealism", in Davidson, 2001: 69–84.
_____ (1998). "Interpretation: Hard in Theory, Easy in Practice", in *Meaning and Interpretation*, ed. D. Prawitz, Stockholm: Kungliga Vitterhets Historie och Antikvitets Akademien, 71–86.
_____ (1998a). "The Irreducibility of the Concept of the Self", in Davidson, 2001: 85–92.
_____ (2001). *Subjective, Intersubjective, Objective*, Oxford: Clarendon Press.

---

[15] That it is necessary to have the concept of *belief* in order to have beliefs or to mean anything might well also strike one as *empirically false*; children under the age of four normally do not yet have a 'theory of mind' sophisticated enough for second-order belief, yet it seems extremely difficult to maintain that they have no beliefs or do not mean anything by what they say. Even clearer counterexamples might be provided by certain high-functioning subjects with autism (cf. Glüer and Pagin, 2003).

—— (2001a). "Externalisms", in *Interpreting Davidson*, eds. P. Kotatko, P. Pagin, G. Segal, Stanford: CSLI, 1–16.

—— (2001b). "Comments on Karlovy Vary Papers", in *Interpreting Davidson*, eds. P. Kotatko, P. Pagin, G. Segal, Stanford: CSLI, 285–307.

Føllesdal, D. (1999). "Triangulation", in *The Philosophy of Donald Davidson (The Library of Living Philosophers, Vol. 27)*, ed. L. Hahn, Chicago: Open Court, 719–28.

Glüer, K. (1999). *Sprache und Regeln*, Berlin: Akademie Verlag.

Glüer, K., and Pagin, P. (2003). "Meaning Theory and Autistic Speakers", *Mind and Language*, 18: 23–51.

Heil, J. (1992). *The Nature of True Minds*, Cambridge: Cambridge University Press.

Pagin, P. (2001). "Semantic Triangulation", in *Interpreting Davidson*, eds. P. Kotatko, P. Pagin, G. Segal, Stanford: CSLI, 199–212.

Talmage, C. (1997). "Meaning and Triangulation", *Linguistics and Philosophy*, 20: 139–45.

Verheggen, C. (1997). "Davidson's Second Person", *The Philosophical Quarterly*, 47: 361–9.

CHAPTER 40

SHARED CONTENT

HERMAN CAPPELEN
AND ERNEST LEPORE

A general and fundamental tension surrounds our concept of what is said. On the one hand, what is said (asserted, claimed, stated, etc.) by utterances of a significant range of sentences is highly *context sensitive*. More specifically, (Observation 1 (O1)), what these sentences can be used to say depends on their contexts of utterance. On the other hand, speakers face no difficulty whatsoever in using many of these sentences to say (or make) the exact same claim, assertion, etc., across a wide array of contexts. More specifically, (Observation 2 (O2)), many of the sentences in support of (O1) can be used to express the same thought, the same proposition, across a wide range of different contexts.

The puzzle is that (O1) and (O2) conflict: for many sentences there is evidence that what their utterances say depends on features $F_1 \ldots F_n$ of their contexts of utterance; while, at the same time, there is also evidence that two utterances of these sentences in contexts C and C' express agreement, despite C and C' failing to overlap on $F_1 \ldots F_n$.

Here's a simple illustration. What an utterance of (1) says depends in part on the contextually salient comparison class, standards of measurement, and other such things.

(1) Serena is really smart.

These data support (O1) for the comparative adjective 'smart'. Yet, suppose all we tell you is that Venus uttered (1). We predict the following:

- There is a sense in which you can understand what Venus said, *viz.* that Serena is really smart.
- You can repeat what Venus said, i.e. do what we're about to do right now, *viz.* say the same as Venus did: Serena is really smart.
- You can indirectly report Venus by uttering (2):

(2) Venus said that Serena is really smart.

What's puzzling is how you can achieve all this without extensive knowledge of the contextually salient aspects of Venus' original utterance of (1). How can you do it without knowing exactly which comparison class, measurement method, etc., Venus' utterance picked out? Why does it seem not to be a requirement on your saying what Venus said that your context of utterance overlaps in relevant ways with hers?

Before elaborating, we want to say why this tension between observations (O1) and (O2) interests us.

First, there's a *Very Big Picture Issue* we want to draw attention to: contemporary philosophy of language has to a large extent lost sight of some fundamental facts about how we communicate *across* contexts. We can communicate and understand each other despite an overwhelming range of differences (in perceptual inputs, interests, cognitive processing, background assumptions, conversational contexts, goals, sense of relevance, etc.). This fact should be at the forefront of any reflection about communication, but it hasn't been.

Second, we want to use data in support of (O2) to raise objections to a range of so-called contextualist semantic theories constructed in response to data in support of (O1). Contemporary philosophy (and linguistics) is filled with well-supported observations of instances of (O1). On this basis alone, various categories of expression are, though hitherto unrecognized as such, inferred to be context sensitive. Examples from an extensive list include not just comparative adjectives like 'smart', but also quantifier expressions (e.g. 'every'), vague terms (e.g. 'red'), semantic expressions (e.g. 'true'), epistemic (e.g. 'know'), moral (e.g. 'good'), and psychological (e.g. 'believes') attributions, to name a few. Yet in *all* these cases, much like with 'smart', (O2) is well evidenced. These linguistic items can be used, in indirect reports, in ways that appear context *insensitive*.

The bottom line is that (O1) and (O2), at first blush, are incompatible, and so, no semantic theory that postulates context sensitivity based on (O1) is acceptable unless it shows how doing so is compatible with (O2). Most theorists, even those who acknowledge (O2), neglect to provide such explanations.

The paper divides into three parts. In Section 40.1–40.3, we present in greater detail the puzzle (or tension or whatever you want to call it); in Section 40.4–40.9, we discuss several failed solutions; and in Section 40.10, we present and defend our favored solution.

40.1 CONTEXTUAL VARIABILITY IN WHAT-IS-SAID

How much variability is there in what can be said (asserted, claimed, etc.) with a single sentence in different contexts? For any sentence S, to answer this question, we must look to see whether speakers agree that, when uttered in differing contexts, what

S says varies. The consensus for many sentences S is (O1): *viz.* what S says depends on a context of utterance. (O1) is trivial for sentences which contain overt indexical or demonstrative expressions. What distinct utterances of 'I'm happy' or 'That's a boy' say differs contingent upon who is being indexed or demonstrated. However, as the above data render obvious, (O1) is no less trivial for distinct utterances of (1) (a sentence devoid of any obvious context sensitive expressions). What distinct utterances of (1) say differs contingent upon the contextually relevant comparison class or norm.

Watching Serena Williams playing tennis, entirely absorbed in her game, after a particularly clever play, Venus' utterance of (1) might say Serena is a really smart tennis player; however, Serena's agent's utterance of (1), in a context where the topic is astute negotiators in professional sports, might say that she is a really smart negotiator. The intuition is that what utterances of (1) say depends on which comparison class or norm a speaker intends or is contextually salient.

Quantifier sentences provide another easy illustration. In Alex's apartment, (3) can be used to assert *Alex rearranged all the furniture in his apartment*.

(3) Alex rearranged everything.

However, looking over a paper Alex has written, where he rearranged the sections, (3) can be used to say *Alex rearranged all the sections of his paper*. An obvious conclusion to draw is that what (3) says varies with context. More generally: since nothing special attaches to the quantifier expression 'every' or the comparative adjective 'smart' in these examples, what's said by quantifier or comparative adjective sentences varies across contexts.[1]

Exploiting these sorts of thought experiment, philosophers (and linguists) conclude that sentences not only containing comparative adjectives and quantifier expressions, but also those containing propositional attitude verbs, knowledge attributions, epistemic modals, counterfactual conditionals, vague terms, moral terms, aesthetic terms, weather and temporal reports, to name a few, can all be used to say different things in different contexts. (To limit discussion to a reasonable length, we assume some familiarity with the relevant literature. For the easiest and most compelling cases we recommend Cappelen and Lepore (2005), ch. 2.)

According to some[2] (including us), this observation generalizes: intuitions about context shifting generalize to all expressions. What began as a modest, though surprising, extension of the list of expressions whose usage can provoke intuitions about differences in what's said ultimately leads to a radical view that every expression can be so used (see Cappelen and Lepore (2005), ch. 3–5).

We turn to the second observation, which concerns content sharing.

[1] There's another way to run these kinds of thought experiments: Describe an utterance of (3) in a context C and elicit the judgment it is true. Then describe an utterance (simultaneous) of (3) in another context C' and elicit the intuition it is false. On this alternative, we don't try to elicit direct intuitions about what the speaker said, but simply intuitions about whether what was said (no matter what it was) is true or false. If these judgments differ, then this has to be because differing contents were expressed.

[2] Neo-Wittgensteineans like Bezuidenhout (1997, 2002); Carston (1998, 2002); Moravcsik (1990, 1998); Recanati (2001, 2004); Searle (1978, 1980); Sperber/Wilson (1986); Travis (1985, 1989, 1996), etc.

40.2 THE EASE OF CONTENT SHARING

Speakers, more often than not, succeed in mutual comprehension despite a diversity of beliefs, intentions, interests, goals, audiences, conversational contexts, and perceptual inputs. Not only do we easily understand each other despite such differences, we can even *share* content. We can say or think what you said or thought even though our contexts are radically different. In what follows, we want to remind readers of some obvious features of content sharing.

Here is a quote from an interview with John Kerry on National Public Radio in the summer of 2004:

(4) Dick Cheney and several other members of the Bush administration knew that Saddam Hussein posed no serious threat to the United States.

Had you heard this radio program, the following would be true about you:

a. You would understand what Kerry said.
b. You could tell us what Kerry said in either one of two ways:
   b1. You could repeat it, i.e. by uttering (4); if you uttered (4), you would have said what Kerry said in uttering (4). In fact, we'll do that right now: Dick Cheney and several other members of the Bush administration knew that Saddam Hussein posed no serious threat to the United States.

Using (4), we just said what Kerry said. Assuming our utterance sincere, etc., we expressed agreement with Kerry. Call two utterances of the same sentence that say the same, *disquotational same-saying* (DSS).

b2. You could indirectly report Kerry by uttering (5):

   (5) Kerry said that Dick Cheney and several other members of the Bush administration knew that Saddam Hussein posed no serious threat to the United States.

Using (5) you succeed in saying something true about what Kerry had said. Call an indirect report where the complement clause is identical to the reported sentence (as in (5)) a *disquotational indirect report* (DIR).

(a) and (b) are simple achievements; we can understand, DSS, and DIR each other without remembering or knowing any of the particulars about the context in which the reported utterance was made. In particular, we do not need extensive knowledge of:

• the reported speaker's intentions;
• the intentions of the reported speaker's audience;
• the nature of the conversation the speaker was engaged in;
• the assumptions shared among participants in the original context;
• what was contextually salient in the original context of utterance;
• the perceptual inputs of those participants in the original context.

It is indisputable that speakers do not typically research such issues in order to DSS or DIR each other.[3] About such facts, they can remain ignorant, confused, mistaken and *still* understand each other (and DSS and DIR each other).[4] (O2) summarizes these points perfectly; let S be a sentence (without any obvious context sensitive expressions) for which (O1) is well documented. When S is used to DSS or DIR someone, it exhibits a high degree of context *insensitivity.*

We hope our illustrations are clear enough, but since this is an important part of our argument and also the point where we tend to meet great resistance, we will elaborate further below. For now we hope the data we have in mind are sufficiently transparent.

40.3 THE PUZZLE: SHARED CONVENT VS. CONTEXTUAL VARIABILITY

We're now in a position to represent clearly the tension this paper aims to explore and reconcile. In all the cases thus far mentioned, theorists find themselves faced with the following predicament: they first fasten on to a sentence S. On the one hand: intuitions are that what's said by utterances of S shifts across contexts, where S is thereby alleged to contain an unobvious context sensitive expression e. Call those features of context that fix the semantic values of an utterance of e (as it occurs in S) F. (For what goes into F, see above.) On the other hand: speakers in contexts not overlapping with respect to F (call these Relevantly Different Contexts (RD-Contexts)) can still use S to express the same content. That is, if C and C′ are RD-Contexts, and if A utters S in C, then B can truly utter,

A said that S

or she can utter just,

S

and in so doing succeed in saying what B said.

Or: consider many different utterances u_1-u_n of S in RD-contexts; B can in an RD-

Context say something true by using:

They all said that S

Or: take speaker A in two RD-Contexts; she can say something true using.

I once said that S

---

[3] There are contexts in which we do; legal contexts spring to mind, but these are obvious exceptions.
[4] Of course, there are exceptions. See Cappelen and Lepore (1997) and (2005).

Furthermore: Even in cases where for one reason or another we do not find DDS natural, we seldom research the specific intentions and circumstances of the original utterance.

We hope the general structure of this tension is transparent. Here's an illustration.

40.3.1 Illustration of Puzzle

Reconsider (4).

(4) Dick Cheney and several other members of the Bush administration knew that Saddam Hussein posed no serious threat to the United States.

(4) contains context sensitive expressions, at least *according to various contextualists*, namely, 'several', 'no', 'knew', and 'serious'. There is extensive evidence that what sentences with these words can be used to say varies with context. (4), by virtue of containing *four* such words, exhibits complex variation depending on the context domain for 'several', 'no', and the epistemic standards for 'know', and the comparison class and measurement standards for 'serious'. In other words, what Kerry said with his utterance of (4) depends on an exceedingly complex set of contextual factors.

If this is true, then in order for someone to use (4) to iterate what Kerry said, she needs to be in a context where the relevant contextual variables fix exactly the same semantic values. That, however, doesn't seem required. We can grasp Kerry's content (i.e. understand him) and re-express his content, using (4) even though the contextual parameters of our context of utterance might differ from those in Kerry's.

40.3.2 Example of Theory That Can't Deal with Puzzle: Stanley and Szabo on Quantifiers

To see the significance of this puzzle and, more specifically, the ways in which (O2) is overlooked, we turn to an influential semantics for quantifiers. Stanley and Szabo (2000) defend the view that domain restrictions on quantifiers should be accounted for within a semantic theory. According to them, noun phrases harbor a hidden argument place that takes as its value in context a domain restriction. The domain of a quantifier, then, is the intersection of the class picked out by the nominal attached to the quantifier and the domain restriction. So, with an utterance of 'Every bottle is F', the domain of 'every bottle' consists of the intersection of the set of all bottles and the set picked out by the contextually determined domain restriction. (If that, for example is, the set of things in room 401, then the domain consists of bottles in room 401.) The domain restriction gets fixed in context. That's how they account for (O1) for sentences with quantifiers: the domain restriction varies, and hence, what's said varies from one context of utterance to another.

Actually, their view is a bit more refined: they write, 'The domain contexts provide for quantifiers are better treated as intensional entities such as *properties*, represented as functions from worlds and times to sets' (Stanley and Szabo, 2000: 252). So, a sentence of the form 'Every F is G' has as its logical form 'Every F[p] is G' and an utterance of this sentence is true just in case every F that has the property p is G.

If this view were correct, then two utterances u_1 and u_2 of a sentence S containing a quantifier phrase can express the same proposition, can make the same claim, *only if* the context for u_1 delivers the same property as a value for the domain variable as the context for u_2 does. To see how difficult this is, consider this example (originally from Stanley and Williamson (1995)).

(6) Every sailor waved to every sailor.

Note that there can, intuitively, be two different domains attached to the two occurrences of 'sailor'. As Stanley and Szabo note, 'This sentence can express the proposition that every sailor on the ship waved to every sailor on the shore' (Stanley and Szabo, 2000: 259).

We're not interested in the phenomenon of intra-sentential domain shift as such, but the slight complexity of this case makes it a convenient example for our purposes. Consider two sailors on the ship, Popeye and Bluto. After the sad departure, Popeye observes, 'That was such a nice occasion. Every sailor waved to every sailor.' Immediately afterwards, Bluto concurs: 'That's right. Every sailor waved to every sailor.'

In such a circumstance the following is often obvious: we treat these two utterances as expressing agreement. Popeye and Bluto agree that every sailor waved to every sailor.

If Stanley and Szabo (and almost all others) were right about the semantics for quantifiers, their concurrence would be a minor miracle. Consider all the possible properties that could be picked out as a domain restriction for the first occurrence of 'every sailor' in Popeye's utterance:

- Person on the ship
- Living creature on the ship
- Person standing on the deck
- Person standing or sitting on the deck
- Person that Bluto saw on the deck of the ship
- Person I saw not asleep on deck
- People over there
- Etc.

There are literally infinitely many other possibilities, most of which would pick out the same set, but some of which would not. Then there is another infinite set of possibilities for the other occurrence of 'every sailor'.

Our point is this: If Stanley and Szabo were correct, Bluto can make the same claim as Popeye, i.e. agree with Popeye, *only if* his utterance picks out the exact same properties for the two occurrences of 'every sailor'. Though it's not impossible for this to happen, its likelihood is, to put it mildly, rather slim.[5] Even though they were both

---

[5] There's a familiar line of argument going back to Wettstein's (1981) to the effect that there's no way to choose between one or the other of these domains. (See also Blackburn (1988); Schiffer (1995); Neale (1990); Lepore (2004); Cappelen and Lepore (2005).) That's not our point here. We're being charitable

on deck, they didn't have the exact same sensory inputs, they didn't share the same background beliefs; they most certainly will have focused on different aspects of the situation, etc. No two people on the deck of a ship overlap in all these respects. Since these are the factors that determine domain restrictions, Popeye and Bluto are quite likely to have expressed different propositions,[6] and hence, not to agree with each other.

And that's not the end of the story: remember, Popeye and Bluto are both sailors; they were, we imagined, on the ship together. We, i.e. C&L, are not sailors and were not on that ship. Nonetheless, we can tell you what Popeye and Bluto both said, *viz. that every sailor waved to every sailor.* And you, the reader, can understand what we said. It's all quite easy. Of course, if Stanley and Szabo were right, and we had to figure out the exact property picked out by Popeye's and Bluto's respective utterances, and you, the reader, had to figure out what we had figured out, then we couldn't do that. Were Stanley and Szabo right, we could, for all practical purposes, relinquish the idea that we ever share content using sentences involving quantifiers.[7]

Stanley and Szabo's theory is not a particularly egregious example of a semantic theory that in a rush to account for (O1), fails to account for (O2). It's representative of much of what goes on in semantics today. We draw the same conclusions, e.g. about Crimmins and Perry's treatment of belief reports as context sensitive (Crimmins and Perry, 1989; Crimmins, 1992); Lewis' treatment of counter-factual conditionals as context sensitive (Lewis, 1973; cf., also, Bach, 1994: 128–9); contextualist epistemic and moral accounts (DeRose, 1992, 1995; Cohen, 1991, 1999; Unger, 1995; Dreier 1990), right on down to the global contextualist positions of Travis (1987, 1996); Searle (1980); and Recanati (2004). Each account in an effort to respect (O1) either ignores or blatantly disrespects (O2).

How, then, should we respond to the puzzle in order to reconcile these two observations?

40.4 Overview of Solutions

The possible solutions divide into several rough categories:

1. *Deny (O1):* There are two ways to do this:

   1.a Deny that speakers have beliefs/intuitions that content varies between contexts.

   1.b Agree that speakers have beliefs/intuitions that there's content variability, but argue that this common sense view is wrong.

---

towards Stanley and Szabo; we grant them that there is a way (though we don't know how, and Stanley and Szabo never tell us), for Popeye's utterance to pick out a unique property. Given that assumption we ask: How can we ever ensure that Bluto picks out the *same* domain as Popeye? He has to do that in order to say what Popeye said.

[6] Problem: Stanley and Szabo insist that they are not doing foundational semantics (2000: 225).

[7] We hope it is clear how to generalize the point made above so it applies to all quantifier expressions, comparative adjectives, etc.

2. *Deny (O2)*: Again, there are two options:

   2a Deny that speakers have beliefs/intuitions that content is invariant across contexts.

   2b Agree that speakers have beliefs/intuitions that speakers can share contents across varied contexts (and do so using the same sentences), but argue that this common sense view is wrong.

3. *Compromise Strategy*: Show that there's no incompatibility between (O1) and (O2). What we have presented is the mere appearance of a puzzle or dilemma, but once these two observations are properly contextualized and interpreted, they are not incompatible.

This leaves quite a range of possible solutions to our puzzle. Since this is not a book, we can't explore them all to the extent we would like (though, we are writing a book on this, so for those interested, stay tuned). In the sections which follow we address various potential solutions, including various ways of denying (O1) and (O2), Similarity Theory, Subject Sensitivity, Relativism about Truth, and finally, our own, Pluralistic Minimalism. We used to try to fit these various proposed solutions neatly into the above five options, but most interesting solutions tend to take a little from each possible solution, and so, they do not fit neatly into any one single category. In what follows we'll not spill any ink trying to relate solutions to options (1)–(3), but instead leave that as an exercise for the reader.

40.5 DENIAL OF (O2)

The options we just surveyed leave a wide range of possible solutions to the puzzle. We'll begin with (2a) and (2b). However, we want to offer a brief justification for why we don't think we need to pursue options (1a) and (1b).

About (1a), note that as formulated (O1) and (O2) are *atheoretical*; they don't invoke a theoretical notion of 'what is said'. They are intended simply to register that we don't encounter a lot people who resist the initial reactions ascribed to these examples above. There is a wide consensus that different utterances of sentences containing, for example, comparative adjectives, or quantifiers, or even 'know' and 'good', vary in content, *in some sense of 'content' and in some sense of 'vary'*, as in (O1). (We believe there is also a wide consensus that we can repeat and report what others say with such sentences, as in (O2); more below.)

About (1b), all we have to say is that we don't know a lot of philosophers who would pursue this strategy (though we suppose there is a way of interpreting Subject Sensitivity as endorsing (1b) for some locutions; see Section 40.7 below), and so, we won't discuss it here.

40.5.1 Solution 1: Denial that we Have O2 Intuitions (i.e. (2a))

One objection we often encounter is that our examples in support of (O2) fail. Those who raise this objection aim to show that the cases where there's genuine variability

(i.e. where (O1) holds) are cases where there's no DIR or DSS in relevantly different contexts (i.e. are cases where (O2) fails). They'll say things like: For quantifiers
and comparative adjectives, (O1) holds, but (O2) does not. Where (O2) holds, (O1)
doesn't.

40.5.1.1 *What Does Denying (O2) Involve?*

First, it is important to be clear on the nature of this disagreement, i.e. to be clear on
what exactly the differences are between our claim and our opponents'. So, let S be a
sentence containing a comparative adjective or a quantifier phrase:

We claim: The following often happens:

S1: A utters S in C, B utters S in C′, C and C′ can be relevantly different, and yet A
and B say the same (make the same claim, i.e. agree (they can DSS each other)).

S2: A utters S in C. B utters 'A said that S' in C′, C and C′ can be relevantly different,
and yet B succeeds in saying something true (i.e. they can DIR each other).[8]

Our opponent's claim: Both S1 and S2 are impossible; there are *no* cases such as
those described in S1 and S2.

To understand the puzzle/tension that concerns us it is important to realize that all
we need (to generate the puzzle) is a single instance of S1 or S2. As it happens, we
think instances of S1 and S2 are ubiquitous. But even if there were only a few cases,
the phenomenon would be no less interesting and no less puzzling. Remember, if S
contains a context sensitive term, and if C and C′ are relevantly different contexts of
utterance (i.e. the semantic value of S when uttered in C differs from when uttered
in C′) and if either S1 or S2 obtains, then there is, as we claim, a fundamental tension at the heart of our notion of what's said. On the one hand, we're postulating
context sensitivity in S to explain how what's said varies from context to context.
On the other, our notion of what's said recognizes some kind of stability across such
relevantly different contexts. We're trying to find a theory that accounts for both.

With that clarification out of the way, we focus on what would constitute a legitimate objection to (O2).

40.5.1.2 *What Would Count as Evidence Against (O2)?*

Expressions fall into three classes with respect to S1 and S2:

Class 1: Sentences containing them can never be DIR-ed or DSS-ed in relevantly different contexts. Examples: 'I' and 'here'.

Class 2: Can always be DIR-ed and DSS-ed in relevantly different contexts. Examples
(though these are not uncontroversial): 'and', 'know', and 'red'.

Class 3: Can sometimes (i.e. in some contexts) be DIR-ed and DSS-ed, and sometimes not. Examples (we claim): Comparative adjectives, quantified noun
phrases, 'left', 'enemy', 'local', etc.

---

[8] We are, of course, assuming that S is either free of obvious indexicals or that the reader makes the
obvious adjustments to control for their occurrence.

The third category is typically overlooked, but it provides by far the most interesting challenges; and it might even be that all instances allegedly in Class 2 are really, when you think hard about it, in Class 3 (though we don't base any of our arguments here on that assumption).

You obviously can't counter-example the claim that an expression is in Class 3. The claim is only that speakers *sometimes* DIR and DSS utterances of such expressions in relevantly different contexts. That claim cannot be refuted by showing there are *some* relevantly different contexts in which we do not do so.

So, then, what would constitute an argument against the claim that an expression is in Class 3? As we see it, there are but two kinds of arguments:

a. You can have some general theory from which it follows that Class 3 expressions are impossible.
b. You can dispute the examples we present as evidence of their Class 3 status. For every example we present, you can show that our intuitions are confused, idiosyncratic or in some other way possible to explain away.

We won't consider (a) here. Our goal is to refute theories that have this implication, so any appeal to a theoretical framework would simply beg the question against us. With respect to (b), we also don't have that much to say, because we don't know exactly what other philosophers will say in response to our examples. We'll restrict our comments to one rather general remark about how *not* to respond to our examples (and certainly leave open the possibility that we're overlooking some ingenious reply).

40.5.1.3 *How not to Respond to Examples of Class 3 Expressions*

There is a trick in constructing examples to best illustrate (O2). Our claim is that we often treat two utterances as having expressed the same content, and when we do so, *we ignore the details of their respective contexts of utterance*; we ignore factors about the context of utterance that we would have focused on were we 'in the context' or were our interests only in one of the utterances, and not in comparing them. We are trying to imagine ourselves in a situation where the differences between u_1 and u_2 are *neither* salient *nor* relevant. We want examples where the participants are not focusing on or indeed don't care about or might be ignorant of the details of two utterances u_1 and u_2 of S. To do so we need examples that mimic this kind of situation. Examples that are frontloaded with detailed descriptions of what the individual speakers of u_1 and u_2 had in mind, what they wanted to communicate, how they should be interpreted, are, for obvious reasons, ill-suited for this purpose.

Here's one such example (a typical one) from Hawthorne's *Knowledge and Lotteries* (the goal of the example is to show that you can't DIR comparative adjectives across relevantly different contexts):

. . . the following disquotational schema for 'tall' is clearly unacceptable:

Disquotational Schema for 'Tall': If an English speaker S sincerely utters something of the form 'A is tall' and 'A' refers to *a*, then S believes of *a* that *a* is tall.

Suppose I am a coach discussing basketball players. Meaning 'tall for a basketball player' by 'tall', I cannot report an ordinary English speaker as believing that Allen Iverson is tall on the grounds that such a person sincerely uttered 'He is tall', where 'He' referred to Allen Iverson. (Hawthorne, 2003: 106)

This example explicitly tells us that the speaker did *not* intend to say the same as the reporter. By so doing, Hawthorne has created a context in which it is almost impossible for us to see the two utterances as saying the same. He has drawn our attention to, and hence, rendered salient and relevant the *differences* between these two utterances. These differences, however, blind us to their common content.

The lesson to draw from this and like 'counter-examples', for those wanting to explain away our (O2) intuitions, is to *not* try to explain these intuitions away by re-describing the contexts of utterance we appeal to; that is, don't change the focus or the interests of the participants. To do so in the context of discussing (O2) is cheating. We, quite frankly, suspect that any attempt to rebuff (O2) examples will involve exactly this kind of cheating. We have, however, no proof of that, and we keep an open mind on the issue.

So, then, what kinds of examples are good for illustrating (O2)? To begin with, is our example involving the two sailors, Popeye and Bluto. When describing their utterances, we emphasized what they had in common: they more or less were made at the same place and at the same time; the two sailors were participants in the same conversation; and their interests were in sailors who wave at each other, etc. Only afterwards did we go on to tell you about their differences: they saw somewhat different aspects of the relevant situation; they had somewhat different reactions to what they saw, etc. That is, only after we had characterized what they had in common did we let on that there's a whole range of differences between them that might lead you to think the domains picked out are different. This situation is not peculiar. This is exactly the relationship most of us stand in most of the time to those with whom we are agreeing or interpreting or reporting.

As soon as we've filled in more, we stop being so inclined. But that does not mean our initial reaction was wrong; it just means that once you've gathered more information, your relationship to the two utterances is suddenly significantly different from what it was before. As we see it, you're not getting closer to the truth about the two utterances; your interest in, and cognitive reactions to them, change in a way so that it becomes almost impossible to focus on the shared content. Increased knowledge of particular contexts undermines our sense of it same-saying other utterances.

40.5.2 Solution 2: Denial of Shared Content (i.e. (2b))

According to (2b), some speakers think they can say *the same thing* using S in different contexts but contextual considerations show they can't. They think they share content across contexts, but they're fundamentally confused.

Contingent on how widespread contextual variability extends, the point generalizes: no two people ever say the same, no two people ever agree or disagree on the same content, no two people ever *fully* understand each other (never understand exactly what the other has said). You cannot understand exactly what we're saying in this article (indeed, you don't even fully understand this sentence).

How plausible is this strategy? We think not very and will offer several objections/challenges to it.

Criticism 1: Explain Why we Developed Defective Reporting Practices

Anyone who claims the intuitions behind (O2) are false must explain how we came to develop linguistic practices in which we invariably make false claims. Anyone who wants to claim that all reports are false must explain why this practice didn't evolve into one in which we used 'said that' to make, on the whole, true judgments; if there's no shared content, it would be remarkable that 'said that' required it.

Criticism 2: Apparent Methodological Inconsistency

We are being asked to accept intuitions about variability in what was said as evidence for (O1) (obviously, that's the evidence that what was said varies between contexts), but at the same to deny intuitions that support shared content across contexts. But why should we treat one set of intuitions differently from another? That's an entirely unjustified asymmetry in relationship to intuitions.

Criticism 3: Account for Implications for Non-Linguistic Practices

Our practice of sharing content is inextricably intertwined with other practices that figure centrally in our non-linguistic lives.

- **Coordinated Action:** Often, people in different contexts are asked to do the same thing, e.g. pay taxes. They receive the same instructions, are bound by the same rules, the same laws and conventions. For such instructions to function, we must assume a wide range of utterances express the same content.
- **Collective Deliberation:** When people over a period of time, across a variety of contexts, try to find out whether something is so, they typically assume content stability across those contexts. Consider a CIA task force concerned with whether Igor knows that Jane is a spy. They are unsure whether or not he does. Investigators, over a period of time, in different contexts study this question. If what they are trying to determine, i.e. whether Igor knows that Jane is a spy, changes across contexts, contingent, for example, on their evidence, what is contextually salient, the conversational context, etc. collective deliberation across contexts would make no sense.
- **Intra-Personal Deliberation:** Suppose Igor, on his own, is trying to determine whether p is so. Suppose its being so makes a difference to his life, but he's unsure. Sometimes he thinks the evidence, on balance, supports p, sometimes not. It depends on how he looks at the evidence, on what he takes to be the relevant considerations. Just as in the inter-personal case, this presupposes a stable content he's deliberating about.

- **Justified Belief:** Much of our knowledge of the world is based on testimony. Hearing a trustworthy person assert that p can provide good reason to believe that p. If we think everything Jason says is true and he says naked mole rats are blind, we have good reason to believe naked mole rats are blind. But this is possible only if we can say what he said, *viz.*, that naked mole rats are blind. We need to understand (and remember) what he said. We have to be in a position to agree with it. This is possible only if content can be shared across contexts.
- **Responsibility:** We hold people responsible for what they say, ask, request, claim, etc. We can do so only if we, in another context, can *understand* what they said (suggested, ordered, claimed, etc.), *say* what they said, and *investigate* what they said.
- **Reasons for Actions:** A closely connected phenomenon is this: What others say often provides reasons for action. What people said in another context can provide reason for action only if we can understand what they have said, investigate it, trust it, etc.

These inter-connections and mutual dependencies between content stability and non-linguistic practices are significant because any theory that implies content is *not*, strictly speaking, shared across contexts or, at least, isn't shared in the conversations in which we think it is, must account for the devastating implications that this view has for these non-linguistic practices. To endorse a view that implies that what we do in all these cases is based on a fundamental confusion that we have about the nature of our own language is an awfully high price to pay to protect contextualism.

Of course, we could be fundamentally mistaken about ourselves in just these ways, but at least this much is clear: if you are inclined to bite this bullet, you had better provide an alternative account of these non-linguistic practices.

These criticisms are more challenges, we suppose, than conclusive objections. Perhaps there is a way around them. We turn to the chief attempt to do so; an attempt that aims to reconcile (O1) and (O2) in letter if not in spirit.

40.6 SOLUTION 3: COMPROMISE BY APPEAL TO SIMILARITY

An impatient reader might ask: What's the problem! So what if we can't share content across contexts? Isn't similarity sufficient? We can make (O2) compatible with (O1) if we hold the view that in order for two speakers A and B to say the same they only need to make utterances *similar* in content. Here's a representative passage from Bezuidenhout (1997):

Since utterance interpretation is always in the first place colored by one's own cognitive perspective, I think we should reject the idea that there is an intermediate stage in communication which involves the recovery of some content shared by speaker and listener and which is attributed by the listener to the utterance. In communication....... [w]e *need recognize only speaker-relative utterance content and listener-relative utterance content and a relation of similarity holding between these two contents . . . This does not mean that we have to deny that lateral interpretation requires the preservation of something. But this something need simply be a relevant degree of similarity between the thought expressed by the speaker and the thought expressed by the listener.* (Bezuidenhout 1997: 212–13; emphasis our own)

Likewise, Sperber and Wilson (1986) write:

. . . It seems to us neither paradoxical nor counterintuitive to say that there are thoughts that we cannot exactly share, and that communication can be successful without resulting in an exact duplication of thoughts in communicator and audience. We see communication as a matter of enlarging mutual cognitive environments, not of duplicating thoughts. (Sperber/Wilson 1986, pp.192-3)

Related points are made by Heck (2002); Recanati (2004); and Carston (2002).

These are all instances of what we call the Similarity View (SV)—a view, as far as we can tell, that has never been elaborated; therefore, much of what we have to say is speculative. According to SV:

Sentences like 'A said that p', 'A said what B said', 'I agree with what A said', 'I understand exactly what I said', and the other such locutions do *not* require for their truth content *identity* across contexts. All they require is content *similarity* across contexts. The details can be elucidated in various ways, one version of which is:

- 'A said that p' means the same as 'A said something similar to p.'
- 'A said what B said' means the same as 'A said something similar to what B said.'
- 'A and B agree' means the same as 'A and B endorse similar thoughts.'
- 'A understands what B said' means (something like) 'A grasped a proposition similar to the one expressed by B.'

And so on for other cases. According to SV, we do not make false claims when reporting or repeating others. Our practice has, wisely, factored in that there is no cross contextual content identity. In this way (O1) and (O2) are rendered compatible.[9]

FIVE CRITICISMS OF SV

Some of our criticisms might be distinct versions of the same criticism (depending on how criticisms are individuated); each would be easier to present were a precise version of SV available. Before turning to criticism, however, we want briefly to record a possible methodological inconsistency in the discussion suggesting replacing (O2) with SV. For, if intuitions about utterances saying the same are not intuitions about

---

[9] Alternatively, we could phrase SV so that reporting and repeating are based on a false assumption, *viz.*, that contents are shared (in any sense) across contexts. Claims like 'A said that p', 'I agree with A', and 'He's ordered me to do . . .' are *all* false. This version of SV denies any intuitions/beliefs about what others say is ever correct. For the reasons cited above, we find this view unattractive. Further, our objections to SV apply (in modified form) to this view as well.

genuine sameness of content, then what evidence can there be for variability of content, i.e. for (O1)?

Remember, the intuitions that support (O1) are intuitions to the effect that utterances u_1 and u_2 say different things. But if saying the same is no evidence of having the same content, why should saying different things be evidence of differences in content?

What the similarity theorist needs is a way to connect differences in saying to differences in semantic content, and she needs to do that in a way that's compatible with her account of same-saying. She needs something like (P):

(P) u_1 and u_2 have the same semantic content only if they say the same.

It *does* follow from (P) that if two utterances say something different, they have different semantic contents. The central challenge for any version of SV, then, becomes this: How, according to SV, can you get evidence for the relationship between semantic contents and same-saying? The SV theorist needs some *independent* way to access semantic content, fix it, and then, compare semantic content with what was said. But no such method has been presented, and we expect, it never will be.

As you'll see below, we're sympathetic to the idea that intuitions about saying are not, in general, evidence for semantic content. But *we* can hold that view because we have a theory about how speakers access semantic contents and also about how semantic content and speech act content are to be compared.

We turn now to criticisms of SV.

Criticism 1: When SV is made Explicit it's Absurd

Try to render SV explicit as follows:

- Let u and u′ be two utterances of 'A is tired' in two contexts C and C′.
- Each expresses a proposition: u express the proposition *that A is too tired to go running;* u′ express the proposition *that A is too tired for any kind of strenuous physical activity.*

We (i.e. C&L) are in a café in NYC. Call our current context (i.e. the one in which we are performing these speech acts) NYC. In NYC we affirm (referring to the utterances of u and u′) either (S1) or (S2):

(S1) They said the same.
(S2) They made the same claim.

Suppose NYC is a context in which these two propositions are indeed similar. We assume there are such contexts, but even if there aren't (we can't imagine why not), that doesn't matter for our argument: articulate two propositions different but similar to each other in a context C and run the argument on those propositions. Recall, according to SV, (S1) and (S2) are true if the propositions expressed by utterances u and u′ are similar according to the standards of NYC. But then it follows from

SV that our utterances of (S1) and (S2) are true in NYC. But since u says *that A is too tired to go running* and u' says *that A is too tired to engage in any kind of strenuous physical activity*, it also follows that, contrary to assumption, they *didn't* say the same thing. One, after all, said she was too tired to go running; and the other said she was too tired to engage in any kind of strenuous physical activity. These are different. Maybe they say something *similar*, but they surely do not *the same*.

In other words, as soon as we insist on making explicit the alleged similar propositions, and comparing them, it becomes obvious that expressing these propositions constitutes at most saying something similar (whatever that might mean), but *not* saying the same.

Here is another way to put this point (if it seems repetitive, we apologize): Suppose an utterance u of 'A is tired' expresses, say, for the sake of simplicity, the proposition *that A is tired*. According to SV, a different utterance u' needn't express the same proposition in order to say the same as u. But how can that be? If u' doesn't express the proposition *that A is tired*, it presumably expresses another one, say, the proposition *that A is too tired to go jogging*. But saying *that A is tired* isn't the same as saying *that A is too tired to go jogging*. Or, at least if it is, we need an argument to relinquish intuitions to the contrary.

Criticism 2: SV doesn't Explain Our Distinction between Saying *Exactly* What Someone said and Saying Something *Similar* but *not Identical*?

If 'A said that p' means 'A expressed a proposition similar to p', then how do we interpret sentences like:

- He almost said that p, but didn't.
- He came very close to saying that p, but didn't.
- What he said was similar to p, but not exactly p.

The easiest way to focus this criticism is to think about (SA):

(SA) She didn't say that p, but she said something similar to p.

In uttering (SA), we don't mean what SV predicts. According to SV, 'said that' means 'said something similar to', so (SA) should mean:

(SAS): S didn't say that p, but said that p.

That is not what (SA) means.[10]

---

[10] Ted Sider, in discussion, suggested that what (SA) really should mean is, 'She didn't say that p, but she said something similar to something similar to p.' If a is similar to b and b similar to c, it doesn't follow a is similar to b, i.e. it doesn't follow that she said something similar to. Sider's objection conflates the meta-language 'said' with the object language 'said.' The view we are considering is presented in English, i.e. in presenting this view we assume that the interpretation of 'said something similar to p' does not mean 'said something similar to something similar to p.' See Segal (1989): 84–86.

In sum: If content similarity is employed to explain what's meant by 'saying the same,' it becomes impossible to explain what's meant by 'saying something similar, but not identical.'

Criticism 3: False Predictions made by SV

There is no *a priori* reason to think there's no context in which the two propositions P and Q are similar.

(P) The US has 49 states.
(Q) The US has 50 states.

But, then, SV predicts that (in some context) it is true to say that someone who said *that the US has 49 states* said *that the US has 50 states*. But that's absurd. No one who said the US has 49 states said the US has 50 states.

The point generalizes: Any two objects are similar in some respect or other. Here is what follows: Take an utterance u by A and an arbitrary proposition p. It follows from SV, *in some respect, that A said that p*. It also follows that in some context, it should be true to report u by uttering 'A said that p.'

Illustration: Let A make an utterance u of a sentence that expresses the proposition *that Uma Thurman has green eyes;* and let p be the proposition *that there are lots of naked mole rats in South Africa*. These two propositions are similar in *some* respects. Therefore, on SV, no *a priori* reason prohibits contexts in which this similarity is relevant. It follows from SV that we should be able truthfully to say: 'In some respects, A said that there are lots of naked mole rats in South Africa.'

The flip side is: Consider a context C in which B utters 'A was tired'. Suppose u expresses the proposition p. Consider a context C′ in which 'A was tired' expresses a different proposition q. Suppose in C′ the standards of similarity are such that p and q are *not* relevantly similar. (There will be some p, q and C′ for which this is so.) Notice that in C′, it is not true to utter 'B said that A was tired' in reference to u. We doubt there are any such contexts. If B uttered 'A was tired', it is true to say B said that A was tired. *Nothing* about the context of utterance can render that false. (See Section 40. 9 below.)

Criticism 4: Claims About Degrees of Similarity and Comparative Similarity are Unintelligible in Connection with 'said that' Claims

We can make intelligible and even true similarity judgments of the form:

- A is more similar to B than to C.
- A is a little bit like B.
- A is like B in some respects.

According to SV, 'A said that p' means 'A expressed a proposition that's similar to p' but that predicts we should not only be able to make sense of, but also make, true judgments of the form:

- A said p more than q.
- A said p a little bit.
- A said p in some respects.

But such judgments are hardly intelligible and certainly play no significant role in our practice of indirectly reporting others.[11]

Criticism 5: Identity is Transitive; Similarity is not

Our final criticism is an old chestnut exploiting the non-transitivity of 'similarity'. If A said the same as B and B said the same as C, then A and C said the same as well. But if A said something similar to B and B said something similar to C, it simply doesn't follow that A said something similar to C. So, the view that 'A said that p' means the same as 'A said something similar to p' is false.

In summary: to be fair, SV has an advantage over blanket rejections of (O1) and (O2) by virtue of respecting these observations. It explains how two utterances of the same sentence can say something the same and something different; it all depends on relevant standards of similarity. Unfortunately, its problems are insuperable.

We turn now to another sort of effort to reconcile (O1) and (O2).

40.7 SOLUTION 4: SUBJECT SENSITIVITY

Hawthorne (2004) tentatively defends a semantics for 'know' he calls 'Sensitive Moderate Invariantism' (SSI). It is a view motivated exactly by the kinds of considerations we have presented, although our presentation was more general in form. It can be understood as a local solution, a local fix, to our puzzle. (A closely related view has been developed by Stanley, 'Context, Interest-Relativity and Knowledge'; Graff (2000) develops a version of this view applied to vague terms; see also Stanley's reply

---

[11] Another criticism, which we will not elaborate on here, but instead refer the reader to *Insensitive Semantic*, concerns the failure of 'said that' to pass key tests for context sensitivity. According to proponents of SV, 'similar' is context sensitive, i.e. what's similar to what depends on the contextually salient features being compared. As a consequence, 'said that' is context sensitive, i.e. 'A said that p' can be true when uttered in one context, and false when uttered in another. But 'said that' is context *insensitive*. We have developed various tests for identifying context sensitivity: *viz.*, Disquotational Indirect Report Test (singular and collective); Collection Test; VP-deletion test, and ICD/RCSA. The locution 'said that' fails to pass any of these tests for context sensitivity. See *Insensitive Semantics*, ch. 7.

(Stanley (2003)). We focus our discussion on Hawthorne's version,[12] but with small modifications it generalizes to these other versions.)

Sensitive Moderate Invariantism is motivated by two lines of argument: on the one hand, it challenges the view that 'know' is semantically context sensitive. Many of Hawthorne's arguments are based on the way we go about reporting knowledge attributions, i.e. on how we say what others have said when they use the word 'know'. He argues these practices are inconsistent with the view that 'know' is context sensitive.

On the other hand, he argues against the view that knowledge attributions are entirely context *in*sensitive. There is evidence, indeed overwhelming evidence, that there is some sort of context sensitivity in knowledge attributions, according to Hawthorne this is not context sensitivity in the sense that different utterances of "A knows that p at time t" have different semantic contents depending on their contexts of utterance. Here Hawthorne's suggestion in summary form:

For suppose instead that the kinds of factors that the contextualist adverts to as making for ascriber dependence—attention, interests, stakes and so on—had bearing on the truth of knowledge claims only insofar as they were the attention, interests, stakes and so on of the subject. Then the relevance of attention, interests, and stakes to the truth of knowledge ascriptions would not, in itself, force the thesis of semantic context dependence. Here is the picture. Restricting ourselves to extensional matters, the verb 'know' picks out the same ordered triples of subject, time, and proposition in the mouths of any ascriber. However, whether a particular subject/time/proposition triple is included in the extension of 'know' depends not merely upon the kinds of factors traditionally adverted to in accounts of knowledge . . . but also upon the kinds of factors that in the contextualist's hands make for ascriber dependence. These factors will thus include (some or all of) the attention, interests, and stakes of that subject at that time.   (Hawthorne 2004, pp. 157–58)

On this view, knowledge attributions are sensitive to the non-epistemic features of the situation in which the subject of the attribution finds herself. The semantics, meanwhile, is *in*sensitive to the context of utterance. (It is sensitive to the *subject's* situation, but insensitive to the ascriber's context of utterance.) This kind of theory is supposed to achieve two ends:

First, it is supposed to preserve stability of content across contexts of utterance. All utterances of 'A knows that p' express the exact same proposition, and hence, say the same. There is no variability in the proposition expressed from one context of utterance to another (assuming, of course, we have adjusted for obvious context sensitivity). That's supposed to accommodate the shared content part of our dilemma.

Sensitive Moderate Invariantism is also supposed to accommodate some kind of context sensitivity surrounding knowledge attributions: What it *takes* for A to be in the extension of 'know' (at a time t) depends on A's interests, concerns, and salient standards at t. If this is the extent of context sensitivity, then, as Hawthorne says,

---

[12] We should say 'one version of Hawthorne's view' since he considers several and doesn't conclusively come down in favor of one over the others.

'the relevance of attention, interests, and stakes to the truth of knowledge ascriptions would not, in itself, force the thesis of semantic context dependence.'

Before raising objections to Sensitive Moderate Invariantism, we should emphasize that Hawthorne discusses a range of options for how to spell out subject sensitivity. He discusses various versions of the view that what is contextually salient to the subject matters. He also considers various versions of the view that the agent's 'practical environment' is relevant to the truth conditions of knowledge claims.[13] He doesn't come down firmly on one side or the other. The objections we raise below, however, do not depend on the details of his account (or if they do, they can be modified to fit any version of this kind of view).

We have two objections and three critical comments on his solution.

Objection 1

We have throughout our discussion tried to emphasize and illustrate that the puzzle is a general one: It has to do with a wide-ranging tension between intuitions we have about contextual variability of what speakers say by uttering sentences, on the one hand, and intuitions we have about content sharing across contexts, on the other. It is, of course, possible this tension could be resolved one way for 'know', another for adjectives, another for epistemic modals, another for 'true', another for moral terms, another for verbs, another for conjunctions, and so on and so on. We do, however, consider it obvious that should a general solution be available, it is to be preferred over a range of local fixes (especially when these come with all kinds of difficulties, as illustrated above). If there's evidence that an underlying misconception generates the appearance of a puzzle, and if removing that misconception resolves the perceived tension across the board, then local fixes aren't necessary. Below, we argue there is such a misconception and that it works across the board.

If we're right, then Sensitive Moderate Invariantism turns out to be not well motivated because it doesn't generalize. None of its proponents has suggested that the solution can be extended to other cases; there has been one attempt to do something related with respect to vague terms (see Graff, 2000), but the proponent of that solution does not advocate extending it to "knows" and one of the two proponents of SSI for "knows" has criticized Graff's application of the strategy. So the proponents of this strategy are in agreement that this is, at best, a local fix.[14]

---

[13] He says that we maybe should allow '. . . what we might call 'practical environment' to make a difference to what one knows. We now have before us the outlines of a second mechanism that may be introduced by the sensitive moderate invariantist. The basic idea is clear enough. Insofar as it is unacceptable—and not merely because the content of the belief is irrelevant to the issues at hand—to use a belief that p as a premise in practical reasoning on a certain occasion, the belief is not a piece of knowledge at that time. Thus when offered a penny for my lottery ticket, it would be unacceptable to use the premise that I will lose the lottery as my grounds for making such a sale. So on that occasion I do not know that I will lose. Meanwhile, when you are offered life insurance, it would be unacceptable for you to use your belief that you are going to Blackpool as grounds for refusal. So on that occasion you do not know that you are going to Blackpool' (Hawthorne 2004: 176).

[14] Hawthorne does not fully endorse the view even for "knows", see ch. 4 of Hawthorne 2004.

Objection 2

SSI doesn't even resolve the tension between O1 and O2 with respect to 'knows'—i.e. it doesn't even provide a *local* fix. SSI, in effect, denies O1 without argument and provides no reconciliation between O1 and O2. Remember; for SSI there's a stable semantic content for all utterances of 'A knows that p at t', no variability from one context of utterance to another. That takes care of O1. The puzzle, however, is how the stability can be reconciled with (intuitive) variability in what is said by different utterances of 'A knows that p at t'. According to SSI, there is no variability in such utterances—they all express the same proposition—they all say the same. The theory doesn't recognize, and hence doesn't account for, the variability of what's said by such utterances. Since it doesn't recognize our puzzle it also doesn't solve it.

Here's how to see the puzzle with respect to 'knows'. 'Knows' is a **Class 3** expression (see Section 40.5.1.2 above): the sentences in which it occurs can be DIR and DSS'ed, in some contexts, but not in other contexts. SSI has no explanation of why we encounter this variability. An example to illustrate the point:

In the discussion of front loading in Section 40.5.1.3 we said that the way to undermine O2 intuitions was to present two utterances of the same sentence by focusing on the differences between context of utterance—i.e. focus on the difference in e.g. the speaker's intentions, their practical goals, their conversational contexts, and so on. When examples are so presented, we argued, you can easily trigger the intuition that the two utterances say different things, don't make the same assertion, and don't express agreement. Two such frontloaded examples;

Naomi is taking some friends to an Italian restaurant she is familiar with; she knows the owner, she has visited on numerable occasions, latest for lunch earlier in the day. One of her friends, not familiar with this particular restaurant and worried about being stuck in a French restaurant, asks Naomi 'Do you know that it is an Italian restaurant?' Naomi answers: 'Yes, I know it's an Italian restaurant'. Her interest is just in calming her friends practical concern about ending up in a French restaurant. She has never thought about skepticism and her epistemic standards are low, adjusted to the practical issues at hand.

Now consider John, a participant in a philosophical seminar, he has just learned about certain kinds of skeptical arguments, he has no practical concerns whatsoever; his epistemic standards are extremely high; he applies these standards to his friend Naomi, just as an example, and utters: 'Naomi doesn't know that it's an Italian restaurant'[15], meaning to say that she doesn't know it by these very high epistemic standards that he has adopted for this particular occasion.

When asked whether Naomi and John in, *some sense*, said different things, made different assertions, our informants are inclined to say they did. In particular, they are inclined to agree that Naomi said something like *She knows (by relatively low, practical standards) that it's an Italian Restaurant* and that John said *she does know (by high philosophical standards) that it is an Italian restaurant*. So in that sense, they

---

[15] Obviously assume tense is the same in the two cases.

might not disagree—the two utterances need not be expressions of disagreement; what Naomi said is compatible with what John said.[16] Another way to get at the intuition of variability is to ask yourself: Isn't what Naomi said, intuitively true? Isn't what John said also intuitively true? Our inclination is to say, in some sense, 'yes'. If so, their knowledge attributions must have different contents. In some sense: Naomi *counts as* knowing in the context of her utterance, but *doesn't* count as knowing in the context of John's utterance.

Based on such examples we conclude: two utterances of 'A knows that p at t' might express the same proposition relative to some contexts of interpretation, and different propositions relative to other contexts of interpretation. SSI can account for the first cases but not the second.

Comment 1

We now turn to another objection that relates specifically to implications of Sensitive Moderate Invariantism as a theory of knowledge attribution. As mentioned, our overarching concern is not knowledge attributions *per se*; we're interested in the general puzzle, and so a solution for 'know' is interesting only in so far as it generalizes. But to see why we doubt it generalizes, it helps to see why it fails for 'know'.

Sensitive Moderate Invariantism has the following peculiar implications:[17] When a subject matter is important to you, when it is of some kind of immediate practical significance, epistemic standards rise; the requirements for knowing something about this subject matter are 'stricter'.[18] As a result, you can end up knowing less of a subject matter, say, penguins, by paying more attention to penguin related issues or by engaging in activities where penguins are important. To wit: If you care enormously about what penguins eat, if it's an important matter in your life, then epistemic standards are high. As a result, it becomes difficult to know, e.g. that penguins eat fish. If, however, you couldn't care less about what penguins eat, then epistemic standards are low, and it is easier to fall in the extension of 'x knows that penguins eat fish'. This aspect of Sensitive Moderate Invariantism opens up a strategy for increasing knowledge, a strategy not really available to humans. If you don't know whether penguins eat fish, but want to know, you might think that the only way to become more informed is through study; you have to gather evidence, try to learn more about penguins. If Sensitive Moderate Invariantism were correct, though, you have another option: You could take a drink or shoot heroin. If as a result you care less about penguins and their eating habits (or change your practical environment in such a

---

[16] Of course, our (i.e. C&L's) position is a bit tricky here: We're presenting these examples to you in very peculiar context, a context that, if our view is right, will affect your intuitions. We've just spent pages trying to convince you that there's a common content, and then we try to turn you around and see that there's no common content; that's bound to be dizzying for a reader and our readers probably should not fully trust their intuitions at this point. So we suggest trying out these kinds of cases in a less loaded environment at a later point.

[17] These kinds of implications are not original to us; Hawthorne mentions them, but seems to consider them reasonable bullets to bite in order to get an otherwise explanatorily powerful theory.

[18] There are many ways to spell out 'stricter' but the differences do not matter for our purposes.

way that these habits become irrelevant), you would know more (of course, on the assumption that p is true). But this is not how to improve your epistemic standing!

Comment 2

Second, Sensitive Moderate Invariantism is inconsistent with widespread intuitions about knowledge attributions. The following seems clearly unacceptable: Suppose A cares very much about whether p is so; it matters a lot in her practical environment. Standards are high, and as a result she doesn't know that p. A is thinking about B, who has the exactly same evidence, with the sole difference being that B doesn't care as much about p-related issues. In such circumstances, A could truly say:

(7) Lucky B, she knows that p (assuming that p is true), but I don't. Not because she has better evidence than I or has done more research on p-related issues or anything like that; but just because B couldn't care less and her practical environment is one in which p doesn't matter.

This simply doesn't accord with the kinds of intuitions we have about knowledge attributions: when epistemic standards rise, you hold others to those standards as well.

These objections apply to sensitive Moderate Invariantism for 'know' specifically but we care about them because they are related to more general points about how to deal with the puzzle.

Comment 3

We earlier emphasized that content stability over time is required to make sense of various aspects of inter- and intra-personal deliberation. This presents a serious obstacle for Sensitive Moderate Invariantism. Consider the following scenario: You're about to hire A and you learn that you can't hire her unless you know she has a Ph.D. Suddenly, it becomes a pressing practical concern for you whether or not she has a Ph.D. As a result, standards are high, lots of possibilities must be ruled out in order to know her educational status. Suppose you end up concluding you do not know whether she has a Ph.D. The following is now possible:

- If it turns out she did have a Ph.D., you might have known she had one before it became a pressing issue.
- You lost that knowledge as soon as it became a pressing issue (because standards rose).
- As soon as you've decided not to hire her, it is no longer a pressing practical issue, so once again you know she has a Ph.D.

Just when it really mattered, you didn't know. Not because your evidence was any better prior to the hiring process; in fact, it might have been worse.

These kinds of implications seem to us to make a mockery of inter-personal deliberation over time (knowledge doesn't just come and go like that, contingent on what you care about) and also of third person attributions (we don't describe people as first knowing, then not knowing, then knowing again under the described circumstances).

Hawthorne might think this cost is an acceptable price to pay for an otherwise explanatorily adequate theory, but we're not sure how he's adding up the pros and cons here.

Before turning to our proposal for how to solve the puzzle, in Section 40.9, we want to consider one more failed effort.

40.8 SOLUTION 5: RELATIVISM ABOUT TRUTH

Versions of relativism recently proposed independently by Richard (2004); MacFarlane (2005) on comparative adjectives and knowledge claims, Egan/Hawthorne/Weatherson (2005) on epistemic modals, Lasersohn (2006) on predicates of personal taste, are all attempts at reconciling (O1) and (O2).

Here's how Richard introduces the problem: Suppose we can't say who's rich unless we've settled on what counts as a luxury and a necessity, and suppose this varies from person to person. This is the correlate to (O1). Richard then raises a version of our puzzle for a contextualist about 'rich'. The worry is that we can't capture disagreements across contexts. Richard says about this contextualist position:

many cases which seem to involve disagreement over who is rich (or what is urgent or dangerous or...) turn out to be cases in which there is no literal disagreement. Suppose, to take an example, that Mary wins a million-dollar lottery. Didi is impressed, and remarks to a friend 'Mary's rich.' Naomi, for whom a million dollars is not really all that much, remarks in a conversation disjoint from Didi's, 'Mary is not rich at all.' It seems to most of us that Naomi is contradicting Didi. But, especially if each remark is part of a longer conversation (with Naomi assessing various people she and her friend know for wealth, Didi doing the same), *it is very plausible that the truth of their claims about wealth turns on whatever standards prevail within their conversations.* This is, in any case, part and parcel of a contextualist view of the semantics of 'rich'. *But then Naomi and Didi don't disagree,* in the sense that one asserts something which is inconsistent with what the other asserts. (Richard 2004: 218)

On the one hand, 'rich' is clearly, in some sense, context sensitive. On the other hand, we seem to assume that utterance of 'Naomi is rich' expresses the same content across contexts and that might at first glance seem inconsistent with the kind of context sensitivity exhibited by sentences containing 'rich'. Richard's solution, if we understand it right, is to account for the context sensitivity by making the truth evaluations sensitive to parameters supplied by the conversational context. These parameters are not part of what the speaker says, but part of the mechanism by which we evaluate the truth of what was said. Richard says:

Once the contextualist accepts the banality that whoever utters 'Mary is rich' says that Mary is rich, he must use a relativized notion of truth to formulate contextualism. Contextualism about 'rich' must be formulated as the view that whether a use of 'Mary is rich' is valid—i.e. is true relative to the conversational context in which it occurs—turns upon the standards of wealth supplied by that context.   (Richard 2004: 233)

In the report (i.e. 'They disagree: one thinks Mary is rich, the other does not'), Didi and Naomi disagree. So, there is something Didi affirms that Naomi denies. Still, within the confines of each woman's conversation, each use of 'is rich' is correct. So, Didi says something true when she utters 'Mary is rich' and Naomi something true when she utters the sentence's denial. This is consistent with the two disagreeing over the truth of a single claim, *if* that truth is relative, so that it may be 'true for Didi, but not for Naomi.'

Lasersohn (2006) motivates his relativism in much the same way:
Our basic problem is that if John says 'This is fun' and Mary says 'This is not fun', it seems possible for both sentences simultaneously to be true (relative to their respective speakers), but we also want to claim that John and Mary are overtly contradicting or disagreeing with each other . . . . How can that be? All we have to do is assign words like 'fun' and 'tasty' the same content relative to different individuals, but contextually relativize the assignment of truth values to contents, so that the same content may be assigned different truth values relative to different individuals. This will allow for the possibility that two utterances express identical semantic content, but with one of them true and the other one false . . . Instead of treating the content of a sentence as a set of time-world pairs, we should treat it as a set of time of time-world-individual triples. We assume that the context will provide an individual to be used in evaluating the sentences for truth and falsity, just as it provides a time and world; hence a sentence may be true relative to John but false relative to Mary. But this will be contextual variation in truth value only; the sentence will express the same content relative to both individuals.   (Lasersohn, 2006; cf., also, MacFarlane, 2005)

If we have understood their position correctly, its solution has two parts:

a. There's a stable content; it involves what Richard calls *notions*. This is what, for example, different utterances of 'Mary is rich' share; they all express the proposition *that Mary is rich*. This is intended to accommodate (O2).

b. There is also, however, variability, not in content, but in *what it takes for a proposition to be true in a context of assessment,* i.e. what it takes to be true relative to Didi's and Naomi's contexts respectively. What it takes for the proposition that these different utterances of 'Mary is rich' express to be true relative to Didi is not the same as what it takes for them to be true relative to Naomi. In this regard, (O1) is not about variability in content (in what speakers say), but rather variability in what it takes for what's said to be true relative to the speaker.

In what follows our goal is not to criticize this strategy as a theory of truth. Truth is a very big and very deep topic, not one we feel comfortable or confident making pronouncements about. We focus only on relativism as a solution to our puzzle about content. So understood, we shall argue, relativism of the form described above, fails for the very same reasons that Subject Sensitive Invariantism fails.

Two Objections to Relativism

Objection 1

In response to Sensitive Moderate Invariantism, we emphasized that a universal solution is preferable to a local fix. Relativism about Truth is not and cannot provide a universal solution to our problem. Universal relativism is internally inconsistent for familiar reasons. Plato's version of the argument against strong truth-value relativism is typically said to go like this: either the claim that truth is relative is true absolutely (i.e. true in a non-relative sense) or else it is only true relative to some framework. If it is true absolutely, all across the board, then at least one truth is not merely true relative to a framework, so this version of the claim is inconsistent. Furthermore, if we make an exception for the relativist's thesis, it is difficult to find a principled way to rule out other exceptions; what justifies stopping here? On the other hand, if the relativist's claim that truth is relative is only true relative to his framework, then it can be false in other, perhaps equally good, frameworks. And why should we care about the relativist's (perhaps rather idiosyncratic or parochial) framework (cf. MacFarlane, 2005).

The universal solution we present below in Section 40.9 is, other things being equal, preferable to this kind of local solution.

Objection 2

Above we argued that Subject Sensitive Invariantism sacrificed (O1) to save (O2). That is in effect what the relativists are doing as well. They have a stable content across contexts of utterance, i.e. different utterances of 'Naomi is rich' have the same semantic content—in that sense they say the same (they can agree and disagree, as in Richard's example). What the relativist cannot account for is the equally clear sense that two utterances of 'Naomi is rich' uttered with different standards of wealth in mind, say different things, make different claims, and cannot be used to express agreement or disagreement.

Examples should be unnecessary to provide by now, but here's a quick one, again notice the heavy front loading to get you, the reader, to focus on the differences in content:

In C1, Naomi whose standards are very high with respect to whom she considers wealthy is thinking about Mary. Naomi doesn't think people count as rich unless they have several multi-dollar houses and apartment, servants etc. Using these standards, she utters 'Mary isn't rich', meaning to communicate that Mary doesn't live up to her exceedingly high standards for when someone is wealthy.

In C2, Didi, who has rather low standards for when she considers someone wealthy, she considers someone wealthy if they own a home and a car, have some savings, don't live from pay check to pay check etc. She does not share Naomi's high standards. Using these standards, she utters 'Mary is rich', meaning to say that Mary's standards of living measures up to her rather low standards.

When presented with this kind of cases, it is very easy get informants to accept that Didi and Naomi don't disagree. They didn't contradict each other. 'Mary is rich' uttered by Naomi says something different from that sentence as uttered by Didi. The relativist cannot explain the clear intuition to the effect that there's a difference in content.[19]

40.9 SOLUTION 6: PLURALISTIC MINIMALISM

The central question guiding us throughout our discussion of the puzzle has an air of paradox: How can two utterances u_1 and u_2 of a single sentence S disagree in what they say, even if they say the same thing? The answer is surprisingly simple. It is, however, difficult to accept without relinquishing precious fundamental assumptions underlying contemporary work in semantics for natural language.

The crucial step is to relinquish what we call *Speech Act Monism*. This is the view that each utterance of a sentence says (asserts, claims, etc.) just one thing (one proposition, one thought). It is Speech Act Monism that generates even the appearance of tension between (O1) and (O2): If utterance u_1 says just one thing, e.g. p, and utterance u_2 says something else, e.g. q, and if $p \neq q$, then how could u_1 and u_2 say the same?

Here's the solution: Drop the idea that an utterance expresses one proposition, i.e. endorse a combination of what we call *Speech Act Pluralism* and *Semantic Minimalism*. (We call the combination *Pluralistic Minimalism*.)

According to Speech Act Pluralism, any utterance can be used to express a whole bunch of propositions. Accordingly, u_1 of S expresses a set of propositions, say, C1, and u_2 of S expresses a set of propositions, say, C2; and it may be that C1 $\neq$ C2, i.e. they don't share the exact same members. This, however, does not prevent an overlap. If C1 and C2 *do* overlap, then there is an obvious explanation of how u_1 and u_2 can both say different things and yet say the same. When we speak of two utterances of S saying the same, we are focusing on the area of overlap, and when we speak of two utterances saying different things, we are focusing on the area of non-overlap.

More specifically, return to u_1 and u_2 of (1) by Venus Williams and Serena William's agent respectively:

(1) Serena is really smart.

u_1 was uttered in a context where Venus is focusing on Serena's intelligent play and we, reporting on what's said, are interested in what Venus had in mind (for more on the importance of the reporter's interests, see below). In consequence, we report

---

[19] For further discussion of relativism and the relationship between relativism and the view we present below, see the discussion between John MacFarlane and us.

Venus as having said that Serena is a really smart tennis player. u_2, however, was uttered in a context where the focus is on athletes who negotiate great endorsement fees. We know this is what Serena's agent had in mind, and it is what the context of his utterance rendered salient, and suppose we care about what's salient in the context and what the speaker had in mind. In consequence, we report Serena's agent as having said that Serena is a really smart negotiator. Here's another fact: *both speakers said that Serena is really smart*. That is, u_1, in addition to saying Serena is a really smart tennis player, also says that Serena is really smart; u_2 in addition to saying that she is a really smart negotiator, also says that Serena is really smart. Of all the propositions expressed by u_1 and u_2, there's at least one overlap (of course, there could be more), and there is also a lot of divergence. Hence, we account for both observations (O1) and (O2).

Which part of speech act content we focus on varies from context to context. Sometimes it is the context specific content: If our interest is in what goes on in that particular context, we focus on the context specific propositions. If our interest is in the common content—that which is abstracted from the peculiarities of specific contexts, we focus on the common content (i.e. that content many utterances of the same sentence share).

40.10 CLARIFICATIONS OF PLURALISTIC MINIMALISM

In what follows, we address a range of worries an uninitiated might have about Pluralistic Minimalism. (We should mention, in passing, that we have written extensively about these issues earlier, so at certain points we will refer the reader to earlier work, but what follows will be largely self-contained.) We present our defense of Pluralistic Minimalism in the form of responses to three imagined objections.

Objection 1: 'Why on earth should I join a club who call themselves Speech Act Pluralists? Is there independent evidence for this view, or is it just some cockamamie theory you guys cobbled together to resolve the alleged puzzle?'

Speech Act Pluralism is independently motivated. Here's how we see the dialectic: There are two opposing theories about speech acts: Monism and Pluralism. Needless to say, neither is *a priori* true. It is not an analytic truth that an utterance of (1) says just one thing or more than one thing. So, we need to rely on theory neutral data. A great deal of our earlier work has been devoted to looking at how people actually describe what people say in uttering sentences. It turns out that for any one utterance there's a wide range of ways in which we can describe what was said (asserted, claimed, etc.) by that utterance. Here's an example of what we have in mind (taken from Cappelen and Lepore (2005)):

Consider this verbatim transcript of an utterance, the so-called 'Smoking Gun' utterance ('. . .' indicates pauses):

When you get in these people, when you get these people in, say: 'Look, the problem is that this will open the whole, the whole Bay of Pigs thing, and the president just feels that,' ah, without going into the details . . . don't, don't lie to them to the extent to say there is no involvement, but just say this is sort of a comedy of errors, bizarre, without getting into it, 'the president believes that it is going to open the whole Bay of Pigs thing up again, and ah because these people are plugging for, for keeps and that they should call the FBI in and say that we wish for the country, don't go any further into this case'. Period. That's the way to put it, do it straight.

Let's reflect on what's said by this utterance. We want a naïve description of what it says—the sort of description you would give if you weren't encountering it with a philosophical axe to grind. Notice first the following:

(a) This quote is typical in that almost none of it includes a grammatical sentence. Indeed, few well-formed English sentences ever get uttered.

(b) As a result, to ascertain what's said, you must first reconstruct utterances to a point where they express thoughts. There are many ways to achieve this end, as illustrated by this quote. No one way is uniquely correct.

(c) To report on this utterance (and see how others would report on it), it obviously helps to know basic facts about it, such as who the speaker and audience are and where the utterance took place. It helps, for example, to know that the speaker was Richard Milhouse Nixon, the 37th President of the United States, that his audience was R. H. Haldeman (his Chief of Staff), that the locution 'these people' refers to one or all of CIA Director Richard Helms and his deputy, General Vernon Walters (a longtime associate of the President's), and FBI Acting Director Pat Gray, that the conversation takes place in Oval Office June 23, 1972 from 10:04–11:39 a.m. (From a transcript of the so-called Smoking Gun Tape)[20]

Observation: Such factors influence how we describe what Nixon said, asserted, claimed, ordered, etc. Our hypothesis is that there's no single way to put all of this together in order to devise a unique description of what Nixon said. There are many different ways to do it, no one of which is more correct than all others.

So, what *did* Nixon say? The current standard reports on this tape go something like this (found in any history book, innumerable contemporaneous news articles, the congressional record, etc.):

Nixon told Haldeman to tell the CIA to tell the FBI not to pursue their investigation into the Watergate Burglary.

Nixon is clearly heard telling his chief of staff, Bob Haldeman, to implement John Dean's idea that the CIA be used to pressure the FBI to limit the Watergate investigation.

Nixon wanted the CIA Director Richard Helms to thwart the FBI's probe of the Watergate Burglary by saying it was a CIA operation.

[20] It's not clear whether 'those people' refers to [CIA Director] Richard Helms, [Deputy CIA Director] Vernon Walters, [FBI Director] Pat Gray, or to all of them. Reports actually vary, and if you read the transcript carefully, no unique answer emerges and there's no reason to think there would be one even if you were able to go back in time and look into Nixon's head.

Nixon told Haldeman to tell Helms that Nixon wanted him to stop the Watergate Investigation.

Nixon told Haldeman to break the law.

These reports all attribute different sayings to the smoking gun utterance; and they constitute but a modest start. Nixon's utterance clearly said lots of other things, e.g.:

He told Haldeman to tell someone at the CIA to tell the FBI that there was a connection between the Bay of Pigs invasion and the Watergate Burglary.

He said that Haldeman should give the FBI few details about the connection between the Bay of Pigs and the Watergate Burglary.

And so on and so on.

What's crucial here (and, in general) is that our intuitions about what speakers say with their utterances are influenced by, at least, the following sorts of considerations:

(a) Facts about the Speaker's Intentions and Beliefs

These reports make assumptions about what Nixon believes, for example, that he thinks 'those people' hold certain positions and that they have certain kinds of power; he has certain beliefs about the CIA and the FBI, the legal system, etc.

(b) Facts about the Conversational Context of this Particular Utterance

The reports of what Nixon said are influenced by information about whom Nixon and Haldeman have been talking, the topic of their conversation, etc.

(c) Other Facts about the World

What's illegal (i.e. that it is a crime for the President of the United States to ask the CIA to ask the FBI to stop an investigation), that getting the CIA to talk to the FBI in certain ways constitutes undue influence, etc.

(d) Logical Relations

The most obvious examples are conjuncts of conjunctions or trivial logical implications. If Nixon said he wanted the CIA Director Richard Helms to thwart the FBI's probe of the Watergate Burglary by saying it was a CIA operation, then it follows he also said he wanted the CIA Director Richard Helms to thwart the FBI's probe of the Watergate Burglary—where the latter follows logically/semantically from the former.

(e) In light of (a)–(d), we can easily substitute co-extensive predicates and referring expressions.

Take, e.g. Haldeman. Since he was Nixon's Chief of Staff, one true report would be: 'Nixon told his Chief of Staff to break the law.

(f) There's no reason to think (a)–(e) exhaust all the factors that influence our intuitions about what speakers say.

The general point illustrated by (a)–(f) is that our intuitions about what speakers say depend on a wide range of considerations not all of which are encoded solely in the meanings of the words uttered. It is only when these considerations are combined with the meanings of the words used that it even makes sense for us to ask what an individual said with his utterance.

This is the kind of evidence and argument we use against Monism and in favor of Pluralism (for an extremely wide range of further examples, see *Insensitive Semantics*). You might remain unconvinced thinking there must be ways around these data, i.e. various ways to preserve Speech Act Monism. If so, we'll have to refer you to other work. A full-fledged defense of Pluralism goes well beyond the scope of this chapter but for some such concerns see *Insensitive Semantics*.

Objection 2: 'Suppose I concede that there's evidence for Pluralism, but how, on this view, does that accommodate the shared content observation (O2)? You speak of an overlap between different utterances of the same sentence (that's how you intend to capture the shared content observation), but how do you *guarantee* this overlap?'

Two utterances of S might express different sets of propositions. We claim that if you adjust for obviously context sensitive expressions (i.e. hold the semantic value of these stable), then these sets will have at least one proposition in common. Call this the semantic content of S, i.e. one way (not the only) to characterize the semantic content of S is as that content which all utterances of S have in common (once we adjust for obvious context sensitivity). The view that there is such a common content is *Semantic Minimalism* ('minimalism' because the contextual influence is minimal).

What's our argument for Semantic Minimalism, i.e. that there is such an overlap between different utterances of, e.g. (1)? In earlier work, we presented three kinds of arguments:

(1) Semantic Minimalism helps explain how we can share contents across contexts. If we accept that theory, we can explain why contents are not contextually trapped. If our arguments above are right, then this is our only protection against what can be called *contextual content solipsism*. Semantic Minimalism guarantees a level of content that enables speakers whose conversational, perceptual and cognitive environments are very different to agree and disagree. This inference is one of the best explanations.

(2) There's a related argument (in some sense the flip side of the last one), but it appeals more directly to intuitions: When we encounter a range of utterances of S in diverse contexts (or just one utterance in a context we are ignorant of), we're often inclined to use S to say what was said by these utterances (i.e. we DSS or DIR other speakers). When we do that, i.e. when we focus on what they all share (or what was said by a single utterance in an unknown context), we have a kind of direct access to the minimal content. It's not something we focus on (or care about) in most contexts, but when we do, it's right there and we have direct cognitive access to it. When someone asks you what A said with his utterance of (1), the obvious answer is (even if you know very little about the context that A was in) is (2):

  (2) A said that Serena Williams is really smart.

This most obvious of answers provides evidence that in such circumstances we grasp minimal propositions directly.

(3) Finally, we argued that the view that there's no common content is internally inconsistent. We will not present that argument here because it requires saying much more about our opponent's position, but for an extended discussion see Chapter 9 of *Insensitive Semantics*.

Objection 3: 'In your third objection to the Similarity View (SV), you argued that since any two objects are similar in some respect or other, it follows from the SV that were we to take any utterance u by a speaker A and any proposition p, there is some respect in which *A said that p*. It also follows that in some context, it should be true to report u by uttering 'A said that p,' why doesn't the same criticism extend to your Speech Act Pluralism?'

Anyone who raises this objection against our position has not understood it. We're *not* saying that every sentence can same-say every sentence. Indeed, we are not offering, contrary to SV, a theory of same-saying. What convinced us to endorse Speech Act Pluralism are the data.

Furthermore, if there is a context in which two utterances u1 and u2 same-say each other, we are certainly *not* claiming that this relationship obtains in virtue of these two utterances expressing propositions that are similar to one another. Recall, on SV, if there is a context C in which two propositions p and q are similar, then they same-say each other. But we never once mentioned similarity as either necessary or sufficient for same-saying. To repeat: we say we have no theory for when two utterances same-say each other (and to be honest, we're doubtful there could be one, though we have no argument for that). We go with the data. In this regard: we have a no-theory theory.

Conclusion

Here are important corollaries of accepting Pluralistic Minimalism. First, a Pluralistic Minimalist must reject the Speech Act Conception of Semantics.

The Speech Act Conception of Semantics is the view that the variability in what speakers say is relevant to semantics because the goal of semantics is, roughly speaking, to account for the content of speech acts performed by utterances of sentences. So, if S is a sentence of L and S is used to say that p (to assert that p), then the semantics for L should explain how that could be. On this view, there must be a close explanatory connection (this connection can be spelled out in various ways) between the semantic content of S and the content of speech acts involving S. As a corollary, if what is said by utterances of S varies between contexts of utterance, then the semantic content of S should be context sensitive.

Pluralistic Minimalists must also reject the *Semantic Conception of Indirect Reports*, according to which If 'A said that p' is a true indirect report of an utterance of S, then the semantic content of p (as it occurs in that report) should be identical to the semantic content of S. In short, indirect reports report on semantic contents.

Here's another way to present the dialectic of this paper: the apparent tension between (O1) and (O2) arises because philosophers tend to (tacitly) accept Monism, the Speech Act Conception of Semantics and the Semantic Conception of Indirect Reports. These closely related assumptions are jointly the source of all these troubles. Of course, giving these up is not equivalent to having a positive theory. The positive theory we suggest to take their place is Pluralistic Minimalism.

Further Work

A great deal of work needs to be done in support of Pluralistic Minimalism before it can be called a full-fledged theory. Here are some challenges we conceive of as further work:

a. How is speech act content determined?
b. Can there be a systematic theory of speech act content?
c. What is the nature of minimal semantic propositions? How do we determine what the minimal content is?
d. Above we claimed that there are propositions such as the proposition that Serena is smart. Can anything interesting or informative be said about such propositions?
e. What constraints does the semantic content put on the speech act content?
f. Above we have talked about how interpreters focus sometimes on one aspect of the speech act content, sometimes on another. How does that focusing take place and how do we shift focus?

In other works, we have addressed some of these concerns, but we see them as essentially open-ended areas of further research.

References

Bach, K. (1994). 'Conversational Impliciture,' *Mind and Language*, 9/2: 124–62: 128–9
Bezuidenhout, A. (1997). 'The Communication of *De Re* Thoughts,' *Nous*, 31, 2: 197–225.
Bezuidenhout, A. (2002). 'Truth-Conditional Pragmatics', *Philosophical Perspectives*, 16: 105–34.
Blackburn, W. (1988). 'Wettstein on Definite Descriptions', *Philosophical Studies*, 53: 263–78.
Cappelen, H. and E. Lepore (1997). 'On an Alleged Connection between Indirect Quotation and Semantic Theory', *Mind and Language*, 12: 278–96.
Cappelen, H. and E. Lepore (2004). 'Context Shifting Arguments', *Philosophical Perspectives*: 25–50.
Cappelen, H. and E. Lepore (2005). *Insensitive Semantics*, Basil Blackwell: Oxford.
Carston, R. (1998). 'Implicature, Explicature, and Truth-Theoretic Semantics,' in R. Kempson (ed.), *Mental Representations: The Interface between Language and Reality*, Cambridge: Cambridge University Press, pp. 155–81.
Carston, R. (2001). 'Explicature and Semantics,' in: S. Davis and B. Gillon (eds.) *Semantics: A Reader*. Oxford: Oxford University Press.
Carston, R. (2002). *Thoughts and Utterances: The Pragmatics of Explicit Communication*, Oxford: Blackwell.

Cohen, Stewart (1991). 'Skepticism, Relevance, and Relativity,' in McLaughlin (ed.), Dretske and His Critics, Cambridge, Mass.: Blackwell.

——— (1999). 'Contextualism, Skepticism, and the Structure of Reasons,' Philosophical Perspectives, 13: 57–89.

Crimmins, M. (1992). Talk about Belief. Cambridge, Mass., MIT Press.

Crimmins, M. and Perry, J. (1989). 'The Prince and the Phone Booth'. Journal of Philosophy, 86: 685–711.

DeRose, K. (1992). 'Contextualism and Knowledge Attributions,' Philosophy and Phenomenological Research, 52/4: 913–29.

——— (1995). 'Solving the Skeptical Problem,' Philosophical Review, 104: 1–52.

——— (2005). 'The Ordinary Language Basis for Contextualism and the New Invariantism', Philosophical Quarterly, 55: 172–98.

Dreier, J. (1990). 'Internalism and Speaker Relativism,' Ethics: 6–26.

Egan, A., J Hawthorne and B. Weatherson (2005). Epistemic Modals in Context, forthcoming in Gerhard Preyer and George Peter (eds.) Contextualism in Philosophy, Oxford University Press: Oxford: 131–70.

Frege, G. (1977). translated by P. T. Geach, as 'Thoughts' in Logical Investigations, ed. P. T. Geach, Oxford, pp. 1–30.

Graff, D. (2000). Shifting Sands: An Interest-Relative Theory of Vagueness. In Philosophical Topics, pp. 45–81.

Hawthorne, John (2004). Knowledge and Lotteries. Oxford University Press.

Heck, R. (2002). 'Do Demonstratives Have Senses?,' Philosophers' Imprint, 2: 1–33.

Kaplan, David (1989). 'Demonstratives.' in Themes from Kaplan. Oxford: Oxford University Press, J. Almog, J. Perry, and H. Wettstein, pp. 481–563.

Lasersohn, Peter (2005). 'Context Dependence, Disagreement, and Predicates of Personal Taste', Linguistics and Philosophy, 28:643–86.

Lewis, David (1973). Counterfactuals, Oxford: Blackwell.

——— (1996). 'Elusive Knowledge,' Papers in Metaphysics and Epistemology, pp. 549–67.

MacFarlane, John (2005). "Making Sense of Relative Truth," Proceedings of the Aristotelian Society, 105: 321–39.

Moravcsik, J. M. (1990). Thought and Language, London: Routledge.

——— (1998). Meaning, Creativity, and the Partial Inscrutability of the Human Mind, Stanford, Calif.: CSLI.

Neale, Stephen (1990). Descriptions, Cambridge, MA: MIT Press.

Recanati, F. (2001). 'What is Said,' Synthese, 128: 75–91.

——— (2004). Literal Meaning, Cambridge: Cambridge University Press.

Richard, Mark (2004). 'Contextualism and Relativism', Philosophical Studies: 215–42.

Schiffer, S. (1995). 'Descriptions, Indexicals and Belief Reports: Some Dilemmas', Mind, 104: 107–31.

Searle, John (1978). 'Literal Meaning,' Erkenntnis, 13, pp. 207–24.

——— (1980). 'The Background of Meaning,' in J. Searle, F. Kiefer, and M. Bierwisch (eds.), Speech Act Theory and Pragmatics, Dordrecht: Reidel, pp. 221–32.

Segal, G. (1989). 'A Preference for Sense and Reference'. Journal of Philosophy, 86: 73–89.

Sperber, D. and D. Wilson (1986). Relevance, Basil Blackwell: Oxford.

Stanley, Jason (forthcoming) 'Context, Interest-Relativity, and Knowledge'.

Stanley, Jason (2000a). 'Nominal Restriction,' in Logical Form and Language, ed. G. Preyer and G. Peter. Oxford: Oxford University Press, pp. 365–88.

Stanley, Jason (2002b). 'Making it Articulated', Mind and Language, 17: 149–68.

Stanley, Jason (2003). 'Context, Interest-Relativity and the Stories', Analysis, 63.4: 269–80.

Stanley, J. and T. Williamson (1995). 'Quantifiers and Context-Dependence', *Analysis*, 55: 291–5.

Stanley, Jason and Szabo, Zoltan (2000). 'On Quantifier Domain Restriction', *Mind and Language*, 15.2: 219–61.

Travis, Charles (1985). 'On What is Strictly Speaking True,' *Canadian Journal of Philosophy*, 15/2: 187–229.

——— (1989). *The Uses of Sense* Oxford: Oxford University Press.

——— (1996). 'Meaning's Role in Truth,' *Mind*, 100: 451–66.

Unger, Peter (1995). 'Contextual Analysis in Ethics,' *Philosophy and Phenomenological Research*, 55: 1–26.

Wettstein, H. (1981). 'Demonstrative Reference and Definite Descriptions'. Reprinted in *Has Semantics Rested on a Mistake? And other Essays*, Stanford: Stanford University Press, pp. 35–49.

....

CHAPTER 41

THE PERILS AND PLEASURES OF INTERPRETATION

....

DONALD DAVIDSON

THERE is a contrast between the difficulties that stand in the way of explaining in detail how we manage to find out what is in other people's minds and the relative ease with which we do it in practice. The first part of the paper is devoted to exploring the obstacles that thwart theory, the second part to describing features of our minds that work in our favor when it comes to practice. At the end it is suggested that the project of fully naturalizing our understanding of other minds—a project philosophers are bound to find enticing—is doomed. We understand others, but we cannot reduce this understanding to a branch of the natural sciences.

The Problem of Other Minds, as traditionally formulated, arises when we ask whether, from our observations of the behavior of another person, we can tell that that person has experiences and thoughts anything like our own. That problem has not been solved; what has happened instead is that the subject has undergone a sort of naturalization.[1] Where before we tried to answer the skeptic, now it is assumed that we know, to a reasonable extent, what goes on in the minds of others. The project then becomes one of describing how we are able to find this out. The analogy with Quine's suggestion for the naturalization of epistemology is obvious. It's more

---

[1] I say a sort of naturalization because the word has been used differently by different philosophers. Here I am not taking naturalization to involve showing, or trying to show, how to reduce talk of mental states to something that can be subsumed under the natural sciences; I do take it to involve shifting from trying to justify our claims to knowledge to describing our normal ways of achieving knowledge.

than an analogy, for viewed as a matter of describing how we arrive at knowledge, the problem of other minds is just a special case.

The shift from trying to answer the skeptic to giving a description is not as great a change of subject as might appear. For while the original problem was a plea for justification, any satisfactory description of how knowledge is achieved must specify what reasons we count as justifying knowledge claims. Nevertheless, the change of venue can be salubrious. The focus on skepticism demands that we assume the skeptic's position represents an intelligible stance and therefore that the supposed problem must be met with a forthright solution. The more modest request for a description of our practices may lead us to recognize that we could never be in a position to doubt our knowledge of other minds or of an external world. This is my view of the matter: if we can think, we already know there are other people with minds like ours, and that we share a world with them.

It would, however, be foolish to underestimate how difficult it is to describe how we detect the motives and thoughts of others, and to comprehend what they say. One thing that makes it hard to devise a theoretical account of interpretation is the complexity of the interdependencies among the various attitudes, and the extent to which the content of a single thought or expression rests on its place in a network of further thoughts and expressions. These interdependencies entail that the understanding of any particular belief, intention, desire, action, or utterance of an agent is always contingent on knowing or correctly assuming a vast amount about the rest of that agent's attitudes. If it were possible to discover the contents of thoughts one at a time, it is at least possible to imagine how a general picture of a mind could be built up. But since grasping the content of any one thought or motive or utterance depends on grasping the content of a multitude, there is a problem how an interpreter can get started.

Concepts and thoughts with propositional content have logical relations to one another. It therefore behooves us, if we are considering attributing a particular thought to someone, to determine if that person is also entertaining at least the most obvious consequences of that thought. Does Carlos believe he sees a live spider in the corner? If he does, there are a great many other things he must believe: that what he sees is a living animal, that it is self-locomoting, that it has many legs, that it is apt to spin webs, that it must eat to continue living, that it will evade what it senses as dangerous, and so on. No doubt spider-thoughts involve many more entanglements with further thoughts than this, though there is no privileged list of such thoughts that provides necessary and sufficient conditions for having spider-thoughts. As interpreters what we demand as an adequate background for having spider-thoughts varies, depending on the circumstances.

There are those who embrace a kind of conceptual atomism, maintaining that it is possible to have the concept of a spider and no other concept (Fodor and Lepore, 1992). This view may reflect no more than a difference in what one counts as a concept. A creature might be genetically programmed to behave in many ways appropriate to the presence of a spider, and it might seem natural to attribute to such a creature the concept of a spider. If to have a concept is simply to be able to discriminate objects or properties of one sort or another, then the most primitive animals have the concepts of heat, color, and moisture; even plants adjust to sunlight, nutrients, and competition. But if having a concept is to place objects in a category, then a creature with concepts is capable of thought, for to place something in a category is to opine that it belongs there, and opinions are prone to error, they are true or false, and are in part identified by their relations to other judgments.

Consider Alex. Alex is a parrot who, when presented with a number of objects he has never seen before, and asked, "Alex, What's the name?", will answer, in English, "Color", if that is the right answer. Alex, we are told, can name many things, ask for them in English, say what color or shape they are, and how many there are, more or less (Pepperberg, 1998). Does Alex have the concepts of the things he "names", or of color, shape or number? The evidence does not support the idea that he does, for the evidence indicates only that Alex responds in ways he has been conditioned to respond. There is no reason to suppose Alex is judging because there is no reason to suppose he recognizes the possibility of error. Alex's performance can be explained much more simply than by assuming thoughts with propositional content.

These reflections reinforce the thesis that propositional thought requires a network of thoughts in order to locate and identify one. I have spoken of thoughts generally, but of course there are many sorts of thoughts: interrogative thoughts, beliefs, doubts, intentions, suspicions, longings, goals, plans; and these are just a few. Thoughts interact. Intentions are formed on the basis of wishes and convictions; an agent calculates the probable consequences of her possible actions on the basis of estimates of the chance of success and the relative strength of desires; we are proud of ourselves because we believe we have traits or accomplishments we admire or prize. This interaction of thoughts of various sorts makes understanding other people trying, for what we observe is the product of many cognitive factors. If we were to ask a child what property a number of objects share and he were to answer "Color" we would under normal circumstances assume he had understood the question, knew English, and intended to use that word to convey the fact that he believed the objects were the same color. Think how much we are assuming! For after all, we could have just trained that child to make that noise under those circumstances, in which case no thought was required. Instead we think the child understands, can speak English, that he gave the answer he did because he made a judgment about a property salient for him and for the questioner, that he wanted to give the right answer, and believed that color was the right answer.

Let me focus on one particular problem, that of understanding the speech of another person. If we could trust speakers always to say what they believe and what is in fact true it would make the task of interpreting their words much easier than it is, though certainly not easy. Not easy, for one thing, because we do not always know what is true ourselves. Not easy even if both we and those we would understand were infallible, for we would need to form a comprehensive and systematic theory of truth for the other's language. But of course we cannot assume people mostly say what they believe to be true. Lying is common enough, but it is not the only, or even the major case, where speakers deviate from the literal truth as they see it. Telling stories, acting a part, making jokes, indulging in irony, inventing metaphors, exaggerating, are some of the many ways we consciously depart from the literal truth. Yet the literal truth conditions of utterances is something we must get at if we are to grasp what a speaker is up to. To make matters worse, a speaker may not intend his words to mean what those words are said to mean in the dictionary, or in the mouths of other speakers. If we want to understand a particular speaker, we must somehow know or find out or intuit what that particular speaker takes to be the truth conditions of his or her utterances. Such knowledge must encompass an understanding of both intentional and unintentional departures from what we may suppose is standard usage; we must also be prepared to cope with slips of the tongue, incomplete and ungrammatical sentences, and so on. How on earth do we ever manage to understand what speakers say?

It's clear enough that we could not understand any utterance if we did not know a great deal about the speaker, the speaker's background knowledge, assumptions, values, education, and general purposes. We must also size up the multitude of intentions with which any given utterance is launched, intentions to amuse, to question, to alert, to proclaim, to demand, to acquiesce. There is not just one such intention for any given utterance; there are many. One can intend simultaneously to ask a question and to amuse a hearer. That's the least of it. Any utterance must have at least all of the following intentions: the intention to shape one's mouth, place one's tongue, and breath in such a way as to produce the desired sounds, the intention to utter sounds that will be understood by the audience as having certain (literal) truth conditions, the intention to utter the words with a certain force (assertion, question, command), the intention to be taken by the audience to have uttered those words with that force, the intention to promote some further, non-linguistic, end such as to get someone to bet on a horse, or convey the information that the house is on fire, or learn what time it is. All but the last of these intentions (the non-linguistic intentions) must be grasped by the audience if the speaker is to be understood.[2]

To return to the question how we can tell that a creature, say a parrot or a child, utters sounds (or makes gestures) with a propositional content. With an animal that we know to be in control of language, we assume we can get a start at assigning a content to its utterances by noting a correlation between its one-word sentences ("Red", "Box", "Round", "Gavagai") and events and objects in the environment which the creature seems to be tracking. The correlation is between what we suppose to be a cause and an observed effect, the cause being the perception of an object, event, or property of an aspect of the environment and the effect the utterance. But how do we pick out the cause which is relevant to understanding the content of the utterance? Repetitions can eliminate some candidates, but they can't begin to reduce the claimants to one. The point is not that inductions can be fallible. We can accept induction for what it is worth and still be uncertain about Alex. What is it that tells us that the stimulus (cause) of Alex's "answer" to the question "What's the same?"

---

[2] I count an action as having a certain intention if it would not have been performed intentionally without that intention. Most intentions do not need to be consciously arrived at, weighed, or considered. Given most typical purposes, we automatically put at least some of the means in train.

isn't the activation of certain rods and cones in his eyes, or the firing of certain optic nerves, or the photons bouncing off surfaces we see as the same color? All of these causes, and endless more, are common to the cases where Alex emitted the sound, "Color". We have no obvious grounds for choosing one of these causes over the others. But then we have no grounds for attributing one content rather than another to his answer, which is tantamount to saying, we have no reason to attribute any thought to Alex.

On the other hand, why do we think we can do better in the case of a rational human with a natural language? This brings me back to where I started: how do we tell the difference between unthinking responses, the tripping of mere dispositions, and the responses of an animal with a reasoning mind? Some years ago I asked my readers to imagine that, while walking through a swamp, I was destroyed by lightning, while quite by chance a perfect physical facsimile of me was created from various chemicals lying around. I called this creation Swampman. My story continued:

The Swampman moves exactly as I did; according to its nature it departs the swamp, encounters and seems to recognize my friends, and appears to return their greetings in English. It moves into my house and seems to write articles on radical interpretation. No one can tell the difference.   (Davidson, 1987)

Of course no one can tell the difference, for the story tells us so. People are simply fooled when they think Swampman is Donald Davidson; but are they fooled when they think the Swampman is thinking? I decided they were. I wrote:

there is a difference. My replica can't recognize my friends; it can't re-cognize anything, since it never cognized anything in the first place. It can't know my friends' names (though of course it seems to), it can't remember my house. It can't mean what I do by the word 'house', for example, since the sound 'house' it makes was not learned in a context that would give it the right meaning—or any meaning at all. Indeed, I don't see how my replica can be said to mean anything by the sounds it makes, nor to have any thoughts.

One reaction might be that this is the old mind–body problem over again: how can we tell whether Swampman is thinking? But I think this is the wrong response. Any view that proved we couldn't be wrong under such cooked-up conditions would be a mistaken view. Of course we can be massively mistaken under circumstances that philosophers contrive (Swampman, brains in vats, omnipotent deceivers). But even Swampman won't fool us forever: if we talk with him long enough, his words will begin to be connected to our world in the usual way, he will come to have real memories, and he will recognize things. Where we will remain confused, because the story says we will, is whether he is I.

The question I raise isn't whether a perfectly designed robot, made, perhaps, of silicon chips and the usual science fiction hardware, could think. There is no good reason to hold that it couldn't. Swampman's trouble was that the connections between what was in his brain and the world were not of the right sort to give his thoughts and words a semantics, a content. A robot might be constructed that would in the course of time make such connections.

I confess Swampman now embarrasses me. Science-fiction stories that imagine things that never happen provide a poor testing ground for our intuitions concerning concepts like the concept of a person, or what constitutes thought. These common concepts work as well as need be in the world as we know it. There are multiple criteria for applying many important concepts, and the imagined cases are ones in which these criteria, which normally go together, point in different directions. We ask, what would we say in such cases? Who knows? Why should we care? Unless the cases actually occur. If they do, we will decide what to say, just as we decided, under pressure from Freud, to take seriously cases where first person authority and behavior differ in the attitudes we are inclined to attribute to people (we call them unconscious attitudes). Swampman simply raises the new mind–body question: using our ordinary intuitions and knowhow, how do we tell when and what a creature is thinking?

I have been speaking of the infinite complexities of thought and the apparently insuperable difficulties these complexities raise for the task of understanding the thoughts and speech of others. In fact we not only overcome the difficulties, at least to a surprising degree, but we do it with apparent ease most of the time. The difficulty is not in the practice but in the theory: we find it hard to explain how we do it, or even how it could be done. I have spelled out elsewhere some aspects of the domain of thought which I think help explain how it is possible.[3] But in any case these explanations are highly schematic and idealized, and bear only indirectly on our actual interpretive practices. Taken literally, they make interpreting the thoughts of others seem ridiculously difficult by comparison with the relatively thoughtless ease with which we daily perform the feat.

Here I want to mention two of the reasons we find interpreting the thoughts, speech, and actions of others as easy as we do. The first reason, on which I shall concentrate, concerns the nature of conceptualization.

We endow objects with powers. Salt is water soluble, that is, it has the power of dissolving in water. Alcohol has the power to inebriate, the sun has the power to burn us. People interest us a lot, and we endow them with many powers, some permanent, some transitory, many somewhere in between. Once in a while we have explanations of these powers, but often the explanations involve appeal to further powers. Powers are causal: something about salt causes it to dissolve in water, something about alcohol causes us to get drunk if we imbibe too much of it. I assume that there are known physical explanations of these particular powers, explanations that enable us to dispense with talk of powers (or dispositions) and causality. But in our everyday lives we would have little use for the ultimate physical explanations of things even if we knew them. We depend on common-sense knowledge of how things are apt to react to what happens to them.

The sense organs of people have extraordinary powers. They allow us to react to our environment in ways suited to our survival. They do this in part by misrepresenting the world. Our eyes, for example, exaggerate the contrast at the boundary

---

[3] Many of the essays in *Inquiries into Truth and Interpretation* (Davidson, 1984) are devoted to this topic, as is "The Structure and Content of Truth" (Davidson, 1990).

between differently shaded areas, which is a help in detecting objects against a background, and our ears cause the same voice to send different signals to the brain depending on whether the voice is behind or in front of us. We know these things from naive observation, and science has shown that these powers of discrimination depend more on the sense organs themselves than on the brain.

The brain is the central processor in higher mammals. While still in embryo it is making connections, some of them with the world quite literally around it, becoming accustomed to the sounds of its mother's voice and language. The neonate has many powers, not only obvious ones such as being pained by sudden loud noises and seeking the breast, but also surprising ones like responding to smiles with smiles. We come equipped to notice bodies, to treat them in the same way in different lighting, at different distances, in different poses. Conditioning is not responsible for all of these traits, or for many more that emerge in the process of maturation, but learning can, of course, add to them.

These many discriminatory powers at some point take us into the realm of conceptualization, though they do not explain the transition from mere disposition to the use of concepts and thought. In thinking about this, it is worth asking where the categories conceptualization deals with come from in the first place. Here I dip briefly into history.[4] Plato held that good philosophizing, and indeed good thinking, requires that our concepts correspond to real divisions in nature. In the *Phaedrus* Plato introduces a principle of the dialectic, "that of dividing things by classes where the natural joints are, and trying not to break any part, the way a bad carver does" (*Phaedrus*, 265E). The demiurge of the *Timaeus* creates everything on earth, but he does not create the eternal forms on which the things on earth are modelled; they are eternal, and given.

The concept of non-arbitrary natural kinds lasted a long time. Leibniz, for example, speaks of "all the different classes of beings which taken together make up the universe" as being based on "the ideas of God". Leibniz, like Plato in the *Timaeus*, thought nothing good had been left out either in the pattern or the material copy, which implied, explicitly in Leibniz's case, a continuum, a continuum of kinds. Spinoza accepted the same view, though Leibniz criticized him for not realizing that not all possibilities could exist, only compossible ones. A skeptical note enters when Locke writes that "the boundaries of species, whereby men sort them, are made by men", but all he doubts is our ability to get "the real essences" of species right: "Our distinguishing substances into species by names is not at all founded on their real essences; nor can we pretend to range and determine them exactly into species, according to essential internal differences" (*Essay Concerning Human Understanding*, Book III, Chapter 6, §20). Buffon at first thought the notion of species was artificial, "since in reality individuals alone exist in nature", but he abandoned this position when he learned of the infertility of hybrids. Species, he decided, are "as ancient and as permanent as Nature herself". John Muir, the American naturalist, tells how his enthusiasm for plants and animals was stimulated by a teacher who

---

[4] In the historical remarks that follow I am indebted to Lovejoy (Lovejoy, 1936).

told him that "the Creator in making the pea vine and locust tree had the same idea in mind. . .plants are not classified arbitrarily. Man has nothing to do with their classification. Nature has attended to all that, giving essential unity with boundless variety, so that the botanist has only to examine plants to learn the harmony of their relations." (Muir, 1988, pp. 224–5)

If nature supplies the kinds without concern for minds that classify, it would be pointless to try to explain conceptualization as based on innate animal propensities; only an already conceptualizing intellect could hope to discover nature's true divisions. But most of us would now take for granted that all classifications are solely the work of intelligent creatures like ourselves. All concepts, we think, are embodied only in the minds, speech, or writings of creatures capable of judgment. Even if the classifications were god-given, the entities to be classified would have had to have been identified by further concepts. In fact, nature does none of the conceptual work for us except by crafting us, through evolution, to conceptualize in ways we need in order to survive or flourish.

Kant believed rationality dictated a single fixed scheme, but his firm distinction between conceptual scheme and experiential content invited the thought that there might be other schemes. When Euclidean geometry turned out to be neither the only, nor even the best geometry for serious physics, relativism became the norm for conceptual schemes. C. I. Lewis and Carnap, both committed to the scheme/content dichotomy, declared that the choice of a conceptual structure (or language) was a matter of convenience. Quine, though he dismissed the analytic/synthetic distinction, took the same view.

Some philosophers go further. If all concepts are human inventions, they argue, why should we think our constructions fit reality at all—a thought that had already occurred to Locke. It is in fact easy to see that this was an idea that was not foreign to Plato, who wanted our concepts to divide at nature's joints, but accepted the possibility that they might not. It now seems to some thinkers only a short further step to wonder whether the real world may not be something we reinvent with each new scheme.

It is a mistake to think that because our concepts, which determine how we perceive and cope with the world, are not dictated by anything more than our needs and interests, truth will forever elude us, or our vision must be incurably warped. Despite the provincial provenance of our ideology, nature is pretty much how we think it is. There really are people and atoms and stars, given what we mean by the words. The infertility of hybrids defines real species, though this matters only to those interested in the relevant concepts. This explains why it is foolish to deny that these divisions exist in nature, whether or not anyone entertains the thought. Even if no one had ever had a concept, there would be species, though of course this is our concept and our word, born of our interests.

Quine discusses what he calls relevant similarity in *Roots of Reference* (Quine, 1974). "If an individual learns at all, differences in degree of similarity must be implicit in his learning pattern . . . Some implicit standard, however provisional, for ordering our episodes as more or less similar must therefore antedate all learning, and be innate" (p. 19). Such similarity, he remarked, is confined to the individual—the episodes are more or less similar *for him*. Moreover, "our innate standards of perceptual similarity show a gratifying tendency to run with the grain of nature", due to the effects of natural selection. Quine does not mean, of course, that nature has any particular grain; what he means is that our innate standards of perceptual similarity work, in the sense that they make for roughly successful inductions.

Quine does not hold that perceptual similarity applies only to creatures with conscious thoughts; it is characterized behavioristically. The first rough condition is this: "an episode *a* is proved to be perceptually more similar to *b* than to *c* when a subject has been conditioned to respond in some fashion to *b* and not to so respond to *c*, and then is found to respond in that fashion to *a*." (p. 17) This is not the final formulation, but I will skip the details, since the final formulation, like this one, makes essential use of the notion of a relevantly similar response (the subject responds in "that fashion").

When I first read these passages I was troubled by the thought that the most basic sort of similarity (perceptual similarity) was being characterized in terms of another sort of similarity (relevantly similar responses). This second variety of similarity could no more be attributed to nature apart from living creatures than the first. I sensed a circle or regress. I was wrong to be worried. There was no circle or regress. Quine was, as he explained, reflecting on how science, with all its categories and concepts intact, might explain how we have come to view the world as full of objects with their powers and properties. (What difficulty did I have in mind? I hope I was not thinking of trying to explain conceptualization without using concepts.)

There is a closely related problem here, though not the one Quine was working on. The problem I was fumbling for is that of explaining what makes the difference between simply showing, by one's behavior, that certain perceptions are found to be similar, and that one has a *criterion* for grouping things found perceptually similar. To put it this way is to depend heavily on a mentalistic notion; the problem is to put the distinction in less subjective terms.

The simple animals, such as the invertebrate octopus or the common wasp, discriminate and learn, but there is no reason to attribute concepts to them, if to have a concept is to be able to judge, that is, *believe*, that something falls under the concept. Having a concept is like knowing what a predicate means, and this a creature can do only if it can think such things as "There's an octopus, Here's something red, It's cold, That shark is dangerous". In other words, no concepts without propositional contents; no predicates without predication. The difference between innate or learned discriminations and having a concept emerges when we try to explain error. If we condition an animal by exposing it sequentially to a number of items, rewarding it when it responds one way, punishing it when it responds in another, it is we who classify the responses and the stimuli, and count certain responses as errors. The animal may be trained more and more to go our way, but there is no evidence in such behavior to support the view that the animal is making judgments, or has the notion of making a mistake.

A creature that has concepts, and hence beliefs, will no doubt also have other attitudes towards propositional contents, such as intentions, perceptions, memories, desires, hopes, and the rest. Such a creature can be surprised, in the sense of suddenly finding that something it previously believed is false. With concepts come beliefs, and with beliefs come the distinction between the true and the false. To have this distinction is to have the concept of *objectivity*, that is, to appreciate the fact that many things are as they are however we think of them. One cannot have beliefs about most aspects of the world without grasping the fact that things may seem, look, or appear to be other than they are.

All these issues arise only after beliefs have a determinate content, and it is simply unclear how the conditioning of responses, no matter how sophisticated, can bestow a content on beliefs or sentences, as long as it is unclear how conditioning can account for error and conceptualization. So we can add the problem of assigning an appropriate content to beliefs to the other problems centering on conceptualization.

These reflections do not directly advance our understanding of conceptualization except insofar as they suggest that any of a number of concepts—the concepts of truth, error, belief, and propositional content—are so closely related to conceptualization and to one another that an insight into conditions for attributing any of them to a creature will lead directly to conditions for attributing the others.

I begin with error, and here I take cues from two sources. One is Wittgenstein, who seems to have expressed, or hinted at, the idea that the only way to make sense of error is in interpersonal situations. "Following a rule" for Wittgenstein I understand here as meaning employing a concept or word. Following a rule differs from the mere touching off of a disposition or habit in that it is possible to go wrong in applying a rule. The norm implied by a rule or concept is established by a social practice; one is wrong in a particular case if one fails to follow the practice. The other cue is in *Roots of Reference*. There Quine says, somewhat mysteriously, "Perception being such a private business, I find it ironical that the best evidence of what to count as perceptual should be social conformity. I shall not pause over the lesson, but there is surely one there" (Quine, 1974: 23).

Here is how I see the social element providing the ground for the concept of error. A single animal can be born with exquisite skills adapted to its needs and environment, and it can learn more, but nothing it does can clearly evince the thought of error. It is we, with our conceptual apparatus in place, who may so count certain of the animal's actions. This in itself is worth reflection. For despite our differences from other people and other animals, we find it easy much of the time to say what they are reacting to: the leopard has singled out the lame zebra in the herd, the vulture has spotted a distant feast. If we find this easy, it must be because we class together aspects of the environment that they do, and we appreciate this fact because we also class together the telltale reactions. Like other beasts, we discriminate moving bodies against a background, and distinguish gazelle from wild dog at many distances, orientations, and light conditions. These similarities in perceptual similarities override considerable differences in sensory equipment: we can tell what bats are chasing, though we lack sonar; we can see what the vulture sees, though only at a fraction of the distance; we can tell what the dog is tracking without its sense of smell. The deaf and the blind detect much of what we hear and see.

This simple sharing of perceived similarities has its advantages in providing advance warning of danger, as when one chimp's lone response to an approaching threat can touch off appropriate behavior in the troop. For the troop, this response to this stimulus, whether innate or learned, depends ultimately on the correlation between other's responses and the shared danger.

In this primitive triangle of two creatures reacting to a common stimulus and to each other's reactions to that stimulus we have necessary conditions for the concept of error to arise. The conditions, to spell it out, are repeated reactions to shared situations found similar by two or more creatures each simultaneously observing the other's reactions, these reactions in turn being found similar by each creature to reactions previously observed in the other in the shared situations found similar. The space needed for error to make sense appears when the correlation breaks down for one creature, but not for the other (or others): one creature responds to a shared situation as before (meaning, in a way the other creature has found similar in the past), but the other does not.

We, observing this social scene, may choose to attribute error, but here we go beyond the evidence if, in attributing error we mean the creature can recognize its behavior as mistaken. Nevertheless it is progress to have identified what is apparently a necessary condition for error to arise, and so for attributing error, conceptualization, and thought. The social hypothesis helps with another problem, that of determining the contents of perceptual beliefs. With a single creature, there is no way to decide what it is reacting to when a stimulus hits. When the frog sticks out its tongue, is the stimulus a fly or the firing of a certain pattern of receptors in the eye? We incline to say the latter, on the ground that the frog makes no distinction between flies and large birds. But even if the frog were wiser than it is, and learned to save its fire when the target is a large but distant bird, we would be in no position to choose a single cause of the reaction; we would have only narrowed down the possibilities. The social situation I have postulated eases this problem. The stimulus that matters is the nearest cause of the shared reactions. When the triangle is working normally, the mutual reactions of the two (or, of course, more) creatures *triangulate* the relevant stimulus, locating it in a public space, and bestowing on it a potential standard of objectivity.

This helps with the problem of assigning a propositional content to thought, but much more is required before a content can be specified. What I think is true is that *if* a creature has the rudiments of thought, then the conditions I have described do determine the contents of the simplest perceptual beliefs. Before this can happen, though, an elaborate conceptual background must be present, a background that includes the concepts I have mentioned, such as the contrast between true and false belief, the concept of an object, of causality, of a public space and time, and of other creatures similarly endowed with language. The simple concept of error is necessary, but it seems likely that a mind cannot accept the idea of error without some notion of how error is to be explained. We know of no way all this can be shared by creatures except through the use of language. Before triangulation can generate thought, the base line between creatures that observe that they share stimuli must therefore be strengthened to include linguistic communication. Here we go in a circle: propositional thought requires language, language requires thought. The interdependence of thought and language poses a difficulty for theory, as we saw, for it denies us the chance of finding an entering wedge. As a result, we can neither say in detail how the transition from the pre-propositional to the propositional takes place, nor can we reduce the propositional to the pre-propositional. In practice, the fact that language and thought depend on each other, and that both are so complex, poses no problem: the transition is effortless; both evolve together.

Ostensive learning of concepts and one-word sentences is an instructive example of triangulation. When a particular lesson starts, the learner cannot, as Wittgenstein points out, doubt the teacher. It doesn't matter whether or not the teacher is in tune with a larger society: from the learner's point of view, a word (sentence) is being given a meaning. The learner has no more to go on than the sample ostensions and her natural inductive flair. She is in the state of a primitive triangulator before error is in sight. Once she tries her new bit of language, the possibility of error arises.

This hasty survey of ways of viewing the process of dividing nature at the joints suggests that from the time of the Greeks we have followed a familiar sequence. Smoothing out a few millennia of development, there seem to be three major attitudes. For the Greeks, and long afterwards, the joints were taken to be in nature, a vast and organized hierarchy of structures to which thinkers should shape their concepts. To view the matter in this way is to miss the way the discriminatory powers of animals have been shaped by their needs.

A second stage transfers responsibility for categorization to the individual. An appreciation of the role of evolution shifted credit for the basic categories from a divine architect to man, and the effect of the shift on thinking about conceptualization was to make the fit between the innate powers of animal discrimination and animal needs seem less magical. Early conceptualization isn't arbitrary, but it is due to nature only in the sense that animals and their needs are the product of natural causes. But seeing things in this light still obscures the crucial role of social interaction in the transition to conceptualization.

The individual is born making certain basic distinctions; and more come with the process of development and learning. But true conceptualization can arise only in a social setting, and in that setting conceptualization and thought emerge in company with the development of language. This is the third stage in our thinking about conceptualization, and it comes closest to explaining conceptualization. But fully explain it it does not. What it does do is help in responding to the second part of the paradox with which I started, the paradox that, despite the impossibility of providing a theory that accounts for the emergence of thought and interpretation, we find interpretation relatively easy in practice.

The main points are two. The first is that the possibility of communication, and hence of understanding others, depends on the fact that our natural powers of discrimination are so very much alike. The same objects, events and properties are salient for most of us; this shows in our behavior, behavior which is, in turn, salient for most of us. This double salience makes triangulation possible, thus providing the ground for objectivity and the appreciation of error. Indeed, it is triangulation that gives meaning to the concept of salience.

The second point has to do with the complex relations and dependencies among the propositional attitudes. I stressed at first how the holism of the propositional mental means that thoughts are located only within a network of other thoughts. But as thought develops, the interdependencies speed progress rather then hinder it, for many of the relations are basically rational, and so as rational creatures ourselves, we are able to project from a part of what we understand about other people much of the rest. Examples of such rational structures are those revealed by inference, by the operation of practical reasoning, and by the ordering of language by a grammar that makes possible a grasp of the meanings of an indefinitely large number of sentences in the basis of what we know about a finite vocabulary.

How can we tell if a creature is thinking? I fear the only answer is too simple to seem philosophically interesting. If we can communicate with the creature on a range of topics concerning our shared environment, that creature is conscious and it is thinking. It is a little more interesting that there is no other way to tell.

References

Davidson, Donald (1984). *Inquiries into Truth and Interpretation*. Oxford: Oxford University Press.

—— (1987). Knowing One's Own Mind. *Proceedings and Addresses of the American Philosophical Association*, 60: 441–58.

—— (1990). The Structure and Content of Truth. *The Journal of Philosophy*, 87: 279–328.

Fodor, Jerry, and Ernest Lepore (1992). *Holism: a Shopper's Guide*. Cambridge, Mass.: Blackwell.

Lovejoy, Arthur O. (1936). *The Great Chain of Being*. Cambridge, MA: Harvard University Press.

Muir, John (1988). *The Story of My Boyhood and Youth*. San Francisco: Sierra Club Books.

Pepperberg, Irene (1998). Parrot. In *Machiavellian Intelligence 2: Extensions and Evaluations*, edited by A. Whiten and R. W. Byrne. Cambridge, UK: Cambridge University Press.

Quine, W. V. (1974). *The Roots of Reference*. La Salle, Illinois: Open Court.

Index